History of Trumbull and Mahoning Counties

HZ Williams & Bro

HISTORY

OF

TRUMBULL AND MAHONING

COUNTIES,

WITH

ILLUSTRATIONS AND BIOGRAPHICAL SKETCHES.

VOL. II.

CLEVELAND:

H. Z. WILLIAMS & BRO.

1882.

CONTENTS.

HISTORICAL.

BIOGRAPHICAL.

CONTENTS.

ILLUSTRATIONS.

Eben Newton

TOWNSHIPS AND VILLAGES

OF

MAHONING COUNTY, OHIO.

CHAPTER I.

CANFIELD.

INTRODUCTORY.

Canfield is the central township of Mahoning county. On the north lies Austintown; on the east Boardman; on the south Green and Beaver; and on the west Ellsworth. In point of agricultural importance this township ranks among the very first of those situated in the southern part of the Reserve. There are no large streams flowing through Canfield, but a large number of swales and small creeks divide the land into a number of varying ridges and undulatory elevations of moderate height. Indian creek, the largest of these streams, enters the southern part of the township almost directly south of the center, and, after flowing northward about one mile, turns to the east and crosses into Boardman township. The number of fresh water springs is large, affording a supply of pure, cold water which seldom fails—a most valuable arrangement of nature for the convenience of dairy farmers and stock raisers.

The soil is an easily cultivated loam of richness and fertility. The township being among the earliest settlements made upon the Reserve, and withal thickly peopled by an industrious and thrifty class, is conspicuous for its large number of well improved farms and other general evidences of prosperity.

In addition to its important agricultural resources, Canfield has considerable mineral wealth. Coal was discovered in 1798, and coal reservations were marked in the original surveys. Bituminous coal is found in nearly all parts of the township in veins from fifteen to thirty-three inches in thickness; while in the southern and southeastern parts extensive fields of cannel coal are found.

There is but one village, which has an air of rural simplicity quite unusual in most places of its size. As in most townships of the Reserve first settled by Connecticut Yankees, the "center" was the point where the first families took up their abode, and about that point has grown up one of those sober, quiet, unpretentious country villages, far more like an old New England village than one of the modern western "towns."

The village of Canfield has the advantage of a pleasant site, the principal part of it being upon a gentle elevation of land overlooking by far the greater portion of the township. Broad street, running north and south, is the principal business street, and includes within itself a park or common extending almost its entire length. Though there is little that can be said in praise of the architecture or general appearance of many of the buildings facing upon this park, yet so large a tract of grassy lawn adds much to the beauty of the village. And a few years hence, when the small trees now growing shall have attained a size entitling them to be ranked as shade trees, this spot will become a charming ornament to Canfield. The remaining streets of the village have, in general, an old-fashioned look. The houses are placed some distance back from the road in some instances, but in others, near to it,—many of them surrounded by orchards or gardens, making a generous mingling of the country in the town which delights by its quaintness.

The old court-house at the head of the common—soon to be transferred into an educational institute—may yet become a source of pride to Canfield's people instead of an eye-sore, as it has been since the removal of the county seat.

Whatever may be the future of the place, the brightness of the past will not speedily be extinguished. Many men of sterling worth and wide reputation have Canfield either for their birthplace or their home. Though some of them have been sleeping for years in the quiet village cemetery, Canfield still remembers them, and points out the acts of their lives as examples worthy of imitation.

OWNERSHIP AND SURVEY.

Township one in range three was purchased from the Connecticut Land company by six persons, who owned in the following proportions: Judson Canfield, 6,171 acres; James Johnson, 3,502 acres; David Waterman, 2,745 acres; Elijah Wadsworth, 2,069 acres; Nathaniel Church, 1,400 acres, Samuel Canfield, 437 acres.

The price paid for this township of 16,324 acres was $12,903.23, being a very little more than seventy-nine cents per acre. But in addition to the number of acres above given, there was annexed to this township, for the purpose of equalizing its value, lot number two in township one in the tenth range. To explain this process of equalization we make the following extract from the manuscripts prepared by Hon. Elisha Whittlesey:

As the whole tract purchased by the Connecticut Land company was in common, it was a principle of justice to equalize the township so that the proprietors of each should have an equal share of the whole, and if the quality of the land was below mediocrity, the quantity was to be increased to obtain the equality in value. A committee was appointed to make this equalization. They had no personal knowledge of the land, and judged of it by examining the field notes or surveys. The surveyors who ran the lines of the townships did not examine the land not on or contiguous to the line surveyed; and the surveyors who subdivided the townships had no knowledge of the land except what they saw on the line; and their descriptions of it in their field notes were made from what they thus saw. On the south line of Canfield and west of the north and south center line is low, wet land, on the margin of a creek, the extent of which was not known to either set of the surveyors mentioned. The tradition is that the equalizing committee, apprehending that the low swampy land which they saw on the south township line might be extensive, annexed lot two in township number one in the tenth range, containing 1,664 acres, to make township number one of range number three equal in value to an average of the land on the Reserve. It was a fact,

however, at that time, that the said township number one, range number three, was above instead of below the average quality of the tract divided. Calvin Cone, Esq., of Hartford, was assessor in Trumbull county during several years, and he said he deemed the township of Canfield to be the best quality of land in the county. This opinion was given exclusive of the annexation. The annexation was a valuable tract of land, and on being re-surveyed was found to contain 1,723½ acres, or 58½ acres more than it was computed to contain when annexed. The proprietors, therefore, may be considered as having been unusually fortunate.

In 1798 the proprietors of the township appointed Nathaniel Church, one of their number, an agent to superintend the surveying of the land into lots and commence improvements. Concerning the journey and the first operations of the party after reaching the township, the following extract from a letter written by Samuel Church to Hon. Elisha Whittlesey gives a graphic and interesting account. The letter bears the date "Salisbury, Litchfield county, Connecticut, November 5, 1837," and is written by a son of Nathaniel Church. Mr. Church writes:

DEAR SIR: Yours of July 27, 1837, addressed to my father, Nathaniel Church, enquiring of him in regard to the early history of the town of Canfield, Trumbull county, Ohio, has been submitted to my perusal. The age and infirmities of my venerable parent have prevented him from making under his own hand a reply to your request—a circumstance regretted by me. But the brief detail of facts here given you is taken from his verbal statement. . . .

He says: On the 20th day of April, 1797,[*] I started from Sharon, accompanied by the following named persons and perhaps a few others not now recollected: Nathan Moore, of Salisbury, surveyor; Eli Tousley, Nathaniel Gridley, Barber King, Reuben Tupper, and one Skinner, of Salisbury; Samuel Gilson, of Sharon, and Joseph Pangburn, of Cornwall, axemen.

I performed the journey on horseback with all my effects contained in my saddle-bags. My men traveled on foot. My associates were cheerful, and at times a little rude, though not uncivil, on the journey. We traveled through the towns of Newburg, in the State of New York; Lupex, Belvidere, in the State of New Jersey; Eaton, Bethlehem, a Moravian town, Reading, Harrisburg, then a small village on the Susquehanna river, Carlisle, Shippensburg, and Shawsburg, in Pennsylvania, at the eastern margin of the Alleghanies. Thus far the country was well inhabited and well cultivated. On our way over the mountains to Pittsburg the roads were dreadful and the settlements sparse. Bedford, Strystown, and Greensburg were about all the settlements we passed. From Pittsburg, or Fort Pitt as it was then most commonly called, to the mouth of the Big Beaver, there were few or no inhabitants. We performed our journey on the south side of the Ohio river, there being no road on the other side. At the mouth of the Big Beaver was a small settlement called McIntosh. From thence to the place of our destination the forest was uninterrupted, with the exception that one or two families had settled and made some improvement at a place since called Greersburg.

[*]Should be 1798.—E. Whittlesey in a note.

We arrived at Canfield on the 24th day of May, 1797,* and pitched our first tent near the northeast corner of the town, our surveyor mistaking this for the center. Our journey from the mouth of the Big Beaver had been performed by the aid of the compass and marked trees. We erected a cabin or hut of poles and bark at the place where we first stopped. Our surveyor soon learned his mistake, and ascertained and fixed the center of the town. While doing this our cabin took fire and was burned up and some of our utensils with it. The lot upon which this cabin stood was afterwards known as the Burnt Cabin lot. Our first repast was made of smoked pork bought in McIntosh, bread made by ourselves and baked in the ashes, and coffee without milk or sugar; and having thus feasted we slept soundly upon our blankets spread upon the ground. Within a day or two we erected another cabin, at the center, and began to survey the road from the center east. Our surveyor after running about half a mile eastwardly from the center pronounced it impracticable to proceed, by reason of the wet and miry state of the ground. I returned with him; and, wading through mud and water over my boots about six rods, found hard ground and we proceeded without further difficulty.

A little eastward of this swale of wet ground, on the north side of our surveyed road, we commenced the first clearing. Having cleared two acres we raked off the leaves with our hands, harrowed it with one horse and a wooden harrow. I planted it with corn, potatoes, and beans. We cleared twelve acres and sowed wheat, and inclosed one field with a seven-rail fence. We cleared and sowed three acres to oats, and on the south side of the road we cleared and sowed twelve acres of wheat,† which proved an abundant crop. We erected a log house in the center and two houses and one barn east of the center. Having done this we cut out the east and west road.

About one month after our arrival at Canfield, Champion Minor, with his wife and two children from Salisbury, arrived with an ox-team. This was the first family which ever visited or settled in the town, and the company made a donation of land to the woman. A few days after the arrival of Minor's family the youngest child died. I went to Youngstown to procure a woman to aid in preparing the body for the grave. The coffin was made of split wood pinned together, and we buried the child decently, but without religious solemnities, about twenty rods from our cabin. Some wild beast nearly disinterred the body on the night of its burial, and we then built a strong fence around the grave. This was the first burial of any white person within the town.

During this first summer I brought all our provisions and other necessaries from Pittsburg through the wilderness on pack-horses, guided on my way by marked trees. A settlement had commenced the year before at Youngstown, and that was the only settlement near us. A few Indians visited us on their hunting excursions this summer. We understood that they came from the vicinity of Sandusky. They appeared friendly. Our party enjoyed tolerable health during the summer, and were generally submissive to my orders, although in my absence some disorder prevailed.

Our men established a code of justice and system of punishment of their own, and when I was absent from them, sometimes put their laws in force by tying the condemned one to a tree with his body naked and exposed to the attacks of mosquitoes. I soon repealed this cruel code.

*1798.—E. Whittlesey.

†There was probably but one twelve-acre lot of wheat, and that on the south side of the road.—ED.

The town was laid off into lots, and most of our men took up lots but did not retain them long, as but few of them remained in the town. One Sunday one of my men, without my leave, went into his lot and commenced labor upon it by clearing. He was soon frightened away and came back to our cabin declaring that the devil had appeared to him. He had probably been frightened by the appearance of some wild beast. After this incident none of my men were disposed to labor on the Sabbath, a practice which I had strictly forbidden.

Champion Minor and his family, Samuel Gilson and Joseph Pangburn remained in the town. I believe all the others returned after cutting through the east and west road, which was the last of our labor. We reached Connecticut in safety the fall of the same year, some of us at least grateful for the mercies which Providence had extended to us."

It may be interesting to our readers to know with what equipments this surveying party were provided, and fortunately the information is at hand:

A bill of articles delivered to Judson Canfield for the New Connecticut:

April 28, 1798.*	£	s.	d.
12 Narrow axes at 8s	4	16	0
1 Broad axe at 15s		15	0
1 Chain		18	0
1 Square and two pair compasses		7	0
1 Draw-shave			6
Half bushel white clover seed	2	8	0
Half bushel herdsgrass seed		16	0
3 lbs. Bohea tea at 4s. 6d		13	6
2 lbs. pepper at 3s. 3d		6	6
6 lbs. ginger at 1s. 6.		9	0

£11 14s 6d

Received the above mentioned articles from Captain Elijah Wadsworth, by the hand of Arad Way. Also 16s. in cash. Sharon, April 28, 1798.

Such was the outfit for a party of twelve men who were to spend several months in a solitary wilderness, fifty miles from any settlement of importance—about $5 to each man in tools, seed, and groceries, and sixteen shillings in cash! Yet the eleven men, who performed the journey on foot, doubtless thought they had as much baggage as was convenient.

The names and residences of this surveying party were as follow: Nathaniel Church, Nathan Moore, Eli Tousley, Nathaniel Gridley, Barker King, Reuben Tupper, and David Skinner, of Salisbury, Connecticut; Carson Bacon, Samuel Gilson, and Joshua Hollister, of Sharon, Connecticut; Charles Campbell and Joseph Pangburn, of Cornwall, Connecticut.

*The date given in Mr. Church's letter must be incorrect. Evidently these articles were for the surveying party, which must have left Sharon after their delivery and not on April 20th, as stated.—ED.

Just here arises the question whether Hon. Judson Canfield was of the party. That he was in Canfield in June, 1798, is show by a transcript of the records of the survey, originally in the possession of Judson Canfield and now belonging to his grandson. On page 123 of this transcript is the following:

A draft of the first division in Campfield on the Reserve, made the 20th of June, 1798, at Campfield, by Nathaniel Church, the agent, and Judson Canfield, clerk, and drawn by Nathan Moore, viz:

Judson Canfield........ 4,081,* drew lot No. fourth.

Judson Canfield.........	2,090	4,081, do. lot No. first.
Samuel Canfield.........	437	
Nathaniel Church	1,400	
James Johnston........	154	
James Johnston........	3,348	4,081, do. lot second.
David Waterman.......	733	
David Waterman......	2,012	4,081, do. lot No. third.
Elijah Wadsworth......	2,069	

N. B.—Not No. 1 is the southwest lot, lot No. 2 is the northwest lot, lot No. 3 is the southeast lot, and lot No. 4 is the northeast lot.

Signed,

JUDSON CANFELD.
NATHANIEL CHURCH.
NATHAN MOORE.

N. B.—The above four lots were the four center lots previous to their being cut up into small lots containing about seven acres each. Each of the above four lots before cut up contained about sixty-three acres, being 186 by 60 rods, including highways; and each lot has been cut up into eight.

When these four center lots were subdivided does not appear, but it must have been during the summer of 1798, as Mr. Church speaks of his men taking up lots in the town, in the letter given above. It is somewhat surprising that he nowhere mentions Mr. Canfield's visit to the Reserve.

THE NAME.

Campfield was the name given the township by the surveyors, and it is so denominated in their maps and notes. An old book of records deposited with the recorder of deeds of Trumbull county contains in manuscript a record of the survey as well as other records. The first page of this book is as follows:

The first book of records of the township number one in the third range in the Connecticut Reserve called Campfield, *alias* Canfield.

April, 1798. Voted that township number one in the third range should be called Campfield.

April 15, 1800. Voted that the above township should be called Canfield.

The last name was bestowed in honor of Judson Canfield, the largest proprietor of land in the township.

---

*The number of acres owned by each is denoted by the figures opposite the name.

SETTLEMENT.

All of the first settlers were from Connecticut —wide-awake, progressive Yankees. We have attempted to classify the early settlers according to the date at which they arrived here. As already recorded, Champion Miner and family made a permanent settlement in 1798. This family, with Samuel Gilson and Joseph Pangburn, made up the population of Canfield during the winter of 1798–99.

1799. Phineas Reed arrived in the spring of this year, whether with or without a family, we are unable to learn. In the fall came Eleazer Gilson and Joshua Hollister.

1800. Nathan Moore and family arrived on the 15th of May, having been forty-five days on the road. This is the only recorded arrival during that year.

1801. James Doud and family, Ichabod Atwood, Calvin Tobias, Abijah Peck.

1802. Captain Wadsworth, Simeon Sprague, Tryal Tanner, Matthew Steele, Aaron Collar, and William Chidester with families, David Butler, David Hatfield, Charles and Henry Chittenden, Benjamin Bradley, Ariel Bradley, Warren Bissel, Daniel Miner. Some of those last named were probably accompanied · by their families.

1803—Abisha Chapman, Jonathan Sprague, Dr. Pardee, Benjamin Yale, William Chapman, Bradford Waldo, Wilder Page, Cook Fitch.

1804—Zeba Loveland, Archibald Johnston, and probably many others.

1805—Herman Canfield and wife, Ebenezer Bostwick and family. This year began the German settlement. Henry Yager, Jacob Ritter, Jacob Wetzel, Henry Ohl, Conrad Neff, Peter Lynn, John Lynn, George Lynn, Daniel Fink, Adam Blankman and Philip Borts arrived during this year; some of them, perhaps, a year earlier. All, however, did not settle in Canfield, but those who did formed an important addition to the population and did much toward developing the agricultural resources of the new settlement.

There are others whose names should have been included in the above lists, could the precise date of their coming have been ascertained. Azariah Wetmore, Jonah Scofield, John Everett and others were among the very earliest settlers.

Many of those whose names appear above remained but a few years, some of them but one

H. G. Sims.

season; and of those who remained and died here information has not always been obtainable.

Nathan Moore was the surveyor of the party which came out in 1798. After his settlement here in 1800 he remained a few years then moved away with his family.

James Doud settled two miles east of the center. He had several children who lived here until they were men and women and then moved. His sons were Herman, James, William, and Samuel. His oldest daughter, Lydia, married Judge Bingham, of Ellsworth; Anna became Mrs. Hall, of Ravenna. Mr. Doud was a drover. He passed over the mountains many times with droves of cattle, but on his last trip he was taken sick and died.

Ichabod Atwood settled in the northwest of the township and afterward moved to Springfield. He had several sons and daughters, none of whom settled here. He built quit a nice frame barn at an early date.

Eleazer Gilson settled east of the center in 1801, afterwards moved to Turner street. His son Samuel was also an early settler. Isaac, Lizzie (Everett), Cynthia, and Maria (Beeman) were the names of others of this family.

Jonah Scofield in 1800 or 1801 settled a short distance west of the center, where he lived and died. His son William went South and died. Pamela married Edward Wadsworth. Frances married John Reed. Both of these resided in Canfield.

Aaron Collar died in 1813 at the age of forty-nine. Lavinia, his wife, died the same year aged forty-six. Several of their descendants still reside in this township. An epidemic in 1813 carried off a large number of the settlers.

James Bradley lived on the farm afterwards owned by Philo Beardsley, and now owned by Noah Lynn. Ariel Bradley removed to Portage county in 1805.

William Chidester came out in company with Tryal Tanner. He settled one and one fourth miles west of the center. He died in 1813, aged fifty-seven. His sons were Hezekiah, Philo, Erastus, Rush, Velorus, Julius, and Royal. Chloe and Betsey were his daughters. Chloe became Mrs. Smith and settled in Ellsworth. Hezekiah married Lizzie Buell, resided in Canfield and reared a large family. Philo also passed his life in this township. Erastus lived

here several years, then moved west. Rush went to Medina county. Velorus died the same year with his father. Julius moved to Medina county. Royal occupied his father's old farm, and died there. He married the widow of Jarvis, who is still living on the old place. William Chidester, the father, was a man of good ability. He was the first justice of the peace in Canfield, and solemnized many marriages in this and surrounding townships in early days.

Ira Spague settled one mile south of the center. His son Augustus occupied the farm after him. Henry Sprague, son of Augustus, is now living on the place.

Reuben Tupper settled on the farm which David Hine purchased later.

Several members of the Sackett family settled in Canfield very early. Simmons Sackett lived in this township until 1863, when he died at the age of seventy-five.

Some of the old settlers attained a remarkable age. Esther, the wife of Captain Philo Beardsley, died at the age of ninety-one. Ethel Starr, a comparatively early settler, died in 1861, aged ninety-two years. John Everett died in 1819, at the age of ninety-two.

Abishai Chapman settled in the northwest of the township, but sold out and moved.

William Chapman owned two lots near the center. He died in 1813, at the age of thirty-six, and was buried the same day as Squire Chidester. His widow married a Mr. Merwin and went to Palmyra to live.

John and Sarah Everett were early settlers. They had but one child, a daughter—Mrs. Sprague. They were old people when they came here and died in early years.

Matthew Steele settled southeast of the center. The family were all grown before the memory of old residents.

Bradford Waldo remained few years in this township, then moved to Portage county. He was noted as a wit, and had a gift for making impromptu doggerel verses, which were sometimes extremely amusing.

Herman Canfield, Sr., brother of Judson Canfield, married Fitia Bostwick. In October, 1805, they settled in Canfield. Six children were born to them, viz: Herman, William H., Elizabeth, Cornelia, and Lora. Lieutenant-colonel Herman Canfield died at Crump's Landing, April 7,

1862, while in the service of his country. He was a lawyer of ability and worth, served as State Senator from Medina county, and held other important positions. William H. Canfield was born in 1806, and died in Kansas in 1874. He studied law in the office of Hon. Elisha Whittlesey. In 1866 he removed to Kansas, and in 1870 was appointed judge of the Eighth Judicial district of that State, and held the position until his death.

James Reed settled in the western part of the township in 1805, moving from Ellsworth. After his settlement his father, also named James, came out and lived with him. He died here at the age of about seventy, and was the fifth person buried in the center graveyard. During the War of 1812 Mr. Reed set up a distillery, and furnished the army with whiskey, which then formed a part of soldiers' rations. James Reed died in 1813; Mrs. Reed survived until 1860, and reached the remarkable age of ninety-eight years. Her children were: Mary (Bowman), born in 1791, still living, in Goshen township; Rosanna, born in 1793, died in 1813; Jemima (Rudisill), born in 1797, died, aged seventy-five; James, Jr., born in 1799, lives in Michigan; Rachel (Turner), born in 1801, resides in Canfield; Eleanor (Turner), born in 1803, lives in Summit county; Anna, born in 1806, died, aged three and a half years; John C., born in 1809, died, aged forty; Hiram, born in 1811, killed when two months old, his mother being thrown from a horse with the babe in her arms; Joshua, born in 1812, resides in Alliance. Mr. Reed, while living in Canfield, attempted to dig a well upon his farm, and came near losing his life in it on account of the "damps" or foul gases there. A colored man known as Black Tobe, hearing that Mr. Reed had abandoned the well, came to him, and urged that he be allowed to finish the job. He was told of the danger, but would not listen, and was finally allowed to enter the well. Before those attending him became aware of his state, he was overcome and sank down in a suffocating condition. He was lifted out, but all attempts to revive him proved ineffectual, and he died the victim of his rashness.

John and Magdalena (Neir) Harding came to this township about the year 1805. Their sons were John, George, and Jacob, all of whom died in this county. The daughters were Mollie (Harroff), Katharine (Ohl), Mary (Neff), Betsey (Kline), Sarah A. (Oswald), and Rebecca (Hood). Mrs. Kline and Mrs. Oswald are the only survivors of this family.

Jacob Oswald was among the early settlers of the township, located on what is now the Samuel Stitel farm. He moved to Liberty township, Trumbull county. His son Charles returned to Canfield in 1826, and passed his life in the township.

The Lynns of Canfield and other portions of this county, are descended from Nicholas Lynn, who emigrated to America from Germany previous to the Revolutionary war. He was a soldier in the war, and after its close married and settled in Berks county, Pennsylvania. It is said that he was the father of fourteen children, but the history of only eleven can be traced—five sons, Philip, Jacob, Peter, George, and John, and six daughters. Philip and four of the daughters, Mrs. Snyder, Mrs. Reaser, Mrs. Sheibly, and Mrs. Kock, remained in Pennsylvania, and their descendants are numerous in Berks, Perry, Lehigh, and other counties, ranking high in social and civic positions. The family of the oldest son, Philip, consisted of three sons and several daughters. One of the sons, John, came to Canfield and resided near Cornersburg. After living here several years, building a saw-mill, etc., he sold out and returned to Pennsylvania. One of his grandsons, Solomon W., is a resident of Austintown.

Jacob, the second son, came to Ohio about 1830, and died in this township in 1837, at the age of seventy. His sons were Jacob, Jesse, John, and Philip; his daughters, Mrs. Jacob Heintzelman, Mrs. Christian Heintzelman, and Mrs. Miller. Two are now living, Mrs. Jacob Heintzelman, and Jesse, the second son.

The three younger sons of Nicholas Lynn came to Canfield in 1805, and settled on adjoining farms. George died in 1833, aged fifty-eight; John in 1835, aged fifty-six, and Peter in 1858, at the age of eighty-six. Peter Lynn had three sons, Adam, William, and Peter, and three daughters, Mrs. Fullwiler, Mrs. Shellabarger, and Mrs. Infelt. All are dead excepting Adam Lynn, Esq., for many years a justice in this township. George Lynn's family numbered five sons, David, John, George, William second, and Levi, and two daughters, Mrs. Nathan Hartman, and Mrs. S. W. Lynn. All are living except William, who died in 1851, aged thirty-five. His son, William C. Lynn, a resident of the Black Hills region, is six feet eight inches tall, and correspondingly well developed. John Lynn, youngest son of Nicholas, had three sons, John N. O., David second, and G. W., and three daughters, Mrs. George E. Harding, Mrs. Joseph Hartman, and one who died young. Three members of this family are living.

Barbara, youngest daughter of Nicholas Lynn, came to Ohio about 1806. She married Abraham Kline. Her husband soon died, and she lived a widow fifty-seven years, until death called her home. She was a woman of great benevolence, and having gained a competence, bestowed it freely upon religious and charitable organizations. Among other bequests, she gave $1,000 to Heidelberg college, Tiffin, Ohio. She died in 1873, aged seventy-eight.

Susanna, also a daughter of the Revolutionary ancestor, married a Mr. Bailey and settled in Ohio about 1820. She had three sons and two daughters. One of the daughters married John Corll, and another, Samuel Rupright. Only one of Mrs. Bailey's children is now living, her son, Jacob, now a resident of Indiana. The Lynns are thrifty and worthy people, friends to law and order, and zealous in the support of education and religion. In 1804 David Hine, from Warren, Litchfield county, Connecticut, came to Canfield on foot; purchased land and began some improvements upon it, in 1806. The same year he brought his family with an ox team. His farm was situated one and one-half miles west of the center. In 1810 Mr. and Mrs. Hine returned to Connecticut to visit their friends, and remained until the spring of 1811, when they again came to Canfield. David Hine died in 1859, in his seventy-eighth year. His wife, Achsah (Sackett) Hine, died in 1832, aged forty-seven. Their family consisted of seven sons and three daughters, namely, Myron, Warren, Chester, Benjamin, Charles, David, Jr., William, Cynthia, Mary, and Betsey. All arrived at maturity. Three sons and two daughters are still living, Warren, in Canfield; Charles, in Warren, Connecticut; William, in Canfield; Cynthia, wife of C. S. Mygatt, Canfield; and Betsey, wife of William Cumstock, Canfield.

In 1806 came Elisha Whittlesey, doubtless the greatest accession the township ever had. He was in public service almost constantly from the date of his settlement until his death, in 1863; and all trusts, whether of town, county, State, or Nation, were discharged in a manner which never failed to please and satisfy. His biography, and likewise that of his honored and esteemed associate, Judge Eben Newton, will be found in this work. It may be proper to mention here the names of a few distinguished men who were students in the law office of Mr. Whittlesey: Hon. Joshua R. Giddings, Hon. Benjamin F. Wade, W. C. Otis, General Ralph P. Buckland, and Columbia Lancaster, afterwards of Oregon, received a portion of their legal training in Canfield.

In 1806 the Turner family came to the northwestern part of the township. The road on which they lived was long known as "Turner street" and is frequently mentioned thus by old residents at the present day. Adam Turner and his wife Margaret came from New Jersey. They had five sons and three daughters, viz: John, Elsie, Conrad, Mary, James, George, Robert, and Charity. John settled in Canfield for a time, but moved to Sharon, Medina county, where he died at the age of eighty-six. Elsie married Giles Clark and resided in Hubbard, Trumbull county; died in Clarksville, Pennsylvania. Conrad bought his brother John's farm in the northwest of the township; sold out, moved to Medina county, and died at the age of eighty-two. Mary married James Reed, formerly of Pennsylvania, and died in this township.

George died in Medina county, and Robert in Michigan. Charity married Henry Edsall, and resided in Canfield. Of these eight children there are no survivors. James, the third son, was born in 1796, and died July 17, 1873. In 1819 he married Rachel Reed, who is still living. She bore five children, four of whom arrived at maturity. Three are still living. Fidelia married Ward E. Sackett, and after his death became the wife of Julius Tanner, of Canfield. Charles R. married Flora Sackett for his first wife. She bore three children, two of whom, Jemima Estella and Hattie S., are living. For his second wife he married Harriet Sackett, who bore one son; he was accidentally shot by a playmate at the age of nine years. Charles R. Turner was born in 1822 and died in 1874.

James C. resides on the old homestead in Canfield. Betsey M. is the wife of Judson W. Canfield.

Benjamin Manchester, whose ancestors came from England to America in 1638, was born in Newport county, Rhode Island, in 1786. Thomas Manchester, the progenitor of the Manchester family in this country, was one of the company that purchased the Island of Aquiday, afterwards called Rhode Island, from the Indian sachem, Miantonomah, in 1639. Benjamin Manchester moved with his parents to Washington county, Pennsylvania, in 1797. In 1805 he married Phebe Hannah Doddridge, born in 1788. In April, 1809, they settled on a farm in the southern part of Canfield township. They reared four children, three of whom are now living: James, born in 1806, resides in Illinois; Philip, born in 1808, resides in Indiana; Isaac, born in 1810, now living in Canfield; and Mary Ann, born in 1812. She married George Ranck, of Wayne county, Indiana, and died in 1852. The wife of Benjamin Manchester died in 1813. In 1821 he married Margaret McGowen, who also bore four children—Phebe Jane, Eliza, Robert, and Martha. Eliza and Martha are dead. Phebe Jane, the widow of Elijah Jones, lives in Missouri. Robert resides in Canfield. Benjamin Manchester was a soldier in the War of 1812. He held various township trusts, and was one of the township trustees twenty-seven consecutive years. He was a man of the strictest morality and integrity. He died in 1857.

TAXES IN 1803.

Thirty-six dollars and ninety-three cents was the amount of taxes raised in the township of Canfield in the year 1803. Many who paid less than a dollar doubtless lived to see their taxes increased, "some thirty, and some sixty, and some an hundred fold." The list is as follows:

CANFIELD, RANGE THREE, TOWN ONE.

	Amount of Tax.
Atwood, Ichabod	$ .50
Bradley, James	1.04
Bradford, James	.64
Bissel, Warren	.20
Collar, Aaron	1.52
Crane, Calvin	.52
Chidester, William	.54
Chittenden, Timothy	.53
Chittenden, Charles	.58
Doud, James	.56
Doud, Polly	.25
Everett, John	.53
Faulkner, Henry	.25
Gridley, Nathaniel	.82
Gilson, Samuel	1.10
Gifford, James	.10
Gifford, Peregrine P.	.10
Gifford, Richard	.38
Hollister, Joshua	.14
Hulbert, Raphael	1.06
Harrington, Jacob	.24
Hine, Homer	.03
Johnson, Archibald	.80
Loveland, Zeba	.12
Merwin, Zebulon	.52
Miner, Champion	.20
Moore, Nathan	.48
Neil, John	.21
Page, Wilder	.56
Pardy, David	.03
Pangburn, Joseph	.22
Reed, Phineas	.58
Reed, James	.47
Steele, Matthew	2.30
Scovill, Jonah	.24
Simcox, John	.10
Sprague, Ira	.24
Tobias, Calvin	.28
Tupper, Reuben	.52
Tanner, Tryal	1.60
Wilcox, Isaac	.52
Wadsworth, Elijah	15.26
Waldo, Bradford	.14
Yale, Benjamin	.02
Total	$36.93

FIRST EVENTS.

The first burial in the township took place July 21, 1798. A little child, the daughter of Champion Minor, was buried in lot forty-four, second division, about three-fourths of a mile east of the center. Two rude stones mark the head and foot of the grave. The first person buried in the cemetery east of the center was Olive, the wife of Charles Chittenden. She died September 30, 1801.

The first male child born in the township was Royal Canfield Chidister, born June 22, 1802, about three rods east of the center of the township.

The first log-house built in the township was on the southeast corner of lot fifty-one in the second division. The first clearing was made on lot fifty-two, second division.

The first frame house in the township was built in 1802-3 by Elijah Wadsworth. It was two-story, 30 x 40 feet.

The first marriage ceremony ever solemnized in this township was that of Joseph Pangburn

Henry Van Hyning

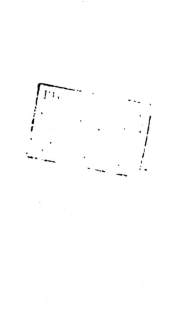

Mrs Sophia Beardsley.

and Lydia Fitch. They were married April 11, 1801, by Caleb Baldwin, Esq., of Youngstown.

February 11, 1800, Alfred Woolcott, surveyor, led to the hymenial altar Mercy Gilson, daughter of Eleazer Gilson, of this township. For want of some person qualified by law to solemnize the ceremony, they were obliged to go to Pennsylvania to be married.

POST-OFFICE.

In 1801 the first mail route to the Reserve was established through the influence of Elijah Wadsworth, who was then appointed postmaster at Canfield. He was again postmaster in 1813.

THE FIRST MILLS.

The first saw-mill in the township was erected on lot number three in the fourth division, in the northwestern corner of the township. Work was begun in the spring of 1801, by Jonah Scoville. In the summer of the same year he sold it to Ichabod Atwood, who completed the mill during the succeeding fall and winter, and commenced sawing in the spring of 1802.

The second saw-mill was erected in 1802, on the southeast corner of the "Brier Lot." It was owned, one-half by Elijah Wadsworth, one-fourth by Tryal Tanner, one-eighth by William Sprague, and one-eighth by Matthew Steele. Jared Hill came from Connecticut to build it. Sawing was commenced in 1803. The land on which the mill stood belonged to Judson Canfield, from whom it was rented in 1802, by Mr. Wadsworth, for seven years. The consideration for the use of the land was thus expressed in the lease: "One pepper-corn yearly, to be paid if demanded."

In 1810 a carding machine was erected by a company. The machinery was propelled by horse-power. Wool was sent to this mill from Cleveland, Painesville, and other distant points.

A saw-mill and grist-mill was in operation in 1828, on the stream known as the "South run." It was run by a man named Oister.

PHYSICIANS.

The first of these useful members of society who ministered unto the sick and afflicted in Canfield was Dr. David Pardee. He came to the settlement in 1803, but remained only a short time. Little is known concerning him except that he was considered very much of an oddity.

3*

In 1807 Dr. Shadrach Bostwick moved from Deerfield to Canfield. He was born in Maryland, in 1769; moved to Massachusetts, and thence to Deerfield, Portage county, in company with his father-in-law, Daniel Diver, in 1803. He held two important positions, physician and Methodist minister. In both he was earnest and faithful. Though by no means deeply skilled in the healing art, he always strove to the best of his ability to effect cures, and the patient always knew that the doctor's sympathies were with him. For many years Dr. Bostwick continued to give both medical and spiritual advice to the people of Canfield and adjoining settlements. When he arrived in the township there was but one Methodist family among its inhabitants, but he lived to see a large and prosperous society as the result of his labors. He died in Canfield in 1837.

Dr. Ticknor was a physician in Canfield as early as 1814. He married Getia Bostwick, and practiced here with good success several years. He held some kind of a naval commission and was subject to orders to leave at any time.

Dr. Ira Brainard came to Canfield about 1817 and died here in 1825. He studied medicine with Dr. Allen in Kinsman, and had a large practice in this region.

Dr. Chauncy R. Fowler, whose long and extensive practice in this county has secured a wide reputation, was born in Poland, this county, September 25, 1802, being a son of Jonathan and Lydia (Kirtland) Fowler, the first settlers in the township of Poland. He studied medicine with Dr. Manning, of Youngstown, and in October, 1823, commenced practice in Poland, where he continued until 1826, when he removed to Canfield, where he has since resided. Dr. Fowler was married in 1826 to Mary D. Holland, daughter of Benjamin Holland, of Youngstown. She died in 1865, having borne four sons and one daughter, viz: Dr. Charles N. Fowler, of Youngstown; Henry M. Fowler, editor of the Dispatch, Canfield; Russell C. Fowler, who died in 1858; Dr. Jonathan E. Fowler, who died in 1870, and Hannah Jane, wife of Dr. A. W. Calvin, of Canfield. Dr. Fowler has been actively engaged in the practice of medicine in this county longer than any other physician, his practice in Canfield and adjoining townships covering a period of more than fifty-five years. That he has been successful the high esteem with which he is regarded by the large community which has employed him affords most convincing evidence.

Dr. J. M. Caldwell has been engaged in the practice of medicine in Canfield for about forty years past. He was also in the drug and grocery business for some time. Dr. Caldwell was born in Ireland, attended medical lectures in Philadelphia and graduated there over fifty years ago.

Dr. Lewis D. Coy, eclectic physician and surgeon, is a native of this county, and though a young man is fast gaining a lucrative practice. He settled in Canfield in 1879.

Dr. A. W. Calvin, for several years an esteemed physician of Canfield, died in 1881. A sketch of his life will be found elsewhere.

Dr. E. K. Prettyman, eclectic physician, is a native of Delaware. He practiced in Pennsylvania some years and settled in Canfield in 1880.

FORMER MERCHANTS.

The first store was established in 1804 by Zalmon Fitch, in partnership with Herman Canfield. This is said, on good authority, to have been the second permanent mercantile establishment upon the Reserve. Mr. Fitch continued the business in Canfield until 1813, when he moved to Warren. While in Canfield he also kept tavern.

Comfort S. Mygatt, one of Canfield's earliest merchants, was born August 23, 1763. About the 1st of June, 1807, from his home in Danbury, Connecticut, he dispatched a team consisting of two pair of oxen and two horses, with a large wagon loaded with household goods, for Ohio. One week later he started with his family with four horses and a fifth horse to hitch on when necessary, which was often the case. He overtook the first team in Shippensburg, Pennsylvania, and from there the two journeyed in company. On the 4th of July all were in Pittsburg together, and on the 7th they arrived in Canfield, the first team having been five weeks on the road and the one which brought Mr. Mygatt and family four. The family, at the time of their arrival, consisted of Mr. Mygatt and wife, four daughters, two sons, and two step-sons —ten persons in all. July 16, 1807, a son was born—Dr. Eli Mygatt, now an honored citizen of Poland. Soon after reaching Canfield Mr. Mygatt entered into partnership with Herman

Canfield and Zalmon Fitch, under the firm name of Mygatt, Canfield & Fitch, and opened a store of dry goods, groceries, and general merchandise. The partnership was dissolved after about two years, and the business was continued by Mr. Mygatt during the remainder of his life. He died in October, 1823. In 1811 Mr. Mygatt and his wife rode on horseback from Canfield to Danbury, but returned in a two-wheeled carriage, driving one horse before the other. The journey, a distance of five hundred and thirty miles, occupied eleven days.

In 1828 the merchants of Canfield were three, Alson Kent, Eli T. Boughton, and William Hogg.

Boughton came here a young man. He was a tailor by trade. As a merchant he continued to do a fair business for many years. He died in Canfield. His first wife was a daughter of Comfort S. Mygatt, and his second the widow of Ensign Church.

Alson Kent came to this place from Ravenna, and was in business several years.

William Hogg came from Petersburg and was a fairly successful merchant. A store built by him is now a dwelling, owned by Charles French.

C. S. Mygatt, son of Comfort S., was born in Canfield in 1815. In 1833 he began business with the firm of Lockwood, Mygatt & Co., dealers in general merchandise. From that date until 1860 he was in business here as a merchant, part of the time in partnership. Mr. Mygatt is still a resident of his native town.

Among others who have been merchants in Canfield, and are still residents of the place, are William Schmick, John Sanzenbacher, and Pierpont Edwards. For particulars see their biographies.

CANFIELD'S MERCHANTS.

Below we briefly mention the firms now doing business in Canfield, beginning at the store situated on the corner northwest of the center of the township and proceeding south to the courthouse, crossing the street and asking the reader to accompany us down on the other side:

W. H. Kyle, dealer in hardware, etc., began business in 1878 in the corner store formerly occupied by C. S. Mygatt as a grocery. Betts & Sons manufacture and deal in pumps in a part of the same building.

Truesdale & Kirk, who have an extensive stock of dry goods and general merchandise, began business in Schmick's block in 1876. The senior member of this firm, Dr. J. Truesdale, began keeping a general store in 1859 in Odd Fellow's block, having James McClelland as partner, the style of the firm being McClelland & Truesdale. Three years later McClelland went out, and Dr. Truesdale continued business alone till 1867, and then formed a partnership with Charles E. Boughton, the name of the firm being Truesdale & Boughton. The partnership continued three years, and in 1870 Mr. J. C. Kirk became the Doctor's partner. Mr. Kirk is a native of Berlin township, this county, and began his business life as a clerk in 1866, at the age of seventeen.

Hollis & Brother, dealers in stoves and hardware, have been in business since 1860. G. H. Hollis began in 1857, and was joined by his brother, R. S. Hollis, in 1860. They were burned out in 1867, after which occurrence they built the store they now occupy. Lynn Brothers, dealers in drugs, groceries, and notions, commenced in 1873. The firm consists of Messrs. G. F. & E. D. Lynn, both young men and natives of the township. They are doing a good business. The store which they occupy had been previously used by Gee & Blythe, who were in the same business.

Samuel Ewing opened his meat market in 1878 in the shop owned by the widow Lynn.

G. Fishel, dealer in confectionery, tobacco, cigars, ice cream, etc., commenced in 1877.

George Bartman, repairer and dealer in clocks, has been at work in this place over twenty years.

G. Rupright, grocer, bought out John Miller in 1864. He moved to Canfield village from a farm in the southeastern part of the township.

A. G. Arnold began the furniture business about fifteen years ago. He is now agent for Eli Creps, and does business in the store built and now owned by Robert Hole, of Salem.

G. W. Shellhorn, manufacturer and dealer in boots and shoes, came to Canfield in 1853 from Summit county, and purchased of Henry Hoffman the store formerly occupied by G. G. Weare.

J. O. Corll, druggist, began in November, 1879, having bought the store of Dr. W. M. Corll. He keeps a large stock of first-class goods, both drugs and groceries, and aims to meet all the wants of his rapidly increasing list of customers.

H. B. Brainerd, tailor, came to Canfield in October, 1828, and began working at his trade, which he still continues to follow. Mr. Brainerd was born at Saratoga Springs, New York, in 1808. He came to Ohio in 1811 with his father, George Brainerd, who settled in Boardman. There are four survivors of this family, viz: Henry, Liberty, Trumbull county; Mrs. Eliza Davidson, Boardman; John H., Cuyahoga Falls, Summit county; and Horace B., Canfield. George Brainerd, the father, died in 1870 at the age of ninety-two. Mrs. Brainerd died in 1824 aged forty-four. H. B. Brainerd served his apprenticeship in Cleveland when that place was but a small village. He acted as insurance agent in Canfield about thirty-five years.

S. K. Crooks began the harness business in 1861. This he still continues in connection with dealing in grain and feed. He occupies the store formerly John Metzal's meat shop. The building was erected for an office and occupied for some time by John Wetmore, revenue collector.

John Dodson, dealer in groceries, books, stationery, etc., commenced business in Canfield in 1859. He has moved several times, but has been in his present store since 1868. The building was formerly a cigar factory. In 1881 Mr. Dodson began building a large and commodious store, two stories, 59x19 feet, which he intends to occupy as a store as soon as it is completed, at the same time carrying on business in his present quarters.

Ira H. Bunnell, manufacturer and dealer in saddles, harness, and trunks, commenced in 1870 in the building he now occupies. Mr. Bunnell was born in Canfield township in 1822. His father, Charles A. Bunnell, came here quite early and was a carpenter by trade. Mr. Bunnell has served as justice of the peace several years.

At present there is but one store in operation on the east side of Broad street until Main street is reached, and that one is the grocery and saloon of J. P. Saddler, who began business in 1880.

Pierpont Edwards had a well-filled store north of the Congregational church, but closed out his business in 1881.

M. V. B. King, druggist, Church block, corner of Main and Broad streets, has been in his present business since May, 1878. He succeeded I. W. Kirk, grocer and postmaster. Mr. King was appointed postmaster in 1879.

Edwards & Dyball, dealers in dry goods and general merchandise, commenced in May, 1881, succeeding P. Edwards. They occupy a store in the Independent Order of Odd Fellows' block.

TAVERNS.

Who kept the first tavern in Canfield we have not learned. In early days every house was a "house of entertainment," and new arrivals were made welcome and treated to the best the house afforded.

Cook Fitch came to Canfield in 1802. For some years he kept tavern north of Main street, on the east side of the road—the fourth house north of the corner where the brick block stands. He was a quiet, straight-forward man, and kept a good house, which was a stopping place for the Cleveland and Pittsburg stages.

The brick hotel, now known as the American house, was built by Joel Keck. M. L. Edwards kept hotel a number of years in a frame hotel, afterwards burned, which occupied the site of the American house. The American, under the management of Ira M. Twiss, is proving very popular.

L. L. Bostwick enlarged his father's dwelling, converted it into a public house, and acted as landlord a number of years. The house is still known as the Bostwick house.

Besides the American and the Bostwick, Canfield has two other hotels : Canfield house, H. Hoffman, and the Union house, Christian Patterman.

BANKING.

Canfield has no National bank, or savings institution. Van Hyning & Co. commenced banking in 1871. The stock company originally consisted of fourteen members, which number is now reduced to seven. In 1873 they erected the bank building which they now occupy. The names of the stockholders are as follow: Henry Van Hyning, president ; Peter Gee, cashier; Eben Newton, Hosea Hoover, Warren Hine, Giles Van Hyning, and S. W. Brainerd.

TANNERY AND BELT MANUFACTORY.

The leading manufacturing interest in Canfield is represented by the firm of J. Sanzenbacher

& Co. The history of this industry, briefly sketched, is as follows: In 1865 John Sanzenbacher bought of F. A. Brainard his tannery, and commenced work in it. The tannery at the time of its purchase had a capacity for dressing about five hundred hides per year. Mr. Sanzenbacher enlarged the building, and doubled the amount of work done. About 1865 he ceased tanning, and commenced the manufacture of leather belting. In 1867 he disposed of the building and machinery to Royal Collar. In 1869 Mr. Sanzenbacher again engaged in the making of belts in the house which he had formerly occupied as a dwelling. In October, 1869, he formed a partnership with Pierpont Edwards, who is still a member of the firm. Frank Schauweker was one of the firm from 1872 to 1876. In 1872 was erected the tannery and belt factory now in operation. The capacity of the works was about five thousand hides per annum, but in 1879 an addition was made to the main building, 81 x 42 feet, and the amount of work considerably increased. Until 1876 all of the stock was worked up into belts. Since that time the manufacturers have been, making a speciality of harness leather. This firm sends and receives more freight than all the rest of the town combined. They pay to the railroad company about $2,000 a year on freight received. Employment is given to twenty men on an average, and the pay roll amounts to $200 per week. The proprietors have thus far found a ready market for all of their products, and their establishment has gained a reputation for first-class work.

CLEWELL'S SAW-MILL AND LUMBER YARD.

In 1854 J. H. Clewell and Eben Newton purchased of John Wetmore his saw-mill and lumber yard and began business. Mr. Clewell soon bought out Judge Newton's share, and then went into partnership with Warren Hine for several years. Mr. Hine sold his interest to Frederick Whittlesey, who continued the business with Mr. Clewell a short time. Since 1867 the business has been carried on by Mr. Clewell alone. He has recently built an addition to the mill and is doing a larger business than ever, manufacturing and dealing in all kinds of house furnishing lumber.

STAR FLOURING MILL.

This mill was built in 1879 by J. and C. W.

Edmund P. Tanner

Harroff. From them it was purchased in 1880, by Stafford & Calvin, who are doing a good business. About twenty barrels of flour are produced daily.

CARRIAGE MAKING.

Matthias Swank was extensively engaged in the manufacture of wagons and carriages for a number of years. Beginning in 1835 he continued the business until his death in 1881. At one time he employed from fifteen to twenty men and turned out a large amount of work yearly. His son, E. C. Swank, now carries on the business at the old stand on East Main street.

THE COUNTY SEAT AND ITS REMOVAL.

The county of Mahoning was created by act of the Legislature in the winter session of 1845-46, and Canfield, its geographical center, fixed upon as the county seat. This good fortune was a source of much satisfaction and pride to the citizens of Canfield. It gave increased value to real estate, and made the town of more importance every way. The court-house was erected in 1847-48. The first court was held in it in 1848. The jail was built in 1850.

For a time all was harmonious; Canfield was happy; the county was satisfied, and men came to Canfield, very naturally and properly, to transact their legal business, to patronize the merchants and hotel-keepers, to arrange for caucuses and conventions, and carry out political programmes. Meanwhile Youngstown was getting on in the world at a rapid rate. In 1860 the town had about three thousand inhabitants; in 1870, eight thousand. With prosperity Youngstown became avaricious. Canfield had no iron furnaces and her growing rival was soon far, far ahead in point of wealth and commercial importance. Youngstown became gleeful, Canfield grew despondent. What were the reasons? Let us glance back a little and investigate. Possibly one might have seen in Youngstown and vicinity little groups of magnates occasionally conferring together in whispers. Had Canfield heard those whispers? Did she suddenly become aware of the familiar fact that big fishes eat up little ones and fear for her own safety? Perhaps. But Youngstown did not long talk in whispers. Her word became murmured, then boldly spoken, then shouted, "We're going to have the county seat!" She at

length proclaimed it in stentorian tones. Canfield was a little taken aback, to be sure, but then, she was possessed of Spartan pluck, and assuming as fierce an attitude as was possible she defiantly uttered the words, "Let's see you get it!"

Youngstown got it; Canfield survived the shock as well as could reasonably be expected. We need not here repeat the arguments that were made pro and con, or otherwise stir up troubles now irrevocably settled. In 1874-75 the Legislature took action upon the matter; in 1876 Youngstown became the county seat of Mahoning.

INCORPORATION.

Canfield village was incorporated by act of the Legislature in 1849, Warren Hine, John Clark, H. B. Brainerd and John Wetmore incorporators. The first election was held in April, 1849. L. L. Bostwick was chosen mayor; H. B. Brainerd, recorder; and Charles Frethy, John Clark, William B. Ferrell, M. Swank, and Thomas Hansom, trustees. A list of the mayors and recorders follows:

Mayors—1850-51, John Wetmore; 1852, Nathan Hardman; 1853-57, J. B. Blocksom; 1858, William B. Dawson; 1859-67, F. G. Servis; 1868-71, H. G. Ruggles; 1872-77, M. H. Burky; 1878, M. V. B. King; 1879, J. S. Roller; 1880-82, S. E. Dyball.

Recorders—1850-51, Thaddeus Foot, Jr.; 1852-53, H. B. Brainerd; 1854, B. S. Hine; 1855-57, E. G. Canfield; 1858, William Neir; 1859, H. H. Edsall; 1860, G. G. Weare; 1861-65, John M. Edwards; 1866-69, T. L. Carroll; 1870-71, C. S. Mygatt; 1872, H. B. Brainerd, C. S. Mygatt; 1873-74, J. C. Kirk; 1875-76, I. H. Bunnell; 1877, W. H. Mygatt; 1878-82, C. S. Mygatt.

CEMETERIES.

Soon after the settlement began, a graveyard was laid out east of the center, which is now the principal cemetery of the township. The spot is a pretty one, and its appearance has been much improved of recent years by the labor of loving hands. Here repose the bones of the founders of Canfield; peaceful be their rest after their generous toil! In this quiet spot has been laid all that was mortal of several men whose talents and energies achieved for them during their lifetime, honor, respect, and applause. The resting place of men whose reputation is widespread and National, the Canfield cemetery should ever be fondly cared for and protected by the living.

Many costly monuments have been erected during the past few years, and they present a marked contrast to the rude stones and half effaced inscriptions which mark the graves of the earlier settlers. This is fitting and proper; and is but another indication that the wealth and prosperity, for which they formerly labored, have been realized. It is less difficult for sons and daughters of to-day to procure a costly monument for the graves of their departed parents, than those of sixty years ago to purchase the lowly and humble headstones, which are here so numerous. After all, what does it matter to the dead, whether a lofty column of polished granite stands above them, or only a plain slab of unlettered sandstone.

> "The leaves of the oak and the willow shall fade,
> Be scattered around and together be laid ;
> And the old and the young, and the low and the high,
> Shall moulder to dust and together shall lie."

The next largest and next oldest graveyard is situated about one mile north of the village, and has been the burying place of the German population since their first advent to the township. Here, too, are many tasteful stones and monuments; and the shadow of the church where they were faithful worshipers for many a year, many—the aged, the sick, and the infirm—have at length found peaceful repose, while not a few in the morn of life and the bloom of youthful promise have been laid away. But "All that breathe will share their destiny."

There is another graveyard in the township, near the spot where the old Disciple church stood, northwest of the center.

CHURCH HISTORY.

THE CONGREGATIONAL CHURCH.

This is the oldest religious organization in Canfield. The church was organized April 27, 1804, on "the accommodation plan," by Revs. Joseph Badger and Thomas Robbins, from the Connecticut Missionary society. John and Sarah Everett, Nathaniel and Hepsibah Chapman, Jonathan Sprague, Lydia Doud, Mary Gilson, Mary Brainard, and Lavina Collar were admitted to membership.

The first baptisms recorded took place October 14, 1804, when three persons were baptized, Jarvis Weeks and Ammial, children of Aaron and Lavina Collar, and Maria, daughter of Jonathan and Sarah Sprague.

Services were held in private houses and school-houses until a church building was erected. The records are not continuous, but from them it is learned that Revs. Horace Smith and Mr. Curtis in 1818 and in 1822 were supplying the congregations of Ellsworth, Boardman, and Canfield. From 1818 to 1828 the names of Revs. Dwight, Coe, Vallandingham, Hughes, and Sullivan, are mentioned as ministering here.

In 1820, as the result of a subscription to which citizens of all denominations contributed, a house of worship was erected in the village on the east side of the Public square—a good substantial frame building which is to-day the finest church in the town. The building committee were Comfort S. Mygatt, Cook Fitch, William Stoddard, James Doud, Edmund P. Tanner, David Hine, and Erastus Chidester. The terms of subscription are somewhat peculiar, some agreeing to pay the amounts opposite their names in labor, others in building materials, others in produce, etc. Aaron Collar subscribed $75, to be paid "one-third in produce, one-third in boards, and the remainder in whiskey." The largest subscriptions were as follow: Comfort S. Mygatt, $500; heirs of E. Wadsworth, $225; Elisha Whittlesey, $200; James Doud, $150; Eli T. Boughton, $125; Cook Fitch, $100; Aaron Collar, Rhoda Wadsworth, David Hine, $75 each; and Jerusha Boughton, Edmund P. Tanner, Myron Sackett, William Dean, Adam Turner, Philo Beardsley, Herman Canfield, Mabel Scofield, Thomas Jones, $50 each.

Rev. William O. Stratton was the officiating clergyman from 1830 to 1835. In the latter year occurred a division which resulted in the organization of the Presbyterian church in Canfield. The Presbyterian portion withdrew and organized a church of their own, while the Congregationalists became the owners of the church property. The names of the pastors who have served here are as follow: William Beardsley, 1836; David Metcalf, 1837; Edward Evans, 1839-44; Davis R. Barker, 1845-47; L. B. Lane, 1848-49; Willard Burr, 1849; John A. Allen, 1857-59; S. W. Pierson, 1860-62; J. W. C. Pike,

1863-64; Tertius S. Clark, 1866-69; Mortimer Smith, 1870-71; Samuel Manning, 1871-74; W. S. Peterson, 1875-76; R. A. Davis, 1880; R. G. McClelland, 1881.

There have been several intervals during which the church had no pastor. During the most of its history the pastors of this church have preached here a portion of the time only. Latterly, however, the pastors have served here all of their time.

The membership is about thirty at present. There is an interesting Sabbath-school of fifty or more.

THE PRESBYTERIAN CHURCH.*

This church was originally established on the plan of union adopted by the general assembly of 1801. It was organized April 27, 1804. The church consisted of nine members, and they adopted the confession of faith and covenant that were commonly received in the Congregational churches in the vicinity as their standards of doctrine and discipline. It had been their practice to hold meetings on the Sabbath from the early settlement of the town, and clergymen of all orthodox denominations were invited to preach when present. Most of the inhabitants having received a religious education usually attended, and when they did not enjoy preaching they habitually attended their lay meetings, which were regarded as interesting and useful. Meetings were first held in a large log schoolhouse that stood on the corner of a burying-ground. Afterwards in the summer seasons they met in partially finished houses and in barns, until a house was finally erected for the use of both meetings and schools northeast of the center. During these early periods of their existence a great degree of brotherly love existed in the church. In the autumn of 1831 the church was visited with an interesting and precious revival of religion which resulted in adding some twenty-five members. This precious revival continued from August until December. This church enjoyed the labors at different periods of the following ministers: Rev. Messrs. Badger, Robbins, Chapman, Wick, A. Scott, I. Scott, Leslie, Derrow, Hanford, Curtis, Field, Dwight, Cooke, Coe, Smith, Duncan, Wright, Hughes, Beal, Vallandigham, Stone, Sullivan, Lathrop,

*By Rev. William Dickson.

Bouton, Treat, Woods, Satterfield, Sample, Stratton, and McCombs. Mr. Stratton was the first minister that was installed pastor of this church. They frequently attempted to obtain a settled minister, but failed, although they were remarkably united in their counsels and prompt in the payment of their pecuniary obligations. Mr. Stratton first preached as a licentiate in connection with the presbytery of New York. September, 1827, he returned to New York, and was there ordained and finally installed pastor of the church in October, 1828.

The congregation remained under the government of the plan of union in 1801 until 1835. The presbytery of Beaver, with which it was connected by a special resolution, requested those churches under their care, that were organized under that plan, to change their organization to that of regularly constituted Presbyterian churches. The presbytery repeated their recommendations or injunction, and the pastor (Mr. Stratton) and the Presbyterian portion of the church and congregation felt themselves constrained in conscience, and in obedience to the authority of their presbytery, to carry out the recommendation, although they were soon led to believe it would result in their separation from the Congregational part of the society, with whom they had been long happily connected. From them they accordingly separated, and on the 22d day of January, 1835, the pastor and fifty members organized themselves into a regular Presbyterian church, adopting the confession of faith and catechism of the Presbyterian church in the United States as their exclusive standards of doctrine and discipline. The congregation met for divine worship in the house of Mr. C. Frithy during one season, their numbers constantly increasing. With great energy and personal effort they united together and erected the house of worship they have since occupied. On the first Monday of January, 1838, Rev. William O. Stratton, the pastor, submitted to the congregation a request that they would consent to a dissolution of his pastoral connection with the congregation. The congregation, however, not considering the reasons assigned sufficient, and unwilling to part with him, did not give their assent. Mr. Stratton resolved to travel as an agent for the Western Theological seminary for some months, and during his absence engaged the Rev. William McCombs to supply his pulpit. On his return the following June, Mr. Stratton applied to the presbytery for the dissolution of his pastoral connection, which, with the consent of the congregation, was accordingly done.

In August of the same year a unanimous call was made out for Mr. McCombs, which he accepted, and in April, 1839, he was installed pastor of the congregation. After a successful pastorate of several years Mr. McCombs resigned, and then the church secured as his successor in the pastoral office Rev. James Price, an eloquent and able minister. Mr. Price was succeeded by Mr. J. G. Reaser, now of St. Louis, Missouri. Dr. William G. March succeeded Mr. Reaser, and, after a successful pastorate of about twelve years, resigned to take charge of the Presbyterian church of Marysville, Ohio. Rev. J. P. Irwin succeeded Mr. March, and remained pastor of the church for about eleven years. The present pastor is Rev. Dr. William Dickson, who was brought up in the congregation which he now serves as pastor.

THE GERMAN REFORMED LUTHERAN CHURCH.

This church was organized a few years prior to 1810. The first meetings were held at the houses of Peter Lynn, George Lynn, and other members. Among the first members were John Neff, Conrad Neff, Peter and George Lynn, John Lynn, Jacob Ritter, Philip Borts, John Harding, Henry Ohl, Jacob Frank, Simeon Gilbert, Benjamin Butt, Philip Stitel, Charles Gilbert, Philip Arner, Martin Dustman, Henry Neff, David Ohl, Henry Brunstetter, Henry Crum, and others, for the most part with their wives and families. The first pastor of the Lutheran congregation was Rev. Henry Stough. His successors have been Revs. Henry Hewett, Becker, Fixeisen, Long, Smith, Allbright, and Miller. Of the German Reformed the pastors have been Revs. Peter Mahensmith, Charles Zwisler, Henry Sonnedecker, J. B. Ruhl, G. M. Allbright, and J. B. Zumpe.

The first church building erected in Canfield was the German Reformed and Lutheran, built in October, 1810, of hewn logs, 40x50 feet in dimensions. It was situated one mile north of the village. The house remained in an unfinished condition three or four years. It was then completed and continued to be occupied by the two congregations until April, 1845, when it was destroyed by fire. A new and more substantial house was built during the summer and autumn on the side of the road opposite the site of the old one. In 1857 the congregation placed a pipe organ in this church at a cost of $800, which is believed to be the first organ of its size ever placed in a country church in this county.

Father Mahnensmith and Father Hewitt ministered in the church for many years. Father Becker also served a long term. In the early years of the settlement the Canfield church was the religious home of the church-going Germans for miles around.

For fifty years or more the services were conducted exclusively in the German language. The needs of the rising generation have caused change, and of late years the services are half the time in English.

The membership originally was probably about fifty. Hundreds have been members, many of whom are now dead, and many more in other parts of the country. The present number of members is one hundred and ninety.

Mrs. Barbara Kline, a member of the society, bequeathed an endowment fund of $500 to this church, the interest of which can be used annually in making repairs about the cemetery or church building. Another member, Philip Lynn, bequeathed $680 to be used in repairs or in building a new church.

Thus the congregations can make all ordinary and necessary repairs for years without resorting to a tax upon the members.

ST. STEPHEN'S EPISCOPAL CHURCH.

Previous to 1834 Canfield, Poland, and Boardman Episcopalians formed but one church. In that year a subscription paper was headed by Curtis Beardsley with $100 and circulated by him for the purpose of obtaining funds with which to build a church at Canfield village. Alson Kent, Stanley C. Lockwood, and Curtis Beardsley were chosen as building committee. Work was commenced in 1835, and the house completed in 1836, at a cost of $1,450. The land on which it stood was donated by Hon. Judson Canfield. September 27, 1836, the church was consecrated by Bishop Charles P. McIlvaine, of the diocese of Ohio, by the name of St. Stephen's church, Canfield, Ohio. The leading members of this church at the time of its

J. M. Nash

Sherman Kinney

organization were: Curtis Beardsley and family, Stanley C. Lockwood and family, Joseph Bassett and family, Azor Ruggles and family, Mrs. Mary Tanner, Mrs. Kezele Wadsworth, Miss Olive Landon, Abiram Squier and wife, Lyman Warner and wife, Miriam Squier and her mother, Mrs. Galetzah Hunt, Joseph R. Bostwick, Mrs. Mary Mitchell, and others.

The ministers were the same who officiated at Boardman. The church continued in a prosperous condition for several years. A large number of members were lost by death and removals, and the church building being considered unsafe, on account of defects in its architecture, in 1866 it was sold at auction and torn down. Since that time the church has had no regular preaching, though several ministers have officiated here occasionally.

A Sunday-school was organized in 1829 by Curtis Beardsley, superintendent, who continued to act in that capacity thirty years.

METHODIST EPISCOPAL CHURCH.

From a historical sketch of this church in Canfield, prepared by Dr. Jackson Truesdale in 1869, the following extracts are made:

No early records of the society are known to exist. Canfield, as well as the whole Northwest Territory, was embraced in the boundaries of the Baltimore conference up to the formation of the Ohio conference in 1812, when it formed a part of that and so continued until 1825, when it fell within the limits of the Pittsburg conference. It is now one of the appointments of the Erie conference. It is not known who first preached a Methodist sermon in Canfield, but the honor doubtless belongs either to Rev. Henry Shewell or to Dr. Shadrach Bostwick. The former settled in Deerfield in 1802 and the latter in 1803, and made and filled many appointments throughout the new settlements. Whether Methodist preaching was regularly sustained in Canfield from 1803 to 1820 cannot be learned; but it is probable that ministers sent to labor on the Western circuits preached more or less stately here. As nearly as can be ascertained, the names of these early preachers were as follow: Revs. Shadrach Bostwick, David Best, J. A. Shackleford, R. R. Roberts (afterwards bishop), James Watts, C. Reynolds, A. Daniels, T. Divers, Job Guest, William Butler, J. Charles, I. M. Hanson, J. Decellum, James Ewen,

Thomas J. Crockwell, J. Somerville, James McMahan, John Solomon, Oliver Carver, Lemuel Lane, John Waterman, Shadrach Ruark, Curtis Goddard, John P. Kent, D. D. Davidson, Ezra Booth, Calvin Ruter, and John Stewart.

In 1820 James McMahan and Ezra Booth were sent by the Ohio conference to the "Mahoning circuit." This year the first society was organized in Canfield, consisting of Rev. S. Bostwick, wife and sister, Comfort Starr and wife, Ansel Beeman and wife, and Ezra Hunt. In 1821 the well-known Rev. Charles Elliott and Dennis Goddard traveled the circuit. In 1822 it went for the first time by the name of Youngstown circuit, and was traveled by William Tipton and Albert Richardson; in 1823 by Samuel Adams and Sylvester Dunham; in 1824 by John Somerville and Alfred Brunson; in 1825 by Edward H. Taylor and W. R. Babcock; in 1826 by Robert C. Hatton and Robert Hopkins.

Up to this time preaching and society meetings were held in a little frame school-house which stood a little east of the center. In 1826, with some outside help, the society erected a commodious house of worship at an expense of about $1,200. It was located near the site of the present building on the land of Dr. Bostwick. The building was of brick with galleries on three sides, and was known as the "Bethel chapel." The principal contributors towards the erection of the house were Dr. Bostwick, who gave something over $350; Edward Wadsworth, $180; Elihu Warner, Philo Chidester, John Moore, Ezra Hunt, Josiah Wetmore, Erastus Chidester, Mabel Scoville, Elisha Whittlesey, Eben Newton, George Wadsworth, J. R. Church, and several others who contributed sums of $75 and under.

The ministers who served the society from 1826 to 1836 were R. C. Hatton, Samuel Adams, Billings O. Plympton, Edmund W. Seehon, Richard Armstrong, A. Brunson, T. Carr, Cornelius Jones, John Luccock, Philip Green, Caleb Brown, David Preston, John L. Holmes, John W. Hill, B. Preston, Thomas Stubbs, and H. Elliott.

In 1836 the Erie conference was formed, and Canfield included within its limits.

In 1837 Dr. Shadrach Bostwick died at his residence in Canfield, having lived here thirty years. He is mentioned in the History of the

Methodist Church as a good man and a useful preacher.

From 1836 until the present time Canfield has at different periods been a part of Youngstown, Poland, and Ellsworth circuits, and at times has given name to the circuit in which it was embraced.

In 1860–61, the old Bethel chapel having become somewhat dilapidated from age, the society, after some misgivings as to their ability, concluded to tear down the structure, and partly with the same material erect a new one. The first cost, exclusive of labor performed by members gratis, was from $1,600 to $1,700. The building committee were Hosea Hoover, Horace Hunt, and Jackson Truesdale. The principal contributors were Hosea Hoover, Jackson Truesdale, Samuel, William, and Abram Cassiday, Chester Hine, Hon. Eben Newton, Horace Hunt, Abram Kline, Fanny Church, and others. The new church was dedicated with appropriate ceremonies in June, 1861, by Rev. Samuel Gregg, the presiding elder of Ravenna district. A good cabinet organ was purchased in the winter of 1865–66. Mrs. Rhoda Hine was mainly instrumental in procuring the means with which to purchase it. In the summer of 1869 a dwelling house was purchased for a parsonage at a cost of $1,500. The society is now in a prosperous condition. There are about one huundred members.

THE DISCIPLES.

As the Disciples of Canfield were originally an off-shoot from the Baptists, it is necessary, in writing their history, to take a glance at their predecessors. January 12, 1822, a Baptist church was formed at the house of David Hays. Thomas Miller was the officiating clergyman, and Deacon Samuel Hayden, William Hayden, and John Lane, of Youngstown, and Elijah Canfield, of Palmyra, were present as council. The church was moderately Calvinistic, but progressive in spirit. For some years meetings were held in a small log building near the spot where the Disciples afterwards built a church. The principal members were David Hays and family, William Dean and family, Myron Sackett, H. Edsall, James Turner, and Mr. Wood. William Hayden became a preacher and ministered to this church. In the winter of 1827–28 Walter Scott came into the community and in a memorable sermon, preached at the house of Simeon Sackett, set forth the plea of the ancient Gospel and gained many converts to his then new and novel doctrines. The most of the Baptists became converted, and during this winter were organized into a Disciples church. A comfortable frame building was soon erected in the northwestern part of the township, and the new church increased in members and influence. In 1830 a large addition was received by the admission of several who had hitherto styled themselves Bible Christians.

As many of the Disciples resided near the village this church gave permission to them to form a separate organization. Therefore, in 1847, about twenty associated together in that relation, and soon built, at the center, the neat and comfortable little church which is still their place of worship. J. W. Lamphear organized this church. J. M. Caldwell and Andrew Flick were chosen elders, and Walter Clark and John Flick deacons. Among those who have labored here we find the names of Elders Pow, Applegate, Belton, Phillips, Errett, Hillock, White, Green, Van Horn, Rogers, Morrison, and Baker.

In 1867, the most of the original members of the church in the northwest of the township having gone to their reward, after struggling in feebleness for a while the remaining members united with the church at the center. This union took place October 6, 1867.

The church is now prosperous and is receiving many additions. It has some very earnest members whose efforts have been of great service in securing harmony and promoting the welfare of the organization.

SCHOOLS.

The first school taught in the township was in the winter of 1800 and 1801, Caleb Palmer, teacher. The term was three months. The school-house stood about a mile and a quarter east of the center.

Miss Getia Bostwick was an early school-teacher and taught in an unfinished room in the house of Judson Canfield. Benjamin Carter was also one of the early teachers.

Miss Olive Landon, for many years a faithful laborer in the schools of Canfield township, taught in early years in a small log building about two miles south of the center. She was a very efficient teacher, well versed in the art of governing and educating.

In 1806 Elisha Whittlesey taught school in the house where Caleb Palmer taught the first school in the township.

For many years schools were few and the advantages of the rising generation for obtaining education were consequently small.

The Mahoning academy while in existence did much to advance the condition of the common schools by providing them with competent teachers.

The village schools were often conducted in a slip-shod manner, and not until 1867 was grading carried out in any systematic manner. Up to that year the village school had been for a long period in two divisions, and, of course, good work could not be done, no matter how faithful the teachers were, while there was so large a number of classes that but a few minutes could be given to each recitation.

A meeting was held July 27, 1867, to consider whether the district would adopt the union school law or not. The question was decided in the affirmative by a unanimous vote. A board of education was elected, as follows: J. W. Canfield and J. Sonnedecker for three years; W. G. Marsh and I. A. Justice for two years; G. R. Crane and P. Edwards for one year. At the next meeting W. G. Marsh was chosen president of this board, J. W. Canfield treasurer, and I. A. Justice secretary.

September 9, 1867, S. B. Reiger was chosen principal of the high school, Miss Sarah E. Edwards assistant, Miss Amanda Wilson to take charge of the second grade, and Miss Paulina Test teacher of the primary department. It was voted that tuition be charged pupils attending the school when they resided outside of the district. The academy building was occupied for school purposes until a new house could be erected.

In 1870, plans for a new school building having been completed, work was begun upon it. In the spring of 1871 it was ready for occupancy. The building is of brick, two stories, large and well-furnished, and forms an ornament to the town. The structure, grounds, and furnishings cost about $30,000, including interest upon bonds.

The principals of the school have been as follow: S. R. Reigel, 1867-68; W. R. Smiley and Ashael Cary, 1869; Milton Fording, 1870-75; Charles J. Fillius, 1875-78; E. C. Hitchcock, 1878; B. E. Helman, 1879-80. In the fall of 1881 H. S. Foote took charge and is making the school interesting and profitable. His assistant, Miss Ellen Scobie, who has labored in this school several years, has won golden opinions for her work. Messrs. Fillius and Helman did much to raise the standard of the school and improve the course of instruction.

When the new normal school begins its work, it would seem that Canfield's educational advantages will be great.

MAHONING ACADEMY.

This was a flourishing institution, which perished in the time of the war. An organization was effected in 1855, the academy building erected in 1856, and the school incorporated in 1857. David Hine, A. M., a graduate of Williams college in Massachusetts, was the leader in establishing the school; he became its principal, and continued in that position until the institution was abandoned. Mr. Hine was a native of this township, and a man of fine literary attainments. He proved a popular and faithful instructor, and some men who are high in professional ranks remember with gratitude their early teacher. Associated with him for a time was Mr. P. T. Caldwell, a young man of ability and scholarship.

From a catalogue issued in October, 1860, it is learned that the number of pupils in attendance during the year was two hundred and forty. Connected with the school was a literary society known as the "Adelphic Union."

The old academy building is now owned by Judge Newton, and occupied by Richard Brown as a dwelling.

NORTHEASTERN OHIO NORMAL SCHOOL.

A corporation was formed in 1881 after much discussion of the subject by a number of the friends of education, and it is expected that the school will be put in operation during the year 1882. A board of nine trustees has been elected, viz: Hon. G. Van Hyning, Hon. J. R. Johnston, Rev. William Dickson, Dr. A. W. Calvin, H. A. Manchester, Esq., David Clugston, George F. Lynn, Hiram N. Lynn, and Russel F. Starr.

Hon. Eben Newton, to whom the court-house and the land it occupies reverted when it ceased to be used by the county, has generously donated the property to the trustees. It is the intention to have the building thoroughly repaired and fitted up in a manner suitable for the wants of such a school. Canfield is an excellent location for an institution of learning, and no doubt this institution will be grandly successful.

NEWSPAPERS.*

The first printing office in Canfield was established May 9, 1846, by James and Clate Herrington, of Warren. They were practical printers, and when the county seat of Mahoning was located here, the Mahoning Index, a Democratic newspaper, was started. In January, 1849, the Index office was sold to John R. Church, a leading man in the Democratic party. Under Church's administration, the paper was edited by several prominent persons, among whom were: J. M. Edwards, H. H. McChestney, and A. T. Walling, the latter now being a congressman from the Pickaway district. The Index office was run by John R. Church until September, 1851, when it was burned and nothing at all saved from the ruins.

In the winter of 1852 the Mahoning Sentinel was established by an association, Ira Norris editor. The Sentinel was also Democratic in politics. Mr. Norris continued as editor until 1854, when a change in the ownership of the paper took place. H. M. Fowler had printed the Sentinel for the association up to the time of this change. John Woodruff purchased both the office and the materials, but in 1855 John M. Webb became sole editor and proprietor of the paper and continued the publication until 1858, when W. B. Dawson purchased it. Mr. Dawson continued to publish the Sentinel until the spring of 1860. John M. Webb then re-purchased it and moved the office to Youngstown.

In the spring of 1860 Hon. Elisha Whittlesey induced John Weeks, of Medina, to come here and start the Herald. The Herald was a small sheet, subscription price $1 per year, and Republican in politics. Its publication was continued with a number of changes until 1865. At one time it was owned by John Weeks, then by Thomas Menary, Menary & Musser, John S. Roller, and others. In 1865 Weeks re-purchased the paper and took as a partner Ed. E. Fitch.

*Prepared by H. M. Fowler, editor of the Dispatch.

Mr. Fitch finally purchased Mr. Weeks' share and changed the name of the paper to the Canfield Herald. He enlarged it in 1870, and in 1872 sold out to McDonald & Son. They changed the name to the Mahoning County News, and after running the paper eighteen months disposed of it to W. R. Brownlee, who made the News Democratic. In the spring of 1875 Brownlee sold the establishment to Rev. W. S. Peterson, who soon afterward removed to Warren.

Canfield was then without a newspaper from August 3, 1876, till May 1, 1877. At the latter date H. M. Fowler started the Mahoning Dispatch, an independent family journal, devoted to the interests of the working classes. The Dispatch is a five column eight-page paper. It soon attained to eight hundred regular subscribers. In May, 1880, C. C. Fowler became its local editor, and from that time until January, 1882, the circulation was increased to twelve hundred and thirteen subscribers, the largest number of *bona fide* subscribers ever on the books of any newspaper in Canfield.

THE ONION SOCIETY.

What a name for an organization of any sort! Yet the objects of the society were as original as its title, as will be seen from the following, which is copied directly from the secretary's book:

CONSTITUTION OF THE ONION SOCIETY IN CANFIELD.

Article I.

SECTION 1. The oldest person who is, or shall hereafter be, a member of this society, shall be president; and in case of his absence the next oldest shall be president *pro tem.*

SEC. 2. There shall annually be elected a clerk by the members of the society at their first meeting after the cooking of the new crop, which election shall be by ballot.

SEC. 3. There may be an officer appointed by the president when he shall deem the interests of the society require it, known and to be called the cup-bearer, whose duty is sufficiently made known by the title of the office.

Article II.

SEC. 1. The president shall preside at the meetings of the society, preserve order, and see that all the members are duly refreshed.

SEC. 2. The clerk shall record in a book to be kept for that purpose all the votes and proceedings of the society, and such miscellaneous matters as the society or the president may direct. He shall take and keep an accurate roll of the members of the society, which, together with the records shall be produced at each meeting.

Article III.

SEC. 1. Fully persuaded that all well-regulated societies must depend upon a voluntary association of its members, we adopt it as a fundamental principle that no person shall be compelled to become a member of this society.

Dr. A. W. Calvin

SEC. 2. Any member of this society may be at any time suspended or expelled for unbecoming conduct, as a plurality of the members shall deem proper.

Article IV.

SEC. 1. As the object of this association is to feast on the delicious vegetable the name of which stands prominent in the entitling of the society, onions, with their grand helpmate, pork, shall form the principal bill of fare, except that in case of emergency fresh beef or other meat may be substituted for the pork.

SEC. 2. The time of inviting the members shall be optional with the member giving the entertainment, unless for good cause. The president or the society may appoint a meeting, in which case he or they may warn a meeting whenever they please.

SEC. 3. Notice shall be given at least fifteen minutes to each member to repair to the table.

SEC. 4. The members are to be prepared when the lady furnishing the entertainment announces the supper to be ready.

Article V.

SEC. 1. Knowing that on the cultivation of the onion the prosperity of the society much depends, and feeling desirous to give all reasonable encouragement to industry and a suitable tribute to merit, it is ordained that the member who shall first entertain the society on onions of his own raising shall be entitled to a seat for that evening at the right hand of the president.

SEC. 2. Honorable mention shall be made at our meetings of the member who shall raise the largest onion; and on any member requesting a view of his garden, it shall be the duty of the president to attend; or he may appoint a committee, or he may summon the society *en masse.*

We recognize the Onion society in Danbury, Connecticut, as our parent institution.

July 23, 1818. At a meeting of the Onion society of Canfield, at the house of Cooke Fitch, the foregoing constitution was adopted by a unanimous vote of the members present.

The following is a roll of the members of the society with their ages in 1818: Eleazer Gilson, 65; Judson Canfield, 57; Comfort S. Mygatt, 55; Shadrach Bostwick, 49; Herman Canfield, 45; Cyrenus Ruggles, 42; Roger Searl, 42; Cooke Fitch, 42; Joseph Coit, 35; Elisha Whittlesey, 35; John H. Patch, 33; Frederick Wadsworth, 33; William Stoddard, 31; Eli T. Boughton, 31; Eli Booth, 27, Edward Wadsworth, 26.

It would appear that the society had been in existence some time previous to the adoption of the above constitution, as in the roll of members the following note is found: "Elijah Wadsworth, former president of this society, deceased December 30, 1817, aged sixty-nine years in November preceding."

The Onion society grew rapidly, and its reputation became wide-spread. All the leading men of the town came to have a share in its pleasantries and social festivals. Sober judges, busy merchants, merry doctors of law, medicine, and divinity, captains, majors, colonels, generals, as well as untitled farmers, met frequently to feast upon the savory esculent, and enjoy an hour of genuine hearty fun. Meetings were held at the houses of various members more or less frequently, and the utmost good-will and hilarity marked the proceedings. Distinguished visitors from neighboring settlements were often in attendance. Upon the records may be found the names of Joshua R. Giddings, Judge Tod, Colonel Rayen and other prominent men.

The proceedings were characterized by the utmost outward decorum, if we may judge from the records, but with a deep vein of humor underlying all. Committees were frequently appointed to decide who carried off the honors of the table—*i. e.,* ate the biggest supper, and their reports soberly (?) recorded. A seat at the right hand of the president was the reward for a brilliant gastronomic feat.

The Onion society continued in existence many years. The last recorded meetings bear the date 1833. Many are still living who cannot fail to have pleasant reminiscences of their connection with this society.

TEMPERANCE SOCIETY.

In 1832 occurred a general awakening on the subject of temperance. It is said to have originated in sport by a young man proposing to "get up some grand excitement," but as the movement progressed, serious earnestness was the spirit which characterized it. A temperance society was organized, and continued in existence some twenty years, and during that period a large number of names were enrolled upon the pledge. Elihu and Elisha Warner, Charles Frethy, and Edmund P. Tanner were especially active members. The better portion of the community aided the organization, and much good work was accomplished. At times an enthusiastic interest was felt. Among those who were wont to address the meetings we notice that the names of the village preachers have a prominent place.

SOLDIERS' AID SOCIETY.

During the war for the Union the ladies of Canfield showed their patriotism by organizing a society for the aid of the soldiers, and through their labors and generosity much valuable material aid found its way into Federal camps. The society was organized October 30, 1861, and its officers were: Mrs. S. R. Canfield, president; Mrs. E. Newton, vice-president; Miss M. M. Pierson, secretary; Mrs. J. B. Blocksom, assistant secretary; Mrs. F. G. Servis, treasurer; Miss Susan Tomson, assistant treasurer. For their generous efforts they were blessed by the hearts of hundreds of soldiers.

ODD FELLOWS.

A charter was granted January 18, 1850, to Canfield lodge No. 155, Independent Order of Odd Fellows, to the following charter members: William W. Whittlesey, Walter M. Prentice, E. J. Estep, James Powers, and John G. Kyle. The lodge was instituted May 1, 1850, by Most Worthy Grand Master William C. Earl. The first officers were as follow: Walter M. Prentice, N. G.; James Powers, V. G.; E. J. Estep, secretary, and William W. Whittlesey, treasurer. The following were initiated as members on the evening the lodge was instituted: John H. Mill, Nathan Hartman, Walter Blythe, L. L. Bostwick, and William Schmick.

In 1857 the lodge purchased of William Lynn the three-story brick building on the upper floor of which is their hall. The lower floors are rented for a store, offices, etc. The hall is of ample size, and is fitted and furnished tastefully.

Up to the present writing there have been received into the lodge by initiation and by card two hundred and fifty members. The present membership is ninety-three. Several former members of this lodge have withdrawn and joined lodges organized in neighboring towns.

The lodge is in a prosperous condition financially and its membership of a high character. The total amount of property belonging to it is valued at $6,500. From the first this organization has been prosperous. The present officers, elected in July, 1881, are as follow: John Martin, N. G.; J. K. Misner, V. G.; George F. Lynn, secretary; Hosea Hoover, permanent secretary, and J. Truesdale, treasurer. The two officers last named have held their respective offices for a period of twenty-one consecutive years.

THE OIL BUSINESS.

From 1854 to 1863 the cannel coal of the southeastern part of the township was considerably worked for "coal oil." In 1858-59 four large establishments were erected in the south-eastern quarter of the township for the manufacture of oil, at an expense of about $200,000, but the discovery of naturally flowing oil wells drove them out of existence. These establishments were built by Eastern capitalists and for a time the business was carried on "with a rush." The four companies were as follow:

1. The Hartford company; works cost $20,000; the buildings were burned in June, 1860, and rebuilt at an expense of $20,000.

2. The Mahoning company, originally the Buffalo company; cost of works, $75,000.

3. The Mystic, afterwards the New London company; cost $18,000.

4. The Phœnix company; $75,000.

In 1861 the managers of these companies in the order above given were C. H. Parsons, John Wetmore, Mr. Thompson, and A. H. Everett. The Phœnix, the largest of the works, made about seventy-five barrels of oil per week, had thirty-two retorts, and employed thirty-one men. The coal was drawn from the mine by steam-power.

ANECDOTES, INCIDENTS, AND TRADITIONS.

In 1805 occurred one of those mysterious phenomena for which man has striven in vain to account. Archibald Johnston, a settler of 1804, was a man of an intelligent, strong mind, void of bigotry or superstition. He had purchased Nathan Moore's farm and was preparing to move onto it. Returning home one evening he saw what appeared to him to be a burning bush, and something in the vision strongly impressed him that he would die in just six weeks. He told his friends of his conviction, and no arguments could remove it from his mind. He died upon the designated day.

The old well at the center of Canfield is a land-mark. It was built at the exact center of the township for the benefit of the inhabitants of the town. Mr. J. W. Canfield, while looking over some of his grandfather's papers recently, came across the bill for building the well. There were a large number of items in it, but not a great number of articles were specified. One word occurred with such frequency as to cause Mr. Canfield to remark, "It is astonishing how much whiskey it took to make a well in those days!" The chief items of expense, in fact, were a certain number of gallons of whiskey, followed up by many a line of ditto, ditto.

What has been said concerning the wildness of other townships will apply equally well to Canfield in early days. Deer were so numerous that an old lady now living says it was almost as common to see one as it is to see a dog now-a-days. The children were often obliged to be lulled to sleep while the howling of the wolves rang in their ears. Bears were often destructive to stock, though it seems that the young people were never molested by them. James Reed caught a young cub and tamed it. He kept the bear tied to a stake until it was a year old, when it broke loose and escaped.

In the days when the discussion of the slavery question was the all-absorbing topic, Canfield became possessed of a strong anti-slavery element on the one had, and on the other an equally strong pro-slavery party. Of course the bitterest of feeling sprang up between the two, and many hostile, though bloodless, encounters resulted.

The mobbing of Rev. M. R. Robinson, in Berlin, in 1837, is alluded to in the history of that township. On the morning after his rough treatment he appeared early at the house of Mr. Wetmore, south of the village of Canfield, and knocked at the door. Mrs. Wetmore looked out of the window and saw a startling sight. The figure of a man, hatless, with disordered clothing, feathers filling his hair and moving about in the wind, caused the good lady to think, at first, that the devil himself had appeared. However, the family aroused, listened to the stranger's story, and at once took measures for his relief. His soiled garments were removed and William Wetmore provided him with a change of raiment. It being the Sabbath he went with the family to church and there made announcement that he would lecture in the afternoon. The story of his treatment got abroad and a large audience greeted him.

During the same year a Methodist preacher named Miller announced an anti-slavery lecture for one evening, in the Congregational church. Many inhabitants of Canfield thought they had had enough discussion of this subject and proposed to teach Miller a lesson. The result was a disgraceful scene, of which many of the participants afterwards became heartily ashamed.

The evening for the lecture arrived and Miller was present with his wife and son. He had not proceeded far in his speech when he was greeted by a shower of rotten eggs, while hooting and jeering resounded through the house. But this apostle of justice to all the human race was a man of pluck and could not be silenced in this way. He directed his son to come and stand over him with an umbrella, to ward off the unsavory missiles; and thus protected he finished his speech. It had been arranged to seize the speaker as he was leaving the house and then treat him to a coat of tar and feathers. The materials, already prepared, were at hand. But Miller walked from the pulpit and passed down the aisle between two ladies, reaching the door in safety. He sprang into the buggy with Mrs. Miller and drove away at a rapid rate. Attempts were made to catch him as he was entering the carriage, but he was too quick for his persecutors. A fellow caught hold of the hind end of the buggy as it started away and hung on for some distance, but Mrs. Miller made such good use of the whip about his head and ears that he was glad to desist. The son took to the woods and effected his escape. When we consider that the greater part of the above described scenes were enacted in the house of God, we can form some idea of the public sentiment which then prevailed.

But Canfield was not without a strong body of Abolitionists whose conduct was as heroic as that of the opposing element was reprehensible. Among those who befriended and assisted the persecuted fugitive slaves was Jacob Barnes, now deceased, who resided two miles east of the village. His house was a station on the underground railway. In a large covered wagon which he owned he carried many a load of negroes from his house, journeying by night, to Hartford, Trumbull county, where the next station was located.

A MURDER.

In 1826 occurred an unfortunate affair in which a poor fellow lost his life. Archibald McLean, a worthless, drunken shoemaker, became involved in a dispute with Adam Mell and stabbed the latter with a shoe-knife. Mell died from the effects of the wound the next day. His death took place in February, 1826. The stabbing was done in the house occupied by Mell in the village. McLean had his trial, was convicted, and sentenced to the penitentiary for life.

BIOGRAPHICAL,

The following sketches of some of the first proprietors of the township of Canfield are principally compiled from information collected and recorded by Hon. Elisha Whittlesey:

NATHANIEL CHURCH

was a descendant of the fifth generation from Richard Church, one of the colonists of Plymouth, Massachusetts, who, though not a passenger in the Mayflower, joined the Pilgrims as early as 1631. It is supposed that he afterwards removed to Hartford, Connecticut, as the name of Richard Church is found there upon the public monument erected to the memory of the first settlers of the town. Nathaniel Church was the son of Samuel Church, and was born in Bethlehem, Connecticut, November 16, 1756. His father died when he was but three years old. At a suitable age he was apprenticed to a weaver, but finding his master one difficult to please he deserted his service soon after the breaking out of the Revolutionary war and joined the patriot army. He was wounded in the battle of White Plains and his injuries were pronounced mortal. He recovered, however, though his wounds ever troubled him. He did not rejoin the army, but as soon as he was able to resume his trade as a weaver he went to Canaan, Connecticut, and was there employed by Captain John Ensign, a clothier. October 4, 1781, he married Lois Ensign, youngest daughter of his employer. She died in about two years, leaving two sons, Ensign and Samuel. In 1793 he was again married, to Dorcas Nickerson, who died in 1799. From this marriage there were also two children, Luman and John. He was a third time married in 1800, to Mrs. Ruth Johns, who bore five children—Nathaniel, Frederick, Lois, William, and Ruth. His third wife survived him and died in 1842. Mr. Church was prominently engaged in manufacturing and assisted in the erection of a paper-mill in Salisbury. This mill having burned, he retired to a farm on the banks of the Housatonic, where he died November 10, 1837. He was an active and ardent politician and was twice elected a member of the House of Assembly from the town of Salisbury. He was a devoted Christian of the Methodist denomination.

Samuel Church, his oldest son, became a distinguished lawyer in Connecticut and chief justice of the supreme court in that State. He was the father of A. E. Church, a distinguished mathematician and a professor in the United States Military academy at West Point.

Ensign Church was born in Salisbury in 1782, and married Jerusha Wright in 1805. He and his wife left Connecticut in May, 1805, and arrived in Canfield the 4th of June following. In 1812 he was appointed deputy quartermaster under General Simon Perkins, and was discharged in 1813, broken down by fatigue in the service. He died April 17, 1813. He was the father of two children, one of whom died in 1818; the other became the wife of Hon. Eben Newton. His widow afterwards married Eli T. Boughton, of Canfield, and died here in 1869 at the advanced age of eighty-four.

John R. Church, a son of Nathaniel Church, came to Canfield in 1818, and for several years was a successful business man and associate judge. He died April 11, 1868.

GENERAL ELIJAH WADSWORTH

was born in Hartford, Connecticut, November 14, 1747, and removed to Litchfield in the same State previous to the year 1770. Tradition has it that he was a lineal descendant of Captain Joseph Wadsworth who secreted the charter of Connecticut in the famous Charter Oak, in Hartford, on the 9th day of May, 1689. Elijah Wadsworth built and owned the house in Litchfield, which about the year 1790 he sold to Chief Justice Adams, the first chief justice of Connecticut. This house was subsequently owned and occupied by Dr. Lyman Beecher as his residence during a pastorate of several years. In this house were born Harriet Beecher Stowe, Henry Ward Beecher, and others of the family.

February 16, 1780, Mr. Wadsworth married Rhoda Hopkins, who was born at Litchfield, Connecticut, November 1, 1759, and died in Canfield, June 21, 1832. The fruits of this union were five children: Henry, Rhoda, Frederick, Edward, and George. All were born in Litchfield. Henry, born October 11, 1781, died in Bradleysville, Connecticut, November, 1830; Rhoda, born February 17, 1784, married in

Litchfield in September, 1802, Archibald Clark, of St. Mary's, Georgia, and died in St. Mary's, August 2, 1830; Frederick, born March 7, 1786, died ——; Edward, born May 3, 1791, died in Canfield, August 5, 1835; George, born April 5, 1793, died in Canfield, August 6, 1832.

When the first news of the battle of Bunker Hill reached Litchfield, Mr. Wadsworth volunteered to go to Boston, but for some reason went no further than Hartford, and thence returned to Litchfield, where he assisted in raising Sheldon's regiment of light dragoons, and served in that regiment during the whole of the Revolutionary war. Sheldon's regiment was one of the first squadrons of horse that joined the revolutionary army, and was with and under the immediate command of Washington, and had frequent and at times almost daily skirmishes with the enemy. Frederick Wadsworth, in a biographical sketch of his father, says:

Sheldon's regiment or that part of it then in actual service, was at West Point when Major Andre was taken prisoner, and General Arnold made his escape. I have often heard my father narrate the circumstances of the capture, trial, and execution of Andre. He always spoke enthusiastically in his praise, but did not give his captors that credit for disinterested patriotism which history awards to them. My father was one of the guard set over Major Andre the night after his capture. I never could understand why Arnold was not secured. I have heard my father say that after Andre was taken, Major Jamison, one of the majors of Sheldon's regiment, was ordered by Colonel Tallmadge who then had command of the regiment, to take a squadron of horse, surround Arnold's house, and not suffer him to leave it; this duty was performed by Major Jamison so far as to surround Arnold's house, but still he was permitted to make his escape.

Mr. Wadsworth entered the service as a lieutenant, but before the close of the war he held a captain's commission. Captain Wadsworth was one of the earliest members of the land company which purchased the Western Reserve from the State of Connecticut in 1795. He was one of the original proprietors of the townships of Canfield and Boardman in Mahoning county, Johnston in Trumbull county, Conneaut in Ashtabula county, Palmyra in Portage county, and Wadsworth (named after him) in Medina county.

He spent the summers of 1799 and 1801 on the Reserve, and attended to the surveying of Salem (now Conneaut), Palmyra, Boardman, and Johnston, returning to Connecticut in the fall of each year. In 1799 he succeeded Nathaniel Church as the agent of the proprietors of Canfield township. His services in establishing the

first mail route upon the Reserve in 1801 are fully detailed elsewhere.

The spring and summer of 1802 Captain Wadsworth likewise spent upon the Western Reserve; then returned to Connecticut, and on the 15th day of September of the same year left Litchfield with his family, in a wagon drawn by two horses, leading one extra horse. Twelve days before he started he sent Azariah Wetmore ahead with a wagon and his yoke of oxen. He overtook Wetmore before arriving at Pittsburg, and they continued in company until they reached Canfield on the 17th of October, Captain Wadsworth and family having been thirty-three days on the way, and Mr. Wetmore forty-five. Thenceforth until his death, Canfield was his home.

Captain Wadsworth was postmaster in Canfield from 1801 until his resignation in 1803, and was again appointed postmaster in 1813. At the first general election after Ohio became a State, the second Tuesday in February, 1803, he was elected sheriff of Trumbull county. At the session of the Legislature of 1803-4, the Legislature divided the State into four military divisions and elected him major-general of the fourth division, which comprised all the territory south of Lake Erie to the south line of Jefferson county. It required great exertion to organize the militia in this vast district. War was declared by the United States against Great Britain on the 19th of June, 1812, and on the 16th of August General Hull at Detroit surrendered the Northwestern army to the British. By this surrender the whole northwestern frontier was exposed to incursions from the enemy. The fourth division embraced the entire northwestern frontier of the State, the Cuyahoga river being then the limit of frontier settlement. News of Hull's surrender was brought to General Wadswords on the morning of August 21st by Charles Fitch of Ellsworth, who had been at Cleveland on business, and hearing of the disaster returned express. General Wadsworth sent expresses to his brigadier-generals to detail troops from their respective commands for defending the frontier, and ordered Captain James Doud and his company of cavalry into the service. The remainder of the day was spent in obtaining the ammunition on sale in Canfield and neighboring towns, and making preparations for a tour of military duty.

Sunday morning, the 22d, General Wadsworth, with Elisha Whittlesey, one of his aides, and the above mentioned company of cavalry, left Canfield about 10 o'clock for Cleveland, where they arrived the next day about 4 o'clock P. M. On the 24th of August he sent Governor Huntington express to Washington with the first authentic and reliable account of the surrender of General Hull.

Immediately after this General Wadsworth took up a position at old Portage, on the Cuyahoga, six miles north of the present site of Akron, in readiness to meet the enemy at that point with a detachment of his command. Soon after we find him at Camp Avery, near where Milan, Erie county, now is. He soon received orders, however, from Governor Meigs and from the Secretary of War to protect the frontiers, and to organize a brigade of fifteen hundred men from his division, put them under the command of a brigadier-general, and report them over to General Winchester or other officer commanding the northwestern army. This was completed the following November, and under the command of Brigadier-general Simon Perkins they were reported to General William H. Harrison, at that time commanding the Northwestern army. General Wadsworth then retired from the service and returned to his home in November, 1812.

At the beginning of the war General Wadsworth was sixty-five years of age, with a constitution which had been hardy, robust, and vigorous, but at that time considerably impaired. His anxieties and exertions greatly injured his health, and it was never good afterwards. In the summer of 1815 he had a shock of the palsy which paralyzed his left side and rendered him almost entirely helpless until his death. He died December 30, 1817, aged seventy years, a veteran of two wars, a hero of the "times that tried men's souls." In the Revolutionary war he lost the little property he had previously accumulated, and returned with nothing save a quantity of Continental currency, which soon became worthless. The only reward he obtained for his services in the War of 1812, except the approval of his conscience, was a judgment against him for $26,551.02 for purchases he had made to subsist his troops. To the honor of Congress and the Nation, however, this judgment was dis-

charged by an act of Congress, but not until he had been dead for years, as the act was passed March 3, 1825.

HON. JUDSON CANFIELD

was born in New Milford, Connecticut, January 23, 1759. He was the second son of Colonel Samuel Canfield, an officer in the Revolutionary army and a member of the Connecticut State Legislature for twenty-six sessions. Colonel Canfield was distinguished by great energy of character and clearness of intellect. He died in 1799 in the seventy-fourth year of his age. Judson Canfield was educated at Yale college and graduated therefrom in 1782. Two years later he was admitted to the bar, and in 1786 he settled in Sharon, Connecticut, where he successfully pursued his profession. The same year he was married to Mabel Ruggles, daughter of Captain Ruggles, an officer of the Revolution and a man distinguished for high moral character and refinement.

Mr. Canfield was a member of the popular branch of the State Legislature, from the town of Sharon, at almost every session, from 1802 to 1809, when he was elected a State Senator for each successive year until he removed from the State in 1815. From 1808 to 1815 he was also an associate judge of the county court for the county of Litchfield.

After his removal to Ohio he devoted himself mainly to farming and disposing of his lands. He died February 5, 1840. His children were Henry J., Julia, Elvira, Elizabeth H., and Caroline Elena.

Henry J. Canfield was born January 4, 1789, died November 27, 1856. He married Sally R. Ferris in 1825; she died January 23, 1881. The children of this union were two, Julia E. and Judson W. Julia married D. C. Ruggles, and died in 1857.

THE BEARDSLEY FAMILY.

Curtis Beardsley was the fourth son of Captain Philo Beardsley, a Connecticut soldier in the Revolutionary war. He was born in Kent, now New Preston, Litchfield county, Connecticut, March 1, 1797. March 10, 1816, being then but nineteen years of age, he was united in marriage to Miss Sophia Hanford, who was one year younger than himself. The tenth day of the following April this youthful couple left their native State for their future home in the new West. In company with Mr. Beardsley's brother Philo, in a wagon drawn by two horses and a yoke of oxen they journeyed from Connecticut to the Western Reserve, arriving in Boardman May 4, 1816. The following day, which was Sunday, they spent with Josiah Beardsley, a brother, at his home in that township. On Monday they reached Canfield, and took up their abode in a little log cabin with puncheon floor and without a pane of glass. The land taken up by Mr. Beardsley was uncleared, but he at once set to work, and during the first season cleared ten acres and sowed it to wheat. For his seed wheat he was obliged to pay the enormous price of $2 per bushel, but when harvest time came he found that he could not get three shillings per bushel in cash for his grain.

Hard and untiring labor, strict economy, and wise management were practiced by both husband and wife, and in due course of time they found themselves in the possession of a pleasant home and a fine farm. Children came to bless and encourage them in their work, and kind Providence smiled upon their efforts. Mr. Beardsley became a prominent and honored citizen of Canfield, enjoying during his long life the highest respect and esteem of friends and neighbors. December 6, 1876, he passed peacefully from this life to the life above.

Mr. Beardsley was remarkable for firmness of purpose, and integrity and uprightness of principle; yet, more than this, he was an exemplary, unobtrusive Christian. He was ever animated and sustained in his true and useful life by the partner of his toils and fortunes, who having previously become interested in the Episcopal church, united herself after coming here, with that little band afterwards known as the St. James' church, Boardman, though including Poland and Canfield, which they found already organized; and in 1822 he himself became a member and was soon after chosen a vestryman of the same.

In 1829 Mr. Beardsley organized a Sunday-school in Canfield and continued as its superintendent thirty years. In 1834 he became the leader of a movement which resulted in the building of a church edifice in Canfield; and it was to his efforts more than to those of any other man that St. Stephen's church owed its origin. He was elected junior warden of this church, became its senior warden, and for more than thirteen years previous to his death, as its only male communicant, the whole burden of the temporal affairs of this church rested upon this aged and declining servant of God. Residing at a distance of three miles from town, and more infirm in health than he was willing to acknowledge, he was seldom absent from services when held in Canfield, and when there were none here often rode eight miles to attend those of the church in Boardman.

Mr. Beardsley was a man of deep convictions, and although never obtrusive, was inflexible in maintaining them. He united great strength of character with the most scrupulous integrity, and during all his years sustained a high standing in the community.

Mrs. Sophia Beardsley, one of the few surviving old residents of Canfield, was born in Norwalk, Connecticut, May 12, 1798. She was the only child of Joseph Whitman Hanford and Elizabeth (Smith) Hanford. She is descended from an old New England family, her great-great-grandfather having emigrated from England to Connecticut in the early years of its settlement. His name was Rev. Thomas Hanford. In 1648 he began preaching in Norwalk and was the first Congregational minister in that town, where he continued to preach forty-one years.

Left an orphan by the death of her mother when less than two years of age, Sophia Hanford was brought up by her grandmother. Her father was a merchant and a seafaring man and died in 1824, aged sixty-two years. Though married young and surrendering the pleasures of cultivated society for a home in the wilds of Ohio, Mrs. Beardsley never repined at her lot and nobly co-operated with her husband in his efforts to gain a home. Faithful in her outward life as well as in her deep religious life, she has always acted up to her convictions of duty, and numerous friends testify to her worth. She has borne eight children, only three of whom are now living. Mrs. Beardsley is now spending the evening of her days with her daughter in the village of Canfield, with which she has been familiar almost from its infancy. She is now in her eighty-fourth year and seems as cheerful and bright as a youth. For sixty-four years she has been a communicant of the Episcopal church and ever one of its most active female members.

We append a record of the Beardsley family:

Philo Beardsley, born 1755, died 1826; married Esther Curtis, born 1764, died 1856. Children: Birdsey Beardsley, born 1785, married Sarah Mecuen. Anna Beardsley, born 1787, married John Taylor. Josiah Beardsley, born 1789, married Mary Merwin. Sarah Beardsley, born 1791, married Milo Stone. Philo Beardsley, born 1794, married Lois S. Gunn. Curtis Beardsley, born 1797, married Sophia Hanford. Almus Beardsley, born 1799, married Amanda Cogswell. Agur Beardsley, born 1801, married Eliza Bennett.

All are dead, Curtis Beardsley being the last. Four of the brothers settled in Mahoning county, Josiah in Boardman, Philo and Curtis in Canfield, and Almus in Ellsworth.

Descendants of Curtis Beardsley and Sophia Hanford. Children: Henry H., born May 1, 1818, died May 4, 1818. William Hanford, born December 13, 1819, married Mary Edsall June 10, 1846; children, Nelson S., Edwin H., Charles R., Henry E., and Hattie M., all living, two married. William H. Beardsley resides at East Claridon, Geauga county; Nelson S., professor of penmanship Delaware Normal school, Ohio, married Esther O. Hulin, two children, Willis Reed and Emmett Hulin. Edwin H. married Carrie Dana, two children, Nelson Vernon and Minnie. Mary L., born November 13, 1821, married Augustus L. Van Gorder May 12, 1847, died at Warren, Ohio, July 18, 1859, husband also dead; children, Anna S., Henry L., William C., George Dubois, Charles M., Frank B.; Anna, George, and Frank are deceased; William C. Van Gorder married Ella Crane, two children, Edgar C. and an infant daughter. Anna S., born August 26, 1824, died May 4, 1844. Eliza M., born March 19, 1827, died January 7, 1879. Sarah M., born July 22, 1832, married Pratt Allen Spicer, April 26, 1854, died December 25, 1857; one child, Ella I., resides in Marshall, Michigan. Lucy E., born November 5, 1834, resides at Canfield. Henry C., born March 12, 1838, married Mary J. Hine July 4, 1863; two children, Rhoda Hanford, and Edward Henry, residence old Beardsley homestead, Canfield.

Concerning the deceased members of this family we make the following extract from obituary notices published in local papers:

Died, Warren, Ohio, July 18, 1859, Mrs. Mary L. Van-Gorder. She was the oldest daughter of Curtis and Sophia Beardsley, of Canfield. For twenty years a communicant of the Episcopal church, during that time she adorned her profession by a consistent walk and conversation. In her last illness she exhibited a meek and patient disposition, and under all suffering appeared resigned to the will of her Heavenly Master. She calmly awaited death without fear of the dread messenger, and fell asleep in Jesus repeating the words of the beautiful hymn:

"There sweet be my rest till He bid me arise
To hail Him in triumph descending the skies."

Anna S. was a lovely and sweet dispositioned daughter, who had a large circle of friends, both young and old. Speaking of her death the local paper says:

Seldom has the hand of death made a more painful breach in the hopes and enjoyments of a family, or given a more affecting warning to an extensive circle of relatives and acquaintances, and to all in the joyous period of youth, that "we know not what shall be the morrow."

Eliza M. possessed a quick and scholarly mind, and at a youthful age began teaching school, in which occupation she continued more than thirty years. She was a remarkably efficient and successful teacher, possessing the rare talent of imparting knowledge in a manner that at once enlisted the attention and commanded the respect of the pupil. From the age of eighteen until her death she was a communicant of the Episcopal church and a devoted Christian.

Mrs. Spicer was, from a child, of a serious and contemplative mind. She early united with the church, became a zealous member, and found in Christ the sweet peace which passeth all understanding. Though compelled to part from earth in the morning of her married life, she accepted her fate with resignation and died with calmness of spirit, leaving her sweet babe in the care of Him who hath promised to protect the orphan.

JOHN SANZENBACHER AND FAMILY.

John Sanzenbacher was born in the kingdom of Wurtemberg, Germany, May 5, 1827. His parents were Jacob and Barbara (Schuger) Sanzenbacher, both natives of Wurtemberg. Jacob Sanzenbacher was born August 1, 1799, and is

John Danzenbacher

Mrs J. Sanzenbacher.

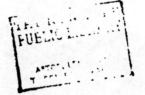

still living, a resident of New Springfield, Mahoning county. Mrs. Barbara Sanzenbacher was born February 12, 1804, and died December 24, 1878. She was the mother of five sons and two daughters, but of this number only two children remain—John and his brother Jacob. The latter resides in Southington, Trumbull county. John was the second child and the oldest son.

In 1833 he emigrated to the United States with his parents, and lived near Unity, Columbiana county, Ohio, until 1836, when the family moved to Beaver county, now Lawrence county, Pennsylvania. There his boyhood was passed upon a farm until August 19, 1844, at which date he was bound out to Mr. R. Fullerton for three years and six months to learn the trade of tanning and currying. At the end of this period he came to Mahoning county, and worked at his trade for William Moore, in Boardman, for ten months. He next went to New Middleton, in this county, where he worked about nine months, then returned to Boardman, and was employed by Mr. Moore for six months.

In the winter of 1849-50 he purchased of F. A. Brainard his tannery in Canfield. April 9, 1850, he came to Canfield, and commenced business with a capital of about $500, out of which he made a payment to Mr. Brainard of $40. Six hundred dollars was the price paid for the tannery.

December 24, 1850, having got a little start in his business and having concluded to take a wife, he was united in marriage to Miss Sarah A. Oswald, of Canfield township.

March 3, 1862, in company with Pierpont Edwards, he engaged in the drug and grocery business but continued to carry on tanning. About the year 1865 he formed a partnership with F. Krehl, of Girard, in the tanning and currying business. In 1867 he sold out to Mr. Krehl, and also disposed of his interest in the drug store. The same year he purchased a farm one mile east of Canfield, to which he moved June 20, 1867. In 1868 he erected a fine large barn and made other improvements upon the place.

Mr. Sanzenbacher began the manufacture of leather belting in 1865 and carried it on for one year in connection with his other business. In 1866 he quit tanning, and in the spring of 1867 disposed of his tannery and machinery. But in 1869 he again resumed the manufacture of belting, and October 20th of that year took P. Edwards as a partner under the firm name of J. Sanzenbacher & Co., which is still the style of the firm. During the summer of 1872 this firm erected a large building, where they still continue the business. From the time their new establishment was erected until the present they have been doing a large business both in tanning and in belt making.

Mr. Sanzenbacher is a man of quiet, social, and agreeable manners, and enjoys the highest esteem and confidence of the better portion of the community. He is regarded as the friend of every worthy cause, and is never backward in matters of public interest.

Mrs. Sarah A. Sanzenbacher, the worthy helpmate and companion of the subject of this notice, was born in Canfield township, November 25, 1832. She is the youngest daughter of Charles and Sarah A. (Harding) Oswald, of Canfield township. Her father died September 20, 1862, in the fifty-eighth year of his age. Her mother is still living in her seventy-sixth year, and makes her home with Mr. Sanzenbacher's family. Mrs. John Sanzenbacher is the youngest daughter of a family of three sons and three daughters. She has but one sister living, Mrs. Amanda Mahnensmith, Gilman, Iowa, and no brothers.

To Mr. and Mrs. Sanzenbacher have been born six children, all of whom are living in Canfield. Following is the family record: Harriet Louisa, born October 26, 1851; married March 31, 1870, to John Neff, of Canfield; has five children viz: Sadie, Ensign, Martin, Calvin, and an infant son. Rebecca Caroline, born August 30, 1856; married Irvin Callahan May 20, 1875. Charles J., born August 25, 1860. John H., born December 16, 1864. David L., born November 11, 1869. Martin L., born July 14, 1871.

THE TANNER FAMILY.

Tryal Tanner was one of the first settlers of Canfield. He was the son of William Tanner; his father died when Tryal was eleven years old, and thenceforth he lived with his uncle, Justus Sackett, in Warren, Connecticut, until he became of age. He then went to Cornwall, Connecticut, and engaged in farming. He served five years in the Revolutionary war, holding the rank of lieutenant, but resigned shortly before the close of the war. For his services in behalf of his country he was paid in Continental currency, and as an illustration of the value of that money it will be sufficient to state that he once paid $80 for a tea-kettle.

Soon after leaving the army he married Huldah Jackson, purchased a farm in Cornwall, settled there, and remained until his removal to Ohio. To Mr. and Mrs. Tanner were born three sons and six daughters, whose names were as follow: Archibald, Edmund Prior, Julius, Nancy, Peggy, Laura, Bridget, Panthea, and one daughter who died in infancy.

In 1801 Mr. Tanner exchanged his farm with Judson and Herman Canfield for four hundred acres of land in the new settlement of Canfield, four hundred acres in Johnston, and $400. This proved a good bargain. In addition to this land Mr. Tanner took an eight-acre lot in one of the divisions of the center of Canfield. In the spring of 1801 he visited his new property, built a log-house on the center lot, and commenced work on his farm by clearing thirteen acres and sowing it to wheat.

In 1802 Mr. Tanner and family came to Canfield and moved into the house which he had erected the previous year. They journeyed with William Chidester and family, making up a company of twenty-two persons in all. Mr. Tanner had one wagon drawn by two yoke of oxen and two horses; also two extra horses, one with harness to be used in the team when necessary, the other with a side-saddle for his wife to ride. The party started from Connecticut April 22, 1802, and arrived in Canfield on the 13th of the following May.

During his former visit Mr. Tanner had engaged two men to fell ten acres of timber and get it ready for logging. They, however, completed but six acres, and it was the summer job of Mr. Tanner and his sons to finish this clearing and sow the land to wheat. They began operations immediately. The three sons, who were aged respectively sixteen, fourteen, and twelve, assisted their father. He could handle the butt-end of a log alone, while all three of the boys united their strength to lift the smaller end. They worked "with a will," and

with eagerness, and soon had the satisfaction of seeing the forest show the results of their labor. During the summer they girdled thirty-five acres of trees, thus preparing them for future destruction. The winter they employed in cutting out small trees and underbrush.

In 1803 they sowed wheat among the trees which were still standing and raised about half a crop. They sowed grass seed with the wheat and the following year raised an abundance of hay. Thus they lived and labored, and soon their farm began to assume a comparatively improved appearance. In those days in the wild woods plenty of work and very little time for pleasure were the rules.

In 1806 Mr. Tanner built a frame house on his eight-acre lot, in which he lived until his death. He died November 22, 1833, aged eighty-two. His first wife died December 31, 1803. The following year he married Mary Doud, who survived until July 13, 1843, when she died at the age of eighty-seven.

Tryal Tanner was a good specimen of the hardy pioneer, tall and sinewy, and capable of great endurance. Toward the end of his life his sight failed by degrees and he became almost blind. He was a man of strong will and great determination, very tenacious of his own views. He was a member of the Episcopal church, and one of the leaders in founding the first church of that denomination on the Reserve. Through his life he sustained a high social standing and was much respected and esteemed.

Archibald Tanner, the oldest son, was a man very much like his father,—hardy, bold, and energetic. He was engaged in boating on the Ohio for several years, then settled in Warren, Pennsylvania, where he became a prosperous merchant and prominent citizen.

Edmund Prior Tanner, the second son of Tryal Tanner, and the longest survivor of the entire family, was born in Cornwall, Litchfield county, Connecticut, in 1788, on the 22d of February. He received all of his schooling in Connecticut; for after coming to Ohio his life was the busy life of a pioneer farmer's son.

November 16, 1809, he was united in marriage with Fanny Chapman, daughter of William and Sylvia Chapman, of Vernon, Trumbull county. He lived with his father for a time, but in the spring of 1810 moved into a house of hewed logs, which stood on the site of the present dwelling of his son, Julius Tanner.

Soon after the breaking out of the War of 1812 he was called into the service and was absent from home two months and eighteen days.

Mr. Tanner was always deeply interested in everything that concerned the educational, moral, and religious status of the community. He was a friend to those deserving sympathy and never refused his support to worthy objects. During the exciting days when slavery was under discussion he did not hesitate at all times to denounce the infamous traffic in human lives and became noted as a strong Abolitionist. He lived to see that word of reproach become one of honor, and to hear his actions spoken of as noble, whereas they were once bitterly denounced. The underground railway received from him assistance and encouragement.

For nearly sixty years he was an earnest and devout member of the Congregational church. He held the office of deacon many years, and was earnest and faithful, full of Christian spirit and prayer for the welfare of the church. His worth and benevolence endeared him to a large circle and his character was a model worthy of imitation. For several years he was so crippled by rheumatism as to be unable to walk without crutches, but he loved the house of God and Sunday usually found him in the sanctuary.

Sixty-three years of happy wedded life had passed before Mr. and Mrs. Tanner were called upon to part from each other. Death removed the aged and honored husband October 24, 1872, in the eighty-fifth year of his age. Of his life it can truly be said that it was one of usefulness. He was a keen observer and took a heartfelt interest in the topics of the day. Fond of reading and study he continued until the last to keep well informed upon current affairs. During his last illness he appeared cheerful and hopeful and fell asleep firm in the faith and hope of a blessed immortality.

His widow survived until September 24, 1875, when she went to join him. She was born in Barkhampton, Litchfield county, Connecticut, March 5, 1791, and was, therefore, also in her eighty-fifth year at the time of her decease. Early in life she united with the church, and ever continued a zealous and confiding disciple of the Lord. She was a woman of benevolence and a faithful helpmate to her worthy husband. She was the mother of eight children, four of whom are living. The family record is as follows: Mary, born August 30, 1811; married Lyman Warner, September 11, 1832. Huldah, born December 5, 1812; married James Jones, September 11, 1832. Jane, born February 15, 1814; married David Hollister, September 11, 1832; died March 19, 1834. Bridget, born September 26, 1816; died September 22, 1833. Julius, born October 6, 1818; married November 4, 1840, to Mary Wadsworth; married Fidelia T. Sackett, December 12, 1855. Electa Chapman, born August 6, 1820; married Pierpont Edwards, October 31, 1838; died in September, 1840. Sylvia Smith, born July 31, 1822; married Charles E. Boughton, March 22, 1843. William Chapman, born July 12, 1824; died March 26, 1825. Mrs. Warner resides at Lowell, Massachusetts; she is a widow and has one child, a daughter. Mrs. Jones resides in Canfield; has three children living, one deceased. Mrs. Boughton resides in Canfield. One son is living, and one was killed in the war.

Julius Tanner, only surviving son of Deacon Edmund P. Tanner, has resided in Canfield all his life. His residence is the old homestead farm. His first wife died April 15, 1855, leaving three children living and one dead—Edward Wadsworth, William Henry (deceased), Henry Archibald, and Mary Ida. All are married. Edward married Kate Shaffer; resides in Meadville, Pennsylvania. Henry married Carrie Harrison; resides in Pittsburg; he has two children. Ida married John Delfs, and resides in Canfield; has two children, one living.

By his second marriage Mr. Tanner is the father of three children—Fanny Chapman, died at the age of seventeen; Edmund Prior, and Horace Boughton. The sons reside at home. Mrs. Tanner had one son by her former marriage, Myron W. Sackett, now residing in Meadville, Pennsylvania.

DR. A. W. CALVIN.

In the full strength of vigorous manhood, in the midst of a successful professional career which was rapidly raising him in the esteem of a community where he was already trusted and honored, Dr. Calvin was suddenly prostrated by a dread disease, and after an illness of brief duration, died on the 18th of December, 1881, in the thirty-fifth year and seventh month of his age.

Of his boyhood it is perhaps sufficient to state that it was like that of most farmers' sons.

Aaron Wilbur Calvin was born in Green township, Mahoning county, May 18, 1846. He was a son of Robert and Jane Calvin, who were well-known in this vicinity, and both of whom have been dead less than two years, the husband preceding the wife about three weeks. Nurtured by Christian parents by whom the seeds were sown which subsequently developed into the character which gave him such a hold upon the affections of all who knew him, he with the rest of the children was accredited with a good name.

His education was begun in the district school at Locust Grove, and afterwards prosecuted at the old academy in Canfield. After acquiring an ordinary amount of learning, he turned his attention for a brief period to the profession of teaching. He was married, February 15, 1866, to Miss H. J. Fowler, a daughter of Dr. C. R. Fowler. After his marriage he resided in Canfield until 1868, when he removed to Crawford county, Illinois, where he remained two years. In 1870 he returned to Canfield, and began the study of medicine with his father-in-law, Dr. Fowler, and in 1873 graduated from the Cleveland Medical college. After graduation he began the practice of his profession in Canfield, and continued the same up to the time of his death. During his married life he was blessed with three children: Mamie, Emma, and Florence, who are now aged respectively fifteen, eleven, and six years. These, with the bereaved wife and three brothers and four sisters, are left to mourn his loss.

As a citizen and a man Dr. Calvin received the respect and confidence of all. Always generous and obliging, he made hosts of friends, and was able to retain them. As a student he applied himself with more than usual vigor, and completed his course of study in much less time than is usually allotted to the ordinary pupil. As a physician he was learned in theory and skilled in practice, yet he was a constant student, searching in every field for means of increasing his knowledge and usefulness. He was a faithful and tender nurse, and to this fact owed much of his success. But above all he was a conscientious man. He took no unwarranted risks; none of his patients were ever troubled with the fear of being experimented upon at the risk of life. He had begun to gather about him, just prior to his death, circumstances of prosperity above the ordinary man of his age. He had just reached that period of life where he might begin to enjoy the fruits of his faithfulness and industry, when he was smitten by the hand of death.

The above statements are gathered from a discourse delivered by Rev. C. L. Morrison on December 25, 1881, and they present a fair and impartial view of one who was beloved, honored, and esteemed by a large circle of intimate acquaintances.

JUDGE FRANCIS G. SERVIS.

A man of noble and genial nature, charitable, and friendly toward all who needed friendship and sympathy; never failing to extend a helping hand to those in distress; full of enthusiasm himself, he gave, both by example and precept, aid and encouragement to the struggling and aspiring; endowed with an honorable ambition, laboring manfully and unceasingly to make his influence widespread and useful, he was snatched away just as he had reached the goal of his hopes.

Judge Servis was born in Hunterdon county, New Jersey, August 1, 1826, and died in Canfield, Ohio, March 6, 1877. His father, Abram P. Servis, was born in Amwell township, Hunterdon county, New Jersey; he died in Berlin township, Mahoning county, Ohio, February 28, 1858, at the age of seventy-four. He married Sarah Pegg, a native of the same county and State as himself. They came to Palmyra township, Portage county, arriving May 29, 1827. Mrs. Servis died the following August. She was the mother of two children, Mary A. and Francis G. The former survives in Deerfield, Portage county.

Francis G. Servis was married September 11, 1853, to Martha E. Patton, youngest of three daughters of John and Mary (Taylor) Patton. John Patton was born in Ohio April 3, 1806;

married in 1828, and died May 8, 1880. His wife, a native of Beaver county, Pennsylvania, was born in 1810, married in 1828, and died in October, 1832, aged twenty-two years. Martha E. Patton was born in Beaver county, Pennsylvania, December 15, 1831, and by the death of her mother was left an orphan at the age of ten months. Mr. and Mrs. F. G. Servis, having no children of their own, adopted two daughters, Florence Geer and Minnie V. Piert, the former at the age of five years and the latter at the age of three. Florence is now the wife of Frank W. Freer, Ashland, Ohio. Minnie is single and resides at home with Mrs. Servis.

Judge Servis's father was a man in humble circumstances, who, after coming to Ohio, settled on a small farm, and divided his time between labor upon his farm and law practice in the lower courts. He had few early opportunities, but made the most of the facilities afforded him, and, having a natural aptitude for legal pursuits, he was skillful in the management of his cases. He is said to have been quite successful, and this no doubt, led his son to adopt the same profession. The young man, however, was obliged to depend entirely upon himself for means to acquire an education. He passed his boyhood laboring at various occupations, gaining what knowledge he could from the limited advantages afforded by the district schools and studying with zeal in his spare time.

In 1850 Judge Servis came to Mahoning county and entered the probate office of William Hartzell, then probate judge, as his deputy. While performing the duties of this position he pursued his legal studies under the instruction of John H. Lewis, Esq., at that time a leading lawyer of Mahoning county bar. In 1853 Mr. Servis was admitted to the bar upon the certificate of Wilson & Church, in whose office he had completed his studies. Soon after he opened an office, and ere long enjoyed a good practice. The acquaintance formed with citizens of all parts of the county during the years of his clerkship was of great service to him; the young man had many friends, and rose in his profession with almost marvelous rapidity. By diligence in his business, by faithfulness in promptly and punctually discharging every duty entrusted to him, he gained the confidence and respect of all his clients. When embarked on

the full tide of a prosperous practice, neither greed for gain nor any other unworthy ambition ever entered his heart. On the contrary, he rendered valuable assistance to many just entering upon the difficult task of building up a law practice, who, like himself, were obliged to begin at the foot of the ladder. A distinguished member of the Mahoning bar, after the death of Judge Servis, spoke of his friend and brother in the profession as follows: "I came to Canfield compelled to rely for a livelihood on my own exertions, and I should have found this a hard matter to accomplish had it not been for the helping hand extended to me of Judge Servis. I had no clients, but he had many. He worked from dawn of day till late at night, and many and many a time has he come to me and told me where I could make a cent, a dime, or a dollar. I can never forget the kindness done me in those days by this noble-hearted man. Illustrating his kindness, let me speak of what I myself know. A few years ago, while he was in Montana, the banking firm of which he was a member made an assignment, and by the stress of circumstances he individually was compelled to do the same. I was his assignee, and when I came to look up his assets, I found that there were hundreds, nay, thousands of dollars loaned out to needy widows or unfortunate men, from which not a dollar could ever be realized. He loaned knowing that he would never get a dollar back; he gave out of his warm sympathy never expecting a return save that which came from the affectionate regard of those whom he helped."

Concerning his abilities as a lawyer, a prominent member of the bar said:

He was strong as a statutory lawyer, and in this respect had not an equal in the State of Ohio. He had the statutes at his fingers' ends and at his tongue's end, and could turn to any one he wanted without a moment's delay or hesitation. When you add to this his strong common sense, he was an antagonist in a law suit to be dreaded and an attorney to be desired and sought after.

Judge Servis exerted a great, and at times a controlling influence in the politics of the county for nearly a quarter of a century. Up to the time the war broke out he was a Democrat, but when Sumter was fired upon he espoused the Union cause with fervent patriotism, and faltered not in this course until he laid down his life. Considering his activity in politics he rarely held office. Indeed, he seemed more desirous of helping his friends than of advancing his own interests. He was twice elected prosecuting attorney of Mahoning county, and discharged the duties of that office with great credit to himself and advantage to the public.

During the war he was draft commissioner for Mahoning county, and in the discharge of the responsible duties of this trying position he displayed energy, courage, and ability that commanded universal admiration.

In 1872 he was appointed associate justice of the supreme court of Montana, and entered upon his duties in the fall of that year. In the summer of 1875 he resigned this position, returned to Canfield, and resumed his practice. In Montana he was held in high esteem by men of all parties. The press and bar of that Territory, with absolute unanimity, paid the highest tributes to his memory as to his ability, integrity, and judicial character generally.

In 1876 Judge Servis was elected circuit judge of his district. Concerning this period of his career the Youngstown Register says:

There is no doubt that he has cherished for many years an honorable ambition to hold the office to which he has just been elected, and upon the performance of whose duties he has not been permitted to enter. Since his election last October he has without any doubt overworked himself that he might reflect honor upon the great public dignity to which the people had called him. Of the judicial reputation and honorable fame he justly anticipated winning from a service upon the bench, among those with whom he had maintained life-long friendship and associations, cruel Death has robbed him.

Both in public and in private life Judge Servis was ever the same—a genial, generous, whole-souled man; and at his death the entire community mourned the loss of a valued and trusted friend.

HENRY VAN HYNING.

The name Van Hyning originated in Holland and was brought to this country by some of the earliest of the New York colonists.

Henry, son of Henry and Hannah (Brower) Van Hyning, was born in Saratoga county, New York, May 1, 1797. His mother, who was his father's second wife, was a grandchild of ——— Bogardus, a missionary from Holland. To the first wife of Henry Van Hyning, Sr., three sons were born, and to the second four sons and six daughters, of whom only two survive, Henry and

Sylvester. The latter lives in Norton township, Summit county.

In the spring of 1804 the family started for Ohio. The family then consisted of the father, mother, and nine children. Mr. Van Hyning made a canoe and took it with the heavier part of his goods to French creek, thence into the Allegheny, to Pittsburg. There he was met by the family, who had journeyed by land, and after putting the goods aboard wagons, all started for Canfield. They came via Beaver and arrived in Canfield township the latter part of August, 1805, having stopped in Susquehanna county nearly a year, and remained until the latter part of October. During their stay in Canfield the youngest son, Sylvester Van Hyning, was born.

Meantime the father had been to Northampton, then in Trumbull, but now in Summit county, and had selected and purchased land for a farm. He hitched up his teams with two wagons and started for his new home, traveling by the way of Ravenna, and cutting a road a portion of the distance. From Ravenna he proceeded to Warren and there purchased a barrel of pork, a barrel of flour, and a barrel of whiskey, doubled his teams, and in due time reached Northampton. There were then but two white families in that township. All was dense forest and Indians were numerous. After six years of pioneer life in Northampton, Mr. Van Hyning sold out and removed to Wolf creek, now Norton township, where both he and his wife died. The father lived to see the fourth generation and attained the remarkable age of one hundred and two years. He served in the French and Indian war and all through the Revolution.

In the last-named war he was a captain, and commanded a company of picked men, selected from a brigade. Of the eighty members of this company not one was less than six feet in height, the captain being among the tallest of them. Captain VanHyning was under General Gates, and participated in the battle which resulted in taking General Burgoyne. During his residence in Northampton he was a justice of the peace; the greater part of the time for several townships, all of which were included in one election district. He also held the same office in Wolf Creek district, being one of the first elected there.

Henry VanHyning, Jr., passed his early years

amid the pioneer scenes of the Western Reserve. He is one of the few men now living in Ohio who had Indians for his neighbors and associates. He found them friendly and well disposed, learned to talk their language, and frequently went hunting with them.

He obtained all of his school education in the log school-houses of pioneer days, usually attending a few months in the winter. At home he frequently studied by the light of hickory bark, and, in fact, picked up the most of his learning in this way.

At the time of the War of 1812, though not subject to military duty, he went into the service as a substitute for his brother, who had been drafted immediately after Hull's surrender, and served about three months in scout and outpost duty against the Indian raiders.

While in Norton Mr. VanHyning was a justice of the peace for several years, and was engaged in other public business, settling estates, etc., most of the time. In 1855 he removed to Cleveland, thence to Newburg after a year or two. He remained in Newburg until he removed to Canfield in 1871. Mr. VanHyning was principally the means of getting a bank established in Canfield, and has been its president ever since it was founded.

He has married twice—first on August 14, 1820, to Miss Almira Taylor, a native of Connecticut. She bore him three children, two sons and one daughter—Julius, Giles, and Henrietta. The daughter died in Newburg at the age of twenty-three; Julius is a farmer in Napoleon, Henry county, Ohio; Giles is a prominent member of Mahoning county bar, practicing in Canfield.

Mrs. VanHyning was born January 15, 1799, and died March 14, 1864.

November 30, 1864, Mr. VanHyning wedded Julia Randall. She was born in Northampton, Massachusetts, April 2, 1815. She died March 27, 1881.

Mr. VanHyning is a man of sterling integrity, an esteemed citizen, and a useful member of society. His long life and active business career have made him familiar with many men, and all speak of him in the highest terms.

COLONEL SHERMAN KINNEY.

Sherman Kinney was born in Washington, Litchfield county, Connecticut, September 4, 1817, being a son of Theron and Ruth Ann (Meeker) Kinney. Sherman is the oldest of a family of eight children, two sons and six daughters, of whom all are living except two daughters. His parents removed to Ohio when the subject of this sketch was about fourteen years old, settling in Boardman township where the father died in 1863, aged seventy-two. Mrs. Kinney is still living in Boardman. Sherman Kinney received a common school education. When in his thirteenth year, under the instruction of his father, he began to learn the carpenter and joiner's trade, working summers and attending school winters. After about four years he began working with his uncle, William Meeker, also a carpenter, and continued with him until he was about nineteen. His father then gave him his time during the remaining years of his minority, and Mr. Kinney began work for himself, and has since been following his trade. He made the study of architecture a specialty, and having a love for his pursuit he soon became well skilled in designing, which he has practiced as a department of his work from 1840 up to the present time.

From the beginning of his business life Mr. Kinney has been successful. He has worked industriously, zealously and faithfully. Of recent years his business has been large and ever increasing. He has taken many important contracts and in every instance his work has given the best of satisfaction.

From 1852 to 1859 Mr. Kinney was a contractor and builder in the city of Cleveland and conducted quite an extensive business with his usual success.

In 1860 he came to Canfield, where he has since resided. As a business man he enjoys the respect and confidence of his fellow-citizens, and maintains a high social standing. Mr. Kinney is a Republican, but he has always been too busy to take a very active part in politics. In military matters he has been honored by several appointments.

In 1841 Mr. Kinney was chosen a captain of militia, and served several years. At the breaking out of the war a company, principally of Canfield men, was raised and Mr. Kinney was chosen captain. Under the first call for troops—seventy-five thousand men for three months—this company attempted to get into the army, but did not succeed, though many of its members subsequently enlisted in other companies.

At the time of the organization of the State militia during the war the militia of Mahoning county was divided into three regiments, and Mr. Kinney received an appointment as colonel of the Second regiment of Mahoning county, and served in that office about two years.

Mr. Kinney was married in 1838 to Miss Marcia M. Titus. This lady was born in Washington, Litchfield county, Connecticut, December 10, 1820, and was the daughter of Onesimus and Nancy Titus. The parents moved to Boardman township in this county in 1821 and spent the remainder of their days on the farm where they first settled. They reared five children who arrived at maturity, Mrs. Kinney being the second child. Three of this family are now living, one son and two daughters. Mrs. Titus died in 1863 aged sixty-seven; and Mr. Titus in 1875 at the age of eighty four.

Mr. and Mrs. Kinney have no children living. Their only child, Henry, born September 8, 1849, died October 13, 1856. This couple have many friends and no enemies.

It has been truthfully said, "On their own merits, modest men are dumb," and Colonel Kinney is one of most modest and unassuming of men. Nevertheless, his long experience in active business has made his circle of acquaintances a large one, and every one bears cheerful testimony to his worth and usefulness. By faithful attention to his business and unwearied industry he has won success and prosperity.

NOTES OF SETTLEMENT.

George J. Lynn was born in Berks county, Pennsylvania, December 26, 1775. He came to Ohio in the fall of 1803 and purchased land in Canfield township, then Trumbull county, and settled in the midst of the forest. He erected a rude log cabin in which he and a sister kept house until his marriage in the spring of 1807. His wife was Miss Catharine Grove, a representative of a pioneer family. The subject of this sketch was a poor boy and started in life with but seven cents in money and the clothes he had on. But he patiently and successfully met every difficulty which beset his pathway and eventually accumulated quite an extensive property. • He died November 14, 1833, mourned by his relatives and a host of friends, by whom he was familiarly known as "Uncle George." He was the father of five sons and two daughters, as follow: David, John, George, William, Levi, Mary, and Elizabeth. Levi and William are dead, both leaving families. Mrs. Lynn survived her husband until March 15, 1866. They are buried in the cemetery near Canfield.

David Lynn, the eldest son of the subject of the previous sketch, was born on the old Lynn homestead April 25, 1808. His occupation has always been that of a farmer. He was united in marriage February 17, 1834, to Miss Mary Ann Harding. To them were born nine children, as follow: George, John, George E., Almedus, D. E., Elizabeth C., Lucy A., Mary, and Mary Jane. George and Mary Jane died in infancy; the remainder are living. Mr. Lynn is one of the prosperous and substantial farmers of his township and has held various offices of trust. He and his wife are members of the Presbyterian church of Canfield.

George Lynn, third son of George J. and Catharine Lynn, was born on the old homestead where he now lives, in Canfield township, March 21, 1813. During his active business life he has followed farming. He has been twice married, first to Rachel Moherman, who became the mother of five sons, viz: Freeman T., George F., Ensign Daniel, Orlando M., and Walter J.

Henry Thoman, Canfield township, Mahoning county, was born in York county, Pennsylvania, in 1790. He learned shoemaking when a young man, though he has followed farming principally. He married Mary Marter, who died in 1860, having borne ten children, viz: Harriet, Daniel, Catharine, Lewis, Henry, Margaret, Isaac, Samuel, Jesse, and Amanda. Six are living,—Lewis, in Kansas; Harriet (Crouse), in Crawford county; Catharine (Morris) and Margaret (Wining) in Columbiana county; Samuel and Amanda (Heintzelman), in Canfield township. Mr. Thoman is now passing the evening of his ripe old age at the home of his son Samuel. The family came to Beaver township, Mahoning county, in 1828. In 1877 Mr. Thoman and his son Samuel moved to Canfield. Samuel Thoman was born in Beaver township in 1833. He has followed a variety of occupations, having been a carpenter, a tinner, a millwright, a merchant, and a farmer, by turns. He has also resided in what is now Mahoning county. In 1854 he married Elizabeth Heintzelman, of Beaver township. They have had six children: Ora Alice, Alvin, Viola, Melvin, Cora L., and an infant daughter. Ora Alice, Melvin, and the youngest are deceased. The family belong to the Reformed church.

Prior T. Jones, farmer, Canfield township, Mahoning county, was born in Ellsworth township, in 1836. In 1860 he married Ellen R. Bond, of Edinburg, Portage county. They have four children,—Lester. L., Harry T., James B., and Amy Belle. Mr. Jones is a son of James Jones, who was born in Ellsworth in 1807 and died in Canfield in 1870. He married Huldah Tanner, and lived in Ellsworth until 1852, then moved to Canfield. While in Ellsworth he carried on tanning some years. His widow still lives in Canfield. She has borne four children, three of whom are living: William died in Kansas in 1857 about twenty-four years of age; Prior T., Fanny (Turner), and Laura reside in Canfield. A sketch of the Jones family will be found in the history of Ellsworth.

George F. Lynn, member of the firm of Lynn Brothers, druggists, Canfield, Mahoning county, was born in Canfield township, March 20, 1845, a son of George and Rachel Lynn. He followed the dry goods business seven years, commencing in 1866. Since 1873 he has been engaged in the drug business. He was married November 9, 1872, to Lena N. Taylor, of Canfield. Mr. Lynn, for a young man, has been honored with a large number of local offices. He has been township clerk nine successive years; secretary of the Mahoning County Agricultural society one year, and treasurer of the same two years. He was nominated for county auditor in 1880 by the Democrats, and ran about four hundred votes ahead of the rest of the ticket; he was a member of the Democratic Executive committee several years, and was chairman of the central committee in 1879, and exerts much influence in the Democratic party. He is one of the incorporators of the Northeastern Ohio Normal school, Canfield, and is secretary of its board of trustees.

He has served several years as councilman of the incorporated village of Canfield.

J. C. Turner, farmer and coal operator, Canfield township, Mahoning county, was born in 1832 on the old Turner homestead, his present residence. In 1869 he married Fanny Jones, daughter of James and Huldah Jones, of Canfield. They have two children living, one deceased—Elsie, Laura Electa, and Sylvia (deceased). Mr. Turner is proprietor of a coal bank, from which he is shipping several car loads of coal daily. He has been working the mine about three years. At present he employs from thirty to forty men, and is the most extensive coal operator in the township. For Turner family see Canfield township history.

Warren Hine, stock dealer and farmer, Canfield, Mahoning county, was born in Warren, Litchfield county, Connecticut, in 1810. In 1811 his parents returned to Canfield, their home, and here Mr. Hine has since lived. He has followed agricultural pursuits and is a large dealer in stock; he has been buying and selling for many years and is well known throughout a large region. Mr. Hine was married in 1836 to Rhoda Tichner, a native of Salisbury, Connecticut. They have no children of their own, but have reared two in their family, namely, Kate and Warren. During the war Mr. Hine warmly espoused the Union cause and was earnest in getting recruits for the army. Formerly a Whig he is now a Republican. Mr. Hine is a wideawake citizen and a friend to every good work. He was one of the earliest supporters and organizers of the Mahoning County Agricultural society. For his parentage see chapter on Canfield township.

Lewis D. Coy, physician, Canfield, Mahoning county, was born in Green village, Mahoning county, in 1848, the son of Wesley and Dorothea (Bush) Coy, of Green village. He studied with Dr. Tritt, of Green; attended Eclectic Medical institute, Cincinnati; graduated therefrom May 9, 1876. He then located in Green village and practiced till April, 1879, when he settled in Canfield, where he now enjoys a large and increasing practice. In April, 1881, he was appointed physician at the county infirmary. This, with his outside calls, keeps the doctor very busy. In 1868 he married Laura C. Bowell, of New Albany, Ohio, who has borne two children,

Olive F. and Warren. Dr. Coy served in the late war; enlisted January, 1864, in company C, Sixth Ohio cavalry, and served until the close of the Rebellion. He is a member of the Lutheran church.

John H. Clewell, lumber dealer, Canfield, Mahoning county, was born in Northampton county, Pennsylvania, in 1806. He worked as a tinner and locksmith some years. In 1835 he came to Ohio and resided in Green village, Mahoning county, where he was engaged in buying and selling stock. In 1837 he moved to Canfield and kept the hotel known as the Clewell house on the site of the present American house. This business he continued until 1848. He then went to Philadelphia, where he kept hotel about one year. In May, 1850, he returned to Canfield and began the manufacture of sewing machines. In 1854 he engaged in the lumber business, which he still continues. At first his work was making bed-pins and broom-handles. In the first days of the oil well excitement he manufactured pump-rods for the oil well pumps. He now manufactures and deals quite extensively in all kinds of house-furnishing lumber. Mr. Clewell was married in 1830 to Elizabeth Koehler (born in 1808), daughter of Nathaniel Koehler, of Lebanon, Pennsylvania. To them have been born four children: Harriet Adelia (Whittlesey), Canfield; Stephen Albert, Stillwater, Minnesota; Delorma M., Ravenna, and Mary L. (Super), Athens. Mr. Clewell is a member of the Odd Fellows.

John J. N. Delfs, tanner, Canfield, Mahoning county, was born in Hamburg, North Germany, in 1849. In July, 1872, he emigrated to America, and after remaining a few months in New York city went to Hartford, Connecticut, and worked at his trade. From Hartford he went to Holyoke, Massachusetts, thence to Rockwell, Connecticut, from Rockwell to Cleveland, from Cleveland to Pittsburg, and from the latter place to Canfield in 1877. The following year he married Miss Ida M. Tanner. They have had two children—Roy and Fannie. Only the son is living. Mr. Delfs belongs to the order of Odd Fellows. Mrs. Delfs is a member of the Congregational church.

Allen Calvin, miller, Canfield, Mahoning county, was born in Green township, Mahoning county, in 1842. He is a son of Robert Calvin.

He lived at home until of age, then went to Southern Illinois, and was there nearly all of the time for eighteen years engaged in milling. In 1880 he returned to Mahoning county, and began milling in Canfield. Mr. Calvin was married in 1868, to Miss Julia E. Reese, of Annapolis, Crawford county, Illinois. She was a native of Pennsylvania; she died in November, 1874, leaving two children living—Eva Laura and Joe V. Another, Cora Lee, is dead. Mr. Calvin is a Democrat politically.

William Schmick, retired merchant, Canfield, Mahoning county, was born in Reading, Berks county, Pennsylvania, August 21, 1812. When fifteen years of age he began to learn the trade of making hats, and worked at this trade until 1840. In September, 1833, Mr. Schmick came to Ohio, and began working at Green village, now in Mahoning county. There he continued fifteen years. During this time he was elected a justice of the peace, and served three terms. In the fall of 1848 he was elected sheriff of Mahoning county, and moved to Canfield, which has since been his home. In 1850 Mr. Schmick engaged in business as a merchant and continued until 1861, when he gave up his store to his sons. From 1853 to 1861 Mr. Schmick served as postmaster in Canfield. Four years, 1857-61, he was deputy United States marshal of the Northern district of Ohio. He was cashier of the bank in Canfield four years (1870-74). He has been a very active and successful business man. During recent years he has not been in active business, though he continues to take deep interest in all that relates to the prosperity of his town or county. In 1881 he was nominated by the Democrats of Mahoning county, without his knowledge or consent, for State Senator, but of course in a strongly Republican district an election could not be expected. Mr. Schmick was married in 1837 to Mrs. Rhoda Trevett (nee Brookhart) of Frankfort, Hampshire county, Virginia. To them have been born two sons, William Henry and Charles Nelson. Both are prosperous business men of Leetonia, Columbiana county, where they are engaged in banking and mercantile business; also doing an extensive business in iron manufacture, being the proprietors of a rolling-mill, two blast furnaces, etc.

Hosea Hoover, Canfield, Mahoning county,

was born in Kendall, Stark county, Ohio, November 27, 1814. He is the oldest son of Jacob and Elizabeth (Shellenberger) Hoover, who came from Pennsylvania to Ohio at an early date. His father died in 1835; his mother is still living. The family consisted of eight children, of whom five are living—Hosea, Canfield; David, Marlboro, Stark county; Hector, Alliance; Mrs. Mary Tribbey, Ravenna; and Frances, Alliance. Mrs. Hoover, the mother, is still living at Alliance, at the ripe age of eighty-eight years, in good health, and in full possession of her faculties. The names of her children who are deceased are Hiram P., died at Petersburg; Humphrey, died at Alliance; John, died in Stark county. After the death of his father, Hosea being the oldest of the children, the care of the family devolved largely upon him, and for many years all his earnings were contributed to its support. Mr. Hoover has resided in this county nearly all of his life; his parents moved to Springfield township, now in Mahoning county, when he was about four years old, and he has since resided in Mahoning. When a young man he learned carpentry and joining, and worked at that business until 1854. In that year he was elected treasurer of Mahoning county; moved to Canfield with his family in 1856. Having been re-elected in 1856, he thus served two terms with great credit to himself and satisfaction to the citizens who elected him. Mr. Hoover was employed in the drug business about nine years. He served as deputy collector of internal revenue in this county for four years and eight months. He was married January 26, 1842, to Mary Seidner, daughter of Christian Seidner, of Springfield township. Mr. Hoover is an active member of the Odd Fellows, which organization he joined twenty-six years ago. He has been a member of the Methodist church forty-six years, and has contributed liberally toward its support.

Pierpont Edwards, manufacturer, Canfield, Mahoning county, was born in New Milford, Litchfield county, Connecticut, July 7, 1812, the second of a family of seven children. His grandfather, Edward Edwards, of Welsh parentage, was born in London, July 16, 1743, and died in this country October 19, 1823. Edward Edwards sailed from Bristol, England, April 6, 1764; arrived in New York the 27th of May following, and settled in New Milford. His wife,

Martha, died June 3, 1824, aged eighty-two. The father of Pierpont Edwards was Martin Luther Edwards, born May 18, 1781, and died September 14, 1870. His mother was Sarah Hoyt, who died February 25, 1851, at the age of sixty-seven. Her father was Nathan Hoyt, who was driven out of Norwalk when it was burned by the British during the Revolutionary war. M. L. Edwards and family moved to Warwick, Orange county, New York, in 1821, and resided there until the spring of 1827, when the whole family started for Ohio in a two-horse wagon. They were three weeks on the way. They settled in Canfield permanently, excepting one year afterwards spent in Boardman and one in Steubenville. Pierpont Edwards followed chair-making and painting a number of years with his father, and afterwards by himself. In 1838 he was married to Electa Chapman, daughter of Edmund P. and Fanny Tanner. She died September 22, 1840, aged twenty years, and an infant son died the 11th of the following month. November 8, 1842, Mr. Edwards married Mary Patch, formerly of Groton, Massachusetts. She has borne three sons and three daughters. The oldest, Albert Tanner, died October 4, 1863, in his twentieth year. The remaining five are living—Sarah Electa, George Rufus, Lucy, Ellen, and Martin Luther. In 1851 Mr. Edwards' house and shop were burned. He then engaged in selling stoves, clothing, etc., and for a few years was in the drug and medicine business with the late Dr. W. W. Prentice and his brother, Dr. N. P. Prentice, now of Cleveland. During the late war he was in partnership with J. Sanzenbacher in the drug and grocery line. His health failing he dissolved partnership and sold out. In 1866 he built a new store and commenced dealing in groceries and notions in 1867. This business he continued until May, 1881. In 1869 he formed a partnership with J. Sanzenbacher and began the business of tanning and manufacturing leather belting, which business is still carried on in the name of J. Sanzenbacher & Co., who are assisted by George R. Edwards and Charles Sanzenbacher, sons of the partners, and I. Callahan, Mr. Sanzenbacher's son-in-law, who have an interest in the business. This industry is more fully noticed under the head of Canfield township.

Stephen W. Jones, Canfield, Mahoning county, was born in Stockbridge, Massachusetts, July 29, 1799. He passed his early life farming, and has followed that business principally, though with the usual characteristics of a Yankee he has turned his hand to almost every kind of mechanical labor, such as carpentry, wagon manufacturing, furniture making, etc. In middle life he became much interested in scientific studies, especially geology, and has followed up his investigations zealously through many years. In 1853 he was sent to the Holy Land by the Society for the Amelioration of the Condition of the Jews, looking to the colonization and improvement of the Jews of that portion of the world. He was there during the Crimean war and saw many of the trying scenes of those troublous times. In 1855 he returned to his home in Massachusetts and resumed farming and mechanical work. In 1864 he sold his farm and for four years was engaged in various occupations. In 1864 he was among the mines of Nova Scotia five months, being employed as a geological expert. Returning to Boston he was immediately engaged by a mining company to investigate the newly discovered oil regions, and followed this work some time, traveling a portion of each year. He journeyed hundreds and frequently thousands of miles yearly, often on foot, and made explorations in New York, Pennsylvania, Ohio, Virginia, Kentucky, etc. In 1868 he moved to Salem, Columbiana county, Ohio. His wife died that year and he again became a wanderer, visiting and residing in various localities. In 1871 he settled permanently in Canfield, his present home. Mr. Jones possesses a keen, investigating mind, and his travels and studies have enabled him to acquire a large amount of valuable scientific information. His travels have extended over all the northern States east of the Mississippi and through Canada and the provinces. He has published many articles in the press, and his opinions are regarded as of weight and value by scientific men. At the advanced age of eight-two his mind is remarkably active and his capacity for mental and physical labor great. He possesses a rare and valuable collection of minerals from all parts of America, as well as many choice relics gathered in the Holy Land. Mr. Jones was married, March 3, 1824, to Dalesa Crosby,

of Stockbridge, Massachusetts. She died in 1869, having borne one child, Sarah Elizabeth, born in 1825 and died at the age of twenty-three. January 13, 1872, he married Almira Mygatt, youngest daughter of Comfort S. Mygatt, one of the early merchants of Canfield.

Judson W. Canfield, farmer and county surveyor, Canfield, Mahoning county, was born in Canfield, December 5, 1828. He is the only son of Henry J. Canfield. He was educated in the schools of his native place, studied surveying with his father and S. W. Gilson, and began its practice in 1849. He has served three terms of three years each as county surveyor and is now serving a fourth term. As a practical surveyor Mr. Canfield sustains an enviable reputation. He was assistant provost marshal of the Nineteenth district during a portion of the war period, and was also assistant assessor of internal revenue several years. In addition to his other duties Mr. Canfield manages a large farm. On the 28th of February, 1853, he was married to Betsey M. Turner, daughter of James Turner, of Canfield. They have five children, namely: Julia A., Maude M., Walter H., Judson T., and Colden R. For Mr. Canfield's ancestry see the chapter on Canfield township. The first map of Mahoning county, made in 1861, is the work of Mr. Canfield.

John Dodson, merchant, Canfield, Mahoning county, was born at Stepney Green, near London, England, in 1808. In 1852 he emigrated to America, settling in Cleveland and engaging as a clerk in 1853. In 1859 he removed to Canfield and engaged in merchandising, which he continues to follow. Mr. Dodson was married in England in 1832 to Eleanor Sullivan. She died in 1854 in Canfield, having borne no children. In 1865 he married Melissa R. Skyles, a native of Pennsylvania, by whom he has two children living and one dead, viz: Victoria (deceased), Tom Vass, and John Warren. Mr. Dodson is a successful business man.

J. O. Corll, druggist, Canfield, Mahoning county, was born in Canfield township, November 20, 1857. He is a son of William Corll. He was educated in the schools of Canfield, and commenced business for himself in 1879. Mr. Corll is a young man of enterprise and is fast laying the foundation for a successful business career.

S. E. Dyball, dentist and merchant, Canfield, Mahoning county, was born in Orange, Cuyahoga county, May 2, 1856. He was educated in the schools of his native county; studied dentistry at Chagrin Falls, came to Canfield and began its practice in May, 1877. He soon found his business rapidly increasing and is now kept busy constantly. In the spring of 1881 he joined Mr. M. L. Edwards in a partnership in the dry goods business. Mr. Dyball was married October 31, 1877, to Lora J. Antisdale, of Chagrin Falls. He is a member of the Independent Order of Odd Fellows lodge. At the spring election, 1880, he was chosen mayor of the village of Canfield, which office he still continues to hold.

Dr. Jackson Truesdale, merchant, Canfield, Mahoning county, was born in Austintown township, in 1820. He is a son of John and Mary (Reed) Truesdale, of Poland township. His parents died when he was between four and five years of age, and thenceforth he was cared for by his grandmother until about twelve years old, at which time he became a member of the family of his uncle, Dr. Joseph Truesdale, of Poland township. He attended the select schools of Poland, and about the age of sixteen began studying under private tutors at Oberlin, and afterwards at Allegheny college. At the age of seventeen he commenced teaching in the district schools of this county, and in 1840 went to Kentucky, where he continued in the same employment. He taught three years or more in Kentucky and Tennessee, employing his spare time in the study of medicine. In 1844 he returned to this county and continued his studies under his uncle's tuition; attended medical lectures at the Cleveland Medical school; began the practice of medicine in 1846 at Lordstown, Trumbull county, removed thence to Frederick, Milton township, Mahoning county; from Frederick to North Benton, thence to North Jackson, and to Canfield in 1855. While residing in Jackson Dr. Truesdale was elected justice of the peace and served several years, and in 1854 he was elected county auditor of Mahoning county. At the expiration of his first term he was reelected and administered the duties of that responsible office during another term to the entire satisfaction of the citizens of the county. In 1859 the doctor embarked in mercantile enter-

prise, in which he still continues. Dr. Truesdale has been married four times; first to Julia Tanner, of Kentucky, she lived only a few months and died of consumption; second to Lola M Tyler, of Lorain county, who died after being married three or four years, leaving two children, Henry T. and Lola M. Henry entered company E, second Ohio cavalry at the age of sixteen; was captured by the enemy, and after nine months' imprisonment died at Andersonville. He was a noble young man and his untimely death was a heavy blow to his parents. Lola is the wife of Edgar Cummins, of Lorain county, where she resides. Dr. Truesdale was next married to Hannah Eckis, of Milton township, who lived about sixteen years after her marriage. There were no children. In 1865 he married the lady who now presides in his home, Lucy Allen Ripley, of Berlin, daughter of Edwin Ripley, and granddaughter of General Ripley. The fruits of this union have been three children, two of whom are living, viz: Eddie (died in infancy), William J., and John. Dr. Truesdale is a prominent member of the Independent Order of Odd Fellows lodge, from which he has received the highest honors within its gift. He has been a member of the Methodist church from boyhood.

Isaac Manchester, the third son of Benjamin Manchester, was born in Canfield in 1810, and was married October 2, 1834, to Eleanor, daughter of Hugh Wilson, who emigrated from county Down, in the north of Ireland, and settled in Canfield at an early day. She died October 18, 1867. To them were born six children, who are now living, viz: Hugh Alexander, born March 5, 1837; Robert Asa, born August 13, 1838; William John, born September 27, 1840; Mary Margaret, born April 22, 1844; Benjamin Oscar, born November 11, 1847; Hannah Jane Elizabeth, born July 20, 1854. They are all married. The oldest two live in Mahoning county, and the others all live in the State of Indiana. Benjamin Oscar is, at present, city clerk of Elkhart. H. A. Manchester and Miss Rose A. Squire, who was born September 27, 1838, were married November 8, 1859. She was the daughter of Asher Canfield Squire, who was a native of Connecticut, and moved with his father to Canfield, Ohio, at a very early day. Her mother was Mary, daughter of Thomas Jones, who moved from Maryland and settled in Ellsworth township in 1804. H. A. and Rose A. are the parents of six children, Mary E., born June 20, 1861, an intelligent and amiable girl, who died September 22, 1880; Laura E., born December 5, 1862; Fanny C., born July 8, 1865; Isaac Asher, born July 22, 1867; William Charles, born December 25, 1873; Curtis Asa, born November 6, 1876. H. A. received a liberal education at the Poland and Mahoning academies. He commenced teaching school at the age of eighteen, and has followed that profession more or less every year since. His general practice has been to teach in the fall and winter months, and to cultivate his farm in the spring and summer. He has taught the district school where he now lives, and in which he was raised, for twenty-three winters. He is now, and has been for the last six years, a member and clerk of the board of county school examiners. He has also been moderately successful and thrifty as a farmer, having acquired, by the aid of a most industrious and economical helpmeet, a farm of over two hundred acres in the southwest part of the township. He has been elected to fill, at different times, nearly every important local and township office. He is now one of the justices of the peace of the township, and has held the office for the last fourteen years. He was the Democratic candidate for Representative in the State Legislature at the last election, and though defeated, as the county is largely Republican, in his own township he received the entire vote of his party and nearly one-half of the whole Republican vote.

Jacob Barnes was a native of New Haven, Connecticut, born in 1785. In 1813 he married Nancy Carroll, who is still living. She was born in Surry county, Virginia, in 1790. The family moved to Canfield in 1826. There were twelve children, eight of whom arrived at maturity, and seven are still living—Ann (Doud), Chicago; Jacob H., Bement, Illinois; Jane (Ellett), Alliance, Ohio; Lois (Hine), Leetonia; Nancy (Neff), Humboldt, Kansas; Theophilus and Sarah, Canfield. Mr. Barnes was a pronounced anti-slavery man, and his efforts to assist the fugitives are of considerable local notoriety. He died in 1848. His widow now resides in Canfield village.

T. G. Barnes, son of Jacob and Nancy Barnes, was born in Canfield township, August 8, 1828. He has always followed farming, and has always lived upon the farm where he was born and of which he is now the owner, which consists of seventy-one acres. He married October 14, 1857, Miss Alice A. Cowden, the result of which union was three children, two sons and one daughter—Williard S., Gertrude C., and John J., all of whom are living.

Darius J. Church, of Canfield township, Mahoning county, was born in that town in 1825. He received a good common school education, and afterwards followed general merchandising, in which business he was successfully engaged for many years. In 1852, two days after the election of President Pierce, he was married to Miss Electa Morrel, of Orangeville, Wyoming county, New York, and by this union is the father of two children—Fannie, born July, 1853, now the wife of John T. McConnell, a merchant of Mineral Ridge, Mahoning county; and Fred Church, of the firm of Church & Coffee, of Youngstown, born September, 1854.

R. J. Crockett, farmer, Canfield township, Mahoning county, was born January 3, 1837. He was the second son of James and Sarah Crockett, who were the parents of ten children who grew up and were married. The subject of this sketch came from his native State, Virginia, when but two years of age with his parents to Ohio, the family settling in Portage county. At the outbreak of the rebellion he enlisted in company A, First Ohio light artillery, and served for four years. He participated in some of the severest engagements of the war, Shiloh, Chickamauga, Kenesaw Mountain, Mission Ridge, Stone River, etc. He received a wound in the arm near the shoulder by a ball from one of the enemy in one of the engagements, but the injury did not prove serious. At the expiration of his term of service he returned to his home, then in Stark county. He had learned the trade of carpenter and joiner, and he now took up that business and followed it for a few years. He then went to Ellsworth, Mahoning county, and was married to Miss Caroline Lour. To them have been born three children—Perry J., Frank, and Florence E. Mr. Crockett is the owner of a finely improved farm, the result of industry and economy. James Crockett, his father, was a soldier in the War of 1812.

Lewis Cramer, farmer, Canfield township, Mahoning county, second son of W. F. and Agnes C. Cramer, was born in Beaver township, Mahoning county, in 1837. His father and mother were natives of Germany, born respectively in the years 1793 and 1795. They emigrated from Germany with their family, consisting of four daughters and one son and the father of Mr. Cramer, in the year 1830. They came to what is now Mahoning county and settled in Beaver township. He cleared up and improved a farm which he occupied until 1855, when he moved to Berlin township where he resided until his death, 1860 or 1861. His wife survived him some twelve years. Lewis Cramer, when sixteen years of age learned the trade of carpenter and joiner and followed it with industry for sixteen years. He afterwards became a farmer and still continues in that occupation. He was married in 1867 to Miss Mary Ann Kenreigh and has two sons, Noah M. and William F. Mr. Cramer is a farmer of thrift and enterprise, as is plainly evidenced by his surroundings. Himself and Mrs. Cramer are both members of the Lutheran church.

David Clugston, of Canfield, Mahoning county, fifth son of Thomas and Mary Clugston, was born in Franklin county, Pennsylvania, in December, 1829. He was married in 1851 to Miss Lavona McKelvey, of Portage county. Mr. Clugston is a blacksmith by trade and is associated with Thomas C. Scott, under the firm name of Clugston & Scott, in that business in Canfield. He is an enterprising citizen, taking an active interest in educational matters. Himself and wife are both members of the Disciple church of Canfield.

J. S. Collar, manufacturer of lumber, Canfield township, Mahoning county, fourth son of Ira A. and Sarah E. Collar, is a native of Mahoning county, born in 1849. At an early age he began work in the mill with his father in the manufacture of lumber, which business he has successfully followed. He was married in 1873 to Miss Christina Toot and has two children—Carrie D. and Ella May.

William Y. Comstock, farmer, of Canfield township, Mahoning county, was born in Williamstown, Berkshire county, Massachusetts, January 12, 1816. He came to Portage county, Ohio, in 1832. September 1, 1842, he married Miss Betsey Hine, of Canfield, by whom he has three daughters, viz: Chenia W., born March 21, 1847, Carrie S., born October 26, 1853, Mary H., born April 22, 1858. Mr. and Mrs. Comstock are members of the Presbyterian church of Canfield. They are now residing upon the old Hine homestead.

Hiram Dean, farmer, of Canfield township, Mahoning county, is a native of Connecticut, born in the year 1799, and came with his father's family to Canfield. He married in 1821 Miss Ruby Mason, by whom he has had seven children, four sons and three daughters: Austin, Mason, Priscilla, Benjamin, Mary, William, and Minerva. Mason and Mary are still living. The rest are deceased. Benjamin died at Murfreesboro, Tennessee, during the war of the rebellion. Mr. and Mrs. Dean are prominent and zealous members of the Disciple church.

Orvill Edsall, eldest son of Henry Edsall, was born on the old homestead, where Amos Swank now lives, east of Canfield, December 13, 1825. He was married in April, 1852, to Lydia Ritter, daughter of Henry Ritter, now eighty-seven years of age and living in Berlin township. For several years after his marriage Mr. Edsall resided in Canfield, where he kept a grocery and provision store for some time, and then moved to the farm where he now lives. Mr. Edsall has a family of one daughter and two sons, viz: Julia, Charles H., and Edwin. One child is deceased —Hiram, who died in infancy. Julia married Charles Wetmore and has one child, Frank.

Benjamin L. Hine, fourth son of David and Achsah Hine, was born upon the old homestead in Canfield township, December 17, 1814. He assisted his father in carrying on the farm until twenty years of age, when he went to take care of his uncle Justus Sackett's farm, which he superintended for seven years while his uncle was absent dealing in stock. He then returned to his father's home near Canfield and took charge of the old farm for three years. He then purchased sixty acres near by, and as he prospered added to his original purchase, the farm containing one hundred and forty-two acres at the time of his death. He married Miss Silia W. Comstock October 5, 1841, and had one son and one daughter, Henry M. and Lucy E. He died October 20, 1872. His widow still survives and lives with her son Henry, who owns the old farm. He was born October 17, 1843; married January 1, 1866, Miss Clara Williams, and has two children—Charles H. and Frances Irene, two having died in infancy. Lucy married, January 3, 1870, Henry Cozad, by whom she had one child. Her husband lived but two years, and she subsequently married again and now resides in Akron, Ohio.

William Hine, the youngest child of David and Achsah Hine, was born upon the old Hine homestead in Canfield township, January 9, 1828. He married, September 30, 1851, Miss Mary A. McClelland, which union has been childless. From boyhood Mr. Hine has been engaged in agricultural pursuits and is now situated upon finely improved farm in Canfield. He is a representative of a pioneer and respected family. He and his wife are members of the Presbyterian church at Canfield.

Horace Hunt, farmer, Canfield township, Mahoning county, eldest son of Ezra Hunt, was born in Boardman township, that county, in 1805. Ezra Hunt came from Milford, Connecticut, about the beginning of the present century to Boardman township in company with Elijah Boardman, for whom the township was named. Mr. Hunt purchased a lot of Boardman on which he built a log cabin. About the year 1804 he married Miss Dema Sprague, daughter of an early settler. They encountered the various hardships and privations incident to pioneer life, and now sleep in the burying-ground at Canfield. They had a family of five sons and one daughter as follows: Horace, Charles, Emeline, Orvill, Richard, and Harmon. Orvill, Richard, and Emeline are dead. Richard died while in the army, at Nashville, Tennessee, during the war of the Rebellion. Horace remained on the farm with his father until twenty-five years of age, and also worked at the trade of carpenter and joiner. As early as sixteen he began teaching school. In 1833 he married Miss G. Ruggles, and has had five sons and one daughter—Cornelius C., Alfred A., Chauncey M., Alice M., Azor R., and Henry M. Alfred and Chauncey enlisted in the army in the war of 1861–65. Alfred fell in battle at Atlanta, Georgia, and lies buried in a Southern grave. Chauncey returned to his home at the close of the war in a shattered physical condition, but with careful nursing by a kind mother finally recovered. He now resides in Warren, Ohio, and is manager of the Kinsman Machine works. Horace Hunt is still residing on his first purchase. He and his wife are members of the Methodist Episcopal church of Canfield.

Eli Harding, farmer, Canfield township, Mahoning county, is the fifth child and third son of John and Elizabeth Harding, of the preceding sketch, and was born on the old homestead, near Canfield, December 20, 1821. He was raised upon the farm and remained with his father until he was twenty-five years of age. In 1849 he married Miss Rosa Yager, whose parents were early settlers in Mahoning county. They have a family consisting of one son and three daughters, all of whom are living, namely: Betty, John A., Julia A., and Charlotte. Mr. Harding is an enterprising citizen and prosperous farmer.

George E. Harding, farmer, Canfield township, Mahoning county, was born September 1, 1819. He is a representative of a family who were among the earliest settlers of that township. His grandfather, John Harding, came to the township with his family as early as 1805 or 1807, and settled on the farm now occupied by the subject of this sketch. He died in his seventy-ninth year, after a long life of toil and usefulness, his wife surviving him some years. After their death the homestead was bought by John, the second son, who was born in Lehigh county, Pennsylvania, in the year 1787. He came to Ohio with his parents. At the age of twenty-four he married Miss Elizabeth Crumrine. He had a family of five sons and three daughters, viz: Mary Ann, Elizabeth, John A., George E., Eli, Peter, Lucy Ann, and Jacob. Elizabeth, John A., and Jacob are deceased. John was killed by a hay fork striking him upon the head while unloading hay. The father and mother are both deceased, Mr. Harding surviving his wife nine or ten years. They were good citizens, earnest Christians, and useful members of society. George E. Harding, the fourth child and second son, as before stated, occupies the homestead which for so many years has been in possession of the family, and is one of the enterprising farmers of the community. He married, in 1850, Miss Elizabeth Lynn, and has a family of six daughters and one son, viz: Emma E., Fannie Alice, Melissa S., Anna S., Ida, Celia, and George L. One daughter (Mary Ellen) is dead.

Peter Harding, youngest son of John and Elizabeth Harding, was born on the old Harding homestead, near Canfield, October 18, 1824. He assisted his father in carrying on the farm until twenty-five years of age. Three years later he purchased sixty acres adjoining the old farm, and when thirty years of age he married Miss Amanda Diehl. They have four children as follow: Mary E., Willie G., Clara B., and Frankie I. Mary E. is the wife of J. A. Ebert, a farmer of Ellsworth township, and has one son and two daughters, Flora B., Scott Wilson, and Lizzie E. Mr. Harding is among the substantial and enterprising farmers of his township.

Jonathan Kline was born in Northampton county, Pennsylvania, in 1796 or 1797. His father was Abraham Kline, who came to Ohio in the early settlement of the county and located where the city of Youngstown now stands. Here he reared his family, consisting of three sons and three daughters. He was an active man and a large property-holder, dealing largely in stock, in which he was very successful. He was born in Northampton county, Pennsylvania, in 1769, and died December 1, 1816, at the age of forty-seven. Jonathan Kline at the age of twenty-five was married to Elizabeth, daughter of Philip Arner, having settled two years before upon a portion of his father's estate in Canfield township. He followed in the footsteps of his father, superintending his large estate, consisting of one thousand acres, and also dealt largely in stock. He was the father of five sons, viz: Solomon, Gabriel, Peter, Caleb, and Heman; all living but Caleb who died at the age of four years. Mr. Kline died in 1871, leaving a family of four sons and a widow, and numerous friends to mourn his loss. His widow is still living on the old place in Canfield. Peter Kline was born August 25, 1830, and in 1853 married Hannah Beard. The fruit of this union was one son, Jonathan Allen. Mr. Kline, like his father and grandfather, turned his attention to farming and stock-raising and is the owner of one of the best improved farms in his township. Heman Kline, the youngest son of Jonathan and Elizabeth Kline, was born in 1844, and at the age of nineteen married Miss Martha Folk, and settled in Berlin township on the farm where he now lives. He has three children, Charles H., Warren C., and Ida May.

John Kirk, farmer, Canfield township, Mahoning county, son of John and Ann Kirk, was born in Pittsburg, Pennsylvania, May 15, 1827. He came with his parents to Jefferson county, Ohio, in the year 1829. His father having died he remained with his mother until the twenty-third year of his age, when he married Miss Mary Pow, whose parents were early settlers in Mahoning county, owning the farm now owned by the subject of this sketch. To Mr. and Mrs. Kirk have been born three daughters—Elizabeth, Jane, and Barbara. Jane is the wife of M. S. Frederick. Mr. Kirk has given a good deal of attention to the raising of stock, and is the owner of a well-improved and good farm. Mrs. Kirk is a member of the Disciple church.

George D. Messerly, oldest child of John and Susannah Messerly, was born in Beaver township, now Mahoning county, in 1836, on the old Messerly homestead. He remained at home assisting his father upon the farm until his marriage in 1861. He married Miss Mary Ann Miller, and has one daughter and two sons—Hattie E., Joseph, and Charlie A.; Joseph died in infancy. Mr. Messerly is a thrifty and prosperous farmer, owning two hundred and forty-eight acres in the eastern part of Canfield township. He and his wife are both members of Paradise Reformed church, in Beaver township.

John C. Miller, manufacturer of lumber, Canfield township, Mahoning county, was born in that county in 1847. He remained upon the farm with his father until his marriage in 1869. His wife was Sarah E. Collar, by whom he has one child, Rollis R. In 1877 Mr. Miller and J. S. Collar formed a co-partnership for the manufacture of lumber, under the name of Miller & Collar. Their saw-mill is situated about two and a half miles south of Canfield.

Henry M. Meeker, carpenter and joiner, Canfield, Mahoning county, was born March 3, 1837. His father, Marion Meeker, was born in Connecticut in 1806; came to Mahoning county, then Trumbull, Ohio, in 1822. During his lifetime he was engaged in various pursuits; first a farmer and stock dealer and later proprietor of the Americal hotel, of Canfield, or more commonly known as the Meeker house. This he conducted until his death in 1865. His wife, whose maiden name was Cynthia D. Cleland, survived him several years, dying in March, 1872. They had a family of nine children, six sons and three daughters—Mary A., Anthony Wayne, Henry M., Marion, William C., Louis M., Maria H., Ora J., and Winfield Scott. William C. and Winfield are deceased. Henry Meeker, the subject of this sketch, is the only one of the family now residing in Mahoning county. At the age of seventeen he learned his trade, which he has since followed. He enlisted early in the war of the Rebellion in the Second Ohio volunteer cavalry, but became disabled and was discharged after a service of a year and a half. Returning to Canfield he married, in 1867, Miss Jennie Slaugh. To them was born one daughter, Minnie E. Mrs. M. is a member of the Disciple church.

John K. Misner, farmer, Canfield township, Mahoning county, was born in Berlin township, said county, in 1836. His father, George Misner, is a native of Pennsylvania, where he was born in 1813. He came to Mahoning county with his parents, Benjamin and Mary, about the year 1820, and settled in Berlin township. He married before reaching his majority, Miss Hannah Swartz, and raised a family of ten children —four sons and six daughters, as follow: Harriet, Zimri, John K., Lucy M., Frances, Isabella, George, Hannah, Jane, and James. One daughter, Lucinda, is deceased, dying in infancy. In 1837 the father removed with his family to Trumbull county, subsequently removed to Indiana, where he lived several years, then returned to Trumbull county, and at present resides in Southington township in that county. John K. Misner was married February 1, 1860, to Miss Lystra A. Beeman, and has a family of two sons and two daughters—C. E., Etta A., Charlie J., and Celia. Mr. Misner is one of the enterprising farmers of his township, owning one of the best improved farms, his farm containing one hundred and ninety acres, and situated two miles northwest of Canfield village.

Conrad Neff, with his wife and family of six children, emigrated from Berks county, Pennsylvania, to the then far distant West in 1802, and settled in Canfield township, then Trumbull county. Mr. Neff was among the earliest of that noble band of pioneers who invaded the wilderness of Canfield, and after untold hardships and privations made it to "blossom as the rose." Mr. Neff began with but little besides his own strong hands, and a determination to conquer the obstacles that lay in the way to success. He was a hard-working and an industrious man, and succeeded in acquiring a good property. He died at an advanced age, his wife surviving him but a few years. The estate afterward came into the possession of John and Conrad, his sons.

John Neff was born in 1797, and came with his father's family to Ohio, and always afterward resided upon the Neff homestead. At the age of twenty-four he married Elizabeth Kline, a representative of an early family in the township. To them were born five children—four sons and a daughter, as follows: Eli, Mary, Edward, Martin, and John. John, our subject, was an active and prosperous farmer, and dealt largely in live stock, principally in the buying and selling of cattle, in which he was very successful. He died in the spring of 1861, one week previous to the breaking out of the rebellion. He left surviving him a family of three children, and his wife, who died sixteen years later. They are buried in the cemetery at Canfield.

Martin Neff, son of John and Elizabeth Neff, was born on the old homestead March 24, 1828. His occupation through life has been that of farmer, having given considerable attention to stock-raising and the buying and selling of stock. April 5, 1848, he was married to Miss Catharine Wilson, the result of which union was five children, namely: John E., Caroline, Elizabeth J., Mary A., and Lewis, all living but Elizabeth. Mr. Neff is the owner of his father's old home, and is pleasantly situated on one of the best improved farms in that locality. He is one of the most substantial and respected citizens of his township.

John E. Neff, the oldest child of Martin Neff, was born on the old home farm February 24, 1849. March 31, 1870, he married Miss Harriet Louisa Sanzenbacher, and has a family of four sons and one daughter, as follows: Sadie, Ensign, Martin, Calvin, and Cyrus. Mr. Neff owns a fine farm of one hundred and twenty-five acres near Canfield, and is one of the most enterprising and prosperous young farmers of the township, giving considerable attention to the buying and selling of stock. He and his wife are members of the Methodist Episcopal church at Canfield.

Azor Ruggles, one of the early settlers of Canfield township, was born and brought up in Brookfield, Litchfield county, Connecticut, the date of his birth being May, 1769. He was a millwright and in 1810 came to Ohio on horseback for the purpose of doing some work for Judge Canfield. After remaining a year he returned to Connecticut and in 1813 brought out his family, consisting of his wife and six children. The journey was made with two wagons and teams and consumed one month. The oldest daughter drove one of the wagons. Mr. Ruggles first located on the farm where John Sanzenbacher now lives, remained one year and a half and settled permanently about two miles south of Canfield, where he died December 10, 1843. He was twice married. His first wife was Mary Peck, whom he married in Connecticut, and by whom he had six children, viz: Alice, Harriet, Julia, Charles, Galetsy, and Hepsey. Of these three are living, Charles, Galetsy (now Mrs. Horace Hunt), and Hepsey, who is unmarried and occupies the old homestead. His first wife died in 1828 and in 1832 he married Miss C. M. A. Mitchell, by whom he had two children, Robert M. and Mary Helen, now Mrs. James Mackey, of Youngstown. His second wife survived him and she afterwards became the wife of Dr. Manning, of Youngstown. Miss Hepsey Ruggles, who is now seventy-one years of age, has in her possession a couple of pillow cases made by her mother before her marriage, in 1790, and a picture frame made of the rim of the wheel on which the material used in the making of the pillow-cases was spun; also a rocking-chair in which her mother rode all the way from Connecticut when the family moved to Ohio.

Jacob Resch, tanner, Canfield, Mahoning county, only son of John and Catharine Resch, is a native of Germany, born December 26, 1835. In 1852, at the age of seventeen, he started out to seek his fortune and sailed for America. He learned the tanner's trade, and soon after his arrival in this country commenced business at Newton Falls, where he remained for a short time, when he removed to Berlin Center where he carried on the business for ten years. He settled in Canfield in 1870 and has since been engaged in the manufacture of leather. He married, in 1857, Miss Mary Goeppinger,

and has a family of nine children, named as follows: John, Charles, Frank, Albert, Fred, Mary, Laura, Louisa, and Lilly. Mr. Resch has a leather and finding store in Youngstown. He is a member of the Lutheran church, as is also his wife.

Jacob F. Stambaugh, coal dealer, Canfield, Mahoning county, second son of William and Sarah Stambaugh, was born in Liberty township, Trumbull county, Ohio, February 3, 1845. He assisted his father upon the farm until fifteen years of age, and at the age of eighteen he enlisted in company B, One Hundred and Fifty-fifth regiment, one hundred day service, in the late war. After the expiration of his service he returned to Youngstown, Ohio, and until thirty years of age was engaged in various pursuits. In 1875 he was united in marriage to Miss Elizabeth Milliken, and has had two children, Frederick and Roy. In 1880 Mr. Stambaugh went to Canfield, and the same year engaged with others in mining in Green township, Mahoning county. The parents of Mr. Stambaugh were early settlers in Trumbull county.

Mathias Swank (deceased) was born in Lehigh county, Pennsylvania, in the year 1812. Soon after attaining his majority he married Margaret Strone, by whom he had three children, one son and two daughters: Hannah, Mary Etta, and Emery. His wife died January 8, 1867, and he afterwards married Miss J. E. Wetmore. There were no children by this marriage. Mr. Swank's business was principally that of carriage manufacturing, which he carried on successfully for a period of nearly forty years, settling in Canfield in 1835. He died July 1, 1881, leaving a devoted wife and many friends to mourn his loss. He was an active, enterprising business man, a good neighbor and citizen. His remains were interred in the cemetery in Canfield. Mrs. Swank still lives at the old home in Canfield.

Thomas C. Scott, blacksmith, Canfield, Mahoning county, second son of Hiram B. and Elizabeth Scott, was born in Stark county, Ohio, September 24, 1845. At the age of twenty-three he went as an apprentice to learn the trade which he now follows, with David Clugston, and subsequently entered into partnership with him, and the firm is now known as Clugston & Scott. He married, in 1872, Miss Mary C. Parshall, and has three children—Charles William, Ernest David, and Sophia Elizabeth. Mr. Scott was in the hundred-day service in the war of the Rebellion. He and his wife are members of the Disciple church of Canfield.

Julius Tanner, farmer, Canfield township, Mahoning county, eldest son of Edmund P. and Fannie Tanner, is a native of the township in which he resides, having been born October 6, 1818, on the farm which he now occupies—the Tanner homestead. He has been twice married. His first wife was Mary Wadsworth, daughter of one of the earliest pioneers of the township. By this marriage there were four children, three sons and one daughter, named as follows: Edward W., Henry W., Henry A., and Mary I. All are living except Henry W. The mother died in 1855, and Mr. Tanner subsequently married Mrs. Fidelia Sackett, widow of Ward Sackett. By his second wife he has three children—Fannie C., Edwin P., and Horace B. Fannie is deceased. Mr. Tanner is one of the substantial and esteemed citizens of his township. He and his wife are members of the Congregational church of Canfield.

Ira M. Twiss, superintendent county infirmary, Canfield township, Mahoning county, was born in that county, Poland township, October 7, 1837. His father, John Twiss, with his wife and one child, emigrated about the year 1820 from Connecticut to Ohio and settled in what is now Mahoning county, Boardman township. There he reared a family of five sons and three daughters, viz: Frederick, Mary, Seymour, Minerva, Samuel, Sarah, Ira, and Titus. Three of the children are deceased, to wit: Frederick, Minerva, and Sarah. Only two of the children are now living in Mahoning county, viz: Titus, of Boardman, and Ira, of Canfield. Mr. Twiss, the subject of this sketch, had followed agricultural pursuits until his appointment as superintendent of the county infirmary in the spring of 1878. This institution is pleasantly situated about two miles northwest of Canfield, the farm containing two hundred and thirty acres of land, with good buildings. Soon after attaining his majority our subject was married to Almira Osborn. The result of this union is one son—Curtis W.

John Williams (deceased), a native of Pennsylvania, emigrated with his family from Bedford county in wagons to Ohio about the year 1820. He came to Mahoning county and settled in

Canfield on what is commonly known as the Atwood place. Here he lived and reared a family of two sons and three daughters named as follow: James, Betsey (Scott), Banner, Nancy (Dean), and Rachael (Porter). Mr. Williams was an industrious and hard-working man, and was in the War of 1812. He died at his home in Canfield at the age of sixty-five. His wife survived him four years.

Banner Williams, farmer, Canfield township, Mahoning county, second son of John Williams, was born in Pennsylvania in 1813 and removed to Ohio with his parents. He was united in marriage in 1841 to Miss Clarissa Lew, who died two years afterward. He married for his second wife Miss Margaret McDonald, by whom he has had four daughters and one son, viz: Clarissa, James, Mariette and Mary Ellen (twins), and Flora. Mariette is deceased. She was the wife of James Van Horn and left three children. Mr. Williams has always been engaged in farming and stock raising, and has given special attention to the growing of wool. Mrs. Williams is a member of the Disciple church.

Azariah Wetmore (deceased), one of the earliest pioneers in Canfield township, Mahoning county, came from Connecticut in 1801. He was then single, and came out with the Wadsworths, driving an ox team, the second team of oxen brought into that locality. He made his home with the Wadsworths and helped to clear the same fall some four acres where the village of Canfield now stands. In a few months he returned to Connecticut, but came back the next year. He afterwards purchased one hundred and twenty-five acres of land south of the present village of Canfield, where his son George now lives. He married in 1806 Miss Balinda Sprague and had a family of three sons and five daughters, as follows: Caroline, Harriet, Cornelia, Sarah, Betsy, William, Henry, and George.

William Wetmore, farmer, Canfield township, Mahoning county, eldest son of the subject of the preceding sketch, was born in 1816. At the age of twenty-two he married Miss Susan Edwards, daughter of an early and prominent family, and has had three children—Walden, Luther E., and Henry P. Walden is deceased. Mr. Wetmore is an industrious, intelligent, and influential citizen.

Thomas J. Wise, coal operator, Canfield, Mahoning county, second son of John and Mary Wise, was born in Mahoning county, February 8, 1849. He remained on the farm of his father until sixteen years of age, when he became a clerk in a store. In the fall of 1880 he engaged in operating in coal, the mine being situated in Green township, Mahoning county. The mine is one of the most promising in that locality, and preparations are being made to work it extensively. Mr. Wise was married in 1872 to Miss Jennie R. Thorn, of Allegheny City, Pennsylvania. They have only one son, James T.

Eli Yager, farmer, Canfield township, Mahoning county, was born on the farm where he now lives, in 1832. The Yager family were among the earliest in that neighborhood. Henry Yager came with his family from Pennsylvania to Canfield township, now Mahoning county, in 1800 or 1801, and resided there until his death. His wife survived him about ten years. After their death the homestead was bought by Daniel, the third son. He was born on the farm now owned and occupied by his son Eli, whose name heads this sketch, in 1811. He married Elizabeth Carr, by whom he had three children—Eli, Edwin, and Mary. Edwin is deceased. The mother died in 1871. Eli Yager has always lived on the farm which he now occupies, a period of nearly half a century. He was married in 1865 to Miss Rebecca Corll, and now has two children—Eda P. and Irvin C. Mr. Yager is an industrious and prosperous farmer, his farm being one of the most highly cultivated and improved in the neighborhood. He and his wife are both members of the Reformed church.

CHAPTER II.

POLAND.

GENERAL DESCRIPTION.

This township is the southeastern township of the Western Reserve, and is therefore township one of range one of the Reserve. It is bounded on the north by Coitsville, on the east by Pennsylvania, on the south by Spring-

field, and on the west by Boardman. It was settled almost as early as any part of the county, and by the year 1810 contained quite a large population which came principally from Pennsylvania.

The surface is quite uneven, especially in the northern half, which is cut by the deep and narrow valleys of the Mahoning and the Yellow creek. The Mahoning flows in a southeasterly direction through the northeastern part of the township, entering at Struthers, and passing out into Pennsylvania about one-half mile north of the center road. Yellow creek winds its sinuous course through Poland village, and flowing northeast enters the Mahoning at Struthers.

There are many coal deposits, some of them of superior quality. Iron ore is found in considerable quantities on Yellow creek and elsewhere, and the very best of limestone in the vicinity of Lowellville. All of the land was heavily wooded originally. The youth of the present day would doubtless shrink in dismay from the task, if told that such forests must be extirpated before they could have homes and farms of their own.

The soil is deep and fertile, and many excellent farms are included in the township. The farming community appears to be industrious, well contented and prosperous. The other industries furnish abundance of work for all the laborers, and the general prosperity of Poland township is fast increasing. By the last census the population, including the villages, was 2,513.

SETTLEMENT.

Unlike many of the townships Poland was colonized by quite a large number during the first two or three years of its history. The first arrival was Turhand Kirtland, of Wallingford, Connecticut, afterwards known as Judge Kirtland, one of the foremost citizens. He came to the Reserve in 1798, and arrived within the present limits of Poland township, accompanied by Esquire Law and six other men, on the first day of August. He acted in the capacity of agent for the Connecticut Land company. During that year he surveyed the townships in the Reserve now known as Burton and Poland, and also assisted Judge Young in surveying Youngstown, returning to Connecticut to pass the winter. In May, 1799, he was again in Youngstown, stopping with Robert Stevens. He also spent the summer of 1800 upon the Reserve.

A few years later Mr. Kirtland and his brother Jared brought their families to Poland and took up their abode in the village. Turhand Kirtland was State Senator in 1814, and also served as associate judge. He was long and favorably known as an active business man and a public-spirited citizen. Through his dealings in his office of land agent he became acquainted with a large number of the pioneers, all of whom bore witness to his popularity and influence. His son, Dr. Jared P. Kirtland, was likewise an honored citizen during his residence in the county. He served as Representative three years.

Judge Kirtland kept a diary of events during the earliest years of his settlement, which has been furnished for our use by Hon. C. F. Kirtland, of Poland, and from it many of the early incidents in this history are taken.

Jonathan Fowler, of Guilford, Connecticut, was the first white settler in the township. Mrs. Fowler was a sister of Judge Kirtland. They came from Connecticut to Pittsburg by land conveyance, thence by water down the Ohio, and up the Big Beaver and Mahoning rivers in a canoe. The family, consisting of Mr. Fowler, his wife, and an infant daughter, arrived in Youngstown in the latter part of May, 1799. Judge Kirtland was then stopping there, and took them to Poland in his wagon. They all lodged for the night by the side of a fire, with no shelter save the open sky and a big oak tree, on a spot a few rods west of Yellow creek on the lot afterwards owned by Dr. Truesdale. Let the mothers of the present day try to picture to themselves this scene: A deep and lonely forest, the abode of wild beasts and lurking savages; the silence of midnight broken only by the crackling of the camp-fire, the rustle of the leaves in the breeze, and the faint sound of the flowing stream. In this lonely spot is a woman with her babe in her arms, and two men and their rifles are her only protectors! Without a roof above their heads, with no human beings within miles of them, unless perchance some wandering Indians, we cannot imagine that this party passed the night without gloomy thoughts and forebodings, and speculations as to what might occur. The fortitude of Mrs. Fowler demands our admiration, and deserves to be remembered by

coming generations. Shortly after their arrival a cabin was erected from logs previously made ready by Esquire Law, and into this the family moved and made it their home. Their daughter, Rachel B. Fowler, who married Thomas Riley in 1820, was born February 16, 1800, the first white child born in the township. Jonathan Fowler was drowned in the Big Beaver April 12, 1806, while engaged in boating merchandise upon the river. He was the father of Dr. Chauncy Fowler, of Canfield, and the grandfather of Dr. C. N. Fowler, of Youngstown.

John Struthers, from Washington county, Pennsylvania, bought four hundred acres of land and a mill site on Yellow creek, near its mouth, August 30, 1799, negotiating with Judge Kirtland for the same. On the 19th of October, in the same year, Mr. Struthers and his family arrived and settled upon this purchase, now the site of the flourishing little village called by his name. Here, in August, 1800, Ebenezer Struthers was born, the first white male child born in the township. Alexander Struthers, a lieutenant in the War of 1812, died in the service of his country at Detroit, in the latter part of the year 1813. Hon. Thomas Struthers, of Warren, Pennsylvania, well known in this vicinity, was born at the home of his father, John Struthers, in 1803, and is now the only surviving member of the family. His brother John, who lived upon a farm adjacent to the old homestead, died a short time ago.

For a few years after the coming of these pioneers the land was taken up very rapidly. The most of the settlers came from Washington and Franklin counties, Pennsylvania, and from that vicinity. Forests were cleared away, log cabins were erected in various parts of the township, and initiatory farming operations were begun upon the farms which are now as rich and productive as any in the county.

From the most reliable information that is now attainable, the following facts regarding early families have been gathered. The account is not so complete as the writer would have been glad to make it, but every precaution has been taken to have it as full and authentic as possible. At this late date many of the early families have no living representatives here, and there is consequently much uncertainty regarding the exact dates of their coming:

In 1800 John Arrel purchased land in the township and settled where his son Walter S. Arrel now resides. A complete family record is given elsewhere in this work.

John McGill came from Pennsylvania the same year and bought two hundred acres where the village of Lowellville now stands. He lived and died upon the farm. His sons were: James, Joseph, Fenton, Robert, John, and William. There were also several daughters. John and Robert died some years ago at Lowellville, and probably none of the original family are now living.

John Miller, from Franklin county, Pennsylvania, bought two hundred acres in lot fifty-seven near the east or Pennsylvania line. He probably located here as early as 1800. He married in the township and brought up one son and two daughters. His son Isaac still lives in the township.

About 1800 Stephen Frazier settled on the west line of the township near the Stambaugh farm.

In 1800 or 1801 William Buck and family settled in the same neighborhood.

James Adair, from Washington county, Pennsylvania, settled on lot twenty-four, and later took up a farm near the river. Among his children were William, Alexander, and James, for many years residents of the township.

John Dickson settled in the township in 1801. His sons now occupy the old farm.

Rev. James Duncan was an early settler on the north side of the Mahoning, adjoining the State line. He was the first pastor of the church at the center and also preached on McBride's hill, in Pennsylvania.

Thomas and John Jordan with their families settled on the Youngstown road, in the western part of the township about 1800. Later they sold out and moved away.

Samuel Lowden was an early settler on the north side of the Mahoning. He lived and died a single man. There was some mystery surrounding his departure from earth and by some he was supposed to have been murdered.

Rev. Nicholas Pettinger came into the township and settled in 1801. He was the first pastor of the Presbyterian church.

Francis Henry settled on the Yellow creek below Poland village in 1801 or 1802. Among his children were William, James, John, and Francis. William settled in the township and remained for a short time. James removed to Austintown. Francis lived upon the old place until he was an aged man.

Robert Smith, from Franklin county, Pennsylvania, settled on the south line of the township in 1802. The family consisted of six sons and four daughters. James, Robert, John, Stewart, Joseph, and Samuel were the sons. The two last named still live in the township.

Benjamin Leach settled west of Yellow creek about 1802. A few years later he sold to Arthur Anderson.

Patrick McKeever was an early settler on the north side of the Mahoning, and passed his life in the township. His farm adjoined that of Samuel Lowden.

The widow Cowden and her sons, Joseph, William, Reynolds, and Dr. Isaac P. Cowden, were among the early settlers. William located in the southern part of the township, and Reynolds settled near him. Dr. Cowden settled on the place where his son Samuel now resides. He was the first settled physician in the township, and had a large practice in this vicinity. He died in 1855 in his eightieth year. He rode day and night over miles and miles of bad roads in early times. He was honored and respected by old and young.

Francis Barclay, from Franklin county, Pennsylvania, settled one and one-half miles southeast of the center in 1802, and afterwards moved to the Pennsylvania line. He married Elizabeth Wilson, and brought up a large family. Ten sons and three daughters arrived at maturity. Alexander is the only one of these children now living in the township. James was for many years a resident of Poland village. He died in March, 1875.

William McCombs, a native of Washington county, Pennsylvania, settled in 1802 on the farm where his son William M. now lives. He died in 1854, leaving a wife and nine children.

Peter Shoaf settled in the southeast part of the township, on the Pennsylvania line, at an early day. Thomas Love came about 1802. His son William, the only surviving soldier of the War of 1812 in this township, is still a resident here.

Robert Lowry, a native of Ireland, and his

sons, Robert, William, and Johnston, settled in the township in 1802. William died in 1827. His son, J. J. Lowry, now occupies the old farm.

James Russel and family, from Pennsylvania, were early settlers. Mr. Russel located one mile south of Poland Center. He had three sons— Robert, John, and Joseph—and two daughters, all of whom lived and died in the township, excepting Robert and Joseph, who died in the West. Major John Russel was "a" well known citizen.

Thomas McCullough settled in the township in 1803, and brought up a family, which is still well represented in the township.

William Guthrie, from Franklin county, Pennsylvania, purchased in 1800 the farm of two hundred acres on which he settled in 1804. He brought up two sons and two daughters. The sons, James S. and John, are still living, the former eighty-one years old and the latter seventy-three. William Guthrie died in 1848, and his wife in 1849.

Ludwig Ripple located on the east side of Yellow creek at an early date. He died on the place, and after his death the family, which was quite large, scattered.

James Stewart and family, from Franklin county, Pennsylvania, settled near Struthers. His son John lived and died upon the place. ·

Gilbert Buchanan came about 1803 with his sons, Walter, Isaac, and James, and settled on the southeast center lot. Isaac and James lived with their father. Isaac never married. James married but had no family. Walter settled just west of Lowellville and brought up a large family, which moved away after his death.

John Hineman and his sons, John and Samuel, were early settlers on the south side of the river, but did not long remain.

The name Truesdale is well known in this county. The progenitor of the Ohio branch of this family was John Truesdale, of Scotch-Irish blood, born in Ireland in 1745. He came to America with his father, John, in 1771; was a revolutionary soldier; married Hannah Robinson and settled in what is now Perry county, Pennsylvania; removed thence to Washington county, in the same State; and in 1804 to Poland township, settling on a farm between the village and the center. Here the family resided nine years, and then moved to a farm about a mile south-

west of the center of Austintown. John Truesdale died in 1819 aged seventy-four; Mrs. Truesdale in 1849. Their children were John, James, Jane, Mary, Hugh, William, Nancy, Alexander, Samuel, Margaret, Robinson, and Joseph. Nancy and Samuel died young. Ten grew to maturity. Mary married but died without issue. John and James were twins and were born in 1782. Soon after coming to Poland, John married Mary Reed, and settled for life in Austintown. With three other brothers he served in the War of 1812. Both he and his wife died in 1825. Their children were: James, William, Mary, John, and Jackson. William, a successful business man of Peoria, Illinois, died in 1881. James settled in Canfield. He married Orpha Parker, of Kinsman, now Mrs. Elijah Bond. He died in 1845. John died in Hartford, Trumbull county, in 1849. Jackson is a well-known citizen of Canfield. James, the second son of John Truesdale, married three times. The name of his first wife is forgotten. His second was Jane Buchanan, of Poland, and his third Susan Jordan, of Austintown, where he passed the greater portion of his life. By his first marriage he had three sons, William, John, and James. By his third, a daughter, Mary. William and James are dead. John lives in Wisconsin and Mary (Clemens) in Liberty, Trumbull county. James, the father, died in 1862, in his eighty-first year. Jane, the third child of the original family, remained single and died in Ellsworth in 1851, aged sixty-eight. Hugh, the third son, born in 1790, died in Poland in 1862. He held the office of justice of the peace many years, being first elected when twenty-one years old. He married, first, Anna Riley, and second, Mrs. Rachael Walker. Rachael (Cowden), Julianna (Bingham), and Margaret (Kennedy), daughters by the second marriage, are still living. William, John's fourth son, born in 1795, died in Austintown in 1826, on the old homestead. He married Mary Jordan and had four children, viz: Clark, Priscilla, John R., and Calvin. William was an officer in the artillery service of the War of 1812. He was justice of the peace from twenty-one years of age until the end of his life. Of his children Clark and Priscilla died young. John R., born in 1821, died in Canfield in 1879, a worthy citizen. Calvin studied medicine with his uncle, Dr.

W. S. Arrel

Mrs. W. S. Arrel

Truesdale, of Poland, and is now a prominent physician in Rock Island, Illinois. Alexander Truesdale, born in 1798, died in Youngstown in 1874. He married Hannah Leech, of Austintown, who bore the following children: Olive (Weher), Canfield; John Addison, Thomas Jefferson, James Madison, and Hannah Maria (Woodruff), all dead; William Wallace, Benjamin F., Lucy Jane (Jacobs), Charles R., and Joseph Alexander. Benjamin F. and Joseph A. are dead. Charles R. is the prosecuting attorney of Mahoning county. Margaret, the youngest daughter of John, born in 1799, died in Ellsworth in 1868. She married Jonathan Eastman and had eight children,—William, James R., Sarah, Almon, Joseph, John, Mary Marilla, and Mary Melissa. James, Sarah, and Marilla are dead. Robinson Truesdale was born in 1801 and died in Youngstown in 1866. He was a colonel of militia. For his first wife he married Catharine Borden, of Hartford, and for his second Belinda Avery. By his first marriage the children were George, Charles, Amelia, Mary, Clinton, Dwight first and Dwight second. George, Mary, Clinton, and Dwight first are dead. Dwight and Charles are leading business men of Cincinnati. Colonel Truesdale was a good and useful citizen. Joseph, the youngest son of John and Hannah Truesdale, was born in 1804 and died in 1871. He studied medicine with Dr. Jones, of Hartford, Ohio, and graduated at the Ohio Medical college, in Cincinnati. He succeeded Dr. Jared P. Kirtland in the practice of his profession in Poland village, and was an honored and welcome guest in many a household whenever sickness visited its members. His practice in Poland and adjacent townships was large and everywhere received with favor. In 1847 and in 1856-57 he was a member of the State Legislature. He married Eliza, daughter of Judge Hays, of Hartford, Trumbull county, and reared a large family, six of whom are living: Sarah M. (Riley), Pulaski, Pennsylvania; Ellen E. (Smith), London, England; Lucy C. (Rockwood), Chicago; Dr. Seth H., Mount Jackson, Pennsylvania; Charlotte E. (King), and Fred, Chicago.*

William Brown settled in Poland township

* NOTE.—Though the history of this family properly belongs to several townships, we have included it all here, to avoid separating what should be connected.

at an early day. His son now occupies the farm.

Stephen Sexton, from Washington county, Pennsylvania, settled near the northwest corner of the township in 1803. He purchased two hundred acres of land at $2.50 an acre. He brought up four sons and three daughters. Joseph Sexton, born April 7, 1796, is the only one living at this date. His sister Nancy, wife of John Justice, died in the spring of 1881 in her eightieth year. Mr. Sexton recalls the following facts which may be interesting to the younger readers of this volume. He has known of his father giving eighteen bushels of wheat for a barrel of salt; of selling oats at ten cents per bushel, to get money to pay taxes, and has seen the taxes on two hundred acres paid with a five dollar bill. He remembers well of hearing a store keeper refuse to take wheat at twenty-five cents per bushel in payment of debt.

Isaac Walker and his father Nathaniel were early settlers in the northeast of the township. Rachel, the wife of Isaac, came on horseback from Pennsylvania to Poland on a visit in April, 1811. She was married to Mr. Walker in November of the same year. He was elected captain of a military company in the fall of 1812, and in February, 1813, started with his company for the seat of war. Soon after reaching Fort Stephenson he was stricken with camp fever, and died April 5, 1813. Mrs. Walker remained in possession of the farm until her death, March 20, 1870. Isaac Walker was the father of one daughter, now the wife of John Stewart, Esq.

James Blackburn settled on the Center road early. His sons James and John, also early settlers, lived and died in the township.

James McNabb was an early settler. His son James lived upon the old place until his death in the year 1865. His widow still resides there.

The Moores were early settlers and are elsewhere mentioned.

William Campbell and family moved from Pennsylvania and settled on lot number twenty-four. The sons, John, Allen, William, and James, none of whom are living, were all residents of this township.

William Reed and family, from Washington county, Pennsylvania, settled just southwest of the center of the township. James, William, and Samuel were among the children. Several of the grandchildren of William Reed, Sr., are residents of the township.

Andrew Dunlap came from Pennsylvania and settled three-fourths of a mile southeast of Poland village. He married the widow of Jonathan Fowler and brought up several sons and daughters, among whom were Chauncy and David.

John McConnell, a native of Ireland, settled at Poland Center. He brought up a family of six sons and two daughters, none of whom are living. He was killed by being thrown from a wagon. His son John built a tannery on the farm, afterwards one at Poland village, where he worked at tanning and shoemaking for some years, then married and moved away. Thomas McConnell, a son of John, Sr., settled near Poland Center. He was the father of six children, three of whom arrived at maturity, and one of them—John McConnel—is still living near Poland village, and is now in his eightieth year. Nicholas lived and died in the township, brought up two children, who are yet living. Jane, a daughter of John, Sr., became the wife of Robert Walker. Both are dead.

William McConnell, not a relative of John McConnell, settled near the Center, and brought up a large family, all of whom moved away.

Brian Slavin settled west of the Center about 1806 and reared a large family.

John McCulley, who came from west of Pittsburg, settled quite early at Poland village and was the first blacksmith in the place. He sold out and went to Portage county in 1833. He was married, after coming here, to Sarah Jewell, a native of New Jersey. This marriage took place February 16, 1808, in a log house on Water street. A marriage was a rare event in those days, and people came from far and near to witness the ceremony. The house was too small to contain more than a small portion of the visitors, so they built up a huge fire out of doors and stood patiently by it until the interesting exercises were over.

RECORDS.

No doubt the early records of this township, if they could be found, would give some very interesting history. But they are lost, and the names of the early township officers are consequently not to be ascertained.

AN ANCIENT TAX-LIST.

In the year 1803 Poland had a larger number of inhabitants than any other of the ten Western Reserve townships now included in Mahoning county. Poland that year paid a tax of $48.24, which was about $8 more than the tax of Youngstown, then the next largest of the townships above mentioned. We give the list of tax-payers for 1803:

POLAND, RANGE ONE, TOWN ONE.

	Amount of Tax.		Amount of Tax.
Adair, William	$ 41	Kirtland, Jared	$ 5 08
Brierly, George	83	Kirtland, Isaac	41
Buchanan, John	60	Keys, Jonas	40
Burgess Heirs	41	Leach, Benjamin	40
Blackburn, John,	40	McGill, John	84
Buchanan, Gilbert	39	McConnell, William	30
Beach, William	41	McConnell, John	39
Gray, John	27	McCullough, John	41
Cowden, William	20	McCombs, John, Jr	20
Cowden, Joseph	40	McCombs, John and	
Craycraft, Joseph	40	William	40
Campbell, William and Brice	—	McCullough, Thomas	40
		McIvers, and Lowdon	20
Chapin	41	McGill, Fenton	40
Dunlap, William	80	Moore, William	78
Duncan, James	40	Miller, John	80
Dawson, Thomas	20	Nelson, Archibald	20
Dawson, Jacob	40	Ripple, Henry	40
Dickson, John	84	Smith, Robert	1 60
Earl, John	80	Struthers, John	80
Earl, David	40	Sheerer, John	20
Embrie, James	40	Shoaf, Peter	80
Fowler, Jonathan	68	Stewart, William	38
Frazer, Jonathan	1 23	Sexton, Stephen	40
Gordon, Thomas	41	Truesdale, John	39
Guthrie, William	40	Vance, Andrew	40
Hinneman, John	40	Wishard, John	22
Henry, Francis	20	Webb, James	40
Jordan, John	40		
Kirtland, Turhand	17.55	Total	$48 24

INCEPTION OF THE IRON INDUSTRY.

The manufacture of iron, now the chief industry of the Mahoning valley, had its birth in Poland township, and Dan Eaton, that odd compound of good sense and whimsical notions, was its father. As there is much uncertainty as to the exact date at which this important industry began, we reproduce the testimony of those who are best informed upon the matter. Thomas Struthers, now of Warren, Pennsylvania, says:

I cannot obtain evidence of the exact date when the first blast furnace on the Reserve was started into operation. Daniel Heaton (afterward abbreviated to Dan Eaton, by act of Assembly) I am satisfied built the stack, and made contracts for ore, and wood for coal for a blast-furnace, in 1803; and the recollection of my older brother is that he had it in operation that year. The only doubt as to the correctness of his recollection arises from the fact of a suit found on record by John Hayes and Dan Heaton vs. James Douglass, June term, 1808, claiming damages for the imperfect construction of a furnace bellows, contracted for September 1, 1806. This may have been to replace the original one, however. It was located about one and one-fourth miles from the mouth of Yellow creek, in the township of Poland, then Trumbull, now Mahoning county. It is certain that Robert Montgomery and John Struthers, my father, built and put in operation a blast-furnace on the same stream, and on the farm on which the furnace of the Struthers Iron company now stands, in the year 1806. These furnaces were of about equal capacity, and would yield about two and a half or three tons each per day. The metal was principally run into molds for kettles, caldrons, bake-ovens, flat-irons, stoves, hand-irons, and such other articles as the needs of new settlers required, and any surplus into pigs and sent to the Pittsburg market. These were, I believe, the first blast-furnaces built in the State of Ohio, certainly the first on the Reserve. The former, it is said, had for one side the natural rock of the bluff, against which it was built, and for that or other reasons was fickle in its working, and probably did not last long. I have no recollection of ever seeing it in blast. The latter continued to work until 1812, when the men were all drafted into the war, and it was never started up again.

David Loveland, who was born and always lived near the site of the old furnaces, when in his seventy-fifth year wrote concerning them as follows:

The manufacture of iron in the Mahoning valley, now one of its most important interests, was first commenced near the mouth of Yellow creek, a short distance from Struther's station, and about five miles southeast of Youngstown, by two brothers, James and Daniel Heaton. These brothers were of an enterprising and experimenting disposition, and their faces will easily be remembered by many of the older settlers in and about Youngstown.

In 1805 or 1806 they erected, on Yellow creek, near the Mahoning river, a charcoal furnace, which soon went into active operation. Connected with, and belonging to, the furnace proper were about one hundred acres of well-timbered land, which supplied the charcoal and much of the ore for the works. The "blast" was produced by an apparatus of rather peculiar construction, and was similar in principle to that produced by the column of water of the early furnaces. It consisted of a square wooden box set in a cistern, with an opening at the top for the ingress of water, and one in the side to conduct the air or "blast" to the furnace. The surplus water escaped underneath. The water, flowing in through a pipe at the top of the box, was accompanied with air, which, being compressed by the continual flow, was forced through the side opening, and conducted from thence by a pipe to the furnace stack. The "blast" thus obtained has always, I am informed, been considered objectionable on account of its damp and chilly character. At any rate it was the case in the present instance.

After this furnace had been in operation for some time James Heaton transferred his interest in the property to his brother Daniel, and went up to Niles where he built another furnace. Dan continued at the old works and manufactured considerable iron, much of it consisting of stoves, large kettles and other castings, the appearance of which might be considered rude in these days.

While thus engaged Robert Montgomery (with whom I think was then associated David Clendenin, our member of Congress elected in 1814) built a furnace on the same creek about a half-mile* below Heaton's. It was constructed substantially in the same manner as the Heaton furnace, except that the blast was much better, being generated by a water-wheel, walking-beams, and two wooden cylinders.

Soon after the last named furnace went into operation Montgomery purchased the Heaton furnace property paying for the same $1,000 in land, and giving a mortgage for the balance of the purchase money. It went out of blast almost immediately after it changed hands. It then got into the courts, and after being in litigation for several years, was re-transferred to Daniel Heaton, its original owner, who about that time or shortly afterward had his name changed by act of the Legislature to Dan Eaton. It was never started up again, however, after its sale to Montgomery, and in all, never made iron for more than three years. Both furnaces went to ruin after the year 1812.

This, in brief, was the inception of our now great branch of trade.   .   .   .   Though the writer might justly distrust his early recollections, he would add that they have often been verified by subsequent acquaintance and inter-communication with the Heatons and many of the older settlers and early pioneers of this region, and it is with pleasure that he now has the opportunity of testifying to the merits of those two brothers, James and Daniel Heaton, who, with indomitable will, first gave life to an industry which from a wilderness has created a city almost continuous for a score of miles along the valley of the Mahoning.

Bowen and Isaac Heaton established a furnace on Yellow creek, about one-half mile from its mouth, about the year 1836. Associated with them were Dr. Joseph Truesdale, Bostwick Fitch, Horace Elliot, and —— Stofer. They had a stone stack, run the furnace by water, using charcoal as fuel. They used the ore found on the creek. They made considerable iron, castings, etc., but the establishment soon became a total failure through the action of water and frost upon its foundations.

AN EARLY DEBATING SOCIETY.

The best evidence we have that the pioneers of this township were zealous friends of education, is the knowledge that schools were established almost as soon as there were settlers enough to support them. Here we wish to introduce another fact which clearly indicates the characteristic desire for self-improvement possessed by the youth and men of those times.

A debating society which met evenings at the house of John Struthers, and probably at the houses of other members, was in existence in 1803. The names of those who organized it were John Struthers, Thomas Struthers, Alexander Struthers, Robert McCombs, William Mc-

---

* About a mile and a half, it should be.

Combs, Samuel Wilkinson, William Campbell, James Adair, William Adair, and John Blackburn. Similar societies were kept up for some years, and during the long winter evenings the sturdy boys and gray-haired men discussed questions of greater or less importance. These meetings were a source of pleasure to all the members, and doubtless many a young man gained skill and practice in the art of debate as well as some knowledge of parliamentary rules which enabled him in future years to preside at public meetings with ease and dignity—an acquirement which is of no little value to any citizen. The old-fashioned debating society was an educator which imparted valuable instruction to many young men.

THE FIRST MARRIAGE.

The following is from the writings of James Brownlee, Esq., published in the Collections of the Mahoning Valley Historical society:

The first marriage ceremony was near 1800, and took place on the farm then owned by John Blackburn. John Blackburn and Nancy Bryan had agreed to get married. The trouble was to get some one to marry them, as they were determined to have the wedding before the surveyors left after finishing the survey. No minister, no justice of the peace, in fact no one authorized to marry. They finally agreed that Judge Kirtland, having some kind of authority in Connecticut, where he emigrated from, should officiate. When that was settled upon it was discovered that no previous announcement had been made, as required by law, by posting notices ten days. Dr. Charles Dutton said he could remedy this. So he wrote four notices and posted one on each side of the log cabin. Then Judge Kirtland looked up his Episcopal prayer-book, which contained the marriage ceremony. The company in waiting, a stool was placed in front of the judge, and on it a white cover. Upon this the judge had placed his book. A slight delay occurring at the moment when all appeared to be ready, some one proposed that they should take a drink of whiskey all around before they were married. There were about seventy persons in attendance, and this was agreed to unanimously. While the judge was taking his drink some one stole the prayer-book, leaving him without a guide. But he said if they were agreed to it they should say so. They were both agreed; and thus ended the ceremony.

In 1802 Esquire Struthers at his house united in marriage a Mr. Kearney and a Miss Brierly. Kearney lived a half mile southeast of Poland village, on land now owned by Mr. C. F. Kirtland, and his bride in the same neighborhood. In the evening after the happy pair had returned from the 'squire's, the neighbors far and near assembled at Kearney's to pay their respects to them. During the festivities of the evening an accident occurred which dampened them to some extent. After the bride had retired to the second story of the log house, which was reached by a ladder, the men, in endeavoring to assist the groom up the ladder, let him fall to the floor, breaking his leg.

FIRST DEATHS.

A man named Hineman died in Poland village in 1801. He was buried on land now owned by James McNalley. This was probably the first death in the township. A Mrs. Stone died in February 1802, and was buried near the road leading to Boardman center, near where Mr. Scoville now lives. This is thought to have been the first female person that died in Poland.

A PANTHER STORY.

A story is related concerning Tom McClees, the miller at Struthers' mill. Struthers had a large dog and McClees took it one day to go out hunting for deer. Aroused by the barking of the dog, he hastened to the spot from which the sound proceeded and discovered a large panther up a tree. He fired and brought the animal down. The panther rolled over a steep bank, and the dog after him, the panther landing uppermost. McClees took the beast by the tail and pulled him off the dog; then with the aid of the dog and a club dispatched him. He killed two more panthers the same day. This took place near Indian Rock in the Nebo gully.

"I know not how this thing may be;
I tell the tale as 'twas told to me."

EARLY SCHOOLS.

A school was started at Struthers at an early date. Perly Brush was one of the first, if not the very first teacher in the township. Other early teachers in that school were Rev. Mr. Cook, James Anderson, and others. The school was kept in a small log house, and was probably opened as early as 1801.

Later a school-house was built and a school opened at Poland Center. The house was small, but many a time as many as one hundred persons were gathered there at singing schools and other meetings. Forty scholars was about the number in attendance.

Concerning her school days, Mrs. John Stewart has written as follows:

My first day's experience in attending school is strongly fixed in memory. The school-house was at the Center, and two hundred acres of unbroken forest lay between our house and it, making it a serious undertaking for a child of six years. On the first morning of my attendance, May, 1819,

Elias King

Mrs Elias King.

my mother said she was going on horseback to the village, and that she would carry me on the horse behind her, which she did. On her return she brought me a copy of Webster's Spelling Book, and made arrangements for the teacher to board with us for some time on my account. He was an estimable young man, James Campbell by name, gone to his reward. The school-house was built on the southeast corner of the cross-roads; built of round logs, with a clapboard roof, held on by weight poles. I do not remember to have seen a nail about the premises. On the north side was a window of four lights of eight-by-ten glass. It was set high above the reach of the smaller juveniles, a wise arrangement for the protection of the glass. It afforded sufficient light for the teacher's desk under it. On the other three sides of the house were spaces made by cutting out a log, all except sufficient to hold up the corners. In this was a sash for eight by ten, one light high, but no glass. In the winter the sash was covered with writing paper, saturated with grease applied to it by a hot flat-iron. These windows let in what was considered sufficient light for school purposes, and by the time the winter school was over there was but little paper left. The writing desks were large slabs, flat side up, supported by pins set into the wall in holes made by a large auger. The seats were of narrower slabs, with supports made of dogwood saplings put into holes made near the ends by those same augers. There was a ten-plate stove in the center of the room, inscribed on each of the side-plates, "Dan Eaton, Hopewell Furnace." The stove was set on blocks of wood, protected by one brick at each corner, between the wood and iron. The cast-iron supporters made for it were hanging on a wooden pin driven into the wall for want of sufficient iron to make two rods to hold them together. The stove-pipe was formed of what was called "cot and clay." Its circumference was nearly that of a flour barrel, as it had several barrel staves around it which were held on by hoops that I suppose had once been on the ends of flour barrels. The pipe ran through the upper floor, and the smoke had to find its way through the roof.

MILITARY.

The militia were enrolled in 1802. John Struthers was elected captain and Robert Mc-Combs first lieutenant. There were eighty-seven names upon the roll, and at the first roll call every man was present. In 1805 the eastern part of the township formed one company and the western part another. The two companies met at the village on the same day for drill. There being some rivalry between the two companies it was proposed that there be a test to ascertain which had the best marksman, each company to select its best man, and he to have but one shot. The eastern company chose Tom Clees, and the western a man by the name of Garner. The distance was sixty yards, off-hand, with a rifle. McClees fired first, then Garner; each hit the exact center, consequently there was no victory.

A partial list of those who were soldiers from
9*

this township in the War of 1812 includes the following names:

John and James Strain—John died during the war; Alexander Buchanan, who volunteered and died when not quite eighteen years old; Elijah Stevenson; Alexander McKeever was killed in a skirmish; Captain Isaac Walker and Alexander Struthers also died in the service; Major John Russel, William Brown, John Arrel, Isaac and Walter Buchanan, Eli McConnell, Francis Henry, William Reed, James Jack, John Sexton, William and Johnston Lowry, Hugh Truesdale, Alexander Truesdale, John and Alexander Cowden, William Love. Mr. Love is still living, the only survivor.

POLAND VILLAGE.

This is a quiet little country village, prettily situated on the Yellow creek, about the middle of the west line of the township. It was first known as "Fowler's" taking its name from the tavern of Jonathan Fowler, built in 1804. Well supplied with shade trees, without the noise, dirt, and bustle of large places, Poland wears an air of repose especially alluring to those who wish to find rest and health.

In former years the village was a busy one, and its stores, mills, and hotels did a thriving business. It was at one time far ahead of Youngstown as a trading place. It was quite an important place in the days of staging, as the stages to Pittsburg both from the north and west passed through it. The building of the canal, passing at a distance of two and a half miles from the village, and later of the railroad, somewhat changed the current of business life, and Poland suffered because of its location. The changes wrought by time and the important accessories of labor and steam seem to have determined that the village, one of the oldest in the county, should not become a place of any great commercial importance; and so Poland remains to-day an attractive country village with a quiet and orderly population. It has an institution of learning favorably known and liberally patronized, two churches, several good doctors, but no lawyers, two hotels, three dry goods stores, four groceries, one bank, one hardware store, two tin-shops, two drug stores, two wagon shops, a turning shop, one photographer, three shoemakers, three blacksmiths, a harness shop, a flouring-mill, and a saw-mill. By the last census the population of the corporation was three hundred and ninety-nine.

INCORPORATION.

Poland village was incorporated August 7, 1866. A petition signed by sixty-three voters had been presented to the county commissioners and was acted upon favorably. The first mayor was Andrew Campbell; recorder, Seth H. Truesdale, elected to serve until April, 1867, when the following officers were chosen: John A. Leslie, mayor; B. B. Stilson, recorder; C. B. Stoddard, W. J. Ogden, Adam Case, John Barclay, Henry Burnett, councilmen; Michael Graham, marshal.

The officers at present are mayor, marshal, recorder, treasurer, street commissioner, and six councilmen.

POST-OFFICE.

The post-office at Poland was established at an early date. Jared Kirtland was probably the first postmaster. He was succeeded by Andrew Burgess. Other postmasters have been Hugh Duncan, H. K. Morse, E. F. Drake, Jackson Moody, Adam Case. George Allen, the present incumbent, has been postmaster for twenty years.

PHYSICIANS.

Dr. Ira Brainard was the first physician who located in the village. He remained about two years, and about 1822 removed to Canfield, where he died in 1823. Dr. Jared P. Kirtland, a graduate of the Philadelphia Medical college, settled in Poland in 1823. In 1829-30 he was a member of the State Legislature, and again in 1834-35. In 1832 he was appointed a State geologist. He became one of the faculty of the State Medical college at Cincinnati, and was afterwards a professor in the Cleveland Medical school. He died in Cleveland a few years ago. Dr. Eli Mygatt, who still resides here, entered into practice with Dr. Kirtland in 1829, and had a large and successful practice for many years. Dr. Joseph Truesdale settled in Poland in 1831, and practiced until his death in 1871. He was a graduate of the Cincinnati State Medical college, and an honored man in his profession. He twice represented the county in the Legislature. Dr. Davis, an eclectic physician, now of Cleveland, practiced here about six years. Dr. Calvin Truesdale, a nephew of Dr. Joseph Truesdale, studied with his uncle and graduated from the Cleveland Medical school. He practiced in Poland some years, leaving in 1854. He is now one of the leading physicians of Rock Island, Illinois. Dr. Onesettler, a native of this county, practiced six or seven years, beginning about 1865. There have been other doctors in Poland, each of whom remained only a short time. The present practitioners here are Dr. H. R. Moore, Dr. I. D. Bard, Dr. C. R. Justice, and Dr. A. C. Elliot, dentist.

A LAW COLLEGE

was started some years ago in the house now owned by B. F. Lee, Esq. Judge Chester Hayden and M. A. King, of New York State, were the originators of the enterprise. They brought several students with them, and conducted the school about five years, but abandoned it on account of a lack of support.

POLAND UNION SEMINARY.

In order to understand fully the history of this seminary it is necessary to go back more than fifty years, and trace from the small beginnings the slow, gradual, but certain growth and development of the educational interests of this community. The early settlers of this section fully realized the necessity of education, and had a due appreciation of its advantages. Convinced of this necessity, Rev. Mr. Bradley, a Presbyterian minister, opened a select school about the year 1830, where the classical languages and higher English branches were taught. Thus was the seed sown which soon germinated. In 1835 Mr. John Lynch, a young man of limited means and a pupil of Mr. Bradley's, put up the building now occupied by Mr. Clark McGeehon as a dwelling, and opened an academy, which was maintained for about ten years, when Mr. Lynch, because of financial failure, was obliged to discontinue the academy.

For a period of about four years the educational interests of Poland seemed to be at a standstill. The cessation of growth was only apparent, however, for in 1848 Mr. B. F. Lee, a student fresh from Allegheny college, laid the foundation of an academy on the west side of the town, and began his school in the fall of the year 1849. Almost immediately another academy was opened on the east side of Yellow creek, under the especial care and patronage of the Presbyterians. Rev. Jacob Coon, Rev.

Algernon Sydney MacMaster, D. D., and Professor George S. Rice were at different times at the head of this academy, which was very successful for about six years, when the building took fire from an imperfect chimney-flue and was burned, and the school in consequence soon thereafter discontinued.

Mr. Lee selected a natural and picturesque mound for the location of his academy, erected a suitable building, and employed a competent corps of teachers, to-wit: Professor M. R. Atkins, principal; Miss E. M. Blakelee, preceptress; Miss Elmina Smith, assistant; and Miss Mary Cook teacher of music. It is with the founding of this school, known as Poland institute, that the history of Poland Union seminary properly begins.

At the end of six years Mr. Lee led a movement to provide better accommodations for the growing academy, with a prospective endowment from the Pittsburg and Erie Annual conferences of the Methodist Episcopal church. The Methodist Episcopal church of Poland, generously assisted by the citizens, erected, on a pleasant site not far from the building put up by Mr. Lee, a three-story brick edifice, 60 x 80 feet. The school was moved from its pleasant quarters on the mound to the more commodious building. The conferences being able to secure only a portion of the proposed endowment, it never became available, and the school was sustained by contributions from the citizens and tuition from the students.

The former building was purchased by Judge Chester Hayden and M. A. King, Esq., of New York State, and used by them for a law school, with which General Leggett was for a time connected. Many promising young lawyers were graduated from this school, among whom were Judge C. E. Glidden, Judge Van Hyning, H. G. Leslie, Esq., William C. Bunts, Esq., and General I. R. Sherwood. After a number of years of general success, the proprietors, thinking the city a better point, removed the institution to Cleveland.

The college, as the school in the brick building was now called, struggled to maintain an existence, as all such institutions must, in a new country, for want of means, but it was kept alive and growing by the constant and earnest efforts of the citizens, Mr. B. F. Lee always taking a prominent part, giving liberally of his time and means, down to the year 1862, when the various religious denominations of the town united and raised funds for the improvement of the building. At this time the school was chartered as Poland Union seminary.

In 1871 the school was offered to the presbytery of Mahoning upon condition that the presbytery make an earnest effort to secure an endowment of $15,000. When $10,000 were secured the seminary was to pass into the control of the presbytery. Immediate action was taken by the presbytery and the board of trustees to secure the endowment, by appointing Mr. B. F. Lee financial agent, who, in canvassing about one half of the territory, secured the $10,000, which was invested as a permanent endowment, and the presbytery assumed control of the school, fraternizing, however, with other religious denominations.

Since the removal of the school to the brick building, the following educators have been at its head: Professor J. E. Cummings, Professor A. T. Copeland, Rev. G. B. Hawkins, Rev. J. N. Reno, Professor M. C. Butler, Professor H. J. Clark, Rev. William Dickson, D. D., and William H. Tibbals, M. A., the present principal. Miss E. M. Blakelee was preceptress from the beginning in 1849 to 1880, except for a period of six years.

The seminary is now well established as one of the permanent literary institutions of the State, with an endowment of $15,000, $5,000 having been added by a recent bequest of Mr. George P. Miller, deceased.

It has had among its students many young men and women who have filled, or are now filling, places of trust and responsibility, among whom may be mentioned Revs. T. L. Sexton, D. J. Satterfield, Maxwell Cornelius, David Nesbit, T. S. Scott, R. D. Scott, D. V. Mays, H. P. Wilson, H. W. Lowry, W. D. Sexton, Hon. William McKinley, Member of Congress; Abner McKinley, Esq., Cecil Hine, Esq., Judge Van Hyning, W. B. Williams, Esq., H. G. Leslie, Esq., Hon. I. F. Mansfield, Hon. A. E. Lee, William J. Calhoun, Esq., John McClure, Esq., and James Kennedy, Esq.; W. S. Matthews, M. D., H. G. Cornwell, M. D., B. F. Hahn, M. D., J. M. Hamilton, M. D., S. D. Clarke, M. D., A. P. Kirtland, C. E., Julian and Hugh Kennedy, and the Morse Brothers, bridge builders and engineers.

The seminary provides two courses of study, a literary course for young ladies and young men who wish a practical education for general business, embracing a normal course, preparing them especially for teaching, and a college preparatory course. Graduates from this school have entered at Yale, Michigan university, Allegheny college, Oberlin, Westminster, Western Reserve, Wooster university, and others.

The number who have entered the profession of teaching from this seminary gives evidence of the excellent advantages it affords those who wish to prepare themselves for this profession.

The present instructors are William H. Tibbals, M. A., principal; Miss Ida M. Tarbell, B. A., preceptress, and Miss Adelaide Simpson, M. E. L., assistant.

POLAND FARMERS' DEPOSIT AND SAVINGS BANK.

This institution was chartered in 1875, and opened for business October 1st, the same year, with a capital of $50,000, increased now to $100,000. The first officers were: R. L. Walker, president; Clark Stough, cashier; Dr. Eli Mygatt, vice-president, succeeded by Samuel Hine, and later by C. F. Kirtland; directors, R. L. Walker, C. F. Kirtland, Eli Mygatt, Clark Stough, Alexander Walker, James Smith, Samuel Hine, Samuel McClurg (deceased), and William Arrel (deceased). C. N. Kirtland and Walter Arrel have been appointed in place of the two deceased.

FOUNDRY.

An iron foundry was built on the east side of Yellow creek in 1843 by Colonel Robinson Truesdale and George Kirtland. A part of it was carried away by the freshet of 1844. In 1860 the building was removed to the hill where it now stands. It was run by Allen, Woodruff & Co. until 1846, then by Allen & Woodruff until about two years ago. They manufactured stoves and various kinds of castings.

DISTILLERIES.

A large number of small stills were run by farmers in various parts of the township. John Hunter has quite a large distillery in the village, situated just below the bridge. This did quite a large business for a number of years. A great deal of the "ardent" was made and used in early times, yet the people were never noted for intemperance.

VARIOUS ENTERPRISES.

Elkanah Morse, from Wallingford, Connecticut, settled at Poland village in 1815, and was the originator of several manufacturing enterprises, which largely contributed to the prosperity of the town. In company with Henry T. Kirtland he built and managed an oil-mill, a saw-mill, a cloth-dressing and fulling-mill, and later a grist-mill. In company with Mr. Botsford he was engaged in the manufacture of combs for a number of years on Water street. He had a broom factory at the house where H. K. Morse now lives, and was the proprietor of a tin-shop where spoons and various kinds of German-silverware were manufactured. In connection with his other business he had a large farm, a store where four or more peddlars received their supplies, etc. The various industries mentioned afforded employment to from thirty to forty men and helped to make business lively.

John McConnell built the first tannery at the village and run it for some years. It was afterwards owned by James Shepard, and later by Robert Hartley. It was run by steam for some years, but is no longer in operation.

HOTELS.

Jared Kirtland erected and kept the first tavern. It was built in 1804. Many are living now who recollect the quaint old sign with the picture of a bull's head upon it, and the date 1804 painted beneath. It was a large house for those times and did a big business before the days of canals or railroads.

Jonathan Fowler built the stone hotel, now known as the Sparrow house, the same year. After his death it was run by Mr. Reed. It is now kept by Mrs. Jane Sparrow, who with her late husband took possession twenty-one years ago.

On the ground where the Union house now stands John McGill kept a small tavern for some years; after him Chester Bidwell.

STORES.

Probably the first store-keeper in the village was James Hezlep. He kept in a corner room of the tavern when it was owned by Reed. He continued to do a good business here for some years, and became sheriff of Trumbull county.

After leaving Poland he was in trade at Youngstown for a while.

Morse & Hall had a store in a room of Turhand Kirtland's house at an early date.

Henry T. Kirtland became a proprietor and afterwards built a frame store, and later a brick store on the ground where Stough's store is now situated. The old brick store stood there some fifty years.

Mr. Stough does a successful business in the same place, and is now one of the leading business men of the village.

Joseph McCombs opened a store on the creek near the bridge as early as 1812. He was in business here several years.

Richard Hall set up as a store-keeper about the same date.

The Duncans were also among Poland's early merchants and did quite an extensive business for some years.

Morse's store was situated on the corner opposite the store now occupied by Mr. Haynes. Later he built the Haynes store.

The first store-keepers got little money. Whiskey was perhaps the nearest thing to legal tender. They were obliged to take produce, grain, cattle, horses, and almost anything else that they in turn could use for buying goods.

Hezlep built the store now occupied by Z. P. Curry.

THE FIRST STORE

in the township was built and run by the proprietors of the old Montgomery furnace, near the mouth of the Yellow creek. It was there that the first settlers went for their supplies long before a store was started at the village.

MILLS.

The first grist-mill in the township, and one of the first on the Western Reserve, was built by John Struthers on Yellow creek in 1800. He also built a saw-mill there early.

Jonathan Fowler built the first grist-mill at Poland village in 1801. It was a small log building and was situated in the middle of the creek, reached by a foot bridge. He had also a saw-mill upon the same stream, built the same year. The log grist-mill was replaced by a good frame structure. After Fowler, Turhand Kirtland, John Reed, and later John Hunter, owned both the saw-mill and the grist-mill.

Peter Shoaf, on the Pennsylvania line, had a saw-mill and grist-mill on Spring run at quite an early date. It was run by his sons for some years, then sold to John Hunter of Poland.

James McGill had the first mill at Lowellville.

James Stewart built a flouring-mill on the north side of the Mahoning, where the village of Newport was laid out. The building, a substantial stone structure, was torn down by the Pennsylvania and Ohio Canal company.

The building now known as the Poland Flouring-mill was built by William Little in 1844.

North of the village, on the creek, Kirtland & Morse built a grist-mill, which, after running for a time, was found not a paying investment by the owners. It was sold, removed to Youngstown, and was the predecessor of the Diamond mills in that city.

COOPERS.

John Hineman was probably the first cooper in the township though he did not do a large amount of work. John Arnold settled near Poland village and was engaged largely for several years in making barrels and doing other kinds of coopering. Probably he made as many whiskey barrels as any man in this part of the country. His sons followed their father's trade.

POLAND PRESBYTERIAN CHURCH.

The congregation was organized May 3, 1802, by Rev. William Wick, pastor of the congregations of Youngstown and Hopewell, and a member of the Erie presbytery. The following named persons were present at the organization: William McCombs, Josiah Walker, William Campbell, Thomas Love, John Gordon, William Buck, Thomas Gordon, James Adair, Jesse Rose, John Jordan, William Dunlap, John Hineman, John Blackburn, John Truesdale, Robert Smith, John Arrel, John McCombs, Isaac McCombs, and others whose names are not now remembered.

October 23, 1804, Mr. Nicholas Pettinger was installed pastor over the congregations of Poland and Westfield. March 20, 1810, Mr. Pettinger obtained leave of the presbytery to resign his charge of the congregation of Poland.

October 25, 1810, Rev. Alexander Cook was appointed to supply Poland one-third of his time. He continued to supply the congregation until April, 1812. In June, 1815, the congregations of Poland and Westfield obtained leave of the presbytery to prosecute calls for Mr. James Wright, a licentiate of the Ohio presbytery, and on the 26th of June, 1815, Mr. Wright was ordained and installed pastor over these congregations. January 10, 1832, Mr. Wright accepted a call for the whole of his time from Westfield. January 16, 1834, Mr. John Scott accepted a call for two-thirds of his time from the congregation of Poland. April 3, 1834, he was ordained and installed pastor of the Poland and Liberty congregations. Mr. Scott was dismissed from these charges April 13, 1836. Mr. William McCombs supplied the congregation of Poland during most of the year 1837. June 25, 1839, the presbytery of New Lisbon met, ordained and installed Mr. Edward Nevin pastor of the congregation of Poland. He was dismissed April 20, 1840. The Rev. Jacob Coon supplied the congregation the most of the time from 1841 to 1843. Rev. Joseph Kerr, a member of the Steubenville presbytery, was installed pastor over the congregations of Poland and Liberty November 21, 1843, to be two-thirds of his time at Poland. In 1854 Mr. Kerr was dismissed from the Poland congregation. Rev. Algernon S. McMaster entered upon the duties of pastor of the Poland congregation November 19, 1854, and filled the position most acceptably until his dismissal, April 24, 1878. Rev. Samuel H. Moore, the present pastor, was installed September 25, 1879.

A flourishing Sabbath-school has been maintained for many years.

Soon after the congregation was organized a log-house, on the common in front of the present location of the church, was erected and used for several years. It was then replaced by a frame. The present church, a fine brick structure, was erected in 1855.

The number of members in 1811 was sixty. In 1881 it was two hundred and eighteen.

POLAND METHODIST CHURCH.

A society was formed in 1832 with eight members, a majority of them being ladies. Of these there are yet living Mr. and Mrs. William Logan and Miss Sarah Blackman. The first sermon preached in the village was by Rev. Charles Elliott, at the school-house. Mr. Elliott came there one wintry Sabbath, dug the wood out of the snow, built the fire himself, and waited for his hearers to collect. The church was organized by Rev. Mr. Preston, a converted sailor belonging either to the Pittsburg or the Erie conference.

The membership increased rapidly for several years. Services were at first held in the school-house, and in pleasant weather in orchards, groves, etc. The first church edifice was built in 1834. Among those who assisted most in building it were the Logan, Wallace, and Detchon families, Josiah Beardsley and his wife. The latter was a host in herself, ever active in getting funds and assistance with which to build up the kingdom of Zion. About 1863 the church was rebuilt and much improved. It is now a large, well-furnished, and comfortable building. Until about 1850 all of the preachers were circuit ministers. The church had generally been supplied with men of good ability, who were faithful and efficient workers—of course with some exceptions. About 1850 it was made a station, and Rev. William F. Day became the pastor for two years, that being then the limit of time allowed by the conference for remaining in one place.

There have been several series of revival meetings, the most of them quite successful in adding members. Owing to deaths and removals the membership is not at present as great as it has been. There are now about one hundred and fifty members, and the society is in a prosperous condition.

A good Sabbath-school has been maintained since the church was organized. Of course the society has had its periods of prosperity and adversity; but it has always contained many faithful ones who would never give up or desert.

The relations between the Presbyterians and the Methodists are now harmonious and friendly, and both are doing good work in adding to the kingdom of the Master.

CEMETERIES.

The oldest graveyard in the township is that adjoining the Presbyterian church at Poland. It was established in 1804, and in it repose the bodies of many of the first settlers and a large number of their descendants.

The graveyard at Poland Center is also quite ancient.

The new cemetery at Poland is prettily situated and tastefully laid out. It was established through the efforts of an association of the citizens formed January 14, 1865.

These three, with the new one commenced at Lowellville, are the only public burying places in the township.

LOWELLVILLE.

This thriving village is situated on both sides of the Mahoning, which is here spanned by a large and strong iron bridge. Its site is pleasant and even picturesque. High hills are on either hand, and from their tops can be obtained a view of some of the richest and most attractive scenery of the Mahoning valley.

The history of this place does not run back very far. Its growth may be said to have begun with the completion of the Pennsylvania and Ohio canal. The Lawrence branch of the Pittsburg, Ft. Wayne & Chicago railroad runs along the south side of the river, and on the north side is the Pittsburgh & Lake Erie road.

Lowellville has two churches, a good school building, three dry goods stores, five groceries, a hardware store, a drug store, two wagon shops, three blacksmith shops, one hotel, a harness shop, two shoemaker shops, besides the mills and the furnace. In 1880 it had a population of eight hundred and seventeen. Business is brisk, and there is plenty of work for everybody. Property is constantly increasing in value, and with the large amount of limestone and coal in this vicinity, no reason can be assigned why the place may not continue developing year by year. With two railroads now and the speedy prospect of another it looks as though the future of the town were assured.

INITIAL ITEMS.

The village was laid out about 1836 by Mr. Wick and others. The first store was opened about the same time by Calvin Bissel. Other store-keepers, coming in soon after, were S. H. McBride, Hugh Wick, Davidson & McCombs, Hunter & Watson, Brown & Shehy.

The post-office was established as early as 1840 with S. H. McBride postmaster. His successors in the office have been Dr. John Butler, John D. Davidson, Henry Smith, and J. B. Nessle, the present incumbent.

John McGill built the first grist-mill at Lowellville. It was run by his sons until the canal was built. Robert McGill had the first saw-mill in the place.

Wilson & Crawford started a tannery about 1844, which was sold to William Moore in 1850. He rebuilt and refitted it and carried on the business until 1874. It is not now in operation.

In 1838 William Watson and John S. Hunter bought a water privilege of George Hunter and erected a large grist-mill which they operated until 1866 and then sold to Anderson & Co. They operated it for a short time and sold to C. McCombs & Co. The mill is at present owned by Mr. McCombs.

THE LOWELLVILLE FURNACE.

Wilkes, Wilkison & Co. started the furnace in 1846. They had a hundred and fifty-six acres of land in one lot and forty acres in another, as well as considerable capital invested. It is believed that the Lowellville furnace was the first one in the valley that produced iron from uncoked coal, making use of the coal from Mount Nebo. They obtained a great deal of iron ore from Mount Nebo, the Graham and Galloway farms, the James Dickson farm, and the Robert McGill farm. About 1853 the company sold their works to Alexander Crawford & Co., of New Castle, Pennsylvania, who continued the business until 1864, then sold a hundred and fifty-six acres of land and the furnace to Hitchcock, McCreary & Co., for $100,000. In 1871 Hitchcock, McCreary & Co. sold to the Mahoning Iron company, which run the works a short time, then they passed into the hands of McCreary & Bell. February 11, 1880, these gentlemen sold to the Ohio Iron & Steel company of Youngstown, who now operate the works, doing a larger business than ever before. The officers of this company are Thomas H. Wells, president; Henry Wick, vice-president; Robert Bentley, secretary and treasurer. The amount of capital stock is $35,000. About forty men are employed. The company makes a specialty of the finer grades of foundry iron. They have their own beds of limestone near by, from which they secure the limestone necessary for use in the works.

It should be stated that in 1872 the furnace was built over and improved. Changes and improvements are also contemplated by the present owners.

HOPE MILLS.

James Brown built the mill which now bears this name. It was situated a few rods above the bridge and was run by steam for about two years. In 1859 it was moved to its present site and run by water power. The mill is now owned and run by Mr. Brown's heirs. They do a large amount of custom milling, grinding wheat and corn. They also put up and ship flour. Frequently thirty barrels per day are produced.

PLANING-MILL.

This mill was started by Lewis & Drake in 1871. In February, 1872, it was leased by J. D. Dickson & Co., who run it until November, 1880. Since that time Mr. Dickson has managed it. He is engaged in manufacturing all kinds of house finishing lumber.

COAL.

A great deal of coal has been taken from the banks in this township first and last. The most important was the Mount Nebo mine. About 1828 this was opened by Elijah Stevenson and worked on a small scale for some ten years. John Thomas and William James worked it after him for some years. John Kirk then bought the mine and commenced shipping coal in 1845. Kirk sold to a company which failed, and the property reverted to him. He again disposed of it to Doan & Howells, of Philadelphia, who did quite an extensive business for six or eight years, shipping the coal by canal to Cleveland. This firm also purchased a coal bank from the Adairs which they worked at the same time. George Smith was their manager. They gave employment to fifty or more men. The coal was found to be of a superior quality.

The Lowellville Furnace company also worked the Mount Nebo mine quite extensively to obtain coal for use in their iron works. The mine was finally abandoned because the water had become too deep for successful operations. Other coal mines have been worked in the vicinity of Lowellville, but there is no great amount of business in that line in the township at present. It is believed, however, that an abundance of coal remains, and may be mined successfully when desired.

QUARRIES.

Limestone has been quarried quite extensively. The Pence quarry was the largest and did a big business for the past ten years, but is now worked out. The Moore and Arrel quarries contain a large amount of stone of excellent quality. A brisk business has been done in this line for some years past. The quarries having been operated to a greater or less extent for the last twenty-five years. McCombs & Johnson were quite extensively engaged in the business. The Moore quarry is now in operation.

PRESBYTERIAN CHURCH.

The Free church people, who differed from the Presbyterians on the question of slavery, withdrew from neighboring congregations, and in 1850 succeeded in erecting a church building at Lowellville. Among the leading members were John and William McFarland, Andrew McFarland, James S. Moore, John S. Hunter, and John Book.

After the slavery question was settled the most of the Free church returned to the sects to which they originally belonged; so that the Lowellville congregation is now entirely Presbyterian. Those who preached here after the organization of the church were Revs. J. D. Whitham, Bushnell, James Bingham, George McElhaney. The membership is quite small.

THE METHODIST CHURCH.

Rev. John Prosser created the revival which resulted in the building of this church. Dr. John Butler and John Bissel were also active and leading members. The building was erected about 1840. The membership has always been quite small. Preaching and Sabbath-school are maintained regularly.

PHYSICIANS.

Dr. John Butler settled at Lowellville in 1838, and practiced until his death, some ten years later. The next physician was Dr. Joseph Cowden, who removed West and died. Dr. Scroggs practiced a few years, then removed to Beaver, Pennsylvania, where he now resides. Dr. Amberson practiced four or five years, moved to New Castle, Pennsylvania, and died there. Dr. Foster practiced here about five years. He went to Allegheny City, Pennsylvania. Dr. John Kirker practiced in Lowellville four or five years. During the war he served as a surgeon, and at its close located in Allegheny City. Dr. Cloud was in Lowellville a short time, moved to Columbus, and is now deceased. The present practitioners

James S. Brown

William Brown, the father of the subject of this sketch, was born in Pennsylvania, September 28, 1788; came to Trumbull county (now Mahoning) in an early day and located on the farm now occupied by his son, James S. He married Miss Ann Porter, April 15, 1813. Their children were James S., born January 4, 1814; David, born June 30, 1816, and died March 7, 1824; Martha, born June 24, 1822, married Wyoming N. Fry, and resides in Suffield township, Portage county. William Brown served in the War of 1812. He died April 20, 1833. James S. Brown was married to Mary Ann Printz, who was born in Canton, Ohio. Her parents were Joseph and Susan (Blosser) Printz, who were united in marriage September 23, 1830. They had the following children: Henry, born June 21, 1831; Mary Ann (now Mrs. Brown), August 20, 1832;

Mary A. Brown

Barbara, January 29, 1834; Isabel, September 22, 1835; Jacob, March 17, 1837; Samuel, November 27, 1838; Ambrose, February 3, 1843. Mr. Brown is a Democrat in politics, yet he recognizes a higher duty in the use of the ballot than mere attachment to party, and endeavors to vote for the best candidates. He has resided all his life on the old homestead, having been born there. From actual experience he knows what pioneer life is, and his memory carries him back to the days when the present beautiful and thrifty neighborhood where he lives was covered with the original forest, interspersed here and there by small clearings and rude log cabins. He has always been a hard-working and industrious man, and is now, in his old age, blessed with a comfortable home. Mr. and Mrs. Brown are Presbyterians in their religious faith.

of the place are Dr. R. H. Stewart, Dr. R. W. Weller, Dr. J. N. Cowden, and Dr. Reynolds Cowden.

GRAND ARMY OF THE REPUBLIC.

Reno Post No. 87, Grand Army of the Republic, was organized June 28, 1881, with the following officers: William Leggett, commander; Porter Watson, senior vice commander; T. E. Grist, junior vice commander; J. W. Van Auker, adjutant; W. C. Rowland, quartermaster; Dr. R. W. Weller, surgeon; Rev. Snyder, chaplain; I. J. Nessle, officer of the day; J. C. Mapes, officer of the guard.

An organization of the Grand Army of the Republic was in existence some years ago, but it went down.

CEMETERY.

In the spring of 1881 ground for a cemetery was purchased on the hill on the north side of the river, which is being laid out into lots, and otherwise fitted for a burial place.

POLAND CENTER UNITED PRESBYTERIAN CHURCH.

A society of Seceders was formed in 1804, and some years later, probably in 1810, a large meeting-house of hewn logs was erected. Among the early members were: William Cowden, Reynolds Cowden, Joseph Cowden, Isaac P. Cowden, Robert Lowry, Johnston Lowry, William Strain, Richard McConnell, Thomas McConnell, and others.

About 1826 a brick church was erected. Squire David Houston took the job of building it. In 1849 the present house was built. Nearly twenty years ago the church was merged into the United Presbyterians.

The first preacher was Rev. James Duncan, a farmer, from below Lowellville. Rev. Robert Douglas was the next pastor. Rev. David Goodwille preached in this vicinity, though not in this church alone, fifty years. He was succeeded by Rev. James M. Henderson, Rev. T. W. Winter, and Rev. W. T. McConnell, the present pastor. There are now about sixty-six members. A Sabbath school has been kept up a number of years.

NEWPORT

was laid out for a village about the same time as Lowellville. Lots were sold at one time as high as in the latter place. But Newport did not grow and no village marks its site.

STRUTHERS.

This little village was laid out about sixteen years ago. Its growth commenced with the advent of the Lawrence railroad in 1867. It now has a railroad station on each side of the river, and perhaps a third railroad will soon be added.

The village contains the large furnace of the Struthers' Iron company, a hotel, two stores, and a saw-mill. A post-office was established about the year 1866, Richard Olney postmaster. His successors have been Rufus Parker and A. G. S. Parker, the present incumbent.

Mr. Olney kept the first store. The saw-mill, built about the time the railroad was completed, was erected and is now owned by Thomas Struthers. Mr. Struthers also built the hotel in 1873.

The Catholic church was erected about the time the furnace was built.

THE FURNACE

of the Struthers Iron company was built in 1869. The casting-house and smoke-stack were blown down in July, 1881, but have since been rebuilt. The furnace when in active operation produces about sixty-five tons of iron per day, and affords about fifty men employment. It is owned by Thomas Struthers, T. W. Kennedy, John and H. T. Stewart, and John and Daniel Stambaugh. Mr. Kennedy is manager, and H. T. Stewart secretary and treasurer.

BIOGRAPHICAL SKETCHES.

THE KIRTLAND FAMILY.

Turhand Kirtland, the first representative of the family who came to the Western Reserve, was a native of Wallingford, Connecticut, born November 16, 1755. He was a carriage manufacturer by trade, which he followed in Wallingford until his removal to Ohio. In 1798, having gathered together a few thousand dollars, he came to Ohio and purchased considerable land in different portions of the Reserve, and also acted as agent for the Connecticut Land company for the sale of their land. He located at first at Burton (now Geauga county), but spent much of his time in Poland and Youngstown, engaged in examining, surveying, and selling land. He kept a diary during the early years of his residence in Ohio, in which he gives a minute account of his proceedings and observations. The writing of a letter in those days was an event of sufficient importance to make a record of it. In a few years he removed from Burton to Poland and settled on a farm, his brother, Jared Kirtland, having started a tavern at what is now Poland village. He died August 16, 1844.

Mr. Kirtland was a man of more than ordinary energy of character, and ability, and served his county in many positions of trust and honor. He was elected to the State Senate from Trumbull county in 1814, was associate judge of the court of common pleas for a long time, and was justice of the peace in Poland for some twenty years. He left at his death a large property. He was twice married. His second wife was Mary Potter, of New Haven, Connecticut, born February 10, 1772, died March 21, 1850. They reared a family of children, as follows: Jared P. Henry T., Billius, George, Mary P., and Nancy, of whom only Billius and George are now living.

Dr. Jared P. Kirtland was a noted physician and an able man. He practiced medicine for many years in Poland, and represented the county, then Trumbull, in the Ohio Legislature in 1829, 1831, and 1834. He was a professor in the Cleveland Medical college, of Clevleand, Ohio, during the latter part of his life, and had previously held a similar position in the Ohio Medical college, Cincinnati. He has a daughter living in Rockport, Cuyahoga county.

Henry T. Kirtland was a prominent business man of Poland for a great many years, being engaged in merchandising. He was born in Connecticut November 16, 1795; married in 1825 Thalia Rebecca Fitch, who died October 1, 1826. In April, 1828, he married Mary Fitch, a sister of his first wife. He died February 27, 1874, in Poland, and his wife, Mary, December 24, 1877. By his first marriage he had one child, Hon. C. F. Kirtland, of Poland, a Representative in the Legislature from Mahoning county, session of 1872 and 1873, and by his second marriage three children, of whom the only survivor is Mr. C. N. Kirtland, of Poland.

Billius Kirtland was born in Poland, Ohio, August 29, 1807. In 1830 he married Ruthanna Frame, who was born in Chester county, Pennsylvania, in 1809. They have had nine children, only three of whom survive. Alfred resides in Blairsville, Indiana county, Pennsylvania, and is superintendent of the West Pennsylvania railroad. He graduated at the Van Rensselaer Polytechnic institute, of Troy, New York, taking a course in surveying, and for some time was assistant civil engineer of the road of which he is now superintendent. Emma married Samuel Hines and lives in Poland, and Lucy married Rev. Dallas B. Mays and resides at North Benton.

Mr. and Mrs. Kirtland belong to the Methodist Episcopal church and are among the most prominent and highly respected citizens of the county. Mr. Kirtland is an enthusiastic student of chemistry, and has spent about fifteen years of his life in investigating that science. George Kirtland is living in Poland, engaged in farming and in the manufacture of ink. Mary was the wife of Richard Hall, for many years a merchant in Poland, and Nancy was the wife of Elkanah Morse, a manufacturer and miller of Poland.

WALTER S. ARREL.

One of the earliest settlers in what is now Mahoning county was John A. Arrel, the father of the subject of this biographical sketch. He was born in Franklin county, Pennsylvania, November 6, 1773. He married Margaret Stewart, who was a native of the same county, born in the same year, June 25th. He moved to Poland township in 1800, and settled on the farm where Walter S. Arrel now lives, which he purchased in 1799. Mr. Arrel began his settlement in the woods, there being at that time only here and there a cabin with a small clearing, and he cleared up and improved a farm of two hundred acres, which, when he moved onto it, was covered by the original forest. Mr. Arrel was well and favorably known throughout the region, and was identified with many interests designed for the public good. He was the father of eight children—Martha, born May 6, 1798, died November 29, 1860; Margaret, November 10, 1800. David, May 6, 1803; James, November 19, 1805, died August 16, 1857; John, January 1, 1808; George, January 4, 1811, died March 14, 1877; William, January 27, 1814, died November 14, 1878; Walter S., June 10, 1816. Margaret, David, John, and Walter are still living. John A. Arrel died August 10, 1848, and his wife February 10, 1833.

Walter S. Arrel is the youngest child, and was born on the old farm where he still lives. He has always resided in the county, attending strictly to his business, and has accumulated a fine property, being the owner of six hundred acres of excellent land in one tract, besides other lands. He is also engaged to some extent in milling. In addition to extensive farming, which has been his chief occupation, Mr. Arrel has at different times dealt largely in stock and wool. His business capacity and enterprise are well known and need no comment. He is now erecting a fine brick residence in Poland village, to which he has removed, and where he will spend the remainder of his days in the enjoyment of his industry.

In politics Mr. Arrel is a strong Republican. He was formerly a Whig, and when the Abolitionists formed a party, and chose J. G. Birney as their candidate, he was one of seventeen citizens of Poland township who cast their votes for him.

Mr. Arrel was married March 16, 1871, to Miss Martha Duff, daughter of Oliver and Jane (Tait) Duff. Her parents were married November 16, 1826, and reared their family in Pennsylvania. Oliver Duff was born in Pennsylvania, July 10, 1799, and died August 7, 1857. Mrs. Duff was born in Ireland, July 4, 1805, and came to this country when two years old. Their children were William and Martha (twins), born February 11, 1828; Samuel, February 10, 1830; Robert, January 16, 1836; Alexander, September 11, 1840. William married Maria Henly, and resides in Hillsdale, Lawrence county, Pennsylvania; Samuel is unmarried; Robert married Maria J. White, and resides at Mount Jackson, Pennsylvania; Alexander married Lizzie Poole, and lives in Cass county, Michigan.

ELIAS KING.

Elias King, son of John and Margaret (Davidson) King, was born near New Lisbon, Columbiana county, Ohio, April 15, 1811. John King, the father, was a native of Lancaster county, Pennsylvania, and died in Allegheny county at the age of eighty-four. His children were Hugh D., William, John, and Robert (deceased), Elias, Thomas (deceased), Mary Ann (deceased), Margaret, and Annabella C., living in East Liberty, Allegheny county, Pennsylvania; Elizabeth (deceased), and O. J., a resident of Kansas.

The boyhood of Elias King was spent in Allegheny county, residing there until he was twenty-two or twenty-three years of age, when he went to Lawrence county, in the same State. Although he only became a resident of Mahoning county in 1870, yet he has resided the most of his life in the Mahoning valley, his home previous to his removal to Ohio being only about a mile from the Ohio State line. He was brought up on a farm but received a good common school education, and was engaged in teaching school a short time. He was engaged in mercantile pursuits for a couple of years in Edenburg, and was also engaged for some time in the manufacture of brooms. He operated a grist-mill near Edenburg some two years. Finally purchasing a farm in Mahoning township, Lawrence county, Pennsylvania, he moved and lived upon it for twenty years, whence he removed to Lowellville, Ohio, where he has since resided. After coming to Lowellville he was engaged in the drug business for five or six years, since which time he has been living a practically retired life.

Mr. King's mercantile ventures were pecuniarily unfortunate, having passed through the panics of 1837 and 1873, yet he still possesses enough of this world's goods to allow him and his family to live in comfort and plenty the balance of their days. January 2, 1838, he married Eleanor Cavett, daughter of John Cavett, of Westmoreland county, Pennsylvania. She was born July 27, 1820. The fruit of this union was two sons and two daughters, as follows: Margaret, John, Mary Jane, and Hugh Davidson. Mary Jane, now Mrs. Cowden, is the only survivor, and resides with her parents. Margaret died at the age of sixteen months, John when two years old, and Hugh Davidson at the age of fourteen years and nine months. Mrs. Cowden was born in Lawrence county, Pennsylvania, October 27, 1846. January 3, 1867, she became the wife of Dr. Isaac P. Cowden, a physician of Lawrence county, Pennsylvania, who died February 3, 1877, in the thirty-fourth year of his age. Mr. King is a Republican in politics, and was former-

ly a Whig. During the early anti-slavery agitation he was an active Abolitionist. Mrs. King is
an active and valued member of the Presbyterian
church, and both are worthy members of the
community, and esteemed by all who know
them.

NOTES OF SETTLEMENT.

William Frame, a native of Chester county,
Pennsylvania, was born June 29, 1776. He
moved from Baltimore, Maryland, to Poland,
Ohio, in 1827, and settled where Struthers station now stands. In early life he was a miller,
and followed that vocation to some extent in
Ohio, though his chief occupation was farming.
He was for some time a justice of the peace in
Poland. He died in 1842, aged sixty-six years.
His wife, whose maiden name was Rebecca
Marsh, a native of New Jersey, survived him
about six months. They were the parents of
three sons and six daughters: Eliza Allen, resid-
ing in Kansas City, Missouri; George (deceased) Ruthanna, wife of Billius Kirtland, of
Poland; Thomas (deceased); Janet M. Allen (de-
ceased); William S. M. (deceased); Mary M.
Meacham, residing in Iowa; Rebecca Meacham
(deceased), and Catherine Allen, of Oberlin,
Ohio.

James Dickson, farmer, Poland township, Mahoning county. The subject of this sketch is
one of the oldest residents of Mahoning county,
being now eighty-three years of age. He was
born near Chambersburg, Franklin county, Pennsylvania, October 28, 1798. His father, John
Dickson, was a native of Ireland; came to America when thirteen years of age, and settled in
Pennsylvania with his parents. He came to
Ohio in 1801, and settled in Poland township on
the farm where his sons, James and George, now
live. He was emphatically one of the pioneers
of the Western Reserve, and did much toward
the improvement of that part of the country in
which he lived. He followed farming until his
death, which occurred in 1826, his wife and
eleven children surviving him. Mrs. Dickson
died in 1841. James Dickson was married in
1831 to Miss Martha Gilbraith, daughter of Samuel Gilbraith, of Poland township. They have
had six children—John A., Sarah, Ann M.,

Martha H., Samuel E., and James M. John
and Martha are deceased. Mr. and Mrs. Dickson are the oldest couple in Poland township.
They are both members of the United Presbyterian church.

George Dickson, farmer, Poland township,
Mahoning county, was born in Poland April 20,
1808. He has always lived upon the home farm
with the exception of two years, which he spent
in Pennsylvania. Farming has been his chief
occupation, though in connection with this he
has been engaged in the manufacture of grain
cradles quite extensively. He was married, in
1833, to Miss Isabel McBride, daughter of John
McBride, of Pennsylvania. They had nine children, six of whom are living. Mrs. Dickson
died July 14, 1861, and he married, March 24,
1864, for his second wife, Mrs. Esther G. Walker,
daughter of John Gibson, of Youngstown, Ohio.
Mr. and Mrs. Dickson are members of the
United Presbyterian church.

Samuel Smith, farmer, Poland township, Mahoning county, was born in that township
September 17, 1820. His father, Robert, was a
native of Franklin county, Pennsylvania, and
came to Ohio in 1802. He settled in Poland
township, the country then being but little better
than a vast wilderness. Mr. Smith, by dint of
industry and economy succeeded in making a
fine farm, and after a life of labor and usefulness,
during which he saw much of the hard conditions
of pioneer life, died in 1835, in his seventieth
year. He left a family of six sons and four
daughters, besides his widow, who died in 1846.
Samuel Smith has always resided upon the old
home place, and in 1847, the next year after his
mother's death, he married Miss Margaret Blackburn, daughter of Robert Blackburn, of Poland
township. This union was blessed with two
children, J. S. and Robert F. Robert is dead.
Mr. and Mrs. Smith are members of the Presbyterian church. Mr. Smith is a stanch Democrat and one of the substantial men of the
township.

J. A. Smith, farmer, Poland township, Mahoning county, was born in said township September 23, 1838. Robert Smith, his father, was a
native of Pennsylvania and came to Ohio in
1802 with his parents and settled where his son,
the subject of this sketch, now lives. He died
in 1860, his wife and one child surviving him.

Mrs. Smith is still living with her son. Mr. Smith, our subject, was married, in 1862, to Miss Mary Ann Gault, daughter of Robert Gault, of North Jackson.

David Arrel, farmer, Poland township, Mahoning county, eldest son of John and Margaret (Stewart) Arrel, was born in said township, May 6, 1803. He has always lived in the township and has witnessed many changes. He was married, in 1830, to Miss Martha Moore, daughter of William Moore, of Poland township. They have had four children, viz: William M., Margaret, John, and George F. Mrs. Arrel died in 1872. She was a member of the Presbyterian church. Mr. Arrel is also a member of the same church. He has always been an active, industrious man and is now spending the evening of his days with his son.

John Stewart, Poland township, Mahoning county, was born in Coitsville township that county, May 28, 1807. His father, John Stewart, was a native of Adams county, Pennsylvania, and came to Ohio the year it was admitted as a State, in 1802. He settled in Coitsville township and was engaged in farming until his death in 1833. John Stewart, his son, has resided in Mahoning county the most of his life, and has been engaged in business in various places. He was at Lowellville five years and at New Castle, Pennsylvania, one and a half years. At the latter place he was interested in milling. He was united in marriage to Miss M. G. Walker, daughter of Captain Walker, of Poland township, on the 5th of January, 1836, and has had seven children, six of whom are still living. Mr. Stewart has filled many places of public trust within the gift of his county and township. He has been justice of the peace many years, and has also been a county commissioner. He was a colonel of militia in the old militia days. Mr. Stewart and his wife are members of the Presbyterian church.

James Davidson, farmer, Poland township, Mahoning county, was born in Beaver (now Lawrence) county, Pennsylvania, June 7, 1820. James Davidson, Sr., his father, was a native of Carlisle, Pennsylvania, and followed farming as an occupation. Mr. Davidson, our subject, came to Lowellville, Mahoning county, in September, 1851, and was for a long time engaged in the shoe business, though he is now engaged in farming. July 3, 1859, he married Miss Rovinah Nessle, daughter of Isaiah Nessle, and has four children—Maggie, Mary, Thomas, and Daniel A. Mr. Davidson's political affiliations are with the Republican party. He and his wife are both members of the Presbyterian church.

Dr. Eli Mygatt, physician, Poland, Mahoning county, was born in Canfield, Mahoning county, Ohio, July 16, 1807. His father was Comfort S. Mygatt, an early and prominent resident of Canfield, who is spoken of elsewhere. Dr. Mygatt, the subject of this brief sketch, has resided all his life in what is now Mahoning county. He studied medicine at Canfield with Dr. Fowler, who is still living, and attended the Western Medical college at New York, and has a diploma from the Cleveland Medical school. He has had an extensive practice over the county in which he has resided for many years, beginning with Dr. Kirtland, at Poland. Dr. Mygatt was married in 1831 to Miss Lois Y. Kirtland, daughter of Jared Kirtland, of Poland, brother of Judge Kirtland, one of the earliest and most prominent of the pioneers of the Reserve. To Dr. Mygatt and wife were born six children—Jared P., Mary S., Sarah M., William L., Hannah O., and Lucy E. Lucy and Mary only are living. Mrs. Mygatt died February, 1881. She was a member of the Presbyterian church, and a devoted Christian. In politics Dr. Mygatt is a Republican.

Samuel McCullough, Jr., was born in Poland township in 1844. His father, Samuel McCullough, Sr., was born in the same township, where the family were early settlers, and has always resided on the old homestead. Samuel McCullough, Jr., is a farmer by occupation. He was united in marriage in 1874 to Miss Mary J. Stewart, daughter of Samuel Stewart, of Knoxville, Iowa. They have three children, John E., George S., and Arthur R. Mrs. McCullough is a member of the Presbyterian church. In politics Mr. McCullough is a conservative.

William R. Cowden, farmer, Poland township, Mahoning county, a representative of one of the oldest families in the township, was born in Poland township April 5, 1841. His father, Isaac P., was also a native of the same township, having been born and raised on the place where his son now lives. The grandfather, William Cowden, was among the pioneers of that section, coming at a very early day from Pennsylvania. Isaac P. was a farmer, and died in 1869. William R. Cowden has always lived on the old homestead, and has about one hundred acres of excellent land. He was married in 1867 to Miss Almira J. Glenn, daughter of William Glenn, of Beaver county, Pennsylvania. They have one child, Martha E., born May 1, 1868. They are both members of the Presbyterian church.

John G. Cowden, farmer, Poland township, Mahoning county, an older brother of the subject of the preceding sketch, was born in Poland township, August 4, 1838, and still resides within a short distance of his old home. Mention has been made of his immediate ancestors in the former sketch, and it will not be necessary to repeat it here. He was married October 10, 1861, to Miss Mary Ann, daughter of John Smith, of Springfield township. They have two children, Nannie E., and Joseph. Mr. and Mrs. Cowden are members of the Presbyterian church.

John L. Dobbins, insurance, etc., Poland township, Mahoning county, was born in said township July 15, 1831. His father, Hugh Dobbins, was a native of Washington county, Pennsylvania, and came to Ohio in 1804 with his parents and located upon the farm where the subject of this sketch now resides. The Dobbins family were among the early pioneers of the county, and have taken a prominent part in the development and improvement of that part of the county. Hugh Dobbins died in 1866, leaving a family of five children surviving him. J. L. Dobbins is one of the active business men of Poland, being engaged in insurance, in farming, and is also a dealer in agricultural implements. He is unmarried.

James S. Guthrie, farmer, Poland township, Mahoning county, one of the oldest citizens of the county, was born in Pennsylvania February 28, 1800. His father, William Guthrie, was a native of Ireland, and emigrated with his parents to America in an early day. They settled in Pennsylvania, where they lived until 1804 when they moved to Ohio and located in Poland township. They were indeed pioneers in the wilderness, there being when they arrived but two or three cabins within a circuit of several miles. William Guthrie was a weaver by trade, though he taught school considerably. He died in 1849. Farming has been the chief occupation of James

S. Guthrie, though he has also been engaged a good deal in the wool business. He was married to Miss Elizabeth Pauley in 1825. She is a daughter of John Pauley, of Coitsville township. They have had seven children, three of whom are living. Mrs. Guthrie died nearly forty years ago. Mr. Guthrie, for one of his years, retains his vigor remarkably well.

James S. Moore, farmer, Poland township, Mahoning county, one of the oldest residents of the township, was born in Franklin county, Pennsylvania, October 28, 1804. His father, William Moore, was a native of Pennsylvania, and emigrated to Ohio in 1805 and located in Poland township on the farm where his son, the subject of this sketch, now resides. The country was then, of course, very new and all kinds of game plenty. William Moore died December 13, 1854. James Moore has always followed farming with the exception of a few years during which he was engaged in the mercantile business. In 1838 he was married to Miss Hannah R. Truesdale, daughter of Hugh Truesdale, of Poland, and has had seven children, viz: Rachel A., William B., Hugh R., F. M., Mary E., Rebecca J., and Julia A. Mr. and Mrs. Moore are both members of the Presbyterian church, he having been an elder for many years. His sister, Rebecca Moore, still resides on the old home place, and has assisted in taking care of her parents and her brother's children.

George Liddle, farmer, Poland township, Mahoning county, was born in Poland, March 5, 1812, on the farm where he now lives. His father, George, was a native of England and emigrated to this country in September, 1806. He landed at Baltimore after a tedious passage, and at once came to Ohio and settled in Poland while his brothers settled in Boardman. He died in 1852. George Liddle, the subject of this notice, married in 1841 Miss Mary E., daughter of James Kennedy, of Coitsville township. They have had twelve children seven of whom are now deceased. Mr. and Mrs. Liddle are members of the United Presbyterian church.

A. D. McClurg, farmer, Poland township, Mahoning county, was born in Boardman township, said county, in 1834. His father, Samuel McClurg, was a native of Pennsylvania, but came to Ohio when he was nine years old with his father, James, who came originally from Ireland.

The family settled in Poland township, then Trumbull county. Samuel McClurg followed farming all his life and died on the 4th of July 1877, leaving two children, A. D., and Richard J. Mrs. McClurg died in 1834. Mr. A. D. McClurg has always been a resident of the county, engaged in farming. He was married, in 1860, to Miss Maggie A. Kerr, daughter of Matthew Kerr, of Boardman. They have had three children, viz: Ella J., Lella J., and Minnie B. Ella is deceased. Mr. and Mrs. McClurg are members of the Presbyterian church. Politically he is a Republican, and at present is county commissioner.

B. F. Lee, farmer, Poland township, Mahoning county, was born in Poland township May 7, 1815. His father, Christopher Lee, was one of the earliest settlers in Poland township, coming there from Shippensburg, Pennsylvania, as early as 1805. He resided there until his death in 1835. He was a farmer by occupation and had a family of thirteen children. Mr. B. F. Lee was educated at Meadville, Pennsylvania. After being there three years he returned to Poland and started the institution of learning known as the Poland institute. He was married September 17, 1845, to Miss Pauline King, daughter of Amos King, of Erie county, Pennsylvania. They have had nine children, seven of whom are living. Mr. Lee has been engaged in various occupations; has been a merchant, also a wool buyer, and is now interested in railroads. He is an active, enterprising man, and is always ready to help along a good work. He and his wife are members of the Presbyterian church.

Carson R. Justice, M. D., druggist, Poland, Mahoning county, was born in Springfield township, December 15, 1851. His father, James Justice, came from Pennsylvania to Ohio in 1801, and settled in what was then Columbiana county, now Mahoning. He was thus one of the earliest of the pioneers. Dr. Justice studied his profession at Poland, and graduated at the Cleveland Medical college in 1878. Since then he has practiced at Poland in connection with his drug business. Dr. Justice is a member of the Presbyterian church, and politically is a stanch Republican. He is an active and enterprising business man.

Charles S. Haynes, merchant, Poland, Ma-

honing county, was born June 9, 1830, in Vernon township, Trumbull county. David Haynes, his father, was a native of Connecticut, whence he came to Ohio with his parents about 1810. He died in 1870. His wife is still living with a daughter at Rock Island, Ill. Charles S. Haynes has always lived in the section where he now resides. He was engaged in farming until 1872, when he engaged in the mercantile business at Poland. He was married in 1858 to Miss Lucy M. Meeker, daughter of William Meeker, of Boardman township, and has two children—Calvin T. and Lillie Belle, twins, born December 10, 1863. In politics Mr. Haynes is a sound Republican.

J. N. Cowden, M. D., physician, Poland township, Mahoning county, was born in Beaver county, now called Lawrence county, Pennsylvania, October 29, 1840, but was raised in Portage county, Ohio. His father, James S. Cowden, came from Washington county, Pennsylvania, in 1818, and located in Poland township, and was one of the pioneers of that section. He was a blacksmith by trade, though he was engaged in milling chiefly. Dr. Cowden studied medicine with E. A. Wilcox at Mt. Jackson, Pennsylvania, and attended lectures at the Ohio Medical college in 1862. He now has an extensive practice. He was married December 31, 1863, to Miss Julia M., daughter of Lyman B. and Eliza D. Dickerson, of Yates county, New York. They have had two children—James L. and Charles C. Dr. Cowden is a Free Mason, an Odd Fellow, and a member of the Sons of Temperance. Mrs. Cowden is a member of the Disciple church.

J. D. Bard, M. D., physician, Lowellville, Mahoning county, was born in Franklin county, Pennsylvania, August 4, 1814. William Bard, his father, was a native of the same county, and was engaged in the law and in mercantile business for a number of years. He came to Ohio in 1819, and settled in Liberty township, Trumbull county, and followed farming as long as he was able. He died in 1875. Dr. Bard, the subject of this sketch, studied medicine with Dr. John Loy three years, and attended lectures at the Cleveland Medical college. He began practice in 1838 at Middletown, Ohio, but two years subsequently went to Winchester, Indiana, where he remained one year and then removed to Pulaski, Indiana. There he resided between ten and eleven years. He then came back to Trumbull county, Ohio, and continued in practice in Liberty township for twenty-three years. He then removed to Poland, where he still lives. He has been eminently successful in his practice. November 2, 1841, he married Elizabeth, daughter of James and Elizabeth Miller, of Chester county, Pennsylvania. Mrs. Bard was born February 4, 1816, in Washington city. They have had eight children, five of whom are living. Dr. and Mrs. Bard are members of the Methodist Episcopal church.

A. G. Botsford, deceased, was born in Newtown, Connecticut, in 1805. He came to Ohio about the year 1825, and located in Poland township. He was married September 16, 1828, to Miss Eliza Lynn, daughter of James Lynn, of Wheeling, West Virginia, and had a family of five children—J. E., of Louisville, Kentucky; J. S., of Youngstown, Ohio; T. G. of Poland; Mary, wife of H. O. Bonnell, of Youngstown; J. K., deceased. The father died in 1870, and the mother May 25, 1881. They were both members of the Presbyterian church. T. G. Botsford lives on the old homestead at Poland, but is engaged in business in Louisville, Kentucky.

Henry Hubbard, manufacturer of tinware, Poland township, Mahoning county, was born in Hartford county, Connecticut, May 26, 1805. His father, John Hubbard, was a native of the same State, and lived and died there. Henry Hubbard came to Ohio in 1826, and located in the township where he has since lived. He has been for many years in the manufacture of tinware. He was married February 10, 1828, to Miss Eliza Ann Robinson, daughter of David Robinson, of Glastonberry, Connecticut. They have had eight children, four of whom are still living. Mrs. Hubbard died several years ago. Mr. Hubbard is a Congregationalist in belief and a Republican in politics.

James Smith, farmer, Poland township, Mahoning county, was born in Franklin county, Pennsylvania, August 15, 1810. His father, Joseph, was a native of the same State, and in 1827 moved to Ohio, and settled in Poland township, where he resided until his death. He died in January, 1841, leaving a family consisting of a wife and four children, to mourn his loss.

James Smith has been engaged in various occupations, but is now living upon the old home place, and is evidently enjoying the evening of his days. In politics he is a Republican, and was formerly an anti-slavery man. He has always been what might be termed a reformer. He has never married.

Henry Heasley, farmer, Poland township, Mahoning county, was born in Youngstown, Ohio, November 1, 1845. His father was Henry Heasley, who was born in Westmoreland county, Pennsylvania, and came to Ohio about 1828, locating at Youngstown. He was a cabinetmaker by trade and resided at Youngstown twenty or twenty-five years, then moved upon the farm where his son now lives in Poland. He died in 1868, his widow and eight children surviving him. Henry Heasley, our subject, was married in 1874 to Miss Mary Clark, daughter of John Clark, of Poland. They have two children, Henry and Susan. Mr. and Mrs. Heasley are members of the Presbyterian church.

William Cole, farmer, Poland township, Mahoning county, was born in Morristown, Lamoille county, Vermont, February 11, 1826. His father, Ebenezer Cole, was also a native of Vermont, and came to Ohio in 1832. He settled in Poland township, upon the farm where William Cole, his son, now lives. He followed farming for about forty years, then went to Salem, where he died February 22, 1876, in his eighty-fifth year. He left a family of six children, three children having died previously. His wife died in 1847. Mr. Cole was in former years a Free-will Baptist preacher, though he followed farming chiefly in Ohio. William Cole has resided in Poland, upon the old homestead, since his boyhood. He has a farm of two hundred and thirty-two acres and is engaged in general farming and in the nursery business. He married, February 25, 1846, Miss Elma, daughter of Mahlon Parritt, of Hillsville, Pennsylvania, and has had three children, viz: Olive, born December 10, 1846; Alice, June 22, 1848; Emma, March 17, 1850. Mrs. Cole died October 9, 1853.

John W. Van Auker, farmer, Poland township, Mahoning county, was born in Youngstown, Ohio, August 10, 1834. Absalom Van Auker, his father, was a native of Delaware, and came to Ohio about 1829. He located at

Wooster, where he resided but a short time, then moved to Youngstown. He was a farmer, and died in 1836. John W. Van Auker, our subject, has always resided in the county, with the exception of two years, during which he lived in Wisconsin. His principal occupation through life has been that of farming and mercantile business. He was married August 16, 1854, to Miss Silvia A. Jackson, of Mahoning county, daughter of Joseph Jackson. They have had seven children, six of whom are living. Mr. Van Auker was in the Nineteenth Ohio volunteer infantry, and saw nearly four years of service. He is a Republican, and is an active, enterprising man. Mrs. Van Auker is a member of the Presbyterian church.

Samuel H. McBride, deceased, was born in Mercer county, Pennsylvania, April 29, 1809. His father, John, was a native of Washington county, and followed farming. He died about the year 1853. Samuel McBride came to Ohio in the spring of 1836, and located at Lowellville, Poland township. He was married in the fall of the same year—October 3, 1836—to Miss Phebe Harris, daughter of Barnabas Harris, of Coitsville township. Mr. McBride engaged in the mercantile business at Lowellville, and continued in it until 1875, when his health failed him, and, in consequence, retired from business. He died March 5, 1881, highly esteemed by all who enjoyed his acquaintance. He was a member of the United Presbyterian church. Mrs. McBride still resides in Lowellville, where she lived so many years with her late husband. She is the mother of three children—Leander, John, and Rose.

John B. Nessle, merchant and postmaster, Lowellville, Mahoning county, was born in 1818, in Montgomery county, New York. He learned the shoemakers trade when about sixteen years of age, and in 1837 found his way to Lowellville, Mahoning county, (then Trumbull) Ohio. He followed his trade upwards of twenty years, subsequently went into merchandizing in which he still continues, and was appointed postmaster of Lowellville in 1861, which position he still holds. He was married in 1839 to Miss Jane, daughter of John Pettigrew, of Lowellville, the fruit of which union was eight children. His first wife dying in 1870, Mr. Nessle was again married, in 1873, to Mrs. Stevens, a daughter of

Levi Beardsley, of Pennsylvania. Mrs. Nessle is a member of the Methodist church. Mr. Nessle is a Free Mason and a sound Republican. His father was Isaiah Nessle, a native of New York, who died in 1868 or 1869.

James B. Brown, farmer, Poland township, Mahoning county, was born in Ireland, February 20, 1820, and came to America with his parents in 1835 or 1836, landing at New York after a pleasant voyage of four weeks. The family went to Philadelphia, where they stopped about six weeks, and then went to Pittsburg where his father was engaged in merchandizing for four years. The family then removed to Ohio and settled in Poland township where the subject of this sketch still lives. His father died in 1849. Mr. Brown was married in 1855, to Miss Mary, daughter of James Buck, of Poland township, and has four children: Eliza, Jennie, Willie, and Emma.

Simon D. Brown, miller, was born in Trumbull county, Ohio, March 9, 1842, though he has always lived in Mahoning county, with the exception of two years. In his boyhood he was quite delicate, but as he grew older he gained in physical strength and is now a healthy man. He is now engaged in milling at Lowellville, Mahoning county, and does an extensive business. He married a daughter (Clara) of John Reed, of Poland township, October 2, 1879, and has one child, Ralph, born October 22, 1880. Mr. Brown's politics are Republican.

Robert B. Martin, farmer, Poland township, Mahoning county, was born in Lancaster county, Pennsylvania, February 19, 1835. His father, H. R. Martin, came from Pennsylvania in 1841 and settled in Springfield township, where he lived until his death, September 8, 1879. He was a tailor by trade in Pennsylvania, but after his removal to Ohio he followed farming. R. B. Martin was married, in 1862, to Miss Rachel, daughter of James McCord, of Lawrence county, Pennsylvania. They had three children, viz: Mary D., Alice J., and James C. Mr. Martin is a Democrat in politics.

H. R. Moore, M. D., physician, of Poland, Mahoning county, was born in said township January 24, 1842. His father, James Moore, is still living in the township, and is among its oldest residents. Dr. Moore studied medicine with Dr. Truesdale in Poland, and graduated at

11*

the Ohio Medical college, Cincinnati, after two years' study, in 1866. He has succeeded in building up a good practice in the Mahoning valley and is well liked. He was married in 1866, to Miss Maggie Woodruff, daughter of George Woodruff, of Poland. They have had three children—Lizzie, Kittie, and George C. Kittie is deceased. Dr. Moore and wife are Presbyterians in their religious faith. He is a Greenbacker in politics.

James G. Cavett, farmer, Poland township, Mahoning county, was born in Westmoreland county, Pennsylvania, May 25, 1804. He came to Ohio in 1854, and located in Poland upon the farm where he still lives. He was engaged in the tanning business in Pennsylvania, but since coming to Ohio has followed farming. He was married in 1830, to Miss Amanda Smith, of Franklin county, Pennsylvania. They have had three children—Jane M., John H., and Elizabeth, the last named being deceased. Mrs. Cavett died in 1867. She was a member of the Presbyterian church, as is also her husband.

John H. Cavett was born in Westmoreland county, Pennsylvania, December 2, 1835, and came to Ohio in 1854, with his parents. He married April 7, 1857, Miss Elizabeth Rigler, of Pennsylvania. They have two children, Lizzie E. and James B. Mr. and Mrs. Cavett are members of the Presbyterian church. He is a firm Republican in politics, has been township clerk five terms, and is held in high esteem by his fellow-citizens.

J. H. Davidson, merchant, Poland, Mahoning county, was born at Shippensburg, Pennsylvania, June 22, 1826. Samuel Davidson, his father, came from Pennsylvania in 1831, and located in Coitsville township, where he engaged at farming. He died November 21, 1871, at the age of seventy-nine years, six months and fifteen days. His wife died June 5, 1871, aged seventy years, eight months and twenty-eight days. They were both members of the Presbyterian church, and he was one of the first to move in the organization of the Free Presbyterian church at New Bedford, Pennsylvania. J. H. Davidson has been engaged in various occupations; worked at blacksmithing several years, and was engaged in prospecting for oil and coal from 1859 to 1874. He went to Poland in 1866 and started in merchandizing in 1875. He

was married in 1853 to Miss Emily Clark, daughter of Henry Clark, of Hubbard, and has two children, Mary E. and Charles H. Mr. and Mrs. Davidson are members of the Methodist church. Mr. Davidson enlisted, April 27, 1864, in the One Hundred and Seventy-first Ohio National guard, serving one hundred days, when he was mustered out.

Dr. Alexander C. Elliott, dentist, Poland, Mahoning county, was born in Beaver county, Pennsylvania, December 20, 1831, and came to Ohio in 1865 and located in Poland township. He studied dentistry at Rochester, Pennsylvania. Dr. Elliott was in the war of the Rebellion four years—three years in the First Pennsylvania cavalry, and one year in the First Pennsylvania veteran cavalry, and was wounded in the right leg at St. Mary's church, near Malvern Hill, Virginia. He was married in 1866 to Miss Isabella, daughter of John Young, of Columbiana county, and has one child, Clarence, born August 3, 1868. Dr. Elliott and his wife are members of the First Baptist church of Youngstown.

Leander D. Robinson, farmer, Poland township, Mahoning county, was born in Lawrence county, Pennsylvania, in 1843. His father, Samuel, was a Pennsylvanian, a farmer by occupation, and died in 1858. L. D. Robinson came to Ohio in 1874, and is engaged in general farming. He married, in 1866, Miss Annie, daughter of Robert Graham, of Poland township, and has one child—Lillie May. He was in the One Hundred and Fifty-fifth regiment, Ohio infantry, in the rebellion, and also in the One Hundred and Thirty-fourth Pennsylvania. He and his wife are both members of the Presbyterian church.

R. W. Weller, M. D., physician, Lowellville, Mahoning county, was born in Beaver, now Lawrence, county, Pennsylvania, May 17, 1838. His father, John Weller, is a native of New Jersey, and is still living at the advanced age of eighty-one years. Dr. Weller studied medicine at the University of Wooster, graduated in 1876, and has since been in practice at Lowellville. He built up a good practice, and is well liked. He was first lieutenant in the Pennsylvania "round head" regiment (One Hundredth); enlisted August 27, 1861, and was mustered out October 15, 1864. He is now a member of the Grand Army of the Republic, and is also a Free Mason. He married, in 1865, Miss Lavenia Monroe, daughter of Joel Monroe, of Lawrence county, Pennsylvania, and has two children—John and James. Dr. and Mrs. Weller are members of the Presbyterian church.

CHAPTER III.

BOARDMAN.

PHYSICAL FEATURES.

The surface of this township is gently undulating, and in many portions nearly level. There are some hills, but none that are very steep. The soil is mostly fertile, and well adapted to a variety of crops. The western and northwestern part of the township is watered by Mill creek and its tributaries. Yellow creek flows for over two miles through the southeast of Boardman, thence entering Poland township near the village. Altogether, the natural aspect of this township is one of beauty, with just enough of hills and valleys, fields and woodlands, to please the eye by presenting to its gaze a varied and lovely landscape. A ride from Boardman center in either direction, north, south, east, or west, takes the traveler through as pleasant a farming region as can be found in this part of the State. Although a considerable portion of the land still remains uncleared, there are several large productive farms, with neat and pretty houses, large and convenient barns, showing that the owners are men of activity and thrift. The southwestern quarter of the township is the least improved, and contains but few inhabitants. Here stands the Big Oak, on a path believed by the old settlers to have been made by deer. This oak is a stern monarch of the forest, five and a half feet in diameter, and seventeen feet in circumference three feet from the ground, as has been ascertained by actual measurement. It has fifty feet of trunk and does not rise above the neighboring trees, or it might have been prostrated by the wind years ago. Probably this venerable tree was a sturdy youth at the time America was discovered! It is still at some distance from any improved land.

In the northern part of the township, on the farm of J. B. Kistler, and in that vicinity, there are extensive coal deposits, which it is believed may become a source of profit to their owners ere many years have elapsed.

VILLAGES.

Properly speaking Boardman has no village. Boardman center, the only point which bears any resemblance to one, contains about a dozen houses, a carriage shop, and a post-office. It is in a delightful situation, and if it should grow in future years, no pleasanter location for a town could be found. A small portion of Poland village on the eastern border is included within this township.

INDUSTRIES, ETC.

Boardman is essentially a farming community. In former years there have been a few stores, some tanneries, several saw-mills, but never any manufacturing enterprises of much importance; and to-day farming is the principal business, and almost the only business carried on in the township. The only store in the township is that kept by Uriah Stafford on the south line of the township at Steamtown, which village, however, is all included in Beaver township except the store and post-office.

Stewart Snyder has a carriage and blacksmith shop at the center.

Elias Eyster, wagon-maker, has a shop one and a half miles north of the center, and near him is the blacksmith shop of Cyrus Simon.

Joseph Miller is also a blacksmith at Zedaker's corners, in the shop formerly occupied by John Westbecker.

William J. Hitchcock and W. Moherman each have steam saw-mills in the Boardman woods.

George Simon has a steam saw-mill near his residence. In former years he manufactured shingles and barrel staves in quite large quantities. Now he saws lumber only.

EARLY SETTLEMENT.

Elijah Boardman, accompanied by six able men, among whom were Nathaniel and Ebenezer Blakely, and a man named Summers, came to this township in 1798. Mr. Boardman was a resident of New Milford, Connecticut, and was a member of the Connecticut Land company. He spent the entire summer here, making surveys and establishing land-marks, while the men whom he had brought with him were making clearings and preparing for other comers. These pioneers brought two yoke of oxen, which they left at Youngstown to be wintered. Five of the number returned to Connecticut on foot; the other, one of the Blakelys, remained and became a permanent settler.

The township was named for Elijah Boardman. A stone set by him to mark the center of the township was unearthed a few years ago, and his initials, E. B., discovered upon it.

From 1800 to 1811 settlers came in rapidly, the majority coming from Connecticut. A few natives of Pennsylvania also found their way hither.

In 1810 the population of the township was about 850, nearly as large as it is at the present writing.

Upon the township records, containing a list and description of ear marks in the year 1806, there appear the following names, showing that these men were property holders here at that date: Abner Webb, Linus Brainard, William Drake, Haynes Fitch, Eli Baldwin, George Stilson, John Davidson, Joseph Merchant, Oswald Detchon, Eleazer Fairchild and his sons—John, Amos, and Daniel—Elijah Boardman, Francis Dowler, Richard J. Elliot, Peter Stilson, Samuel Swan, David Noble, Warren Bissel.

The same book also shows the following names at the dates given:

1807—Isaac Blackman, James Moody.

1808—Beach Summers, David Fitch, Ethel Starr.

1809—Andrew Hull, Herman Stilson, Jacob Frank, Elijah Deane.

1813—Simeon Mitchell, Eliakim Stoddard, John Northrop.

Francis Dowler, and his son John, the former a native of Ireland, settled in this township in 1801.

John and Charlotte Davidson settled near the center in 1805. They were forty days on their way hither from Connecticut.

Haynes Fitch and his sons Jedediah and David came in 1804, and settled on the farm where Alexander Gault now lives.

Ethel Starr settled on the west of Indian creek about 1807. He lived to be quite aged.

Isaac Blackman was an early comer, who settled on the Poland road one-half mile from the village. In 1808 he built a good frame house, which is still standing, being now used as a stable. Afterwards he sold out and moved to Poland.

Eliakim Stoddard came about the year 1804, and settled on the south road, one and a half miles from Boardman center.

Major Samuel Clark came in 1810, and settled where his son William L. Clark now resides. He was one of the first postmasters, and used to bring the mail from Poland once a week in his pocket. He served as justice of the peace in 1828 or 1829, and was a worthy man and a prominent citizen. He was commissioned lieutenant, captain, and afterwards major of militia. His wife was Anna Northrup. She, like the major, was a native of Connecticut. Major Clark died in 1847 in his sixty-first year. Mrs. Clark died in 1860, aged sixty-seven years.

Richard J. Elliot came in 1804 or 1805. He was a member of the Legislature in 1808 and 1809. At his last election he received every vote in his district, an honor probably never accorded to any other candidate either before or since. He resided on the farm cleared by William Drake.

Oswald Detchon, a native of England, was among the very first settlers. He located three-fourths of a mile east of the center.

The Stilson brothers, Peter and George, came in 1800. Peter Stilson settled on the south side of the road leading to Canfield, near the present residence of Eli Reed. He had four sons, Herman, Anson, Luther, and Philip, all of whom lived here several years.

David Noble came in the year 1804 or 1805. He settled on the south road about a mile from the center.

David Woodruff, a very early settler, located on what is now the J. B. Kistler farm in the northern part of the township. After his death his sons sold out and went West.

Captain Warren Bissel previous to 1806 settled one-half mile west of Poland, on the road leading to Canfield.

Henry Brainard came in 1800 and settled about one mile from the center on the road running west. He had several sons, one of whom, Dr. Ira Brainard, was probably the first and only settled physician in this township. Dr. Brainard practiced here a few years, then moved to Can-

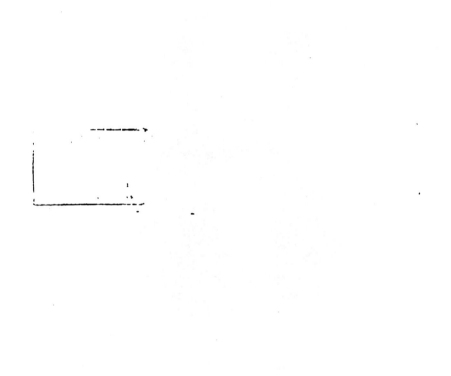

Billius Kirtland

Mrs. B. Kirtland.

Billius Kirtland

Mrs. B. Kirtland.

field. The children of Henry Brainard were Solomon, George, Linus, Ira, and Henry, and three daughters who became Mrs. Dowd, Mrs. Nathaniel Blakely, and Mrs. Hermon Stilson.

William Drake made a clearing in the southwestern quarter of the township in 1800. In a small log hut on that farm occurred the first wedding in Boardman. A man named Cummings married Drake's sister. There also was born the second female child born in the township, that child being the widow Allhands, of Youngstown township, now deceased.

James Stall settled quite early in the northeastern part of Boardman, on the eastern line of the township.

Eleazer Fairchild was an early settler. He located on what is now Eli Reed's farm. He had several sons, Eleazer, Amos, Daniel, and perhaps others.

Among those who came to Boardman as early as 1801, and from that time until 1810, were several families by the name of Simon, from Washington county, Pennsylvania. Of these, probably Adam Simon came first. He settled on the farm now owned by Michael Simon. Soon afterward came Jacob Simon. Michael Simon came a few years later with several sons and daughters, all of whom settled in the northern part of the township. Among his children were Adam, Peter, Jacob, Abraham, and Henry. There were two Jacob Simons, Jacob, the son of Michael, being known as "Schoolmaster Jake" —thus distinguishing from "Mill Creek Jake," who settled farther to the westward. All of the Simons brought up large families, and many of their descendants still reside here.

George Zedaker and his son John came from Washington county, Pennsylvania, in 1802 or 1803. J. P. Zedaker, a son of John Zedaker, now lives upon the farm where they located. John Zedaker was a soldier in the War of 1812, and was the last survivor in Boardman of the soldiers of that war. He died several years ago.

Isaac Hankins, an early comer, settled on Benjamin McNutt's farm, in the northern part of the township. About the year 1815 he sold his farm to "Preacher" Hewett and moved away.

George Pope, an early settler, also located on a part of the McNutt farm, which he bought from Hankins. Later he moved to the northwestern part of the township, and settled near

Mill creek. He attained the age of ninety-eight years. He was a native of Virginia.

Other early settlements were made in the Simons neighborhood by a man named Feester, Martin Dustman, who settled near the north line of the township, and Henry Dustman, on the farm now owned by Samuel Moyer.

Andrew Hull settled quite early on the farm now belonging to Thomas Matthews.

John Northrup came about 1811. He was a carpenter by trade. He resided at the center for a short time, then moved south of there, and afterwards went West.

John Twiss came in 1818, Charles Titus in 1819. The latter is still living.

Amos Baldwin, a native of Connecticut, moved here from Washington county, Pennsylvania, in 1811, and settled on Mill creek. His son, Asa Baldwin, born in 1798, still resides in Boardman. Amos Baldwin moved to Trumbull county, where he died in 1850 at the age of eighty-six. He brought up seven sons and two daughters. Three of his sons, John, Garry, and Asa, settled in Boardman.

Asa Baldwin, a brother of Amos, came in 1811, or perhaps a year or two before. He settled on the Agnew farm.

Thomas and Elizabeth Agnew settled on the farm where their son, Ralph Agnew, Esq., now lives, in the year 1824, coming here from Pennsylvania.

Henry Foster, a wheelwright, was a resident of the township for many years. He came here with his father previous to 1808.

Elijah Deane, an early settler, settled near Foster.

Philip and Catharine Stambaugh settled in the northeastern corner of the township in 1811, where their son Philip is still living. He was born February 16, 1796, and is the oldest man in the township. Mr. Stambaugh, Sr., took up about two hundred acres of land in the four townships, Boardman, Youngstown, Coitsville, and Poland, paying for it at the rate of $7 and $8 per acre.

Eli Baldwin came from Connecticut in 1801, being then about twenty years of age. He acted as the agent of Elijah Boardman, who owned the greater part of the land in this township. Mr. Baldwin was a very prominent man, active in all public affairs. He was the first captain of militia, the first justice of the peace, and, it is believed, the first postmaster in the township. He represented this district in the Legislature several terms, and served as associate judge one term. He settled in the northern part of the township in 1809 or 1810, where he passed the remainder of his days.

About 1801 came the DeCamps, the Shields and Woodruff families, elsewhere mentioned. All these settled in the northwestern part of the township.

Abraham Osborn settled near DeCamp at an early date.

Josiah Walker settled on Yellow creek in 1803. His sons live on the same farm now.

Nathaniel Blakely was one of the first settlers, a schoolmaster, and a justice of the peace in early days.

Isaac Newton settled at Boardman center in 1811.

William and Pamelia Fankle came about the year 1816, and settled in the southeast of the township, one mile from the Poland line. Three of their five children are yet living, Silas in this township, and Edward and Della F. in the west.

David Porter, and his wife, Mary Walker, both natives of Adams county, Pennsylvania, settled near the southern line of the township, about one mile from the southeast corner, in 1815. The log house where they lived is still standing— one of the few remaining mementoes of early days. They had five children, three of whom are living—David, their youngest, in this township, Mrs. Martha M. Slaven and Harvey Porter, in Kansas. David Porter, Sr., was killed by a falling tree, June 19, 1819, thus leaving his wife and little children to provide for themselves, and undergo the harsh experiences of pioneers. David occupies a portion of the original farm.

FIRST ELECTION.

The first township meeting for the election of officers was held April 7, 1806. Haynes Fitch was chosen chairman, Henry Brainard and David Woodruff clerks. The following officers were chosen for the year: Eli Baldwin, township clerk; Henry Brainard, George Stilson, and Adam Simon, trustees; Eleazer Fairchild and Michael Simon, overseers of the poor; James Hull and Abner Webb, fence viewers; Nathaniel Blakely, lister and appraiser; Jedediah Fitch, appraiser; Isaac Hankins, Nathaniel Blakely,

and David Fitch, supervisors of highway; David Fitch, constable; and James Moody, treasurer.

Previous to the above date the township had been included in Youngstown. It was organized as Boardman township in 1805.

JUSTICES OF THE PEACE.

The first justice was Judge Eli Baldwin. His successors have been Nathaniel Blakely, James Moody, Asa Baldwin, John Woodruff, Parkus Woodruff, Shelden Newton, and Ralph Agnew, who holds the office at present.

PRIMITIVE TAXES.

The amount of taxes levied in Boardman, in 1803, was $17.47. Taxes could not have been very oppressive that year. We give a list of the taxes and tax-payers for 1803:

BOARDMAN, RANGE TWO, TOWN ONE.

	Amount of tax.		Amount of tax.
Brainard, Sinas	$ 0 40	Dustman, Henry	$ 0 10
Brainard, Solomon	15	Fisher, Benjamin	20
Blakesley, Ebenezer	61	Fairchild, Eleazer	1 83
Blakesley, Nathaniel	62	McCorkle, Archibald	20
Baldwin, Caleb	3 33	Stephens, John	47
Baldwin, Eli	24	Scroggs, Allen	40
Cook, Isaac	24	Simon, Michael	1 77
Canada, James	30	Stilson, George	07
Comyns, Joseph	20	Stilson, Peter	16
Chamberlain, Noah	41	Stall, James	62
Davis, Ebenezer	40	Simon, Andrew	50
DeCamp, Lewis	62	Somers, Beach	30
Dice, Edward	56	Thornton, John, Jr.	81
Dice, William	40	McMahan, John	16
Detchon, Oswald	1 30		
Total			$17 47

EARLY INCIDENTS AND ADVENTURES.

From the writings of Shelden Newton, Esq., for whose assistance in preparing this township history the writer desires to express the heartiest thanks, are gathered many of the facts and incidents which follow.

Seventy years ago Boardman was wild and desolate; there were no good roads, and all of the low ground was covered with logs, or corduroy crossings. Sugar was worth forty cents per pound, and was a luxury to be used sparingly or not at all. The crop of maple sugar in 1811 was almost a total failure; but the following season about forty thousand pounds were made in the township, as was ascertained from figures gathered on election day—the first Monday in April—of that year.

In December, 1805, George Stilson and a boy name Whitney were at work in the forest getting out timber with which to build Stilson's tavern, when suddenly they heard the sharp report of a hunter's rifle, and were astonished to see a bear rushing almost directly toward them. Stilson had a worthless cur lying on his coat near by. Now, he thought, was excellent opportunity for training his dog. According the dog was urged on, and ran directly in front of the bear and attempted to seize it. But he soon found himself in the close embrace of the huge animal. The dog gave two or three sharp yells, and then his voice was heard no more. Stilson seized his axe and advanced toward the bear. As he came within a few feet of him, the bear, no doubt divining his intentions, dropped the almost lifeless dog and started for his assailant. Stilson took to his heels, dropping his axe in the excitement of the moment, and soon bear and man were making lively circles around a large poplar tree. The boy Whitney stood on the fallen timber and shouted, "Run, Uncle George; run or he will catch you." Just at this moment, when the case looked hopeless, and Stilson's breath became quite short, the hunter's dog came up and seized the bear by a hind leg, thus diverting bruin's attention from his intended prey. The hunter, Donaldson, soon arrived upon the scene and shot the bear. A team was brought to the place, the dead animal was hauled to the center and dressed, his meat weighing three hundred pounds. Everybody who wished could obtain a piece of the meat.

Boardman was considered the best of hunting ground for deer in those early days. Curtis Fairchild, a noted huntsman, killed one hundred and five deer in one season, besides trapping thirteen wolves. The skin of a deer was worth seventy-five cents; the meat, nothing. A bounty of $6 each was paid by the county for the scalps of wolves.

Bears and wolves were numerous and troublesome. One night in December, 1811, Eliakim Stoddard was aroused about ten o'clock by the squealing of his hogs. Seizing his axe he went to the pen and there saw a huge bear attacking his best hog. Stoddard was intending to creep up unnoticed and strike the bear with his axe, but the bear was on the alert for intruders and at once rushed at him. Stoddard retreated to the house, while the bear returned to the pen, seized the hog, drew it across the road and

across a small stream to a point about ten rods from the house and there proceeded with his meal undisturbed. The hog was a long time in dying, and of course its cries were hideous. Stoddard did not wish to leave his wife and children alone while the bear remained in the vicinity. What was to be done? Nobody lived within a mile of him. He resolved to await events; and, about twelve o'clock, was rejoiced to see the bear depart into the forest. He then fastened up the house as securely as possible, and proceeded to the center to arouse the neighborhood. As soon as it was daylight a party of men with dogs and arms started in pursuit of the bear, which they chased all through the day, and until after sunset. The hunters took lodging at the nearest house, and the next day commenced the chase anew. After leading them a long race the bear was finally treed and despatched, though it took three shots to bring him down.

THE WAR OF 1812

drew from Boardman every man able to do military service. Few, if any in the township, volunteered, but all were drafted.

Three drafts were made, each taking one-third of the militia. Regarding these times, Shelden Newton, Esq., writes as follows concerning the second draft:

The company was again called out. Captain Bissel and a Government officer were present. The orderly sergeant, Isaac Blackman, with his spontoon—its handle stained red with poke-berry juice—paraded the company, marching them around in single file, calling on the members to fall into ranks. When he had them all in, he brought them up before the tavern "front face." The officers of the company and the Government officer held a few moments' consultation. The captain then ordered the company to call off in the usual form, "right, left; right, left," to the end. Then the Government officer told them they must march the next day at two o'clock, with three days' rations in their knapsacks. In this draft were David Noble, Asa Baldwin, Thomas Moody, and a score of others.

From that time until the hour of starting there was no sleep in the neighborhood. It required the constant vigilance of all to get the men ready. Cooking had to be done, knapsacks made, clothing prepared, etc. All were ready and left at the appointed time. In a few short days came another express, saying that the enemy were then crossing the lake, and were in sight of Cleveland. This was on Saturday, and every man must start on Monday. The captain and all other officers had gone in the second draft. Thus for two nights Boardman was left entirely destitute of men. Not an able-bodied man was left. I now recollect of only two men who were too old to do military duty. They were John Davidson and Henry Brainard. However, the scare on Lake Erie proved a false alarm, and the last draft were ordered home.

Charles A. Boardman went out as adjutant under Colonel Rayen. He was afterward transferred to another regiment. William Ingersol, a chum of Boardman, went with him, and was soon appointed forage master, and proved to be very efficient in obtaining supplies.

At the battle of the Peninsula, near Sandusky, three of Boardman township's soldiers were volunteers: Jacob Frank, George Moherman, and John Dowler. Frank was a stout, courageous man, ready to deal blows right and left, regardless of his own safety. Moherman was as reckless a warrior as ever aimed at an Indian. Dowler, a William Penn in principle, would not choose to harm any living being; but when the shrieks of the women and children of the frontier almost reached his ears, he did not hesitate about the rightfulness of his action, but shouldered his rifle and started. These men were under Captain Cotton, of Austintown, an efficient officer. There were two hundred men, all volunteers, in that skirmish with the Indians. When they had entered the peninsula, it was found that they had plenty of business on their hands. Indians rose from the grass on all sides, fighting became general, and still more Indians appeared. Moherman was then in his element. Frank proceeded too far from his companions, and found himself alone and surrounded by savages. He was shot through the arm and commenced to run. There was a large block-house on the peninsula, which was the means of saving many lives. The captain ordered a retreat, which had already become quite general, and was being carried out in a very straggling manner. Moherman, a leader in the fray, obeyed quite reluctantly. When he had retreated a few steps he found a dead Indian, and determined to have his scalp; but other Indians dashed toward him, and he ran into the high grass and escaped. When a few rods away he stumbled over the body of a wounded red man not yet dead. Now was his opportunity; he seized the Indian by the hair, and with one circle of his knife cut loose the scalp, caught it in his mouth and tore it from the head, and hurried on as rapidly as possible. When some distance further on, he came across Abraham Simon, one of his neighbors from Youngstown, mortally wounded. Moherman offered his assistance, but Simon told him to take care of himself. Moherman, however, resolved to save his comrade, and, stooping down, placed the arms of the wounded man about his neck, took his own gun in his hand, and hastened again toward the block-house, bearing Simon upon his back. Near the house he came to a fence, and while he was climbing it an Indian shot Simon through the head, killing him almost instantly. Moherman gained the retreat in safety, still carrying the scalp, of which ever after he was very proud. He brought it home with him, and afterward sold it to a Philadelphia merchant for ten dollars.

When the retreat commenced Dowler caught an Indian in the act of taking a scalp from one of his comrades. The man was dead and the savage was proceeding to scalp him before loading his gun. The Indian ran at once, directly away from Dowler, who fired upon him, and, not wishing to know that he had killed an Indian, turned and fled in safety to the block-house.

Times were hard, and the soldiers and their families were obliged to undergo many bitter experiences and privations, even after the close of the war.

From 1814 up to 1820 money was exceedingly scarce. Wheat brought twenty-five cents per bushel in paper money. Butter was five cents per pound, and eggs four cents a dozen in "store pay." Three year old steers sold for $10 per head, cash. People drank rye coffee and had no tea. They manufactured every article of clothing except leather for shoes. This had to be bought, consequently many went barefooted a large portion of the year. Deer skins were good, serviceable articles, and half of the men wore buckskin breeches. Charles A. Boardman made a fine pair of pantaloons from this material. After the skins were prepared and dressed he obtained some kind of blue liquid with which he stained them, thus making the best and most showy garments in the country. He wore them for two years or more, and during that time taught school for $2.40 per month and "found himself."

CHURCH HISTORY.

At this date (1881) there are four religious societies and three church edifices in the township, two of them being at the center, and the other in the northern part. The Universalists held meetings in 1820, but never built a church. A

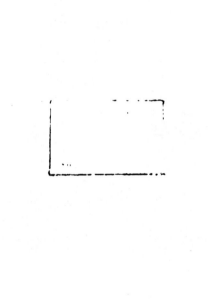

Sheldon Newton

dozen years ago there were four churches at Boardman center—Protestant Episcopal, Presbyterian, Methodist and Disciple. Now only the Methodists and the Episcopals maintain their organizations. The buildings which belonged to the other denominations are devoted to other than religious purposes.

ST. JAMES' CHURCH, PROTESTANT EPISCOPAL.

This church, the oldest in the diocese, dates back to July 20, 1809. At that date was issued a petition urging that the inhabitants of Boardman, Canfield, and Poland meet August 12, 1809, for the purpose of forming a regular Episcopal society, and the organization was effected the same year. We give below the names of the signers of this paper:

Turhand Kirtland, Ensign Church, Charles Chittenden, Josiah Wetmore, Samuel Blocker. Joseph Platt, Ethel Starr, Francis Dowler, John Liddle, John Dowler, Eleazer Fairchild, Ziba Loveland, Arad Way, Eleazer Gilson, Russell F. Starr, Eli Platt, John Loveland, Lewis Hoyt, Joseph Liddle, Jared Kirtland. For a time only laymen officiated in the church, with occasional assistance from traveling missionaries. In March, 1817, the society was organized as a parish, according to the canons, and received the name St. James' Episcopal church. Following is a list of missionaries and rectors who have labored in this church: First, Rev. Jackson Kemper, 1814, afterwards bishop of Wisconsin; succeeded by Revs. Jacob Morgan Douglas, Roger Searle, Philander Chase, afterwards bishop of this diocese and later of Illinois, M. T. C. Wing, afterwards a professor in Kenyon college, John L. Bryan, Joshua L. Harrison, Intrepid Morse, Joshua T. Eaton, William Grandville, C. F. Lewis, Joseph Adderly, C. S. Doolittle, A. T. McMurphy, Abraham J. Warner (longest service of any, 1864-78), C. F. Adams. The last named served but one year, and left on account of illness. At present the church is without a rector. It numbers fifty-six members, twenty-four communicants.

The school-house and private dwellings were used as places of worship until 1828, when the present church edifice was completed. In 1824 the church had sixty members. In 1853 a movement was made to build a parsonage, and successfully carried out a year or two later.

There has also been connected with this parish a Ladies' Missionary society, the organization of which dates back nearly fifty years.

BETHLEHEM CHURCH.

This is a union church belonging to the two societies, the Lutherans and the German Reformed. Through the efforts of the Simons families and others a log house was built at a very early date and used as a place for worship for many years. The first preacher was a man named Stough. Later Rev. Henry Hewett, who married a daughter of Michael Simon, was the pastor. This church is located on the north line of the township, one mile from the eastern corner.

The first graveyard of the Germans was on the farm of Adam Simon. After the first church was built a cemetery was established near by, in which the remains of Henry Dustman were the first to be interred.

Regular services are held alternately by the two societies, but the membership of each is quite small. The present house was erected in 1845. The log house was erected as early as 1810, and was the first house of worship built in the township.

THE CONGREGATIONAL CHURCH,

called also the Presbyterian church, was established by Rev. John Field, a missionary from Connecticut, May 28, 1813. In 1849 the organization ceased to exist, on account of removals to other parts of the country and the death of several of its members. The first officers of this church were Samuel Swan and Charles A. Boardman, church committee, and Charles A. Boardman, deacon.

Rev. Warren Taylor was the only settled minister. He was installed in 1844 and remained one year. Other preachers were either missionaries or pastors of other congregations who preached here a part of the time.

METHODIST EPISCOPAL CHURCH.

At what date this organization began the historian is unable to learn. Oswald Detchon was one of its prime movers and most prominent members. The first meetings were held in a log school-house upon his farm. Dr. Adams, of Beaver, was among the early preachers. The present house of worship at the center was probably built about 1835. Among those whose means and influence contributed largely toward

12*

building it may be mentioned the following names: Thomas Agnew, Major Samuel Clark, and Josiah Beardsley.

THE DISCIPLES.

A church of this denomination was organized about the year 1854 by Herman Reeves, an evangelist. A church building was erected some two years later. The membership was never large, and through deaths and removal of members, the organization ceased to exist some ten years ago. The house was sold to the township and is now used as a town hall. The preachers in this church were Revs. Reeves, Ephraim Phillips, John Errett, D. J. White, and James Calvin.

AN EARLY SOCIETY.

An organization known as The Female Tract Society of Boardman, Canfield and the Western Reserve, held its first meeting February 18, 1818. It contained a large number of members in all parts of the Reserve, but has been extinct for many years.

CEMETERIES AND BURIAL PLACES.

The first burials in the township were made upon the farm of Adam Simon. The German cemetery was soon afterward laid out.

One or more interments were made near Poland, at an early date, opposite where the house of William Hultz now stands.

The cemetery near the center was laid out in 1805, and the first burials there were in that year or the year following.

THE FIRST SCHOOLS.

About as soon as the pioneers were established in their new homes, preparations were made for the education of their children. A log schoolhouse, the first in the township, was built a few rods west of the center, probably in 1803 or 1804. Nathaniel Blakely was the first teacher. Mrs. Mitchell, wife of Simeon Mitchell, who settled at the center in 1810, also taught several terms. Boardman was favored with excellent teachers in early days. In place of the log building a two-story frame school-house was erected in 1809. This was called the academy, and was used for school, church, and other meetings for thirty years or more. It is still standing one and a half miles east of the center, where it was moved years ago, and is now used as a stable.

A log school-house was built by the Simons almost as early as the one at the center. German alone was taught for several years, but English was gradually substituted. Jacob Simon taught this school for some years, and was afterwards succeeded by his sons and the sons of Adam Simon. The house was situated on the farm of the latter.

The first schools were all private, or tuition schools.

TAVERNS.

George Stilson built the first frame house in the township in 1805, on the spot where Jesse Baldwin's house now is. Here he kept tavern for about twenty-five years. He was succeeded by Perry Baldwin, Herman Crane, Samuel Elliot, Alex. McKinney, and Arthur Patrick. Since the death of Mr. Patrick in 1860 Boardman has been without a hotel.

Joseph Merchant came from Connecticut in 1804, and soon afterward settled one-half mile south of the center. About the year 1814 he began keeping tavern about eighty rods east of the center. In 1823 Asa Baldwin carried on the same business at the same place for about one year. Mr. Baldwin's sign was an original one, and had the merit of attracting attention and customers. One side read as follows:

> Nothing on this side,
> Not much on the other;

and the opposite side,

> Nothing in the house,
> Or in the barn either.

The house was quite popular; from which it may be inferred that the "advertising dodge" didn't tell the exact truth.

POST-OFFICES.

The first, and until recently, the only post-office in Boardman, was that at Boardman center. The exact date of its establishment can not be ascertained, but it was in existence in 1810. The first postmaster and his successors were as follows: Eli Baldwin, Major Samuel Clark, William Ingersoll, Samuel Swan, H. M. Boardman, Arthur Patrick, S. O. Stilson, and Edward Davidson, the present incumbent. Boardman now receives four mails, one from each direction, daily.

A post-office named Woodworth was established a few years ago, in the southern part of the township. Uriah Stafford is the present postmaster.

THE FIRST MILLS.

The first grist-mill in Boardman was a small affair. It was a log building, but was soon replaced by a good one. It was situated on Mill creek, near Lanterman's falls, and was known as Baird's mill. It was run for many years by Thomas Shields. Eli Baldwin afterwards owned it. The flood of 1843 carried it almost entirely away. This was one of the first mills in the Reserve, and probably the very first.

The first saw-mill was built one and a half miles from the center, in a southeasterly direction, on a small tributary of Mill creek. Elijah Boardman and Richard Elliot were the proprietors. It was probably built in 1808. DeCamp's was the next mill erected, on a small stream in the northwestern corner of the township. Neither of these saw-mills was run very long.

Eli Baldwin had a saw-mill, a grist-mill, and a cloth-mill upon Mill creek, at a later date. The saw-mill was destroyed by fire and the grist-mill torn down and removed years ago.

The Zedakers built a cider-mill in 1818.

A saw-mill built by the Walkers' is still standing but unused.

THE FIRST STORE

was opened in a room of Stilson's tavern by Charles Boardman and William Ingersoll. They continued in the business but a short time, however. Later, Calvin Brainard kept store on the corner where G. E. Lanterman's house now stands.

DISTILLERIES.

Many people operated small stills but none were of much importance, except the distillery of Eli Baldwin. He commenced distilling in 1809 or 1810 and conducted the business for several years, manufacturing considerable quantities of liquor. This distillery was located near the north line of the township on the Youngstown road.

TANNERY.

A tannery was built by James Moody just north of the center. He came in 1804 and began working at his trade in 1805. At first he ground bark by rolling a heavy stone over it, afterwards introducing improvements. He continued in the business over forty years and was considered a good workman. His buildings, —house, barn, mill, and bark-house—were first made of logs and replaced later by frame buildings.

MISCELLANEOUS.

The first white child born in the township was James D. McMahon, born October 31, 1799. For his history see Jackson township.

Horace Daniels was born in Boardman in March, 1800. His parents came in 1799. In 1823 he drove the first stage westward on the old Pittsburg & Cleveland stage line.

The first sermon was preached in the old school-house at the center in 1804, by Rev. Mr. Badger, a Presbyterian missionary from Connecticut.

The first blacksmith was Andrew Webb, who came about 1804. In company with Samuel Swan he made scythes and sold them for $2 each. Eastern manufactured scythes were then worth $2.50. Webb first had a shop at the center, and afterwards moved one mile west where he continued working at his trade for some years.

George Brainard, a blacksmith, came in 1812, and worked at his trade in a shop near the center for some thirty years. He sold out and went to Austintown.

John Davidson was probably the first shoemaker in the township.

Elijah Deane, who settled on the farm now owned by James Hughes, was also one of the first shoemakers.

The first cheese made in this township, and perhaps the first made on the Western Reserve, was made by Peter Stilson in 1804. He carried a few hundred-weight to Pittsburg and sold it there.

BIOGRAPHICAL SKETCHES.

THE BOARDMAN FAMILY.

Henry M. Boardman, son of Elijah and Mary Anna Boardman, was born in New Milford, Litchfield county, Connecticut, January 4, 1797. Elijah Boardman, for whom the township of Boardman was named, was a member of the Connecticut Land company and owned extensive tracts of land in different portions of the Western Reserve. He came here in 1798 and spent the summer establishing land-marks and making surveys, but did not settle. Henry M. Boardman married, December 13, 1818, Sarah Hall Benham, daughter of Rev. Benjamin Benham, pastor of St. John's parish at New Milford, and the next year removed with his wife to Boardman. He located at the center of the township, first occupying the house which is now the dwelling of his son, Frederick A. This house had been erected two years before by Isaac Newton, who at first occupied and cultivated land for the proprietor, Elijah Boardman. The house was constructed entirely of oak, and so strongly and substantially was it built that after the lapse of sixty-five years it is apparently as firm and substantial as ever. Mr. Boardman occupied this dwelling but a short time. In 1820 he built and occupied the house on the corner opposite, in which he resided until his death.

The life of Mr. Boardman, like those of nearly all the pioneers, was of a commonplace character. From the very nature of their circumstances and surroundings there could be little in their careers which would furnish a biographer with materials for anything more than a brief and simple narrative. Their lives were a continuous round of toil, often of deprivation, and sometimes of suffering. He who looks for exciting interest, spirit, or variety in the "simple annals" of the pioneers must look in vain. Mr. Boardman was a farmer by occupation and he did not neglect his business for other things. But his principal characteristic was his interest in the moral and religious welfare of the community and his devotion to his church. The religious element in his nature seems to have been predominant.

The next year after his settlement in Boardman (in 1820), to supply the existing want of pastoral services, he united with a few neighbors in organizing a parish at the center under the title of St. John's church. Of this parish he was clerk for twenty-five years, and as lay reader, licensed by the bishop of Ohio, he conducted public services both at Boardman and at Canfield, generally twice every Sabbath. For many years he was senior warden of the parish, and as a delegate he represented it at the annual diocesan convention. He took an active part in the erection of the church building, drawing with his own teams much of the timber used in its construction, and he contributed in addition to this materials to the value of more than $500. Mr.

Boardman was well equipped for an efficient worker in the church, which he was, being a man of more than ordinary ability, of excellent principles, and of deep, earnest piety. Possessing a retiring disposition he always declined appointments to offices of honor and trust, although frequently urged to accept them. The only office which he was induced to accept was that of captain of light infantry. This position he filled for some time and he performed the duties with such general acceptance that it was determined to promote him to the rank of major-general. But he at once declined the proffered honor. He frequently acted as arbiter in the settlement of disputes and disagreements, and took great pleasure in being instrumental in effecting an amicable settlement.

Mr. Boardman's death was the result of an accident received while getting into his buggy. He died December 17, 1846, two days after the accident occurred. His wife survived him many years, dying February 8, 1870, aged seventy-four. They were the parents of four boys, viz: Frederick A., Elijah G. (who died May 11, 1853), William J., and Henry W., residing in Cleveland, the former an attorney.

Frederick A. Boardman, who is prominently identified with the interests of Mahoning county, was born in Boardman, September 1, 1820, and has always resided at the center. He has been extensively engaged in agricultural pursuits, but is at present practically retired from active pursuits. He was married March 20, 1848, to Mary Ann Williams, who was born in New Milford, Litchfield county, Connecticut, November 3, 1817. Mrs. Boardman's father, Jehiel Williams, was a noted physician of New Milford, where he practiced for more than fifty years, and died at the age of over eighty years. Mrs. Boardman is a zealous and efficient member of St. John's church. Henry Mason Boardman, the only child of Mr. and Mrs. F. A. Boardman, was born June 18, 1849. He was graduated at the Polytechnic institute of Troy, New York, in the class of 1871. He is married and resides in Brooklyn, New York, engaged in the drug business.

———

G. A. Boardman

Mrs. Mary A. Boardman

HON. SHELDEN NEWTON.

Shelden Newton, son of Isaac and Olive (Warner) Newton, was born in Washington, Litchfield county, Connecticut, February 24, 1804. When he was seven years of age (in 1811) his father removed with his family to Boardman, now Mahoning county, settling at the center. Isaac Newton worked land for Elijah Boardman for some twelve years, engaged in dairying, and erected the dwelling house in which Mr. F. A. Boardman now lives in 1817. In 1824 he moved on to a farm one and one-half miles south of the center, where he resided until his death. He died January 31, 1850, aged eighty years. His wife, Olive, died October 9, 1830. They were the parents of two sons, the subject of this sketch, and Timothy, who died in Boardman, in December, 1846. Shelden Newton's advantages in early life for the acquirement of an education were of the most meager character, attending the ordinary district schools a few months in the winter only till he was sixteen. Being the elder of the two sons, the larger share of the work upon the farm fell to his lot. October 16, 1836, he married Rachel Hahn, of Boardman, born December 5, 1814. After his marriage he resided in Poland some three years, and worked by the month for Dr. Kirtland. In 1845 he removed to Boardman center, and has always since resided there, engaged in farming, save when attending to his public duties, of which he has had his full share. He was elected justice of the peace in 1840, and held the office for thirty-six consecutive years, with the exception of an interval of only eighteen months. He was elected county commissioner of Mahoning county in 1867, and again in 1875. He was elected to the State Legislature in the fall of 1873 on the "removal" ticket, and served on several important committees, being a member of the committee on new counties, State library, and roads and turnpikes.

Although Mr. Newton had few school privileges when young, there are few men of his age better informed on current topics or endowed with a more accurate and retentive memory. Politically, he is a strong Republican. Mr. and Mrs. Newton have two children living, North and Olive. The former married Marietta Kirk, and resides at Boardman center, and the latter, now the wife of Hiram Thorn, resides in Brooklyn, New York. The oldest son, Warner, served in the Union army during the whole period of the war of secession, and gave his life for his country. Enlisting at Youngstown in April, 1861, in the Nineteenth Ohio volunteer infantry for three months, he afterwards went out as private with the Second Ohio cavalry. He was promoted to captain of company E, and was wounded March 29, 1865, at the battle of Five Points, near Richmond, Virginia, and died April 9, 1865.

JACOB H. BALDWIN.

The subject of this sketch, Mr. Jacob H. Baldwin, was born at Queensburg, Washington county, New York, October 13, 1792. His life, until 1811, was spent here and in Morceau, Saratoga county. In November of 1811, in company with his father and other members of the family, he came to Boardman (then in Trumbull county), Ohio, where the remainder of his life was spent. In 1815 he married Miss Florinda Walter, daughter of David Walter, of Palmyra, Portage county; and in April, 1816, removed to Baldwin's Mill, Youngstown, and engaged in partnership with his uncle, Eli Baldwin. They had for neighbors and customers Thomas Packard, John Woods (father of Dr. Woods), Benjamin Ross, William Smith, James Taylor, Joshua Kyle, Robert Kyle, Wendell Grove, Jedediah Fitch, Camden and Paine Cleveland, James Hillman, Dr. Henry Manning, and others. In 1819 he was appointed by James Mackey, John H. Patch, and William Bushnell (county commissioners) collector of taxes, in which capacity he visited every tax-payer in the county. In 1820 he was again appointed county collector, and also was appointed by John Harmon, of Zanesville (who was marshal of Ohio), to take the United States census. This he did, finding the population of Trumbull—consisting then of thirty-five townships—to be, in all, 15,542, including Warren and Youngstown. In 1821 he was appointed county auditor by the General Assembly of Ohio, the office having been created at that time, in which office he continued for seventeen years, having been elected by the people eight times—two years each term. During much of this time his family resided in Youngstown and Boardman. In 1840 he was appointed by the court of common pleas appraiser of real estate for taxation. He began this work at Poland in the month of May, and finished in October, having visited personally every farm in the county, and appraised all the small lots in the towns and villages. During these years his acquaintance throughout Trumbull was necessarily greater than most men, and the memory of those days and the events of the time were indelibly impressed upon his mind. In 1842 he was elected a member of the Legislature of Ohio, and served one year in the House of Representatives. In 1844 he was elected a Presidential elector, and cast his vote for Clay and Frelinghuysen for President and Vice-President. In the year 1850 he was appointed by Jones, of Mount Vernon, marshal of the State of Ohio, to take the census in district one hundred and forty-three, north division of Trumbull county, which included the townships of Champion, Southington, Farmington, Bristol, Bloomfield, Mesopotamia, Greene, Mecca, Gustavus, and Kinsman. James Hoyt had the remainder of the county in his division. Afterwards he was appointed assistant assessor in Warren, and served a part of the term, when he resigned, and James Hoyt was appointed his successor.

SETTLEMENT NOTES.

S. P. Blackman, farmer, Boardman township, Mahoning county, was born in Poland in 1844. His parents, Heman and Phyllis Blackman, were residents of Poland. Heman Blackman came to this county from Connecticut in 1807. Mr. Blackman has always followed farming. He was married in 1866 to Kate A. Shaffer, daughter of George Shaffer, of Springfield township. They have four children, born as follows: Fannie, May 23, 1868; Asa, February 1, 1870; Perry, July 29, 1871; Clark, December 3, 1874. Mr. Blackman is a Republican. He has resided in Boardman township since 1866.

George Baldwin, farmer, Boardman township, Mahoning county, was born in Boardman township, September 30, 1825. His father, Garry Baldwin, came here from Fort George, Washington county, New York, in 1811. His mother, Harriet Meeker, was a native of New Preston, Connecticut, and came here in 1823. Garry Baldwin died September 7, 1869, aged sixty-nine. Mrs. Baldwin is still living, at the age of seventy-five. George Baldwin lives upon the old farm. He has one hundred and forty-two acres, and does a thriving business. His land is good, his home is pleasant and pretty. He built a large barn in 1880, 36x50 feet, by far the best in the township. Mr. Baldwin was married January 31, 1856, to Eliza Detchon, born in this township January 11, 1833. They have three children: Hattie M., born January 3, 1860; Henry J., born November 27, 1864; Stanton, born August 16, 1869. Mrs. Baldwin is a member of the Disciple church. Mr. Baldwin is one of our most successful farmers, and occupies a high social position. In politics he is a Republican.

Captain Charles C. Chapman, farmer, Boardman township, Mahoning county, was born in Ellsworth, April 27, 1833. He worked at carriage trimming ten years; was ten years a merchant at Youngstown; enlisted in November, 1862, in company G, One Hundred and Twenty-fifth Ohio infantry, and served until December, 1865. He was promoted from a private to second lieutenant, then to first lieutenant, and afterwards to captain. He was in some of the severest engagements of the war, including the battles of Chickamauga, Atlanta, Kenesaw mountain, etc. Mr. Chapman bought the farm on which he now resides, in 1877. Mr. Chapman was married in 1857 to Julia Campbell, daughter of William Campbell, of Trumbull county. She died in 1867, aged about thirty-five years. He was married a second time, in 1871, to Mrs. Sophia E. Thomas of Youngstown. They have one child, Ada A., born September 13, 1874. Mrs. Chapman is a member of the Methodist church. Mr. Chapman is a Republican. He held several local offices while in Youngstown; was constable, city marshal, and deputy United States marshal. He is a member of the Odd Fellows.

Henry B. Dowler, farmer, Boardman township, Mahoning county, was born in Boardman township February 29, 1820; hence has had his birthday but fifteen times, at this date. His grandfather, Francis Dowler, a native of county Cavin, Ireland, was among the earliest of those who took up land in this country. He came here in 1801, as did also his son John, the father of Henry. Francis Dowler died in 1846, aged ninety-six years. John Dowler died in 1839, aged fifty-four. His wife was Nancy Packard. They had seven sons and three daughters; four sons and two daughters are still living, viz: William F., Henry B., Francis A., Thomas J., Nancy P. (Kentner), and Betsey A. Mr. H. B. Dowler, excepting from 1847 to 1857, while he was in the South engaged in making and selling fanning-mills, has always resided in the county. He resides upon the farm which his grandfather settled. Mr. Dowler has never married. He is an old-style Jacksonian Democrat, a prominent farmer, and a respected citizen.

Norman Davidson, farmer, Boardman township, Mahoning county, was born in Washington, Litchfield county, Connecticut, August 7, 1803. His parents, John and Charlotte Davidson, came to Boardman township in 1805 and settled in the midst of the forest near the center of the township. John Davidson had two sons and a daughter; of these Norman Davidson is the only survivor. He is one of the few old settlers now living. Mr. Davidson has a fine farm of a hundred and forty-five acres, with neat and tasty buildings. He was married, January 13, 1831, to Eliza Brainard, who was born June 23, 1805, in Washington, Litchfield county, Connecticut. They have had three children, one of whom is living. Sarah A., born May 2, 1833, died December 3, 1834; Charlotte, born February 2, 1836, died July 29, 1864; Edward, born January 4, 1839, is married and resides at home. Mr. and Mrs. Davidson have been members of the Episcopal church for many years. They bear an excellent reputation in the community where they have so long resided. Mr. Davidson is a thorough Republican. He has held several local offices, such as assessor, trustee, justice, etc.

Alexander Gault, farmer, Boardman township, Mahoning county, was born in Jackson township, May 26, 1838. His father, John Gault, still living in Jackson, is among the old citizens. His grandfather, who died in the War of 1812, was among the early settlers in this county. Mr. Alexander Gault resided in Jackson until 1867, when he came to Boardman and purchased the farm on which he now is. He was a soldier in the Rebellion; enlisted in September, 1862, and served until November, 1865,

and saw some of the severest battles. He was in company F, Forty-first Ohio volunteers. Mr. Gault was married in 1867 to Miss Anna E. Forsythe, a native of Muskingum county, this State. They have one child living, one deceased—Mary Sylvia, born August 30, 1870; Robert J. S., born July 20, 1873, died June 21, 1880. Mr. and Mrs. Gault are members of the United Presbyterian church. Mr. Gault is an earnest Republican.

James Hughes, farmer, Boardman township, Mahoning county, was born in Pembrokeshire, South Wales, November 10, 1831. He came to this country in 1840 with his parents, who settled in Palmyra, Portage county, Ohio. There Mr. James Hughes remained until 1847, when he came to Youngstown and engaged in mining. In 1872 he bought the farm on which he is at present. He has an excellent farm of one hundred and eighty-one acres, and does a large business. Mr. Hughes was married December 31, 1857, to Lydia H. Jackson, daughter of John Jackson, of Youngstown. Mrs. Hughes died November 19, 1876, in the thirty-ninth year of her age. They had six children, all living—John K., Minnie, Weltha, Dan, Sammie, and James; all reside at home. Mr. Hughes is a Republican and a member of the Presbyterian church.

G. E. Lanterman, farmer, Boardman township, Mahoning county, was born in Austintown township March 22, 1841. His father, John Lanterman, was a native of this county, and his grandfather, Peter Lanterman, among the earliest settlers in Austintown. Mr. Lanterman was left an orphan at the age of two years by the death of his father. His mother died when he was sixteen, and from that time forward he acted for himself. In 1861 he went West to Virginia City, thence crossing the plains to California; he was seven months on the way. He spent three years in the West, then returned to this county, and after living four years in Austintown he bought the farm on which he now resides. He has one hundred and fifteen acres of excellent land with the best of buildings and improvements; he deals considerably in stock. Mr. Lanterman was married in 1864 to Miss Elizabeth Kistler, daughter of John B. Kistler, of this township. They have six children living, one deceased: German U., Bettie A., John S., Mary I. (died when about six weeks old), Jennie

D., Blanche G., Frederick A. Mr. Lanterman is a straight-out Democrat and an active business man. His wife is a member of the Lutheran church.

Richard J. McClurg, farmer, Boardman township, was born in Boardman June 22, 1840. He is the son of Samuel McClurg, a native of Allegheny county, Pennsylvania. Samuel McClurg settled in this county quite early and lived here until the time of his death, bringing up a family of three children, of whom two, Richard and Andrew, are living. Richard lives on the home farm, which contains one hundred and eighty acres of excellent land with good buildings and improvements. Mr. McClurg was married in 1866 to Miss Kesia McCullough, of Springfield. They have two children—George, born July 25, 1871; Samuel H., born November 16, 1878. Mr. McClurg and wife belong to the Presbyterian church. Mr. McClurg is a sound Republican. He is a prominent citizen; has been township trustee, etc.

Thomas Matthews, farmer, Boardman, Mahoning county, was born in Allegheny county, Pennsylvania, August 17, 1813. He came to this county when nine years of age with his parents, Thomas and Jane (McClurg) Matthews. Mr. Matthews bought his present farm about thirty-eight years ago. He has one hundred and sixty-five acres of excellent land; is engaged in mixed farming and sheep raising. He was married, in 1842, to Cynthia Shannon, daughter of Major John Shannon, of Pennsylvania, a soldier of the War of 1812. They have three children living and three deceased—William S., born October 30, 1843, now a successful physician at Youngstown; Bruce S., May 1, 1846; Charles W., March 31, 1851; Ellen J., February 20, 1855, died April 1, 1855; Ellen D., June 2, 1857, died December 16, 1863; Cora C., December 10, 1858, died January 29 1866. Mr. and Mrs. Matthews are members of the Methodist church. Mr. Matthews is a Republican and an esteemed citizen.

Eli Reed, farmer, Boardman township, Mahoning county, was born in Canfield township in 1816. His parents, James and Mary (Turner) Reed, came to this county in 1806, Mr. Reed from Washington county, Pennsylvania, and Mrs. Reed from New Jersey. They brought up a family of five children, three of whom are yet living, two sons and a daughter. James Reed died October 13, 1854, in his sixty-sixth year. Mary Reed died April 8, 1863, in her eighty-fourth year. Adam and Margaret Turner, grandfather and grandmother of Eli Reed, settled in Canfield in April, 1806, coming from New Jersey by team. Adam Turner was born September 5, 1763, and died September 3, 1837. Margaret (Mizner) Turner was born June 11, 1766, and died October 28, 1840. Eli Reed was married, in 1843, to Margaret Thomas, of Canfield township. They have five children living, four deceased, including a daughter that died in infancy—Amanda M., born July 24, 1845, now the wife of Samuel Steele of Youngstown; Alvin T., September 27, 1847; Sibyl C., August 15, 1849, died October 24, 1851; Florus A. and Flora C., July 4, 1853, Florus dying October 9, 1853, and Flora May 18, 1855; Hattie E., September 29, 1856, is the wife of Almon Alderman, Evart, Michigan; Oscar W., March 13, 1859; Clinton E., June 1, 1864. Mr. Reed has been a Republican since the organization of the party. He has been assessor two terms and trustee three terms. He is a worthy and respected citizen.

Michael Simon, farmer, Boardman township, Mahoning county, was born in Boardman township July 13, 1820. His father, Adam Simon, was one of the earliest settlers in the county, having come here from Washington county, Pennsylvania, about the year 1800. He was father of six children, three of whom are living, viz: Andrew, Reinhart, and Michael. The two first-named reside in Wood county. Michael Simon was married, in 1846, to Rosini Gentholtz, a native of Wittenberg, Germany. They have seven children living, five deceased, viz: Ezra A., born March 26, 1848; Lenora C., born March 26, 1848; Cornelius A., born February 25, 1850; Catharine E., born December 15, 1851, married Mr. Stempel, died September 19, 1873; Rebecca M., born April 1, 1853; Caroline S., born May 5, 1855; Julius A., born October 24, 1856; Elmer E., Bishop C., Ira C., born July 21, 1861. Bishop died August 22, 1861; Ira died February 12, 1862; and Warren, born May 3, 1868. Mr. and Mrs. Simon belong to the Lutheran church. Mr. Simon is a Republican. He is a leading farmer and respected citizen.

Joseph Cort

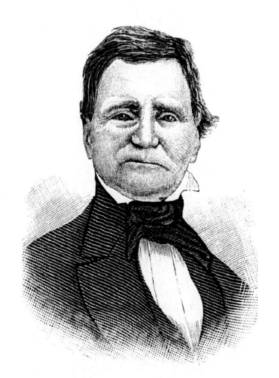

J. H. Shields, farmer, Boardman township, Mahoning county, was born in Boardman township November 12, 1840. The farm on which he was born and where he now lives was purchased in 1798 by Thomas Shields, and has since been in possession of the Shields family. Thomas Shields bought two mill-sites and several hundred acres of land, then returned to his home in Augusta county, Virginia, where died shortly after. His sons, Thomas, James, and William, came in 1800 and settled on the farm. Thomas Shields was a miller by trade, and the first miller west of Rochester, Pennsylvania. James and William were in the War of 1812; Thomas was exempted from service on account of being a useful and necessary member of the community —a miller—and the only man exempted in his neighborhood. William Shields had two sons. The family moved to Indiana about 1848. James had no children. Thomas had five sons and a daughter. All are now dead, nearly every one reaching the age of seventy years. Andrew Shields, son of Thomas, was the father of J. H. Shields. He married Jane Price, of Youngstown township. They had two sons and two daughters, viz: J. H., Lois H. (Hopkins), Louisa M. (Anderson), and Wallace, who died young. Andrew Shields died in June, 1880, in his seventy-second year. Mrs. Shields is still living. J. H. Shields married, in 1863, Miss L. H. Starr, of this township. They have three children living, one deceased, viz: Maud M., born in 1866; Budd S., born in 1867; Mary J.; Allora C., born in 1873. Mary J. was drowned July 9, 1879, aged eight years. She fell from a log while attempting to cross the creek when the water was high. Mr Shields is one of our largest and most prosperous farmers. He manages six hundred acres of land and deals quite extensively in cattle and sheep.

T. M. Twiss, farmer, Boardman township, Mahoning county, was born in Boardman township, November 28, 1833. His father, John Twiss, came here from Connecticut in 1818, and brought up a family of eight children, of whom Mr. T. M. Twiss is the youngest. Mr. Twiss has made farming his principal business; he also deals considerably in stock. He has a farm of one hundred and seventy-three acres, good land well improved. Mr. Twiss was married in 1860 to Mary Hyde, of Orangeville, Trumbull county.

She died in 1864, in the 27th year of her age. Mr. Twiss was again married, in 1874, to Mrs. Carrie Minnis, of Mercer county, Pennsylvania. Mr. Twiss is a Republican. He has been township trustee and assessor. Mrs. Twiss is a member of the Methodist church.

CHAPTER IV.

ELLSWORTH.

SURFACE AND SOIL.

Ellsworth, or township one in range four of the Western Reserve, has a varied surface and a fertile soil. The Meander and its branches cut the eastern portion by a number of narrow valleys, quite deep and winding, forming ridges and knolls of varying dimensions. The main branch of the stream enters the eastern side of the township about a mile below the Canfield road, flows westerly about one mile and a half, then turns abruptly to the north, and winding northward and to the east, passes into Jackson township about three-fourths of a mile from the southeastern corner of Jackson. The western part of the township is quite smooth, and contains many wide tracts of level land.

The soil is fine clayey loam, somewhat sandy in places. It is well adapted to wheat, and the farmers generally secure a good crop of this cereal. The township was originally covered,— and much of it is to-day,—with a heavy growth of white oak, sugar maple, beech, basswood, walnut, hickory, etc. The underlying lime rock and sandstone crops out in several places, the latter affording a good quality of stone for building purposes.

SETTLEMENT.

This township was settled mainly by Connecticut and Pennsylvania people. Captain Joseph Coit, whose biography will be found elsewhere, came in 1804 and began making improvements. From the most reliable information we are able to obtain, it appears that the settlement of the township began in that year. The family of James Reed was the first in the township. Mrs. Reed was the first white woman who entered the township, and lived here six months without ever seeing the face of a female excepting her daughters.

From Mrs. Polly Bowman, an old lady past the ninetieth year of her age, now residing in Goshen township, is gathered the following information regarding her father's settlement:

James Reed came to Ellsworth from Westmoreland county, Pennsylvania, in 1803, and remained during the summer. He made a clearing, built a camp, and raised a crop of corn that year. While he was encamped on one side of the Meander, an Indian occupied a camp opposite, across the stream. Mr. Reed began operations on what is now called the Harclerode farm. Before he came here to live he had made several trips from his home in Pennsylvania to Canfield, carrying supplies to the settlers on pack-horses.

Toward the latter part of February, 1804, Mr. Reed and two of his daughters returned to the camp. They came with a pair of oxen and a cart, following a course of travel marked by blazed trees, and cutting a road for the team when necessary. Mr. Reed then went back for the remainder of his family, leaving his daughters in the care of a man who worked for him. They reached here in April following. The camp was a log structure, with three sides, the fourth being open and used as an entrance. The ground was the floor, and into it was driven forked stakes for bed-posts. Here the family lived until a house could be erected. During the spring of 1804 they made a considerable quantity of maple sugar.

Mr. Reed brought out some stock, including several hogs. Six of the hogs, being averse to living in a wild country, escaped and made their way back to Pennsylvania, where they were found by Mr. Reed's father one morning sound asleep in their old nest. They had made the whole distance of sixty miles alone, guided only by instinct or memory.

One night a fat hog belonging to Mr. Reed was killed and partially devoured by a bear, very quietly it would seem, as none of the family were awakened by any noise. Indians were frequent visitors at the house, but were never troublesome. Bears were often seen. Polly Reed, then a girl of about eleven years, was after the cows one night when she saw a huge black fellow just across the ravine. He reared upon his hind legs as soon as he saw her, while she, much

frightened, ran to the house crying for aid. Deer were numerous, and the children sometimes found the young fawns lying in the bushes near the house.

Mr. Reed lived in Ellsworth a little over a year, then sold his farm to John and Nicholas Leonard, and moved to Canfield township, where he died in 1813.

In 1804 a clearing was made one mile west of the center by two men from Connecticut, one of them named Penuel Cheney. These men did not settle here, but returned to their own State. The land was bought by William and Harvey Ripley in 1806.

Joseph Coit had eight acres cleared at Ellsworth center in the summer of 1804. He also erected a log-house the same year.

Thomas Jones settled on the east line of the township in 1804, his family being the second that arrived in this township. He was born in Maryland, and died in Ellsworth in 1852, at the age of ninety-two. His wife, whose maiden name was Sarah Wilson, died in 1865, aged about ninety. They were the parents of fifteen children, ten of whom arrived at maturity, seven sons and three daughters. Three sons and two daughters are still living. Their names are: Mary, Margaret, Thomas, James, Joseph, John, Samuel, Rosanna, Elijah, and Matthew. Mary married Ashur Squier, and is still living in Canfield; Margaret married James Bruce, and died in Randolph, Portage county; Thomas married Rachel Webb, and died in Edinburg, Portage county; James married Huldah Tanner, and died in Canfield; Joseph married Ann ——, and died in Portage county; John married Nancy Calhoon for his first wife, for his second Desire Phelps, and lives in Ravenna; Samuel married Betsy Calhoon, and lives in North Jackson; Rosanna married Columbia Lancaster, and now lives in Washington Territory; Elijah married Phebe Manchester, and died in St. Clair county, Missouri; Matthew married Eliza Manchester, and he now lives in Missouri.

Philip Arner, a native of Pennsylvania bought land and erected a cabin in 1803, and returned to his home. He came back to Ellsworth in 1804 with his family and settled east of the Meander.

George Broadsword, one of the first settlers, located on the place where Martin Allen now lives. He brought up a family of fourteen children, and all but two of them are living. The names of his sons were Peter, Daniel, John, David, Anthony, Matthias, and Levi. The daughters became Mrs. Abigail Allen, Mrs. Rachel Wagoner, Mrs. Mary Winans, Mrs. Charlotte Rhodes, and Mrs. Lucy Parker. The oldest two, Betsey and Eliza, remained single. The sons are all living except David, and all the daughters except Mrs. Wagoner. Anthony, Matthias, and Mrs. Winans reside in this township.

John Huston came in 1804 to buy land, but did not purchase that year. He built a log house in 1807 and remained until about 1813, then sold to John Baker. In 1817 A. W. Allen bought the place of Baker.

Hugh Smith, who had been here previously, came from Maryland in 1806 and settled on the main branch of the Meander. He brought up five sons and three daughters. Two sons and two daughters are now living in the western part of this State. Mr. Smith died quite suddenly in 1821 or 1822. He was going toward the barn one evening in a cheerful mood, singing the hymn commencing with the lines,

> Oh, when shall I see Jesus.
> And dwell with him above.

A few minutes later he was found dead between the house and barn.

In 1805 William Ripley, Hervey Ripley, Elisha Palmer, and one or two others, came from Scotland, Windham county, Connecticut, and commenced improving land west of the center, which they had previously purchased. In 1806 William Ripley returned to Ellsworth with his wife, Susan Bingham, and settled at the center. Hervey Ripley died here in 1813, aged forty years. William Ripley was a justice of the peace for many years, a member of the Legislature in 1826 or 1827, and afterwards a State Senator.

Daniel Fitch and wife, from Norwalk, Connecticut, came in 1806, and settled one-half mile north of the center. They had four sons and four daughters, several of whom are dead. None of the survivors reside in this township. Daniel Fitch died in 1826.

In 1806 Thomas Jones and family, from Maryland, settled in the eastern part of the township. Mr. Jones had seven sons and three daughters. He lived to be an old man. After his death the family moved away.

The Fitch brothers, Richard, William and Charles, came from Salisbury, Connecticut, in 1806 with their families. Richard settled at the center, and cleared the farm north of there, where his son Richard now lives. William and Charles remained eight or ten years and then moved to Tiffin, Seneca county, Ohio. William afterwards returned and settled two miles north of the center, where he resided several years, thence removing to Ashtabula county, where he died at the age of ninety-four. Charles died in Chicago, aged eighty years.

Philip Borts came from Pennsylvania in 1805 with his family and located near Philip Arner. He had two sons and three daughters. He became one of the wealthiest men in this region, and gave a farm to each of his children. One of his daughters married George Harding, whose son, G. W. Harding, now lives on the old Borts homestead, and has the finest house in the township.

John Leonard and family settled near the Meander about the year 1806. Mr. Leonard had several sons and daughters. One of his sons, James, now lives in Portage county. John Leonard died at quite an early date.

Nicholas Leonard settled one mile from the centre. He had a large family, seven sons and five daughters. Abram, the youngest son, resides in Wood county, and a daughter, Mrs. Dorothy Swartz, in Ashtabula county.

Andrew Fitch, an early settler, located at the centre. He married Lucy Manning. He lived here until quite old, then returned to Connecticut and died there. He had one daughter, who is now living, the wife of Silas C. Clark, of Washington, District of Columbia.

James Parshall settled on the southwestern corner of section twenty-four at an early day. He had several sons and daughters, none of whom are now residing here.

Thomas and Robert McKean settled on the diagonal road running northwest from the center. Thomas died quite early. He brought up a family of three sons and one daughter. Robert McKean lived here until his death in 1843. He had four sons and four daughters.

James McGill and family settled on section twelve, where Thomas Young now lives, resided there several years, then sold and moved to Poland.

Peter Walts settled on the Meander previous to 1810, and resided there some years, moving thence to Medina county.

Wolf and Painter, Broadsword and Razor, were some of the fierce sounding names belonging to Ellsworth's early citizens.

John and Robert McCreary settled on section nineteen. Robert remained single. John had two daughters, both of whom died quite young. Janet married John Howard and two of her sons reside in the township.

Michael Crumrine settled on the west side of the Meander. He had four sons, one of whom died here. The others remained some time, then moved to Berlin township.

James Byers settled here quite early and raised a large family. He moved into Berlin township and was killed by a falling tree.

William Logan, the first cooper in the township, died during the War of 1812.

The Spauldings, David and Philo, came about 1813. David settled one-fourth of a mile west of the center. Philo settled in the southwestern part of the township. He died in 1876, in his ninetieth year. His son Moses is still living in Ellsworth.

John Bingham, from New London county, Connecticut, settled on section eight in 1816. He married a daughter of Richard Fitch, who is still living in the township.

Asa Witter Allen was born in Windham, Connecticut, June 3, 1795. He came to Ellsworth in 1817 with a one-horse buggy, and was seventeen days on the road. He married Sophia Hopkins, who was born in Vermont in 1799. Both are still living. Two sons and three daughters are also living. Mr. Allen lived in Ellsworth township until 1864, and then moved to Perry township, Columbiana county, where he now resides.

FIRST EVENTS.

The first child born in the township was Thomas Jones, Jr. His parents were from Maryland. They settled near the eastern line of the township. Jeannette, daughter of Hugh Smith, was the second child born in the township, and Mary L. Fitch, daughter of Richard Fitch, the third. These births all occurred in 1806.

The first death was an infant child of Mr. Bell, the miller. The parents were here a short time only. The second death is believed to have been that of William Logan. They were both buried in the cemetery near Ellsworth center.

The first marriage in the township took place at the house of Richard Fitch a year or two after he settled here. Lydia Buel, a sister of Mr. Fitch's wife, was married to Hezekiah Chidester of Canfield township.

The first frame dwelling house of any size was erected by General William Ripley, as late as 1820 or 1821. This house is still standing about one-half mile west of the center. Richard Fitch had previously erected a framed addition to his tavern as early as 1810 or 1812.

The first Sabbath-school was organized the second Sabbath in October, 1818, and is said to have been an excellent school in all respects. Daniel W. Lathrop was its instigator.

Mrs. Smith, wife of Hugh Smith, was the first person who offered public prayer in Ellsworth.

Ira F. Powers was the first volunteer for the Rebellion from this township. He enlisted July 4, 1861, in the Eleventh Ohio infantry.

A company of cavalry composed of members from Boardman, Poland, Canfield, and Ellsworth was organized as early as 1810. Richard Fitch was the first captain, succeeded by Joseph Coit.

ORGANIZATION.

The first entry upon the township records of Ellsworth is as follows :

It is hereby certified that the board of commissioners at their March meeting, 1810, did apart and set off from the townships of Canfield and Newton a new township and election district by the name of Ellsworth, with all the privileges and immunities of a township as by law designated, within the following lines, to wit : Beginning at the southwest corner of the county of Trumbull, thence north on the county line to the northwest corner of township number one in the fifth range of townships, thence east on the township line to the northeast corner of number one in the fourth range, thence south to the southeast corner of number one in the fourth range, thence west on the county line to the place of beginning; in fact, comprising townships number one in the fourth and fifth ranges.

ELI BALDWIN,
Clerk *pro tem.* of Commissioners.
WARREN, 22d March, 1810.
A true copy.
JOSEPH COIT, Township Clerk.

Ellsworth, as then organized, included the townships of Ellsworth and Berlin. Berlin was set off from Ellsworth and erected a separate

Martin Allen

Mrs Lucy M. Allen.

township by the county commissioners March 4, 1828.

FIRST ELECTION.

The first election was held April 2, 1810. The following officers were chosen: Joseph Coit, clerk; Andrew Fitch, Daniel Fitch, Hugh Smith, trustees; William Ripley, James Parshall, overseers of the poor; John Leonard, Robert McKean, fence viewers; Daniel Fitch, lister; Daniel Fitch, William Fitch, appraisers; Jesse Buel, constable; Peter Watts, George Painter, James McGill, supervisors; Hervey Ripley, treasurer.

At the first election after Berlin was created a separate precinct the following were chosen as the officers of Ellsworth township, April 7, 1828: William Ripley, Jacob Dustman, Robert McKean, trustees; Walter Smith, Asa W. Allen, overseers of the poor; John Bingham, Harvey Allen, fence viewers; John C. Webb, John Miller, constables; Andrew Fitch, treasurer. Also a road supervisor for each of the eleven districts.

OTHER RECORDS.

Richard Fitch qualified as a justice of the peace June 19, 1810; Robert McKean (or McCane, as the name is spelled upon the old records), was commissioned as justice March 13, 1813, resigned June 23, 1815; William Ripley was commissioned August 21, 1815, October 17, 1818, October 29, 1821, December 11, 1824, March 17, 1828; Henry Boyd, June 6, 1826; Thomas Fitch, April 30, 1831; George Matson, May 7, 1832. Later than this date the records are not complete.

The first selection of jurors, or the first of which there is any record, occurred March 2, 1812. William Ripley and Richard Fitch were chosen grand jurors; William Logan, Andrew Fitch, and Thomas McKean, traverse jurors.

That the people of this township in early days were rigid in their determination to prevent the spread of pauperism in their midst will appear from the following entry upon the records:

To Jesse Buel, constable of the township of Ellsworth, greeting:

Whereas, it appears from information by us received, that —— —— is likely to become a township charge; these are therefore to command you to warn the said —— —— to depart from this township.

Given under our hands at Ellsworth, this sixth day of June, 1811.

CHARLES B. FITCH, } Overseers of the Poor.
PETER WALTS,

JUNE 8, 1811.—Served the within warrant by reading it to the within-named person, at the house of William Fitch, in Ellsworth.

JESSE BUEL, constable.

A true copy.

JOSEPH COIT, township clerk.

Many similar entries appear on the records for years following. The persons warned, however, were not obliged to quit the township; but if they afterwards become so poor as to require aid, the township officers were relieved from the responsibility of furnishing it. Often these severe measures doubtless served to "foster home industry." Sometimes the most worthy citizens were "warned," on account of the complaints of those who bore them some ill-will.

For many years the township elections were held at the house of Richard Fitch.

The town hall was built in 1818 by private subscriptions. Thenceforth religious meetings, schools, elections, etc., were held there.

EARLY INCIDENTS.

February 3, 1818, three feet of snow fell in one day. Some who are yet living remember wading through it when it reached higher than their waists.

The most of the families coming from Connecticut in 1806 were not provided with cabins, so they stopped at Captain Coit's until homes could be built for them. Coit was then a single man, and required little room; besides, he was at work the greater part of the time making improvements on his land in the northern part of the township. While thus engaged one day his house took fire and was destroyed, together with his watch, money, books, and clothing. Mr. Coit came home toward evening, and gazed unmoved upon the destruction the flames had made. He found the women in tears, and almost in despair. He, however, seemed in excellent spirits; and, seating himself near the ruins, began singing in a rich, full voice the air, Contentment, the first verse of which is:

"Why should we at our lot repine,
  Or grieve at our distress?
Some think if they should riches gain,
  They'd gain true happiness.
Alas! how vain is all our gain,
  Since life must soon decay;
And since we're here with friends so dear,
  Let's drive dull care away!"

In the early part of the summer of 1806, William Ripley had his leg broken by a log falling on it, while he was helping to raise the cabin of Daniel Fitch. The fracture was a severe one, and he was unable to work the greater part of that summer. There were then no physicians nearer than Youngstown.

At an early day, Captain Coit offered a poor fellow named Alexander Crawford ten acres of land in this township, if he would dig a well for him and put it in working order. Crawford accepted the job, and toiled alone until he had excavated a good well, twenty-eight feet deep, throwing the dirt up from one scaffold to another until it reached the top. He then exchanged work with a neighbor, and got assistance in stoning it. He received a deed of the land as pay for his labor. Land soon commenced to rise in value, and a few years later he sold the ten acres and with the proceeds bought an eighty-acre lot in Hancock county, this State, which he made into a good farm.

A story is told concerning Mrs. Hugh Smith, which shows that she was a lady possessed of strength of mind and courage which is seldom equalled. She heard a noise in the hog-pen one evening, and, on investigating the cause of it, discovered a large bear attacking a lusty porker. She seized a club and pounded the bear until he was glad to retreat without any pork for supper.

An incident which occurred during the War of 1812 was often laughed about and talked over by the early settlers. Some half-breed Indian hunters who had spent the night hunting coons, returned to the vicinity of the settlement about daylight, and to amuse themselves began firing at a mark. The whole neighborhood was aroused by the reports of their rifles, and much consternation ensued, as it was thought the Indians were attacking the settlers. Houses were fastened up and valuables hidden away. At length two experienced hunters were prevailed upon to go and learn the cause of the alarm. They mounted horses and proceeded to the spot where the firing had been heard, but by the time they arrived there the hunters had gone and no "Indians" were visible. When the whole affair was thoroughly understood there was much hearty laughter over "the great Indian raid."

EARLY SCHOOLS.

The first school was taught in 1811 by Miss Clara Landon, of Canfield. The school-house, or rather the building used as such during that year and several years thereafter, was the small log house east of the center, mentioned in connection with the history of the Presbyterian church. The next teacher was Miss Matilda Sackett, of Tallmadge, succeeded by Jesse Buel, Hiram B. Hubbard, and others. Asa W. Allen taught school here in the winter of 1817 and 1818, and had all the scholars in the township—not over twenty. He states that there was a bench extending along the side of the house, also one chair in the room, which of course belonged to the teacher. There were three small windows, each one containing as much paper and wood as there was glass, and perhaps more.

For several years the Center district was the only one in the township, and in the rude school-house just mentioned some of Ellsworth's smartest men received their first drill in "readin', 'ritin', and 'rithm'tic."

PRESBYTERIANS.

For many years the most, if not all, the preaching in Ellsworth was by ministers of this denomination. Rev. John Bruce was the first preacher. He was born in New York in 1771, and studied theology with Rev. T. E. Hughes. In 1809 he was licensed, and commenced preaching in Ellsworth, where he remained five years He afterwards preached one year in Newton, and died there in 1816. The first meeting house was situated just north of the center. It was built of hewn logs and had no floor. This was used as a place of worship for a short time. A similar log structure was erected a few years later on the hill just east of the bridge across the Meander, where Mr. Bruce continued preaching as long as he remained here. Services were frequently held in open air as well as in barns, school-houses, and private dwellings. In 1817 meetings were held in a small log-house, with a huge fire-place in it; this was situated near the center, upon a spot just east of where the Methodist church now stands. The building was erected for a dwelling house, but had been used as a school-house for some years before this date. The present Ellsworth church was organized as a union church of the Presbyterians and Congregationalists, March 26, 1818, under Revs. William Hanford and Joseph Treat, missionaries. It started with fourteen members, whose names are given below: Henry and Margaret Boyd,

Christian and Elizabeth Bowman, Catherine, wife of John Bowman, Joshua and Mary Bowman, Joseph and Polly Bruce, Daniel and Elizabeth Fitch, Daniel W. Lathrop, Thomas and Nancy Fitch. Sixteen more members were added during the year, and in succeeding years the number increased. The first church officers were Henry Boyd and Daniel W. Lathrop, committee, and Daniel W. Lathrop, clerk. The first preachers were all missionaries, and many different ones labored here. The town hall was used for a place of public worship from the time it was built in 1818 until the present church was erected in 1833. The church has had but four installed pastors, whose names are Rev. William O. Stratton, Rev. William Hoyt, Rev. Warren Taylor, and the present pastor, Rev. William J. Reese, who has been here since 1878. When vacancies have occurred, as has frequently been the case, missionaries or "stated supplies" have carried on the meetings. At present the church has about eighty members, and is in a prosperous condition.

THE METHODISTS.

Rev. Nicholas Gee, a native of New York, moved to Ellsworth township in 1823. He was licensed to preach in 1824, and a society was probably organized about that date, though concerning this no information is attainable. Mr. Gee acted as a local preacher here for some years. The first meetings were held at private residences and at the school-house in district number three, until about 1835, when the church in that district was completed and dedicated. Mr. Gee and C. A. Bunts gave most toward building it. Among the most prominent members of Mr. Gee's church were the Gee family, Nicholas Leonard and family, Mrs. Hugh Smith and family, John Hoyle and family, C. A. Bunts, and others. The church is still standing, but no organization has been maintained since 1856.

In 1839 a society was formed at the center. A church was commenced that year and finished in 1840. This building was erected through the efforts of Mr. Gee, Mr. Bunts, Dr. Hughes, John Smith, L. D. Smith, and others, assisted by their brethren in neighboring townships. This church was used until the new one was completed in 1880—dedicated February 17, 1881. It is a neat brick structure, well fitted and furnished in excellent taste. The society numbers

about fifty members at present. It is out of debt and in a prosperous condition. Jacob Lower, Miller & Ripley, Jefferson Diehl, Eli Diehl, John Cronick, and others, gave liberally towards building the new church.

CEMETERIES.

Of these there are but two in the township, one at the center and the other near the old Methodist church on section twenty-four. The graveyard near the center is the oldest, and for many years was the only burying-place in Ellsworth.

The inscription upon the monument of Captain Coit is as follows:

Joseph Coit, born in Norwich, Connecticut, August 18, 1783; died May 31, 1857. He came to Ohio in 1804, and with his location commenced the settlement of Ellsworth.

FIRST TAVERN.

Richard Fitch opened a tavern in a small log-cabin built in 1806 on the site of the present hotel. He made a framed addition some years later, and about 1824 put up quite a large house which is still standing. He continued to entertain travelers until 1837, and was then succeeded by Charles and Andrew Fitch. The house was in the hands of many different individuals during the succeeding years. For ten years past it has not been a hotel, until it was opened to the public by Mr. Rose in 1881.

POST-OFFICE AND MAIL.

The first postmaster was Lucius W. Leffingwell, who settled in the township in 1818, and was probably commissioned postmaster the same year. The mail was obtained once a week by a carrier who went after it on horseback. When the stage line through this place began running, the mail was obtained twice each week. As Mr. Leffingwell lived at some distance from the center, he could not conveniently perform the duties of postmaster, so he appointed Joseph Coit as his deputy. Mr. Coit was also the school-teacher, and whenever the mail-carrier signified by tapping on the window of the schoolroom that the presence of the postmaster was required at his office the classes were left until the mail could be disposed of. As would naturally be expected, the boys held high carnival during the teacher's absence, but sobered down mysteriously and suddenly as he again approached. The second postmaster was Joseph Coit, who held the position until 1857. His successors were John C.

Fusselman, Samuel McKean, James Green, Oliver A. Bingham, A. R. Hammond, Andrew McKinney, John McKinney, and W. J. McKinney, the present incumbent. Ellsworth now has an eastern and a western mail daily.

DISTILLERIES.

The first distiller in the township was a Mr. Stanley, the father of German Stanley. His still was situated just below Hoover's mill. He worked it several years. Charles C. Chapman, a Methodist preacher, also had a still on the same stream, built a few years later. Both of these did quite an extensive business. George Leonard operated a small still on the Meander for a short time.

TANNERY.

Walter Smith came about the year 1816 and began business as a tanner on the stream a short distance north of the centre. He did a good business here for several years, and acquired considerable property. Mr. Smith followed tanning until 1856. He was an active business man, a worthy and prominent member of the Presbyterian church.

MILLS, STORES, ETC.

The first grist-mill in the township was built by General Perkins, of Warren, and Eli Baldwin, of Boardman. It was situated near the site of the present one, and was built of hewed logs. In 1819 or 1820 it was replaced by a frame building and operated for some years. The same parties also owned a saw-mill upon the same stream. Another grist-mill was built at an early date in the northern part of the township. This was known as Hoover's mill, and was built by Ezekiel Hoover, on a branch of the Meander. It was situated just north of where the Methodist church now stands. A saw-mill near it was also operated for some time. A. W. Allen owned two saw-mills on the Meander about 1835.

The first store was opened by Adams & Lloyd, of Philadelphia, in 1822, in a log house, near the spot where Mr. McKinney's residence now is. Soon afterwards they built a good store which was destroyed by fire some years later. These gentlemen were here about five years. The next merchants were O. A. and L. Bingham, who continued in business about ten years. Their successors have been T. U. Kelley, Jesse

B. Fitch, William Ripley, Jr., Spaulding & Morse, A. and J. McKinney, and McKinney Brothers.

In 1836 a store was built on the corner where Kirkbride's blacksmith shop stands and run for some ten years by Church & Fusselman. About 1850 E. A. Green built a store on the corner next to the hotel, where he traded three years. He was succeeded by Stofer & Hole, who were in business four or five years. McKinney Brothers are now the only merchants in the township.

PHYSICIANS.

The first physician who practiced in the settlement of Ellsworth was Dr. Shadrach Bostwick, of Canfield. The first resident physician was Dr. Chauncy C. Cook. He settled here about the year 1824, and remained three years. He moved to Youngstown and died there. Dr. Robert G. Huntington came about 1827 and remained until his death in 1838. Dr. Mordecai B. Hughes came in 1839 and remained until his death in 1852. Dr. G. W. Brooke came that year and still practices here. Ellsworth has always been favored with good physicians, well-read and skilled in their profession.

NOTES.

The first blacksmith was probably Thomas Fitch. He came to Ellsworth about 1814, and opened a shop a short distance east of the center, where he continued to work until 1840. He then sold out and engaged in farming and afterwards went West.

The first shoemaker was probably William Porter, who lived about one-half mile west of the center. He was quite an early settler.

The following men from Ellsworth were soldiers in the War of 1812: Nicholas Courtney, William Fitch, Joseph Coit, John Lower, —— Parshall, and perhaps others.

SEMI-CENTENNIAL CELEBRATION.*

On the 4th of July, 1855, the citizens of Ellsworth celebrated the semi-centennial anniversary of its settlement. The officers of the day were Dr. G. W. Brooke, president, and Granville W. Sears, secretary.

The Declaration of Independence was read by P. Allen Spicer, Esq. Rev. Loomis Chandler delivered the historical address. Hon. Eben

---

*This account was furnished by Dr. G. W. Brooke.

Hervey Ripley

Newton, Rev. E. C. Sharp (of Atwater), Samuel Smith, C. A. Bunts, and many others delivered brief addresses. Dr. James W. Hughes, of Berlin, read a poem. Letters of regret on account of inability to be present were read from Hon. Elisha Whittlesey, Hon. Milton Sutliff, and K. Upman, Esq.

The singing was led by Captain Joseph Coit. To "start the tune" he used an old-fashioned pitch-pipe, which is still in the possession of the family. All of the old settlers of the township then living, and many from surrounding townships, were present. The day was very fine, the attendance large, and many pioneer incidents were rehearsed with great zest.

BUSINESS INTERESTS.

The following is believed to be a complete business directory of the township: McKinney Brothers, merchants, center; H. H. Rose, carriage painter and hotel keeper, center; W. H. Kirkbridge, blacksmith, carriage maker, and carriage painter, center; P. B. Hughes, blacksmith, center; Jonathan Hull, cooper, center; Samuel McKean and Nelson W. King, wheelwrights, center; Albert Dakin, cabinet-maker, center; Roland Davis and Eli Davis, shoemakers, center; Eli and J. H. Diehl, distillers, section ten. Eli Diehl, grist-mill, section eight; D. R. Stahl: smith, saw-mill, section one. Thomas Rose works a coal mine on section twenty-one, and Frank Winans, on section fifteen. There are other small coal banks in the township.

The principal stone quarries are owned by Eli Diehl, Eli T. Arner, and G. W. Harding.

REFLECTIONS.

The first settlers are dead and gone. Nearly eighty years have elapsed since the first clearing was made in the now thriving township of Ellsworth. What the pioneers accomplished and what they suffered few of the present inhabitants know or can tell. But if we judge them by their works, we shall certainly form a high opinion of their worth. Ellsworth has maintained good schools ever since there were enough children here to form a class. Churches have been kept up, and pious men are still teaching those who soon shall come upon the stage of active life to keep the way their fathers trod. Ellsworth center has two good, substantial edifices, either of which would be a credit to a much larger place,

where divine services are regularly held. There are no saloons or other resorts where crime is manufactured.

On every hand we see indisputable evidence that the people are awake and at work. The mowing machine and harvester are now driven over fields which, in the memory of some who are living here, were frequented by bears, wolves, deer, and other denizens of the primitive forest. The steam threshing machine moves along roads which not long ago were solitary foot-paths, or tracks where only horseback riders or slow-going ox-teams could pass. Log cabins have been replaced by substantial farm houses, surrounded by orchards, shade trees, and rich and beautiful fields. Neat white barns, large and commodious, in every neighborhood show that the farmers understand their business, and are increasing in wealth and prosperity.

The allurements and vices of large towns are at a distance from this prosperous community; and safe in Christian homes, supplied with good books and papers, with examples of uprightness and refinement constantly before them, the rising generation is growing up to take the place of fathers and mothers who soon must pass away. The next fifty years will doubtless show a great change upon the face of the country; but in the characters and hearts of the people there will surely linger the brave and generous spirit of the hardy pioneers, ever active in promoting public welfare and morality as well as private interests.

The first settlers, many of them, were men and women of culture and education, who fully understood the great truth that the only hope of any country lies in a refined, enlightened, and civilized people. For this reason, though in the midst of a wilderness, they taught their children honesty, virtue, and temperance, and, above all, made them ladies and gentlemen in the best sense of the word.

POEM.

Written for the semi-centennial celebration of the settlement of Ellsworth township, by Dr. J. W. Hughes, Berlin center, Mahoning county, Ohio.

> Hail, father! mother! friendship greets you here,
> Each well-known face to-day is doubly dear,
> While grateful feelings own His sovereign power,
> Whose gracious arm has kept us to this hour;
> As back our thoughts with deep emotions flow,
> To dwell on Ellsworth fifty years ago.

14

Nor changed the scene, since you whose features bear
The trace of years and toil engraven there,
From New England's cherished homestead came
The western forest's dreary wilds to tame:
No path to guide you but the woodman's "blaze,"
Nor shelter, till the cabin you could raise;
To years of toil and weariness resigned,
Ease, friendship, luxury you left behind,
Amid privations such as few endure,
A future home and comforts to secure.

Where now the stately farm house meets the eye,
And wavy fields in cheerful sunshine lie,
One wide, unbroken forest spread around,
And silence reigned in solitude profound;
Where forth his brood the lordly turkey led,
Or timid deer in tranquil safety fed,
Till started by the wolf's discordant howl,
Or midnight hootings of the sun-blind owl.
No humble school-house reared its unhewn walls,
No sacred temple echoed mercy's calls,
No Sabbath bell the lonely settler heard,
No hymn of praise the slumbering echo stirr'd,
Save when at eve, the grateful pioneer,
Waked some loved strain to busy mem'ry dear.

But soon the tide of emigration gave
Increasing strength with each succeeding wave.
New settlers, lured by hopes of future gain,
Or kindred ties, that seldom plead in vain,
Increased the numbers at first so few,
While social comforts with those numbers grew.

Soon here and there in quick succession rose
The needed school-house and the school-boy's woes;
Nor these alone—religion next demands
A house for God, and there the temple stands.
Long may it stand, and long may his holy word,
With heartfelt joy, within its walls be heard!
Here may no selfish partisan intrude,
Discordant themes with worldly aims imbued,
Nor zeal unwise, with hidden mischief rife,
Mar Christian peace, nor fan fraternal strife.

Ye township's fathers, whom we greet to-day—
Ye honored mothers—no less dear than they—
Revered, beloved—of "length of days possesst,"
Your children here rise up and "call you blest."
But while with heart-felt joy we mingle here,
And thoughts arise and mem'ry claims a tear
For those, the partners of your early toil,
Who silent sleep beneath their chosen soil,
Or hence removed to some far distant clime,
No more shall meet you on the shores of time.

Here let us briefly call our thoughts away
From local themes to hail our Nation's day.
Far down the vista of receding years
On hist'ry's page a patriot group appears :
No nobler names in any land or clime
Adorn the annals of recorded time.

Life, fortune, honor, pledged to freedom lie :
Fearless, tho' few—resolved to win or die.
No minion there to base dishonor sold—
No sordid slave to ignominious gold ;

No mock philanthropist self-lauded stood,
Invoking strife, and calling "evil good";
No fierce oppressor, drunk with lawless power,
Insatiate reveled—courting ruin's hour.

Alas ! that nations should like parents rear
Unworthy sons an honored name to bear ;
That brethren to a common fortune born
Should link their birthright with undying scorn,
And scathe and blast the noblest heritage
That ever nations had in any age.

Say not the bard to human progress blind
Sees not the onward, mighty march of mind :
He sees it—feels it—owns it all and more,
The near abyss—the rocky leeward shore—
Beyond it all he sees the threatening rod,
And reads—"The world by wisdom knew not God !"

And speak I warmly ? I should inly feel
The curse of treason o'er my conscience steal,
Could I to-day before this audience stand,
And breathe no tribute to my native land ;
Desert who may—prove recreant who will,
With all her faults, I love my country still.

BIOGRAPHICAL SKETCHES.

JOSEPH COIT.

The man most prominently and effectively identified with the early settlement and improvement of the township of Ellsworth was without doubt he whose name heads this sketch. Joseph Coit was born in Norwich, Connecticut, August 18, 1783. He was the eldest child of Thomas and Sarah (Chester) Coit. His father was a merchant of Norwich, and in early life the son was employed in the store. He received a good education, being for some time a pupil of John Adams, a celebrated teacher of Norwich, and father of the late Dr. William Adams, the distinguished pastor of Madison Square Presbyterian church, New York city. Mr. Coit had mastered the science of civil engineering, and his uncle, Daniel Coit, being the owner of a large amount of land in the Western Reserve, he was induced by his uncle to come West and act in his interest as a surveyor and as agent for the sale of his land. He made his first journey to the Reserve in 1803, when he accompanied General Moses Cleaveland who came to treat with the Indians for the extinguishment of their title to the land on a portion of which the city of Cleveland now stands. This journey was made on horseback, and consumed twenty-eight days.

At this time he selected a place for his own settlement at the center of Ellsworth, then an unbroken wilderness. He soon returned to Connecticut, but came back the next year to take permanent possession. Taking four men from Canfield he cleared up eight acres that season and on the 4th of July surveyed and laid off the first village lots in what is now Ellsworth center. He was for a time employed in the office of General Perkins, at Warren, giving his attention mostly to collections. Besides his agricultural labors he was considerably employed in surveying and selling lands, always taking an active part in the various improvements of the township. He served in the War of 1812 as cornet of a company of dragoons. He was frequently called upon to fill various civil offices. He was postmaster and deputy postmaster at Ellsworth center for about thirty years. In 1817 and 1818 he was tax collector for Trumbull county. The onerous duties of this office will be better understood when the extent of territory then embraced within the limits of Trumbull county is considered in connection with the fact that it was the duty of the collector to visit every house for the collection of the tax. The tax books for those years are still in possession of his widow, and they are models of official book-keeping, showing Mr. Coit to have been a systematic business man and correct accountant. He was elected county surveyor of Trumbull county in 1821, and county commissioner in 1844. He also served as county commissioner of Mahoning county toward the latter part of his life. Always moral and exemplary in his life, he did not make a public profession of religion until the last year of his life. His death occurred May 31, 1857, resulting from cancer upon the face. Mr. Coit was married June 15, 1838, in Hartford, Connecticut, to Elizabeth Mygatt, daughter of Thomas and Lucy (Oakes) Mygatt. Mrs. Coit was born in Weathersfield, Connecticut, February 22, 1802, and is still living with her daughter at Ellsworth center, where she and her husband first settled on coming to Ohio. One child only was born of this union, Fannie M., born April 2, 1844, now the wife of Chester Allen, whom she married on her twenty-fourth birthday.

THE RIPLEY FAMILY.

General William Ripley was among the earliest settlers, and for years one of the most prominent residents of Ellsworth township. He was born in Windham, Connecticut, in May, 1782; was brought up on a farm and enjoyed few privileges for mental training. He, however, possessed more than ordinary native ability, and in mature life was elevated to positions of trust and honor. He married, March 31, 1805, Susan Bingham, of Windham (born November 30, 1784), and the same spring he came out to the Western Reserve, leaving his bride in Connecticut. He purchased, in connection with his brother Hervey, three hundred and twenty acres of land of the Connecticut Land company, a short distance west of Ellsworth center. This farm, or a part of it, is now occupied by his son Hervey. General Ripley that season cut off ten acres and put up a log cabin, and the next fall returned to Connecticut. In the spring of 180 he returned with his wife to Ellsworth. After occupying his farm for a few years, on account of threatened hostilities by the Indians he moved to the center, where he resided a number of years. In 1820 he erected the large frame residence now occupied by his son, and moved into it November 30th of the same year, and lived there until his death. He was a general of militia, hence his military title. He was justice of the peace in Ellsworth for fifteen years, and was a Representative in the State Legislature two terms and served one term as State Senator. He died December 7, 1860, and his wife May 1, 1868. They were the parents of seven children, as follows: Adaline, Edwin, Emily, Susan, Hervey, William, and Bingam, of whom only Emily (now Mrs. Fitch), living in Wisconsin; William in Chicago, and Hervey, are living.

Hervey Ripley was born at Ellsworth center, February 23, 1816. He received an ordinary education at the common schools of his neighborhood, and January 7, 1838, was married to Henrietta H. Sackett, daughter of Moses and Cordelia (Fox) Sackett, of Ellsworth. Mrs. Ripley was born in Warren, Connecticut, December 5, 1816, and came with her parents to Ellsworth when a small girl and settled south of the center where Mr. Arner now resides. With the exception of three months Mr. Ripley has resided in the house which he still occupies with his family for a period of sixty-two consecutive years. Mrs. Ripley departed this life April 13, 1874. She was a member of the Presbyterian church, as is her husband, and was an estimable woman, and a devoted wife and mother. She left surviving her her husband and nine children, her own death being the only death which has occurred in the family. The names of the children are as follow: Judith P., widow of Walter Smith, residing with her daughter, Mrs. Miller, in Ellsworth; Thomas, in Alliance, Ohio; Warren L., at Ellsworth center; Ward S. and Edgar, in Olathe, Kansas; Florence E., at home; Emma C., at home; William, at Burton, Ohio, and Margaret V., at home. Four of the sons served in the Union army during the war of the Rebellion, viz: Thomas, Warren, Ward, and Edgar, the latter in the one hundred day service; Thomas was in the Third Iowa infantry, and was discharged at the expiration of six months on account of sickness. Warren and Ward were members of the Forty-first Ohio volunteer infantry, and served all through the war, participating in the battles of Pittsburg Landing, Nashville, Lookout Mountain, and Stone River, and came out unhurt. Walter Smith, the husband of the eldest daughter, was a member of the same regiment and died at New Haven, Kentucky, in February, 1862.

MARTIN ALLEN.

Martin Allen was born in Windham, Connecticut, on the 25th day of August, 1807. His early days were spent in farm labor and attending the common schools. Having decided upon the study of medicine, after his common school education was completed, he attended Plainfield academy for a while with a view of training himself, by a thorough preparatory course, for the career he had marked out. After teaching for a time he at length decided that a professional life would not suit him, and resolved to devote himself thenceforth to farming. About this time he determined to make his home in the West, and in 1829 came to Ellsworth township and located upon the farm which he still occupies. After his arrival here he continued teaching for several years, following the usual custom of district school-teachers, of teaching during the winter

months and farming in summer. Those of his pupils now residing in the neighborhood are unanimous in their testimony as to his popularity and worth as an instructor.

March 21, 1832, Mr. Allen married Miss Lucy M. Fitch, of Ellsworth township—a union which has resulted in a long and happy married life and the rearing of a large family. Mr. Allen, by economy and enterprise has prospered abundantly, and is now the owner of a pleasant home, a well selected library, and a large, well cultivated farm. His home is beautifully situated, and its surroundings afford evidence of the care and taste of its owner.

Mr. and Mrs. Allen both united with the Presbyterian church about the same time (1843) and have ever remained constant, faithful members. For many years Mr. Allen has been a ruling elder and one of the main supporters of this church.

Martin Allen is a man of cultivated tastes and of more than ordinary ability. The friends of the family are many, and in simple justice it should be stated few men enjoy the respect of their fellow-citizens in as high a degree as Mr. Allen. Modest and unassuming he has always refrained from seeking notoriety of any kind, much preferring the pleasures of home life and the enjoyment of the rewards of industry and social kindness. A contented mind, and a heart filled with a spirit of Christian resignation are indeed the greatest boons a man can have.

Mr. Allen was the third son and the fourth child of Enoch and Betsey (Witter) Allen, who were married in 1794. They had five children: Asa Witter, born 1795; John, 1797; Eliza, (died young; Martin, 1807; and David, 1809. Enoch Allen was born in Windham, Connecticut, May 23, 1768. His father, Asahel Allen, was born in the same place in the year 1742. The Allen family were among the earliest of the New England colonists. Martin Allen is a direct descendant of Samuel and Ann Allen, of Bridgewater, Somersetshire, England, who located at Braintree, Massachusetts, ten miles south of Boston, in the early part of the seventeenth century.

To Mr. and Mrs. Martin Allen have been born twelve children, of whom eight are now living. The names of the survivors are as follows: Lloyd, born July 14, 1833, married Fannie M. Beardsley, resides in Ellsworth; Mary Eliza, born

James Williams.

Almyra Williams.

August 26, 1837, married Robert A. Kirk, Canton, Ohio; Jesse Fitch, born August 13, 1841, unmarried, at home; Chester, born February 1, 1843, married Fannie M. Coit, in Ellsworth; William Hoyt, born January 3, 1845, married Ella Brooke, Ellsworth; Henry Bingham, born April 26, 1847, married Emma R. Weaver, Salem, Columbiana county; Lucy A., born November 5, 1848, at home; Jettie W., born April 6, 1851, at home; Enoch, Enoch Fitch, Betsey Ann, and an infant son are deceased.

JAMES WILLIAMS.

John Williams was among the pioneers of Canfield township, and bore with fortitude the experiences of pioneer life. He enlisted in the army during the War of 1812, immediately after Hull's surrender, and served as first lieutenant. He married Mary Smith. The names of their children were James, Rebecca, Elizabeth, Banner, Nancy, and Rachel. Rebecca (deceased) married Jacob Bower; Elizabeth married Almedius Scott, and resides in Canfield; Banner married first Clarissa Lew, and second Margaret McDaniels, and resides in Canfield; Nancy the wife of Ormon Dean, resides in Lordstown; Rachel married John Porter, and resides in Palmyra, Portage county.

James Williams, the oldest child of John and Mary Williams, was born in Bedford county, Pennsylvania, November 8, 1809. He was married November 17, 1836, to Miss Almyra Cook. She was born in Columbiana county, August 28, 1818. Their children are as follows: Henry A., married Irene Greathouse, and lives in Oregon; Mary E., the wife of George Bennett, resides in Illinois; Delos E., married Esther Jane Bennett, and resides in Ellsworth; Homer married Mary Brooke, and resides in Canfield; Alice J., married Samuel S. Gault—her home is in Ellsworth; Lewis died at the age of two years.

Mr. Williams worked at the trade of a carpenter and joiner for about forty years of his life, but is now retired from active business, having secured a competency sufficient to support himself and wife during the remainder of their days, besides amply providing for all their children.

Although Mr. Williams never sought office, his fellow-citizens, have shown their confidence in his integrity by electing him to the office of justice of the peace three times.

No better tribute of respect to this worthy couple can be paid than the universally prevalent sentiment of their associates and friends, that their lives have been distinguished by acts of kindness and benevolence toward many a one in need of friends and help.

NOTES OF SETTLEMENT.

Dr. George W. Brooke, son of Basil and Rachel (Morris) Brooke, was born in Goshen township, then Columbiana (now Mahoning) county, Ohio, April 29, 1828. He began the study of medicine in 1846, under Dr. James W. Hughes of Berlin township, and attended lectures at the Cleveland Medical college, where he graduated in the spring of 1851. He immediately commenced practice under the supervision of his preceptor in Berlin, removing in the spring of 1852 to Ellsworth, where he has since been engaged in his profession. He married in 1852 Miss Theda A. Carter, of Darien, Genesee county, New York. The children born of this union are Ella E., Clara R., Mary Q., Georgie, and Theda Carter. Mrs. Brooke died December 29, 1874, and he married September 21, 1878, Miss Mary E. Williams. Dr. Brooke was a Republican presidential elector in 1860, and cast the electoral vote of the Nineteenth Congressional district for Abraham Lincoln. He was elected a representative in the State Legislature in 1877, and re-elected in 1879.

Richard Fitch, Ellsworth township, Mahoning county, is the son of Richard Fitch, Sr., one of the early pioneers of Ellsworth township. Richard Fitch, Sr. was born in Salisbury township, Litchfield county, Connecticut, and emigrated to Ohio in 1806. He settled in Ellsworth, in section thirteen. His wife was Lucinda Buell, a native of Connecticut. They had a family of two sons and eight daughters, three of whom are living, viz: Sally, Antoinette, and Richard. The latter was born on the homestead in section thirteen. In 1838 he was married to Nancy F. Webb, by whom he has had six children, two of whom are deceased, having died in infancy. The rest live in Ellsworth. Frank, the oldest son, was born September 20, 1842, in Ellsworth township. May 2, 1867, he was married to Miss Martha B. McNeilly, and has had five children— Lizzie M., Jesse B., Charles P., and Bertha B., who are living, and John S., who died at the age of twenty-three months. Frank Fitch enlisted in 1864, in the One Hundred and Fifty-fifth Ohio national guard, serving one hundred days. Richard Fitch, Jr., the subject of this sketch, was justice of the peace of this township for fifteen years. He is a member of the Presbyterian church.

William Dean (deceased) was born in Litchfield county, Connecticut, in the year 1774. He emigrated from that State with his family in company with his father's family in the year 1810 and settled in Canfield township, then Trumbull county. The country was then very wild; Indians were not uncommon and frequently visited the cabins of the settlers while passing over their lost hunting-ground. There were also plenty of wild animals and game, wolves, deer, and bear being far more plenty than sheep and cattle. Not long after their settlement in their new home, mother Dean was called away, her husband surviving her but a few years. William Dean married Miss Parthenia Bailey and had a family of eight children, six sons and two daughters, viz: Orpha, Hiram, Orsemus, James, Benjamin, William B., Orman, and Balinda; of these James, Benjamin, and Balinda are deceased. By his second marriage he had one daughter, Rebecca. Mr. Dean followed farming during his life, and by dint of industry and good management acquired a good property. He died at the old homestead in 1847 at the age of seventy-three years. He was married three times. His third wife is still living.

William B. Dean, farmer, Ellsworth township, Mahoning county, son of William Dean, the pioneer above mentioned, was born in Litchfield county, Connecticut, in 1810. In October of that year his parents emigrated to Ohio, or New Connecticut as the Reserve was then called. William B. Dean grew up on the farm and was trained in the severe school of pioneer times. In 1832 he was married to Phebe Diehl. They have one child, Ward, born January 18, 1834. Mr. Dean settled in Ellsworth in 1835 and cleared the farm on which he lives.

In the year 1840 a part of the family of James Dixon, consisting of five sons and one daughter, emigrated to this country from Ireland. They came to Ohio and settled about a mile south of the present fair grounds. John Dixon, the third child, was born in county Down, Ireland, in 1809. He married in 1838 Elizabeth Kirkpatrick, by whom he had eight children, viz: James, Agnes, Mary Ann, Eliza, Margaret, Mary Agnes, Robert, and Martha. Agnes, Mary Ann, and Mary Agnes are deceased. Mr. Dickson is now seventy-two years old but is still active and can do his day's work in the harvest field. Himself and wife are members of the Presbyterian church.

Philip Arner (deceased) was born in Pennsylvania in 1776; was married in 1801 to Miss Susan Broadsword, and had five sons and three daughters, as follows: Peter, Elizabeth, Chloe, Lewis, Mary, Caleb, Daniel, and Eli T., two of whom are deceased. Mr. Arner came to Ellsworth township, now in Mahoning county, in 1802, and bought one hundred and sixty acres of land on Meander creek, the farm now being owned by his son Daniel. He made a small clearing, the first in Ellsworth township, and built a log cabin and then went back for his family, whom he brought out in 1804. He was an industrious man, worthy citizen and was held in high esteem by the entire community. He lived to an advanced age.

Eli T. Arner, farmer, Ellsworth township, Mahoning county, youngest son of Philip Arner, was born in Ellsworth, May 8, 1825. In 1846 he married Miss N. Orcleroad, and has three children—Susan, Ella, and Jessie. Mr. Arner is a thorough and successful farmer, and possesses a well improved farm.

Charles Fenstemaker (deceased) was born in Pennsylvania in 1817. He came to Ohio with his father, and settled about one and a half miles from where his widow now lives. He resided upon his father's farm until the year 1837, when he married Miss Abby Antony. He then bought and settled where his family now lives. Mr. Fenstemaker, by industry, prudence, and economy acquired a good property and pleasant home. He had two sons and three daughters— Anna, Elizabeth, Susanna, Ira and Aaron. The three daughters are deceased. Mr. Fenstemaker died in 1880. He was a member of the Presbyterian church, as is also his widow.

Jonathan Howard, farmer, Ellsworth township, Mahoning county, third son of William and Mary Howard, was born in Poland township, then Trumbull county, now Mahoning, March 30, 1811. His father was born in Maryland in 1774. He came to Ohio in 1802, and settled in Poland township. About 1816 he moved to Ellsworth township. April 6, 1802, he married Miss Mary Rose, by whom he had thirteen children, as follows: Susan, Mary, John, Jesse, Jonathan, William, Rebecca, Jane, Louisa, Melvina, Isaac, Albert C., and one that died in infancy. It is a singular circumstance in the history of this family that the circle of twelve children was not broken by death until the youngest was forty years of age. Jonathan was some five years of age when his parents moved to Ellsworth. He married, in 1849, Margaret Hoover, and has one son, Frank C., born September 11, 1852. He lives at home with his parents.

Albert C. Howard, farmer, Ellsworth township, Mahoning county, youngest child of William and Mary Howard, was born in Ellsworth, November 5, 1826. He married, March 3, 1857, Miss Susan Teegarden, by whom he has had two children, a son and daughter, viz: Martha, born January 17, 1858, who died March 10th of the same year, and L. U., born February 24, 1859, now a student in Mount Union college, having attended some four terms. Albert Howard taught school for a number of terms in Jackson, Newton, and Green townships, and has studied medicine to some extent, but has never practiced.

J. M. Howard, farmer, Ellsworth township, Mahoning county, was born in section twenty, Ellsworth township, in 1833. When about two years of age he went to live with his grandparents (McCreary), who resided in the same neighborhood, and of whom a brief sketch is given elsewhere. Mr. Howard was married in 1859 to Sarah M. Rose, of Jackson township, and has one child, Jeannette. He owns and occupies the farm previously owned by his grandfather McCreary.

Philo Spaulding (deceased) was a native of Connecticut, where he was born June 26, 1786. In 1808 he married Miss Amanda Bingham, by whom he had six sons and two daughters, as follow: Augustus, Moses, Amos, Newman, Isaac, Jeremiah, Paulina, and Jerusha. In 1813, with

his family of wife, daughter Paulina, and sons Augustus and Moses, he came to Ohio making the journey in an ox-cart. He settled in Ellsworth township, now Mahoning county. Two years afterward he located upon the farm where his son Moses now lives. He began there in the woods and by hard work and under the difficulties incident to pioneer life built up a good home and reared his family. His wife and companion of his pioneer days died in 1835, and in 1837 he married Mrs. Elizabeth Kidd. By the second marriage there were no children. He died in 1876 at the advanced age of ninety years, surviving his wife twenty years.

Moses Spaulding, farmer, Ellsworth, Mahoning county, son of the subject of the preceding sketch, was born in Connecticut December 21, 1811. He remained upon the farm with his parents until his marriage, which took place October 8, 1834, to Miss Harriet Ann Dakin. The result of this union was eleven children, as follow: Horace, Caroline E., Emily, Julia, Homer, Susan, Charlotte, Horace (2), Ella, Ida, and Mary. Horace (1), Julia, and Homer are dead. The latter enlisted in the war of the Rebellion, although only fifteen years of age, and was severely wounded in his first engagement at the battle of Shiloh. He rallied for a time and was brought home where he received the kindest attention and care, but the wound proved a fatal one and he died December 2, 1862, his loss being a severe blow to his parents. Mr. Spaulding is an enterprising farmer and has accumulated a good property. Himself and wife are members of the Presbyterian church.

James McNeilly (deceased) was born in Ireland, July, 1804. He married Elizabeth Trimble in 1824, and in 1827 emigrated to America; came to Ohio and settled in Mahoning county, then Trumbull, Jackson township. He remained there about three years and then moved to Ellsworth and located in section twenty-three, where he lived until his death. His children were John, Robert, William, Margaret, Eliza, Samuel, Mary, James P., and Martha, all of whom are living but John.

James P. McNeilly, farmer, Ellsworth, Mahoning county, son of James McNeilly of the above sketch, was born February 1st, 1844, in Ellsworth township. At the age of twenty-seven he was united in marriage to Miss Jerusha Fitch, by whom he has had two children, Frances F. and Fannie A., one of whom died at the age of sixteen months. Mr. McNeilly enlisted in the One Hundred and Fifty-fifth Ohio National guard in 1864, and served one hundred days. Himself and wife are both members of the Presbyterian church.

Samuel A. McNeilly, farmer, Ellsworth township, Mahoning county, was born in Ellsworth in 1839. In 1860 he married Miss Mary W. Smith, and has a family of four children, viz: Walter T., Helen V., Mary E., and Charles S. Mr. McNeilly has a good property in Ellsworth center. He and his wife are members of the Presbyterian church.

John McCreary (deceased) was born in county Down, Ireland, in 1770. He emigrated to America in 1787, and settled in New Jersey. Shortly afterwards he moved to Erie, Pennsylvania. In 1801 he married Miss Jane McFarland, and two years afterwards he came to Ohio, and settled in section nineteen, Ellsworth township, now Mahoning county. He cleared up and improved a fine farm, on which he lived until his death in 1839. He left surviving him a wife and two daughters, Mary and Jeannette.

Samuel Knauff (deceased) was born in Green township, now Mahoning county, in the year 1822. He lived with his parents until his marriage, which event occurred in 1850. He married Miss Barbara Hardman, and began married life on the farm now occupied by the widow. The family consists of five sons and five daughters as follows: Anna, Henry, John, Lida, Erin, Mary, Amos, Lovina, Amanda, and Ensign. Mr. Knauff died in 1872, and was buried in Green township beside his parents, who died many years ago. He was a member of the Lutheran church.

William J. McKinney, postmaster, Ellsworth center, Mahoning county, was born in Pittsburg, Pennsylvania, August 4, 1852, and came to Ohio with his father in the latter part of the year 1858. He was married to Miss Hannah Mygatt, but has no children. He was appointed postmaster at Ellsworth center in 1874, and also elected township treasurer the same year. He is a merchant at Ellsworth center.

George W. Harroff, farmer, Ellsworth township, Mahoning county, was born in Augusta county, Virginia, July 11, 1833. He married in 1865, Miss Mary McLaughlin, who died December 22d of the same year, while on the way to Ohio, and was buried at Wellsville. He was again married, early in 1867, to Miss Mary Diehl, by whom he had one child, Mary S. C. His second wife died December 22, 1867. Mr. Harroff was married a third time, to Miss Sarah Diehl, sister of his second wife, March 20, 1868, by whom he has had one child, George A., born February 14, 1869.

Henry C. Beardsley, farmer, Ellsworth township, Mahoning county, was born in the State of Connecticut, December 2, 1823. He came to Ohio with his father, Almus Beardsley, and settled in the woods in Ellsworth township. Henry C. Beardsley married, in 1851, Miss Elizabeth Smith, and has had eight children. Four daughters and two sons are now living, viz: Laura, W. L., Ora, Lucy M., Edith, and Arthur. Mr. Beardsley still resides on the old homestead. He is a member of the Presbyterian church. In politics he is a Republican.

Henry Boyd, grandfather of Dr. F. Wilson, came to this county in 1830; settled in Ellsworth township first, afterwards in Berlin; was a member of the State Legislature in 1847, and it was probably on his recommendation that the lines bounding the county were run. He was a justice of the peace for many years; an elder in the Presbyterian church; was a man of influence and highly esteemed. He died in Lima, Ohio, in 1864.

CHAPTER V.
BERLIN.

GENERAL DESCRIPTION.

Berlin is township one of range five, Connecticut Western Reserve, and was, until the formation of Mahoning county, the southwest corner township of Trumbull county. Berlin has Milton on the north, Ellsworth on the east, Goshen and Smith on the south, and Deerfield, Portage county on the west. In natural beauty it is unsurpassed by any portion of the county. The winding Mahoning washes a portion of the western borders of the township. The surface in its vicinity is more or less broken, and with

R. K. Hughes

Mrs. Martha A. Hughes.

woody banks and verdant valleys, the river helps to make a scene of picturesque loveliness. Mill creek waters the southwestern quarter of the township. One of its tributaries has the suggestive name of Turkey Broth. Turkey Broth creek is a small stream rising in the northeastern part of the township, and flowing southwesterly until it reaches Mill creek. Several small runs empty into it.

The land of Berlin is mostly very nearly level, and consists of a succession of broad swells with wide and very slight depressions intervening. The surface is so nearly uniform that an observer, upon almost any of the gentle rises of land, can obtain a view of nearly all parts of the township. The soil is deep and fertile; very little clay or sand, but a good strong loam, well adapted to fruits and cereals. A traveler along almost any of the roads in the township can scarcely fail to note and admire the beautiful fields on every hand.

Berlin center, a straggling settlement of twenty or more houses, is the only village, and is pleasantly situated on a slight elevation a short distance east of the geographical center of the township.

Belvidere, where Schilling's mill is located, advanced far enough toward the dignity of a village to receive a name, and apparently its ambition was satisfied. Shelltown in the northeast is a thickly settled community. At Christy's corners, in the southwestern part of the township, quite an extensive business has been carried on for a number of years in the manufacture of pottery.

The township was but sparsely settled until about 1824 for the reason that the greater portion of the land was not offered for sale until that time.

ORGANIZATION.

The township, which for several years had been a part of Ellsworth, was erected a separate township and election precinct by the county commissioners in March, 1828.

THE FIRST ELECTION

of township officers took place at the schoolhouse near the center April 7, 1828, Matthias Glass, Salmon Hall, and Joseph Stall being judges of election, and Peter Musser and Joseph H. Coult, clerks. The following officers were

elected: Nathan Minard, Thompson Craig, Samuel Kauffman, trustees; Salmon Hall, treasurer; Joseph H. Coult, clerk; John Stuart, constable; William Kirkpatrick, Christian Kauffman overseers of the poor; Joseph Davis, Joseph Leonard fence viewers; Edward Fankle, Benjamin Misner, Abraham Craft, supervisors.

SCHOOL DISTRICTS.

In 1828 the township was divided into four school districts. Four years later the number had increased to nine. The old township records give the following names of the inhabitants of the four school districts in 1829. Where the name is illegible in the old book, or where the spelling is of doubtful authenticity, a question mark (?) is placed after the name:

District Number One.—Joshua Minard, John Vosburg, William Kirkpatrick, Edward Fankle, John Crumrine, John Ween (?), Benjamin Leonard, Nathan Minard, Adam Morningstar, Henry Morningstar, Adam Morningstar, Jr., John Ludwick, John Kimmel.

District Number Two.—John Smith, Henry Powell, William Bishop, Ephraim Horner, Elisha Fogg, Adna B. Silver, Joseph Huntley, Enoch Sharpe, Isaac Sharpe, Hoffman Brown, James Ramsey, Jacob Strong, John Shatto (?), David Parshall, Henry Houck, Joseph Davis, John Thomas, Samuel Leonard, John Leonard, Joseph Leonard, Jacob Starling, Isaac Phipps, Andrew Hull, Joseph Poll (?), Peter Helsel, Joseph H. Coult.

District Number Three.—George Ripple, Eli Rush, John Craig, James Packard, John Carter, John Stump (?), William Parker, Eleanor Packard, George Boom (Baum ?), Jacob Welty, William Leonard, George Foster, Abraham Craft, John Foster, Salmon Hall, John Best, Henry Rummell, John Rummell.

District Number Four.—Daniel Myer, John Rummell, John Phillips, Jonathan King, John Cline, Peter Glass, Adam Schilling, David Misner, Samuel Misner, Samuel Phillips, Phillip Wise (?), Jacob Stump, Henry Fulk, Matthias Swartz, Benjamin Misner, George Hartzell, Abraham Hawn, William Glass, Christian Kauffman, Samuel Kauffman, David Mauen (?), William Mell, Jacob Eib, Matthias Glass, Adam Zedaker, Daniel Greenamyer, Peter Musser, Moses Ross, Jacob Greenamyer, James Winans, James Byers, William Stull (?), Emmanuel Hull.

This is doubtless a complete list of the property holders and tax-payers of the township for the year 1829.

The first justice of the peace was Peter Musser, appointed in 1828. His immediate successors were Joseph H. Coult, William Hartzell, James B. Boyd (resigned), and D. A. Fitch.

Garrett Packard, the first white settler of Berlin, came from the vicinity of Winchester, Virginia, to Austintown in 1803. Two years later he moved to Deerfield, where he resided until March, 1809, at which date he settled on a farm on Mill creek, in the southwestern part of Berlin township, having previously purchased the land of General Perkins. He had sold his place in Deerfield and was contemplating a move to this purchase when he was taken sick, and for some time was unable to do any work. His Deerfield neighbors generally combined their efforts and erected a log cabin upon his land,—rude and primitive to be sure, but it served to shelter the family. The structure was of rough logs, three sides, the fourth side serving as a door, over which blankets were hung in cold weather. The spaces between the logs were filled with moss. Like many pioneer dwellings, this had no floor except the earth.

Soon after the arrival of the family in the township, Mrs. Packard gave birth to a son, who is now a well-known citizen of Champion township, Trumbull county,—Thomas Packard, born March 27, 1809, the first white child born in Berlin. Garrett Packard's was the only family in the township for several years. At the time of the War of 1812 he was the only man residing in what is now Berlin. He was drafted and was in the service three months. He died November 20, 1820, aged about forty-five, his death being the first that occurred in the township. Mrs. Packard, whose maiden name was Eleanor Hendrickson, survived until May 13, 1830, and died in Austintown while visiting the home of her son-in-law, John McCollum. She was fifty-four years of age. Below we briefly mention each of the ten children of the family : Betsy became the wife of George Baum, and resided in Berlin township. They had seven children, six of whom arrived at maturity. Five are still living, three sons and two daughters. Mrs. Baum died in Atwater, Portage county, in 1877. Polly be-

came the first wife of John McCollum, and died in Milton in 1867. She was the mother of six children, three sons and three daughters. Two sons and two daughters are still living. James H. was killed in 1829 when about twenty-five years old by the fall of a pile of boards which he was drying by means of a fire. It was a rainy day, and he probably lay down by the fire and fell asleep. The board kiln being loosely built, fell over upon him, and when his friends came to look for him they found only his bruised and mangled body beneath the pile of lumber. Jane became the wife of Daniel Parshall, and resided in Milton township. She died in 1843. Her family consisted of two sons and three daughters, all of whom are living, excepting one son. Esther married Jesse Rose, son of David Rose, resided in Jackson and afterwards in Champion. She is now a widow and lives in Washington county, Iowa. She has no children. Charlotte was the second wife of Joseph H. Coult. She had one son and one daughter. The son is living. Mrs. Coult died in Ellsworth in 1854. Thomas resides in Champion. Asby went West when a young man, and is now a resident of Johnson county, Iowa. He is the father of two sons and five daughters. One son and four daughters are living. John W. resides in Columbus, Ohio. His family of three sons and three daughters are all living excepting one son. Garrett resides in Johnson county, Iowa. He has two sons and three daughters living.

Jacob Weldy was the second settler. He came with his family from east of the mountains, but at what date we are unable to learn. He located in the northwestern corner of the township. His son Jacob lived upon the old place after him. Samuel also lived and died in Berlin. The family was a large one.

George Baum was the next comer. His father emigrated from Germany and settled in Salem. George came to Berlin when a young man. About 1815 he married Betsey Packard. This was the first marriage that occurred among the residents of "Hart and Mather's." They went to Ellsworth and the ceremony was performed by 'Squire William Ripley. Baum settled in the southwestern part of the township on the next farm east of Weldy. None of his children reside in the township.

Abraham Hawn came to the township about 1820, and located two miles north and a little east of the center. He brought up a family of six children. Two of the sons, Peter and Matthias, died in Berlin; Jacob lives in Akron; Michael D., in Berlin. His daughters were: Christina, who became the wife of Joseph Cline, and died in this township, and Mrs. Susanna Smith, Deerfield.

Joseph H. Coult was the first settler at the center. His family was the fourth or fifth that came to the township. Coult acted as land agent for Amos Sill, the proprietor of the greater part of the township, and sold the land to the settlers. He came about 1823. He made the first clearing at the center and built the first frame house in the township. In 1842 he sold his place to Thomas Hawkins, who still resides upon it. Mr. Coult moved to Ellsworth and thence to Atwater.

Matthias Glass settled in the northwest of the township about 1822. His sons were John, William, Matthias, Peter, Jacob, Solomon. There were also several daughters.

Reuben Gee, Joseph Davis and David Parshall bought land and settled in the township about 1824. Gee remained but a short time. Joseph Davis is remembered by some of the old settlers as a very religious man, and an earnest friend of the church and preachers. His son James resided in the township for a while. David Parshall settled about one mile west of the center on the south side of the road. He sold out and moved.

From 1824 to 1830 the settlers came in rapidly, but of the families who came during that time comparatively few are represented in the township. The early as well as the later settlers were chiefly Pennsylvanians, quiet, unobtrusive, but progressive people. Their characteristic thrift has borne its fruit, and Berlin, the youngest of the Mahoning county townships, will compare very favorably with some sections where improvements were begun much earlier. We have space to mention a few early comers.

Jonathan King was born in Pennsylvania in 1804. In 1823 he came to Springfield township, this county, where he worked for some time. In 1825 he married Lydia Keck, and in 1826 settled in Berlin township. They had ten children. Seven arrived at maturity, and five are still living. Mr. King first settled two miles north of the centre and a little east, and there made the first improvements on the farm where his son Joseph now lives. Mr. King has probably been a resident of Berlin longer than any other man now living in the township.

John Cline, a native of Pennsylvania, settled in Boardman township quite early; thence moved to Canfield, and in 1828 settled in the northern part of Berlin. He was the father of seven sons and four daughters. Three sons and one daughter are still living, viz: Jonathan, George, and Conrad, and Mrs. Sarah Hawn, the oldest of the family. All are residents of this township.

George Ripple was an early settler west of the center.

Salmon Hall settled on the west side of the Mahoning.

The Misner family settled in the northern part of the township.

Henry Houck located on the road west of the center.

David and Tobias Hartzell were early settlers.

William Kirkpatrick settled east of the center on the farm now occupied by Jonathan King. He kept tavern at the center a few years. His name was changed to Kirk on his petitioning the Legislature. His sons, William, James, and Isaac were residents of Berlin for a time. James died here.

Emanuel Hull, an early settler in the northeast of the township, lived and died on the farm now owned by his son George, and his daughter Mary. Michael, his son, also resides in the northeastern part of the township.

John Kimmel settled on the east line of Berlin township in 1828. He brought up five sons and four daughters. Four sons and two daughters are yet living. Daniel, one of the sons, lives on a part of the old homestead.

George Best came to Berlin township in 1830 and settled northwest of the center, where he now resides. He has brought up a family of eight children, six of whom are living.

Horace Rowland has been a resident of the township since 1831. He began in the woods in the southeast of Berlin. Later he moved east of the center and bought the farm on which Michael Crumrine had made the first improvement.

Zimri Engle has resided in Berlin since 1832.

In 1833 John Burkey came from Petersburg and settled in the northeast of the township. He brought up a family of eleven children, nine of whom are living, five sons and four daughters, Peter, Solomon, and Sophia (Hull) being residents of this township.

John Carson came to Berlin in 1832, and in 1834 settled on the farm he now occupies, in the northwestern corner of the township. Adam Zedaker had been living on the place and had made some improvements before Mr. Carson purchased it.

Lawrence Shively came to the northwestern part of Berlin in 1833. His family of ten children are all living. Mr. Shively moved to Milton in 1848, and resided there several years. He is now living in Berlin.

About the year 1800, Peter Hoyle came from Virginia and settled in Ellsworth township, where he lived until 1836. At that date he settled in the eastern part of Berlin. He brought up five sons and two daughters. All are now living excepting one daughter. George and Peter are residents of this township.

BERLIN

was the name given the township at the instance of Matthias Glass. He, being a German, desired to have his adopted home bear a name which would remind him of the Fatherland. Previous to the organization, the township was known to the early settlers for miles around as Hart and Mather's, from the names of two men who were originally proprietors of a tract within it. General Perkins owned a thousand acres or more in the southwest corner, and it was of him that Packard and other early comers purchased their land. About two-thirds of the township was owned by Amos Sill, and sold by his agent, Joseph H. Coult, who was the first settler at the center.

TURKEY BROTH CREEK

was so named by Garrett Packard. His journey with his family from Austintown to the place where he settled in Deerfield, a distance of nineteen miles, occupied three days. The first night he stayed at the house of Philip Borts, in Ellsworth; the second night encamped beside the creek, and while there shot a wild turkey and made broth, using water from the stream, which

has since borne the name he bestowed upon it. The third day Packard arrived in Deerfield.

HARD TIMES.

A majority of the settlers of Berlin came after surrounding townships were considerably settled, and thus had some advantages over the first pioneers upon the Reserve. Stores had been established and mills were in operation, and neighboring settlements were beginning to assume some of the habiliments of civilization. Yet pioneer life everywhere is attended with privations and hardships; and these the early residents of Berlin did not escape. In the matter of game, however, they were especially fortunate. "Hart and Mather's" was long a favorite hunting-ground for sportsmen from miles around. The number of deer that have been slaughtered within the limits of the township, if it could be ascertained, would no doubt cause open-eyed astonishment among the youth of to-day.

But notwithstanding the fact that there was enough meat running about in the forest, the people subsisted largely upon corn bread. In the busy season the farmer could not leave his field to go hunting.

Thomas Packard, in a conversation which the writer had with him, while speaking of his boyhood in Berlin and the difference between now and then, incidentally made allusion to a "hominy block," which formed a part of the household furniture of his father. On being asked an explanation of those mysterious words, Mr. Packard said:

You know there were few mills in this part of the country in those days, and the few small affairs that had been erected were frequently rendered useless in a dry season. Such seasons—and likewise at times when people were so much occupied with planting or sowing that there was no opportunity for going to mill—the hominy block was in requisition. I remember ours perfectly well. It was a large, solid block of wood, in the end of which a hollow had been cut and smoothly shaved. This cavity would hold nearly half a bushel. By means of this hollow block and a large and heavy stick, smooth and round, corn and wheat were converted by pounding into substitutes for meal and flour. This hominy was usually cooked by boiling; it was healthy food, and tasted well, too.

A NARROW ESCAPE.

In early days Indians were probably as numerous along the Mahoning as in any part of this region, and here, too, they continued to remain some years after the white man appeared and made his home in the forest.

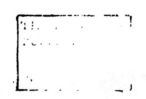

Jonathan King

Mrs Lydia King

While Garrett Packard was living in Deerfield, both he and his wife were at work in the field one day, when Mr. Packard chanced to get a splinter in his finger. His wife came to his assistance, stood by his side, and picked it out with a pin. Soon afterwards an Indian emerged from the woods close at hand bearing a gun. Said he, "While you were standing near together, I was there by yonder tree. I could have shot you both, and laid one on the ground there, and the other there," indicating the place by his finger. "But then me think, white man never harm me; why me kill him? So me no shoot." Both thanked the Indian heartily for his thoughtful consideration and self-restraint—for so good a mark seemed to have much impressed the savage. He was invited to the cabin to dinner, and from that day forward remained a warm and earnest friend of the family.

MILLS.

About the year 1825 Matthias Glass built a saw-mill and grist-mill on the Mahoning, a short distance above Frederick. The first grist-mill was destroyed by fire. Isaac Wilson purchased the mill-site of Glass and put up the flouring-mill which is still standing. His sons, J. B. and J. S. Wilson, ran it for some years. It was then purchased by its present owner, George Schilling. This is the only grist-mill ever built in Berlin township.

In 1826 David Shoemaker built a saw-mill on Mill creek, in the southwestern part of the township. It was sold to Jacob Sheets, who run it several years.

About the same date Joseph H. Coult put up a saw-mill on Turkey Broth a short distance north of the center. Coult sold it to Jonathan King, King to Henry Morningstar, and Morningstar to Joseph Cline.

TANNERY.

A man named McKean carried on tanning and shoemaking at the center, some forty-five years ago. His tannery was on the Turkey Broth, west of the center.

MERCHANTS.

The first store-keeper in Berlin was Joseph Edwards, who commenced business in 1833 on the southeast corner at the center, where Dr. Hughes now lives. He lived in a small log house and kept his goods in a small frame build-ing. Garrison & Hoover were the next merchants, followed by Daniel A. Fitch. David McCauley came next and moved the store to the northeast corner, where it now stands. John Ward, Warren & Webber, R. H. King, Hughes Brothers, A. G. Ramsdell, and B. T. Stanley have since occupied the store. For a time there were two stores at the center. Richards & Cotton kept one in the building now occupied by J. M. Brown. It then stood on the southwest corner lot. William Porter had goods there after Richards & Cotton, and employed a man named Linton to sell them.

In addition to these stores William Kirk kept goods for sale in his tavern. Joel Booth also had a store opposite the blacksmith shop some thirty years ago. Kirk's place of business was the old unoccupied building now standing west of the town-house.

TAVERNS.

Probably Peter Musser, in the northern part of the township, kept the first tavern. William Kirk kept several years in a building now standing just east of the town-house. George Taylor kept public house a number of years where R. H. King now lives.

WILSON'S STORE.

Isaac Wilson put up a store at Belvidere in 1839, soon after he bought the mill privilege there. His sons sold goods there for some years. Jacob W. Glass purchased the store from them. Morgan Reed, Langstaff, and others have carried on merchandising there in later years. For some time the building has not been used as a store.

PHYSICIANS.

Dr. James W. Hughes was the first regular physician in the township. He settled in Berlin in 1834, and practiced successfully until his death in 1869. His son, Dr. W. K. Hughes, succeeded to his practice and continues to be the physician of the township. Other doctors have located at the center, but they have mainly been residents only a short time.

POST-OFFICES.

The first post-office in Berlin township was established about 1828, Peter Musser postmaster. Amity was the name of the post-office. Musser kept tavern on the old stage road in the northern part of the township, very near the line.

He soon moved and the office was discontinued. Frederick post-office, of which mention is made in the history of Milton township, is now kept in Berlin. The Berlin post-office (at the center) was established in 1833. The mail was then received but once a week. Joseph Edwards was the first postmaster, succeeded by Daniel A. Fitch, David Routsawn, Thomas L. Dutton, Cyrus O. Warren, R. H. King, Lizzie Hughes, A. G. Ramsdell, and B. T. Stanley. Daily mails.

EARLY SCHOOLS.

In another portion of this chapter will be found a list of the inhabitants of the original school districts of the township, interesting not only in connection with the school history, but valuable as showing who were the heads of families in the township at the time this record was made.

But schools had been maintained previous to the organization of the township. A little log school-house was erected on the banks of the Turkey Broth, near the center, at a date which was probably not far from 1824. Sarah Gee was one of the first teachers.

Martha McKelvey and afterwards Eliza McKelvey taught school in a deserted log-cabin in the southwestern part of the township at an early date. In the northern part of the township a school-house was built quite early. English and German were taught alternate weeks or alternate terms. Alexander Hall was one of the first teachers in this school.

THE FIRST WEDDING

at Berlin center took place at the house of Joseph H. Coult, now the residence of Thomas Hawkins, on a cold and wintry night in December. The parties wedded were William Ripley and Miss Allen. The guests were the nearest neighbors, some from Benton and some from Ellsworth. As there was no wagon road between Ellsworth and Benton, the visitors from the latter place came on horseback, carrying torches in their hands for the purpose of keeping wolves at bay. The next morning it was noticed that the wolves had followed the party some distance and left tracks all around the house and even on the doorsteps.

AN INCIDENT OF SLAVERY DAYS. *

Marius R. Robinson, a Presbyterian minister

*Contributed by F. P. Thorn, Ellsworth.

residing in Salem, Ohio, came to Berlin in June, 1837, having been invited to deliver a lecture on the slavery question. He was one of the early Abolitionists, and was about thirty-one years of age at the time of his visit to Berlin. Here he became the guest of Jesse Garretson, a Quaker merchant. It being impossible to secure any public building for a lecture he spoke in Mr. Garretson's dwelling on Friday, June 2d.

Another meeting was announced for the following Sunday, when the lecturer proposed to vindicate the Bible from the charge of supporting slavery. The South at that time largely controlled public opinion in the North and forbade the agitation of the slavery question, therefore the announcement of an "abolition" lecture threw the village into a state of fierce excitement.

About ten o'clock Saturday evening Mr. Robinson was sitting in the store with Mr. and Mrs. Garretson, when several men rushed in and seized him, saying, "You have got to leave this town to-night; you have disturbed the peace of our citizens long enough." A struggle ensued, Mr. Garretson and his wife making desperate efforts to protect him, but they were overpowered; the lecturer was taken out, stripped of his clothing and covered with tar and feathers. While some of the men were holding him, waiting for others to bring the tar and feathers, Mr. Robinson made several attempts to talk, but was prevented by being struck at each effort. He was bleeding freely from a cut or wound in the arm, near his left shoulder. After the tar and feathers had been applied, his clothes were put on again and he was carried in a wagon a distance of about eleven miles to a point about one mile south of Canfield, and there left in the road. Although a stranger in that locality he found his way to the house of Mr. Wetmore, where he was kindly cared for.

Twelve of the men who committed the outrage were arrested and had a preliminary trial before a justice of the peace at Ellsworth; but while Mr. Robinson's attorneys, Milton Sutliff and Robert Taylor, of Warren, and Joshua R. Giddings, of Ashtabula, were preparing the case for the court of common pleas, a compromise was effected, each of the parties charged paying Mr. Robinson the sum of $40.

The effect of this affair was wide spread. Salem became known throughout the whole country as a "hot-bed of abolitionism;" and it was this incident and Mr. Robinson's subsequent work that made it so, or contributed largely toward that result. Mr. Robinson was an able man and devoted the remaining years of his life to fighting slavery as a lecturer and as editor of the Anti-slavery Bugle, until the institution was swept out of existence by the war.

CHURCH HISTORY.

The history of the churches of Berlin is not a record of brilliant successes. Probably the township contains, in proportion to its population, an average number of devout people ; but the mistake has been made of trying to support too many churches, and consequently we have several failures to chronicle.

THE GERMAN CHURCH.

The Germans held meetings at the house of Abraham Hawn for several years. In 1828 those belonging to the Lutheran and German Reformed denominations erected a small house for public worship, north of the center about two miles. The building served both as a church and a school-house. It was built of hewn logs, and was perhaps 22x28 feet. They next erected a frame building in 1836, with gallery, lofty pulpit, etc.—in short, an old-fashioned Dutch church. This house continued to be used until 1872, when the church now standing was erected.

Prominent among the early Lutherans were Abraham Hawn, Jonathan King, John Eckis, John Eckis, jr., John March and Henry Houck.

Among those who were members of the Reformed church we mention Henry Rummel, Jacob Greenamyer, Peter Kimmel, and Daniel Kump.

The Lutherans and the Reformed have always occupied the church in common. For some years all of the preaching was in German. In 1842 occurred a great revival. The membership of the Reformed church has been growing gradually less until they no longer support a pastor, and the meetings are now conducted wholly by the Lutherans. The first preacher of the Lutherans was Rev. Henry Hewett, who supplied the pulpit many years. Revs. John C. Ellinger, Samuel Seachrist, J. W. Sloan, William B. Roller, George Moore, Peter Smith, and I. J. Miller have been his successors. The pastors of the Reformed congregation have been Rev. J. P.

Mahnensmith, first ; Revs. Hess, Bechtley, Sigler, Grether, Mechtley, Otting, and others.

The Germans have the neatest and by far the prettiest church building in the township, and are evidently in a good condition, both financially and morally.

THE METHODISTS.

The Methodists formed a society previous to 1830, and for some years held meetings in school-houses and private dwellings. They commenced with very few members, prominent among whom were Joseph Davis and wife, Samuel Leonard and wife, David Parshall and wife. In about 1839 a house for public worship was erected at the center, through the efforts of the church people, assisted liberally by the leading citizens of various beliefs. Early preachers were Revs. Nicholas Gee, Stubbs, Prosser, Ingraham, Clark, and others.

Until within the past two or three years the society has held regular services each Sabbath. Now services are held once in two weeks. The church has about fifty members at present.

THE UNITED BRETHREN.

This denomination once had two churches in the township, and now has none. Had the two concentrated perhaps the church might have been alive now. The motto, "United we stand, divided we fall," applies to churches, as well as to political parties.

About 1835, the United Brethren organized and held meetings at the houses of Jacob Strong and Joseph Davis, south of the center. A few years later they built a house two miles west of the village. Among those who preached here were Charles Carter and Father Biddle. Prominent among the first members were Jacob Strong, Joseph Davis, and Jonathan Davis. About 1851 the United Brethren and Evangelical Association built a union church at Shelltown. Active members: Michael Hull, John Hull, Madison Traill, and Alexander McNutt. The society was small and short-lived. Carter's Zion drew away several members, and the few that remained were not able to pay a preacher.

MOUNT CARMEL EVANGELICAL CHURCH.

This is a small society, and is known from its location as the "Shelltown church." About the year 1850 the church was organized under the preaching of Rev. Barnhart. Among the early and prominent members are mentioned Jacob Shellenbarger and wife, Jonathan Cline and wife, Andrew Cline and wife, Mrs. Mock, and Catherine Hull. A year or two after its organization the society joined the United Brethren in their efforts to build a union church. A small house was erected, which these two denominations, and occasionally the Methodists, continued to use until 1873, when the Evangelical Association purchased of Jonas Barringer the house which was built for the use of the Zion church.

As the preachers of this denomination are itinerants, they have been quite numerous. The church comprises perhaps twenty-five members, and has service once in two weeks.

ZION CHURCH.

Charles Carter, a dissenter from the United Brethren, among whom he had been an elder and a preacher for several years, began preaching in Ashtabula in the interests of a new denomination of which he was the author and leader, if not the object of worship. Having succeeded in starting a church in Ashtabula he came here and by vigorous efforts secured enough members to form a class, which he styled the Zion church. Meetings were held in the house belonging to the United Brethren until an earnest protest from the members compelled the Zionites to seek new quarters. About 1870 a church was built—principally through the means of Jonas Barringer. But the disciples of Carter soon became weary and the organization died out. The house passed into the possession of the Evangelical denomination as is elsewhere mentioned. We would be glad to tell our readers the tenets and doctrines of the Zion church but we regard them as past finding out, as diligent inquiry failed to give us any light.

THE CHRISTIANS.

In 1867 the Christians, or Bible Christians, of Berlin, organized and formed a church. There were twelve members enrolled February 26, 1867. The number was increased to twenty-four during that year. Elder Miles Harrod was the organizer and became the first pastor of the church. In 1868 a house for public worship was erected.

The preachers in this church have been: Elders Harrod, Winget, Cameron, Middleton, McCowan, and Dunlap. There are about thirty members at present. They have no regular services now.

CEMETERIES.

There are three small burying grounds in the township. That adjoining the German church is probably the oldest, though the graveyard near the center was probably laid out nearly the same time with it. In the German graveyard the earliest recorded death that is legible is that of Noah Boyer, died December 27, 1831. Doubtless interments were made much earlier, but the all-effacing fingers of time have already blotted out some inscriptions that were placed upon rude headstones of sandstone.

BERLIN BUSINESS DIRECTORY.

The following is believed to be a correct list of all occupations carried on in the township, other than farming:

B. T. Stanley, merchant, center. J. Mock & Son, carriage and blacksmith shop, center. A. Willsdoff, tannery, center. R. H. King, hotel, center. J. M. Brown, saloon, center. John Lally, shoemaker, center. Blacksmiths: George Humphrey, west; B. F. Kirkbride, southeast. Saw-mill and grist-mill: George Schilling & Son, northwest. Steam saw-mills: David King & Son, south; E. H. Miller & Son, northeast; Cline Brothers, northeast. Cooper: Samuel Jolly, west. Planing-mill and cabinet shop: Daniel Kimmel, east. Manufacturers of pottery: Stewart Christy's heirs; Andrew Dustman, Christy's corners.

BIOGRAPHICAL SKETCHES.

DR. JAMES W. HUGHES.

No class of men experienced more fully the trials incident to pioneer life than the early physicians of the Reserve. Their work required that they should be men of vigorous body, capable of great endurance, for such was the difficulty of travel that none but hardy natures could bear the constant exertions required of them. The roads and forest paths were in a state that forbids description. Houses were few and far apart, and could only be reached by traveling on foot or on horseback. Besides, the people were generally poor and some families even destitute. There were no markets where agricultural prod-

Alonzo Strong

William Strong, the father of the subject of this sketch, was born in Durham, Connecticut, and in 1806 removed with his wife, whose maiden name was Abigail Crane, to Atwater township, then Trumbull county, now Portage county, Ohio. There Alonzo was born in 1805 in Connecticut. William Strong, his father, was a soldier in the War of 1812, and was seized with a fatal fever, of which he died in 1814, and he was buried on the shore of Lake Erie.

Mr. Strong is the only survivor of the three children, one being a daughter named Eliza, and the other a son, Luzerne. After the arrival of the family in Ohio he was sent back east to attend school, and remained some two years. He then returned to Ohio and was bound out to Joseph Hartzell for eight years. After his term of service with Hartzell expired he learned the trade of cloth dressing but worked at it only about six months. He learned the carpenter's trade which he followed some six years, but finally engaged in farming on the place where he now lives. In 1828 he married Miss Christina Lazarus, by whom he had six children, as follow : Lovina, who married Elijah Whinnery, and resides in Salem, Columbiana county; William A., who married Miss Annie Marshall, and resides in Alliance; Levi (dead). Fred-

Elizabeth C. Strong.

erick (dead), Julia, unmarried, and a child that died in infancy. Levi was in the war of the Rebellion, enlisting in 1862, and in 1863 was taken prisoner. He was taken to Richmond, then to Andersonville where he died. Mrs. Christina Strong died in 1842, and in 1845 Mr. Strong was married again, to Elizabeth Whinnery, whose parents were early settlers in Columbiana county, removing from Pennsylvania in 1804. By his second marriage he has had nine children, as follow: Serena, wife of William Heckler, resides in Illinois; Edward and Edwin, twins, Edward is living and Edwin is deceased; Lovisa, wife of Alvin Smith, resides in Illinois; Ashley, who married Miss Annie Malmsbery, and resides in North Benton; Ophelia, unmarried; Leora E., wife of Henry Koch, lives in Columbiana county; Alonzo C., and Wendell P. Edwin, the only deceased member of the family, was drowned at the age of eighteen months.

Mr. Strong cultivates a large farm of two hundred and fifty acres, and gives particular attention to the raising of sheep. He has served one term as justice of the peace.

ucts could be exchanged for money. As a consequence the physician received little hard cash to remunerate him for his hard and fatiguing labor. Their self-sacrificing spirit cannot receive too great a tribute of praise. These men, generally liberally educated and thoroughly skilled, spent their lives amid the humble scenes of pioneer settlements, administering to the sick and afflicted, when, if they had chosen, they could easily have gained a lucrative practice in old settled communities, and at the same time maintained the highest standing in the upper circles of society. But instead, they adopted the life of a pioneer and labored arduously, riding night and day in the service of others.

Dr. James W. Hughes was one of the first settlers of Berlin. He was a native of Montgomery county, Maryland, and a graduate of the medical college of Washington, District of Columbia. In the year 1832 he came to Goshen, where he practiced two years, after which he came to Berlin, which was then but newly settled, and entered upon the practice of his profession, which he continued until his death in 1869. In 1834 he married Miss Paulina S. Brooke, who still survives. Their four children are Wallace K., Adaline V., Elizabeth H., and James B., all living except James B., who died July 25, 1881, at the age of thirty-five. Dr. J. W. Hughes died of paralysis. He was long a member of the Methodist Episcopal church, and did much toward supporting it. He was successful as a physician, and was a well known practitioner throughout all surrounding townships. Dr. Hughes was a man of much information, well versed in current literature, a frequent contributor to the religious and secular press and to medical journals. As a speaker he was gifted with more than ordinary ability. He was deeply devoted to his profession, and achieved in it a useful, honorable career.

During the war of the Rebellion Dr. Hughes not only gave liberally of his means, but gave the benefit of his medical skill gratuitously to the families of soldiers of his acquaintance. This is but one example of his many benevolent acts.

Dr. Wallace K. Hughes, oldest child of Dr. James W. Hughes, was born in Berlin township, now Mahoning county, Ohio, July 18, 1835. He passed his boyhood at home, and attended the

16*

district school until of sufficient age to begin the study of medicine under the tuition of his father. After having pursued his studies for some time, he attended lectures at the Cleveland Medical college, and graduated therefrom in 1859.

After graduating he returned home and began practice. In the fall of 1862 he received his first appointment as assistant surgeon, and started to join the Thirty-eighth regiment, Ohio volunteers, which was then at Nashville, Tennessee. Owing to obstruction of the railroad between Louisville and Nashville, he was unable to report to his regiment, and by order of the surgeon-general he reported to General Wright, commanding forces at Covington, Kentucky. Here he was placed on detached service, and remained about five months, during which time he organized an hospital, afterwards known as the Greenup-street hospital, at the corner of Greenup and Front streets. From this place he was transferred to Camp Dennison. After three months' failing health he was compelled to resign, and he returned home in the spring of 1863. The 21st of May the same spring he married Miss Martha F. Smith. In the following fall he received a request from the surgeon-general desiring him, if he felt able and willing, to return to military duty. Having expressed a willingness to return, the doctor was appointed assistant-surgeon of the Twelfth Ohio volunteer cavalry, and entered upon his duties. Afterwards the surgeon retired, and Dr. Hughes was promoted to that position, and filled it most acceptably until the close of the war. He was mustered out November 25, 1865. He was with the force that captured Salisbury prison, and was also with the forces under General Stoneman that followed Jefferson Davis in his failing fortunes, from Virginia, through North and South Carolina to Macon, Georgia, where he was captured.

Dr. Hughes is a member of Perry lodge No. 185, Free and Accepted Masons, Salem, Ohio. As a physician he is deservedly popular, and enjoys an extensive practice.

Mr. and Mrs. Hughes have never been blessed with children, but they adopted a boy, Oscar, who died April 2, 1879, aged eight years. Upon him they bestowed the deepest affection, and his loss was severely felt.

Mrs. Hughes was born in Berlin township, November 22, 1834. She is the fourth child of Dr. and Mrs. Lavina Smith. Her father is one of the first settlers of Berlin township, and located on the farm now owned by David King. Those of the family now living are: Mrs. Esther Porter, residing in Missouri; Mrs. Elizabeth Beardsley, residing in Ellsworth; Mrs. Mary King and Mrs. Hughes, Berlin. Her father married for his second wife Abigail Meach. Their three children are all dead.

JONATHAN KING.

Jonathan King was born in Armstrong county, Pennsylvania, January 5, 1804. His father, George King, was a native of the same State and married Sarah Sylvis, by whom he had a family of seven children, viz: Jonathan, the subject of this sketch; Christina (Frankfort), deceased; Elizabeth, deceased; Mary (McCulloch), deceased; Henry, a resident of Berlin; Anna (Wahl), and Phebe (Ramsdell), both of whom are residents of Indiana.

At the age of fifteen Jonathan King was apprenticed to a potter. He served a full apprenticeship but was dismissed without receiving the customary "apprentice suit" of clothes.

During the following winter he went with his uncle, John Wile, on a raft of saw-logs to Pittsburg to trade for flour for his mother. Failing to get flour sufficient in exchange for the saw-logs to last till harvest, and having no money he returned home. But not discouraged he started with several others with a four-horse team for the West, stopping in Springfield township, Mahoning county (then Columbiana county), Ohio, where he engaged to work during the summer for wheat, which was paid in advance, and sent back to his mother with the persons with whom he came. In the fall of the same year he returned to Pennsylvania and removed his mother, brothers, and sisters to Springfield township, Ohio.

In 1825 he was married to Lydia Peck, and in April, 1826, removed to Berlin township, Mahoning county (then Trumbull), Ohio, where he had purchased a farm the fall previous.

He settled upon his farm and devoted himself with diligence to the work of building up a home. His busy days and years of toil bore

fruit, and now in his old age (seventy-nine years) he can review his well spent life with the satisfactory reflection that none of his time has been wasted.

By strict integrity and economy Mr. King acquired considerable property, though he started with nothing but nature's endowments.

Before the days of railroads he was a noted teamster and made frequent trips from Pittsburg to Cleveland, and from Cleveland to the mouth of Huron river, usually driving six horses. At one time he made a trip from Pittsburg to Erie, Pennsylvania, for which he received $75. But such was the condition of the roads at that time that the entire amount except $2.60 was required to pay the necessary expenses of the journey. The life of a teamster in those days was one of hardships, and none but the most vigorous could long endure it..

In 1842 Mr. King was elected a captain of militia and held the office until the company disbanded.

He was the father of ten children, four of whom died in infancy and youth. The remaining six are as follow: David, who married Miss Mary Smith, and resides in Berlin; Catharine, married to George Kail, moved to Michigan, where she died; Joseph, married to Miss Lucinda Greenamyer, and resides in Berlin on the farm upon which his father first settled; Susannah, married to J. B. Shively, and resides in Berlin; Sarah, married to R. B. Engle, and resides in Salem, Ohio; Hannah, married to J. B. Hughes (who served two terms as auditor of Mahoning county, and is now deceased), and resides in Youngstown.

Mrs. King was born August 13, 1806, in Lehigh county, Pennsylvania, and moved with her parents to Springfield township, Mahoning county, Ohio, in 1808. She died February 22, 1875.

In religion, Mr. King was a firm adherent to the Protestant faith, and of deep conviction, zealous in good works and liberal in his contributions to the cause of Christ. He and his wife have both been lifelong members of the Evangelical Lutheran church. Politically he stood with the Democratic party, voting for General Jackson at the time of his second election, until the abolitionist Hale came before the people for their suffrages, when he voted for him. After the organization of the Republican party he

George Carson

voted with it until 1881, when his strong temperance principles compelled him to cast his ballot for the Prohibition candidate.

Mr. King is one of the most social and agreeable of men. His cheerful disposition and his sterling worth make him a favorite among the old and young.

The King family possess considerable native ingenuity and skill in the use of tools. Jonathan King is quite proficient in blacksmithing, carpentry, etc. His grandson, W. H. King, son of Joseph King, of this township, is the inventor of the King wind-mill, now so widely used throughout the Western Reserve. The manufacturers of threshing machines are indebted to David King for many suggestions and improvements in grain separators and clover hullers. David King began threshing when seventeen years old, and still follows the business. Joseph King has also been the proprietor of a threshing machine for a number of years, running one now with a steamer.

David, and his son, Mervin W., are the proprietors of a steam saw-mill, which is doing an extensive business. David also owns a half interest in the planing-mill, in the eastern part of the township, known as the Kimmel & King mill, which is also doing an extensive business

Honesty and sobriety characterize the entire family.

ALONZO STRONG.

William A. Strong, the father of the subject of this sketch, was born in Durham, Connecticut, and in 1804 removed with his wife, whose maiden name was Abigail Crane, to Atwater township, then Trumbull, now Portage county, Ohio. There Alonzo was born the following year, in 1805. William Strong, his father, was a soldier in the War of 1812, and was seized with a fatal fever, of which he died in 1814, and he was buried on the shore of Lake Erie.

Mr. Strong is the only survivor of three children, the others being daughters, named Eliza and Lucerne. After the arrival of the family in Ohio, he was sent back east to attend school, and remained some three years. He then returned to Ohio, and was bound out to Joseph Hartzell for eight years. After his term of service with Hartzell had expired, he learned the trade of cloth dressing, but worked at it only about six months. He learned the carpenter's trade, which he followed some six years, but finally engaged in farming on the place where he now lives. In 1829 he married Miss Christina Lazarus, by whom he had six children, as follows : Lavinia, who married Elijah Whinnery, and resides in Salem, Columbiana county ; William A., who married Miss Annie Marshall, and resides in Alliance ; Levi, dead ; Frederick, dead ; Julia, unmarried, and a child that died in infancy. Levi was in the war of the Rebellion, enlisting in 1862, and in 1863 was taken prisoner. He was taken to Richmond, then to Andersonville, where he died. Mrs. Christina Strong died in 1842, and in 1845 Mr. Strong was married again to Elizabeth Whinney (or Whinnery), whose parents were early settlers in Columbiana county, removing from Pennsylvania in 1804. By his second marriage he has had nine children, as follows : Serena (or Lorena), wife of William Hicker, resides in Illinois ; Edward and Edwin, twins—Edward is living and Edwin is deceased ; Lovisa, wife of Alvin Smith, resides in Illinois ; Ashley, who married Miss Annie Malinsby, and resides in North Benton ; Ophelia, unmarried ; Leora E., wife of Henry Koch, resides in Columbiana county; Alonzo C., and Wendell P. Edwin, the only deceased member of the family, was drowned at the age of eighteen months.

Mr. Strong cultivates a large farm of two hundred and fifty acres, and gives particular attention to the raising of sheep. He has served one term as justice of the peace.

GEORGE CARSON.

George Carson was born in Dauphin county, Pennsylvania, August 19, 1812. His parents were John and Catherine (Wentz) Carson, who removed to Trumbull county, Ohio, in 1832, and first settled on the farm now owned and occupied by James Weasner, in Berlin township. After residing there a number of years he moved to Milton, where he died at the age of seventy-four years. Mrs. Carson survived her husband a couple of years. They raised a family of seven sons and five daughters, named as follow: Sarah (dead), John, in Berlin; George in Berlin;

Sophia (Hiser), in Michigan; Jacob, in Portage county; Harriet, dead; William, in the West; Samuel, in Michigan; Robert, in Milton; David, in Michigan; Susan (Vaughn), in Ashtabula county.

George Carson was brought up on the farm. He was married in 1835 to Miss Catharine Gross, daughter of John and Christina Gross, who was born in York county, Pennsylvania, July 17, 1818. After his marriage he settled near Schilling's mills, in Berlin, where he resided until his removal to a farm at Berlin center, some eighteen years ago. The same fall he was elected justice of the peace and has held that office continuously since with the exception of only a few months. Mr. Carson, besides his farm at the center of Berlin, still owns a part of the farm on which he originally settled, near Schilling's mills.

Mr. and Mrs. Carson have had eleven children, one dying young. The others are as follow: Catharine married Cornelius Mott and lives in Portage county; Harriet married John Cessna and lives in Weathersfield township; Uriah married Mary Jones and lives in Lordstown; David has been married twice and lives in Deerfield, Portage county; Emily married Lawrence Shively, in Berlin; Minerva married Frank Keiser, both deceased; Ella married Jeremiah Shively, and lives in Berlin; Elmer married Addie Newton, and lives at Berlin center; William F., single, of Deerfield center, Portage county, is fitting himself for the medical profession; Clara married Amos Hoyle, and lives in Berlin. Uriah volunteered at the first call for troops in 1861, going out with the Nineteenth Ohio volunteer infantry and served three years. He was also out in the one hundred days' service as member of the One Hundred and Fifty-fifth Ohio National guard. David was also out in the same regiment.

Mr. Carson has always been an intelligent and industrious farmer and has prospered in his business. He and his wife are members of the Christian church.

———

HORACE ROWLAND

was born in Litchfield, Connecticut, February 18, 1805. He is the elder of two sons of David and Anna (Taylor) Rowland, the other son being Orrin. Mr. Rowland came to Berlin township in 1831, and located on the farm now owned by John Cronick, where he resided for twenty-five years. He then removed to the farm where he now is. He married, December 15, 1829, Miss Fidelia Caldwell, who was the youngest child of James and Esther (Pierce) Caldwell, who were born respectively March 20, 1760, and October 11, 1766. Their family consisted of the following children, viz: Betsey, born March 10, 1790; James, March 14, 1791; Margaret, June 9, 1792; Beulah, September 18, 1793; Samuel W., December 27, 1794; Oby, March 12, 1796; Milo, April 20, 1802; Lovina, November 29, 1804; and Fidelia, October 11, 1807—all now dead except Mrs. Rowland. Mr. Caldwell was a native of Scotland, and he and his wife were members of the Episcopal church. Mr. Rowland has accumulated a goodly share of this world's goods through his industry and economy, and is now living in comfort and independence. Mr. and Mrs. Rowland have no children. They are worthy members of the Methodist Episcopal church, their connection with the church extending over a period of about thirty years.

———

Rev. I. J. Miller was born in Springfield township, Mahoning county, February 22, 1850. He is the son of George and Elizabeth (Wilhelm) Miller and grandson of Henry Miller, who with his father moved into the woods in the west central part of Springfield when but a boy, about the year 1800. His early days were spent on the farm and in the district school. At the age of eighteen he began school-teaching, teaching during the winter and prosecuting his studies during the spring and fall at Poland Union seminary. Subsequently he took a regular course of theology in the Theological seminary in connection with Wittenberg college, Springfield, Ohio. He was licensed to preach the gospel by the East Ohio synod of the Evangelical Lutheran church at Canton, Ohio, October 18, 1875, and ordained to the gospel ministry by the same synod at Ashland, Ohio, September 11, 1876. August 1, 1876, he took charge of the Berlin pastorate, consisting of two congregations—one situated in Berlin township, the other in Lordstown, Trumbull county—of which he still continues to be the pastor (January 26, 1882). He has two brothers,

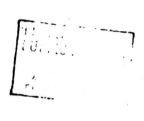

Horace Rowland

Mrs. Fidelia Rowland.

viz: Eli and A. C., both of whom are graduates of Wittenberg college and seminary, and are regularly ordained ministers of the Lutheran church. Also six sisters, three of whom are married to ministers of the same church, viz: J. F. Sponseller, Elias Minter, and W. M. Smith. He was married to Miss Louisa Spait, of Beaver township, and has two children, viz: Clarke E. and Cora A., aged respectively eight and six years.

Hezekiah Parshall, farmer, Berlin township, Mahoning county, was born in Springfield township, Columbiana county, now Mahoning, in the year 1812. His father, James Parshall, was a native of Orange county, New York, and came to Ohio in 1812 and settled in Milton township. His wife was Margaret Bacht, who bore him fourteen children. Mr. Parshall was one of the pioneers of that part of the county. He was a man of industry and reared a large family. They both died many years ago and are buried in Milton. Hezekiah Parshall was married, in 1839, to Miss Maria Shaffer, and has had a family of seven children, as follow: Mary, Susanna, Martha, Sophina, Solomon, Lewis, and James, all of whom are living but Sophina, who died at the age of five years. Mr. and Mrs. Parshall are members of the Lutheran church of Berlin.

John Eckis, the first of the family who came to Ohio, was born in Maryland in 1774, and about 1800 settled in Springfield township, then Columbiana county, now Mahoning. He settled in the woods, being among the first of the pioneers, built him a log-cabin, and there lived for upwards of twenty-five years, when he removed to Milton and purchased the place now owned and occupied by his son George. His wife was Catharine Lind, by whom he had the following children: Nicholas, John, Jacob, George, Daniel, Mary, Joseph, Susan, Catharine, Hannah, and Samuel. Joseph, Susan, Catherine, and Hannah are deceased. Mr. Eckis died in 1861, at the advanced age of eighty-seven. George Eckis, the fourth child of John and Catharine, was born in 1806 in Springfield township, now Mahoning county. At the age of twenty-six he was married to Miss Elizabeth Kale, and has had six children, viz: Tobias, Joshua, Eliza, Frederick, Mary, and George, all living but Eliza, who died at the age of thirty-eight. Mr. Eckis is a farmer by occupation, but

is able to work but little on account of his age. He and his wife are members of the Lutheran church. Tobias Eckis, the eldest son of George and Elizabeth, was born in Milton township, now Mahoning county, in 1833. He lived at home with his parents until he was thirty-four years of age when he married Miss Sarah Forder, by whom he has two children, George and Charles; another died in infancy. Mr. Eckis lived in Milton some three years after his marriage, when he bought the place where he now resides in Berlin township. He and his wife are members of the Lutheran church.

Robert Kirkbride was born in Bucks county, Pennsylvania, in the year 1800. He married, in the year 1824, Miss Sarah Shaw, and in 1832 removed to Ohio and settled upon the farm now owned and occupied by his widow in Berlin township, Mahoning county. There he resided until his death, and raised his family, consisting of nine children, two of whom are now deceased. Three died in infancy. The names of those who grew up are as follows: Nancy, Ferdinand, Mary, Benjamin F., Watson, James, Joseph, Asher, and Mahlon, all living but Mary and Asher. The latter enlisted in the One Hundred and Fifth Ohio volunteer infantry in 1862, and served until 1864, when he was mortally wounded at the battle of Lookout Mountain, and died in a few hours. The mother is still living, at the age of seventy-six.

Benjamin F. Kirkbride, the fourth child of the subject of the preceding sketch, was born in Pennsylvania in 1831. In 1853 he married Miss Lucinda Hoadley, who died in 1877. By this marriage there were no children. In 1878 Mr. Kirkbride was married to Miss Ellen Dickson, by whom he has had one child—Mabel. He followed farming until he attained his majority, when he went to blacksmithing, at which he still continues. Mr. and Mrs. Kirkbride are members of the Presbyterian church.

Houston Porter was born in 1822, and in 1847 was married to Esther Smith, who was a native of Connecticut, but came to Berlin township at an early date. The parents of Mr. Porter were among the early pioneers. He lived for fourteen years on the old homestead, and then bought the farm now owned and occupied by T. Campbell, where he lived sixteen years, and then removed to Missouri, where he now resides. He is the father of fourteen children, namely: Lovina C., Cecil S., Augusta A., Theda E. and Theron W. (twins), Wilbur O., Leroy W., Almedus, Ella S., Birdie F., Ida L., Effie M., George W. B., and Ulysses S. G. Theron W., Ida L., and Almedus are deceased. Lovina C., the eldest child, who was born in Ellsworth in 1848, became the wife, in 1876, of Elias Beckman, of Sweden. Mr. Beckman came to America in 1869, and first went to Illinois, where he remained two years. He then came to Ohio. He is now engaged in the tailoring business at Berlin center. Mr. and Mrs. Beckman have three children, Martha F., Cora L., and Arthur Garfield.

Eli Myers, the youngest child of Daniel and Anna Myers, was born on the farm where he now lives in Berlin township, Mahoning county, in 1837. His father, Daniel Myers, was a native of Pennsylvania, and came to Ohio with his parents in 1802, and settled in Springfield township, the county then being a dense wilderness. He afterwards moved to Berlin township, where he also settled in the woods, on the farm now occupied by his son Eli. He was married at the age of twenty-five to Anna Mary Rummel, and had a family of nine children, as follows: Christina, Susanna, Elizabeth, Margaret, Lucinda, Henry, John, Peter, and Eli. They are all living with the exception of Susanna and Lucinda. Mr. Myers was a hard-working and prosperous farmer, and lived to the good old age of eighty-two years. Mr. Eli Myers was married to Miss Barbara E. Reichards in 1859, and has eight children, as follows: John, Emery J., Henry, Clark, Elina, Serena, Martha J., and Anna Mary, all of whom survive. Mr. Myers has always followed farming, and is now (1881) serving his first term as justice of the peace. He and his wife are members of the Lutheran church.

Henry King was born in Armstrong county, Pennsylvania, in 1811. He came to Ohio in 1823 and settled in Springfield township, where he resided some four years. He was then deprived by death of his mother, whose loss was a severe blow to the family. He was then employed for three years by a man by the name of John Carns, and afterward learned the cabinet trade, at which he worked until he was twenty-one years of age. He then went to Fremont,

Ohio, and worked at the carpenter and joiner trade. An epidemic breaking out there he returned to Berlin and settled on the farm on which he now lives. He was married in 1836 to Miss Julia Ann Shrontz and has had seven children, viz: Royal, Wesley, Emeline, Isaac, Zephaniah, Margaret, and Lucy, all living but Isaac and Zephaniah. At the time of Mr. King's settlement there was only a small clearing on the place. He built him a log cabin and in connection with farming worked at the joiner trade, which he followed for about thirty years, when he was compelled by reason of his age to lead a less active life. He lived for three years in Deerfield, and while there, in 1873, his companion departed this life. She was a devoted wife and mother. Mr. King is one of the oldest and best known citizens of this township. He is a member of the Methodist Ediscopal church and a worthy citizen.

Adna B. Silver was born in New Jersey in 1800; married in 1821 to Miss Lydia Allen, and had a family of five children, viz: Sarah, Joseph, Elizabeth, Allen, and Mary, all of whom are living except the son Joseph. Mr. Silver came to Ohio in 1827 and settled in Berlin township, Mahoning county, on the farm now owned and occupied by his daughter Mary Linton. He erected his log-cabin in the woods, as the country was yet new. He was the pioneer blacksmith in that region, and made most of the implements which his neighbors used in clearing their farms. His wife died in December, 1868.

CHAPTER VI.
AUSTINTOWN.
PHYSICAL FEATURES.

Austintown is township two of range three of the Connecticut Western Reserve. It is bounded on the north by Weathersfield, Trumbull county, on the east by Youngstown, on the south by Canfield, and on the west by Jackson. The surface is quite level, excepting along the streams. The soil is similar to that in other parts of the county, is easily tilled, and produces good crops. Portions of it are stony, but there is a large number of excellent farms with good timber and pasture land. The Meander and several small creeks flowing into it drain the western half of the township. The eastern half has four small streams, the largest of which is known as Four-mile run, flowing towards the Mahoning. Four-mile run rises southeast of Austintown center and flows north and north-easterly until it leaves the township near the corner. Meander creek winds along the western border of the township, a part of its course being in Jackson, and enters Weathersfield township not far from the northwestern corner of Austintown.

The villages of the township are Austintown, West Austintown, and a part of Mineral Ridge.

ANCIENT WORKS.

On the farm of J. H. Fitch, near the village, was pointed out to the writer a spot which the early settlers believed to have been an Indian burying-ground. It is a space about three rods square, and at the time of its discovery by the whites, was loosely covered to the depth of several inches with small stones, which looked as though they had been thrown upon it. When these had been removed, beneath them were found stones closely packed together, the most of them being flattish in shape and set up edge-wise. These stones vary in size, some being no larger than a man's fist, while others are as large as a man's head. They are so closely im-bedded that it is a difficult task to remove them. Much of this curious structure yet remains un-disturbed and is believed to extend downward a depth of several feet. Why they were placed there and what they conceal still remains a mys-tery. On the trees which stood near the spot were noticed marks made as if by a hatchet, showing that the prehistoric people had a path to the place, marked, as were the white man's first roads, by blazed trees.

On the farm of Abraham Strock, west of the place above described, there is a work of similar nature, and likewise one on the Weaver farm, near West Austintown. The two last mentioned are somewhat smaller than that on the Fitch place. Some enterprising archæologist might find here material worthy of his investigation. These mounds or graveyards are all three situated near the Limestone run and were the densest part of the forest.

The early settlers say that the Indians had a lead mine somewhere on the Meander, from which they obtained large supplies of ore for the manufacture of bullets. They kept the spot a secret, however, and diligent search has failed to reveal it to the white man.

TIMBER.

The township was originally covered with a dense growth of timber. From the Meander to the center or the Salt spring tract, there was a magnificent growth of white oak. On the low lands were maples, and in various parts of the township, chestnut, beech, hickory, ash, cucum-ber wood, poplar, etc.

EARLY RECORDS.

The first records of the township have all been lost or destroyed. Only those of recent date are now in possession of the township clerk, there-fore the first officers' names cannot be given.

Among the first justices of the peace were James Russell, John Carlton, and William Trues-dale. The township was named after Judge Austin, of Warren, who was its land agent.

SETTLEMENT.

From the fact that many of the first settlers located here for only a short time, and then moved away, and owing to the meagre sources of information, the following account is not as complete as we should have made it, could we have found anybody at all well versed in the township's early history.

John McCollum bought the first land in the township in 1798 and erected a cabin upon it the same year. This cabin was on the farm now owned by his son Harvey, and was situated about one-half mile west of the township line, between Austintown and Youngstown. Here he moved his family in 1800. John McCollum was born in New Jersey, December 25, 1770. He married Jane (Hamson) Ayers, June 10, 1798. She was born in New Jersey, September 27, 1767, and married Robert Hamson, by whom she had five children: Elizabeth, Rachel, Michael, Jane, and Susan. By Mr. McCollum she had eight children: David and Mary (twins), Robert, John, Daniel, Anna, Ira, and Harvey. Mrs. McCollum was a woman of industry and economy, and largely assisted in paying for the farm by taking weaving to do. In the midst of an almost impenetrable wilderness, whose silence was unbroken save by the howling of wolves and the wild cries of bears, this worthy couple lived and completed their self-appointed task of securing a home for themselves and their children. John McCollum died April 7, 1849, a short time after his wife, who died March 19, 1849. Mr. McCollum was in the War of 1812 for a short time, under Colonel Rayen. He was for many years a Baptist, afterwards joining the Disciples. He was a life-long Democrat in politics.

Wendall Grove, from Pennsylvania, settled where his son, John Grove, now resides, in 1801.

Jacob Parkus settled on the farm of Jacob Leach at an early day. He sold out to Benjamin Leach, who spent his life in the township. John and Abraham Leach, brothers of Benjamin, also settled in the eastern part of the township, and remained several years.

James Russell was an early settler on land now owned by the widow Arms. After he left the place Jacob Miller, then Theophilus Cotton, owned the farm. Russell was a captain of militia in early times.

John Carlton settled on land now owned by the Webbs. He moved to Lordstown, thence to Brookfield.

The Webb family came to the township in 1819.

Edward Jones was an early settler on Fourmile run, who lived and died in the township. He brought up a large family. His son Seymour lived upon the old place until his death, some three years ago. Caleb Jones, a brother of Edward, was an early settler in the same neighborhood.

John Lane was an early settler on a farm part of which is now owned by Thomas James. He located in the woods, lived and died here. Henry, one of his sons, lived on the old place after him; moved to Missouri, and is now dead.

David Dillon was an early settler on the farm now owned by Jonathan Edwards, of Youngstown. He was the first captain of militia in this township. He sold out and moved west in this State, where he died. William, Aaron, Asa, Jonathan, Jesse, Cyrus, and Eli were his sons. Several of them are yet living in different parts of Ohio.

Robert Russell, in 1806, settled on Stony ridge, in the southwestern part of the township.

His parents came with him. After locating here, Robert was married to Miss Hamson. James, who resides in Jackson township; John, on the old place; Hamson, and Samuel, who died a few years ago, were his sons.

John Duncan was an early settler on the Hammon farm, in the southeastern part of the township. He sold to Gaily.

Among the earliest settlers were George Gilbert and family, who took up a farm adjoining the Russell farm on the east. There was a large family. George, the oldest son, settled in the western part of the township; his brother Jacob lived upon the old place. Both are now dead. Others of the family settled in different parts of the county.

Henry Ohl located where D. Lawrence now resides, in 1803. The sons and daughters are now all dead, excepting, perhaps, one daughter. Several members of the family resided for some time in the township and vicinity. Henry, one of the sons, lived on a farm near the old place some years, and died in Canfield. David and Michael were drafted for the War of 1812, but got only as far as Youngstown when they were returned. Henry Ohl, Sr., was a blacksmith, and had a shop on the farm. He was possessed of a good property, and was considered a shrewd, careful business man. Michael, David, Jacob, John, Abraham, Henry, and Jonathan were his sons, and Eve, Mary, and Polly the daughters. When the family came to the township the road had just been "slashed out," and they were obliged to clamber over the fallen logs to reach their home. In very early times the women were sitting one day on the porch of their two-story log house, when their little dog came out from under the porch, barking fiercely. On investigating to learn the cause of his excitement, they discovered a monster rattlesnake upon the stone steps. Eve, a female gifted with a different spirit from the first lady by that name, procured a stick, killed the serpent, and hung its body upon the gate. The reptile was so long that it touched the ground on both sides of the gate.

James J. Russell, from Pennsylvania, came about 1806. He died in 1870. He was a soldier of 1812. He was the father of ten children, six sons and four daughters, seven of whom are yet living, only two of them in this township, viz:

David Anderson.

Hannah L. Anderson.

Mrs. Jane Moore and Mrs. Davis Randolph.

John Truesdale was an early settler about one-half mile southwest of the center. He brought up a large family, none of whom are now living. His sons, John, James, and William, all married, lived, and died in the township upon the old farm.

Robert Fullerton settled on the southwest corner lot of the center, cleared up a farm and brought up a large family. His oldest son, Andrew, lived for a time in Austintown, then moved to Pennsylvania. The two next in age, Samuel and Joseph, sold their interest in the property to their youngest brother, Robert, who owned the whole farm a number of years. He died in Girard. None of the original family are now living.

William Wick, an early settler in the eastern part, had the first bearing orchard in Austintown.

Anthony and Henry Weatherstay were early settlers near the Four-mile run. Their sons and daughters are all now either dead or moved away.

Jacob Wise was an early settler in the same neighborhood. His sons, John and Jacob, still live in the township.

Jacob Harding, son of John Harding, an early inhabitant of Canfield, located on the place now owned by his son John, in 1808. The farm had been somewhat improved and cleared previously by a family of negroes by the name of Sisco. Jacob Harding had one son and four daughters. The son and three of the daughters are still living.

Archibald Ewing settled on the farm now occupied by his son John at about the same date. His children were Alexander, Thomas, William, John, Archibald, and Anna. Archibald lived and died in the township. Alexander and Thomas moved to Columbiana county, and William to Pittsburg.

The Cotton family were among the first settlers. Joshua, a captain of militia, lived and died in the township. Theophilus settled on part of the old farm, resided there several years, then moved north. John took a part of the old farm, sold out and moved away.

James Henry lived and died upon a farm about one-half mile south of the center, and brought up five or six children. One of the

daughters, Mrs. Mary Grove, still resides in the township.

Frederick Moherman in 1803 settled in the eastern part of the township. His sons, Daniel and Winchester, still reside in the township, and are reckoned among its prosperous farmers. Three sons also reside in Jackson.

Thomas Reed settled on the road running south from the center quite early. His widow is still living upon the old farm with her son Stephen. Amos also lives on the same road.

Henry Strack settled in the south part of the township; lived and died upon the farm now owned by Henry Crum, second. His sons were Henry, Samuel, John, William, Joseph, and Jacob. Several of his descendants now reside in the township.

Jacob Harroff settled in Canfield, then moved to this township. By his first marriage the children were John and Elizabeth, both of whom died in Portage county. By his second marriage the sons were Jacob, Andrew, William, and Lewis, all of whom lived and died in Austintown. Susan, Leah, and Rachel were the three daughters.

Henry Crum was an early settler at Smith's corners.

Abraham Wolfcale and his sons, John and Abraham, were quite early settlers on the road east of the center.

Henry Brunstetter was an early settler in the southeast of the township.

George Fulk settled north of the center road in the western part of the township. The family scattered and died.

The Harshmans were also early settlers. Jacob, David, and Matthias resided in the township several years.

John Jordan, a native of Ireland, came to the township in 1813. Previous to his coming here he had resided a few years in Poland township. His farm was the one adjoining on the west that now owned by his son, J. S. Jordan. His family consisted of five sons and five daughters. Two of the sons are yet living—James Jordan, in Crawford county, Pennsylvania, and J. S. Jordan. The father died in 1824, and the mother some years after. Abraham and James lived upon the old farm some years.

The Whitman tract, a part of the Salt springs tract, contained eight hundred acres, and be-

17*

longed to the Whitman heirs in Connecticut. Samuel Whitman cleared up a part of it, and settled at the center. Until about forty-five years ago no other clearing had been made upon the land.

In 1812 Frederick Shively settled upon the place where his son George, one of the oldest residents of the township, is now living.

The first white child born in Austintown township was John McCollum, son of the first settler. The date of his birth was 1803. He settled in Milton township, where he died in the fall of 1881.

EARLY DAYS.

Every cabin was a factory where clothing was manufactured. Busy hands kept the spinning-wheel and loom buzzing and slamming early and late. The number of mouths to feed and bodies to clothe was large in almost every household. Shoes were used sparingly, for new pairs might not be forthcoming when the old were gone. Often the girls and women could be seen walking to church barefooted, carrying shoes and stockings, which they put on when near the house. Tow and linen, buckskin, and similar goods, "home made," were the clothing worn by males of all ages. The girls' best dresses were frequently spun and woven by the wearer. An old resident remarks that the young ladies were just as pretty in those days as now; but could one of our fashionably dressed belles have stepped among them, some might have gone wild with envy and excitement.

Bears and wolves abounded, and it required the utmost vigilance to protect stock from them. Sheep, especially, often fell a prey to their ravages. At night the howling of the wolves could be heard in all directions. Deer were often shot, and furnished the early settlers an amount of meat of no small importance.

THE FIRST CHURCH

was a small log building, built by the Presbyterians on the Webb farm in the northern part of the township. It must have been built nearly seventy years ago. Later they erected a small frame church mentioned elsewhere.

THE FIRST SCHOOLS.

Of these little can be learned. They were usually kept in some log-cabin, which the thrifty old settler had abandoned for a more comfort-

able home. The children of those days had small advantages for gaining an education. As the schools were all conducted on the tuition plan, only those parents who were able to pay could send their children.

One of the first school-houses was situated near the spot where the Disciple church now stands. It was made of hewed logs, and contained a huge stone chimney. Asa Dillon and Elias Wick taught there years ago. Few of their pupils are now living.

A school was taught in a log-cabin on the Shively farm at an early date. Mr. John Grove, born in 1813, says that John Fullerton was the first teacher he remembers.

The spelling-book and the Bible were the principal text-books used. School-boy nature was then much the same as now, but mischief was not so openly carried on, for the rod was used unsparingly.

In 1812 there were several schools taught in log-cabins in various parts of the township. Isaac Alley was an early teacher in a cabin on the farm of Jacob Parkus.

TAXES LONG AGO.

We give below a list of the tax-payers of Austintown in 1803, and the amount of their taxes for that year. The whole amount ($9.22) could not have been enough to pay the expenses of assessing and collecting, unless, as was probably the case, county officers were content with a less salary than those of the present day.

AUSTINTOWN, RANGE THREE, TOWN TWO.

	Amount of Tax.		Amount of Tax.
Bayard, William.....	$ 15	McCollum, John.....	$ 33
Bayard, Benjamin	25	Musgrove, John......	32
Britton, Nathan	20	Moherman, Frederick.	30
Duncan, John........	52	Packard, Thomas....	69
Ewing, John.........	60	Packard, Daniel......	20
Ewing, Archibald.....	32	Roberts, Gilbert......	20
Grove, Wendell.......	40	Sanford, George.....	64
Guy, Matthew........	40	Sisco, James.........	12
Hayes, William, and		Sisco, Benjamin......	20
Samuel Ferguson.....	60	Sisco, William.......	32
Kirkpatrick, Robert...	32	Templeton, William..	48
Moore, Samuel......	16	Walker, Nathaniel...	30
McAllister, Alexander.	40	Withington, William.	40
Morgan, Thomas.....	40		
Total			$9 22

CHURCH HISTORY.

The inhabitants of Austintown have always held various religious beliefs. On account of death and removals the membership of the different churches is now quite small. There are, however, many earnest and sincere Christians in the township who have labored long and bravely to keep alive the religious interests.

THE DISCIPLES.

Elder Bently, of Warren, Walter Scott, of Pittsburg, and William Hayden, of this township, started what was known as the reformation, which resulted in the building of this church. The Disciples organized in 1828, and soon afterwards erected a church building in the northeastern part of the township on Four-mile run, which was used until the present house was built, in 1860 or 1861. John Henry and William Hayden were the first elders. Ira McCullom, Mrs. Jane Henry, the Hayden family, John Lane, and several of the Lantermans, Dillons, Lanes, and others were among the earliest members. William Hayden and John Henry were among the first preachers. Alexander Campbell often preached in the church. The Disciples have now about one hundred and twenty members, and hold services regularly.

THE BAPTISTS

were formerly quite numerous in this part of the township. They had an organization and held meetings in the Osborn school-house in Youngstown, also in a log church situated at the four corners between Austintown, Canfield, Boardman, and Youngstown townships. Many of them became members of the Disciples, and soon after the latter denomination built their church they disbanded.

THE PRESBYTERIANS

also had an organization and a church quite early. It was known as the Rehoboth Presbyterian church. They built a house one mile north of the center, which was afterwards moved to Ohltown on the north line of the township, where it remained until recently.

THE COVENANTERS,

or Reformed Presbyterians, built a house at Austintown center in 1844. The building was erected by the combined subscriptions of citizens of all denominations, with the agreement that it was to be used by any denomination when the Covenanters did not want it for their meetings. Among the principal subscribers were James Jordan, Abraham Jordan, Scott Jordan, Caldwell and William Porter. James Truesdale and John Truesdale were both elders and prominent members. The first regular preacher was Rev. McCrackoran. Since his time the preaching has been by various ministers sent by the presbytery. Formerly the church was quite large, there being about one hundred members shortly after the house was built.

EVANGELICAL.

The Evangelical church, West Austintown, was organized about 1841, and the house erected about 1853. The first meeting was held in Jacob Harroff's barn. The first prayer-meeting was at the house of Mrs. Catharine Gilbert. Meetings were held in private houses, barns, school-houses, groves, etc., for some time. Among the early members were Valentine Boley, Christina Gilbert, George Ohl, Conrad Lodwick, George Shaffer, Mary Kisner, and Betsey Ripple.

The first preacher was Rev. Joseph Long. Revs. Staley, Stofer, and Swartz were also early preachers in this church.

The society is small at present, as the most of the old members have died and their places have not been refilled.

THE UNITED BRETHREN,

West Austintown. A class was formed about 1859, comprising about ten members, among them being Sylvanus Pennell and wife, Leah Shaffer, Ira Wilcox and wife, Matthias McMahan and wife, and others. The first pastor was Rev. J. Knight. Other pastors—J. K. Sweihart, H. F. Day, David Kosht, and others. First presiding elder, Eli Schlutz. The house was built in 1863. The church now has about forty-five members, and maintains regular service.

THE EVANGELICAL EBENEZER CHURCH,

at Smith's corners, was organized in 1861, and the house of worship erected in 1861-62. John Gilbert, Henry Smith, and David Strock were the building committee. The principal subscribers were: J. P. Snyder, David Strock, Michael Buck, Jonas Naff. Number of members in 1862, seventeen. The church was dedicated December 21, 1862, Bishop Joseph Long, Presiding Elder J. L. Sibert, Revs. G. S. Domer and S. Wantersal being present. The first preachers were G. S. Domer and S. Wantersal for the years 1862 and 1863. Other pastors— J. D. Hollenger, Abraham Leohnar, J. J. Barnhart, Isaac Roller, John Domer, ——— Weaver, John Carmony, and Mr. Haupt, the minister now in charge. The church is small. Services are held every two weeks.

WEST AUSTINTOWN.

This thriving little settlement, a station on the Niles & New Lisbon railroad, has been built since the completion of that road in 1869. The first store was kept by D. B. Blott. He was afterwards in company with Homer Williams, and later with Wesley Ohl. Calhoun & Hardman kept store, in the building now occupied by Wesley Ohl, for about four years, commencing in 1871. The Anderson block was built by Robert McClure in 1871. The hotel was built the same year by James Kane, of Youngstown. He run this as a hotel until 1875, and still owns the property, but rents it. Wesley Ohl's store was built in 1871 by Calhoun, Hartman & Baldwin. The store occupied by Mr. Booker was built by him in 1871-72, but has been enlarged twice. He has been in business as a hardware dealer since 1872; has carried a stock of drugs during the past year.

The post-office was established in 1870, Winsor Calhoun postmaster, succeeded by Wesley Ohl, the present incumbent.

The stores in West Austintown are now as follows: Wesley Ohl, J. T. McConnell, general merchandise; Anderson & Brother, groceries; James Booker, hardware and drugs.

The physicians of West Austintown have been many, considering the short time since the village started. Dr. J. T. McKinley, now of Niles, opened an office here about 1870. He did not reside here, but in Jackson; had a drug store in West Austintown, and considerable practice, much of which he still continues. Dr. G. E. Rose, who had been a student in the office of Dr. McKinley, bought out the drug store and practiced here some five years, then moved to Birmingham, Erie county, having disposed of his stock of drugs to B. F. Phillips, of North Jackson. Dr. Kline was the next physician, for a short time. Dr. L. B. Ruhelman, of Green, next practiced about two years, then moved to North Lima. Dr. S. T. Keese, of North Jackson, has practiced in this place three or four years; he opened an office here last spring. Dr. I. W. Bard, of Mineral Ridge, located here in 1881.

AUSTINTOWN CENTER

is a thriving little country village or "cross-roads," pleasantly and prettily located. It was not settled so early as other parts of the township, although more than sixty years have elapsed since the first house was located here.

The first store was kept on the southwest corner by Alexander Thompson, probably as early as 1822. Soon after him Dr. Alfred Packard started a small store on the corner where Corll's tavern stands. Dr. Packard sold out to James Hezlip, who started Caldwell Porter in business in 1830. Caldwell Porter afterwards moved to the southwest corner, where he continued business until about 1848. He came here a poor Irish boy, but by his unwavering industry, energy, and scrupulous attention to business, he became quite wealthy. A few years after he settled here he returned to Ireland and married, and then came back to his store. He was widely respected during his residence here, and his successful business career may well be pointed out to the young as an example of what pluck and strict attention to business are able to accomplish. From Austintown he went to Cincinnati, and there, too, he prospered. He is now dead. Few country merchants can point to a more prosperous record than that left by him on the minds of the people of Austintown.

Judge Rayen started a store here—date not known, perhaps 1830—on the corner where the Doncaster house is, and employed Cornelius Thompson to keep it. About 1834 he built the brick store on the northwest corner. The business changes have been so many that it is not very easy to trace them. John Cotton kept store on the southeast corner in 1831-32. Joseph McCaughtesy kept a public house, and later a clothing store on the same corner. He put up the greater part of the present hotel, and was quite a successful business man for several years. William Porter was in company with his brother a short time, then bought him out, and continued as a merchant here until 1857. Austin Corll kept a tailoring and clothing establishment for several years. Isaac Hoover and Levi Crum, who acted as clerks for William Porter, were merchants in this place a number of years. John Lanterman kept in brick store a short time.

Who kept the first tavern we are unable to learn. Alexander McKinney, Snyder, Whitsal,

Robert Fullerton, and others, have kept the house now owned by Corll.

The business of the place at present is represented by the following: Meander house, Eli Corll; Doncaster house, J. P. Hill; Fitch, Smith & Co., and Abram Forney, general stores; E. Creps, undertaker and furniture dealer. There is also a blacksmith and wagon-shop, a shoemaker's shop, and a harness shop.

The post-office was probably established as early as 1820. Theophilus Cotton was the first postmaster. His successors' names cannot be learned.

The first physician was Dr. Peer. Dr. Alfred Packard was the only one who resided here for any great length of time. He was a son of Thomas Packard, an early settler in the southeastern part of the township.

COAL MINES.

The first mine opened at West Austintown was the Harroff slope, where operations were begun in 1870 by John M. Owen, John Stambaugh, and others, under the name of the Harroff Coal company. The Harroff slope having become exhausted, in the fall of 1880 this company sank a shaft and commenced mining on the Jordan farm. The shaft is one hundred and seventy-one feet deep. They employ about sixty-five men and produce about one hundred and thirty tons of coal per day.

In 1871 the New Lisbon Coal company opened the Pennell mine and are still working it successfully. The slope is about four hundred and fifty feet and the coal of prime quality. This company employs about seventy-five men and mines about two hundred and fifty tons per day.

The Anderson Coal company opened a bank on the Anderson farm in 1878, which they worked for a short time, but as it was not successful the mine was abandoned.

Dalzell & Co., of Niles, have commenced work on a new bank just north of West Austintown during the present summer of 1881.

The Tod, Wells & Co. bank, on the farm of Henry Kyle, near Mineral Ridge, was opened and a shaft sunk about 1858, and has been quite successfully and largely operated up to the present time. Morris, Robbins & Co. leased the mine and operated it for some time, but it is now in the hands of Tod, Wells & Co.

The Ohltown bank, Harris, Maurer & Co., was opened about 1868, and worked quite extensively until 1880, when it was exhausted.

The McKinney shaft on the Tibbetts farm near Mineral Ridge was begun in 1871 by Henry Smith & Co., and afterwards worked by Powers & Wick, and Warner, Arms & Co. During the last five years it has not been in operation.

The Thornton bank was on the old Cleveland farm. Operations were commenced in 1870 by Case, Thornton & Co., under the name of the Ohltown Coal company. Some of the bank is still worked by the John Henry Mining company, who sank a shaft about three years ago. They employ about sixty men and produce about one hundred tons daily.

The Leadville shaft on the Lanterman farm was commenced some eight years ago. A great deal of capital has been expended upon this mine, but the water in it has always been troublesome. During the summer of 1881 a fire in this shaft caused great damage.

The mines just mentioned are only the most important. There are many small banks which have been operated on a small scale. The mining interest in Austintown is of great importance. The supply of coal will doubtless continue to hold out many years.

OTHER BUSINESS INTERESTS.

The township contains many deposits of iron ore, both of the kidney and black-band varieties. Before the days of railroads ore was taken out and hauled to the furnaces in considerable quantities.

Limestone of good quality has been quarried in many parts of the township, and the supply is almost inexhaustible. Several lime-kilns have been in successful operation. There are also quarries of sandstone and of flagstone yielding good material.

A mill for crushing and grinding limestone, to be used as a fertilizer, has recently been set up in the southern part of the township by Calhoun & Co.

The first and only furnace for the reduction of iron ore in this township was the Meander furnace, built by William Porter and others near Ohltown.

The only grist-mill, so far as is known, was built by William Irvin on Four-mile run, near the northeastern corner of the township. Although it was a small affair, it did considerable work for several years.

There were no saw-mills at an early date. The first one was built some thirty-five years ago in the eastern part of the township, south of the center road. It was built by Andrew J. Brickley. A few years later Harvey McCollum built a saw-mill on the same stream or "run," near the township line. These, with the steam saw-mills of recent date, are believed to have been the only ones in the township.

John Justice, recently deceased, operated a tannery north of the center on the Ohltown road for many years. Robinson Young also had a tannery in the southwestern part of the township for some years.

Many of the early settlers operated small copper stills, which they turned to account by using up their surplus grain, and putting it into a more salable form.

Henry Ohl built a mill upon his land at an early date for the manufacture of linseed oil. It was upon a small stream on the D. Lawrence place. There was a dam and a mill race some eighty rods in length. A part of the latter is still visible. This oil mill was one of the first built in this part of the country, but it was not a success.

Robinson Young settled in the township in 1826, and soon afterwards built a tannery, which he operated in company with his brother William. They boarded at Archibald Ewing's for seventy-five cents per week each. The tannery contained about twelve vats. The Youngs cut and closed boots and shoes and had them bottomed, and in this way disposed of their leather. Robinson Young used to work on the shoe-bench with the Bible open before him, diligently studying its pages. It is said that he learned the book almost by heart in this way.

GRAVEYARDS.

Of these there are five in the township. That known as the Brunstetter graveyard is the oldest, and was laid out as early as 1823. The first burial made there was the body of John Doane, a grandson of Robert Russell, one of the earliest settlers. Doane died when quite a young man. William Truesdale was the next person buried there, probably in 1823. The next year twenty-two children were carried off by dysentery in less than two weeks, and all were buried in this graveyard.

The graveyard adjoining the Disciples' church is probably the next oldest.

BIOGRAPHICAL SKETCHES.

WILLIAM PORTER.

William Porter, Austintown township, Mahoning county, was born in county Donegal, Ireland, May 22, 1801. He was educated in the common schools. In 1837 he came to Mahoning county, and was a merchant for twenty years. In 1857–58 he built the Meander furnace, and was engaged in smelting for two years. Through unfortunate endorsements, in less than three years he lost his fortune, and since that time has engaged in no active business.

In September, 1843, Mr. Porter was married to Mary Nesbat, a native of Mercer county, Pennsylvania. They have had four children, the youngest dying in infancy—James N., superintendent of a coal company in Jefferson county, Pennsylvania; Charles W., druggist, Niles, Trumbull county; and Isabella, who married Robert McCordy, president of the First National bank, Youngstown.

In politics Mr. Porter is a Democrat; in religion a Presbyterian. His wife is a Covenanter. During the past year, though over eighty years of age, he assessed Austintown township. Mr. Poter is a hale and hearty old man, enjoying the respect of all who know him.

DAVID ANDERSON.

David Anderson was born in Londonderry, Ireland, August 12, 1816. He was the youngest of three children of David Anderson, farmer. His mother died when he was a boy, and after that event finding home life distasteful, he left his father, a well-to-do citizen, and his two sisters, Margaret and Jane, and started alone for the land of the free. To one accustomed to the refinements and comforts of home, never having been away from home a day in his life, crossing the broad Atlantic to gain a living in a strange land was an undertaking of great moment. He landed in Philadelphia in 1832 and remained there seven years. His first work was setting curb-stones; next he went into a wholesale grocery, in which he remained several years. In April, 1839, he came to Youngstown, Ohio, and engaged in a general merchandise store with a partner, the firm being Anderson & Wick. The firm in a few years became somewhat involved and the partnership was dissolved. Mr. Anderson, by reason of his known integrity and business capacity, was enabled to go into business for himself, which he did, and he afterward paid every dollar of his indebtedness. He carried on his business for one year at Austintown, and then for thirty-seven years kept a general assortment store at Jackson, Mahoning county. This store he closed out April, 1881, being then the oldest merchant in the valley. Some twenty years ago he traded his stock of goods for a fine farm in Lordstown township, Trumbull county, and sold his interest in a foundry he had purchased and commenced business again with his previous success and with his old patrons. April 10, 1842, he married Julia Phillips, who was born in Warren township, and was a step-daughter of 'Squire Robert Carr. About sixteen months after her marriage she died—August 8, 1843. February 10, 1847, he married Hannah L. Shaw, a native of Lawrence county, Pennsylvania, the result of which union was four children, viz: W. S., an attorney of Youngstown, Ohio; Julia E.; Margaret J., who married Charles K. Phillips, who was killed three years ago by a hay-fork falling upon him, and David Fitch, resides at home. The wife and mother died October 14, 1879, aged sixty. Mrs. Anderson was a daughter of Dr. William Shaw, a leading physician of New Castle, Pennsylvania, and was born and brought up in that town, where she resided until her marriage. She was a member of the Presbyterian church, a good and faithful wife and mother, highly esteemed by all who knew her.

Mr. Anderson is at present largely engaged in farming and stock raising. He has the management of about nine hundred acres of land. But his enterprising business spirit will not admit of his devoting his entire attention to agriculture, and he intends to again engage in mercantile business. For many years Mr. Anderson has been a member of the Presbyterian church.

NOTES OF SETTLEMENT.

Charles Gilbert, farmer, Austintown township, Mahoning county, was a native of Pennsylvania. About the year 1821 he came to Mahoning county, where he remained four years, and then bought a farm north of Warren, on which he lived until his death. He was of German descent, his grandfather having come from Germany. His father, George Gilbert, came to Ohio several years in advance of him. Charles Gilbert married Magdalene Miller, a native of the same State, by whom he had nine children— Mary, Hannah, Benjamin, Elizabeth, Manly, Susan, Margaret, David, and Catharine. Hannah, widow of Thomas Reed; Benjamin, who resides in Warren; Susan, who married Martin Bear and resides in Hicksville; and Margaret, who married James Morgan, and now lives in Western Ohio, are still living. Mrs. Gilbert's parents were also from Germany.

William H. Burford, undertaker, Mineral Ridge, Ohio, was born in Swansea, Glamorganshire, Wales, March, 1813. He was educated in the Swansea academy, and the Carmarthen academy, also at the Academy of Bristol, England. At one time he studied with the intention of entering the ministry, but afterwards gave it up. He was apprenticed to a linen draper at Carmarthen, and after thoroughly learning the trade, he procured a situation at London, and worked in that and other places for a number of years. He had determined to emigrate to this country and locate in Texas, but did not at that time. Preferring some other trade to the one he had adopted he learned that of cabinet-making. He finished this trade when about twenty-seven, and for about three years subsequent was engaged as a teacher in the country schools, and was usher in the grammar school at Swansea for a time. February 6, 1849, he was married to Mary E. Jenkin, by whom he has three children—William R., born February 5, 1850; Sarah Louisa, November 27, 1859; Maggie E., June 17, 1862. Two years after his marriage he emigrated to America, finally settling in Scranton, Pennsylvania, where he resided some six years. In the fall of 1856 he came to Mineral Ridge. Here he engaged in his business of the manufacture of furniture, and undertaking, in which he still continues. He is a member of the Episcopal church and of the society, "Temple of Honor." In politics he is a Prohibitionist. Mr. Burford is the pioneer business man of Mineral Ridge.

Stephen Anderson (deceased) was a native of Ireland. He was born June 21, 1799, and came when a small child with his parents to America. His parents were among the early pioneers of Trumbull county, having settled in Liberty township about 1802. Stephen was raised upon the farm and after he became old enough he was given the management of a large farm and a saw-mill. He married on his nineteenth birthday —June 21, 1818—Elizabeth McKinley of Trumbull county, and had a family of ten children: James, Eliza, Margaret, William, Nancy, Hannah, Mary, Silas, John and Alvin. James and Mary are deceased. He was a member of the Presbyterian church, as was also his wife. In politics he was a Democrat. He died July 9, 1872, and his wife December 7, 1879.

Silas Anderson, grocer, West Austintown, Mahoning county, son of Stephen and Elizabeth Anderson, was born in Liberty township, Trumbull county, February 2, 1836. He worked upon the farm and in the saw-mill until he was about twenty years of age, the last two working for himself. He then engaged for two years in the livery business at Austintown. During the next few years he operated in coal, engaged principally in prospecting, leasing and drilling. He then moved upon the farm where he now lives, near West Austintown. Some four years ago he started a grocery store at West Austintown, and soon after purchased the brick block in which his business is located. May 7, 1861, he was united in marriage to Mary, daughter of William Hawser, who was born March 24, 1843. They had five children, three of whom are living, viz: Edward, born January 18, 1865; Manning, born February 1, 1867; Laura, born July 9, 1880.

Levi Crum, dealer in wool, etc., Austintown township, Mahoning county, was born in Austintown township February 7, 1832. He is the fourth of nine children of John Crum, born in Pennsylvania, but who came to this county when four years of age. John Crum's father, Henry Crum, Sr., was a native of Pennsylvania, and a farmer by occupation. He was a soldier in the War of 1812. He was the father of five children: John, Jonathan, Lydia, Henry, and Samuel. Only Jonathan and Henry are now living.

John Crum was a farmer and stock-dealer, a man well and favorably known as a successful business man. His wife was Catharine Fenstemaker, of Bedford county, Pennsylvania. They had nine children, viz: Eli, Gideon, Mary, Levi, Susan, Margaret, Sarah (deceased), Amanda, and John (deceased). Mr. Crum was a Presbyterian, and in politics a Democrat. He died November 14, 1873, in his seventy-second year. His wife died October 3, 1875, in her seventy-fifth year.

Levi Crum remained at home until of age, then engaged in clerking for four years, after which he bought out Joseph McCaughtery and kept a general merchandise store for eight years. Then he had J. H. Fitch as his partner for eight years, and afterwards A. Forney for three years. About five years ago Mr. Crum sold out to Forney & Raver and since then he has been in the wool business. On the 7th of February, 1857, he married Meno Winters, who came from Germany when ten years of age. This marriage resulted in two children, one of whom died in infancy. The oldest, Lillie F., was born September 6, 1858. She married William S. Fairman, of Youngstown. Mr. Crum's wife died in January, 1864. March 20, 1866, he married Eunice Grove, nee Ousborne. She had two children by her former marriage, Minnie and Lulu Grove. Mr. Crum is a Presbyterian, and in politics a Democrat. He is a thorough business man, and his integrity and genial disposition have gained him many friends.

Adam Flick, farmer, Austintown township, Mahoning county, son of Frederick and Mary Flick, old time residents of Tuscarora valley, in what is now Juniata county, Pennsylvania, was born in said State, April 6, 1783. September 2, 1806, he married Elizabeth Polm, daughter of John Polm. To them eleven children were born: John, born April 3, 1807; Jacob, March 24, 1809; Benjamin, January 28, 1811; Samuel, February 25, 1813; Sarah, January 7, 1815; Thomas, March 2, 1817; William, December 4, 1818; Margaret, December 8, 1820; Susan, December 28, 1822; Nancy, March 12, 1825, and Mary, May 25, 1829. Margaret, Mary, and Susan, died in infancy. Benjamin, Jacob, and Samuel have died within the last six years. Jacob married Henrietta Rumsy, of Austintown, and removed to Mercer county, Pennsylvania;

William Porter

Mrs Wm Porter

Benjamin married Jane Gibson, daughter of Robert Gibson, of Trumbull county, and lived for a number of years at Farmington ; Samuel married Mary, a sister of Henrietta Rumsy, and afterward moved to Lordstown ; John married Mariah McCoy, and resides in Lordstown ; Sarah, wife of Samuel Cook, lives on the home place ; Nancy, wife of Michael Diehl, lives in Wells county, Indiana. Adam Flick, with his family, came to Austintown township in 1824, and lived for the first four years on the Buck farm. He bought for $3.50 per acre one hundred acres of wild land, upon which he built a log house in the fall of 1828, and moved into it in the following spring. At once began the task of clearing away the forest and making fertile fields in the wilderness, and raising therefrom, not only food for the family, but the means with which to pay for the farm. They came with one wagon and three horses, two of which died soon after their arrival. Years of steady toil had its effect upon the stubborn forest, and Adam Flick lived to see the wilderness become almost a garden, and the region round about possessing all the advantages of civilized life. His life, which was one of many hardships, closed April 28, 1851. His wife could read English and German with ease, although her attendance at school lasted but about six months. She did her part fully in making a home in the wilderness, and died February 29, 1843.

Thomas Flick, farmer, son of Adam Flick, was born in Pennsylvania, March 2, 1817. He, like his father, received but little schooling, but by observation has succeeded in gaining much valuable knowledge, which has made him a first class farmer and business man. His brother William had but little better school advantages. Together they have added to the old farm, and now have over two hundred acres, which is one of the best managed farms in the county. They deal largely in horses and cattle. Both are Republicans, practical farmers, and worthy men. They have lived in the same school district over fifty-seven years.

Frederick Moherman, one of the earliest pioneers of Austintown township, was a native of Maryland. On account of the destruction of property during the Revolutionary war, he and an uncle moved to Washington county, Pennsylvania. He was then about sixteen years of age,

and remained in Pennsylvania several years, when he and a family by the name of Park came to Austintown to look at the country. He subsequently came out again, and then purchased a hundred and fifty acres in the southeast corner of Austintown township, erected a cabin and made a clearing. He then returned to Washington county, Pennsylvania, and married Mary Horn, and the next spring he moved out and settled in Austintown, where he spent the remainder of his life. When he settled there the Indians had not disappeared, and the wild animals were far more plenty than neighbors. There were no roads for miles around, and no mills. With these surroundings he and his young wife began housekeeping. They both lived to witness vast changes wrought, and to see the wilderness become a prosperous region. They had nine children, as follows : John, Abraham, Daniel, Robert, Ann (now Mrs. Woodward, of Lordstown), Betsy, who died when about twenty; Austin, who resides at Ashland, Ohio; Rachel, who married George Lynn, of Canfield, and Winchester, who lives on the old homestead. Daniel lives near him in Austintown, and the three other brothers live in Jackson.

Robert Moherman, the fourth son of Frederick Moherman, was born in Austintown township, Mahoning county, February 11, 1809. He received his education in the pioneer subscription schools, but after he got to be of a size to work, he was permitted to attend even those but little. When about twenty-seven he began clearing and improving the farm on which he now lives, boarding with a family that occupied the place some nine years. In October, 1840, he was married to Catharine, daughter of Robert McCain, of Ellsworth township. This marriage was blessed with four children: Robert, John, Seth, and Mary Ellen. who became the wife of Ogden Rose. Mr. Moherman cast his first vote for Andrew Jackson ; he is now a Republican.

Wendell Grove, deceased, was a native of Northumberland county, Pennsylvania. He was a carpenter by trade, but principally a farmer by occupation. From Northumberland he went to Beaver, Pennsylvania, where he married Miss May, by whom he had five children: Katie, David, Benjamin, Susan, and Elizabeth. This wife dying, he married Jane Coon, of Juniata county, Pennsylvania. They had eight children:

Jacob, Andrew, Maria, Eve, John, Abraham, Joseph, and Reuben, of whom Jacob and the two daughters are dead. Between the birth of the second and third child, they removed to their new home in the wilderness, settling in Austintown township, where he purchased about two hundred acres of land at $1.25 an acre. This farm is now occupied by his son John. About two years prior to his moving here with his family, he came and cleared a piece of land and made other preparations for his removal. He arrived at his new home on the third day of April, 1800. There were no neighbors nearer than five miles, and wild animals were numerous and often troublesome. He was a great hunter, as well as a hard working farmer. He had been in the war of the Revolution, and lived to the great age of ninety-nine years and six months. He witnessed, during his long life, which closed in Springfield township, December 19, 1849, great and important changes—greater than many are permitted to see. His wife survived him until March 27, 1857. Both were members of the Lutheran church.

John Grove, farmer, Austintown township, was born in Mahoning county January 4, 1813. He is the fifth child of Wendell Grove. He remained upon the farm with his father until he reached the age of twenty, when he went to Youngstown and learned the carpenter's trade, which he followed for some six years. For several years he was engaged in various occupations until at length he bought the old homestead, where he now lives. He now has two hundred and thirty-two acres of land under good cultivation. His farm is managed as a stock farm. He married, January 11, 1838, Mary McCullick, a native of Canfield township. They have had five children—Rosina, Orlando R., Melvina, Florence E., and C. G. The third child died when quite small.

Rogers Hill was born in Sussex county, Delaware, January 31, 1799. When he was five weeks old his parents removed to Redstone, Pennsylvania, where they remained two years, when they moved to the forks of the Beaver in Columbiana county, where they remained until Rogers was of age. He was the oldest of ten children of Robert and Patience Rogers Hill, both natives of Delaware. Grandfather Rogers was an Englishman and a sea captain. On his father's side they were from Holland. Rogers Hill took up shoemaking, which he followed for twenty-one years in Pennsylvania and Ohio. September 20, 1820, he married Eliza Chambers, a native of Pennsylvania and daughter of W. Chambers, also a native of Pennsylvania. Her ancestors were from Ireland. Their children are John, Robert, William, Eliza, Jane, Joseph, George, Matthew, Patience, Mary, Ann, Alvira, and James. The mother died February 4, 1873. April 9, 1874, he married Phœbe Anderson of Hubbard, Trumbull county. From Little Beaver he removed, in 1833, to Ohltown, where he resided several years engaged in farming. He then moved to the mouth of Little Hocking in Washington county, where he remained thirty years, attending a wood yard. September, 1872, he returned to Austintown township.

James P. Hill, hotel-keeper, Austintown, Mahoning county, youngest child of Rogers Hill, was born in Wood county, now West Virginia, March 4, 1845. He attended the common schools of his native State and for one year the Iron City college of Pittsburg. When nineteen he was apprenticed to a blacksmith and served three years. After working at his trade one year he went upon the Ohio river as cabin watchman on a boat which ran between Cincinnati and Louisville, in which he continued for some time, and then established a wagon shop at Parkersburg. In this business he continued a year and then came to Austintown, where he carried on his trade for a short time and then commenced the business in which he is now engaged. Some two years since he went to Jackson and kept the Jackson house. In the spring of 1881 he purchased the Northwestern house at Austintown, and is still located there, and is now proprietor of the Doncaster house. He was married, October 18, 1870, to Lucy Strock, born October 21, 1846, and daughter of Abraham Strock, of Austintown township. They have four children, viz: Guy, born February 5, 1872; Minnie, August 28, 1874; Edna, December 24, 1876; Earl, November 27, 1879. In politics Mr. Hill is a Democrat.

Lewis Harroff, Jr., farmer, Austintown township, Mahoning county, was born in said township May 13, 1833. He is the third child of Lewis Harroff, Sr., who was a native of Pennsylvania and who came to Mahoning county when but two years of age, settling first in Boardman township. His father, Jacob Harroff, was a shoemaker by trade, and before his marriage was a soldier in the Revolution. He married Kittie Kline. They had eight children—Polly, Susan, Jacob, Andrew, William, Lewis, Leah, and Rachel. By a former marriage there were two children—John and Betsy. Lewis, Sr., being a son of poor parents was permitted to attend school but little and never learned to read or write. He early began farming, which occupation he has since followed. May 11, 1827, he married Mary Gilbert (who died in October, 1880), daughter of Jacob Gilbert, by whom he had five children—Catharine, Sarah, Mary Ann, Lewis, and William. The two oldest girls died during early childhood. Mary, wife of John Franklin, died a few days before her mother, who died in October, 1880. The sons still reside in the township. Lewis Harroff, Jr., had but limited school advantages. At the age of twenty he apprenticed himself to John Gilbert, a cabinet-maker of Austintown, and served there two years, but never worked at the trade afterward. The next three years he worked in a carriage shop at Taylor's corners, and there began carpentering, at which he has been more or less engaged up to the present time. In 1870 he moved upon the farm where he now lives. November 11, 1859, he married Rebecca Brunstetter, daughter of Henry Brunstetter. She was born May 9, 1836. To them have been born three children, one of whom is dead, viz: Perry, who was born February 4, 1859, and died December 30, 1863; W. Henry, born February 24, 1865; and Minnie Pearl, March 13, 1880. Both Mr. and Mrs. Harroff are members of the Evangelical church. He is a Republican, though never a politician, having never sought or held office. He is a straightforward man, well and favorably known.

Seymour A. Jones, deceased, was born in Austintown township, Mahoning county, October 17, 1821. His wife and children are still living here. He was a farmer by occupation, an earnest Republican in politics, and in religion a member of the Disciples' church. His first wife was Martha Burnett, by whom he had four children, viz: Mary, Virgil, Samantha Jane, and Edson Scott. His second wife, whom he married December 9, 1856, and who is still living,

was Mary, daughter of William and Susan (Earnest) Powers, of Perry county, Pennsylvania. She was born June 20, 1833. Her parents came to Ohio when she was about one year old. Her father was a merchant for several years when a young man, but went to farming later on account of his health. Mrs. Jones is the oldest of six children, the names of whom are as follows: Mary, John, Belle, Almira, William, and Lucius Foster. Mrs. Jones is the mother of ten children,—George, William, Kittie, Birdie E., Lucy E., John, Grant, Minnie A., Thomas, and Etta May. Mr. Jones died July 10, 1878.

T. F. James was born in Somersetshire, England, May 15, 1834. He was educated in the public schools of his native country, attending only until about twelve years old. From that time until he was eighteen he was engaged in mining. In 1852 he came to Austintown township, where his work was the same as in England until fifteen years ago, when he began farming about a mile east of Mineral Ridge, where he is at present engaged in raising fine stock. April 5, 1858, he married Margaret Blunt, daughter of Edward Blunt of Weathersfield township, Trumbull county. She was born May 15, 1838. This marriage was blessed with eight children, Susan, Celia A., Hannah, Maggie, Sadie, Will, Edward, and John. Mrs. James is a member of the Disciples' church. Her father, Rev. Edward Blunt, was born in North Wales in 1805, and lived to the age of sixty-six. For twenty-four years prior to his death he lived and labored at Mineral Ridge. He preached for some years for the Welsh Methodist church in Pennsylvania. After coming to Ohio he became a convert to the Disciples' faith, and joined the Welsh Baptist church. He was a zealous Christian.

Solomon W. Lynn, farmer, Austintown township, Mahoning county, was born in Canfield township, then Trumbull county, December 29, 1817. His father was John Lynn, a native of Berks county, Pennsylvania, a weaver by trade, but during his residence in Ohio followed farming. He came here in the early settlement of the country, and erected a saw-mill upon his farm, known as the 'Squire Lynn farm. When Solomon was about six years of age his father returned to his old home in Pennsylvania, where he resided until his death. By his wife, Barbara

Will, he had seven children, three girls and four boys. The girls all died when they were quite small, and in a few days of each other. Of the boys, all are now deceased except the subject of this sketch. When about thirteen his father died, and he worked upon a farm for some three years, when he was apprenticed to learn the shoemaker's trade, at which he worked for two and a half years. He eventually came to Pickaway county, Ohio, but afterwards moved to Canfield, Mahoning county, where he followed his trade. He carried on his trade for twenty-three consecutive years. In 1844 he moved to Canfield, and in 1849 to the farm where he now lives. August 30, 1849, he married Elizabeth, daughter of George Lynn, a brother of John Lynn's father (our subject's grandfather), Philip Lynn. She was born in Canfield, June 28, 1822. They have two children, George W., born August 14, 1850; Mary E., September 19, 1856. Mr. Lynn's politics is Democratic.

Benjamin Leach, a native of New Jersey, came to Austintown township, Mahoning county, in the year 1819, and bought the Jacob Parkhurst farm of one hundred acres, which was partially improved and for which he paid $1,800. He was a blacksmith by trade, but after coming to Ohio he engaged principally at farming. Within a year or two after his arrival he erected the house in which his son, J. B. Leach now resides, and which at that early day was considered the best house in the county. July 12, 1802, he married Dinah Brown, by whom he had four children, Harriet, Julia Ann, Susan, and Dinah. The mother of these children died May 27, 1812. Of these children only Julia and Susan are living. February 1, 1814, he married Hannah Raynor, who was born in New Jersey. She became the mother of five children, Tryphena, Mary, Jacob B., Stephen F., Elias D., of whom all are living but the oldest. These parents were members of the Presbyterian church. The father died a few years after coming to Ohio.

J. B. Leach was born near Morristown, New Jersey, February 8, 1819. During the first year of his life he came with his parents to Austintown township, Mahoning county, where he has lived ever since. His education was obtained in the common schools of that early day. Soon after he attained his majority he came into possession of the old homestead and has lived upon it all his life. In 1846 he married Adaline Eckman, daughter of John Eckman, then a resident of Warren. They had four children, Benjamin, Emory, Jennie, and Margery, of whom all save Benjamin are living. His wife dying October 16, 1852, he, on January 20, 1859, married Olive Jones, daughter of Asa Jones, a stone-mason by trade, and an old resident of Austintown township. This marriage was blessed with two children, Charles and Anna. Mr. Leach was a Democrat until the breaking out of the war, and since then has been a Republican. He has held various township offices and was three times justice of the peace, and for three years recorder of Mahoning county, being in office twenty-five successive years.

Jacob Maurer, farmer, Austintown township, Mahoning county, was born near Reading, Pennsylvania, January 19, 1811. He is the oldest of the sons of Peter Maurer, who in his native State of Pennsylvania followed the trades of a weaver and miller, but after coming to Ohio engaged in farming. Jacob Maurer worked at shoemaking until he came to Ohio, and has since been a farmer. He went with his parents about the year 1832 to Pickaway county, where he remained some seven years, coming to Austintown township at the end of that period. In 1831 he married Magdalena Sies, a native of Northampton county, Pennsylvania, born February, 1811. They had eight daughters and three sons, who are all living except one son and one daughter: Mary A., Marietta, Alexander, Perry C., Elizabeth, Louisa, Susan, Adaline, Lucy, and Melissa. Mrs. Maurer died June 7, 1877. Mr. Maurer is a conscientious Christian, a member of the Lutheran church, and a man of worth. He is a Democrat in politics.

John Maurer, deceased, was born near Reading, Pennsylvania, January 13, 1813. He was the second son of Peter and Barbara (Weis) Maurer, both natives of Pennsylvania. Their children were Jacob, John, Susan, Elizabeth, George, and Peter, who died young. John Maurer went with his father to Pickaway county, Ohio. When about twenty-four years old he came to Austintown, where he engaged in farming. He was married December 4, 1839, to Lucy A. Buck, daughter of David and Mary Buck, who came to this county from Seneca county, New York, in 1839. She was born July 22, 1821. They have two children, Alfred, born November 22, 1840, and Eliza J., born January 27, 1844, now the wife of William Ohl. John Maurer was an earnest Democrat and took a great interest in political matters. He was an industrious man and from nothing made a handsome property. He was an honored and respected citizen. He died February 26, 1873.

Perry C. Maurer, coal operator, Mineral Ridge, Ohio, was born in Austintown township, December 3, 1840. He was educated in the common schools and at Canfield academy. During his school days he also taught in the district schools, his first term before he was eighteen. He was engaged for one year as a clerk at East Lewiston. He next went to Idaho, where he spent the summer. He afterwards acted as a clerk for one year for James Crandon & Co., at Niles, then went to Homewood, Pennsylvania, and had charge of a furnace. In 1867 he engaged in the mercantile business with Charles Warner, and later with J. B. Warner. In 1869 he began business as a coal operator in company with Jenkin Harris, James Ward, and others. He has lately opened a mine at New Lisbon, which yields one hundred and twenty-five tons daily. His other mines yield even larger quantities. November 29, 1865, Mr. Maurer married Rachel Anderson, daughter of James Anderson. She was born in this county, May 14, 1847. She died April 30, 1876, leaving three children—Ivan Anderson, Lalla Rookh, and Grace Edna. He was again married June 27, 1877, to Nettie A. Marshall, daughter of Isaac H. Marshall, of Weathersfield, Trumbull county. She was born May 22, 1854. Mr. Maurer is a member of the Presbyterian church. In politics he is a Democrat.

James McGrew, deceased, was born in Gettysburg, Pennsylvania, January 1, 1810. When he was about eight years old his mother, Mrs. Letitia Porter, came to Poland, Mahoning county, thence going to Girard, Trumbull county, and afterwards to Ashtabula county. After coming to this State she married James Reed. James McGrew was apprenticed at the age of sixteen to learn the blacksmith's trade. He worked at his trade about twenty one years at Howland corners, Weathersfield township, Trumbull county. In 1846 he bought the farm on which his son

now lives, and for the rest of his life was engaged in farming. December 15, 1831, he married Margaret Pennell, daughter of Robert Pennell. She was born April 1, 1816. She bore him seven children—Letitia, Ann, Rosetta, Robert, Sarah Jane, John, Mary M., and John C. Mrs. McGrew died May 29, 1851. Mr. McGrew was married May 12, 1853, to Margaret S. Dougherty. She was a native of Pennsylvania, and was born August 20, 1822. She died August 19, 1866, leaving five children, the oldest and the youngest of whom are deceased—Grover F., Emma R., Alva F., James H., and Eva A. Mr. McGrew was married December 24, 1867, to Katie Spencer, born in Hartford, Trumbull county, October 9, 1814. She died November 1, 1872. On September 17, 1874, he married Nancy Faunce, of Cortland, who survives her husband. Mr. McGrew died April 24, 1878.

J. C. McGrew, farmer, Austintown township, Mahoning county, was born in that township, March 19, 1848. He was married June 4, 1872, to Susan Miller, daughter of William Miller, a former resident of Mahoning county. Mrs. McGrew was born October 18, 1851.

John Miller, Sr., immigrated to Ohio from Pennsylvania in 1812, and settled in Canfield township. He was educated in the common schools of his native State, and, when a young man, learned the carpenter's trade. He was a first-class workman, but, after coming to Ohio, worked entirely at farming. He remained in Canfield township seven years, and then removed to the northeast part of Austintown township, the same county, and settled in the woods near the spot where the residence of Jacob Miller now stands. As a " deadening " had been made, and the land allowed to grow up with trees again, the work of clearing was exceedingly difficult. He married Elizabeth Stittle, by whom he had the following named children: Samuel, Sarah, Jacob, Martha, William, John, Susan, Levi, Lydia. Susan, Sarah, John, Levi, and Jacob are yet living. He was a member of the German Lutheran church. He died in the fall of 1867, having lived to see the wilderness transformed into fine, productive farms.

John Miller, Jr., was born September 14, 1816, in Canfield township. He was educated in the common schools and early began farming, which has been his lifelong occupation. He staid with his father until the age of twenty-three, when he began farming for himself on the same farm on shares for a time, and then bought half of it, upon which he still lives. February 11, 1845, he married Maria Lanteiman, daughter of William Lanterman, of Austintown township. She was born June 28, 1822, and died February 18, 1878. She was an estimable Christian woman and a member of the Disciple church. Five children were born to them, viz: Austin, born May 31, 1846; Sophia, December 21, 1847; Joseph, October 13, 1849; Laura, April 2, 1852; John, March 29, 1854. Mr. Miller is a member of the German Lutheran church.

Oen Naff, farmer, Austintown township, Mahoning county, was born in Lehigh county, Pennsylvania, March 12, 1827. His mother died when he was about six weeks old, and he was brought up under the care of his grandfather, Christian Meassamer. When Oen was about six years old his grandfather moved to Jackson township, and resided there until the time of his death. Oen is the only child of George and Eva (Meassamer) Naff. His father still resides in Lehigh county, Pennsylvania. When Mr. Naff was eighteen years of age he began learning the cabinet maker's trade, at which he worked many years. Since 1850 he has been engaged in farming. He moved upon the present farm in 1860, and has a pleasant home. Mr. Naff was married January 3, 1850, to Madelina Hood, daughter of David Hood. She was born in Mahoning county, June 5, 1828, and died February 17, 1859. She was the mother of two children, whose names are Mary Magdalene and John Wallace. Mr. Naff was again married, March 4, 1860, to Maria Buck, who was born March 5, 1825. She was the daughter of David Buck. They have two children: George Oliver and Lucy Alice. Mr. Naff is an active member of the Republican party.

Michael Ohl was a native of Northampton county, Pennsylvania. When a young man he came with his father, Henry Ohl, to Mahoning county, and settled in Canfield township. The family of children were Michael, Jacob, Henry, David, John, Abraham, Eve Hood, Maria Waggoner, and Mary Shatto. Shortly after their arrival Michael married Eva Moyers, who came to Mahoning county with her husband's family.

They first settled in the southwest corner of Austintown township, where they lived some twelve years, and then moved to that part of the township where Ohltown is now located. He was a cooper by trade, and worked at this some in the new country, but his principal occupation was farming, in addition to managing a saw- and gristmill. He owned the land which is now occupied by Ohltown, which he laid out over fifty years ago, and to which he gave his own name. He was the father of the following named children: Charles, Catharine Hood, Elizabeth Dustman, Henry, David, John, Eve Campbell, Aydelott, Michael (who was killed at Warren during the building of a bridge), Samuel, Abigail, McDonald, Andrew, Mary Kraus, and Julia Rose. Mr. Ohl was hotel-keeper at Ohltown, and also engaged at distilling. He died October 21, 1857, at the age of seventy-four. His father, Henry Ohl, died September 7, 1849. Eve Ohl died July 11, 1860.

David Ohl was born in Austintown township, Mahoning county, December 22, 1818. He received his education in the common schools and aided his father until he became of age, when he began learning the millwright's trade with his brother Charles. After working with him three years he began building mills. He was engaged at this business for thirty-five years. Directly after his marriage he began farming where he now lives. January 15, 1846, he married Elizabeth A. White, daughter of James White. She was born in Weathersfield township, Trumbull county, April 29, 1828. They have had seven children—Ezra, Albert, Julia Ann, Michael, James, Olander, and Jennie (Samantha Jane). Mr. and Mrs. Ohl are old-time members of the Methodist church.

Wesley Ohl, merchant, West Austintown, Mahoning county, was born in Austintown township, June 19, 1843. He is the oldest child of George Ohl, son of David Ohl, a Pennsylvanian by birth, who came to Mahoning county, then Trumbull, in an early day, and was a prominent farmer and stock dealer in his day, and was engaged in driving stock to the East over the mountains. George Ohl acquired a good education at the public schools, and for a number of years was engaged in teaching, attending to his farm at the same time. Farming was his chief occupation through life. He was born in

Austintown township; married Lydia Graber, a native of Bucks county, Pennsylvania. This union resulted in two children, the eldest dying in infancy. He was a member of the Evangelical Association, and a Republican in politics. He and his wife are both dead. Wesley Ohl remained upon the farm until 1872, when he engaged in the mercantile business with D. B. Blott. This partnership continued two years, since which time Mr. Ohl has carried on the business alone at West Austintown. He married Miss Carrie, daughter of William Hauser. They have one child, Elva Irene, born October 7, 1878.

Davis Randolph, Esq., Austintown township, Mahoning county, was born in Juniata county, Pennsylvania, July 25, 1810. He is a brother of William Randolph, of Windsor, Ashtabula county, and a son of John and Mary (Davis) Randolph. His mother was of Welsh descent. The old stock of Randolphs came from Virginia. Davis received but a limited common school education. He learned the shoemaker's trade with his brother, with whom he came to Austintown and commenced business, in which he continued about twenty-five years. Mr. Randolph is an influential member of the Democratic party. He has held nearly all of the township offices, and since 1859 has been justice of the peace. He married Elizabeth McCarter, of Mahoning county, November 30, 1837, by whom he had one child, Elizabeth McCoy, October 21, 1841. His wife died February 14, 1842. On January 16, 1843, he married Caroline Russel, of Austintown, daughter of James Russel, a soldier of 1812. They have seven children born as follow: James Clark, January 19, 1844; Mary Jane, February 12, 1845; Jonathan Russel, October 28, 1846; John Clayton, May 30, 1848; Charles, November 6, 1854; Cornelia Emeline, May 6, 1856; Luella C., May 4, 1862. Each of the oldest three of the sons served two years in company E, Twelfth Ohio cavalry, enlisting before they were of age. Mr. Davis is a member of the Disciple church and is a man who has gained honor from a long life of steadfast integrity.

Thomas Reed, farmer, Austintown township, Mahoning county, was born in Loudoun county, Virginia, September 24, 1789. His father, James Reed, was an old time resident of Poland township. He married Hannah Gilbert, born September 11, 1807, daughter of Charles Gilbert, a native of Pennsylvania. Her mother was Magdalene Miller, a native of the same State. To Mr. and Mrs. Reed were born seven children: Peggy, born June 27, 1825; Betsy, December 1, 1826; Polly, March 9, 1829; Stephen, November 26, 1830; Nancy, October 10, 1832; Hannah, November 3, 1835; and Amos, May 27, 1839. Peggy, Nancy, Hannah, and Stephen, still make their home with their mother on the old farm. Mr. Reed was a Covenanter in religion, and in politics a Republican. He was a practical farmer and a worthy citizen. His death occurred February 18, 1865.

James Raver, a native of Allentown, Lehigh county, Pennsylvania, was born April 2, 1823. He was the son of William Raver, who came to Austintown township when James was thirteen years of age. After living here a few years he removed to Lordstown township. James and his father were both coopers by trade, but were principally engaged in farming. William Raver was the father of seven children, Lovina, James, Eliza, Lewis, William, Catharine, and Maria, all living at the present time. He married Catharine Bailey, who was born in Canfield township, May 13, 1821. Their children, Levi, Lewis W., Sarah A., and Mary Sophia, are living, with the exception of Mary. After the death of his first wife he married Clarinda Dustman, a native of Canfield, by whom he had one child, Henry F., who died at the age of six years. In 1852 James Raver moved into Canfield township, where he has since been engaged in farming.

L. W. Raver was born in Lordstown township, Trumbull county, May 11, 1849. He is the second child of James Raver. When seventeen years of age he was apprenticed to learn the plasterer's trade, serving two years, and during the winters he also learned harness-making. He worked at the former of these seven summers and at the latter six winters. He then with Abraham Forney engaged in mercantile business for three years, when he sold out and soon afterward went into the drug business with Dr. C. B. White. This partnership lasted but one year. He then for a few months went into the furniture business. He is now keeping a general store with J. H. Fitch and Joseph Smith. March 16, 1873, he married Melvina Wilson, daughter of William Wilson, born December 5, 1848. They have three children, James O., Allen Thurman, and Harry Rush.

Robert Russell, Austintown township, Mahoning county, was born in Loudoun county, Virginia, August 23, 1784. When he was two years of age his father, Robert Russell, Sr., moved into Washington county, Pennsylvania, and in 1802 into Lake county, Ohio. In 1806 or 1807 he came into Austintown township, Mahoning county. At this early date there had not been a road laid out in the entire township. He was a farmer by occupation, and lived to see the wilderness converted into fine farms possessing the comforts and refinements of civilized life. He married, May 17, 1809, Rachel Hampson, who was a daughter of Robert and Jane Hampson, and was born in New Jersey, October 24, 1786. They reared nine children, all living to celebrate their parents' golden wedding, and even their sixtieth anniversary. Mr. Russell lived an exemplary life, and was a member for fifty years of the Disciple church at Four-mile run. He was ever a friend to the poor and needy. His useful life closed January 31, 1879, and his wife died February 20, 1872.

Hampson Russell, farmer, Austintown township, Mahoning county, son of Robert Russell, the pioneer, was born August 24, 1822. His education was received in the pioneer schools of his native township. He early began the work of farming upon the home farm, and at the age of twenty-five moved upon the farm where he now resides, two miles southwest of the center of the township. In May, 1849, he married Elizabeth Reed, daughter of Thomas Reed, of Austintown township. She was born December 1, 1826. This couple have but three children: Charles Warren, born May 24, 1852; Amos Calvin, May 14, 1856; Thomas Robert, June 20, 1860. Mr. Russell is a member of the Disciple church and his wife is a Covenanter. He is a Republican in politics.

Abraham Strock, farmer, Austintown township, Mahoning county, was born in Perry county, Pennsylvania, April 7, 1813. He is a son of John Henry Strock and a twin brother of Zachariah R. Strock. His father was born in Northumberland county, Pennsylvania, October 14, 1781. He married Catharine Rice, a native of Pennsylvania, by whom he had eleven children:

Benjamin, Elizabeth, Mary, Isaac, Abraham, Zachariah, Catharine, Anna, Susan, Joseph, and Julia. Of these the sons are all living and the daughters all dead. John H. Strock was a Presbyterian and a Democrat. He died in the forty-ninth year of his age, December 14, 1830. The father of John H. Strock was Joseph Strock, a native of France, who came to this country an orphan boy nine years old. After coming here he was bound out to pay for his passage. He was married in Pennsylvania and had seven sons and four daughters. He came to Mahoning county and settled in the southern part of Austintown township. Abraham Strock has resided here since his father came in 1815. He began learning carpentry and joining when fourteen years old and worked at those trades forty-seven years. He has erected so many churches that the title "the old church-builder" is often applied to him. September 7, 1834, he married Sophia Wetzell, who was born in Pennsylvania, December 18, 1807. They had seven children: Sarah, William H., Eliza, Caroline, Benjamin, Lucy, and George. Mrs. Strock died August 11, 1869. Mr. Strock was one of the first Abolitionists in this county and is now an earnest Republican. Since retiring from active business he has studied a variety of subjects, upon each of which he is well informed.

Joseph Smith, a native of Mercer county, Pennsylvania, was born May 27, 1853. When he was about two years old his father, Henry Smith, moved into Jackson township. After remaining here a few years he moved to Smith's corners, Austintown township. Joseph received his education at this place, attending school winters and working on the farm summers. When eighteen years old he began clerking for J. H. Fitch & Co. He remained here for one year and then worked for J. H. Fitch until April 1, 1880, when he bought an interest in the stock of goods and the firm of Fitch, Smith & Co. was formed. He married Elizabeth Wetzel, daughter of Jacob Wetzel, an old-time hotel proprietor of Austintown.

Daniel Thornton, who was a native of Long Island, came to Youngstown township, Trumbull county, now Mahoning, in the year 1817. After remaining here five or six years he went back to his old home, but not being satisfied there returned to this county. He served in the

War of 1812 before he was eighteen, first three months as substitute and afterward a time for himself. At the close of the war he began learning the ship-carpenter's trade, serving an apprenticeship of three years. He followed this trade in the Island until his removal to Ohio. Just before leaving Long Island he married Hannah Rogers, a native of that island. She became the mother of three children—Jesse A., merchant of Germantown, Pennsylvania; Mary, who died in infancy; and Hiram, of Austintown. He was a Democrat through early life but eventually became a Republican.

Hiram Thornton, third child of Daniel Thornton, was born in Youngstown township, Trumbull county, now Mahoning, January 18, 1823. His school advantages were very limited as there was no school in his district until he was of age. But by reading and observation he has become well informed. He is a natural mechanic, understanding several different trades. His early life was spent upon the farm. At the age of seventeen he began making whiskey, at which occupation he continued for five years, at the end of which time he began carriage- and wagon-making, which he carried on for about eleven years. Since then he has been engaged in various pursuits, among others that of operating in coal. He is now superintending mines for H. Baldwin, of Youngstown. He married, August 5, 1849, Matilda Smith, daughter of William Smith, of Austintown. She was born in England, August 31, 1830. To them have been born fifteen children—Daniel, Mary, Stephen, Joseph, Henry, Elizabeth, Sarah, William, Walter, Lovina, Ida, George, Myron, Ella, Edward, of whom Daniel, Ida, and George are dead. He is a Republican and a worthy and respected citizen.

William Tibbit (deceased) was born in Maryland, June 25, 1805. When he was still an infant his father, Jerry Tibbit, moved to Youngstown. Here he lived until he was eighteen, when his father, who was a saddler and harness-maker in Youngstown, moved to Austintown, where he resided until his death engaged in farming. William Tibbit received his education in the Youngstown schools. He remained with his father until he was twenty-four, assisting in the shop and on the farm. He then bought the business and carried it on for about seven years,

meanwhile purchasing the farm on which his widow and family now reside. He moved upon this farm in 1836, and engaged afterwards at farming. November 28, 1833, he married Thankful Almyra, daughter of Judge Camden Cleaveland, a native of Connecticut. Judge Cleaveland emigrated to Liberty township, Trumbull county, about 1800, and when his daughter, Mrs. Tibbit, was about four years old moved to Youngstown, where he taught school for several years. He afterwards operated the Cleaveland mill on Mill creek. He married Elizabeth Adams, daughter of Asahel Adams, who was also a pioneer in this region. Judge Cleaveland had a family of two boys—Camden H. and Mason A. (who died young), and five girls: Eliza P., Thankful Almyra, Olive A., Charlotte M., and Harriet M. Judge Cleaveland was a brother of Moses Cleaveland, after whom the city of Cleveland was named. William Tibbit was a member of the Presbyterian church, and a member of the Republican party. He was an unassuming man, a conscientious Christian, a kind father and husband, and a good citizen. He died October 14, 1856. He was the father of eight children, six of whom are living—Nancy E., Charlotte M., Asahel C., Laura E., John Ferris and Mary Ann.

Jacob Wolfcale, farmer, Austintown township, Mahoning county, was born in the same township October 23, 1819. He is the third of the children of Abram Wolfcale, a native of Virginia, who, with his brother John, and his father, John Wolfcale, Sr., came into this country at an early date, and bought tracts of land on part of which their children are now living. Abram Wolfcale was a cabinet-maker and carpenter by trade. He also carried on a farm. He was born January 14, 1785. He married Elizabeth Brooks, who was born in Maryland October 6, 1792. They had five children—Margaret, Jonathan, Jacob, Polly, and Elizabeth. Of these Polly died in infancy, and Jonathan when about forty years of age. Margaret married Roswell Matthews, and lives upon the old homestead. Jacob Wolfcale is a blacksmith by trade, but is engaged in farming. He was married July 17, 1843, to Lavina Oatstein, a native of Mahoning county. They have seven children living, three deceased. The names of those living are: Owen, Abram, William, Milo, Elizabeth, Filena, and Mary. Mr. Wolfcale is a Democrat. He has surrendered the care of his farm to his sons and is now enjoying the quiet which a life of activity has earned him.

Ira Wilcox, farmer, Austintown township, Mahoning county, is a native of that county, born March 9, 1816. His father, Isaac Wilcox, was a native of Maryland, and was in the War of 1812. Isaac Wilcox was married to Catharine Kussurd, and shortly afterward came to Canfield township, now Mahoning county. About twenty-five years later he removed to Virginia. He was a class leader in the Methodist church, and for a long time a justice of the peace in Canfield. He had four children: Ira, Reuben, Eli, and Hannah. Eli died when but fourteen years old. Hannah married Jacob Umstardt, and died many years ago. Reuben is living at Rootstown, Ohio. Ira Wilcox, when about twelve years of age, was apprenticed to the shoemaker's trade, at which he served until he was eighteen, in the meantime working upon the farm of his employer. He followed his trade some eighteen years. After his marriage he resided in Jackson township for a short time, then returned to his former home. In 1839 he bought a small part of his present farm, which was then in the woods. He has since added to his first purchase until he now has a fine farm. April 11, 1835, he married Rebecca Gilman, who was born in (now) Mahoning county, November 16, 1816, and is a daughter of Jacob Gilman. Mr. and Mrs. Wilcox have nine children, as follows: Christina, Daniel, Isaac, Sarah, Ira, Jr., Mary, Cecilia, Anson B., and Ella. Their church relationship is with the United Brethren in Christ.

Jacob Wise, deceased, was born in Lehigh county, Pennsylvania, January 21, 1786. He came to Trumbull county in 1810, and bought one hundred acres of land at $3 per acre. Several years later he purchased what is now known as the Peters farm, one hundred and thirty-three acres, and afterwards he bought one hundred and twelve acres on the tract where the Tod mine was opened. Coal was mined there over fifty years ago. In 1810 Jacob Wise married Susanna Weitzel, who lived only about one year after giving birth to a child named Jacob, born June 24, 1813. In 1815 Mr. Wise married Priscilla Pyle, who was born in Little York, Pennsylvania, in 1797. They had thirteen children—John, Mary, Eliza, Sarah, Hannah, Priscilla, Lydia, Solomon, Jonathan, Rebecca, Adaline, Rachel, and Elias, who died when quite young. Priscilla, Rebecca, Mary, and Solomon are also deceased. Jacob Wise was a soldier in the War of 1812. Both he and his wife were members of the Presbyterian church. He died October 24, 1854, and Mrs. Wise September 7, 1862.

John Wise, farmer, Austintown township, Mahoning county, was born in Trumbull county, August 13, 1816. He is the second son of Jacob Wise. He was married October 1, 1844, to Mary Carn, who was born in Canfield, February 18, 1820. Her father, a tailor by trade, came from Pennsylvania. The union gave them two children, Zenas, an attorney at Pine Bluff, Kansas, and Thomas Jefferson, a coal operator at Canfield. Mrs. Wise died May 24, 1854. Mr. Wise was married a second time February 1, 1855, to Rachel A. Morris, born in Monmouthshire, England, February 26, 1828. They have two children, Lucy, born February 7, 1856, the wife of E. Grover Marshall, Weathersfield township, Trumbull county, and David, born May 30, 1865, now residing at home. Mrs. Wise is the seventh of fourteen children of William Morris, who emigrated to America in 1839, and settled in Schuylkill county, Pennsylvania, where he was a coal operator some years; he then moved to Weathersfield township, Trumbull county, and was there a superintendent of mines.

CHAPTER VII.
JACKSON.
GENERAL DESCRIPTION.

This township, named in honor of Andrew Jackson, is township two of range four of the Western Reserve, and is bounded on the north by Lordstown, Trumbull county; on the east by Austintown; on the south by Berlin; and on the west by Milton. The Meander creek drains the eastern part of the township, pursuing its zigzag course northward partly in this township but mostly in Austintown. A number of small streams enter the creek from the westward, rendering the surface broken and uneven. There are no long or very steep hills, but quite a number of undulations such as may be found in prairie countries. The western half of the township may be briefly described as level. Many broad fields, acres in extent, are apparently as flat and even as the surface of a calm lake. Likewise in the southern part of the township, the fields which have been formed from the ancient swamp-land are almost uniformly smooth.

There is a large average of woodland interspersed with acres of cultivated fields, this combination producing an effect very pleasing to lovers of natural beauty. When the green mantle of spring is spread over all, or when the magic painter, Autumn, with divinely skilled hand has touched the forest trees, transformed their foliage with countless tints of crimson, gold, and scarlet, these groves assume a beauty which is indescribable.

The soil is generally deep and rich, and is well adapted to wheat and corn. But little of the land is stony and all is easily cultivated. The farm-houses are good and comfortable, though by no means large or imposing in appearance.

There is but one village in the township,—North Jackson, which is not north geographically but situated at the very center. The post-office has been called by this name to distinguish it from the many other Jacksons in this country.

Farming is the principal business. There has never been a railroad through the township, but one is now in process of construction and other lines have been surveyed. The Alliance, Niles & Ashtabula road will pass diagonally through the western and northern portion of the township, and with its completion there may be an inception of other industries.

TIMBER.

The western and much of the northern part of the township were originally covered with a dense growth of hard wood, principally oak and hickory. On the Meander there were many sugar-maples. In the southern part of the township there were several kinds of soft wood found in some tracts including considerable poplar. Beech and ash grow in various parts of the township.

COAL.

A fair quantity of surface coal has been mined in several places, but the deposits are not extensive. As yet no banks containing paying quantities have been opened.

SETTLEMENT.

The first pioneers were nearly all of the Scotch-Irish race, and moved to the township from Pennsylvania. Samuel Calhoun was the first actual settler. He located on the south line of the township in 1803, and there passed the remainder of his days. His sons were Andrew, Samuel, and Matthew; his daughters Nancy, Betsey, Isabel, Sally, Anna, Martha, and Esther. Andrew Calhoun lived in the township, on the eastern part, through his life. Anna became the wife of David Leonard, and is still living in Ellsworth township. The name is spelled Calhoon by some of those who bear it.

William Orr, from Washington county, Pennsylvania, settled in 1803 or 1804 upon the farm which remained in possession of the Orr family many years. He built a frame house at an early date, which was probably the first in the township. It was a story and a half in height, perhaps twenty-four feet wide, and somewhat longer. There was a stone chimney in the middle of the house; it was both large and wide, and took up a considerable amount of room. William Orr died in 1815, in his sixtieth year. His wife Mary died in 1849, in her ninetieth year. Their family consisted of eleven children, viz: James, Margaret, John, Humphrey, William, Thomas, Russel, Anna, Abraham, Isaac, and Mary. John, Humphrey, William, and Russel settled in Milton and died there. Thomas lived in Jackson for a time, then returned to Pennsylvania. James moved to some distant part. Abraham and Isaac are the only survivors of the family. The former lives in Trumbull county and the latter in Illinois. Anna was the wife of John Johnston. Margaret married John Ewing.

Andrew Gault came to the township in 1803, and made a permanent settlement in 1804. His sons were Ebenezer, Robert, and Andrew; his daughters Rachel, Betsey, and Ann. Robert and Andrew settled in the township, Andrew upon the old place. Rachel married Andrew Duer and settled in Ellsworth. Betsey married Robert Gibson. Ann became the wife of Robinson Young, and lived in Austintown.

About 1804 Samuel Riddle, from Pennsylvania settled in the southeast part of the township. His house stood near where Mr. Kimmel's now stands. His children were David, James, Andrew, John, Samuel, Catharine, and Ann. David married Betsey Van Emmon, and settled one mile and a half northeast of the center. He brought up a family of two sons and four daughters. James married Jane Bell of Pennsylvania, and lived upon the old homestead. His family consisted of ten children. Andrew married Matilda Taylor and settled on the Meander, in Ellsworth. He was the father of three sons and two daughters. John became a doctor and practiced some time in Wooster. He married Rhoda Winters and had four daughters. Samuel married Mary Campbell, and settled one mile west of the old place. He brought up two sons and two daughters. The daughters are dead. His sons live in Jackson. Catharine married John McCready, and lived in Bedford, Pennsylvania. Ann married Nicholas Van Emmon and resided in the western part of this township.

Robert Kirkpatrick was among the earliest settlers, and probably came to this township soon after the families just mentioned. He was a native of Ireland, of Scotch-Irish blood. Five of his children arrived at maturity, viz : Martin, Isaac, Josiah, Martha, and Eleanor. Martin and Isaac lived and died in Ellsworth, where their father purchased farms for them. Josiah passed his life upon the old farm. Martha became Mrs. McGeorge, and Eleanor Mrs. Wilson. Martha is the only survivor. Robert Kirkpatrick first settled in Austintown near Smith's corners, but soon afterwards made a permanent settlement in Jackson, on the Meander. He died in 1847, in the seventy-ninth year of his age. Catharine, his wife, died in 1856, at the age of eighty-seven. Josiah, the youngest son, died in 1878, aged sixty-four.

John Ewing, and his brother Archibald Ewing, natives of Ireland, came with their mother and sister in 1803 or 1804. They first settled in Austintown, and Archibald took up and lived upon the old Ewing farm in that township. The first night after their arrival the family passed beneath the shelter of a walnut tree. The sister mentioned became Mrs. Robert Kirkpatrick. John Ewing located in Jackson upon the farm now owned by Mr. Kimmel. He married Margaret Orr, and reared a large family. A sketch is given elsewhere.

John and Eleanor Morrison settled in 1805 on the place where the widow Lynn now lives, southwest of the center. James, Jane, John, Nancy, Thomas, Martha, and Mary Ann were the names of their children. The sons moved away quite early—James to Holmes county ; John to the northern part of Trumbull county ; and Thomas to Pennsylvania. Mary Ann was married to David Johnston, and is living in Jackson. She is the only member of the family now in this county.

In 1805 or 1806 Nicholas VanEmmon settled one mile and a half west and a mile south of the center of the township. His wife died here, after bringing up a large family. He married again and moved away. None of the children settled in the township.

From 1810 to 1820 there were scarcely any permanent settlements made in the township. Quite a number came and remained a short time, but a few years' experience with the swamps and the bad roads disgusted them, and they either returned to civilization or pressed on toward the newer settlements, declaring that such a country wasn't " fit for a white man to live in." The process of development was consequently a slow one.

A man named Crooks was living on the farm west of the Lynn farm in 1811, but moved away soon after. Two of the sons afterwards came back and settled in the northern part of the township, where they remained a few years.

Thomas Dinwiddie was also a resident of the township at that date, upon the farm now owned by James Oswald. He moved away later.

James and Martha Patterson were early settlers on the north side of the road, one-half mile west of the center. They had no children. In 1823 they moved to Wayne county.

David McConnell settled in the northwestern part of the township about 1817, but sold out after making a few improvements.

John Graves settled near Joseph Pierce about 1819. His farm was east of Mr. Pierce's. He made considerable improvement. Joseph McCorkle bought the farm from him, moving to it from the eastern part of the township. Mr. McCorkle died on the farm and his widow is still living there.

George Ormsby settled in Jackson previous to 1820 and lived to be an old man.

Joshua T. Cotton, who was a captain in the War of 1812, moved to Jackson township about 1818. He married in Youngstown Miss Williamson, and brought up a large family. From Jackson he moved to Indiana, where he died. Captain Cotton was a true specimen of the hardy pioneer as well as a good and brave soldier.

About the same date John Pearsall settled one and three-fourth miles east of the center. He moved to another farm in this township, then to Milton, and finally to Pennsylvania.

Joseph Pierce and wife, the father of Joseph Pierce, one of the oldest residents of the township, moved from Youngstown to the northwestern part of the township in the fall of 1818. Mrs. Pierce died the following winter. Joseph Pierce, Jr., came from Warren to this township in 1819, with an axe as his only property. It proved a very serviceable tool, for miles of road had to be cut in order to reach his land. He used to work from before daybreak until nine and ten o'clock at night in the clearings. His energy and industry won him a home which he still lives to enjoy.

Thomas Duer settled on the west side of the township about 1820 and died soon afterward. His son Joseph passed his life on the old place.

John McMahan, of Pennsylvania, moved from his native State to the northern part of Boardman township in 1799, and remained until 1806, when he settled on a farm in Austintown. He served three months in the War of 1812, and died while on his way home. He was the father of five sons and one daughter—James D., Benjamin, John, Thomas, Harriet, and Joseph. James and Benjamin settled in Jackson in 1820. John went West and has never been heard from. Thomas settled in Lordstown, removed to Pennsylvania and died. Harriet, the wife of John Cory, lives in Champion, Trumbull county. Joseph died in Morgan county, Ohio.

In 1820 the widow of John McMahan, Sr., removed from Austintown to Jackson with her sons. She died in 1855, aged about eighty-three years.

James D. McMahan, who is perhaps the oldest man living of those born upon the Reserve, was born in Boardman township October 31, 1799. He was one of the pioneers of Jackson.

He married Betsey Cory and had a family of eight children, four of whom are living—John, on the old homestead in the northern part of Jackson; Thomas, one mile east of Warren; Silas, in Champion township, and Mary in San Francisco, California. Mrs. McMahan died in 1868. Mr. McMahan has since been living with his sons. For a man of his years he is wonderfully bright, active, and cheerful.

Benjamin McMahan settled in Jackson and died in 1878. He was married three times. His first wife bore three children, his second one, and his third four. All these are living excepting one.

John Cartwright settled about 1827 on the farm northwest of Abraham Moherman's, but moved away a few years later.

Abraham Moherman, son of Frederick Moherman, one of the first settlers of Austintown, came to Jackson in 1827 and settled one mile and a half west of the center where he now lives. He was married in the township to Anna, daughter of Daniel Rush, and has a family of four children living.

John Moherman settled some time after his brother. He married Mary Cassiday, now deceased, and has four children living.

Thomas Woodward settled on the farm where he now lives in 1828.

Robert Turnbull moved from Austintown to Goshen township, and in 1828 located at Jackson center, where he made the first clearing in what is now the village. His house stood on the corner where the drug store now is. Squire Turnbull is well remembered by the old residents, and is generally described as having been a "smart man." He was married twice; first to Celia, daughter of John Wolfcale, of Austintown. One son by this marriage is now living in Portage county. His name is Cyrus. For his second wife Mr. Turnbull married Anna Ormsby, of this township. One of the sons, Lewis, was killed in a saw-mill in Indiana. The family was a large one.

Jonathan Osborn bought land in the township in 1828, and settled here permanently in 1836.

William Young, a native of Pennsylvania, bought his farm in 1830, paying $5 per acre for it, when land in the northern and western part of the township was worth $3 to $4 per acre.

From 1825 until 1835 the Pennsylvania Dutch

flocked to the township in large numbers. The Schlabach, Wetherstay, Lodwick, Wannemaker, Ebert, Shoeneberger, Iry, Shively, and other families were the earliest and most prominent. The limits of this article forbid us to go into particulars regarding the settlers of this date; for though they may be regarded as pioneers inasmuch as they began in the woods, we cannot in strict propriety call them early settlers.

By 1840 the settlement had grown almost to its present dimensions. The census of that year showed a population of 1,124. The Germans with their characteristic thrift and sturdy industry have been largely instrumental in adding to the wealth of the township.

One reason why the township was not settled faster may be found in the fact that a considerable portion of the land it contains was not put in the market by the proprietors until long after many other townships had become thriving and populous.

TAXES IN 1803.

Here is a list of the tax-payers of Jackson for the year 1803:

RANGE FOUR, TOWN TWO.

	Amount of tax.		Amount of tax.
Calhoun, Samuel	$ 20	Starnford, James	$ 24
Gault, Andrew	32	Riddle, Samuel	1 59
Orr, William	32	McInrue, Joseph	40
Total			$3.07

FIRST EVENTS.

Andrew Gault, born in 1804, was the first white male child born in the township, and James Van Emmon the second. Mary Ewing (Mrs. Andrew Gault) was born in 1807, and is said to have been the first female child.

Probably the first marriage was that of John Ewing and Margaret Orr, which took place in 1805 in a little log-cabin on the Orr place, now known as the Goldner farm. The ceremony was performed by 'Squire Chidester, of Canfield.

The first death was that of Mary, daughter of William and Mary Orr, who died February 18, 1805, in the fourteenth year of her age. Her grave is in the old burying ground adjoining the Covenanter church.

EARLY SCHOOLS.

The first school-house in the township was on the east line in the southeastern part. It was made of logs, the cracks daubed with mud, and the roof covered with loose boards weighted down. The floor was made of split timber and there were a few hard benches. The house was placed on a side-hill or steep bank. John Fullerton and a man named Ferguson were probably the first teachers. Fullerton was the schoolmaster of the settlement for many years. The second school-house in this district, or rather in this neighborhood, was a small log house, and was situated on the hill northeast of the Covenanter church, where it stood several years. In one corner of the school-room was a stump—its roots still in the ground and the floor fitted around it—which had been sawed off and made into a seat. This was called the "dunce block," and for a refractory urchin to be placed upon it was deemed the most humiliating punishment that could be administered.

Matilda Taylor probably taught the first summer school in this part of the township.

One night while Fullerton was the teacher he and some of the larger boys succeeded in getting a wagon fixed upon the roof of the school-house; and when the wrathful owner of the conveyance appeared and demanded that the mischief-makers should be punished, the pedagogue gravely assured him that he would do his best to find out who they were and treat them as they deserved.

A third school-house of hewed logs was built at the cross roads west of the Covenanter church.

The house in which William Young now lives was the first framed school-house in the district.

Among the early teachers in the northwestern part of the township were Orman Deane, Hayes Bell, and Amelia Streeter.

In the Jackson Centre district previous to 1840 English was taught a part of the term and German the remainder. Soon after Samuel Jones settled he was elected a school director and made a canvass of the district to find out how many were in favor of substituting English alone. He found only three opposed to this plan, and those three had no scholars. The change was accordingly made and the German language ceased to be taught in the township.

In the first schools the "three R.'s" were all the branches in which instruction was given. The spelling book and Bible were text books for all scholars, whether old or young. Geography and grammar were not introduced for many years, and their admission into the schools at all was bitterly opposed by the conservative, old-fashioned parents. They were considered innovations unnecessary and worthless. "We got along without studying them—why can't our children?" This style of argument has always met the friends of education, but we are thankful that it no longer carries conviction with it.

EARLY MILLS.

The first grist-mill in the township was built by Samuel Riddle, Sr. It was on the Meander, in the southeastern corner of the township, and must have been erected more than seventy years ago. It was a small affair, and was made as cheaply as possible. It was succeeded by a mill situated just southeast of the old site. This second mill was built by a man named Amos Stoddard, and was run by the Riddles several years. It was owned later by a man named Butler, then by Benjamin McMahan, but was destroyed by fire some years ago.

The Riddle saw-mill was built near the first grist-mill mentioned above, but was in Ellsworth township. It was probably erected as early as 1810. A saw-mill situated on a little run northwest of the center, was standing in 1830. It was known as Haynen's mill, afterwards as Camp's mill. It ran until 1850 or later. No trace of its site is now visible and the stream, for a mill-stream, is decidedly a diminutive one.

James Crooks operated a carding- and fulling-mill, about a mile and a quarter north of the center, some fifty years ago. Horace Platt owned the mill after him. About the same time a saw-mill was built by the McMahan's on the same stream, north of the carding-mill. It was run by different parties until within a few years.

Reuben Craver put up a saw-mill on Morrison's run, and Andrew Gault bought it. William Young built a saw-mill on the same stream in 1844. It is still standing but disused.

CHURCH HISTORY.

The early settlers of Jackson were a church-going people, and had a place for public worship at a very early date, so early that in these days one can but wonder where the worshipers came from and how they managed to pay a preacher. But it is not reasonable to suppose that the congregations were large, or that the preacher received more than a meagre salary. People rode horseback or walked to church and came from all the region around.

THE OLD LOG CHURCH.

The first church building in the township was a structure of hewn logs, and was situated on a hill near the west line of the township, on the south side of the road running east and west. It was probably built in 1818, or perhaps a little earlier. The house contained a few rude seats and had no floor except some loose boards. An aged resident of Jackson remembers that he attended services there and sat upon a sleeper which formed a part of the building. This primitive house of worship was used but a short time. It was erected and used by the Presbyterians of Jackson and Austintown. Rev. Joshua Bier was the minister. He is described as a good and pious old man, who adhered rigidly and uncompromisingly to the strongest and most old-fashioned doctrines. As a preacher he had only ordinary talents, but his earnestness and sincerity always secured the attention of his hearers. On account of an unfortunate family trouble he severed his connection with his little flock, and the old church ceased to be a meeting-house.

THE COVENANTERS.

As early as 1818 the Reformed Presbyterians or Covenanters of the southeastern part of the township organized and formed a church, and were supplied by a minister who also presided over the congregation of the same denomination at Little Beaver, Pennsylvania, thirty miles distant. Mr. Williams, an aged missionary, preached in the settlement occasionally before the organization was effected. Rev. Robert Gibson was the first regular preacher, and supplied the congregation three or four years. Meetings were held in barns in summer and in dwelling-houses in winter. After Mr. Gibson resigned his charge, there was a vacancy which continued several years. About 1830 Rev. George Scott was ordained pastor, and soon afterwards was erected a small frame house, perhaps 25 x 30 feet in its dimensions. It was plain and cheaply furnished, containing movable seats, and was never painted either inside or out. This building was used as a church for many years, but was finally taken down and carried to the center, where its materials were used in constructing W. B. Mansel's wagon-shop.

In 1833 occurred the division in the church which resulted in the formation of two schools of Covenanters. Mr. Scott resigned his charge, and joined the new school, which built a church in Austintown later. Another vacancy ensued until Rev. James Blackwood became pastor. The church having been reorganized, a branch of the same church at Greenville, Pennsylvania, some forty miles distant, having been added to the charge, which still included Little Beaver and Jackson, Mr. Blackwood resigned on account of poor health and the large amount of labor his pastorate demanded. Until about 1847 the church remained unsupplied, but at that date Rev. Samuel Sterrett began his ministrations, and continued as the pastor over twenty years. Soon after he entered upon his labors here, the church building now standing was erected—a very neat little country church of ample size for the accommodation of its congregation. Rev. R. J. George became pastor in 1870; succeeded by Rev. T. C. Sproul until 1879. The church is at present without a pastor and its membership small. Under Mr. Sterrett Greenville was thrown from the charge, and later Little Beaver. The two last ministers were supported by the Jackson and Poland branches, Poland branch having been added in place of those that were dismissed.

The old church has had many periods of adversity. Its prosperity was once quite marked. Commencing with but a handful of members, it grew to over seventy, then began to diminish. Archibald Ewing, John Ewing, Robert Kirkpatrick, Andrew Gault, William Knight, William Young, Robinson Young and their families were the principal and earliest members. The first elders were Archibald Ewing, Andrew Gault, and James Truesdale.

THE METHODIST CHURCH.

The first preaching by this denomination was begun in 1823 by Rev. Charles Elliot. In 1824 a class was formed consisting of eight members. The first meetings were held at the house of John Erwin.

Private houses and school-houses were used as places for worship for some years, then the building which is now Mansel's wagon shop was purchased and occupied until the present building was erected north of the center in 1847.

Among the earliest Methodists who worshiped in this township were John Pearsall and wife, Richard Osborn and wife, Mrs. Susanna McMahan, J. D. McMahan, George Ormsby and wife, John Erwin and wife, and Mrs. Kincaid.

The early preachers were "circuit riders," who filled a large number of appointments and often preached every day in the week.

LUTHERAN AND GERMAN REFORMED CHURCH.

The early meetings of these societies were held in private houses. In 1835 an organization was effected and the corner-stone of the present building laid. The house was built by the united efforts of the Lutherans and German Reformed inhabitants of Jackson. The house is situated a short distance north of the center, and is a quaint, old-fashioned building, square, with high pulpit and galleries. It was dedicated in 1836, the sermon on that occasion being preached by Rev. Mr. Holder.

The first pastor of the Lutherans was Rev. F. C. Becker, who has since served. The first German Reformed pastor was Rev. J. P. Mahnenschmidt.

The Fulks, Shoenenbergers, Klingensmiths, and others were among the leading members at the time of the organization. The first trustees were Samuel Klingensmith (Lutheran) and Peter Fulk (German Reformed); first elders, Martin Goldner (Lutheran) and Mr. Schlabach (Reformed).

The Sunday-school is made a union school and supported by both denominations.

Father Becker, the venerable pastor of the Lutherans, resides in Lordstown, and notwithstanding the many busy years he has spent in his holy calling, he is still vigorous and as attentive to his work as in his youthful days. Mr. Becker is father of most of the Lutheran church organizations in this section.

THE DISCIPLES.

This denomination has a comfortable little house situated just south of the center. The church was organized in the fall of 1852 by Rev. C. Smith, with fifty-two members. For a time it was in a flourishing condition, but it gradually passed into a state of somnolence, and in 1874 was resurrected and reorganized by H. C. Carlton, with thirty-four members. W. B. Dean, Joseph Pierce, James Russell, George and Christian Shively have been most active in this church, and have contributed largely toward its support.

The church edifice, small but comfortable, is situated at the center. There are now from sixty to seventy members. The pastors have been Revs. Smith, Wakefield, Reeves, Calvin, Green, Carlton, Bartlett, and Bush.

FIRST PRESBYTERIAN CHURCH.

This church was organized in November, 1871, by members of the churches at Orr's corners and Ohltown. There were twenty-one members from the Newton church at Orr's corners, who petitioned to become members of the new church, and fifteen from the Rehoboth church, Ohltown, were admitted to membership by letter. Five persons, not at that time members of any church, were received upon profession of faith.

The church building, a neat and tastefully made house, probably the best country church in the county, was completed the same fall. The dedication took place December 28, 1871, Rev. John McMillan preaching the sermon on that occasion. Among those who were the largest subscribers to the building fund were William Riddle, Samuel Riddle, David Anderson, Miles Marshall, David Calhoun, David Johnson, and Samuel Johnson.

The church received several additions to its membership shortly after its organization, and now numbers over ninety communicants. The house was refurnished in 1881, and is now a very pretty and very comfortable church. There have been two settled ministers. Rev. Robert T. McMahan was the first; Rev. James W. Reese, who is now in charge, the second.

GRAVEYARDS.

The oldest burial place in the township is in the southeastern part near the Covenanter church. Here, in an uneven piece of ground, neglected, and overgrown with weeds and briers, the bones of the first settlers and many of their descendants repose.

There is a small graveyard in the northwestern part of the township, less than a half acre in area, which contains about twenty grave-stones. The earliest death there recorded is that of Lydia, wife of Anthony Stogdill, who died June, 12, 1832, aged thirty-seven.

North of the center are two graveyards adjoining the Methodist and the German churches.

IN EARLY DAYS.

We can find no traditions of mighty hunters; but here must have been an ample field for sportsmen. Deer were very numerous, and there were a large number of their trails leading through the township toward the salt springs. Killing wolves was pursued, not for sport, but as a matter of serious business, with a two-fold object in view, namely,—to preserve the flocks from their depredations, and to obtain the bounty for their scalps. Mr. Joseph Pierce relates that in one night seventeen sheep,—all of his flock but three,—were destroyed by these hungry marauders. John Pearsall, an early settler in the eastern part of the township, was chased one night by a pack of wolves. He was unarmed at the time, but by seizing a heavy club and making good use of it he was enabled to reach home in safety.

One night in the winter of 1819 Mrs. Pierce, mother of Joseph Pierce, lost her way while going to the house of her neighbor, McConnell, and took by mistake a path which led toward the salt spring, in Weathersfield. When the family became alarmed because of her absence they aroused the neighbors and hastened to search for her. She was found about midnight some miles from home. She contracted a severe cold from this exposure and never recovered from its effects.

Johnny, a little eight-year-old son of David McConnell, got lost one day while going from Pierce's house to his home. It was in the spring of the year and a very wet season, the lowland being entirely covered with water. The whole neighborhood was aroused and men and women commenced searching for the lost boy, wading through water and mud. Trumpets were blown and all joined in shouting, hoping that the boy would be guided to his friends by the sounds. After several hours Johnny was found near Jackson center by some of John Irwin's family. He had reached a creek so swollen by rains that he could not cross it, and had sat down by a tree to rest, where it is supposed he fell asleep. A heavy rain came on and awakened him suddenly. He began crying and thereby attracted the attention of the Irwins, who came to his rescue and restored him to his anxious parents.

The roads of Jackson township were long in condition which rendered travel on foot or

20*

horseback anything but pleasurable. Wagons were not much used, and many of the pioneers got along for years without one. The State road running east to Youngstown was cut out early in the present century, but for a long time it remained impassable for any kind of vehicles. West of the center there was a long strip of "corduroy" road—formed by laying round logs in the mud. From 1830 to 1840 many improvements were made in the highways previously marked out, and new roads built. Mr. William Young says that when he came to the township there were plenty of paths running through the woods, but no roads worthy the name. He was instrumental in having the north and south road west of his place constructed, and also assisted in making the north and south center road. For several years the first named road, now a much frequented thoroughfare, was not traveled enough to keep the grass down.

The swamps and swales of the southern part of the township were often covered with water for weeks at a time.

Canfield and Warren were the nearest trading places for the early settlers. There were very few articles bought at the stores, however. Sugar, clothing, etc., were manufactured at home. Salt, leather, tea and coffee were necessarily procured of the merchants. Few families took a newspaper, and letters were rarely sent or received.

JUSTICES OF THE PEACE.

From the fact that no township records are in existence, excepting those of a comparatively recent date, we can give no names of early township officers. It is generally agreed that Andrew Gault was the first justice, and John Pearsall the second. Robert Turnbull, William L. Roberts, Thomas Woodward, Jonathan Osborn, Jonas Ebert, David Camp, Jackson Truesdale, Samuel Johnston, Samuel Jones, William Anderson, Moses Felnagle, G. W. Osborn, and perhaps others, have held the office.

THE VILLAGE.

Jackson center, or North Jackson—it is the same place whichever name you use—is a thrifty little country village containing a goodly number of white houses, as well as four churches, four stores, a hotel, a saloon, three blacksmith shops, a tannery, two saw-mills, a flax-mill, a wagon-

shop, a harness shop, and a tailor's shop. A daily mail is received from West Austintown.

MERCHANTS.

Colwell Porter, Austintown's most successful merchant, started the first store in 1834, and employed a man named Housel to keep it. The goods were kept in a part of 'Squire Turnbull's log house. Afterwards Gideon Anthony managed the business, the firm being Porter & Anthony A man named Koons had a store in 1834, which he sold to Augustus Grater about the time Porter sold his interest to Anthony. Grater & Hoffman were in business on the southeast corner some years. David Anderson commenced in 1843, and afterwards sold to John Cartwright. About the same time Turnbull & Welkers had a store on the northwest corner of the center. David Anderson again commenced in 1856 on the southeast corner, and Anthony & Flaugher on the southwest corner. Anderson & Fusselman formed a partnership under the name D. Anderson & Co., and in 1862 the firm was changed to Anderson, Shaffer & Co.; the firm is now G. W. Shaffer & Co. Welkers sold to Moherman, Osborn & Lynn. Lynn retired, and the firm then became Moherman, Osborn & Moherman, afterwards changed to William & A. Moherman. They were followed by Dickson & Kirk, who were burned out in 1874. Fulk & Anderson commenced in 1866; Anderson withdrew, and the firm of Fulk, Wetzel & Wannemaker commenced business in 1868; Wetzel and Wannemaker retired, and Gideon Fulk continued until his death in 1873. Daniel B. Blott is now the proprietor of the store. G. W. Osborn and Osborn & Jones were in business as drug and hardware merchants a short time between 1865 and 1870. Shields, Orr & Co. had a furniture store for about one year. B. F. Phillips, who carries an extensive stock of drugs, medicines, notions, and jewelry, has been in the place since 1878. The two dry goods stores are well stocked, and their owners are receiving a large and well-merited patronage. Samuel Jones opened a hardware store in 1880. Considering the size of the place, there is a large amount of trading done at North Jackson.

PHYSICIANS.

The doctors who have resided for a short time in Jackson have been many. It is evidently a good place in which to begin the practice of medicine. Dr. Isaac Powers was the first physician, and remained less than a year. Dr. James F. Porter came in 1839, and was a successful practitioner for some years. Dr. Jackson Truesdale, Drs. Davis, Davidson, Gilmore, Connor, Burger, McKinley, Keith, Wilson, and others have each been here for short periods. Dr. Wells Spear was here some twenty years ago, and remained long enough to make an excellent reputation.

The present physicians are Dr. H. H. Webster and Dr. E. D. Hughes. Both are constantly increasing their practice, and rising in the respect of the people.

INDUSTRIES.

It was some time after the stores were opened at the village before there were any other industries.

In 1848 the steam saw-mill now owned by D. D. Jones was erected by Gideon Anthony and John Wannemaker. The mill now operated by Gault & Fullerton was built by Henry Prince at a later date.

The tannery of Miles Marshall & Sons was built by Mr. Marshall and Samuel Jones in 1848. Mr. Jones was in business with Mr. Marshall for about two years. The original building has been enlarged and its proprietors are doing a good business.

The hotel was built about 1844 by Benjamin Wannemaker, who was its landlord for some years, then sold to Samuel Wannemaker. In 1860 the house was purchased by its present proprietor, Cyrus Koons, who has enlarged and improved it.

In 1870 Samuel Wannemaker put up a building west of the center where he dresses flax, presses hay and straw, etc.

THE FIRST TAVERN.

Robert Turnbull kept a house of entertainment, but perhaps not a regular tavern. Jacob Probst, who also worked at his trade of tailoring, was keeping tavern in 1837 in the building now used by W. B. Mansel as a wagon-shop. Mr. Mansel, as will be seen from these pages, owns two buildings that once were churches, as well as a tavern and a school-house. The old tavern, the Methodist church, and the school-house are the same building, however.

OTHER MATTERS.

Robert Turnbull was the pioneer at the center, and built the first house. He came about 1828, and died in 1852. David Urick was the second settler at the center, coming soon after 'Squire Turnbull. He lived where 'Squire Jones now resides. He was a carpenter by trade, a good workman, and helped to build many houses in the township. Abner, one of his sons, is still a resident of Jackson.

Solomon Stroup moved from Pennsylvania to Jackson in 1833, and is still living here. He says he thinks there were but two houses at the center at the time of his coming. The growth of the place was slow. In 1840 there were seven or eight houses in the village.

Eli Marberger was the first blacksmith at the center. He was the strongest kind of a Democrat as well as a good citizen and an industrious worker. The post-office was kept in his shop for some years. He was elected justice of the peace, but resigned after serving a very short time. Mr. Marberger sold out and went to Niles.

THE POST-OFFICE.

The first postmaster at North Jackson was Robert Turnbull. The office was established in 1834 or 1835. Dr. James Porter, D. Anderson, Eli Marberger, Gideon Fulk, and G. W. Shaffer have succeeded in the office.

NORTH JACKSON HIGH SCHOOL.

A general feeling of interest in educational matters seems to have come upon the citizens about the year 1856. A select school was formed soon after, and Robert A. Kirk became the teacher. The building now used as a paint-shop was used as a school-room for a few terms. In 1860 the academy was erected, and thereafter, until recently, there have been regular terms of school. O. P. Brockway was the first teacher in the new house.

About four years ago the building was purchased of the stockholders by the trustees of the township, to be used as a town hall, but with the understanding that the citizens of the township should have the privilege of using the house for a select school whenever they desired.

BIOGRAPHICAL SKETCHES.

THE OSBORN FAMILY.

Nicholas Osborn, when a young man, emigrated to this country from England and settled in Virginia. He married in that State Margaret Cunnard, and reared a family of children, as follows: Jonathan, Sarah, Abraham, Richard, John, Elizabeth, Anthony, Mary, Joseph, and Aaron. His occupation was farming and milling. In 1804 he sold out and came to Trumbull county, Ohio, now Mahoning county, and purchased a large tract of land, one thousand acres of which was in Youngstown township and five hundred acres in Canfield, and he had in addition to these still other tracts. With him came Abraham, Anthony, Joseph, and their families, Aaron, then single, and the family of William Nier. John and his family came a short time before the rest. Joseph Osborn was born in Virginia in May, 1775, and when twenty-two years of age he married Margaret Wolfcale, daughter of John Wolfcale, who was born October 7, 1774. They became the parents of ten children, viz: Sarah, Mary, Mahlon, Jonathan, John W., Alfred, Abner, Thomas P., Elizabeth, and Joseph. On the 25th day of December, 1804, Joseph Osborn moved upon a part of the one thousand acre tract, which contained a log house erected by a man by the name of Parkhurst. The floor consisted of a few loose boards, and the door and windows were simply openings cut out of the sides of the house. There was no ceiling, and the fire-place had no hearth. Upon that place he resided and toiled until his death, which occurred February 17, 1846. His wife died July 20, 1854. Jonathan Osborn, a son of Joseph and Margaret Osborn, was born in Loudoun county, Virginia, May 28, 1804. The same year his parents removed to Ohio, and settled on the land which had been purchased in Trumbull county, as previously mentioned. Jonathan had but few early advantages for the acquirement of an education, but he has become, by reading and observation, a well-informed man. He remained upon the farm until after he was twenty-one. When he started for himself he had only a two-year-old colt. For the first five years he worked for Judge Baldwin, commencing at $2 per month. During this time he bought two hundred acres of land, paying $2.30 per acre for it. January 28, 1836, he married Mary Ann Goff, daughter of Humphrey Goff, then of Youngstown. She was born February 15, 1818, near Lewistown, Pennsylvania. This marriage was blessed with six children, viz: George W., Margaret J., Albert M., William N., Mary Alice, and Jonathan W. William and Jonathan died in early childhood. Mr. Osborn resides on a finely improved farm in the northwest part of Jackson township.

NOTES OF SETTLEMENT.

Andrew Calhoon was born in Pennsylvania October 5, 1777. In the first settlement of the country he and his father, Samuel Calhoon, came to Jackson township, now Mahoning county, bought them land and made preparations for the arrival of the mother, Nancy Calhoon, and Samuel and Matthew, and their ten sisters. Their only neighbors were the wild animals. Their greatest drawback was the heavy timber which occupied the soil, but the soil when exposed to the sun produced abundantly and there was no danger of starvation. But the wheat and corn had to be taken many miles during the first years of the settlement of the county in order to be ground for food. In a few years, however, neighbors began to come in, fields expanded, and the log cabins gave place to more commodious dwellings. Andrew Calhoon married Elizabeth, daughter of James Marshall, of Weathersfield, Trumbull county. She was then eighteen years of age. The result of this marriage was twelve children, namely: Isaac, Nancy, Lydia, David, Elizabeth, Matilda, Andrew, Samuel, James, Malissa, Belinda, and one that died in infancy. All of those named lived to maturity, although Nancy and Lydia are now deceased. Andrew Calhoon died October 5, 1833. His wife lived a widow something over forty years and died December 28, 1873.

David Calhoon, son of the subject of the preceding sketch, was born in Jackson township, Mahoning county, December 18, 1814. He attended only the pioneer schools where the "three R's" (reading, 'riting, and 'rithmetic) were taught. He remained on the home farm until he was of age and then bought a part of the

Jonathan Osborn

farm where he now resides in Jackson, which was then heavily timbered. He has since added to his first purchase and now has about two hundred acres. April 16, 1840, he married Rebecca Riddle, who was born in western Pennsylvania January 17, 1818, and when about two years old came with her parents to Jackson township. By this marriage there were seven children, to-wit: Andrew C., Samuel S., David B., John M., Elizabeth J., Sylvester J., James W., all living at this writing. Mr. and Mrs. Calhoon are members of the Presbyterian church.

Andrew Gault, Jr., youngest of seven children of Andrew Gault, Sr., was born in Jackson township, Mahoning county, December 7, 1804. Andrew Gault, Sr., was a native of Ireland and when about seventeen years of age he emigrated to America and after a time settled in Washington county, Pennsylvania. April 22, 1788, he married Eleanor Chesney, by whom he had seven children. In 1803 he emigrated with his family to Trumbull county, Ohio, and settled in Jackson township, where his grandson, James G., and his mother now live. He died January 8, 1832, surviving his wife, who died April 27, 1829. Andrew Gault received a good education for the times, attending, besides the common schools, select schools and the Canfield school. He helped to clear the farm on which he lived and devoted his life to his chosen occupation, that of farming. March 31, 1831, he married Mary Ewing, daughter of John Ewing, of Jackson township. She was born May 22, 1807. The result of this marriage was ten children, viz: Eleanor, Margaret, John E., Andrew R., Robert A., Margery Ann, James G., Sarah J., Mary C., and Rachel E., all of whom are living except Eleanor and Margery. It is said that Andrew Gault, our subject, was the first white male child born in Jackson township, and that his wife was the first female child. Mr. Gault was an intelligent but unassuming man and a Christian. He was a member of the Covenanter church. He died at the age of about sixty-six.

Robert A. Gault, son of the above, was born on the old homestead in Jackson, August 26, 1839. In 1861 he enlisted in company F, Forty-first Ohio volunteer infantry, serving four years and two months in the Army of the Tennessee and was in the battles of Pittsburg Land-

ing, Murfreesboro, Dallas, etc. He entered the service as a private but rose to the position of captain. In 1867 he was married to Miss Martha Johnson and has three children, viz: Cassius, Homer J., and Edith E.

James G. Gault, youngest son of Andrew Gault, Jr., was born in Jackson township August 21, 1842. In 1864 he went out in the one hundred day service, enlisting in company G, One Hundred and Fifty-fifth Ohio National guard. In 1869, June 15th, he married Mary Ellen Ewing, who was born November 24, 1844. They have three children, viz: Charles C., Lois M. B., and Grace Irene.

Robert Gault, Jr., was born in Green township, Mahoning county, on December 8, 1814. He is the only child of Robert Gault, Sr., who was born in Washington county, Pennsylvania, on March 31, 1789. Robert Gault, Sr., was the oldest child of Andrew Gault. Robert Gault was educated in the schools of Pennsylvania, and thus had probably better advantages than his younger brothers, whose chances for "schooling" were in the pioneer schools. He aided in clearing up and making a home and a sustenance on the tract of land which now constitutes the homestead. He and his father, when he was grown, purchased a farm of one hundred and sixty acres, on which the subject of this sketch now resides. In the fall of 1813 he married Charlotte Bowman, daughter of Phillip Bowman, a pioneer of Green township. He was a German by birth and immigrated from Maryland to Iowa. Prior to his immigrating he was one of the soldiers of the Revolutionary war. A few months after their marriage Robert Gault, Sr., was drafted in the War of 1812, and started for Detroit. At Cleveland he was taken ill, but for fear of being called a coward he proceeded with his company toward Detroit, but on the way was taken worse and died at Rocky River, Ohio, at the house of Widow Miner, October 29, 1814. Mrs. Gault, meanwhile, had gone to her father's in Green township, Mahoning county, where soon after her husband's death she gave birth to her only child by this husband. She afterwards married Joseph Hudson and moved to Iowa. When Robert Gault, Jr., was two years old he went to live with his grandfather, Andrew Gault. With him he grew up. On December 9, 1835, he married Margery Ewing, daughter of John

Ewing, of Jackson township. She was born in Jackson township on June 3, 1816. This marriage was blessed with twelve children—John, born December 27, 1836; Alexander and Margaret Sarah (twins), May 26, 1838; Mary, December 14, 1839; Andrew, November 14, 1841; Caroline, July 8, 1843; Martha J., March 8, 1845; Gideon, November 6, 1846; Samuel S., March 11, 1848; William, March 28, 1850; Gibson J., December 6, 1852, and Robert E., March 7, 1855. Caroline died August 31, 1844. Andrew enlisted in 1861 in the Forty-first regiment, Ohio volunteers, and was in the Army of the Cumberland. He was wounded in the arm at a skirmish at Dallas, Georgia, while retreating. This necessitated amputation, from the effects of which he died July 8, 1864. Both Mr. and Mrs. Gault are members of the United Presbyterian church.

Samuel Riddle, the subject of this sketch, was born in Washington county, Pennsylvania, July 8, 1794. His father, whose name was also Samuel, came to Jackson township, now Mahoning county, about the year 1803 or 1804. He settled on the Meander where he erected one of the first mills in that locality, which was long known as Riddle's mill. Samuel Riddle, our subject, was married June 18, 1818, to Polly Campbell, daughter of William Campbell, who was born in Pennsylvania March 28, 1792. By this marriage there were six children, viz: William C., Martha J., Margaret, Samuel, and a pair of twins that died in infancy. Both the daughters are now deceased. Margaret was the wife of Gibson Ewing. Samuel Riddle died March 30, 1869, and his wife Polly November 2, 1854.

William C. Riddle, the oldest of the children of the subject of the preceding sketch, was born in Jackson township, Mahoning county, then Trumbull, May 13, 1819. He remained at home upon the farm until he was twenty-seven, when he married and settled upon a farm two miles southeast of North Jackson, where he lived until five years ago, when he moved to that village. June 27, 1848, he married Martha J., daughter of John and Margaret Ewing, of Jackson township. She was born August 12, 1823. Though living in town Mr. Riddle superintends his farm, which is situated a short distance from his present residence. Himself and wife are members of the Presbyterian church.

Samuel Riddle, a younger brother of William C., was born in Jackson township, May 16, 1827. He derived his education at the district schools, which he attended for the most part during the winter season. When he was seventeen he taught his first school, and subsequently continued school teaching for six winters, and taught the school he formerly attended the winter after his marriage. Some six years after his marriage he bought the farm on which he now lives, east of North Jackson. He was united in marriage April 17, 1851, to Mary Spear, daughter of Alexander Spear, of Hartford, Trumbull county, who was born at Mount Jackson, Pennsylvania, August 12, 1824. For over twenty years he and his wife have been members of the Presbyterian church of Ohltown and of North Jackson.

John Ewing was a native of county Donegal, Ireland, and when about seventeen years of age his mother (his father having previously died) with two sons and two daughters emigrated to America. They first settled in Penn's valley, Pennsylvania, where for seven years he worked a farm on shares. In 1803 John Ewing came to Jackson township, now Mahoning county, where he bought a piece of land and erected the second house in the township. His older brother, Archibald, came out at the same time and settled in Austintown. The county was then almost a complete wilderness, with few neighbors (if settlers living miles apart and separated by dense woods can be called neighbors), the nearest mill being near Darlington, Pennsylvania; it was with these surroundings and under these circumstances that the subject of this biography began to build up a home. But his industry and energy brought prosperity, and he added to his original tract from time to time until he had a large property. When he commenced farming labor was worth only $4 per month. He married Margaret Orr, daughter of William Orr, then of Jackson but a native of Pennsylvania. They had a family of twelve children, as follow: Mary, Eleanor, Ann, Margaret, Alexander, Margery, Sarah, Gibson, Catharine, Martha J., John, and Rebecca, all of whom lived to adult age. Margaret, Sarah, Catharine, and Rebecca are now deceased. The father died July 13, 1842, aged seventy-one years. His wife survived him. He was drafted in the War of 1812 and started for the field, but the news from Hull's army caused him with others to return to their homes. He was an honest, upright man, and a good citizen, warmly attached to his adopted country, but owing to some peculiarity of his disposition never became naturalized. He and his wife were members of the Reformed church.

Alexander E. Ewing, oldest son and fifth child of John Ewing, of the preceding sketch, was born in Jackson township, Mahoning county, October 2, 1814. He remained with his father on the farm until he was twenty-seven, when, in 1842, he moved on the farm where he now lives which was then covered with forest. On May 19, 1842, he married Mary Ann Cook, daughter of James Cook, of Lawrence county, Pennsylvania. She was born March 14, 1821. They had five children: Margaret J., born March 24, 1843, died June 7, 1860; William J., born May 11, 1845; James C., born May 7, 1847; Gibson C., born February 24, 1851; and Mary Ellen Tirzah, born August 17, 1859. Mr. and Mrs. Ewing are members of the Reformed Presbyterian church. Mr. Ewing is the oldest resident of this township who was born in it.

Gibson Ewing, second son and eighth child of John Ewing, was born in Jackson township, Mahoning county, July 23, 1818. He attended the common schools of his boyhood days a short time during the winter months, but he acquired learning easily and made such progress that for five successive winters after his nineteenth year he taught school. He remained at home until he was nearly twenty-five engaged at farming, when not teaching, and on May 19, 1842, married Margaret Riddle, who was born in Jackson township September 18, 1823. This union resulted in eleven children, five dying in infancy. The following lived to maturity, viz: Samuel J., born July 17, 1844; Martha, born August 7, 1846; James R., born October 4, 1852; Rutherford B., born October 9, 1858 (died January 23, 1881); Mary A., born May 18, 1861; Sarah M., born November 3, 1863. Samuel was in the army in the war of the Rebellion in company F, Forty-first regiment, and was shot at the battle of Murfreesboro, on Stone river. Mrs. Ewing died January 10, 1872. She was a member of the Reformed Presbyterian church. Mr. Ewing is now connected with the United Presbyterian church of Youngstown.

William Shafer was a native of Virginia, born in 1813. When he was yet a boy his father, Samuel Shafer, emigrated from northern Virginia and settled a little over a mile southwest of Austintown center. He was the father of eight children, viz: Henry, John, William, Samuel, Daniel, Edward, Maria, and Eliza Jane. Schoolhouses in that early day being very scarce, William and his brother attended school for a time in Jackson township. William received but a meager education in these schools, working meanwhile upon the farm. A few years after his marriage he bought one hundred acres of land in Champion township, on which there had not been a stick of timber cut. The first winter they lived in a log house which was built without a fire-place and which was destitute of a stove. He lived upon that place, clearing and improving it, and working also at his trade, that of stone-mason. He married Elizabeth, daughter of George Gilbert, of Austintown. He was a soldier in the War of 1812. This marriage resulted in a family of five children, viz: Elizabeth, Henry, Jonathan R., Cornelius, and Phebe J., of whom all are living except Cornelius, who died in the winter of 1880–81. William Shafer died in 1855 in the forty-second year of his age.

Henry Shafer, oldest son of the subject of the foregoing sketch was born in Austintown township, Mahoning county, October 28, 1835. His parents having settled in the woods when he was a child, where the nearest school-house was over two miles distant, and there being so much hard work required upon the farm he enjoyed slender advantages for the acquirement of an education. He remained upon the farm until he was about twenty years of age, when he learned the carpenter's trade, and has made this a part of his business since, though farming is his chief occupation. In October, 1860, he was married to Louisa, daughter of Abraham Strock, of Austintown township, by whom he has had six children, as follow: William, Frank B., Leander D., Lewis A., George W., and Charles Caster, of whom William and Lewis are dead. Mrs. Shafer died November 2, 1879. She was a member of the Christian church.

Jonas Wannemaker was born in Lehigh county, Pennsylvania, December 12, 1821. His father, Daniel Wannemaker, was also a Pennsylvanian and a miller by trade. He married Catharine Kistler, whose father was a Revolutionary soldier and died of camp fever near Philadelphia. By this marriage there were seven children—Nathan, Sophia, Abbie, Daniel, John, Benjamin, and Jonas. Abbie and John are dead. When the subject of this sketch was about twelve years of age his father died and some three years afterward his mother and her family, except the oldest child, emigrated to Trumbull county, and located in Southington township. Mrs. Wannemaker there married Daniel Murrboyer, of Warren township. When the subject of this sketch was seventeen he began clearing a farm of one hundred and eight acres, which fell to him and his brother Benjaman from the estate. For some four years after he was twenty-one he worked most of the time at carpentering with his brothers, Daniel and John. Since that time he has been engaged at farming. About thirty years ago he purchased and moved upon the farm where he now lives. January, 1847, he married Hannah Ebert, of Jackson, by whom he has had ten children—Mary, Charles A., Thomas, Wesley, William Henry, Sarah A., Lottie C., Elmer D., Jonas F., and L. Dell. Mary died in infancy and Charles at the age of twenty-two. Mrs. Wannemaker died May 23, 1879. She was and he is a member of the Methodist Episcopal church.

Tobias Kimmel was born in Somerset county, Pennsylvania, in 1802. When quite a small boy his father, Isaac Kimmel, came to Youngstown township, Trumbull county, now Mahoning, where he remained for a number of years and then removed to Coitsville township. He was a farmer by occupation. Tobias Kimmel when a young man learned the blacksmith trade and for a number of years carried on a shop in Youngstown. About 1824 he moved to his farm which he occupied some eight years, when he moved to Poland township where he resided until his death. His wife was Rebecca, daughter of William Smith, of Mercer county, Pennsylvania, who became the mother of the following named children, all living to mature age, viz: Abraham, William, Philip, Smith, Dwight, Mary, John, Sarah, Ruth Ann, and Tobias M. Philip died at the age of twenty-two. After his wife's death Mr. Kimmel married Lida Shearer, nee McBride, who is still living. Mr. Kimmel died January 20, 1880.

Smith Kimmel was born in Coitsville township September 9, 1830. He derived his education in the common schools, and farming has been his chief occupation although for a number of years he has carried on a blacksmith shop with his brother Abraham in Coitsville township. December 21, 1852, he married Julia Ann, daughter of David Struble, of East Hubbard. This marriage has been blest with eight children, to wit: Martin A., David A., Alice N., Mary E., Frank E., Charles E., Gilbert B., and Arthur D. Alice is deceased. In 1864 Mr. Kimmel was called out with his company and regiment—company C, One Hundred and Seventy-first Ohio National guard—and served one hundred days under Heintzleman. While in the service he contracted a fever from which he has never wholly recovered. He resided in Coitsville township until six years of ago when he purchased the John Ewing place, in Jackson township, where he now resides.

James Hervey Webster was born in the State of New York. He was a mason by trade and also carried on a farm in Chautauqua county. When a few years old he moved to Sandusky county, Ohio, where he married Mary Ann Tucker, daughter of Nathaniel and Mary Tucker, now living at an advanced age in Sandusky county. Soon after their marriage they moved upon a farm in Chautauqua county, New York, where he remained until his death, which occurred April 1, 1870. He was an old-time Whig and afterward a Republican. He was the father of ten children, of whom three died in infancy, Jason, Herbert T., Henry H., Ella A., Ralph D., Israel J., and Nelson R. The mother of these children afterward married Philip R. Snider, and is now living near Port Clinton, Ottawa county, Ohio.

H. H. Webster, M. D., was born in Portland township, Chautauqua county, New York, July 30, 1849. He is the third child of James H. Webster, a sketch of whose life has been given. Dr. H. H. Webster was educated in the common schools, and through the influence of his brother, Dr. H. T. Webster, for five years a practicing physician of Jackson, he began studying medicine, and graduated after attending three courses of lectures at the Eclectic Medical institute of Cincinnati, in the spring of 1873. He located first at Niles with his brother, where he remained until August, 1874, when he went to Montville, Geauga county, where he remained until January 11, 1879, when he came to Jackson and bought out his brother, and has since practiced in that town and vicinity. February 18, 1875, he married Martha Jones, daughter of Samuel Jones, of Lordstown township. She was born May 18, 1850. They have two children, Samuel J., born October 25, 1876; Hervey, born November, 1877. Mrs. Webster is a member of the Disciple church. Dr. Webster is a member of the society of Free and Accepted Masons.

Thomas Woodward, a native of Milford township, Mifflin county, Pennsylvania, was born December 17, 1799. He is the fifth child of Jehu Woodward, who married Rachel Rummins, of Mifflin county, Pennsylvania. They had the following children: James, Ruth, Joseph, Lydia, Thomas, William Leonard, Jehu, Elizabeth, Rachael, Joel, and Ezekiel. When Thomas was seventeen years old he was apprenticed to learn the carpenter's and cabinet-maker's trade, serving two years, after which he worked at his trade about two years. In April, 1823, he came to Austintown where he remained a year, then went to Youngstown where he built houses which are yet standing. He then bought land which constitutes his present farm. This was a dense forest at that time, out of which he made a fruitful farm and comfortable home. He married January 10, 1823, Margaret Shively, daughter of Frederick Shively, of Austintown. She was born in Tyron township, Cumberland county, Pennsylvania, August 17, 1805. They had thirteen children: Jehu, Leonard, John, Abraham, Elizabeth, Margaret, Rachel, Joel, Angeline, Mary, Ezekiel, Melissa Olive, and Almina, of whom Leonard, Rachel, Margaret, and Ezekiel are dead, the two former living to be grown. He has been a Democrat from Jackson's time; has held several township offices, and was for eleven years justice of the peace of Jackson. He is one of the oldest residents of the township. Mrs. Woodward has been for years a member of the Methodist church. He is an upright man enjoying the esteem of all who know him.

William Young was born in Little Beaver township, Beaver county, Pennsylvania, January 14, 1804. He was the fourth in a family of nine children of James and Esther Young. He re-

mained with his father until he was about sixteen, and on starting out in life he went to Buffalo where he worked out six months teaming. He spent the winter at home threshing with a flail for the tenth part, and in the spring he went up the Allegheny river, and for three years was at work on the canals in Pennsylvania and Ohio. September 8, 1830, he married Sarah McGeorge, a former school-mate, and on the third day after their marriage he and his young bride started on horseback for Trumbull county, Ohio. He purchased the farm on which he now lives and moved upon it in 1837. There was but little clearing done and a log house and barn constituted the improvements. He has since added to his original purchase until he owns over three hundred and twenty acres in the southeast part of Jackson township. His farms are now managed by his three sons. By his first marriage he had eight children: William, Hatton, Adaline, Julia A., James, John, Mary, and Clark, of whom the oldest and youngest are dead. His first wife died October 27, 1854, aged fifty-two, and July 5, 1855, he married Margaret Anderson, of Poland township, by whom he had two children: Emily and Margaret. His second wife died April 9, 1858, aged nearly forty-two, and he married a third time, May 5, 1859, Ellen Wallace, from near Petersburg, Mahoning county. His third wife died April 4, 1880, aged sixty-two. He had by this marriage one child, W. M. Wallace. Mr. Young is a member of the Reform Presbyterian church. His daughter Adaline married John Truesdale and is now living in Richland county, Wisconsin; Julia married Daniel Gibson, and now resides in Beaver county, Pennsylvania; Mary became the wife of Charles Anthony, and lives in Nodaway county, Missouri; Margaret married Sylvester Calhoon, and resides in Sumner county, Kansas; and Emily resides at home with her father.

James Russell was born in Austintown township, Mahoning county, July 1, 1815. His father was Robert Russell, who settled in that township in 1806. The subject of this sketch derived his education in the schools of that early period, the teachers of which, in many instances, taught both English and German. He worked upon the home farm until he was twenty-six years of age, when he moved to the farm in

Jackson where he now lives, which now consists of two hundred acres. May 4, 1841, he married Catharine, daughter of Henry Foos, one of the pioneers of Austintown and a soldier of the War of 1812. He moved into Austintown just at the close of the war. Mrs. Russell was born October 21, 1820. They have a family of seven children, as follows: Clark, Austin, Henry, Robert, Newton, Almeda A., and James Monroe. Mr. Russell has always attended strictly to his own affairs; has never been a witness at court and has never been a litigant, either as plaintiff or defendant, which few can say. He and his wife are members of the Disciple church, and are worthy citizens.

Gideon Fusselman, a native of Lehigh county, Pennsylvania, removed from that State to Ohio in the year 1814, and settled in Warren township, Trumbull county, on the Storer farm which was then owned by John Fusselman, Sr. In about a year he removed to Canfield and established a tannery (he being a tanner by trade) one mile north of the center. This was conducted by him until his death. In about 1812 he married Eve Schriber, also a native of Lehigh county. They had five children, John C., Mary, Sarah, Catharine, and Elizabeth, all of whom are living. Gideon Fusselman died August 30, 1844, in Lehigh county, Pennsylvania, while on a visit to that place. His wife died January 22, 1878, at the age of eighty-three years.

John C. Fusselman was born in Lehigh county, Pennsylvania, February 25, 1813. He was the oldest child of Gideon Fusselman who removed to Ohio when John was about a year old. He received a common school education and staid upon the farm with his father until June, 1830, when he began clerking for J. R. Church at Canfield in a general merchandise store, remaining here five years. He then went into partnership with Mr. Church in Ellsworth in merchandising, where he remained until 1840. He then clerked for William Ripley one year, when he went into business for himself until 1856. He then came to Jackson and began the same business with D. Anderson, which continued six years. Then the firm of Anderson, Shaffer & Co. was formed. April, 1881, Mr. Anderson retired, and the firm Shaffer & Co. continue the business, with a full assortment of goods usually kept in a country store. On Au-

gust 11, 1837, J. C. Fusselman married Catharine Houts, daughter of William Houts, then of Green township, Mahoning county. She was born September 24, 1815. This union was blessed with seven children—Louisa Ann, Lottie B., Frank A., Mary, Ella H., John R., and Ralph, who died at three years of age. He and his wife are both members of the Methodist church. For twenty years prior to 1856 he was justice of the peace of Ellsworth township.

D. B. Blott, was born in Jackson township, Mahoning county, October 6, 1837. He is the second child of Benjamin Blott, a native of Pennsylvania, who was born January 16, 1812. He is a farmer, residing a short distance south of North Jackson. D. B was educated in the common schools, and attended also for a short time Hiram college. At the age of fifteen he was apprenticed to learn the bricklayer and stone mason trade, serving two years—afterward working at his trade for ten years, when, on account of poor health, he was obliged to stop work for about three years. Then for six years he kept a store in Lordstown. After this he kept a store for several years at West Austintown. He now keeps a store at Jackson, where he carries a line of assorted goods. He married Lucinda Bailey, daughter of Jesse Bailey. They have five children, Charley C., born 1863; Seamon Edward, 1865, William A., 1869, Marietta, 1874, and Emory B., 1876.

Robert McClure, a native of county Donegal, Ireland, was born November, 1816. His father, Robert McClure, died when he was three years old, when he was taken by his paternal grandfather, who was a farmer. He remained with him until 1839, when he sailed to America, coming in the same ship with William Porter, of Austintown. He came at once to Austintown and began as day laborer here and there, and for five months worked on the extension of the Erie canal. A few years afterward he bought the land where he now resides. He at one time owned over two hundred acres of land, but by unfortunate indorsements he lost a part of this. He owns one hundred acres under good cultivation. May 14, 1846, he married Eliza Anderson, daughter of Arthur Anderson, of Poland township. She was born in that township November 20, 1819. This marriage was blessed with eight children, William, a physician of Cleveland;

Mary, who married William Turner, of Austintown; Arthur, who died in early childhood; John S., an attorney of Chicago; Emily; Nettie; Nancy, a teacher of Youngstown; Robert, a teacher, who, with Emily, are still at home. He is a member of the Presbyterian church, and his wife is a Covenanter.

Peter Ivy was born in Perry county, Pennsylvania, March 8, 1805. He was a son of Samuel Ivy, and twin brother of William Ivy, who at last accounts was living in Clark county, Ohio. His father, Samuel Ivy, died when he was an infant, and his mother married Michael Waggoner, and soon after the family removed to Cumberland county, Pennsylvania, whence in the fall of 1822 they immigrated to Stark county, Ohio, where they remained about four years, during which time Mr. Waggoner died, when Peter brought the family to Austintown, where he had gone in the spring of 1823. After farming there a few years, Peter moved in 1831 upon the farm where he now lives, which he purchased the previous year, and upon which he made a small clearing and erected a cabin. He has now over a hundred acres under cultivation. August 13, 1826, he married Sarah Miller, daughter of Jacob Miller, a Virginian, who, in advanced life, became a resident of Austintown township. She was born in Augusta county, Virginia, September 12, 1798. She became the mother of seven children, Mary, Christian, John, Alfred, William, Elizabeth, who died when small, and Sarah. The oldest child died before it was named. She was a Presbyterian in belief, and an estimable lady, who, after a long and useful life, died September 8, 1879. He cast his first vote for Jackson.

John Lynn, son of Nicholas Lynn, was born in Berks county, Pennsylvania, and emigrated to Ohio with his brothers, Peter and George, and settled in Canfield township, Trumbull county (now Mahoning), about the year 1806. They settled in the same neighborhood. John, in company with his sister Barbara, purchased the farm originally owned by Ira Wilcox, and they lived together a number of years. Late in life he married Sophrona F. Burgart of Ellsworth township, by whom he had six children, viz: Sarah Ann, who married Joseph Hartman; John N. O., David, Elizabeth, who married George E. Harding, George, who died in infancy, and

Mary, who died when two years of age. Mr. Lynn died in 1835, at the age of fifty-six years. He was a member of the German Reformed church. His widow afterwards married Solomon Gordon, of Canfield.

John N. O. Lynn was born in Canfield township, August 8, 1826. When he was about twenty years of age he and his brother and two sisters began the management of the farm, which he continued for seven years. He afterward moved to Atwater township, Portage county, where he lived eighteen years engaged in farming, which has been his lifelong occupation. In April, 1875, he returned to Mahoning county, and has since resided at North Jackson. April 29, 1855, he was married to Elizabeth, daughter of Abraham Moherman, who was born March 15, 1835. They have no children, but are raising two—Chester and Mary. He and his wife are members of the Disciples church.

David Lynn, second son of John Lynn, was born December 31, 1829. He adopted the occupation of his father, cultivating the soil and dealing to some extent in stock and fruit growing. At the age of twenty-five he married Miss Mary Ann Peters, by whom he had four sons—Willis, Emory, Homer, and Alfred. While engaged attentively at his business he has not neglected the education of his children, his oldest son graduating at Heidelberg college, Tiffin, Ohio, in the class of 1878. Mr. and Mrs. Lynn are members of the Reformed church.

CHAPTER VIII.
COITSVILLE.[*]
INTRODUCTORY.

This is township two of range one of the Connecticut Western Reserve, and forms the extreme northeastern corner of Mahoning county. Coitsville is thus bounded: on the north by Hubbard, Trumbull county; on the east by Pennsylvania; on the south by Poland; and on the west by Youngstown. The township contains the little village of Coitsville Center, which, however, is situated a little south of the geo-

[*]Mainly from facts collected by John Shields.

graphical center of the township; also a portion of the little mining village known as Thorn Hill, now in a condition of decline.

The land of the township is excellent for farming purposes, the soil being generally a deep and fertile loam. The nearness of Youngstown gives the farmers the advantage of a ready market, and as their land is constantly rising in value, we find them generally well-contented and prosperous.

The surface is quite variable. In the eastern and southern portions of the township are a number of steep hills of considerable elevation, reaching back some distance from the Mahoning river. This stream cuts across the southeastern part of the township, and its green banks and fertile bottom lands here form some of the finest natural scenery in the whole county. From the big hill east of Struthers can be obtained a view of the Mahoning valley surpassingly rich in its extent and beauty. Busy hamlets overhung by dark clouds of smoke impress the spectator with the greatness of the industries of the valley; while vast expanses of woodland, interspersed with many richly cultivated farms adorned with fields of waving grain which surround the comfortable farm houses and barns; the sleek cattle grazing in the meadows; the busy farmers in their corn-fields, or driving along the roads with wagons heavily laden with the fruits of their toil, all show that the agricultural community is as thrifty and as active as the manufacturers. Could one of the men who in 1798 entered this beautiful valley and found it as silent and as wild as ever primeval forests were, its solitude invaded only by the prowling savage, the stealthy beasts of prey or flocks of birds—could such a one now rise from his years of sleep in the grave and behold this bustling scene, his astonishment, surprise, and amazement would doubtless equal the feelings of Rip Van Winkle on his return to his former home.

Excepting the Mahoning, the streams in this township are small and unimportant. Dry run pursues a winding course and drains a considerable portion of the surface. Other small streams are numerous.

Coal has been mined to some extent in former years, but at present no mines of importance are in operation. Thorn Hill and vicinity formed a busy mining community, but the banks were deserted for other and more promising ones not situated in Coitsville. Agriculture is the mainstay and support of nearly all the inhabitants of the township.

PURCHASE AND SURVEY.

Previous to the year 1798 Daniel Coit, of the State of Connecticut, purchased from the Connecticut Land company township number two in the first range, and gave to it the name of Coitsville. It does not appear that he ever became a resident of the township, but authorized Simon Perkins, of Warren, to act as his general agent.

In 1798 Mr. Coit sent on a party to survey his land and put it in the market. John Partridge Bissel was the chief surveyor and also the sub-agent for the sale of the land.

ORGANIZATION AND FIRST ELECTION.

In 1806, December 4th, the following was given at Warren, Trumbull county:

ORDERED, by the board of commissioners for the county of Trumbull, that number two, in the first range of townships in said county, be set off as a separate township, by the name of Coitsville, with all the rights, privileges, and immunities by law given to and invested in any township in this State, and the first meeting of said township shall be held at the house formerly occupied by John P. Bissel, in said township.

Attest:
                     WILLIAM WETMORE,
                     Clerk Commissioners *pro tem.*

The first election was held April 6, A. D. 1807, Alexander M'Guffey, chairman, John Johnson and Joseph Jackson, judges of the election. The following officers were chosen: Joseph Bissel, township clerk; William Huston, Joseph Jackson, and William Stewart, trustees; John M'Call and Timothy Swan, overseers of the poor; William Martin and Ebenezer Corey, supervisors of highways; David Cooper and John Stewart, fence viewers; James Stewart and Alexander M'Guffey, appraisers of houses; Alexander M'Guffey, lister; James Lynn, constable; John Johnson, treasurer.

INTERESTING TOWNSHIP RECORDS.

The records of the township for a few years following its organization show a number of interesting facts. Here is one which we copy from Towship Record Book No. 1, page 98:

At a meeting of William Huston, Joseph Jackson, and William Stewart, trustees for the township of Coitsville, at the dwelling house of Joseph Bissel of said town, on April 27, 1808, ordered, that every person subject to pay a county tax, according to the act passed by the General Assembly of the State of Ohio, December 24, 1807, to kill ten squirrels, and in addition to the ten squirrels, each person to kill two squirrels for each cow and four for each horse; and if a person have but one cow she is exempt.

Attest: JOSEPH BISSEL,
                                 Township Clerk.

Same page:

At a meeting of the inhabitants June 27, 1808, voted that the squirrel act be continued to the 1st day of August next, before returns are made to the collector of county taxes.

Attest: JOSEPH BISSEL,
                                 Township Clerk.

There are several records made of warning poor people, likely to become township charges, to quit the township.

TAXES IN 1803.

From ancient records we learn that the entire amount of taxes assessed upon Coitsville in the year 1803, was $14.95. A copy of the list is given.

COITSVILLE, RANGE ONE, TOWN ONE.

	Amount of tax.		Amount of tax.
Augustine, Daniel	$0 57	Pauley, James	$0 65
Bissell, Joseph	71	Robb, Matthew	44
Cooper, David	60	Shehy, Roger	80
Casper, Cramer	86	Shields, James	46
Fitch, Andrew	61	Smith, James	20
Given, John	32	Stewart, William Jr.	40
Gillan, Matthew	20	Thompson, John Jr.	81
Houston, William	64	Thompson, George	70
Harris, Barnabas	40	Weeks, William	60
Loveland, Amos	1 56	Wilson, Robert	32
Meers, James	20	Wilson, Daniel	30
Martin, William	20	White, James	40
McGuffey, Alexander	64	White, Francis	24
McBride, Samuel	40	Welch, James	20
McCall, John	32		
Potter, John	20	Total	$14 95

EARLY SETTLERS.

To Amos Loveland belongs the honor of having made the first permanent settlement in the township. He was a Revolutionary soldier and served three years. He came to Coitsville in the spring of 1798, joined the surveying party and spent the summer assisting them. In the fall he returned to his home in Chelsea, Orange county, Vermont, having purchased all the land in Coitsville situated on the south side of the Mahoning—a tract of four hundred and twenty-six acres, mostly level, rich, and fertile. In December, 1798, with his wife and six children, he left Chelsea for his new home. Mr. Loveland started from Vermont with two sleighs loaded with bedding, furniture, farming utensils, etc., each sleigh being drawn by two horses They traveled in this way until they reached the Susquehanna, which they crossed on the ice at Whitestown; the snow disappearing soon after, Mr. Loveland traded his sleighs for a wagon, transferred his goods into it and continued his journey. April 4, 1799, he arrived with his family upon his farm. They began housekeeping in a small log cabin which he had erected the previous year. This cabin was about eighteen feet square; it had no glass windows, and its door was made of clapboards with two sticks across, two of them being hinges fastened by wooden pins. Not a nail had been used in the construction of this dwelling. A puncheon or split log floor covered about half the ground included within the log walls. There was no upper floor, and no chimney except a stone wall built up about five feet to keep the fire from the logs. In this cabin, of course with the addition of some improvements, the family lived six years, and then erected a larger and more convenient one.

During the first year the family depended largely upon the results of hunting for their food, with occasional supplies obtained from the few neighboring settlements. Mr. Loveland cleared up his farm and resided upon it until his death, which occurred at the age of ninety. Mrs. Loveland died when ninety-three. Her maiden name was Jemima Dickerson. The Lovelands were the first family in the township, and to them were born the first male, as well as the first female child born in Coitsville. Cynthia Loveland was born in June, 1799, and died in 1815. Her brother David, born a year or two later, was the second child born in the township. He spent the whole of a long life upon the old homestead, and his heirs still own some three hundred acres of the original farm. Elizabeth Loveland, one of the daughters, became the wife of William McFarlin and the mother of six sons and six daughters. She died June 16, 1881, aged ninety years, ten months and nine days. She enjoyed the distinction of being a resident of the Western Reserve longer than any other person, having resided continuously in the Mahoning valley over eighty-two years.

John P. Bissel, the surveyor of 1798, purchased a farm including the center of the township, made a clearing, and built a log-cabin. In 1800 he emigrated from his home in Lebanon, Connecticut, with his family, consisting of three sons and six daughters, and settled on his purchase. The family remained in Coitsville until 1805 or 1806 when they removed to Youngstown in order that the children might have better school advantages. Mr. Bissel was the first acting justice of the peace in Coitsville. He died in 1811. His daughter Mrs. Mary Kyle resided upon the old homestead from the time of his father's death until her own. She died in 1880, in the eighty-third year of her age.

Asa Mariner, then a single man, was one of the surveying party. In 1798 he purchased a farm a little northwest of the center of the township, upon which he settled in 1800. He married Sally Beggs and reared a numerous and respectable family. This couple lived to a good old age, honored and respected. Mr. Mariner was a member of the Disciple church, his wife of the United Presbyterian. The old farm is still in the possession of two of the sons, Major James Mariner and his brother Ira.

Rev. William Wick was a pioneer of Coitsville. He was a native of Long Island, New York, but came to this county from Washington county, Pennsylvania. September 1, 1799, he preached a sermon in Youngstown, said to have been the first sermon preached on the Reserve. About 1801 he purchased a farm on the State line which is now occupied by the Beggs family. Mr. Wick was ordained a preacher of the gospel by the Presbyterian church and installed pastor of the congregations of Youngstown and Hopewell, now Bedford, Pennsylvania. All the Coitsville Presbyterians of the old school attended his church. He continued in his relation as pastor until death called him home in 1815. He was a very popular preacher and was instrumental in persuading persons of moral and religious character to settle in Coitsville. During his pastorate he preached fifteen hundred and twenty-two sermons and solemnized sixty-nine marriages. He was the father of eight sons and five daughters. Of this family eleven lived to mature age. Some of his sons attained some eminence in the political world. William was Secretary of State in Indiana and James a judge of the court of common pleas in Mercer county, Pennsylvania. The family were noted for being fine singers and proficients in penmanship.

Barney Harris, the first blacksmith in Coitsville township, came from Washington county, Pennsylvania, and settled on section eleven previous to 1802. He brought up ten children, three sons and seven daughters. George, the only son now living, resides with his family in Iowa. Three daughters with their families still in this vicinity. Mrs. Harris was a daughter of Andrew Poe, noted for his encounter with an Indian near Georgetown, on the Ohio river. Mr. A. B. Wilson, a grandson of Barney Harris, resides on the old Harris farm. David Wilson came from Washington county, Pennsylvania, in 1803 or 1804. He had two sons and three daughters. Of this number only one son, David, is now living—a resident of Bedford, Pennsylvania. Mr. Wilson was a wheelwright by trade. In early years the little spinning-wheel was an indispensable article in every household, and Mr. Wilson engaged in its manufacture, and for many years gave employment to several men in his shop, where he made wheels, reels, and coffins. The improvements made in spinning machinery as time progressed destroyed one branch of this business, but he continued the undertaking business for many years. Mr. Wilson erected a grist-mill to be run by ox-power, but after a few years' trial it was pronounced a failure and abandoned. He erected a brick house in 1815, which is still occupied by his descendants.

Alexander McGuffey and family moved from Washington county, Pennsylvania, to Coitsville in about the year 1800. His father and mother, who were natives of Scotland, also came with him. The family were zealous Presbyterians. Alexander was a farmer, and settled near Sand Hill. His son, Rev. William McGuffey, became widely known as the author of a series of school books known as McGuffey's Eclectic Readers. William was brought to Coitsville in infancy. His mother—an excellent woman—used to delight in recounting the hardships they endured during the first years of their residence here, and how she used to place William in a sugar-trough while she assisted her husband in clearing up the farm. William received his common school education in Coitsville, the writer of these sketches being one of his school-mates. Our school-house was a cabin built of round logs, situated at the corners of the farms now occupied by Thomas Brownlee, Rev. H. S. Boyd, Al. Wilson, and Ambrose Shields. William McGuffey afterwards taught school in the same place. He began the study of the dead languages under John McCready, who taught a select school near Pulaski, Mercer county, Pennsylvania, in 1817; completed his college course and graduated from the college at Oxford, Ohio. He was licensed as a preacher by the presbytery, but was never the settled pastor of any congregation. Instead, he devoted his life to the advancement of education. He died in his seventy-sixth year at the residence of his daughter in Dayton, Ohio. But his memory will be long perpetuated by his works. William McGuffey was a man of genial temperament, a pleasant and affable speaker.

David and Rebecca (Armstrong) Cooper settled in the township in 1800. Five of their children still reside in Coitsville. He was a native of Maryland; his wife of Pennsylvania. Mr. Cooper was a member of the surveying party of 1798.

James Lynn settled early on section eleven. His farm is now the Dalby farm. About the same time with him John Johnson settled on section ten.

Sampson Moore, about 1802, settled on section ten. He lived and died in this township, and brought up his family here. None of his sons became settlers of Coitsville.

William, James, John, and David Stewart came here at different dates. All were early settlers. David settled west of the village. William, James, and John took up farms in the northwestern quarter of the township. David Stewart, son of William, lives on his father's old place. Robert Stewart, son of William, lives on section three. John and James settled near William. Mr. Rush owns a part of James' farm, and the Grays a part of John's.

Thomas Early was among the first settlers in the western part of the township. The Fitch family, elsewhere mentioned, were among the early settlers on the Mahoning.

David Brownlee, his parents, and his sister Margaret, were early settlers near the south line of the township. John Brownlee, who lives near the Pennsylvania line, is a son of David. The family consisted of ten children, of whom three sons and one daughter are still living, John being the oldest.

Matthew Robb was an early settler on the William Price farm. He afterwards sold this and built where Mr. McCartney lives.

Daniel Augustine, a sober, industrious, honest German, settled in the township in 1802. His family is still well represented in this township. It is related of him that he was once offered $15 for a cow which he had for sale. He refused the price; said that $13 was all that she was worth, and all he was willing to take.

William Bell was an early settler in the northeast of the township, lived and died here. Some of his sons remained for a time, then moved away. One, John Mason Bell, lived upon the old place until his death.

In the same neighborhood was Ebenezer Corey, whose family are all gone from the township.

A man named Thompson was an early settler on Ambrose Shields' farm. He sold to Timothy Swan, who lived and died there.

Joseph and Mary (Goe) Beggs, natives of Ireland, settled in Coitsville, west of the village, in 1802. Their son, James Beggs, Esq., born June 17, 1799, is still a resident of the township. Joseph Beggs was a soldier of 1812.

John Johnson, from Mercer county, Pennsylvania, settled in the eastern part of the township in 1803. He married Jane Caldwell, of Beaver county, Pennsylvania, and brought up a family of nine children. Only two are now living, Samuel in Iowa, and John in this township. David Johnson, one of his family, died in April, 1881.

James Shields, a native of Ireland, came to Coitsville in 1802 and purchased a farm of two hundred and thirty acres east of the village. The same year he married Margaret Walker. He died in 1854 aged eighty years. He reared three sons and five daughters, all of whom settled in Coitsville and had families, except one daughter who died young. All of the original family are now dead excepting John, the oldest son, and James, the youngest. The latter resides in Loveland, Colorado. James Shields, Sr., built and operated the first distillery in the township. It was erected in 1803. He operated it for a few years, but not finding the business profitable, sold out and thenceforth devoted himself to employments more useful and beneficial. Ammi R. and Prudence (Burrows) Bissel settled a little north of the village in 1806. Their son, Partridge Bissel, born in 1803, is still a resident of the township. Ammi Bissel was a brother of John

P., and came from Vermont. He was the father of five sons and two daughters. He was the first carpenter in the township, and was energetic and active in his work. He was a good neighbor and an honest man.

The Widow McFarlin (*nee* Margery Anderson) came to this township from Ireland about the year 1804, with a family of four sons and two daughters, all of whom married after coming here. Isabel, the oldest, married James McGill; Mary married Robert McKean, settled in Ellsworth and died there; Alexander settled south of the center of Coitsville. He was accidentally killed by the falling of a tree. He had seven sons and two daughters, most of whom settled in this vicinity. William settled on the top of the hill on the Hazelton road. He reared a large family. Eleven children arrived at years of maturity. But one son is living, Anderson, at Coitsville. Four of his daughters are living, viz: Mrs. Lydia Mahan, Liberty, Trumbull county; Miss Jemima McFarlin, Niles; Mrs. Matilda Price, Coitsville, and Mrs. Lavina Harris, Youngstown. Andrew settled in the southern part of the township, but later moved to Indiana and died. He had a large family. His sons are all dead. Several daughters are living in Indiana. James settled on the road leading west from the village and died there. He had several children, none of whom remain.

The first shoemaker, Stephen Allerton, came from New Jersey, and settled south of the center, early in this century. He was honest and a good neighbor, but intemperate in his habits.

The first tailor was John Potter, a very early settler. He was a good citizen, and a strict Presbyterian. His farm was on the Hubbard and Lowell road. He had a large family, but not a branch of it remains here at the present day.

The oldest man in this township is Alexander Beggs, born in Ireland about the year 1789. He settled in Coitsville in 1822.

The first marriage ceremony was performed about 1803, uniting Ebenzer Corey and Polly Thompson in the bonds of wedlock.

The first death was that of an infant son of John P. Bissel, and occurred in 1801.

HARD TIMES.

The year 1811 brought hard times for many of the pioneers of Coitsville. Mr. Bissel died in that year. His financial affairs were found in a bad condition, which brought disaster to many of those who had purchased their lands from him. Some had paid for their lands, received their deeds, and were, consequently, safe. Others who had not got their lands paid for and received their titles were caught up. No matter how much they had paid, all fared alike and received a small percentage on the money which they had paid. The land had to be re-purchased or abandoned. It was supposed, had he lived to settle up his own affairs, the result would have been different. Another cause of discouragement was a series of very rainy seasons, which flooded the low, flat lands, and caused them to be unproductive. This caused a bad report to be put into circulation concerning the town, and many emigrants to pass us by. Again, the War of 1812 was upon us, and many of the men subject to do military duty were drafted or volunteered, and went into the service. There were few left at home except women and children, old men, cripples, and invalids.

Farmers, who had spent years of hard labor upon their lands, were asked to give them up. At many a fireside there was dejection and despondency. Some men abandoned their claims and left. Others exchanged their farms for other property; but a majority withstood their difficulties and trials. Many of those who had lost their lands made new contracts for them, and succeeded, finally, in retaining them.

In a few years the dark cloud broke and passed away. The fields yielded good crops, and there was an abundance of food for man and beast. The war terminated, and the Coitsville soldiers came home without the loss of a man, it is believed. If there had been mourning there was now rejoicing. The claims for the re-purchased farms were liquidated, the fee simple titles on record, and soon every farm had its occupant, and vacant lots were no more to be found in the township.

HIGHWAYS.

The first public highway laid out in this township is the east and west road, known as the Mercer and Youngstown road. It is one-half mile south of and parallel to the east and west center line. It was established and opened in 1802. Soon after that date the road known as the Yellow Creek road, leading from Poland village to Hubbard, was opened through the township. In 1827 the Youngstown and Mercer road became a post-road from New Bedford, Pennsylvania, westward.

ENCOUNTER WITH A BEAR.

Patrick Thompson, in 1803 or 1804, was returning home from Youngstown, and stopped at J. P. Bissel's to transact some business which detained him until near evening, when he proceeded toward home. When he arrived on the farm of Josiah Dalby, near the State line, he discovered a cub bear in his path. Determining to make its acquaintance, and it offering no violent opposition, he took it up in his arms. It, however, soon became dissatisfied with his nursing, and with loud cries notified its mother; she, being within hearing distance, hastened to its rescue with mouth open and bristles up. Thompson seeing that a fight was imminent strove to get rid of his new acquaintance. But cub refused to break up friendly relations so abruptly and clung to his arm with a regular bear hug. After some effort he loosed its grip, and to use his own language, he "threw the little devil into its mother's face."

The battle now began, and Thompson seeing his danger of defeat attempted to climb a tree near by, but as often as he began to ascend the bear would catch him by the feet and pull him back, and with such energy did she make her attacks that she tore the bottoms from his shoes, and so lacerated his feet that he was ever afterward a cripple, although he lived many years after this event. Up to this time victory seemed to be on the side of the bear; a few more crunches at his feet and she would have had it all her own way. But fortunately, at this juncture, Mr. Thompson obtained a large splinter, and again making the attempt to climb the tree she again made for him. He made a drive at her with the splinter, and luckily sent it deep into one of her nostrils. She then resolved to have a truce until she could get rid of the splinter; she would strike it with one paw, then with the other, until she effected her purpose. By this time friend Thompson was high in the tree, and neither party was disposed to renew the fight. Bruin soon retired with a sore nose. Thompson became faint from loss of blood. It was now in the night. A heavy rain commencing to fall, he

squeezed the water from his linen hunting-shirt into his mouth, which revived him somewhat. His hallooing was heard at the house of the Rev. Mr. Wick, and they came to his relief. When they arrived the bear and her family had left. This was the only known encounter with a wild bear in this township.

THE STRUTHERS TRAGEDY.

In February, 1826, Miss Drucilla Struthers left her father's residence in Coitsville for the purpose of going to the post-office at Poland village, where she expected to get a letter from her affianced lover, then residing in Washington county, Pennsylvania. Her younger sister, Emma, accompanied her down to the Mahoning river, which was very high at that time, intending to ferry her across, and then return home. The skiff in which they were to cross was fastened nearly opposite the mouth of Yellow creek, and directly opposite to the present village of Struthers. The young ladies were daughters of John Struthers, who settled in Poland township in 1799, held the office of sheriff of Trumbull county, and other responsible offices, and was well known and respected by the pioneers of this county. They were sisters of the Hon. Thomas Struthers, who was the proprietor of the thriving village of Struthers.

When the young ladies came to the bank of the river Emma laid off her shawl and bonnet on the shore, and they embarked on their fatal voyage. Emma was good with an oar, and practiced in rowing and managing a skiff.

At this point the known history of their lives ends. It is involved in mystery that can not be unraveled. No human eye saw them on their fatal voyage, as they were not spared to relate the events of that awful hour, of what happened or befell them; why they were unable to propel their craft across the stream; what were their feelings and actions when they discovered their dangerous and helpless situation; how many plans they devised to regain a landing; how hope and despair alternated each other in quick succession; how their terrors increased as their disappointments were repeated; and as they approached the dam over which they were soon to be precipitated how their souls sank within them, when they beheld the foaming waters beneath them and hope gone; what thoughts agitated their souls as they made the fatal descent, their craft overturned, and the dark waters received them.

Alexander Cowden heard their cries, but did not apprehend at the time that they came from persons in distress. David Brownlee reported having crossed the river a short time previous in that skiff, and that one of the oars or rowlocks was defective in some way, which doubtless was the cause of the disaster.

When they were missed an active search was commenced. The next day the remains of Drucilla were found fastened to a bush which grew on the river bank, one and one-half miles below where they embarked. Six weeks elapsed before the body of Emma was discovered. It was found at the head of an island near the Dickson farm.

Mr. J. R. Cowden has favored us with the above facts. He was one of the searching party from the first and until the body of Emma was found.

RELIGIOUS HISTORY.

A majority of the early settlers of Coitsville were church-going people, yet there was no church edifice erected in the township until 1838. The inhabitants went to church in two different States, Ohio and Pennsylvania; in four different counties, Trumbull and Mahoning in Ohio, Lawrence and Mercer in Pennsylvania; and in eight different townships, Coitsville, Poland, Youngstown, Liberty, and Hubbard in Ohio, and Shenango, Pulaski, and Mahoning in Pennsylvania. Many still continue members of churches in these various places. The Methodists for some years held meetings in barns, school-houses and dwellings. In 1835 they effected an organization, James McKinley, class-leader. This organization took place after a series of revival meetings held in Tobias Kimball's barn, in which Revs. Green, Preston, and others took part. They had no church building until 1838. Then Isaac Powers, late of Youngstown, presented to the society a lot of land for a church site and cemetery, the lot lying on the old Youngstown and Bedford road, where the Poland road intersects it. John Bissel and James McCartney were very active in securing funds with which to build and complete the meeting-house. James McCartney, Abraham Jacobs, and John Bissel were the first trustees. Upon this land, deeded to the society in 1839,

the house was erected; and a living, working congregation worshiped there in peace and unity. But when the agitation of the slavery question struck this little band, division and bitterness came with it. Troubles increased until in 1847 some Godless incendiary applied a torch to the church, and it was destroyed. The guilty wretch has never been detected. In 1848 a new building was erected upon the same site, superior to the old in style and finish, and there the Methodist Episcopals continue to hold their services.

The Presbyterians organized a congregation in 1836. A commodious edifice was erected at the village in 1836 or 1837, and Rev. William Nesbit became pastor. John Jackson and John Lynn were elected ruling elders, and soon after Thomas McGeehan and George Harris were elected, and their names added to the session roll. Mr. McGeehan is the only member of the original session now left, and he is nearly fourscore years of age. Since Mr. Nesbit, who remained several years, a number of clergymen have officiated as stated preachers: Revs. Dickson, McCombs, Dobbins, Kerr, Price, McCready, and Rice. The present incumbent is Rev. Krush; the present session, Thomas McGeehan, George Gray, and Joseph Hanna. The roll of communicants shows twelve males and twenty-five females. Is it not a question worthy of our consideration whether the above proportion of males and females will hold good in Heaven as well as here?

In 1870 the old house was taken down and rebuilt in better style, and in a more substantial manner. The constitution of this church is dated 1839, and to it are attached the names of William Reed, John and Davis Jackson, J. I. Hirst, George Harris, Samuel Jackson, Andrew McFarlin, Ebenezer Corey, and James Kerney.

Of the early settlers the Lynns, Swans, Johnsons, Moores, Martins, Bells, Coreys, Monteiths, Murdocks, Jacksons, and Wicks were Presbyterians; the Allens, Stewarts, Coopers, Houstons Milligans Beggses, Dicksons, McGuffeys, McBrides, Reeds, Thompsons, and others were United Presbyterians; the McCartneys, Bissels, Kirks, Kimmels, Vails, McFarlins, Jacobses, and others were Methodist Episcopal. Various other denominations were also represented by Coitsville people.

THE FIRST MARRIAGE

in the township was that of Ebenezer Corey and Polly Thompson, about the year 1803. The wedding festival took place in and about a little log cabin, which was standing until within a few years, on the farm of Ambrose Shields. This couple lived together until three children were born. Then the husband died. The widow afterwards married James Crooks and had a large family.

EARLY SCHOOLS.

The first school in Coitsville was taught in a log cabin on the farm of Joseph Beggs early in the present century. The cabin was a short distance west of the center. Jeremiah Breaden, the father of Dr. Breaden, was the teacher. Many of the scholars resided at a long distance from the school-house. There were few roads, and many were guided through the woods by blazed trees. Some of the members of that school were afterwards representatives to the Legislature; David Houston being one of this number.

The first school-house proper, was a little log building, damp and uncomfortable. It was situated in the northeastern part of the township, and was built about 1807 or 1808. The only branches taught were reading, writing, and arithmetic. The Bible was the class book for reading. The more advanced pupils read in the Old Testament and were called the Bible class. The younger readers used the New Testament. The Bible, Webster's Spelling-book, and Welsh's arithmetic, were the only text-books. When a scholar had mastered the rule of three his education was considered finished, though some of the boys did not stop when they had accomplished this much, but finished the book. The old log school-house was removed about 1815 and replaced by a comfortable frame house, which was used for school purposes until destroyed by fire, about the time the State Legislature took our schools under its protection.

Several other school-houses were built and used in the township, but none were so permanent as the Harris school. In winter male teachers taught and were paid by assessing a certain rate per scholar. Summer schools were usually taught by ladies whose wages were raised by voluntary subscriptions. The township is now divided into seven school districts, and is well supplied with good school-houses.

MILLS.

The first saw-mill in the township was erected by Asa Mariner, one and one-fourth miles northwest of the center, on Dry run. There was also a corn-cracker run in connection with the saw-mill.

The next mill was the McFarlin mill in the south of the township. The building of mills continued until there were seven saw-mills in operation on Dry run, all propelled by its waters. But as the lands were cleared the water of the stream diminished, the mills became less useful each year, until all were abandoned. In later years steam saw-mills took the place of the old water mills. There have been ten of these operated in the township at different times and places. Now there are but two.

There was a good grist-mill erected by Asa Mariner, but it departed with the old saw-mills. There have been three mills in the township which were run by horse- or ox-power—Wilson's, Buchanan's, and Brownlee's—but they were in operation but a short time.

DISTILLERIES.

Here, as elsewhere, distilling was considerably carried on in early times. James Shields had the first distillery. Seven others were afterwards built, some of them of little importance; but four of them, namely, Loveland's, Brownlee's, William McFarlin's, and James McFarlin's, pushed their business with energy for some years, consuming about twenty-four bushels of grain daily at least one hundred and fifty days out of the year, thirty-six hundred bushels per annum, and putting upon the market nine thousand gallons, more or less, of ardent spirits.

MORALS.

Never was a drinking saloon in Coitsville successfully operated. A few attempts were made to start them, all resulting in failure, except in the northwest part of the township in a little mining village. When the coal was dug out the miners left, and the grog-shops failed for want of customers.

No one was ever accused of murder here except William O. Moore, who was tried and found guilty of murdering his sister-in-law, Sarah Stewart, and sentenced to State prison for life. The beginning of the trouble was the violation of the seventh commandment. Moore served a number of years in prison, then was sent home to die of consumption. Contrary to expectation, he grew fat and enjoyed his liberty some years. Except Moore only one other person has ever been sent to the penitentiary from this township. He was a tramp and horse thief, named Fairbrother, and had been in Coitsville only a few months.

BURIAL PLACES.

The cemetery near the Methodist church was located in 1836 or 1837. The first interment was that of a son of John Bissel, a merchant at the village. This burial was made in 1837.

The cemetery adjoining the Presbyterian church at the village was gotten up by private enterprise. Samuel Jackson purchased a piece of ground and donated it to the church for burial purposes in 1878.

The remains of most of the old settlers of Coitsville are buried in the Deer Creek Church cemetery, New Bedford, Pennsylvania.

THE VILLAGE.

Coitsville has two stores, two wagon shops, two blacksmith shops and a tannery. There is at present no hotel. Andrew McFarlin kept the first hotel, the "Temperance house," some years. John Bissel had the first store in the place in in 1831 or 1832.

The carriage works of Mr. D. P. Cooper are worthy of special mention. The proprietor is a young man of enterprise, and seems determined to win success. He is already doing a very good business.

EARLY JUSTICES OF THE PEACE.

John P. Bissel, D. Monteith, William Houston, and James Shields were justices of the peace previous to 1818.

POST-OFFICE.

The first post road from New Bedford, Pennsylvania, to Youngstown was established in 1827. Mail was received once a week. William Bissel was appointed postmaster at Coitsville; John Shields, Andrew McFarlin, James Milligan, Thomas McGeehan, David Jackson, and Anderson McFarlin were his successors in office. Mrs. Joseph Hanna is the present incumbent.

TANNERIES.

The first tannery was operated by David Shields. It was a failure and was soon abandoned. In 1832 William Stewart and R. W. Shields commenced the business at the village and the tannery started by them has been successfully operated up to the present time. Mr. Stewart became owner by purchase of Mr. Shields' interest in 1855. In February, 1875, the building was destroyed by fire together with a large amount of stock and the machinery, the loss amounting to about $5,000. A new and much larger building has been erected, 86 x 40 feet and two stories high, and Mr. Stewart is doing a good business in company with his son D. C. Stewart.

INCIDENTS OF THE 1812 WAR.

William Crawford, who had first settled in the northeast of the township, was drafted into General Wadsworth's division of the northwestern army early in the fall of 1812, and marched to Camp Avery on the Huron river about six miles from the lake. On Sabbath evening, September 28th, a runner came into camp with a dispatch from Sandusky bay stating that a company of Indians had landed on the peninsula. A call for volunteers to proceed to that point was made instanter, and some sixty or seventy responded, Crawford among the number. They were put in command of Captain Cotton, and started for their destination in the night. They arrived at Cedar Point, on the bay, about daylight Monday morning, crossed over the bay, and reached the peninsula about sunrise. On their way they had been joined by others until they numbered abou ninety men. They then marched inland three or four miles, and discovered satisfactory evidence that there was a large number of Indians on the peninsula.

For some reason they decided to retrace their way to the four boats in which they had crossed, which boats they had left in charge of eight men. They had not gone far on their returning march when Indians concealed in the high grass began firing upon them. Captain Cotton ordered his men into line of battle. Crawford hastened to the captain and remonstrated, telling him that they would all be shot down if thus exposed. An order was then issued allowing each man to do as he chose—"paddle his own canoe, take care of himself and pick off a redskin at every opportunity." The firing was briskly kept up for a short time, then ceased, ap-

James Milligan

parently by mutual consent. In this skirmish three of the soldiers were killed and three wounded. The dead were buried, and the wounded cared for, then the march toward the boats was again begun in good order. They had proceeded but a short distance, however, when the enemy again began to fire upon them. The fire was returned with spirit and with good effect, every soldier taking care of himself as in the previous encounter. The captain ordered a retreat. But Crawford and his friend John Burrell, another Coitsville man, were too eagerly engaged in the fight to hear the order. While concealed in the grass he noticed a movement near him and creeping a little closer, saw an Indian loading his gun. Crawford fired and the Indian lay stretched in death. Presently another savage was seen some distance away, nearly concealed from the soldier's sight by intervening grass and a tall weed near him. Crawford fired; the weed doubled down and so did the Indian.

Burrell first noticed that the company had retreated and notified Crawford of the fact. They at once made haste to overtake their comrades and soon came to a tangled pile of fallen timber, at each end of which an Indian met them. Mr. Crawford used to say that he never could tell how he got over those fallen trees, but he passed them safely, and so did Burrell. Soon they came up with a soldier carrying his brother, who was mortally wounded. They assisted him in carrying the dying man to a cabin where they lifted up the floor, placed him beneath it and continued their flight. They soon came to a house at which Captain Cotton and about half of his men had halted; the other half had gone on to the boats, taking with them all of the wounded, eight in number. On arriving at the shore they found that the Indians had sunk two of their boats, while the men left on guard had taken the other two and escaped. They, however, came back, and the soldiers were transferred to Cedar Point. The wounded were then placed in the boats and sent on to the camp which they reached in safety. Tuesday Crawford said to Burrell that he would as lief be shot by the Indians as starved to death, and as he had had no food since the previous morning, he proposed to reconnoiter and see if some means of relief could not be discovered. Burrell accompanied him. They went down to the bay and discovered an

old canoe concealed in the grass. They immediately returned to their companions and told them of their good fortune. Two experienced men were selected to go down the bay in the canoe and give notice at the camp of their situation. This plan succeeded admirably and in due time reinforcements arrived with material aid and all were brought off in safety.

RELIGIOUS EXCITEMENT.

A strange, mysterious visitation came upon the Presbyterian churches about 1805–06. The excitement is said to have originated in Kentucky and spread northward through western Pennsylvania and northern Ohio, agitating many Presbyterian congregations. Hopewell, one of Rev. William Wick's charges, where most of the Coitsville people attended church, was touched by its influence. Its subjects were mostly young people and generally females. They first became excited in regard to their future state and their condition here as sinners against Heaven in the sight of God. Sobbings would convulse them; spasmodic jerkings and twitchings then ensued; finally they fell down prostrate and to all appearances unconscious. In this state they would remain for a long time, but when the congregation was dismissed they appeared to waken and gain their usual mind. At the time there was great controversy as to the cause of these remarkable occurrences, some holding that it was the influence of the Holy Spirit, while others held that it was the work of an evil spirit. Some assigned mesmerism as a reason; others fanaticism. But soon all traces of the excitement vanished to return no more.

NOTES OF SETTLEMENT.

James Milligan was born in county Tyrone, Ireland, March 15, 1806, and came to this country with his parents, John and Margaret, when a lad of twelve years. Three brothers, John, Dixon, and Robert, came also at this time. The oldest brother, William, remained in Ireland with his grandfather Milligan. He was at length employed by a wealthy shipping company as clerk, and afterwards taken into partnership. He died April 2, 1882, having amassed a fortune of $2,000,000. Dixon settled in the western part of Ohio, where he became a successful physician. He died in February, 1874. Robert died in 1875. At the time of his death he was prominently connected with the Kentucky university. He was the author of several works on the Bible, and held a high position as an educator. John lived a quiet and honorable life on the homestead, and died January, 1876. Isabel, Thomas, and Samuel were born after the family came to America. James possessed a great memory, and the recollection of his boyhood days was very vivid. The voyage across the ocean was an intensely interesting event to the keen Irish lad, and many were the anecdotes he could relate in connection with it. The family settled in the northwest part of Coitsville township about two and one-half miles from the present city of Youngstown. In 1826 James married Catharine, sister of William McGuffey, author of school readers bearing his name, and afterwards engaged in the dry goods business in Vienna. He afterward returned to his first place of residence, where he held the office of justice of the peace for three terms. In 1846 he was elected commissioner of Trumbull county. He was a Democrat in politics, and an influential member of the party. He was an active member of the Methodist Episcopal church, which he served in many capacities. In 1850 his entire family was prostrated by typhoid fever, at which time his wife and two children, Margaret and Alexander, died. The surviving children were Isabel, John, Sarah, and Mary. He married again Nancy M. Reed, daughter of William Reed. By this marriage there were two sons, Dixon and James. He was a public-spirited and influential man, and his death, which occurred March 30, 1881, was sincerely and widely lamented.

John Shields, Coitsville township, was born September 1, 1804. His father, James, a native of Ireland, came to the farm where Mr. Shields now resides in 1802, from Beaver county, Pennsylvania. He was born November 26, 1773, died January 19, 1854. His wife, whom he married in 1802, was Margaret Walker, of Mercer county, Pennsylvania. She was born October 1, 1783, died February 14, 1852. They brought up a family of eight children, of whom two sons are yet living, John and James. The latter resides in Loveland, Colorado. A daughter, Mrs. Mary Davidson, of Coitsville, died July 6, 1881, aged seventy-eight years. John Shields was married in 1829 to Sarah Davidson,

of Youngstown, born May 17, 1809. They have had four children, and the three sons are yet living, each of their farms being near the old homestead. Names of children: James Davidson, born January 24, 1831; Ann Jane, June 5, 1834; John Gailey, June 15, 1843; Ambrose, August 18, 1849. Ann Jane died January 17, 1868. Mr. Shields and all of the family are Republicans, temperance men, and members of the United Presbyterian church. Mr. Shields has been honored by election to the following offices: county commissioner, coroner, justice of the peace, postmaster, etc. He has been an elder in his church for over forty years. His oldest son, one of our leading farmers, was married December 12, 1865, to Mary Gilchrist, of Coitsville. The other sons are also married. J. D. Shields has a splendid farm residence, and the best barn in the township. The Shields family is one of activity and integrity.

William Stewart was born in Coitsville, May 18, 1808. He is the son of William Stewart, a native of Adams county, Pennsylvania, who came to this county previous to 1804, and settled in the western part of Coitsville township, where he lived and died, bringing up five sons and three daughters. Four sons are still living, Elijah, Robert, William, and David. Elijah resides in DeKalb county, Illinois; the others in this township. William Stewart, Sr., was one of six brothers who came to the Western Reserve in early times and settled in Trumbull and Mahoning counties. All brought up families and lived to be old. Mr. Stewart, when eighteen years of age, learned the business of tanning, in which he is still engaged. He established his tannery at Coitsville in 1832, and is still doing business there. He married Jane Brownlee in 1833. Four of their children are living: Mary E. (deceased), Huldah, Morilla, David C., and Florence; all married except Huldah. Mrs. Stewart died in 1863, aged forty-eight years. She was a devoted member of the United Presbyterian church for several years. Mr. Stewart is well and favorably known as a business man; has held several township offices.

John S. Brownlee was born at Turfoot, Lenwickshire, Scotland, March 6, 1806. He came to America in 1830, and settled in Coitsville township, where he still resides, in 1831. He has a farm of over two hundred acres and a very pleasant and comfortable home. Mr. Brownlee was married April 19, 1830, to Janet Patterson, who was born in Strathhaven, Scotland, September 11, 1811. They have had eight children, three of whom are living, Margaret W., Ellen F., Jane F., John A., James P., Randal Scroggs, and William W. The second child, a daughter, died in infancy. Jane, Randall S., and William W., are yet living. Mr. and Mrs. Brownlee are members of the Presbyterian church. They are among the most respected citizens of Coitsville.

Robert Davidson was born in Youngstown in 1807. His father, James Davidson, a native of Ireland. settled in Youngstown previous to the year 1800. He was married before coming to the county to Margaret Croskery, a native of Westmoreland county, Pennsylvania. They brought up eleven children, eight of them still living, Robert Davidson being the fourth child. Mr. Davidson bought the farm on which he now lives in 1831, and moved there the following year. He has been twice married—first in 1832 to Anna Shields, daughter of James Shields, one of the first settlers in Coitsville ; she died in 1835. In 1839 Mr. Davidson married Catharine Lackey of Lawrence county, Pennsylvania. They have three children, Anna, Mary, and Frances. Mary is the wife of James Cowden, of Wheeling, West Virginia, and Frances is the wife of D. C. Stewart of Coitsville. Mr. and Mrs. Davidson have belonged to the United Presbyterian church for many years. Mr. Davidson has been an elder in this church for over forty years. He is a sound Republican and a worthy citizen.

John H. Reed, farmer, was born in Coitsville township in 1816, and has always resided here. His parents, William and Martha Reed, were among the early settlers. They brought up a family of five children, three of whom are living, viz: John, William, and Nancy (widow of James Milligan). John H. Reed lives upon the farm settled by his father. The farm contains at present one hundred and seventy-two acres. Mr. Reed was first married in 1838 to Jane Kimmel, daughter of Philip Kimmel, of Coitsville. They had seven children, three of whom are living: Lycurgus S., born September 22, 1839, died March 14, 1864; Martha M., August 12, 1841, died August 28, 1859; Philip K., July 4, 1845, died July 19, 1859; William H., February 24,

1849; Susan W., April 20, 1853; Elizabeth T., Edward F., (twins), June 26, 1856. Elizabeth died November 14, 1871; Mrs. Reed died February 24, 1862. In 1863 Mr. Reed married Mrs. Samantha McFarlin, daughter of William McClelland, by whom he has two children: Althea, born April 23, 1865, and Pluma, June 20, 1866. Mr. Reed is a Republican. He has held the office of township trustee. He does an excellent farming business.

John F. Robison was born in Mercer county, (now Lawrence county) Pennsylvania, February 17, 1829. He came to Mahoning county in 1857, locating in Coitsville township. He purchased his present farm in 1863; has one hundred and fifteen acres in Coitsville, with good buildings and improvements, and owns also seventy-six acres with buildings, etc., in Poland township. He raises grain, cattle, sheep, etc. Mr. Robison was married March 25, 1854, to Hannah McWilliams, of Lawrence county, Pennsylvania. They have six children, Almina, Ellen, George L., William J., Elmer and Edward Lee (twins), and Audley O. Mr. and Mrs. Robison are members of the Presbyterian church. Mr. Robison is a sound Democrat.

Anderson McFarlin, a descendant of some of the very earliest settlers in the county, was born in Coitsville April 12, 1828, and has always resided here. He is the owner of a good farm of one hundred and ninety acres situated near the center of the township. Mr. McFarlin was married April 26, 1849, to Sarah Kirk. Mrs. McFarlin is the daughter of Andrew and Elizabeth (Baldwin) Kirk. Andrew Kirk came at an early date from Washington county, Pennsylvania; he was originally from New Jersey. Elizabeth Baldwin was the daughter of Caleb Baldwin, one of the first settlers in Youngstown. Mr. McFarlin is one of a family of twelve children, and Mrs. McFarlin the youngest of thirteen. Their children are William E., Alice K., Vina J., Mary E., Bettie B., William K., Frank M., Thomas E., and Charles A. William E., Alice K., and Charles A. are deceased. William K. is now engaged on the new through-line railroad in the capacity of civil engineer. Mr. McFarlin has been a Republican since the party was formed. He was postmaster at Coitsville for seventeen years. The family are well known and highly respected in this county.

Robert Lowry, Coitsville township, was born in Poland township August 12, 1818. His parents were William and Mary (Houston) Lowry. William Lowry was a native of the north of Ireland, who settled in Poland township about the year 1806, and brought up three sons and six daughters; two sons and four daughters are now living. His wife, Mary Houston, of Scotch parentage, was born in Lancaster county, Pennsylvania. Her father, William Houston, came to this county about the year 1800. Robert Lowry was the fifth child of William Lowry. He settled in Coitsville township in 1842. He was married September 22, 1842, to Margaret Stewart, daughter of William Stewart, of Coitsville township. They had four children, all living: Mary Jane, wife of D. C. McBride, Mahoning township, Lawrence county, Pennsylvania; William S., Pulaski township, Lawrence county, Pennsylvania; Theoressa J., wife of J. W. McNabb, Pulaski township, Lawrence county, Pennsylvania; Sarah E., wife of W. S. Allen, Coitsville township. Mrs. Lowry died July 1, 1873, aged fifty-six years. Mr. Lowry was married a second time May 18, 1876, to Miss Anna Madge, daughter of Robert Madge, of Lackawanna township, Mercer county, Pennsylvania. Mr. and Mrs. Lowry are members of the United Presbyterian church. Mr. Lowry is a sound Republican. He has held several offices: was justice of the peace for twelve consecutive years, commencing in 1856; county commissioner from 1866 to 1872, and has held several township offices.

J. M. Jackson was born in New Bedford, Pennsylvania, August 5, 1828. His father, John Jackson, settled in Coitsville township in 1803. J. M. Jackson has followed a variety of occupations. When young he taught school for several years; then was a merchant. He now owns a saw-mill, which does a good business, and is one of our largest farmers. Mr. Jackson settled in Coitsville in 1864. From 1844 to that date he had been in business in Trumbull county. He owns two hundred and twenty acres in this township. Mr. Jackson was married March 9, 1852, to Rebecca L. Roberts, daughter of Thomas N. Roberts, Hubbard, Trumbull county. They have two sons and two daughters—Marietta, Sidney Delamar (a successful attorney in Youngstown), Eliza Jane, and John Calvin. Mr. Jack-

son has been quite prominent in local affairs, and has held the offices of justice of the peace, county commissioner, township clerk, trustee, etc. He is one of our solid and energetic business men. He served in the army a short time as captain in company C, One Hundred and Seventy-first Ohio volunteers, enlisting April 28, 1864, for the one hundred days' service.

F. D. Kirk, Coitsville township, was born in that township July 11, 1846. His parents were Andrew and Sylvina Kirk. His father is still living. Mrs. Kirk died eight years ago. Mr. F. D. Kirk is one of our active farmers; has ninety acres of good land; raises stock, and intends to go into sheep-raising. In 1880 he received over $150 in premiums at fairs, mostly on pigs. Mr. Kirk was married, in 1869, to Miss Almira J. Bailey, daughter of C. T. Bailey, of Coitsville township. They belong to the Methodist Episcopal church. Mr. Kirk is a Republican, and a strong temperance man. He was in the army. He enlisted in January, 1864, serving until the close of the war in company G, Seventy-eighth Pennsylvania volunteers, under General Thomas.

Nicholas Jacobs (deceased) was born near Girard, Mahoning county, January 13, 1810. His parents were Abraham and Elizabeth (Kimmel) Jacobs, who came here at quite an early date. After his birth they returned to Washington county, Pennsylvania. In 1832 Abraham Jacobs and his son Nicholas returned to Mahoning county, and settled near together in the northern part of Coitsville township. Nicholas Jacobs was married January 19, 1832, to Isabella Brown, of Washington county, Pennsylvania. They had two children, Lewis J. and Francis P., both now residents of Youngstown. Mrs. Jacobs died February 18, 1836, aged twenty-two years. Mr. Jacobs was again married September 12, 1837, to Phœbe Kirk, of Coitsville township. Six children: Sheldon, Charles, Louisa, Caroline, Alice and Phœbe. Charles died in the army, at Chattanooga, September 30, 1863, aged twenty-two years. Phœbe died September 9, 1851, aged one year. The others reside in the county. Mrs. Phœbe Jacobs died April 11, 1850, aged thirty-one. His third wife, whom he married October 1, 1850, was Mrs. Juliana Calvin, née Briggs. She was born in Dighton, Massachusetts, September 25, 1820. She was married in 1842 to Robert Calvin, of Beaver county, Pennsylvania, by whom she had two children, Josephus and Gustavus; the latter a resident of this township, and Josephus of Hollidaysburg, Pennsylvania. Mr. Calvin died February 11, 1845, aged twenty-seven. Mr. and Mrs. Jacobs had seven children: Mary, Spencer, Myron, Jessie, Clarinda, William, and Charles G. Jessie died December 2, 1870, aged fourteen; Clarinda September 28, 1861, aged two. The others reside in Coitsville township. Mr. Jacobs died December 14, 1880, nearly seventy-one years of age. He had been an earnest member of the Disciples' church for about forty years of his life. He was well known in this county, and highly respected.

Andrew Garner Fitch came to this county from Lebanon, Connecticut, and settled in the western part of Coitsville township, on a farm which had been taken up previously and somewhat improved by a man named Robinson. His wife was Mary Levenwell. They had nine children, none of them now living. Samuel Fitch was the fifth child, and the longest survivor of the family. He was twelve years of age when he came to the county, having been born in 1789. Samuel Fitch and his brother Henry were soldiers in the War of 1812. The wife of Samuel Fitch was Mary T. Simpson, a native of Maysville, Kentucky. They had five children, Mary Jane, Elizabeth B., Julia A., Joseph T., and Caroline S. Only Elizabeth and Julia are now living. They reside at the old homestead. Mrs. Fitch, their mother, died in 1848, aged fifty-two years. She was for many years a devoted member of the Presbyterian church. Mr. Fitch died in 1875. He lived to a ripe old age, and was always an honored and respected citizen. He was an earnest friend of the Union, and though he had no sons to send to the army, he gave liberally of his means to aid in the cause.

John Cooper, lumber manufacturer, Coitsville township, was born September 15, 1815. His parents were David and Rebecca (Armstrong) Cooper, the former a native of Maryland, and the latter of Washington county, Pennsylvania. David Cooper came to Coitsville in 1798 and helped to survey the Western Reserve. He then went back to Maryland, and in 1800 returned to Coitsville, took up four hundred acres,

and spent the remainder of his life here. He died in 1855 in the ninety-fifth year of his age. He was a man of strong constitution, active industry, and business ability. He was married about the year 1806, and was the father of twelve children; eleven arrived at maturity and five are yet living, viz: John, David, Eliza, William, and Robert, all residents of Coitsville township. Mrs. Cooper died in 1852 aged sixty-six years. John Cooper lives upon a portion of the original farm. He is engaged in the lumber business and has been running a saw-mill since 1849. The Cooper family is one of the oldest in the township, and comprises some of its best citizens.

John White, farmer, Coitsville township, Mahoning county, was born in county Monaghn, Ireland, in 1820. He came to America in 1835, and after three or four years settled in Coitsville. Mr. White is a large farmer; he has at present two hundred and seventy-six acres of land in a good state of cultivation. He built a large and convenient house in the spring of 1877. Mr. White is engaged in mixed farming, raises cattle, sheep, and grain. He was married November 24, 1853, to Eliza Dickson, daughter of George Dickson, of Coitsville township. They have five children, born as follows: Hugh J., November 11, 1854; George D., November 4, 1856; William B., December 22, 1858; John B., October 24, 1860; Robert F., February 22, 1863. Mr. and Mrs. White are members of the Presbyterian church. Mr. White is a Democrat. He has been township trustee and judge of elections, and is a most worthy and respected citizen.

William H. Wick, farmer, Coitsville, Mahoning county, was born in this township in 1827. His parents, Daniel and Elizabeth (Armitage) Wick, were old residents, having come to the place where Mr. Wick now resides in 1815. Daniel Wick had previously been a resident of Austintown, having come there from New Jersey about 1796. He was a soldier in the War of 1812. He died June 18, 1863, in his seventy-seventh year. His wife, Elizabeth Armitage, whom he married in 1813, was born in Huntingdon county, Pennsylvania, and came to Jackson township, Mahoning county, when a child. She was a daughter of Benjamin Armitage. Her mother's name was Drake, a descendant from Sir Francis Drake. Mrs. Wick died February

23*

5, 1869, aged seventy-six years. She was the mother of six children, all of whom are living, Mr. W. H. Wick being the youngest. William H. Wick was married March 7, 1855, to Sarah A. Williams, daughter of William Williams, of Wayne county, Ohio. They have five children; Mary Ella Pearl, born March 7, 1857, wife of Albert Martin of Lawrence county, Pennsylvania; Louie Evangeline, born May 19, 1860; Lizzie Carrie, born August 31, 1865; Grace Gertrude, born March 3, 1869; Vernon Victor, born May 21, 1876. Mr. Wick has always been a stanch Republican. He has been township trustee, and has held other local offices. He does an extensive farming business, owns one hundred and eighty acres; and is one of the most active and successful farmers in the township.

CHAPTER IX.

MILTON.

Milton is township two of range five, and is the northwest corner of Mahoning county, having Newton, Trumbull county, on the north, Jackson on the east, Berlin on the south, and Palmyra, Portage county, on the west.

The Mahoning river—that marvelously crooked stream, which flows northward through the western part of the county, but after passing into Trumbull county and going through all manner of twisting and turning returns to the territory named after it and flows through its eastern portion in a southeasterly direction—is here a narrow and very pretty stream, cutting the western half of the township into two very nearly equal portions. The bottom land along the river is quite broad in some places and generally of more than average fertility.

Going from the eastern side of the township to the west, you will notice that there are a number of broad ridges of land of gradual slope and gentle elevation with numerous runs cutting them. Nearer the river the ridges are not so broad but are higher; none of the surface is exactly level, and little is very hilly. Limestone and sandstone are exposed in a few places.

The soil is a clayey loam, with a few fields that are composed almost wholly of heavy clay. Most of the soil, however, is fertile and easily worked; well watered, both by springs and brooks, and seems especially adapted for grazing.

On the east bank of the river and about one mile south of the north line of the township is a sulphur spring. The water is deep and cool and flows constantly. It has sometimes been recommended for medical uses.

Coal has been obtained in small quantities in the southeast and southwest portions of the township. Several attempts have been made to find oil in years past, and at the present writing wells are being drilled with the same object in view.

The township contains no villages except one almost as extinct as Herculaneum, and a portion of the little settlement at Price's mills. The population is small, many farms being without houses or occupants. The farmers are generally comfortably situated, contented, and happy.

The timber is principally white oak and hickory; there is a little ash and not much maple.

EARLY TOWNSHIP OFFICERS.

No township records of an early date are in existence. We learn that John Johnston of Milton, and Bildad Hine of Newton, were elected justices of the peace, in 1814, by the joint townships, Newton and Milton. A year or two later Milton became a township and voting precinct by itself. Justices of the peace prior to 1840: John Johnston, Daniel Vaughan, Robert Price, Johnston, Vaughan, William Strander, Milton Rogers, John Matherspaw, James Moore, John Eckis, Jr., and Peter Kinnaman.

SETTLEMENT.

The first settlement in the township was made about the year 1803 in the vicinity of Pricetown. In the course of three or four years quite a number of families had come to the township and located along the river on both sides of it.

About the same date (1803) a settlement was commenced on the eastern side of the township. For some years the central and southern as well as the southeastern portions of the township lay unimproved.

It is claimed that Nathaniel Stanley, one of those belonging to the western or river settlement, was the first actual settler. He took up and improved land just south of the old Judge Clarke farm on the east side of the river, a short distance above Pricetown. He sold out to Jacob Cole quite early and moved north into Newton township.

Aaron Porter, said by his sons to have been the second settler in the township, came from Pennsylvania in 1803, and located west of the river on the farm where Henry Winfield now lives, afterwards (in 1812) moving to the farm where his sons, Enoch and Joseph Porter, reside. He brought up a family of twelve children, three of whom were born in this township. Porter was a strong man and of great endurance. He reached the age of ninety-six. The names of the surviving members of his family are : Margaret, wife of John Jones, Medina county; Robin, in Indiana; Nancy, widow of Joseph McKenzie, Huron county; Enoch and Joseph, Milton township.

In 1803 John Vanetten and family came from Delaware to the western part of the township. The second dwelling built by him, a two-story log house with a large stone chimney, is still standing. They came with a wagon, and after their arrival three weeks elapsed before a cabin was completed. During this time they slept in the wagon and cooked and ate in the open air. The family at this time consisted of Mr. Vanetten, wife, and three children. When all was in readiness for the erection of the cabin, owing to the scarcity of men in the vicinity, the women were called in to assist in raising the logs to the proper height. Some time after coming here Captain Vanetten procured a pair of spoon-molds, which his wife used for years in making spoons for the settlers, and for use in her own family. Old pewter plates furnished the material. If a spoon was broken the pieces were carefully saved until they could be run over and made into a new spoon. Captain Vanetten was married in Delaware to Anna Lebar. They had ten children in all, whose names were as follows: Margaret married Daniel Parshall, and died in this township; Daniel died in Crawford county, Pennsylvania; Mary married Joseph Depew and died in Allen county; Elizabeth became the wife of Jacob Parshall and died in Michigan; Sally is living, the wife of John McKenzie of this township; Jacob is living in Wood county; Ann married Hugh Patterson and died in Milton; John

died in Wood county; Jonah died in Indiana; Aaron died in Oregon. John Vanetten, Sr., served as a captain in the War of 1812. He lived to the age of seventy-seven. His wife died at the age of sixty-eight.

Samuel Linton was an early settler on the farm now owned by the Ewing heirs. His sons were Samuel and Adam. The latter lived and died in Milton. Samuel is sill living in Berlin township. There were also three daughters.

Samuel Bowles was one of the earliest settlers of the township, and came here about 1803. He settled in the eastern part of Milton, on the farm now owned by Josiah Fenton. In 1823 he moved with his entire family to Portage county.

In about 1804 three brothers by the name of Winans, Isaac, James, and Jacob, moved from Delaware to the eastern part of the township, and each took up a farm. They all lived to be old men. Isaac died on the farm where he settled. His children were Jacob, Isaac, John, Sarah, Eleanor, Phebe, Rebecca, Hannah, and Susan. Jacob lived on a part of the old place and died there; Eleanor married Russel Orr, of Milton, and after his death moved to Illinois, where she died at a ripe old age; Phebe married Andrew Moore, and lived and died in Milton; Susan became the wife of John McCollum, and died in this township.

James Winans also died in Milton. He brought up four sons—Jacob J., Isaac, Henry, and James, all of whom settled in this township but Isaac and James. Isaac is still living. He was a preacher for several years, as was also his brother Henry. The daughters of James, Sr., were Polly, Jemima, Anna, Susan, and Hannah; all dead. Polly was the wife of Jesse Delong, of this township.

Jacob Winans passed the most of his life in this township, but died in Pennsylvania. His son Jacob is still a resident of Milton. His daughter Rachel married a Porter, and is still living in the township. Jemima, one of the girls, marred Robert Short, and lived here many years.

Jesse Holliday was one of the first settlers, and a very enterprising business man, although he had more energy than capital. He remained but a few years, and none of his family became permanent residents.

Reuben S. Clarke was one of the first settlers

at Pricetown, and died upon the farm which he took up and improved. He was associate judge at quite an early date. His sons were John Quincy and Reuben. The former remained on the farm with his widowed mother until her death. Reuben went to Iowa. There were several daughters, but none of them settled in Milton. The Clarke farm began at the township line and extended up the river on the east bank.

Daniel Stewart settled south of Orr's corners, on land now owned by Daniel Eckis, at an early date, probably 1804. He sold and moved to another part of the township, but afterwards returned to the original farm and died there. None of the family are left in Milton.

John Delong was an early settler south of Orr's corners. He had two sons, Jesse and Aaron, who settled in the township and remained several years.

Joseph Depew was an early settler on the farm east of the river afterwards owned by Stephen Case. From Depew's hands the farm passed to John Gibson. Parkus and Joseph Depew, sons of Joseph, passed their lives in this township. One of their sisters became Mrs. Craig.

A man named Munson was an early settler on the river but moved away before making much improvement.

John Brunton made the first improvements on the farm now owned by Leonidas Carson.

James and John Craig were early settlers east of the river. John moved to Berlin and died there. James died in this township and his family scattered.

Thomas L. Fenton settled early at Pricetown and carried on his trade of blacksmithing. About 1817 he moved to the eastern part of the township and settled on a farm just west of the old Johnston farm. He had three sons—Hiram C., Jesse, and Josiah. The youngest lives on the farm; the other two are in the West. His daughters were Mary, Lucy Ann, Jane, Christina, and Harriet. Three of them are living: Mrs. Jane Johnson, Newton Falls; Mrs. Christina Kale, Milton; and Mrs. Harriet Flaugher, Jackson.

George Snyder settled east of the river about 1805 and cleared up a farm, which he afterwards sold to Shepard. It is now owned by John Scott. Snyder moved to Green township.

In 1805 John McKenzie settled on the farm now owned by Frank Keefer. His son John still resides in the township and is one of its oldest inhabitants.

Samuel Daniels settled on the Vaughn farm west of the river about 1806, but later moved with all his family.

John Pennel was an early settler in the eastern part of Milton. He afterwards bought a farm in the northwestern part where he died quite early. His family scattered.

Peter DeCourcey settled in the township previous to 1809. Three of his sons remained here some time but did not become permanent residents.

Robert Russell came from Poland township to the eastern part of Milton when a young man. He married after coming here a daughter of Alexander French, and reared a family of ten children, two of whom survive, James and Enoch, of this township.

Alexander French settled in the northeastern part of the township about 1809. He had only one son, William, who lived here some years and then emigrated to Allen county, Ohio, where he died. His daughters were Margaret, Martha, Jane, Ann, Betsey, and Sarah. All married here except Martha, who remained single. Betsey is still living, the wife of John Shearer, of Newton.

Thomas Reed settled in the eastern part of the township, north of Orr's corners, about the year 1810. Two of his sons—Benjamin and John—resided here some years. Two of his daughters were also residents of the township—Catharine, the wife of Thomas L. Fenton, and Mary, wife of James Chalfant. Both died years ago.

William Parshall, son of Samuel Parshall, was an early settler west of the river, and kept store a few years opposite Captain Vanetten's house. He moved to New Castle, Pennsylvania.

John Johnston settled on the east line of Milton township in 1811. He was of Irish descent and was born in Pennsylvania in 1773. He was married in his native State to Margaret Robinson. They had six children living at the time they settled here, and two were born afterwards. The names were as follow: Mary, John, Margaret, David, Samuel, Elizabeth, Thomas, and Francis R. Mary married Alexander Gilmore and lives in Newton. She has brought up five children, two of whom are living. John settled in Jackson and brought up five children by his first wife and four by his second. He died in 1868. Margaret married James Moore and resided in the township. Both are dead. Mrs. Moore died in 1881, leaving two children living and four deceased. David settled on the west line of Jackson, where he now lives. He has a family of seven children living. Samuel settled on the west line of Jackson and has seven children living. Elizabeth married Alexander Moore and now resides in Milton, and has four children living. Thomas resides in Milton, on the east line, a mile and a half north of the center road. He has eight children living. Francis R. occupies the old farm. He is the father of eleven children, only two of whom are living. John Johnston, Sr., died in 1842, and his widow in 1849. When he came to this township he moved into a small log cabin, perhaps sixteen feet square, which had been erected by a previous settler. There was a puncheon floor, made from roughly split logs, and a stick and mud chimney. For a few weeks this small cabin, containing but one room, in which was a loom in addition to other household furniture, was inhabited by two families. Alexander Campbell lived there while he was building a cabin for himself. He came to Milton about 1810, and remained a resident of the township until 1823, when he moved to Lordstown, where he died some years later.

Five members of the Orr family, sons of William Orr, of Jackson, settled in Milton at different dates. They were John, Humphrey, William, Russell, and Isaac. Many of their descendants continue to reside here.

Henry Lingo settled in 1813 on a farm northeast of the center. His sons were Allen, Joseph, Robert, Samuel, John, Henry, and Hamilton. His daughter Susan became the wife of Robert McKenzie. Several of the sons lived and died in this township.

Robert Price, afterwards Judge Price, came to the little village now called by his name, in 1817, and was one of its prominent men for several years.

Robert Rose, one of the oldest residents of Mahoning county, and perhaps the oldest man within its borders, was born near Bath, Virginia, April 7, 1786. When about fourteen years old he came to Poland township with his father, Jesse Rose, who settled in the eastern part of Poland, near the Pennsylvania line. Jesse Rose moved from Poland to Ellsworth and died there. His family consisted of eight children, Robert being now the only survivor. David, Robert, Jesse, and James were the sons; Mary, Nancy, Rhoda, and Hannah the daughters. David and Jesse settled and died in Ellsworth. James settled in Jackson but moved west. Mary became the wife of William Howard and lived in Ellsworth. Nancy married John Brothers and lived in Pennsylvania. Rhoda married John Rose and lived in Mecca, Trumbull county. Hannah married Ebenezer Cole and lived on the old farm where her father settled, in Poland. Robert Rose was married in Poland to Catharine Shoaf, who bore eight children. For his second wife he married Catharine Wortenbarger. About the year 1816 Mr. Rose moved to Milton township, took up and settled upon a farm in the southeast, on the old Palmyra road, where he resided until about thirteen years ago, and has since been living with his sons in Berlin township. Mr. Rose is one of the few surviving veterans of the War of 1812. His oldest brother was also a soldier of that war. The writer made a visit to Uncle Robert, as he is familiarly called, one pleasant day in November, 1881. One of his "boys," a gray-haired man, directed us to the place where we found the old gentleman. He was in the woods, at least three-quarters of a mile from the house, in his shirt-sleeves and was busily engaged in gathering hickory-nuts. Few men reach their ninety-sixth year, and very few attain to Mr. Rose's age and retain full possession of their faculties. We found Mr. Rose's memory of early events clear, distinct, and accurate. His hearing is but little impaired. His mind is active, and his face and conversation cheerful. In his early years he was a very Hercules in physical strength, and even now, considering how near he is to the age of a centenarian, his vigor is remarkable.

Calvin Shepard came out with Judge Price from New Jersey, and worked for him some years. He married Isabella Beck and settled on land now owned by John Scott. There were eight children, seven of whom are living, none of them in this township.

Frederick Byers, from Pennsylvania, came to

the township about 1824, and settled just west of the river, on the farm now owned by Robert Weasner. His son Frederick occupied it after him a number of years. Mr. Byers, Sr., caused the village to be laid out which is called by his first name.

John Eckis came from Maryland to Springfield township in 1801, and in 1826 moved to Milton, and was a pioneer of the southeastern part of the township. Even at that date there was no improved farm west of his place, until the river was reached.

John McCollum recently deceased, came to the township in 1828, and took up an unimproved farm in the southeastern quarter.

From 1830 to 1840 the township grew rapidly in population. In that period both Frederick and Pricetown were flourishing villages. But the advent of the New York and Ohio canal, turning business and travel aside, gave these places a staggering blow; and a few years later the railroad came through and finished them; for the iron horse, like the canal mule, "passed by on the other side" of Milton. In 1840 the census returns gave the township a population of twelve-hundred and seventy-seven. Each succeeding decade has witnessed a gradual falling off, until now the entire population is between seven and eight hundred, making this the smallest township in the county.

PRICE'S MILLS.

Price's Mills, or Pricetown, was once a flourishing place, but is so no longer. It is situated on the line between Milton and Newton, and as nearly all of its business enterprises were carried on in this township, we include a sketch of them here.

Jesse Holliday came to this place among the very first of the settlers, and in 1804 erected a grist-mill, carding-mill, and saw-mill. The grist-mill was a good size for those days; two stories in height, perhaps 34x40 feet, and contained two run of granite stones. The wheel was an undershot, twenty-two feet in diameter. The saw-mill had an old-fashioned "flutter wheel." These mills were on the sites of the present grist-mill and saw-mill. The carding-mill was just north of the grist-mill. Holliday run these mills until 1816, and then sold them to John Price. A year or two later they came into the possession of Robert Price, who

operated them many years. In 1834 Price put up a stone flouring-mill. It was badly built and fell down a few years later. It was rebuilt by Dr. Jonathan I. Tod, son-in-law of Judge Price, who in the meantime had purchased the entire mill property. The mills remained in possession of Dr. Tod and his widow until 1861, when they were purchased by Mr. Calender, father of the present owner. The saw-mill now standing was also built by Price.

In 1837 Dr. Tod built a foundry on the west side of the river. It was in operation five or six years, and was then changed into a linseed oil manufactory. It disappeared some years ago. In 1842 Dr. Tod erected a foundry on the east side of the river. Calender bought it and changed it into a flax-mill.

J. M. Calender erected a frame building north of the grist-mill in 1866, and transferred the machinery of the grist-mill to it. He converted the stone mill into a woolen factory, where spinning, weaving, cloth-dressing, etc., were successfully carried on until about the time of his death. In 1875 the machinery of the grist-mill was restored to the stone building.

The first tavern in the place was kept by Thomas L. Fenton, on the northwest corner of the Newton side. Robert Weasner, Peter Bell, Peter Smith, and Noah Smith have since kept tavern in the place. Bell built a second building for a hotel.

Who kept the first store we are unable to learn for a certainty. Booth & Elliot, and Elliot & Ingersol have been mentioned as the first storekeepers. Robert Price began business as a merchant in 1817. Jonathan I. Tod, William Porter, Carpenter & Avery, Porter & Bronson, Porter & Moffat, James M. Calender, Fiester & Porter, Charles Curtis, and Noah Smith have all been engaged in the mercantile business here. John L. Greer kept a second store for a time, while Carpenter & Avery were in business. Some of the firms mentioned did a large business. But the place is now scarcely able to support one small grocery.

AN EXTINCT VILLAGE.

Frederick, or Fredericksburg as it is frequently called, was a flourishing little village on the river, near the south line of the township, forty or fifty years ago. Now a few dilapidated old houses and a church, windowless and almost roofless, remain to mark its site. But in days gone by, those primitive days which shall return no more forever, when the stages from Pittsburg and Cleveland passed through Frederick daily, the little village was at the zenith of its prosperity.

The first merchant in the place was a man named Swift. This is all that is known of him. Peter Kinnaman, from Petersburg, this county, began keeping a store in a part of Lebaugh's tavern in 1834. Soon after he built a store and occupied it some years. John Eckis was the next merchant in the place. Carpenter & Avery had a small store for a time. Matthias & George Christy and Mattox & Raymond were merchants in the later years of the village.

Louis Lebaugh kept the first and the principal hotel. The stage stopped at his door. His house was on the north side of the road and opposite the corner. Moses Everett kept another house of entertainment west of the bridge, on the south side of the road. Frederick Myers was the landlord of a long two-story building, situated west of Everett's, between it and the corner. His tavern was a large one for those days. The three houses were all open to the public at the same time.

A distillery was operated by Dyer Fitch for a short time. Mecca, or lubricating oil, found in the vicinity, got in the water used so much that it spoiled the liquor, and the business had to be dropped.

A tannery was successfully worked for a time by a German named John Kreitzinger. In addition to these industries the busy little place included among its inhabitants the following named artisans: William Cowell, hatter; Daniel Mauen, tailor; McWilliams and William Shoemaker, wagonmakers, as well as several blacksmiths and shoemakers.

CHURCH HISTORY.

At present there are but two church buildings in the township, the Methodist and the Presbyterian. The Disciples once had two churches, but they no longer have an organization. The Germans go to church in Berlin.

THE PRESBYTERIANS.

In 1807 or 1808 a Presbyterian church was organized by the citizens of Newton and Milton, and a church erected in Newton near Price's mills. Rev. James Boyd was the first pastor of the congregations of Newton and Warren. He died in 1813 and is buried in the old graveyard at Pricetown. Rev. Joshua Beer was the next pastor. There were then several supplies for a number of years. Rev. William O. Stratton was a settled pastor for a number of years, commencing about 1836. During his ministry the old church ceased to be used, and a new one was built at Orr's corners about 1847, which is still called the Newton church. Rev. J. B. Miller, Rev. Thomas P. Spear, Revs. Sharp and Taylor have presided since. When the Jackson church was built in 1871, it drew away a large portion of the members of the Newton church, and left it in a weak condition. It is now without a pastor. We append names of some of the prominent and active members of this church in early years: Nathaniel and William Stanley, Thomas Gilmer; elders, John Craig, Thomas McCoy, Nicholas Van Emmon, Isaac Winans, Jacob Winans, second, Emanuel Hoover, Sr. and Jr., Robert Russell, John Johnston.

THE METHODISTS.

The Methodist church was organized about 1812. Meetings were held in the school-house at Orr's corners, often on week-days, for the accommodation of circuit preachers whose duties were multifarious. Rev. Billings O. Plimpton, Dr. Bostwick, Nicholas Gee, Ira Eddy, Rev. Prosser, and others were early preachers. The prominent members of the church were the Winans, Vaughns, Tillinghast Morey, Isaac Mitchell, and others. About 1830 the organization built a brick church at Baldwin's corners in the northeastern part of the township. This building was destroyed by a gale in 1849. A few years later the present church, a small frame building, was erected. The church keeps up its organization and has regular preaching in connection with other societies.

From an old History of Methodism in the West we make the following extract:

During the summer of 1810 Mr. Tillinghast Mowry [Morey] moved from Connecticut and settled in Milton, one mile west of the center, where his house became a welcome home for Methodist preachers who were sent to labor on Hartford circuit, and was for many years a preaching place. Father Henry Shewel, residing in Deerfield, Ohio, after toiling through the week with his hands would on Sunday find his way through the woods to the new neighboring settlements to break the bread of life to the hungry souls in the wilderness. He established a preaching appointment at Mr. Mowry's and a class was formed comprising Tillinghast

Mowry, leader, and wife; Jacob Allen and wife, Joseph Depew, Margaret Hudson, Mr. Cole and wife, and perhaps others. The appointment was soon added to Hartford circuit and supplied with circuit preaching.

THE DISCIPLES.

The Disciples organized as early as 1830. William Hayden and Walter Scott began preaching here about 1827, and baptized several persons. Many of the Methodists joined them. They held their meetings in the Orr's corners schoolhouse for a time, then built a small church one-fourth of a mile east of the corners. Their organization went down more than twenty years ago. Early preachers: Webb, Flick, Shaffer, and others. Early and prominent members: Isaac Mitchell, Thomas L. Fenton, John Thatcher, Joseph Pierce, Amos Pierce, Joseph Pierce, Jr., and Jacob Winans, Sr.

The Disciples also built a church at Frederick, the frame of which is still standing. This church was organized through the efforts of Herman Reeves, who became its first pastor. The house was erected in 1852. Reeves, Shaffer, Griffin, Phillips, Hillock, Chapman, Megowan, and others were preachers in this church. Matthias Christy and William Cowell were the first elders; Christy also preached occasionally. John Carson, M. Smith, and Aaron Fink were elders and prominent members. The church was organized with thirty or forty members, and the number increased to nearly one hundred. Many members moved, and the war and its issues caused divisions which resulted in the dissolution of the organization.

BURIAL PLACES.

The first settlers were all buried in Newton near Price's mills. There are three small public burying places in this township, of which the one west of the river and a little north of the center road is probably the oldest.

POST-OFFICES.

The first post-office was established at Price's mills, or Pricetown, about the year 1808. Although Milton is the name of the post-office it has been kept in Newton township almost if not quite as much as in Milton. The office was originally on the route between Warren and Ravenna. The first postmaster was probably Judge Reuben S. Clark, succeeded by Robert Price, Jonathan I. Tod, Frank Porter, Noah Smith, and J. M. Calender, the present incumbent.

The post-office at Frederick was established previous to 1830. John Shoemaker, Sr., was probably the first postmaster. His successors: Peter Kinnaman, John Eckis, John Shoemaker, Jr., David Byers, Lydia A. Steffey, Robert Weasner, Madison Traill, John Carson. Since Mr. Carson took the office, about fifteen years ago, it has been kept in Berlin township. The mail is received twice a week.

PHYSICIANS.

Dr. Tracy Bronson, who lived just over the line in Newton township, was the practicing physician in Milton for many years, and is remembered with gratitude and affection by many of his old patients.

Dr. George Ewing had quite a large practice in the township. He settled on a farm but continued attending to the calls of his patients up to the time of his death. There have been many other physicians in the township, but none that have been permanent residents.

THE FIRST SCHOOLS.

For several years teachers were paid by subscription, their wages in summer terms being four or five dollars per month, and nine or ten in winter, not all in cash but frequently in grain or orders on the store-keepers.

Daniel Depew, an aged man, was one of the first school-teachers in a log-cabin situated east of the river. A very few of his pupils are still living. Other early teachers in different parts of Milton were Tillinghast Morey, Robert White, Margaret Depew, Nancy Best, Peggy Stevens, Gain Robison, Joseph Duer, Phebe Canfield, and Billings O. Plimpton, afterwards quite celebrated as a Methodist preacher.

John Johnston taught school two winters, 1811–12 and 1812–13, in a little log schoolhouse which was situated on the center road about three-fourths of a mile west of the Jackson township line. The school-house contained an immense fire-place in a chimney at one end of the room. The house was perhaps sixteen feet square; paper was used for glass in the windows, and the door was pinned together with wooden pins in place of nails. Probably twenty scholars attended this school while Mr. Johnston taught. The cabin just described was used as a school-house until about 1818, when a building of hewed logs was erected on the lot where the present school-house stands.

The method of instruction in these early schools was somewhat different from that which is now in use. First, the pupil was taught the alphabet; then spelling, reading, writing, in succession, and finally arithmetic. Many of the old settlers never attended a school in which grammar or geography was taught.

IN THE WILD WOODS.

As late as 1806 three Indians, rejoicing in the euphonious names of Nicksaw, Cayuga, and Cadashua, were living on the west bank of the river on the best of terms with their white neighbors. They subsisted chiefly by hunting and fishing, though they raised a little corn on the river bottom. There are those now living who remember having seen these Indians at their homes.

Game of all kinds was abundant. Squirrels and other small pests attacked the corn and wheat, and wolves were ever ready to make way with lambs and other young stock. It was no uncommon thing for a farmer to wake up in the morning and find that a bear had killed his hog, or a wolf destroyed some of his sheep.

The last known instance of a bear in the township was in 1835. At that date Joseph Mead tracked one across Milton into Newton where it was killed.

MISCELLANEOUS.

Probably the first bridge across the Mahoning above Warren, was a trestle-work bridge on the line between Newton and Milton. This broke down in 1822 while Joseph Depew was crossing it with three yoke of oxen. Four of the oxen were killed by the fall, but the driver and the head yoke got out uninjured. This bridge was soon replaced by another of similar construction, which the breaking up of the ice in 1831 destroyed. Soon after the bridge now standing was built in a more substantial manner.

Captain Vanetten had a distillery in very early times. During the War of 1812 it was run by his wife, who, the captain declared, could make more and better whiskey from the same amount of grain than he could. There were numerous stills in all parts of the settlement. James Orr built a distillery and an ashery near Orr's corners

about the year 1817. Soon after he sold the distillery to his brother John. John Hineman built a distillery in the northeastern corner of the township about the same date. Some years later John Reed built a third near the location of the first.

John Johnston and James Moore started a tannery in 1823. It was situated about one-half mile north of the center road on Johnston's farm. It was worked until 1839, when it was moved by Samuel Johnston to his farm in Jackson, where he carried on the business until about 1870. Robert Laughlin started a tannery some time after this. In 1827 James Moore built another one-fourth of a mile west of Orr's corners.

A grist-mill and a saw-mill were built by Jesse Holliday and Joseph Hoover on the Mahoning, about two and one-half miles south of Price's mills, in 1824. A carding machine was operated in connection with these mills for some time. The grist-mill was sold to a man named Brian and later to John Nolan. While he was the owner it was destroyed by fire and rebuilt. A few old timbers still remain to mark the spot where it stood. John and George Forder some years later had a grist-mill and saw-mill on their land.

A BEAR STORY.

Aaron Porter was a famous hunter, and the history of his experiences and achievements would make an interesting book. Early and late, in every season and all kinds of weather, he busied himself in the pursuit which he so dearly loved. With his moccasins—he never would wear boots while hunting—and his rifle, he could often be seen striding through the forest, either going in quest of adventure or returning victorious after a day's exploits. He was a man of strong limbs and powerful frame, capable of enduring almost any amount of physical exertion. Miles were nothing to him. With an easy, swinging, rapid gait he would traverse the woods hour after hour, apparently with no thought of fatigue or desire for rest. The man who would attempt to follow "Uncle Aaron" all day would have been considered rash indeed.

We will here note one of his many hunting episodes, as told by his son. One day while Porter and his son Samuel were hunting near the north fork of the Mahoning, while ranging the woods they suddenly came across an old In-

24*

dian and a young brave who had treed an old she bear and her cubs, and were attempting to secure them. The animals had taken refuge within a large hollow tree and were some distance from the ground. Porter came where the red men were, and at once comprehending the condition of affairs, made signs to the Indians that they should allow him to cut the tree down. The old hunter shook his head, and intimated that the bear would run away. Porter pointed to two dogs which were following him; but the Indian uttered a contemptuous "Ugh!" and declared that the dogs were "too light." As they were only small water spaniels, his reasoning was apparently well founded. The Indians soon lighted a fire at the base of the tree, and as the smoke found its way up the cavity where the bear was, she began to scramble upward in a very lively manner, until she reached an opening just large enough to put her head through. As soon as the black nose was visible to the hunters, and while its owner was in full and complete enjoyment of fresh air, the old Indian fired. The bear fell back into the tree and there was much noise and commotion among the cubs. Porter then asked the Indian if he should cut the tree, and, receiving an affirmative reply, set to work and soon the trunk went crackling to the earth; and lo! out rushed the bear which the Indian thought he had killed, and bounded away at a lively rate. Uncle Aaron fired off his gun to excite the dogs, and all started in hot pursuit of the running game except the old Indian, who stopped to secure the cubs, and then followed as fast as his limbs could carry him.

The dogs, which were well trained, and had participated in many a bear-hunt before this one, soon brought the animal at bay, by biting her hind legs and otherwise worrying her. Porter, as usual, caught up with the dogs before the other hunters, but he could do nothing, as his gun was empty. Before he had time to reload his son came up, and taking his gun, uncle Aaron walked up close to the bear's head and shot her. Soon the young Indian arrived, and he, too, poured his rifle's charge into the bear, which Porter's shot had already killed. The old Indian next appeared and took his turn at shooting. By this time the animal was "dead enough to skin;" as all the hunters unanimously agreed; and the Indians, with deft and skillful fingers,

soon had the hide removed. The old red man then cut off a large piece of the shoulder, which he offered to Porter. The latter declined it by shaking his head. The Indian, however, insisted; made signs of eating, pointed to the meat and then to his mouth to declare that it was good; and Porter, to please him, accepted the gift and wrapped it carefully in some bark, that he might carry it home without the inconvenience of being daubed with bear's grease. The young Indian next cut off some of the meat and wrapped it up as Porter had done. The old warrior then took the remainder of the carcass, entrails and all, put the cubs, which were still alive, into it, wrapped the whole securely in the bear-skin, making a bundle plenty large and heavy for one to carry, shouldered it and marched toward his wigwam, doubtless well pleased with the result of his hunting, and thankful for the white man's assistance.

NOTES OF SETTLEMENT.

John McKenzie, the fifth child of John and Elizabeth McKenzie, was born in Pennsylvania in the year 1803. He came to Ohio with his parents in 1805, who settled in Milton township on the farm now owned by Frank Keefer. They were the first settlers in that locality, and the country was then a wilderness. At the age of twenty-one the subject of this sketch was married to Miss Sally Vanetten and has had a family of ten children, viz: Royal, Anna, Simeon, Harriet, Maryette, Martin Van, Jeannette, Addison, and Alice. One child died in infancy Maryette, Anna, and Jeannette are also dead.

Robert Russel was born in Pennsylvania in 1778. His father's family, consisting of his wife and five children, came to Ohio in 1803 and settled in Poland township on a farm now occupied by Mrs. Sullivan. The father lived to the good old age of ninety years. Robert Russell followed shoemaking for over fifty years. He married in 1814 Miss Anna French and had a large family of sons, named James, Alexander, John, Robert, Enoch, Joseph, Robert, Enoch (second), Joseph, and Ebenezer. The only survivors are James and Enoch. James, the eldest of the family, was born in 1815. In 1843 he married Miss Kate Gillmer and has two children, Ann Elizabeth and Sarah Margaret. Mr. Russell has always followed farming and stock raising, and now occupies the old homestead. He and his wife are both members of the Presbyterian church of Newton.

Russell Orr was born in Pennsylvania in 1798. He came to Ohio with his parents, who settled in Jackson township, now Mahoning county, at an early date, on the farm now occupied by Mr. Goldsmith. Russell Orr removed to Milton township in 1824, where he lived until his death. He was married in 1820 to Eleanor Winans, and became the father of ten children, to-wit: Ellen, Rodney, Gates, James, Casselman, Susan, Mary, Jacintha, Olive, and Russell, all of whom survive except James. Mr. Orr died at the age of forty-one, and his wife at the age of seventy-nine. Rodney Orr, the second child, was born in Jackson, in 1823. At the age of thirty he was married to Miss Elizabeth Moore. In 1862 he enlisted in the Forty-first Ohio volunteer infantry.

John W. Osborn, whose family still live in Milton, was born in Youngstown township, Mahoning county, June 8, 1806. His father was Joseph Osborn, who was born in Virginia in 1776, and died on his farm in Youngstown township in 1846 at seventy years of age. The original settler of the family was Nicholas Osborn, further mentioned elsewhere. He was a native of England, born in 1729, emigrated to Virginia, and located on a farm in Loudoun county; married and resided there until the death of his wife. In the fall of 1804 he moved with his family to Youngstown township, then Trumbull county, Ohio, purchasing one thousand acres of land in the southwest corner of that township, which he afterwards divided among his children, with whom he made his home. He died June, 1814, at the age of eighty-five years. John W. Osborn was raised on a farm, receiving a common school education, such as the district schools of the time afforded. While a young man he learned the cabinet and carpenter trade, which he followed more or less for a number of years. He married, in 1835, Mary Harclerode, of Ellsworth, and resided in that township about two years. He then purchased a farm in Milton, to which he moved in 1837. He thenceforth resided in Milton, principally engaged in farming, until his death, which occurred December 12, 1874. He owned at his death a good farm, on which his widow still lives, at the age of sixty-eight years. There were born to them three boys and four girls, all of whom are living.

Robert Carson, twelfth child of John and Catharine Carson, was born in Pennsylvania in 1828 and came to Ohio with his parents in 1832. At the age of twenty-two he was married to Miss Martha Patterson, by whom he has had three children: Willis S., Eva, and Orra. Willis S. is deceased. At the age of thirty-three Mr. Carson started in the flax business in which he continued some fifteen years. He now follows farming. He has been justice of the peace twelve years and is at this writing still holding that office.

Leonidas Carson was born in what is now Mahoning county in 1835. He lived upon the farm with his parents until he was of age when he married Miss Rebecca Weasner. This union resulted in six children as follow: Lucy, Hannah, George, Mary, Ellen, and Jessie; all living. Mr. Carson was first lieutenant of company G, One Hundred and Fifty-fifth Ohio National guard, and served one hundred days. He is now extensively engaged in the raising of bees and the production of honey, in which he is quite successful. He and his wife are members of the Disciple church of Deerfield.

Richard Woodward was born in Pennsylvania in 1800. He was reared at home until he was sixteen years of age, when he went to learn the trade of weaving (the weaving of double coverlets) at which he continued five years and then went into business for himself. At the age of twenty-two he was married to Miss Nancy Roberts and had six children: Jonah, Mary A., Caroline, Ann M., John, and Joseph, of whom Ann and John are deceased. Mr. Woodward came to Ohio in 1835 and settled on the farm now owned and occupied by his son Joseph. He died at the age of sixty-eight and is buried in Jackson. Joseph R., the youngest child, was born in Milton township in 1844. In 1867 he married Miss Sarah Phillips and has five children, viz: Daniel N., Arlinna B., Joseph E., Homer, and Anna M.; all living but Daniel, who died at the age of twenty months. Mr. Woodward and wife are members of the Disciple church.

William Weasner was born in New Jersey in 1786. He came to Ohio in 1841, and settled in Milton township, on the Morey farm, where he lived until his death in 1864. He married, in 1826, Miss Mahala Boyd, and had a family of twelve children, viz: Susan, Rebecca, Robert, William, James, Margaret, Sarah, Horace, Hannah, Lewis, Jeffrey, and Grace; Susan, William, and Lewis are deceased. Mrs. Weasner is still living.

Robert Weasner, third child of William and Matilda Weasner, was born in New Jersey in 1836. He was married, in 1857, to Miss Rachel Best, by whom he has had three children—Alva H., Maud A., and Lee Etta; Maud A. is deceased. Mr. Weasner is a farmer by occupation and has held the office of justice of the peace for thirteen years, and still retains it. He and his wife are prominent members of the Lutheran church of Berlin, and Mr. Weasner has been superintendent of the Sunday-school of the church for about fifteen years. He enlisted in the Nineteenth Ohio volunteer infantry in 1861, served nine months when, on account of physical disability, he was honorably discharged.

Hiram Taylor was born in Middletown, Springfield township, now Mahoning county, in 1830. When he was four years of age his parents removed to Austintown township. When twenty-five years of age he married Miss Martha Justice and settled in Ohltown and engaged in the business of carriage making, which he carried on for about twenty years. He resided in Trumbull county about six years when he bought the old homestead in Austintown. He occupied this two years and then purchased the place where he now lives. Some twenty-four years after his marriage his wife died, and in 1881 he married Miss Mary Chessman, of Salem. He now follows farming in connection with his trade. Himself and wife are members of the Presbyterian church.

Nathaniel Smith was born in Sussex county, New Jersey, in 1812. He resided with his parents until he was twenty years of age, when he was married to Miss Mary Welsh. They have had eleven children, named as follow: Emory, Nathan, Z. T., H. E., Catharine, Elizabeth, Sarah, Orpha, Ezra, Charles, and Anna. The three last-named are deceased. Mr. Smith came to Ohio in 1843 and settled in Milton township on the place where he now lives. He has been justice of the peace eleven years. He and his wife are members of the Disciples church.

Thomas L. Fenton, a native of Pennsylvania, and his wife, Catharine Reed, came to Ohio in

an early day, and first settled on a farm now owned by Robert Walker, in Milton township, in Mahoning county. He was a blacksmith by trade, which he followed in connection with farming. After occupying this place for some time, he moved to the place where his son Josiah now lives. He was the father of eight children, viz: Hiram, Jesse, Josiah, Mary, Lucy, Jane, Christina, and Harriet. Lucy and Mary are dead. Mr. Fenton survived his wife three years, and died at an advanced age. Josiah Fenton, the third child, was born on the farm where he now lives in 1817. At the age of twenty-eight he was married to Hannah Corll and and has had thirteen children, viz: Chauncey, Urinas, Samuel, Albina, Mary A., Alverett, Charles, Josiah, Landa, Arvilla, Herman, Cora, and Bert.

Daniel Reichard was born in Guilford township, Franklin county, Pennsylvania, in the year 1815. He came to Ohio in 1845, and settled on the farm where he now lives. At that time there was about five acres cleared on the place, and a rude log cabin. In this the family resided until 1870, when he erected the substantial residence which he now occupies. At the age of twenty-one, he began teaching school, at which he continued for some six years, when he went to farming. He was married in 1841 to Miss Rebecca Benedict, by whom he had four children, John B., Alfred, Daniel, and Rebecca, who died in infancy. Mrs. Reichard died in 1848, and in 1850 he married Eliza J. Forder. By this marriage there were eleven children, Franklin, Octavia, Hattie J., B. F., Helen M., Randolph, Clarence, Clara, George W., Pulaski, and Ruhama V. Octavia and Clara are dead. Mr. Reichard has been justice of the peace three years.

John Greenamyer was born in Columbiana county in 1809. He remained with his parents, Jacob and Catharine, and worked at farming until he was twenty-one when he went to learn the carpenter's trade. This trade he followed until he was thirty-six years old, when, in 1845, he began farming, removing to the place where he now lives in Milton township. At the age of twenty-four he was united in marriage to Miss Mary Kale, by whom he had thirteen children, as follow: Samuel, John, Solomon, Lucy Ann, Caroline, Reuben, Hannah, William, Martin,

Delvina, Benjamin, Edwin, and one died in infancy; Reuben and Delvina are also deceased. Mr. Greenamyer and his wife are members of the Reformed church.

David Beard was born in Springfield township, now Mahoning county, in 1825. At the age of eighteen he went to learn the trade of shoemaking which he followed twelve years. He then engaged in the grocery business at Canfield some seven years, after which he purchased the place in Milton, Mahoning county, where he now lives and has since followed farming. In 1859 he married Miss Mary Heintzleman, and has five children, as follow: James B., Ida H., Dorothea A., Theron A., and Lucy E. Mr. Beard was elected treasurer of his township in 1855, which office he held two years. He and his wife are members of the German Lutheran church.

Ancil Johnson was born in Milton township, Mahoning county, on the place where he now lives in 1849. In 1873 he was united in marriage to Miss Elizabeth Strock, by whom he had four children: Lisle, and three that died in infancy. Mr. Johnson has always given his undivided attention to farming, and is an industrious and successful agriculturist.

CHAPTER X.

BEAVER.

Before 1811 this township was known as township three, range two, but in that year was organized with the name Beaver. Since 1846 it has formed a part of Mahoning county. It is bounded on the east by Springfield, north by Fairfield, and west by Green.

The surface is moderately level with a general drainage to the north and east. In parts it is slightly broken by low hills, and along the streams are some lands too low and level for cultivation, being subject to overflow. There are also a few small swamps. The township was originally covered with a heavy growth of oak, ash, maple, beech, elm, and a limited quantity of pine. Timber still remains in considerable quantity.

Mill creek, the principal stream flows, through the township northward west of the center, receiving the waters of a number of small brooks. On account of its low banks but little water-power is afforded. The head of Big Bull creek is in the southeastern part of the township, but its volume here is no greater than a brook. Nearly every section has enough springs to furnish water for domestic use, or it may easily be obtained by digging wells.

Building stone and coal abound, and sand may be procured in several localities. The soil is variable, being a light loam or sandy clay, generally free from stones and easily cultivated. The inhabitants are mostly occupied with the ordinary farm pursuits, but lately increasing attention has been given to dairying and the raising of live stock.

THE PIONEERS.

One of the first settlers was Major Jacob Gilbert, a native of Maryland, who settled on the farm now occupied by Michael Wieland about 1802. The Wielands of this township descended from one of his seven children, a daughter, who married Adam Wieland. Major Gilbert took an active part in the War of 1812, and was one of the prominent men of the township in his day.

About the same time John Shanefelt, also a soldier of 1812, settled near Gilbert on the homestead afterward occupied by his son John.

Adam Little was an early and prominent settler near the center of Beaver.

The first settler in the north of the township was an old bachelor named "Billy" Stewart, who lived alone many years in a small log cabin. Still farther west Abraham Miller was the pioneer.

On section one, the first settler was Peter Stevens, who had a lease on a small tract of land. He is credited with being the discoverer of the coal in this locality, which he mined, in a small way, for two cents per bushel.

Farther south, on section thirteen, settlement was made in 1803 by Christopher Mentzer, and soon after Christian Clinker settled in the neighborhood of North Lima, with his sons, Abner, Josiah, Samuel, and Isaac. Not far from here were, also, as early as 1804, Frederick and Michael Dutterer, and in the southern part of the township, among the pioneers of that period, were John Harman, Henry Neidigh, and Frederick Sponseller.

John Coblentz, from Frederick, Maryland, settled on the south side of section twenty-five in 1804. His family consisted of four sons and a daughter, who married John Elser, who has resided on this section since 1827.

Other early and noteworthy settlers were John Crumbacher, George Hoke, Balzer Mowen, John Neidigh, Jacob Crouse, Christian Crebs, David Gerringer, Peter Eib, Isaiah Bachman, George Augustine, Michael Shaefer, George Hively, Christian Fox, Adam Movingstar, Mathias Glass, William Heckman, Henry Myers, George Pontius, Abraham Stouffer, Abraham Boyer, Jacob Whitter, David Coy, Jacob Mellinger, John Metz, John Rukenbrod, Jacob Overhaltzer, Henry Snyder, and Jacob Rupert.

Settlements were rapidly made and many changes took place. This can best be seen from a list prepared twenty years later.

The freeholders living in the township in 1830 were as follows: On school district number one—Christian Ackerman, John Frankfelter, Andrew Hahn, George Lonefelter, Ebenezer Stahl, William Sullivan, David Sprinkel, Jacob Witter, John Bennett, Jacob Gilbert, John Gilbert, Jacob Paulin, W. Sheckel, John Shanefelt, Jr., Frederick Shanefelt, Adam Wieland.

On the second district—John Blosser, Daniel Cohler, Patrick Dilley, Andrew Forney, John Fox, Jacob Linn, Jacob Miller, Abraham Miller, Henry Sponseller, Joseph Sprinkel, Frederick Smith, Jacob Wansettler, John Chub, Aaron C. Cain, John Fellnagle, Jacob Fellnagle, John Heller, Adam Little, George Messerley, William Shepler, Peter Steffey, Michael Shank, Ferdinand Shantz.

On district number three lived John Bachman, George Bachman, Jacob Boyer, Abraham Boyer, Benjamin Bechtel, John Coy, Adam Frankfelter, Reuben Grimes, Tobias Heverly, David Hoover, William Kendricks, Michael Kulp, Henry Kulp, John Kulp, Daniel Mackley, Frederick Roos, Mathias Topper, Martin Wilderson, John Bright, John Calvin, George Foreman, E. Gardner, John Harmon, Charles Hammer, Philip Houck, Abraham Myers, John Myers, Henry Myers, John Nold, John Shoemaker, Henry Thomas, Peter Yoder.

On district number four were John Aultman,

John Bieber, Peter Blosser, Solomon Crouse, Jacob Crouse, William Crouse, Frederick Fellnagel, John Glass, John Hahn, Jacob Jokis, Michael Huyler, Michael Keek, Christopher Mentzer, Jacob Mentzer, William Miller, Catharine Augustine, Jacob S. Buzard, John Cohler, John Clinker, Isaac Clinker, Michael Dutterer, John Fasnacht, David Gerringer, Jacob Harman, R. P. Justice, G. Hutchin, F. Leitzey, Adam Myrice, David Metzler, Jacob Mowen, John Mowen, Peter Mowen, Balzar Mowen, Daniel Shilling, Michael Wieland, William Eyster, Jacob Reephard, James Simpson, Jacob Shoemaker.

In district number five lived George Bush, Frederick Frankfetter, Adam Fisher, Mathias Gilbert, Andrew Little, John Shanefelt, David Shanefelt, Gabriel Erb, George Fox, John B. Fox, Jacob Lenhart, John Simons, Henry Wohford.

On the sixth district were Alexander Anderson, John Borlan, Samuel Detweiler, John Fox, Peter Fox, Jacob Haltereth, Gotlieb Hedler, Jacob Landis, Mary Mellinger, John Royer, David Stephens, George Bachman, Jacob Bachman, Joseph Frederick, Peter Hendricks, William Heckman, George Haltereth, Jacob Knob, Tobias Miller, Jacob Oberholser, Jacob Oberholser, Jr., Solomon Sloop.

District number seven had the following freeholders: Joseph Borlan, Jacob Baker, David Coy, Samuel Coy, John Esterly, Jacob Hill, Peter Kleckner, Henry Kendig, Augustine Miller, George Bloom, Christian Shiely, John Stiver, Frederick Stiver, Michael Unger, Christian Beringer, Frederick Beringer, E. Crumbacher, Jacob Detweiler, William Hooker, Peter Hibble, Baltas Kutcher, H. B. Myers, Jacob Paetner, Christian Rinkinberger, Abraham Shaeffer, Abraham Stauffer, Frederick Ungelbower.

In district number eight lived William Cox, Widow Coblentz, Jacob Cope, Frederick Dutterer, Michael Dutterer, George Dutterer, John Elser, George Glaser, John Glackler, Jacob Glackler, John Harman, Jr., Solomon Harman, Henry Harman, George Candle, Mary Lipply, Catherine Myers, George Rukenbrod, Michael Rukenbrod, John Rapp, Sr., John Rapp, Jr., Frederick Sponseller, George Sponseller, Michael Sponseller, John Schnurrenberger, Conrad Snyder, Amos Worthington, John Zeigler.

CIVIL LIST.

The township was organized for civil purposes in the year 1811, and in the following year Beaver was added to the tax list of the county, the assessment for 1812 being $35.25.

The first election was held April 1, 1811, the judges being Christian Clinker, Frederick Sponseller, and Peter Eib. The following were elected: Trustees—John Crumbacher, Christian Clinker, Frederick Sponseller; clerk, George Hoke; treasurer, John Harman; lister, Adam Little; house appraiser, John Coblentz; constable, Jacob Gilbert; overseers of the poor, Balzar Mowen, David Geringer; fence-viewers, John Neidigh, Sr., Christopher Mentzer; road supervisors, Christian Crebs and Jacob Crouse. Peter Eib and Adam Little were justices of the peace.

MINING AND MANUFACTURING.

Coal may be procured in almost every section of the township, and is profitably mined in the central and northeasten parts. One of the most extensive mines is that of Azariah Paulin, in section one, which yields fifteen hundred to two thousand tons yearly. South from him David Sprinkel has a mine in which is a vein of cannel coal five feet in thickness; and a little southwest are mines operated by Catterhead & McGill, Inser & Shaefer, and others. On section six coal was mined about twenty-five years ago to supply a furnace for the manufacture of coal oil. Near the center of the township there are coal banks on the farms of Daniel Crouse and Abraham Yoder, and farther west, south of East Lewistown, are a number of mines yielding good coal.

On Mill creek, section fifteen, the first mill was put in operation about 1805 by Matthias Glass. A small affair, it was displaced by one of greater capacity by Jacob Crouse. In 1849 the present mill was built by Anthony Smith and steam power added. Subsequent owners have been Solomon Elser, John Faulk, Henry Nerr, and since 1877, Hasness, Thoman & Co. It is a three-story frame, and has three run of stones.

Abraham Stauffer had grist- and saw-mills further south, on Mill creek, but they were abandoned about 1840.

North of the old Glass mill Peter Glass put up a saw-mill, which was operated many years by Solomon Crouse.

On Turkey Broth creek, in section nine, Jacob Detwiler put up a water-power saw-mill, which was changed to steam by John Fellnagel, and is now in operation.

Quite a number of steam mills are now in operation in the township.

At the village of North Lima a steam gristmill, erected a few years ago by John Spait, is now in operation.

In the early history of the place, Jacob Esterley had a tannery near the site of the present hotel. Another tannery was established in 1852 by Solomon Clinker.

Here were formerly distilleries carried on by Lewis Ruhlman, John Fasnacht, Anthony Smith, Samuel Summers, and John Fisher. The village has a carriage shop and a number of mechanic-shops.

NORTH LIMA

is a pleasant village, located chiefly on the south half of section fourteen, and was founded about 1826 by James Simpson. The original plat contained only a few lots along the county road. Additions have been made by John Northrup, Martin Hasness, Samuel Crouse, and J. S. Buzard. The village did not grow fast, and owes its existence wholly to the demand for a local trading point. The population is about three hundred. There are three fine churches and two handsome school-houses. The one in the west district is of brick, 32x40 feet, and was built in 1868 at a cost of $2,500. The east house is of the same material, 36x48 feet, and cost to build in 1871 $2,700. There is also a village hall, the old Evangelical church having been altered for this purpose in 1876.

As early as 1828 a man named Hartzell sold goods in a small way in the village; other small traders were John Glass and John Northrup. The first regular store was opened by the Niell Brothers in a building where is now Raus' tinshop. John G. Leslie was their clerk, becoming their partner when the store was moved down street. Others here in trade were Crouse & Northrup, Buzard & Co., J. H. Donalb, Mentz, Hahn, Fell & Co., Miller, Ruhlman, George Buzard, and J. Ernst.

In the buildings on the opposite corners have been stores by Truesdell, Baldwin, Kirtland, Felger, Haller, Buzard, Henkle, Shaefer, Heindle, and Witter. The village has also had a few small grocery stores.

In 1830 John Glass opened the first public house in a building since used for that purpose. Among the landlords which followed were John B. Fox, John H. Rowell, William McKeown, E. Ruhlman, M. E. Dutterer, John Weaver, and Amos Clinker.

The post-office was established about 1828, with Jacob Gilbert as postmaster. A man named Stillson carried the mail, going afoot to Liverpool. Owing to the difficulty in getting the mail the office was discontinued about 1831. It was re-established in 1834, and the postmasters since that period have been J. G. Leslie, Samuel Rohrbaugh, J. G. Buzard, John H. Donald, Samuel Rau, George Buzard, and Henry Buzard. It has three mails per day.

About 1831 Drs. Manning and Willet came to the place to establish a practice in medicine, but did not remain long. They were followed for a short space of time, by Drs. Correll, Blocksom, Eddy, Campbell, Truesdell, etc. In 1846 Nathan Hahn became the first permanent physician, remaining until his death, in 1874. Contemporary practitioners were Drs. Stewart, Dawson, Davis, Bowman, etc. Dr. S. S. Schiller came in 1870, and Dr. H. H. Hahn in 1876.

Two miles west of North Lima is the village of

EAST LEWISTOWN.

It has a very handsome location on sections sixteen and twenty-seven, and but for the advantage enjoyed by North Lima in being the older village, would have become the more important place. Village lots were laid out about 1830 by Peter Goder, Sr., John Nold, Henry Thoman, Sr., and George Houck; but it was not until 1836 that building commenced, when the place grew rapidly, attaining, in a few years its maximum. It contains about forty buildings, and a schoolhouse of attractive appearance, erected in 1867, at a cost of $3,300.

Jesse Motter opened a store in the village in 1839, in the house occupied by H. Thoman as a residence, and was in trade until 1845. Meantime another store was conducted on the southwest corner of the square by Hoover & Rudisill. The village has had as merchants Jacob S. Thoman, Daniel Thoman, T. G. Northrup, Frederick Fellnagle, Franklin Dunn, Smith & Buzard, Abraham Miller, and George Buzard.

A man named Morrow kept the first public house about 1843, in a building opposite the Thoman residence. Ten years later Conrad Stigletz opened an inn on the square, which he kept till 1863. He was followed by George Heindle. About the same time a tavern was kept on the north side of the square by Isaac Thoman, which was continued only a short time.

The post-office was established about 1851, and had Philip Fetzer as the first postmaster. It then had a semi-weekly mail; at present it is supplied daily from Columbiana. The other postmasters of this office have been Daniel Thoman, Josiah Rohrbaugh, Isaac Thoman, David Wonderlin, and George Buzard.

The first to practice the healing art was an herbalist, a Dr. Pappenaugh. Dr. Ethan A. Hoke was the first regular physician.

The hamlet of Woodworth, locally called Steamtown, is situated on the Boardman line, there being but a few houses and a steam sawmill on the Beaver side.

SCHOOLS AND CHURCHES.

The township has taken great interest in education, and given particular attention to supplying an excellent class of school-buildings. It is stated, on the authority of a State official, that Beaver leads all the other townships in this respect.

There are eleven districts, and every one of them is provided with a commodious and handsome brick house, with belfry, inside blinds, and modern furniture, costing from $2,700 to $3,500, whose attractive appearance reflects great credit upon the people of the township.

A small log meeting-house was built in 1808, by the Lutheran and Reformed congregations. Mount Olivet Reformed congregation was formed in 1810. Paradise church was built on section nine in 1849. The old Overholtzer Mennonite church was erected in 1825 and the present one in 1871. The Dunkers built their present church in 1872. Calvary Evangelical church at North Lima was organized in 1836, and their present edifice erected in 1876. A Methodist church, not now in existence, was organized at North Lima in 1840.

CHAPTER XI.

GOSHEN.

The township of Goshen (number seventeen, range four) contains thirty-two square miles. Its principal streams are the Middle fork of Beaver creek, which rises in Perry, flows through the eastern part of Goshen, and a branch of the Mahoning river, which rises in section nineteen and flows in a general course northerly through the western portion of the township, and leaves it about a mile east of the northwest corner.

The township of Goshen has an undulating surface, and yields to the landscape outlines of quiet beauty in infinite variety. The soil is fertile and well adapted to grazing and the raising of small fruits.

FIRST SETTLEMENTS.

Anthony Morris came in 1804, and settled in section thirty-one. His wife was Hannah French. He was overseer of the poor in 1812. His daughter Sarah married James Bruff, who came in 1822.

Barzilla French also settled on part of section thirty-one.

Thomas French first came to Damascus in 1805, and his brother Elijah soon after. Thomas married a daughter of Jonas Cattell, who located in Salem.

Horton Howard entered several sections of land in Goshen for a man named Hoopes and acted as his agent. The tract was bought by Benjamin Wright in 1847 and divided among his five daughters.

David Venable came to Goshen in 1805 and settled as a tenant on the farm of Jonas Cattell.

Isaac and Thomas Votaw came from Winchester, Virginia, in 1806. Isaac purchased two hundred and forty acres on section nineteen and died in 1820. He had two sons, Benjamin and David, and was trustee of the township in 1812–18. Thomas Votaw settled in section six, and served as supervisor and trustee. He had three sons, Thomas, Samuel and Isaac. Descendants of both Isaac and Thomas live in the township.

Robert Armstrong was an early settler and held various township offices. His descendants still live in the township.

About 1806 Stacy Shreeve came with his wife

from New Jersey and settled in section nineteen. John, his son, lives on the old homestead.

Joseph Kindele, a brother-in-law of Shreeve, also located on section nineteen in 1806.

James Brooke came from York State in 1806, and settled in section seven. A daughter of Mr. Brooke married Dr. James Hughes and resides in Berlin.

Isaac Ellison came from Virginia in 1806 and married a daughter of James Cattell, locating on section seven. Zachariah Ellison, father of Isaac, came in 1816 and settled in section nineteen. He married Mary, a sister of Isaac Votaw, and died at the age of eighty.

William and James Cattell came before 1810. William settled about a mile west of Goshen. James had a large family of daughters and settled on section nineteen.

Samuel Davis, of Salem, entered section twenty as early as 1804, receiving a deed from the Government dated November 1, 1808. He gave the southeast quarter of the section to his daughter Rachael, who married Lewis Townsend, a brother of Mrs. Dr. Benjamin Stanton, of Salem. The northeast quarter was given to William Davis, a son, who was killed on the mountains a few years after, when the property passed to his children.

Joshua Morris came in about 1810 and located a farm a little north of William Fawcett. He sold it in 1818 to James Hemingway, from New Jersey, whose son James was clerk of the township from 1827 to 1842.

Aaron Stratton, elder brother of Michael and Stacy, came from New Jersey in 1808 and settled in section twenty-three, on Beaver creek, where he soon after built a grist-mill, which well accommodated the country round. The property was sold in 1834 to Emor F. Weaver, and afterwards to Samuel Mathers.

Henry Hinchman came from New Jersey about 1808 with a large family of children,— John, Henry, Aaron, Hannah, Elizabeth, Grace, and Mary,—and settled on section thirty-six. His son Henry lives in the township. Aaron published a newspaper in 1842, which he printed in his father's house. He afterwards removed to Salem.

Benjamin Butler, Hannah his wife, and their children, Lawrence, Ellen, Hannah, John, Meribah, Ann, and Sarah, came from near Philadelphia, by the way of Lancaster, Harrisburg, and Pittsburg, in a two-horse wagon, and were about four weeks on the route. They arrived at Salem in April, 1811. Mr. Butler was poor and settled on the farm of Robert French, in section thirty-six, where he lived a year. He then moved into the present township of Goshen and occupied land owned by Aaron Street, near the western boundary, and lived there two years. A Friend gave him an opportunity to buy and build, and he purchased one hundred and sixty acres on section eighteen, where Elihu Cobb lives, and moved into a building of round logs which he there erected. He lived in this until August, 1828, when he died.

John Butler, son of Benjamin, purchased a farm adjoining the Friends' meeting-house, and in 1825 built a two-story cabin, of hewn logs, in which he began housekeeping in August of that year. His wife was Priscilla Fawcett, whom he married at the Friends' meeting house in Salem. In 1829 he purchased the farm he now occupies, which was at that time all woods. Here he built, in 1830, a log house with a shingle roof, but, his wife dying in that year, he changed his plans, and did not move to the farm until his second marriage, in 1834. While living with his father on the farm in section eighteen, it fell to his lot to do the "milling." He generally carried to mill about two bushels of grain. The mill was nearly due east from the farm, on a branch of Beaver creek, was known as the "Stratton mill," and was probably built about 1809.

Mr. Butler, a prominent member of the Society of Friends, was appointed one of the associated executive committee of Friends of the Central Indian Superintendency of the United States.

William Fawcett, with his wife, came from Virginia in 1811, and purchased one hundred and sixty-four acres on section thirty-two.

Samuel and Thomas Langstaff in 1812 settled on section eighteen, where now is a hamlet called "Boswell."

Joseph Wright came from New Jersey in 1810, settled first on section thirteen, and moved therefrom to section fourteen. He lived to old age, and served the township in various offices almost continuously until the time of his death.

Benjamin Malmsbury came from New Jersey with his wife and children about 1812, and bought one hundred and sixty acres on section thirty-six.

Bazel Perry and his wife came from Maryland in 1811 and settled on section five, east of Thomas Votaw. He was not an aspirant for position evidently, for in 1813 he declined the honor of an election to the office of constable.

Benjamin Lloyd settled on the southwest quarter of section twenty-one.

Caleb Shinn settled in the township very early, where some of his descendants remain.

Richard Templin, from Lancaster county, Pennsylvania, a moulder by trade, settled in section thirteen about 1825. His son John moved to Patmos about 1831, and settled on section three. John King, from the same place, and also a moulder, settled on section one in 1831, where Joshua Bowman lives. His son Joseph lives in Patmos.

Jesse Straughn, in October, 1820, came from Bucks county, Pennsylvania, and lived a while with John Straughn, his brother. In 1822 he settled on section thirty-four, of which he bought seventy-four acres. Daniel Straughn, father of John and Jesse, some years earlier settled the east half of section thirty-four, and gave it to his children.

Stacy Stratton (a brother of Michael and Aaron Stratton, who came in 1806) came from Burlington county, New Jersey, and settled first on Mr. Cattell's farm, on the Ellsworth road.

Adam Fast, in 1816, purchased the southwest quarter of section one, and was probably the first person who settled in that part of the township. Jacob Leyman, from Lancaster county, Pennsylvania, who married the daughter of Mr. Fast, received from him this piece of land in 1821.

Peter Gloss, about 1820, bought land in the southeast quarter of section twelve, where he built a factory and manufactured wooden bowls. He afterwards settled upon the Cessna farm.

Josiah and Jacob Bowman (sons of Philip Bowman, who settled in Green township,) about 1831 settled on the northeast quarter of section one. This part of the section was entered by a man named Bowers in 1816.

Drade Husk entered and settled upon the northwest quarter of section two, which was afterwards purchased by Raphael Campbell.

William Bradshaw, in 1832, came from Bucks

county, Pennsylvania, and bought one hundred and six acres of section nine. This land was entered by William Swenn as early as 1820.

Among other early settlers may be mentioned Noah Deed, Christian and David Countryman, Isaac Evans, Enoch Gaus, Joseph Mirl, Nathan Brown, Benjamin and Joshua Owen, Thomas Johnson, Levi Rakestraw, Charles Curl, and Abraham Keffer.

ORGANIZATION.

Goshen was incorporated September 11, 1810. The first volume of records contains, as the first minute of proceedings, under date of December 30, 1810, an account of the appointment of Thomas Watson to the office of constable by the trustees. The names of the trustees are not given.

January 8, 1812, "the township officers met on the first Second day of March," and settled the town accounts. April 6, 1812, the following resolution was passed at a meeting of the inhabitants :

Resolved, That Isaac Votaw, Michael Stratton, Thomas Conn, Thomas French, and Joel Sharp be a committee to view the southeast quarter of section number sixteen, and to conclude on a suitable piece of ground for to set a house for to hold elections in, and to warn the inhabitants to meet and raise a sufficient house for that purpose, and to have the house to hold the fall election in.

The following officers were chosen at this meeting: Joseph Wright, township clerk; Michael Stratton, Isaac Votaw, Levi Jennings, trustees ; Anthony Morris, Isaac Barber, overseers of the poor; Thomas French, Josiah Stratton, appraisers of property ; Robert Armstrong, Asa Ware, fence-viewers; Barzilla French, Stacy Shreeve, Thomas Votaw, Thomas Conn, Abram Warrington, supervisors ; George Baum, treasurer; Joseph Kindle, constable.

There seems to have been some difficulty in securing a constable, for, on April 10, 1813, out of thirty-three persons named for that office, thirty were summoned, of whom twenty-eight refused to serve, and were fined. The following is the list of the names chosen : Isaac Ellison, Bazel Perry, Henry Hinchman, Christian Countryman, Joseph Hoile, Simeon Jennings, Isaac Gaus, William Johnson, Levi Rakestraw, Joshua Owen, Enoch Gaus, Joseph Mirl, Joel Sharp, Charles Stratton, Nathan Brown, Robert French, John Webb, Noah Reed, David Countryman, Robert McKim, Evan Gaus, Levi Hoile, Joshua

Morris, William Faucett, Richard Webb, Abraham Barber, Thomas Johnson, Jonathan Votaw, Benjamin Owen, Samuel Votaw, Charles Curl, Abraham Keffer.

VILLAGES.

Damascus, situated on the line between Butler and Goshen townships, was platted and laid out by Horton Howard in 1808. It contains about four hundred inhabitants, and on the Goshen side has one church (Wesleyan), a post-office, academy, steam saw-mill, woolen-mill, and several stores and shops. The post-office was established in 1828 with James B. Bruff as postmaster.

Patmos was first settled by Benjamin Regle, John Templin, William Ware, and Levi A. Leyman. James W. Templin opened the first store in 1850. Levi A. Leyman was the first postmaster, appointed in 1850, and continued in office twelve years. While Leyman and Captain Coit, of Ellsworth, were cogitating upon a name for the new post-office which should be different from any other in the State, they noticed an open music book near by upon whose pages appeared the good old time " Patmos." The word was spoken and the name adopted, and " Patmos " it remains. The postmasters who have succeeded Mr. Leyman have been Mrs. Catharine Roller, William Bradshaw, and J. W. Templin. The settlement contains a post-office, store, saw-mill, blacksmith shop, carriage shop, and a dozen dwellings.

Boswell post-office was established in 1850, John Martin first postmaster.

Garfield post-office was established in 1875 at Garfield station, on the Pittsburg, Fort Wayne & Chicago railroad. S. A. Fogg was appointed postmaster.

SCHOOLS AND CHURCHES.

The Friends at an early day formed by far the largest part of the population of the township, and instituted schools, which they kept up even after the organization of the township into school districts. There were at one time nine schools under the care of a visiting committee appointed by the " monthly meeting," whose territory comprised the townships of Butler and Goshen. Several of these were family schools.

The first school in the town was opened in the winter of 1812 at the log meeting-house in

Goshen, a settlement near the west line of the township. The house was in size about 15 x 24 feet, and was built for both school and "meeting" purposes. The first teacher was Samuel Votaw, a son of Isaac Votaw, an early settler in the northwest section of the township.

A school was opened a little later near the Stratton mill, and was taught by Daniel Stratton. The teachers who served at the school in the Goshen neighborhood after Mr. Votaw were Martha Townsend (now Mrs. Martha Stanton, living at Salem), who taught in the fall of 1814; William Green, an Irishman; William Titus, a Yankee; and Joshua Crew, who let the pupils do as they pleased; Benjamin Marshall, who taught three winters; John Butler, who taught ten winters; Isaac Trescott, Solomon Shreeve, Jesse Lloyd, and Stephen Roberts.

At Damascus a school was first taught by Joshua Lynch, afterwards by James Bruff, John P. Gruel, Jacob Hole, Simeon Fawcett, Lydia Maria Stanley, and others.

Professor Israel P. Hole, with his brother Jacob, afterwards established a school in a large two-story building of brick, situated is spacious grounds on the Goshen side. This they continued for three or four years, when the Friends purchased the property for a "quarterly-meeting school." Jesse Lloyd, William P. Pinkham, and Otis Beal were the principal teachers.

There was a school in the Votaw settlement in its earlier years, mostly taught by females. Elizabeth Blackburn taught during several summers. James Hemingway taught in the Benjamin Malmsbury neighborhood.

A log school-house was built and a school supported by subscription about 1825, in what is now district number one, half a mile east of Patmos. Andrew Templin was the first teacher. The town has eight school districts.

The first church or "meeting-house" was built by the Friends. It was burned in 1842. In 1852 their present brick church was erected. A Methodist class was formed about 1820. Their present building on section eight was built in 1863. Two miles east of Patmos is the Bethel Methodist Episcopal church, built in 1847, and another Methodist church exists at Damascus.

A newspaper called the Self-Examiner was published at Goshen a short time in 1842.

CHAPTER XII.
GREEN.

Green township is bounded on the north by the townships of Ellsworth and Canfield, east by Beaver, west by Perry and Goshen, and north by Salem and Perry, in Columbiana county. Its surface is undulating, broken only by the valleys lying along the middle fork of Beaver creek, which fork flows in a general southeasterly direction through the township, passing into Salem township about a half mile west of the corporation of Washingtonville. Another fork of Beaver creek rises in the northeast part of the township, and flows southerly through the second tier of sections from the east, and passes out on the south border at Washingtonville.

The soil of the township is well adapted to the cultivation of trees, small fruits, and grain. The valleys and slopes are heavily timbered with oak, chestnut, and beech. Woodlands and cultivated fields abound, and form on every hand pictures pleasing to the eye.

EARLY SETTLEMENTS.

The early settlers of Green were for the most part Germans, attracted to the then far West by the excellence of the land.

Section one was unoccupied for many years. It was finally bought by Eben Newton, of Canfield, whence it was known as the "Newton tract."

The first settlers of section two were Henry Pyle and wife, who came from Germany about 1804. A daughter of Pyle married David Loveland, and her descendants still live in this section. "Loveland," a station on the Niles & New Lisbon railroad, is in this section, and has a post-office, saw-mill, Evangelical church, etc.

Section three remained in possession of a man by name of Rhodes until 1829, when it was sold to John Beard, Casper Kenreich, Nicholas Knauff, and John Goodman.

Section four was first settled by Henry Beard, with his wife and five children, who came to this county in 1804 from Germany and much of the section still remains in possession of his family and their connections. A union church stands on this section.

Of section five James Webb entered the south half, paying $1.25 per acre; and John Beard, son of Henry, purchased the north half.

Section six was first owned by Philip Bauman who exchanged for it land he owned in Redstone, Pennsylvania, and afterward divided it among his children.

In 1804 section seven was entered by Michael Durr and his two sisters, Elizabeth and Mary.

Section eight had for its first owners a man named Rupert, John D. Cook, and James Webb.

Jacob and Philip Cool, George and Jacob Countryman, John Hafely and Van Amier were the first settlers on sections nine and ten.

Section eleven remained unsettled many years, its owners living in the East. Jacob Miller and Michael and George Culp were the first to open the way.

The west part of section twelve was settled by Philip Houts, a German, who divided it among his children. On the place was a large spring, where Houts built a distillery, which was in operation for many years, until about 1830. A school-house stands in the northwest corner of the section.

Sections thirteen and twenty-four were purchased by Joshua Calvin for his sons, who came from New Jersey, with their families, arriving April 27, 1816. A school-house stands on the southwest corner of section thirteen, and a Baptist church and burying-ground on section twenty-four.

Section fourteen was entered by a stranger who sold it to Abram Garber. The Niles & New Lisbon railroad has a station on this section called Greenford.

Section fifteen was settled in 1808 by Lewis Baker, a native of Kentucky, who married Elizabeth, daughter of John Zimmerman, who entered section thirty-four.

Section sixteen was the "school lot," and was sold in 1849 to John D. Cook, —— Bly, Wesley Coy, M. Kenreich, and others.

Section seventeen was entered by Job Cooke, and divided among his sons. A couple of small coal banks have been opened in this section.

About 1810 James Wilson entered section eighteen, and divided it among his children.

Abram Warrington located section nineteen about 1811, and divided it between the four sons of Edward Bonsall, who had married Warrington's daughter Rachel. The sons were Edward, Ivan, Joshua, and Isaac. Edward started a

nursery forty years ago, which is still in operation. One coal mine in this section yields about forty thousand bushels annually.

About 1808 Elisha Teeter entered section twenty for his sons—John, Jonathan, William, and Wilson. In 1822 the first steam mill in this part of the country was erected by Wilson Teeter. A coal bank opened by the Teeters fifty years ago is, with one exception, the largest in the township. It contains a vein three feet thick and extends half a mile under the surface.

Sections twenty-one and twenty-two were held as "reserved lands" for many years, but were finally settled by Jeremiah Callahan, Philip Bush, Jacob Wilhelm, Caleb Roller, John Stahl, and others. A Disciple church and graveyard are situated on section twenty-one and a schoolhouse stands on its north side.

In 1816 section twenty-three was sold to Michael Roller and Michael Dressel by a man from Pennsylvania who had previously entered it.

In 1804 sections twenty-five and twenty-six were entered, it is believed by John Harness and Jacob Momert, who years after sold to the Stouffers, Rollers, Knopp, and others. A school house stands on the southwest quarter of section twenty-six.

Some time in 1804 Peter Weikert and John Carr, neighbors in Adams county, Pennsylvania, started westward on horseback to view the country for the purpose of finding homes for their families where soil and climate were both good. Pleased with section twenty-seven Weikert entered it at Steubenville, while Carr went farther west. Section twenty-seven is still in possession of the Weikert family. One son, Dr. Andrew Weikert, is a practicing physician at Green village.

In 1804 Elias Adgate and William and James Callahan, all brothers-in-law, from Redstone, Pennsylvania, entered section twenty-eight, and divided it among themselves, each afterward dividing his share among his children. Two other brothers of the Callahans, Jeremiah and Jesse, settled in this section for a short time previous to 1812.

Section thirty-three was entered by Samuel Davis in 1803. He received a deed from the Government signed by Thomas Jefferson, dated March 10, 1807. He disposed of it by gift and sale. About 1819 John Briggs built a grist-mill on the creek, and a few years later another was built by Aaron Holloway, which is still standing, a short distance below the first.

John Zimmerman, of Lancaster county, Pennsylvania, entered section thirty-four in 1804 and moved upon it with his family the next year. Subsequently he divided it among his five sons and three daughters.

From Huntingdon county, Pennsylvania, came three brothers in an early day, Michael, Baltzer, and Caleb Roller. Michael entered section thirty-five in 1804, divided it among his sons, Jacob, William, Thomas, and James. Land was given for a church and burying-ground in a very early day by the Rollers. Part of Washingtonville is located in sections thirty-five and thirty-six of this township.

Baltzer Roller entered section thirty-six in 1803. His son, Colonel Jacob B., served the district as State Representative for twenty-one years. He was in General Harrison's army and at Fort Meigs. While stooping to drink at a spring in the woods near the fort one day, a ball from an Indian's rifle grazed the back of his head. He grasped his gun and fired at the retreating Indian, but missed him.

ORGANIZATION.

Green township was incorporated June 3, 1806, and was then in Columbiana county, where it remained until attached to Mahoning county, upon its organization in 1846. It originally contained thirty-six square miles, but was reduced to thirty-two by the organization of Perry township in 1832.

GREEN VILLAGE

is situated near the center of the township, on sections fifteen and twenty-two, and was first laid out by Lewis Baker, Jacob Wilhelm, and Jacob Cook. Abram Stofer (or Stauffer) kept the first store. Samuel Hardman, David Weikert, and J. M. Hole succeeded him. The first post-office was established in 1831, and William Van Horn was the first postmaster. He has been succeeded by David Weikert, William Roller, Daniel Beam, N. P. Callahan, A. S. Griffith, and Henry Shray.

The village contains three churches, Lutheran, German Lutheran, and Swedenborgian, a post-office, school-house, drug-store, two dry goods and grocery stores, a tannery, steam saw- and planing-mill, grist-mill, two blacksmith shops, two

wagon shops, two shoe shops, and one millinery store. In the village are two practicing physicians.

WASHINGTONVILLE.

This town was laid out about 1832, principally through the exertions and influence of Michael Frederick, and is situated in the townships of Green and Salem. It contains two churches (Methodist and Evangelical Lutheran), a post-office, school-house, three hotels, two blacksmith shops, four grocery stores, one dry goods store, one drug store, two carriage shops, two shoe shops, about seventy-five dwellings, and has a population of eight hundred.

The first hotel was opened by Michael Frederick, about 1833. The first store was opened in what is now Railroad Tavern, by Jacob Stoffer, who was appointed postmaster upon the establishment of the post-office, in 1836. He was succeeded as postmaster by Jacob Borton, Henry Estep, George R. Hillburn, John B. Stover, Samuel Greenwold, and John R. Stover.

Peter Miller was the first blacksmith who opened a shop. Before removing to Washingtonville he resided one year at New Lisbon, where he built the first brick house. About 1828 John Miller, a blacksmith, began the manufacture of edge-tools, which he continued for about ten years.

NEW ALBANY.

New Albany is situated about two miles and a half west from Green village, and contains a store, post-office, blacksmith shop, and twenty-two dwellings. The first steam mill in the county was built at this place by Wilson Teeter and Edwin Webb, by whom the town was laid out. The post-office was established prior to 1853. The first postmaster was Henry Thulen, who was succeeded by Joshua Webb, Daniel Beam, Charles Taylor, Lemuel Hixson, Solomon Russell, David Coy, and Lewis Pow.

SCHOOLS.

Soon after the settlers came to the township an effort was made among the widely scattered families to assemble the children for purposes of education. Elisha Teeter gave for school and burying purposes a piece of ground situated on the east side of section twenty, and a log school-house was built, about 20 x 24 feet in size, with a puncheon floor and a door with wooden hinges.

The children from sections seventeen, eighteen, nineteen, and twenty attended school at this house. The first teacher was Edward Bonsall, who was succeeded by Rachel, his wife, and Priscilla Fisher, wife of William Fisher—both daughters of Abram Warrington. John Cowdin, Patrick Smith, and Daniel Stratton were also teachers before the adoption of the district school system.

The first school-house for children living in the north middle part of the township was on the New Lisbon road, on section ten. This was a log-house built by Henry Pyle. It was fitted with slab seats, and with desks fastened against the walls with wooden pins. In 1814 Samuel McBride was hired to teach. George Pow succeeded him. No school was taught there after Mr. Pow retired until the district schools were opened, in 1827. The children from other sections, far and near, attended school in this log building.

The first school in the center of the township was held in the log church west of Green village. A log school-house was built on section thirty-four, on land belonging to Jacob Stofer. Henry Zimmerman was the first teacher of this school, about 1815. William, Rachel, and Samuel Schofield, sons and daughter of David Schofield, afterwards taught in a second log school-house, built on the same ground.

At Washingtonville a school was opened about 1818 in the log church built by Michael and Baltzer Roller. John Roller and Henry Gilbert were among the first teachers.

Owing to the imperfect records of schools in the early days but little information can be obtained respecting them.

The following is from the earliest existing records (in 1844):

Twelve schools taught in township; number of teachers, 10; number of children between the ages of four and twenty-one years, 338 males, 346 females; number of children enrolled, 295 males, 241 females; average daily attendance, 169 males, 131 females; amount paid to teachers of common schools from public fund—to males, $367.83; to females, $125. Amount paid from other sources—males, $23; females, $23.50. Branches taught: reading, writing, arithmetic, English grammar, geography.

The township has an Evangelical Lutheran church at Washingtonville, and one at Green village; a German Lutheran church; a Swedenborgian church at Green; Concord Presbyterian church on the line of Goshen and Green; a Baptist church; a union church on section four; a Disciple church on section twenty-one, with a burying-ground attached; and an Evangelical Association church at Loveland station.

The Niles & New Lisbon railroad traverses the township in a general north and south course, and has three stations in the township—Loveland, Green village, and Washingtonville.

CHAPTER XIII.
SMITH.

The township of Smith is of range number five township eighteen north from the Ohio river. It is bounded north by Deerfield, in Portage county, and Berlin township, in Mahoning county; east by Goshen, in Mahoning county; south by Knox township, Columbiana county; and west by Lexington, in Stark county. The general surface of the land is undulating, and in the northeastern part hilly, where the greatest elevation is attained. The center, within the radius of two miles from the town-house, is the most depressed portion of the township, the land gradually rising as the township lines are approached. The township is drained by the Mahoning river and its tributaries. The Mahoning proper passes northwesterly across the southwest corner of the township, which it again enters on section six, at the northwest corner, crossing it in a northeasterly direction.

EARLY SETTLEMENT.

Probably the first white man in Smith township, by whom any material improvements were made, was James Carter, from Pennsylvania, in the year 1803. His advent was entirely an accident. Carter having purchased land on what is known as the Western Reserve (of which the north line of Smith township forms part of the southern boundary) entered and cleared a portion, and built a log house on what he supposed to be his own lands. The same year William Smith purchased from the government section three, containing six hundred and forty acres, and went with his family to occupy the same in 1804. On his arrival he found that Carter had by mistake built his cabin on his (Smith's) land. Smith paid Carter for the improvements he had made, who soon after left to occupy the lands he had in fact purchased. Although the first improvements were made by Carter in 1803, and the first house built by him at that time, the distinction of first permanent settlement properly belongs to William Smith and his family. William Smith died in 1841, aged seventy-three years; his wife died in 1845, aged seventy-two years. Both were interred in the family burying-ground on the hill, near the present village of North Benton.

James C. Stanley, of Hanover county, Virginia, was one of the pioneers of Smith township, and probably the second settler. He came in the year 1805, and located on section twenty-four, which he had purchased from the Government, and which lies about four miles southeast of William Smith's section, in what was afterwards called the "Stanley neighborhood." He brought with him a wife and eight children. The house built by the pioneer James C. was the second in the township, and the first south of the center line.

In the year 1811 Edmund, oldest son of Thomas Stanley, of Hanover county, Virginia, in company with John White (a colored family servant), came to Smith and built a log house in the eastern part of the township, preparatory to the coming of the family. Thomas Stanley arrived with his family in the spring of 1812. His children were John, who died in 1877; Elijah, who died in 1836; Frances, who married Isaac Votaw, and died about 1818; Edmund, who died in 1842; Millie, who married Joshua Crew, and came with the Stanley family or a few weeks later. Joshua Crew died about the year 1845, after which his wife went to Iowa, where she died about 1868. These were the children of Thomas Stanley by his first wife. His second wife was Priscilla Ladd, and their children were Isaac, Thomas Binford, Sarah, who married Thomas Woolman, and Micajah. Micajah Stanley married Unity Coppack, by whom he had eight children.

John Detchon, son of Oswell and Annie (Carr) Detchon, pioneers of Trumbull county, came to Smith in 1822. In 1824 he married Maria Hoadley, seventh child of Gideon Hoadley.

Gideon Hoadley, with his wife and children,

settled in the township in 1823. In 1824 Henry Hartzell's family settled here.

In 1812 Levi Rakestraw and his wife Rebecca (Bryan) came from New Jersey and located in Goshen township, where they lived until November 10, 1825, when they moved to Smith township, where they spent the remainder of their lives. Joseph Snods came from the same State in 1824 with his wife and three children. His son William now lives in Smith township.

One of the most prominent of the early settlers was Benjamin Votaw, who settled permanently in Smith township in 1829. He operated the first mill in the township before his settlement, built on Island creek about 1823 by James Smith, son of Judge William Smith, the pioneer.

Samuel Oyster was the first settler of the western part of Smith township, locating on section thirty-one in 1826. He raised a family of fourteen children.

Among the old families of the township was that of Nathan Heacock. He settled near Salem, Columbiana county, in 1816, coming from Bucks county, Pennsylvania, and in 1825 came to Smith, bringing a family of ten children.

Peter Wise came from Pennsylvania to Smith in 1832 with a large family.

In 1810 James Cattell, of New Jersey, located in Goshen township, and in 1833 moved to Smith, where he died in 1860.

James M. Dobson came to Smith in 1833 with his wife and one child—John.

George Atkinson was a resident of Goshen in 1816, and one of his sons, William, afterward became a resident of Smith.

Other early settlers were Solomon Hartzell, Jacob Paxson, Job Lamborn, Christian Sheets, William Johnston, Hugh Wright, and John Thompson.

There were families among the early settlers whose history is not recorded. Of these some are dead, others have left the township, and no authentic record of the date of their settlement, death, or departure can be obtained. On information from the oldest living residents, the names of many have been obtained as follows: Mathias Hollowpeter, Jonathan Hoope, John Cowgill, the Cobbs, Hugh Packer, John Trago, Abram Haines, Leonard Reed, Abram and Samuel Miller, Adam

McGowan, William Matthews, John Hillerman, Amos Allerton, John Schaffer. These were probably settled in the township prior to 1830; yet it is possible that some were later, as in 1828 there were but twenty-three voters in the township.

ORGANIZATION.

Smith township was organized at a meeting of the Columbiana county commissioners in the month of March, 1821, upon the petition of Judge William Smith, one of its pioneers, in honor of whom it was named. The books of the township, containing records of the first meetings and of the election of the first officers, are lost or destroyed. Notice of the organization was found in the old commissioner's journal. James C. Stanley was probably clerk of the first town-meeting.

NORTH BENTON.

The village of North Benton was surveyed and laid out on the 27th and 28th days of March, 1834, under the proprietorship of William Smith, Dr. John Dellenbaugh, and James Smith. The map or plat was recorded March 31, 1834. Although not till then formally laid out, yet as early as the year 1830 a number of buildings had been erected, and the village was a general gathering place for the people in that vicinity. North Benton was named in honor of Thomas Benton, a "hard-money" Democrat of the time, who had many friends and admirers in that community. "North" was prefixed in order to distinguish it from another place of that name. The first hotel was built in 1832 by one Fitch, and called the "Benton Exchange."

The village has a population of about two hundred and fifty, comprising about seventy families, and has two churches, a school, several stores, and business interests of various kinds.

WESTVILLE.

In the year 1831 the town or village of Westville was named and partially laid out, under the proprietorship of Aaron Coppack, and then was composed of a portion of sections thirty-five and thirty six. The map was recorded September 27th of the same year. In 1835 an addition was made, and portions of sections one and two of Knox township included within the village limits. This was done under the direction of Aaron Coppack, Samuel Coppack, Joseph Cobbs,

and Edward Randolph, proprietors. The plat was recorded October 15, 1835. The village continued to grow until about 1850, and became a convenient trading centre, having a saw-mill on section thirty-five and a general country store. Since that time there has been no material increase in population.

BELOIT.

This hamlet, although never regularly laid out or incorporated as a village, is indebted for its existence to the building of the Pittsburg, Fort Wayne & Chicago railroad, in the years 1848-49. It was originally called "Smithfield Station," and a post-office established there under that name. In about 1863 the name was changed to Beloit, there being then another Smithfield village in the State. Within the limits of what may properly be called Beloit are a church, saw-mill, two stores, a wagon manufactory, and a blacksmith shop. The village has a population of about one hundred and fifty.

EAST ALLIANCE.

East Alliance, as it is called, is but one of the suburbs of Alliance, Stark county, resulting from the growth of the latter place. In 1879 East Alliance was made the second election district of Smith township.

CHURCHES AND SCHOOLS.

Smith township has four churches. The first erected was in 1829 by the Friends on section thirty-four. This building was also used for a school, taught by Hannah Courtney. A Methodist Episcopal church was erected at North Benton in 1840. A Presbyterian congregation formed in Deerfield, Portage county, moved to Smith, and elected a church near North Benton in 1851. A union church was built in 1859 on section twenty-six, but was sold to the Presbyterian society in 1870.

The first school of the township was taught in an old log-house on the site of North Benton, but by whom is not known. Margaret Davis taught the school at a very early day. The township was originally divided into four districts, but now comprises ten. The annual cost of the maintenance of schools is about $2,500.

CHAPTER XIV.

SPRINGFIELD.

The township is bounded on the north by the south line of the Western Reserve; on the east by the State of Pennsylvania; on the south by the township of Unity; and on the west by the township of Beaver. It is designated in the Government survey as town nine, in range one. It was one of the oldest townships in the county, having been organized for civil purposes in 1803. In 1846 Springfield was attached to Mahoning county.

The general surface of the township is broken by hills of moderate height, between which are intervales and lowlands, originally somewhat swampy. The whole township was covered with a fine growth of the common woods, and a liberal supply of timber yet remains. Building-stone may be obtained in various localities, and coal is unusually abundant.

The principal streams are Honey creek and several small creeks, flowing southeast from the central and the western parts of the township; and the Little Yellow creek in the northwest, having a northerly course. Numerous springs abound, and the natural drainage is generally sufficient to afford an arable surface. The soil varies from a sandy loam to a heavy clay, along the streams being more or less of an alluvium. The whole is fertile and well adapted to the products of mixed husbandry. The people are chiefly engaged in agriculture.

PIONEER SETTLERS.

The early history of Springfield is somewhat obscure. None of the original settlers remain, and what little recorded history they had has been destroyed. The recollections of the descendants of those who came to the township as pioneers are not clear, and their statements concerning that period are contradictory. It appears, however, that the township was permanently settled about 1801, and that Peter Musser was the first to establish himself in what is now Springfield. He came from York county, Pennsylvania, and having considerable means purchased the four sections in the southeast corner of the township, living a little north of the present village of Petersburg. Here he built small grist- and saw-mills, and made other desirable improvements. He died in 1808, leaving a family of four sons and two daughters. The oldest son, John, succeeded to the mill property, but after a few years removed to Missouri. Peter was the proprietor of the village site, and the founder of Petersburg. He removed to the northern part of the State. The third son, Jacob, lived in the village, selling there the first goods. He enlisted in the army of 1812, and afterwards in the regular army of the United States, serving as drum-major; he finally settled in Missouri.

One of Musser's daughters was married to Israel Warner, who came with his father-in-law in 1801, and settled on the farm now occupied by his son Ellis. Other sons of Warner were John, George, Peter, David, Israel, William, and Jacob. Some of these yet live in Springfield and the adjacent towns. Israel Warner was a captain in 1812. The other daughter of Musser married Jacob Rudisill, and lived north of the Warner homestead.

James Wallace was one of the first and foremost settlers and is yet well remembered as a merchant. Having been elected judge of Mahoning county, he removed to Canfield. To that place, also, removed Hosea Hoover, one of Petersburg's early settlers, who was elected county treasurer.

On the farm now occupied by C. B. Wilson John Pontius was the original settler, and was followed by his son John. East of the village, on the farm yet occupied by his family, Henry Miller settled at an early day; and north of the place the Bock, Beight, and Dressel families were among the first settlers.

In the western part of the township Daniel Miller, from Adams county, Pennsylvania, was the earliest settler, coming in 1802, and settling on section eighteen.

The same year C. Seidner and his son-in-law, C. Mentzer, came from Hagerstown and settled south of Miller. A few years later this locality was settled by Jacob Shafer, George Macklin, Jacob Christ, John May, Hugh Chain, John Robinson, and Peter Shreiver.

Section six was settled in 1801 by Adam Hohn, who soon after put up a saw-mill there.

Section four was settled before 1863 by George Stump and his sons George, Henry, Abraham, and John, and section five was settled in 1802 by John Summers of York county, Pennsylvania. One of Summers' sons-in-law, George Elser, settled on the same section in April, 1806, where he died in 1847.

In the northeastern part of the township the early settlers were: John Shoemaker, about 1804; Henry Myers, on section twelve, in 1803; Peter and Henry Raub and Peter Benedict, on section eleven, about the same time; and before 1806 settlements had been made by men named Empie, Taylor, Barnard, Parsons, and Messerly.

In the neighborhood of New Middleton were the Burkey, Kuhn, Schillinger, Gray, Cublin, and Schiller families, some time before 1810, and after that period Joshua Hahn, Simon Martin, the Welker, Beard, and Ilgenfritz families took place among the prominent settlers. Immigration was so great between 1805 and 1815 that it is impossible to gather up the names of all who became pioneers of Springfield.

CIVIL LIST.

The records of this township from its organization in 1803 until 1868 have been lost in some way, making the compilation of an accurate civil list impossible and necessitating the omission of much valuable and interesting matter.

THE COAL INTERESTS

of the township deserve brief mention. Although coal generally abounds in the township but little effort has been made to develop its riches outside of the territory in the northwest part of the township along Little Yellow creek. East of that stream mining was carried on to some extent on the Ruhlman, Kurt and Heine farms; but the principal product is on the west side on section seven, where three mines are in successful operation, whose united output is two thousand five hundred tons per year. The first mine in the township was opened by the Summers family and is still worked.

PETERSBURGH.

The oldest and most important village in the township was founded before 1810 by Peter Musser, on section thirty-six, and named in his honor Petersburgh. It now has a population of five hundred, and is a busy, bustling little place.

The post-office was established first with name of Musser's Mill, and in 1811 Jacob Musser was postmaster. It subsequently received the present name and has had the following officials:

Peter Musser, F. Spaeth, Colonel James Miller, Martha Miller, O. H. P. Swisher, Robert Wallace, C. C. Swisher, Lewis Sholl, Gideon Schiller, George Herr, T. S. Guy, and Henry Myers. Mail is received twice a day.

It is said that Jacob Musser sold the first goods in the place in the building now the residence of J. P. Swisher, the oldest frame house in Petersburgh. James Wallace was the first to engage regularly in trade, opening a store where is now the post-office building, about 1815. He converted that house into a hotel and opened a store on the north side of the street, where he remained about thirty years. W. C. Dunlap was a cotemporary merchant, opening a store where is now S. Ernst's residence. The principal merchants that followed them were: Robert Forbus, Spaeth & Swisher, J. G. Leslie, O. H. P. Swisher, David and John Shearer, James Mathews, Ernst & Hahn, Hoover & Seidner, and others. The place now has three good general stores, a drug store, harness shop, furniture store, and boot and shoe store.

A foundry was established by R. C. Bean in 1870, and is still carried on in the manufacture of plows, light castings, and in repair work. The village has two tanneries employing steam power. The first tannery was carried on by John Embrie and has gone through a number of hands since. The place has also two carriage shops, as well as other indispensable mechanical industries.

As early as 1803 Peter Musser put in operation saw- and grist-mills, a little north of the village, on the site of the present old mill on Honey creek. John Musser, John Pontius, and D. Whitmyer were among its subsequent owners. About 1825 a mill was put up near the State line on the same stream, by John Miller, which was operated by him and his family until a few years ago. Between these sites John Musser put up a mill, which was operated until 1860.

In 1874 a steam flouring-mill, having three runs of stones, was erected near the center of the village by Maurer & Edler Brothers. It is now successfully operated, but by other men. A steam saw-mill, erected west of the village in 1870 by Ernst & Rauch, is still in operation; and in the village a saw-mill, planer, and machines for making bent work were put in operation in 1875 by Failer Brothers & Miller.

The first public house was kept by Peter Musser on his farm, now owned by A. Kneasel. The next was kept in the J. P. Swisher residence by Kinneman, Douglas, Pontius, and others. James Wallace was a well known landlord for many years. Henry Kale opened a public house where the Lochiel house stands, and was succeeded by Kelley, Mathews, Conrad, George Kneasel (who changed the house to its present comfortable condition), and others.

Dr. Luther Spellman was probably the first physician to locate permanently in the village. Dr. B. F. Adams died here. Others in practice have been : Drs. Jehu Stough, John D. Coffin, John Wise, John McCook, Ferdinand Casper, P. H. Swisher (since 1828), George W. Pettit, P. W. Welker, and perhaps others.

Richard Smith practiced law here a short time. Jacob Musser was the justice of the peace from 1845 to 1875, and was succeeded by William F. Stoll.

Dr. G. W. Pettit, physician, Petersburgh, Mahoning county, son of Samuel Pettit, was born in New Lisbon, Columbiana county, March 21, 1828. Samuel Pettit was a native of Chester county, Pennsylvania, and came to Ohio in 1808 with his parents, who settled at New Lisbon. He died in 1873. His widow is still living. Dr. Pettit studied medicine with Dr. McCook at New Lisbon and graduated at the Cleveland Medical college in 1852, having practiced for two years previous. He began practice, after receiving his degree, at Marlborough, Stark county, where he remained ten years. He then came to Petersburgh, where he now lives. He has an extensive practice, and is a successful physician. He was united in marriage in 1855 to Miss Emily, daughter of Ebenezer Stevens of Stark county. They have had three children, two of whom are living. Mrs. Pettit is a member of the Methodist church.

Solomon Ernst, merchant, Petersburgh, Mahoning county, was born in Springfield township, Mahoning county, then Columbiana, April 20, 1830. He is a son of Peter Ernst, who was a native of Maryland, and came to Ohio in 1826 or 1827 and located in Springfield township. He was by occupation a farmer. Solomon Ernst followed farming until he was twenty-one or twenty-two years of age, then engaged in mercantile business at Middleton where he re-

mained ten years. He then came to Petersburgh where he now is, conducting a dry goods and grocery store. He was married in 1857 to Miss Louisa, daughter of Henry Welk, of Springfield township, and has one child, John. Mr. and Mrs. Ernst are members of the Reformed church.

NEW SPRINGFIELD

is located on the southern part of section twenty-nine, and is a pleasant little village of three hundred and fifty inhabitants. It was laid out some time before 1825 by Abraham Christ, who platted twenty-eight lots around the present square or " diamond." Additions have since been made by Jacob Fulgerson, Christian Harker, John Wagner, and David Spiltner, until the village spreads over a considerable area. Its moral welfare is watched over by two churches, and it is supplied with a good school-house.

The first store was opened in a building near Shale's distillery by Joseph Davis. On the square, Thomas Knight erected a building for a store about 1828, and conducted business there about twenty years. Nicholas Eckes, Jacob Spaeth, William May, William Phillips, Schillinger and Eckert & Peters, Tobias Elser, George Smith, and George Slutter are among those who have been engaged in active business here.

The village has a daily mail from Columbiana. The postmasters have been Nicholas Eckes, George Smith, S. F. Hadley, John Peters, Tobias Elser, and George Slutter.

Among the keepers of public houses are remembered John Peters, William May, S. F. Hadley, Joseph Thompson, and a few others who sometimes entertained strangers without having regular inns.

Christian Seidner and John May have operated saw-mills on the brook southeast of the village ; and below, on the same stream, Solomon Crouse had an early grist-mill. The location is now occupied by steam and water-power grist- and saw-mills. In the village a steam saw-mill put up prior to 1860 by Diser, Shale & Felger is still in operation.

The first distiller was Joseph Davis, many years ago. A grain and fruit distillery are now running in the village.

A tannery was at one time carried on by Conrad & Shawacre.

In 1872 William May and Adam Seidner

built a foundry in the lower part of the village. In 1878 it was removed to its present location, where, by the aid of steam-power, stoves, plows, and agricultural implements are produced.

The New Springfield Bent works are the outgrowth of a small business established by George Felger & Son near the square. In August, 1877, their shop was destroyed by fire, together with the dwellings of J. S. Shearer and S. F. Hadley. A large building was then erected on the outskirts of the village, in which the business has since been carried on, with the aid of steam-power.

Besides the industries mentioned, the village has carriage shops, tin shop, harness shops, and a half dozen other shops, where the ordinary trades are carried on.

Professional men have not been very numerous. The first physician was Dr. Louis Zeigler, followed by A. King, Dustin, Hamilton, Heinman, William Stafford, and R. E. Warner. Horace Macklin is the only practicing lawyer ever located in the village. Three sons of George Miller, Isaiah, Eli, and Aaron, have become ministers of the Lutheran church.

NEW MIDDLETON,

a bright little village of two hundred and fifty inhabitants, is located on section ten, chiefly on Youngstown street. It was laid out before 1825 by Samuel Moore, and additions have been made by William Brotherton and John Miller. David Shearer put up the first frame house just north of the mill.

A small store was opened about 1830 by Joshua Dixon, in a house now occupied by D. Metz. He was followed in trade by Adam Powers and David Shearer. Later came Brungard & Davison, at the stand where was afterwards Tobias Hahn. The store was burned in 1851, and was rebuilt by Hahn. It was afterwards occupied by Henry Miller, Tobias Hahn, and at present contains the store of John F. Smith. South of this building Henry Miller put up and occupied a good business house, which was burned in 1870, when occupied by Brungard & Brother. Seven years later Tobias Hahn opened a large store near by, which, in August, 1878, was robbed and burned by the burglars to prevent detection. Besides the store mentioned, there are in trade J. G. Smith, H. A.

Whelk, and R. L. Floor, the latter having a drug store.

The establishment of the post-office cannot be clearly determined. Among the postmasters have been David Shearer, T. Hahn, David Johnson, Henry Miller, and Abraham McCurley. The office has a daily mail from Youngstown.

As physicians are remembered Drs. Elisha Murray, Greble, Connor, Henry, Zimmerman, and Frank, R. L., and John Floor.

The first public house was kept by Samuel Moore, before 1830, in a building which stood on the site of J. G. Bacher's residence. In the old house Adam Powers, John B. Miller, William Forbus, and David Johnson were among the keepers. The latter built the present house after the destruction of the old one, in 1851. At this stand Oliver Stanford was the last landlord. South of this place was another public house, in which Shearer, Dixon, Cox, and others, kept entertainment. At one time the village had four taverns.

About the first attempt at manufacturing in the village was made in 1841 by Welker, Pease & Co., who put up a carding-mill which was operated by horse-power. In after years there was a distillery in this building; and still later machinery was supplied to carry on the manufacture of linseed oil. Steam-power was then employed. In 1871, while the property of T. Hahn, the building was burned to the ground.

In 1849 Welker & Brungard put up a steam saw-mill. In 1870 a stock company of twenty members was formed to build a steam grist-mill in the village. After the lapse of several years this property passed into the hands of Fred. Fouser, and was destroyed in the conflagration of August 27, 1878. The present mill was soon after built by Mr. Fouser, and is now successfully operated. The village has a full complement of the ordinary mechanic-shops.

On section six, Adam Hahn, the original settler there, had a saw-mill on Yellow creek before 1805; later, his son Andrew had a mill, and at present the Printz family have here in operation a steam saw-mill.

John Ratliff

TOWNSHIPS AND VILLAGES

OF

TRUMBULL COUNTY, OHIO.

CHAPTER I.

HOWLAND.

GENERAL FEATURES.

Howland, the fourth township in the third range, lies east of the adjoining township of Warren, between it and Vienna. Bazetta is north and Weathersfield south of it. The city limits of Warren encroach slightly upon its western line.

The Mahoning river cuts across a small corner in the southwest of Howland. Mosquito creek, here a stream of considerable size, flows through the township from north to south, dividing its surface into two very nearly equal portions. The land is rolling. On the cast side of the creek a crest of considerable height rises gradually, being two hundred feet above the level of the stream, and on the west side about one hundred and fifty.

East of the creek the soil is somewhat sandy and gravelly; on the west side it contains more or less clay. The improvements in this township are very marked. Good farms, with many cost'' and beautiful houses, large and convenient barns, well-fenced fields and carefully tilled gardens, show that the residents of this township are possessed of wealth, enterprise and good taste.

The towns of Warren and Niles afford convenient and ready markets, and abundant railroad privileges for farmers and shippers of produce. Real estate is constantly appreciating in value. No agricultural community in Trumbull county is more fortunate in its location than Howland township.

PIONEER SETTLEMENT.

Excepting one family, the first settlers of Howland were Pennsylvanians.

The honor of making the first settlement in this township belongs to Captain John H. Adgate, who penetrated the wilderness of this section, bringing his family with him in 1799. He owned one thousand six hundred acres of land in the southwest of the township and here he built the first cabin and made the first clearing. Captain Adgate's children were Sally, Belinda, Caroline, John H., Nancy, Charles, Ulysses, and James. Benoni Ockrum, a Stockbridge Indian, also lived with this family. John H., Jr., remained some years on the old homestead, then moved away. Several of his sons reside in Howland.

Soon after Captain Adgate came John Earl, Michael Peltz, John Daily, James Ward, John Reeves, Jesse Bowell, John Ewalt, and Joseph Quigley, most of whom made permanent settlement in 1802.

John Earl settled on the farm now owned by C. Milliken. Sixteen strong, active, and healthy boys and girls were his children. The sons were Ebenezer, Edward, Moses, John, George, Washington, William, and Charles. There were eight daughters. Our informant remembers the name of seven of them—Rebecca, Susan, Betsey, Nancy, Mary, Sarah, and Olive. The father moved to Lordstown after several years' residence here.

Michael Peltz, a genuine specimen of the *genus homo* commonly denominated Dutchmen, moved away about 1814, or soon after. He acted as a drummer on several occasions when there were military parades. It is related that when the first tidings of the opening movements of the War of 1812 reached Howland Michael got hold of the news. Not knowing what was meant by it he determined to consult the 'squire, who he doubtless supposed held the concentrated wisdom of the township, and having found 'Squire Heaton he asked: "'Squire, vat dey means by all dis talk, eh? Have de Pritishers done some dinks pad?" Like every Heaton the 'squire was fond of a joke, and answered the Dutchman thus: "Yes, bad enough, I think. They have set Lake Erie on fire and burned the whole it." Michael believed the 'squire—who would question a statement from such an authority?—and with his eyes distended with astonishment went home to his "frau" and narrated to her the wonderful doings of "de Pritishers." "You old fool," said she, "you tinks the Pritishers can purn up a lake? A lake is wasser! Go out and feed dem pigs." And crestfallen and humbled he obeyed.

Jesse Bowell moved from Green county, Pennsylvania, to Howland in 1801 or 1802. He married Rebecca Hank, and they had the following children: Calvin, David, John, Bazil, Hannah, Rebecca, and Jesse. Mr. Bowell went to the War of 1812, and returned home to die soon after. Mrs. Bowell afterwards married John Cherry, from Washington county, Pennsylvania, a Howland settler of 1807, and had by him two children, Daniel and Margaret. Three members of this family are now living, John Bowell, in Washington county, Pennsylvania; Daniel Cherry, in Howland, and Mrs. Margaret Mason, Weathersfield. David died young; the others all reached years of maturity. Bazil, Jesse, and Hannah (Luse) died in Niles; Rebecca (Luse) died in Illinois; Calvin died in Mahoning county. Mr. Cherry died in 1846, aged sixty-three; Mrs. Cherry in 1864 at the age of eighty-seven.

John Daily settled on the Kinsman farm, but moved away early. James Ward did not remain later than 1814.

John Reeves, Sr., was a permanent settler, having located on lot twelve in 1803. His son John still lives upon the old farm. Other sons were Jesse, Abner, Ephraim, and Samuel Q. There were three daughters, Sarah, Eugenia, and Nancy.

John Ewalt settled on the farm which is now the property of his son Harris. He reared a good sized family. Harris, and Z. T., of Howland; Jacob, of Bazetta, and John, who resides near Pittsburg, are his sons. One of the daughters, Mrs. Abigail Wainright, is also living in Pittsburg.

Joseph Quigley settled on the Deacon Smith farm, now the Ratliff farm, but moved away early.

William Kennedy in 1805 settled on the farm now belonging to Ebenezer Brown. He was a miller, and worked in Warren, Liberty, and other parts of the county. His son Samuel M. lived and died in Howland. Another son, William A., is still living in the township.

Dr. John W. Seely in 1806 settled where Milo McCombs now lives. This farm was first improved by Jesse Bowell about 1802. Among Dr. Seely's sons were Richard L., Dr. Sylvanus, and William.

Isaac Heaton and James, his brother, settled in the southeastern part of Howland in 1805. James sold out to Abraham Drake and went to Weathersfield. Isaac, universally known to the settlers as 'Squire Heaton, lived and died in Howland. He had but two children—a daughter, Maria, and a son, Dr. Heaton, who practiced in Warren with distinguished success. 'Squire Heaton, being the magistrate of the township, of course had many disputes to settle. But he always strove to adjust matters and have the disputants settle their difficulty, if possible, without resorting to legal proceedings. Once a young lawyer from Warren took exception to one of the 'squire's rulings and said to him, "Why, 'squire, that isn't law!" "Law, law? what do I care about law? All the law I want is here," returned the 'squire laying his hand upon his old leather-covered Bible. He was a man of good judgment and sound common sense, though of limited education.

Abraham Drake settled in 1805. His sons were Abraham, Jacob, Aaron, and George, all of whom are dead. Jacob lived on the old homestead. Abraham and Aaron also resided in the township. George moved to Wooster.

Barber King settled in 1806. He was from Massachusetts and was the only Yankee of the settlement. He had five sons: Jonathan, James, Samuel, William, and David B., and two daughters, Anna and Sarah. The sons all settled, lived, and died in this vicinity. Sarah is still living. William lived on the old homestead, where his son James F. now resides.

William Wilson in 1806 settled on land now owned by James F. Kennedy. He moved away about 1812.

Thomas Crooks, another settler of 1806, died early. His widow brought up the family, which was a large one. Thomas, Robert, and John, her sons, remained in Howland, and died here. William died in Bazetta. Henry and Samuel moved away. There were also two daughters.

William Medley, an early settler in the northeast of the township, had a family of sixteen children. One of his sons still resides in Bazetta, and one in Vienna. Other members of this family are scattered widely.

John and Uriah Williams were settlers of 1803. Uriah lived in the southeast of the township, near the springs. His son John, still living, is one of the oldest residents of Howland. One daughter, Mrs. Drake, is still living in Warren.

John Williams lived on the Perkins farm, west of the creek. His sons were Joseph and Benjamin.

ORGANIZATION.

In 1812 the commissioners of Trumbull county organized township four, range three, into a separate township and election district. Who the first township officers were cannot be learned, as the early records have been lost. Howland was named from the purchaser, James Howland, who paid $24,000 for Howland and Greene townships.

FOOD AND CLOTHING OF PIONEERS.

Fortunate indeed was it for the pioneers that they possessed the rare quality, contentment, which the luxurious tastes of modern times have in no small measure destroyed. They were enabled to live up to that sound precept of Horatian philosophy which advises men to "preserve an equal mind in adversity," and blessed with such a mind, they were thankful in prosperity and patient under afflictions. At their rude firesides they ate the bread which their toil had earned, and though it was coarse, it was wholesome, and far ahead of many articles of modern cookery in nutritious qualities. Plenty of exercise rendered digestion healthy, and good appetites made every article of food relish.

Corn-bread was a staple article of food—would that it still were. Johnny-cake, as it was called, was usually baked in this wise: the dough having been spread on a smooth board, kept especially for this purpose, was placed before the hot, roaring fire, and some young member of the family directed to watch it. The side next the fire would quickly bake, then the board was turned around and the other side received the heat in turn. Careful tending and a good fire soon finished the job, and the johnny cake, beautifully browned and steaming hot, was placed upon the table with good fresh milk in bowls, and big spoons. There was a supper fit for a king.

Potatoes, buckwheat cakes, or biscuits, often venison and sometimes bear-steak, were about the only kinds of food, always excepting the johnny cake. Dutch ovens were perhaps the most useful kitchen utensils—excepting the johnny-cake board. The Dutch oven was an iron kettle which was provided with a cover capable of holding a heap of fire coals. The oven was placed upon the coals, and the heat thus applied to both top and bottom usually resulted in what housekeepers called a good bake, while none of the savory odors of the cooking food could escape. Stoves, ranges, and all other modern improvements in kitchen utensils are good and useful enough, yet probably as well-tasting dishes were prepared in Dutch ovens as any now produced by masters of the culinary art.

In the matter of clothing, too, eighty years have wrought wonderful changes. During the first years of this settlement every article of clothing worn by men, women, and children was manufactured in the homes of the wearers. Mr. John Ratliff, son of a Howland pioneer, says that until he was sixteen years of age he never saw a dress-coat of broadcloth or similar material upon any man.

Every farmer kept a few sheep, the wool of which was carded, spun, and woven by the hands of the female members of the family. Cotton was bought just as it was taken from the bale, carded with hand cards, and spun into warp. Wool, after undergoing similar processes, made the filling, and the cloth made from these two materials in old-fashioned looms was cut and made into garments for winter wear. Long frocks reaching below the knee were made for men and boys. Butternut bark or the bark of some other tree furnished the dye-stuff which was used in coloring the cloth.

Summer clothing was usually made from cloth of tow and linen warp and cotton filling. Why did not women buy calico for dresses? Perhaps it is sufficient answer to this question to state that calico was fifty cents per yard and butter only six cents a pound. These home-made garments were worn to church and all other gatherings. Could a lady in a fashionable suit such as are now worn have been seen among the country maids and matrons of those days, she would have seemed like a creature from another land if not from another world.

Buckskin was considerably worn by men; but as it was usually but imperfectly tanned, after a short season of use and a few wettings it became stiff and hard and had to be laid aside.

EARLY SCHOOLS.

The first school-house was built on the 4th of July near where Ward lived, on lot eighteen. A term of school was taught in it the same year by Ruth Alford. This old building was a simple structure of logs. Its benches were rude and primitive, formed from slabs without backs or other appliances for the rest of the arms and body. Boards upon wooden pins driven into the wall formed the pupil's writing desk. In those days a boy or girl, after a hearty breakfast of johnny-cake and bacon, required no support for an aching back—a thing to them unknown. And as for comfortable heating furnaces, to dry wet clothing or warm cold fingers and cold feet, these were provided in the shape of a huge fire-place which extended entirely across one side of the house. This was kept in full blast by long, heavy logs, which were rolled into it from time to time. The simplicity of this style of heating apparatus, however, yielded after a while to the aristocratic notions of Mr. Heaton, who supplied the building with a rudely formed cast-iron stove, manufactured at Heaton's furnace.

Other log-houses were built early, among them one in the northwest of the township, and another in the King neighborhood. John Ewalt taught in the former about 1812. About 1814 Montgomery Anderson taught in the King district.

One after another, as they were needed, buildings for school purposes were erected until ten had been built in the township. Not many years ago the township was redistricted, and now there are in all but six school-houses, three on each side of Mosquito creek.

CHURCHES.

The first religious meeting in this township, or the first in which a sermon was preached, was held at the house of John Reeves in 1803. A Baptist minister conducted the services.

Rev. Joseph Curtis, pastor of the Warren church, organized a Presbyterian church about 1815, with thirteen members. In 1820 a log building was erected in the northeast of the township, which served both as church and school-house. In this building a Methodist church of about ten members was organized in 1821. After Rev. Curtis left Warren, the Presbyterian organization ceased to exist. We cannot learn that the Methodists ever had regular preaching here.

The Disciples' church of Howland was organized in 1828. The Drake family, Jacob, Simeon, Aaron, and George, were its mainstay and support. They were devout and sincere Christians of noble character. In 1830 this denomination built a church edifice near the forks of the road on Simeon Drake's farm, at a cost of about $3,000. The only church building in the township at present was erected by the Disciples in 1862, at the center, and cost about $1,700. Among the early and faithful laborers in the Disciples' church were the preachers Campbell, father and son, Scott, Bentley, Hayden, Bentley, Henry, Bosworth, Hartzell, and others. The proximity of Howland to Warren accounts for the fewness of churches.

DR. SEELY.

About the year 1806 Dr. John W. Seely settled in this township and began the practice of medicine. He was a competent physician, and skilled, especially in surgery. Genial and affable toward every one, he sustained an honorable reputation and lived a useful life. For many years he had a large practice throughout this part of the county, and his memory is still revered by those who knew him. Soon after the opening of the canal he was seized with an apoplectic fit, and died at Akron while on a journey. His son, Dr. Sylvanus Seely, continued the practice of his father, residing in Howland, and afterwards in Warren. His death was from the same disease which carried off his father.

FIRST EVENTS.

The first child born in this township was Samuel Q. Reeves, March 10, 1804.

The first marriage was in 1803, when Jack Legg and Conny Ward embarked upon the sea of matrimony. 'Squire Loveless performed the ceremony.

It is not remembered who built the first frame house. The first frame barn was erected by Barber King in 1822 on the farm now owned by his son Franklin. The second frame barn was built in 1826 by John Ratliff. Both are still standing.

Dr. Seely built a stone dwelling house in the southeast of the township at an early date.

The first store was opened about 1831 by John Collins, at the corners.

Isaac Heaton was the first justice of the peace in this township.

PUBLIC OFFICERS.

In its early history, this part of Trumbull county was represented in the State Legislature by Dr. John W. Seely. Howland has also furnished the following county officers: John Ratliff, associate judge; John Reeves, treasurer; Z. T. Ewalt, treasurer; and Harris Ewalt, infirmary director.

THE BIG STORM.

Here, as in other portions of the county, the great snow storm of February, 1818, occasioned great inconvenience and some hardships. Houses were rendered almost invisible; traveling was almost impossible; and even for the farmer to get from his cabin to his barn became an undertaking involving no small amount of labor. Fortunately wood was plenty and good fires cost nothing. If people had depended upon stores for their supplies of food in those days, what suffering and famine this storm would have caused.

Perhaps the wild animals suffered more than the inhabitants. Deer could scarcely move through the snow-drifts to their usual haunts, and the prowling wolf became nearly famished while engaged in a fruitless search for prey.

WILD ANIMALS AND HUNTS.

In early times bears and wolves were very plenty, and stock had to be carefully watched to save it from destruction. Sheep had to be kept closely penned at night, for they might as well have been slaughtered by their owners as to be left in a place where it was possible for bears or wolves to reach them. Mr. Ratliff one morning turned out his sheep, and before they had gone more than a few rods from his house a wolf was among the flock and soon had a sheep down. At night the howling was sometimes frightful. In one part of the forest a wolf would raise a cry, those near him would repeat it at intervals, others farther away would answer, and soon the sounds became so loud, so terribly dismal, that to the mind of a superstitious person who had never before heard them, they would have suggested that pandemonium must be close at hand.

With so many fierce wild animals in the forest one would almost think it strange that men were not oftener attacked by them; but the reason for the comparative good behavior of the bears and wolves is to be found in the abundance of wild game which then inhabited the woods. Wild turkeys, partridges, and other of the feathered tribe, as well as rabbits and other small animals were frequently captured by their stealthy enemies; and only a desire to regale their palate with a taste of pork or mutton enticed the beasts of prey from their haunts toward the settler's clearing. They came to know that the white man's rifle was a deadly weapon, and doubtless he was more feared on this account; for whether beasts reason or not, it is certain that they observe and remember.

Next to wolves and bears the settlers were annoyed by a wild hog—once domesticated but now a savage—which made sad havoc in the corn-fields along the creek bottom. He had long been at large, and the amount of mischief he caused assumed such magnitude that it was determined that he ought to be exterminated. To effect this a grand hunt was undertaken by men and boys with dogs. The hog was routed without difficulty, and then began an exciting chase. At length he was run into a swamp, and then ensued a desperate encounter with the dogs, in which he succeeded in killing three or four of them. At last he was captured, and, after the tusks had been knocked out, allowed to escape. A few days thereafter it appears that he was attacked by a bear, and from the appearance of the ground upon which they had fought, the conflict must have been a terrible one. Both were victors; hog and bear were found dead a short distance from each other on the scene of conflict. Bear-ishness and hoggishness, obstinacy and fortitude had met ; the result satisfied man, their enemy.

Hogs and cattle were allowed the freedom of the woods. One night in the spring of 1812 as John Ratliff was driving his hogs into the pen he discovered that one was missing. Suspecting that it had gone to satisfy the hunger of a bear he sent for his neighbor, Noah Bowen, quite a noted bear hunter, and the next morning Bowen. Ratliff, and his son John started into the woods, following the tracks made by the hogs, to dis-cover and punish the cause of the mischief. Bowen's best dog soon got on track of the bear and began to bark. "The dog is pretty near him," said Bowen, as the barking increased. The three hastened .fter the dog, and having followed about a mile discovered the bear high up in a tree, sixty or sixty-five feet from the the ground, resting upon a limb. Bowen brought his rifle to bear, putting a bullet through the animal's eye. From his lofty perch the bear fell tumbling to the earth, dead. He was a huge, heavy fellow, over three hundred and fifty pounds in weight.

AN EPIDEMIC.

Doubtless the pioneers of Howland thought that they had enough disadvantages to contend with, even when in the full enjoyment of health and strength. But in the winter of 1811–12 many were attacked by a raging epidemic fever. Among those who fell victims to this scourge and died were Mrs. William Anderson, Mrs. John Cherry, and three sons of the Norris family.

Much suffering and anxious watching was endured in many a household, even where the disease did not result fatally.

ACCIDENTS.

At the raising of a log barn on the Perkins farm, in 1811, for a man named Bentley, Law-yer Webb, of Warren, was the victim of a severe and most painful accident. He was a young man and had just come to Warren from the East, and in company with others attended the raising to see the fun. The walls of the barn were up and material was being raised for the roof by means of long poles or "skids," upon which the timbers were slid upward ; each end of the log being in a forked stick was raised simultaneously by the builders. The skids had been peeled in order to facilitate the work of getting the weight-poles to the top. A log which was being raised thus suddenly slipped out of the fork, which held one end and came down rapidly. Webb was beneath and saw it falling. He ran backward to get out of the danger, but fell over a log lying upon the ground and the descending weight struck one of his legs, break-ing it in a frightful manner, so that the bone pro-truded from the flesh. Dr. Seely was summoned, and found it necessary to amputate the limb abov .he knee.

Another accident, which came near being a fatal one, occurred about 1835. One Sunday in that year Archibald Reeves went into the woods hunting. In the course of his rambles he discovered a spot where, evidently, a bear had been at work, tearing a rotten log and scratching the earth. While examining these traces he heard a sudden noise like the cracking of a twig or the shell of a nut, and, peering through the bushes discovered a small patch of long black hair, moving about slightly among the twigs. Supposing of course that the hairy object was a part of the body of a bear, he took aim and dis-charged his rifle. The dimly outlined form fell, and much to Reeves' surprise, cries of a human being in distress reached his ears. He hastened to the spot, and discovered that, instead of a bear, he had shot his neighbor, John Rutledge, who, unbeknown to Reeves, was likewise engaged in a Sunday bear-hunt. Rutledge was helpless, and to all appearance mortally wounded. Aid was summoned and he was borne to the nearest house. Dr. John B. Harmon, of Warren, was sent for to attend to the sufferer. When he arrived, he ordered Rutledge's frock and shirt to be removed, and this being done, the bullet dropped out of the clothing upon the floor. It was found upon examination that the ball had struck the shoulder-blade, then glancing had passed around to the front of the body and passed out through the flesh of the upper arm. Dr. Harmon said that if the bullet had struck a very little lower a fatal wound must have been the consequence. He dressed the shoulder and, in due time, the wounded man recovered.

MILLS.

The first mill, a rude affair, of very limited capacity, was built about 1815, by Septimus

Cadwalader, on a small branch of Mosquito creek in the northern part of the township. No one would now judge that the water-power was ever sufficient to run a mill. The mill was of logs, small, and provided with but one run of stones. Though it could do but little work and that little very imperfectly, yet this mill was a great convenience to the settlers for some ten or fifteen years, until the establishment of other and better mills in this vicinity caused it to be deserted by customers.

The first saw-mill was built in 1814 by Samuel Kennedy, and was located on the same eam. It was remodeled several times, and is now owned by James Kennedy. It has not done any work for several years.

STONE QUARRIES.

West of Mosquito creek in the northwest of the township, and underlying the surface is an extensive bed of flag-stone of the best quality. This stone bed runs nearly the whole length of the township, from north to south, beginning with the Austin quarry and extending through the Ewalt and Davis quarries south of it. This stone is most valuable, being among the best to be found anywhere in the country. The strongest acid will not affect it, and its hardness is so great that it wears but slowly. The rock is found at depths ranging from eight to twelve feet below the surface in the Austin quarry, but in other portions of the bed it comes much nearer the top of the ground. Generally there are three layers of the stone with shale rock or soap-stone between. The hardest of the stone lies deepest. After being exposed to the atmosphere the rock hardens very rapidly.

Warren is especially fortunate in having this valuable natural deposit of flagstone so near. The sidewalks of this beautiful little city are mostly laid with this material. The stone splits or shales into thicknesses of three to five inches, and can readily be broken into pieces of such length and width as are desired. Its surface is usually quite smooth.

Of the quarries operated that of Messrs. Austin & Co. is the most extensive, and affords employment to several men throughout the year. The stone from this quarry is much used in this part of the State, and makes sidewalks of unsurpassed excellence and durability. Besides the large flagstones material is here found for paving, gutter, and cross-walk stones. The supply is great, and it will take many years to exhaust it.

The Howland springs are located on a tract of land originally owned by John Hank, a settler who came from Pennsylvania in 1802. He bought the ground, made some improvements, and afterwards sold to Dr. John W. Seely. The property has since changed owners several times, and is now owned by Shedd Brothers, of Youngstown, who have improved and beautified the grounds, making the place quite a noted summer resort. Good buildings and accommodations for pleasure-seekers attract many visitors each summer. The water of the springs is believed to possess medicinal and health-giving properties.

———:—

BIOGRAPHICAL SKETCHES.

JOHN RATLIFF.

Among the surviving pioneers of Trumbull county few are more deserving a place in this history than Judge Ratliff. He was born in Westmoreland county, Pennsylvania, December 17, 1799. His grandparents came to this country from England, but at what date is not known. His father was John Ratliff, and his mother Mary Vandyke, both of whom were natives of Delaware, where they lived until about the year 1798. They moved to Westmoreland county and thence to Beaver county in 1801, near the Pennsylvania and Ohio State line. On the 1st day of April, 1811, his parents removed to Trumbull county, Ohio, arriving at their destination in the northwest part of Howland township on the 3d day of the same month. There the subject of this sketch grew to manhood, surrounded by all the difficulties attending a pioneer settlement. In 1818 he married Elizabeth Wilson, daughter of Robert and Elizabeth (Hyde) Wilson, who were natives of Ireland but came to this country when quite young. In April, 1821, he was elected township clerk of Howland and served in that capacity for a period of eighteen years. About the year 1823 there was a regiment of volunteer riflemen organized in Trumbull county. The township of Howland raised a company of about eighty men, who were uniformed and equipped with good rifles. At the first election of officers

Richard L. Seeley was chosen captain but was afterwards promoted and Judge Ratliff was elected captain, serving seven or eight years, shortly after which the regiment was disbanded. About the year 1839 he was elected justice of the peace and served in that capacity six years, when, in 1845, he was elected one of the associated judges of the common pleas court of Trumbull county, which office he filled with ability until the change in the State constitution in 1851. His associates on the bench were Edward Spear, of Warren, and Asa Haines, of Vernon, the presiding judge being Hon. Benjamin F. Wade.

September 1, 1844, Judge Ratliff became a member of the Disciples church of Warren, and in the following year was elected by the congregation one of the overseers of the church and officiated in that capacity till about 1870, when he was released from the duties of the office on account of his age. May 3, 1855, the Disciples church in Warren became an organized body under the laws of Ohio for the incorporation of churches and he was elected one of the trustees and still holds such office.

He is the father of seven children. Two died in infancy. The others are as follow: Isaac, now living in Howland; Robert W., of Warren; Ann (deceased), wife of Josiah Soule; Mary (deceased), wife of Henry Hoagland; and Lydia Maria, wife of Daniel L. Jones, of Warren, with whom the subect of this sketch makes his home. Mrs. Ratliff died in Warren March 16, 1875, aged seventy-seven.

Judge Ratliff's occupation through life has been that of farming. He has been unusually blessed with good health, and, possessing a naturally vigorous constitution, he is to-day, notwithstanding his advanced age, a hale and hearty old gentleman. At this writing (March 17, 1882) he is eighty-two years and three months old.

JAMES FRANKLIN KING.

James Franklin King, widely and favorably known throughout this part of Ohio as a stock dealer and farmer, is a descendant of one of the earliest settlers of the county. His grandfather, Barber King, was a native of Connecticut, and was employed in that State as an iron worker.

He made the acquaintance and courted Irene Schoville, a lady of aristocratic family, whose parents objected to her marriage with a laborer; and the old Connecticut statutes made it a crime for a man to lead a lady to Hymen's altar without her parents' consent. But Cupid has never been easily bound by statutes, and when in earnest always finds a way of evading them. In this instance Miss Schoville rode to her affianced's house, gave him a place behind her on her horse, and rode to a magistrate's office, where they were lawfully married. Mr. King joined the second company of surveyors sent out by the Connecticut Land company in 1797, and while thus employed selected a place for settlement near the present site of Canfield. The following spring he removed with his wife from Connecticut and made an improvement on the lot which had been selected. They lived there two years, then removed to a lot at the present village of Girard. After a residence on this lot of about six years, having made considerable improvement, General Perkins proposed an exchange of one hundred acres in Howland for the lot on which Mr. King lived. After viewing the ground the proposition was accepted, on condition that the center of the one hundred acres should be a certain strong, clear, flowing spring. Beside this spring Mr. King built his house in Howland, and moved into it in June, 1806, on the day of a total eclipse of the sun. The house stood on the ground now occupied by J. F. King's residence. Mr. King was a plain, unambitious farmer. He lived to the age of sixty-nine years. Mrs. King lived to the advanced age of eighty-six years. During the Revolution she was taken prisoner at Wyoming by the Indians and held captive for six months. The family of Barber and Irene King consisted of seven children— Jonathan, James, Samuel, William, Bliss, Anna, and Sarah. Sarah (Mrs. William Brinton) is the only member of the family living. They all settled in Howland township except James, Anna (Mrs. Jabez Bell), and Sarah Brinton.

William King, father of James F. King, was born April 9, 1798, and died October 8, 1866. He was married in 1820 to Mary B. Kennedy, a daughter of Samuel and Jane Kennedy. She was born in 1801, and died January 3, 1869. Mr. King was a man of great energy and pro-

James F. King

gressive ideas; his wife was plain, unassuming and industrious. They were both members of the Presbyterian church and were remarked in their neighborhood for sympathy and kindness in cases of sickness. Their family consisted of four children—James F., Irene (deceased), Orvilla (Mrs. William Chamberlain), and Jerusha (Mrs. Charles Hunt).

James Franklin, whose portrait appears on an adjoining page in this volume, was born March 12, 1822. He owns and resides on the old homestead of his grandfather and father, and where he was born and raised. He attended the district school and received a fair English education, but it was farm work that mainly occupied his attention. Soon after thoroughbred shorthorn cattle had been introduced into the county, in 1841, by Thomas and Frederick Kinsman, Henry B. Perkins, and the Cowdens of Gustavus, Mr. King saw the opportunity of building up a successful industry. The first importations of cattle had been from New York. Mr. King accompanied Messrs. Kinsman and Perkins to the Bluegrass region in Kentucky in 1850, at which time he made a purchase of short-horns, and has since continued to supply his herds with stock cattle from that region and from southern Ohio. He has for about forty years given close and intelligent attention to the breeding and raising of stock cattle. He keeps on his farm about one hundred head. Of late years Mr. King has been dealing to some extent in thoroughbred Southdown sheep. He has been identified with the Trumbull County Agricultural society as an officer ever since its re-organization in 1846, and for eight years was president. Under his management the annual fairs were made of special interest to the general farmers. He aimed to make the annual exhibitions what they professed to be—agricultural fairs. He is a man of good executive talent, being energetic, correct and decided. Mr. King married in 1862 Miss Cornelia J. Andrews, daughter of Samuel and Lorena (Hutchins) Andrews, of Howland township. They have a family of two children.

DRAKE FAMILY.*

Abraham Drake, of Monmouth, New Jersey, was in the habit of going with others to Schooley mountain, in that State, in the fall of the year, for the purpose of hunting. On one of these occasions he became acquainted with a Miss Stark, a relative of Colonel John Stark of Revolutionary fame, and married her. He bought two hundred acres of land near Haskelstown, New Jersey, where they settled, and to them were born three sons, viz: Abraham, Aaron, and Sylvenius. Abraham, the oldest, was born in in 1756. In 1788 or 1789 he married Sarah Bell, of Sussex county, New Jersey. To them three daughters and six sons were born, viz: Elizabeth, Sarah, and Meriam, Jacob, Simeon, Aaron, George, Abraham, and Amos. And for some years they lived near the above-named town, but the father dying, and having willed all his property to his son Aaron, Abraham and Sylvenius were dissatisfied. Abraham endeavored to persuade Aaron to allow him to have the house and a small piece of land belonging to his father's estate, and on which he then lived, and which would enable him to maintain his family by his occupation, being a weaver, but in this his efforts proved to be of no avail, and on returning home from this mission, late one evening, sadly disappointed, and as no other avenue seemed open to him whereby he might support his family, he said to his wife, "We will go West," and with this decision, which was characteristic of the man, he soon bid his friends and native place a last farewell, for he never returned, and the writer believes never heard of them afterward. He removed his family to Jefferson village, Morgan township, Washington county, Pennsylvania, where they stayed some six months, while he went on to Ohio to look for a place to locate their future home. This was in the year 1804 or 1805. He purchased three hundred and twelve acres of land in Howland township, for which he paid $655, and settled on that part of it which is the farm now owned by his grandson, Amos Drake. Here they began by earnest and unceasing toil to supply their wants from their own productions, amid the privations and hardships incident to the times. It was even no small task to guard the few domestic animals, which they had or could get,

*Prepared by Amos Drake.

from the attacks of wild beasts. Well does the writer remember the log pen in which the sheep were secured at night to keep the wolves from them, and also of the trap made of logs in the woods, to catch those prowling invaders, yet with all of their vigilance sheep were frequently killed, and bears would kill the hogs and calves, and the deer would persist in feeding upon their wheat in the fall and spring.

And yet amid these scenes with willing hands they soon began to gain for themselves a comfortable home. But when it seemed they most needed each other's presence to assist and cheer them in their efforts death took from the home the wife and mother. She died May 16, 1808, aged forty-two, leaving the husband and eight children, the youngest a son only a year old.

The household duties henceforth devolved upon the daughters, Elizabeth and Sarah. In 1813 he built the house (yet standing) in which he afterwards lived until his death, July 17, 1818, aged sixty-two years, and here would my pen fondly linger to pay a tribute to one whose industry, honesty, and uprightness of character were proverbial. The impress of the virtues of that father and mother was seen upon their children in after years, and made them moral, upright, unassuming, faithful men and women.

Elizabeth having married, the care of the family fell on Sarah, which duties she faithfully performed for some years, she and Jacob keeping and living on the homestead. Simeon and Aaron settled on a part of the land which belonged to their father; George and Abraham settled on the west side of the creek in this township. Elizabeth moved to Poland, now Mahoning county, all following agricultural pursuits. George in 1844 removed with his family to Howard, Knox county, Ohio. Sarah in 1833 sold her interest in the homestead to Jacob, and built a house on the farm of Abraham, where she lived until April 1851, when she ceased to keep house, and lived with Aaron and his family until April, 1860, when she returned to the old home, and lived with her nephew up to the time of her death October 26, 1864, aged seventy-two years. She and her brother Amos were not married—he dying July 30, 1821. Meriam died in infancy in New Jersey. The following are marriages of the the sons and daughters of Abraham and Sarah Drake; the number of children born to each mar-

riage; the death and age of parents, and the number of children now living.

June 11, 1811, by Dan Eaton, justice of the peace, James Stull, of Poland, and Elizabeth Drake, of Howland. To them were born three daughters and one son. Death and age of parents unknown. One daughter survives.

January 3, 1822, by Isaac Heaton, justice of the peace, Simeon Drake and Lucretia Williams, of Howland. No children, she dying soon after marriage; age unknown.

May 8, 1825, by John Hank, justice of the peace, Aaron Drake and Mary Williams, of Howland. To them were born five sons and three daughters. He died August 22, 1855, aged fifty-six years; his widow, three sons, and one daughter survive.

June 9, 1825, by R. L. Seely, justice of the peace, Simeon Drake and Olvina Hank, of Howland. To them were born four sons and one daughter. The father died March 12, 1859, aged sixty years; the mother February, 1880, aged seventy-six years. Three sons survive.

June 15, 1826, by Alford Brunson, justice of the peace, George Drake and Nancy Smith, of Hubbard. To them one son was born. The mother died May, 1827. The son survives.

May 30, 1829, by Adamson Bently, minister, George Drake and Mary McElroy, of Washington county, Pennsylvania. To them were born two daughters. The mother dying in 185–; the father February 23, 1871, aged sixty-eight years. One daughter survives.

May 17, 1830, by A. Bently, minister, Abraham Drake and Jane McElroy, of Washington county, Pennsylvania. To them one son was born; the mother dying October, 1842; the son surviving.

May, 1844, by A. S. Hayden, Abraham Drake and Phebe Moffit, of Solon. To them was born one daughter; the father dying May 24, 1849, aged forty-four years. His widow survives.

April 11, 1826, by Joseph W. Curtis, minister, Josiah Drake and Agnes Anderson, of Howland. To them were born two sons and one daughter, viz: Amos, Alva, and Agnes. The mother died September 19, 1831, aged thirty-six years.

February 12, 1833, by John Henry, minister, Jacob Drake and Artlissa Lane, of Austintown. To them were born a son and daughter, viz: George and Emily. The father died September

A. A. Drake

28, 1842, aged forty-six years; the mother August 22, 1846, aged thirty-seven years; his daughter Agnes October 4, 1846, aged fifteen years.

The following are the marriages of the sons and daughter of Jacob Drake referred to and the number of children surviving:

April 24, 1851, by Isaac Errett, minister, Amos Drake, of Howland, and Lavinia J. Hull, of Champion. To them a son and daughter were born—Charlie W. and Ida M.—who reside as above written.

September 6, 1860, by Mathias Christy, minister, Alva A. Drake and Lide J. Grove, both of Howland, where they still reside.

Emily went to Clinton county, Iowa, in 1847, where she married Dr. S. D. Golder. They settled in Charleston, Missouri. To them four sons and one daughter were born. The mother died January 31, 1875, aged forty-one years. The daughter and three sons survive.

George went to Colorado in 1860, where he married Martha A. Brown. To them two sons and one daughter were born. An infant son survives.

Alva A., second son of Jacob and Agnes Drake, was born in Howland township in the year 1829. After obtaining a fair English education he devoted himself to agricultural pursuits. In 1860 he married Miss Lide Grove, daughter of Jacob and Rachel Grove, of Austintown, and later of Howland. Mr. Grove was born in Beaver, Pennsylvania, in 1802. While but a child his parents removed to Austintown, and there he married, in 1830, Rachel Woodward. He removed to Howland in 1850, and died April 16, 1881. Mrs. Grove died March 31, 1880. They had two children—John C. and Lide. The former died in 1861, leaving two children—Minnie and Lulu. Mr. Drake settled on the farm on which he now resides in 1865. He is an extensive and practical farmer and dealer in fine Merino sheep. He has accumulated two hundred and fifty acres of land, which is in good condition. While he is enterprising and industrious he is at the same time liberal and companionable. He held the office of justice of the peace in Howland township, and on account of reliable judgment in business matters was chosen real estate appraiser. He is a representative of one of the oldest and most respect-

able families in the township, as the preceding family sketch will show.

KENNEDY FAMILY.

Samuel Kennedy (Howland), the pioneer of this family in Trumbull county, was born in Chester county, Pennsylvania, in 1764, from whence he moved to Ohio in 1814, and settled on the Kennedy homestead in Howland, where he lived until his death, which occurred in 1816. On this farm he erected the first saw-mill in the township on Kennedy run, on the east part of the farm. This mill was operated from that time until about 1873.

He was married to Jane Kennedy, and to them were born the following children: Montgomery K. (deceased), Nancy, now living in Howland, Elizabeth (deceased), Mary, mother of J. F. King, Tabitha (deceased), James, now on the home-farm, Maxwell (deceased), Thomas and William, of Bazetta; and Ann, widow of M. J. Iddings, of Howland.

James Kennedy was born in Northumberland county, Pennsylvania, in 1807, and came with his father to Ohio, when he was but seven years old. From his boyhood to his present advanced age he has been a resident of Howland, and always prominently identified with all the public interests of the township. In early times every settler from necessity became expert in the use of a gun; but Mr. Kennedy was, and is now rated, as an extra good shot. He relates that he succeeded in killing forty-two wild turkeys in forty-four shots; and now exhibits a target about two inches in diameter in which eight bullet holes cluster about the center. He was also a mechanic and manufactured articles of furniture and cutlery with considerable skill.

He was married in 1831 to Miss Alice Scott, who was born in 1809. Their children are William Wallace, of Newton Falls; George W., of Howland; James Lawrence, of Warren, and John Scott.

The Kennedy family of Howland was represented in the late civil war by George W. Kennedy, who enlisted August 22, 1861, in company C, Second Ohio cavalry. The regiment immediately went into camp at Cleveland, where they spent the winter. Afterwards were ordered west to Platte City, Missouri, and were employed mostly as scouts in the Indian country. The first skirmish in which they were engaged was at Independence, Missouri, afterwards being engaged in a battle at Cow-skin prairie, and, also, at the second battle at Pea Ridge. In 1862 or 1863 they returned from the West and in following campaign were engaged as scouts in Kentucky and Tennessee; was through the memorable campaign of the wilderness under Grant; also at the seige of Knoxville, Tennessee. He was considerably disabled by his horse falling on him at Somerset, Kentucky, breaking a leg and three ribs.

In the fight at Piney Creek church his horse was shot from under him while in command of his company, to which he succeeded on account of the cowardice of his captain while under fire, he holding the rank of sergeant at the time. At the famous battle at Winchester, Virginia, he had another horse disabled, and was present when General Phil. Sheridan appeared after his famous ride—"saving the day at Winchester."

After following the regiment through many hard campaigns he was discharged September 18, 1864, on account of injuries received as above mentioned. On his return home he was married November 11, 1865, to Eliza Bailey, who was born July 25, 1837. They now have one child, Jimmie Frank, who was born April 5, 1868. After his marriage, he settled on the east part of the homestead farm and operated a saw-mill. He afterwards returned to Sharon, Pennsylvania, where he kept a hotel; also, afterwards engaged in same business at Warren. He removed to the present farm in Howland in 1877, where he now resides—having served his township as assessor, school trustee and supervisor.

John Scott Kennedy was born in 1850, and was married in 1876, to Jennie King, who was born in 1855. They have one child, Grace.

He is now a member of the firm of M. C. & J. S. Kennedy, marble and granite works, Cortland, Ohio; was census enumerator of 1880, and had the honor of presenting the best set of books in the census district; he has also held the office of town assessor for two years, having been elected to that office while absent from home. He now resides on the home-farm in Howland.

NOTES OF SETTLEMENT.

John Reeves, Sr., was born in Westmoreland county, Pennsylvania, June 6, 1781; married April 16, 1801, Sarah Quinby, who was born in Washington county, Pennsylvania, April 30, 1786. They moved to Howland in the spring of 1803, he having been out the fall previous and purchased one hundred and sixty acres in lot twelve. He brought his goods by water in a canoe down the Monongahela and Ohio to Beaver, thence up the Beaver and Mahoning to Warren, while his wife made the journey on horseback. During the War of 1812 Mr. Reeves was drafted but furnished a substitute. Shortly afterward he removed to Washington county, Pennsylvania, where he kept a tavern on the National pike some three years. He returned again to the farm but did not remain long, removing to and residing in Beaver county, Pennsylvania, about three years. He then moved to Sharon, Mercer county, where he operated a carding machine, grist- and saw-mill some three years. He then returned to the farm where he lived until his death November 20, 1851, aged seventy years. His wife lived until February 3, 1880, aged ninety-three years and nine months.

Provisions were very scarce in the early settlement, and on one occasion Mr. Reeves went to Beaver to procure them, leaving his wife with a child and a neighbor's girl to take care of the stock. On a very dark night during his absence the wolves attacked the small flock of sheep near the barn, some ten rods from the house, killing all but one, which Mrs. Reeves courageously rescued from the rapacious beasts. She, with the aid of the girl, pulled the wool from the dead sheep and afterwards carded and spun it, and had it woven into coverlets, some of which still remain as relics in the family.

Francis Andrews was born in Vienna township in 1818, and was married first in 1840 to Ann King, who was born in 1820, and died in 1852. To them was born Kennedy K. in 1841. Mr. Andrews was again married in 1854 to Esther Ann Kennedy, who was born in 1836. Their children were Daniel and Anna, both deceased, and Linda now living at home. He has been mostly engaged as a farmer and dealer in Durham cattle; also buying and selling horses, and was previously engaged in the dairy business. He settled on the farm on which he has since resided, in 1843, where he now lives in the retired enjoyment of the fruits of a busy life.

Isaac Ratliff was born February 6, 1818, on the farm on which his son James now lives. He was married in 1839 to Phœbe King, who was born in 1821. To them were born the following children : Mary, William (who died in the army in Kentucky in 1862), and James, and Josiah. Mr. Ratliff has been mostly engaged as a farmer, but has served as a supervisor for a number of years. About 1865 he began quarrying stone in the quarry which he afterwards sold to the Harmon Austin Stone company.

James Ratliff was born in 1845, and was married to Barbara Snair, who was born in 1846. To them were born the following children : William, John, Anna (deceased), and Judson. Mr. Ratliff has been engaged in various occupations—working in stone quarry, farming, and is now engaged with his brother Josiah in operating the steam saw-mill. He is known as one of the rising young men of this township, throughout which he is well and popularly known.

Josiah Ratliff was born in 1847 and married to Eliza Wilson, who was born in 1847. Their children are as follows: Mina and Bertie. He enlisted in 1864 in the One Hundred and Ninety-sixth Ohio volunteer infantry, and served about one year, doing garrison duty at Fort Delaware, and in the Shenandoah valley. Mr. Ratliff returned from the army and settled to the peaceful pursuits of a farmer's life in Howland township. He has served his township as trustee, and at present is engaged with his brother James in running the steam saw-mill near their residence in the northwest part of the township.

John Reeves, Sr., came from Westmoreland county, Pennsylvania, in the fall of 1803, and purchased the well known Reeves homestead farm, being part of lots twelve and thirteen, Howland township. He moved in the spring of 1804 and settled on this farm, having brought his goods down the Monongahela and up the Ohio, Beaver, and Mahoning rivers in a common canoe. He was born June 5, 1781, and died in 1851; was married April 16, 1801, to Miss Sarah Quinby, who was born April 30, 1786. Their children were Arthur, Samuel, Abner, Jesse, Ephraim Q., Joseph P., John, Lewis, Sarah (now Mrs Reno, of Chicago), Eugenia (now Mrs. Little, of Chicago), Nancy (now Mrs. I. N. Dawson, of

Warren), and Hannah B., deceased. John Reeves, Jr., the seventh child, was born Tuesday, March 21, 1815, and was married in 1839 to Harriet Mason, who was born September 11, 1820. To them were born the following children: Ellesif, Abner M., Sarah, Mary, James, and John. Mr. Reeves was elected treasurer of Trumbull county in 1856, and served two years; has been several times elected justice of the peace of his township. During the late war he was actively engaged in enlisting soldiers, having recruited company B, One Hundred and Fifth Ohio volunteer infantry, in about nine days, and of which he was commissioned captain. He is now one of the well known, leading men of his township, engaged as a farmer on the homestead farm.

James Bolin was born in Weathersfield, Trumbull county, Ohio, December 7, 1819; son of John and Delilah (Williams) Bolin. John Bolin came to Ohio in 1817, settling in Weathersfield, and cleared up the place now owned by his sons James and John. He raised a family of five children, three of whom survive—James, John, and Mrs. Maria Kyle. He died in January, 1841. His wife came to Trumbull county with the family of James Heaton in 1801. James Bolin married, January 3, 1844, Miss Elizabeth Drake, who was born in Pennsylvania March 7, 1812. They have one son and two daughters, as follows: Warren S., born December 28, 1845; Candace, September 19, 1847; Maria E., wife of William Van Wye of Weathersfield, June 4, 1851. In the spring of 1861 Mr. Bolin settled on the place where he now lives, in Howland, on which Samuel Drake settled about 1816.

Milo McCombs was born in Weathersfield, Trumbull county, February 3, 1818, son of James McCombs. He removed to Howland township in the fall of 1855, settling on the place now owned by his son Nelson J., the old Dr. Seely place. He married for his first wife Harriet Nelson, who died in 1851, and in 1853 he married Rebecca Hake, who is still living. He died in June, 1879. Nelson J., his oldest son, was born in Weathersfield June 24, 1842, and married, October 4, 1870, Miss Charlotte Sowers, born in Cuyahoga county in March, 1843, and has a son and a daughter—Harry C., born October 27, 1873, and Mary Bell November 23, 1878.

John Williams was born in Howland township October 1, 1806. His father, Uriah Williams, was a native of Pennsylvania, where he was married. He came to Ohio with his family in 1801 and settled in Howland on the farm now occupied by his son John. The family consisted of three sons and seven daughters, of whom three are living. His death occurred in 1814. John was the youngest son. He was raised on the farm and his father's death threw upon him at an early age considerable responsibility in the management of the place. He obtained a good education for that time, and taught school one term. He was married in 1842 to Miss L. Scott, by whom one son, Lewis, was born December 13, 1852; a carpenter by trade. Mrs. Williams died January 3, 1865. He was married again September 13, 1866, to Mrs. Elizabeth Kyle, daughter of James W. Russell, who was an early settler in Austintown. By her first husband Mrs. Williams had one child—Laura E. Kyle, wife of M. L. Hyde. Mr. Williams settled on his present farm in 1842. He was active during the war in the Union cause.

Z. T. Ewalt was born in Howland township September 6, 1816. His father, John Ewalt, was born in New Jersey in 1776, came to Ohio in 1801, and settled in Howland township in 1802 on the place now owned by his son, Harris Ewalt, where he died about 1858. His family consisted of ten children, five of whom are living. He was a member of the Society of Friends, as was also his wife. Z. T. Ewalt was reared on his father's farm and resided at home until twenty-seven years old. He spent the year 1841 in the West. He was married April 20, 1843, to Belinda Adams, who was born in Little Beaver, Pennsylvania, September 6, 1823. Their family consists of six children, four of whom are still living, viz: John A., Madison county, Ohio, a Presbyterian minister; Z. T., Jr., resides in Howland; Florence I., wife of S. B. Reed, resides in Windham, Portage county; Olive B., resides in Howland. Mr. Ewalt settled on his present farm in 1843. He has filled several township offices, including justice of the peace, to which he was first elected in 1863, and served twelve years; was county coroner eight years, and again elected justice of the peace in 1881. In politics he was a Whig and is now a Republican.

William W., the only son of Samuel M. and Tabitha Kennedy, was born in Howland township, March 27, 1836. His father, Samuel Kennedy, was born in Westmoreland county, Pennsylvania, in 1798. He came to Ohio with the family and settled in Howland township. His family consisted of two children—William W. and Mrs. Ann E. Gilbert, who resides on the homestead. Samuel Kennedy was much esteemed as a neighbor and citizen. He died February 21, 1875. William W. Kennedy married, September 25, 1877, Miss Addie Ewing, by whom one son was born—Samuel E. Mrs. Kennedy died August 6, 1878. Mr. Kennedy was married again April 19, 1882, to Miss Barbara Jones. He resides on the homestead in Howland.

John Lane was born in Austintown, Mahoning county, Ohio, May 29, 1812; married, February, 1840, Miss Anna Westover, and soon after was appointed superintendent of the county infirmary, filling that position some three years. He purchased a farm in Champion, where he lived some thirty years, with the exception of a year and a half in Vienna. In 1870 he purchased the Simeon Drake farm, where he afterwards lived. He had a family of four children. Austin W., born February 20, 1841, enlisted, in 1861, in the Fourteenth Ohio battery, and was in the battle of Shiloh. Being prostrated by sickness he was soon removed to Cincinnati under the care of his father. He died April 29, 1862. Chester, born March 5, 1843, died September 7, 1844. Frank B., born April 2, 1855, died October 20, 1859. Irenus L., the only survivor, was born in Champion township, January 3, 1853. He attended a normal school at Orwell, and Hiram college some five terms; also took a commercial course at Eastman's Commercial college, Poughkeepsie, New York. In the spring of 1875 he took charge of the home place. He married, June 8, 1876, Miss Maggie D., daughter of Adam Dawson, of Howland.

Jonathan Folsom was born in Essex county, New York, July 31, 1814. His parents were Jonathan and Betsey (Leonard) Folsom. Jonathan, Sr., was a native of New Hampshire, born April 18, 1784. He came to Trumbull county, Ohio, in 1833, and settled in Weathersfield, clearing up a place now owned by John Parks. He died in 1850, and his wife the same year.

Jonathan Folsom, the subject of this sketch, was united in marriage in 1836 to Milly A. Dunlap, by whom he has two children living, viz: Nathan D., superintendent of Trumbull county poor-house; O. W., a resident of Hiram. Mrs. Folsom died August 5, 1841, and he married for his second wife, December 16, 1841, Miss Jane Scott, whose parents settled in Vienna township at an early date, removing to the place now occupied by the subject of our sketch in 1828. He died in 1863. Mrs. Folsom was born in Vienna, March 10, 1818. Six children were born of this marriage, of whom four are living, as follows: Cyrus B., born November 8, 1842, a merchant of Youngstown; Emma C., October 20, 1844, wife of S. A. Corbin, of Warren; Elizabeth J., January 22, 1847, wife of Lewis H. Thayer, a merchant of Youngstown; Olive L., April 26, 1849, at home. Mr. Folsom continued to reside in Weathersfield until 1863, having purchased the old homestead, when he moved to Howland.

J. R. Chamberlain, now a resident of Howland, was born in Ontario county, New York, August 25, 1833. His family came to Ohio in 1834 and settled in Vienna township. After passing through the course of the common schools and Vienna academy he attended Poland academy two terms, and then engaged in teaching for several years, teaching in winter and farming in summer. He was married November 21, 1860, to Tryphena Hibler, daughter of Jacob Hibler, an early settler of Hubbard township. They lived in Vienna and Brookfield townships until 1870, when the place on which they now reside was purchased. Both Mr. and Mrs. Chamberlain are members of the Presbyterian church in Vienna.

CHAPTER II.

WEATHERSFIELD.

GENERAL DESCRIPTION.

Weathersfield is one of the townships on the southern line of Trumbull county, and is township three of range three of the Reserve. It is south of Howland and north of Austintown. Liberty adjoins it on the east and Lordstown on the west. The soil is of good quality and the surface generally level—in portions low and wet.

Weathersfield is well watered, and though it has great mineral wealth its agricultural advantages are of no inferior order. The Mahoning river enters the township a short distance from the northwestern corner, and flows southerly until west of Niles, where it makes an abrupt turn toward the east; thence pursuing a southeasterly course, just east of Niles it reaches a point south of the center line of the township, then makes a graceful bend to the northward, gradually winding easterly and southeasterly until it enters Liberty township about three-quarters of a mile below the center line. At Niles the Mahoning receives the waters of Mosquito creek from the north and of the Meander from the south. The former stream enters Weathersfield almost directly north of the center of the township, and flows southerly, with few deviations, until its confluence with the Mahoning. Meander creek crosses the county line at Ohltown, about one mile and a quarter from the southwestern corner of the township, pursues a general course toward the northwest, though with numerous turnings, and joins the river a few rods below the mouth of Mosquito creek.

The famous salt spring, known to the whites years before any settlements were made in Ohio, is situated about one-half mile south of the Mahoning and a mile west of the village of Niles.

This township includes the important manufacturing town of Niles, and the enterprising mining village of Mineral Ridge.

Weathersfield has sixteen churches, a larger number, we venture to assert, than can be found in any township of its population in the State.

ORGANIZATION.

Township three of range three was organized into a township and election district by the name of Weathersfield in 1809. No record of the first township officers can be found.

THE SALT SPRINGS.

Samuel Holden Parsons, of Middletown, Connecticut, obtained a grant of about thirty-six thousand acres under an order of the General Assembly of the State of Connecticut and received a deed of it bearing the date February 10, 1788, signed by Samuel Huntingdon, Governor. This was the first grant of land made by the State of Connecticut, and was made before any survey of the lands of Ohio by the former State.

The description of the land as given in the deed was upon the hypothesis that the townships were to be laid out six miles square, and reference was made to townships and ranges as if the boundaries were already run. The tract included within its boundaries very nearly what is known as the "great salt springs tract," in which are the salt springs of Weathersfield. The salt springs tract having been granted to General Parsons, was held by him or his heirs at the time of the purchase of the lands of the Reserve by the Connecticut Land company, and formed no part of its purchases.

The salt springs were known to the whites as early as 1755, and marked on the Evans map of that date. They contained but a very small percentage of saline matter, which, however, was sufficient to attract the deer for miles around. Deer licks and Indian trails leading to the principal springs were discovered by the first settlers.

General Parsons, after receiving his grant, came on and established salt works, but while returning to Connecticut was drowned at Beaver falls, and his works were abandoned. The early settlers have transmitted to us accounts of their discovery of old kettles in which the boiling was done, and huge heaps of ashes, showing that considerable labor had been expended here.

Doubtless the abundance of deer in the vicinity of this spring originally brought the locality to the knowledge of the whites by attracting hunters hither.

SETTLEMENT.

Doubtless the first settler of this township was Reuben Harmon, as his name only appears upon the duplicate tax-list of Trumbull county as a resident tax-payer of township three, range three, in the year 1801. Of course other transient residents had been at the salt springs before him. He came to Ohio from Vermont in 1797, having purchased five hundred acres of the salt spring tract, and engaged in the manufacture of salt. Early in 1800 he returned to Vermont and in August came with his family. He was the father of Heman R. Harmon and Dr. John B. Harmon, both of whom became prominent and well known citizens of this county.

The settlers of this township nearly all came from Pennsylvania, and many of them, after several years' residence here, moved further West, leaving no record either of their coming or their going, except the marks of their sturdy industry upon the forests, fields, and meadows.

The first settlers were very naturally attracted to the salt spring, possibly with dimly outlined visions of wealth in their heads as a result of the manufacture of salt. But they soon learned that the value of the waters of the spring had been vastly over-estimated, and came to rely upon the results of the chase and the products of the land as a means of livelihood.

The lands along the river next attracted attention and soon each bank was sparsely lined with cabins, sending up their blue smoke from little clearings made in the depth of the heavy forests. The northeast of the township was also settled early, doubtless on account of the elevation of its land and its consequent adaptability to agriculture.

John Tidd lived at the salt spring as early as 1802. He was the step-father of Thomas Bristol, the potter. Two potteries, for the manufacture of glazed earthenware, were in operation near the spring in 1816. They were run by Orrin Dunscom, and Bristol. They made use of the clay found in the vicinity of the spring, but the discovery of better clay elsewhere put an end to the business after a few years.

Among the first settlers were the Heatons, who were here in 1806 and probably some years before that date. There were five brothers, James, Dan, Bowen, Reese, and Isaac. The latter settled in Howland.

James settled on the east side of the creek at Niles, and lived here in a small log cabin. Three of his children, Lewis, Warren, and Maria (Robbins), reached mature years. All settled and died in Weathersfield.

Dan Eaton, not Heaton, as he went to the trouble of having his name changed by act of the Legislature from Daniel Heaton to Dan Eaton, settled east of the creek on the A. G. Bentley place. His sons were Jacob, Bowen, and Isaac; his daughters Hannah, Ann, and Amy. All of the sons moved away excepting Jacob, who died here.

Dan Eaton was the pioneer iron manufacturer of the Mahoning valley. He was one of the oddest mortals that ever lived. A pronounced, deist and a most outspoken unbeliever, he was, nevertheless, friendly to ministers of the gospel and entertained many of them in his hospitable home. He was social with old and young, but his opinions, like himself, were odd,—very. Among his neighbors he called every man "brother," and every woman, "sister." His knowledge of politics was sound for those days. In 1813 he was elected as State Senator from Trumbull county, and again in 1820 he received an election to the popular branch of the Legislature. Old Dan lived a pure and simple life and arrived at a ripe old age honored and respected. He was a "good hater," and shams and evils of every kind received no encouragement from him. His animosity was strongly aroused against intemperance, and he never failed to give the whiskey traffic a blow whenever opportunity allowed. He had peculiar financial ideas, and during the last years of his life gave much attention to a plan for the issue of National currency, which was afterwards adopted in part in the issue of greenbacks. Dan's idea was original with him. He believed that the Government and not banks should issue the paper currency of the Nation, making it a legal tender, and in order to keep up its value should allow a low rate of interest, say one per cent., to the holder of its notes. He talked up his theory with everybody, and secured quite a lengthy list of names to a petition which he circulated recommending and urging his views.

Bowen Heaton, Dan's brother, did not settle permanently in the township. Reese Heaton settled upon the Luse farm. In 1836 he removed to Illinois with his family. The Heatons were rough-mannered, sturdy men; good citizens in the main, but each had his individual traits and peculiarities. The name, once so familiar in the township, is now known here no longer. Not a single Heaton or Eaton now remains in Weathersfield. But in the corner of the cemetery upon the hill, are many tombstones upon which the name is inscribed; so many that a settler of 1835 upon first visiting the spot gave utterance to this exclamation: "Why, this township is all settled by Heatons, and they are all dead!"

Aaron Bell was an early settler, but sold out to Miller Blachly. Miller Blachly settled about one mile from Niles, a little northeast of the town. He had three sons, Eben, Miller, and Bell; and three daughters, Phebe (Dunlap), Eleanor, who remained single, and Sarah (Bradley). Eben became a doctor, and practised several years in Niles and Warren. He married Minerva, only daughter of Dr. John Seeley. Miller, Jr., was also a physician and practised here. Bell married and settled in Weathersfield. All moved to Wisconsin. Miller Blachly was a very good man, but positive, and sometimes even obstinate in adhering to his opinions. He was a devoted Presbyterian and a strong temperance advocate. In early days the roads in his neighborhood were very bad, and sometimes teams stuck in the mud and could not move their loads. Mr. Blachly was usually ready to lend his team to assist over the difficult places; but when a man who was hauling a load of grain to a neighboring distillery asked for such assistance, he obtained only a very stern refusal.

Andrew Trew, by trade a weaver and a maker of cloth, settled early in the northeastern part of the township. His children were Nancy (Bell), who lives in Pennsylvania; Robert, deceased; Eliza (Burley), Howland; Nelson, deceased; Jane (Blachly), Kansas; Lettie (Osborn), Bazetta; Margaret (Ewalt), Howland; and Phebe and John, deceased. Mr. Trew was the first postmaster in the township. He did a large amount of weaving in early times, making woolen and tow cloth, flannel, etc.

William Carlton, an early settler of the southeastern part of the township, had three sons, William, Joseph, and Bryson, one of whom, William, is still living near Girard.

About 1809 John Horner settled on the farm now owned by H. T. Mason. His children were: David, who remained and died upon the old farm; John, who now lives in Pennsylvania; Jane (Hultz), who died in Pennsylvania; and Joseph, who removed to Hardin county.

John and Isaac Clay settled in the eastern part of the township, but left after several years' residence. Matthew Atchison settled on the Clay farm. His children were Jane (McMichael), David, Anna (McLain), John, Charles Steen, and Minerva. The latter is now living in Pennsylvania. David died in Vienna. John and Charles S. went to Iowa.

Aaron Loveland was among the first settlers. His farm was situated in the northeast part of the township. Two of his daughters are still living in Vienna township at an advanced age—Mrs. Munson and Mrs. Williams. The other children are all dead. Jacob Hake and Isaac Pope were also early settlers in the same neighborhood.

Augustus A. Adams located on the east line of the township and reared a family, none of whom now remain in the township.

John Bolen was an early settler, who lived north of Niles, on Mosquito creek. He was the miller at Heaton's old mill.

Several brothers by the name of St. John were among the earliest settlers. They have no descendants here. Their names were James, Thomas, Charles, and George. They were employed about the Heaton forge.

Nathan Draper, a native of Connecticut, settled on lot five of the salt spring tract in this township in 1807. His family lived the first summer in a bark hut or wigwam, which stood on the bank of the Mahoning, near where the iron bridge crosses that stream, one mile west of Niles. He married Hannah Cartright in 1792. Their children were John, Benjamin, Elihu, Sally, Katie, Polly, and Milly Ann. John and Benjamin had no families. Elihu married Rachel Dunlap and reared five boys and four girls. Two of his sons, Warren and Nathan, enlisted in the Nineteenth Ohio volunteer infantry, and served through numerous campaigns. Sally (Armstrong), Katie (McMullen), Polly (Dunlap), and Milly Ann (Heaton), each raised large families. The descendants of the Draper family are now scattered from Pennsylvania to Minnesota.

Peter Reel settled on the farm now owned by Peter Stillwagon in the northwestern corner of Weathersfield in 1801. Samuel, one of his sons, remained here until his death. John Reel, a brother of Peter, took up a farm near him. David was an early settler in the same neighborhood.

Robert Fenton settled about one mile east of Niles, on the T. N. Robbins farm. His children were Samuel, William, Mary Ann, Margaret, Joseph, and John. In 1837 the family moved to Putnam county.

The Reese family were here early, but none are now remaining.

William Dunlap located on the south side of the Mahoning, and there lived and died. His sons were Jonathan, Josiah, William, Stephen, Chauncy, and Perry. Two of them died here, William and Stephen. Chauncy and Perry are living, Chauncy in Vienna and Perry in Lordstown. The daughters became Mrs. Draper, Mrs. McCartney, and Mrs. Gibson.

John McConnell settled in the south of the township on the farm adjoining William Dunlap's. His sons were Alexander, John, Matthew, James and William; his daughters, Polly, Rebecca and Rebecca. All married and had families.

Joseph Hunter, John and James White were the names of other early settlers in the township.

David Moser moved to this township in 1817; Jacob Hake in 1812; Isaac Pope in 1816; Aaron Loveland in 1812; Frederick Plot about 1820; Daniel Evert in 1820.

Isaac Marshall settled on a farm adjoining the land of William Dunlap and John McConnell. His brother John settled in the same neighborhood. Two sons of the latter, John and Houston, are still residents of Weathersfield.

Bariah Battles in 1814, bought eighty acres, which is now included within the corporation limits of Niles. He was from Crawford county, Pennsylvania. In 1816 he moved here with his family, which consisted of eleven children. Five sons and a daughter are still living, viz: Rebecca (Dray), Allen county; Caleb, Akron; John, Niles; Edward, Howland; Asa, Hancock county. Bariah Battles died in 1838, at the age of seventy-seven. His wife (nee Mary Jones) died in 1855, aged eighty-six. John Battles, one of the oldest residents of the township, was born in 1807, and came to Weathersfield with his parents. He married Sarah J. Leavings, of New York State, by whom he had seven children, all of whom are living: Mary Jane (Schwindler), Lucy (Dunlap), John E., Sarah (Allison), Laura (White), Franklin B., and William. Mr. Battles worked at iron manufacturing from the age of twenty years until 1854. With Jacob Robinson he ran the Heaton furnace from 1849 to 1854.

Michael Ohl moved from Austintown to Weathersfield in 1815, and settled on the Meander at the place where the little village of Ohltown grew up. His sons were Charles, David, Samuel, Henry, John, Michael, and Andrew. Henry went west and died. Michael died in this township. The others are all living. His daughters were Catharine (Hood), Liberty; Abbie (Mc-Donald), Weathersfield; Julia (Rose), Weathersfield; and Eve (Adelhart), dead.

James McCombs settled in the southern part of Weathersfield at an early date. His sons were Milo and John. The latter is cashier of the First National bank of Warren. The former is dead. James McCombs was drafted in the War of 1812. Robert McCombs settled in the same neighborhood. His sons were John, William, James, and Andrew. John is in the West. William died in the lake mining region. James is still living.

Martin Barnhisel located in the eastern part of the township. Of his children, Rachel (Wilderson) lives in Newton; Eliza (Hood), Liberty; George died in Wisconsin; Mary (Fee) lives in Warren; Sarah (Shadel), and Caroline (Bell), Liberty.

John Edwards, father of S. C. and William Edwards, settled within the present limits of Niles in 1823. In 1830 he moved one mile from the village.

Josiah Robbins settled in this township about 1826. He married Maria, daughter of James Heaton. Their family consisted of four children, all of whom are living except Jesse,—James, Josiah, Jesse. and Frank. His first wife died in 1835. In 1836 Mr. Robbins married Electa Mason, who bore three children, who are still living,—Ambrose, Maria, and Charles.

John Tibbetts settled in the northeast of the township about 1830. His children were Henry and Sarah, dead; Jeremiah, California; Austin and Charles, Weathersfield, and Ann (Gettis), Liberty.

George Young, a comparatively early settler located one mile east of Niles. All the family moved to another part of the State except John, who died here.

Warren Luse settled in the northeast of the township. He married Hannah Bowell, and had three children, Rebecca (Tibbetts), deceased; Jesse and Clara (Sykes), Weathersfield.

Ambrose Mason moved from Essex county, New York, to this township in 1835, and settled one mile east of Niles. There were eight children, viz: Lucy (Woodworth), Cleveland; Amanda (Goodrich), Lockport, New York; Eliza (Crandon) and Dean Edson, deceased; Electa (Robbins), Hiram T., Henry H., Niles, and Harriet

(Reeves), Howland. Mr. Mason died in 1870, in his ninetieth year. He was the first postmaster at Niles, and one of the first merchants. Mrs. Mason (*nee* Jemima Turner) died in 1866, aged eighty-one. Both were devoted members of the Disciples church.

Thomas Brooks, John White, John Battles, William McConnell, and John Marshall, have been residents of Weathersfield longer than any other men now living in the township.

Thomas Brooks, now seventy-three years of age, is the oldest resident of this township.

Dr. A. M. Blackford came to Niles to practice medicine in 1846; and practiced ten years. He has been connected with various interests of the town, including the iron industry. In 1848 he opened the first drug store in the place. Dr. Blackford was born in Fayette county, Pennsylvania, in 1813. He was educated for the ministry of the Presbyterian church at Madison college, and continued as a preacher ten years. His health then failing, he began the practice of medicine. He afterwards entered upon the duties of the clerical profession, but was compelled to retire at the end of five years. Dr. Blackford is still a resident of Niles. He married Eliza, daughter of Thomas Russell of this place.

EARLY SCHOOLS.

Concerning the early schools little can be learned. An old log school-house, with greased paper for windows, was situated south of the river at Niles. On the brow of the hill near the site of the grist-mill, was a school-house where the children of the little settlement surrounding Heaton's furnace attended school. Heman R. Harmon was an early teacher here.

POST-OFFICES.

The first post-office in the township was established in the northeast of Weathersfield about 1825, Andrew Trew, postmaster. This office, which was known as Weathersfield, continued until 1843, when a post-office was established at Niles, Ambrose Mason being postmaster. His successors have been H. H. Mason, —— Morgan, J. W. Leslie, Josiah Robbins, Sr., C. W. Robbins, Josiah Robbins, Jr., William Campbell, and H. H. Mason, the present incumbent.

The second post-office was the Ohltown office, of which Michael Ohl was the first postmaster.

This post-office was formerly on the old stage route to Ashtabula, and then received a mail from each way daily; now a tri-weekly mail is received from Mineral Ridge.

An office was established at Mineral Ridge in 1860, Azariah Hughes, postmaster. It was kept in Mahoning county, and a semi-weekly mail was procured from Niles. It was discontinued after a few months on account of political differences and a lack of support. Leading citizens wanted a Democratic postmaster, but no one in that party could be found who was willing to perform the duties of the office. A semi-weekly mail was not sufficient for the business men of the place, and a prominent business man had his own mail brought from Niles daily. This largely diminished the receipts of the office, and the postmaster became tired of his position and returned the mail bags to the Government post-office department. In 1863 the office was re-established with a daily mail, and J. L. Pierce was appointed postmaster. A few years later the office became Mineral Ridge, Trumbull county. M. L. Campbell, Mrs. Sarah Wilson, and E. J. Ohl have since been postmasters.

TEMPERANCE WORK.

Dan Eaton and Miller Blachly were the leaders and incorporators of a temperance society in the time of the Washingtonian temperance movement. A number of good earnest workers joined them, and the society, which began about 1830, continued in existence several years. Meetings were held at school-houses and private dwellings.

Dan Eaton, when about to build a barn, announced that whiskey should have no part in the work of raising it. Accordingly, after the timber had been prepared, as was customary in those days, he invited his neighbors to come and help him get the frame up. But no one would come unless whiskey was to be furnished, and Dan adhered resolutely to his determination that none should be used upon his premises. He was therefore compelled to hire men to do the work for him, and the barn was built without the aid of whiskey. It was probably the first building erected in the township in which the ardent liquid was not a prominent feature at the "raising."

EARLY MILLS.

The Heatons built a saw-mill and grist-mill on Mosquito creek very early. Both were in operation in 1816. The present grist-mill at Niles was built by the Heatons in 1839.

Probably the second mill in the township was that of Michael Ohl, elsewhere mentioned.

Mills were often stopped during the dry season and when this happened the settlers were obliged to go to the Cuyahoga for milling. Roasting-ears from the corn-field served in part to supply the want of meal.

AN UNPERFORMED MIRACLE.

In the early years a poor, half-crazy old fellow named Dobbins, a Methodist and great talker, one day asserted that he had as much faith as ever any of the apostles had, and that he believed himself capable of performing miracles through this faith. "Can you walk upon the water?" asked one of his listeners. "Walk on the water? Yes. Peter tried it, but couldn't. He hadn't faith enough. I have faith and can perform the act." A number of idlers and boys collected and dared him to try it. He yielded to their wishes, and proceeded to the river at once. Here he uttered a short prayer, removed his shoes and stockings, and drew near to the water's edge. The excitement in the crowd was now at a high pitch, when suddenly the old man paused and asked: "Have you all faith that I can do this thing?" A voice in the crowd: "No, you ——— old fool!" "Well, then we might as well abandon the undertaking. Faith on your part is necessary as well as on mine, for without faith we can do nothing." So the promised miracle was never performed.

MORMON MEETINGS.

Although old Dan Eaton was one of the most outspoken of unbelievers, yet his house was always open to religious meetings of whatever character. A Mormon missionary named McClellan, and Sam Smith, a brother of Joe Smith, labored in Weathersfield in the winter of 1833-34, and held meetings at Dan Eaton's house. They secured a number of converts, but so far as can be learned none followed them hence.

DISTILLING.

So far as can be learned there were only a few small stills operated in this township in early times. Simon Hood, Jacob Wise, and James McCombs had copper stills, and made whiskey in small quantities.

CEMETERIES.

The first burial-place in the township was situated near the salt spring. A number of interments were made there, but all of the bodies were subsequently removed to other cemeteries and nothing now remains to indicate the location of the old graveyard.

The graveyard at Ohltown was established quite early.

The Union cemetery, northeast of Niles, is the principal cemetery of the township. Interments were made here as early as 1804. The grounds are beautifully situated on the slope of a hill, and are large and tastefully kept. They are adorned by a number of beautiful evergreens and other evidences of the care bestowed upon them. The earliest inscription which we discovered upon a cursory examination was that upon the stone erected to the memory of Hannah, daughter of James and Margaret Heaton, who died February 2, 1806, in her sixth year. James Heaton died in 1856, aged eighty-six years. Dan Eaton died in 1858, aged eighty-five. His wife, Naomi, died in 1818, aged thirty-eight. Upon an old-fashioned stone near the little monument which marks the grave of Dan Eaton, is the following quaint and curious epitaph :

NAOMI EATON,

Wife of Dan Eaton, was born December 2d, U. S. 4, and on the 5th of November, U. S. 43, became like unto a potter's vessel that was stripped of its glazing and its gilding, but as she believed the work wou'd not be lost but wou'd be moulded in another form and become fit for the Master's use.

We doubt if another instance of the use of the year of the United States instead of *Anno Domini* can be found in all the tombstone literature of the country.

We notice here the recorded death of another of the pioneers, William Bell, died in 1808, aged sixty-eight years. His wife, Priscilla, died in 1814, aged sixty-eight.

. There are also several small graveyards in the township.

NILES.

This is one of the busiest towns in northeastern Ohio. The iron industry has built it up, and is still its main support. Niles is situated in the northern part of Weathersfield township, its southern limits reaching a little below the center. The incorporated portion includes at present a territory extending a mile and a half east and west and a mile and three-fourths north and south, with an estimated population of four thousand. It is most favorably situated as regards railroad facilities, being on the Mahoning branch of the New York, Pennsylvania & Ohio, and forming the northern terminus of the Niles & New Lisbon branch of the same road. The Ashtabula & Pittsburg and the Painesville & Youngstown roads also pass through this place. Two new railroads are building, on both of which Niles will be a station—the Alliance, Niles & Ashtabula, and the Pittsburg, Youngstown & Chicago. When these roads are completed and put in operation we may expect to see a new impetus given to the business of the town and its thrift and prosperity much augmented in consequence. All present indications augur a prosperous future.

The village was laid out in 1834 by James and Warren Heaton, but only on a very limited scale, as the original plat was made to include only a small part of the present town lying west of Mosquito creek and north of the river between it and the New York, Pennsylvania & Ohio railroad. Numerous additions have since been made on all sides.

The name Niles was given to the village by James Heaton in honor of the editor of Niles' Register, a journal published at Baltimore, Maryland. Mr. Heaton was a subscriber of this paper and held a very exalted opinion of the abilities of its chief editor. He was fond of quoting the Register, and usually agreed most fully with the opinions which it expressed editorially. Therefore he called the town after the name of his favorite journalist. Who says that the influence of the press is not wide-spread?

Previous to 1834 the village had no existence, and only a few huts and shanties in the vicinity of the furnace marked its future site. Warren Heaton built a house in 1832 on a lot which is at present included within the village limits.

In the winter of 1834-35 a few buildings were erected, among them the dwelling houses of Thomas Evans and Samuel Dempsey. The village grew slowly until 1842 when the establishment of Ward's rolling-mill brought a considerable number of workmen into the place. By 1850 the population had increased to nearly or quite one thousand persons. From that date until 1873 the place grew steadily. The panic and the consequent failure of the leading business firm gave Niles a blow from which it has only recently recovered.

BUSINESS BEGINNINGS.

Although Niles, as we have stated, was an unknown place previous to 1834, yet by its former name of Heaton's furnace, the place had been known far and wide for years. In 1809 James Heaton built a small refining forge on Mosquito creek for the manufacture of bar iron, with charcoal, from the pig iron made at the Yellow creek furnace. Here were produced the first hammered bars in the State. In 1820 he rebuilt this forge which continued in operation many years. It was run by the same water-power with the furnace, and was situated near it. In 1812 the famous Mosquito creek furnace was erected a few rods east of where the public school building now stands. This was a cold-blast, charcoal furnace, run by the water of the creek. The stack was about thirty-six feet high and the bosh seven or eight feet. This furnace was owned and operated by James Heaton for many years, and was in the possession of the Heatons until it went out of blast in 1854. In 1830 the furnace was leased. Campbell, McKinley & Dempsey operated it for a considerable period. From 1849 until 1854 it was run by Robinson & Battles. In its first years its product would not average a ton of iron per day. Its capacity was somewhat increased, but five tons per day would have been considered a large yield at any period of its history. Castings for stoves, andirons, kettles, and other household utensils were made and found a ready market. The Heatons acquired considerable property through this industry, but not a fortune; for great wealth from the manufacture of iron is not to be had through the use of such primitive means as they employed. Native ore was always used in this furnace, chiefly the kidney ore found in Weathersfield, Austintown, and vicinity. This, briefly,

was the inception of the great industry which has contributed so largely to the building up of Niles.

A store was kept for the supply of the furnace hands as long as the furnace was in operation. The first store excepting this company store was kept by Robert Quigley on the northern corner of Mill and Main streets. He built and began business there in 1836. After a few years he sold out and went to Pennsylvania, where he was connected with the management of a furnace. In the time of the gold excitement Mr. Quigley started for California, but died on his way there. The second store in Niles was started by Robbins & Mason in 1839. H. H. Mason, son of Ambrose Mason, one of the proprietors, was their successor and continued the business until 1864.

The first hotel was kept by Jacob Robinson about 1836, in the house built by Mr. Dempsey. This house, much enlarged, is now the Sanford house. In 1837 Robinson built a hotel opposite Quigley's store, on the west side of the street, and kept it for many years. The present Commercial house was formerly the dwelling of James Ward. Previous to Robinson's public house, a grog-shop or tavern was kept in a log cabin on the south side of the river by a man named Parker.

The first brick building for mercantile purposes was built by James Crandon and occupied by him as a store until recently. It is the store on Main street now occupied by C. P. Moore, dealer in flour and feed.

The Mason block, the first block of any importance, was erected in 1867 by the combined efforts of five different parties.

INCORPORATION.

The following petition was addressed to the commissioners of Trumbull county August 27, 1864:

To the Commissioners of Trumbull county, State of Ohio:

We, the undersigned, inhabitants and qualified voters of Weathersfield township in said county, not embraced within the limits of any city or incorporated village, desire that the following described territory within the township of Weathersfield be organized into an incorporated village, to wit:

Beginning at a stake or corner on the farm of John Fee near the dwelling of H. H. Mason, and running west one mile to a stake or corner on the land belonging to the heirs of John A. Hunter, deceased, near the dwelling of S. H. Pew, thence due south one and one-fourth miles to a stake or corner on the farm of John Battles, thence east one mile to a stake or corner on the farm of C. S. Campbell, thence north to the place of beginning—an accurate map or plat thereof is hereunto annexed—and that said village be named and called Niles, and that A. M. Blackford be authorized to act in behalf of the petitioners in prosecuting this claim.

This petition having been granted the organization was effected. The first election was held January 23, 1866, when the following officers were chosen: H. H. Mason, mayor; James Draa, recorder; James Ward, Jr., William Davis, David Griffiths, Richard Holton, and Henry Shaffer, council.

In 1867 J. B. Noble was chosen mayor to fill a vacancy.

The mayors and recorders have been as follows: Mayors: 1868, John Ohl; 1869, F. Caspar, to fill a vacancy; 1870, J. H. Fluhart; 1872, M. D. Sanderson; 1874, Ephraim Thomas; 1876-78-80, William Davis. Recorders: 1868, A. C. Allison; 1870, M. G. Butler; 1872-74, George W. Mawby; 1876-78, B. D. Smith; 1880, George L. Campbell.

FIRE DEPARTMENT.

The village of Niles has one of the best volunteer fire departments in the State. The chief engineer, who is paid by the village, devotes his whole time to the care of the department. Two teamsters and a fine span of horses are kept on hand constantly.

The fire department was organized in 1870. Messrs. Ward and Carter procured a second-hand engine from Pittsburg, which was used until 1875, when a fine steamer was purchased. T. D. Thomas was the chief officer for ten years, and managed affairs with skill and efficiency. George W. Bear has since been in charge. The company are well drilled and well equipped, efficient and faithful.

PHYSICIANS.

Niles is well supplied with good and reliable physicians. Dr. F. Caspar is the oldest resident physician, and has been in constant practice since 1860; Dr. A. G. Miner comes next, having labored here many years. The other physicians of the town are Dr. A. J. Leitch and partner, Dr. Z. W. Shepherd, and Dr. I. B. Hargett. The two last named are homeopaths.

ATTORNEYS.

J. N. Cowdery and C. H. Strock look after the legal interests of the village.

NILES SCHOOLS.

The Union school district was organized in 1869, and the following school board elected: Josiah Robbins, Jr., and T. C. Stewart for three years; S. D. Young and William Davis for two years; W. C. Mason and William Campbell for one year. Mr. Robbins was elected president, and Mr. Stewart secretary of this board.

At a meeting held May 22, 1869, it was voted: First, that the board be empowered to procure a site for a school-house. Second, that the board be empowered to build upon said site such a school-house as will, in their estimation, be adapted to the wants of the district. Third, that a tax of $15,000 be levied in said district for the building of said school-house, and that said money be raised in three successive annual instalments of $5,000.

In 1870 two new members of the board of education were elected: George S. Baldwin and W. Campbell for three years. May 18, 1870, it was voted to accept the proposition of C. E. Cooley & Co., of Cleveland, to build the house for $27,950, taking the bonds of the district at eight per cent. in payment. Previous to this action, however, a vote was taken to make an additional levy of $10,000 for erecting the house. The building was completed and ready for occupancy in 1871. Some of the principal expenses are included in the following items: For the school site, one acre and sixty rods of land, $1,375; school desks and school furniture, $2,000; bell, $573; besides the cost of the heating apparatus of the building, the wages of workmen employed in setting up the furniture, the heaters, etc. Twenty-three thousand dollars in bonds were issued, and all paid up May 15, 1875.

The school building is by far the best in the county. It is large, built in a good style of architecture, forming an ornament to the town and a monument to the enterprising spirit of the citizens of Niles. The house is of brick, three stories and a basement. There are four school rooms on the first floor, and the same number on the second. The grammar and high school use the upper floor, which is also a public hall for entertainments of various kinds. It is furnished with a good stage, scenery, etc.

In October, 1869, Rev. T. Calvin Stewart was elected as acting superintendent of the public schools of the district, to devote at least two days of each week to the schools, at a salary of $400 per year. In 1871 L. L. Campbell was elected superintendent and principal, and proved a very faithful and efficient teacher. In 1872 his salary was increased to $1,200. He continued as superintendent until 1875, when he was succeeded by Miss M. J. Stewart for two terms. C. E. Hitchcock began his labors as superintendent in the spring of 1876; continued the balance of that year and through the school year of 1877-78. T. H. Bulla, who had been the high school teacher under Mr. Hitchcock, was elected to the superintendency in September, 1878, and still continues to discharge the duties of that responsible position in a most capable and satisfactory manner. His present salary is $1,100 per year. The school has been ably managed by faithful teachers ever since the union district was formed. Among those whose long service in the schools of Niles is a sufficient testimonial of their ability and fidelity as teachers, we mention Mrs. Nellie B. Sanderson, Miss Lottie Bowell, and the Misses Thorne.

At present the schools are well graded, with courses of study admirably arranged. Nine teachers and a superintendent are employed in the brick building, outside of which there are two primary schools. The school population of the district as ascertained by the enumeration of 1881 was 1,337.

The janitor of the school building, Mr. J. R. Davis, has taken faithful care of the school property for many years, and deserves honorable mention in this connection.

MERCANTILE.

Niles is well supplied with shops and stores. We have space to notice only a few of the principal firms and the dates at which their business was established.

Gephart & Co., Main street, dry goods.

S. A. Russell, Main street, grocer; began business May 1, 1881, in the store formerly occupied by Gephart & Co. He has a large and first-class stock of all articles in the grocery and provision line.

A. Ristedt, merchant tailor, Main street, 1881; successor to Radle & Ristedt. Large stock.

Mrs. O. S. Crandon, groceries and provisions, Lewis & Fear building, Main street; successor to James Crandon, who began this business in 1877.

George B. Robbins, dry goods and clothing, former banking room, Main street; fall of 1880.

E. C. Moore & Co., wholesale and retail dealers in flour and feed, Main street; fall of 1880.

Dalzell & Co., dry goods, clothing, groceries, etc., successors to J. M. Bowman & Co., corner of Main and Mill streets; established in November, 1874.

Cook & Co., drugs, notions, stationery, cigars, etc., Mason block, Mill street, 1878; successors to Moore & Blachly. Mr. Cook, the head of this firm, is an enterprising young man and his business is constantly increasing.

Young Brothers, grocers, Mason block, Mill street, 1878. The senior partner, Mr. S. D. Young, has been in the mercantile line in Niles since 1865.

C. W. Thomas, Mill street, 1877. Mr. Thomas began business opposite the post-office, Furnace street. He carries a large and well selected stock of books, stationery, toys, music, musical instruments, picture frames, etc., and his store is deservedly popular. He has occupied his present location since 1881.

Taylor Brothers, dealers in buggies, sleighs, sewing machines, stoves, tin and hardware, corner Furnace and Mill streets, 1876. The business was formerly conducted by R. G. Sykes, then by Sykes & Taylor, now by G. J. and T. N. Taylor.

Church & Coffee, Exchange block, Furnace street, 1880; successors to McConnell & Church, who began business in 1878. Church & Coffee run a large dry goods and grocery establishment, occupying two separate store rooms, each with its own corps of clerks. Their stock is extensive, and embraces everything usually found in a first-class store. They employ a larger number of clerks than any other mercantile house in town, and are doing a fine business.

C. W. Porter, drugs, school-books, stationery, lamps, cigars, and notions, Exchange block, Furnace street. Mr. Porter has a commodious store, well filled with a great variety of articles. He began business in 1875, with Dr. A. J. Leitch, under the firm name of Leitch & Porter. In October, 1879, Mr. Porter purchased Dr. Leitch's interest.

John C. Kerns, jeweler, Furnace street, 1873.

James Bowden, boots and shoes, Mill street, 1871.

C. W. Brieder, dealer in stoves, tin, and hardware, Furnace street, has been in business in Niles since 1874. He began in company with William C. Mann & Co., under the firm name of W. C. Mann & Co. W. C. Mann went out, and the firm then became Brieder & Co. This partnership was dissolved in 1878, since which time Mr. Brieder has conducted the business. In 1880 Mr. Brieder bought the hardware stock of John Dithridge, his former partner, and added it to his own. He is doing a large business in roofing, job work, etc.

We have mentioned some of the principal business houses. In addition to the above stores there are a large number of groceries and provision stores, and saloons innumerable. The commercial prosperity of Niles is advancing rapidly.

HOTELS.

Niles has two hotels at present, the Sanford and the Commercial. Both are overrun with business.

In 1868 L. W. Sanford purchased from Joseph McCaughtery the hotel known as the American house. Some five years later he changed its name to the Sanford house. He has made some improvements, and his hotel bears an excellent reputation. Connected with the house is a good livery-stable, Sanford & Pierce, proprietors.

The Commercial house has been in charge of E. R. Miller since April, 1880. This was formerly known as the Iron City house. Good livery attached.

BANKING.

Banking was begun in Niles, in 1869, by Wick, Bentley & Co. The firm was soon changed to Bentley & Crandon, and in 1871 was succeeded by the Citizens' Loan & Saving Association. The association continued to conduct the business until October, 1880, when it was succeeded by A. G. Bentley & Co. This firm do a large general banking business.

INDUSTRIES.

THE WARD ROLLING MILL.

This mill, one of the most extensive in the Mahoning valley, has played a prominent part in the history of Niles, and during its existence has brought both prosperity and disaster to the town.

The works were begun in 1841 by James Ward, Sr., and finished and put in operation in 1842. We have the statement made by a prominent citizen of Niles, whom we consider the very best of authority upon the subject, that the first rolled iron ever made in the Mahoning valley was produced in 1842 at this mill. This important fact should add another laurel to the memory of the enterprising spirit of the man whose business career was so long inseparably connected with the growth and development of this thrifty town. James Ward & Co. operated these works successfully from the time they were built until the death of their originator in 1864. In 1866 the works were rebuilt. Since then they have been much enlarged and the capacity greatly increased by the introduction of much costly machinery of the most improved patterns. James Ward & Co.—the James Ward being the son of the original proprietor—carried on the business successfully a number of years until the great financial panic came, when the firm failed and consequently nearly every business interest in Niles received a shock from which the recovery has been slow and painful. The mill is now running under the control of the Ward Iron company, and turning out larger and more valuable products than ever before. James Ward is the general manager. He is a man well fitted by nature and training for the important position.

The works comprise twenty puddling furnaces, six heating furnaces, and five trains of rolls. The products are bar, plate, and sheet iron, the annual capacity being about fourteen thousand net tons. Over two hundred men are employed in this rolling-mill, and the pay-roll amounts to about $15,000 per month.

THE RUSSIA SHEET IRON MILLS.

Mrs. L. B. Ward is the proprietor, and James Ward general manager of these works. The mill was built in 1864, but since that date many changes, repairs, and improvements have been made. The works consist of twelve puddling and four heating furnaces, and three trains of rolls. The products are sheet iron in widths from twenty to forty-nine inches, shingle bands, Sykes' improved metallic roofing, plate iron, etc. The annual capacity is about four thousand five hundred net tons. About two hundred and twenty men are employed and the pay-roll amounts to between $10,000 and $14,000 per month. This mill was formerly a part of the works of James Ward & Co.

THE ELIZABETH FURNACE.

This furnace was erected in 1859. It had one stack 65x14½ feet. After a few years its name was changed to the Mahoning Valley Iron company's works. It was removed from Niles to Youngstown some time ago.

THE THOMAS FURNACE.

This furnace was built in 1870 by William Ward & Co., and operated by them until 1875, when it passed into the hands of the trustees of the creditors of the original owners and remained out of blast until 1879. It was then purchased by John R. Thomas, who gave the plant a thorough repair, preparatory to putting in blast. Since that time the furnace has been in successful operation, turning out about one thousand tons of iron per month. The furnace is fifty-six feet high and fourteen feet at the boshes. The motive power consists of one blast engine and two large steam pumps for water supply—with two batteries of boilers of three large boilers each. The owners are at present placing another large, new blast engine to work in connection with the one now in operation, and making other important improvements in the plant.

GLOBE FOUNDRY AND MACHINE WORKS.

These works were built in 1858 by Thomas Carter and run by him until 1873. James Ward & Co. then managed the business for about two years. In 1875 John Carter took charge and has since been operating the works. He manufactures and deals in iron and brass castings, engines, pumps, and machinery, also Carter's patent ore pulverizer; and, in fact, makes and repairs all kinds of machinery used in coal banks, blast furnaces, etc. Employment is given to about fifty men on an average. The original buildings have been enlarged several times and at present a larger business than ever before is carried on.

NILES IRON WORKS.

In 1865 the project of building a rolling mill in Niles was conceived by William Davis, George Harris, and James Harris. They were joined by Corydon Beans and Thomas Jose, and on the 10th of August the works were completed and set in operation. After the company had been organized, A. M. Blackford, and subsequently James Russell, became members of it. Business was carried on under the firm name of Harris, Davis & Co. The mill cost $50,000. The works at first consisted of three boiling furnaces, three heating furnaces, one sheet mill, and one ten-inch train of rolls. While under the management of this firm, the capacity of the works was considerably enlarged. The product was six tons of sheet iron, or sixteen tons of sheet and bar iron per day. In 1870 Mr. Davis disposed of his interest, and the firm then became Harris, Blackford & Co. This firm failed and made an assignment. The works then came into the hands of C. H. Andrews & Co., who rebuilt and enlarged the mill in 1872. The works have since been run by the Niles Iron company, producing bar, sheet, rod, skelp and band iron, the annual capacity being twelve thousand net tons. L. G. Andrews is president of this company and L. E. Cochran secretary. The puddling department has been removed to Youngstown, and we understand that the remainder of the works will follow.

FALCON IRON AND NAIL WORKS.

These works were built in 1867, and then had twelve single puddling furnaces, three heating furnaces, forty-four nail machines, and three trains of rolls (one eight, one eighteen, and one twenty-one inch). The products are nails and guide-iron. The capacity was formerly eleven thousand tons annually, but has been increased. Two puddling furnaces are now building, and a new train of rolls has been put in. The officers of the original company were James Ward, superintendent, and J. Key Wilson, secretary and treasurer. In 1875 the company was reorganized. The present officers are John Stambaugh, president; Henry Wick, vice-president, and Myron I. Arms, secretary and treasurer. Two hundred hands are employed, and the pay roll amounts to about $12,000 per month. The products of the Falcon Iron and Nail company go to all parts of the country.

NILES BOILER WORKS.

These works, the only manufactory of the kind in Trumbull county, were built in 1871 by Jeremiah and George Reeves, who still continue to operate them. They manufacture all kinds of portable and stationary steam boilers, oil tanks, blast furnace stacks, and sheet-iron work.

They also deal in brass goods, pipes and fittings. The Reeves Brothers employ thirty-five men in their works, and sixty men in the States of New York and Pennsylvania, who set up work shipped from the factory. They have in progress the erection of additional works which will double the present capacity and necessitate a large increase in the number of workmen.

NILES FIRE-BRICK WORKS.

These works were built in 1872 by John R. Thomas, the present manager, and excepting about one year, have been in operation since that time. In 1876 Mr. Thomas invented a composition for fire-brick and obtained a patent upon it. Since then the improved bricks have been manufactured in large quantities and shipped to nearly all parts of the country where fire-brick is used. The manufacturers make a specialty of fire-brick of various shapes and sizes suitable for rolling-mills and blast furnaces.

The present capacity is between two and three thousand per day, but the owners expect to greatly increase the amount of brick manufactured at an early date. About fifteen men and boys are at present employed.

SAW-MILL AND PLANING-MILL.

In 1878 the Erwin Lumber company built a saw-mill 100 x 40 feet, with a planing-mill 60 x 50 feet. The mill was run one year by this company. The proprietors are now C. P. Souder and David Erwin,—firm name C. P. Souder & Co. The mills give employment to six men and manufacture all kinds of building lumber. These mills are near the New York, Pennsylvania & Ohio depot.

NEWSPAPERS.

The history of the press in Niles represents a career of numerous, though not unusual or unnatural, vicissitudes.

The first paper started in this place was the Niles Register, begun in the summer of 1867, by Edward Butler and E. E. Moore, publishers, and Rev. William Campbell, editor. It was of about the same size as the paper at present published here. After six months it was suspended on account of a lack of support.

In the spring of 1868 J. H. Fluhart began the publication of the Niles Independent, and ran it with varying success until June, 1871, when M. D. Sanderson succeeded him as editor and pro-

prietor. Mr. Sanderson and his immediate successors had all of the paper printed at home, and made it a very neat local journal. November 1, 1872, Fred C. McDonald assumed the management of the Independent, and at the end of one year sold out to Dyer & Sanderson. This firm changed the name of the paper to the Niles Home Record, and continued publication until November, 1874, when as a result of the panic and of the failure of the leading business of the village, they were compelled to suspend. Previous to the panic the paper attained a circulation of about nine hundred copies, and appeared to be on the road to prosperity. October 1, 1875, M. D. Sanderson revived the paper and brought it out as the Trumbull County Independent, a six-column quarto. He published but four numbers, then sold out to N. N. Bartlett, who continued to publish under the same name and in the same form. Soon after entering upon the management of the paper, Mr. Bartlett took J. H. Fluhart into partnership.

In May, 1876, the present proprietors, McCormick & Williams, bought the paper from Bartlett & Fluhart. The Independent is now a seven-column folio, well printed, and liberally patronized by business men as an advertising medium. It is independent in politics, and devotes the most of its space to local news and the encouragement of home industries. The proprietors are young men and bid fair to make the paper permanently prosperous. Under their management the circulation has largely increased.

NILES CHURCHES.

METHODIST CHURCH.

In 1814 a Methodist class was formed at the house of Ebenezer Roller, who lived where the village of Niles now stands, by Rev. Samuel Lane, a circuit preacher. It was a small class, but was soon enlarged, and from it the Niles Methodist Episcopal church has grown. From the fact that there are none of the early members of this church now living, we are able to give but little information as to the progress and growth of this church.

The churches, like everything else in Niles, felt the evil effects of the panic, but this church has been steadily gaining ground since good times returned. It is mainly supported by workingmen. The present membership is one

30*.

hundred and thirty. The church edifice now in use was erected in 1870. Though its exterior is unpretentious and devoid of any trace of beauty, the audience-room is tastefully furnished, large, and capacious.

PRESBYTERIAN CHURCH.

In 1838 application was made to the presbytery of Beaver by certain inhabitants of Weathersfield and vicinity for the action of that body to recognize them as a congregation, and to take measures for organizing a church to be known as Weathersfield church. After some initiatory steps in that presbytery, since by the division made by the synod of Pittsburg the petitioners resided within the presbytery of New Lisbon, the petition was committed to the latter presbytery and granted by it. The congregation was taken upon the rolls of the New Lisbon presbytery in 1839, and Rev. William O. Stratton was appointed to organize into a church so many among them as were members of sister churches at the time, or who wished to connect themselves with the church. The following persons were received at a regular appointed meeting at the brick school-house in Niles, as members in good and regular standing: Miller Blachly and Phebe, his wife, Eben Blachly, Anna Blachly, Robert Quigley, Catharine Reiter, Andrew Trew, Margaret Biggart, Elizabeth Biggart, Miller Blachly, Jr., and Mary, his wife, James McCombs and Elizabeth, his wife, and Eleanor Bell. Eben Blachly and Miller Blachly, Jr., were appointed to the office of ruling elders, and at the same time were ordained and installed. In February, 1842, William Dunlap, third, was ordained a ruling elder. This office has since been held by Ebenezer G. Stewart, George Campbell, William Ward, Robert Moffatt, Ephraim Thomas, J. C. Southard, and A. J. Leitch. Revs. Stratton, Kerr, Dickey, and others, including several stated supplies, acted as pastors until July 11, 1867, when Rev. T. Calvin Stewart was installed, and continued as pastor until 1876. During his pastorate seventy-one members were added on examination and forty-three by certificate. Rev. S. T. Street was pastor from 1877 to 1880, and Rev. A. A. Mealey in 1880–81. At the present writing there is a vacancy. The church numbers one hundred and fifty members, and has a commodious and well-furnished house of worship.

DISCIPLE CHURCH.

This church was organized in 1840 by Elder John Henry, an evangelist. The members at the time of organization were as follows: Elder Joshua Carle and his wife Margaret, Elder A. Jackson Luse and his wife Eleanor, Deacon Jacob Robinson and his wife Dorcia, Deacon Samuel Burnett and wife, Deacon Lewis Heaton and his wife Milly Ann, Nancy Carle, Mrs. Battles, Josiah Dunlap, Polly Dunlap, William Winfield, Seymour Hake, and others. Early members: Elihu and Rachel Draper, Benjamin and Louisa Goodheart, J. R. and Elizabeth Noble, John and Laura Draper, Stephen and Hannah Dunlap, Noble T. and Adeline Robbins, Polly Sheeler, Elizabeth St. John, Ambrose and Jemima Mason, Matilda L. Cleveland, Jerusha Stoddard, Hiram T. and Margaret C. Mason.

The church edifice was erected in 1843–44, and dedicated in 1844, with services conducted by Rev. John Henry. The ministers who have labored here are as follow: Revs. Hervey Brockett, John Henry, John T. Smith, John Applegate, William Winfield, William Higby, F. S. Whitzler, Theobald Miller, Thomas Hallock, Gideon Applegate, Walter Hayden, Mathias Christy, S. B. Teagarden, Orrin Gates, J. M. Monroe, W. H. Rogers, C. C. Smith, E. W. Wakefield, N. N. Bartlett, C. L. Morrison, and L. W. Shepherd, the present pastor. The present membership is over one hundred. The present church officers are: Elders, Benjamin Leach, Hiram T. Mason, and Lewis Reel; deacons, Hiram Ohl, George Battles, and Lewis N. Young.

PRIMITIVE METHODISTS.

The society of this name in Niles is the only one of the kind in the county. The doctrine is like that of the Methodist Episcopal church, but the method of the church government is different. The church was organized in 1873 by Rev. M. Harvey, its first pastor. In 1879 a neat little house of worship was erected in the neighborhood of the Russia mill. At present there are about thirty-one members, nearly all of whom are employed in the Russia Iron works. There is a Sunday-school of about eighty members, and nine teachers. The church property is valued at $1,100. Rev. Thomas Large is the pastor. His predecessors have been Revs. Harvey B. Whillock, J. A. James, John Mason, and Thomas James.

BAPTIST CHURCH.

This church was organized with a small number of members in 1868. A house of worship was erected in 1872–73. The first pastor was Rev. I. T. Griffith, who remained in charge but a short time. In 1874 Rev. D. C. Thomas took charge, and continued as pastor three years. He then went to Nebraska for one year. Then returned and resumed the pastorate, and still remains in charge. The membership is twenty-eight, and is made up of mill employes.

CATHOLIC CHURCH.

St. Stephen's Roman Catholic church was formed by Rev. E. M. O'Callahan of Youngstown, by whom the building was erected. Rev. J. Kulhn succeeded him for a short time. Then Rev. A. R. Sidley, who remained two years. The priests who have since had charge of this church, named in the order of their succession, are as follows: Rev. E. Conway, B. B. Kelly, T. Mahony, M. A. Scanlon, and the present pastor, J. Monahan. The church embraces about one hundred families at present. Connected with it are three schools conducted by four of the sisters of the Humility of Mary, of New Bedford, Pennsylvania.

WELSH PRESBYTERIAN CHURCH.

This church, known also as the Calvinistic Methodist, has a neat little church edifice, erected in 1872 at a cost of about $6,000. The church had been organized previous to this date, and had held meetings in the building of the Cumberland Presbyterians—a society which is now extinct. In 1872 there were about sixty members of the Welsh Presbyterian, and the number at present is about the same, though there were one hundred and fifty a short time before the panic. The first pastor was Rev. John Moses, succeeded by Rev. T. C. Davis, of Pittsburg, and Rev. Ebenezer Evans, the present minister. The deacons are D. H. Davis and Reese Davis.

SECRET SOCIETIES.

MASONIC.

Mahoning lodge No. 394, Free and Accepted Masons, was granted a charter June 22, 1867. Previously, however, T. C. Van Antwerp, of Leavittsburg, had held a school of instruction, drilling the proposed members in the precepts of the Masonic order; and for six months previous to the receipt of the charter the lodge had been working under a dispensation from the Grand lodge. There were sixteen charter members, viz: James C. Southard, S. D. Young, I. M. Butler, Josiah Robbins, Jr., George Harris, William Davis, E. J. Warner, H. B. Gilman, T. B. Tait, Thomas James, S. A. Corbin, J. G. Butler, Jr., Evan Davis, J. R. Noble, James Crandon, Lewis Gebhart.

The first officers were J. C. Southard, W. M.; Josiah Robbins, Jr., S. W.; and William Davis, J. W. One hundred and twenty have been admitted to membership since the charter was granted. The present membership is sixty-six. The lodge occupies a neat and convenient hall, comfortably and tastefully furnished, and is in every way prosperous.

Present officers: S. D. Young, W. M.; C. W. Talbitzer, S. W.; L. W. Sanford, J. W.; J. K. Wilson, treasurer: L. S. Cole, secretary; William Farr, S. D.; George Reeves, J. D.; William Templeman, tyler.

ODD FELLOWS.

Falcon lodge No. 436, Independent Order of Odd Fellows, was instituted in January, 1870, with the following charter members: F. Caspar, H. Scott, J. K. Wilson, John McElroy, A. D. Ferguson, and J. L. Wills. The first officers were Ed. Scott, N. G.; F. Caspar, V. G.; J. K. Wilson, secretary; Lewis Gephart, permanent secretary, and Samuel Evans, treasurer. Over one hundred and fifty have been admitted to membership in this lodge. In August, 1871, a number of members withdrew and started a lodge at Mineral Ridge. The present membership of the Falcon lodge is about seventy. In 1881 the lodge purchased the building in which the meetings are held. The lodge is prosperous financially, owing no bills, and with money in the treasury.

THE FORESTERS.

Court Providence lodge No. 5782, Ancient Order of Foresters, was instituted at Niles December 28, 1862, with fifty charter members and the following named officers: Daniel Fisher, C. R.; Evan S. Williams, S. C. R.; George S. Williams, treasurer, and John Meredith, secretary. The lodge has a good membership and is prosperous.

MINERAL RIDGE.

This place is appropriately named. Extensive coal deposits are found in the vicinity and near the village some of the principal mines of the Mahoning valley are located. The blackband iron ore, whose use during recent years has rendered the iron products of the valley justly famous, is found underlying the coal in strata varying from one to ten inches in thickness. Thirty years ago Mineral Ridge was a farming community. But after the mines began to be largely developed, and especially since the advent of the railroad in 1869, the population increased rapidly. During the panic there was a temporary check, but the ground lost was speedily recovered. Mineral Ridge is now an incorporated village of some twelve hundred inhabitants, as well as several hundred who reside just outside of the corporation limits. It is situated on the south line of Weathersfield township, and the unincorporated portion of the village extends over the county line into Austintown township. The main street is something like a mile and a half in length, but is not thickly lined with houses. There are two fine brick buildings in the village—the Odd Fellows' block and the public school. Six churches indicate that the moral atmosphere of the place ought to be pure.

Mineral Ridge is situated immediately south of Niles, and from the latter place is the first station on the Niles & New Lisbon railroad. Main street runs along the ridge of land which gives the village its name.

INCORPORATION.

Mineral Ridge became an incorporated village in 1871. Joseph Stuart was the first mayor elected, and he has been continued in office up to the present time.

COAL AND IRON.

The first coal was mined at Mineral Ridge in 1835, the mine being situated on Coal run, on the south side of the village, on the farm of Michael Ohl, in Austintown township. In 1833 Roger Hill, a Pennsylvania coal miner, moved to Mineral Ridge. He showed Mr. Ohl the coal exposed in the run, and advised him to open a mine. Two years later Mr. Hill commenced work for Mr. Ohl, and drifting into a hill, found a seam of coal four feet in thickness. He selected a smooth, square and heavy piece, and carried it home to test its quality. The piece would not burn, and Hill pronounced it bastard cannel coal, or blackstone. Other parts of the seam proved to be of good quality, and the blackstone was left unworked, forming the floor of the mine. The coal found a ready sale for blacksmithing and household use.

John Lewis, a miner, originally from Monmouthshire, England, had settled at Mineral Ridge in 1854. One day while sinking a hole in the floor of his working place to set up a prop he was struck with the similarity of the "blackstone" to the blackband ore he had mined in the old country. He stated to Messrs. Ward & Co., his employers, his opinion of the coal floor,—that it was a valuable deposit of blackband ore. He was directed to mine and calcine a quantity of it. The results proved the correctness of the miner's knowledge. All the old coal openings were now re-opened and searched for the blackband, and it was lifted in every working place, old and new.

It was not until 1868, however, that the real value of the ore was fully appreciated. The art of calcining and using it prudently in connection with the lake ores, in the blast furnace, was not well understood. Since that time, however, the iron made from a judicious mixture of the blackband of the Mahoning valley has taken a front rank in the markets of the United States and is everywhere known and prized as " American Scotch."

The first coal shipped from Mineral Ridge to Cleveland was shipped in 1857 from the mines of Rice, French, Cook & Co. The coal of this region has always maintained a good reputation, and is especially adapted for rolling-mill purposes, and the generation of steam as well as for house fuel.*

The blackband ore continues to be mined along with the coal, and is a most valuable product. Its principal use is in foundry iron, which it renders of a superior quality.

The Cambria mine was opened in 1850 by Morris & Price. The Peacock mine was opened in 1853 by Rice, French, Cook & Co. The John Morris & Co. shaft was opened in 1856 by Tod, Wells & Co. The Ashland mine was opened the same year by Jonathan Warner.

* Condensed from the report of the State inspector of mines.

The principal mines now in operation at Mineral Ridge are as follow: Austin shaft, Tod, Wells & Co.; Cambria, W. T. Williams & Co.; Weathersfield; Osborn slope, Osborn Coal Co.; Peacock, W. I. Metcalf.

MERCHANTS.

The first store at Mineral Ridge was opened by James Ward & Co., to supply men who were working their coal-bank. It was kept by E. Smith, on the lot now owned by Jonathan Warner. The first store excepting this company store was opened in 1862 by J. L. Pierce, who continued in business about six years. He has been railroad station agent at this place since the road was opened to the public.

Below we give the names of the principal merchants who are now doing business in the village, and also the date at which they commenced:

General stores: Joseph Stuart, 1863; Daniel Wilcox, formerly in partnership with Ira and Isaac Wilcox, 1864; C. F. Whitney, 1876; McConnell Brothers, 1878; J. B. Lewis, 1878; E. M. Morgan, 1878; C. D. James, 1879; A. J. Garry, successor to Spill & Son, 1880. Hardware dealers: W. & W. H. Johnson, 1869. Undertaker: M. E. Burford, 1872. Dealer in drugs, medicines, notions, etc.: E. J. Ohl, successor to S. C. Wilson, 1876. McConnell Brothers have the largest and best filled store in the village. They occupy both of the large store-rooms in the Independent Order of Odd Fellows block, and have a large and complete stock of dry goods, groceries and provisions, boots and shoes, etc. Messrs. E. J. Ohl and J. B. Lewis also have good assortments of all articles in their respective lines.

In addition to the above, there are several saloons and a few small stores. Mineral Ridge merchants appear to be prosperous.

PHYSICIAN.

One physician, Dr. L. A. Bard, attends to the wants of the sick and afflicted.

MINERAL RIDGE FLOURING MILL.

This mill is now owned by W. I. Metcalf. It was built in 1873 by Dunlap, Ohl & Co. A large amount of custom milling is done here, and flour and feed are shipped and kept on hand for sale. A mill upon the same site was moved to this place from Canfield, and after being operated several years, was destroyed by fire.

MINERAL RIDGE FURNACES.

In 1858-59 Jonathan Warner, in company with Captain James Wood of Pittsburg, erected the first furnace at this place, called the Ashland furnace, for using the Mineral Ridge coal and blackband ore for the manufacture of pig-iron. This furnace was run quite successfully. In June, 1862, Mr. Warner bought of Captain Wood his interest, and in 1863 or 1864 bought the Porter or Meander furnace in Austintown and moved it here. Early in 1866 a company was formed and incorporated under the name of the Mineral Ridge Iron and Coal company. The stockholders were Milton Sutliff of Warren, Lemuel Wick of Cleveland, Joseph H. Brown of Youngstown, and Jonathan Warner of Mineral Ridge. Mr. Warner was made manager and general agent, and held the position until July or August, 1868, when the company sold out to William H. Brown of Pittsburg, who afterwards formed a new company known as the Brown Iron company. In 1870 the furnaces passed into the hands of James Ward and wife of Niles, from whom in 1871 they were re-purchased by Mr. Warner, and run until after the failure of Cooke in 1873, and up to 1874 or 1875, when Mr. Warner and those in interest with him were obliged to stop business and take advantage of the bankrupt law. Since then these furnaces have been sold and torn down and are now numbered with the things that are no more.

ODD FELLOWS.

Mineral Ridge lodge No. 497, Independent Order of Odd Fellows, was instituted August 23, 1871, by Horace F. Beebe, D. G. M., of Ravenna. The following are the names of the charter members: J. Jones, J. B. Lewis, Eli J. Ohl, R. Lloyd, Ed. Foulk, James Matthias, James Morris, William Jones, Thomas J. Roberts (deceased), John Miles (deceased), John Elias, E. G. Ohl, Robert Roberts, W. J. Williams, and Thomas T. Jones. The first officers were J. Jones, N. G.; J. B. Lewis, V. G.; E. J. Ohl, P. S.; and R. Lloyd, C. S. The number of members admitted since the lodge was formed has been two hundred and twenty-eight. The present membership is one hundred and forty. In 1874 this lodge built the fine large brick block now known as the I. O. O. F. block, at a cost of $16,500. The building is fifty-four feet high, three stories, and 40 x 70 feet on the ground. The first floor is fitted for two large store-rooms; the second contains a public hall with good scenery, a stage and five hundred and eight chairs. The third story is all occupied by the lodge rooms. There is ample room and a good hall 40 x 50 feet. The lodge is now very prosperous.

FIRST PRESBYTERIAN CHURCH.

About 1858 a few of the inhabitants of this place formed a Sabbath-school, and held prayer-meetings in the district school-house. Both were well attended and considerable interest was aroused. In September, 1862, Rev. J. H. Scott was invited to come here and preach; he accepted and became the instrument of much good. From the school-house the band of worshipers changed the place of holding their meetings to a building temporarily fitted up for the purpose. January 11, 1863, a church of eleven members was formally organized by the committee of Trumbull presbytery, consisting of Revs. W. C. Clark, S. B. Wilson, A. Cone, and H. L. Hitchcock, D.D., of the Western Reserve college. Dr. Hitchcock preached a sermon on this occasion, taking for his text Phillipians II: 14-15. The following persons were received into the new organization: By letter—Mrs. Ellen E. Scott, from the First Presbyterian church of West Liberty, Iowa; Miss Mary A. Brook, from the Presbyterian church of Niles, Ohio; Mrs. Lucy A. Prevost, from the Methodist Episcopal church of Minersville, Pennsylvania; George Otterman, from the Methodist Episcopal church of Girard, Ohio; Charles H. Jackson, Jonathan Warner, and Mrs. Eliza Warner, from the Presbyterian church of Youngstown; and by profession, Alexander Brown, Maria Lewis, Harriet E. Scott, and Mary A. Clark. After organizing, the church proceeded to elect an elder; Mr. Jonathan Warner, formerly an elder in the Youngstown church, was elected to the office and has since held it.

Early in 1863 preparations for the erection of a church edifice began. Friends in adjoining towns subscribed what they could, and a little help was received from Youngstown and Cleveland. Mr. Jonathan Warner did far more than any other person towards completing the struct-

ure; indeed it may be said that his liberal giving and encouragement started the project and carried it successfully through. The house completed, the church was between $1,400 and $1,800 in debt. It is one of the finest houses for a village of the size of Mineral Ridge to be found in this section of the State. On January 26, 1865, the church was dedicated to the service of God and the new pastor, Rev. B. F. Sharp, was installed over the congregation which then numbered over one hundred persons. At this time a collection was taken up and new subscriptions made, sufficient in amount to wipe out the entire church debt. A parsonage has since been built and the church still remains debt free. The pastors, since Mr. Sharp left, have been Revs. Williams, Dalzell, Graham, and the present pastor, Rev. J. M. Mercer, who has labored here since 1878. Rev. Mr. Scott and Rev. Dalzell, left their charge on account of ill health, and together with Mr. Williams they have since gone home to their rewards.

Several interesting revivals have blessed the labors of the different pastors. Especially was this true of the pastorate of Rev. J. J. Graham. As many as sixty-three persons were added to the church during one of these interesting seasons.

The church is and has been in a flourishing condition. A pastor is sustained and employed for all his time. At present about one-half of the members come from the surrounding country; hence the church is more certain of a prosperous condition in the future than if it depended for its support upon the population of Mineral Ridge alone, as, in a mining town, many are constantly going and coming. The present membership is considerably more than one hundred, notwithstanding numerous removals and a large number of deaths of members. In the donations to the boards of the Presbyterian church of the Mahoning presbytery, this church ranks as the eleventh, and it is proposed to make this record even better in the future. For these facts we are indebted to Mr. Warner and the pastor.

METHODIST EPISCOPAL CHURCH.

This church was organized in 1867, with three members, but was soon increased by the addition of thirty or forty names to the books. In 1868 a house of worship was erected and dedicated by Bishop Kingsley, December 23d. From the books we learn that the society was clear of debt at that time. The house is neat and comfortable, well furnished, both in the main room and basement. A church parlor is one of the improvements recently made—cost $300.

The first members of this church were W. T. Williams and wife, Mrs. Mary Hartman, Edwin Warner and wife, Joseph and Mary Clark, George and Mary Greenville, Jonathan Hofius, David Jones, John and William Browning, and others. The first pastor was Rev. R. M. Bear, under whose labors the church was organized. After the house was built Rev. Manasseh Miller was sent to this circuit, which comprised Ohltown and Mineral Ridge. A glorious revival resulted from his work. Revs. E. H. Prosser, T. B. Tait, and James Shields succeeded him. In 1876 Mineral Ridge was transferred to the Jackson circuit, and Revs. George Crooks and John Beethan sent to labor here. In September, 1880, this was made a station, and Rev. C. E. Locke, the present pastor, appointed. The number of members is ninety. An interesting Sabbath-school numbers one hundred and sixty. The society is out of debt, and every way prosperous.

DISCIPLES CHURCH.

This church was organized with twenty members on the 2d day of January, 1870, in the old school-house. They continued to meet in the school-house for public worship until September, 1872. The church edifice was erected in the fall of that year, at a cost, including the lot, of $3,000. It was dedicated September 29, 1872. The first church officers were: J. L. Pearce and L. L. Campbell, elders; John Crum and Evan Owens, deacons. The first pastor was Elder J. M. Van Horn. His successors have been J. S. Ross, R. T. Davis, D. J. White, N. N. Bartlett, and George Musson. The number of members is now one hundred and ten.

CATHOLIC CHURCH.

This church was organized and the house erected about the year 1871. The membership is quite large. The priest who officiates here also has charge of the East Palestine and Salem churches.

WELSH CHURCHES.

The Welsh of this township seem to take a great interest in religion, and have a church wherever there is a sufficient number to support it.

The Welsh Baptist church at Mineral Ridge was built in 1858, and is a comfortable building, of ample size for the accommodation of its members.

The Welsh Independent church was built soon after the Baptist. At present it has a good sized congregation and is prosperous. The house has recently been enlarged.

MINERAL RIDGE SCHOOLS.

In 1870 Jonathan Warner and L. L. Campbell called a school meeting and steps were taken to form a union district in this village. In December of that year a vote was taken which resulted in the formation of such a district. Before that time Mineral Ridge had only a common district school system.

In 1872 an elegant school building was erected 62x62 feet on the ground, built of brick, two stories, with a basement for heaters and rooms for the scholars to occupy during the noon intermissions. There are four school-rooms, two recitation rooms, and halls above and below. The lot upon which the house stands is over two acres in extent. The site, building, and furniture together cost about $18,500.

In 1873-74 H. B. Clark was principal of the school. Mr. L. L. Campbell took charge in the summer of 1874, and continued as superintendent until March, 1881. Through his efforts the schools were all properly graded and put in efficient working order. Much credit is due to him for his untiring and generous labor for the good of the school. It was with the regrets of every patron of the school that he resigned his position. Mr. B. A. Bowe is the present superintendent.

Upon an average from fifteen to twenty pupils from outside the district attend the high school. The rates of tuition are $1.25 per month for high school scholars, and $1 per month for intermediate.

OHLTOWN.

This is a quiet little village in the southwestern part of the township, a mile and a half west of Mineral Ridge. It was laid out by Michael Ohl, its first settler. There are some thirty houses, two small stores, kept by T. J. Moore and J. A. Rumsey, a blacksmith's shop, and the grist-mill of Flick Brothers.

Michael Ohl built a grist-mill and a saw-mill in this place soon after settling here in 1815. The mill was a small affair, and had but one run of stones at first, but another was afterwards put in. The grist-mill was torn down and a new one erected upon its site. The second mill was burned. The mill now standing was built by Mr. Ohl in 1843 or 1844.

Michael Ohl kept the first store in the place, in a part of his house. He also built an oil mill, which was abandoned after a few years, as the business was found not to be a paying one.

OHLTOWN METHODIST EPISCOPAL CHURCH.

The following facts were obtained from Father Joseph Turner, now deceased, and recorded upon the church book :

The first class was formed about the year 1838, consisting of fifteen members, Joseph Turner being class leader. Of this number but two survive, viz : Rachel Turner and Ellen Patrick. Ohltown was made an appointment of Liberty circuit, and the following preachers were sent to labor here :

Hiram Norris, Ditton Prosser, Stephen Hubbard, Hiram Kellogg, Thomas Guy, Ahab Keller, Nelson Brown, George Brown, A. Reeves, J. H. Vance, W. N. Reno, W. F. Day, Albert Norton, Stephen Heard, J. W. Hill, R. M. Bear, Ezra Wade, Frederick Vernon, William Hayes, J. H. Vance, up to and including 1866.

In 1867 the circuit was divided, and Mineral Ridge and Ohltown formed a circuit. The same preachers labored at both places until 1880, when Ohltown was added to the Jackson circuit. J. J. Excell and G. W. Anderson have been the appointees since that date. The society has a comfortable house and a membership of about sixty.

OTHER CHURCHES.

The German Reformed people formerly had a church in this place, but their organization continued but a few years. They built a house about 1845, which they afterwards sold to the Methodists.

The German Reformed congregation was converted into an organization of the Cumberland Presbyterians, under the labors of Dr. A. M. Blackford. After a brief existence this organization also died out.

The regular Presbyterians also had a church in this place, and built a house about 1845. Rev. Koons was the first preacher and was succeeded by Revs. March and Spear, pastors, besides several supplies. They sold their house to a body of Primitive Methodists, who kept up a church for three or four years.

OHLTOWN SELECT SCHOOL.

This school was started about 1857, principally through the efforts of Michael Ohl, Jr. Almon McCorkle was the first teacher. The school was in existence a few years only. It was kept in the old Methodist church.

WEATHERSFIELD.

This is a little mining community in the southeastern part of the township, containing some twenty or thirty houses, the most of them very dilapidated in appearance. The first coal bank here was operated some thirty-eight years ago. Mining was carried on, on a small scale, for several years; but about fifteen or twenty years ago banks were opened and operated largely, one hundred and seventy-five or more men being employed in them. But the banks were soon worked out—that is, the principal ones, and now less than half of that number find employment here. The place has neither store or post-office.

WEATHERSFIELD CHURCHES.

There are two Welsh churches here. The Welsh Baptist church was built in 1866. Meetings have been kept up regularly ever since. Rev. Edward Jenkins was the first pastor and Rev. John James is at present in charge. The membership is small. A tasteful little cemetery is situated near the church.

The Welsh Calvinistic Methodist church was organized previous to 1867 and a house was built at that date. Rev. T. C. Davis was the first pastor. Meetings have been held ever since the organization, though not always at regular intervals. The church now numbers about sixty members. Rev. J. L. Jeffreys is the pastor.

BIOGRAPHICAL SKETCHES.

JAMES WARD.

It is but proper that a sketch of the life of the man to whom more than any other the industrial development of Niles is due should be included in this work. The following sketch was published in a book containing an account of the principal manufactures and manufacturers of Ohio:

James Ward was born November 25, 1813, near Dudley, Staffordshire, England. When four years old he came with his parents to Pittsburg, where he received an ordinary school education which concluded when he was thirteen years of age. He then began work in earnest, aiding his father in the manufacture of wrought iron nails. This he continued until he was nineteen, when he commenced to learn engineering and remained engaged in that business until 1841. In 1843 he moved to Niles and was connected with the rolling-mill business of James Ward & Co., continuing the same until his death, July 24, 1864.

James Ward was looked upon by business men, even when a boy, as possessing all the elements suitable for the avocation he pursued, and many predicted that in time he would attain the first rank in his business and stand at its head. This prophecy was abundantly fulfilled.

Mr. Ward was married in 1835 at Pittsburg, to Miss Eliza Dithridge, of that place, daughter of William and Elizabeth Dithridge. The issue of this marriage was seven children, all of whom are dead except James Ward, Jr. Mr. Ward is supposed to have been the first man to practically use pig iron made from raw coal, also the first to practically utilize the blackband ore of this region. The furnace built by him in 1859 was operated a number of years.

He left a name known not only in his immediate vicinity, but as wide-spread as the country, an honorable and liberal man, endowed with great enterprise and business capacity, and was cut down while yet in his prime. He had garnered wealth and reputation without creating the envy which so usually accompanies these possessions. He won golden opinions from all, and there are none who knew him who do not respect his memory and appreciate his character.

31*]

SETTLEMENT NOTES.

John McConnell (deceased) was born in Washington county, Pennsylvania, April 3, 1778. February 25, 1802, he married Miss Nancy Travis, and had a family of five sons and five daughters—Alexander, born April 5, 1803; John, born September 3, 1804; Polly, January 8, 1806; Rebecca, October 19, 1807; Peggy, April 2, 1809; Matthew, November 26, 1810; Elizabeth, August 17, 1812; James, June 6, 1814; William C., February 2, 1816; Martha J., January 24, 1818. John, Rebecca, Peggy, Matthew, and Martha J. are deceased. Mr. McConnell, with his family, consisting then of his wife and oldest son, came to Trumbull county, Ohio, in 1804, settling in Weathersfield township. He erected a log-cabin in the woods, building it one day and moving into it the next. He resided there until his death, which took place September 27, 1853. His wife died February 26, 1841, and he was married again to Mrs. Lovinia Rice, who lived until January 17, 1881, reaching within less than a month the great age of one hundred and three years. The old homestead is now occupied by William C. McConnell. He has been married three times. His first wife was Harriet McCombs, by whom he had six children—Sally, Olive, John T., William J., Charlie, Kittie H. After twenty-five years of married life his wife died. He married for his second wife Miss Sarah J. Simpson. By this marriage he had one son, Clyde W. The mother died December 26, 1867, and he again married Mrs. Eusebia Campbell, widow of Calvin S. Campbell. She had one son by her former husband, George C.

Josiah Robbins was born in Youngstown, Mahoning county, Ohio, August 21, 1802, son of Josiah and Elizabeth (Newport) Robbins. Josiah Robbins, Sr., settled in Youngstown township in 1799, on the place now owned by James Smith, which he cleared up and on which he lived until 1850. He was for many years a justice of the peace and was a member of the Swedenborgian church. He raised a family of four sons and four daughters, of whom but two are living: Mrs. Matilda Cleveland, of Niles, and Mrs. Eliza Heaton, of Illinois. He died in 1855. Josiah, Jr., married in 1827 Maria, daughter of James Heaton. She was born in 1806. To that marriage were born four sons, three of whom are living. Mrs. Robbins died in 1835, and in 1836

Mr. Robbins married Electa, daughter of Judge Ambrose Mason. She was born in Moriah, Essex county, New York, January 28, 1815. By this marriage there were born two sons and one daughter, all of whom are living. Josiah Robbins, Jr., settled on the Heaton homestead, now occupied by William B. Mason, in 1827. He was engaged in the furnace business in connection with his brother-in-law, Warren Heaton, for ten or twelve years, until 1843, when he was elected to the State Legislature for one term. He took an active part in the cause of temperance and was a strong and influential anti-slavery man. His home was frequently visited by that able and stalwart abolitionist, Joshua R. Giddings, and furnished a refuge for fugitives from slavery. He was engaged for many years in the lumber trade. He was also engaged in farming, owning four hundred acres, upon which the greater part of Niles is situated. In company with a son and a Mr. Lawson, he erected a flouring mill at Princeton, Illinois, in 1854, and one also in Chicago. During the latter part of his life he was engaged in market-gardening, which he followed merely as a pastime. He did much for the improvement of Niles, building many of the principal buildings there, including the post-office. He was postmaster for eleven years, holding the position at the time of his death, which occurred December 11, 1873, at the age of seventy-one years, four months, and twenty days.

The Dunlap family, of which William Dunlap, Sr., was the first representative in Trumbull county, were among the earliest settlers here. William Dunlap, Sr., emigrated from Washington county, Pennsylvania, to Poland township, then Trumbull county, Ohio, about 1800. He afterwards purchased seven hundred acres of land in Weathersfield, and moved to that township about 1806. His sons settled around him on this tract. He had a family of six sons and four daughters. He died in Liberty township at the residence of his daughter, Mrs. Carlton, at the age of about ninety-six. His son William married Rachel Frazee, of Poland, and lived on the farm, which is now occupied by the widow of the late Stephen Dunlap, son of William, Jr. William and Rachel Dunlap were the parents of nine children, of whom three are yet living, to-wit: Rachel (Lewis) and Perry in Lordstown, and

Chauncy in Vienna. Stephen Dunlap was born November 30, 1813, in Weathersfield, on the farm, where he lived until his death December 18, 1881. He married in 1840 Hannah McMullen, of Brookfield, who was born in 1822. Mrs. Dunlap still resides on the old Dunlap homestead. She has three children, as follows: George in Wisconsin, B. F. in New York city, and Emma at home.

Benjamin B. Robbins was born in Youngstown, Ohio, December 11, 1830. He was the eldest of three sons of N. T. Robbins, who settled on what is still the family homestead, in 1834. The two younger sons are still living, T. N. in Niles, and J. D. in Cleveland. B. B. Robbins was united in marriage September 29, 1853, to Miss A. E. Carle, daughter of Joshua and Margaret (Oliver) Carle, who was born in Smithfield, Jefferson county, Ohio, on the 1st of March, 1834. After their marriage they settled on the place where the family still reside. Mr. Robbins was a farmer by occupation and a successful and prosperous man. He was noted for his benevolence and generosity. He died November 21, 1881. He was the father of five sons and two daughters, six of whom are living: George B., born September 2, 1854, a merchant of Niles; Noble T., February 22, 1856, a graduate of the Albany, New York, law school; Frank C., May 30, 1858, in trade with his brother George; Henry J., February 17, 1862, on the home place; Maggie N., January 30, 1865; Ollie E., April 17, 1868.

Abram Van Wye (deceased) was born in Washington county, Pennsylvania, in 1797. In 1819 he married Charity Laird and had a family of twelve children, as follows: Charles, John, Lydia, Mary, Nancy, Catharine, Amanda, William, Joseph W., Darthula W., Almyra S., and Sabina H., of whom six are living. In the spring of 1834 he emigrated to Ohio and settled in Weathersfield township, Trumbull county. His original purchase comprised one hundred and fifty acres of land, but at the time of his death he owned four hundred acres. He was well and favorably known throughout this region. He died May 2, 1854, his wife surviving him about ten years. Charles, the oldest son, who owns the family homestead, was born March 28, 1820; married Miss Katie Draper, and has had ten children — Abram, Elihu, William,

George, Charles, Alice May, John, Kit, and two unnamed, dying in infancy. His first wife died in 1873, and he afterwards married Rebecca Caldwell (her maiden name). No children by this marriage. Joseph W., the fourth son, was born on the old homestead in Weathersfield, April 16, 1837. In 1877 he married Alla Troxel and has had one daughter—Almyra. Mrs. Van Wye had been previously married and had one son—Freddie. He purchased the farm on which he now lives in 1872. He was in the war of secession three months as member of company B, Eighty-fourth Ohio volunteer infantry. Abram Van Wye was born in Weathersfield township, November 19, 1845. He was in the service of his country during the war of the Rebellion, a member of company C, Nineteenth Ohio veteran volunteer infantry, and participated in a number of severe engagements, among them the battles of Kenesaw Mountain, Peach Tree Creek, Atlanta, etc., but came through without a scar, and returned to peaceful pursuits. Mr. Van Wye married Sarah Leach. They have three children, all living—Warren, Frank, and Anna. William Van Wye was born upon the homestead farm July 7, 1850. He has always followed farming, and now resides upon a portion of the old homestead. In October, 1873, he married Maria E. Bolin, by whom he has one child—Lizzie Bolin Van Wye.

Jonathan Warner was born in Sodus, Wayne county, New York, February 10, 1808. When fifteen or sixteen years of age he went to Oswego, where he was employed as a clerk in a store. He afterwards returned to Sodus and engaged in mercantile business. He was married November 22, 1829, to Eliza Landon, who was born in Oneida county, New York, April 6, 1810. Mr. Warner continued in business in Sodus until about the year 1843, when he removed to Youngstown, Ohio, where he carried on the same business many years. He afterwards engaged in the iron business, and with Mr. Philpott built the first furnace at Brier Hill in that section, and operated there some two years. A short time previous to the war of 1861–65 he removed to Mineral Ridge, where he has since resided. He had acquired large coal and iron interests at Mineral Ridge, built two blast furnaces, and afterwards carried on an extensive business there many years. He finally sold his furnaces for a large figure, taking in part payment several thousand acres undeveloped mineral lands in the Lake Superior region. He organized the Republic Iron company, of Marquette, Michigan, of which he was president several years, and in which he is still a stockholder. Mr. Warner was the first to discover the unprecedented richness of the mine originally called Smith Mountain, and inaugurated the movement for its development. In 1872 he bought back his furnace at Mineral Ridge. The panic came the next year, and proved disastrous to his business, and he was compelled to make an assignment. He subsequently went to North Carolina and leased a gold mine, which proved unremunerative, and after remaining there a couple of years he returned to Mineral Ridge, where he has since led a substantially retired life. Mr. Warner's career has been one of great activity, and he has done much for the material development of the region in which he has lived. He has also been a generous donor to moral and religious enterprises. Mr. and Mrs. Warner are the parents of five children, who are all living, as follows: Mrs. Myron I. Arms, of Youngstown; Edwin J. and Jacob B., of Denver, Colorado; Charles M. and William H., of Mineral Ridge.

Isaac Marshall was among the early settlers of Weathersfield township, where he purchased fifty-four acres of land. He was born in 1785 and 1808 married Jane Megee, who was born in 1784. They had a family of four boys and five girls, as follows: John, Benjamin, Huston, Miles, Sally, Betsey, Jane, Mary, and Lucinda. Isaac Marshall died March, 1858, and his wife September, 1868. He was drafted in the War of 1812 for three months.

John Marshall was born March 14, 1810; married in March, 1836, Mary A. Nelson, born October 5, 1813. Their children were John Calvin, a son who died in infancy, Margaret Jane, Sarah Samantha (deceased), Electa Ann, and Linus Ida. John Marshall attended the pioneer schools of Weathersfield. The building was of the rudest kind. It was built of round logs daubed with mortar; the floors were laid down loose, a fire-place on one side, split logs for benches, boards fastened onto pins driven into the walls for writing desks, and windows of greased paper. Such is a brief description of the earliest school-houses, and all the schooling he ever got was obtained in such a house. There was no church building in his township until as late as 1833.

George McCartney, oldest son of Andrew and Eleanor (Wilson) McCartney, was born in Liberty township, Trumbull county, Ohio, September 7, 1811. His father was a native of Indiana county, Pennsylvania; came to Ohio first about 1806. He was then a single man, and tended saw-mill at Mill creek for Judge Baldwin. He married Eleanor, daughter of James Wilson, of Youngstown township, and settled within one mile of where Girard now is. James Wilson, the father of Mrs. McCartney, was one of the earliest pioneers of Youngstown township. He was a Revolutionary soldier, serving during the entire war. About three years after his marriage Andrew McCartney removed with his family to Indiana county, Pennsylvania, and occupied the old homestead nineteen years. He then returned to Trumbull county and bought a gristmill at Girard, and afterwards built a saw-mill, fulling-mill, and carding machine, which he operated for many years. He was made justice of the peace in Liberty township and served nine years. He died March 30, 1858, in the seventy-fifth year of his age. His wife survived him about ten years. They had six sons and two daughters. George McCartney obtained his schooling in the log school-house of those days. He was brought up to milling and tended his father's mills until the building of the Pennsylvania & Ohio canal necessitated the abandonment of the grist-mill. He married first, March 22, 1836, Mary Eckman, and continued to live at Girard. His wife died October 9, 1847, leaving two daughters and one son—Elizabeth, wife of Jacob Stambaugh, Eleanor, wife of John Rush, of Girard, and Andrew J. McCartney, of Youngstown. May 25, 1848, Mr. McCartney married Mrs. Mary Ann Brooks, who died December 10, 1851. He was married a third time to Elizabeth Osborn, of Youngstown township, born in 1815, who is still living. By this marriage one daughter was born—Mary L., now wife of Calvin Marshall. About 1839 Mr. McCartney located on the farm where he now lives. There was then but three acres cleared and a small log cabin on the place. He has lived to see a vast improvement in the appearance of the county, and is enjoying the fruit of an active life.

Camden A. Cleveland was born in Liberty township in 1803. February 24, 1830, he married Matilda, daughter of Josiah and Elizabeth (Newport) Robbins, born in Youngstown, December 31, 1804, and settled in Austintown township, where he cleared up a farm, and where he lived until his death, which occurred in 1839. They were the parents of three children—Eliza L., wife of Samuel Campbell, died in 1867; Albert A., a resident of Youngstown, and at present engaged in mining in Colorado; Alice M., wife of Hiram Ohl, of Niles. Mrs. Cleveland removed to Niles, where she lived nine years, and then returned to Austintown until 1872, when she again moved to Niles, where she has since resided.

Samuel C. Edwards was born in Jefferson, Greene county, Pennsylvania, March 30, 1811. His parents, John and Jane (Rook) Edwards, removed with their family from Pennsylvania to Weathersfield township, Trumbull county, in June, 1823. In the spring of 1830 he removed further north and purchased fifty-seven and one-half acres at $2.50 per acre, which he cleared up and improved. He died in February, 1855, aged seventy years. His widow removed to Niles, and died at her son Samuel's residence, at the age of eighty-nine years, six months, and nineteen days. Of the eight children born to them five are still living—Samuel C.; John, who resides in Mecca; William, who occupies the old homestead; George, who lives in West Geneva, Michigan; Mary Jane, wife of John Reel, living in Girard, Ohio. Samuel was married March 15, 1839, to Miss Ann Jane Wilson, by whom he had four sons and three daughters—James L., John F., George E., William C., Amanda, Esther, and Alice. Alice and George are deceased. George lost his life February 3, 1881, by an explosion in Ward's iron mill in which he was employed as engineer. His first wife died August 23, 1854, and he afterwards married the widow of Aaron Kingsley. They had seven children—Mary, Martha, Luther, Phila A., William H. H., Sarah S. J., and Franklin. Mr. Edwards has been during his life engaged in different pursuits. While young he learned the shoemaker's trade, but in later years he has given his principal attention to farming.

William Arnold was born in Washington county, Pennsylvania, November 30, 1802. He came to Weathersfield, Trumbull county, Ohio, in the year 1827. He married Miss Catharine Justice, of Springfield township, Columbiana county, born in Beaver county, Pennsylvania, in 1804. To Mr. and Mrs. Arnold were born two children, James E., now residing in Iowa, and Mrs. James McRoberts. Mr. Arnold purchased his farm, consisting of one hundred and four acres, paying for it out of his earnings in a sawmill, his wages being $9 per month, at the rate of $4 per acre. He cleared up the farm, and occupied it until his death, April 10, 1857. Mrs. Arnold is still living, making her home with her daughter.

John Park, son of Elijah and Margaret Park, was born in Wells, Rutland county, Vermont, May 22, 1794. He was married December 5, 1816, to Miss Sophia Broughton, and has had a family of five children, four sons and one daughter, named as follows: Samuel, Cephas, John H., Rachel Ann, Servetus W., all born in Vermont but the youngest, who was born in Moriah, New York. Mr. Park removed from Vermont to Essex county, New York, where he resided some five or six years, when he came to Ohio in the spring of 1831. He was accompanied by Jonathan Folsom, and with him purchased five hundred and fifty-two acres in Weathersfield township, near Niles. The tract was afterwards divided, our subject getting one hundred and eighty-four acres off the south part. He brought out his family in the fall of 1831. That section was still quite new, the nearest post-office being Hake's corners. His wife died January 3, 1854, and the following year he married Miss Mary Ann Cline, by whom he had three children, one son and two daughters— Mary, Seth, and Cora. Of the children by his first marriage all are dead except Cephas, John H., and Servetus. John H. occupies the old homestead. He was married May 1, 1845, to Mary Weisell and had the following children: Edwin, Minerva J. (dead), Rachel A., Rebecca R., John, C. E., and Samuel H. Mrs. Parks died June 14, 1880. Mr. Parks, Sr., is still living in a pleasant home adjoining the homestead at the advanced age of eighty-seven.

Thomas B. Wilson, with a wife and five children, came from Perry county, Pennsylvania, to Weathersfield, Trumbull county, Ohio, in 1833. He was married in 1812, immediately on his re-

turn from the war, and had a family of the following children: Margaret, Anna, James, Mary, Caroline, Rachel, and Elizabeth. He was a hatter by trade, but did not follow it after coming to Ohio, but successfully pursued farming until the time of his death, which occurred in April, 1869. His wife, whose maiden name was Agnes Thompson, survived him, dying in June, 1878. The old homestead is owned and occupied by their son James.

Jacob May was born in Columbiana county, Ohio, August 6, 1814. He was brought up on a farm and has always followed farming as an occupation. He moved to his present farm in Weathersfield township, Tumbull county, in 1835, purchasing one hundred acres. He now owns two hundred and ninety-three acres and is one of the substantial farmers of the county; is the owner of property in Niles and also in Girard. In September, 1834, he married Miss Elizabeth Floor, and had a family of eleven children, as follows: Samuel, Mary, Freeman, Daniel, Katie, John, Zenas, William, Amanda and Lucy (twins) and Lines, all living but Freeman.

H. H. Mason was born in Essex county, New York, January 3, 1819. He came to Ohio in April, 1835, with his parents and settled near Niles, Trumbull county. During the next four years he was employed as clerk for William H. Goodhue and William McFarland, each a year and a half, and for Smith & McCombs one year. In 1839 he returned to Niles and engaged in mercantile business in which he continued until 1864. August 16, 1880, he was appointed postmaster at Niles, which position he still holds. His father, Ambrose Mason, was the first incumbent of the office, appointed in 1842, and as assistant to his father he distributed the first mail received there. He was married, February 22, 1842, to Miss Adaliza T. Kingsley, and has six children, four sons and two daughters.

Hiram T. Mason, third son of Ambrose and Jemima Mason, was born in Essex county, New York, in 1816; came to Ohio with his parents in 1835; married in 1839, Miss Margaret Cherry, by whom he has had three sons and two daughters, as follows: A. C., Albert H., Jesse E., Alice A., and Clara A. A. C. and Alice are deceased. A. C. died in the army during the Rebellion, and is buried at Chattanooga, Tennessee. He was captain of company C, One Hundred and Fifth Ohio volunteer infantry. Mr. Mason, our subject, was elected county commissioner in 1861, and served six years. He is a prominent member of the Disciples church, and has been deacon in his church for twenty years and an elder for ten years.

James Ward, Sr., was a native of Staffordshire, England. He came to America in 1815, and in 1841 located at Niles, Trumbull county, Ohio, and in company with his brother William, and Thomas Russell, under the firm name of James Ward & Co., erected the first rolling mill established at Niles, and in 1859 built the first blast furnace. Mr. Ward was one of the most prosperous and enterprising citizens of the Mahoning valley, and Niles owes its growth and prosperity principally to him. He died in 1864. His widow, Eliza Ward, is still living, residing with her son James. They had a family of seven children, of whom Mr. James Ward, of Niles, is the only survivor, the well-known iron manufacturer of Niles. He married Miss Elizabeth, daughter of William H. Brown, of Pittsburg, Pennsylvania, and has five children, James, William H., Charles S., May B., and Lizzie B.

E. J. Ohl, druggist, Mineral Ridge, Trumbull county, was born in Ohltown, Weathersfield township, Trumbull county, in 1847. He is a son of Henry Ohl. When six years of age he went with his parents to Allen county, Indiana, where his father engaged in farming. At the age of fifteen and one-half years Mr. Ohl enlisted as a private in the Thirtieth regiment of Indiana volunteers. This regiment witnessed some hard engagements, among which were the battles of Shiloh, Lookout Mountain, and at Atlanta. January 1, 1863, Mr. Ohl's company went into the battle of Stone River with thirty-one men, and twenty-one of these were killed and wounded. His term of enlistment expired September 29, 1864, and he returned to Trumbull county. After four months he enlisted in the One Hundred and Ninety-sixth Ohio volunteers, and was commissioned second lieutenant of company K by Governor Brough. The members of this company presented Lieutenant Ohl with a fine gold watch in token of their esteem. When the war closed he returned to Ohltown. In 1867 he engaged in mercantile business in partnership with Andrew Ohl, at Mineral Ridge. In 1875 the store, of which he was the sole proprietor, be-

ing destroyed by fire he engaged in farming for one year. He was then appointed postmaster at Mineral Ridge, and still manages the office in connection with the drug business. In 1875 Mr. Ohl recruited a company of the Ohio National guard and was elected captain. In 1877 he was appointed lieutenant-colonel, and 1880 colonel. Colonel Ohl has also held a number of local offices. In 1866 he married Sarah J. Herring, of Weathersfield township. They have five children—Sadie Olive O., William Arthur, Mary Ida, Harry Carlton, and Nellie Herring. Mr. Ohl is one of the charter members of the Mineral Ridge Independent Order of Odd Fellows' lodge.

J. T. McConnell, merchant, senior member of the firm McConnell Brothers, of Mineral Ridge, Trumbull county, is a son of William C. and Harriet McConnell. He was born in Weathersfield township, Trumbull county, in 1848. He began business with John Leavitt at Mineral Ridge, under the firm name John Leavitt & Co., and continued in this partnership about six years. In 1878 McConnell Brothers bought out Mr. Leavitt and have since been in the business. They have by far the largest and best furnished store in the village, and their custom is constantly increasing. In 1876 Mr. McConnell married Fannie L. Church, of Canfield, by whom he has two children, Freddie and Willie. He is a member of the Niles Masonic lodge.

W. J. McConnell, junior partner in the above named firm, was born in Weathersfield township in 1852, and began mercantile life in 1878. In 1879 he married Jennie Jones, of Mineral Ridge, and has one child, Blanche.

William Davis, mayor of Niles, Trumbull county, was born in Bilston, county of Stafford, England, May 8, 1817. In early life he began to work in a rolling-mill, and continued until he emigrated to America in 1842. Landing in New York in June of that year, he proceeded to Pittsburg and worked in a rolling-mill from 1842 to 1846. In April, 1846, he moved to Franklin, Venango county, Pennsylvania, and there held the position of guide-roller and nail-plate roller until 1851, when he removed to Niles. Here he worked at a heating furnace for James Ward & Co. In 1859 he became superintendent of the mill, and continued in that capacity until the death of James Ward, Sr., in 1865.

He then went to Youngstown to manage the mill of Brown, Bonnell & Co. But having formed the purpose of establishing a rolling-mill in Niles, in company with George and James Harris, Mr. Davis was released from his engagement, and the mill, since bought by C. H. Andrews & Co., was erected and operated by Harris, Davis & Co. Mr. Davis continued a member of this firm until 1870, when he sold out. He then bought William Fisher's boot and shoe store, and was in that business about three years. October 4, 1872, Mr. Davis was thrown from a buggy in Warren, and received a compound fracture of his ankle, which compelled him to use crutches for three years. Since 1876 he has been acting as mayor of Niles, and is now serving his third term in that office. In 1839 he married Mary Ann Jones, a native of England, who still shares his home. They have ten children living and two sons deceased. Names and residences: John M., New Castle, Pennsylvania; William W., Canfield; James R., Jefferson C., Thomas R., Niles; Alexander M. B., Youngstown; and Joseph M., Niles. Daughters: Mrs. Susie Wood and Mrs. Sarah A. Spencer, Youngstown; Miss Lida Ward Davis, Niles.

Sexton Sykes, deceased, was a native of the State of Vermont, born in 1809. He lived in New York State several years. When a young man he came to Ohio and settled in Green township, now in Mahoning county. He was elected the first recorder of deeds of Mahoning county in 1846 and served two terms. He then went to California and engaged in mining and keeping boarders. He died in Placerville, California, in 1853. He was married in 1836 to Rachel, daughter of David and Elizabeth Gilson, of Columbiana county. She was born in 1809 and now resides in Canfield, Mahoning county, where her home has been since 1846. She is the mother of six children, all of whom are living, viz : Phebe, Niles, Trumbull county; Melissa, married James Lowry, resides in Boardman; Celestia, married James Shorten, resides in Cincinnati; Robert, married Anna McIntyre, lives in Holmes county; Loretta, married Daniel Strickler, resides in Salem, Columbiana county; and Raymond G., married Clara Loose, resides in Niles, where he is engaged in the manufacture of iron roofing.

John Carter, proprietor of the Globe Foundry and Machine works, Niles, Trumbull county, was born in Niles in 1853 and has always resided in the place. When young he began work in the foundry and machine shop of his father, Thomas Carter, and later succeeded him in the management of his business. Mr. Carter is doing a large and prosperous business.

E. I. Moore, book-keeper at Russia Iron mills, Niles, Trumbull county, was born in Niles in 1854, and is a son of Irwin and Mary N. Moore. He was educated at Oberlin college. After finishing his school work Mr. Moore acted as book-keeper and then as cashier of a bank for five years; he then engaged in the drug business in Niles in company with Dr. McKinley for one year, then served one year in the bank. In 1879 he was engaged as book-keeper for L. B. Ward, a position which he still holds.

William Spill was born in Thornbury, England, November 5, 1822, the oldest son of William Spill, Sr., and Ann Brett. The family removed to Wales about 1837, where he worked as tallow-chandler. He was engaged as superintendent of coal banks for some three years. He married in 1845, Jane Hanson, a native also of England, and has two sons now living in Warren, George and Thomas. His first wife died in 1853. He married in 1859 Mary Williams, his present wife, born in Wales in 1822. Mr. Spill came to this country in 1852 and to Ohio in 1854, having lived for two years in Maryland. He first located in Weathersfield township and engaged at his old occupation, coal mining. In 1866 he removed to Mineral Ridge, where, with his son George, he was engaged in merchandising some twelve years. He removed to Warren in 1880 and has since lived a retired life.

Dr. A. J. Leitch, son of Robert and Eliza Leitch, was born near Belfast, Ireland, in 1848, and came to Niles, Trumbull county, Ohio, with his parents in the spring of 1852. He adopted the medical profession, and after a course of reading graduated from the Cleveland Medical college in 1871. He commenced practice the same year in Niles in partnership with Professor H. G. Landis, of the Starling Medical college, Columbus, Ohio, with whom he continued some four years. He then engaged in the drug business, in which he was engaged until the fall of 1879, when he formed a partnership in the practice of medicine with Dr. A. P. McKinley, of

Niles, the firm being McKinley & Leitch. February 17, 1881, he was united in marriage to Miss Ella M. Ward.

Dr. F. Caspar was born in Strasburg, France (now Germany), in 1816; came to the United States in the summer of 1831 and located in New Lisbon, where he was educated. He studied medicine with Dr. George McCook, of New Lisbon, and subsequently attended lectures at the Jefferson Medical college, Philadelphia. He commenced practice in 1840 at Petersburg, now Mahoning county, and remained there until 1853 when he removed to Canfield, where he was engaged in the practice of his profession seven years. In 1860 he removed to Niles, where he has resided since. In 1839 he was married to Miss Mary Ann Russell, daughter of William E. Russell, a former prominent attorney of New Lisbon. Mrs. Caspar was born in Steubenville, Ohio, in 1822. To this marriage six children were born, of whom three sons and one daughter survive. Joseph Caspar, the father of Dr. Caspar, was a soldier under Bonaparte, serving three or four years.

Warren Lewis (deceased) was born in Clarksville, Pennsylvania, September 12, 1800. He married, November 26, 1829, Miss Hannah M. Bowel, daughter of an early settler in Howland, the family settling there about 1802. After his marriage he returned to his home in Pennsylvania, but subsequently came to Ohio and purchased a farm in Weathersfield township, Trumbull county, where he located and reared a family of six children, named as follows: Henry, Rebecca M., Mary, Charlotte, Jesse B., and Clara, wife of R. G. Sikes. Henry, Rebecca, Mary, and Charlotte are dead. Rebecca was twice married, first to James M. Robinson, by whom she had one daughter. Her second husband was Jerry Tibbits. Mr. Lewis died October 24, 1859, and his wife September 28, 1864. Jesse B. Lewis was in the Union army in the war of secession, and was wounded at Atlanta in the right arm, which finally necessitated amputation. He married Miss Ella M. Woodward, of Cleveland, by whom he had one child, Ella E., who died in infancy. His wife died August 13, 1872, and he was again married January 1, 1874, to Miss Frances Lamphear, and has two sons by this marriage, Warren S. and Raymond J. Mr. Lewis occupies the old family homestead.

Andrew McRoberts (deceased) was born in Ireland in 1804. In 1832 he married Miss Mary McClure, by whom he had eight children, viz: James, John, and Georgiana, who were born in Ireland, and Caldwell, Mary Ann, Jordan, Helen, and Rachel, born in Mahoning county. In 1837 Mr. McRoberts purchased a farm of fifty acres in Austintown township, Mahoning county, where he made settlement. He removed to Lawrence county, Pennsylvania, in 1852, where he resided until his death, in 1863. His widow is still living, and resides in New Castle, Pennsylvania. James, their eldest son, married, October, 1858, Miss Laura M. Draper, by whom he had four children, as follows: Ida, Alice, John, and Mary. His first wife died May 31, 1870, and he subsequently married Miss Isabella White. He was in the service during the war of the Rebellion nine months. He now resides on the old Draper homestead near Niles.

Samuel H. Stillwagon, only son of Josiah and Jane Stillwagon, was born in Butler county, Pennsylvania, in 1850. He came to Weathersfield township, Trumbull county, Ohio, in 1865, the farm now owned and occupied by him being purchased by his uncle, William Milford. June 11, 1872, he was married to Miss Kittie Hake. They have had two children, Freddie and Millie. The latter died April 21, 1880. Mr. Stillwagon is the owner of two hundred and eighty-five acres, the home place comprising nearly two hundred. Himself and wife are members of the Disciples church. His father died February 29, 1852. His mother still survives, and resides with him.

John R. Thomas, manufacturer of fire-brick and iron, Niles, Trumbull county, was born in Aberdale, county of Glamorgan, South Wales, in 1834. In 1866 he emigrated to America. While in Wales he was engaged in the manufacture of fire-brick, a business which he has followed nearly thirty years. In 1866 Mr. Thomas went to California, returned thence to Wales, and in 1868 came to Youngstown. He has since resided in that place and in Niles. Mr. Thomas is connected with two of the leading industries of Niles, being a member of the Thomas Furnace company, and the Niles Fire-brick company. In 1855 he married Margaret Morgan, a native of Brynllor, county of Carmathen, South

Wales, and has five children living, viz: John M., of Albany Law school, New York; Thomas E., William A., Margaretta and Mary Ann, of Niles. Mr. Thomas is a member of the Masonic order. In politics he has always been a Republican. He is one of the successful and honored manufacturers of the Mahoning valley.

E. E. Ferris was born in the town of Buckingham, Ottawa, Canada, September 28, 1842. He came to Trumbull county, settling in Weathersfield township, in 1869. He married September 8, 1875, Miss Savilla Moser, and purchased, where he now lives, in 1876. He owns altogether one hundred and forty-four acres of land.

C. W. Brieder, hardware merchant, Niles, Trumbull county, was born in New York city in 1849. When fifteen years of age he began learning the printing business in Youngstown. This he followed about three years, and then began the hardware business, which he still continues. In 1871 he moved to Niles. In 1873 he married Lizzie L. Sheible, of Niles. Mr. Brieder is a member of the Independent Order of Odd Fellows.

C. W. Thomas, merchant, Niles, Trumbull county, was born at Clark's Cove, near Pittsburg, in 1857. He has followed clerking and dealing in merchandise. He was in business with his father, D. C. Thomas, in Newburg, Ohio, in 1872–73. In December, 1873, Mr. Thomas came to Niles and was in business with his father until 1877, and has since been in business for himself. In 1880 he married Miss F. E. Talbitzer, of Niles, by whom he has one child—Carl D.

S. A. Russell, merchant, Niles, Trumbull county, was born in Huron county, Ohio, in 1851. He was employed upon a farm until eighteen years of age, then entered a grocery store in Elyria, Ohio, as clerk, and remained three years. In 1873 he came to Niles and learned the drug business, clerking for W. L. Gaston & Co. Then for four years he clerked for James Crandon, grocer, and in 1881 engaged in the same business for himself. In 1875 he married Miss Lena Scheible, of Niles, and has two children—Leroy and Hattie. He is doing a good business.

C. W. Porter, druggist, Niles, Trumbull county, was born in Austintown township, Mahoning county, in 1850. In 1867 he engaged in the drug business for E. A. Smith at Warren, and continued there until 1871, then was in the same business in Meadville, Pennsylvania, until 1874. In 1875 he began the same business in Niles and still continues to follow it. Mr. Porter was married in 1879 to Miss Ella Leslie, of Niles. He is prospering finely in his business.

Fred. J. Church, merchant, Niles, Trumbull county, was born in Canfield, Mahoning county, in 1854, son of Darius and Electa Church, and a descendant of Nathaniel Church. Mr. F. J. Church was educated in Canfield and at the age of nineteen began the mercantile business with his father. In 1878 he removed to Niles and became a member of the firm McConnell & Church. In 1880 this firm was changed to Church & Coffee, who have the largest store in Niles.

A. B. Cook, druggist, Niles, Trumbull county, Ohio, was born in Chardon, Geauga county, in 1856. His father, A. Cook, and his grandfather followed the drug business. Mr. A. B. Cook commenced working in his father's store in Chardon in 1871, and continued until 1878, when he removed to Niles and began business in partnership with his father under the firm name of Cook & Co. Mr. A. B. Cook conducts the business and is successful. He was married in 1881 to Miss Mary Wagstaff, of Niles.

Hiram Dunlap, fifth son of James and Catharine Dunlap, was born in Brookfield, Trumbull county, Ohio, in 1819. In 1848 he married Miss Lydia Van Wye, the result of which union was three children, one son and two daughters, as follow: James A., Emma J., and Lydia C.— James being the only survivor. Mrs. Dunlap died September 7, 1854, and he married for his second wife Miss Amanda Hartzell, by whom he had seven sons, viz: Franklin H., Willie L., Edward H., Elmore W., Henry G., Thomas J., and Ferdinand C., all living but Thomas.

CHAPTER III.

HARTFORD.

This township was known under the surveys of the Connecticut Land company as number five, first range, in the Connecticut Western Reserve. It was called Hartford, after the State capital of the same name. According to draft book, page 225, draft seven-three was drawn by Urial Holmes and Ephraim Root. This draft drew all of Hartford township, containing seventeen thousand three hundred and seventeen acres of land. The Connecticut Land company executed a deed April 22, 1798, to Root and Holmes for a consideration of $12,903.23, being less than seventy-five cents per acre.

The township was surveyed into lots by Raphael Cooke. It was bounded on the east by the Pennsylvania State line; on the north by Smithfield, afterwards named Vernon; on the west by Westfield, afterwards named Fowler; and on the south by Brookfield.

According to Stowe's map of Trumbull county in 1800, numbers four and five in range one and two, and also numbers six, seven, eight, and nine in range one, two, and three, were known as Vernon.

Elections were held at Burg Hill, number five, for this territory of Vernon, which is now divided into sixteen townships, lying in Trumbull and Ashtabula counties.

Burg Hill, located in the north part of the township of Hartford, may have received its name from the fact that it was the business point and place for elections and militia musters for many years early in the century.

The earliest records to be found show that a separate township organization must have been in existence in 1811. Elam Jones was elected township clerk at the April election of that year.

Legal papers bearing date as late as 1814 were drawn in some cases, as if the names of Vernon and Hartford were both used to designate this township.

The deed of Holmes and Root to Titus Brockway, drawn in 1803, in which they reserved one acre of land for a "green," on which to build a "meeting-house," speaks of the township as "Hartford." In a deed of Edward Brockway to his son Titus, drawn in 1802, the township is called Vernon, "in the territory of the United States, northwest of the Ohio river."

The first deed by said Urial Holmes and Ephraim Root was made September 23, 1799, to Edward Brockway, conveying 3,194 acres and a fraction of land, being lots seven, eight, fifteen, sixteen, twenty-one, and twenty-two, for a consideration of $500, being less than sixteen cents an acre. According to tradition he exchanged his farm of two hundred acres in Hartford, Connecticut, for nearly one-fourth of the township, and perhaps this formed a part of the consideration in addition to the amount mentioned in the deed. A number of others exchanged their farms for land here.

GENERAL FEATURES.

The soil is clayey through the central portions, but becomes less so as you approach the principal streams—Yankee run on the west, and Pymatuning in the northeastern part of the township. The first named takes its rise in the marsh and runs in a southern direction in the western part of the township, until it meets the Little Yankee, which runs nearly east from Fowler to its junction with the main stream. Near the south line it runs to the east, crossing the Brookfield and Hartford road at Burnett's mill, and a short distance further leaves the township.

Yankee run is said to have been so named by the Indians because they found the body of a white man at the forks of the stream. Mill brook rises in the north central portion of the township, and runs north into Vernon. The Pymatuning was first called Smith's creek, after General Martin Smith, later Venango, the latter name appearing in old deeds which were made out by pioneer proprietors early in the century, and also in maps of a similar date. For many years it has been called Pymatuning. By some this is supposed to be an Indian name, by others it is claimed to be of French origin. This stream furnishes the water-power which has been so long utilized at Orangeville. Hewitt run rises on the farm which bears the same name, and the larger stream in that vicinity was known on early maps as Brockway run, named after Edward Brockway, the pioneer settler, and as its course nearly all lay within lands purchased by him, it should still bear his name. They are both tributaries of the Pymatuning. McCullough run rises in the central and south central portion of the township. The two branches unite on the farm of T. A. Bushnell, and run thence nearly due east to the State line. It was named after a pioneer settler who resided near its mouth.

In the west central portion of the township is a sandstone ridge known as the ledge. It extends for some distance from north to south, being an abrupt precipice of rocks, of varying height, with some small caves. At different places the rock appears to show the action of water, as if it had at one time been the bank of a stream, and near the road a rocky ravine extends a short distance from east to west. It has been a favorite local resort for school pic-nics, and is not entirely devoid of interest to older persons who have not been accustomed to the rocks and hills of New England, or some similar region. Across the run to the southwest, on the McFarland farm, a similar formation occurs, but of less extent. This stone has been quarried for many years, and is quite valuable for building and bridge-purposes.

The land at Burg Hill is a circular knob or knoll comprising some fifty or more acres, and rising to an elevation of perhaps fifty feet above the general level, and is noted for the large number of springs near its base. The hill itself appears to be composed of conglomerate rock, with a thin covering of surface soil. Since the building of the railway the post-office and the store have been moved a little north to the station of the same name, within the township of Vernon. It is now sometimes called Old Burg Hill, and was formerly the residence of Colonel Richard Hayes and his three sons, Seth, Alvin, and Richard.

There are a few things of local interest, which since the first settlement of the township have been to some extent objects of curiosity to our citizens. The first to which we will refer, is known as the old road. It is located near the center of the northeastern part of the township, perhaps a mile or more west of Orangeville. It is nearly a half mile in length, and its general direction is from northeast to southwest. A portion of the road, or whatever it may have originally been, varies but little from a straight line; the remainder is more winding, but retains the same general course. It has the appearance of having been at some time thrown up like a turnpike. At some points it seems as if the depression was still visible which was made by the removal of earth in constructing.

The embankment is generally the highest on the southern portion, which is also the highest ground, and as you go to the northeast the land gradually descends, and at a short distance from the New York, Pennsylvania & Ohio railroad, it entirely disappears. At one point, south of the Orangeville road, it resembles a railroad embankment where it has been cut through by a stream of water. The first settlers found it covered with forest trees as large as at other places. Tradition says that whenever deer were started by hunters in that vicinity, they always made for the old road, if possible, and used it as a runway during their flight.

It seems to us it must have been of artificial construction. It could hardly have been a fortification, however, and it does not seem to meet any of the requirements of military science. A gentleman who has resided in the vicinity some seventy years, informed the writer he had heard it suggested that it was made as a boundary line between two Indian tribes, but it would seem to have been constructed by a more civilized race.

A boulder of large size, sometime in the history of the world, took up its residence in this vicinity, and is another of our few local curiosities. There are many others of the same class, but so much smaller as to receive but little attention. It is located near the top of Brockway's hill, on the south part of the farm formerly owned by the late Calvin Cone, and has been variously estimated to weigh from seventy-five to one hundred tons. It is surrounded by material which has evidently formed, at some period, part of the rock itself, but from the action of the elements has been reduced in size.

There are a few places in the township where we find a bed of gravel, resting upon the ordinary surface soil, and having all the appearance of being artificial, but no possible reason can be assigned for their construction, and no similar material is found in the vicinity. One bed that has been carefully examined, on A. P. Kepner's land, is some forty feet in diameter, about three feet deep in the center, growing thinner as you approach the circumference or outer edge. It certainly shows no correspondence to drift deposit, and cannot well be classed as kames.

On the farms of Luther and John Fitch, and also on the farm of William Rathbun, at the time of settlement were quite a number of excavations very similar in general appearance. They resembled wells, which having been dug and left for years had partially filled up. In early days they were so deep in some cases as to require fencing to protect stock from danger. They were known in the neighborhood as "old wells." No examination has been made to determine their original purpose.

Coal has been found at various places in the township, and a few thousand tons have been recently mined at the ledge, but none has yet been found in sufficient thickness to warrant extensive operations in mining.

FIRST SETTLEMENT.

The first settlement was made in 1799, by Edward Brockway, Isaac Jones, and Asahel Brainard, who spent their first night by a large tree, then standing about one-fourth of a mile north of the center of the township, nearly opposite the residence of the late Elijah Woodford, now owned by Oliver Perrine.

They commenced a clearing on the farm long owned by the late William Bond, Edward Brockway cutting the first tree. After having built a cabin and sowed a field of wheat, Brockway and Jones returned East and brought out their families in the summer of 1800.

Brainard remained alone through the winter, engaged in clearing land. His nearest neighbor was Martin Smith, of Vernon. Settlement had been made previously at Vienna, Youngstown, and Warren. It was during this winter that two Indians, Flin and Kanoshua, came to Brainard's cabin, and after partaking somewhat freely of whiskey, left apparently on good terms, but soon after fell into an altercation, in which the former was killed. He was shot near the residence on the dairy farm of D. R. Chapman. After the transaction it was feared that trouble with the Indians might grow out of it, and Smith being best acquainted, started for their village near Greenville, Pennsylvania, to notify them and put the best face possible on the matter, but had proceeded no farther than Orangeville, when he met them coming. The Indians having collected from the various encampments, a consultation was held, and after due deliberation, it was decided that "Indian no kill him, but whiskey kill him." He was soon after buried by them with the usual ceremonies, near the east line of the farm on which the first cabin was built. The survivor, instead of departing for parts unknown, as it was feared he might, leaving the blame to rest on others, had informed his friends of the matter, who were coming to bury their dead. A few years later some medical students exhumed his remains, and his bones were kept by them for a long time in the office of Dr. Wilcox, at Burg Hill.

Isaac Jones settled at Burg Hill on the farm now owned by Osman Hull. Charles Merry came the same year with his family, and settled within the present limits of Orangeville.

William Bushnell, the pioneer settler in the south part of the township, bought three hundred and twenty-seven acres in lot thirty, of Holmes and Root, for a consideration of $816, the deed being dated December 31, 1800.

He came into the township with his family in June, 1801, and located on the diagonal road about half way up the hill. His first place of shelter was made by felling a large chestnut tree, taking off the bark, placing one end on the body of the tree and the other on the ground, thus making a shed under which the family found shelter for nine days, during most of which time a rain storm kept them closely "housed."

Titus Brockway also came into the township in 1800, and was land agent for Holmes & Root. He located in the central part, on the farm now in the possession of his grandson, U. H. Brockway. His first cabin was built on the opposite bank of the run, a little north of the present residence. It is said he was an unmarried man at this time, and with a hired man kept "bachelor's hall." Also, that Urial Holmes found it convenient at times to share his cabin, and partake of the plentiful game with which the immense forest abounded. One day they were so fortunate as to kill a bear. Thinking to have a little joke they put it into the hired man's bed, and with much gravity awaited the time for him to retire. We are left to imagine his surprise, and perhaps fright, and the uproarious laughter of the jokers.

In 1803 Daniel Bushnell located on lot thirty, near the present residence of John Craton.

Samuel Spencer located in Burg Hill.

Captain Thomas Thompson came from Farmington, Connecticut, in 1803. He purchased some five hundred acres, including two of the center lots of the township, and a portion of a third one, and located about one-fourth of a mile south of the center, where H. Bennett now resides. William C. Jones probably came in 1802, and located on the farm now occupied by A. D. Fell.

Asahel Brainard, previously mentioned, located at an early period on the farm where Jacob Kepner now resides, one-half mile south of the center.

Aaron Brockway first settled in Vernon in 1798, but in 1801 or 1802 changed his location to Hartford.

Asa Andrews purchased about one thousand acres of land and settled on lot twenty-seven, where John McFarland now resides.

In 1803 Robert McFarland and family settled on lot three on the State line, near the residence of his grandson, Thomas W. McFarland.

The following named persons also came into the township during 1804 and 1805. All but two or three of them were married men and brought their families: Richard Hayes, Thomas Bushnell, Asahel Borden, Andrews Bushnell, Asa Andrews, Jehial Hulburt, Samuel Tuttle, Captain Alexander Bushnell, Shaler Fitch, Asahel Borden, Jr., Elam Jones, Chester Andrews, Jehial Hulburt, Jr., William Rathburn. These were nearly all residents of Hartland, Connecticut. In 1804 a colony of some ten families left Hartland at the same time. The occasion of their departure from Connecticut was considered of so much importance that a meeting was held, a farewell sermon preached, and then the general leavetaking took place, as their old friends and neighbors bade adieu to their late homes and started on their journey of six hundred miles for the State of their choice. Some of them were men far past the prime of life, Revolutionary fathers; one had borne a part at Bunker Hill, that sad, yet glorious day, when Warren fell; another, barefooted at Valley Forge, had camped with Washington, yet rather than part with children and grandchildren, they concluded to forego the comforts of civilization, and endure the fatigues of a six weeks' trip to New Connecticut, as it was then called, to build up homes in a wilderness, not only for themselves, but for coming generations.

DUTCH RIDGE SETTLEMENT.

The southeastern portion of the township was first settled by families of German lineage from Cumberland county, in eastern Pennsylvania.

John Kepner was the pioneer settler. According to tradition, he commenced a clearing in 1805 and built a cabin. The next spring it was burned, and a hewed log-house was then built, which stood until 1880, when it was replaced by a fine frame house erected by his grandson, Lucius Kepner. His deed was made July 2, 1806, for six hundred and thirty-six and one hundred and thirty-nine one-hundred and sixtieth acres of land in lot nine. The consideration was $1,785.

John Pfouts came in the fall of 1806 and settled on the farm now owned by his son Isaac Pfouts. The first cabin stood some forty rods southwest of the present residence. Frederick Shull located where Seth Carnes now resides. Michael Quiggle settled on the farm now owned by Orvis Shatto.

Later, settlement were made by Hull, Reeder, George and John Snyder.

INDIAN HUNTING CAMP.

The remains of a large Indian hunting camp were in existence for several years after the first settlement, on the west side of lot twenty-four, on the farm formerly owned by General Andrews Bushnell. Some of the lodges were apparently new, with all the appearance of having been occasionally occupied; others were quite old and dilapidated.

A DEN OF SNAKES.

During the year 1804, while Samuel Spencer was residing at Burg Hill, some travelers having called for water were directed to a spring near the house, but soon returned, having discovered a rattlesnake den at the head of it. The neighbors were called upon for assistance, and in digging them out it was found necessary to use a yoke of cattle to remove the stone surrounding the den. It was quite cool weather in early spring, and they had just begun to stir, and were not fairly active. The boys used flails in dispatching them. One hundred and seventy of the spotted reptiles were dug out and killed. Soon after Mrs. Spencer found one under the bed, which she dispatched; another fell from overhead to the floor, and last, not least, one day on going into the pantry and taking down a basin, she found one curled up within it—an uninvited guest, truly! What would our modern belles say to an adventure like this? I am afraid his snakeship would have had a better chance for his life than in the hands of Mrs. Spencer.

Early in the century the banks of Brockway run were quite a harbor for rattlesnakes. Edward Brockway was bitten by one of them, and came near losing his life in consequence, but by the aid of an old Indian's prescription, he finally recovered. He, however, became the sworn enemy of the whole fraternity of snakes, and soon an agreement was made by those living in the vicinity, to hunt for snakes, whenever they crossed the stream at the proper season. It was his custom, when going to and returning from church, to stop and hunt for them.

The northwestern part of the township, from the "marsh" for some distance south on the run, seems to be the favorite home of the massassauga. Formerly large numbers were killed. Even in later years fair crops of them have sometimes been harvested. Some forty or fifty have been killed on one farm, in a single year. The war still goes on, and it may be a long time before they are entirely extirpated.

OTHER EARLY SETTLERS.

The following named persons came into the township during its early settlement, most of them probably from 1804 to 1811: Titus Hayes, Russel Borden, Linus Hayes, Lester Hayes, Philo Borden, Nehemiah Andrews, Davis Fuller, Horace Flower, Sylvester Borden, Martin Gangyard, Ebenezer Chapman, Elijah Woodford, Thomas Dugan, David Lane, Lebbeus Beach, Levi Giddings, and Isaac Olmstead.

EARLY EVENTS.

Linus Hayes and Jerusha, daughter of Thomas Bushnell, were married September 11, 1805. They were the first couple married within the township. Previous to this time, however, in 1801, Titus Brockway, of this place, was married to Minerva Palmer, of Vernon. Harriet Merry, daughter of Charles Merry, was born in 1801, and died August 24, 1864. She was the first white child born in the township. She married John Burnett. They resided some years in Vernon and then removed to Ravenna, Ohio, where she died, and was buried at Burg Hill.

William Bushnell, son of Colonel William Bushnell, born June 11, 1802, was the first white male child born in the township. He married Jane Potterfield June 19, 1828. They both died at the same time and were buried in one grave.

The first death was that of a child of Isaac Jones, from small-pox. It was buried at Burg Hill, near the residence of Osman Hull. Mrs. Samuel Tuttle died soon after and was buried at Vernon. Lucy Andrews, a child of two years, was the next, and was the first person buried in the graveyard at the center. The site was selected after her death, and the grave was surrounded by an enclosure of logs in the forest. She died October 11, 1805. Mrs. Jerusha Hayes, wife of Linus Hayes and daughter of Thomas Bushnell, died in 1806, and was the first adult buried here, the next being Mrs. Daniel Bushnell, who died July 7, 1809.

Edward Brockway was elected as the first justice of the peace, in honor of having been the first settler and cutting the first tree, but not wishing to serve, Titus Brockway, his son, was elected and served as the first justice, and was also the first postmaster.

The oldest framed house in the township now standing, and said to have been the second, if not the first one built, is the present residence of Seth Thompson, Jr., standing on the top of the hill on the diagonal road. It was built by Colonel William Bushnell, who sold it to Russel Borden, and a few years later it passed into the hands of the Thompson family, who have occupied it nearly seventy years.

The first dwelling house at the center of the township was built by Seth Thompson, Sr., in 1810. It was a log house and stood north of the "green," where James Stewart now resides, and the second was built some years later by Joseph A. Gould, on the west corner, who also built a blacksmith shop near it.

The first apple-tree which bore fruit in the township was planted by Titus Brockway, and is still standing, a little north of the residence of U. H. Brockway. The first crop consisted of one peck of apples, which were carefully put into the cellar, and when they were visited by their neighbors, two or three were brought up and exhibited, then carefully pared and cut into pieces enough to go around. So the peck furnished most of the people a sight and taste of the apples. Soon, however, fruit became so plenty it had but little market value. Peaches were a drug in the market at a shilling a bushel, and large quantities were taken to Lester Bushnell's still, at the foot of Brockway's hill, to be made into peach brandy. Cider, at the nominal price of fifty cents per barrel, was taken to the same place to be made into "apple-jack," and then stored in the cellar, to be used in treating friends on extra occasions, as parties, weddings, etc., especially after the ten or twelve barrels of cider, "all ripening in a row," in the cellars of most farm-houses, had run low.

At this time the privations and hardships of the early pioneers were growing less; fields of corn and wheat gave evidence of present abundance and a prospect of future luxury.

Additions were yearly being made to the settlement by emigration from the older States, of friends and neighbors, who hoped to better their condition by making a home in the West. Thus a few years swiftly passed away, with little to vary the monotony of frontier life, save an occasional foray upon the sheepfold by wolves, or being awakened from sleep by the squeals of a luckless pig, taken away from his sty by bruin, and borne away to make a toothsome repast for himself, varied by his pursuit and capture, to pay him for his pains. Frame houses and barns were already beginning to take the place of log ones; orchards being set out, clearings enlarged, and roads improved, until the 18th of June, 1812, when the war cloud which had for a long time hung over the Nation, culminated in a declaration of war against Great Britain.

The necessary demands upon the pioneers for military service after Hull's surrender, and their location near the frontier, served to check emigration and general improvement until the close of the war.

The epidemic which prevailed so extensively through the whole Western country during the year 1813, visited this township, and carried off fifteen persons, mostly elderly people, all the deaths of the year except two or three, resulting from it. Among the deaths were Asa Andrews, Jehiel Hulburt, Titus Hayes, Russel Borden, and Mrs. Lucy Fitch, widow of John Fitch, the inventor of steamboats, whose descendants by one branch are still residing here.

A BEAR STORY.

In November, 1817, a large black bear was caught in the woods of Daniel Bushnell. He was in the habit of visiting Mr. Bushnell's corn field at pleasure, going in and out at the same place until the corn was harvested. At length, finding no more corn he went to an adjoining field, where he helped himself to a fat hog weighing near two hundred pounds. After killing it and eating as much as he desired he attempted to get it over the fence into the woods. Finding it too heavy to lift he covered it with leaves and left it in the corner of the fence for his next meal. Mr. Bushnell's son George (now Dr. Bushnell) finding the hog thought it best to put a stop to bruin's depredations, and obtained the assistance of two good hunters, William Waters and T. H. Thompson. They tied the hog to the fence and set two bear traps. At night he came, pulled the hog away from the fence, breaking the straps by which it was tied, dragged it over the traps, sprung them, and then ate his meal. The next night they chained the hog to the fence, and set the traps again. He came, and crawling up on the side rails of the fence avoided the traps, reached the hog and again got his supper. They then put the hog on the woods side, fastened it tight to the fence, staking around it with heavy stakes driven into the ground, and leaving a door just large enough for him to enter, planted or buried a twenty-pound trap outside and another of twelve pounds inside the door. That night he came, pulled up the traps with the log chain with which they were fastened, turned them over and sat down on them. The next night was nearly a repetition of the last. Then moss from old logs was crowded under the pan of the traps to make them hard to spring, but this scheme availed nothing. He still sprung them and secured his supper as usual. They then built a pen of logs, about four feet by eight, with the door end between two trees, securely fastening it to them with pins and withes. The other end was staked and withed as well as notched together. A door was made of split puncheons and the pen was finished with a log floor, and logs on top. They then fastened the hog to a stick, one end of which was put through the back end of the pen, somewhat like the spindle to a box-trap. A pole was then placed over the pen to the end of the puncheon door (which was raised above the entrance) and with a cord at the other end was tied to a top-piece which had one end put in a place in one of the logs, and the other into a notch in the stick or spindle, to which the hog was fastened—a huge log box-trap. The traps and chains were then put at the door to remove his fear of danger in the pen. At night he came, and this time his bearship was outwitted. He walked in and was caught.

He was kept in the pen a portion of the next day for exhibition, and many of the people of the township came to see him, as he had become quite noted among them for his sagacity and cunning. He had gnawed some of the logs half off and would steadily continue to do so, unless he was watched by some one to take his attention. He would spit, snort, and scratch on the logs of the pen, jarring it until the tops of the trees to which it was fastened would shake.

Those who approached the pen would receive such a salute as would sometimes make them start and jump, to the great amusement of the spectators. Towards noon the bear was shot and taken on an ox sled to the house. His live weight was variously estimated from four hundred to four hundred and fifty pounds. He dressed three hundred and fifty pounds. His skin weighed thirty pounds. In his spine was found a half-ounce rifle ball, and a scar of another shot through the ribs, also an ounce ball and a buckshot in his neck. Thompson and Waters took the skin and one-half the meat for their share. Daniel Bushnell had the remainder, which furnished him sixty pounds of oil, in addition to the meat. His family had doughnuts fried in bear's oil all winter, and bear meat in place of the pork he had intended to use. The meat is said to be between beef and pork in appearance and taste. Strangers on eating the meat would sometimes pronounce it beef and sometimes pork, but always good meat, at the same time pehaps remarking they never could eat bear meat. After the meal they were generally informed of what they had partaken, when they would exclaim in great surprise: "Bear's meat! impossible!"

This same historical bear is well remembered to this day (1882) by the postmaster, H. B. Thompson. At that time the roads were full of stumps which had been blackened by frequent attempts to burn them out. He, a little fellow of four years of age, returning from school, was leisurely wending his way homeward down the diagonal road swinging his dinner basket and occasionally turning around to look back. He remembers well on one occasion of seeing an unusual number of black stumps behind him, but did not understand the reason till next day it was explained to him by the excited children at school, who informed him that some men working on Davis Fuller's barn, near the road, happening to look after the boy saw old bruin walk out of the woods on the roadside and leisurely trot on a short distance behind him. Some of the men ran for their guns while the others kept watch. In the meantime the unconscious little fellow was walking on, occasionally looking back, at which times bruin would immediately sit down, then as the boy again walked on he would arise and follow. When the men had procured their guns, however, and started in pursuit, he suddenly increased his speed and taking to the woods was soon lost to them. One can readily imagine the pleasure the boy experienced when he visited the trap and saw the old fellow caught at last.

BEAR HUNT.

A Mr. Hummason having recently arrived from Connecticut on a visit, was anxious to have a bear hunt, and Colonel William Bushnell, as anxious to gratify him, started with dogs and gun to accompany him. On reaching Yankee creek, below Asahel Borden's, they went north on the bottom lands, and very soon were so fortunate as to strike a bear track. They followed it, and soon the dogs treed a white bear a little north of Bates' corners on the hill. Before the men reached them, however, it came down, and was at length run into a thicket or wind-fall, near Parson's corners. Bushnell fired and wounded the bear. Hummason, much excited, got upon a log to get a better sight of the animal, when he slipped and fell. The wounded bear immediately pounced upon him. Bushnell did not wait to charge his gun, but turned in the powder from the horn, and in his haste got in too much. He went within three feet and fired at the head of bear killing him instantly, but burst his gun and injured himself. It was three months before Hummason recovered sufficiently to return home. This was the only white bear ever known to have been killed in this region. The skin was taken to Philadelphia, stuffed, and placed in a museum.

RING, OR WOLF HUNT.

The first settlers, having suffered in the destruction of their flocks from the incursions of the wolves, as well as their cousins, the bruin family, who made their chief rendezvous in the cranberry marsh in the southeast corner of Johnson (rattlesnakes and cranberries, with an unlimited amount of the former, being the principal production), organized at different times, conjointly with the citizens of the adjoining townships, what was called a wolf, or ring hunt. Those in each township who wished to share in the sport met together and elected a captain for the occasion. These four men were to have entire control, and make all needful rules for the day. Before the time set for the hunt the captains proceeded to lay out a line around the swamp by blazing the trees, usually comprising a circle of one-half or three-quarters of a mile in diameter. On the day appointed the men were to start at the highway leading from the center of one township to the other, and at a given time or signal move forward to the inside line, keeping as nearly equally apart from each other as possible, and drive all the game before them. By the time the line was reached the game, deer especially, would become aroused, passing rapidly around to find a place of escape, serving the while as a target for the men on the line. Sportsmen were allowed to shoot square across or at right angles to the line, but not otherwise for fear of accidents. Occasionally some old denizen of the forest would make for a weak or unguarded portion of the line, and succeeded in making his escape. After all were shot that sought to make their exit, the captains would select some of their most careful men to go and shoot all the game found with the lines. The game was then collected and sold at auction to buy whiskey to treat the hunters. At one hunt fifty deer were killed, besides bears and wolves. At another time nine wolves were among the trophies of the day. On the last occasion of the kind one man was severely wounded. In the fall of 1821 (according to George Hallock's diary), at one of these hunts four black bear, six wolves, two hundred deer, a number of turkeys, and considerable other wild game was killed.

33*

THE OLD CHURCH.

The old church was erected in 1819–20 by John Northrop and Oliver Stanford, of Boardman, for $1,310, materials being furnished, one-third of the amount to be paid in grain, cattle, and labor, and the balance in money. Daniel Bushnell, Titus Brockway, Richard Hayes, Andrews Bushnell, and Seymour A. Moses were the building committee. Contract signed December 1, 1818.

It stands on the "green." The main part of the building is forty-five feet square, and according to the original contract, still in existence, was built in the Doric style of architecture, had two rows of small windows, and two large Venetian windows, one in each end, and originally had a high pulpit, a gallery on three sides, square pews, a broad aisle in the center, with two narrow ones on either side, a tall spire and weather vane, all after the old Connecticut fashion. It was built by the Congregationalists, with some assistance from the people of the township, with the understanding that it might be used for all town purposes, and be free to all denominations when not in use by themselves. In addition to the names of the building committee, among the largest subscribers were Thomas Thompson, Davis Fuller, Chester Andrews, William Bushnell, Elam Jones, Calvin Cone, Philo Borden, Seth Thompson, Shaler Fitch, Asahel Brainard, and Aaron Brockway. These were followed by the names of nearly all the men in the township; the young men subscribing an amount sufficient for the erection of the steeple, which was not included in the original contract.

This was the first church built in the county. In 1846 it was repaired and materially changed. During the decade following, the churches having united, and the "old church" being no longer used for religious purposes, it has been devoted entirely to schools.

During its early history it was used for all public purposes, political as well as religious. Within its walls in years past theories of all kinds have been promulgated.

LATER SETTLERS.

After the close of the War of 1812, emigration to the West largely increased, and the following named persons, most of them with families, settled in the township within a few years:

Calvin Cone, Seymour A. Moses, John Banning, Lory Norton, Spencer Parsons, Romanta Norton, Daniel Spencer, Elihu Bates, Nathan Spencer, Azel Tracy, Joseph A. Gould, Amos Jones, Ambrose Hart, Dr. J. C. Wilcox, Thomas Dutcher, Theron Plumb, Alva Hart, Gad Hart, Chester Fancher, Oris Mason, William Waterhouse, Robinson Truesdale, Titus Rowe, Paul Wellman, Hosea Mowrey, Isaac Taylor, Louis Canfield, Levi Canfield, Jarvis Gates, Luman Canfield, Matthias Gates, Richard Gates, Amos Hart, Captain Asa Hutchins, Julius Miner, Jeremiah Leaming, Andrew Messersmith, Arial Chapman, Isaac Leaming, William Hull, Benjamin Reeder.

Calvin Cone was one of the pioneers of Gustavus in 1804, and changed his residence to this place in 1817.

Captain Asa Hutchins came from Vienna in 1816.

William Hull was a pioneer settler of Vernon in 1805, changing his residence to Hartford in 1821.

At a still later date came William Bond, William McCord, Norman E. Austin, Ira Fowler, the Bakers, Bennetts, Beebes, Hulls, Truman Parks, Billings O. Plimpton, Milton Holcomb, and Asa Newman.

At this time almost every family made the material for their own clothes. The clatter of the loom, the humming of the great wheel, or the buzzing of the little wheel, sometimes called "grandmother's piano," gave life and bustle, as well as business, to the whole household. Currency was so scarce that families were compelled to live within themselves, and barter became the usual rule in business. It was difficult at times to raise money for the payment of taxes; property being sold at almost any price to obtain the necessary funds to pay the county treasurer. School "marms" taught at seventy-five cents a week, or less, even, and were sometimes partly paid with "store orders," or "white backs," as they were sometimes called, and with these they purchased calico at fifty cents per yard for their "Sunday best." Butter at six cents per pound, pork and beef from two to three cents, did not allow of large store bills. Men and boys, to some extent, used buckskin breeches for everyday wear. They had one merit, at least, that of being durable if not elegant.

In the summer of 1828 the township was visited by the typhoid fever; some thirty deaths occurring within a few weeks, nearly all young people, the family of Colonel William Bushnell losing seven members in a short time. It commenced in Brookfield, came north into this township, and spread to some extent from this place. For a time it seemed to baffle the skill of the best physicians in the country. Those first taken with it and having the most care and attention, nearly all fell victims to the scourge. Dr. Kirtland, of Poland, Dr. Manning of Youngstown, Dr. J. C. Wilcox, and Dr. Asahel Jones, of this place, were in constant attendance for some weeks.

ANTI-SLAVERY MOVEMENT.

About 1832 the anti-slavery agitation commenced in this community. A society was soon formed, and for a long time Hartford was a prominent place for all lectures of that class. As a result of this agitation a branch of the memorable underground railway was run through the township, with many farm-house stations on its route, from which no fleeing bondsman were ever turned away.

MILLS.

Jeffery Bently bought of Holmes & Root, for a consideration of $100, two acres of land in lot twenty-three, near the south line of the township, the deed bearing date September 7, 1803. Upon this lot, according to the wording of the deed, mills had previously been built by him. The property was soon after sold to Titus Brockway and Daniel Hummason, for a consideration of $700, deed bearing date April 9, 1805. The first grist mill was so poorly constructed that the grain when ground, had such a peculiar appearance a facetious pioneer named it the "maggot mill." Improvements continued to be made, with some additions of land to the original purchase, until finally Hummason sold his one-half interest to Brockway, December 12, 1808, for a consideration of $1,500.

Previous to the building of this and the Orangeville mill, some families made mortars in the tops of stumps, and with a pestle and spring pole pounded their grain; others boiled wheat for food when the supplies ran low, and could not be renewed.

For a short time the pioneers were compelled to go to Beaver and Neshannock to mill, or supply their wants with more primitive means. In 1822 both mills were burned. It was supposed to have been the work of an incendiary. They were immediately rebuilt, however, with the saw-mill at the first location and the grist-mill a short distance farther south. The second grist-mill was burned in 1826, and was never rebuilt. The saw-mill is still standing, which was built at this time. This property soon after passed into the possession of Titus Brockway's son Edward, who sold it to its present owner, Joseph Burnett, in 1855. Water was the motive power for mills of all kinds early in the century.

About 1817 Asa Hutchins built a saw-mill on Yankee run, west of Burnett's mill, but it never did much business and soon went to decay. At a later date Alexander Spears built one, still farther west, on the same stream, which was used many years. On the west township line one was built by Mr. Foot at an early period. At the head of the ravine at the ledge a saw-mill stood, some forty years ago, owned by Daniel G. Andrews. On Brockway run west of Orangeville Lymon A. Moses built a mill, which was afterward owned by Bradford Hewitt, and at a later period was run by steam-power. On McCullough run Wilson Bushnell and Harry Parker built one, and only the remnant of a mill-dam and race are now to be seen. On the ridge George Snyder built a mill of the same class. It was also used as a steam-mill for some time. It has been removed.

So little reliance could be placed on the water saw-mills, and steam as a motive power for making lumber being unused, a project was started for using oxen for this purpose. Such a mill was built in 1821 and 1822, after original plans by the proprietor. It was situated on lot nineteen, a half mile east of the center, on land now known as the Tracy farm.

The steam-mill south of the center was built in 1849 by Jarvin Gates and Jay Parsons. It was bought soon after by Daniel Parsons, who sold to Benjamin Finn, Jr. It is now the property of Hummason & McCullum. It has attained to an unusual age for a steam saw-mill, having been in existence thirty-two years.

INDEPENDENCE DAY.

The first celebration of our National independence in this place is said to have taken place July 4, 1802, all the inhabitants in this vicinity assembling for the purpose.

In 1805 the day was spent by the pioneers in clearing the common, and was certainly a practical as well as patriotic way of spending the day.

In 1813 the day was celebrated with more formality at the barn of William C. Jones, which is now owned by his grandson, Robert C. Jones. An oration was delivered by Rev. Harvey Coe, and a dinner was provided at the tavern of David Lane.

In 1824 a celebration on a large scale was held at the center, and in 1842 the occasion partook more of a political character on account of the anti-slavery agitation, and that in 1861, on account of the breaking out of the war, engendered a military spirit and resulted in the organization of local military companies.

Our National centennial was celebrated in Hartford at Institute hall, in the "old church" building, by a Centennial tea party, which was an occasion of much interest.

SCHOOLS.

Like all people of New England origin and education, the pioneer had no sooner laid the foundation of a church than a school was established in the same vicinity.

In 1804 the first school in the township was taught at Burg Hill by Miss Bartholomew, consisting of twenty-four scholars from Hartford and Vernon.

As soon as the "green" was cleared from trees and brush, in 1805, the first school-house was erected. It was a frame building and stood nearly east of the town hall site. It was the first public building and nearly the first framed one in the township. After some four removals it now stands on the farm of William Mitchel. It has some historic interest connected with it, as for a time it was the only school-house, and for many years served also as church and town-hall. The first summer school was taught by Miss Amanda Finney. The following winter, school was taught by Wells Andrews. Among the early teachers we may mention Philo Borden, Ambrose Hart, Chester Andrews, Joseph Truesdale, George Hallock, Miss Hannah Bushnell, Miss Sally Gates, Miss Lura Bushnell, and Miss Olive Hickox. Theodore Trade at one time taught a school for two seasons in this school-house, numbering one hundred and six scholars. Besides his day labors his evenings were occupied with special schools for writing and spelling, for all of which he was paid the then large salary of $17 per month.

For a time there were but two school districts in the township, one at Burg Hill and one at the center. The first log school-house at Burg Hill stood opposite the residence of the late Seth Hayes. Soon the increase of population, however, made others necessary. The first school-house in the "Mill district" was of logs, and stood on the township line where the Methodist Episcopal church now stands. It was probably built in 1808, and the first school was taught by General Charles Woodruff. The second school-house stood under the "old elm tree" north of the mill-dam, and the first teacher in it was Miss Lavinia Flower, in the summer of 1816, followed by Thomas Bushnell, Jr., the next winter.

The first school-house in the east district was also of logs, and stood upon the corner opposite the residence of John B. Jones. The first two terms were taught by Miss Electa M. Jones. The first school on the ridge was taught by Miss Pluma More. The first school-house in the west district stood on the Bates farm about one-half mile north of Bates's corner. Among the names of those who have since taught in various places in the township may be mentioned Buel Barnes, Sarah M. Jones, Dr. William Bushnell, now of Mansfield, Ohio, Joseph Marvin, James Beebe, James L. Gage, whose wife was the well known Mrs. Frances D. Gage, Bethuel Beaman, Ira L. Fuller, Stephen Watkins, Miss Maria Austin, Miss Hannah Hutchins, Miss Amanda L. Beer, Miss Mary J. Leslie, A. R. Bushnell, Miss Mary Hoadley, Amos Thomas, N. G. Hyde, Riley Hull, and Marshal Woodford.

In 1827 a two-story brick school-house was erected at Burg Hill, the upper part of which was used for many years by the Free-will Baptist society. The first schools in this building were taught by George Hallock and Miss Sarah M. Jones.

In 1828 a two-story brick school-house was built at the center. These two buildings were used for some twenty-five years, when for some good cause they were demolished, and the present less pretentious and more modern houses were erected.

At the present time the common schools of the township are nine in number. Number one is known as Hartford special school district, number five as Orangeville special school district; the remaining schools, comprising four sub-school and three fractional school districts, are known as Hartford school districts. The school enumeration for 1880 in this township was four hundred and thirty-three. The amount paid for the support of common schools for the same year was $2,413.16.

The first school of a higher grade was taught by John Crowell in 1824, in the house now standing, long known as the residence of Captain Thomas Thompson. At a later date the Rev. Wells Andrews, Miss Caroline Andrews, Miss Lorain Marvin, and Miss Ann Brigham were also engaged at various times in teaching.

About 1840 a young ladies' school was taught for a number of terms by Miss Caroline Billings, and after a lapse of forty years is frequently referred to by citizens of the township as one which has left a lasting impression.

Seth A. Bushnell taught in 1843; Rev. Horace Palmer a little later. About this time Mr. and Mrs. Curtis taught at Burg Hill. In 1847 and 1849 John Lynch taught four months in the upper room of the old brick school-house, and gave general satisfaction. During the next summer a room was fitted up in the lower part of the old church for school purposes, at an expense of some $400. Dr. George W. Bushnell, Paul Wellman, Dr. Robert M. Beebe, George Hallock, and William Truesdale were chosen as a board of trustees.

In the winter of 1849 an act was passed by the General Assembly to incorporate the Hartford high school, and the board organized under the provisions of this act. In September, 1849, John Lynch commenced teaching in this new schoolroom, and in the winter following had over one hundred scholars under his charge. Miss Mary Conant, E. M. Cotton, Isaac W. Case, T. A. Bushnell, and F. V. Hayden were his assistants. He left to take charge of the union schools of Ashland, and still later was principal of the schools at Circleville, Ohio. Mr. Lynch possessed a peculiar faculty as teacher, which has never been equaled by any of his numerous successors, and is held in high esteem by all classes. List of principals and assistant teachers: Andrew

Patterson, F. V. Hayden, 1850–51; Cornelius Powers, Mrs. Minerva Powers, 1851–52; Henderson Judd, Mrs. Sarah C. Judd, 1852–53; A. K. Warren, Miss Emeline Warren, 1853–54; A. B. Lyon, Miss M. J. Goodrich, 1854–55; J. R. Kennedy, 1855–56, Edward Whiting, Miss E. Post, 1856–57; Erastus M. Cravath, Miss Mary J. Andrews, 1857–59; E. H. Merrill, Miss J. A. Bushnell, 1859–61; A. H. Brown, Mrs. M. E. Brown, 1861–62; J. G. Knight, 1862–63; Miss Jerusha A. Bushnell, 1863–64; Mrs. Ophelia Forward, 1865–66; John Hamilton, 1866–67; Ransom Davis, 1867–68.

In 1871, the old church being no longer required for religious meetings, it was entirely devoted to school purposes, and repaired at an expense of some $2,000, the lower floors being devoted to school-rooms, and the upper part converted into a hall for public exercises. A board of nine trustees was chosen by the subscribers of the school fund, viz: Homer B. Thompson, Peter Carlton, Edwin Bennett, Rev. George W. Anderson, Seth Thompson, Rev. J. B. Davison, T. A. Bushnell, Dr. James Irwin, and Benjamin Fenn. These trustees became incorporated under a general law of the State, made and provided for such cases, and the school was named Hartford Academic Institute.

The list of teachers since the reorganization has been as follows:

Mr. and Mrs. James W. Cheney, and Miss Ermina J. Day, 1871–72; J. W. Bowen and Miss Ermina J. Day, 1872–73; Mr. P. D. Dodge taught for three years, from 1873 to 1876, with Miss Hattie Linn as assistant for two years, and the third year with Miss F. M. Rogers and Miss Etta Gorseline; Mr. E. P. Madole, with Miss M. C. Hulbert and Miss Albertson, 1876–77; Mr. L. G. Spencer, with Miss Martha Hyde, in 1877–78, and also in 1879; C. B. Shaw, in 1879–80; Peter Vogel, 1880–81; Mr. and Mrs. J. H. Rice, 1881–82.

For over thirty years, this school of a higher grade has been maintained by tuitions and private contributions, and during that time has been of great benefit to this community and neighboring townships. It has in these years had its time of prosperity and adversity, but as long as the spirit of the pioneer fathers exists among the inhabitants, it will doubtless be sustained and supported.

MILITARY.

Among the pioneers were a few men who had served in the Continental army at various periods during the Revolutionary war, all buried at the center, except William C. Jones, who is buried at Burg Hill. He took part at the battle of Bunker Hill, and also served under Gates at Saratoga. Captain Alexander Bushnell, who received his commission while serving under Washington; Titus Hayes, who endured the hardships of the winter at Valley Forge; Edward Brockway, who took part in the capture of Burgoyne at Saratoga; Thomas and Daniel Bushnell, who served in their father's company for a time near the close of the war.

At the first military election, held May 7, 1804, William Bushnell was elected captain, Daniel Hummason first lieutenant, and Ebenezer M. Combs ensign. This company at that time formed a part of the Second regiment, Second brigade, Fourth division, Ohio militia, under Major-general Wadsworth. At a little later period it became the Third regiment, Third brigade of the same division, and was so designated during the War of 1812.

The following imperfect list of soldiers in the war is given. It includes a few who settled here since that period, and also two or three who resided here many years, and were long identified with the township but have since removed: Colonel Richard Hayes, Seth Thompson, Thomas McFarland, Hosea Mowrey, Davis Fuller, John Pfouts, Alexander Bushnell (3d), Selden Jones, Michael Quiggle, Selden C. Jones, Elijah Woodford, Jehiel Hurlburt, Wilson Bushnell, Archibald McFarland, Peter Quiggle, Ezra Hart, Harry Parker, Asa Andrews, A. W. Moses, Lieutenant Andrew Bushnell, Alva Hart, Captain Asa Hutchins, Elisha Bennett, Elijah Sawyer, Mathias Gates, Lester Hayes, Frederick Shull, John Groscost, Sherman Andrews, Joel Hall, William Bates, George W. Cassiday, O. S. Goodrich, Jacob DeWitt, John Kepner, Luman Brockway, Ambrose Hart, Lester Bushnell.

Azariah W. Moses was the last surviving member of Colonel Hayes' regiment in the township.

In 1823, by permission of Andrew Bushnell, brigadier-general First brigade Fourth division, Ohio militia, a company of light infantry was organized here, and for some years, under the command of Captain Philo Borden, Captain

Robinson Truesdale, Captain Azel Tracy, and perhaps other officers, it was maintained with a good degree of military pride. The company was ordered out for guard duty at the execution of Gardiner by Sheriff Mygatt.

In 1835, during the border troubles, the State militia were called upon by Governor Lucas, through the proper officials, for volunteers to "march at a moment's warning to the northern frontier of Ohio, to protect our fellow-citizens residing within its constitutional limits, from the lawless aggression and outrage of the authorities of Michigan."

They probably all volunteered, as was customary in such cases. The matter was soon settled, and their brief vision of military service passed away. The company was made of good material, and at a later date would doubtless have made a good military record. After this the company and regimental musters were all that served to keep alive the military spirit, and even these in a few years were abandoned.

The following is a list of those who died in the war of 1861-65: Lieutenant Calvin C. Hart was killed at Murfreesboro December 31, 1862. Christopher A. Bennett was also wounded at Murfreesboro and died January 10th. Charles Bennett was wounded at Brown's Ferry October 7, 1863, and died December 8, 1863. Asbury Hewitt was wounded at Resaca and died at Atlanta, and was buried by the rebels. Albert McFarland was killed at Murfreesboro. George Norton died in hospital at Louisville, Kentucky. Milo Bushnell died in hospital at Gallipolis, Ohio, April 17, 1863. Daniel W. Brockway died in Cleveland April 12, 1864. Virgil Holcomb died June 24, 1863, at Reedsville, Tennessee. Owen Spencer died at Manchester, Tennessee, August 16, 1863. Stewart Grosscost died in Andersonville prison. William Shirey was killed at Murfreesboro December 31, 1862. William Law died in hospital September 29, 1864. Harry Messenger, a member of the Seventy-sixth Pennsylvania regiment, was killed in July, 1863. Elliot S. Gilky, a member of the Fifty-seventh Pennsylvania regiment, was killed May 7, 1864, in the battle of the Wilderness. George Dutcher, a member of the Seventy-sixth Pennsylvania regiment, was wounded at Bermuda Hundred by a grape shot, and died in hospital at City Point, Virginia. H. H. Brown was known to have died

of starvation in Andersonville prison September 14, 1864. Frank Curtis, J. Pelton, S. Mountain, Luftus Murray, Harrison Allen, Melker Mellinger, John Decker, and William Paden also either died in battle or hospital during the war.

Lieutenant Davis Fuller has since died from disease contracted while in the army.

LADIES' AID SOCIETY.

Soon after President Lincoln's call for troops in April, 1861, the ladies of the township, anxious to bear their small share in the exertions and privations to be imposed by the war, organized a society for the purpose of sending needed aid to the soldiers of our army in camp or hospital. The first meeting was on June 5, 1861, at the session room of the Congregational church. In records still preserved it is shown that Mrs. Joel Miner was elected its first president, Miss Malinda Brockway and Miss Fanny Jones, vice-presidents; Mrs. A. G. Hart, secretary, and Mrs. D. Parsons, treasurer. A committee was then appointed to canvass the township to solicit donations of money and goods. It consisted of Mrs. D. S. Tracy, Miss Harriet Jones, Celia Gallespie, Mary Fitch, Jerusha Bushnell, Mrs. Gad Hart, Carrie Brockway, Mary Hoadly, Laura Olmstead, Mrs. Seth Hayes, Mrs. M. Cook, Jane Hale, Helen Hart, Ellen Bushnell, Matilda Lafferty, Mrs. E. Space, Mrs. Jerome Hall, Miss Elizabeth Myers, Miss Rebecca Jones.

With this competent and energetic corps of officers and committee, commenced the three years and a half of patient, unremitting, and persevering labor which followed. Each week the society met once, if not more, and much work was given out to those who found it not convenient to attend. After the first six months the society was reorganized as a branch of the Cleveland Aid society, and thenceforward received directions for work from it. After this time the officers were as follows: Presidents, Mrs. Benjamin Fenn, Mrs. Daniel Parsons, Miss Eliza Spear, Miss Jerusha Bushnell, Mrs. James Mattox. Secretaries, Mrs. Albert Hart, Mrs. Robert Johnson, Miss Mary Beebe. Treasurers, Mrs. D. Parsons, Mrs. J. Mattox, Mrs. Jay Baker, Miss E. Spear, Mrs. Augustus Drury. The disbursements amounted in all to $18,000, part of which was sent through the Cleveland branch of the sanitary commission, and part sent direct to the army. Beside this, quite an amount of sanitary stores and money were left on hand, at the close of the war, which in time was divided between the Freedmen and sufferers by the Chicago fire. Among the earnest workers of this society were Miss Lizzie Beebe, Mary Bushnell, Mary Bennett, Anna Bates, Rhoda Moses, Mrs. Elmer Moses, Miss Jerusha Fuller, Esther Wier, Ida Thompson, Malinda Kepner, Mrs. Eliza Bennett, Mrs. Solon Gilky, Mrs. Calvin Hart, Mrs. Homer Thompson, Miss Deborah Borden, Anna Hart, Sophia Bennett, Kate Bushnell, Mrs. Henry Chamberlain, Miss Sarah Bushnell, Janett Spear, Miss Caroline Dutcher, Lavina Gallespie. The officers of the Orangeville society, also in this township, consisted of Mrs. Charles Hull, Mrs. Shelden Palmer, presidents; Mrs. Edward Jones, Mrs. Jesse Hahn, vice-presidents; Mrs. Augustus Moffitt, Mrs. Henry Reed, secretaries and treasurers. Estimate of disbursements, $15,000.

A society was also formed at Burnett's mill, but soon after was united with the center society.

PUBLIC HOUSES.

The first public house was kept by Aaron Brockway at Burg Hill, as early as 1802 or 1803. David Lane soon afterward engaged in the same business, and followed it for many years. He was located on the south side of Burg Hill, the old military headquarters, and near the old parade ground, where now stands the residence of his grandson, Henry Lane.

" In days long gone 'his' was deemed of goodly inns the chief."

The sparkling spring near by, freely as of yore, yields to thirsty man and beast refreshment pure, but,

"Never more the sign board swinging, flaunts its gilded wonder there;
Never, as with nearer tinkle through the dust of long ago,
Creeps the Pennsylvania wagons up the twilight, white and slow."

This pioneer host is said to have been very obliging and very funny. As people often halted at the spring near his house to water their horses, he would kindly assist them, and of course receive the usual thanks. It is said of him that he always counted a "thank you" worth a shilling (12½ cents), and a "thank you, sir" worth a quarter of a dollar, and he used to say some days he made several dollars just by obliging people passing by.

Once in early days a band of sneaking Indians entered the kitchen and appropriated for their own use a baking intended for special company, without even a "thank you," much to the discomfort of the weary housekeeper. That time the joke seems to have been on the landlord, and he was consequently "out of pocket."

It was often customary in those days to have a peculiar sign. His had represented upon it a horse, and a plumb line suspended from the center above it, accompanied with the following quotation: "Amos 7th Ch. 7th, 8th v."

Later, Samuel Hewitt and Lester Lane were engaged on the "Hill" in the same business.

The first public house at the center of the township was built by Elam Jones, and opened in 1829. In 1846 he retired, and was followed by Cornelius Silliman. Later by William Christy, J. B. Nelson, and the present proprietor, Daniel Parsons.

About 1841 G. C. Reed opened a second public house a little south of the center. He sold to Jehiel Lane, who was succeeded by Alva Merriam; later by Solon Gilky, who, after a time, converted it into a private residence.

POSTAL MATTERS.

The first postmaster was Titus Brockway; Philo Borden, however, acting as his deputy for many years. Edward Brockway held the office a short time while his father was a member of the Legislature. Later the office has been held successively by James Miller, Elam Jones, G. C. Reed, L. C. Jones, John Yeatman, J. H. C. Johnson, Jay Baker, and H. B. Thomas, the present incumbent.

At Burg Hill the first postmaster was Erastus Olin, the office being in Hayes & Plumb's store building; it was, however, soon removed to the railroad station of the same name in Vernon.

A weekly mail for years supplied our citizens with news of the outside world. About 1830, however, postal facilities were increased, and mail was carried in a four-horse Concord coach. The route became an important one between the lake and the river, for the conveyance of passengers as well as mail. After the financial crash of 1837 mail service was reduced, to be again increased at a later date. For a long time it was a tri-weekly mail between Conneaut and Youngstown. A weekly mail between Warren and Franklin, Pennsylvania, and later a tri-weekly from the former place to Greenville, Pennsylvania, passed through here, but was discontinued after the building of the Atlantic & Great Western railway. The north and south route was also shortened, so that it now extends only from this office to Burg Hill station, from which point daily mails are received.

MERCHANTS.

The first store was opened in 1814 at Burg Hill by James Heslep, who sold out in a few months to Colonel Richard Hayes. At this time goods were brought from Philadelphia in large Pennsylvania six-horse covered wagons, carrying nearly three tons. Colonel Hayes soon learned that the new country must pay its debts in a currency which could transport itself to the seaboard and accordingly engaged in buying large droves of cattle, some numbering as high as five hundred head, which were driven by him over the mountains to Philadelphia market. It is said that Benjamin F. Wade was employed on two or three occasions to assist Colonel Hayes' son Alvin in driving these cattle to the eastern markets.

Goods were also bought to some extent by dealers who would go among the farmers and purchase butter, cheese, and produce, take it to Pittsburg in wagons and exchange it for dry goods and groceries, school books and almanacs, or anything their customers saw fit to order. About two weeks were required to make the round trip. Frequently farmers for themselves and neighbors would carry their produce to Pittsburg and make the needed exchanges.

Colonel Hayes continued in buying until his death in 1837. Seth Hayes, his son, succeeded him in business.

Ralph Plumb was for many years a partner of Seth Hayes. He was an active, energetic business man. He is now a resident of Streator, Illinois. Plumb was succeeded in the partnership by Thomas Vernon.

On West street Draton Andrews carried on a small store for some years.

Horace Flower sold goods in the south part of the township for a short time.

About 1820 Ambrose Hart opened a store in a two-story log-building, which then stood on the north and south center road near the southwest corner of lot eighteen. At a later period he removed to the center of Brookfield, and with

Alva Hart and Seth Thompson as partners continued in the same business.

About 1829 Alva Hart returned to Hartford and with his brother, Gad Hart, built the store building now standing near the northeast corner of the public square, and opened the first store at the "center." Gad Hart soon after sold to his brother and engaged in farming. Alva Hart continued in trade until 1846, a part of this time with S. H. Benton and Salmon N. Hart as partners. In 1837 G. C. Reed opened a store in a building standing near the present location of the east church. Later L. C. Jones, Milton Graham, G. L. Woodford, M. Christy, Jay Baker, Joel Miner, J. L. Pierce, A. R. Gates, and H. B. Thompson have each been engaged in merchandizing at various times and places.

PHYSICIANS.

The first resident physician was Dr. Daniel Upson. Previous to his settlement Dr. Jeremiah Wilcox, of Vernon, practiced here. Upson soon after removed to Hudson, Ohio, and was succeeded by Dr. Jeremiah C. Wilcox, who practiced some twenty years and then removed to Richfield, Ohio.

Dr. Asahel Jones, a student of Dr. Wilcox and a cotemporary also followed the profession for some years until the time of his decease.

Dr. George W. Bushnell, still residing here, and Dr. Robert M. Beebee, deceased, then followed with many years of successful practice. Dr. Daniel W. Atherholt and Dr. James Irwin are the present medical practitioners.

At Orangeville Dr. Asahel Brainard commenced practice in 1837, and resided here until his death in 1881. He was a son of Asahel Brainard, the pioneer, who came into the township in 1799.

Dr. G. W. Hamilton settled here in 1864, and is at present the only physician in the village.

CONGREGATIONAL CHURCH.

The Rev. Joseph Badger, who was sent out by the Connecticut Missionary society, first visited Hartford late in December, 1800, and soon after preached in Vernon. The people of the townships, five families in Vernon and three in Hartford, collected to attend the meeting. The three families in this township were doubtless those of Edward Brockway, Isaac Jones, and Charles Merry.

Some preliminary steps were taken as early as 1802 toward the formation of a church society, but it was not until September 17, 1803, that Mr. Badger met the following persons for that purpose: Edward Brockway and Sarah, his wife, Mrs. Sarah Bates, Timothy Crosby, Titus Brockway, Plumb Sutliff, Sarah Palmer, and Sarah Smith. They adopted the commonly received Congregational confession of faith and covenant, and were constituted a church of Christ.

On the following Sabbath the first season of communion was held in a grove, there being no building that would accommodate the people. Rev. Mr. Tait, of Mercer, Pennsylvania, preached the sermon, and assisted in the communion service. About forty communicants were present.

In 1804 a four-days' meeting was held in the barn of Thomas Thompson, which stood where the steam saw-mill now stands, near the present residence of Henry Bennett. Some additions were made to the church as the result of this meeting. Wells Andrews, who afterwards became the pastor of the church, was one of the number.

This was probably the first Congregational church formed within the present limits of the county, as the Warren church was not organized until October 19th of the same year. This church was known as "The Church of Christ in Hartford, Vernon, and Kinsman." The church adopted the "plan of union" as proposed by the general assembly of the Presbyterian church of America, and approved by the general association of Connecticut known as the "accommodation plan."

Meetings were held in rotation in these townships, the citizens of each attending church in the other as often as convenient. The barn of Thomas Thompson was used as a place of worship for a time, afterwards the school-house, until the erection of the church in 1819. The society had no settled pastor, but enjoyed the occasional labors of Revs. Badger, Darrow, Robbins, and Leslie for the first twelve years of its existence.

In 1813 the church had increased to eighty members, and at this time made the acquaintance of the Rev. Harvey Coe, of Granville, Massachusetts, and invited him to become their pastor.

On the 4th of April, 1814, he was installed at the residence of Dr. Wilcox, in Vernon, the school-house, the usual place of holding meetings, not being large enough to accommodate those in attendance. The Rev. John Seward preached the installation sermon.

The church had been until this time under the care of the presbytery of Hartford, which embraced ministers of western Pennsylvania as well as those living on the Western Reserve, and belonged to the synod of Pittsburg. Among these ministers were Revs. Badger, Barr, Leslie, Darrow, Wick, Hughes, and Tait. This presbytery seems to have been merged into Grand River presbytery about 1814.

For some nine years Mr. Coe's pastorate included the three branches of this church.

Titus Brockway and Daniel Bushnell were the first deacons of the Hartford branch of the church, and served in that capacity for many years. Chester Andrews was afterwards elected to fill the vacancy occasioned by the resignation of Daniel Bushnell.

In 1821 the membership had increased to two hundred and ten. A church having been built in Hartford in 1819 of sufficient size to accommodate the people, it became desirable to have greater religious privileges than were possible under the united church of Hartford, Vernon, and Kinsman, and accordingly the following persons, forty-three in number, were dismissed by letter September 15, 1823, for the purpose of organizing a separate church in this township, viz: Titus Brockway, Chester Andrews, Philo Borden, Abigail A. Borden, William Rathbun, Dorothea Rathbun, Asahel Brainard, Polly M. Brainard, Sarah Jones, Phebe Borden, Shalor Fitch, Lovisa Fitch, Joseph A. Gould, Orrey Gould, Lament Bushnell, Lucy Andrews, Davis Fuller, Hannah Fuller, John B. Fitch, Rebecca Bushnell, Phebe Tracy, Phebe Olmstead, Rebecca Woodford, Chester Francher, Thomas Dutcher, Jemima Francher, Daniel M. Bushnell, Betsy Spencer, Alva Hart, Fanny W. Hart, Amoret Border, Polly Jones, Daniel C. Bushnell, Polly Bushnell, Seymour A. Moses, Rhoda Moses, Gad Hart, Lucretia Hart, Lucy Jones, Lorena Wilcox, Hope Beach, Hannah Andrews, Hannah Hutchins.

On the 4th of December, of the same year, they were formed into a church at the meeting-

34*

house in Hartford by Rev. Harvey Coe. About this time Mr. Coe resigned the pastorate of this branch of the church. In 1826 the Rev. Wells Andrews, pastor of the second Presbyterian church of Alexandria, District of Columbia, accepted a call to this church, and for some ten years remained here. He had formerly been a resident, and was a relative of many members of the church and society, and at an early day cleared up a farm, chopping days and studying nights during his preparation for college, being one of the pioneers of the township. This seems to have been the golden age of this church, Mr. Andrews having been able to exert a great influence in the community.

During this period quite an extensive revival occurred, and many additions were made to the church. The Rev. Lucius Foot assisted Mr. Andrews in these revival labors. Revs. Rockwell, Cochran, and Young, each successively filled the pastorate about this period. The church at this time (1837) numbered a hundred and sixty-four communicants. In October, 1840, Chester Andrews, Alva Hart, Seymour A. Moses, Edward Brockway (second), Michael Quiggle, Amos Jones, and others to the number of forty-two persons, withdrew to form a Presbyterian church, which was immediately organized with the Rev. George D. Young as pastor. They first met in the brick school-house at the center. Soon after a room was fitted up in the upper part of Alva Hart's store building, now the post-office, where meetings were held until the building of the new church in 1846. The Hon. Seth Hayes contributed the greater portion of the funds for this purpose. Mrs. Sarah B. Hayes, his wife, contributed funds for the purchase of the bell. It was known at this time as the Presbyterian church. Rev. Horace Palmer, and the Rev. Benjamin Fenn, each had pastoral charge of this society for a time, until it was again united with the original church in 1852.

In 1842 the Rev. John Keep became the pastor of the Congregational church, and remained some four years. He was one of the prominent anti-slavery clergymen at that time, and during his residence here the church took quite an advanced position on the subject of slavery. This church was considered by people generally to hold extreme views on that subject.

In 1842 Philo Borden, one of the pioneers of the township, and his son, Russell Borden, gave to the church three-quarters of an acre of land on which to erect a parsonage, which was accordingly built in 1843, and first occupied by the Rev. John Keep.

The church at this time obtained an act of incorporation, for the purpose of becoming a corporate body, with all the rights and privileges incident thereto.

In 1847 the Rev. Theodore J. Keep accepted the pastoral charge, but owing to ill health was compelled to resign in 1849.

The Rev. Henry Fairchild (at present president of Berea college, Kentucky), was called to fill the vacancy thus made, and during his pastorate in this church, and that of the Rev. B. Fenn in the Presbyterian, the churches were reunited under its original name of "The Church of Christ in Hartford," as before mentioned, in April, 1852. Soon after this period the Rev. Robert Burgess preached for a time, and was followed by the Rev. Benjamin Walker, who was succeeded by the Rev. Joseph Torrence, Rev. J. B. Davison, and Rev. U. T. Chamberlin, who resigned on account of ill health, and died January 10, 1880. At the present time (1881) the church has no settled pastor.

In 1868 the society sustained a great loss in the death of Deacon Edward Brockway, who had become greatly endeared to the church by many years of faithful Christian service. Deacon Norman E. Austin was elected his successor, but in a few years he also died, and the vacancy was filled by Deacon Truman Jones, who was soon called by death to follow his predecessors.

The present officers of the church are Deacon Simeon C. Baker, who has acted in the capacity of deacon for over thirty years, and Deacon Charles Hyde. Mr. James M. Jones is clerk, and the three above named are also the trustees. From a very early day Sunday-schools have been maintained. Deacon Daniel Bushnell was the first superintendent. He gave catechetical and Bible instructions, as was the custom in those times. Out of this grew the present form of conducting Sunday-schools. After other churches were formed for many years three Sunday-schools were kept up, but in time, churches having been formed at different places in the township, the number of attendants at the "center" was greatly diminished, and it was thought best to unite the different schools. This was accomplished about 1860, since which time a union Sunday-school has been conducted, which meets alternately in the Congregational and Methodist Episcopal churches at present. Thomas Miller, superintendent; Frank Stewart, secretary and treasurer.

HARTFORD METHODIST CHURCH.

This society was first organized within the present limit of Vernon by Rev. Obed Crosby, with five members—Obed Crosby and wife, Ewing Wright and wife, and Eunice Brockway, afterwards Mrs. Daniel Bushnell, of this township. It was the first church of this denomination on the Western Reserve, having been organized in 1801. The place of meeting being near the line of Vernon and Hartford, and the members increasing in Hartford more rapidly than in Vernon, it was removed into Hartford and took its name. Their place of worship was in the school-house at Burg Hill until 1836, when they removed to the center of the township, and built the present house of worship, Isaac Winans being elder, and S. Hubbard and W. French preacher in charge during this year. In 1874 the church was repaired at an expense of $1,100.

So many churches of the same denomination having been formed in this immediate vicinity, the membership of this center church has been materially decreased.

Among those who have been prominent members of this church during its later history may be mentioned the McFarland families, Mr. and Mrs. Asahel Borden, Dr. Robert Beebe and wife, Mr. and Mrs. Joel Miner, Mr. and Mrs. Lyman Rathbun, and Mr. and Mrs. U. H. Brockway. The old members have all passed away, and it has been impossible for the writer to obtain a full history of this church.

DISCIPLES CHURCH.

This church was organized May 1, 1830, by William Hayden, with the following named persons as members, viz: Elihu Bates, William Vince, George W. Bushnell, John Bates, Julius Miner, George Fell, John Jones, Sally Vince, Sally Bushnell, and Julia Bates. Two of these, George W. Bushnell and Julia Bates, are still living.

Marcus Bosworth, John Henry, Alexander Campbell, Walter Scott, Harvey Brocket, and Andrew Burns, were the early preachers of this denomination.

This church was organized on West street, and for over twenty years their place of worship was the school-house in that vicinity. In 1853 it was changed to the center of the township.

The membership at this time is about seventy. G. W. Bushnell, Alexander Spears, James Fowler, Samuel Bates, Abner Banning, and A. D. Drury, have been prominent members of this society for many years. Elder Peter Vogle is the present preacher.

BROCKWAY MILLS METHODIST EPISCOPAL CHURCH.

Quite early Brockway mills school-house became one of the occasional preaching places of the early preachers of the Methodist church.

Dr. Charles Elliot and Rev. Alfred Bronson were probably the first (about 1820). About 1822 preaching was regularly furnished by Rev. William Tipton and Rev. A. G. Richardson, who traveled Youngstown circuit, which then included this place.

Subsequently a class was formed, among the members of which were Abner Fowler and Esther, his wife, John Newcome and wife, Benjamin Reeder and Polly, his wife, with other members of their family, Jane and Margaret Lafferty, Abel Walker and wife, David Snyder and family, Michael Bear and family, and also members of the Byers family. For a long time meetings were held on week days and Sunday evenings, as most convenient for the preachers.

About 1850, however, regular Sunday preaching was established by Rev. Ahab Keller, and in 1857 a church was built. It was dedicated in January, 1858, Elder Norton preaching the dedication sermon, Rev. J. W. Hill being preacher in charge. Miss Sarah Fowler, daughter of Abner Fowler, was one of the largest subscribers to the building fund, and during her life was one of the most faithful members.

At present the church numbers some forty members, and has a flourishing Sunday-school under the superintendence of Miss S. C. Burnett.

MASONRY.

The first meetings of Jerusalem lodge No. 19, Free and Accepted Masons, of Hartford, Ohio, were held under a dispensation of the Grand lodge of Ohio, dated February 15, 1812, and issued by Lewis Cass, grand master. Regular meetings were held under this dispensation until 1814.

The following were the officers appointed for their first meeting: Martin Smith, W. M.; Daniel Bushnell, S. W.; Samuel Spencer, J. W.; Joseph DeWolf, treasurer; Richard Hayes, secretary; Sterling G. Bushnell, S. D.; Lebbeus Beech, J. D.; Thomas McMillen, tyler.

At the first meeting recorded under this dispensation, May 20, 1812, Linus Hayes, Plumb Sutliff, Zopher Case, and Gilbert Palmer were initiated.

A number of the early members of this lodge appear to have previously been among the petitioners for the charter of Old Erie No. 3, established at Warren in 1804, and are known to have been members of Turkey Hill's lodge in Connecticut.

Their first place of meeting is not definitely known, but as early as September, 1812, it was at the public house kept by David Lane at Burg Hill.

At a meeting of the Grand lodge held at Chillicothe January 4, 1814, an application for a charter was presented signed by the following members, viz: Martin Smith, Daniel Bushnell, Samuel Spencer, Richard Hayes, Joseph DeWolf, Sterling G. Bushnell, Lebbeus Beech, and Linus Hayes.

A charter was granted dated January 5, 1814, with the above mentioned persons as charter members, and signed by Henry Brush, grand master, and Robert Kercheral, grand secretary.

Soon after this their place of meeting seems to have been for a short time in the township of Vernon at the public house of Ambrose Palmer, but in 1817 they were for a time located at the residence of Titus Brockway, Esq., in Hartford, and afterwards at the residence of Daniel Bushnell, and in 1829 at the public house of Elam Jones, at the center of the township, where they remained till 1844, when they again removed to the public house of G. C. Reed. In 1854 the present lodge rooms were erected by the society where their meetings have since been held.

In 1816 St. John's Day was celebrated at Vernon by Jerusalem, Erie, and Western Star lodges, sixty-three members of the fraternity being present. The oration was delivered by George Tod.

Clergyman present, Adamson Bentley and Harvey Coe. Among the visiting fraternity present were Elisha Whittlesey, Asahel Adams, Seth Tracy, John W. Seely, Arad Way, and Francis Freeman.

It is recorded that this society laid the corner-stone of the brick church in Vernon on August 3, 1826.

The following are the past masters from 1812 to 1881: Martin Smith, Sterling G. Bushnell, Theron Plumb, Horace Flower, Andrews Bushnell, John C. Smith, Garry C. Reed, Marion Hyde, L. C. Jones, D. S. Tracy, Joel Bushnell, Rev. R. W. Crane, Willis Reeder, A. D. Fell, J. D. Burnett, and Brunell Hull. The officers elected for 1882 are Joel Bushnell, W. M.; D. S. Tracy, S. W.; D. H. Artherholt, J. W.; A. D. Fell, treasurer; L. G. Spencer, secretary: C. W. Hawkins, S. D.; James Weir, J. D.; N. A. Reeder, tyler. The number of members that have been enrolled in this lodge is three hundred and eleven, and the present number ninety-three. The society owns the building in which its commodious lodge-rooms are situated. The ground floor of this building is occupied by a store, and the second floor is devoted to lodge-rooms. The society was never in a more prosperous condition.

BURG HILL GRANGE NO. 1107.

This society was organized January 4, 1875, in the school-house at Burg Hill, by O. P. Laird, deputy of the National Grange. The following are the charter members:

Colonel Edward Hayes, Mrs. E. C. Hayes, A. D. Fell, Mrs. H. M. Fell, William H. Bushnell, Mrs. Eliza Bushnell, Job Biggins, Mrs. Sarah Biggins, C. H. Roberts, Mrs. L. B. Roberts, James Fowler, Mrs. Lorinda Fowler, Osman Hull, Mrs. L. E. Hull, Ransom Hull, Mrs. N. S. Hull, H. G. Bates, Mrs. S. E. Bates, R. R. Miner, Mrs. Paulina Miner, Lucius Holcomb, Mrs. Orra Holcomb, George K. Pelton, Mrs. E. P. Mizener, George W. Holcomb, Brunel Hull, W. A. Bacon, Isaac Pfouts, Joel Bushnell, Henry Biggens.

First officers elected: Colonel Edward Hayes, W. M.; A. D. Fell, W. O.; James Fowler, W. L.; O. Hull, W. S.; R. R. Miner, W. A. S.; H. G. Bates, W. C.; George K. Pelton, W. Treasurer; L. B. Hull, W. Secretary; Henry Biggins, W. G. K. Lady officers—S. E. Bates, W. C.;

E. Roberts, W. F.; L. E. Hull, W. P.; H. M. Fell, W. L. A. S.

This grange met at M. C. Graham's hall until 1878. They then built a hall at old Burg Hill, where they have since held their meetings.

CEMETERIES.

There are three cemeteries in the township, the one at the center being the oldest. The site was selected in 1805, after the death of Fidelia Andrews, the land being given by Titus Brockway. She was buried in the forest, and her grave was surrounded by an enclosure of logs.

Among the marble headstones of later years are scattered here and there the old brown flag- and sand-stones, which mark the early graves. On many of these the inscriptions are rudely chiseled, and some are almost obliterated by the hand of time. Beside them grow the roses planted by hands long since folded to rest in other graves.

Here lies the first pioneer, Edward Brockway, and a large number of his descendants are also buried here. The soldier of the Revolution and the soldier of the Rebellion are found here, and near them lies Asahel Brainard, the first settler, who spent the winter alone in this unbroken forest, the only representative of this pioneer family buried in the township. The Hon. Calvin Cone, the Hon. Titus Brockway, Colonel William Bushnell, and the Hon. James Beebe are among the prominent persons interred in this old cemetery, including Captain Alexander Bushnell, Thomas Bushnell, Titus Hayes, Edward Brockway, and Daniel Bushnell, who were soldiers of the war of the Revolution. Here also are buried Thomas McFarland, Davis Fuller, Alexander Bushnell, Elijah Woodford, Selden Jones, Seth Thompson, Hosea Mowrey, John Pfouts, Wilson Bushnell, Michael Quiggle, Matthias Gates, S. C. Jones, Elijah Sawyer, Ambrose Hart, Jehial Hulburt, Lester Bushnell, General Andrews Bushnell, Archibald McFarland, and Elisha Bennett, soldiers of the War of 1812. Also D. W. Brockway, Milo Bushnell, Lieutenant C. C. Hart, Christopher A. Bennett, Charles Bennett, and Lieutenant Davis Fuller, soldiers of the Rebellion.

The burying ground at Burg Hill has been the burial place of the pioneer families of Hayes, Jones, Merry, and Hull. The first grave was that of Eliza Hayes, daughter of Colonel Richard Hayes, who died August 14, 1814. This site was afterwards presented to the township by the Hayes family. Isaac Jones, one of the first pioneers, William C. Jones, a pioneer and a veteran of 1776, Colonel Richard Hayes, Lester Hayes, Luman Brockway, and James Henry, soldiers of the War of 1812, and Robert Mizener, a Vernon soldier of the late war, are buried here.

The west burying ground was given to the township by Deacon Elihu Bates, and the first grave was that of Mrs. Samuel Bates, in 1837. Romanta Norton, Joel Hall, and William Bates, soldiers of 1812 and George Norton, a soldier of the late war, are buried here. This has been the burial place of the Bates, Leaming, Norton, Parsons, Newman, Spencer, Mason, and Hall families, mostly settlers of a later date. John Groscost, a soldier of 1812, was buried on lot one, on the farm formerly owned by him.

At Orangeville no permanent place of burial was selected until 1841, when Augustus Reed made a donation of land for that purpose. Previous to this time most of the interments were at the centre of the township, a few, however, being made near the residence of Mr. Patton. According to tradition, early in the century a man was buried where the shop of Mr. Davis now stands, and also two children by the name of Totman on the south bank of the Pymatuning east of the State line. The first interment in the present cemetery was Ann Catherine, a daughter of Rensselaer Root, who died June 10, 1841. John Cassidy, Jacob Dewitt, O. S. Goodrich, William Carnes, and A. W. Moses, soldiers of the War of 1812, are buried here. Of the late war Harrison Allen, Caleb Leonard, Milton Mellinger, George Wait, and a non-resident soldier by the name of Fitzpatrick, who was killed on the railroad, are also buried here.

ORANGEVILLE.

For many years the northeastern portion of the township has been known by the name of Orangeville.

The construction of the New York, Pennsylvania & Ohio Railway, and the opening of coal mines east of it, has given some impetus to business at this place. No good reason seems to exist why it may not become a point for manufacturing interests of various kinds, much more extensive than at present, if residents will only take hold of the matter in earnest by investing in such enterprises and hold out inducement to others to do so.

The village was incorporated in 1868, and is situated in the northeast corner of Hartford township. It extends one mile from north to south, and seven-eighths of a mile from east to west. One of the principal streets being on the State line, the business interests and history of the place can not be fully shown, without, to some extent, including territory outside of the present corporate limits of the village, yet practically forming a part of it.

The first mayor was R. E. Grey; and A. M. Brockway, N. E. Austin, E. B. Jones, Dr. A. C. Brainard, and S. H. Spear, were elected as members of the first council. Nelson Hyde held the office of mayor for one year, and from that time to the present it has been filled by the present incumbent, George W. Snyder.

A village special school district was organized in 1868, and a fine school-house was soon after built. The school is at present being taught by L. G. Spencer and Miss Bell Pollock. The enumeration of scholars for 1881 was a hundred and ten.

The territory comprised in the village limits forms a portion of the land purchased of Root & Holmes, in 1799, by Edward Brockway. Charles Merry was the first pioneer settler within the present incorporate limits of Orangeville. He settled on what is now known as the N. E. Austin farm, at present owned by Willard C. Hull. He remained but a short time, however, removing soon to Vernon. Not long after, Edward Brockway removed from his first location, and settled on the farm now owned by his grandson, E. B. Jones.

According to the history and atlas of Mercer county, Pennsylvania, the pioneer settler and founder of Orangeville was Jacob Loutzenhiser, who came in 1797 or 1798, probably in the former year. He built a hewed log mill, with an under-shot wheel twenty-five feet in diameter; and on the 19th of April, 1802, sold to Adam Hahn. This was the first mill in Pymatuning township, Pennsylvania. This place was known for several years as Hahn's mills. Judging by all the facts that have come to the writer's knowledge, he is of the opinion, however, that the mill did not go into operation before 1801. According to tradition it was a rude structure, like

others of its day, yet served a good purpose in relieving the pioneers of long trips to mill. A saw-mill was also built at a later period, so that two of the prime wants of early settlers, food and lumber, could be supplied. The era of steam-power having taken the place of water in lumbering, the old saw-mill has passed away. The grist-mill soon gave place to a better structure, which was used for many years. It has since been successively in possession of Keck, A. & L. Moffatt, Hoadley, Clark, and perhaps of some others. In 1869, being in possession of Shafer Brothers, the principal improvements were made at an expense of $40,000 for mill and dam. The present proprietors of the flouring-mill are Hendrickson & Walworth.

The first village lots were laid out in 1818 by Augustus and Levi Moffatt.

The last named was a clothier by trade, and the brothers built the first carding machine, which they afterwards sold to Charles and Richard Hull, who settled here in 1834-35. Augustus Moffatt remained here until his death, engaged mostly in the occupation of farming.

In 1835 his three brothers, Levi, Lot, and Zelotus, built two flat-boats and launched them in the race below the mill. They were loaded with produce likely to find a market on the way, and with their families embarked on a journey by river to the West.

About 1821 a flat-boat was launched here which was loaded with butter and cheese and sent to the New Orleans' market.

A woolen factory was carried on here for some years by Hull Brothers & Hurlburt. This property was purchased by George McFarland, and the business was soon after discontinued. Moffat & Fell were engaged in the foundry business for many years.

The present industries of the villages not heretofore mentioned are a saw-mill owned by G. W. Arnold, one by Dwight Wilson, a stave-mill by W. R. Field, and the carriage factory of S. H. Spear.

The first merchant at Orangeville was Moses Beach. He was followed first by the firm of Hyde, Reed & Bushnell, later by Morris Jones, Horace Baily, Joel Smith, Hurlburt & Co., Ernst & Hahn, Nathan Showers, Sylvester Fell & Son, Shafer Brothers, Nelson Hyde & Co., Lewis Reno, E. & A. Fell, Aurelius Fell, and at the present time Trimble & McIntosh are engaged in trade, and E. R. Fell & Co. in drugs and general merchandise.

The first postmaster was Rensselær Root. The office has since been held by Dr. Asahel Brainard, N. E. Austin, John Scaling (who held it for over twenty years), Nathan Showers, Jonathan Ernst, Eliza Johnson, Shelden Palmer, and G. W. Snyder the present incumbent. The office was established about 1845. The first mail route was a weekly between Warren, Ohio, and Franklin, Pennsylvania. Later it became a tri-weekly from Warren to Greenville, Pennsylvania, which was superseded by railway service after the construction of the railroad in 1862.

BAPTIST CHURCH.

In 1816 Elder Jonathan Sheldon settled in Fowler, and through his instrumentality a church was organized called the Baptist church of Fowler, Hartford, and Vernon. Its meetings were mostly held in Fowler and Hartford, in school-houses and private dwellings, as circumstances dictated.

Mrs. Nancy Lane, of Hartford, is said to have been the first person in the township baptized by immersion, Elder Jonathan Sheldon officiating.

The early records of the church were burned, but according to tradition Elihu Bates, Ruth Beach, Norman Holcomb, Osman Williams and wife, Mary Black, and Joseph DeWolf were probably among the pioneer members of this church.

Among the Baptist ministers who occasionally supplied the church were Elders Freeman, Gorman, Woodworth, and Sydney Rigdon, of Peters Creek, Virginia, afterwards of Mormon notoriety. He resided in Hartford for some months, preaching a portion of the time in the "old church" at the "center."

About 1827 the doctrines of Alexander Campbell began to prevail, and so many of the members embraced the new faith that for some time the church was almost extinct, yet a few held fast to the old tenets.

In 1835 it was reorganized at Orangeville. Mr. and Mrs. Chares Hull, Lyman Phelps and wife, and a number of others from this vicinity united with the church about that time, and as Orangeville was now the most central point for the members, the church began to hold meetings here and took the name of this place. At first meetings were held in the Methodist house of worship, but about 1845 the present church was built. This society belonged to the Beaver association until the formation of the Trumbull association.

In 1843 quite an addition was made to the church as a result of the revival labors of Elder John Winters. In 1844 Elder R. B. Phelps was pastor of the church, and continued until 1848, when Elder T. W. Greer became the minister, and during his pastorate many additions were made to the church. After this time Elder R. B. Phelps again preached for this society for a time. At the present time (1882) Elder T. W. Greer again holds the pastorate of this church. Mr. James Russel has been a prominent member of this church for over fifty years, and at the present time is one of its most stanch supporters. Mr. and Mrs. Robert Luce, Mr. and Mrs. Lyman Phelps, and Mr. and Mrs. Charles Hull have all been prominent members of this church. The present membership is sixty-seven.

ORANGEVILLE METHODIST CHURCH.

This church was organized probably in 1837. Among its first members were Augustus Reed and wife, Charles Reed, Maria Reed, Harriet Reed, Mrs Daniel Totman, Elisha Fox, and George Fell. A small meeting-house was built soon after, and used until the building of the present church in 1872 at an expense of $5,000. At present the church has eighty-seven members.

UNITED BRETHREN CHURCH.

This society was organized in Pennsylvania, and was removed to Orangeville in 1872. The ministers who have served this people since that period are Revs. Cone, Williams, and Bedow. It is now a small but prosperous society. Liberal contributions were made outside of church membership for building purposes, with the understanding that it is to be open at all times for the use of other denominations, and for lectures when not occupied by the said church of the United Brethren in Christ.

OLD PEOPLE.

Mrs. Chloe (Wait) Bushnell, wife of Captain Alexander Bushnell, was born June 20, 1738, at Lyme, Connecticut, and died here October 28, 1832, the oldest person deceased in the township during the first seventy years of its history. Nearly thirty years before she came here with three generations of descendants, and but for an accident might have lived her hundred years. At the time of her death her descendants numbered three hundred and twenty-two, four being of the fifth generation.

Mrs. Sarah (Hyde) Jones, wife of Elam Jones, was born May 18, 1776, at West Hartland, Connecticut, and died August 30, 1870. She retained her memory in an unusual degree, and to her more than to any one else is the writer indebted for his data of our pioneer history. She had been a resident of the township sixty-five years at the time of her decease. She had, during her life, a personal acquaintance with all of our early citizens, and her narrations of incidents in pioneer times were full of interest. She was a daughter of Uriah Hyde, whose family has been noted for its longevity.

Mrs. Elizabeth (Hyde) Hewitt, wife of Samuel Hewitt, and daughter of Uriah Hyde, was born in West Hartland, Connecticut, January 4, 1772. She resided here for many years but removed with her son, S. N. Hewitt, to Vernon. At ninety-eight years of age she removed to Kansas and a few months later to Fayetteville, Arkansas, where she died July 22, 1873, being over one hundred and one years of age.

Mrs. Anna (Hyde) Hull, wife of William Hull, and daughter of Uriah Hyde, was born November 16, 1778, at West Hartland, Connecticut, and died July 11, 1874, being in the ninety-sixth year of her age, and at the time of her death the oldest person ever deceased in the township.

Mrs. Lovisa (Borden) Fitch, wife of Shaler Fitch, was born December 10, 1779, and died June 6, 1871. They emigrated to Ohio in 1804.

Mrs. Mary Kepner Pfouts, wife of John Pfouts, was born September 5, 1771, and died January 9, 1864.

George W. Cassidy was born in Chester county, Pennsylvania, September 15, 1780, and died April 2, 1870. He was a soldier in the War of 1812 and lost his right arm at the battle of Chippewa.

Mrs. Elizabeth (Allerton) Cassidy was born April 5, 1785, and died June 24, 1875.

Mrs. Phebe (Bushnell) Borden, wife of Asahel Borden, was born August 2, 1784, and died December 4, 1875. She was the last of the adult pioneers to pass away.

Mrs. Catharine (Lavley) Roberts was born near Baltimore, Maryland, August 20, 1776, and died here January 10, 1881, at the residence of her son-in-law, Mr. Jacob Barnhart. She had attained the great age of one hundred and four years, four months, and twenty days. In 1794 she was married to Peter Roberts, and for the almost unparalleled period of seventy-eight years they journeyed through life together, he having reached the advanced age of ninety-six years at the time of his death. She always possessed a strong constitution and in her earlier years was accustomed to doing much out-door work and boasted of having been able to reap more wheat than any man, not excepting her husband. She kept house and did all her own work until her husband's death, although she was then ninety-eight years of age. She was the wife of a soldier of the War of 1812, and granddaughter of a soldier of the Revolution. She was undoubtedly the oldest person in the county, and probably on the Western Reserve, if not in the State.

Nathaniel Wilson, for many years a resident here, died in his ninety-second year.

Among the old people still living in the township who have arrived at fourscore years and over, are Mrs. Alexander Bushnell, at the age of 87; Mrs. Seth Thompson, 85; Lory Norton, 84; John Jones, 82; George W. Bushnell, 82; Mrs. Isaac Leaming, 84; Edward Bowmiller, 83; Dorothy Bowmiller, 83; Mrs. Elisha Cannon, 82; Margaret Bear, 82; Michael Pfouts, 80; Bradford Hewitt, 82; Rebecca Craton, 81; Mrs. Louisa Laird, 80; Mrs. Julia Bates, 80; John Adam Sonk, 87. He was born in Bavaria May 10, 1794. In 1814 he was drafted into the German army, and served in the second company of fusileers, Ninth regiment, commanded by Ferdinand of Wurtemburg. He served six years, nine months in active service, and the rest of the time in garrison.

According to the census of 1880 fifty-three persons in the township had passed their threescore and ten years.

MISCELLANEOUS ITEMS.

A library was established early in the century, and for a long time continued in a flourishing condition. Elam Jones was librarian for many years, some of the first books being brought by him from Connecticut in 1805.

The first blacksmith who located here was

Levi Giddings, whose shop stood on the farm of Peter Carlton, on lot twenty-three.

Captain Azel Tracy, a coach and chair maker, from Norwich, Connecticut, came to Ohio about 1818, and soon after located here and engaged in the building of carriages and wagons. His son D. S. Tracy is pursuing the same vocation at the same place.

Early in the century Isaac Taylor built a tannery at Burg Hill. About 1826 the property came into possession of Arial Chapman, who followed the business of a tanner for over thirty years in the same place.

Davis Fuller was the first saddler and harness maker, having located on lot twenty-five in 1806. He followed the business in the same place for nearly fifty years.

Since the settlement of the township four small distilleries have had an existence here. Three of them were built in pioneer times, when whiskey was thought to be one of the necessities of life, and it was considered a breach of hospitality not to pass the bottle to friends when present. At the present time, however, there is none made or openly sold in the township. At an early period the citizens took a decided stand against the manufacture and sale of intoxicating liquors, and the prevailing sentiment, until the present time, has been in favor of temperance, and in strong opposition to the use of alcohol as a beverage.

A carding mill was built at an early period at the foot of Brockway hill by Lester Bushnell. Another was built by C. & R. Silliman, a little north of the center, and was soon after changed into a clock factory by Hart & Truesdale. For some years quite a business was done in the manufacture of wooden clocks. Later it was converted into a sash factory. Near the same place a hat shop was carried on for a number of years by D. Root & Co. Also a chair factory by T. C. Davis & Son.

The pioneer cheese factory of the State, and probably of the country, was started in this township in 1846 by Samuel Cone. He died during the second season of the new enterprise. From this has grown many or all of the modifications that have been made in the dairy system since that time. W. Pellon, Oris Mason, Sydney Mason, Ralph Mason, A. O. Woodford, C. Spencer, L. Fitch, John Fitch, and Peter Carl-

ton have each been engaged in the business since that period. Eli W. Bushnell was engaged in the manufacture of cutlery for some twenty years. A new factory was built on lot nineteen in 1850, which was burned in September, 1859. The business was then discontinued.

Giles M. Hayes, who resides near the west line of the township, has established a factory for using the surplus products of the orchards in making vinegar, apple-butter, and jellies. This enterprise gives promise of being beneficial to the fruit growers in this vicinity.

The township has few or no large farms, and all of her interests are purely agricultural, especially so for the last thirty years. The growth of mining and manufacturing towns around tends to draw away all interests save those strictly pertaining to agriculture.

A portion of the township is well adapted to fruit growing, and although it has been an important business in our past history yet it deserves more attention than has so far been given to it.

According to the census of 1820 the population of the township was six hundred and twenty-five, and it made a good per cent. of an increase during the next decade, but for the last forty years the numeration has gained but slowly. For at least two generations our people have been emigrating to the West. The sons and daughters of the pioneers, inspired by the same spirit which led their parents to leave New England for Ohio, have been following the star of the empire westward until this township has representatives in almost every western city and State. They have been heard in the halls of Congress, in the Legislatures of different States, at the bar, and in the pulpit; they have held positions in the army and navy of the United States; on the mountains and prairie we find them seeking after wealth and fame, worthy sons of honored sires, whom old Hartford claims with pride.

BIOGRAPHICAL SKETCHES,

EDWARD BROCKWAY.

The subject of this sketch, one of the three pioneer settlers, formerly resided in Branford, Connecticut. He removed to Hartland about 1786, and emigrated to New Connecticut in 1800, having in company with Brainard and Jones visited the township, purchased his land, and with them commenced a clearing in August, 1799. He arrived with his family June 19, 1800. He had purchased of the proprietors, Root & Holmes, nearly thirty-two hundred acres of land. At the present time over one hundred families are residing on this property.

He first settled on lot twenty-two, but soon after removed to lot eight. He was a soldier of the Revolution, taking part in the battle of Saratoga. He died March 4, 1813, aged seventy-seven years. He had a family of seventeen children. Three of his sons, Aaron, Titus, and Philemon, settled here. Aaron Brockway first settled in Vernon in June, 1798, with his family, where his wife is said to have lived seven months without seeing the face of a white woman.

Three years later he removed to Hartford. At five different times during his life he shouldered his axe and started anew to make a home for himself and family in the woods, making, as we think, a practical pioneer.

He died in Forest county, Pennsylvania, in 1848. Eight of the daughters of Edward Brockway married and settled in this township. Five of this number married into the Jones family.

Titus Brockway settled a little south of the center, where he resided until his death, September 6, 1840, at the age of sixty-five. He served as postmaster, justice, member of the Legislature, land agent, and was a prominent member of the Congregational church. He had but two sons, Edward, and Daniel Webster, and five daughters, Maria, Julia, Melissa, Martha W., Sophronia, and Caroline.

HAYES FAMILY.

If it is fair to judge a man by the impression he has produced upon the minds of those of his cotemporaries who survive him, then Colonel Richard Hayes, who came to Hartford from Hartland, Connecticut, in the spring of 1804, must have been a man of remarkable energy and power. He early engaged in trade, and was one of the first to see that the new country must pay its debts in a currency which could transport itself, and he therefore organized the cattle trade with Philadelphia, sending over the mountains droves of from three to five hundred head.

When there was any doubt as to the price which ought to be paid, the people would frequently tell him to take their stock along, sell them, and pay what he could afford, and such was his reputation for probity and fair dealing that it is said his returns were never questioned.

When the War of 1812 came on, the Third regiment, Fourth division, Ohio militia, was called out, and we find him in command. The order calling out the regiment came late on Sunday night, and the colonel at once mounted his two sons, Seth and Alvin, as messengers, to notify the captains to report on Monday for orders. All preparations were completed on Tuesday, and on Wednesday morning the regiment marched for the frontier. When we consider that the regiment had to muster from a territory ten by thirty miles in extent, and that stores and transportation had to be provided, the military reader will see that the achievement was a remarkable one. The late Joshua R. Giddings, who was a private in the regiment, once gave the writer a graphic sketch of the colonel as a commanding officer, which we regret that we cannot reproduce, but he described him as a man who could be in more places and think of more things at once, than any man he had ever met.

After the war he held the position of county commissioner and associate judge of court of common pleas, and although not a lawyer, it is said that his decisions were marked by great good sense and fairness. He often used to ride to Warren over a winter road, remain all day in court, and ride home at night, making thirty-six miles in the saddle besides his day's work in court. This life of a pioneer had told upon him, and he died in 1837 at the age of sixty-five years. He left three sons—Seth, Alvin, and Richard, of whom only the last named is living. All of them were active business men and inherited the old colonel's sturdy uprightness of character. Seth Hayes was a member of the

Ohio Legislature in 1836. He was for many years engaged as a merchant, and was noted for his public and private generosity, and had an enviable reputation as an honorable business man, and as a worthy Christian gentleman. He died March 9, 1865.

Alvin and Richard Hayes were never in public life. The former died in 1880, nearly eighty-five years of age, leaving a reputation for integrity and uprightness which any of his descendants may be proud to emulate.

There is a soldier streak in the family. Titus Hayes, the father of Colonel Richard Hayes, wintered with Washington at Valley Forge, and at least three of his sons, Richard, Titus, and Lester, were in the War of 1812, and when the war of 1861 came on, it "cropped out" in the fourth generation. Among the number was Edward, grandson of Richard, and son of Alvin Hayes. When the war broke out he felt it his duty to keep out of it, if possible, as he had a young family, and being an only son his aged father and mother looked to him for care, but after the first battle of Bull Run he saw that it would be impossible for him to do so, and raising part of a company he went into the Twenty-ninth Ohio infantry under Colonel Lewis Buckley. He was unfortunate in the outset of his military career, being taken down with fever while at Camp Chase, and to add to his ill fortune, his regiment was ordered into West Virginia upon the very day he was taken ill. As a natural consequence, when he rejoined his command some six week later, he found it in a *quasi* mutiny, the members of his company having been led to believe that he was not actually sick, but that he had shirked duty. His emaciated and generally used-up condition went far to convince the men of their mistake, and he informed them that he did not intend to resign until the company had been in at least one fight.

They got this fight at Kernstown near Winchester, Virginia, March 22, 1862, and Hayes decided to stay with the company and let the other fellows do the resigning, which proved satisfactory to all concerned. It may be remarked of the Kernstown fight, that it was the only time during the whole war that Stonewall Jackson got a good square thrashing.

Hayes was next engaged at Port Republic, June 9, 1862. There he with a part of his company had the misfortune to be taken prisoner. The company had gone for a stand of rebel colors and got them, but they had gone in too deeply and could not get out. He summered in the Confederate military prison at Salisbury, North Carolina, and on his exchange in the fall of 1862 rejoined his command at Frederick City, Maryland, finding it much cut up from the disastrous fight at Cedar Mountain, August 9, 1862. He was at Chancellorsville, Virginia, May 1, 2, and 3, 1863, where he commanded the left wing of the regiment as acting major, and two months later was at Gettysburg, Pennsylvania, where he commanded the regiment, there being no field officer present for duty, and Captain Stephens, the ranking officer, being disabled very early in the action. He was commissioned major the week following Gettysburg, and lieutenant-colonel in October following. He went to Chattanooga with Hooker's Twentieth army corps, and was in a part of the Wauhatchie affair, and in the battle of Lookout Mountain; was within reach at the battle of Missionary Ridge, but did not participate, being on other duty at the time. He was active in inducing his regiment to re-enlist, and after it did so came home with it on veteran furlough in January, 1864. Returning to the field with it he wintered at Bridgeport, Alabama, and started with the army on the Atlanta campaign, but on the 8th of May, 1864, at the battle of Mill Spring, Georgia, he received a very severe wound through the right shoulder. Major Fifield, regimental surgeon of the Twenty-ninth Ohio, performed for him the difficult, and at that time new, operation of "exsection," removing the whole of the shoulder joint, and other portions of the shattered bone, and a good deal to his own surprise he got well; but as he was unfit for service he was discharged in November, 1864, on account of wounds received in action.

In 1865 he was elected county treasurer, and held that position from September, 1866, to September, 1870, with a good degree of ability. He is now employed in the Post-office department at Washington, District of Columbia, and is satisfactorily filling a responsible position.

———

BUSHNELL FAMILY.

Among the early pioneer families of Trumbull county the Bushnells are probably the most numerous. Captain Alexander Bushnell, the immediate ancestor of the family, emigrated with his descendants. He was born in Lyme, Connecticut, December 2, 1739, and was a descendant of Francis Bushnell, one of the first settlers of Guilford, Connecticut, who landed in Boston about 1630.

He married Chloe Waite, of the same place, February 12, 1761. She was a descendant of Thomas Waite, member of Parliament, one of the judges who signed the death warrant of King Charles I, the Waite family coming to America soon after the restoration in 1660. Their descendants are numerous, and very many of them reside in Trumbull county. They had ten children, all of whom were married in Connecticut, and these families all emigrated about the same period to Ohio.

He was a captain in the Continental army during the Revolutionary war, receiving his commission while serving under Washington. After the close of the Revolution the tide of emigration first set toward northern Connecticut, and he with many others moved to Hartland, Hartford county, in that State, about 1784.

In 1800 the tide of emigration started towards "New Connecticut" in Northern Ohio, and this now greatly increased family were swept by the torrent to the Western Reserve, the first one coming in 1801 and the remainder following soon after. He died March 8, 1818, in Hartford, Ohio. Captain Bushnell's children were Thomas, Daniel, and William, who with their families settled in Hartford; Chloe, the wife of Obediah Gilder, one of the pioneers of Gustavus, where their descendants still reside; Alexander, Jr., who with his family settled in Pittsburg; Sterling G., who with his family first settled in Vernon and in 1820 removed to Richland county, Ohio; Mary, the wife of Hon. Calvin Cone, who was one of the pioneers of Gustavus in 1804, but in 1817 removed to Hartford, where some of their descendants still reside. He served as member of the Legislature from Barkhamsted, Connecticut, previous to his emigration, and was State Senator in Ohio from 1806 to 1809. Hannah was the wife of Davis Fuller, who was a pioneer of Hartford; Lucy

was the wife of Aaron Brockway, who was one of the first settlers of Vernon. They soon removed to Hartford, and about 1835 again removed to Forest county, Pennsylvania. Phebe was the wife of Asahel Borden. They settled on lot thirty in Hartford in 1804, where they both lived to a good old age, she dying at the age of ninety-one, and was the last of this family of pioneers to pass away.

Thomas Bushnell, eldest son of Captain Alexander and Chloe (Waite) Bushnell, was born in Lyme, Connecticut, January 11, 1762. He served during the last years of the Revolution in his father's company. He married Rebecca Andrews, of Hartland, Connecticut, and emigrated with a family of ten children to Ohio in 1804. He located first on lot twenty-four, and in a few years re-located on lot seventeen. He only lived to endure the hardships and privations of pioneer life, not long enough to enjoy its pleasures which follow. He died of fever April 10, 1817. His was the first death in his father's family. He was greatly respected in the community and much beloved by his numerous relatives, and his death was a severe shock and a great loss to his own family.

His children were General Andrews Bushnell; Rebecca, wife of Colonel Horace Flower, who settled first in Hartford, and afterward in Bloomfield; Jerusha, wife of Linus Hayes; Hannah, wife of Colonel Asa Hutchins and mother of Hon. Wells Hutchins, of Portsmouth, Ohio; Matilda, wife of Lester Hayes; Lorena, wife of Dr. Cullin Wilcox; Thomas, Jr., who lived for many years in Bloomfield; Amanda, wife of Samuel Corning; and Eli, who lived and died in Hartford.

General Andrews Bushnell, eldest son of Thomas, was born in Hartland, Connecticut, August 14, 1782, married Sarah Lane, of the same place, and immediately started for New Connecticut as it was then called. He settled on lot twenty-four, in Hartford, where he died June 17, 1851. He was an extensive farmer and one of the pioneer breeders of blooded cattle in northern Ohio. He was also in early life an efficient and accurate surveyor; was for four years sheriff of Trumbull county, and held various other positions of trust and honor. He held a lieutenant's commission in the War of 1812; commanded a company at the Thames where Tecumseh was killed, and did brave and honorable service in the defence of Fort Erie, where he was wounded by a musket ball through the left lung, for which he received a pension the remainder of his life. He was an able and well drilled officer, and after the close of the war was made brigadier-general of militia, which position he held with honor many years. He was a member of the Congregational church, and a Whig in politics until the formation of the Liberty party, which he supported until his death. His children were Jerusha, who died at the age of nineteen years, a young lady highly esteemed and sincerely regretted by the community; David E., who is supposed to have died in Palestine in January, 1840. He was intelligent young farmer of great originality and very studious habits, fond of historical reading and investigation. Restive of farm life he laid extensive plans for foreign travel and research, for which work he had remarkable qualities. He accordingly left home in December, 1838. He landed at Liverpool, traveled through England, France, Switzerland, and Italy, spent some time in Egypt, traveled up the Nile to Abyssinia, visited the missionaries at Beyroot, and left that place January 8, 1840, with a guide, intending to visit Jerusalem and other points in Palestine. The guide soon returned and reported that Bushnell was short of money and had gone on alone, since which time no tidings were ever received, and it is supposed he was killed by his guide for his money. General Bushnell's next child was Mary, wife of Simon R. Estabrook, of Warren; and the youngest, Seth A., for many years a resident of Hartford, now of Oberlin, Ohio.

Eli W. Bushnell, youngest son of Thomas and Rebecca Bushnell, married Electa, daughter of Elam Jones, one of the pioneers of Hartford. He was a resident of the township of Hartford the greater part of his life. He was well known in the county as one of the best mechanics in the State. For many years he was proprietor of an axe-factory, and manufactured edge tools of all kinds. At one time every tool in his establishment was made by his own hands, including anvils, vise, screw-plates, trip-hammers, etc. It was a matter of pride with him to be able to make or repair any tool which was constructed of steel or iron, no difference how large or small. His factory was destroyed by fire in 1859, after

which he was not again engaged in active business.

He was an honest, conscientious man who always remembered to practice the Golden Rule. His heart was ever open for deeds of charity, and the poor and oppressed always found in him sympathy and help. He was one of the advance guards of the old Liberty party, being one of the twelve first voters of that party in his township.

He was long a member of the Congregational church, of which he was one of the deacons. He died September 8, 1862. His children are Thomas A., who resides at the old home of the family; Cordelia A., wife of F. B. Plimpton, political editor of the Cincinnati Commercial; and Sarah Pauline, residing with her brother.

Daniel Bushnell, the second son of Captain Alexander and Chloe Bushnell, was born in Lyme, Connecticut. December 18, 1763, and married first Rebecca Banning, and second Eunice Brockway.

He also served in the army for a short time near the close of the war for independence in his father's company. He emigrated from Hartland, Connecticut, in 1803, and settled on lot thirty, where he resided till he died, August 12, 1842. He was in early life a carpenter, having been the builder of the Congregational church in Hartland, Connecticut, in 1801. He also took an active part in building the Congregational church in Hartford in 1819. He was a devoted and active church member, and in early times, when ministers were not always to be had, he conducted religious meetings and gave catechetical and Bible instructions to the children of the vicinity. He was an enthusiastic and industrious man, and possessed the requisite elements of a first-class pioneer. He was a lifelong and faithful member of the Masonic fraternity. He raised a family of seventeen children, most of whom lived to maturity; some becoming residents of this county and others going west. Their names were Lewis, Lydia, Ziba, Amoret, Daniel Milton, Clarissa, George Willis, Hiram, Rhoda, Elijah Newton, Alexander, Joseph, Joseph second, Rebecca, Philena, and Benjamin. Of this large family but one, George W., is at present a resident of Hartford, though many of the descendants reside in Trumbull county.

Dr. George W. Bushnell, third son of Daniel and Rebecca Bushnell, was born in Hartland, Connecticut, August 11, 1800, consequently was three years of age at the time the family emigrated, and has the most of his life been a resident of Hartford. He married Miss Sally Bates, September 8, 1824.

He endured as a child the privations and hardships of pioneer life, and early learned that patience and industry were indispensable to success. Striving to keep pace with all the necessities of a new country, he learned anything necessary to be learned. First, farming; second, carpenter work being in demand he learned to be a carpenter; shoes being one of the great necessities, he learned shoe-making. Early becoming dissatisfied with the allopathic treatment of diseases, he studied the botanic practice for the purpose of treating his own family. His success at home was such he was soon called upon to treat his neighbors' families. By faithful study and strict attention to his patients, he soon acquired a reputation as a successful physician, and has since devoted his entire time to the practice of medicine. He has made for himself an honorable reputation for skill and integrity worthy of emulation. In view of his worthy labors the Physio-medical Institute of Cincinnati conferred on him the honorary degree of doctor of medicine.

He has been in the field of medical reform for over fifty years; for forty years has not used tea or coffee, believing them to be useless, if not hurtful. He has never used tobacco in any form, considering it a vile poison. Intoxicating drinks he never employed. He has sought to obey the laws of life in all things; "to be temperate in all things," and to practice what he preaches, "the proper use of things proper for use, and the total abstinence from things naturally hurtful."

Dr. Bushnell was an active agent in the first organization of the church of the Disciples of Christ in Hartford, May 1, 1830, and was at that time chosen overseer of the church, which place he filled with credit to himself and advantage to the church. September 3, 1843, the church gave him a certificate of recommendation to go forth as an evangelist teacher, in which capacity he faithfully labored for some years in eastern Ohio and western Pennsylvania.

On June 21, 1846, he resigned his office as overseer of the church on account of the opposition to his anti-slavery sentiments, and finally withdrew July 2, 1847, and united with the Congregational church, where he remained till the Disciple church passed the following resolutions January 15, 1853:

Resolved, That we as a church of the Disciples of Christ in Hartford, Ohio, do consider slave-holding to be man-stealing.

Resolved, That we will have no Christian or church fellowship with slave-holders, or those who hold their fellow-men as chattel property, nor with those who justify and willingly uphold, aid, or abet them in so doing.

Upon the passage of the above resolutions he again united with the Disciples, and was again chosen overseer, which office he continued to fill until May 31, 1881, when he tendered his resignation of office with good will to all, being eighty-one years of age. His remarkable executive powers, his untiring zeal, his undying devotion to his belief of the truth, has made him the most active worker in the church. His services were never for filthy lucre's sake, his labors always having been gratuitous. He has done more work, contributed more money, and done more preaching during the fifty years since the organization of this church, than any other person in it, and is yet a live member of the church, ready to do his part of whatever may be needed, although eighty-two years of age. The children of Dr. George and Sally Bushnell that have arrived at maturity are Curtis W., born October 14, 1825, and died at the age of twenty-nine years; Sarah B., born September 8, 1827, married first Stephen Watkins, and second Charles Davis; Edward, born Febuary 22, 1831, died at the age of nineteen years; Allen R., born July 18, 1833; Amoret, born June 20, 1835, married Addison Ruey; John L., born December 13, 1837; Annie, born December 7, 1841, married Dr. James Irwin; Milo F., born July 18, 1844, enlisted into the United States service June 11, 1862, and died in the United States hospital at Gallipolis, Ohio, April 17, 1863. His father being notified of his danger reached Gallipolis the evening of the 14th, but on the morning of the 17th he died. He caused his body to be embalmed and encased in a metallic coffin, and returned with him to his native place, where he was interred some days later with military honor, the funeral being one of the largest ever attended in the township. All the sons of the family living in 1861 were Union soldiers in the war of the Rebellion.

Allen R. Bushnell, son of Dr. George W. Bushnell, is a resident of Lancaster, Wisconsin. Receiving his education in his native State, he went to Wisconsin in 1854, where he studied law with Judge Stephen R. Payne, at Platteville; was admitted to the bar at Lancaster in 1857, commencing practice in Platteville. In 1861 he enlisted as a private in company C, Seventh Wisconsin volunteer infantry. He was made a first lieutenant and afterward captain, and served with his regiment in the Iron brigade until 1863, when he was discharged for disability, and resumed practice at Platteville. He removed to Lancaster in 1864. He is very little of a politician, but has been district attorney and member of the Legislature.

Colonel William Bushnell, third son of Captain Alexander and Chloe Bushnell, was born in Lyme, Connecticut, May 18, 1766, and married, first, Mary Borden, of Hartland, Connecticut, and second, Mrs. Candace Adams, of Bristol township. He was the first of the Bushnell family to emigrate and was the first settler in the south part of the township of Hartford, his deed being dated December 31, 1800. He came with his family, then consisting of eight children, in June, 1801, and located on what is now known as Thompson hill, on the diagonal road. A portion of his first purchase is still in the possession of his grandson, Austin Bushnell. He was elected captain of the first military company organized in the township, in 1804, and afterwards served as colonel of the regiment. He was among the early commissioners of the county and filled other county and township offices during the early part of the century.

He was a man of great firmness and decision of character, ardent in all his feelings and honorable in all his dealings, and in his day a man much respected.

His children were: Wilson, Daniel Cone, Lester, Fanny, Alexander, Polly, Lovissa, Sophia, William, and Austa, the last two only natives of the township. These all lived to maturity, married, and all settled in the township. In the summer of 1828, when the typhoid fever prevailed, his wife, five children, two grandchildren, and a daughter-in-law all fell victims to the disease. Daniel Cone and Alexander lived for

many years and died in the township, respected and worthy farmers, the latter having been trustee of the township twenty-one years. Lovisa was the wife of Ambrose Hart, for many years merchant at Brookfield. Sophia married Amos Hart and settled first in Hartford, and about 1840 emigrated to Brighton, Iowa. William was the first white male child born in the township; born June 11, 1802. Many of the descendants of Colonel William Bushnell reside in Trumbull and Mahoning counties.

Daniel Cone, born August 20, 1788, married Polly Hutchins and their children were: Upson, who resides in Gustavus; William, of Epworth, Iowa; Dr. J. Hutchins Bushnell, of Washington, District of Columbia; Nelson Bushnell, Esq., of Franklin, Pennsylvania; and Austin, a resident of Hartford.

Alexander, son of Colonel William Bushnell, was born in Hartland, Connecticut, April 14, 1794, and married, first, Nancy Hummason, and second, Martha Bailey. Their children are: Luman, Lester, Candace, Joel, William, Huldah, and Ellen.

Joel married Mrs. Mary G. Bussey, and resides on the farm where his father first settled in 1816, and on land first purchased by his great-grandfather, Captain Alexander Bushnell, from the original proprietors of the township. He is at present justice of the peace and trustee of the township.

THE BORDEN FAMILY.

Among the pioneers who came into Hartford during 1804 were Asahel Borden and his sons Asahel, Jr., and Sylvester. They left Hartland, Connecticut, May 29th, and arrived at their destination July 20th, having been fifty-three days on the journey, traveling with an ox team. A few years later Russel Borden, a brother of Asahel Borden, Sr., and their mother, Widow Mary Borden, also came. She was born in 1731, and was probably, at the time of her death, the oldest pioneer. She died in 1818, at the age of eighty-seven. Asahel Borden and his son Asahel, Jr., settled on lot twenty-four on the diagonal road. He died July 26, 1826, and his wife Jemima (Jones) Borden, died December 22, 1818. Asahel Borden, Jr., and his wife Phebe (Bushnell) Borden, continued to reside at their first location nearly seventy years, and will long be remembered as social and hospitable pioneers. "The latch-string of their log cabin was always out," and in later years their residence was as freely opened to their numerous friends. They outlived all their pioneer associates, he dying in 1869, at the age of eighty-seven, and she in 1875, at the age of ninety-one, being the last one of the early settlers.

They were members of the Methodist Episcopal church nearly half a century. They were always active and energetic people. In early times they are said to have made journeys to Pittsburg and Beaver with oxen, taking their cheese and farm produce to exchange for family supplies; often making journeys to Warren, Ohio, and Mercer, Pennsylvania, on horseback to trade. Once Mrs. Borden made a trip to Mercer and back in one day, the round trip being a journey of over forty miles, bringing home on her horse a tea-set of crockery, groceries, and other articles for the family. Their children were all daughters. Eliza (who was brought a baby on the long journey from Connecticut) married Richard Gates, Elsa married Paul Wellman, Phebe married George Hallock, Jemima married Daniel Loomis, Hannah died at the age of fourteen, Polly married Abel Whitney, Maria married Abner Banning, and Deborah L. still remains at the old home with her sister, Mrs. Banning.

Sylvester Borden married Amoret Bushnell, daughter of Daniel Bushnell, and their children were John, Edmund, Truman, and Amelia, wife of Rev. Robert Crane, of Green.

Russel Borden settled on the farm now occupied by the Thompson family, on the diagonal road, where he died in 1813. His family consisted of Captain Philo Borden, a resident of the township over fifty years, a prominent man in the Congregational church, a teacher many years, and a respected citizen, who married first in Connecticut, Miss Betsy Priest, and second Abigail Thompson; Florilla, wife of Seth Thompson; Fannie, wife of Alva Hart; Polly, died in 1813; and Catharine, wife of Robison Truesdale. This name of worthy pioneers, once so familiar, is now almost extinct in the township.

DAVIS FULLER.

Davis Fuller, one of the pioneers of Hartford, emigrated from Hartland, Connecticut, in 1806, and settled on lot twenty-five. He was a saddle- and harness-maker, and pursued that vocation during his life. He was a soldier in Colonel Hayes' regiment in the War of 1812; an active member and deacon of the Congregational church, also a prominent man in the anti-slavery movement. He died May 5, 1855, at the age of seventy-three. His wife, Hannah (Bushnell) Fuller, died in 1849, at the age of seventy-one. As an incident of pioneer life it may be related that the first Sunday after moving into their log-cabin a peculiar hissing sound was heard under the floor, which was recognized as that of a rattlesnake. "Uncle Davis" having removed a puncheon, discovered the intruder, and with an old-fashioned fire-shovel struck the snake and held him fast while his wife got down under the floor and cut off his head with a butcher-knife. The snake had eighteen rattles and was five feet long.

The children of Davis and Hannah Fuller were Eunice, Samuel, Henry (who died of fever when eighteen years of age, in 1828), Chloe, Harvey, and Alexander. Of this family only Samuel is a resident of the township. He married Eunice Holcomb, and their children were Emeline, who died at the age of five years; Jerusha, wife of Albert Rathbun, and died in Chicago October 27, 1868, at the age of thirty-three; Emeline, wife of Warren Bates, and Lieutenant Davis C. Fuller, who died October 13, 1870, at the age of twenty-nine, from disease contracted in the army.

THE JONES FAMILY.

All the Jones families now residing in Hartford, with the exception of one, are descendants of the same family. The earliest account of this family in America which we have been able to obtain is of Benjamin Jones, who was a resident of Enfield, Connecticut, and in 1706 removed to Somers, Connecticut, and was the first settler in that township. His grandson, Israel Jones, removed from Enfield to Barkhamsted, Connecticut, and was the second settler in that township in 1759, fixing his home on East mountain.

This farm is now, by regular descent, the property of his great-grandson, Hon. Edwin P. Jones.

The children of Captain Israel Jones were Samuel, Thomas, Colonel Israel Jones, Jemima (wife of Asahel Borden, Sr.), Mrs. Joshua Giddings, Mrs. John Billings, William, and Isaac. Many of this family, like their ancestors, became "first settlers," Isaac, William, and Jemima, also Elam, son of Samuel, being pioneers of Hartford; others of this family, including Samuel, Jr., and the Giddings family, being pioneers of Ashtabula county, Ohio.

Isaac Jones, youngest son of Captain Israel Jones, was the first to emigrate, coming from Barkhamsted, Connecticut, with his family in the spring of 1800, and settling on lot twenty-two, near Burg Hill. He was one of the three first settlers in the township. His wife, Abigail, was the daughter of Edward Brockway, who came at the same time. Their children were Mrs. Asahel Brainard, Mrs. Abner Moses, Mrs. Aaron Rice, Selden, John, James F., and Mrs. George Hewit; the most of them residents of Hartford many years.

James F. Jones was the only son of Isaac and Abigail Jones born in Hartford, and is now the oldest man living who is a native of the place. He was born January 31, 1804, resides on lot eleven, and married first Sarepta Wilson, second Mrs. Mary Pfouts. Their children are Malinda, Asahel, Albert, Mary Ann, Lorinda, Florus, Mandana Juliett, Arial Gordon, Calvin Judson, and Willie Dayton.

William C. Jones, son of Captain Israel Jones, emigrated from the same place in 1802, and located on lot twenty-seven, and on the farm now occupied by Amos Fell, where he died in 1841, at the age of eighty-one years. He was a veteran of the Revolutionary war, having taken part in the battles of Bunker Hill and Saratoga. His children were William, Jr., Selden C., Dr. Asahel Jones, Amelia, Sallie, and Allen. From this family are descended Philander Jones and Asahel Jones, Esq., of Youngstown, Ohio; Dr. Allen Jones, of Kinsman, Ohio; R. C. Jones, of Burg Hill; William C. Jones, of Hartford, and Edward B. Jones, of Orangeville.

William C. Jones, son of Selden C. and Laurinda (Brockway) Jones, was born in Hartford, June 29, 1817, and married Elvira Gates, of the same township, December 27, 1843. She was born December 27, 1823. Their children are: Eliza Laurinda, born October 13, 1844, and married James D. Burnett, June 21, 1866; Alice Minerva, born August 25, 1846, and died November 8, 1854; Edna Luella, born July 21, 1850, died November 22, 1854; Asahel Hallock, born January 15, 1852, and married Clara L. Sponsler, May 16, 1875.

Edward B. Jones, also son of Selden C. and Laurinda (Brockway) Jones, is a resident of Orangeville. He was born on the farm where he now resides, May 8, 1822. This farm has been in the possession of his ancestors since 1799, his grandfather, Edward Brockway, having purchased the same of the original proprietors of the township. He first married Miss Mary E. Leonard, October 24, 1850, who died September 8, 1851; she left one son, Edward M. born September 8, 1851, and died October 14, 1852. He was again married to Ellen D. Jones, of Sheffield, Massachusetts, May 14, 1856. She was born August 26, 1827. Their children are: Lizzie E., wife of Willard C. Hull; Ivah L., and Hattie L.

These brothers, William and Edward, early left fatherless, learned lessons of industry, perseverance, and economy, which have enabled them each to acquire a competency, and they are among the most prosperous farmers in the township.

Elam Jones, son of Samuel, and grandson of Captain Israel Jones, was born at the old Jones home, on East mountain, Barkhamsted, September 29, 1774. He was a man of more than ordinary education and acquirements for his day, having received private instructions of Rev. Aaron Church, of Hartland, Connecticut, and followed the profession of a teacher for many years in his native State. He married Sarah Hyde, of Hartland, April 27, 1801. They emigrated from Barkhamsted in 1805, making the journey in six weeks. They settled on lot twelve in Hartford, Ohio. Their children were: Sarah, wife of Jarvis Gates, a resident of Hartford; Harriet, wife of Linus Parker, a resident of Kinsman; Electa, wife of Eli W. Bushnell, a resident of Hartford; Eunice Lemyra, wife of George Hezlep, for many years a merchant of Gustavus; Hannah, wife of Dr. Edward Best, who died at Freedom, Ohio, October 2, 1838;

36°

and Hon. Lucian C. Jones, a resident of Warren, Ohio. In 1828 he built the first public house at the center of Hartford. He was for many years postmaster, and held the office of town clerk twenty years, in early days. He was a surveyor in early life. He served in the War of 1812 in Colonel Hayes' regiment. He died December 2, 1851, at the age of seventy-seven. Mrs. Sarah Hyde Jones died September 30, 1870, in her ninety-fifth year.

McFARLAND FAMILY.

Robert McFarland, the first settler in the east part of Hartford, was from the north of Ireland, and of Scotch descent. He came from Washington county, Pennsylvania, in the fall of 1803, with one son and one daughter. He built a cabin about seventy rods from the State line, and west of the present residence of his grandson, Thomas W. McFarland. In the spring of 1804 the remainder of the family followed to the new home prepared for them in the wilderness of Ohio. He only lived to see his family well established, as he died in May, 1814. Mrs. McFarland's maiden name was Martha Burnside. She lived until 1836, and died at the age of eighty-six. They were members of the Presbyterian church. Their children were Martha, Robert (who was killed by lightning in Washington county, Pennsylvania), Archibald, Jane, Margaret (who was blind and died soon after her father), John, and Polly.

The three sons all settled in the township, John remaining at the old home, Thomas settling a short distance south on the same road, and Archibald locating on lot thirty-seven, in the southwest part of the township. They all lived and died on the farms they had labored so faithfully to clear of trees and convert into fruitful fields, and these farms are each occupied by their descendants. Thomas and Archibald both served as soldiers in the War of 1812, in Colonel Hayes' regiment.

Thomas McFarland was born September 24, 1785, and died October 27, 1862, at the age of seventy-seven. He married first Martha Fell, and second Mrs. Agnes McKnight. Their children were Nathan, Robert, Smith, George, Cynthia, Thomas F., Phebe, and Amelia.

Thomas F., son of Thomas and Agnes McFarland, was born April 13, 1828, and married first, Parthenia Leslie, who died September 23, 1871; and second, Alice B. Brockway. Their children were Wright D., born February 17, 1854, and married Rosie Wallahan; Julia M., born September 17, 1855, wife of Scot Bates; Mary Florence, born July 2, 1857, died August 19, 1871; Selma A., born June 22, 1859, wife of Wright Banning; Bertha, born May 31, 1864; and Agnes Jane, born June 15, 1873.

John McFarland, youngest son of Robert and Martha McFarland, married Esther Fell. Their children were Mary, Archibald, Thomas W., Eliza, Harriet, and Lucinda. He died in 1857, at the age of sixty-five.

Thomas W. McFarland, son of John and Esther McFarland, married Olive Brockway, and resides at the old ancestral homestead of the family, where Robert McFarland first settled nearly eighty years ago. The family of McFarland includes some of the most thrifty and enterprising citizens of the township.

KEPNER FAMILY.

John Kepner, the pioneer settler of the southeastern portion of the township of Hartford, and the ancestor of all the Kepners in this vicinity, was born October 7, 1784, in Cumberland, Cumberland county, Pennsylvania. In 1805 he made his first journey to Ohio on foot, and immediately purchased a tract of six hundred and thirty-six acres of land, being lot nine in the township of Hartford. He brought the gold and silver coin to pay for the same, in two small, homemade linen bags. He soon made a small clearing and erected a log cabin which was burned. This accident was occasioned by Indian fires running in the woods. After this he returned home and spent the winter, but returning in the spring of 1806 he built a second log house, in which for a time greased paper performed the office of glass in the windows. A second time he returned home for the winter and married Elizabeth Dubs, who was born in Cumberland September 4, 1785.

Early in the spring of 1807 they emigrated to their new home in the forest, coming with large Pennsylvania covered wagons over the Allegheny mountains, camping out wherever night found them, and arrived at their new home in time to put in spring crops. Content and prosperity took up their abode with them, and on this farm they lived and died. Their children were: John, born February 15, 1808, and married Lucinda Hull; Sallie, born September 2, 1809, married John Carnes; Benjamin, born August 9, 1811, and died in infancy; Jane, born March 13, 1813, married Eli Myers; Mary, born May 22, 1815, and married Alex. Spencer; Jacob, born June 12, 1818, married Eliza Parsons, and then Mary McKnight; Catharine, born March 18, 1821, and married Charles Banning; Elizabeth, born March 7, 1823, and married John VanGorder; David, born May 23, 1825, and married first Mary Bates, second Laura Simons; Ruhama, born June 20, 1827, and married John Bates; Henry, born May 23, 1825, and married Adaline Lynch.

The father of this large family, as faithful to his country as to his children, served in the War of 1812, in Colonel Hayes' regiment. In the spring of 1833, while assisting to re-roof his barn, he fell and received fatal injuries from which he died March 20th. He and his wife were members of the Lutheran church. She was a woman of uncommon executive ability, and after her husband's death faithfully performed her duty to the large family thus left in her care. She lived to see them all married, and in her last days resided with her youngest son on a portion of the original estate, and died July 6, 1862, at the advanced age of seventy-eight years.

John Kepner, the eldest son of the pioneer, settled on a portion of the original property. His son Lucious, Lorenzo, and Luzerne each have homes and reside on the original Kepner farm.

Jacob, second son of the pioneer, resides on the farm, and in the house formerly occupied by the pioneer, Asahel Brainard, on lot eighteen. He married, first, Eliza Parsons, who died soon, leaving one son—Allen Parsons Kepner. He then married Mary McKnight, and their children are Thomas Eugene, Linda, Florence, Frankie, Emory, Adell, Maud, and Frederick.

David Kepner is a resident of the northwestern part of the township.

Henry, youngest son of John and Elizabeth

Kepner, also retains a portion of the original estate, and his residence stands near the home where his pioneer parents resided. He married Adaline Lynch March 22, 1859. Their children are Sanford H., William L., and John H.

These Kepner brothers, sons of the pioneer, are all industrious and wealthy farmers and respected citizens of the township.

FOWLER FAMILY.

The first settler in the township of Fowler was Abner Fowler, formerly a resident of Southwick, Massachusetts. He was a brother of the proprietor of the township, Hon. Samuel Fowler, of Westfield, Massachusetts, for which place the township was first named; this name afterwards being changed in honor of the proprietor to the name it now bears. In 1798 he came to the township in the employ of his brother as surveyor of his western lands; finally located and remained till death, February 18, 1806, his death being the first in the township. Abner Fowler, Jr., born July 25, 1782, married Miss Esther Jennings, August 18, 1807, in Fowler. She was from Fairfield, Connecticut, and a descendant of the Rev. Peter Bulkley, who came to America in 1635. Their children were Julia, who married Thomas J. Collins; Ira, Sarah, Abner, Harvey, James, and Rhoda, who married Daniel Parsons. Mr. Fowler remained in Fowler till 1816, when he changed his location to Brookfield, where he resided till his death April 23, 1843. He was a very intelligent farmer, a man of the utmost integrity, and of high Christian character. He was identified with the Methodist church in Fowler at its first organization, also, after his removal, with the Brookfield church.

In politics he was a Whig till the formation of the Liberty party, when he took his stand on the side of humanity, and was one of the first five voters of that party in Brookfield. His son Ira Fowler, born in Fowler township, January 21, 1810, married Miss Sarah Ann Williams, May 6, 1840, and settled on lot twenty-three, on the south line of Hartford township, where he now resides. She died May 15, 1841, leaving one daughter, Elizabeth. Mr. Fowler was again married, to Miss Lovina Wheeler, and they have one son, Harvey.

James Fowler, born February 1, 1820, married Miss Lucina Miner ; their children are Esther L., Addison J., Dwight A., Albert R., James C., Sicily, and Ida.

These Fowler brothers, sons of Abner Fowler, Jr., are both residents of Hartford; intelligent farmers, courteous, worthy Christian gentlemen, and highly respected citizens, in whom the virtues of their ancestors are · perpetuated, Ira Fowler and family being connected with and among the leading members of the Methodist Episcopal church near his place, and Mr. James Fowler long having been an elder in the Disciple church at Hartford center.

The Fowler family have a long line of ancestors in America, the first of which, William Fowler, was one of the company which came from London with Rev. John Davenport, Governor Eaton, and others, and arrived in Boston June 26, 1637, and settled in New Haven in 1638. He was a prisoner in Bridewell, England, with other Puritans in 1592. He was at the famous meeting in Mr. Newman's barn in New Haven, where the peculiar constitution and policy of Mr. Davenport, which afterwards characterized the New Haven colony, was agreed upon, and Mr. Fowler subscribed to that agreement. In 1639 he was elected one of the "seven pillars" of the church of Milford, Rev. Peter Pruden pastor. He was elected magistrate yearly till 1654.

GEORGE SNYDER, SR.

George Snyder, Sr., was born March 9, 1799, in Mahatonca, Dauphin county, Pennsylvania. His father, Thomas Snyder, dying when he was about four years of age, he was raised by his maternal grandfather, John Kepner, till he was fourteen years of age, when he went to Harris-·burg, Pennsylvania, to learn the trade of a cabinet-maker. Although in a school-room but three days in his life, he acquired a fair education. He came on foot to Hartford, Ohio, in 1817, and purchased seventy acres of land of his uncle, John Kepner, in lot nine, near Messersmith's corners, for the consideration of $300, on which he immediately built a house. When he was only nineteen years of age he married Elizabeth Carnes, daughter of Godfrey Carnes, a Revolutionary soldier and pioneer of Mercer county, Pennsylvania. Here he erected a shop,

and was the first cabinet-maker in the township; also working at the carpenter business part of the time for some years. Their children, all born on this farm, were Mary, Margaret, Jane, Ruhama, James, A. C., Uriah, and George W.

In October, 1835, he purchased an addition of two hundred and thirty-seven acres of land lying east of his original purchase, for the consideration of $1,513. On this land he erected a saw-mill, which was run by water for twenty years, when he purchased an engine and run the mill by steam till 1858, when he sold the mill and seventy-nine acres of this land to his son James, and the remainder of this tract to his sons, Uriah and Cornelius Snyder, and in 1861 sold his old home of seventy acres, where he first settled, to Benjamin Messersmith, and removed to the center of the township, purchasing the store and property formerly owned by G. L. Woodford, where he resided for a time, and carried on a grocery store. This property he sold to Dr. Daniel Artherholt, and removed to Brookfield township, where he resided for a time, but being afflicted with paralysis he sold his Brookfield property to his son George, spending the remainder of his days with his children, dying March 8, 1880, aged eighty-one years. Mrs. Snyder was born in 1795, and died June 6, 1859, aged sixty-four years.

George W. Snyder, the youngest son, was born in 1839. He spent his early life on his father's farm, and attended district school till he had reached the age of eighteen years. He then spent three years in Hartford academy, and one term in Folsom's Commercial college, Cleveland. He began the study of law in Hartford, in the office of L. C. Jones, now of Warren. He enlisted under the first call for volunteers, in 1861, being the first man in Hartford to offer his serices, but the quota having been filled, he, like many others, was discharged without being mustered in. In 1862 he again enlisted in the Eighty-fourth Ohio volunteer infantry, and served with that regiment four months. In 1867 Mr. Snyder was admitted to the bar, and opened an office in Orangeville. He has been elected mayor of the village five successive times, and since 1879 has been postmaster. Though his whole family belonged to the Democratic party, Mr. Snyder, in 1860, cast his first vote for Lincoln, and has been an active Republican ever

G. W. Snyder

since. He has been a member of every county convention and several State conventions since attaining his majority. He married, in 1871, Julia A. Wilson, daughter of Nathaniel Wilson, of Orangeville. Their family consists of three children, Sharlie L., Blaine Carlisle, and Vera E.

DR. R. M. BEEBE.

Robert McEwen Beebe was born in Winchester, Connecticut, April 28, 1811. His parents were James Beebe, a prominent citizen of Litchfield county, Connecticut, five times a member of the Legislature of that State, and Abi McEwen Beebe, a sister of the Rev. Dr. Abel McEwen, of New London, Connecticut.

He was a member of Yale college class of 1835, but did not finish his course for want of means. Soon after leaving he commenced the study of medicine with Dr. Benjamin Welch, Jr., in Norfolk, and continued his medical studies in Yale and Berkshire Medical schools, graduating from the latter in the class of 1836-37. In 1837 he married Miss Huldah Case, of Norfolk, and in 1838 removed to Hartford. Here he entered immediately on a large and successful practice of medicine, which he continued till his death, November 16, 1864. Few physicians ever enjoyed more of the love and confidence of the community where they lived, or have been more deeply mourned in their death.

The following is taken from a letter written by Hon. L. C. Jones, who was a resident in Hartford at the time Dr. Beebe came to the township, subsequently was a student in his office, and continued to live in the place till 1862:

Professionally Dr. Beebe almost at once took rank among the first physicians in the vicinity. Among his brethren his thorough scholarship and learning in his profession, his urbanity and courtesy, rapidly won for him their good will and high esteem. They soon learned to know that his judgment and conclusions in critical cases of disease were of the highest value, and as a necessary consequence he was oftener called in consultation than any other physician in this part of the county.

As a citizen he was active and zealous in all matters of public interest, and always, notwithstanding the great demands upon his time by his large practice, took a leading part in civil and political affairs.

Among the most marked traits in his character were his liberality and self-sacrificing labors to the poor. The needed relief, both professional and pecuniary, was prompt and ready, cheerful, and without evasion or excuse.

To his self-sacrificing labors in his profession may be attributed in a great degree his early death. He died in the height of his usefulness, in the prime of his life, with the harness on, leaving behind him a reputation for honor, integrity, professional skill, second to none in the county of his residence, which is remembered by none better than the writer, to whom he was the valued friend and counsellor, the sincere and constant friend."

He left a family of four children, one of whom, Robert, follows his father's profession, and resides in Cleveland. Lizzie G. (Mrs. J. Jones) was a poetess of considerable local reputation.

SULLIVAN HUTCHINS

is the second son of Hiram and Eliza (Lane) Hutchins, and grandson of Samuel Hutchins, who was one of the pioneers of Vienna township. Samuel Hutchins was born in Bolton, Connecticut, August 30, 1777, and was raised by Colonel Holmes, the original proprietor of Vienna and Hartford townships, in Hartland, Connecticut. He came to Vienna with Uriah Holmes, Jr., and his company of surveyors in 1798, and for his assistance in surveying Mr. Holmes gave him his choice of a farm in Vienna, which farm was located in lot four in that township. He married Miss Freelove Flower in January, 1803. They are said to have been the first couple married in Vienna. She and her half sister were the first white women to arrive at this new settlement. The teams with which the family came not being able on account of bad roads to proceed farther than Youngstown, they continued the journey on foot alone through the unbroken wilderness to Vienna settlement to procure assistance, and, strange to say, arrived safely and were received with great astonishment and pleasure.

Samuel and Freelove Hutchins' children were: Hiram, born March 24, 1804, who married Eliza Lane; Aurora Amoret, wife of Richard Treat; Mary Amney, wife of Augustus Fuller; John, married Rhoda Andrews and was Representative in Congress from 1859 to 1863; Serena, wife of Augustus M. Reed; Urial H., married Emily Bennett; Lucia, wife of L. Cotton, who died and she again married Norman Andrews; and Betsey, wife of Larman B. Lane, who went as missionary to Siam.

Hiram and Eliza (Lane) Hutchins first settled in Vienna and afterwards removed to Vernon.

Their children who lived to maturity were : Sullivan, Lovisa, John L., and Elmer.

Sullivan Hutchins was born in Vienna February 26, 1834, and married, first, Hannah Akins, of Vernon, April 6, 1859. She died April 7, 1875, and left one child, Hiram Howard, born August 10, 1874, died August 8, 1875. Mr. Hutchins was again married, to Martha Bushnell, of Johnson, Ohio, May 10, 1876. They have Grace Adel, born June 18, 1877. Mr. Hutchins is the only descendant of Samuel Hutchins bearing the name residing in Trumbull county.

WILLIS REEDER.

Willis Reeder was born in Brookfield, Ohio, October 28, 1830, and was the son of Washington and Caroline (Mattocks) Reeder, and grandson of Benjamin Reeder, who came from Geneva, Cayuga county, New York, and settled on lot twenty-nine, in Hartford, July 9, 1817. When he was a boy of thirteen he found employment on the Erie extension canal. In 1845 the family removed to Louisville, Kentucky, and soon he secured a situation on a flat-boat as cook ; subsequently he became a pilot on a coal boat, and continued on the Ohio and Mississippi rivers in that capacity until the outbreak of the Rebellion, when the business becoming unsafe it was discontinued and coal was transported by steamers. In 1862 he became a licensed steamboat pilot running between Pittsburg and New Orleans, and during the last three years of the war of the Rebellion was engaged in the transportation service. After the close of the war he took command of a tow-boat until failing health caused him to retire from river life, and in 1871 he settled on lot forty-three, in Hartford, where he now resides. He married Maryett Bartholomew August 8, 1854, who was a descendant of Seth Bartholomew, one of the pioneers of Vienna township. Their children are Charlie Willis, Ruby Ann, and Frank Carlyle. Mr. Reeder has served two terms as trustee of the township, and three years as justice of the peace. He is a member of Jerusalem lodge No. 19, Free and Accepted Masons, also a member of Mahoning chapter No. 66, Royal Arch Masons. The first ancestor of this family in America, Joseph Reeder, came from London, England, and settled on Long Island some time previous to 1700, and according to tradition in the family his wife was sister to William of Orange, who superseded James II. on the throne of England. Their sons were Joseph, Benjamin, and William. Joseph settled in New Jersey, and his son Jacob settled in Pennsylvania, and his eldest son, Benjamin, who was born May 15, 1769, with his family settled in Ohio. Thus families follow the " star of empire " westward.

BIOGRAPHICAL NOTES.

Peter Carlton was born in Liberty township, October 28, 1821. He is a grandson of Francis Carlton, a Revolutionary soldier, who emigrated from New Jersey in 1799, and was one of the first settlers of Warren, Ohio, and son of Peter Carlton, a soldier of the War of 1812, who was one of the boys present at Salt Springs when Captain George was killed by McMahon, July 20, 1800. Peter Carlton, Jr., married Miss Catherine Caufield, of Brookfield, in 1850, and removed to Hartford in 1857, and settled in the south part of the township, on lot twenty-nine, on the farm where he has since resided. Their children are Mary B., Lizzie A., Jennie D., John B., and Bertha. Mr. Carlton is a much respected citizen and a peaceable, industrious farmer. He was elected justice of the peace in 1866, and has been successively re-elected four times, holding the office fifteen years. Although he is an active worker in the Republican party he has had the support of all parties. He has considerable reputation as a juror, often having served as grand, common pleas, and United States juror. He was one of the corporators of the Harvard Academic institute. He was the only man in the township who attended the inauguration of President Garfield in 1881. He now holds the office of notary public.

William Hull emigrated from Hartland, Connecticut, to Ohio in 1805, and first settled in Vernon, where the family resided till 1821, when they removed to Hartford, and in 1831 located at Burg Hill, on the farm now owned by his son Osman. He married Annie Hyde in Hartland, Connecticut, September 18, 1802. Their children were Harriet, wife of Elisha Beman, of Gustavus; Horace; Clarissa, wife of Alexander Morris; William, John, and Emeline, wife of

Simeon C. Baker. Mr. and Mrs. Hull were members of the Congregational church, and during their life most worthy citizens. They lived to a good old age, he dying November 30, 1857, at the age of seventy-eight years, and she living till July 11, 1874, reaching the advanced age of ninety-five years and eight months. Osman Hull retains the old home, and is now an enterprising and prosperous farmer, in early life, however, having been a mechanic. He married Miss Lorinda Roper, of Braceville, April 22, 1841. They are both earnest Christian workers in the temperance cause. Their sons are Ransom and Brunell. Mr. Hull is in politics a Republican.

Norman E. Austin was born in Goshen, Connecticut, February 20, 1812. In the year 1815 his father, Russel Austin, removed to Geneseo, New York, where Norman's early life was spent. In 1836 Norman E. Austin came to this county and purchased of John Kinsman the farm near Orangeville, which still bears his name. He married Mary C. Hamilton December 24, 1839, and in 1846 came to Hartford to make a permanent home. He brought with him a superior flock of fine-wool sheep, and in 1848 brought the Morgan horse Bulrush. During his life he was a prominent and successful farmer. He served as county commissioner, and at the time of his death was deacon of the Hartford Congregational church. His only child, Lizzie M., married Willard C. Hull, who now occupies the Austin farm. She died June 14, 1862; Norman E. Austin died April 10, 1870. His wife, Mary (Hamilton) Austin, continued to reside on the farm with her son-in-law till her death in the spring of 1881.

Arial Chapman was born in Hartford, Connecticut, in 1800, and was of English descent. His early home was at Cooperstown, New York, but at fourteen years of age he went to Busti, Chautauqua county, in the same State. Here he learned the trade of a tanner, and also married Miss Mary Derendorf, who was born in Columbia, Herkimer county, New York, and was of German descent. They came to Ohio in 1826, settling at Burg Hill in Hartford. Here Mr. Chapman carried on the tanning business for many years. In later life, however, he was engaged in agriculture, and resided at the same place till his death; and here Mrs.

Chapman continued to reside till 1881, when she died at the age of seventy-nine. They were highly esteemed in the vicinity, and will long be remembered. Their children were Dwight R., Margaret, Charlotte, and one adopted son, Albert Reed. Dwight R. was born June 13, 1827, and married Maria, only daughter of William Bond, December 19, 1849. They have one son, Frederick H. Chapman, and five daughters—Louisa, wife of James Morrow; Kate, Lizzie, Lucy, and Blanche. D. R. Chapman occupies the farm where the first clearing was made in the township of Hartford, in 1799.

Charles Hull was a native of the State of New York, and with his younger brother, Richard Hull, came to Orangeville in 1834 and engaged in business as clothiers, which they followed for some length of time. Charles Hull was born September 17, 1805, and married Miss Jane Ann Chapin January 20, 1835. She was born September 10, 1814. They were active members of the Baptist church in Orangeville during their lives, and much respected citizens of the township of Hartford. Their children were Willard C., George, and Emogene. In the later years of Mr. Hull's life he was engaged in agricultural pursuits, and died on his farm in Hartford, a little south of the village of Orangeville, April 30, 1863. Mrs. Hull died in Orangeville, June 11, 1872.

William Bond was a resident of Hartford over forty years, a worthy farmer, who left behind him a reputation for probity, uprightness, and honor. He was born in Sandersfield, Massachusetts, September 22, 1793. His father's family removed to Avon, New York, where he married Miss Lucy Cook, November 27, 1823. She was born in New Hartford, Connecticut, January 28, 1800. They had but one daughter, Maria, wife of D. R. Chapman. They removed to Hartford, Ohio, in 1833, settling on the farm east of Burg Hill, where they resided the remainder of their lives. She died January 18, 1873, and Mr. Bond died January 2, 1874.

Among the citizens of the township of Hartford are a number of the descendants of John Fitch, the inventor. His wife died here in 1813. To him belongs the honor of having constructed the first steamboat. Twenty years before the great experiment of Fulton and Livingston, on the Hudson, a steamboat was constructed and put in operation in Philadelphia, under his sole direction, and was found to go at the rate of eight miles an hour. He was considered, in his day, as quite visionary, and being a poor man found it difficult to command the means to make his experiments. Had his means been equal to the accomplishment of his designs, there can be no doubt that he would now hold undisputed the honor of having given to the country this most noble and useful invention. He at last became discouraged and disheartened, and ended his days by suicide in 1798, and lies buried at Bardstown, Kentucky. This unhappy man, weary of the world and disappointed in all his expectations, still most honestly believed in the correctness of the darling dream of his life, and expressed a wish to be buried on the banks of the Ohio, where the sound of the steam engine would, in future years, send its echoes abroad. For years there was nothing to mark his grave. Some pains has been taken to identify it, and a rough, unhewn, unlettered stone placed upon it as a memorial. For genius and misfortune, neglected in life and unhonored in death, it is perhaps a more fitting monument· than any storied urn which might be placed over his last resting-place. Let honor be given to whom honor is due. Justice to his memory demands that his name be recorded as the successful inventor of steamboats, he having demonstrated their practicability by his experiments beyond the power of denial.

James D. Burnett is a grandson of William Burnett, one of the pioneers of Hubbard township, and son of Benjamin Burnett, who settled in Hartford, in 1844, on the farm one mile south of Orangeville, where he died. Benjamin Burnett was the father of eleven children, seven of whom lived to maturity, and are all, except one son, residents of Trumbull county. James D. Burnett was a soldier of the war of 1861, and was the first man in the township to enlist for the three years service, his name being enrolled May 27, 1861, in company F, Twenty-fourth regiment, Ohio volunteer infantry, and honorably discharged June 18, 1864. He served in the Army of the Cumberland; was at Shiloh, Stone River, Lookout Mountain, Chickamauga, Missionary Ridge, and many small engagements, being under fire thirty-four days while in the service. After the war (June 21, 1866,) he married Eliza Jones, daughter of William C. Jones.

Giles M. Hayes is a prosperous, enterprising young farmer, residing on lot forty near the east line of the township of Hartford; here he located about 1875, and married Miss Emma Barnhart. He is a son of Almon Hayes and grandson of Elias Hayes, late of Harrison county, Ohio, and on his mother's side a descendant of Wilcox Akins, one of the pioneers of Vernon, who came from Norwalk, Connecticut, about 1810.

CHAPTER IV.

KINSMAN.

LOCATION AND OWNERSHIP.

Kinsman—township number seven in the first range—is situated in the northeast corner of the county, adjoining the Ashtabula county line on the north and the Pennsylvania line on the east. On the south is the township of Vernon and on the west the township of Gustavus. The township contains 16,664 acres, to which was annexed by the equalizing board 1,857 acres (lot number eight, tract two) in the eleventh range, being a part of the land on which the city of Akron is now located. The first township line run by the surveyors began at the south line of the reserve, five miles west from the Pennsylvania State line, and deflected so much from a parallel line as to be nearly five miles and a half from the State line at the lake shore, which accounts for the extra six hundred and sixty-four acres. The draft was made in 1798 and is known as draft number eighty-one of that series. The requisite amount to make a draft of a standard township was $12,903.23, and in this draft was assigned as follows: Uriah Tracy and Joseph Coit, $4,838.61; John Kinsman, $8,064.62. Major Joseph Perkins of Norwich, Connecticut, was a joint owner in this township and in other lands drawn in other drafts. In the division of the Kinsman and Perkins interest Mr. Kinsman took this township and Major Perkins the Akron and other lands. Mr. Kinsman also purchased the interests of Joseph Coit and Uriah Tracy, who was then a United States Senator from Connecticut.

PHYSICAL FEATURES, STREAMS, SOIL, TIMBER.

The surface of the township is in general of a level character. The principal streams are the Pymatuning, Stratton, and Sugar creeks, the last two being branches of the first. The Pymatuning rises in Cherry valley, Ashtabula county, enters Kinsman near the northwest corner and flows a southeasterly course through the west half of the township. Stratton creek—named for the first settler on its banks—comes into the township near the northeast corner, takes a southwest course, and unites with the Pymatuning near the south line of the township. Sugar creek rises in Johnston township and flows into Kinsman near the southwest corner, uniting with the parent stream. This creek derives its name from the sugar maple groves found along its course. Much of the soil of Kinsman is of a superior quality, especially the bottom lands along the Pymatuning, where an alluvial soil is found, this stream frequently overflowing its banks and covering the adjacent land for a considerable distance on either side, and those in the vicinity of the junction of Sugar creek and the Pymatuning, which are exceedingly rich and productive. A considerable proportion of the soil of the township is a sandy loam.

The first settlers found Kinsman covered with a heavy growth of timber with the exception of a tract of about one thousand acres in the center of the township, which was destitute of timber, and which the settlers called "the prairie." The principal varieties of timber were the oak, beech, maple, hickory, chestnut, elm, etc. In the south part of the township, in the west part of section twenty-three, was a grove of white pines of about twenty-five acres, presumably the largest grove of the kind on the Reserve.

INDIANS.

In regard to the Indians of Kinsman a writer* says :

There are many indications that Kinsman, at some early day, was a place of Indian resort, where their villages and wigwams were as permanently fixed as the nature of their wandering life would allow. The high ground back of Wayne Bidwell's house, the meadow in front of it, and the ground about the springs by the old ashery, showed marked indications of having once been the seat of an Indian village. The first plowing of the land revealed spots darkened with charcoal, showing the places of their camp-fires; many

*Rev. H. B. Eldred in Mahoning Valley Historical Collections.

37*

flint arrow-heads and stone axes were found; traces of fortifications on the high grounds, and the dancing circle seen on the flats, all conspire to establish this belief.

Although there were no permanently resident Indians in the vicinity of Kinsman after its first settlement, they frequently visited it in small straggling bands for the purpose of hunting, trapping, and trading at Mr. Kinsman's store. Furs, skins, and various articles of their manufacture, as baskets, wooden trays, ladles, curiously worked 'moccasins, sugar, and various trinkets were the commodities in which they dealt. They also brought in the native fruits—June-berries, strawberries, raspberries, whortleberries, cranberries, haws, plums, and crab apples, to exchange for milk, meal, flour, bread—always wanting equal measure, no matter what was brought or what was asked in return. Calico, blankets, powder and lead, flints, whiskey, tobacco, knives, and some little finery, as beads and the like, comprised their purchases at the store. Some of the Indians were sharp at a bargain. Many could talk broken English, and often showed themselves good judges of the character of those with whom they dealt. They were jealous of their rights, and shy of those whites in whom they lacked confidence.   .   .   .

In the year 1800 a larger party of Indians made an encampment on the bottom-lands in Kinsman than were seen in the township afterward. They broke into the cabin which Mr. Kinsman had erected in 1799 for his surveyors, and appropriated camp-kettles and such articles as had been stored there for future use.

ANCIENT REMAINS.

Upon this subject the same writer says :

That part of the township commencing near the mouth of Stratton's creek, skirting along the east bank of the Pymatuning, and west bank of Stratton's creek, first regarded of so little value, was a beautiful alluvial bottom, on which the first settlers noticed the evident signs of an old Indian corn-field. Further up the land rises into an undulating surface of deep gravelly loam, which undoubtedly had been burned over by the Indians for a hunting ground. Freed from timber the elk and the deer, in the grazing season, would come out from the dense forest on either side, to feed on the open grass plat and plain, and thus could be approached, and presenting a fairer mark for the Indian. Bordering on the open prairie, on the farm now owned by Wayne Bidwell, Esq., upon the high ground in the rear of his house, were the remains of what was supposed to have been an old Indian fort. The lines of an embankment and ditch were clearly defined and were often noticed by the early settlers of the town. In the vicinity of this fort flint arrow-heads and stone axes were frequently found. So late as 1866 Mr. Plant, in plowing up an old field on his farm (a part of the prairie), struck a nest of arrow-heads, which were undoubtedly lost or buried there by the Indians. Until the War of 1812 the Indians made their yearly visits to this locality, where they spent weeks in hunting, fishing, and trapping. Spots of earth, dark with intermingled charcoal, were found near the old fort, showing what was evidently an Indian camping ground. The headwaters of the Pymatuning were marked with a very permanent beaver-dam, which had been abandoned by its occupants before the settlement of the country by the whites.

SURVEY AND FIRST IMPROVEMENTS.

Mr. Kinsman first came to the Reserve in 1799, making the journey, in company with Simon Perkins, on horseback across the Allegheny mountains by way of Pittsburg. He reached Youngstown in the latter part of the spring of the above year, where he met Mr. Young, at whose house he made his headquarters a portion of the time while making preparations for settlement. At Youngstown he made arrangements for the survey of the township, which was done under the direction of Alfred Wolcott. On arriving in this township Mr. Kinsman and his party established themselves at the center, putting up a cabin near the southeast corner of what is now the square. The work of surveying was completed during the year 1799. Mr. Kinsman was a large owner of land in different sections of the Reserve, and not until 1801 did he decide as to the place of his location. In the spring of that year he left Connecticut for his future home in Kinsman township. He was accompanied by Calvin Pease, Simon Perkins, George Tod, John S. Edwards, Ebenezer Reeve, Josiah Pelton, Turhand and Jared Kirtland, and others. Reeve was employed by Mr. Kinsman to begin improvements in the township, and, as an inducement for him to leave his Eastern home for this purpose, was to be paid $20 per month during his absence, and the sum of $40 in case he did not like the country and desired to return to his former home, a quite probable contingency. But it was also stipulated that if he liked the country he was to exchange his land in Connecticut for land in Kinsman. The sequel to this agreement will appear further on. The whole party came out on horseback, with the exception of the two Kirtlands, who came with a team and wagon. That they were a merry set of men, and intelligent as well, may be inferred from the following, which we quote from the writer previously mentioned :

The company usually put up over night at the same place. They soon organized into a society called " the Illuminati." All were titled, and in addressing each other the titles were frequently used. To illustrate the use to which the society was put, and show the wit and humor with which they beguiled the tediousness of their journey, a single case will suffice. Mr. Kinsman was the only one of the company possessed of a hired man. Pease set up a claim to the right of property in this man Reeve. Kinsman resisted, and employed counsel to defend his rights. Pease instituted proceedings to recover the property. The case was brought before one of the titled dignitaries of the " Illuminati " and called for hearing from night to night as they pursued their journey. Profound arguments on the case were made, and a lengthy and learned decision was at last given confirming the title to the property in Mr. Kinsman.

On their arrival in Youngstown the party separated, a part going to Warren, Mr. Kinsman and Mr. Reeve to Kinsman, and Pelton to his purchase in Gustavus.

The first improvements in the township were soon commenced by Mr. Kinsman beginning the erection of a double log house in section twenty-three, east of the Vernon road. When the cabin had reached a height of six or seven feet it was abandoned and another erected between the creek and the store of Kay & Burrill. In the fall of 1801 Kinsman and Reeve returned to Connecticut, leaving John Cummings, John and Isaac Mathews, in charge of the place and to prosecute the work of clearing during their absence.

EARLY SETTLEMENT.

While the settlement of the township will date from the improvements made by Messrs. Kinsman and Reeve, above mentioned, Martin Tidd and his son-in-law, James Hill, and David Randall are regarded as the first permanent settlers, since they were the first to take up their abode with their families, which they did in the spring of 1802, Mr. Kinsman having made a contract with them to this effect the previous fall.

In April the three families left Youngstown together, with two teams and wagons. There was probably a good natured strife between the Tidd party, who occupied one wagon, and Randall, as to who should first arrive upon the ground, but an accident happening to Randall, his wagon breaking down at Smithfield (now Vernon), he was detained there over night. Tidd and family, with Hill and wife, proceeded to Kinsman, and thus bore off the honors of being the first permanent settlers. Tidd settled on the hill north of the Seth Perkins farm, getting one hundred acres in exchange for sixty acres in Kinsman. Randall located on the Seth Perkins farm. Tidd and Randall were originally from the Wyoming valley, Pennsylvania. The former lived a short distance below the settlement of Wyoming at the time of the massacre, his house occupying a high bluff on the banks of the Susquehanna river. His house is said to have been used as a block-house, and during the massacre afforded a place of safety for many of the inhabitants in the vicinity. After removing from Wyoming he went to Westmoreland county. In 1798 he came to Youngstown with his family and nephew, Captain Hillman, where he lived until his removal to Kinsman. Tidd possessed the true spirit of the pioneer, though he continued to live in Kinsman until his death, yet he was restless during the progress of settlement and improvement of the country, and was only prevented from "moving on" by reason of his advanced age and out of deference to the wishes of his children, who did not inherit his pioneer spirit. He died at an advanced age.

Randall moved from Pennsylvania down on the Ohio river, settling near Marietta, Washington county, whence he came to Youngstown in 1800. In his frequent removals from place to place he acquired an extensive acquaintance with the Indians, with whom his dealings were always characterized by such exceptional kindliness and honesty as to invariably win their confidence and good will. At the time of the McMahan difficulty at the salt spring, elsewhere related, he went with Captain Hillman to visit the Indians, and endeavor to prevent the retaliatory measures which they seemed determined to inflict upon the whites.

Randall lived but a short time on the Perkins farm, removing to the farm which in 1806 he exchanged with John Allen for land in Ashtabula county. He resided in Ashtabula but a short time, returning to Kinsman and locating on Stratton creek. He continued to live in Kinsman until advanced in life, when he removed to Michigan, where he died at the age of seventy-two.

As a result of the contract between Mr. Kinsman and Ebenezer Reeve, previously mentioned, the latter exchanged his land in Norwich, Connecticut, for land in Kinsman, and in 1802 moved out with his two daughters, Deborah and Hannah, and erected a log house opposite the site of the Sutliff frame house, where he lived until 1807. In that year he built a two-story frame house in front of where the house of Wayne Bidwell was afterwards built. This was the first two-story frame house erected in Kinsman. Here Mr. Reeve spent the rest of his life.

Besides those already mentioned a few families settled in 1802. Paul Rice and his mother settled on land which subsequently became the Webber farm. Alexander Clark began operations upon his farm. Uriel Driggs located east of Driggs' hill.

In 1803 Captain Charles Case came into the township, and assisted in tending the Kinsman saw-mill. He was accustomed to give singing lessons, free of charge, and gained considerable popularity thereby. He removed to Williamsfield, and died there.

The same year settlements were made as follows: William Tidd, John Wade, John Little, Walter Davis, Isaac and John Matthews—with whom their sister Betsy lived—Robert Laughlin, Peter Yetman, George Gordon Dement, George Matthews, Joseph McMichael, Joshua Budwell, and his son Henry, and William Knox settled in the township. Several of these men brought families; others were young men and single. Joseph Murray, a carpenter and a single man, arrived and lived with the Davises.

In July, 1804, after a journey of seven weeks, John Kinsman and family arrived in the township. His family then consisted of himself and wife and four children—John, Joseph, Sally, and Olive. Accompanying him were several persons whom he had engaged to assist him in erecting a house and other buildings for his family. In this party of settlers were Chester Lewis and family, also his mother-in-law, Mrs. Manning, and her son Samuel. Lewis drove an ox team loaded with household furniture and farming implements. Mr. Kinsman came with a number of teams. On his way he bought a stock of goods, and placed them in charge of Joseph Coit, who came out to act as clerk in the store. Louisa Morse, afterward the wife of Isaac Meacham, and Eunice Morgan, afterward Mrs. John L. Cook, came with the company; also Cook and Jahazel Lathrop, carpenters.

In 1804 Plumb Sutliff settled on the creek, but moved to a farm on the center road a year later, where he died, in 1834, aged eighty-three. He married, the year of his settlement, Deborah Reeve, of Kinsman.

William Scott settled on the ridge in 1804.

Deacon William Matthews settled during the same year. He was a Revolutionary soldier. In 1808 he was appointed justice of the peace. Deacon Matthews was one of the most earnest of working Christians, and was largely instrumental in promoting the cause of religion in the new settlement. He was always in attendance upon the religious meetings, whatever the weather, and frequently conducted the services, as clergymen were seldom in the township during its early years.

Thirty families comprised the inhabitants of the township in 1805, together with twenty or thirty young unmarried men, and twelve or fifteen young women, who were single. Some of the settlers whose names have not yet been mentioned were John Neil, Thomas, John, and William Gillis, Stephen Splitstone, Captain William Westby and his sons, James, John, and Ebenezer, William and Andrew Christy, Thomas Potter, Leonard Blackburn, David and Elam Lindsley.

John Allen, of Norwich, Connecticut, came to the township in 1806. The Allen family has played an important part in the affairs of this township.

David Brackin, a native of Ireland, located in this township in 1806. The same year came John Andrews. He married Hannah, the youngest daughter of Ebenezer Reeve, to whom eight children were born. Mr. Andrews was born in Connecticut, in 1782, and died at the age of eighty-one. About 1812 he engaged in business as a merchant. He was a useful member of society, and a warm supporter of schools and churches. As early as 1825 a boarding-school in Kinsman grew up under his patronage, and ten years later, at his house, built for such a purpose, a female boarding school was opened and successfully conducted until 1840.

Isaac Meacham came from Hartland, Connecticut, in 1806, Lester Cone in 1807, Peter Lossee in 1808, Jairus Brockett in 1809, Michael Burns in 1808, Ira Meacham in 1812, Joshua Yeomans in 1814, Obed Gilder in 1815, Ebenezer Webber, John Yeomans, Simon Fobes, and others later.

EARLY EVENTS.

In 1801 Ebenezer Reeve began work on a mill-dam, but it was swept away by the water the following spring. The next year James King, from Pennsylvania, as mill-wright, built and completed a saw-mill for John Kinsman. It was put in operation the same year.

In 1802 Mr. Kinsman brought a small stock of goods for the supply of his family and the settlers. David Randall and Zopher Case were employed to tend the mill, and Joseph Coit subsequently became clerk in the store. Mrs. Randall sometimes ran the mill and spun while the logs were moving through.

TROUBLE WITH THE MILL-DAM.

The mill-dam erected in 1802 proved to be very much of a nuisance. Those who dwelt near it were afflicted with malarial sickness of a severe nature. Zyphus and kindred diseases raged violently in this and neighboring townships. The dam caused back-water in the creek for a distance of three miles on account of the almost level bed of the stream, and so much stagnant water no doubt caused a most unhealthy atmosphere to prevail in the neighborhood. Loud complaints soon began to be heard, and in 1805 Mr. Kinsman was waited upon by a number of representative men of Hartford, Vernon, and other places, among whom were Rev. Thomas Robbins and General Smith, who came to demand that the dam be destroyed. He treated them with hospitality, gave them a good dinner, plenty of brandy, etc., and in reply to their request said that it would but increase the evil to tear down the dam in hot weather; that he and others wished to do some sawing, but that the trouble should be removed early in the spring. The delegates went home satisfied ; but their neighbors were not, and accused them of having been bribed and made drunk, besides making other insinuations not complimentary to the characters of the distinguished gentlemen.

One night some self-appointed regulators came and cut the boards about the flume. Immediate action prevented serious damage, and in a day or two the mill was running as usual. Mr. Kinsman suspected who had done the mischief, but allowed no talk upon the subject, thinking that some of them would soon return to see what their work had effected. He was correct in his surmises. A short time after a man from Vernon, whom Mr. Kinsman had suspected, was seen on the opposite bank of the creek. Mr. Kinsman mounted a horse, forded the stream, and engaged in conversation with the visitor, inviting him to come over to the store. The latter accepted, and the two entered the store together. After Mr. Kinsman had conversed with the fellow sufficiently to satisfy himself that he had the guilty party, he locked the door of the store, collared the man and gave him a sound flogging. Then knowing that he had acted unlawfully, he stepped behind the counter and offered to settle. The

Riverius Bidwell.

Mrs. Eunicia Bidwell.

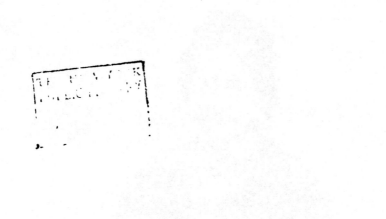

proposition was accepted, and about $3 worth of goods patched up the wounded feelings of the would-be destroyer of the dam. But when the trespasser returned to Vernon he was threatened with another whipping for settling on such easy terms.

Other threats were made, but the dam continued to stand. In 1806 Chloe Gilder, of Gustavus, and Anna Cone, of Gustavus, were riding a horse near this dam when in some way the animal became frightened and Miss Gilder, who was behind, slipped off into the mud and water and was drowned. In March, 1806, the pond was drained and sickness abated. The road now runs on the top of what was the old dam.

The first apples raised in the township came from an orchard planted by David Randall, on the farm subsequently owned by John Allen.

George Gorden Dement built and put in operation a whiskey distillery in the southeastern part of the township in 1803.

The first mechanics among the early settlers were James Hill and Walter Davis, shoemakers; Captain David Randall, cooper; David and Elam Lindsley, Joseph Murray, John L. Cook, Jahazael Lathrop, carpenters.

In 1806 the Gillis brothers erected a saw-mill on Stratton creek, and subsequently a grist-mill.

The first frame house was erected for Mr. Kinsman. It was begun in 1804. The second frame house was built in 1806 by Plumb Sutliff.

A half mile below the Gillis mill Benjamin Allen and Abner Hall built a shop for fulling and cloth dressing. In 1813 a carding-machine was put in Gillis' mill and transferred to Allen's shop in 1814.

About 1806 William Henry, near Hartstown, began work as a tanner. He at first manufactured the lime which he used from shells found in the creek.

In 1813 John Andrews established a store and ashery for the manufacture of pearl ash.

In 1802 the first birth occurred. Twin daughters, Sally and Phebe, were born to Mr. and Mrs. David Randall. Sally afterwards married R. Brown, and Phebe Charles Woodworth, both of Williamsfield.

The same year occurred also the first marriage. Mr. Kinsman, as justice of the peace, united in marriage Robert Henry and Betsey Tidd.

The first death was that of John Tidd, who died in April, 1804, at the age of thirty-two. He was buried in the lot which afterwards became the old cemetery, on the corner near the church. The first death of an adult female was that of Mrs. Walter Davis, October 28, 1805. A child of Samuel Tidd died of a burn in September, 1805. William Westby and son died of typhus fever in 1805. Also a child of Urial Driggs died September 11.

The same year while David and Elam Lindsley were clearing, a limb of a falling tree struck David and fractured his thigh. The wound was cared for by Dr. Wright, of Vernon, and Dr. Hawley, of Austinburg. The broken pieces did not unite and it was found necessary to amputate the limb. The operation was performed by Dr. Wilson, of Meadville, with a common handsaw and a carving-knife.

The first military company was organized in 1806. David Randall was captain, Zopher Case lieutenant, and George G. Dement ensign. Previous to this date the men of Kinsman had trained in Hartford and Vernon.

ROADS.

As in most thickly wooded new settlements, the first way-marks of the town were blazed trees, marking a line from one settlement to another. Afterward these lines were underbrushed. Still later they were cleared of their timber, and some of them at least, worked into highways. There is, however, scarcely a road in the town that follows the first paths traced by the early settlers. The roads commonly lay along the highest and dryest grounds, and had reference to the places most convenient for fording and bridging the streams. Afterwards as the woods were cleared away and the country settled, its thoroughfares were laid out to suit the convenience of the people, and facilitate intercourse between different parts.

The first road of any considerable length that was constructed in this region is what was called the "Old Salt road," laid out in 1804 by Bemis and David Niles. It began on the lake shore at the mouth of Conneaut creek, continuing south to the old county road, thence south through the first range to Kinsman's mill. It took a northerly course from Kinsman's store, along the ridge by the residences of George Mathews, William Scott, and Marvin Leonard, of Williamsfield, somewhere between the present State and center roads, of the first range. South of Lake Erie a settlement had been begun at Monroe.

Midway between Monroe and Kinsman a temporary board cabin was erected, where men and teams might find shelter for the night. Salt was one of the pressing wants of the early inhabitants of Kinsman and adjoining towns, and was one of the principal motives for the construction of this road; hence the name given to the road. Salt was manufactured in Onondaga, New York, and transported in vessels on Lake Ontario to Lewistown, below the Falls of Niagara; from Lewistown it was carted to Buffalo; from Buffalo it was brought to Conneaut in canoes and open boats. It reached Kinsman by means of ox teams, where its price was twenty dollars per barrel.

In 1806 a road from Johnson to Kinsman was laid out, beginning at the east and west center road, on the south side of lot number forty-five, in Johnson, and running thence to the Mercer road, near the house of John Kinsman. The same year a road was laid out from the house of John Kinsman east to the State line, near the house of William Mossman, by the farms of Leonard Blackburn and Thomas Potter. This is known as the Mercer road. In 1807 the State road was laid out. In 1808, a road from the north line of Warren Palmer's farm, in Vernon, was surveyed to the crossing of the Pymatuning creek, near the house of John Kinsman.

The petition, in 1804, for a road from the mouth of Conneaut creek south, shows that it was to terminate at Kinsman's mill, whereas the record of the survey makes it terminate at an oak tree, one mile south of the south line of Kinsman. It is conjectured that the first road was legally established only to Kinsman's mill, and the above piece is to make good the balance of the first survey.

In 1810 the record shows there was a petition to establish a road from Mr. Kinsman's toward Meadville. The record is imperfect, and proper legal action was not had. In 1835 new action was taken, and the road surveyed by Buel Barnes, surveyor, and the lines fixed from the tavern barn, near Mr. Kinsman's, on the line of the Meadville road to the State line, and the whole legalized by the commissioners.

In 1815 the Mill road, so-called, was estab-lished, beginning at the Mercer road west of the house of Thomas Potter, by Gillis's mills to the State road, near the houses of Elizabeth Lewis and Nicholas Krahe.

In 1811 a road was laid out from the vicinity of the Griswold farm east, in Gustavus, to the house of Mr. Kinsman, via the farm of J. Burnham, Esq.

In 1818 a road was established from what was then known as the Clark farm to the northeast part of the township.

In 1819 a road was established by the farms of Simon Fobes and William Mathews to the Meadville road. Also the same year a road from the meeting-house (near Dr. Allen's), in Kinsman, west through the center of Gustavus to the west line of the county.

In 1820 the road from Johnson to Kinsman was altered and straightened. In 1821 the road beginning near the north line of Vernon, by Obed Gilder, was established. In 1822 the north and south center road was surveyed.

SCHOOLS AND SCHOOL BUILDINGS.

The first school in Kinsman was taught by Leonard Blackburn, in a log cabin. He taught a night-school, consisting of a few boys; also during the day, in the winter of 1805-6, in the log cabin of the Neals, on the Joshua Yeoman farm, or in the Yetman cabin, on the Seth Perkins farm. In the winter of 1806-7 his school was in the Neal cabin. It was popular, principally on account of its cheapness. As there were no public funds, and the "Yankee school" charged $2.50 per term for tuition, some of the people were displeased, and patronized the cheaper school.

The first school-house was built of logs, sixteen feet square, seven and a half feet in height, and stood on the bank of Stratton creek, opposite the house of John Andrews on the Randall farm, afterward known as the Daniel Allen farm. It had rough slab benches, and boards fastened to the wall by wooden pins for desks, altogether primitive in its fixtures and surroundings.

The first school taught here was by Jedediah Burnham, Esq., beginning January 1, 1806, and continuing one quarter. He taught also in the winter of 1806-7, at ten dollars per month, and took his pay mostly in grain and barter. He boarded from house to house; his scholars came from all the surrounding settlements. Benjamin

Allen taught the first part of the winter of 1807 –1808. Dr. Peter Allen taught the balance of the winter; also in 1808, assisted by Joseph Kinsman, and the next winter assisted by John Kinsman. Ezra Buell taught in this school-house one or two winters, from 1810 to 1814. Joshua Yeomans taught one winter, as late as 1815 or 1816.

Miss Eunice Allen (wife of Jehiel Meacham) taught the first summer school in 1807. Miss Lucy Andrews, afterward Mrs. Jones, of Hartford, and Miss Bushnell, afterward Mrs. Beecher, of Shalersville, were among the last who taught in that building.

The next school-house was of logs, erected near the township line, north of William Scott's, to accommodate families in Williamsfield. Afterward one was built south, near the site of the present Ridge school-house. The third was also a log house, and stood near where the stone house built by Seymour Potter now stands. Dr. D. Allen attended school there in the summer of 1818. At this time there was a school-house east of McConnell's, on the Pennsylvania line, to accommodate settlers on both sides of the State line.

In 1820 the township was divided into districts, and the whole southwest quarter of the town was organized into district number one. The first frame school-house was erected by subscription, 20x24, feet and placed in the angle of the State and Meadville roads, on the site of the present hotel. The first school taught in it was by Daniel Lathrop (since Rev.), of Norwich, Connecticut, in 1820–21, for $15 per month. The common price for teaching winter schools was $10 per month. The building was a commodious and good one for the times. Afterward it was removed to a rise of ground, a few rods north on the Meadville road, near where the house of Elijah Beckwith now stands. Here it was occupied a number of years under the name of the Village school-house. Here D. Cadwell (afterward known as a distinguished lawyer, provost-marshal of the Northern district of Ohio during the civil war, and district judge of the Cleveland circuit) taught about 1840, and I know not how many others, who in after life filled honorable callings. After the erection of the present school-building, 1853, near L. C. Perkins's, the

old one was sold, and is now the dwelling of R. P. Hulse.

It was several years after the erection of this first frame village school-house that the schools began to be aided by public funds. Only a few of the common English branches were taught in the schools, such as reading, spelling, writing, arithmetic, and, to a very limited extent, geography and grammar.

About 1822 a log school-house was erected north of Esquire King's—not far from the present residence of Gordon Burnside. The second frame school-house was built in 1825, on the ridge, at the crossing, near George Matthews's. The one by David Brackin was built in 1828. The one near Mr. Crocker's, in the north part of the town, on the Meadville road, the one east, by Esquire Laughlin's, and the center school-house, near Henry Lillies's, were built in 1834.

KINSMAN ACADEMY.

This institution was incorporated during the winter of 1841–42, and its academy building erected in 1842, the land on which it stands having been donated by Mr. John Kinsman. The timber for the frame was given in the rough by Esquire Andrews. At the time of building the times were hard and cash scarce. Only $50 in money were paid for building purposes, although many turns and credits were made that answered the same as cash. The building was plain, well proportioned, commodious, neatly and substantially built. John Christy, Albert Allen, and Dr. Dudley Allen, were its first trustees and building committee. The stonework was prepared and laid by Robert and George Braden. P. S. Miner did the carpenter and joiner work, and Zephua Stone the plastering and flues. Its cost was not far from $1,500. In 1863 its rooms were remodeled, at a cost of about $400. It has done good service for the town and surrounding communities.

The following is an imperfect list of its principals and assistant teachers: Charles F. Hudson, assistant; Miss Brown taught in 1842–44; Charles C. Clapp, assistant Miss Clapp, 1844–46; John Lynch, 1846–49; Almon Sampson, 1849–50; Robert F. Moore, 1850–51; John Myers, 1851–52; Miss Owen, 1852–53; Miss H. A. Holt, 1853; Dr. W. R. Gilkey, 1853–55; Miss Hannah P. Parker, 1855; Mr. and Mrs. W. P.

Clark, 1855–58; E. L. Moon, assistant Mrs. Moon, 1858–59; E. P. Haynes and Miss E. C. Allen, 1859–60; Moses G. Watterson, 1860–61; Edwin L. Webber, 1861–62; Mrs. A. A. F. Johnston, 1862–65. Assistants: Miss Josephine C. Field, Miss Celia Morgan, Miss Mary Christy, Miss Louisa M. Fitch. Mrs. Johnston was principal of the academy for a longer period than any other teacher, and was greatly respected and beloved by her pupils.

BIOGRAPHICAL SKETCHES.

JOHN KINSMAN AND FAMILY.*

The ancestors of Mr. Kinsman, on his father's side, are traced from the time of their leaving England, embarking in the ship Mary and John, at Southampton, landing at Boston, settling in Ipswich, Massachusetts, as one of the Puritan fathers, in 1634. From that time the genealogical record is traced by regularly executed recorded wills of the ancestors of Mr. Kinsman down to and including the last will and testament of his father; and whatever of history is shown links them with the patriots of their day and generation. The ancestry of his mother is traced from John Thomas, who came over from England in the ship Hopewell, 1635, a boy fourteen years of age, under the special charge of Governor Edward Winslow, of Plymouth, from whom sprang an honorable and patriotic line of descendants. The name of Mr. Kinsman's mother was Sarah Thomas, sister of General John Thomas, of the American Revolution, one of the generals first appointed by the Continental Congress.

Mr. John Kinsman was the son of Jeremiah Kinsman, a thrifty farmer of Lisbon, Connecticut. Here he lived, working on his father's farm, and receiving such education as the schools of that day afforded, until he was of age. At the breaking out of the Revolution, 1776, being then twenty-three years old, he enlisted in a company of Connecticut militia, destined to take an active part in the bloody and disastrous battle of Long Island. In that battle he was

*From the Mahoning Valley Historical Collections.

taken prisoner and was confined for some time in one of the prison-ships in New York harbor. He suffered greatly from this imprisonment, being inhumanly treated, and never fully recovered from its effects upon his health. With two of his companions he was finally released from the prison-ship on parole and allowed to mess in a room in the city of New York.

While in New York he acquired a knowledge of the hatting business that induced him, immediately on his release and return home, to embark in that business. He at once established a shop, placed in it an experienced workman, Mr. Capron, as foreman, purchased a stock of goods, and devoted his time to the care of the store, furnishing the shop, and making sales of the products. He supplied the army largely with hats, and the trade generally proved to be successful, and was continued in Connecticut, with his farm operations, until after the war.

In 1792 he was married to Miss Rebecca Perkins, daughter of Captain Simon Perkins, of Lisbon, Connecticut.

In 1797, having been elected to represent his native town in the State Legislature, the office was continued to him by successive re-elections for three years. It was here that he became acquainted with many of the officers and stockholders of the Connecticut Land company, and familiar with their operations, and concluded to become one of the proprietors of the company. It was also about this time that he first entertained the idea of a removal to Ohio.

His first trip to the Connecticut Western Reserve was in 1799. He came out to explore the country, and to see and survey some of the lands that had fallen to him in the drafts of the year previous. That year he aided in the survey of the township of Kinsman, and from this time his life and business were very intimately connected with the early history and settlement of the township. His was the ruling spirit of the settlement. His age, experience, enterprise, wealth, and more than all, perhaps, his practical sound judgment, gave him an influence in the affairs of the town which no other individual could pretend to exert.

While naturally firm and decided in his purpose, he was conciliatory in his treatment of others, eminently kind in his feelings and lenient as a creditor.

His first office in Ohio was that of justice of the peace under the Territorial government. Local justices were associated to form the courts called quarter sessions. He was one of those who assisted in constituting the government of the first and subsequent county organizations, providing for county jail, and fixing its limits, etc. Under the State government, in 1806, he was appointed one of the associate judges of the county. Also held the office of postmaster from the time of the first establishment of an office in the town to the time of his decease.

His own increasing business, as well as that of many others, now called for increased facilities of trade and commerce, and was the occasion of the establishment of the Western Reserve bank, the first corporation of the kind in Northern Ohio. Mr. Kinsman was one of its principal projectors, and much the largest subscriber to the stock of the company, taking one-fifth of the $100,000 capital. He did not live, however, to see the organization completed.

His business life was one of great activity and toil, riding often on horseback to Connecticut, New York, and Philadelphia, to purchase goods, also over many parts of the Reserve, looking after settlements and sales of land, occasionally camping out nights. Besides, the building of mills, attention to his store, and the clearing and improving of a large farm, brought upon him exposures and cares greater than his somewhat impaired constitution was able to bear. He died August 17, 1813, aged sixty years. He died intestate, leaving a large estate, for that time, which was administered upon by his brother-in-law, General Simon Perkins.

Mr. Kinsman lived and died in the house which he built on the south side of the square, near where the store and warehouse of Kay & Burrill now stands. A few years after his decease the house took fire in the middle of the night and burned to the ground. The family afterwards occupied the old Sutliff house, a little east of the one burned, until John Kinsman, the eldest son of the deceased, built the house now known as the "Kinsman homestead," which was occupied by the family until by death, marriage, or otherwise, their homes were changed.

The widow, Mrs. Rebecca Kinsman, remained there until her decease, May 27, 1854, aged eighty years. Mrs. Kinsman was a woman of

decided and devoted Christian character, of strong mind, and of large heart. She was active in promoting the religious culture of the place, both in word and deed. She gave freely and largely to benevolent objects; was a liberal benefactor of Western Reserve college in its earlier years, assisted largely towards the building of the Presbyterian and Congregational house of worship, gave the parsonage and grounds to be occupied by the minister of the society, and contributed generously toward an endowment for his support. Her liberal hand, kind advice, and ready relief to those who were in need have often been gratefully remembered and acknowledged.

The family of Mr. and Mrs. Kinsman, when they left Lisbon, Connecticut, consisted of the following children: John, aged ten years; Joseph, aged nine years; Sarah, aged five years, died January 13, 1807; Olive Douglas, aged three years.

John, the eldest of the children, soon took the place of "*pater familias*" in the household, living in the old homestead, which he built. He was married April 28, 1846, to Jane W. Cass, widow of John Jay Cass, and died February 4, 1864.

He was identified with the early settlement of the Western Reserve from his youth; and having uncommon energy and business capacity, he soon became connected with many of the public and business interests of the day, and devoted much of his time and means to the development of the resources of the country, and administered largely of his advice and means to the wants of those around him.

In his extended business large credits, for provisions and supplies, were freely given to relieve the wants of the early settlers, at a time when such credits were deemed absolutely necessary to their success.

Joseph, after remaining with his father in Ohio assisting in the store a few years, returned to Connecticut, fitted himself for college at the academy at Colchester, and entered the freshman class at Yale college in 1816. After three years of close application to study his health gave way, and he was advised by his physician to go South. He spent the winter in the West Indies at St. Thomas and St. Croix, returning with the return of spring. He died of consumption,

June 17, 1819, and was buried in the old cemetery at Norwich, Connecticut. His age was twenty-four years.

Olive Douglas, in 1812, was sent to Norwich, Connecticut, to attend the school of Miss Lydia Huntley, afterward Mrs. Sigourney. From there she went to Hartford, afterwards to Litchfield, where she finished her school education under the instruction of Mrs. Pierce. While in attendance upon Miss Huntley's school for young ladies the intelligence of her father's death was received. An only daughter, she was a favorite of her father's, and his death was to her a great affliction.

Returning from school in 1819, she rode on horseback from Chambersburg, Pennsylvania, to her home. Unaccustomed to this mode of travel the journey was so severe that it produced a spinal affection, from which she never recovered. She married George Swift, Esq., son of Hon. Zephaniah Swift, chief-justice of Connecticut. He was a graduate of Yale college, commenced the practice of law in Warren; occupied, for his first residence, a house on the corner of Main and Franklin streets, where the Anderson block now stands. In 1823 he removed to Kinsman, purchased a farm and built a house upon it, which is now occupied by David Bracken. He continued the practice of law for some time, but in the latter part of his life devoted himself mainly to the farm. He was a great reader and an accomplished scholar, very agreeable and instructive in conversation; was elected a Representative to the State Legislature; was a devoted Christian, and aided much in the religious exercises, and the building up of the church to which he belonged. He died March 14, 1845, of cancer. Mrs. Swift died June 24, 1835, of spinal affection.

Thomas was the first of the family born in Ohio, August 20, 1804. He was one of the most extensive farmers in northern Ohio. His lands, comprising about two thousand acres, were located in the townships of Kinsman and Gustavus. The fine quality of its soil, well watered by springs and spring-brooks, its good timber, and well arranged farm buildings, made his farm one of the most attractive in the State. It was mostly under fine cultivation; a part being devoted to dairy purposes, the number of cows ranging from sixty to eighty each year; the balance to promiscuous farming. His large and well-bred Durham herd constituted at all times a prominent and attractive feature of his business.

His life as a citizen of the town numbers more years than any one that has preceded him, and at his death he was the oldest native inhabitant. His life, from childhood to old age, has been peculiarly marked by kindly relations with all with whom he had to do. Buoyant in spirits, with a strong mind abounding in wit and humor, he drew around him a circle of friends; while his marked integrity, consistent Christian character, and a modesty that withheld him from any aspirations for fame or official position, rendered him prominent as a counselor and adviser with his neighbors and friends.

Frederick Kinsman, the only surviving member of the family, now resides at Warren, Ohio.

————

THE REEVE FAMILY OF KINSMAN.*

Jeremiah Reeve, Sr., was born at Norwich, Connecticut, in April, 1779. His father, Ebenezer Reeve, was born at Southold, Long Island, August 23, 1751, and his wife, Bethia Hudson, at the same place, about five years after. They were married at Southold, Long Island, in the year 1776, and moved to Morris, New Jersey. This place was occupied at about this time by British troops, and the inhabitants were considerably annoyed by them. For this reason my grandfather thought best to sell the farm which his father had helped him purchase, and remove to Norwich, Connecticut. He after this served as a soldier in the war which had then commenced. My grandmother was removed by death, at their home in Norwich, on January 19, 1786, at the age of twenty-nine, leaving three small children, my father, the eldest, being not quite seven years of age.

Of my father's early years I can speak but very little, being at the time of his death only nine years of age. Being the only son considerable pains was taken with his education. He pursued the study of medicine, although never practicing. That he had gifts as a public speaker was shown by his being chosen to deliver an oration at Norwich, his native place, on the 4th of

*By Mary D. Reeve.

July which followed the death of Washington. His allusion to the then recent death of the country's renowned chief and lamented ex-President, was considered by his friends quite a happy effort.

That he was possessed of a sense of the humorous and ludicrous, and perhaps a little of the waggery which prompts to practical joking, seems apparent from an incident related by deacon Charles Wood, late of Kinsman. He was a frequent passenger on boats plying between Norwich and New London. On one of these occasions, when about meeting another boat, the captain of his boat knowing something of his mirthful propensities, said to him, "Now, Jerry, keep quiet and be civil." My father demurely replied, "I will," immediately picking up a section of stove-pipe near him, turned towards the approaching boat through his improvised telescope a long and steady gaze, which had the desired effect of producing the uproarious applause and merriment of both boat-loads. In 1802, my grandfather having traded his farm in Norwich with Judge Kinsman, for land on the Western Reserve, moved with his two younger children, Deborah, afterwards Mrs. Plumb Sutliff, and Hannah, afterwards Mrs. John Andrews, to their new home in Kinsman, Trumbull county, Ohio, my father remaining East a year longer at school. After coming West he engaged in teaching at Hubbard, in this county, where he continued his school for one year. He afterwards engaged in teaching at Wooster, near Marietta, where he became acquainted with and was afterwards married to Miss Mary Quigley, on November 27, 1808. Their eldest and only child, Ebenezer Reeve the second, was born at Kinsman, Ohio, August 9, 1812. His mother died August 9, 1825. His last visit in Kinsman was about the year 1842. He had previous to this been engaged for three years in farming on a farm which he had rented in Kentucky. He promised another visit the next year, but did not come. Several years after this news came to us of his death by drowning in the Mississippi river.

The Reeve family for seven generations occupied the same estate at Southold, Long Island, which descended through the eldest son, who usually, if not in every instance, bore the Christian name of James.

My grandfather was a younger member of a large family of brothers, whose posterity scattered and divided over the Union, and possibly with earlier branches of the family in all parts of the world, without doubt share distinguishing marks which denote a common ancestry.

Chief Justice Tappan Reeve, of Connecticut, was a relative of my grandfather, and a sense of equity manifest in his writings display characteristics of mind and heart which my father and grandfather exemplified in daily life.

The psalmist's description of the man "who sweareth to his own hurt and changeth not," from the knowledge which I have been able to gain of father and son would eminently apply to each.

My father died of typhus fever at Kinsman, Ohio, September 21, 1836.

Sarah McMichael was born at Frederick, Maryland, November 27, 1800. Her children regarded the date as felicitous, the year commencing the century, and the day of the month and the week sometimes being the same as that set apart for our National Thanksgiving day.

My grandfather, Joseph McMichael, was born in Ireland, not far from the year 1750, and was of what is called Scotch-Irish descent. His mother's family had a good estate about three miles from Londonderry, and after his father's death, which occurred when he was quite small, himself and mother returned to their former home.

Annie Masters was born near Dublin, Ireland, some years later. Her father was of English birth, and her mother, Catherine Carroll, of Irish birth, and cousin of Charles Carroll, one of the signers of the American Declaration of Independence. While visiting my grandfather's relatives in London my grandmother became acquainted with a wealthy Scotch family, and engaged with them as a governess for their children, and soon after sailed with them to America, Charleston, South Carolina, being their destination. She remained with them several years, and then engaged as governess in the family of Judge Bey, of Baltimore, Maryland, where she remained until about the year 1795, near or at the close of the Revolutionary war, when she was married to my grandfather. My mother was not quite five years old, and her only brother, Joseph McMichael, Jr., an infant, when her parents removed to Kinsman, Ohio, in 1805.

My grandfather, Joseph McMichael, was a trader, and crossed the Atlantic six times in the course of his business, which was shipping linen to this country and flax-seed back to Ireland. On his third homeward voyage his ship was wrecked, and with the survivors he was carried to London by a rescuing vessel, where his mother's family sent him needed assistance, and after visiting home he crossed the sea the seventh and last time. His death occurred in Kinsman, Ohio, July 28, 1831. That of his wife at the same place, February 27, 1845.

My mother lived to a good old age, and filled out the life of usefulness which had been allotted to her with a cheerful patience, meeting the ills of life and infirmities of age with brave composure and unyielding fortitude. Her death took place April 25th, 1880. My parents were members of the Congregational and Presbyterian church of Kinsman.

Their home was at some distance from the church, and it was no uncommon sight to see them on horseback on their way to church on Sabbath morning, my mother with the youngest in her arms and the eldest seated behind her, and my father with two others disposed in a similar manner. In personal appearance my father was rather tall, well formed, with brown hair, a brown beard, blue eyes, and a very fair complexion. He was a fine singer with an excellent voice for bass. My mother was a trifle below the ordinary height; in childhood her hair was red, but when she grew up it turned black. Her head was handsomely shaped, eyes blue. Her complexion was not as fair as my father's, but very clear and fresh. She was very lady-like and agreeable in her manners, with refined tastes and thoughtful mind. In singing she could not distinguish one note from another, and never attempted singing, although when her children were small, and while she was busy about her work, I have heard her humming in monotones.

My parents were desirous of giving their children the best advantages for acquiring knowledge which the place would afford. Their two eldest, when but "tiny tots," could be seen trudging morning and evening, when the season and weather would permit, on their way to and from school. An infant school, such as is described in Miss Gilbert's Career, written by the late Dr. J. G. Holland, was established in the Kinsman village, a mile and a half from home. My parents' two eldest infants managed to be there to take their part in lessons in astronomy, geometry, and other deep sciences, besides doing their share of the marching, singing, clapping of hands, etc., through the greater share of two summer terms. Were all parents as earnest in procuring educational facilities for their children, laws for compulsory education would be useless.

My parents' family consisted of six children: Mary Deborah, born September 5, 1827; Bethiah Hudson, January 29, 1829; Annie Maria, April 3, 1831; Jane Eliza, October 11, 1833; Jeremiah Reeve, Jr., March 15, 1835; James Albert, May 7, 1837. Bethiah H. Reeve was married to Robert Clark at Paris, Edgar county, Illinois, August 10, 1853, and died at the same place April 9, 1854. Their infant daughter died at Kinsman, Ohio, October 6, 1854. Jane E. Reeve and George C. Harding were married November 10, 1854. Their daughter, Flora Krum Harding, was born at Charleston, Coles county, Illinois, in the summer of 1855, and died at Indianapolis, Indiana, August 20, 1874. Their son, Ben Shillaber Harding, was born at the same place, and was the victim of a railroad accident on the Burlington & Quincy railroad, near Ottumwa, Iowa, December 29, 1879, which caused his instant death. Annie Maria Reeve was married to John T. Edwards, of Chicago, Illinois, at Cleveland, Ohio, June 6, 1859. His widow and a son and four daughters survive the father, who died at Benton Harbor, Michigan, February 7, 1873, where his family still reside.

James A. Reeve and Eliza Woolmer were married at Chicago, Illinois, where they now reside, in December, 1863. Their family consists of two sons and a daughter. Two sons who died in infancy were buried at Benton Harbor, Michigan.

Jane E. R. Harding and John Morris were married at Charleston, Coles county, Illinois, where they still reside, April 16, 1865. Their son, Charles Thomas Morris, was born at Charleston, Illinois, September 13, 1866, and died May 7, 1869. Helen Emily Morris was born September 16, 1870, at Charleston, Illinois. The eldest son and eldest daughter of my parents still reside at Kinsman, their native place.   M. D. R.

SETH PERKINS,

of Kinsman, was born in Hartland, Hartford county, Connecticut, February 29, 1780; removed to Barkhamsted, Litchfield county, Conuecticut, at the age of twelve, and at twenty to Canandaigua, Ontario county, New York, where he resided till April, 1804, when he emigrated to Ohio, with his earthly possessions on his back in a knapsack. He worked by the month through the season, and in October was married to Lucy Thompson, daughter of Thomas Thompson, who came to Hartford, Trumbull county, Ohio, the same year from Farmington, Hartford county, Connecticut. It the winter he made a clearing, and built a cabin on the center line of Fowler, near the Vienna line, where he removed with his wife, then eighteen years old, in the spring of 1805, there being at that time only four families in the township, the nearest one mile distant through an unbroken forest. They endured all the hardships incident to so new a country, and made for themselves a home of comfort, humble though it was. At the time of Hull's surrender in 1812 he went with almost the entire male population of the county, to defend the northwestern frontier at Sandusky and Huron, from whence he returned about the 1st of January, 1813, with impaired health. He still resided on his farm in Fowler, which he had improved to a fine homestead, planted an orchard, which now by its perfectly straight rows shows his taste and care, and the fences being neat and substantial were an evidence of industry and thrift. In the autumn of 1818 he sold his farm to Abijah Silliman, and in April, 1819, removed to Kinsman, where he resided until February, 1846, when, by a fall, which resulted in concussion of the spine, he died three days thereafter. His family at the time of his settlement in Kinsman consisted of himself and wife, six daughters, and one son, and afterward another son and daughter.

DR. PETER ALLEN.

Kinsman has had no citizen more honored and useful in his calling than Dr. Peter Allen. He was born at Norwich, Connecticut, July 1, 1787, the son of John and Tirzah Allen. His father was a respectable and well-to-do farmer of Norwich, and gave his son the best advantages of education which the city at that time afforded. He pursued and completed his professional studies with the eminent Dr. Tracy, of Norwich, emigrating to Kinsman in 1808, and immediately entering on the practice of his profession. He was the first, and for nearly a quarter of a century the only physician in the township and a somewhat extensive surrounding country. Possessed of an uncommonly robust constitution and great energy of character, he endured hardships and performed an amount of labor in his profession which in these days of bridges, good roads, and short rides might seem almost incredible. It was nothing uncommon for him in the early settlement of the country to ride over bad roads and along mere bridle-paths ten, fifteen, twenty or more miles to visit a patient, often fording streams or crossing them on logs or by canoes, exposed to wet and cold, fatigues and discomforts that we are now little able to appreciate. In his day the advantages of medical schools, hospitals, clinics, dissections were enjoyed only by a very few physicians. Notwithstanding the disadvantages with which he had to contend, Dr. Allen attained a high standing in his profession. He performed many difficult surgical operations, such as the operation for strangulated hernia, ligating the femoral artery for aneurism, laryngotomy, lithotomy, removal of cancers, amputation of limbs, and at the shoulder-joint, etc. He stood high in the esteem of medical men, and his counsel was much sought by them in difficult cases of both medicine and surgery. He was an active member of the Ohio State Medical association from its first formation, and was at one time its presiding officer. In the War of 1812 he had the first appointment of surgeon in the army on the northern frontier of the State. He was also a member of the Ohio State Legislature in 1840.

He married Charity Dudley, of Bethlehem, Connecticut, May 15, 1813. Mrs. Allen, a superior and most estimable woman, was for many years a great sufferer. Her death was sudden, she having been thrown from the carriage in which she was riding, by the fright of her horse, June 1, 1840, and lived only a few hours after. In 1841 Dr. Allen married Miss Fanny Brewster Starr, a niece of Mrs. R. Kinsman and General Simon Perkins. She died of consumption in August, 1846. Dr. Allen had but one child, Dr. Dudley Allen, born in June, 1814.

The first office of Dr. Allen was in his father's yard, on the farm now occupied by Isaac Allen, by the maple grove on the banks of Stratton creek. This he occupied until the fall of 1813, when he moved into a double log-house which stood in the yard in which he built his frame house in 1821. This latter was in the time of its erection and is still a beautiful house of elaborate and superior workmanship. It was much admired and cost $3,000, which was then considered an extravagant sum.

His brother, Dr. Francis Allen, was in company with him from 1825 to 1829, and his son from 1837 to 1852, at which time he mostly relinquished practice. The farm on which he lived was purchased in 1812 for $2 per acre.

Dr. Allen is remembered by those who knew him, not merely as a skillful physician, but also as an active and steadfast member of the church of Christ. When his business permitted he was always present in the house of God on the Sabbath. A regular attendant at the weekly prayer-meeting, and in the latter part of his life was an active member of the Sabbath-school.

After having relinquished the business of his profession he was almost the standing representative of the church in meetings of synod, and at the meeting next succeeding his death was spoken of by that body in terms of high regard. Only a few months before his last sickness he represented Trumbull presbytery as their lay delegate in the general assembly, at Dayton. He retained full possession of his faculties though advanced in life, and his Christian example shone bright unto the end.

JEDEDIAH BURNHAM.

The life of Jedediah Burnham, through a period of nearly eighty-seven years, has been intimately and variously connected with the growth and progress of the township of Kinsman. His counsels and acts, whether in the military, civil, or religious organizations of the town, as well as in the administration of all township and county affairs entrusted to him, have been marked with eminent justice, propriety, and wisdom. He came to Kinsman not far from the time that he became of age, and was very soon appointed to office. From that time to the period when the infirmities of age began to press upon him, he was actively employed in the responsible duties to which he was called by his fellow-citizens of the town and county. He was an active member and honored officer of the Congregational and Presbyterian church in Kinsman, from its beginning to the day of his death. Pre-eminently a peace-maker, he was commonly the first one in the town resorted to for the settlement of any misunderstanding or difficulty between neighbor and neighbor, or trouble of any sort that had sprung up in the community.

He was born in Lisbon, Connecticut, in 1785, the son of Dr. Jedediah Burnham, a respectable physician of that place, who in old age, with his wife and daughter, removed to Kinsman, and lived and died in the family of his son. In 1804 Mr. Burnham left the home of his parents and went to Virginia, with the hope of finding in that State a location that would please him. He returned however, without locating, but through an arrangement with Mr. Kinsman he returned to Ohio the next year, and entered the employ of Kinsman. The new house of Mr. Kinsman was being rapidly brought to completion. The first work of Mr. Burnham was to assist in putting in the stone chimney. After that he was busy in various work of the farm until winter, when he was engaged to teach the first regular school of the township. The next spring and summer he was again employed on the farm, and assisted in putting in a crop of oats on the bottom lands south of Wayne Bidwell's. The product was an abundant crop of straw as well as oats, which was mowed and stacked for winter fodder, near Mr. Kinsman's house.

In the winter of 1806 he again commenced the school, with the understanding that Benjamin Allen would take his place as soon as he had finished a job of work in Hubbard. In accordance with this arrangement Mr. Burnham was relieved about midwinter, and went into Mr. Kinsman's store in the capacity of a clerk, where he remained until the breaking out of the War of 1812, when he was called to serve in the army.

In the organization of the township militia Mr. Burnham was first appointed lieutenant in Captain Randall's company, and afterward promoted to captain. Returning from the army, Captain Burnham at once devoted himself to the cultivation and improvement of his farm.

James C. Bishop

He was married to Miss Sophia Bidwell, of Gustavus, 1814. In 1816 he was elected justice of the peace, in which capacity he served uninterruptedly twenty-one years. His official acts were ever marked with justice and propriety; and of all his decisions appealed from during his long administration, it is said that not any (if any, certainly but very few) were reversed by the higher courts.

In 1806 he was chosen collector of the civil township of Green, embracing under that name what is now Kinsman, Gustavus, and Green. Afterward he was appointed county collector, when the law required the collector to call at the residence of every person taxed to make the collection. This arduous duty was performed by himself alone, going on horseback from house to house throughout the county. Afterward he had the office of county assessor, the duties of which were performed in a similar manner, and required about the same amount of time and labor. The duties of his office were attended to with a high degree of exactitude, promptness and fidelity.

He held the office of deacon in the Vernon, Hartford, and Kinsman church, and, after the formation of the Congregational and Presbyterian church in Kinsman, the same office in that until his death. His long, prosperous, eventful, and useful life closed early in the year of 1874.

JAMES C. BISHOP.

James C. Bishop, well known in the northern part of Trumbull county as a dealer in fine stock, is the subject of an illustration on an adjoining page. He was born in New Haven, Connecticut, July 9, 1810. His parents were Ebenezer and Lucinda Bishop. who removed with their family to Herkimer county, New York, in the year 1813. Mr. Bishop built a factory, and engaged extensively in the manufacture of cheese.

In the year 1833 James C. Bishop came to the Reserve, and the following year purchased one hundred and thirty-seven acres near the present site of Kinsman station. After having made a clearing and planted the fall crop, he sold his land and went South, finding employment at the carpenter trade is Mississippi. When spring opened Mr. Bishop returned to his old home in New York on a visit. The trip resulted in his parents selling their farm, and the removal of the whole family to Gustavus township. This was in the spring of 1834. They purchased a dairy farm, and erected a cheese factory similar to those in use in Herkimer county. It was the first of the kind in Trumbull county, though other manufacturers were not slow to imitate its advantageous features.

Mr. Bishop brought with him from New York what was at that time a great curiosity in the north part of this county—a spring buggy. Reuben Roberts, a blacksmith in Gustavus, used the springs for patterns and engaged with profit in their manufacture. James C. operated his father's factory about four years, and then purchased it. He conducted the business with profit to himself and with entire satisfaction to dairymen in the neighborhood for a period of about twenty years. He purchased a second farm in Gustavus and engaged in breeding and trading in fine stock. He brought to the county the first thoroughbred cow, from which was descended many of the best cattle in this part of the State. Two oxen raised by Mr. Bishop were sold in the Pittsburgh market for $300. Mr. Bishop, George Hezlep, and George Cowden were the leading stock dealers in Gustavus township. He was a patron of the Trumbull County Agricultural society, and received premiums on the productions of his farm.

Mr. Bishop married, in 1839, Philena Gates, a daughter of Philo Gates, of Gustavus township. She died in 1845, leaving one son—Chaplin J. Bishop, of Chicago. In 1859 Mr. Bishop sold both his farms in Gustavus and purchased the old Swift farm in Kinsman, which he continues to own. In 1860 he married for his second wife Mrs. Dr. Joseph P. Morford, of Johnston township. Her maiden name was Hannah Dunbar.

Mr. Bishop is a well preserved man; has a clear recollection of past events, and retains the business sagacity of former years.

THE FOBES FAMILY.

Horatio Fobes, youngest son of Joshua and Dorothy Fobes, was born in Ashtabula county, Ohio, February 16, 1812. Joshua Fobes settled in Wayne township, Ashtabula county, in 1802. He raised a family of ten children, of whom six are living. Horatio Fobes, until nineteen, was engaged in farming on the home place, coming to Kinsman in 1831. He commenced with Benjamin Allen the carding and cloth dressing business. He afterwards rented and purchased the business and conducted it until about 1852. He was married in 1835 to Miss Louisa Dodge, of Ashtabula county, but a native of Connecticut. They became the parents of one daughter, Charlotte L., born in 1840, died in 1863. About 1859 Mr. Fobes purchased a half interest in the Bidwell & Fobes flouring mill, which, in connection with Bidwell and other parties he has since operated; was township treasurer for many years.

Lotta Louisa, only child of Horatio and Louisa (Dodge) Fobes, was born in Kinsman in the year 1840, and died Nvember 7, 1863. She was the pride of fond parents, and the beloved of a large circle of friends. In her the charm of a graceful figure was united with the attraction of a a cultured mind and beautiful character. Faithful, gentle, loving, she was death's shining mark. No words can more nearly express a parent's feelings than the lines Byron once wrote beneath a friend's picture:

> Dear object of defeated care,
>   Though now of love and thee bereft,
> To reconcile me with despair
>   Thine image and my tears are left.
>
> 'Tis said with sorrow time can cope;
>   But this, I fear, can ne'er be true;
> For by the death-blow of my hope
>   My memory immortal grew.

RIVERIUS AND EUNICIA BIDWELL.

Riverius Bidwell and his wife Eunicia Bidwell were among the earliest settlers of Gustavus township, the date of their emigration being the year 1812. Mr. Bidwell was born in Connecticut, September 5, 1790. He received a fair English education, and at the age of about nineteen engaged to teach school in a small village near New Haven, where he had planned to pursue his course at Yale college, the village now known as Westville, a suburb of New Haven, was then commonly called Hotchkisstown, it being the seat of the numerous and prominent family bearing the name of Hotchkiss. A friend-

ship between the young schoolmaster and Eunicia Hotchkiss soon ripened into matrimony. They were married in New Haven, Connecticut, June 27, 1810, by Rev. Abram Allen, and two years later sought a home in the wild, cheerless West.

Riverius Bidwell, Sr., father of our subject, lived in Canton, Hartford county, Connecticut. His family consisted of three sons and five daughters, with whom he emigrated to Ohio in the year 1813, and also settled in Gustavus. He died July 22, 1822, aged fifty-nine years. His wife, Phebe Bidwell, died August 17, 1837, aged seventy-six years. Their children were Wayne, died June 10, 1832; Esther (Cone), died in Kinsman January 27, 1816; Achsah (Dyer), died in Canton, Connecticut; Sophia (Burnham), died at Kinsman, January 5, 1851, aged fifty-four; Zehiel, died September, 1864; Phebe Humphrey, died in New York. Marietta, wife of Buell Barnes, is the only surviving member of the family.

Riverius Bidwell, Jr., was somewhat eccentric in habit, but was one of the most pushing, persevering and active men on the Reserve. Under an old law in Ohio taxes were collected by an officer who was appointed for that purpose, at the homes and places of business of the citizens. The office was very laborious on account of the great size of the county and bad condition of roads which connected the sparse settlements. Mr. Bidwell served as collector two years. He walked from house to house till every house in the county had been visited, part of the time being barefooted, always at a brisk gait. After collections had all been made, he walked to Columbus and made settlement with the Treasurer of State. This is but one incident of many which might be written to show his perseverance. He was always ready witted, and rarely found himself in a puzzling situation. He kept the first post-office in Gustavus, but being absent most of the time Mrs. Bidwell transacted most of the business.

Mr. Bidwell was justice of the peace and held other local trusts. He sold his farm in Gustavus in 1834 and removed to Kinsman. He took an active interest and was influential in securing to Kinsman a line of railway. This was about the last work of his busy life. He died February 6, 1870, aged eighty-one years. Mrs. Bidwell, who

Miss Lottie Fobes

is yet living, was born March 24, 1794. She is a woman of great strength of character, is yet strong, and is able to recall with clearness events of eighty years ago.

The family of Mr. and Mrs. Bidwell consisted of three sons and one daughter—Hannah Mariah, born September 20, 1811, at Canton, Connecticut, and died in childhood; Jasper Riverius, born July 25, 1813, and died at the age of twenty years; Caleb Hotchkiss, born September 26, 1815, graduated at Western Reserve college at nineteen years of age, studied law with Whittlesey & Newton, was admitted to the bar, and died at the age of twenty-five; Wayne, the only child living, was born May 6, 1821. He married Mary Hyde, who was born January 11, 1824, in Vernon township.

Both Mr. and Mrs. Bidwell were members of the Presbyterian church and exemplary Christians.

NOTES OF SETTLEMENT.

Charles Burnham, oldest son of Jedediah Burnham, (a sketch of whom is given elsewhere) and Sophia Bidwell, was born in Kinsman, Ohio, March 17, 1817. He remained at home until 23 years of age, and in his younger days was engaged in clerking in Kinsman and elsewhere. He purchased the place where he still resides, the old Ford place, in 1853. He was married June 1st of the same year, to Elizabeth A. Galpin, daughter of Elnathan Galpin, born in 1825. They have three children, as follows: Abbie S., born March 15, 1857; Lizzie G., February 19, 1859; Charles B., February 20, 1861. Mr. Burnham was justice of the peace from 1861 to 1865, and was elected again the latter year, but declined to serve; has also served as assessor three terms. His brother Thomas was a soldier in the Union army in the Rebellion, and was killed at Kershaw mountain, Georgia.

Benjamin Allen was born in Kinsman township, Trumbull county, Ohio, March 23, 1817. His father, Benjamin Allen, Sr., was one of the earliest settlers and prominent citizens of the township, coming in 1805. He was a clothier by trade, and had the first establishment of the kind in Kinsman. He was a Representative in the State Legislature two terms, was justice of the peace, township trustee, and county commis-

sioner, and a lieutenant in the War of 1812. He died in 1851, aged sixty-seven. Benjamin, Jr., was taught the occupation of his father, but afterwards adopted farming as a pursuit. When eighteen he attended the Grand River institute for two years; was engaged in teaching school two terms in Kinsman. Married, January 6, 1841, Charlotte, daughter of Elnathan Galpin of Kinsman, born in Litchfield county, Connecticut, in 1820. They have one son, Arthur B., born January 2, 1858; married November 10, 1880, Albie H. Morehead, born in New Castle, Pennsylvania. Deacon Allen was township clerk for many years; was justice of the peace, but declined to qualify. He has been a prominent member of the Presbyterian church for some forty years.

Lyman P. Andrews was born in Kinsman, Trumbull county, Ohio, May 26, 1822. John Andrews, his father, a native of East Haddam, Connecticut, came to Ohio in 1804. He settled first in Gustavus, where he cleared up a farm east of Gustavus center; afterwards removed to Kinsman, where he engaged in mercantile business. He was the owner of sixty acres of land at the time of his death. He was a sucessful business man, was a justice of the peace, and a member of the Presbyterian church. His oldest son, C. B. Andrews, was a clergyman of the same denomination; went as missionary to the Sandwich Islands, under the auspices of the American Board of Foreign Missions, in 1843; actively engaged there for some thirty years. While returning to the islands he died in 1876. John Andrews married Hannah Reeve, daughter of Ebenezer Reeve, and raised a family of six children, of whom two survive—the subject of this sketch, and Mrs. Caroline Parker, of Cleveland. Lyman P. Andrews derived his education at the common schools of Kinsman, and at Hudson college, which he attended two years. He was married August 3, 1843, to Miss Betsy Fobes, daughter of Aaron Fobes, one of the pioneers of this region. Mrs. Andrews was born in Kinsman about 1826. They have three children—Frank A., born in August, 1853, a resident of Chicago, Illinois; J. Edwards, July, 1856; and Emma S., December, 1861, both at home. Mr. Andrews was a resident of Flint, Michigan, for eleven years from 1867, where he removed for the purpose of educating his children. He removed from the home place in Kinsman to the one he now occupies in 1879. He was elected justice of the peace in Kinsman about 1848, serving six years, and was also an incumbent of the same office in Michigan one term. Enlisted in 1864 in the One Hundred and Seventy-first Ohio National guard, and was commissary sergeant; was taken prisoner by the rebels at Cynthiana, Kentucky; was paroled and finally mustered out of service at Johnson island, near Sandusky, Ohio. He took an active part in the establishment of the Kinsman cemetery, originating it, and is still president of the board of trustees.

Isaac Meacham was born in Kinsman, Trumbull county, Ohio, May 4, 1828. Isaac Meacham, Sr., his father, was a native of Hartland, Connecticut, born in April, 1778, came to Ohio in 1806 and settled on the line of Kinsman and Gustavus townships, Trumbull county, where he cleared up a farm of a hundred and eighty-five acres wholly himself. He was married twice, first in 1808 to Lovisa Morse, by whom he had three children. In 1827 he married Anna Trunkey, and raised a family of four children. He was a successful and industrious farmer, always occupying the place where he originally settled, until his death, which took place in 1861. His wife died in 1860. He offered his services in the War of 1812, and was on duty fourteen days. Isaac, Jr., enlisted in the One Hundred and Seventy-first Ohio National guard, in 1864; married in 1850, Rebecca Baldwin, by whom he had three children, two of whom survive, viz: Charles F., born February 26, 1856, now a resident of Greenville, Pennsylvania, and Harvey S., born September 3, 1857, a book-keeper in Cleveland. His first wife died April 19, 1864. His second wife was Hannah E. Yeomans; died in 1868. His present wife nee Julia E. Peck, to whom he was married December 22, 1869, was born in Crawford county, Pennsylvania, August 27, 1840. They are the parents of two children—William E., born January 2, 1874, and Marian Lulu, born February 24, 1876. Mr. Meacham occupied the old homestead until 1866, when he removed to Kinsman village, where he still resides.

Allen W. Gillis, son of Robert and Mary Gillis, was born in Kinsman, Trumbull county, July 28, 1830; married, in 1852, Miss Harriet Webber, born in Kinsman in 1833. He has three children living, as follows: Byron F., a merchant in New York city; Cora B., residing with her uncle in Ashtabula county; Maud H., at home. His first wife died in 1869, and in December, 1870, he married Mary C. Webb, of Erie county, Pennsylvania. In 1861 he enlisted in company B, Twenty-third Ohio volunteer infantry, and with his regiment was in many engagements, including those of South Mountain and Antietam, serving nearly three years. He was discharged for physical disability. In June, 1864, he again offered his services to the Government, joined the One Hundred and Seventy-first Ohio National guard, and had command of his company at Cynthiana, Kentucky. He was finally discharged as first lieutenant. He settled in Kinsman village after the war, where he now resides.

Robert Gillis (deceased) was born in Maryland in 1801; came to Ohio with his father, Thomas Gillis, in 1806, who put up the first grist-mill in Kinsman, on the creek near the center of the township. The site is now occupied by Hamilton Brothers' mill, the present mill being the third built by the Gillis family. Robert Gillis conducted the mill during his lifetime. February 23, 1825, he married Mary King, daughter of Robert and Isabella King, born in Westmoreland county, Pennsylvania, November 3, 1801. Her parents came to Kinsman in 1809, settling on the place now owned by Gordon Burnside. Robert King was a soldier of the War of 1812, a member of Captain Burnham's company. He raised a family of twelve children, of whom nine are living. Robert and Mary Gillis have had one daughter and eight sons—the daughter, Isabella, was the wife of Lewis Moats, of Mercer county, Pennsylvania, and died at the age of twenty-four; Thomas lives in Jefferson, Ashtabula county; John K. died in California in 1878, where he went in 1852; Allen W., of Kinsman village, of whom a brief sketch is given elsewhere; G. W., now living in Kansas (was a member of the Sixth Ohio volunteer cavalry three years during the Rebellion); Anderson J., now living in Jefferson township, Ashtabula county (was a member of company B, Twenty-third Ohio volunteer infantry, serving three years, afterwards re-enlisted and served until the close of the war); Amos F. enlisted in company B, Twenty-third Ohio volunteer infantry, and served three years; re-enlisting, was promoted to captain and was killed in action at Berryville, Virginia, September 3, 1864, leaving a widow and one daughter now residents of Cleveland. Two children died in infancy.

T. B. Scott, son of James and Sarah (Smith) Scott, was born in Kinsman, Trumbull county, Ohio, January 28, 1849; married October 19, 1870, to Miss Ada Williams, of Bazetta township, adopted daughter of John and Jane Williams, and has three children living, as follows: Jennie Ellen, born July 29, 1872; Sarah Alice, May 25, 1876; Mary Emeline, November 21, 1880. John W. died in infancy. After marriage Mr. Scott continued to reside on the home place some six years, removing to his present place in the spring of 1877. He owns one hundred and eighty acres at the village of Kinsman, and is a prosperous farmer and dairyman. Himself and wife are members of the Methodist church.

John S. Allen was born in Kinsman, Trumbull county, Ohio, November 1, 1813, oldest surviving son of Benjamin and Lydia (Meacham) Allen remained at home until twenty-five, when he was united in marriage October 24, 1838, to Miss Julia E., daughter of Roswell Moore. She was born in Connecticut February 24, 1819. Mr. and Mrs. Allen have had three children, two of whom are living: Darwin F., born June 27, 1839, and Antoinette J., born May 26, 1842, both at home. Darwin was a member of the One Hundred and Twenty-fifth Ohio volunteer infantry, and later of the One Hundred and Seventy-first Ohio National guard; was mustered out in the fall of 1864. September 15th of the same year he was married to Jennie M. Collins, and has one son and one daughter—Fred L., born October 31, 1864, and Theresa E., May 12, 1867. Our subject settled on the place where he still lives in 1838, which was then but partially improved. He was active in militia affairs during his early years; was first elected justice of the peace about 1860 and held that position six years, and was township trustee many terms. Mr. and Mrs. Allen are members of the Presbyterian and Congregational church.

John W. McCurdy was born in Butler county, Pennsylvania, October 22, 1804, oldest son of James and Margaret McCurdy. He was brought up to agricultural pursuits, remaining at home until twenty-six. He married, September 4, 1832,

Mrs. Catharine Thorn, born in Kinsman township November 3, 1804, daughter of George Matthews, who settled there in the spring of that year. He was a prominent farmer and church member; died about 1855. Mr. and Mrs. McCurdy are the parents of four children, three living and one dead, viz: Joseph Thorn, born May 16, 1830, now a resident of Michigan; George, July 29, 1833; Jane, April 22, 1835, died August 5, 1861; James, January 27, 1837, a resident of Missouri, and an artist by profession. After his marriage Mr. McCurdy resided for one year in Butler county, Pennsylvania, coming to Ohio in the fall of 1833. He settled where he now lives about 1840, which place was then entirely wild. Mr. McCurdy was township trustee one term. He has been a member of the Presbyterian and Congregational church for many years.

Joseph Reed, oldest son of John and Elizabeth (West) Reed was born in New York, June 29, 1824. With his parents went to Bath, Steuben county, New York, about 1826, where he went to school. Was engaged in the lumber business in Pennsylvania for some twenty years, being a partner in a steam saw-mill. He was married July 7, 1852, to Rebecca Everhart, born in Blair county, Pennsylvania, April 3, 1831, and is the father of seven children as follow: William A., born July 21, 1853, now a merchant of Kinsman, of the firm of Gee & Reed; Susan E., born July 20, 1855, now wife of George Bennett, of Kinsman; Ella G., born October 10, 1858; May R., May 19, 1860; Augusta D., September 3, 1862; Edith B., August 18, 1864; Minnie B., July 29, 1866. Mr. Reed resided in Pennsylvania until 1869, when he purchased the Galpin place in Kinsman, where he has since lived.

Charles B. Webber, son of Ebenezer and Amanda (Brown) Webber, was born in Kinsman, Trumbull county, Ohio, February 14, 1822. Ebenezer Webber was born in Massachusetts, in 1778; married in 1805, and came to Ohio in 1811, settling on the place now owned by his son Charles B., in Kinsman, in the spring of 1812. He cleared up that place and reared a family of eleven children, of whom five are still living. He died December 15, 1843. Charles B. upon the death of his father took charge of the farm; was married February 21, 1850, to Miss Rachel G. Matthews, daughter of Thomas

Matthews, one of the pioneers of the county. Mrs. Webber was born in Kinsman July 7, 1829. The children of Charles and Rachel Webber are Dwight H., born January 30, 1853, now living in Ashtabula county; Ellen A., October 11, 1854; Alfred P., July 30, 1856; T. B., May 22, 1858; Charles A., February 25, 1861; Frederick G., November 25, 1862; Frank H., December 28, 1864; Theresa H., October 12, 1867. The oldest child died in infancy. After his marriage Mr. Webber continued on the home place, taking care of his mother until her death September 2, 1868. He was township trustee for many years, school director, etc. He enlisted during the Rebellion but was thrown out on account of physical disability. They are members of the Presbyterian and Congregational church.

James W. Storier, son of James and Euphemia Storier, was born in Kinsman, Trumbull county, Ohio, June 11, 1847. James Storier, Sr., was a native of Scotland and emigrated to America in 1845, coming to Trumbull county, Ohio, and settling in Kinsman. He is still living, a successful farmer in Gustavus township. He raised a family of five children, of whom four are living. The oldest son, John J., enlisted in the One Hundred and Seventy-first Ohio National guard, and at the battle of Cynthiana, Kentucky, June 11, 1864, he was instantly killed, on his twentieth birthday. James W. Storier was married March 27, 1872, to Miss Emily Johnson, daughter of John Johnson, of Kinsman, born in Pennsylvania January 1, 1847. He has three daughters, as follows: Nannie, born February 9, 1873; Euphemia, March 13, 1875; Estella, May 22, 1878. He resided on a place then owned by his father-in-law, now the residence of John White, for some two years, removing in the spring of 1874 to the place where he now lives. In the fall of 1881 he purchased the Hugh Miller place, consisting of fifty-two and one-half acres.

William B. Edwards, son of Lewis and Jane (Parks) Edwards, was born in Fayette county, Pennsylvania, July 28, 1825; was brought up in the family of his uncle, James Edwards, and his three sisters, with whom he came to Ohio in the spring of 1848. He settled in Williamsfield, Ashtabula county, on a farm which he still owns. One of his aunts who accompanied him to Ohio, is still living with him at an advanced age. He continued to reside in Ashtabula county until the spring of 1881, when he purchased the Lyman Root place in Kinsman, where he now lives. He married, October 3, 1855, Sarah F. Webb, of Mercer county, Pennsylvania, born about 1833. He was township trustee in Williamsfield one term. Himself and wife are members of the Methodist Episcopal church at the State line. James Edwards, his uncle, died May 10, 1874; was an active member of the Methodist Episcopal church for many years.

Lester Matthews, oldest child of Reuben and Lorenda (Eggleston) Matthews, was born in Kinsman township, Trumbull county, Ohio, October 8, 1842. Reuben Matthews raised a family of five children, of whom three survive. He died in 1851, and his widow in 1864. Lester was married January 1, 1866, to Stella Woodworth, a daughter of Andrew Woodworth, of Ashtabula county. Mrs. Matthews was born in that county in 1849. They have had one daughter, Minnie A., born January 23, 1867; died at the age of ten months. Mr. Matthews occupies the family homestead, the dwelling having been built by his father about 1840. Mr. and Mrs. Matthews are members of the Congregational and Presbyterian church. George Matthews settled in an early day on the property now owned by his sons Ezekiel, Elias, and Reuben's heirs. George Matthews was born December 29, 1773, and his wife, Nancy (Scott), 1775.

L. A. Cole, oldest living son of Harmon and Polly (Blackburn) Cole, was born in Kinsman, Trumbull county, Ohio, August 6, 1834. Harmon Cole was a native of Connecticut, born about 1800, and coming to Ohio about 1818, he settled in Kinsman, where he married Polly Blackburn. He was a cooper by trade, and in later life a successful farmer. He was justice of the peace one term about 1850; died October 2, 1856. Mrs. Polly Cole is still living with her sons, and is yet vigorous in mind and body. L. A. Cole was united in marriage October 3, 1855, to Amanda Simpkins. To this marriage were born three children—Harmon B., a resident of Kinsman township, born October 29, 1856; Mary E., born October 2, 1858, now wife of John Brown, residing in the vicinity of her father's home; Otis A., born April 21, 1861. Mrs. Cole died February 4, 1870. September 7, 1870, he was again married, this time to Miss

Elizabeth Feather, born in Pennsylvania, February 19, 1835. To this union have been born two children, of whom one is living—Harriet Elizabeth, born January 9, 1873. After his marriage he settled on a portion of the family homestead, where he still resides; has been township trustee two terms.

Harmon Cole was born in Kinsman township, Trumbull county, Ohio, August 4, 1826; son of Richard and Priscilla Cole. Richard Cole was a native of Connecticut, born in 1793; coming to Ohio about 1820, and settling on the place now owned by his son Harmon. He cleared up this place, erecting a log house, where the present residence now is, which was built in 1853. He died in the spring of 1880, his wife having died about 1854. Harmon Cole was married, March 15, 1847, to Miss Sivilla Royal, born in Crawford county, Pennsylvania, August 24, 1827, daughter of Peter and Polly Royal, and has had a family of seven children. Four are living, as follows: Orra C., born January 3, 1848, now the wife of A. F. Waid, residing in Kansas; Charles C., born February 15, 1850, a farmer, residing in Ashtabula county, Ohio; Albert S., born March 7, 1856, a resident of Kinsman, and Emma L., born June 27, 1861. Mr. Cole located on the home farm, where he has since resided, consisting of about four hundred acres of finely improved land.

Edwin Yeomans, son of John and Elizabeth (Coyle) Yeomans, was born in Kinsman, Trumbull county, Ohio, February 22, 1823. His father came to Ohio in 1819 and settled on the place now owned by his son, David M. He had a family of ten children, of whom three are living. He died about 1853. His wife survived him until 1881. He was a soldier of the War of 1812, from Connecticut. Edwin remained at home until his twenty-eighth year. In 1853 he engaged in the paper manufacturing business at Cuyahoga Falls, where he resided until returning to the home place in 1880, where he has since resided.

J. M. King was born in Kinsman township, Trumbull county, Ohio, January 17, 1825; oldest son of William and Sarah (McConnell) King. Robert King, the grandfather of J. M. King, was a native of Ireland, coming to Ohio in the first years of the present century. He settled on the place now owned by Mr. Burnside, which

he cleared up and improved. He raised a large family, the son William being the father of the subject of this sketch. Robert King was justice of the peace, probably one of the first that filled that position. He was a soldier in the War of 1812 from Kinsman township. J. M. King was raised in the family of his maternal grandfather, James McConnell, until of age. He was married in 1847 to Harriet L. Christy, daughter of James Christy, an early settler in the county. The result of this union was six children, three of whom are living, viz: Frank C., Clara B., and Nellie. His first wife died in 1857, and in December, 1858, he married Miss L. C. Christy, daughter of John and Hannah Christy, also early settlers. By this marriage he has three children, as follows: George E., Robert A., and Sadie M. After his marriage he rented the farm of his grandfather for three years. He afterwards bought a small place in another part of Kinsman which he improved and occupied until 1864; was a resident of Vernon for some eight years, where he purchased the Palmer farm, which he still owns. In the fall of 1872 he removed to the place where he now lives, near Kinsman village. Himself and wife are members of the Presbyterian and Congregational church.

Gordon Burnside, son of James and Elizabeth (McMullen) Burnside, was born in county Derry, Ireland, March 12, 1826. He emigrated to America in 1849, landing at New York city, whence he came direct to Ohio, reaching Kinsman township in June of that year. For a number of years afterward he was in the employ of others, engaged in farming. He purchased the place where he still lives—the Robert King homestead—in 1855, and January 1, 1857, was married to Miss Elizabeth Anderson, also a native of Ireland, born February 21, 1835. They are the parents of ten children, all of whom are living but one, viz: John, who died in infancy. The others are Samuel J., now a commercial traveler, William W., Robert J., Gordon, Jr., Minnie J., Lena, George Q., Lizzie, and Edith. Mr. Burnside was a member of the One Hundred and Seventy-first Ohio National guard in 1864, and was in the battle of Cynthiana, Kentucky, and at Kelly Bridge; was taken prisoner with his regiment, but after some twenty-four hours detention the command was released on parol, was finally mustered out after serving out his term at Johnson's Island, in the fall of 1864.

James J. Christy, oldest son of Andrew and Elizabeth Christy, was born in Kinsman, Trumbull county, Ohio, July 25, 1818. October 24, 1844, was married to Margaret Hunter, daughter of James Hunter, of Mercer county, Pennsylvania, where she was born November 22, 1822. They have one son and one daughter—Wilbur A., born September 26, 1845, a farmer of Mercer county, Pennsylvania; and Elizabeth J., February 25, 1847, now the wife of James Jack, of Crawford county. Wilbur was a member of the One Hundred and Seventy-first Ohio National guard; served out his term of service, and was mustered out with his regiment in 1864. He married, in 1876, Isa Kinleyside, and has two children, Eleanor S. and Margaret. In 1845 Mr. Christy settled on the place where he now lives, which was originally settled by Joseph Mc-Michael. He has been township trustee several terms; is a member of the United Presbyterian church, of which church, at Jamestown, Pennsylvania, he is still ruling elder. He was formerly a Whig and anti-slavery man, and was active in assisting fugitives.

Isaac T. Allen, son of Daniel and Ruth (Meacham) Allen, was born in Kinsman, Trumbull county, Ohio, November 5, 1828. Daniel Allen was born in Connecticut March 22, 1789, and came to Ohio with his father, John, in 1806, settling on the place now owned by Isaac T., his son. He was a captain in the militia; died February 20, 1859, aged nearly seventy years. His wife died February 6, 1856. Isaac T. Allen was married December 4, 1856, to Sophronia Nackey, born in Butler county, Pennsylvania, September 17, 1836. They have four children living and two dead, viz: Ruth E., born October 24, 1857, now Mrs. D. T. Root, of Kinsman, has one son, Allen D., born March 9, 1881. Daniel F., born May 1, 1859, of Kinsman; Roswell J., July 28, 1866; Joel K., May 9, 1873. Mr. Allen is an extensive dairyman and stockraiser, owning two hundred and fifty-five acres of good land. He offered his services to the Government during the Rebellion; served out his term of enlistment, and was mustered out at Sandusky, Ohio, in the fall of 1864.

William A. Thomas, son of Daniel and Lu-cinda Thomas, was born in Kinsman, Trumbull county, Ohio, February 27, 1834. Daniel Thomas was a native of New London county, Connecticut, born in 1798. He came to Ohio in 1830, locating on the place in Kinsman now owned by his son, the subject of this sketch, which he cleared up and occupied the balance of his life. He died July 27, 1869. His widow is still living with her son. William A., at the breaking out of the Rebellion in 1861, enlisted in the One Hundred and Eleventh Pennsylvania volunteer infantry as private, but having considerable knowledge of military tactics was soon made a lieutenant. He participated in some of the hardest fought battles of the war. The first engagement took place near Harper's Ferry, where he was commanding the company. At Antietam Captain Thomas had command of two companies. In this battle the regiment was decimated fifty-five per cent. He was also in the battles of Chancellorsville and Gettysburg. At the battle of Lookout Mountain he was wounded and incapacitated for further service. He was granted leave of absence to recuperate, and return home for a short time; went again to the front at Nashville, Tennessee, obtaining permission to join his regiment on crutches. He went as far as Atlanta, where he was obliged to remain. He was detailed to serve on court-martial until 1864, when, on account of his injuries, he was discharged. He went on crutches for eight years after the war. August 18, 1862, he was married to Nancy J., daughter of 'Squire Peter Doty, of Crawford county, Pennsylvania, where she was born January 18, 1839; has a family of six children, as follows: Edith Grace, Cornelia J., George H., Clara C., Eugenie G., and Frederick William. One child is deceased. Mr. Thomas was a resident of Andover, Ashtabula county, for some four years. Upon the death of his father in 1869 he took charge of the home place, where he has since resided, having bought the interest of the other heirs. He was justice of the peace for the past three years.

L. W. Roberts was born in Chittenden county, Vermont, April 5, 1833, oldest son of H. P. and Alvira Roberts. With his parents he came to Ohio in 1834, the family locating at Madison, Lake county; was brought up to the trade of carpenter; when nineteen served an apprenticeship of two years at the blacksmithing trade and subsequently worked as journeyman in various places, including Kansas City, for two years; came to Kinsman December, 1855, and the following spring commenced business for himself at Kinsman village. September 16, 1857, he married Mary J., daughter of Alexander and Ellen Waid, who was born in Kinsman July 31, 1834. Mr. and Mrs. Roberts are the parents of five children, viz: James W., born August 3, 1858, an attorney at law recently admitted to the bar; Harriet A., born September 13, 1860; Frank A., August 24, 1867; Perry M., September 19, 1870; Arba L., April 18, 1872. In 1862 Mr. Roberts enlisted in the Tenth Ohio cavalry and made the march to the sea under General Sherman. He was wounded in the thigh in April, 1865. He served until the close of the war and was mustered out at Columbus, Ohio, July 4, 1865. Returning home he resumed his trade at Kinsman, which he continued until 1873; for seven years afterward resided in Jamestown, Pennsylvania, for the purpose of educating his children; returned to Kinsman in the spring of 1880, and purchased a part of the James Laughlin place, where he also established a blacksmith shop, which he continues to carry on, having a large custom.

John Sisley, youngest child of John and Annie (Mattocks) Sisley, was born in Crawford county, Pennsylvania, June 8, 1814; married September 6, 1835, Mary, daughter of Rev. John Betts, of Mercer county, Pennsylvania, where Mrs. Sisley was born June 2, 1815. The fruit of this union was seven children, of whom only two survive—William, born June 7, 1836, died about 1856; Willis, born February 11, 1838, enlisted in 1861 in the Twenty-ninth Ohio volunteer infantry, and was killed June 9, 1862, at Port Republic; Reason, born June 21, 1839, a farmer of Kinsman; Peter R., born November 29, 1841, assisting in the management of the home place. He was married, in 1868, to Mary Clark, born in Pennsylvania in 1848, and has had three sons. All the balance of the family of John Sisley died young. After his marriage he resided in Pennsylvania for some years, locating on his present place in 1853—the Henry Gale place. He owns nearly two hundred acres of fine land. Mr. Sisley is a member of the Methodist Episcopal church. Rev. John Betts, the

father of Mrs. Sisley, was for years a pastor of the Methodist Episcopal church, residing in Greene township where he cleared up a farm. He died there about 1862, upon the place owned by Calvin Betts.

George H. Nickerson, son of Joseph and Rosa (Thomas) Nickerson, was born in Cortland county, New York, May 1, 1833. His grandfather, Edward, was a sergeant in a Massachusetts regiment in the Revolution. In 1862 the subject of this sketch enlisted in company G, One Hundred and Forty-fifth Pennsylvania volunteer infantry, and with his regiment was in the battles of Fredericksburg, Chancellorsville, Spottsylvania Court House, and all the battles around Petersburg in Grant's flank movements. He was taken prisoner and was in the hands of the rebels two weeks, being confined in Castle Thunder and on Belle Isle; was afterwards exchanged and returning to the front; was present at the surrender of Lee, serving till the close of the war with the rank of first sergeant; was mustered out near Pittsburg, Pennsylvania, in the summer of 1865. He has been twice married, first during the Rebellion, while home on a furlough, July 16, 1863, to Miss Eliza C. Wade, daughter of Alexander and Ellen Wade. She died January 25, 1864. He married again January 31, 1867, Elizabeth L. Wade, a sister of his first wife, who was born in Kinsman, Trumbull county, Ohio, January 11, 1832. By this marriage he has had four children, two of whom are living: James A., born October 21, 1867, Arthur J., born September 26, 1871, the only survivor of triplets born on that occasion. Mr. Nickerson came to Trumbull county, Ohio, in the spring of 1870, locating on the place where he still lives. Alexander Wade, the father of Mrs. Nickerson, came to Ohio at an early day, married October 25, 1827, Eleanor McConnell, and raised a family of six children, of whom two survive. He died December 15, 1853. His widow, born June 17, 1806, is still living.

William R. Christy, son of Andrew and Elizabeth (McConnell) Christy, was born June 15, 1828, in Kinsman, Trumbull county, Ohio. Andrew Christy came to Trumbull county in 1806. He was married in 1812; built a hewed log-house, which they occupied until building the present family residence in 1832. They raised a family of eleven children, of whom six are living. He was a soldier of the War of 1812 for a short time. He was born in 1776, and died in 1863. His wife died August, 1863. William R. Christy was married April 4, 1867, to Miss Charlotte Davis, daughter of Walter Davis, and has two sons—Lauren D., born September 25, 1868, and Ward P., born April 24, 1872. Mrs. Christy's mother was Lucena Perkins, daughter of Seth Perkins, one of the pioneers of Kinsman township. Miss Sarah Christy is residing with her brother, William R., and is a vigorous and intelligent lady, the oldest of the family.

Christian Betts, son of Christian and Elizabeth Betts, was born March 13, 1813, in Fayette county, Pennsylvania. His father was a settler of Crawford county, Pennsylvania, as early as 1790. Christian, Jr., was married May 8, 1835, to Eliza Fister, who was born in Pennsylvania September 16, 1815, and has had a family of thirteen children, of whom eight are living, as follows: Sarah, born 1836, now wife of Eli Wakefield; Jacob, November 25, 1838; Mary, September 25, 1840, wife of Joseph Parker; Julia, December 7, 1843, now Mrs. Lewis Sharp; Sylvester, February 4, 1848; Fred D., January 20, 1850; Charles S., September 6, 1855, (married December 24, 1878, to Miss Mary Bush, of Ashtabula county); Adella D., May 10, 1858, wife of Chauncey Bidwell. All reside in Kinsman except Mrs. Wakefield, who resides in Ashtabula county. Cyrus, born April 12, 1841, died October 28, 1860; Wealthy, October 7, 1843, died March 22, 1876. Three others died in infancy. After his marriage Mr. Betts resided in Pennsylvania for some years. In February, 1851, he purchased where he now resides, moving on the place a year after.

John M. Allen, son of Daniel and Ruth (Meacham) Allen, was born in Kinsman, Trumbull county, Ohio, November 5, 1827. He remained at home until twenty-three, when he went to Crawford county, Pennsylvania, for five years, engaged in farming and conducting a sawmill. He married there March 24, 1853, Miss Phebe Leach, who was born in Mercer county, Pennsylvania, July 22, 1828. She died October, 1854, leaving one daughter, now Mrs. Oscar Leland, of Geauga county, Ohio. November 8, 1855, Mr. Allen was again married, his second wife being Jane Eckels, born July 30, 1831. By this marriage he has had eight children, seven of whom are living, viz: George S., born September 1, 1856; Permelia, March 9, 1858; Eva Jane, October 25, 1860; Wilber J., May 24, 1862; Charles A., July 22, 1865; Jessie A., November 23, 1868; Maggie H., April 2, 1872. In the spring of 1855 our subject returned to Kinsman from Pennsylvania, having the year before bought the place where he now lives. In 1864 he enlisted in the One Hundred and Seventy-first Ohio National guard, and participated in the battle of Cynthiana, Kentucky, June 11, 1864; served out his term of enlistment, and was mustered out at Johnson's island at expiration of term of service.

William Christy, son of William and Mary Christy, was born in Kinsman, Trumbull county, Ohio, August 29, 1811. William Christy, Sr., was a native of Westmoreland county, Pennsylvania, born in 1778; came to Ohio in 1805, and settled in Kinsman on the place now owned by his son William. He raised a family of twelve children, of whom but two survive—the subject of this sketch and Mrs. Mary Gibson, of Kinsman. He was a blacksmith by trade, which trade he followed until advanced in years. He died in 1854. He was a soldier in the War of 1812, under Captain Burnham. William, Jr., was married, September 29, 1853, to Phebe Roberts, who was born in Pennsylvania April 29, 1820, and has a family of three children, as follows: Mary Jane, born December 25, 1855, now wife of Levi S. Mowry, and has one child —William R., born January 14, 1881; William H., born February 20, 1857, at home; Robert, born July 4, 1858, residing in Crawford county, Pennsylvania. Mrs. Christy died October 6, 1864. Mr. Christy built his present residence in 1874, and owns one hundred and seventy-six acres, well improved. He gives considerable attention to dairying and stock-raising.

Albert W. Matthews was born in Kinsman township, Trumbull county, Ohio, September 30, 1836. His grandfather, Deacon William Matthews, came to Ohio in 1804, and settled on the place where the subject of this sketch now lives. William Matthews was a Revolutionary soldier. Albert W. Matthews enlisted in the One Hundred and Twenty-fifth Ohio volunteer infantry, in 1862, and with his regiment was in the battles at Mission Ridge, Resaca, Dalton, Atlanta, and Franklin. He served until the close of the war, securing a lieutenant's commission, and was mustered out with his regiment at Nashville, Tennessee, June, 1865. He received a commission after being mustered out as sergeant. After his return home he took charge of the homestead where he still lives. August 30, 1866, he was married to Miss Sarah Johnson, daughter of John and Nancy Johnson, of Mercer county, Pennsylvania, where Mrs. Matthews was born October 5, 1844. They have two children, as follows: William Albert, born March 11, 1870, and Ruth E., June 28, 1871. For one year after his marriage Mr. Matthews was a resident of Nebraska, when he returned to his former home. He has been township trustee several terms. His father, Thomas Matthews, was a soldier of the War of 1812. In 1826 he had a leg amputated on account of injuries received by breaking through the ice on the Ohio river.

David S. Gillis, youngest son of Francis and Mary Gillis, was born in Kinsman, Trumbull county, Ohio, September 6, 1845; married December 24, 1874, to Agnes M. Patrick, by whom he had one daughter, Emma M., born December 4, 1875. His wife Agnes died January, 1879, and October 13, 1880, he married Miss Sarah A. Wood, daughter of Deacon Charles Wood, of Kinsman. By this marriage he has had one daughter, Abbie, born August 26, 1881. Since the retirement of his father he has taken charge of the family homestead, giving considerable attention to dairying and stock-raising.

Francis Gillis, son of Thomas and Mary (Mossman) Gillis, was born in Kinsman, Trumbull county, Ohio, July 8, 1806. His father was one of the early pioneers of Kinsman, erecting the first grist-mill in the township. He raised a family of nine children. Francis was reared a farmer and remained at home until of age. His father gave him one hundred acres east of the homestead. This place, now the residence of his son David S., was then entirely wild, and he cleared it up and improved it. October 26, 1837, he married Mary Ann Sawyer, born in Greene county, Pennsylvania, 1816. They were the parents of six children, three of who are living, John, at home; David S., a farmer of Kinsman, and Malvina C. at home. Subsequent to his marriage he resided on the place now occupied by his son David until the spring of 1881 when he removed to Kinsman

village. His wife died in 1876. She was a member of the Methodist Episcopal church. Mr. Gillis was township trustee many years. He owns over three hundred and seventy acres in Kinsman. John, his oldest son, in 1862 enlisted in the army and served until the close of the war.

John Craig, son of William and Susan Craig, was born in Washington county, Pennsylvania, September 27, 1822. Brought up on the farm and remained at home until his marriage, June 20, 1855, to Mary Brackin, whose father, Ezekiel Brackin, was one of the pioneers of the county. Died about 1864. They raised a family of nine children. Mrs. Craig was born in Kinsman, Trumbull county, May 30, 1832. Mr. and Mrs. Craig have had five children, as follow: Lida, the oldest, died young; Henry Clay, born August 16, 1858; Della M., born October 6, 1860; Fanny Blanche, January 16, 1864; David B., October 14, 1866. After his marriage he continued to reside in Pennsylvania until April, 1874, when he came to Ohio, purchasing the Brackin homestead in Kinsman, where he still resides.

Peter Lossee, youngest son of Peter and Nancy (McLaughlin) Lossee, was born in Kinsman township, Trumbull county, Ohio, May 10, 1812. Peter Lossee, Sr., was a native of New Jersey; came to Ohio in 1808, settling on the place where the son now resides. He raised a family of four children, the subject of this sketch being the only survivor. He died in 1815, his wife surviving him thirty-three years, dying in 1848. Peter, Jr., was married September 10, 1832, to Elizabeth Reed, born in Pennsylvania. Five children were born, four of whom are living, as follows: Jane, born in 1833, and died March 15, 1862; Amanda Morford (widow) in Illinois; Wallace P., born in 1837 in Kinsman; Helen E., at home; Hattie A., wife of Lawrence Leffingwell, of Kinsman. The mother died in 1849, and Mr. Lossee married for his second wife Eleanor, daughter of John Little, an early settler of Kinsman, where she was born April 18, 1814. They were married May 21, 1850. Mr. Lossee has devoted considerable attention to dairying and stock raising; also to buying live stock, and has raised some valuable horses. He sold two that brought $2,500. Mr. Lossee, speaking of early times, says he has seen deer to the number of thirty-five in one herd,

40

and met a bear on one occasion, which the neighbors finally killed. His only son, Wallace P., was a member of the Second Ohio cavalry, serving over four years until the close of the war.

A. H. Porter, son of Daniel and Sally Porter, was born in Washington county, New York, May 2, 1822. Coming to Ohio in the fall of 1844, he located in Andover, Ashtabula county, where he bought a place; was married in 1846 to Miss Ruth Dolph, born in Washington county, New York, in 1824. They have had eight children, five living, as follows: Henry A. and Nellie (now wife of Reuben Foy) of Gustavus township; J. M. and Nettie (wife of John Turnbull) of Kinsman, and Carrie, still at home. Mr. Porter continued to live in Ashtabula until the spring of 1850, when he removed to Kinsman township, Trumbull county, locating at what is known as Porter's corners, building a saw-mill which he still owns. He removed to his present home in the spring of 1866. He was a member of the One Hundred and Seventy-first Ohio National guard in the Rebellion, and was in the battle of Cynthiana, Kentucky; was taken prisoner and paroled. He served out his term of enlistment and was mustered out at Sandusky, Ohio.

Mrs. Rhoda Spencer was born in Trumbull county, Ohio, June 20, 1809; oldest child of John and Elizabeth (Mizener) Waldorf. Her father was one of the pioneers of Hubbard. With her parents she removed to Vernon township in 1812; was educated in the common schools; taught school three terms prior to her marriage. She was married, January 15, 1829, to Warren Spencer, born in 1801. Her husband was a cooper by trade; came to Ohio about 1820, settling in Ashtabula county; came to Kinsman about 1826. After their marriage Mr. and Mrs. Spencer settled on the place now owned by Scott Mizener; settled in the woods, putting up a log house, cleared up and improved the farm, which they occupied until 1860, when they purchased the place formerly the Ben Allen farm, where Mrs. Spencer still resides. Mr. Spencer was an original anti-slavery man, and a Methodist until the division of the church upon the question of slavery. He died November 23, 1863. Mrs. Spencer is a member of the Methodist Episcopal church at Kinsman.

Mrs. Harriet B. Parker, daughter of Elam and Sarah (Hyde) Jones, was born in Hartford township, Trumbull county, Ohio, February 2, 1806. She attended a ladies' seminary at Kinsman; taught school one season at home; married, January 8, 1824, Linus Parker, a native of Connecticut, born in 1778. He was a manufacturer of edged tools, and had quite an establishment in Kinsman. He came with his father to that township in the early years of the present century. He died in 1837. He was a member of the Presbyterian and Congregational church in Kinsman, of which his father, Lovell, was deacon, and was an active member. He had a family of four children, of whom three are living, as follows: Sarah E., born September 27, 1825, widow of William A. Gillis; Rufus H., born December 24, 1827; Lemira J. born September 27, 1835; all residing in Kinsman. The latter completed her education at an academy in Poland, Mahoning county; Hannah P., born October 12, 1837, died November 29, 1855. Rufus H. received his education at a high school in Wayne township, Ashtabula county; was brought up to farming; went to California about 1852, where he was engaged some five or six years in mining and farming. Returning to Ohio, he dealt in lumber and live stock a number of years. After the close of the war he traveled for three or four years wholesaling goods for himself, establishing a store-house in Mercer, Pennsylvania; opened a wholesale family goods house in Sharon, Pennsylvania, and did an extensive trade. He has now a fine home in Kinsman. Mrs. Parker continues to reside on the home place. She is a member of the same church to which her husband belonged.

George Baldwin, son of Jacob H. and Florinda Baldwin, was born in Champion, Trumbull county, Ohio, July 7, 1836; obtained his education in the common schools, and at the high school at Warren, supplemented by an attendance for one term at Kenyon college, Gambier, Ohio. He was engaged at clerking in Warren for one or two years; married, October 1, 1861, to Emma R. Lesuer, born in Bolivar, New York. They have two children: Gertrude F., born May 9, 1864, and Albert L., June 29, 1870. He resided in Warren two years after marriage, then removing to Meadville, Pennsylvania, where he commenced the stove and tinware business. One year afterwards his place of business was destroyed by fire. He removed to Kinsman, Trumbull county, Ohio, in the spring of 1866, where he engaged in the stove trade, buying out the Kinsman foundry, which he conducted till 1870. About 1873 he added to his business that of general hardware, and is doing a prosperous business. He has been a member of the Methodist Episcopal church for the past twenty years, and is superintendent of the Sunday-school.

Dr. Luman G. Moore, only son of Lorenzo and Caroline (Miller) Moore, was born in Kinsman, Trumbull county, Ohio, February 16, 1849. Lorenzo Moore came to Ohio with his parents about 1836, the family locating on the place now owned by John Wallace, where he spent the balance of his days. He died in 1869. His widow, born in 1789, is still living with her son, the subject of this sketch, quite vigorous for one of her age. Dr. Moore was reared upon a farm, attending the common and high schools until twenty; was a student one year at the Ohio Wesleyan university, and also at Michigan university, Ann Arbor, one year; began the study of medicine with Dr. Jones in 1870, continuing three years, during which time he attended a course of lectures at Bellevue Medical college, graduating from Long Island Hospital Medical college, New York, in June, 1873. The same fall he commenced practice at Kinsman, where he has since been located. He was married in May, 1871, to Miss Elizabeth Patterson, and has two children living—Minnie, born June 29, 1879, and Luman G., December 17, 1880. He has been township trustee one year, and township treasurer two years.

Lyman Root, oldest son of Charles and Sally Ann (Laughlin) Root, was born in Mecca, Trumbull county, Ohio, June 2, 1839, and was a student at a seminary in Jamestown, Pennsylvania, at the breaking out of the war. With four companions he went to Columbus, Ohio, and enlisted in the Eighty-fourth Ohio volunteer infantry for three months; was at Camp Laurens, Maryland, and returned home in October, 1862. He re-enlisted in the One Hundred and Twenty-fifth Ohio volunteer infantry for three years, and with his regiment participated in some of the principal battles of the war including Nashville, Mission Ridge, Chickamauga, Lookout Mountain, and Atlanta. He was on detached

duty as mail-carrier for some time, served until the close of the war, and was mustered out at Cleveland, Ohio, June, 1865. He resumed his occupation of farming on the place formerly owned by his grandfather, James Laughlin; was married January 10, 1867, to Miss Irene S., daughter of Thomas Mathews, and has three children: Hubert L., born October 19, 1867; Alice S., February 2, 1874: Ralph, June 2, 1876. He remained on the Laughlin place until buying at Kinne's corners about 1870. He sold out in 1880, and in the spring of 1881 located in Kinsman village, engaging in merchandising, having a general store. He has been justice of the peace for twelve years in Kinsman, and also assessor for two terms.

Daniel C. Clinginsmith, born in Mercer county, Pennsylvania, May 16, 1824; married, April, 1847, Electa J., daughter of Thomas and Eleanor (McLaughlin) Matthews, born October 11, 1823, in Kinsman, Trumbull county, Ohio. Mr. Clinginsmith was a farmer originally, afterward engaged in mercantile business; removed to Wisconsin in 1856, where he engaged in merchandising and was also postmaster. He died September 24, 1870; was worshipful master Free and Accepted Masons at the time of his death, and also member of the Methodist Episcopal church. Mrs. Clinginsmith continued to reside in Wisconsin until the fall of 1879, when she returned to Trumbull county and located in Kinsman village, where she still resides.

Captain E. C. Briggs was born in Newport county, Rhode Island, September 13, 1804; son of Ethan C. Briggs and Mary Littlefield. His father died when he was six, and when ten years of age he ran away from his home and mother; went to New York and engaged as cabin boy on a New York and Philadelphia packet, in which position he continued until fourteen; went before the mast to Patagonia, was subsequently promoted to second mate, still later to that of mate, and finally, when about twenty-four, was placed in command of the packet on which he began as cabin boy. Afterwards he was master of a vessel plying between New York and Baltimore, and later filled the same position on a vessel engaged in the Caribbean sea and the Spanish main. He was married June, 1834, to Anna C. Stanhope. They had four children, two living—James Theodore, and Sarah R., residing in Denver, Colorado. Ethan C., Jr., was born in 1843; enlisted in the war of the Rebellion and with his regiment participated in numerous engagements. At Chattanooga, Tennessee, September 21, 1863, he was captured by the rebels, being wounded in the leg. The limb was amputated and he died a few weeks afterward. Henry Clay, the other son, was thirty-three when he died, December 10, 1880. Mrs. Briggs died in 1863, and the captain was again married February 21, 1867, to Cordelia, daughter of Benjamin Ward. She was born in Hartford, Connecticut, February 5, 1816. Captain Briggs continued the life of a seaman until 1843. For the next four years he was engaged in mercantile business in New York city. Removing to Ohio in 1847 he settled on the place where he still lives in Kinsman, and since then has followed farming. He is a fine specimen of the old style of sea captain, bluff and hearty, and withal hospitable; is vigorous in body and mind, and has never drank a tea-spoonful of liquor in his life.

Wayne Bidwell, son of Riverius and Eunicia Bidwell, was born in Trumbull township, Trumbull county, Ohio, May 6, 1821. Besides his attendance at the common schools he attended school at Oberlin three or four terms. Married, December 31, 1844, to Mary L., daughter of Ezra Hyde, an early settler of Vernon township, where she was born in January, 1823. Mr. and Mrs. Bidwell are the parents of five children, three of whom are living. Jasper R. lived to the age of thirty-one and died in Iowa in 1879; Caleb W. resides on the home place; Ezra H., of Kinsman village; and Chauncey D., of the same place. Cora Lynn died when three years of age. In addition to his farming Mr. Bidwell deals extensively in the buying and shipping of live stock.

J. W. Chase was born in Yates county, New York, November 23, 1817; son of David and Polly (Welsh) Chase. He was raised to the trade of his father, that of carpenter and joiner. With his parents he came to Trumbull county, Ohio, in the fall of 1835, and located in Gustavus township, where he followed his trade, erecting many of the best buildings in that vicinity. In the fall of 1836 he started on a trip South, and made an extended trip through the South and West and also to the northwest as far as Green Bay, Wisconsin, working at his trade at various places. At Fort DesMoines he saw the famous Black Hawk and seven hundred warriors. At Galena, Illinois, he put up the second brick building in the place. Returning home, the next year he again went west, thence south to Vicksburg, Mississippi, making a portion of the trip down the Mississippi in a skiff. At Vicksburg he worked at his trade some six years, the panic breaking him up. He returned to Galena, where he remained one year, then made a trip up the Wisconsin river to the pineries, and engaged in trafficking with the Indians. He finally concluded his wanderings, and on November 10, 1843, was married to Laura, daughter of David Chapman, born in Vernon township, November 14, 1823. They are the parents of three children, of whom two are living—Leroy, born September 1, 1844, residing in Missouri, and Jane Ann, at home. Mr. Chase continued to work at his trade until compelled to give it up on account of rheumatism. He followed farming for a time, conducting the farm of Thomas Kinsman, and run an extensive dairy. Cheese then brought but four cents per pound; subsequently kept a hotel in Crawford county, Pennsylvania, for a couple of years during the oil excitement, afterwards purchasing a farm in Pennsylvania. October, 1861, he enlisted in the Sixth Ohio volunteer cavalry; raised a company and was made first lieutenant. In the spring of 1872 he removed to Kinsman, where he now resides. For the past thirty years he has followed more or less the business of auctioneer. He has also been efficient in detecting horse thieves.

CHAPTER V.

FARMINGTON.

LOCATION AND NATURAL FEATURES.

Farmington township, number six in the fifth range, is bounded on the north by Mesopotamia, on the east by Bristol, on the south by Southington, and on the west by Geauga county. The surface, like most of the townships of the county, is undulating, and the soil is largely clay, though in the northern part a sandy loam is found.

The principal streams are Grand river, Swine creek, and Dead branch. Grand river runs through the township a diagonal course from the southwest to the northeast. Dead branch is a southern branch of Grand river. Swine creek drains the northwestern part of the township.

OWNERSHIP AND SURVEY.

This township contains seventeen thousand one hundred and fifty-seven acres, and was in draft number fourteen, drawn with other lands by Joseph Bowell, William Edwards, Samuel Henshaw, Joseph Pratt, Luther Loomis, David King, John Leavitt, Jr., Ebenezer King, Jr., Timothy King, Fidelio King, and Sylvester Griswold. These owners sold to one another and quit-claimed to others at different times from 1798 to 1811, at which time Solomon Bond owned the greater part of the township.

The survey was made under the direction and personal superintendence of Luther Henshaw, and the township was called Henshaw until it was organized as Farmington in 1817.

SETTLEMENT.

This township was first settled mainly by Connecticut people. Its growth was a slow one and not until long after its organization was it thickly populated.

Lewis Wolcott, best known as Captain Wolcott, and David Curtis, were the first arrivals. They came in the spring of 1806, from Vienna township. Lewis Wolcott, son of Theodore, was a descendant of Henry Wolcott, who came to this country about the year 1630. In the spring of 1805 he made the journey from Connecticut to Ohio on foot, carrying all his earthly possessions in a knapsack. He stopped one year in Vienna, working for Joel Humiston. David Curtis, a son of lawyer Curtis, was the companion of his journeying. Upon their arrival here they built a pole cabin for a summer residence, near the spot where Mr. Kibbee's house now stands at West Farmington.

In the summer of 1806, Zenas Curtis, David or lawyer Curtis, and Elihu Moses brought their families and located. Zenas Curtis built a cabin on the Fuller farm on the State road; the land is now owned by C. A. Mackay. David Curtis built on the old Ransley Curtis farm, where Dr. Meyers now lives, and Elihu Moses on the opposite side of the road from S. H. Loveland's.

The next arrivals are mentioned in the biographical sketch of the Wolcott family given below:

Josiah Wolcott, was born September 17, 1755, and married Miss Lydia Russell, of Weathersfield, May 13, 1779. The children of this union were as follows: Catharine, Daniel R., Horace, Susan, Mary, Josiah W., Erastus, and Edmund P. The mother of Edmund P. died April 19, 1805, aged forty-three years. His father again married; his second wife was Mrs. Nancy Higgins, widow of Dr. Higgins, of Weathersfield, Connecticut; the time of his marriage was February 16, 1806. The names of the children following this union were Lydia R., Caroline, and Charlotte. Their mother died October 13, 1824, aged fifty-eight years. Josiah Wolcott married a third time, the object of his affections being Mrs. Brown, of Warren. They had one daughter, Nancy.

Mr. Wolcott died January 18, 1838, in his eighty-third year. His native place was Weathersfield, which he left about the year 1800, and settled in the town of Bristol, Connecticut. His occupation was that of a farmer. He lived in Bristol until 1806, when he was persuaded, by the glowing representations of a New Connecticut land speculator, one Solomon Bond, to make a purchase of one thousand acres of land in the then unbroken wilderness. He visited his new territory in the fall or winter of 1806 and 1807, in company with his son Horace. Mr. Wolcott's brother Theodore, and his son Lewis, and Gad Hart, came out at the same time. They "rolled" up a log house, perhaps fifteen feet square, without the help of a team; in this place they wintered. The ground on which this bachelor residence stood on northwest corner of centre, was a few feet west of the Wolcott store. This building was raised, inclosed, floors laid, and inside finished without having a sawed piece of timber in it. Here the company passed the winter. At that time the place was nothing more nor less than a wilderness; not an article of food, either for man or beast, was to be had in the township. They brought the straw to fill their bunks from Mesopotamia, and as the forest was so dense that they could not get their straw through, they were obliged to travel down the old path from Mesopotamia to Warren, as far as Grand river, and then come up on the ice to their lodgings.

Mr. Josiah Wolcott returned to his family early in the spring, after a most fatiguing journey, made more so by losing his horse in Pennsylvania; he made the rest of the journey on foot, at the time when the roads were in their worst state. He disposed of his farm and arranged his affairs, and left the land of "steady habits," as it then was appropriately called, arriving with his family and three of his second wife's children, viz: Nancy, Silas, and Polly Higgins. In the meantime his son Horace had put up a log house for the accommodation of the family; the size, perhaps, might be 20 x 22. In this a family of from twelve to fourteen had to find a home, but it was highly prized by all. Now the business was to clear off the timber, and that was undertaken with a will; the boys were working at it every day, except the Sabbath, and on that day services were held at some private house, either at the centre or at some one's house at the west, usually at David Curtis's. Situated as they were, it would seem they had no time for sickness, or no accommodation when they were ill. Yet one of their number, a sister Mary, was during the spring and summer months gradually sinking under the scourge of our race, viz: consumption. Their son, Dr. Silas, attended her, but nothing seemed to produce a good effect, and she died September 2, 1808. A few trees were felled, and a grave dug. This spot was where the present cemetery now is. Her funeral was the first, and her grave the first in the township.*

Mr. Wolcott felt that meetings on the Sabbath must be kept up, and succeeded in carrying out his convictions of propriety in this particular idea. As it was seldom the case that they had preaching, when meetings were not requested at other houses they held meeting in their own place—often had preaching in Parkman, and Judge Parkman and lady frequently attended here. The way of getting to church was on horseback for those who had horses, or with ox-teams.

Mr. Wolcott, considering the help had, had cleared quite a farm before the breaking out of the War of 1812. But from that time he saw the great disadvantage all were laboring under, in not having mills of any kind; and in this state of things two men called upon him, professing to be number one mill-wrights, and persuaded him to undertake the building of a saw- and grist-mill.

They cut and hewed and hauled on to the ground a large quantity of timber, and partially constructed running-gear, etc., but in consequence of indebtedness which was likely to send him to the "lock-up," the main part of his workmen left, and the undertaking was abandoned. The project of mill-building rested for several years. Another mill-wright appeared, who proposed to put up one on the spot where A. D. Kibbee & Co.'s mill now stands; but their mill soon went down, and proved a failure. The scheme went to rest again, and after a space of one or two years a third trial was made, and they succeeded in getting a good saw-mill.

About this time complaints were made by parties who had erected mills above Seats; vexatious suits were commenced and continued in court for some ten years. Several judgments were obtained and paid. Mr. Wolcott being confident that his dam did not back water to the injury of the upper mills, the Legislature enacted a law giving the party wishing to erect or sustain a dam across any stream the privilege to summon a special jury, who should view the premises and decide how high the party might raise a dam without injury to others. This act was complied with, and that put an end to the litigation. Twelve of the best men in Trumbull county gave their verdict to the effect that he had been put to all the costs and vexation of ten or more suits unjustly.

E. P. Wolcott, son of Josiah Wolcott, was born November 17, 1800, in Bristol, Connecticut. His advantages for an education were limited; he however obtained a good practical and business knowledge. He was reared a farmer,—worked at it till he was thirty,—then went to selling goods at Farmington. He married Clarissa Bosworth, of Farmington, November 19, 1829:—result of this union, nine children, seven of whom are living, viz: Julia E., William W., Amelia, Cecilia, Charles F., Addison L., and Mary E. Mr. Wolcott lived some ten years at Chagrin Falls, and while there was justice of the peace. He also held several offices of trust

and honor in this township. He was a member of the Congregational church; in politics, a Republican. It may be said of this gentleman that he was one of the strong supporters of the Congregational church; and the cause of education had in him a warm supporter. He died March 21, 1881.

Captain Erastus Wolcott, fourth son and sixth child of Joseph and Lydia, was born in Bristol, Hartford county, Connecticut, May 2, 1795. His advantages for an education were nothing, in fact, only having had three months' schooling in his life. He was early disciplined in all the details of farm life, which he has followed as an avocation through life. When but eight years old he came here with his father's family. He married Miss Almira Hannahs, of Nelson, Portage county, June 19, 1820. She was born March 9, 1798, in Bethlehem, Connecticut. She was the first teacher in this town. Result of marriage, six children, all living and settled well and doing well;—their names, Orlando K., Luther H., Catharine C., Julius E., Orvis A., and Helen C. Mr. Wolcott has held various offices in his town. Elected captain of State militia about 1825. United with Presbyterian church 1825; he was chosen deacon in 1841, succeeding his father; he was ruling elder at the time of his death. His wife died January 11, 1865. Deacon Wolcott was again married, to Celesta Worrell, of Farmington, January 5, 1866. She was the widow of John Worrell. Captain Wolcott died December 26, 1867.

Horace Wolcott died June 28, 1872, aged eighty-seven years and seven months. We subjoin the names, births, and deaths of his family: Edward C., born October 21, 1809, died April 5, 1864; infant daughter, born June 6, 1810, died June 8, 1810; Louisa, born July 16, 1812, died May 13, 1813; Russell, born May 23, 1814, died October 20, 1865; infant daughter, born September 14, 1816, died September 15, 1816; Julia, born September 23, 1817, died February 21, 1830; Addison, born April 18, 1820, died March 20, 1869; Albert G., born August 30, 1823, living; Sophia, born September 15, 1826, died January 16, 1849; Caroline, born March 18, 1829, living. Mrs. Sabrina Wolcott died July 28, 1865, aged seventy-five. The heads of the above family were united in marriage December 15, 1808. Albert G. is now living in Wyandotte, Kansas, engaged in the lumber business and "real estate." Caroline Bughoff is living at the center, with her only child, Edwin F.

O. K. Wolcott, son of Erastus and Almira, was born May 30, 1823, in this town (Farmington). Educational advantages fair, for those early days. He was united in marriage to Miss Catharine M. Stowe, of Braceville, November 13, 1845. This lady was born May 21, 1821. Result of union, six children, viz: Norman E.,* Cornelia A., Austin E., Miranda C., Julius O.,* and Orvis O. Mr. Wolcott has held several town offices. In 1865 he was chosen county commissioner; he was re-elected in 1868. United with the Presbyterian church April 10, 1859; he was several times chosen superintendent of the Sunday-school. His wife is also a member.

Theodore Wolcott was a member of Captain Benton's company, and made permanent settlement here in 1814. His wife was Rhoda Goodrich. They had nine children—Lewis, Josiah, John, William, Nancy, Newton, Chester, Emily, and Susan. Eight are dead. All resided

---

* Miss Wolcott's death was the result of a serious accident which happened while the family were on their way from Connecticut to Ohio. As the roads were bad the women walked much of the way. As Mary—or Polly—was attempting to cross a stream on a log, steadying herself with a pole, she fell into the water. It being late in the season she took a severe cold, from the effects of which she never recovered. The following epitaph was placed upon the headstone which marks her grave:

" Parents and friends, a long adieu;
I leave this wilderness to you;
My body lies neath this stone—
The arrests of death you cannot shun."

* Deceased.

in Farmington and died here, excepting Emily (Belden), who died in Kansas; William, who died in Parkman, and Chester, who survives. Chester G. Wolcott, youngest son, was born in Connecticut in 1803. He married, in 1843, Louisa S. Hudson, of Orwell. Their only child, Leander H., was killed while in his country's service in his nineteenth year. He was a member of the Ohio National guard, and was killed June 11, 1864, at Covington, Kentucky, while serving against Morgan's raiders. Mrs. Wolcott died in 1867, aged sixty-one. Theodore Wolcott died in 1837, aged about seventy-three. His wife died in 1847 at the age of eighty-eight. Mr. Wolcott was a deacon of the Congregational church from its organization to the time of his death. He was a man of liberality and worth.

O. L. Wolcott, son of Lewis, was born in Farmington in 1823; was married in 1850 to Martha F. Kibbee, and has five children living, one deceased—Ella H. (Chamberlain), Louise S. (deceased), Emma A., Carrie F., Grace L., and Frank B. Mr. Wolcott was county auditor four years, 1859 to 1863; was a member of the State board of equalization from this district, serving the year 1871-72; was then appointed by Governor Noyes as commissioner of railroads and telegraphs and served two years. He is now engaged in farming and stock-dealing.

William Wolcott, son of Newton, was born in Farmington in 1837. In 1866 he married Hattie E. Gillette, who died in 1881, leaving three children—Carrie E., Newton A., and Carroll. In February, 1882, he married Mrs. Sarah Harrison. Mr. Wolcott served four years in company D, Second Ohio cavalry. He has been township trustee two terms.

F. J. Wolcott, son of Lyman B., was born in Farmington in 1859. He is now in partnership with Dr. O. A. Palmer, and C. S. Thompson, and is secretary and treasurer of the Standard Chair company.

Gad Hart, who came on with the Wolcott brothers in 1806, moved with his family to Henshaw in 1807, and took up his abode in the cabin near where the Wolcott store stands, at the center. This was the cabin erected the previous year.

The house built by Horace Wolcott was a little more pretentious than most pioneer dwellings. He hauled boards from Parkman, and made a very comfortable cabin, with floors above and below and a door of boards. But when the family arrived and surveyed it, the women, thinking of the pleasant home they had left in the East, burst into tears.

During the winter months of 1807-8, the Wolcotts purchased their provisions in Mesopotamia, of Esquire Tracy. Sometimes they bought venison of the Indians; and on one occasion a fine buck was purchased for a silver dollar.

At this time the only roads in the township were paths marked by blazed trees. The State road from Warren to Painesville, running across the southwestern part of the township, had been marked out but was not bridged or worked. A little later it was cleared of its obstructions so that ox-teams could travel it. There was a route of travel from Warren via Bristol and Mesopotamia, running diagonally through the northeast of Henshaw, and a bridge across Grand river about one mile and a fourth northeast of the center of the township. The winter of 1807-08 was spent in clearing, and in the spring crops were put in which yielded fairly. During the year the settlement received quite an addition to its members by the arrival of William Wilson, Josiah Wolcott (second son of Theodore), Gad Bartholomew, Ezra Curtis, John Hethman, J. P. Danford, Dennis Lewis, Jacob Bartholomew, and one or two others. Some of these were married and brought their families, others were single.

During the early years of the settlement the nearest place where milling could be done was Parkman. Garrettsville and Bristol were often visited for the same purpose. Frequently the man or boy who went to mill was obliged to make the journey one of two days' duration.

Eben Wildman settled in the eastern part of the township in 1813, and for many years his was the only house in the township east of the center. Several of the name are still residents of Farmington and vicinity.

Dennis Lewis came to West Farmington in 1810, at which time there were but seven families living in this place. His daughter, Mrs. Chauncey Taft, now a widow, is still living, and though seventy-eight years of age, is hale and hearty. It was through the influence of Dennis Lewis that the name of Henshaw was changed to Farmington, also that of Bowlestown to Southington.

Quite a thriving settlement sprang up along the old State road, and log cabins were plentier there than frame houses are now. William Wilson was one of the first settlers on this road, followed by John Young, Daniel and Orrin Taft, and others. From the various Taft families residing here, that part of the township was long known as Taftsburg.

John Young, from Pennsylvania, settled about 1810 on the north bank of Grand river. He had but one child, a son, Eli, who soon after coming here married Catharine Bellows. He was a Quaker and paid his fine instead of going to the War of 1812. Eli Young raised a family of four children, all of whom are living: Sarah (Sager) Bristol; Stephen, on the old homestead; Mary A. (Henry), West Farmington, and Newton, Gustavus. John Young died in 1824.

Orrin Taft came about 1815, and his brother Daniel soon after. Both settled on the State road. Orrin's children were Frederick, Orrin, Julia, Joseph, Lucy Ann, Eliza Ann, Calvin, and Harvey. The two last named are living. Orrin and Frederick died in Braceville. Lucy and Eliza are still living.

Daniel Taft's children were Robert, Mary Ann, Jane, Henry, Harriet, Laura, Caroline, and Lovett. Jane (Green) lives at West Farmington. Harriet and Caroline are also living.

Chauncy, Harvey, and Horace Taft, brothers of Daniel and Orrin, also settled in Taftsburg and reared families. They, however, were later settlers.

In May, 1814, Captain John Benton and his "company," consisting of his own family, Theodore Wolcott and his family, and David Belden with his family, left Connecticut for Henshaw. They were provided with horse and ox teams, and journeyed via Trenton, Philadelphia, Harrisburg, and Pittsburg. At the latter place, then a little smoky village, they bought some flour, which they ate upon their arrival in Henshaw. The company reached here in safety in June, following up the State road from Warren. From this road they were obliged to cut their way through the woods to the center.

David Belden came from Weathersfield, Connecticut. He located where Colonel H. H. Hatch now lives, and afterwards where Shelden Spencer resides, near the river. His family consisted of twelve children, all of whom lived to be married and bring up families, except one son, Daniel.

Chauncey Brockett, from New York State, came to Farmington immediately after the War of 1812, and settled on the river where he cleared up a farm. He died there at about the age of seventy-six. Alanson Brockett, his son, was born in western New York in 1805, and came to Ohio with his parents. He married Anna Maria Moffet and settled on a part of his father's farm. In 1835 he moved to Bristol, settling on the old Moffet farm on West street. The last three years of his life he resided in Bristolville, where he died in 1875. He was twice married, his first wife being the mother of all of his children, fourteen in number, six boys and eight girls. Four boys and two girls are dead.

John Benton moved to this township from Bristol, Connecticut, making the fourteenth family in Henshaw. They journeyed with one yoke of oxen and a horse, and were forty days upon the way. John Benton and his wife (nee Polly C. Upson) were the parents of four children—George Washington, Henry D., Polly (Brown), and Harriet C. (Loveland). Henry D. and Harriet survive, the latter in Dakota. Washington died at Beaufort, South Carolina, and Polly at Council Bluffs, Iowa. H. D. Benton was born in 1810, and has resided in Farmington the most of his life. He married in 1843 Harriet H. Baldwin, of Parkman. They have three children living, one deceased—Herbert U., Edwin H., Marion I. (Underwood). All reside in Iowa. Mary Augusta, the first child, died at the age of seven.

In 1817 Eli Hyde settled in the eastern part of the township; and in 1818 Joel and Ira Hyde, Abijah Lee and others.

Socrates Loveland, a native of Connecticut, moved from the State of Massachusetts to Farmington township in 1818. He was the father of ten children, of whom seven are living, two of them, S. H. and Mrs. Cotton, in Farmington. Mr. Loveland died in 1870; Mrs. Loveland, whose maiden name was Lydia Taft, in 1867.

S. H. Loveland was born in Farmington in 1822 and has resided in this township since, excepting five years in California and Australia. He married Mahala Rood, a native of Connecticut, in 1856, and has two children, Lydia and Henry.

Joel Peck

Mrs. Eliza N. Peck.

Daniel Gates, born in western New York in 1807, settled in east Farmington in 1817. He married, in 1828, Eunice A. Chaffee, of Bristol, and had five children, three of whom survive, viz: Freeman, a prominent manufacturer of Painesville, Ohio; Emily, wife of Rev. J. B. Corey, of Cleveland; and Mary Maria, wife of Dr. A. J. Brockett, of Bristolville. Mr. Gates moved from Farmington to Greene in 1851, and from Greene to Bristol in 1874. He died in Bristol in 1880; his wife in 1879.

Abijah Lee moved to Farmington from Mc-Henry county, New York, in 1818, coming the whole distance of five hundred miles in a sleigh, bringing his mother, then eighty-three years old, his wife and eleven children. The names of his children were as follows: Roswell, Lydia, Isaac, Almira, Harriet, Polly, Simeon, Hannah, Betsey, Seth, and Electa. Of these Roswell, Isaac, Hannah, and Harriet are dead. Simeon lives in Michigan; Lydia, in Ashtabula county; the others are all in Farmington.

William S. Griffith came to Farmington from McHenry county, New York, about the year 1820. Soon after coming here he married Almira Lee, who is still living. Their six children were: James Addison, Chauncy, Milo W., William W., Albert, and a son who died in infancy. Addison died at the age of twenty, and Albert at the age of twenty-one. The three surviving sons reside in Farmington. W. W. Griffith, the youngest of these, was born in 1836. He married Mary Chandler. Mr. Griffith, the father, died in 1864, aged sixty-four years. He taught the first school in east Farmington in the old log school-house, which stood near the présent site of the church.

Alonzo Osmer was born in Chardon, Ohio, in 1821. When four years old he came to this township. In 1842 he married Lydia Folk, of Southington. Their children are: Addison, Orvel C., George H. (deceased), Charles S., Emogene, Mary E., and Julia E. All are married except the youngest.

Ethan Curtiss was born in Connecticut in 1783. In 1808 he removed from New England to Brunswick, in this State, with a family of three boys. About the year 1827 he settled in Farmington. By his first wife his children were Nelson, Lewis, and Giles—all born in Connecticut. The mother of these children, Anna Sedgwick,

was born in Connecticut in 1783. His second wife, Aurelia Strong, bore ten children, five of whom are living. Of the first children, only Giles is living. He resides in Northfield, Summit county. Nelson spent most of his days in Wisconsin. Lewis was born in 1805. In 1831 he married Harriet Lewis (born in Farmington in 1811) who is still living. Mr. Curtiss died in 1874. Their children were named: Miles and Giles (twins), Silas, Nancy, Judson, Martha, Mary J., Ellen, Alfreda, Nelson J. Two, Giles and Judson, are dead.

Nelson J., youngest child of Lewis and Harriet Curtiss, was born in this township in 1852. In 1873 he married Victoria M. Symes, of Farmington. She died in 1875, at the age of twenty-three, having borne one child, Vernie Victoria. In 1877 he married Nettie Lord, who was born in Wisconsin in 1852. Their children are Vinnie May and Fredie Maud. N. J. Curtiss lives upon the old homestead.

LATER SETTLERS.

J. W. and Sarah (Lew) Lamberson came to Farmington in 1832 from Ontario county, New York, being originally from Herkimer county. They settled in the east of the township and reared six children, viz: William D., Charles, Mary Ann, James, Eliza (Harshman), and Luetta (Norton). Two, Mary Ann and James, are dead. The others reside in Farmington, excepting Mrs. Norton, who lives in Bristol. W. D. Lamberson, their oldest child, was born in Herkimer county, New York, in 1826. He came to Farmington with his parents and has since resided here, excepting while he was in the army. He married Emily A. McKay, a native of New York. They have two children living and one deceased: Sarah Catharine (died at the age of eleven), Leora, and Addie May.

Justus Pierce, son of Shadrach Pierce, was born in 1824; in 1847 married Sarah Jane Housel. Their children are: James J., Olive L., Peter H., and Mary J. Peter is dead. Mrs. Pierce died in 1877.

William Fales was born in Buffalo, New York, in 1825; has lived in Ohio forty-five years; was brought up in this county; married Joanna Proctor in 1847, and has seven children living, one deceased. Mr. Fales is largely engaged in buying and selling horses.

Chauncy Hickox came from New Haven

county, Connecticut, to Vienna township, this county, in 1805, and resided the most of his days there. In his old age he lived in Bazetta and died in Mecca at the age of seventy-five. He raised eight children, who arrived at maturity, seven of whom are still living—William, of Bristol; Leverett and Chandler, Farmington; Eliza M., Columbiana county; Abigail (Caldwell), Champion; Mary (Barber), Vienna; Selden, Bristol; Isaac C., the fourth son, died in Kansas at the age of sixty-one. Chandler Hickox, now a resident of Farmington, was born in Vienna in 1809, and has resided in the county excepting two years. He is a carpenter by trade. Mr. Hickox married Ursula Langley, of Hubbard, and has five children living and five deceased. The names of those living are William D., Hattie (Wolcott), Anna (Pierce), Jane (Pierce), Myron E. Millaus R., the oldest son, died in Andersonville prison in 1863. He was in the Second Ohio cavalry. William D. enlisted in 1861 and served through the war. He was also a prisoner at Andersonville.

James M. Harwood was born in Hampshire county, Massachusetts, in 1814. In 1833 he came to Ohio, and settled in Greene township in 1838; was that year married to Hannah Knapp, a native of Massachusetts. Two sons were born of this union—Charles (deceased), and John Avery, resident of Farmington. For his second wife he married Sarah Kinney, who bore one child—Sarah J. (King), now living with her father. He married for his third wife Mrs. Mary A. Pierce, of Farmington. Mr. Harwood has resided in Farmington since 1860.

Robert Kincaid, a brother of William Kincaid whose parentage is given elsewhere, was born in Youngstown in 1817. He married Mary Pierce, of Farmington, and came to this township to live about 1841. The children are four living, two deceased: Cornelia, Christopher, Robert (deceased), Margaret, Allison (deceased), Alice.

Anderson Dana, a native of Connecticut, was for many years a prominent citizen of Farmington, holding the office of justice of the peace and other responsible positions. He died in 1876 at the age of eighty-six years. He was twice married. His first wife, Ann Dennison, bore four children, who are living, viz: Charles A., of the New York Sun; Junius, Maria, and David. For his second wife he married Mary Ann Wright,

who bore three children: Daniel, Wright, and William. The latter was killed in the army; the two former are married and reside in Farmington. Mr. Dana moved to Trumbull county in 1832. His son, Daniel R. Dana, born in 1834, married Miss M. W. Kennedy in 1869, and has one child, Harry R. Mr. Dana began the manufacture of cheese in 1869 in the factory now owned by Wilcox & Griffin, where he carried on the business two years. He began work in the factory which he now operates in 1871. The capacity of this factory is about seventy tons per annum. Mr. Dana makes use of the patent process.

Jared Housel was born in Northumberland county, Pennsylvania, in 1811. In 1812 he went with his parents to Stark county, and after eight years moved to Jackson township, now in Mahoning county. In 1834 Mr. Housel and his father, Peter Housel, came to Farmington. Peter Housel had a family of seven children, all of whom are living. Jared Housel married in 1839 Lucinda Miller, of Farmington. Six children are the result of this union: Mary J., Isaac, George, Survinus, Sophia, and Ira. George and Ira live in Farmington; Mary J. in Bristol; Isaac in Gustavus; Sophia in Kansas. Survinus died in the army at the age of nineteen.

N. A. Gilbert, Esq., attorney-at-law, now of Cleveland, Ohio, is the son of Albert and Esther B. Gilbert, who settled in Farmington township in 1851. He was educated in the common schools, and in West Farmington seminary. He enlisted in 1862, in the Eighty-seventh Ohio volunteer infantry, and afterwards in the Eighty-sixth Ohio volunteer infantry and One Hundred and Seventy-first Ohio National guard, being in the service about fifteen months. After the war Mr. Gilbert read law in the office of Jones & Case at Youngstown, and was admitted to the bar in 1867 at Canfield. He located for practice temporarily at Niles, but after about four months removed to Maysville, Union county, Ohio, and from there in 1871 removed to Cleveland, where he is in full practice. He was married in 1867 to Anna M., daughter of Joseph Allen, one of the pioneers of Bristol township.

J. M. Compton is engaged in the insurance business in West Farmington. He represents the best companies and does a good business.

Mr. Compton is a young man of enterprise and strict integrity, and his business is fast increasing.

EARLY TOWNSHIP ELECTIONS.

Previous to the year 1817, the south part of Windsor, with Mesopotamia, Farmington, and Southington, composed one election district, or precinct. The elections were generally held in Mesopotamia, and Seth I. Ensign for a long time was clerk, and kept the records, which were made in a plain, good handwriting. Also the same territory composed one military district, and they held their trainings alternately in the several townships.

The first election held in the township of Farmington was on the 4th of July, 1817, of which the following record was made:

Poll-book of election held in Farmington township on the 4th day of July, 1817; Josiah Wolcott, chairman, Dennis Lewis and Horace Wolcott, judges of election. Theodore Wolcott was elected clerk; David Belden, Orrin Taft, and John Benton, trustees; Gad Hart, Jacob Bartholomew, overseers of the poor; Joseph Wolcott, Gad Bartholomew, fence viewers; Erastus Wolcott and Ezra Curtis, appraisers of property; Ezra Curtis, lister; Whitney Smith, Zenas Curtis, and Joseph H. Wolcott, supervisors of highways; Erastus Wolcott, constable; and Horace Wolcott, treasurer.

Poll-book of an election held in Farmington on the 5th of July, 1817, for one justice of the peace; David Belden, Aaron Taft, and John Benton, judges of election. Theodore Wolcott and Dennis Lewis were severally sworn, as the law directs, previous to their entering on the duties of office. It is by us certified that the number of electors at this election is twenty-five; and we do hereby certify that Josiah Wolcott had twenty-two votes, and was elected justice of the peace.

Signed by the proper officers. Then comes the following notice:

Notice is hereby given to the qualified electors of Farmington township to convene at their usual place of holding elections, on the second Tuesday of October next, for the purpose of electing two representatives, one county commissioner, and one sheriff.
BENJAMIN AUSTIN,
Sheriff of Trumbull county.
Warren, September 22, 1817.

Then follow the poll-books. The number of electors voting were seven, viz: Orrin Taft, David Belden, Lewis Wolcott, Ephraim White, Theodore Wolcott, Whitney Smith, and Jacob Bartholomew. Lyman Potter and William Ripley had each seven votes for representative; Reuben Clark had seven votes for commissioner; and Andrew Bushnell had seven votes for sheriff.

April 15, 1819, pursuant to an act of Assembly, the trustees contracted with the different persons as follow: Lewis Wolcott, to make nineteen rods of turnpike on State road, and twenty-nine rods of cross-waying, for $25; Orrin Taft, to make nineteen rods of crossing, to chop road sixty rods in length and thirty feet in width, for $10; Daniel Taft, to make twenty rods of cross-waying for $5; Joseph Wolcott to make nine rods of cross-waying, for $5; Roswell Lee, to make nine rods of cross-waying, for $5; Abijah Lee, to make ten rods of cross-waying, for $5.

On October 12, 1819, there was an election at which there were twenty-one votes, as follow: Joshua P. Danford, Chauncey Taft, Socrates Loveland, Josiah Wolcott (2d), John Benton, John Moffitt, John Wolcott, Ezra Curtis, Erastus Wolcott, Jacob Bosley, A. Taft, Josiah Wolcott, Roswell Lee, Theodore Wolcott, Daniel Taft, Ora Kibbee, Dennis Lewis, Abijah Lee, Abiel Jones, Jr., Gad Hart, Ebenezer White. Lemuel Reeves, sheriff; Martin Smith and Benjamin Austin, commissioners; Henry Manning and Harry Lane, Representatives; and voted for a convention.

EARLY INCIDENTS.

It is related of Joshua Danforth that he met a bear in the woods one day, when he had no weapon with him except an axe. Joshua was a great chopper, and when the bear came at him he jumped upon a fallen log and began chopping, making chips fly in bruin's face so fast that the animal soon beat a hasty retreat.

Captain Benton was out hunting turkeys one day, and became so engrossed in the sport that he forgot to take note of his wanderings. Near night he discovered that he was lost, also that he had but one charge of ammunition left and that one was in his gun. He took matters very coolly and began to retrace his steps, hoping thus to arrive at some spot with which he was acquainted. While picking his way carefully, an ominous sound fell upon his ears; he knew well what it was, and he fully realized the peril of his situation. Darkness was gathering; he was alone and lost, and worse yet, the wolves were after him. But he was a bold man, and pressed onward. Soon the sound came nearer; another minute and he could see fierce eyes glaring at him in the darkness. Something must be done, and that speedily. Stumbling over an old log with punk-wood in it an idea entered his head. Discharging the contents of his gun into the punk, the latter was set on fire. Hastily gathering some bark and other combustibles, the captain soon had a brisk fire blazing. The wolves were frightened away, and two of the captain's neighbors, Eden Wildman and Erastus Wolcott, who were in search of him, guided by the report of the gun, found the lost man and conducted him home.

Gad Bartholomew and Lewis Wolcott were fast friends. Each had his eccentricities and peculiarities. Gad kept bachelor's hall for some time after he settled here. His friend Lewis, talking with him one day, asked him if he was not lonely in his house at night. Gad replied that he was frequently; and that he sometimes heard scratching and other odd noises about his dwelling, which sounded unpleasantly. Lewis suggested that the sounds were probably made by a bear, and added, by way of advice, "If you are ever attacked by a bear, climb a tree." One day Gad was out in the woods alone chopping. He got to thinking of Lewis' advice, and wondered if he could carry it into effect if necessary. The more he thought of it the more strongly did he preceive the soundness of the advice; and finally, for the sake of practice, he selected a tree, imagined there was a bear after him, put his arms and feet around it, and scrambled away as fast as he could climb. After some moments of vigorous exertion, as there was no real danger, he became tired, and so stopped to see how far he had ascended. To say that he was astonished at the result of his efforts would give but a faint idea of the state of his mind as he looked about—for lo! he sat flat on the ground just where he had started. He could not climb.

When Gad went back to Connecticut to "buy himself a wife," he took his money (silver) in a buckskin purse in his pocket. Before he had gone very far a heavy shower come on, accompanied by thunder and lightning. Gad was afraid the lightning would strike him because of the silver in his pocket. He, therefore, cut a long pole, tied his purse upon the end of it, and with this novel lightning rod proceeded on his way, feeling quite safe. He succeeded in his mission, and returned to Henshaw with one of the best of wives.

MILITIA.

The following document presents a roll of the militia of Farmington and Southington. Unfortunately the original has no date upon it.

Old residents, however, think that the paper was probably a roll for the year 1821:

A ROLL OF THE FIFTH COMPANY, SECOND REGIMENT, FIRST BRIGADE, AND FOURTH DIVISION OF OHIO MILITIA.

COMMISSIONED OFFICERS.

Captain Ephraim White.
Lieutenant Erastus Wolcott.
Ensign William W. Burley.

NON-COMMISSIONED OFFICERS.

Sergeant Roswell Lee.
Sergeant Stephen Crawford.
Sergeant Isaac Lee.
Sergeant Stephen Osborn.
Corporal Chester Canfield.
Corporal Harmon Hurd.
Corporal Tom Walden.
Drummer Joy Hurd.
Fifer Comfort Hurd.

PRIVATES.

Gad Bartholomew, Harvey Belden, Burrage Belden, David Curtis, Jr., James Chalker, Francis Curtis, Joshua C. Danford, Lemuel Frisby, Jonathan Hethman, Silas Higgins, Horace Norton, Roderick Norton, Leonard Osborn, Stephen Osborn, Gilbert Osborn, Rufus Rice, Benjamin Viets, Jonathan Walden, Horace Wolcott, Josiah Wolcott, Josiah W. Wolcott, Levi Ormsby, James Nutt, John Wolcott, Asahel Belden, Wolcott Belden, Newton Wolcott, John Moffit, Ira Hyde, Eli Hyde, Ithemur Linscott, Daniel Warner, Samuel Horton (Haughton?), Retus Horton, David Hatch, Garrett L. Grossbeck, Chauncy Taft, Asa Walden, Milton Rice, Abiel Jones, Willis Curtis, Elisha Bosley, Elisha Brunsen, Smith Hurd, Chauncy Curtis, Ebenezer White, John Bosley, Orrin Taft, Joseph Rice, Levi Fowler, Eden Wildman, Ezekiel Wilcox, Willard Curtis, Levi Abrams, Philip Griffith, Amos Eastman, Chester Canfield, Elkhara Dibble, Dennis Lewis, Fredom Hurd, Eleazer D. Lamoine, Lawrence Bennet, John Benton, Volney Bemis, Newton Rice, Harmon Hurd, Samuel H. Joy, Martin Rexford, Edmund P. Wolcott, John Hethman, Socrates Loveland, Alexander Crawford, Ransley Curtis, Austin Smith, Harry B. Stannard, Austin Walden, Elisha Walden, Horace Harper, Shelden Curtis, Francis Curtis, David Belden, William Wolcott, William Bolley, Daniel Maltby, ——— Knapp.

EARLY EVENTS.

The first marriage—both parties living here—was Mr. Louis Wolcott to Miss Nancy Higgins, December 1, 1808. She was the daughter of widow Higgins, then the second wife of Josiah Wolcott.

The second marriage was that of Horace Wolcott to Miss Sabrina Tracy, daughter of 'Squire Tracy, of Mesopotamia. This wedding took place December 15, 1808, her father performing the ceremony. Horace had been helping his father build a cattle shed of logs and shakes, up to about 4 o'clock P. M., when he brushed the mud off his hands and said: "Father, I believe

I will not work any more to-day. I am going up to Mesopotamia to be married to-night. Won't you go up?" The father said he guessed not, it was too far. So Horace washed up, put on his best suit (which was not the finest broadcloth), and went on foot to Mesopotamia and was married.

As far as known Caroline Wolcott, afterward the wife of George L. Holmes, was the first child born in Farmington. She was born September 12, 1808. Both she and her husband are now dead. The second child was Joseph H. Wolcott, son of Lewis and Nancy (Higgins) Wolcott. He is now living in Kansas.

The first frame house erected in Farmington township was built by Daniel R. Wolcott, oldest son of Josiah Wolcott, in 1820. It was erected on the south side of the common, or southeast corner of the center, and is yet standing and in good repair. It was for a long time the residence of H. W. Collar, Esq., and was afterwards owned and occupied for a number of years by Captain James Caldwell, and later still, the residence of S. J. Buttles. During the same season, or soon after, a frame house was built in West Farmington, on the northeast corner where the Palmer brick now stands. It was erected by Theodore Wolcott, and afterwards owned and occupied for a long time by Lewis Wolcott, son of Theodore. Theodore Wolcott built a house about half a mile south, where Mrs. S. S. Spencer now lives, and where he lived until his death. About the year 1823 or 1824 a frame house was built on the northwest corner at the center, where T. Hall's house now stands. The frame was put up and enclosed, the roof put on, and the chimney built all in one day. The most of the timber used in its construction was taken from the stump. This house was built for Dr. Abiel Jones. Captain Ira Hyde built the chimney. They had plenty of good old rye whiskey, and when they got through, the captain said he could not see but that the chimney was perfectly straight, but next morning they discovered it was a little crooked.

The first school-house in Farmington was built in the spring of 1816, and located near a pear tree and a spring on the northeast corner at the center. Captain Benton and Josiah Wolcott cut the logs for the school-house one snowy day, and Erastus Wolcott hauled them with an ox team. Captain Benton, although the day was cold, wore a pair of linen pants with holes in the knees.

The first school kept in this house was taught by Miss Almira Hannahs, of Nelson, afterwards the wife of Erastus Wolcott. There was also the same or the next season a log school-house built at West Farmington and located near where the store building, built by Kibbee & Loveland, now stands, and the first school kept in that was taught by Miss Nancy Wolcott, who afterwards became the wife of Silas Higgins.

MANNERS AND CUSTOMS.

The houses of the early settlers were all built of logs, and seldom was a board or a nail used in their construction. Floors of puncheons, chimneys of sticks and mud, hearths of mortar, and lights of hickory bark were some of the usual necessary articles found in the pioneer's dwelling.

Gowns were made from flax, spun and woven by the wearers. When colors were desired butternut and black walnut bark furnished them. The gentlemen wore garments of tow and linen in summer and buckskin or woolen in winter. Shoes and boots were worn very sparingly, as their cost was great. Sociability and hospitality prevailed.

HOTELS.

The first tavern in the township was kept in a log building where William Wilson lived in 1810. Afterwards a frame addition, then a frame house took its place. Huff, James, Joseph Whiting, the Tafts, Herner and others were early landlords. William Kennedy at length bought the property and continued the business. Herner sold liquor and incurred the hostility of the temperance people, and was prosecuted two or three times. Afterwards one or two attempts were made to run a saloon at the center, but the citizens rose in opposition and from that time to this Farmington township has been singularly free from the pernicious influence of the rumseller. There are now two hotels in the township, both at West Farmington—the Lewis house, of long standing, and the house of E. Trunkey, just opposite.

The old red tavern on the State road ceased to be a house of entertainment about 1847.

STORES.

The first store in the township was opened in 1825 on the southeast corner at the center by Mr. Stewart, of Vienna. He was succeeded by Tucker & Crowell; then, about 1833, E. P. Wolcott engaged in the mercantile business, and he and his sons carried it on nearly all of the time for over forty years.

The first merchant at West Farmington was Austin D. Kibbee, who in 1834 kept store in part of his own house. Later he built a store opposite his residence. He was succeeded by Higgins & Wolcott. Kibbee & Wolcott then conducted the business alone for some years. Mr. Kibbee has done more to promote the growth of the village than any other man.

CHURCHES.

The Congregational church at Farmington center was organized on the union plan October 8, 1817, by Revs. Joseph Badger and Abiel Jones, and consisted of eleven members, viz: Abiel and Rebecca Jones, Josiah and Nancy Wolcott, David and Elizabeth Curtis, David and Lois Belden, Eunice Hart, Polly Benton, and Rebecca Jones. The same year Theodore Wolcott, Rhoda Wolcott, and Gad Hart were admitted November 2d. The church grew slowly until 1825. Twenty-six members were added during that year. From 1818 to 1823 inclusive, Rev. Abiel Jones baptized twenty children, and on the 10th of July, 1825, forty children were baptized by Rev. Luther H. Humphrey.

November 22, 1817, Josiah and Theodore Wolcott were chosen deacons. February 4, 1820, David Belden and Gad Hart were elected church committee. About the same date the church was placed under the care of the Grand River presbytery. The first missionaries and preachers were Revs. Badger, Leslie, Darrow, Jones, and others. In 1860 the church became wholly Presbyterian and so continued until 1874, since which time it has been purely Congregational.

The first church edifice was built on or near the site of the present one about the year 1828. It was a frame house 40x50 feet, with a steeple, and continued to be used until 1850. The present house was then erected at a cost of $1,400. The membership is now small and no regular preaching is supported.

The Congregational church of West Farmington was organized April 12, 1834, by Rev. Daniel Miller, and consisted of sixteen male and twenty-three female members, nearly all of whom withdrew from the church at the center of Farmington to join. This church has enjoyed a fair degree of prosperity, and now has a nice house and a good membership.

The Methodist Episcopal church first formed a class in the fall of 1818, in the old log schoolhouse, built the same year, in east Farmington. This class consisted of seven members, viz: Eden Wildman, his wife and wife's mother; Joel Hyde, wife, and daughter; and Mrs. Moffatt. Rev. Ira Eddy was the organizer. The congregation sat on blocks of wood and the sleepers of the house. Rev. Eddy, Jacob Baker, and Father Wilber, were among the first preachers.

About 1830 a frame meeting-house, much like a barn, was erected in east Farmington. A class was organized, which met for several years on the old State road, then concentrated with a class formed at West Farmington later, and built the church at the latter place. The old church at east Farmington was replaced by another built about 1837, and in 1874 the Methodists and Disciples erected the present house of worship. The building at the center, now the town hall, was erected for a Methodist church; but as the congregation were unable to complete it, the township trustees purchased and finished. In 1861 a class in the southeast of the township erected a small church edifice which is still used. The three churches—West Farmington, east Farmington, and southeast Farmington, now form one charge. The Methodists are quite strong and zealously support the preaching of the gospel.

A copy of the first subscription ever taken in Farmington for supporting the gospel by preaching, is given in full below:

Know all men by these presents That we, the Inhabitants of Township No. 6, in the Range 5, called Henshaw, with the neighboring towns, viz: Bristol, Mesopotamia, Parkman, and Bowleston—(Southington), feeling the importance of public instruction by preaching the Gospel for ourselves and children, etc. We do by these presents bind ourselves, our heirs, executors, administrators firmly, to pay the sums annexed to each of our names annually without fraud or delay, for the term of three years, to the Rev. Giles Cowles, beginning as soon as the said Mr. Cowles shall remove his family to the said town of Henshaw to live. The pay to be made in wheat, Rye, corn, oats, potatoes, mess pork, whiskey, etc. The produce of farms as shall be needed by the said Mr.

Cowles and family together with chopping, logging, fencing, etc. We agree, likewise, should any contribute anything within said term of three years, towards the support of the said Mr. Cowles, it shall be deducted according to the sum annexed to each man's name. We likewise agree that the preaching in each town shall be in proportion to what each town subscribes for said preaching. We likewise agree that a committee of one man be appointed in each town to take oversight of said business. We agree further that notwithstanding this subscription shall terminate with the above period; yet his establishment here as a preacher is permanent and yet we may make such regulations and alterations as our circumstances may require, as to our limits, and method of proceeding, etc. Thus we covenant, agree, and bind ourselves, etc., in writing thereof we have hereunto set our hands

HENSHAW, July 26, 1816.

Josiah Wolcott	$30.00
David Curtis	8.00
William Wilson	10.00
Gad Hart	12.
Zenas Curtis, Jr.,	6.
Lewis Wolcott	7.
Josiah Wolcott	5.
Gad Bartholomew	10.
Ezra Curtis	5.
John D. Heathman	7.
Joshua P. Danford	8.
Dennis Lewis	10.
Jacob Bartholomew	.13
Amos P. Woodford	8.
Horace Wolcott	7.00
Subscribers at Bristol	77.25

The price that the within mentioned produce is to be paid in, viz:

Wheat	$1.00 per bushel
Corn	new 50 cents, old .75 per bushel
Rye	.75 per bushel
Oats	.34
Potatoes	34
Flax	12 per lb.
Linnen cloth	34 per yrd
Whiskey	.75 per gall.
Beef	4.00 per cwt.
Pork	6.00 per c "

Chopping, logging, and fencing at the common price.

The Rev. Joseph Badger had been here and preached previous to this time, and as also had other missionaries.

In 1818 Abijah Lee, a Baptist, settled in Farmington with his family. In 1828 a great revival took place in Kirtland under the Disciple preachers, Bentley and Rigdon. Isaac Lee, a son of Abijah, who attended their meetings, was converted and returned to Farmington in 1829. He found Harvey Brockett much awakened on the subject of religion. Lee converted him to the new faith, and Brockett was baptized by him. Benjamin Alton soon came and preached, and in 1830 a church was formed, numbering about twenty members with Abijah Lee leader. This church received from the Baptists Abijah Lee and Daniel Davidson and their wives.

Isaac Lee and Harvey Brockett preached and exhorted successfully, and soon a strong working congregation was gathered into the fold. Other early Disciple preachers who labored here, were Revs. Applegate, Bosworth, Hayden, Collins, Clapp, and Hartzell.

This congregation is now prosperous, and owns one-half of the union church in east Farmington.

MISSIONARY SOCIETY.

The Woman's Foreign Missionary society, Akron district, was organized at West Farmington, June 2, 1879, when the officers of the auxiliary were elected as follow: Mrs. E. A. Lamberson, president; Miss A. Young, Mrs. J. Kennedy, Mrs. J. Hathaway, and Mrs. S. J. Taft, vice-presidents; Miss Augusta Goff, treasurer; Mrs. E. Thompson, recording secretary; Miss E. C. Greer, corresponding secretary.

Number of life members in the society, five; members, twenty-five.

MASONIC.

The Western Reserve lodge No. 507, Free and Accepted Masons, Farmington, Ohio, was granted a charter October 19, 1875, having been previously organized under a dispensation. Following are the names of the charter members: William M. Smith, H. H. Hatch, O. P. Barton, Ervin Johnson, E. T. Barton, C. S. Thompson, F. K. Lewis, A. L. Wolcott, E. B. Williams, C. S. Curtis, and H. H. Pulsifer.

The following were the first officers elected after the lodge received its charter: H. H. Hatch, W. M.; C. S. Thompson, S. W.; D. T. Smith, J. W.; Ervin Johnson, treasurer; E. T. Barton, secretary; F. K. Lewis, S. D.; William B. Loveland, J. D.; William M. Smith, tyler. The lodge now numbers forty members.

PHYSICIANS.

The first physician in the township was Dr. Abiel Jones, who acted in the double capacity of doctor and preacher. Dr. Belden, now of Youngstown, was an efficient practitioner of medicine in West Farmington for a number of years. At present Drs. Latimer and Palmer, both of the Eclectic school, furnish the medical aid required.

THE CEMETERY

is on a knoll of ground midway between the center and West Farmington. It presents a beautiful appearance; is nicely fenced off, and the grounds are well cared for, and it is here many of the pioneer settlers of the township are buried. It is under the control of the township trustees, who have erected a capacious vault.

The soldiers' monument is a beautiful marble structure erected in the cemetery at West Farmington by the citizens of the township in commemoration of the gallant services rendered by the soldiers from Farmington in the late war of the Rebellion. It has the names of those who lost their lives on the field of battle, or who died from wounds in the hospital, inscribed upon it, as follows: Homer H. Stull, lieutenant; William T. True, B. F. Kennedy, Newton F. Wolcott, Calvin Caldwell, Adelbert M. Hart, Ira Wildman, Charles E. Richards, William Dana, Henry Lovell, E. E. Daly, A. Clark Flick, Leander H. Wolcott, George W. Moffit, Virgil N. Weir, Almon A. Lew, Hamlet B. Belden, William Wilberforce Strickland, Judson S. Curtis, Thomas F. Hall, Jesse D. Kinear, Joseph J. Brown, Henry Steel, Robert Mathews, John O. Caldwell, Morris W. Freeman, Sylvanus Housel, Frank G. Palmer, John W. Kingard, Frank Proctor, Edmond E. Kinear, August W. Show, Charles W. Gilbert, Stephen Wildman.

The monument cost $1,400, and was erected and dedicated in 1865, James A. Garfield making the speech on that occasion.

POST-OFFICES.

About 1831 Farmington post-office was established on the State road, Epaphroditus Fuller, postmaster.

As early as 1834 an office was established at the center, Daniel Wilcox postmaster.

About 1847 the Farmington office was removed from the State road to West Farmington, the center office being discontinued. Then began a war between the two villages for the possession of the office, which lasted through many years, but was finally settled by the re-establishment of the Farmington center office. The name of the other office was then changed to West Farmington.

INDUSTRIES.

The first mill in Farmington was a saw-mill built a little southwest of the center, on Grand river, by Deacon Josiah Wolcott as principal,

assisted by Eastman Small, part owner and mill-wright, about the year 1816. This was a rude structure, and in about three years was superseded by another built by Wolcott, principal, and Russell, assistant and mill-wright. It was owned afterwards by Reynolds & Co., then by Kibbee, Malby & Co. In 1861 a flax-mill was added which manufactured about twelve tons of flax straw per year, and gave employment to from ten to twenty-five hands. It was burned down in 1871, and a flour- and grist-mill was afterwards erected with a capacity of grinding about seventy-five bushels of grain per day.

The Bosley mill was an original affair consisting of a saw-mill and then a grist-mill. The Bosleys sold out to Smith & Kibbee, of Warren, and they in turn to Snow, Taft & Co., who added a blacksmith and wagon shop, and made wagons years but eventually failed. It is now owned by William H. & E. S. Higgins. It is in the southwest part of the township.

Both these mills are run by steam and by water. The capacity of this latter mill is about the same as that of the Wolcott mill.

Of the manufactories in West Farmington may be mentioned that of the Standard Chair company. It was started in June, 1881, with a capital stock of $3,500. The officers of the company consist of Dr. O. A. Palmer, president; C. S. Thompson, agent, and F. J. Wolcott, secretary.

The building just erected is a commodious affair, 24x60 feet, two stories in height. The company contemplate building an addition to the main structure, and putting in machinery, and will then give employment to about sixteen hands.

The original cabinet factory, formerly owned by Bowles, was purchased by C. S. Thompson in 1871, and afterward by C. A. Miller in 1873, and is now operated under the name of Miller & Co., whose enterprise gives employment to about fifteen hands and turns out ten tables per day.

Two cheese factories are now in successful operation in this township. For several years there have been three running. Cheese making is one of the principal sources of income to the people of this township.

West Farmington is a thriving little town, having a population of four hundred and fifty. It

Rev. William Kincaid.

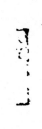

is west of the center, and contains some half-dozen stores, two hotels, two livery stables, two churches, two factories, the Western Reserve seminary, and is the abode of a cultivated and highly refined community. It is on the Painesville & Youngstown Narrow-guage railroad, fourteen miles from Warren. The location of the town is as healthy as is generally found, and there are no saloons of any kind in the place.

The center is somewhat less in size, but it has a town hall, a good store and two or three shops. A good sidewalk connects the two villages.

WESTERN RESERVE SEMINARY.

This institution is located on the Painesville & Youngstown railroad, fourteen miles from Warren, and receives a large patronage from this and adjoining counties. It was originally established in 1831, and known as the Farmington academy until 1849. The building then used is the present hotel owned by E. Trunkey. James Greer was the first president or principal of this institution and was very successful in his management, the attendance averaging some years as many as three hundred students. In 1849 it had so far outgrown the expectations of its founders that it became necessary to erect new buildings capable of accommodating a larger number of students. By liberal donations from the citizens of the vicinity, a fine three-story brick building was erected, and a school started under the name of the Farmington Normal school.

In 1854 the trustees transferred the control of the institution to the Erie annual conference of the Methodist Episcopal church, on the condition that they should maintain a first-class school, in which all sects and denominations should have equal rights and privileges. At this time the name of the institution was changed to Western Reserve seminary and a faculty employed that would compare favorably with any in the country. In 1868 two commodious boarding halls were erected and furnished, which have been a great benefit to the school in enabling students, by means of club boarding, to reduce their expenses to the lowest possible cost. The control is vested in a board of trustees. The laboratory is supplied with large and well selected apparatus for the elucidation of the natural sciences, and the library is well filled with the

works of standard authors in the various departments of literature. The courses of study are comprehensive, and the charter gives the institution power to confer the highest academic honors on those who complete the course successfully.

The faculty consists of Rev. E. B. Webster, M. A., president; assisted by Ernest Moench, M. A., Mrs. E. B. Webster, Professor A. Truman, B. A. Norville, C. W. Harshman, H. L. Steves, and H. B. Steele. There are three structures in the campus. The seminary is a substantial brick, has served for many years, and although old and too small for their increasing demand, yet it is in good repair and presents a very respectable appearance. Its many friends are talking earnestly of erecting a larger one in the near future.

Cory hall, erected by Rev. and Mrs. J. B. Cory for the accommodation of lady students, is 84 x 30 feet, three stories high, and presents a fine appearance. The principal and family reside in it and have general supervision. A large dining-room and kitchen are provided where students are boarded at cost.

Young Men's hall is a building 70 x 34 feet, two stories high. It will accommodate fifty young men. One professor lives in it.

Two well organized and successful societies, the Philomathean and Lumæan, afford excellent opportunities for literary exercises. The president, Rev. E. B. Webster, yet a young man, is a graduate of Mt. Union college, Ohio. He took charge of the institution in the year 1877 under the most adverse circumstances, the school having been run down to the insignificant number of only fifteen students. He summoned his energies, threw himself into the work, and succeeded in opening his first term of school with that number just doubled. By close attention to the duties then devolving upon him he succeeded in regaining the confidence of the former adherents of the institution and opened the first term of his second year in the work with one hundred and thirty students. Since that time the seminary has been increasing its numbers until now the daily average attendance is about three hundred. He is devoted to his work and is assisted by his wife and a well chosen corps of professors.

BIOGRAPHICAL SKETCHES.

JOEL AND ELIZA PECK.

Joel Peck was the son of Jesse Peck and was born in Pompey, Canandaigua county, New York, December 22, 1801. His father, Jesse Peck, was a lad during the Revolution and at the age of sixteen joined the patriot army, in a company commanded by his father. He removed to Farmington, Trumbull county, in the year 1821, and settled on the farm now owned by Mrs. Eliza Peck. The family consisted of four children—Charles, Benjamin, Polly, and Joel, the subject of this sketch.

Joel Peck married January 23, 1822, Eliza Hyde, daughter of Joseph and Eunice (Hall) Hyde. Her father, Joel Hyde, was born January 24, 1773; was married in 1793 to Eunice Hall, in Huntington, Fairfield county, Connecticut, whence they removed to Montgomery county, New York. They had four daughters and one son (who died in youth), viz: Hannah, born in 1794; Sarah, 1796; Mary, 1798; and Eliza, born September 26, 1800. In the year 1818 Joel Hyde with his family in company with his brother Ira and Abijah Lee left their New York home and after a journey of six weeks arrived in Farmington. The three youngest daughters taught school, Sarah in Southington, Mary in Bristol, and Eliza in Champion. Eliza also taught the first summer school in east Farmington. Hannah married in 1818 Levi Abrams, Sarah in 1822 Comfort Hurd, Mary in 1830 Azra Brown, a Methodist minister, and Eliza, as above noted, Joel Peck.

Joel and Eliza Peck had a family of three children—Delia, Allen F., and Fletcher W. Delia was born in 1825, was married to James C. Howard, then of Kentucky, in 1851, and resides in Butler county, Ohio. Allen F. was born in 1829, studied medicine and practiced in Farmington; was married to Cordia Fuller in 1865; was assistant surgeon during the war in a cavalry regiment and afterwards located in Cleveland, where he died in 1878. He was six feet seven inches tall and acquired a good reputation as a practitioner of medicine.

Fletcher W. Peck was born in 1831, was married to Coresta Smith, of Farmington, in 1856, and resides on a farm two miles north of the center. The past, in this timbered country, was a generation of hardy, resolute men, strong both in muscle and courage. The work required to maintain life was an effectual barrier against the weak and timid. It thus occurs that simple truth requires us to say of almost every pioneer that he was industrious, iron-muscled, and a hard worker. Particularly was this true of Joel Peck. He was six feet two inches tall, compact and symmetrical and was never sick until shortly before his death, though for ten years or more his eyesight was seriously impaired by cataract. During his life-time Mr. Peck improved more than three hundred acres of land. Early in life he united with the Methodist church and became one of its most steadfast supporters and valuable assistants to the itinerant clergy. He was an earnest exhorter, and being a licensed local preacher, often conducted the service. When money was wanted he was the main standby. In politics Mr. Peck always voted and co-operated with the most radical anti-slavery sentiment. He was a Whig, Free-soiler, and Republican. He never sought or desired office, and was consequently free to support his convictions with his vote. He died September 25, 1869, in his sixty-eighth year.

Mrs. Peck is a woman greatly esteemed in Farmington, because of her sincerity, kindness of heart and sympathy of feeling. Her church association has always been with her husband. Simple, unquestioning, confident belief is the conforting angel of her declining years. She often spoke fervently and earnestly in religious gatherings. In the home she was always honest and truthful, and has left upon her children the impress of an excellent character. Since the death of her husband Mrs. Peck has managed the farm.

REV. WILLIAM KINCAID.

The grandparents of Rev. William Kincaid were John and Martha (Hill) Kincaid, of Scotch descent, who emigrated from Ireland to this country, and settled near Chambersburg, Pennsylvania, in the last century. From their first location they emigrated to Washington county, Pennsylvania, and settled near Williamsport. About the year 1800 they came to Youngstown, and remained until the end of their days.

John Kincaid was the father of three sons and four daughters, all of whom lived to marry and have families. Robert, the second child, was about twenty-one when the family came to Ohio. He married Margaret Erwin soon after. She was a native of Virginia, daughter of Christopher and Mary Erwin. She reared a large family, ten children in all, seven sons and three daughters. Of this number, four sons and two daughters are still living. William, the fourth child of Robert and Margaret Kincaid, was born April 15, 1812, and passed his early life in Youngstown, his native place. He received a common school education; was brought up a farmer, and has made tilling the soil his business. Mr. Kincaid was married in 1833 to Mary Erwin, daughter of Joseph and Margaret Erwin, of Youngstown. She was born in 1815; died June 15, 1872. This union was blessed by nine children, seven of whom survive. The family record is as follows: Margaret, born October 29, 1834; Sherman, born September 20, 1835; Mary, born June 9, 1837; Robert, born March 4, 1839, died March 10, 1841; Ammiel, born February 27, 1841; Martha J., born December 26, 1843; John W., born March 5, 1845, died September 16, 1864, at Washington, District of Columbia, was in company D, Second Ohio cavalry; Caroline M., born December 27, 1850; William A., January 12, 1855.

The children are all married, and with the exception of Martha, who lives in Ashtabula county, all reside in this county.

In 1831 Mr. Kincaid joined the Methodist Episcopal church, and has since been one of its most devoted adherents. His wife was also a member; she lived a pure, useful life, characterized by Christian benevolence and good works.

In 1845 Mr. Kincaid was licensed as an exhorter in his church, and labored in that capacity nearly four years, when he was licensed as a local preacher, and continued almost constantly to keep regular appointments up to about four years ago. On account of poor health he was compelled to relinquish regular preaching, but he still officiates occasionally. During his work in the ministry he has filled appointments throughout this region—from the Pennsylvania State line westward into Portage and Geauga counties, and north into Ashtabula. His labors have been blessed by the Master. Mr. Kincaid can look back over the long period of years in which he has been a preacher with the satisfaction of knowing that he has been the instrument of promoting the cause which he so dearly loves. He is held in high esteem by a large circle of acquaintances.

SETTLEMENT NOTES.

Joseph Chauncey Hart, Sr., was born in Avon, Connecticut, in 1804; married Hannah Goff, born in West Springfield, Massachusetts, September 11, 1807. They came to Ohio with their family in 1840, and settled in Farmington where they resided until their death. They raised a family of thirteen children, as follows: Hiram S., a blacksmith, of Gustavus; Sarah L. (deceased); J. C., Jr., a farmer, of Southington; Frances (Mrs. Fries), Sarah J. (Taft), Ann Jeanette (Mrs. Maltbie), all of Farmington; J. O., of the clothing firm of Hart Brothers, Warren; A. L., insurance agent, Warren; C. O., of the firm of Hart Brothers, and now county treasurer; V. M., now engaged in stock raising in the Indian Territory; Adelbert M., who was in the army during the Rebellion, taken prisoner, and confined in a rebel prison for sixteen months, died on his way home December 11, 1864, and was buried at sea; M. C., an attorney, of Cleveland; and Arlington M. (deceased). J. C. Hart, Sr., died in Farmington March 19, 1867, aged sixty-three years. Mrs. Rosannah Hart died at West Farmington January 4, 1880, in her seventy-third year. Mrs. Hart, or "Aunt Rosa," as she was familiarly called by her acquaintances, was a woman of more than ordinary endowments, both of mind and heart, the religious element being predominant in her nature. She was energetic and persevering and being blessed with a good physical organization she was well equipped for life's duties. The poor and needy were often made the recipients of her benefactions, and when she died her loss came as a personal bereavement to every one within the circle of her acquaintance.

Dr. Allen F. Peck was born in Farmington, Trumbull county, Ohio, February 5, 1828. He studied medicine and graduated at the College of Physicians and Surgeons, New York city, and also at the Western Reserve Medical college, Cleveland. He practiced his profession in Springfield, Illinois, and in Omaha, and also in Santa Fe, New Mexico. While in the latter place he enlisted in the First New Mexico cavalry, Colonel Kit Carson's regiment, and served three years, being surgeon of the regiment. He was mustered out in the fall of 1864, on account of physical disability. October 19, 1865, he married Miss Cordie A., daughter of Ephraim and Mary Fuller, who was born in Farmington, February 6, 1845. Her father was a native of Massachusetts, born in 1798, and removed to Ohio in 1825, settling in Farmington. He was a major in the militia, and postmaster at Taftsburg, Farmington. He died in 1874. Dr. Peck continued to reside in Farmington after his marriage, engaged in the practice of his profession until the spring of 1871, when he removed to Cleveland, where he resided four years. In 1875 he went to Akron, but returned again to Cleveland in 1877. He died February 21, 1878. Mrs. Peck now resides in Warren with her family, which consists of two children: Frank J., born September 7, 1866, and Cora M., born April 25, 1871. Her second child, Flora L., died in infancy.

CHAPTER VI.

BRISTOL.

INTRODUCTORY.

Bristol is geographically situated as follows: with Bloomfield on the north, Mecca on the east, Champion on the south, and Farmington on the west. The Ashtabula and Warren turnpike runs through the township from north to south, west of the center. The Ashtabula, Youngstown & Pittsburg railroad crosses the eastern half of the township in the same direction, and has two stations for the accommodation of the public—Bristolville and Oakland. The former is a mile east of the village of Bristolville, and the latter an equal distance from North Bristol.

Bristolville, or in local parlance "the center," is pleasantly situated about half a mile from the geographical center of the township, and is a neat, quiet country village of some forty houses. In the center of the village is a tasty little public square, with ornamental shade trees. In the center of the square is the soldiers' monument,

erected to the memory of the patriots of the township who died in their country's service. Two fine churches, well built and well furnished, and a good school building, speak well for the intelligence of the community.

North Bristol is a smaller village, on the turnpike, a mile north of Bristolville, and contains one church, one store, a mill, etc.

The people of the township are industrious, economical, sober-minded, and thrifty. Mixed agriculture, dairying, and sheep and cattle raising are the principal occupations. Good buildings and well-improved farms abound.

The soil is generally a clayey loam, with some sandy or gravelly ridges. The surface is generally very nearly level. The northern and northwestern portions have a few small hills in the vicinity of streams.

The drainage is carried northward by Center creek and Baughman's creek, tributaries to Grand river. The chief source of these streams is in the northern part of Champion. Deacon creek, which rises in that township, flows northward through the eastern part of Bristol until within about half a mile of the Bloomfield line, when it joins a small stream flowing west and northwest, which is thenceforth known as Baughman's creek. All these streams are small and unimportant.

The number of sugar orchards in this township is large. Many acres of apple orchards are also found. Sager's nursery for raising fruit and ornamental trees deserves mention.

SURVEY.

This township was surveyed early in the present century by Alfred Wolcott in behalf of the Connecticut Land company, from whom he received as payment for his services a grant of three hundred and fifty acres of land in the township. He built a cabin at the center during his stay here, which was the first building erected in the township.

THE PIONEERS.

Abraham Baughman was the first actual settler. In 1804 he brought his family and settled on the creek which bears his name. His cabin, the first one erected excepting that of Wolcott, the surveyor, stood about one mile east of the turnpike and about three-fourths of a mile from the north line of the township. The land is now H. Satterlee's farm. Baughman and family removed to Richland county in 1816.

William Sager visited this township in 1802, or perhaps previously. In company with three other men he started from Shenandoah county, Virginia, to find in Ohio a suitable spot on which to settle. On reaching the Ohio river two of his companions refused to proceed farther into the wilderness and deserted him. The other came on with him and in due time both arrived within the present limits of Bristol. They camped one night in the forest, and after selecting a site for Mr. Sager's future home, started on their return trip. They went to Youngstown and from that place followed an Indian trail to the Ohio. Mr. Sager purchased of Wolcott, the surveyor, a piece of land on which he afterwards settled. On the 4th day of June, 1805, Mr. Sager and family arrived in the township. Stopping over night with his brother-in-law, Abraham Baughman, the next morning Mr. Sager, Mr. Baughman, and his two sons, Jacob and Abraham, proceeded to cut a road through the wilderness a mile and a half to Mr. Sager's land.

For a month or more, until a cabin could be constructed, Mr. Sager and his wife, with their one child, slept in his wagon. There was no sawed timber to be procured nearer than at Warren, therefore the cabin was built without the use of boards, as was generally the case with pioneer dwellings. Soon he succeeded in getting his logs together and had a cabin 18 x 20 feet in size. As soon as the lower floor was laid the family moved in. Mr. Sager hewed out a large plank for a work-bench and proceeded to finish off his dwelling. Thus its one room served all the uses of kitchen, sitting room, dining room, parlor, and work-shop. Mr. Sager was by trade a mill-wright, but here he found it necessary to act as carpenter, cabinet-maker, cooper, etc.

William Sager had married Mary Hammon, of German descent, before coming to Ohio, and they had one child, Joseph, born in 1802. Their son Jacob, born in 1805, was the first child born in this township. The names of the six other children were Sarah, John, Solomon, Anna, Rebecca, and William. John, Solomon, and Anna are dead. The others are all living: Joseph, Jacob, William, and Sarah in Bristol, and Rebecca (Hyde) in Farmington. All lived to rear families excepting Sarah, who remains single.

Gabriel Sager, William's father, emigrated from Germany about 1758, first settling in Bucks county, Pennsylvania, and thence removing to Shenandoah county, Virginia, where he reared a family of four sons and four daughters. His certificate of naturalization, issued by the Commonwealth of Pennsylvania in 1765, is now in possession of his grandson Joseph, and is as quaint and old fashioned as any document we have ever seen. Supreme court is printed "supream court," and other deviations from modern standards of orthography are numerous. Mr. Sager being in religion a Mennonite would not take an oath of naturalization but affirmed instead, and was given a paper similar to those issued to Quakers. In 1810 he removed to Bristol, and settled on the farm now owned by Edward Kibbee in the northern part of the township. His son Samuel settled on the same farm about 1811 and remained until 1816, when he removed to Beaver county, Pennsylvania, and lived the remainder of his days there. Gabriel Sager died about 1816 but his wife survived him several years. Their children who came to Ohio were William and Samuel, and the four daughters, viz: Elizabeth, wife of Abraham Baughman; Barbara, wife of William Barb; Margaret, wife of Henry Baughman; and Mary, wife of John Barb. The Baughmans remained but a few years, but both Barb families were permanent residents.

William Barb removed from Shenandoah county, Virginia, in 1801, to Bristol, Trumbull county, Ohio, and located where William Sager now lives. He subsequently exchanged this farm with the owner, Mr. Sager, and settled permanently on the place now owned by Martin J. Barb. He was the father of six children, five boys and one girl, named as follows: Gabriel, William, Jacob, Peter, Abraham, and Mary, all now dead. Abraham, who succeeded to the place after his father's death, was born there in 1809. He married Lydia Ann Curlin and raised a family of seven sons and six daughters, of whom four (sons) are deceased. He died January 7, 1868. Mrs. Barb is yet living and is now in her seventieth year. Their son, M. J. Barb, occupies the homestead where his grandfather settled so long ago and where his father always lived.

John Barb settled on the present Thayer farm

in 1816. He had a family of eight children, three of whom are still living. The names in order of age were: Abraham, Margaret, Elizabeth, Solomon, Polly, Jonathan, Barbara, and David. Those living are Margaret (Parker), Bristolville; Jonathan, Indiana; and Barbara (Thayer), North Bristol. Solomon and Elizabeth (Norton) passed their days in Bristol.

John Fansler settled north of Bristolville in 1806. His family was a large one. Two children died before reaching mature years. The following lived to marry and have families: Michael, John, Solomon, Moses, Samuel, Anna, George, David, and Margaret. Samuel and David now live in Bristol, George in Fowler, and Margaret in Iowa.

John and Sarah Hammon settled in 1806 where their son Jacob now resides. Statistics of their family have been mislaid and we are unable to give them.

Abraham, John, Jacob, and Isaac Kagy came at different dates, Abraham as early as 1820, and located on the east and west road in the eastern part of the township. Samuel and John, sons of Abraham, still reside in the township. Jacob, another of his sons, died in the service of his country. John, Jacob, and Isaac settled in the same neighborhood. Isaac never married. Some of John's children are still living here, viz: John, on the old homestead; Joseph, Jacob, and Michael. The latter lives on the old Abraham Kagy place.

Jacob Norton in 1806 settled in the northeast of the township. His children were Barbara, Henry, Catharine, Zachariah, George, Sally, Michael, David, and William. All lived in this vicinity and reared families. None are now living. Their descendants are numerous, influential and respected. The above were born after Mr. Norton's second marriage. By his first wife he had two sons in Virginia, John and Jacob, who afterwards moved to Ohio.

All of the families above named were of German origin and came to Bristol from Virginia. The township was but sparsely settled until after 1820.

Lyman Potter settled on a farm just south of the present village of Bristolville. After several years' residence he and his family removed from the township. He was the first justice of the peace in Bristol and was well qualified by nature

and education for the position, having received a liberal education with the intention (afterward abandoned) of entering the ministry.

Aaron Fenton, as early as 1805, settled on the farm now occupied by his son Aaron. His children were Daniel, William, Mary, Aaron, Abraham, Lydia, and Enoch. Daniel, William, Abraham, and Mary are dead. William spent his days in Bristol.

John Cox settled in the western part of the township in 1805. In 1816 William Cox came and settled opposite the road from him. William had no children, but John had enough for both. The most of his large family after marrying moved away. Following are the names of his children: Betsey, Abigail, John, Hannah, Peggy, Polly, Amy, Susan, Catharine, Japheth, and Martha. Of these only one, Mrs. Peggy Barb, now lives in Bristol. Timothy resides in Mesopotamia.

Captain Benjamin White was an early pioneer of the northwestern part of the township. He died during the War of 1812. His children were Samuel, Elijah, Patterson, Benjamin, and Polly (Smith). Samuel, well known as 'Squire White, still resides in Bristol.

John Lloyd located in the northwest of this township in 1814. He owned five hundred acres of land in Bristol and one thousand in Kirtland township, which he divided equally among his three children, Thomas, Lester, and Roxana. The Lloyds were from Massachusetts. The farm on which they settled had been improved to a small extent by John and Thomas Martin, who came here about 1807, but remained only a few years.

Emmor Moore settled in 1805 or 1806 on the present Curtis farm, on the turnpike, south of Bristolville. He died of consumption in 1810, and was buried in the township burying-ground at the center, it being the first interment of an adult person there made. The tombstone marking his grave has the oldest date of any in the cemetery. His son William married and settled in Bristol, but deserted his wife and left.

William, John, Thomas, James, and Joseph Cummings, with their sisters, Betsy, Anna, Polly, and Sally, were one of the very first families that settled in the township. They took up a farm near the southwest corner of Bristol. Several of the name still remain in the township.

Robert Miller was one of the first comers. He also located in the southwest of the township, but afterwards moved to the Gordon place on the turnpike. Two sons, James and John, are still residents of Bristol.

William Reed, Abraham Daily, and George Barger, were among the first settlers, but remained only a few years.

The greater part of the above-named settlers were natives of Pennsylvania. In this sketch we have attempted to include all of the pioneers who resided here permanently, or whose descendants now live in the township.

ORGANIZATION.

Township number six in the fourth range was formerly included in the Middlefield election district. In 1807 it was created a separate township and election precinct and named Bristol.

FIRST ELECTION.

The first election of township officers was held on the first Monday in April, 1808, with the following result: Lyman Potter, justice of the peace; Abraham Baughman, John Martin, and William Wilson, trustees; John Cummings, clerk; William Reed, constable; Robert Miller and George Barger, overseers of the poor; Thomas Martin, treasurer; William Cummings, and Abraham Daley, fence-viewers; Emmor Moore and Henry Baughman, supervisors; Joseph Cummings, lister.

NAME.

The township was named Bristol, after Bristol, Connecticut, the home of the surveyor.

BRISTOLVILLE.

The growth of this village was slow, and comparatively few improvements were made until after the turnpike was opened in 1819 and the stage began running in 1828.

Samuel Swetland was the first store-keeper, and after him Henry Hanks came but remained only a short time. Norris, Howard & Kibbee had a store quite early and erected the building which is now E. L. Kibbee's store.

Lyman Potter, who lived at the south end of the village, kept the first tavern for a number of years. A number of others afterwards kept public house in the village.

EARLY SCHOOLS.

The first term of school in this township was taught by Gabriel Sager in the winter of 1810-11. His pupils were members of the Sager families and their relatives. German only was taught.

The first English school was taught by Seth I. Ensign in the winter of 1812-13, in a deserted log cabin one-fourth of a mile north of the Bristolville corners. In 1814-15 Lucy Badger, daughter of the Rev. Joseph Badger, taught school near Bristolville in a cabin west of the creek on the present Cory farm.

The first school-house was built in the fall of 1812 by William Barb, Samuel Sager, William Sager and others, at North Bristol, on ground which is now the mill-yard. It was a primitive log structure and the school-room was lighted by small windows or openings in the wall pasted over with greased paper.

A school-house of logs was built at an early day on the public square at Bristolville.

CHURCHES.

The first church organization in Bristol was the Mennonite, organized by Gabriel Sager at his own house in the northern part of the township in 1810 or 1811. The place is now owned by Edward Kibbee. The Mennonites originated in Holland. Their belief is distinguished by a rejection of infant baptism, refusal to take oaths, and the practice of feet-washing. This society never erected a church building, and ceased to exist after the death of Mr. Sager.

A society of Bible Christians was organized previous to 1820, but they never built a church. Their first preacher was Rev. John Cheney. Meetings were held in school-houses, private houses, and barns. Among the members were members of the Hammon family, Mrs. William Sager, Zachariah Norton, Joseph Chaffee and wife from Bristol, Major Howe and wife, Aaron Smith and wife, George and Michael Norton, William Norton, Charles Thayer and wife, and others, of Bloomfield; and Deacon Abijah Lee and wife of east Farmington, most of whom joined the Disciples.

The Disciples of this township built no church until the North Bristol church was organized in 1868, but attended services in Bloomfield.

The Calvinist Baptists and Free-will Baptists have maintained organizations in this township in former years, but no longer continue to do so, most of the members having joined other churches.

The church organizations in the township at present are four in number, viz: The Methodists and Congregationalists, at Bristolville; the Disciples, at North Bristol, and the Dunkards, in the east part of the township.

THE CONGREGATIONAL CHURCH.

This church was organized June 14, 1817, by Revs. Giles H. Cowles, Abial Jones, and Joseph Treat, under the name of the Presbyterian church of Bristol and Bloomfield. The plan of union was adopted allowing both Presbyterians and Congregationalists to enjoy its privileges. After a few years the church became known as the Presbyterian and Congregationalist church of Bristol, and so continued until a difference of opinion regarding slavery sprung up among its members, when it withdrew from the presbytery and remained independent a few years. At length the difficulty was settled; but meantime nearly all of the old Presbyterian members had died, and accordingly the wishes of the Congregationalists prevailed and the church united with the conference of the Congregational denomination.

At the organization the church consisted of seven members: John Barnes, Lucretia Barnes, Leman Ferry, Lyman Richards, Lucretia C. Richards, Rollin Dutton, and Nancy Dutton. The first church officers elected were John Barnes, standing moderator; John Barnes and Leman Ferry, church committee; and Rollin Dutton, clerk. To the membership the following were added at the dates given: June 15, 1817, Elijah and Elizabeth Bigelow. November 9, 1817, Betsey Barnes. November 15, 1818, John and Sally Morley. February 5, 1820, Margaret Fansler. June 25, 1820, Matthew Current. On the 18th of March, 1821, Shubal and Lydia Hillman, Asa and Olive Smith, Roxana Lloyd, and Mrs. Roxana Lloyd, and Lucinda and Laura Hillman, and Peres R. Hiscock. June 30, 1822, Alpheus Alvord. January 16, 1825, Ira Rose, Gideon L. and Clarinda Sprague, Wilmot Mayhew, Nancy and Lucretia Mayhew. January 1, 1826, Cherry Alvord, Lucy Hiscock, Sophia Baker, and Anson Morley. August 20, 1826, Chloe A. Miller, Orrin Ballard, Holmes Mayhew, Chester and Abigail Hillman, Melvin and Lucretia Mayhew. September 21,

1828, Margaret Ballard and Mary Case. These were all up to 1830. The present membership is over one hundred.

Among the earliest preachers in this church were Rev. Messrs. Cowles, Jones, Joseph W. Curtis, Jonathan Leslie, and Daniel Miller. Mr. Miller was installed pastor and remained and labored earnestly many years.

The first church in this township was erected by the Presbyterians in 1812, five years before they organized. It was of hewn logs and stood on the farm of John Fansler, Sr., now owned by Newell Maltby. The next edifice was a frame building, two stories, which stood on the edge of the old graveyard east of the village common. The upper story was never finished, but the lower was so far completed that meetings were held in it, wooden benches serving as seats. The present house, most tastefully and beautifully constructed, was erected in 1845 or 1846 and dedicated in February, 1847.

THE METHODIST EPISCOPAL CHURCH.

Concerning this organization very few facts are obtainable, but the following statements, gleaned mainly from the oldest living members, are believed to be substantially correct.

A class was formed by Rev. Ira Eddy, in November, 1818, consisting of six members: John Norton and wife, John and Sarah Hammon, and Magdalena and Margaret Cline. Among the first preachers were Revs. Eddy, Green, Hill, Ayer, Crum, Chandler, and Scott. Elder Green (afterwards presiding elder) was on this circuit when it extended from Lake Erie to Warren, and required six weeks for him to travel it and keep his appointments.

Meetings were held in barns, school-houses, and private houses, and for many years in an old log building which stood upon the village common, near the spot where the soldiers' monument is located. Afterwards the two-story school-house, now the tin-shop, was built, and used as a place of meeting. The present church edifice was erected in 1845 through liberal efforts on the part of prominent members. In 1881 this house was remodeled, much enlarged and improved, and is now one of the finest churches to be found in any small village in the State. It contains three rooms besides the main audience room, and all are most conveniently arranged. The original cost of the building was not less than $2,500. Mrs. Dr. Brockett gave the society $1,000 with which to make the recent repairs and improvements. A heavy bell of superior tone now hangs in the belfry, being the fourth bell since the church was built.

The seed planted in the wilderness by the pioneer missionary in 1818 has germinated and borne fruit abundantly. The church now numbers one hundred and eighty-five, being the largest membership of any church in the township.

THE DISCIPLE CHURCH.

This church was organized February 19, 1868, under the labor and superintendence of Rev. J. N. Smith and Rev. N. N. Bartlett. Hiram Thayer and A. A. House were elected overseers; Samuel A. Davidson and Jacob Sager, Sr., deacons, and S. A. Davidson, clerk and treasurer. Subsequently it was deemed advisable to have three deacons, and Henry Clay was chosen as a deacon. June 3, 1868, A. A. House, Hiram Thayer, and William Sager were elected trustees. Later S. A. Davidson was elected an overseer, and Solomon Sager, deacon, to fill the vacancy thus occasioned.

The year of the organization a convenient church was erected at a cost of about $2,000. The church started with a good membership, and soon numerous additions were made.

Rev. N. N. Bartlett was the first pastor. Rev. E. Wakefield succeeded him for one year. Rev. E. B. Wakefield, the present pastor, took charge of this congregation in 1874. Under his ministration the church has been blessed with a high degree of prosperity, and now numbers about one hundred and twenty-five faithful active members. Services are held once in two weeks, the preacher dividing his labors between North Bristol and Bloomfield churches.

The Dunkard church was organized some fifteen years ago, and has a small but convenient meeting-house. John Strohm is one of its principal members and supporters. The membership is small.

CEMETERIES.

The two principal burying places in this township are located at Bristolville, one east and the other west of the turnpike. Interments were made in the township burying-ground east of the public square in very early times. The oldest grave-stone standing bears the date 1810. The new cemetery is large and prettily adorned with shrubbery of evergreens. In the northern part of the township is a small old burying-ground where rest the remains of members of the Sager family and others of the old settlers.

POST-OFFICES.

The first post-office was established about 1825, Gideon Sprague, postmaster. Mail was then brought from Warren once a week by a man on horseback. After the four-horse stage began running the office was moved to the center and Jacob Hammon appointed postmaster. He held the office over thirty years, and found it the source of a great deal of bother and but very little compensation. This being the first office on the road north of Warren, an unassorted mail, heavier than one man could lift, frequently came here. Mr. Hammon was obliged to go through it all, and perhaps find as the result of his researches a single letter or paper for some citizen of his town. The remaining mail was then put upon the coach for the next postmaster on the route to investigate in a similar way. As there was then no hotel in the village, in cold weather all the stage-coach passengers poured into Mr. Hammon's house to warm themselves, and these, together with those who were waiting for mail, gave him no little annoyance. A. A. House was the first postmaster at North Bristol, where an office was established in 1870. E. A. Pierce, his successor, is the present incumbent.

EARLY MILLS.

The first mill in this township was built by William Sager for Abraham Baughman, near where the latter settled, in about 1806. A log saw-mill and grist-mill were erected. One dam served to make a water supply for both. The grist-mill was of peculiar construction, the motive power being a wheel placed horizontally in the water. To get the grain into the hopper it must be carried up a ladder into the second story of the mill, and when ground was removed from a receptacle on the lower floor. One run of stones made from a common rock was used in grinding. The mill ground slowly, but not "exceeding fine." Baughman ran these mills as long as he remained in the township. John Barnes then purchased the property and after him Samuel Baker.

William Sager, about 1816, built a saw-mill upon his farm and did some grinding by the attachment of a small run of stones. About 1828 he built a grist-mill, the frame of which is still standing. His mills were run by the water of Baughman's creek.

About 1830 John Hammon built a saw-mill west of the center, on the present McBride farm. Later the McBrides had a small water-mill for grinding erected there.

As early as 1830 Mayhew & Hillman built and put in operation a fulling- and cloth dressing-mill, near Sager's mills. The business of dyeing, fulling, and dressing cloth was carried on during the fall and winter months for several years.

A turning mill for the manufacture of wooden bowls, wooden plates, etc., was put in operation on the same stream. Colonel Flower, of Bloomfield, was its superintendent.

HUNTING ADVENTURES.

Game of all kinds was so abundant that some of the early settlers obtained all the meat necessary for family use by the aid of dog and gun. In the creeks fish abounded; the forests were full of bee trees; in short, this must have been almost a sportsman's paradise.

William Sager was accustomed to spend considerable time each fall in hunting for "bee trees." Swarms that had come from the older settlements had taken possession of some of the hollow trees; they in turn sent out swarms and occupied many of the suitable trees with their colonies. One day, as Mr. Sager was bee-hunting, he saw that turkeys had been scratching the leaves about. He took out his call-whistle, made from the wing-bone of a turkey, and blew upon it, imitating the noise made by a turkey. Presently he saw a large wolf, which had been attracted by the sound, prowling around under the trees, snuffing the air and looking for turkeys. Mr. Sager discharged his rifle and killed the animal, and in due time received $10 bounty for the act.

One day Sager started to go through the woods to Baughman's, taking his gun as usual. He had not gone far when he saw a deer, at which he fired. The animal dropped and he ran up to cut its throat with his knife, but the deer was not dead and not severely wounded. Just as Sager was upon him he jumped up, and doing so knocked the knife from his hands, then turned and attacked Mr. Sager with all his might, trying to gore him with his antlers. Mr. Sager caught the antlers and held on firmly, but was thrown about by the deer until he was nearly exhausted. He was beginning to despair of being able to maintain his hold and feared that he would be thrown down and trampled upon, but just then his dog arrived, having heard the discharge of the gun and followed his master from home. The dog soon caught hold of the deer's throat; Mr. Sager released himself and dispatched the deer. After this adventure the intelligent dog always accompanied his master on hunting expeditions.

Bears were bold and troublesome. Sometimes a cross old bear with cubs would follow and attempt to attack a man if alone ; but when two men were together the bear usually retreated. Hogs were provided with bells, so that when attacked by bears, as they often were, their owners would hear the alarm.

IN EARLY DAYS

people were frequently lost in the woods here. Nathaniel Moore was out one night hunting raccoons, lost his way home, and was compelled to pass the entire night in the woods. Daylight revealed to him his whereabouts and he returned to his alarmed family.

Flour and meal were very difficult articles to obtain. Until about 1806 there were no mills nearer than Warren, and no roads, such as would now be considered passable, leading to that place. To illustrate the difficulty of obtaining a grist under such circumstances, we will give another incident in William Sager's life. Before any grain had been raised in the township, he heard that a man in Mesopotamia had some wheat to sell. He took his horse and with great difficulty found his way through the trackless region to his neighbor's (?) house, bought two bushels and returned home. Thus one day had been spent in obtaining the grain. Next morning accordingly he started for Warren with his grist, and a whole hard day's work it proved to reach the mill. He had the grist ground in the evening, and the next evening arrived with it at his home. Thus three days were occupied in obtaining a two-bushel grist and having it ground.

Some time before any road to Painesville or the lake was opened, several of the settlers of this township conceived the idea of navigating the Grand river, and measures were undertaken to carry the scheme into effect. The settlers had some maple sugar and other articles which they wished to sell, and having constructed a canoe they undertook a voyage to the lake. The Baughmans, Nortons, and Sagers were the leaders of the project. They began to clear the stream of brush, commencing at the mouth of Baughman's creek, and were occupied several days in this work. At night the boat was fastened to a tree and a guard placed over the merchandise. Two trips were made; but as it was found to be a long and laborious way of getting to the lake, the boat was sold and navigation in these waters ceased.

AN ANCIENT WELL.

William Sager selected for his building spot a place near what appeared to be a small spring issuing from the hillside. But when he proceeded to clear out the spring, he was much surprised to find a shallow well neatly walled up with stones.

OTHER INTERESTING DISCOVERIES

were soon made in the vicinity, among them a lot of ashes about a foot under ground. When Mr. Sager began plowing he found, near the spring, over a quarter of an acre of ground that had a very black appearance and showed many remnants of charcoal, as though the ground had been the bed of a large coal-pit. Some of the pieces remained several years to puzzle and mystify persons of an inquisitive turn of mind.

Mr. Joseph Sager thinks that pottery must have been manufactured here; for he remembers, when a boy, digging in the dirt, as boys are wont to do, that he found a small earthen vessel, which could scarcely have been formed by Nature's art. It was exceedingly brittle, and at once crumbled to pieces. The ground is still black.

Several spots of earth covered over with stones are to be seen in this township, and it is supposed that each marks an Indian grave. The mound-builders have left lasting monuments of themselves in Bloomfield swamp. But this fact scarcely serves to solve the secret of the old coal-pit or pottery; rather it leaves us in doubt whether to assign these works to that race or to the red men. But if the Indians engaged in burning coal, walling up springs, etc., here in Ohio, the evidence of such laborious work ought to remove from our mind the prevailing idea that they were lazy and indolent.

A short distance from Mr. Sager's, near a marsh, could be seen a spot where, evidently, a well has been dug and the dirt thrown out. Do these old works belong to the age of the mound-builders, or are they of more recent origin? This is a question for the curious in such matters to solve. But the fact of their existence is indisputable.

THE INDIANS

were the neighbors of the first settlers of Bristol, and frequently visited their houses. A few years after the arrival of the Sager family Mrs. Sager was washing at the spring one day, having left at the house the baby, Jacob, in charge of her oldest son. Three Indians unceremoniously entered the cabin and began to look about them. They saw some turnips in a corner of the room, and asked for some to eat. As they could speak but little English, or German either, it was only by watching their eyes and their gestures that their wants became known to the boy. He gave each of them a turnip, but they were unprovided with knives and held their turnips, looking around to see if they could discover any thing to eat them with. Finally one of them pronounced the word "messer"—German for knife—and the boy supplied them with the desired articles. They then ate their turnips in silence and with apparent satisfaction, and left the cabin as unceremoniously as they had entered.

A little later, two Indians and a squaw came to the house one day in summer. Evidently they had been traveling a long distance, and they were weary. The two men lay down in the shade of a corn-crib and went to sleep. The squaw chose a sunny spot, lay down and apparently fell asleep, too. She had been carrying a bundle, and the little boy was curious to know what it contained. He tip-toed softly up to the side of the sleeping squaw and was about to lay his hands upon the bundle, when a little dog that accompanied the party began a violent barking. The boy made his way toward the house as fast as his legs could carry him, while the squaw sat up and called to him, "Hiscataw! hiscataw!" The boy thought these words were intended to urge the dog upon him, and, greatly frightened, doubled his efforts to reach the house.

But instead of this she was calling the dog off, and her words at once stopped his barking. The Indians had a hearty laugh over the boy's fright, and in future visits the family often mentioned the incident.

The chief Indian in this locality had a white boy whom he had somehow obtained. He was very reticent when questioned concerning him, and only when under the influence of whiskey would he say anything about him. But when drunk he sometimes stated that he got the boy when he was so high—indicating the child's height by holding his hand about two feet from the floor, and that he found him under an apple-tree. All the Indians left in 1811. Some twenty years after they had gone a man from the southern part of Pennsylvania stayed one night at the house of Joseph Sager, who in the course of the conversation mentioned to the stranger something of the little boy who had lived with the Indians. The stranger asked him to describe the boy, and after he had done so averred that he believed the child was one who had been stolen from one of his neighbors in Pennsylvania, that his parents were wealthy, and would pay almost any price to have him back again. But whether he ever returned to civilization or lived and died among the savages we have no means of ascertaining.

When the Indians approached a settler's house they held their guns by the muzzle as a token that they came as friends. They had the usual Indian custom of carrying their pappooses upon their backs, strapped to a board. When a squaw entered a house she would set her pappoose down by the door and leave it outside, where it was frequently molested by the dogs or hogs that were allowed to run about the place.

FISH.

The first settlers found so many fish in Baughman's creek that many families caught and salted barrels of them for winter use. There was no dam or other obstruction from the lake to Baughman's mill until a mill-dam was built at Austinburg some years after Bristol was settled. William Sager on his first visit to this township found such an abundance of fish in the creek that he declared that a wagon could not be driven through the water without killing some of them.

TEMPERANCE CRUSADE.

The following extract from a county paper dated June, 1858, may prove of interest:

A week or two since fifty women in a party assembled and made an attack on the grocery of one Miller; some dragged the proprietor out of doors and held him down, while others knocked in the heads of his cider, whiskey, vinegar, and rum barrels. Miller has commenced a suit against them.

MISCELLANEOUS NOTES.

The first taxes were assessed on the following plan: Horses twenty cents and cattle eight cents per head. Concerning real estate the records are silent.

The first frame house in this township was built by Jonathan Walkley about one mile south of Bristolville. It is still standing, but no longer used as a dwelling.

The first sermon was preached by Gabriel Sager at his own house. He was also the first regular preacher and the first school-teacher.

The first marriage was that of Jacob Baughman and Barbara Good. The ceremony was performed by Lyman Potter, justice of the peace.

The first practicing physician was Dr. Chandler B. Chapman. He remained a number of years and was highly esteemed in his professional capacity and in society. He afterwards became a professor in a Cincinnati Medical school. Other physicians have been here to tarry longer or shorter periods, and the township now has two good doctors in its midst.

The first store was opened at the center by Salmon Swetland, previous to 1830.

'Squire Potter kept the first tavern, Cyril Green, Lyman Kibbee, and others, succeeding him in the business.

TOWNSHIP BUSINESS DIRECTORY.

General stores: H. H. Pierce, E. L. Kibbee, Bristolville; and E. A. Pierce, North Bristol.

Drug store: E. T. Finney, Bristolville.

Furniture store: A. E. Miner, Bristolville.

Tin shop: R. G. Kelso.

Bristolville post-office, Jacob Norton, postmaster; North Bristol, E. A. Pierce postmaster.

Bristolville physicians: A. J. Brockett, M. D., and F. C. Corey, M. D.

Grist-mills: McBride Brothers & Vradenburg, Bristolville; and Hutton & Freel, North Bristol.

Carriage and blacksmith shop, Eckstine & Reel, North Bristol.

Cheese factories: Jere Barton, North Bristol; Tift & Chryst, southwest part of township.

Steam saw-mills: Strome & Reed have a large saw-mill, planing-mill, handle and spoke manufactory, etc., east of Bristolville station, and carry on an extensive business. Mayhew Brothers have a steam saw-mill and planing-mill at Oakfield station. Two other saw-mills are owned by Sager & Cox, North Bristol; and Osborn & Harclerode, in the southwest of the township.

The above are the principal business interests, not including shoemaker and blacksmith shops.

NOTES OF SETTLEMENT.

Jacob Sager was born in Bristol township October 25, 1805. His father, William Sager, was a native of Shenandoah county, West Virginia, and came to Ohio in 1805 and settled in Bristol township, and was among the early settlers of the township. He settled in the north part of the township and resided upon his farm until his death, which occurred in 1856. There were eight children in his family—five boys and three girls—Joseph, Jacob, Sally, John, Solomon, Annie, Rebecca, and William. John, Solomon, and Annie are deceased. Mr. Sager was a millwright by trade, though he carried on farming in connection. Mr. Jacob Sager has always lived in the township. He was the first white child born in Bristol. He has lived to witness many changes; has seen a dense wilderness change to a thriving community. He was married September 8, 1831, to Miss Leah Kagy, daughter of Jacob Kagy, of Bristol. They have had six children, five of whom are living—Susan, William J., Henry F., Mary E., Sophia, and Jacob A. Mr. and Mrs. Sager are members of the Disciples church, and in every respect are good citizens.

Joseph Sager, a well known resident of Bristol, was born June 1, 1802, in Shenandoah county, Virginia, and came to Ohio in 1805 in company with his father, William. Gabriel Sager, father of William, was a native of Germany, and came to America in an early day. Mr. William Sager made a trip to Ohio in 1801, though it is not known whether he made a purchase at this time or not. In 1805 he removed his family. He made his journey to Ohio in a covered wagon, and lived in this several weeks while a hut was in process of construction. He brought a cow. Mr. Sager cleared up a good farm, upon which he lived till his death, which occurred September 24, 1856. Joseph Sager is one of the oldest residents of the township. He was married in 1829, to Miss Catharine Peters, daughter of Daniel Peters, of Bristol township. There were two children by this marriage: Mary A. and Daniel W. Mrs. Sager died in 1854. In 1856 Mr. Sager was married a second time, to Mrs. Hewitt, daughter of Eli Young, of Farmington, and has one child by this union: Frank J. Both himself and wife are Methodists.

William Sager was born February 14, 1821, in Bristol township, upon the farm where he now lives. He is the youngest son of William Sager. He has always lived in the township. Farming has been his chief business. He has a farm of one hundred and seventy-five acres of good land. He was married in 1844, to Miss Mary M. Norton, daughter of Zachariah Norton, of Bristol. Eight children are the fruit of this union: Flora, Delia, Olive, Julia, Jennie, George, Minnie, William. William died in infancy. Mrs. Sager is a member of the Disciple church. Politically Mr. Sager is a firm Republican. He has held several of the township offices, has been township trustee, assessor, and justice of the peace, thus showing the high esteem in which he is held by his fellow-townsmen.

Isaac Barb, an old resident of Bristol township, was born December 18, 1822, in Bristol township, Trumbull county, upon the farm where he now lives. His father, Gabriel, was born in Shenandoah county, Virginia, and came to Ohio in 1805, when he was eleven years of age, in company with his father, William, who came to the township with the Sager family. There were very few settlers in the township at the time of their arriving. William Barb began in an unbroken wilderness, and succeeded in building up a grand farm, upon which he lived till his death, which occurred in 1839, leaving a family of six children, Peter, Gabriel, William, Jacob, Abram, Mary. Mrs. Barb died in 1854 or 1855. Mr. and Mrs. Barb were members of the Mennonite church. Mr. Gabriel Barb came upon the farm where his son Isaac now lives, in February, 1822. The first tree he cut down came very near killing him. Timothy Cox did the most of his chopping. Abram Kagy was his nearest neighbor. At the time of Mr. Barb's death he had about one hundred acres of land cleared. There were three children in the family, Isaac, Henry, and Elizabeth. Isaac and Henry reside upon the old home place. Elizabeth (Diehl) lives in Nebraska. Mr. Barb was a Mennonite. Mrs. Barb was a Dunkard. Isaac Barb, the subject of this sketch, has a farm of three hundred and fifty acres. He is engaged in general farming. He was married in 1848 to Miss Elizabeth Norton, daughter of Zachariah Norton, of Bristol. They have two children, Joseph S. and Maria. Mr. and Mrs. Barb are church members and are sincere Christians. Mr. Barb has been unable to do work for the last few years on account of lameness. His son carries on the farm.

Henry Barb was born January 14, 1826, in Bristol township, upon the farm where he now lives. His father, Gabriel, was one of the first settlers in the township. Mr. Henry Barb has always been engaged in farming, though in connection with this he has been in a saw-mill, in which he did an extensive business for several years. He has one hundred and sixty-seven acres of excellent land. Mr. Barb was united in matrimony to Miss Jane A. Thompson, daughter of Robert Thompson, of Bristol township. Three children are the fruits of this union, Harriet, Nettie A., George E. Harriet is deceased. Mr. and Mrs. Barb are Methodists.

S. A. Davidson was born in 1800 in New Haven, Connecticut, and came to Ohio in a very early day, over fifty years ago, and settled in Boardman township, Trumbull county, now Mahoning. Here he lived several years, and then moved to Mecca township, Trumbull county, where he resided till 1865, when he moved to Bristol township and resided till his death in 1875. He was a carpenter by trade. He was married in December, 1838, to Miss Martha A. Chaffee, daughter of Rev. J. Chaffee, of Bristol township. They had five children, three of whom are living—Lurena, Orrin E. Flora A. Mr. Davidson was a member of the Disciple church. Mrs. Davidson is also a member, He had been justice of the peace twelve years; also notary public nine years.

Rev. J. Chaffee was born in Massachusetts. He came to Ohio about 1814 and settled in Bristol township, west of the center, and was among the early pioneers. He began in the

wilderness and cleared up a good farm, and lived there till 1824, and then moved to Mecca township, where he resided till 1865; then returned to Bristol and spent the remainder of his days. He died September 3, 1869. Mrs. Chaffee died September 14, 1874. Mr. Chaffee married Miss Theodosia Fletcher, daughter of John Fletcher, of Massachusetts, March 1, 1813. There were nine children in the family—Theodosia, Sally L., Martha A., Joseph G., Eunice P., Mary M., John M., Betsy, and Nancy. Rev. J. Chaffee was a minister of the Disciple church, though he carried on a farm; also worked at shoemaking at intervals.

Hoshea Moffet, a former old resident of Bristolville, was born March 22, 1787, in Connecticut, and came to Ohio in 1828 and settled in Bristol township, Trumbull county. He located in the northwestern part of the township, where he lived till his death, which occurred January 18, 1857, leaving a family of nine children to mourn his loss. Mrs. Moffet died in 1830. He was married November 6, 1801, to Miss Polly Porter, daughter of Alexander Porter, of Connecticut. The names of his children are as follow: Edwin, Lucine, Adaline, Louisa, Orlando, Erastus, Chauncey, Charles, Amanda. Edwin, Orlando, Chauncey, and Amanda are deceased. Mr. and Mrs. Moffet were members of the Methodist church, and enjoyed the esteem and confidence of all who knew them.

Stephen Osborn, an old resident of Bristol township, was born in Litchfield county, town of Colebrook, Connecticut, November 20, 1797. His father, Joshua, was born in Connecticut, and came to Ohio in 1809, and settled in Southington township, Trumbull county, and was among the early settlers of the township. Like the early pioneers he began in the woods and made himself a good farm and lived upon this till his death. He died in 1837, leaving a family of thirteen children—Chloe, Reuben, Mansfield, Dorcas, Sheldon, Roxy, Gilbert, Leonard, Stephen, Amanda, Sterling, Annie, Phœbe. Stephen, Amanda, Annie, and Phœbe are the only surviving members of the family. Mr. Stephen Osborn came to Bristol township in 1830. He first settled upon the turnpike south of the center and here resided about twenty years, then moved upon the farm where he now lives. Many improvements have been made by Mr. Osborn.

Farming has been his occupation, and even at his present advanced age he is able to do much labor in the field. He was married in 1826 to Miss Mary Hillman, daughter of Shubal Hillman, of Bristol. He had four children by this marriage. Mrs. Osborn died in 1834. He then married Miss Amanda Hillman, sister of his first wife, and had four children by this marriage. Mrs. Osborn died in 1855. He married in 1858 his third wife, Mrs. Rebecca Difford, of Bloomfield, who died in 1870. Mr. Osborn has one hundred and thirty-four acres of good land. He has been quite a hunter and trapper in his day, and takes much pride in exhibiting his old wolf-trap at the present day. He is a member of the Methodist church.

Among the first settlers of Bristol was Aaron Fenton, Sr., who removed from New Jersey. He located where his son Aaron now lives. He died many years ago, leaving a family of five sons and two daughters, viz: Daniel, William, Aaron, Abraham, Enoch, Mary, and Lydia (Baird). William, the second son, was born in Bristol in 1811; married Adaline Moffet in 1835, and settled at the center of Bristol, where he resided a number of years, then purchasing the farm which his widow still occupies. He was a carpenter by trade. He died in 1860. Mrs. Fenton was born in Herkimer county, New York, in 1814. Her father was Hoshea Moffet, a brief notice of whom is elsewhere given. To Mr. and Mrs. Fenton were born seven sons and two daughters, as follows: William W., living in Bristol; A. W., deputy collector of customs, Cleveland, Ohio; Shurben, on the farm with his mother; Marshal, in Warren, and Dr. Hoshea Fenton, of Troy, Geauga county; Mortimer and Charles and the two daughters, Mary and Delia, are deceased.

Jacob Norton, an old resident of Bristol, was born in 1820 in Bristol. His father, Zachariah, was a native of Shenandoah county, Virginia, and came to Ohio in a very early day, and settled in the northeastern part of the township. Jacob Norton, the grandfather of Jacob, the subject of this sketch, came from Germany. He was one of the early pioneers of old Trumbull. Like the most of the early settlers he began in the woods and cleared up a good farm, and lived upon it until his death. There were nine children in his family. Mr. Zachariah Norton lived in the township till his death. He was a farmer

by occupation, and like his father made a farm for himself. There were twelve children in his family, ten of whom are living. Mr. Jacob Norton, one of the number, has always resided in the township. He has been engaged in the mercantile business chiefly, though he has been postmaster since 1861, and is still serving in that position. He was married in 1844 to Miss Hannah A. Whitmore, daughter of Beriah and Nancy Whitmore, of Gustavus township. They have one child, Francis B., who is a practicing physician at Newburg, Ohio. Mr. and Mrs. Norton are members of the Methodist church.

C. W. Huntly was born in Canandaigua, Ontario county, New York, in 1813, June 3d. His father, Rufus Huntly, was a native of Connecticut, and came to Ohio in 1832, and settled in Sharon, Medina county, where he lived till his death. He was an early settler in the section where he located. There were twelve children in his family, only six of whom are now living. Mr. C. W. Huntly came to Trumbull county in 1846, and located in Bristol township, upon the farm formerly owned by Jacob Norton. Here he lived till he came to the center. He was proprietor of the hotel at Bristolville about fifteen years, and won the good wishes of the traveling public. He was married in 1834 to Miss Julia A. Fairchild, daughter of Abel Fairchild, of Ontario county, New York. They have had thirteen children, twelve of whom are living. Mr. and Mrs. Huntly are members of the Methodist church, and are sincere Christians. Mr. Huntly served a short time in the late war. He had four sons, who also acted in defense of their country, one of whom died at Vicksburg. Mr. Huntly may well take pride in the war record of his family. Politically Mr. Huntly is a stanch Republican, and is held in high esteem by his fellow-townsmen.

Scott F. Huntly was born April 22, 1847, in Bristol township, Trumbull county, Ohio. His father, Calvin W., came to Ohio in 1846. Mr. S. F. Huntly has lived most of his life in Bristol; was in Michigan nine months. At the present time he is proprietor of a hotel at Bristolville, and is universally liked by the traveling public. He was married in 1869, to Miss Lizzie Mullen, daughter of Samuel Mullen, of Mecca township. Mr. Huntly served nearly two and a half years in the Rebellion, though very young at the time of his enlistment. He enlisted in February, 1862, in the Twenty-third Ohio infantry, and participated in thirteen different engagements, was at Cloyd Mountain, New River Bridge, Cedar Creek, and many others. Mr. Huntley is a carpenter by trade.

Samuel White, an old resident of Bristol, was born April 1, 1808, in Bristol township, Trumbull county, Ohio. His father, Benjamin, was a native of Washington county, Pennsylvania. He came to Ohio in 1802, and was among the pioneers of the county. He first settled in the west part of the township of Bristol. He purchased his land of Richard Iddings, and soon after bought the farm now occupied by Mr. Spitler, through the agency at Warren. He probably owned about one hundred acres. He cleared up a good farm, and built the first grist-mill in the township, which he carried on in connection with his farming for several years. He then went to Middlefield, Geauga county, where he lived till his death, which occurred in November, 1815. Mrs. White died in November, 1875, in her eighty-eighth year. They were married in 1804, in Bristol township, by 'Squire Tracy of Mesopotamia. They had eight children, six of whom are living, two dying in infancy—Samuel, Elijah G., Polly, Jane, Patterson, and Benjamin. Mr. Samuel White has always lived in the township, never having been out of it for a month at a time since he was born. He learned the carpenter trade when he was about eighteen years of age, and followed it till 1840, though he purchased a farm in 1834. He was married October 12, 1835, to Mary Ann Flower, daughter of Horace Flower, of Bloomfield township. Seven children were the fruit of this union, three of whom are living. Mrs. White died February 7, 1851. Mr. White was married the second time in 1854 to Mrs. Malvina Seaton, of Erie county, New York. One child was born to them. Mrs. White is a member of the Congregational church. Mr. White has filled several of the township offices; was justice many years; also has been town clerk and trustee. In politics he is a firm Republican.

Anan Gordon was born February 12, 1823, in Warren, Ohio. His father, Robert Gordon, was born in Washington county, Pennsylvania, June 8, 1796. His grandfather, Colonel Thomas Gordon, came from Scotland in an early day, and settled in Washington county, Pennsylvania. An attempt was made to bribe him to go into Burgoyne's army in the Revolution, but Mr. Gordon remained steadfast in his loyalty to the land of his adoption, and spurned the insult with indignation. In 1799 he came to Ohio and located in Poland township, and was one of the first in the township. He cleared up a good farm and lived upon it several years, then moved to Ashtabula county, where he resided till he removed to Lordstown, Trumbull county. He died in 1840. Mr. Robert Gordon came to Warren about 1817, from Ashtabula county. He was a brick-maker by trade and lived in Warren till his death. There were twelve children in his family, six boys and six girls, all of whom lived to maturity. Mr. Anan Gordon has always lived in the county. In 1850 he went to Bazetta township, where he lived twenty-one years, and was engaged in farming in the meantime. In 1861 he came to Bristol, where he has since resided. He was married February 15, 1849, to Miss Ruanna Bell, daughter of Jabez and Anna Bell, of Bazetta. There were two children by this marriage. Second marriage September 29, 1859, to Miss Harriet Nutt, daughter of Chauncey Nutt, of Southington township. Four children by this marriage. Third marriage March 30, 1876, to Mrs. Frances F. Lightfoot, daughter of Michael Chandler, of Parkman, Portage county. Mr. Gordon has two hundred and thirty-three acres of fine land. He is engaged in general farming.

Gideon Bowers was born May 21, 1831, in Bristol township. His father, John Bowers, was born in Shenandoah county, Virginia, and came to Ohio in 1829, and settled in Bristol township, west of the center, but soon after moved to the eastern part of this township upon the farm where he now lives. Mr. John Bowers began in the dense wilderness and made for himself a good farm. There were six children in his family—Leah, Levi, Gideon, Lydia, Sarah, Mary. Levi is deceased—was killed by the falling of a tree in 1848. Mr. John Bowers and lady are still living. Gideon Bowers has always resided in this township; farming has been his occupation. He was married in 1858 to Miss Sarah Crozier, daughter of James Crozier, of Mecca township. They have four children—Charles J., Hattie A., Jay L., George Washington. Mr.

and Mrs. Bowers are members of the Methodist church, also Hattie. Mr. Bowers is a sound Republican.

Jacob Eckstine, a well known resident of Bristol township, was born in Germany August 3, 1818. His father, Michael Eckstine, was also a native of Germany and came to America in 1820, landing in Baltimore, Maryland, where he resided a short time, then went to Virginia, Shenandoah county, and located and lived until 1834, when he moved to Ohio and settled in Bristol township, upon the farm where his son Jacob now lives. He began in an unbroken forest and built up a good farm and lived to enjoy the fruit of his labor until his death, which occurred July 23, 1861. Mrs. Eckstine died January 17, 1864. There were two children, Jacob and Mary. Mary died in West Virginia. Mr. and Mrs. Eckstine were members of the Lutheran church. Jacob Eckstine has always lived upon the old home place ; has made farming a life occupation. He was married in 1848 to Miss Leah Bowers, daughter of John Bowers, of Bristol township. Five children have been born to them: Mary J., Amos, Cyrus, Charles, Sarah Ann. Sarah, who is the oldest of the family, is deceased. Mr. and Mrs. Eckstine are hospitable people and merit and enjoy the good wishes of all who know them.

A. J. Brockett, M. D., son of Alanson and grandson of Chauncey Brockett, early settlers in Farmington, was born in Bristol, Trumbull county, Ohio, in 1836. He was the first child born on what is called West street, where his father had settled the year before. Dr. Brockett read medicine with Dr. C. T. Metcalf, of Bristolville, now of Warren, for three years from 1858 to 1861. In the spring of the latter year he graduated at the University of Michigan, Ann Arbor. In the spring of 1864 he went into the army as surgeon of the First regiment Ohio volunteer infantry, serving until mustered out with the regiment. He afterwards, as assistant surgeon, had charge of the Eighty-eighth Ohio volunteer infantry at Camp Chase, Columbus, until the close of the war. He then returned to Bristolville and bought out Dr. Metcalf and has been engaged in the practice of his profession there since. He is president of the Trumbull County Medical society. In the spring of 1882 he formed a partnership with his younger brother, Dr. O. H.

Brockett, a recent graduate of Cleveland Medical college. He married January 10, 1878, Amelia J. Noyes, who died February 21, 1879. July 14, 1880, he married Mrs. Mary Maria Pond, a daughter of Daniel Gates, an early resident of Farmington.

Dr. Frank C. Corey, a rising physician of Bristol, was born October 7, 1853, in Bristol. His father, Frank H., was a native of Vermont and came to Bristol in 1850. Dr. Corey studied medicine at Mt. Vernon with Dr. J. C. Gordon, and graduated at Cleveland Medical college in 1874. He also attended one course of lectures at Philadelphia. Dr. Corey practiced in Mt. Vernon about thirteen months, then came to Bristol, where he has since practiced. He was married in 1877 to Miss Ida M. Bennett, daughter of Edwin Bennett, of Hartford township. They have one child—Loule L. Mr. and Mrs. Corey are members of the Congregational church Politically he is a Republican.

Newell Maltby was born in Tompkins, New York, in 1832, and moved with his parents, Nathaniel H. and Betsey (Patchen) Maltby to Bristol township in 1841. They settled on the farm now owned by Newell Maltby who is the youngest of eight children, only three of whom are now living. His mother died in 1836, and his father in 1855, at the age of seventy-three. Mr. Maltby was married, in 1856, to Jane Pierce, a native of Vermont, daughter of Thaddeus Pierce, who settled in Bristol in 1854. Their children are Mellie J., and Hattie Dell.

E. D. Baldwin was born in Crawford county, Pennsylvania, March 26, 1846. His father, Isaac S. Baldwin, was a native of Vermont, though he moved to New York when he was very young and remained there until he was thirteen years old, then moved to Pennsylvania where he still resides. Mr. E. D. Baldwin came to Ohio in 1877, in October, and settled in Bristol township upon the farm where he now lives. He is engaged in general farming and has one hundred and thirty-seven acres of good land. He was married in 1877 to Miss Elizabeth McMahan, daughter of Thomas McMahan of Howland township. Mr. and Mrs. Baldwin are members of the Congregational church and are good citizens.

CHAPTER VII.

BROOKFIELD.

This township is known as town number four in range one, and is bounded on the north by Hartford, east by the Pennsylvania State line, with Hubbard on the south and Vienna on the west. Save the coal interest which in recent years has been one of considerable importance and a source of great profit to many land owners, Brookfield is purely an agricultural community. It was first settled by a class of people, mainly New Englanders, who were noted for their intelligence and morality. The settlement first began at or near the center of the township, and as families collected at that point a nucleus was formed for the growth of the little village, the largest in the township, known as Brookfield center.

The main water-course is Big Yankee creek, which takes its rise a short distance north of the central part of the north boundary, in Hartford township, and flowing from this point in a southeast direction empties into the Shenango river in the southeast corner of the township. This creek with its tributaries drains the northwest, the west, and central parts of the township. Little Yankee creek enters the township at the northwest, and flows southeasterly across the southwest corner, where at a point west of the center it enters Hubbard township, but after reaching Hubbard center it turns northeast, and again enters Brookfield at the southeast corner and flows into the Shenango. The Lake Shore & Michigan Southern railroad extends across the southwest corner, following in this township the general course of Little Yankee creek, and has its main station at the crossing of the main east and west center road, about two miles west of Brookfield village, and near Payne's corners.

The New York, Pennsylvania & Ohio railroad barely enters the township across the southeast corner. Various coal-road branches are extended to the coal banks in the different localities.

The surface of the township is generally rolling; the soil generally clay, but in the northwest part somewhat more gravelly soil is found. The Yankee creek bottom lands, consisting of a black loam, are especially productive. The southern part of the township is somewhat broken, and in this part are situated the coal mines.

ORGANIZATION.

The township from its organization up to 1810 formed, with Vienna, one election precinct. On May 14th of the above year the qualified electors of the township were notified to meet at the house of Constant Lake, for the purpose of electing the usual township officers for the new township of Brookfield. The election board consisted of Diament Whitier, chairman; William Cunningham and Anthony Patrick, judges; Henry Gandy and Jacob Hummason, clerks. The following officials were then chosen by ballot and were declared elected "according as the law directs:" William Cunningham, Anthony Patrick, and John D. Smith, trustees; Isaac Flower, Jr., treasurer and constable; Jacob Hummason, clerk and lister; Henry H. Gandy, appraiser; Diament Whitier, Timothy Alderman and Clark Rathbun, supervisors; Robert Hughes and Benjamin Bentley, overseers of the poor; Johnson Patrick and James Montgomery, fence viewers.

On the 8th day of November, 1810, Isaac Flower, Jr., appeared before Robert Hughes, associate judge of the county, and took the required oath as the first justice of the peace of Brookfield. It is stated as a probability, however, that Judge Hughes officiated as justice of the peace here before the township was formally organized, but the first elected justice of Brookfield was Isaac Flower, Jr., as above stated.

POPULATION AND INDUSTRIES.

The population of the township in 1870 was 2,657; in 1880, 2,569, showing a decrease.

Coal mining is carried on quite extensively in various localities. Coal was first discovered and used for domestic purposes prior to 1838, in which year General Joel B. Curtis opened the first mine from which coal was shipped. Several mines are now operated in the township.

In former years, about 1826, John Myers and Franklin Peck built the only woolen-mill in which wool was carded into rolls, and cloth was fulled. The machinery was propelled by oxen on a tread-wheel. William Montgomery afterwards came in possession of this mill, and continued its operation until some time in 1847.

Lawrence Smith erected the only blast furnace in the township about 1836. It was a quarter-stack, and was located near the center. The furnace had a foundry attached at which were manufactured plows, stoves, and hollow-ware. The ore was obtained principally from the farm of Timothy Roberts, in Hubbard, and charcoal was used exculsively for smelting and also for melting the pig and scrap-iron for casting. It was obtained from the lands of James and Robert Christy. The works passed into the hands of Hart, Miner & Norton in 1839, who operated a few months, after which it was blown out and lay idle for some time until purchased by Galbraith & McCleery, of Pennsylvania, who after a short time sold to William Wheeler. But the enterprise proved disastrous to all these parties and the works were abandoned. The only flour-mill was built by Daniel Arthurholtz on Big Yankee run, on lot number fifty-six in the northeast part of the township. It is now operated by Asa Arthurholtz. The mill is now doing a good general custom work, and has two run of buhrs, propelled by both steam and water-power.

VILLAGES.

Brookfield center is the only village in the township. The leading kinds of business, such as dry goods, groceries, etc., are well represented. Its only hotel is conducted by Thomas A. Ballou.

The religious element is well represented by the commodious church buildings of the Presbyterian, Disciples, and Methodist Episcopal churches. The town and school buildings are well located and amply sufficient for the demand of the place, which taken altogether is a prosperous, intelligent, and quiet neighborhood.

PROPRIETORSHIP.

The original owner of the soil of Brookfield was Samuel Hinckley, of Northampton, Hampshire county, Massachusetts. He was represented in the sale of the lands by Dr. Solomon Bond, of Enfield, Hartford county, Connecticut.

The proprietor donated the lands at the center, commonly known as "the green," and the survey of the place was made in 1806. He also donated the original burying-grounds at the center, embracing one acre of land in lot number twenty-nine. The deed for this land was made to James Montgomery, John Briggs, and John D. Smith, township trustees, and is dated April 16, 1823. Soon after the grounds were im-

proved by private subscription and became the public burying-place in the township. Here are gathered in their last sleep many of the pioneer farthers and mothers of Brookfield. The history of their lives and deeds, to a great extent, has forever perished with them. To save what time has not wholly obliterated and to rescue the names of the pioneers from oblivion is the aim of the historian.

EARLY SETTLEMENT.

The first white man who came into this township for the purpose of settlement was James McMullen, Sr. The inducement held out to him to come into this then unbroken wilderness was an offer of one hundred and sixty acres of land in lot number seventy-eight in the east part of the township. He arrived in the year 1796, and erected his log cabin near a spring a few rods southeast of the present school-house.

This cabin was a very rude structure, built of unhewn logs notched and fitted together at the ends and "chinked" with mud. The floor was made of split logs familiarly known as puncheons. McMullen had a family of seven sons, namely: Thomas, Samuel, John, Martin, James, William, and Doctor (the latter receiving this unusual name on account of his being the seventh son). Samuel was married to Elizabeth, daughter of William Chatfield, in whose cabin the marriage ceremony was performed by Rev. Thomas G. Jones. This was the first marriage in the township. The cabin stood immediately south of the present residence of James Bentley, lot sixty-seven. William, a son of James McMullen and his second wife, was born in the log cabin above mentioned and was the first white child born in the township.

Rev. Thomas G. Jones built a log cabin in 1802, about one-half mile south of McMullen, and in company with his brother Benjamin brought the first stock of goods into the township and started the first store in the above-mentioned cabin. The cabin had but two rooms, one for the store and the other for the family. And the store room was back of the family room, and had no outside door, the customers being compelled to pass through the family room to get to the store. The shelving of the first store in Brookfield was constructed by driving large wooden pins in the logs upon which puncheon logs were laid. Here the early settlers did their trading, and it is supposed that the facilities of Jones' store were amply sufficient to meet all the demands of the settlement at that time. Mr. Jones was a minister of the Baptist denomination, and he sometimes held religious services at the houses of the settlers; but at this time the general services were held over the line in Pennsylvania. To him, therefore, must be accorded the honor of first introducing the gospel into Brookfield.

John Briggs settled on the north road two miles north of the center about 1806. In the latter year, or previous, several of the prominent settlers arrived. Anthony Patrick lived on the farm now owned by Benjamin McMullen. Benjamin Bentley settled on the present farm of his son James, and built his cabin home about one half mile north of the present farm residence. The first frame barn built in the township was erected by Mr. Bentley on this farm in 1808. This seems to have been considered at the time a great step in the way of building improvements, and called together quite a number of men from distant neighborhoods. It took two or three days to raise the building that two or three men could now soon put in position. To accommodate the many persons who came to his assistance on this occasion, Mr. Bentley killed several sheep and a large ox, and generously supplied the many other wants of his friends.

Johnson Patrick lived adjoining Mr. Bentley on the west, and William Chatfield south of the latter on the south part of lot sixty-seven.

Jacob Ulp lived southeast of Chatfield, and Ethan Newcomb joined Mr. Bentley on the north.

Thomas Thompson settled north of the center on the west side of the road, lot number forty, and Thomas Patten lived north of Mr. Thompson. Samuel Patrick lived on the north part of lot number fifty-one.

Judge Robert Hughes settled off the center road south on lot number twenty-five; Henry Gandy south of the center near the coal bank on lot number forty-seven.

The first death in the township of which there is any record, was that of Mrs. Henry Gandy. The body was interred in the woods, a short distance south of the present Whitacre coal bank.

Matthew Thompson settled on lot number forty-four, south of Brookfield, and Samuel

Clark south of him on lot number forty-five.

Dr. Thomas Hartford lived with Constant Lake, previous to 1806, on lot number forty, one mile north of the center, and was the first physician in the township. Dr. Upson settled at the center soon after, and became a well-known practitioner.

Robert Montgomery settled on lot number twenty-six, south of Judge Hughes. Isaac Flower on the northeast corner at the center, where he opened the first store at the center. Jacob Hummason settled on the southwest corner at the center.

In 1811 the road districts were designated and the supervisor elected received the names of the persons whom he had under his charge, and the following assignments are appended to show the extent of the Brookfield settlement in that year. The district assigned to Jacob Ulp included the road leading from his house to Brockway's mills, also the road running east on the center line from Yankee run to the Pennsylvania line, and embraced the following persons with himself: Thomas G. Jones, Benjamin Jones, James McMullen, Nathan Birge, Geo. Middleton, John Tribby, John Patterson, Philip Yarnell, and Daniel Groscost.

James Wilson was assigned to the road leading west from the center to Simeon Wheeler's and from thence south on the township line to the Liberty township line, and included the following persons, with himself: William White, Philip Quigley, David Wheeler, Samuel Munson, Jonathan Kerr, James and Robert Montgomery, James Haw, James Kerney, John D. Smith, Robert Hughes, Timothy Alderman, A. Alderman, and Daniel Williams.

Henry H. Gandy was assigned to the road leading from the center south through the township; also the road leading east from the center to Yankee run, embracing the following persons, with himself: Walter Clark, Collins Youngs, Henry Reidsilly, Jacob Harris, Amos and Charles Bradford, John Woods, John Patrick, Jacob Hummason, Isaac Flower, Jr., and Ebenezer W. Comes.

William Cunningham's district included the road leading from the center north to Brockway's mill and from thence on the triangle road leading to Simeon Wheeler's, and included the following persons: David Bacon, Constant Lake,

Clark Rathbun, Samuel Patrick, Benjamin Bentley, Ethan Nathan, John Briggs, Reuben Campbell, James Thompson, Henry and John Hull, James Russell, Jacob Reeder, Richard Creamer, Thomas Pattens, Joseph R. Porter, Jonathan Alderman.

SCHOOLS.

The first school was held in a small log schoolhouse near Big Yankee run, on the east and west center road—lot number seventy-seven. The teacher was Miss Lois Sanford, of Connecticut, familiarly known as "Aunt Lois." This school, as may be imagined, was not only very rude in its accommodations, but also in the appliances for imparting instruction.

David Shepherd is remembered as one of the early teachers who taught in a house at the southeast part of the center ; also, afterward, Jacob Hummason, on the west side of "the green." The latter teacher had been a merchant in the East, and was considered quite a good teacher. These schools soon gave way to the district school system, of which the township now has eleven, with nine separate districts. District number one, embracing the village, supports two schools in separate buildings, and enumerates ninety scholars. District number eleven, located in the southeastern part, also supports two schools.

INDIANS.

The early settlers in this township, especially along Big Yankee run, were often annoyed by the Indians as they wandered up and down the stream. The boys of these strolling parties became very familiar with the white boys of the settlement, with whom they often engaged in many friendly trials of physical strength and skill. The white boys could generally throw their red skin antagonists, but when it came to foot-racing the Indian boys could out-distance them.

The Indians were generally friendly but were in the habit of going over into the neighboring towns of Pennsylvania to exchange their furs for whiskey, on which occasions they frequently became engaged in quarrels which often ended in fights, causing no little alarm among the whites. On one of these occasions an old Indian, well known in the neighborhood by the name of Flinn, who was generally disliked on account of his sullen disposition and love of whiskey, butchered his squaw near the east bank of Big Yankee run. The Indians seemed to care little or nothing for the crime committed, and the murdered squaw was buried along the roadside near the present school-house on the east side of the creek. The funeral was celebrated in the usual Indian custom and nothing more was thought of the deed, and old Flinn pursued his usual vagabond life up and down Yankee run. But it is related that a white man by the name of Carr determined to avenge the murder and accordingly watched his chance, and one day as he was going along the banks of the creek he saw the murderer in the act of stooping over to tie his moccasin and he immediately sent a bullet through his brain and then fled to his cabin. Soon after the Indians found the body. They suspected the whites of the murder and made threats of retaliation, but as they had no proof of the person guilty of the deed nothing more came of it. No one knew who had killed the old Indian until years afterward when the mystery was cleared up by a confession from Carr. Several well known chiefs, among them "Cadashaway" and "Kiogg," were frequent visitors in the neighborhood.

THE BROOKFIELD AGRICULTURAL SOCIETY.

This society was organized in the year 1865 by five stockholders, namely: Samuel Shilling, Albert Christy, Allison Chew, James C. Struble, and James Clark. The first officials were Samuel Shilling, president ; Albert Christy, vice-president; A. Adams, secretary; and John Shook, treasurer. The first exhibition was given in September, 1865, and the annual sessions have been held regularly since. The past years have been successful, the exhibits comparing favorably with other like societies, and the attendance has been very large. During the first years the stock paid good dividends, and in 1874 the exhibits numbered nineteen hundred and fifteen; of later years, however, the attendance has not been so large on account of the more complete exhibitions held in neighboring cities, which naturally attract attention from the smaller societies. The present board is composed of the following gentlemen : Thomas A. Ballou, president ; Peter Carlton, vice-president; John Cole, treasurer; A. C. Burnett, secretary; John L. Doud, A. Price, W. H. Bushnell, Jesse Hall, Jr., H. H. Carey, and A. Seaburn, directors.

THE PRESBYTERIAN (OLD-SCHOOL) CHURCH.

The early organization of the Presbyterian church at Vienna center had among its members many of the early settlers of Brookfield, who as soon as the country became more thickly settled organized a society of their own. Concerning this organization the following original paper is still to be found among the records of the church at Brookfield:

BROOKFIELD, April 1, 1816.

We, the people, inhabitants of Brookfield, or others adjacent, taking into serious consideration the great importance of establishing a gospel ministry in this place, do hereby form ourselves into a church or congregation and to be known as the Presbyterian church or congregation of Brookfield, and do hereby promise and engage to give all pecuniary aid or the assistance that may appear necessary for the support of the same. In witness whereof we have hereunto set our hands the day and year above mentioned.

(Signed)

ROBERT HUGHES,   JAMES MONTGOMERY,
JACOB ULP,   JAMES KERNEY,
MATTHEW THOMPSON,   ROBERT MONTGOMERY,
JOHN LAFFERTY.

On the day following the date of the above document the church was organized by Rev. James Satterfield, of Mercer, Pennsylvania, acting under authority of the Hartford presbytery. The original members were James and Martha Montgomery, Robert and Martha Hughes, Matthew and Sarah Thompson, Jane Montgomery, and James Kerney, from Washington county, Pennsylvania; Jacob and Elizabeth Ulp, New Jersey; Abigail Lafferty, Mary Lafferty and her daughter Mary, Ann Lafferty and her daughter Ann, and Nancy Lafferty. The officials of the church were as follows: Matthew Thompson, Robert Montgomery, and Jacob Ulp, trustees; Robert Hughes, clerk, and Matthew Thompson, treasurer.

During the year 1817 the first house of worship was built, and was on the northwest corner of what is now the cemetery. This was a frame building, and the nails used in its construction were all made by Isaac Flower by hand. In the winter of 1817 Rev. John Core, a licentiate of the Hartford presbytery, was requested to become the pastor, and the following spring he was ordained at Youngstown and installed pastor of Youngstown, Vienna, and Brookfield.

On January 18, 1818, Robert Hughes, Matthew Thompson, and Jacob Ulp were elected elders (perpetual). On April 8, 1820, James Dunlap and Robert Hughes were elected ruling elders, and on August 13th of the same year, John Hughes was ordained and installed, with James Dunlap, as ruling elder. In the autumn of 1819 Rev. Core resigned the pastorate of Vienna, but how long he remained the pastor of Youngstown and Brookfield jointly is not known. A statement, however, appears of a settlement with him as pastor dated September 10, 1825.

The congregation on April 8, 1833, decided to secure the services of Rev. James Anderson, a licentiate of Washington presbytery, and during this year the church received nineteen additions. The sessions of this church and of Hubbard met together at Hubbard, and in all probability one minister served both charges.

At the session of the church held in May, 1837, Rev. William Woods then being pastor, upon the question of a division of the denomination into the Old- and New-school, which took place the next year, it was decided to remain with the old school.

At the meeting of the session, December 30, 1843, Rev. Joseph Smith officiated as moderator and administered the Lord's supper, at which time there was an addition of sixteen members. At the meeting of the congregation on April 4, 1844, the membership of the session was increased by the election of the following elders: Ambrose Hart, John Kerney, and William Jewell, who were ordained and installed as ruling elders the following April, by Rev. Joseph Kerr.

September 11, 1845, Rev. Ward was installed as pastor, and during his ministry occurred the only case of discipline in this congregation from its organization to the present, a period of over sixty years. The pastorate of Mr. Ward was one of much prosperity, spiritually, to the congregation. He continued as pastor until 1849, and was succeeded in that year by Rev. Jacob Coon, who was succeeded in 1853 by Rev. H. Webber. In the following year the record shows a membership of sixty-two. In 1855 Rev. A. McCurdy administered the Lord's supper and in 1856 Rev. W. G. March was moderator. In this same year, August 23d, Dr. John E. Stewart, Samuel Shilling, and John Long were elected ruling elders, but only the former two were installed. Rev. N. B. Lyons was installed as pastor in June of this year, and probably served until 1860.

In 1866 Rev. G. S. Rice was the stated supply for a time.

The name of Rev. W. C. Falconer appears on the records as moderator in 1868. The few years following the congregation did not prosper, the membership declined, and regular preaching was discontinued until the winter of 1871-72, when a revival occurred in the Methodist Episcopal church, and the religious fervor awakened the few remaining members of this church, and an effort was made to secure the regular ministration of the Gospel in their own house, which during the following summer was thoroughly repaired.

In the meantime Rev. Willis Weaver, a licentiate of the Mahoning presbytery, now a missionary to Bogata, South America, preached here half his time.

In September, 1872, an engagement was made with the present pastor, Rev. J. Rea Stockton, who served as supply until the spring meeting of the presbytery, the congregation then numbering twenty. In 1873 the pastor was installed, and Thomas M. Gordon elected elder.

Since his pastorate began the church has received many additions, and the Sabbath-school has been reorganized, and is now in a flourishing condition. John A. Stewart, Frank B. McKay, and Francis M. McKay were elected elders in June, 1881.

THE METHODISTS.

The Methodist Episcopal church of Brookfield has had an existence for many years, but the writer found it impossible to obtain any definite information concerning its history The early members are all gone and they have left no records concerning its organization and growth from which reliable data could be procured.

THE DISCIPLES CHURCH.

The organization of this society was effected by Rev. N. N. Bartlett, February 22, 1874. The first official board was composed of Jesse Hoagland, Henry Patterson, and A. Taylor, elders; R. S. Hart, H. Hamilton, and J. W. Groves, deacons. The charter members of the society, including the above officials, are S. C. Hamilton, Susan Groves, Mary and Flora Taylor, Lucy Struble, Caroline Seaburn, Mary Groves, Mary A. Toward, Catharine, Hannah, and Carrie Jones, E. A. Clark, Mary Christy, Emily, Kate, and O. Hart, Elsie Mason, G. W. and Sarah Burton, J. and Mary McMullen, O. J. and Hester Burnett, Mystilla Jones, L. and Mary Randall, A. and Esther McCollum, Emily Patterson, Lorain Hatch, Elnora Day, James Haney, and Lavina Montgomery. The society first held services in the town hall at Brookfield until 1876, when the present church building was erected. From the time of organization to the present the society has been served by the following preachers: Henry Patterson, N. N. Bartlett, H. D. Carlton, P. Vogle, Elder Peckham, O. A. Richards.

The Sabbath-school was organized June 30, 1881, with A. Taylor, superintendent; W. P. Kerr, assistant; Dora Hart, secretary and treasurer; J. J. Gettins and Cora McClain, librarians; and J. Broadbent, organist.

The school now has an enrollment of eighty-six scholars, and is in a flourishing condition. The church has a membership numbering ninety-three; forty-one having been received by immersion and letter during the past year. The organization is yet new, but the indications of the present bid fair for continued prosperity and the accomplishment of much good work for the moral welfare of the community.

NOTES OF SETTLEMENT.

Dr. Elijah Flower was one of the most widely known and popular of the early physicians of Trumbull county. He was born in Burlington, Hartford county, Connecticut, in 1782, and removed to Ohio in the fall of 1813 with his family, consisting of his wife and one child, Mrs. E. D. King, then not quite two years old. His father, Horace Flower, had moved out previously and settled in Vienna, and his daughter Lavinia is said to have been the first white child born in that township. Dr. Fowler settled in the center of Brookfield, and resided there until his death. He had practiced his profession in Connecticut, having studied medicine with Dr. Everett, of Burlington. His professional life was one of great activity. He enjoyed an extensive practice in Trumbull and Mercer counties, and was deservedly popular, not only on account of his professional skill, but also for his eminently genial disposition and social qualities. He died February 2, 1839. His wife was Sylvia Hart, daughter of Bliss Hart, of Connecticut, of whom and family a sketch may be found on another page of this work. Sylvia Hart was born in Burlington, Connecticut, April 1, 1790, and was married to Dr. Flower November 8, 1810. They were the parents of eight children, of whom only two survive—Mrs. E. D. King, living in Warren, and Mrs. A. Chew, living- in Mercer county, Pennsylvania. The deceased children were Amanda (first wife of Dr. T. Garlick), Lucy (wife of Pierce Wallahan), Sylvia (second wife of Dr. Garlick), Orlando, Emeline M., and Peter Allen.

E. D. King was born in Montgomery county, Maryland, November 20, 1804. His father, Edward King, was a native of the same place, and removed with his family to Youngstown, Ohio, in 1806. He resided in Youngstown until his death which occurred at about the age of forty-five years. His occupation was principally that of a butcher. He married in Maryland, Catharine Pool, and reared a family of five boys and five girls; four are now living. His wife survived him a number of years and died in Youngstown. E. D. King came to Ohio with his parents in 1806, being then the youngest of five children. He was brought up to farming until twenty years old, then engaged in the boot and shoe business in Youngstown as an employe of George Hardman. He remained with him some four years, then commencing the same business for himself in which he continued for over twenty years. In 1847 he engaged in the dry goods business at Brookfield with his brother-in-law, A. Chew, in which he continued for three years. For the subsequent three years he kept the hotel at Brookfield center, and afterwards, until 1872, was engaged in farming in Brookfield and Vienna. In that year he removed to Warren and has since that time led a comparatively retired life. Mr. King was a justice of the peace in Brookfield for six years and was elected to the same office in Vienna, but did not serve. In 1855 he was elected county commissioner, serving three years. He married in 1827, Maria, daughter of Dr. Elijah Flower, of Brookfield, born in Connecticut in 1811.

Jacob Ulp came from New Jersey to Brookfield in 1804 and settled on the farm where his sons now live. He married Elizabeth Scheiner and raised three sons and two daughters. All are living except one daughter, viz: William and Amos, Brookfield; Enoch, Hickory township, Mercer county, Pennsylvania; Eliza (Clark) Girard, Pennsylvania. Susan is dead. Jacob

Ulp died in 1860 aged eighty-three; Mrs. Ulp died in 1836 aged about sixty-two. William Ulp was born in Brookfield on the farm where he now lives in 1810. He married, first, Elizabeth Carkuff, a native of New Jersey. She bore four children, all now living: Timothy Dwight, Enoch, William, and Adelaide. Mrs. Ulp died in 1845 aged thirty-two. Mr. Ulp married for his second wife Nancy Wright, a native of Massachusetts. Five children, Eliza, Jane, Leonidas, Ella, and Ida. Amos Ulp was born in Brookfield in 1813, and is still a resident of the township. He married Rachel Conover and has three children—Robert, Charles, and Alfred.

Robert Montgomery, from Washington county, Pennsylvania, settled in Brookfield in 1804. He raised a family of seven children, who arrived at maturity: Robert, James, William, Hugh, Morgan, Eliza Jane, and Mrs. John Kearney. All are now living except William and Mrs. Kearney. Eliza Jane married Wyatt McKay, of Mercer county, Pennsylvania. Mr. McKay died in 1874, aged about fifty-four. He was the father of six children, four of whom are living: Myrtilla Jane, S. A., F. B. and F. M. (twins), Nannie, James. The daughters are both dead. The sons are living, located as follows: S. A. married Maggie McMichael first, and second, Mary Clark. He is now in Sharon in the book and news business. F. B. married Mary Gillmer and resides in Brookfield; F. M. married Arie Long and resides in Brookfield; James is attending school in Valparaiso, Indiana, fitting for the legal profession; Wyatt McKay settled on the old Montgomery farm, where his widow still resides. Mr. McKay was an active business man and a prominent citizen of Brookfield.

James Bentley was born in Sharon, Pennsylvania, in 1798. In 1806 he came to Brookfield with his parents, Benjamin and Mary Bentley, who settled north of the center road. They raised eight sons and two daughters. All are dead but James and Aholiab. The latter lives in Portsmouth, Ohio, where he has been engaged in the iron business. Benjamin Bentley, the father, died in October, 1818, aged sixty-two. His widow died about 1867, aged eighty-six. James Bentley lives on the old farm. He married Temperance Buttles, a native of Connecticut, in 1823. She moved from Connecticut to Brookfield in 1817 with her parents, Benoni and

Mary Buttles. Mr. and Mrs. James Bentley have five children living, two deceased: Amos B., Missouri; Anson G., Niles; Martin V. died, in Iowa; Benjamin F., Brookfield; Joel B., Missouri; Caroline (Woodbridge), Iowa; Eveline (Devol), dead. Mr. Bentley served as justice of the peace two terms. In 1840 he took the census of the south half of Trumbull county before Mahoning county was formed. Mr. Bentley is in the enjoyment of vigorous health and has a vivid recollection of pioneer times.

William Squires was born in Burlington, Connecticut, in 1810, and came to Ohio with his parents, Jason and Elizabeth (Wilmot) Squires, when eight years old. They settled in Vienna, on the farm where William lived. William Squires in 1834 married Sarepta Woodford, who survives him. They had six children: Jason, Willard, Sidney, Docia, Lucia, and Nellie. Mr. Squires died August 22, 1879. Mrs. Squires is the daughter of Isaac and Statira (Cowles) Woodford, who settled in this township among the first arrivals. Only four of their children are living, viz.: Isaac, Emeline (Truesdell), Laura (Smith), and Mrs. Squires.

Abiel Bartholomew came to Vienna from Waterbury, Connecticut, arriving in October, 1804. His son Ira came with him. Ira married Boadicea Church. They raised five children: Abiel, Mary, Eli, Rachel, Erastus. Abiel resides in Vienna, Eli in Indiana, Mary (Fuller) in Vienna. Rachel and Erastus are dead. Abiel was born September 14, 1805. He married Lorinda Maria Tyrrell in 1830. They have seven children: Rebecca, Mary Antoinette, Epenetus R., Boadicea, Ira, Celesta and Austin. All are married and have families. Mr. Bartholomew is the oldest native of the township now living in Vienna.

James Stewart settled in Coitsville in 1802, coming from Pennsylvania. He was twice married. By his first wife he had four children, all of whom are dead. For his second wife he married Jane Buchanan. Eight children were born to them, five of whom are living: Polly, James, Joseph, Alexander, and David. David Stewart was born in Coitsville in 1828. In 1849 he married Aurilla Gray, of Coitsville. They have three children living—John M., George H., and Luella. Mr. Stewart first settled in Liberty township, moved thence to Hubbard, and in

1867 moved to his present location in Brookfield. Mr. Stewart is a member of the United Presbyterian church. Mrs. Stewart died in August, 1878, aged forty-nine. She was a member of the same church. Both the sons are married. John resides in Brookfield. George is in the hardware business in Hubbard.

Phineas Wheeler was born in Erie county, Pennsylvania, in 1826, and came with his parents, William and Margaret Wheeler, to Brookfield when young. Of William Wheeler's children eight are yet living, five sons and three daughters. Phineas, the fourth child, married Emily Jones in 1859. She is a daughter of John E. Jones, of Brookfield. Mr. and Mrs. Wheeler have but one child, Earl. Mrs. Wheeler belongs to the Methodist Episcopal church. Mr. Wheeler is a Republican in politics.

James Christy, a native of Sussex county, New Jersey, settled in Brookfield in 1816. His wife was Elizabeth Struble. They had nine children, six of whom are living, Robert, Emeline, David, Seth, William, and John. James Christy died in 1861 in his seventy-third year. Mrs. Christy died about seven years later. Robert Christy was born in New Jersey in 1811, and has lived in Brookfield since 1816. He married Amanda Reno in 1837. They have six children—Albina, Minerva, J. N., Elizabeth E., Charles R., and J. P. Mr. Christy is a member of the Presbyterian church. His wife is a Methodist.

Dr. Robert P. Hays was born in Venango county, Pennsylvania, in 1840. He studied medicine with Dr. Robert Crawford, at Cooperstown, Pennsylvania. He attended medical lectures at the University of Pennsylvania, Philadelphia, and graduated in March, 1866. In May of the same year Dr. Hays settled in Vienna, where he now enjoys a large practice. He is a member of the Masons and of the Temple of Honor, and in politics a Prohibitionist. Dr. Hays was married in 1876 to Miss Lavinia C. Bacon, of Vienna. They have one child, a daughter—Frank—three years old.

Among the Welsh residents of Brookfield David S. Jones, who lives on a farm in the southwest of the township, is one of the most prominent. At the time of our visit he was absent, visiting his native land, therefore we are unable to give a personal history of him.

John and Lucy Bentley were among the early

settlers of Mercer county, Pennsylvania, adjoining Brookfield. Their son Elam Bentley was born in 1811. He married first Rachel Dilley, and after residing two years in Hubbard moved to Brookfield and there spent the remainder of his days. By his first wife he had six children, three of whom are living, James Lauriston, John Emery, and Cornelius. In 1860 he married Elizabeth Thomas, a native of Hartford, who survives him. One child, Mary Louie, is living; Lucy Anna died in 1881 aged ten years. Mr. Bentley died in 1873. He was a member of the Baptist church. Mrs. Bentley is a member of the Methodist church.

Samuel D. Gettis came to Ohio from Carlisle, Pennsylvania, and settled with his parents, James and Margaret Gettis, in Liberty township, at an early date. S. D. Gettis married, first, Eliza Tully, by whom he had three children, two of whom are living—Lorinda, Emeline, and Mary Jane (dead). Mr. Gettis married for his second wife Ellen Branning. Three children by this marriage are living—John, Eliza M., and Lina. Lorinda Gettis first married Austin Alderman. One child by this marriage—Lyman G., dead. Mr. Alderman died in 1857. His widow married Joseph Hart, and by him had one child—Mary Elizabeth. Mr. Hart died in 1860. Mrs. Hart still resides upon the homestead in Vienna.

Isaac D. Price, son of Isaac and Christiana (Hibler) Price, was born in Hubbard in 1836. His father was a native of Hubbard and his mother came to that township from New Jersey when young. Mrs. Price is still living. Mr. Price died in 1867. Six of their children are living, three sons and three daughters. I. D. Price in 1867 married Nancy Hall, daughter of Jesse and Jane Hall, old residents of Hubbard. In 1873 Mr. Price settled in Brookfield. He is the father of three children—Isaac, Clara J., and Mary F. Mr. and Mrs. Price are members of the Disciples church. In August, 1862, Mr. Price enlisted in the Ninety-fourth Ohio volunteen infantry, and served two years. He was taken prisoner in September, 1862, near Lexington, Kentucky, but was released on parole after two days. He was in the battles of Richmond, Chickamauga, Lookout Mountain, etc.

R. R. Miner, son of Julius and Lucy (Rowe) Miner, was born in Hartford, Trumbull county, in 1822. His father, from Hartland, Connecti-

cut, came to Ohio in 1820; settled in Vernon; lived there several years, removing to Hartford, and died there at the age of seventy-seven. Mrs. Miner was a daughter of Titus Rowe, who settled in Hartford in 1820, and there lived and died. R. R. Miner is the third son of a family of nine children, of whom two sons and four daughters are living. He was married in 1850 to Paulina L. Lewis, daughter of Levi Lewis, of Vienna. They have three children living: Eugenia (Groves), Sharon; Cornelia (Sanburn), Brookfield, and Clara, at home. Mr. Miner has lived in Brookfield about twenty-seven years.

Peter Cook was born in the province of Bavaria, Germany, in 1830. In 1852 he came to America, and remained in New York one year; settled at Sharon, Pennsylvania, in 1853, and on his present farm in Brookfield in 1865. He married Margaret Dininger, also a native of Germany, in 1855. They have nine children living: Leonard J., Sophia R., Martha L., Theodore H., Godlove G., Alfred C., Jonathan S., Martha, Selina. Mr. and Mrs. Cook belong to the Lutheran church.

James Lafferty was an early settler of Brookfield. He was a native of Ireland. His sons were James and William; his daughters, Jane, Rebecca, Martha, Margaret, Orpha, and Lettie. Of this family only three are living—Martha, Orpha, and Lettie. William Lafferty lived in Brookfield on the home place. He married Mary Arthurholt for his first wife, and for his second Fannie Eacrett. By the first marriage there were six children, three of whom are living—Orpha, Drusilla, and William Andrew. The children of the second marriage are Ella and Edward, both living. Mr. Lafferty died in 1875 aged fifty-eight. He was a member of the Methodist Episcopal church and a respected citizen.

J. G. Treat, son of J. H. Treat, was born in 1855 in Weathersfield township. He is now engaged in keeping a livery stable at Cortland. He followed the same business two years in Vienna, and moved from that place to his present location in the spring of 1882.

BIOGRAPHICAL SKETCHES.

BLISS HART AND FAMILY.

The Hart family is a very numerous and honorable one, and highly distinguished for piety, industry, and patriotism, of which the principal subject of this sketch is a worthy representative. Bliss Hart, one of the pioneer settlers of Brookfield township, was the third son of the Hon. Simeon Hart, and his wife Sarah (Sloper), of Burlington, Connecticut. He entered the Continental army in 1777, at the age of fifteen, was in a number of hard-fought battles, and after much hardship, privation, and suffering, was discharged May, 1780. In May, 1783, he married Sylvia Upson, a lady of good family, and of first-rate intellectual endowments, a brilliant conversationalist. Witty, beautiful, and warm-hearted, she was worthy of her husband, who was a man of strong powers of mind, and was much respected, and had much influence in the church, town, and society of Burlington, which he represented at six sessions of the General Assembly; was a magistrate, and was a member of the convention to form the constitution, but having gone security for a large amount for a friend he was obliged to sell his real estate at a heavy sacrifice, and in the year 1823 removed with his family, which at this time consisted of himself and wife, and a son, Oliver Ellsworth, and a daughter, Amanda (their other children having previously married), to the south part of Brookfield township, where he purchased four hundred and fifty acres of land, upon which he set about building up a new home, clearing, erecting buildings, planting fruit trees, etc., so that in a short time the wilderness bloomed and blossomed as the rose.

Mrs. Hart was a woman of much native strength of character, kind-hearted, and sympathetic, very energetic, with an indomitable will, thrifty and industrious, possessed of a genial and sunny disposition. She was a fit help-meet for her husband under the changed circumstances in which they were placed, and instead of repining at the adverse dealings of Providence, she went to work with a will, to help redeem their fallen fortunes. Heaven smiled upon their earnest endeavors, and plenty soon crowned their hospitable board, while good cheer and happiness reigned.

The broken soldier, kindly bade to stay,
Sate by the fire, and talked the night away,
Wept o'er his wounds, or, tales of sorrow done,
Shouldered his crutch, and showed how fields were won.

It is related, as an instance of Mrs. Hart's pluck, that a rabid dog came into their door-yard one day when there was no one at home except herself and her two little grandchildren. She saw that the animal was on its way to the barnyard, and with wonderful presence of mind, without a moment's hesitation, ran out through the wood-yard and picked up a stout hickory club, which fortunately lay there, and armed with this weapon of defense, drove the savage animal away, and down the road, without its having offered to attack her or showing any resistance. Mr. and Mrs. Hart were among the "pillars of the Presbyterian church, never absenting themselves from its services, except in case of severe sickness in their family. Mrs. Hart was noted for her ministrations by the side of the sick bed and also for her benevolence, verifying the Scripture that it is more blessed to give than to receive." After a long life of active usefulness, beloved by all who knew her, "like a shock of corn, fully ripe," she passed to her rest, August 20, 1854, at the advanced age of eighty-nine years, and was interred in the old burying-ground in Brookfield by the side of her husband, who departed this life March 6, 1831, aged seventy years. Their children were Oliver Bliss, Sylvia, Experience, Levi, Amanda, Oliver Ellsworth, Rosalinda, Melissendia, and Robert Sloper, the first and last of whom died young; the others lived to grow up and have families of their own. All of them, except Experience, finally removed to Brookfield, and settled there. Upon the death of Bliss Hart the old homestead reverted to his son, Oliver Ellsworth Hart, who afterward married Susannah White Danforth, of Palmyra, New York, a cultured, Christian lady, of excellent family, lovely in disposition, and exemplary in character. Five children were the fruit of this union, two sons and three daughters, all of whom were born and brought up, at the old homestead, except one son, who died at the age of three years. In middle life Mr. and Mrs. Hart were called to their long home. Surrounded by their children and friends they died in the triumph of a living faith, and were buried in the village graveyard in Brookfield. A beautiful monument marks their graves.

Simeon O. Hart, the surviving son of Oliver Ellsworth Hart and his wife, is a young man of good natural ability, who has had good educational advantages, and has improved his mind by extensive reading, observation, and travel. He studied law at the Cleveland Law school; but his health failing he has never entered upon its practice. In politics he is a Republican. At the age of fifteen years he united with the church of the Disciples, of which he is still a constant member. He is known and respected in business circles for his integrity of character. He is the owner of considerable real estate in Trumbull and Mahoning counties, and in other parts of the country.

Harriet Eliza Hart, granddaughter of Bliss Hart and his wife Sylvia (Upson), and daughter of Oliver Ellsworth Hart and his wife, Susannah White (Danforth), early evinced a love of learning, and an aptitude for the acquisition of knowledge. With a miser's greed she sought knowledge, and eagerly devoured the contents of every book or newspaper which fell into her hands. She especially delighted in books of poetry, history, and biography. She was diligent and painstaking while in school, and always stood at the head of her class. At an early age she contributed to the press both prose and poetry. It is related as an instance of her readiness with the pen, that a leading member of the Mahoning county bar, having read an article in one of the newspapers dated at Brookfield, under the signature of H., inquired of a friend of his, whose home was in Brookfield, what legal gentleman they had in their town capable of writing such a paper as the one published in last week's Review? His friend informed him that the author of the contribution was Miss Hart. The president of a college where she studied, says in speaking of her: "She possesses a mind of the highest order, as to powers of reading and forcible, elegant, persuasive expression. I feel sure that providence calls her to serve her generation and age in some needed work, where her superior culture and deep sympathy with the needy can be brought into active daily recognition." She is an active temperance worker, and occupies advanced ground upon all questions relating to the uplifting of humanity. True to her convictions, she permits no lion in the way to turn her aside from duty's path. Doing with her might what her hands find to do, she will go on her way, laboring for the advancement of every good cause, until death shall crown her victor.

Orenus Hart, the oldest of the ten children of Bliss and Sylvia (Upson) Hart, married Sabra Lewis in Connecticut. They had five children, viz: Charles (deceased), Robert S., Blucher B. (deceased), Adeline (deceased), and Henry, who died in Andersonville prison. Orenus Hart was born in 1785, and died in his eighty-sixth year. His wife died at the age of eighty-nine in November, 1877.

Robert S. Hart, only living representative of the family of Orenus Hart, was born in Burlington, Connecticut, June 29, 1814. In 1838 he married Mary Ann Christy, a native of New Jersey. She died in 1871, leaving seven children, six of whom are now living—Orenus, born 1839; Seth, born 1842; Dennis B., born 1843; John, born 1850; Florence (Forward), born 1852; George, born 1853; Emeline, born 1854, died 1880. Emeline married Samuel Seaburn, and left one child, a daughter. The children are all married. All live in Brookfield except Dennis B., who resides in Portage county, and Florence in Wayne county, Iowa. Mr. Hart served three years as justice of the peace. His son Seth was in the One Hundred and Fifth Ohio volunteer infantry, and was under Sherman during his march to the sea. In 1873 Mr. Hart married Mrs. Mary E. Scovill, nee Roberts, a native of Vienna. Mr. and Mrs. Hart belong to the Disciple church. Mr. Hart recalls the manner of the journey from Connecticut to Brookfield. His father and his uncle Bliss journeyed with ox-teams, and were six weeks upon the road. They came via Albany, Buffalo, Erie, Meadville, and from Kinsman down the first range of townships to Brookfield. His father taught school at the center in the winter of 1822–23, in a small frame schoolhouse which stood on the present site of the Disciple church. The scholars sat on benches made from slabs. This was the only school in Brookfield at that time, and between fifty and sixty scholars attended it.

Chauncey Hart, eldest son of Ard and Millicent (Roberts) Hart, was born in Burlington, Connecticut, June 9, 1802. He married in

Burlington, December 17, 1823, Millessendra Hart, daughter of Bliss Hart, born in Burlington December 17, 1803. They removed to Trumbull county, Ohio, in 1825, and settled in Vienna township, where they resided about seven years. Subsequently they resided in Hartford for a time, but in the spring of 1835 they located in Brookfield, where he lived until his death, September 18, 1844. Mrs. Hart afterwards became the wife of Samuel Baldwin and resided at Ravenna, Portage county, Ohio, surviving the death of her second husband. Chauncey and Millessendra Hart were the parents of the following named children: Helen M., born August 17, 1824, now wife of Henry H. Long, residing in Hubbard; William E., born April 9, 1826, residing in Cleveland; Alphonso, born July 4, 1830, a lawyer, residing at Hillsborough, Ohio —ex-State Senator and ex-Lieutenant-governor of Ohio; Orlando, born July 29, 1832, residing at Ravenna; Edgar L., born April 13, 1825, a merchant of Cleveland.

William E. Hart remained on the farm until eighteen, taught school and was employed as clerk in a store until 1852, when he began a general mercantile business at Newton Falls. Remained there until 1866, doing a prosperous business, and removed to Cleveland. In the spring of 1868 he engaged in the wholesale grocery business under the firm name of Thompson, Hart & Co. He continued in that business until 1875, when his impaired health compelled his retirement from business. He married in 1852 Miss Rachel H. Wheelock, born in Portage county, and has a son and a daughter—Frank W., born September 9, 1853, a member of the firm of Hart & Co.; and Clara A., born December 2, 1857.

Edgar L. Hart was educated at a private school in Youngstown, where he resided with his mother until 1850; taught school two years (from fourteen years of age to sixteen). In 1852 he entered the employ of his brother, William E., in the dry goods trade at Newton Falls. He was then a student at Bryant & Stratton's Commercial college, Cleveland, taking a full course and acquiring a practical knowledge of mercantile business. He then entered the employ of H. S. Day, of Ravenna, where he remained until 1860, when he went to Cleveland and engaged as salesman for Morgan, Root & Co. After the establishment of their wholesale house he became a partner in the millinery and notion department, which connection he retained until January, 1881. He then formed a partnership with F. W. Hart and A. Van Tuyl, and purchased the millinery branch of the business, erecting the building on Bank street, 48 to 50, where they are now located. This is probably the most extensive house for the sale of millinery, silks, and fancy goods in the State, a business of half a million dollars per annum being transacted. Mr. Hart is unmarried.

CHAPTER VIII.

HUBBARD.

INTRODUCTORY.

East of the Mahoning in the southern tier of townships of this county the country for several miles presents a broken surface consisting of a succession of low hills, knolls, ridges and valleys. From the tops of the principal elevations the observer obtains a fine view of picturesque scenery in which the results of the handiwork of Nature and man's creative industry are harmoniously blended. Fertile fields, green woodlands and sparkling streamlets delight the eye, and the subdued sounds of industrial activity greet the ear. At the foot of the hills are busy towns and hamlets, whence arise such dense clouds of black smoke that one would almost fancy himself near the workshops of the Titans and Vulcans of antiquity. Toiling locomotives, dragging heavy loads of coal and ore, wend their way through the valleys, and from numerous hillsides arise the puffs of smoke and steam which attest that the coal-beds beneath the earth are being made to yield up their hidden wealth. Everywhere the steam-engine is at work, even

> Down in the depths of the fathomless mine
> Its tireless arm doth play,
> Where the rocks never saw the sun's decline
> Or the dawn of the glorious day.

Hubbard township contains some of the most extensive coal deposits of the Mahoning valley. Two railroads, branches of the New York, Pennsylvania & Ohio and the Lake Shore & Michigan Southern, pass through the township, having their termini in Youngstown. Numerous coal roads branch off from these and run to the various banks in Hubbard. The coal and iron interests of this township have contributed largely towards increasing the wealth and prosperity of the inhabitants.

Hubbard also contains much good farming land. The soil is variable, consisting of clayey, sandy, and gravelly loams. As the most of the surface is high and rolling, the soil is well-drained and arable.

Little Yankee run is the chief stream in the township. Crossing the township line about three-fourths of a mile east of the northwestern corner of Hubbard, it flows southerly and southeasterly, past the village of Coalburg to a point very near the center of the township and just north of Hubbard village, where it makes a U-shaped turn and flows easterly a mile; then bending to the northward passes over into the southeast of Brookfield township, where it enters the Shenango river. The stream in its course through Hubbard township is very crooked; and the New York, Pennsylvania & Ohio railroad, which follows up its valley from Hubbard village, crosses the Little Yankee five times in the township.

Hubbard township is the southeastern corner of Trumbull county, and adjoins the Pennsylvania line on the east. Brookfield is the next township north of it; Liberty lies on the west, and Coitsville, Mahoning county, on the south. Hubbard is the third township in the first range of New Connecticut.

OWNERSHIP, ETC.

Nehemiah Hubbard, Jr., an original member of the Connecticut Land company, was the owner of the land of township three, range one, and it was sold out to settlers by his agent, Samuel Tylee.

The township was organized into an election district in 1806, and named after its original owner. No records of early elections can be found.

SETTLEMENT.

Hubbard was first settled by people from Connecticut, New Jersey, Virginia, and other eastern States; a few Pennsylvanians were also among the pioneers. Very few of the original families are now represented in the township. The growth of population was very slow. In 1834 there were only about one hundred voters in the township.

Samuel Tylee and family were the first settlers. They came from Middletown, Connecticut, and arrived in Hubbard September 1, 1801. Mr. Tylee chose as a site for his cabin a spot northwest of the present corners of the village, and there began the life of a pioneer. He married Anna Sanford, and they had a family of five children when they came here. Mr. Tylee acted as agent for Nehemiah Hubbard for the sale of the land of the township to settlers, for many years. He was born in Litchfield county, Connecticut, in 1766, and died in Hubbard in 1845. His first wife bore ten children, and his second, Elizabeth Ayres, one. The names of these children were Anna, Laura, Samuel, Mary, Sanford, William, Julia, Hannah, Maria A. and Olivia. Five are still living, viz: William, in Kansas; Hannah (Bussey), New Orleans; Maria (Clingen), Hubbard; Eliza (Hagar), Hubbard; and Olivia (Barnheisel) San Francisco. Samuel Tylee was the first justice of the peace in the township and also a very prominent business man, whose enterprise contributed not a little to the prosperity of the settlement.

Sylvester Tylee, brother of Samuel, settled on the northeastern corner lot at the cross-roads in 1802. The village became known as Tylee's corners. His children are all dead. Their names were Clarissa, Samuel, Alfred, Marietta, Rebecca, and Homer.

William Burnett, from Sussex county, New Jersey, settled in this township about the year 1801. He lived to the age of ninety-four. His son Silas, born in December, 1802, was the first white child born in the township. William Burnett was twice married, and reared eleven children to mature years. Those now living are: Silas, Warren; Rachel (Bowen), Iowa; Zilla (Brockway), Iowa; Joseph, Hartford; and by his second wife, William and Peter, in Pennsylvania.

Enos Burnett, Silas, Edward, and Stephen were also early settlers and nearly all passed their lives in the township.

As definite dates of the several settlements cannot now be ascertained, we mention below several representatives of the pioneers, most of whom came to the township between 1802 and 1808:

Jeremiah Wolf, from New Jersey, settled on lot seventy-two in the southeast of the township, being among the first arrivals. His sons John and Cephas still live in Hubbard. His daughter Elizabeth, now Mrs. McGill, of Poland, is said to have been the first white female child born in Hubbard. He was a nail-maker, and made the nails used by 'Squire Tylee in the first frame house erected in the township.

Jesse Hall, from New Jersey, was an early settler in the northern part of the township. So many New Jersey settlers were located on the road running north from the center that it was long known as "Jersey street." Jesse Hall, Jr., is the only survivor of the original family now in the township.

John Ayres was another of the Jersey settlers. His son John lived and died on the old homestead. The family name is not represented in the township at present.

Cornelius Dilley, another of the pioneers, had two sons who passed their days in Hubbard— John, on the old homestead, and Thompson in east Hubbard.

Martin Swartzwelter and his father, of New Jersey, settled in the northwest of this township. His son Thomas lives on part of the old farm.

Samuel Leslie, father of James, of Irish descent, or of Irish nativity, was also one of the pioneers of the northwest of Hubbard.

Matthew Mitchell, a native of Ireland, settled in the west of Hubbard in 1806, coming hither from Pittsburg. His son, Nathaniel Mitchell, Esq., is now the only survivor of the family of two sons and three daughters.

William Porterfield, from Washington county, Pennsylvania, was an early settler in the northwest of the township, on a place which had been somewhat improved by a man named Chamberlain. Robert, the oldest son of William Porterfield, now lives on the old place.

John Jewell, also from Allegheny county, Pennsylvania, settled in the Porterfield neighborhood. His son, Alexander M., now living in Warren, raised his family in Hubbard.

Joel Smith was among the first who located in the southwest of the township. He moved away quite early.

John Gardner, another inhabitant of the southwest of Hubbard, reared a family of four children, John, James, Andrew, and Elizabeth. All lived and died in this township excepting John, who died in Coitsville.

Amos Smith settled in the southwest of the township. His sons, William, Amos, Nathan, and Joel, lived in this township and reared families.

George Frazier lived on the farm adjoining that of Amos Smith, Sr. His son George brought up his family here. Hugh died on the old place; John went West.

Stephen Doughton lived on a place adjoining the Porterfield farm. His son David reared a family of four children here, and died on his way to California of cholera, in 1852.

David Bailey, from Connecticut, settled on the south lot of the township, on the road leading to the center. His sons were David, Seth, Tryan, and Ritter. He also had four daughters.

William Parrish was one of the early Maryland settlers. His son John, who is one of the oldest residents of Hubbard, still lives upon the old farm.

The Roberts and Clark families were among the first of the Yankee settlers in the southern part of the township. The names are no longer to be found among the residents of Hubbard. Edward Bussey, about 1803, settled north of the Porterfield farm.

A. K. Cramer, a native of New Jersey, settled in east Hubbard in 1816. His father, Captain Frederick Cramer, was under the immediate command of Washington during six years of the Revolutionary war. Mr. Cramer came here a young man and married Susan Price, by whom he had four children, Elizabeth, Sarah (deceased), Naomi, and Susan. By his second wife, Matilda Pierce, seven children were born: J. P., Hannah, S. P., A. K., J. H., Matilda, and A. W. Two of these, S. P. and A. K., reside in Hubbard and are engaged in the drug business. A. K. Cramer, Sr., was one of the organizers and main supporters of the Baptist church. He was justice of the peace two terms and township clerk thirty consecutive years. In 1865 he moved to Iowa. He died in 1873 aged seventy-seven. Mrs. Cramer died in 1877 aged seventy-three. Of their sons, S. P., was township clerk for years, and justice of the peace one term. A. K., Jr., has been twice elected justice and three times mayor.

EARLY EVENTS.

The first frame house in Hubbard township was erected in 1808 by Samuel Tylee. It is still standing in Hubbard township.

The first justice of the peace was Samuel Tylee, who also served in later years. George Frazier, Joel Smith, and Thomas Robinson were also among the early justices.

George Frazier built the first brick house in the township.

EARLY SCHOOLS.

Several log school-houses were built in the township previous to 1810. The first was probably that built on the farm of John Gardner in the southwest of the township. Who the first teacher was is not to be ascertained. Joel Smith, a middle-aged man, was a very early teacher in the old school-house just named. Among his pupils were a number of well-grown boys and not too fond of study. The practice of barring out the schoolmaster was then almost universal, and was usually tried the morning following Christmas. One day Smith came to the school-house in the morning—the preceding day had been Christmas and a holiday—and found that his pupils were inside but every entrance was barred by heavy logs. He demanded admission but this was refused. He then procured a rail and pried out some of the chunks which were fitted in between the logs. Failing to make an entrance sufficiently large to admit him, he went to a neighboring house for advice and aid. The neighbor returned with him, and the two men then climbed upon the roof, made a hole through it and got inside upon the loft, which was laid with loose boards placed across heavy beams. Tearing up this flooring, they were preparing to descend when several stout boys seized a heavy wooden table, raised it upon their shoulders and held it firmly against the opening. The teacher jumped upon the table determined to get it out of his way, when at a given signal the boys let go and teacher and table made a rapid descent into the room and sprawled over the floor. Both were somewhat bruised but not seriously injured. The schoolmaster was seized, put out of doors and his castle again barricaded from the interior. There was no school that day.

A. G. Babcock and Timothy Doty were the names of early teachers in a school-house situated on the road west of the village

EARLY INDUSTRIES.

'Squire Tylee erected the first grist-mill about 1809. It was on Yankee run, a mile and a half northeast of the village. It was built of logs and had two runs of stones. He also had a saw-mill near the grist-mill built about the same time. Both were afterwards replaced by frame buildings.

The first distillery in the township was erected on the farm of 'Squire Tylee.

About 1810 a carding-mill, situated near the State line, was run by William Elliott. About 1824 'Squire Tylee erected a carding- and cloth-fulling-mill on the present village lot of 'Squire Mitchell. This mill was run by horse-power.

The first tannery was built by Jehiel Roberts, early in this century, a little south of the center of the village. Jesse Clark, who married the widow Roberts, carried on the business after him.

The first store was opened by Dr. John Mitcheltree, who came to the township about 1806, and commenced business soon after. This store was in Pennsylvania; but as the end of the log-cabin in which the merchant lived was in Hubbard, probably the latter has the best claim to the establishment. His store was in the east end of the cabin, so that while doing business in Pennsylvania, he was a resident of Ohio.

Dr. Mitcheltree was the first physician. He was born in Ireland, but came to this country young, and here learned the art of medicine. For many years he was the only doctor in the township. From his store and his practice combined he accumulated sufficient property so that he was accounted a wealthy man in those days.

Sylvester Tylee was the first postmaster. The office was established previous to 1812. He also kept tavern and a few groceries.

The first store at Tylee's corners was kept in his own house by Samuel Tylee as early as 1818.

HUBBARD VILLAGE.

This enterprising little place is too young to have much history. Up to 1861 it was merely a country cross-roads, with few houses or inhabitants. But when the coal-fields began to be largely developed the corners rapidly became a village, and in the course of ten years nearly two thousand inhabitants were comprised within the present limits of the village. The houses were

A. M. Jewell

Rebecca C. Jewell.

nearly all put up in haste, and many of them still stand unimproved in appearance. Main street is long and thickly dotted with houses and stores for nearly a mile and a half.

The largest mercantile establishment in Hubbard is that of George M. McKelvey & Co., who have been in business in this place since September 1, 1877. The furnace and coal companies have an interest in the store, and from it the workmen receive supplies. Mr. G. M. McKelvey, the head of the firm, was born in Indiana county, Pennsylvania, in 1849. He was a merchant in Youngtown ten years before coming to Hubbard. In politics he is Republican; in religion, a member of the United Presbyterian church. He is married, and has two children.

D. J. Edwards, at present the clerk of the Ohio House of Representatives, is another of the successful and respected merchants of this place.

A summary of the business of the village shows the following: twelve stores of all kinds, one hotel, numerous saloons, seven churches, one National bank, three physicians, two lawyers, one newspaper, one grist-mill, one rolling-mill, two blast furnaces, etc.

INCORPORATION.

Hubbard village, comprising a tract about one mile square, was incorporated in 1868. It now has an estimated population of about two thousand. The mayors, since the incorporation, have been: Nathaniel Mitchell, L. R. Prior, John Cramer, Add. Randall, Alexander Campbell, J. D. Cramer, and A. K. Cramer. The latter is now serving his third term. The officers consist of mayor, six councilmen, clerk, treasurer, marshal, and one street commissioner.

IRON MANUFACTURE.

Next to the coal business the manufacture of iron has contributed most to the prosperity of Hubbard.

Hubbard furnace, number one, was erected in 1868; number two, in 1872. Both are owned by Andrews & Hitchcock. Eighty to ninety men are employed. The daily capacity of both furnaces in one hundred and ten tons.

Hubbard rolling-mill was built in 1872 by the Hubbard Rolling-mill company. It is now owned by Jesse Hall & Sons, who were partners in the firm from the start. The mill has twelve puddling furnaces, one sixteen-inch muck train

46*

of rolls, one twelve inch bar mill, and one eight-inch guy mill. Product, merchant guide iron. Capacity, one hundred and fifty tons of muck bar per week. Employment is given to about two hundred men.

HUBBARD FLOURING-MILL.

This mill was built by W. A. Loveless and run by him for some time as a planing-mill. Five years ago it was converted into a grist-mill and run by Long Brothers & Co. The proprietors are now Long & Shook. The mill has a capacity of fifty barrels per day.

HUBBARD NATIONAL BANK.

This institution was organized in 1873 as Hubbard Savings bank, with A. M. Jewell president, and G. M. Dill cashier, and continued as a savings bank until 1878, when it was converted into a National bank with a cash capital of $50,000. The present officers are A. M. Jewell, president; R. H. Jewell, cashier; and the following directors: A. M. Jewell, D. J. Dennison, S. L. Kerr, H. H. Long, A. T. Mizner, G. H. Kerr, and S. Q. March.

NEWSPAPERS.

The first newspaper in Hubbard was established by A. D. Fassett, and run by him from July, 1868, to November, 1872. For a few months it was called the Standard, and was printed in the Courier office at Youngstown. In the winter of 1868-69 Mr. Fassett bought a press and type and began the Miners' Journal, which was at first a five-column folio with but small circulation. It afterwards attained a circulation of two thousand eight hundred, and was the organ of the coal miners of Ohio. In November, 1872, Mr Fassett bought the Courier office in Youngstown, moved his paper thither, and continued its publication, changing the name to the Miner and Manufacturer, making it a daily —the first daily published in the Mahoning valley. The Hubbard office was sold to W. T. McGaughey, who ran a local newspaper for a time, then sold out. The paper was continued a while, then suspended. Ford Wharton next published the Hubbard Signal for a year or two.

The Hubbard Enterprise was started in the fall of 1877 by F. J. Horton, editor and proprietor. In 1880 W. R. Wadsworth assumed the management of the paper, provided new type and enlarged the paper. Under his control the circulation of the Enterprise has trebled. The paper is a four-page seven-column sheet, largely devoted to home affairs, county matters, and manufacturing notes. It is independent in politics. The enterprise receives a considerable amount of advertising and turns out good job work. The paper is neatly printed and is a very wide-awake local journal.

HUBBARD SCHOOLS.

In 1868 measures were taken to establish a high school in the village which should be free for all the scholars of the township. A school building was built by the township and finished in 1870, since which time the school has been in successful operation. The house and furnishing cost about $10,000. The superintendents of the high school have been S. Q. March, Alexander Campbell, J. L. Gillmer, D. A. Wilson, and the present teacher, Mr. March, who began his labors in the fall of 1881. The school has been in charge of competent instructors and has accomplished good work, making it a blessing to the entire community.

By act of the Legislature of 1873 the schools of incorporated villages became union schools. The Hubbard village union schools are in four departments and, apparently, well managed. The free high school building is partially devoted to the use of the village schools.

METHODIST EPISCOPAL CHURCH.

In 1803 Rev. Noah Fidler, of the Erie conference, formed a Methodist class in Hubbard, consisting of Revs. Amos Smith and William Veach—both local preachers of excellent reputation—and their wives, Mr. Parrish and wife, Mr. Frazee and wife, Amos Snyder, Thomas Snyder, Joshua Snyder, William Burnett, Enos Burnett, and a few others. This class met for a number of years a mile and a half west of the center. Subsequently another class was formed about the same distance east of the center. Both were ultimately merged into the Hubbard village church.

In 1810 Rev. Jacob Gruber held a camp-meeting in the eastern part of Hubbard, near what has since been known as the Veach meeting-house, which resulted in adding fifty members to the church.

In 1854 both the east and west churches being nearly or quite abandoned, all the Method-

ists of the township united and built a church at the village at a cost of about $2,200. Rev. S. K. Paden was on the circuit at that time. James A. Johnson and Jacob Marsteller each paid $150 towards building the new church. The west church was sold for a school-house. The Veach church is still standing and occasionally used.

The church is now in a flourishing condition, with one hundred and fifty members.

PRESBYTERIAN CHURCH.

This church was organized about 1804. The exact date is not known, and as the early members are all dead and the early records all lost little information concerning it is attainable. Rev. James Satterfield was a Presbyterian preacher and devoted fifty years to ministerial labors. During nearly all of this time he was either an occasional or a regular preacher in the church of Hubbard. Other early preachers were: Revs. McDermott, McCready, and Rockwell. Among the early members were: Sylvester Tylee, Samuel Tylee, William Clingham, Thomas McMoran, William Porterfield, John Jewell, Charles Stewart, and Robert Love, with their wives and families. John Jewell, Sylvester Tylee, and William Clingham were the first elders.

The first church edifice in the township—a rude structure of hewn logs—was erected by this denomination. It stood at the south end of the old graveyard north of the village. After several years' use it was replaced by a frame building which was used until the present house in the village was erected in 1857.

The present membership is one hundred. The pastor, Rev. J. H. Wright, was ordained and installed in 1873. Several revivals have occurred during his pastorate.

THE BAPTIST CHURCH.

The Baptists had an organization, or at least held meetings very early, and probably were in existence as a church long before the present organization was formed, in 1819. The information concerning the Baptists is very limited. The names of some of the earlier members will be found in the sketch devoted to the Disciples.

The Baptists were few in numbers at first and for many years struggled against difficulties. But faith and perseverance enabled them to overcome all obstacles and to-day they are most prosperous. They have about two hundred and thirty-five members. A fine church edifice was erected by this denomination in 1870 in the village of Hubbard, at a cost of about $7,000.

This church erected the building which is now the parsonage of the Lutherans and used it as a place for public worship many years.

THE DISCIPLES CHURCH.

In 1819 a Baptist church was organized at the house of Jesse Hall, who for fifteen years had been a member of the Baptist church in Sharon, Pennsylvania. Mr. Hall, A. K. Cramer, Archibald Price, James Price, Walter Clark, and Silas Burnett, with their families, were prominent members. Jesse Hall was an influential man among the Baptists, deacon, counselor, and chief supporter. For some time the church met at his house. When the "Christian Baptists" began their work, and Walter Scott, the evangelist, came most of the members gave him a cordial welcome. His forcible preaching brought all of the Baptist church, eight or ten excepted, into the Disciple fold. The church thus formed had about forty members. Jesse and John Applegate were appointed overseers and served with faithfulness for about twenty-five years. Oliver Hart and Warren Burton succeeded them. Orenus Hart and David Waldruff served in the same capacity, followed by James Struble, H. Green, and A. K. Cramer, Jr., acting elders. The church increased in members, strength, and zeal. Applegate soon became a preacher and served in his own church twenty years or more, besides traveling much abroad. Others preached here, among then Revs. Scott, Bentley, Hayden, Henry, Hartzell, the two Bosworths, J. T. Smith, Brockett, Perky, and J. W. Lamphear. In later times W. T. Horner, William S. Winfield, Willard Goodrich, Matthias Christy, Harmon Reeves, C. C. Smith, and J. A. Thayer, co-operated in extending the usefulness of this church. In August, 1837, the Trumbull county yearly meeting was held in Hubbard, and was one of the largest assemblies of the kind ever gathered on the Reserve. To this meeting came Campbell, Bentley, the Bosworths, Henry, Hartzell, G. W. Lucy, Clapp, Applegate, Rudolph, J. J. Moss, and A. S. Hayden, nearly all of whom preached, exhorted, and held evening meetings.

Thirteen converts were made. Two years later a meeting held at Youngstown resulted in several accessions to this church. For a few years meetings were held in a building belonging to Jesse Hall, which he finally gave to the trustees with the ground on which it stood. Subsequently they erected a valuable edifice in the northern part of the township. The church continues prosperous with a large membership.

Most of the above facts are collected from the writings of Rev. A. S. Hayden.

CATHOLIC CHURCH.

An organization was made and the church supplied by priests from Hickory corners a few years previous to 1868. At that date Rev. E. O. Callahan, of Youngstown, built the church, which is probably worth $3,000. After him Rev. Peter Becker of Youngstown officiated here. The first resident pastor was Rev. John T. Schaffield, who came in 1870. He erected a parsonage and organized a school. In 1880 he was succeeded by Rev. J. Klute, who enlarged the school-house and gave the sisters charge over the schools.

The organization is known as St. Patrick's Roman Catholic church, and has a membership represented by one hundred and twenty families of Irish, Germans, and Italians.

WELSH CONGREGATIONAL CHURCH.

The church of this denomination organized and built a house in 1865. Dependent upon workingmen for its support, the members have been quite variable. There are now about fifty members. The preachers of this church have been Revs. J. Edwards, Thomas Davis, D. E. Evans, David Powell, and some supplies. Rev. David Davis is now preaching here one-half the time.

WELSH BAPTIST CHURCH.

This church was organized in 1863 with forty members. Their first meeting-house was a building rented from the Protestant Methodists, an organization now extinct. The church was built in 1841, and about three years ago the Baptists purchased it. At one time the Welsh Baptists numbered over one hundred members. They now have about thirty-five. The pastors have been Rev. David Hopkins, Theophilus Jones, Edward Jenkins, and Thomas M. Matthews.

THE LUTHERAN CHURCH.

St. John's church (German Lutheran) was organized in 1867 by Rev. Frederick N. Wolf, with a membership represented by twenty-five families. Previously, however, meetings had been held, beginning in 1864. Mr. Wolf was the first pastor, succeeded in 1869 by Rev. H. T. H. G. Hengist. Rev. G. F. H. Meiser became pastor in 1870. In that year the organization was completed and a church council chosen. Rev. H. A. Smith became pastor in 1872, and remained until 1880, when he was succeeded by Rev. L. A. Detzer, the present pastor.

The church edifice was erected in 1871 at a cost of $3,074.

A school, supported six months of each year, is connected with this church. This school was organized by Mr. Smith in 1871, and taught by him and Gustav Birdemann. Rev. L. A. Detzer is now the teacher. He has upwards of eighty pupils, and gives instruction both in English and German.

COALBURG CHURCHES.

The churches of Coalburg are three in number—Methodist Episcopal, Welsh Baptist, and Welsh Congregational. The Baptist church was built in 1870, the Methodist in 1871, and the Congregational in 1872. All are still kept up, though with diminished membership, and only occasional preaching, except in the Methodist church, which is supplied regularly in connection with Brookfield. All of these churches are dependent upon mining people for their support.

CEMETERIES.

The principal cemetery of this township is located a short distance north of Hubbard village. Interments were made here very early, as the old-fashioned grave-stones would attest, even if no inscriptions were upon them. These stones are common flag-stones obtained from the creek-bed, rudely carved and rudely lettered. Many departures from modern methods of orthography are observable. The oldest stone in the graveyard was erected

To the memory of
JEHIEL ROBBARTS,
who departed this life
January 16, 1809,
aged thirty years.

Roberts was a shoemaker, and was drowned by breaking through the ice into the Mahoning river, while he was carrying a bundle of shoes to some of his customers. The shoes were found lying upon the ice, and led to the recovery of his body.

Another of these old grave-stones chronicles the following history:

In memory of
ANNA TYLEE,
who departed this life
February 2, 1818,
aged 45 yrs.
The first female citizen in Hubbard.

Of early settlers buried here, Ida, wife of Barney Lyons, died in 1812, aged thirty-eight; Barnabas Lyons died in 1841, aged eighty; Amos Ayres died in 1817, aged fifty-two; Samuel Price, aged seventy-six, died in 1827; Cornelius Dilly died in 1824, aged fifty-three; Mary, wife of Enos Burnett, died in 1813, aged forty-nine; John Burnett died in 1843, aged forty-six; Silas Burnett, born in New Jersey, in 1791, died in Hubbard in 1878.

In the northern part of the township adjoining the Disciples' church is another graveyard of more recent origin.

ODD FELLOWS.

Hubbard lodge No. 495, Independent Order of Odd Fellows, was instituted August 22, 1871, with the following charter members: M. B. White, A. P. Flaugher, D. J. Edwards, C. H. Huff, Caleb Davis, D. Struble, William Campbell, Samuel Walters, Alfred Crooks, John Wadle, David Wallace, Daniel Jones, John Thomas Jenkins, and Frederick James. A public installation of officers was largely attended by members of other lodges. The following were the first officers: M. B. White, N. G.; D. J. Edwards, V. G.; D. Struble, R. S.; John Wadle, P. S.; C. H. Huff, treasurer. The lodge has steadily prospered ever since its formation.

TEMPLE OF HONOR.

Enterprise Temple of Honor No. 21, Hubbard, Ohio, was organized August 16, 1874, with seventeen members. This society has accomplished much good work in promoting temperance. The lodge is now in good condition, has forty-seven members and occupies a well-furnished hall.

FORESTERS.

Court Lily of the Valley No. 6624, Ancient Order of Foresters, of Hubbard, was organized in 1881 with about twenty members. Its membership is now eighty and constant additions are being made. The society is in a most flourishing condition. Its present officers are: E. O. Jones, C. R.; Isaac Green, sub-C. R.; W. R. Wadsworth, P. C. R.; James J. Davis, F. S., and L. E. Davis, treasurer.

COALBURG.

This is a small village in the northwest of Hubbard township. It was built up by the mining business and has declined with it. At one time Coalburg had a population of about eight hundred, several stores, and was a thriving place. It was hastily built and has few good buildings. The population is now about three hundred. The first store was started about 1863 by William Powers & Co. Jacob Sanders was the first postmaster. Coalburg is a station on the Lake Shore & Michigan Southern railroad.

COAL OPERATIONS.

The coal interests of this township are on the wane. The best mines have long since been worked out. A vast amount of wealth has resulted from the working of these mines during the past twenty years, operations having been carried on very extensively during the greater portion of the time.

Jackson Brothers opened the first banks in 1861. These were known as the Veach mines, situated in East Hubbard. E. P. Burnett owned the most valuable coal fields in the township, and after opening a mine leased it to Andrews & Hitchcock, who are still operating it. After coal railroads had been built to various parts of the township, mining went forward with an impetus until very recently. The enterprising firm, Andrews & Hitchcock, are still operating quite largely. P. Jacobs & Sons are now opening mines in the southeast of the township and preparing for an extensive business.

The first coal operations in the vicinity of Coalburg began in 1863. Powers & Arms leased coal fields from Jesse Hall, Madison Powers, and others, and after working them a short time leased to Brown, Bonnell & Co., who, under the name of the Mahoning Coal company, have carried on the business very extensively. They built the railroad from Youngstown, which has since become the Lake Shore & Michigan Southern branch, now extended northward to the main line. Some of the banks once yielded three to four hundred tons of coal per day and gave employment to hundreds of workmen. The Love, Burnett, and Cramer banks, operated by Andrews & Hitchcock have each been very productive. All are now more or less exhausted, though the annual coal production of this township still amounts to a large number of tons.

BIOGRAPHICAL SKETCHES.

WILLIAM BURNETT.

Closely identified with the history of Hubbard township is the name of Burnett. In 1801 William Burnett and uncle Enos came from Sussex county, New Jersey, and settled here. His family at that time consisted of three sons: James, Benjamin, and John. Two little graves were left behind. The whole of the long journey was made in wagons over the poorest roads, or where there was no road at all. After perils and hardships which we can imagine but not describe, they reached Beaver late in the fall. As no road was opened farther and the severities of winter so near at hand, they decided to spend the winter there. In early spring he came on to Hubbard, the point for which he started. A farm was purchased, small clearing made, and log cabin put up. Surrounded by woods, Indians, and wild beasts, the struggle for life and property began. Soon after they were settled in their new home a fourth son, Silas, was added to the family circle. This was the first male child born in Hubbard township.

After ten years of labor which were crowned with more than ordinary success, his wife died, leaving him with seven children, the oldest being but fourteen, to continue the struggle alone.

During the next year, memorable in our National annals, he was drafted to serve in the War of 1812. For this service he afterwards received two quarter sections of land which he sold for a mere nominal price. The following year he married Barbara Huff, who died in 1863. Four children from this union survived her, one,

Washington, having been killed at the age of twelve, by the running away of a team which he was driving. Mr. Burnett died just one week after his wife, April 12, 1863, at the ripe age of ninety-one years and four months, having lived over sixty years near the spot where he first erected his log cabin. Having given a necessarily brief sketch of this pioneer's life, we cannot refrain from glancing back at the early history of our country at the time when he made his entry into this busy world, December 8, 1771.

During a hundred and fifty years the work of settlement in the colonies had been steadily going on, and they numbered three millions. They had just passed through the period known as the French and Indian war, and now the country is ablaze with excitement over the oppression of Great Britain. The struggle for freedom had begun. "No taxation without representation" was the cry. Three years after his birth the famous "Boston tea party" was held. When five years old, the great Liberty bell proclaimed freedom throughout the land in tones that made tyrants tremble. How often this subject was discussed in that humble home just as we now discuss the perpetuity of these institutions. At the close of the war the subject of this sketch was old enough to engage in the general rejoicing. During the campaign in New Jersey Washington spent several weeks near his home, where he frequently saw and conversed with him. Being twenty-one years old, he undoubtedly cast his first vote for him when he was re-elected in 1793. It seems to us a great privilege to vote for Washington, Jefferson, Jackson, and so on through the list of worthies who so honorably filled the Presidential office. His last vote was cast for Stephen A. Douglas in 1860. Born when our Nation was struggling for an existence, his life went out during the struggle for its continuance. There are now living in 1882, as his descendants—four sons and two daughters, also fifty-six grandchildren, one hundred and seventy-nine great-grandchildren, sixty-two great-great-grandchildren, a total of three hundred and three persons.

Joseph Burnett, son of William Burnett, was born in Hubbard township May 2, 1808, and resided with his father till his majority. From 1829 till the time of his marriage he was engaged as a distiller of liquor. In 1838 he married

Cassandra Courtney, of Virginia. Their family consisted of eight children, five of whom survive. From 1839 to 1855 he resided in Weathersfield township, and engaged in sawing timber. In 1855 he purchased what is known as the Brockway mills property, situated in the south part of Hartford township, where he now resides.

Although engaged in distilling in his early life, he has always been a strictly temperate man, and as an indication of the growth of temperance sentiment we might say that his eldest daughter Cythia is an active worker in the temperance cause as a lecturer and writer, and his only son, Albert Burnett, is a strong prohibitionist.

A. M. JEWELL.

A. M. Jewell, son of John and Jane (Miller) Jewell, was born in Hubbard township, Trumbull county, Ohio, June 18, 1808. His parents removed from Allegheny county, Pennsylvania, and settled in the west part of Hubbard on the farm now occupied by Stephen Doughten, in the spring of 1805. John Jewell died in Hubbard in 1859. His wife survived him many years, dying in Warren, January, 1873, in the ninety-second year of her age. A. M. Jewell was married in 1829 to Rebecca C. Love, born in Westmoreland county, Pennsylvania, December, 1806, and came to Trumbull county with her parents when she was but three or four years of age. The family settled in Hubbard. Mr. Jewell has been engaged in active business life, principally in farming and trading in live stock, and has been very successful. He eventually purchased the home farm, which he occupied until 1870, when he sold it, and moved to Warren the next year, where he now resides. He is a stockholder in the First National and Mahoning National banks of Youngstown, and also in the Trumbull National, of Warren, having been connected with the first named since its organization. He is largely interested in the bank at Hubbard, and is its president, his oldest son being the cashier. He has six children living, one having died when young, viz: Robert H., in Hubbard; Sarah J. Kerr, in Hubbard; John D., in New York city; William A., in Mississippi; Mary A., at home with her parents, and Louisa (Veach), in Allegheny City, Pennsylvania.

SETTLEMENT NOTES.

Jesse Hall was born in Hubbard township, Trumbull county, Ohio. His father, Jesse Hall, was a native of New Jersey, and came to Ohio in 1801, and settled in Hubbard township, about two miles north of the village, and was one of the earliest settlers in the township. He died in 1843, leaving a family of ten children, and widow—Hannah, Esther, William, Margaret, Jacob, Sarah, Elizabeth, Mary, Christian, and Jesse. Sarah, Christian, and Jesse are the only surviving members. Mrs. Hall died in 1861. Both she and her husband were members of the Disciple church. His son Jesse has always lived in the township, upon the old homestead until 1874. He has been engaged in iron manufacture and operating in coal in addition to his farming. He was married in 1833 to Hannah J. Sheline, daughter of David Sheline, of Carroll county. They have nine children— Caroline, Miriam, David, Christiana, Nancy, William, Clara, Harriet, and Jesse. Mr. and Mrs. Hall are members of the Disciple church.

Nathaniel Mitchell, an old resident of Hubbard, was born in Chester county, Pennsylvania, in January, 1805. His father, Mathew Mitchell, a native of Ireland, came to America in 1803. He resided in Philadelphia a short time, then went to Pittsburg, and came to Ohio in 1805, and settled in Hubbard, in the western part of the township. He cleared up a good farm and resided here till 1827, then moved to Liberty township, where he lived till his death. He died in June, 1831. There were five children in his family. Nathaniel is the only surviving member. Mrs. Mitchell died in October, 1874, in the ninety-sixth year of her age. Mr. Nathaniel Mitchell has always lived in this township, and is one of the oldest settlers. He has made farming his principal business. He was married, in 1831, to Miss Elizabeth Murdock, daughter of Abram Murdock, of Coitsville. They have had five children, two of whom are living—Mary J. and Maria. Mr. and Mrs. Mitchell and daughters are members of the Presbyterian church. Mr. Mitchell has been a justice of the peace for thirty-six years, and is

probably the oldest 'squire in the county. He has been township trustee, town clerk, treasurer, etc.

Robert Porterfield, farmer, Hubbard township, Trumbull county, was born May 12, 1799, in Westmoreland county, Pennsylvania. His father, William, was a native of Cumberland county, Pennsylvania, and came to Ohio in December, 1804, locating in Liberty township, where he lived about eighteen months. He then removed to Hubbard, where his son now resides. William Porterfield died September 14, 1831. His wife died October 7, 1838. The family consisted of seven children—John, Robert, Jane, William, James, Sarah, and Mary. John, Jane, James, and Sarah are dead. Mr. and Mrs. Porterfield were among the earliest members of the Presbyterian church in the township. Robert Porterfield has resided in this township since 1806. He was married November 1, 1838, to Hannah McMurray, daughter of William McMurray, of Liberty township. They had six children: William H., Mary A., James M., Araminta M., Hannah M., and Charlotte J.—all living at home except Mary, who is deceased. The family belong to the Presbyterian church. Mr. Porterfield has served as coroner in this county.

Cornelius Price, farmer, Hubbard township, Trumbull county, was born in Hubbard township, July 8, 1812. His father, Archibald Price, was a native of New Jersey and came to Hubbard in 1807, and settled in the northwestern part of the township, and was a pioneer of that neighborhood. Four brothers of Archibald Price came to Ohio and settled in this county. Their names were James, David, John, and Jacob. Archibald resided upon his farm until his death in 1847. His widow survived until 1873. The family consisted of ten children—Samuel, Frederick, Cornelius, Elizabeth, Sarah, Mary, Abram, Archibald, Hannah, and James. Samuel, Frederick, and James are deceased. Cornelius has always been a farmer, and a resident of this township. In 1837 he married Anna Burnett, born in 1819. They have four children—Mathias S., Harriet L., Smith B., and Clara M. Mr. Price is a member of the Disciple church. Politically he is a Democrat.

Lewis S. Burnett, farmer, Hubbard township, Trumbull county, was born in Hubbard township, April 9, 1836. Smith Burnett, his father, a native of New Jersey, came to the eastern part of the township at a very early date. His father settled on what is now the Beach farm, where he passed the remainder of his days. Smith Burnett died in the township in 1846 or 1847. The family consisted of twelve children, whose names were Harriet Ann, Marietta, Edmund, Lucy, St. Clair, Malinda, Jane, Lewis, Seymour, and Sarah. One child died in infancy. Harriet, Marietta, St. Clair, and Sarah are dead. Mrs. Burnett died in 1870. L. S. Burnett is a carpenter by trade, but carries on farming. He was married October 23, 1856, to Miriam Hall, daughter of Jesse Hall, of this township. They have had seven children, six of whom are living: Lois L., Charles S., Almon L., Hattie L., Sarah J., Loretta, and Jesse. Sarah is deceased. Mr. and Mrs. Burnett and their oldest daughter are members of the Disciple church.

Judson Ray Noble, Hubbard township, Trumbull county, was born in Kent, Litchfield county, Connecticut, March 17, 1805, and came to Ohio with his father, David Noble, the same year. David Noble settled in Boardman. His log cabin stood where the Methodist church now stands. He died in 1816, February 24th. Mrs. Noble died in April, 1836. Their children were Roxilana, Austin B., Judson R., William N., Calvin L., and David T., all living except Roxilana. J. R. Noble lived in Boardman until he was about twenty-five years of age, when he went to Youngstown and worked at carpentry a few years. He then moved to Niles, where he resided until 1870. He married, December 31, 1829, Mary Ann Robbins, daughter of Josiah Robbins, of Youngstown. By this marriage two children were born—Sabrina S. and Calvin. Calvin died young. Mrs. Noble died in 1847. In February, 1850, Mr. Noble married Elizabeth Price, daughter of Archibald Price. She was born May 26, 1814. They have three children —Mary, Hannah, and Anna. Mrs. Noble has been a member of the Disciple church forty-five years. Mr. Noble united with the Disciples in 1842. He has served as justice of the peace; was court crier twenty-four years, and constable several years in Niles.

George W. Randall, farmer, Hubbard township, Trumbull county, was born October 20, 1821, in Hubbard township. John Randall, his father, was a native of Washington county, Pennsylvania, and came to Ohio with his father, William, in 1806, and settled on lot forty-eight in the southeast of the township. John Randall began farming on lot forty-nine and resided there until his death, which occurred in 1872. There was not a death in the family until Mrs. Randall died in 1871. The family consists of nine children, viz: Amos, George, William W., Nancy L., Joel S., Angeline, John, Austin, and Addison. The parents belonged to the Methodist church. George Randall has resided in the township all of his life excepting one year which he spent in Pennsylvania. In 1843 he married Anna M. Burnett, daughter of James Burnett. This union was blessed with six children, five of whom survive: Ariminta, Albert O. and Orpha A. (twins), Charles M., Mary R., and Jennie M. Charles is dead. Mr. and Mrs. Randall and two of the children are members of the Methodist Episcopal church.

G. R. Stevenson, M. D., a well known resident of Hubbard, was born in Jefferson county, Ohio, in 1838. His father, David, was a native of Ireland. The family is of Scotch descent. Mr. Stevenson studied medicine with Dr. Gibson in Illinois and graduated at Rush college in 1858, and has since been in practice in different localities. He came to Hubbard in 1867. He has a large and lucrative practice. He was married in 1859 to Miss Amanda Dentler, of Lawrence county, Pennsylvania. One son by this marriage. Mrs. Stevenson died in 1860. Mr. Stevenson's second marriage occurred in 1868, to Miss Ellen Bell, daughter of William Bell, of Mercer county, Pennsylvania. Three children were born of this union. Mr. and Mrs. Stevenson are members of the United Presbyterian church.

CHAPTER IX.
VERNON.

In the year 1800 Trumbull county was divided into two election districts, of which Vernon, Youngstown, and Warren constituted what was known as the southern district, and the house of Ephraim Quinby, Esq., at Warren, was made the place for holding the elections of the district thus formed. Vernon at this time embraced a large expanse of territory from which several of the adjoining townships were subsequently formed.

The formal organization of Vernon township as now constituted was effected in 1806. Previous to the organization the township was known —locally, at least—as Smithfield, so called in honor of Martin Smith, one of the first settlers of the township, and why it was changed to Vernon is not now known. At the time, however, Mr. Kinsman, of Kinsman township, a zealous friend of Mr. Smith, taking the action as an insult to his friend, tendered him a farm in Kinsman if he would remove from a township where such an indignity had been offered him. Mr. Smith, however, treated the matter lightly, and remained in the township upon whose soil he was one of the first to cast his lot. For the name which it now bears there is no local circumstance to suggest an assignable reason.

PROPRIETORSHIP.

The original proprietors of the lands now embraced in Vernon township were Gideon Granger, who owned the entire north half; Jeremiah Wilcox, the west part, and a Mr. Shepherd, the east part of the south half. From these men the original settlers made their purchases; the earliest settlements being made on the northeast part of the Wilcox tract.

LOCATION AND BOUNDARY.

Vernon is located in the northeast part of the county in town six (east), and range one, and is bounded on the north by Kinsman, east by Pennsylvania, on the south by Hartford, and west by Johnston.

SURFACE FEATURES, SOIL, ETC.

The surface of the township rises gradually into rolling highlands from both sides of Pymatuning creek, and is more or less undulating throughout. On the east side of the creek the highlands roll away in rich table lands of clay loam highly productive of wheat and other cereals common to this section of the State. Throughout the western part the soil consists mostly of clay, but inclined to be more damp and heavy but generally productive. The Pymatuning valley extends along the course of the creek by the same name, with a variable width

of less than one mile, the soil of which is a sandy loam and affords the best farming land of the township.

DRAINAGE AND RAILWAYS.

Pymatuning creek, the most important stream, enters the township from Kinsman at the central part of the north boundary line and winds through the central part and leaves the township at the southeast, emptying finally into Beaver. Sugar creek, a smaller stream, extends across the northwest corner.

The Mahoning coal road extends across the northwest, and the Atlantic & Great Western railroad runs through the southern part with the main station at Burg Hill.

POPULATION.

The original settlers of Vernon were mostly from the State of Connecticut, and the present inhabitants are largely the lineal descendants of the pioneers, though New York, Massachusetts, Pennsylvania, and other eastern States are represented.

The larger farms are mostly in the north and west part of the township, gradually growing smaller as they approach the north and south centre road. Along this road the former settlements were made, and the present centre of population is distributed; growing in density, however, from Vernon center toward Burg Hill, which is now the central point of business interests and trade.

The census of 1860 gives Vernon a population of 964, which is reduced in 1870 to 930, but increased again in 1880 to 1,018.

The prospective outlook for Vernon in point of equality in respect to future standing with the other townships of Trumbull county, is to say the least, fair. Her people are quiet and steady in all their ways and for the most part peaceful, industrious and provident. The industries belong mostly to the agricultural department, though there are some branches of manufacture. The manufacture of cheese is the most important; there are at this time four factories for this purpose in the township.

The one flouring mill and several saw-mills, together with some attention to raising cattle for the dairy, and also sheep, will embrace the industrial operations.

47*

EARLY SETTLEMENT.

In the spring of 1798 Thomas Giddings and Martin Smith, the first white men to come within the bounds of the township for the purpose of making a settlement, paddled up the languid current of the Pymatuning in a canoe, having rowed all the way from Pittsburg. Their course in the creek was often obstructed by the accumulation of drift and logs, and they frequently were compelled to cut away the obstructions before they could proceed, and becoming entangled in the drifts they were at times obliged to swim or wade ashore. The craft which they thus slowly and tediously propelled toward their destined settlement in the wilds of the Reserve was laden with bacon, flour, and that other necessary article of consumption—a barrel of whiskey. They finally landed at a point south of the present center bridge, on the land now owned by Havilah Smith, where between two trees they built a fire and probably remained one night. Here they stored the provisions as securely as possible and began the exploration of the wilds of the then dense forests of Vernon. They naturally followed the course of a little branch whose clear waters flowing into the Pymatuning led them to suppose that it flowed from a spring of good water, which was then a very necessary adjunct to a new settlement. Following the devious and unknown course of the little brook they found its fountain-head in a spring near the present residence of Thomas Jennings— lot number two of the Wilcox tract. The following day they proceeded to the south line of the township (then marked by blazed trees) at a point near the present residence of Samuel Merry, and cutting a pole for a measuring stick proceeded to lay off toward the north what they supposed to be the land of Mr. Wilcox, of whom they had purchased. This brought them to the spring above mentioned, where they concluded to build a log-house for temporary shelter while they cleared a place for more extensive improvements.

They began at once to cut the logs and roll them together without hewing, and thus constructed a rude building. The first tree fell before the axe of Thomas Giddings and was rolled in position as the foundation for the first human habitation in Vernon. The sides of this building were thus made of unhewn logs, while the roof was made of thatched brush and leaves. It now appears that by some means they had either brought a horse with them, or, perhaps, bought it from a party who had made settlement south of them in Vienna or over the line in Pennsylvania, but they had no harness. This necessity, however, was soon supplied by stripping the bark from an elm tree, from which they constructed the necessary gearing. Two poles were then procured and lashed together for shafts, which extended long enough to drag on the ground, and thus answer for a rude sled on which the provisions, including whiskey, were dragged from the first landing place on the Pymatuning to the more secure shelter of the new house. While they were engaged in chopping in the clearing the sounds of their axes naturally attracted the attention of the Indians, who would come to them and invariably ask for whiskey. Mr. Giddings would tell them that he had none and would try to appease the appetite of his red neighbors with bread and such other eatables as he might have, but the presence of the barrel of whiskey (on which Mr. Giddings always sat as a guard during these interviews, and on the head of which the Indians would tap and say "heap full") was a standing witness against him, and in this way gave him much annoyance, so much so that he finally rolled it under a large brush heap and hid it from view.

Soon after the settlement of Giddings and Smith, Aaron Brockway, Colonel Holmes and Mr. Ely came, the former bringing his family, and his wife was the first white woman in the settlement. The first permanent cabin was then erected for Brockway in July, 1798, and was built by Giddings, Smith and Ely, and stood near the present burial grounds at Vernon center. At the raising of this cabin beside some men who came up from the settlement in Vienna, there were six Indians and one white woman. Martin Smith, after sowing a field of wheat returned to Connecticut with Colonel Holmes, for his family, with which he returned the following spring. He was accompanied on his return by Joseph DeWolf and Paul Rice, coming by way of Pittsburg and bringing valuable acquisitions consisting of two horses and an ox team. After leaving Beaver on the return they were compelled to cut their way through the woods and underbrush to Vernon.

At harvest time they cut the wheat that Smith had sown, and after threshing a grist took it to the mill at Beaver, which required an absence of nine days, and before they succeeded in obtaining wheat flour the settlers subsisted on wild meat and corn pounded in a hollowed stump with a spring-pole and pestle. In the fall of 1799 Caleb Palmer and his son Warren, with Dr. Wilcox, and the family of Joseph DeWolf arrived in the settlement. The beginning of the year 1800 found only the families of Smith, Brockway, and DeWolf in the Smithfield settlement. Afterward immigration may be said to have set steadily in, and the township soon showed evident signs of general settlement.

In the spring of 1800 Rev. Obed Crosby came and his family arrived the following year. In June of this year Jeremiah Yemans, a lad of about nineteen years of age, was in company with several other men and boys bathing in the the Pymatuning, and being unable to swim he got beyond his depth and sank. He was seen to rise the third time, but there seems to have been no one there with sufficient courage to go to his assistance. The alarm that was given brought Martin Smith to the scene of the accident, and he immediately entered the water to find the body. After making several dives he finally succeeded in bringing the body to the shore and it was carried to the house of his sister, Mrs. Aaron Brockway. It appears that at this time the arrival of the first native born settler of Vernon was seriously expected at the house of Mr. Brockway, and on this account the dead body of the brother was laid in an out-house. That same evening a very heavy thunderstorm arose, and amidst these unfavorable circumstances the little stranger was born. But it was not permitted to live, and the little community was called upon to attend this double funeral and open the first grave in the new settlement. The following morning the selection was made for a cemetery, which was located on the grounds donated by Mr. Brockway on his farm, about a half-mile south of the center on the west side of the center road.

The first person born in the township who lived to maturity was Zachariah Palmer, who was born in the fall of 1800.

In June, 1800, Abner Moses came with his children—Abner, John, and Polly. After them the families of Caleb Palmer and his son War-

ren, also Thomas Giddings after a brief absence, returned to the settlement with his newly married wife. In 1801 the settlement consisted of the above families and their cabins ranged along the present center road. Thomas Giddings lived nearly opposite the present residence of Havilah Smith, which was then the site of the cabin of his father Martin. Caleb Palmer's cabin stood where William Thompson now resides; Joseph DeWolf where Mr. Fulton's house now stands; Obed Crosby where A. Woldrof lives; Abner Moses near the present residence of Dr. King; and Aaron Brockway where Matthew Davis now lives. These were all log cabins of the rudest kind with no floor but "mother earth." They served as temporary lodgment for the hardy pioneers until the forests that surrounded them were subdued and the cleared fields answered in abundance to their industry, and the old logs were removed and more commodious residences took their places.

In the early times Andrew Burns was the hatter and carried on his trade east of Joseph De-Wolf, with whom John Langley, then a lad of ten years of age, worked at scraping the fur from coon, muskrat, and other skins, of which was constructed some wonderful head-gear for the gentry of the times, especially for the militia officers, whose high-cocked hats and waving plumes were startling to behold and no doubt struck terror to the hearts of their foes at very long range.

It was not often that a beaver was caught, and then generally by the Indians, and a hat made of this fur brought to the revenue of the pioneer hatter the sum of $10.

Some time prior to 1810 Percy Sheldon came with his wife and one child and settled on the farm on which he lived and died.

Plumb Sutliff about the same time took up the farm south and adjoining Sheldon. Samuel Sutliff also settled on the farm where he lived until his death in 1840. Dr. Amos Wright settled on the land south of Plumb Sutliff, now owned by Ralsa Clark. In 1803 Luther and Thomas Thompson made the first improvement on the east side of the Pymatuning, on the farm now owned by James Brown.

Morgan Banning was also an early settler on the east side south of Thompson. Ewing Wright settled near the present Baptist church.

He was a blacksmith, and also manufactured bells.

The first wedding in the township occurred about 1802 under rather singular circumstances. It appears that Josiah Pelton, of Killingsworth, Connecticut, had made purchase of a section of land in Gustavus, and after a visit to the wilderness he proclaimed that he would give one hundred acres of land to the woman who would first make her home there. This offer was quickly accepted by his son Jesse in behalf of Ruhamah DeWolf of Granby, Connecticut. She came with her father to Vernon, where the marriage ceremony was performed by Martin Smith, Esq. She remained in Vernon till a clearing was made and a log cabin erected on her farm in Gustavus. The cabin was raised by the men of Vernon on July 4, 1802. Mrs. Pelton did not move to the cabin until December of that year, and her husband, while at work on the farm, brought all his bread from Vernon. On his visits back and forth he met with many incidents, among which it is related that at one time he came across a panther in a tree on the bank of the Pymatuning. He had no gun with him, but leaving his dog and a "paddy," made of his hat and coat, to guard the animal, he returned a distance of about three miles for his gun. On his return he succeeded in killing the animal, which measured nearly seven feet.

The first saw-mill was built by Joseph DeWolf in 1800, on Mill creek, and was located about one mile northwest of Vernon center.

General Martin Smith was the first justice of the peace, in 1800, and his commission was signed by Arthur St. Clair, and dated at Chillicothe. Titus Brockway was constable this same year. The marriage of the latter to Minerva Palmer was the second wedding in Vernon.

Joseph DeWolf framed the first barn for Martin Smith. It was covered with white oak boards two feet wide, rabitted on the plate. On them was a cleat four inches wide, fastened with spikes made by the blacksmith. John Boswell constructed the first loom for Mrs. Rutledge, sister of Mrs. Aaron Brockway, who lived where Richard Brown now lives. At the completion of this structure the neighbors from far and near, especially the women, gathered to see if the machine would work, as it was something much needed in the settlement. The timbers for the loom were hewn out roughly with a common axe, and were sufficient for the construction of an ordinary house in these days, but it proved to be a good one, and the garments of the early settlers were nearly all produced from this rude loom.

SCHOOLS.

The first school-house was built about 1801–2 on lot number four of the Wilcox tract, on the site of Samuel De Wolf's present residence, in which Electa Smith first taught in the summer of 1802, with eight scholars. Amos Wright taught the next winter, and his sister Sarah the following summer. Mr. Gilpin taught as early as 1803–4, and after him Ebenezer Chapman at Vernon center. The books used in this school (1812) were the well known text books which comprised the curriculum of the early schools, Lindley Murray's grammar, and Webster' speller. Mr. Chapman had many peculiarities, but was in general a good teacher. He is remembered as being very watchful of his scholars, and even in his devotional exercises, which he conducted regularly every morning, he did not forget the Scriptural injunction "to watch as well as pray," for in the midst of his devotions he would suddenly open his eyes and detect the impious pioneer youngsters in their tricks. When thus detected the punishment that followed was very severe ; so much so that the law was frequently appealed to for the purpose of settling many difficulties thus arising.

The cause of education has not been neglected in Vernon. The various districts, six in number, are all supplied with the ordinary requirements of the common schools. In late years a graded school of two departments has been established at Burg Hill.

THE PRESBYTERIAN CHURCH.

Rev. Joseph Badger, the Connecticut missionary to the Reserve, made the first efforts toward the organization of the "Church of Christ in Hartford, Vernon and Kinsman," as early as 1802. In the following year, Friday, September 16, 1803, a meeting was called at the house of Martin Smith, at which Rev. Badger presided, and the following persons formed the first organization, namely, Edward Brockway and Sarah, his wife ; Timothy Crosby, Aaron and Sarah Bates, Titus Brockway, Plumb Sutliff, Susannah

Palmer, and Sarah Smith. On the following day the above persons, with the exception of Aaron Bates, adopted the commonly received Congregational confession of faith and covenant, and were constituted a Church of Christ. On the Sabbath following, there being no building large enough to accommodate the people, the first communion was held in a grove. Rev. Tait, of Mercer, Pennsylvania, preached the sermon, followed by an address by Rev. Badger, after which the communion was dispensed to about forty persons. The society then adopted the "plan of union," proposed by the general assembly of the Presbyterian church and approved by the general association of Connecticut. The "plan of union" was evidently regarded as a temporary arrangement, but proved a disappointment to both Presbyterians and Congregationalists. It did not make the churches Presbyterian nor Congregational, but rather stood in the way of both. The admixture of these different elements often proved disastrous to the welfare of the organized work of spreading the gospel, by the different religious views being tenaciously held and exercised by sticklers to church polity.

Rev. Harvey Coe was pastor of the church thus formed, having been installed April 4, 1814. The following is the first subscription for his support by the people of Vernon: Aaron Bates, $10; Henry Bignal, $5; Wilson Clark, $1.50; Samuel Sutliff, $7.50; Martin Smith, $10; Stephen Linsley, $8; Elam Linsley, $3; Isaac Gibbs, 50 cents; Ezra Hyde, $3; William Hull, $2; Charles Clark, $4.50; Tully Crosby, $2; Luther Thompson, $8; Calvin Smith, $2; Benjamin W. Tanner, $2; Jeremiah Wilcox, $12; William Chapman, $8; S. G. Bushnell, $5; Festus DeWolf, $2; Ira Case, $5; Charles Merry, $1.50; John Moses, $3; James King, $2; H. V. W., 75 cents; I. C. Wilcox, $4; William Brown, $1.50; Charles Trunkey, 75 cents; Asahel Banning, $3; Thomas Beckwith, $3. The subscriptions of Chauncey H. Wilcox, Horatio DeWolf, and Henry C. Aiken cannot be deciphered. The total amount was $120.50. The church was under the charge of Hartford presbytery up to the time of Rev. Coe's pastorate, of which Revs. Badger, Bar, Leslie, Darrow, Wick, Hughs, Tait, etc., were members.

Rev. Coe continued as pastor for sixteen years, the first nine of which embraced the congregations of Hartford, Vernon, and Kinsman. His pastorate was very successful, especially in the year 1820, in which time one hundred and eleven were added to the several congregations, embracing in their numbers many heads of families and many of the leading members of society. The number of baptisms recorded during his ministry is over four hundred; two hundred and fifty-four were added to the church; one hundred and seven marriages were solemnized. The amount received for his services in solemnizing marriages were, Adam Wright, of Mercer, Pennsylvania, gave $10; seven others $5 each, some $3, the remainder $2 and under, and one in a border State generously promised a peck of potatoes.

A large proportion of the cases of discipline in the church were occasioned by the free use of intoxicating drinks, and more were expelled from the church for this cause than for all other causes combined. Special effort to arrest this evil was made by the church in 1829, and a temperance society was organized.

The large two-story brick church that now stands at Vernon center was built by this organization about 1825, but it is now deserted and fast falling to decay. The members of the old church, many of them, with their pastor, have long since passed away, but their works still live —not in plaster and stone, perhaps, but in the work of moral reform, the basis of true prosperity, for which they labored long years ago.

THE FREE-WILL BAPTIST CHURCH.

This society was organized by Elder Ransom Dunn, March 9, 1840, and was called the Hartford and Vernon Free-will Baptist Church of Christ. The original members were Wilcox and Lucinda Aikins, Amos, Herman, William, and Rosella Eastman, Horace and Lucinda Hayes, Loyal and Betsey Thompson, Orin and Electa Nephew, Loring, William, and Lucinda Miller, Edmund Burr, Mary S. Chase, Eunice Burr, Sally Hull, Cynthia Crawford, Ursula Beecher, Eliza Gilbert, Eliza Canfield, Edward Root, Peter Miller.

The first quarterly meeting was held April 11, 1840, at which the following officers were elected: Amos Eastman, deacon; Horace Hayes, clerk; and Wilcox Aiken, secretary.

At this meeting it was resolved to send a representative to the next session of the Ashtabula

quarterly meeting and request admission to that
body; and Amos and William Eastman and Benjamin Perham were elected delegates.

In September, 1840, Rev. Ransom Dunn accepted a call as pastor to the church. In 1841
Wilcox Aiken and Amos Eastman were elected
deacons; Horace Hayes, treasurer; W. Aikens,
B. Perham, P. Miller, and O. Nephew, visiting
committee.

The following May Edward Root was granted
" power to hold meetings and improve his gift as
God shall direct."

The present church building at Burg Hill was
erected in 1871. The first meeting was held in
it May 26, 1871, and the house was dedicated
May 28th. The dedicatory sermon was preached
by A. K. Matton assisted by Elder E. H. Higbee. The church is located near the Hartford
line in central part of the township and the
membership reside in both Vernon and Hartford.
Elders Higbee, A. H. Case, Jeremiah Phillips,
the present pastor, have served this congregation.

UNITED BRETHREN CHURCH.

This society was organized about 1860 by
Rev. Silas Casterline, in the house of Weston
Smith, about one-half mile west of the present
church building. Among the original members
were Edmund and Sapronia Burr, John and
Sarah Smith, Richard, Minerva, Jesse, Lydia,
Calvin, and Mary A. Mizner, Sullivan and Anna
Ralph, Weston and Julia Smith, Bissell Spencer,
Ransom, David and Hannah Ralph.

The present church building was erected about
one year after the organization and is located in
the southwest part of the township on the west
side of the west road. The trustees were Edmund Burr, John Smith, and Calvin Mizner.
The former of these also held the office of class-
leader and John Smith was also steward. Among
those who have served this congregation as ministers are W. H. Miller, H. F. Day, David Traver,
Samuel S. Evans, A. Berzee, D. F. Reynolds,
Rev. Riley, J. E. Brown, R. Watson, N. Lewis,
D. W. Sprinkle, and B. A. Bonewell. The congregation now belongs to Fowler circuit and
numbers about forty members. The union Sabbath-school held in the church numbers about
fifty, with Eva Williams superintendent.

Owing to recent changes in the circuit the
society is now without a pastor and the general

condition of the organization is not so good as
in former years.

THE METHODIST EPISCOPAL CHURCH (BURG HILL).

In the spring of 1800, Rev. Obed Crosby, a
local preacher of this denomination, came to
Vernon from Hartland, Hartford county, Connecticut. In the following year he brought his
family, and some time during this year he organized a class consisting of himself and wife, Ewing Wright and wife, and Eunice (Brockway)
Bushnell. The first quarterly meeting was held
in Rev. Crosby's barn, and on this occasion the
eccentric presiding elder, Jacob Gruber, preached,
and the organization thus completed is said to
be the first Methodist organization on the Western Reserve.

The society met for some time at the house
of Rev. Crosby, and afterwards in the log barn
belonging to Colonel Richard Hayes, which
stood on lot number twenty-eight in Hartford. In
1804 a log school-house was built on the same
lot, in which services were held until a frame
school-house was built on lot twenty-two (Hartford) in 1809. This house was moved across
the street in 1822, near a spring a short distance
south of the Orangeville road. Services were
held in this house until the brick school-house
was built in 1827-28, on lot twenty-two (Hartford), where services were held until the Methodist Episcopal church was built at Hartford.

Regular services were not held at Burg Hill
until Rev. A. N. Craft organized a class in 1866.
The class numbered about sixty and met at the
Burg Hill school-house. The first Methodist
Episcopal church building was erected in June,
1872, and dedicated September 7, 1876. Rev.
Niram Norton preached the dedicatory sermon
from Luke VII: 5, and Rev. R. M. Bear
dedicated the church. The building is of modern
design, located at Burg Hill.

About 1816-20 a class of this denomination was formed at school-house number four,
on lot number three (West Shepherd tract),
and this was a preaching place for some
twenty years. John Waldorf, John Fell,
Chauncy Jones, and Anson Coe were prominent members here. The brick church at the
center was used by this class until 1867. Among
the ministers who have preached to this denomination here were the Revs. Joseph Shane, Robert
R. Roberts (afterward bishop), Asa Shinn (after-

ward a prominent leader in the "Mutual Rights" movement, which culminated in the formation of the Methodist Protestant church in 1828). Noah Pidler was the first regular traveling minister who preached at Burg Hill. Andrew Hemphill, David Best, Caleb Reynolds, Job Guest, James Charles, Thorton Fleming (who was presiding elder until 1810), James Ewen, James Watt, James Ewing, Thomas J. Crockwell, John Summerville, Jacob Gruber (presiding elder until 1813). In the meantime many other eminent ministers of the church have preached here. Burg Hill was formerly supplied with preachers from the Baltimore conference until October, 1812, and from the Ohio conference until 1825. The circuit required a six week's journey, and the allowance of an unmarried minister was $80 per year, which was double that amount for a married minister. The present membership numbers about forty-five, belonging to Burg Hill and Orangeville circuit, of which Rev. Dunmire is the pastor. The society has had a long and arduous struggle with many difficulties, but now takes position among the leading religious organizations of this locality, and has "come up through many tribulations" with the pioneers of Vernon.

OTHER CHURCHES.

The Disciples or Campbellites organized a society in 1870–71, which met for a time in Reeder's hall.

The Methodist Protestant organized a class of about ten members in 1879 at the center, of which Rev. George Stillwagon is pastor.

The Universalists secured the use of Reeder's hall in the fall of 1881, and now hold regular services under Rev. A. A. McMaster, pastor.

THE ANTI-SLAVERY MOVEMENT.

The question of human slavery in the United States early agitated the lovers of "freedom and equality before the law for all men," in Vernon. The church organizations early incorporated in their creeds the radical emancipation view of this question. This is especially true of the Free-will Baptist church at Burg Hill, as a reference to its records will prove, and, in fact, most if not all the leading citizens of the locality generally were early champions of the "bondmen." The famous "underground railroad" had a good paying branch through Vernon, and many able and efficient conductors were located at convenient stations along the road.

The great question has been settled at last, and the incipient stages of an unparalleled struggle, together with the actors in them, belong to the past in which they are buried, and the operations of the "railroad" were shared so generally by all, that the naming of special ones might be deemed unjust to forgotten meritorious services of others.

In the rural graveyard immediately south of Burg Hill stands a plain tombstone with this historic inscription:

Mary P. Sutliff (*nee* Plumb) died March 7, 1836, aged 23 years. The first secretary of the first Female Anti-slavery society of Vernon.

On earth the friend of the needy; in heaven Jesus is her friend.

FLOUR- AND SAW-MILL.

The only flouring-mill in the township is now operated by Ransom Hull at Burg Hill, and was erected by him in 1874. The building is a two-story frame, 22 x 27, with a basement for machinery. It has two runs of stone propelled by a twenty-horse steam engine, and has a capacity of ten barrels of flour and from three to four tons of chop. The saw-mill was built by O. Hull & Son, in 1867, and has a capacity of three thousand feet per day.

VILLAGES.

Burg Hill is the most important point of general business in the township, and is located on the Atlantic & Great Western railroad. Old Burg Hill, whose name the new station retained, is located in Hartford, a short distance south. The building of the railroad induced the removal to the present location. Since then the village has gradually increased in importance and now forms a pleasant and well-to-do community. Various departments of trade usually found in small villages and at railway stations are found here. At present the business directory is one general store, one furniture store, two hotels, one saloon, one harness shop, one tin store, one drug store, a union school and two churches.

Vernon center, the former point of trade in the township, still retains a post-office and the town house. Since the abandonment of the Presbyterian church, a society of the Methodist Protestant church has been recently organized.

INDIANS.

The early settlers in the valley of the Pymatuning were often very much annoyed by visits from the strolling Indians who passed up and down the creek. They never allowed an opportunity pass for drunken revels when by entreaty or barter they could procure whiskey. The romantic idea of the Indian character as the "noble red man" was not apparent in those who were known to the settlers of Vernon.

"Yankee Jim" and "Cadashaway" were two well known Indians who frequently visited the settlement. It is related of them that they once killed three elks in this neighborhood and took nothing but the tongues. The antlers being afterwards found were kept for a long while in the settlement for ornaments.

THE INDIAN FUNERAL.

At one time a tribe of Indians were encamped south of Vernon and two of their party visited Martin Smith to procure some whiskey. The old 'squire, after a great deal of persuasion and fair promises that they would not become intoxicated, at least in the neighborhood, finally acceded to their desires. The Indians started homeward with their much coveted "fire-water," but on their way forgot their promise to the 'squire and indulged freely, so much so that they both become intoxicated, and, as usual, began quarreling, which resulted finally in a fight in which one stabbed the other to death.

Soon after Asahel Brainard, of Hartford, came upon the body of the dead Indian in the woods and became very much alarmed for his own safety, fearing that the Indians would accuse him of the murder and take summary vengeance. He reported the case to Squire 'Smith, and soon the Indians also received word of the murder and speedily apprehended the criminal. The body was brought in funeral procession by the tribe to 'Squire 'Smith's cabin, and Joseph DeWolf, at the request of the Indians, made a rude coffin of puncheon slabs, in which the body was placed. It was then taken eastward near the banks of the Pymatuning where the grave was dug. During all this time the author of the crime was present as a prisoner and self-confessed murderer of his comrade, but made the plea that "whiskey did it;" and was compelled, as a punishment, to hold the feet of his dead victim in both his hands during the ceremony of burial. At the grave a general powwow was held, and quite a number of the tribe were present. The squaw of the murdered Indian put into the coffin a pair of moccasins, hunting shirt, his rifle, knives, pipe and tobacco, and finally a lighted coal of fire for the use of the dead Indian in the "happy hunting grounds." After these superstitious rites were performed the tribe took their departure down the Pymatuning, and the settlers who had gathered to witness the strange spectacle returned to their cabin homes.

Time has long since removed all marks of the lone Indian grave, and the memory of it has now almost passed into the realms of legends with many stranger though truthful incidents of the early times in Vernon.

BIOGRAPHICAL SKETCHES.

EDMUND A. REED.

Edmund A. Reed, son of Allen and Silva Reed, was born in Connecticut, September 21, 1821. While yet a child his father died, and his mother in 1830 removed with the family to Trumbull county, and settled in Vernon township. The family consisted of three sons and two daughters—Chester, Edmund A., and Charles reside in Vernon; the daughters were Mary Ann (Mrs. Allen), and Harriet E. (Mrs. Barnes), who is dead.

Mrs. Reed was poor, and the sons had to rely upon their own efforts both for subsistence and a start in life. Edmund A., the subject of this sketch, attended district school in the winter and worked by the month in summer. After he had advanced far enough he taught school, by which means he increased his annual income. Though without money Mr. Reed had the good fortune of possessing an earnest purpose, and the will to attain the object of his reasonable ambition.

In 1847 Mr. Reed was married to Eliza M. Smith, daughter of Havilah M. Smith, of Vernon township. General Smith, grandfather of Mrs. Reed, was one of the first settlers of Vernon, and her father was the second child born in the town. Soon after his marriage Mr. Reed

E. A. Reed.

Samuel Merry

began the management of a farm, and has ever since devoted himself to that employment. Having a well trained mind and natural business capacity he soon became a local leader in politics and public affairs generally. He has served through the whole list of town offices, and for twenty-one successive years filled the position of justice of the peace. In 1866 the northeast part of the county presented his name to the Republican county convention for county commissioner, an office to which he was chosen at the subsequent regular election. He filled the position with profit to the county and credit to himself for four years.

In 1877 Mr. Reed was chosen to represent Trumbull county in the General Assembly of Ohio. He is spoken of by his associates as an unostentatious and quiet, but diligent and attentive member. During both terms of his service he was a member of the committee on schools and school lands, and on the committee on Federal relations. During his second term he was chairman of the committee on new counties.

Mr. Reed introduced and succeeded in having passed a bill for the re-survey of the State line between the Reserve and Pennsylvania. The location of this line had been a vexed question ever since the first settlement of Ohio. There had been no survey since the establishment of the western boundary of Pennsylvania by Virginia and Pennsylvania surveyors, in 1786. In 1796 the Connecticut Land company surveyors accepted the old Pennsylvania line, which was indefinitely marked by a cleared line through the forest. Difficulties grew chiefly out of questions of jurisdiction in criminal cases, the disputed ground being a sort of refuge where outlaws could evade arrest. Mr. Reed's bill authorized the Governor to appoint three commissioners to represent Ohio and a concurrent bill passed by the Pennsylvania Legislature authorized a similar commission from that State. The Ohio commissioners were H. B. Perkins, James Mackey, of Youngstown, and Mr. Rickey, of Steubenville. The resurveyed line deviated slightly from the formerly acknowledged line, but the chief benefit of this measure was to establish a recognized boundary.

Mr. Reed is a man of clear insight into affairs, an intelligent observer, and a practical student. These are qualities which distinguish him from the class commonly called average farmers, which is unfortunately too large.

Two children are living, Charles E. and Harriet E. Allen died in his twenty-second year.

SAMUEL MERRY.

The Merry family, of which Samuel Merry is the oldest representative in this county, is of English descent. The genealogical record has been traced to Samuel Merry, of Hartford county, Connecticut, who was one generation removed from his English ancestors. He had a family of ten children, with whom, in 1789, he removed to Herkimer county, New York, being one of the earliest pioneers in that valley. He died at Herkimer village, August 19, 1827, aged seventy-seven years. Hannah Merrill Merry, his wife, was born in Hartford, Connecticut, September, 1747, and died at Litchfield, Herkimer county, New York, August 19, 1814. Their children were Samuel, Jr., Enos, Charles, Epaphras, Francis, Lucy, Edmund, Ralph, Harriet, and Hannah.

Charles Merry, the third son of Samuel Merry, was born in Hartford county, Connecticut, in 1774, and was fifteen years old when his father moved to New York. Pioneer life is much the same everywhere—ceaseless toil, privation and discouragement. The decade spent in Herkimer county was just the sort of preparatory drill Mr. Merry needed for life in the new West opened up by the Connecticut company's purchase. In the spring of 1800 he started for the Reserve, going on foot with a pack weighing twenty-four pounds on his back. He did not follow the traveled roads which had been cut out by previous emigrants, but took a straight course through an unbroken wilderness, swimming streams and sleeping in the open air. One night he slept in an Indian hut. This was probably the most uncomfortable night of his journey, for, although there was no occasion for alarm, he thought it prudent to keep one eye on his host. His pocket compass finally guided him to Hartford township, where Timothy Brockway, his father-in-law, had previously settled.

Mr. Merry had married in New York Martha Brockway, whom he left at the old home in

Herkimer county until he could prepare a home for her here. Having selected a piece of land in Hartford township he made a clearing, built a cabin, and planted spring crops. He was well satisfied with his first summer's work, and having planted a fall crop returned to New York for his family, which at that time consisted of a wife and one son. In the following spring he settled in Hartford, where he remained about five years and then removed to Vernon, where he died.

Charles and Martha Merry had a family of eleven children, seven of whom lived to mature age: Erastus, Harriet, Aber, Samuel, Francis, Matilda, and Charles.

Samuel Merry, the subject of an illustration on another page, was born in Vernon, January 27, 1807. His early life was spent on his father's farm, and odd hours occupied in coopering until he had mastered the trade. During the winter he manufactured large numbers of cider barrels, whiskey barrels, and pork casks. The price of the former at that time was four and the latter five shillings.

Mr. Merry married January 1, 1836, Mary Crossman, of Onondaga county, New York, and began housekeeping on the farm on which he continues to reside. They have had a family of eight children. Judson L. resides in Arizona; Ellen (Mrs. James T. Weir), in Vernon; Courtland D., in Vernon; Delia C (Mrs. John Morrison), in Ashtabula county; Charles T., in Vernon; Theodore T. and Willard P., in Burg Hill, and Mrs. W. P. Crowell.

Mrs. Samuel Merry died December 17, 1881. She had joined the Baptist church in New York and during all her life was a Christian woman. Mr. Merry united with the Methodist Protestant church and remained a member until the church was removed. His father, Charles Merry, was one of the most prominent of the pioneers; was paymaster of militia from 1811 until 1817, and held various other local trusts.

JOHN I. KING, M. D.

The subject of this sketch was born in Harrison township, near Platteville, Grant county, Wisconsin, November 13, 1848. His father, John, son of James King, Sr., and Eliza Jane Smail, were married May 11, or 13, 1847, near Jamestown, Pennsylvania, each being about twenty years of age. They went to Wisconsin in April, 1848, where young King was born. April, 1849, his father started for California to try his success in the gold mines. He died a short time after reaching Negro bar on the American river, California, the first day of January, 1850, lacking a few days of being twenty-three years of age. He was born in Vernon township, Trumbull county, Ohio, January 13, 1827, and his wife April 8th of the same year in West Salem township, Mercer county, Pennsylvania. Mrs. King married for her second husband Harvey H., son of Chancey Jones, Sr., of Harrison county, Wisconsin, February, 1851, by whom she had two children, Eliza, born December 11, 1851, and Harvey, born December 9, 1853. March 29, 1854, Mr. Jones with his family started by the overland route for Washington Territory. After a trip of varied and thrilling experience they reached their place of destination on the White river, King county, twenty miles from Seattle, an important town on Puget sound, October 24, 1854. Here young King endured the privations and inconveniences incident to a newly and sparsely settled country. He had to walk two miles to attend school, along a blazed path through a dense forest at the risk of being killed by Indians or mangled by panthers.

Sunday, October 28, 1855, his mother and step-father were murdered in cold blood by a party of about fourteen Klikitat Indians. After the massacre he carried his little half-brother and led his half-sister about three miles in hopes of finding some of the whites near where he used to attend school, which was done at the risk of their lives, but all had become alarmed and had fled. The houses were deserted and some of them ransacked. The outlook was gloomy indeed. They had been driven from the breakfast table, had had no dinner except a few potatoes they had dug from the ashes of the milk-house where they had been stored. It was getting late in the afternoon of a short October day, the children were becoming tired and hungry and begging for food; the roots he had dug for them to eat did not fully satisfy the cravings of a long-fasting stomach. The youngest, not quite two years of age, was inconsolable, and his sobs and cries added the danger of detection to the already harrowing complication of adverse circumstances. He could not be made to comprehend why he was being kept away from his mother, and his piteous pleadings to be taken to her and for something to eat made the heart of young King sick and faint. To add to the dismal prospects he discovered an Indian coming directly towards them, but from his manner he was certain they had not been observed. There was no time to be lost, and hastily securing the children he returned and started to meet the approaching Indian, whom he recognized as a friendly one whom he had often seen before and knew by the name of "Curly." They all were taken to his wigwam, and his squaw set out a great quantity of dried whortleberries and smoked fish. Ample justice was done to her hospitality. Nothing she or young King could do could induce the two younger children to treat her with anything but shyness and looks of fear and suspicion. Tired nature demanded her rights and he soon had the satisfaction of seeing them sound asleep, and never will he forget the mingled feeling of pride, sympathy and sorrow experienced as he looked upon his sleeping charge. Curly took them down the White river in a canoe the next day and delivered them up to the proper authorities. Their uncle John Small was in California, where he heard of the massacre, and immediately came to Seattle and took charge of the children. Some time in June, 1856, they left Seattle on the Government man-of-war Decatur. The vessel came near foundering in a gale off the mouth of the Columbia river. At San Francisco the children received the most generous attention, and a benefit was given them in the American theater. Thence they went to New York by the way of the Isthmus of Panama, and from there were taken to Wisconsin. Eliza and Harvey were left with relatives in that State and young King was brought back to Ohio and placed in the care of his uncle, Rev. David King, and his wife, in September, 1856. He joined the Methodist Episcopal church the 9th of November, 1862. He never saw his half-sister and half-brother after he parted with them in 1856. Eliza died October 6, 1864, and Harvey October 4, 1864, of diphtheria. They had not seen each other for three weeks, and had lived three miles apart.

Young King's boyhood days were spent as most, and no pains were spared to secure to him the advantages of a common as well as select school education. He attended the Allegheny college, Meadville, Pennsylvania, in the years 1867-68-69-70, and 1871. He began the study of medicine in July, 1867, and entered his name as a student in the office of David Best, M. D. in Meadville, Pennsylvania, in January, 1870. He attended two courses of lectures of six months each in the medical department of the University of Michigan, at Ann Arbor, in the years 1871 and 1872, and received his degree of doctor of medicine from Bellevue Hospital Medical college, New York city, February 27, 1873. In April of the same year he established himself in Greece City, in Butler county, Pennsylvania oil regions. In November, 1874, he located at his old home at Burg Hill, Vernon township, Ohio, where he is still [1882] engaged in the practice of his chosen profession.

January 31, 1875, he lost his uncle, Rev. David King, aged sixty-five, and September 9, 1878, his aunt, Jane King, wife of David, aged seventy-four. He takes this opportunity of paying grateful tribute to their memory. To their teaching and example he renders the most profound admiration and respect. Truthfully can it be said they tried to live as they thought others should live, and preached nothing they were not willing to practice. Mr. King was united in marriage to Miss Emorinda C. Brown, April 18, 1802.

Chancey Jones, Sr., was born in Barkhamsted, Litchfield county, Connecticut, May 11, 1780. His brothers were Israel, Pliny, and Horace, and his sisters Clarissa, Mima, Rebecca, and Orpha. At eleven years of age he removed to Herkimer county, New York; came to Vernon about 1802-3, and married Ursula, daughter of Rev. Obed Crosby, August 28, 1804. His house stood on lot six, southeast part. He subsequently lived near number four school-house. His house was the stopping place for the weary itinerant Methodist preacher. He took an active part in church affairs. He moved from Vernon to Illinois in 1838, and near Platteville, Wisconsin, in 1839. He died there in 1859; also his wife in 1876. His children were: Sterling, born in 1804, and died in infancy; Chancey, born in 1807, married Elizabeth Brown in 1830, and died in 1853; Obed Crosby, born in 1810; Clarissa, born in 1813, married Jesse Waldorf in

1833, and her children were Ursula, Elizabeth, and Laura Etta; Horace, born in 1818, and died in infancy; Jerusha, born in 1822, and died in infancy. Harvey, born in 1825, married Mrs. John King in 1851, and their children were Eliza Olive and Harvey Percival, both dying in 1864. He and his wife, Eliza Jane, were both murdered by the Indians on White river, King county, twenty miles from Seattle, Washington Territory, Sunday morning, October 28, 1855. His body was burned in his house, which the Indians set on fire. Orpha was born in 1828, and died in infancy.

Chancey Jones, Jr., was born in Vernon December 19, 1807, and married Elizabeth, daughter of James and Hannah Brown, when he was twenty-three years of age. He settled on the east side of the Pymatuning creek, near number four school-house in Vernon, where he remained until 1837, when he went to the West, and finally located in the township of Harrison, Grant county, Wisconsin, in 1840, where he died September 19, 1853. His children were Orlando Sterling, born in 1831, married Sarah Elizabeth Munger in 1852. Their children were Alice, who married W. C. King, and Chancey, who married and had two children, a son and daughter, who died in infancy. Obed King, born in 1833, married Harriet Elizabeth Guernsey in 1856. Their children were De Forest and Charlotte Elizabeth; for his second wife he married Susie M. Janney in 1867, and had two daughters and a son. Hannah Orpha was born in 1836, and died in 1846. James Horace was born in 1846, and married Ortha A. McFall in 1864. They had five children. All except James H. were born in Vernon.

Rev. Obed Crosby was born in Hartland, Hartford county, Connecticut, in 1753. He was married to Jerusha Phelps in Hartland in 1782. She was born in Connecticut in 1757. He was in the Revolutionary war under General Washington. He came to Vernon in the spring of 1800 and erected a log house on lot seven, Wilcox tract, near the site of J. M. Dickerman's, and boarded with Thomas Giddings while building it, and also held meetings and preached occasionally, but where is not definitely known. He returned to Connecticut, and the next spring (1801) brought his wife and three children to Vernon. They came by the way of Pittsburg,

Pennsylvania, in an open wagon drawn by a yoke of oxen. Shortly after leaving that place one of the oxen died and a cow was yoked to take its place. They were six weeks on the trip from Connecticut. He formed the first Methodist Episcopal society ever organized in Vernon (1801). He lived in his round log house six months and then moved into his new house on the exact site of A. Waldorf's on lot four, West Shepard tract. This was the first hewn log house in Vernon and a fine structure for its day; had a large room, two bed rooms, and a pantry down stairs and a chamber; had a board gable. The nails used were hand-wrought in Pittsburg. He died during the prevalence of a malignant type of typhoid fever January 13, 1813. His wife died February 20, 1839. They lie side by side in the burial ground just south of the center of Vernon. His children were Ursula, born August 16, 1785; died near Platteville, Wisconsin, August 25, 1876. Polly died in infancy. Ezra died near New Castle, Pennsylvania. No dates of birth or death. Ezra had a son, Obed. Jerusha, born in 1790, died in Vernon, Ohio, February 11, 1839.

James King was born in the county of Tyrone, Ireland, in 1781. He had brothers Robert, William, John, and a sister Mary. His mother, Mrs. Jane King, married John Brackin, by whom she had three children, Ezekiel, David, and Elizabeth. John Brackin left Londonderry, Ireland, in 1800, with his family, and landed at Wilmington, Delaware, after a four weeks' voyage, and came to Strabane, Washington county, Pennsylvania. Robert King first went to Kinsman, Ohio, and the rest followed in 1804. James worked for Mr. Kinsman in that township and subsequently bought of him a farm in the north part of lot twenty-three, Kinsman, now owned by J. R. Russell. In 1805–6 he married Jerusha, daughter of Rev. Obed Crosby, of Vernon, by whom he had eleven children, three boys and two girls dying in infancy. A short time after his marriage he traded his farm in Kinsman for one in Vernon, with his brother-in-law, Ezra Crosby, and became identified with the interests of this township thereafter. He held various offices of trust; was considered one of the best farmers in the township. The jokes he played were many and of a practical kind and often repaid. One of his neighbors at one time in his absence turned a drover's herd into a field of clover nearly ready to be cut. He told him it was all right, as it was to be plowed under, then went to Mr. King and told him some one had taken possession, and he better see about it. Mr. King, as soon as he had had a talk with the drover, could trace the joke back to his informer. He watched his opportunity and soon had a chance to play a prank on him. This and many other ones were played and repaid in the best of humor. He was county commissioner in 1837. His wife died in 1839. He was a member of the Seceder church in Kinsman at his death, which occurred May 9, 1842. His children were Obed, born 1807, married Mary Phelps, 1833, who had one child—died in infancy. He died in 1840. David, born 1810, died 1875. George, born 1819, married Sarah Waldorf, had children, Obed C., died aged ten, and Will C., born 1853.* James, born 1813, an artist of much promise, died 1842. William, born 1822, died in Platteville, Wisconsin, in 1865. John, born 1827, died 1850. See sketch of J. I. King, M. D. The others died in infancy.

Rev. David King was born in Kinsman township, August 22, 1810. When about twenty-four years of age he professed religion in Wayne, Ashtabula county. Attended Allegheny college, Meadville, Pennsylvania, in the years 1834 and 1835. Was licensed to exhort in 1834 and to preach in 1836. Was missionary among the Sioux Indians about Fort Snelling and St. Paul, Minnesota, from 1836 to 1842 inclusive. Was financial agent for Allegheny college in 1850–51 and 1853; was married in 1851 in Pittsburg, Pennsylvania, to Mrs. Jane Settlemires. He died in Vernon, January 31, 1875. He was noted for his zeal and peace-making. He was not great, but good, and died respected, the world being better for his having lived in it.

NOTES OF SETTLEMENT.

General Martin Smith was born in Connecticut in 1762; removed to the Reserve in an early day and was among the first settlers of Vernon township. He was a soldier in the Revolutionary war. He followed merchandising in an early

* Platteville.

day and was also by occupation a surveyor. He was grand master Mason and in early times the Masonic lodge held their meetings in his house. He married Sarah Kellogg, born in 1763, and had a family of eleven children. They were prominent members of the Presbyterian church and their home was the usual stopping place of the pioneer preacher and missionary. He died in Vernon in 1853; his wife July 22, 1834.

Harvilah Smith, son of the subject of the preceding sketch, was born in Vernon, Trumbull county, Ohio, January 3, 1801, said to be the second white male child born in that township. His birthplace was on the farm where he still lives near the center of Vernon. His memory is still quite good and he retains a vivid recollection of the experiences of pioneer life. He says he can well remember when a small boy of lying awake in bed at night listening to the wolves tearing the bark from the logs of the cabin. Of the four hundred acres comprising the Smith homestead there is not a field in which he has not assisted in clearing it of the native forest. He married, in 1824, Hannah Clark, born in Connecticut in 1802, and who removed to Vernon in 1813. They have children as follows: Erastus, Eliza, Julia, Alexander H., Charles H., Lottie, and Hannah.

Luman Hobart, son of Martin and Chloe (Jennings) Hobart, was born in Pennsylvania in 1812, February 7th. His father was a native of Massachusetts, born October 13, 1779, and his mother a native of Vermont, born in 1783. They settled in Vernon, Trumbull county, Ohio, in 1834, on the land now owned by Isaac Morford. Ten years later they removed to Michigan, and in 1855 removed to New York State, where they died. They had a family of eleven children, their names all beginning with L, viz: Lorin, Lyman, Lester, Luman, Lucy, Lemuel, Lois, Lucius, Leonard, and Lewis; one died in infancy. Martin Hobart was a commissioned officer in the War of 1812. Luman Hobart came to Trumbull county with his parents in the fall of 1834, and has always since resided in Vernon township. He married, July 4, 1837, Rebecca Splitstone, born in Vernon July 11, 1818, and has a family of six children: Mary L., born in 1838, now wife of A. Brockway, residing in Mercer county, Pennsylvania; Oscar F., born 1840, married, March 7, 1872, Elvira Mifford, of Oneida county, New York, and has two children, Idelma R. and Sylvia J.; Clinton, born 1842, married Marilla Johnston, of Pennsylvania; Thomas C., born 1844, married Lizzie Storier, of Vernon; Dudley, born 1846, married, October 16, 1872, Lydia Bates, of Mercer county, Pennsylvania, and has three children, Sadie L, Albert C., and Ella May; Lima O., born 1850, married J. V. Bates, of Pennsylvania. Three of the sons, Oscar, Clinton, and Corwin, were members of company G, One Hundred and Seventy-first Ohio National guard, served four months and were discharged with their regiment. In 1852 Mr. Luman Hobart made a trip to California, being one hundred and nine days in reaching San Francisco, owing to sickness and other drawbacks, and followed mining about two years near Grass valley. On his homeward trip in October, 1854, when out about twenty-four hours the vessel struck a rock and sank. There were a large number of passengers aboard and many lives were lost. Mr. Hobart fortunately saved his life, but lost nearly all of his effects.

John Langley.—This venerable gentleman is one of the oldest residents of Trumbull county, as he was one of its earliest pioneers. His residence in the county spans a period of over eighty years. He was born in Baltimore county, Maryland, July 29, 1791. He came to Trumbull county in 1801, and lived with his uncle, Andrew Burns, until he was twenty-one. He was drafted in the army in the War of 1812, and served three months under Captain Fobes, when he was discharged on account of sickness. He then began the improvement of his land, situated east of the center of Vernon. He put up a hewed log house and barn, and in 1814 put in a small piece of wheat. In 1816 he married Mary Waldorf, who came with her parents to Hubbard township in an early day. She died in Vernon December 28, 1871. Mr. Langley is the father of two sons and two daughters, viz: John W., George W., Rhoda, and Lucinda. John W., born October 11, 1817, married Ellen Millikin, and has four children. George W., born April, 1820, married in 1844 Margaret Millikin, born December 29, 1821, in Ireland, and has a family of four children, viz: Jasper, born March 10, 1846, married Movilla Fell and has two daughters; Emery, April 1, 1850, married in 1875 Ellen Biggins, born in England

in 1854, and has two children, Flora and Willie; Alfred, March 1, 1855; Lucinda Dott—his sister's daughter—born February 3, 1866. Rhoda Langley, the third child of John and Mary Langley, was born July 25, 1824, died July 4, 1861. Lucinda, born December 20, 1831, died March 10, 1866. Mr. Langley, the subject of this sketch, was present at the first quarterly meeting held by the Methodist Episcopal church in Trumbull county. The presiding elder was Jacob Gruber, and the meeting was held in the barn of Obed Crosby.

Francis Haynes, son of Asa Haynes, Jr., was born in Connecticut, December 24, 1811, and came to Ohio with his parents in 1817, the family settling in Vernon township, Trumbull county. Colonel Haynes was born in Connecticut March 29, 1791, and married in 1810, Sarah Rice, born in the same State the same year. They had three children: Francis, Eliza J., and Sylvia. Colonel Haynes was an associate judge for several years. He died January 28, 1879, his wife April 28, 1857. Francis Haynes married in 1835, Mary A. Davis, born July 19, 1812, in New York. They have a family of five children, viz: George F., Orlando W., Mary L., Amaret A., and Fayette M. The three sons served in the late war. Asa Haynes, Sr., the grandfather of the subject of this sketch, settled in Vernon in 1818. They raised a family of ten children, all of whom lived to raise families.

William E. Chapman, son of Erastus and Lydia (Leonard) Chapman, was born in Vernon, Trumbull county, Ohio, in 1827. His grandparents, William and Sylvia (Smith) Chapman, of Connecticut, came to Trumbull county, Ohio, in 1805, and settled in Vernon township. They had a family of four children: Erastus, Fanny, Electa, and Sylvia. Erastus, the father of William E., was born in Connecticut in 1794, came to Ohio with his parents, and subsequently married Lydia Leonard, born in Massachusetts in 1799, and had eight children. Erastus Chapman died in Vernon in 1869. William E. Chapman was married in 1848, to Charlotte Clark, born in 1829, and she died in 1857. He was again married in 1859 to Mary A. Sheldon, born in 1838. He had two children by his first marriage: Erastus C. and William R.

Ralsa B. Clark was born in Hartford county, Connecticut, in 1796, and came with his parents to Vernon, Trumbull county, Ohio, in 1814. His father, Eber B. Clark, was born in Connecticut in 1774, and his mother, Wealthy A. Holcomb, in 1775; she died in 1861. They had a family of eleven children. Ralsa Clark was united in marriage in 1823 to Dorothy B. Holcomb, born in 1799 in Connecticut. They have had eight children, four of whom are living. Mr. Clark, now one of the most wealthy farmers of the county, started in life a poor man; his prosperity and success are the result of his industry, foresight, and economy. Laura S., a daughter of Mr. Clark, was born in Vernon, Trumbull county, Ohio, in 1839, married in 1860 Jasper D. Mattocks, now a resident of Toledo. They had two children, a boy and girl.

Joseph P. Williams was born in Vernon township, Trumbull county, Ohio, January 18, 1818. His parents, Asmond and Mary (Sheldon) Williams, removed to Vernon in 1815. Asmond Williams was born in 1790 and his wife in 1789. He died in 1865 and she in 1869. They reared a family of nine children—four are living. Joseph P. married Vienna Proper, who was born in Venango county, Pennsylvania, in 1822. She died in 1865. He is the father of three children: Sarah U., Amanda B., and Joseph P. Mr. Williams is a farmer and dairyman.

Alfred F. Waldorf, son of John and Elizabeth Waldorf, was born in Vernon, Trumbull county, Ohio, in 1818. His grandfather, John Waldorf, Sr., was a native of New Jersey, born 1750, and came to Ohio in 1802, and died in Hubbard township, Trumbull county, in 1810. He had a family of six children. His son John, Jr., father of the subject of this sketch, was born in New Jersey in 1786, settled in Vernon township, Trumbull county, in 1809, and died there in 1835. He married Elizabeth Misner, daughter of Nicholas and Rhoda Misner. She was born in New Jersey in 1789, and died in Vernon in 1876. They had a family of thirteen children, of whom four are living. Alfred F. was united in marriage in 1842 to Annis L. Wadsworth, daughter of Henry and Laura Wadsworth, born in New York State in 1823. Mr. and Mrs. Waldorf have a family of six children, as follows: Laura A., John H., Gertrude, Emma, Ada M. and Ida M. (twins). Eugene is dead. Mr. and Mrs. Waldorf are members of the Free-will Baptist church.

George K. Pelton was born in Gustavus, Trumbull county, Ohio, in 1818. His maternal grandfather, Joseph DeWolf, was born in Hartland, Connecticut, in 1762, and settled in Vernon township, Trumbull county, one mile south of the center, in the spring of 1800. He came out a short time in advance of his family, who followed with an ox team. On the way one of the oxen died, and the cow, which they were bringing with them, was yoked up in his place and the journey completed in this way. Joseph DeWolf married Sarah Gibbons (born in 1764), and had a family of thirteen children. He was a soldier in the war of independence, serving through the whole struggle. As a pioneer he battled not only with the forests of Vernon, but frequently with the wild beasts as well. On one occasion he had quite an adventure with a wounded deer. On going up to cut its throat it sprang up and at him, knocking him down. On regaining his feet he ran for a log that lay up some distance from the ground. Whenever the deer would spring at him he would roll down under the log and the deer would land on the other side of the tree, and he would then roll back and climb upon the log. This proceeding was kept up for some time, finally wearing the animal out, but not without himself receiving many bruises. Mr. DeWolf died in Vernon in 1846, and his wife two years later. They were highly esteemed by the entire community in which they resided so long. Their oldest daughter, Ruhamah, was born in Connecticut in 1783 and became the wife of Joseph Pelton, a native of Saybrook, Connecticut, and died in 1872. Mr. Pelton served in the War of 1812. They had eleven children. George K. married in 1848 Mary A. King, daughter of William King, of Kinsman. She was born in 1821 and died in 1874. Two children is the result of this union—Myra and John S., both at home.

Ira Case, son of Abner and Hannah Case, of Barkhamstead, Connecticut, was born March 15, 1782, came to Ohio about the year 1805 and settled in Vernon, Trumbull county, where he lived until his death which took place May 25, 1837. His wife was Ursula, daughter of Uriah and Mehitabel Hyde, born June 10, 1786, in Lyme, Connecticut, died in October, 1864. They had a family of seven children, namely: Julia, born August 10, 1808, married Norris Humphrey, and died January 26, 1870; Imri, born March 4, 1810; Uriah N., born August 26, 1811, of Orangeville; Hannah M., born March 6, 1813, wife of George Fell (second), of Vernon; Eveline, born July 12, 1819, died about 1860; Lucy C., born May 7, 1821, died in 1879; George S., born April 1, 1826, of Vernon. He married Mary Hoagland, of Brookfield, born October 15, 1836. They have had five children, as follows: Ida L., born July 27, 1856, died in Colorado July 14, 1880; Jesse H., born December 7, 1858; Mary E., born March 26, 1862; Cora D., born December 5, 1865, died September 5, 1866; Minnie D., born August 26, 1869.

James M. Dickerman, son of Isaac and Ann Dickerman, was born in Massachusetts in 1826; came to Ohio in 1854 and settled in Bloomfield township, Trumbull county. Later he moved to Vernon township and at present is proprietor of the hotel at Burg Hill. His wife Harriet was born in Massachusetts in 1828. In 1862 he enlisted in company B, One Hundred and Fifth Ohio volunteer infantry, and served nine months.

CHAPTER X.
BLOOMFIELD.
GENERAL FEATURES.

Bloomfield, the seventh township in the fourth range, is in the northern part of Trumbull county, adjoining Ashtabula county. It lies between Greene on the east and Mesopotamia on the west, and is north of Bristol. The largest stream in the township is Grand river, which enters near the southwestern corner, and pursues a general northerly direction parallel to the western township line, crossing the center road, and passing out of the township into Mesopotamia a short distance north of this road. Several small streams, tributaries of this river, drain the western portion of the township. Baughman's creek enters the river in the southwest; about a mile north of its mouth a small run empties, and perhaps a half mile further, Center creek flowing west from its headwaters in the tamarack swamp, adds its waters to those of the river. North creek rises north of the center of the township, and flowing southwesterly, joins the river near the township line. Still another small creek, known as Haine's run, flows through the northwestern portion of this township. The streams are mainly in the western half of the township. A large portion of the land in the eastern half is covered by the tamarack swamp, which extends from north to south almost entirely across the township, east of the Ashtabula & Pittsburg railroad. The eastern and western portions—the tamarack swamp and the valley of Grand river—are low-lying and wet. The river bottom is often flooded by rains which appear to affect other localities much less. Through the township from north to south extends a swell or ridge of land rising gradually from the swampy regions on either side, and generally very nearly level on its broad crest. The soil of this slight elevation varies from sandy and gravelly loam on the west to clay on the east. Along the turnpike are many fine farms, with first-rate buildings and improvements. This is an excellent farming region, well suited for wheat. Dairying and sheep-raising are carried on quite profitably.

The township was late settled, and even now contains but a small number of inhabitants, there being less than two hundred voters. The tamarack swamp has not yet been subjugated, but labor is now being expended upon it with a view toward making its fertility and richness available for the farmer. When this result has been accomplished the agricultural resources of Bloomfield will be greatly enlarged. Another swamp in the southwest of the township is the black ash swamp, containing three or four hundred acres lying near Grand river. These swamps have proved a drawback to Bloomfield, but they soon must yield, subdued by the labor of the progressive agriculturist.

The only village in the township is the center, or, to give its post-office address, North Bloomfield, situated a half mile west of the geographical center. This is one of the pleasantest rural villages in the county. Beautiful shade trees line its streets, and a level grassy lawn of nearly five acres in the center of the village lends additional beauty to the place. Forty or fifty houses, three stores, and a few other shops, and two churches are comprised in North Bloomfield.

RONGHAL OWNERS.

Peter Chardon Brooks, of Boston, was the proprietor of large tracts of land in this portion of the Reserve and this township was held by him until 1814. He then sold it to Ephraim Brown, of Westmoreland, New Hampshire, and Thomas Howe of Williamstown, Vermont. Although the purchasers were of nearly the same age, Howe was Brown's uncle and the playmate of his boyhood. It is said that the first business transaction between the two took place when the uncle and the nephew were both less than ten years of age, and was of a most unique nature. Howe rented a hen of Brown for the season, and, at the expiration of the time agreed upon, returned her with half her chickens. Two or three years after purchasing the township, Howe sold out to Brown, reserving one thousand acres in the southern part.

SURVEY.

Soon after purchasing Howe and Brown engaged S. I. Ensign, of Mesopotamia, to survey this township—not an easy task, considering the then swampy condition of the land. The township is divided into one hundred and seventy lots, containing from fifty to one hundred acres each. These lots are numbered from north to south, beginning with lot one in the northwestern corner of the township.

THE FIRST SETTLER.

Leman Ferry, of Brookfield, Vermont, started for his new home in the western wilds about the 10th day of January, 1815, and reached his destination about the 20th of February following. He started with two teams, one a sled drawn by two yoke of oxen, the other a sleigh drawn by a span of horses. The teams conveyed his household goods and his family. Mr. Ferry was accompanied by his hired man, Mrs. Ferry, and two sons and three daughters. When west of Buffalo it was found impracticable to proceed further with the ox-sled on account of the scantiness of snow. Therefore Mr. Ferry exchanged the sled for a wagon and continued his journey, but kept the sleigh along, the horses dragging it over bare ground much of the way. He entered this township from the northward, guided only by spotted trees in the latter part of his journey. There was then no house between Rome center and Bristol township, and no road

through Bloomfield. Arriving in the vicinity of his purchase Mr. Ferry found shelter for his family in a deserted log cabin situated just over the line in Bristol, until he had time to erect a shanty upon his own land. Leman Ferry, Jr., his oldest son, was at this time twenty-one years old, and with his assistance and that of the hired man a comfortable dwelling was soon finished. At first no chimney was built, but a smoke-hole was cut through the roof instead. The fire was built against the green logs in the end of the room until these were burned away somewhat, then a kind of stone fire-place was made by heaping up stones against the logs. Here the family lived and worked. When spring came, a number of men came on to make clearings, and as many as twenty at a time boarded at the house of Mrs. Ferry. Benches made of split or hewn logs were ranged round the room for seats, and at night beds were made up on the floor. Mr. Ferry had never built a log-house before this, and therefore was not especially skilled in that kind of carpentry; and the roof of the building, which was covered by "shakes," or long shingles, held down by weight-poles, was not properly constructed. One day Mr. Ferry's son Noble, then a small boy, climbed upon the roof to rescue a cat which had got up there and was afraid to come down. When he was about midway of the building, the whole roof suddenly started, shingles, and weight-poles all together, and carried the boy to the ground, burying him in the debris. The hired man, who was chopping wood back of the house, saw the fall and with the assistance of young Leman Ferry soon extricated the bruised and frightened child. Fortunately no bones were broken, and the victim of the accident still lives to relate the incident.

The summer following his arrival and settlement Mr. Ferry returned to Conneaut, where he had left his sled, taking back the wagon he had purchased in order to reach Bloomfield. The wagon he sold for six barrels of salt at $10 per barrel, hauled the salt home on the sled, and sold it out to the settlers at the price he had paid.

Leman Ferry died in 1825, aged sixty. Mrs. Ferry lived to reach her ninetieth year. They were the parents of seven children, of whom the youngest five came to Ohio with them. The children were Editha (Pinney) and Lucy

(Lamphere); Leman, Polly, Chloe, Lucinda, and Noble B., of whom only the youngest survives. Leman, Jr., married Susan Hillman, and afterwards moved to Garrettsville, where he died. Polly married Dr. Andrew Clark and lived in Newton township. Chloe married William Mc-Clintock and resided in Bloomfield several years. She died at Garrettsville. Lucinda married first Samuel Tinan, of Rome, and second Thomas Bushnell, of Bloomfield. N. B. married Abigail Flower, and lives upon the old homestead. His wife died in 1875. They had ten children; nine are now living, the youngest son with his father.

EARLY SETTLERS.

The spring and summer after Mr. Ferry's settlement a number of others came and began improving their farms, and a few brought their families during that year. In the spring of 1815 Willard Crowell, Israel Proctor, Samuel Eastman, and David Comstock came to this township from Vermont on foot.

Ephraim Brown, from Cheshire county, New Hampshire, was one of the first settlers and most prominent citizens. He settled at the center in 1815, in a log cabin built a short time previously by Major Howe. The site of the cabin is now covered by the residence of his son, E. A. Brown. Ephraim Brown married Mary B. Huntington, and at the time of their arrival in the township their family consisted of four children; five were afterwards born to them. The names of the children were Ephraim Alexander, George W., Mary, Charles, Elizabeth H., James M., Marvin H., Fayette, and Anne F. E. A. Brown now resides upon the old homestead. He was in business in Pittsburg from 1829 to 1845, principally as a wholesale dry goods merchant. George W. died in Bloomfield; Mary (Wing) still lives in the township as also Elizabeth; Charles died in Georgia in 1880; James died in Massillon; Marvin resides in Painesville, and Fayette in Cleveland, Annie F. in Bloomfield. Ephraim Brown died in 1845, and his widow in 1862. Mr. Brown was the first postmaster, the first merchant, and the second justice of the peace. With Major Howe, and Judge Austin, of Austinburg, he was among the originators of the Warren and Ashtabula turnpike.

Lewis Clisby was the second settler at the center, arriving soon after Mr. Brown.

Jared Kimball, from Vermont, settled north of the public square in 1816, and here lived and died. None of his family now remain. His daughter, Mrs. Teed, also lived in Bloomfield. Mr. Kimball was the first justice of the peace, and a very worthy man. Of him the following is related: A poor man living in the township had rented a piece of grass land which he was to mow and have a portion of the hay for his work. He mowed the hay and stacked it. Soon after the owner of the land set a fire, which after working some time in the turf, at length reached the renter's haystack and destroyed it. The man sought to recover damages and the case was brought before 'Squire Kimball. 'Squire Brown made a plea stating the law applicable to the case, but 'Squire Kimball said, "Here is a law which applies," and quoted from the Bible, "If a man set a fire which catch in the stubble and destroy his neighbor's grain, verily that man shall make restitution." Judgment was accordingly rendered in favor of the poor man. 'Squire Kimball was a Presbyterian deacon and a firm believer in the doctrines of his church.

David Comstock, who came in 1815, worked for Major Howe, and was noted as one of the greatest wood-choppers of the time. He married a sister of William McClintock and settled in the northern part of the township, afterwards moving to the center. They had no children. Mrs. Comstock was a resolute woman, and probably such a frightful creature as a mouse, which is now capable of frightening ladies nearly to death, had no terrors for her. In her husband's absence she kept house, and one day when a bear attacked a hog in the pen, she took down the rifle, went out and succeeded in driving the intruder away, though she could not kill him.

Amasa Bigelow, a brother of Mrs. Leman Ferry, settled near Ferry in 1816. His son Elijah made the first improvements upon the place. The four sons were Daniel, Timothy, Amasa, and Elijah. Amasa and Elijah did not reside permanently in Bloomfield. Daniel and Timothy passed their lives here. One daughter, Jemima, married John Weed.

Samuel Eastman was an early settler in the northern part of the township west of the turnpike. He married Sophia Meecham, of Greene township. He was a most eccentric character.

Jared and Cyril Green came to the township

in 1815, and settled on lot forty-six. Jared was then unmarried. Cyril married Polly Sherman, and she came with him. Cyril lived until 1874, when he died in his eighty-first year. He was favorably known as an enterprising, public-spirited man. Two years after the arrival of Jared and Cyril Green, their father, Jared Green, came out and settled. Besides the two above mentioned, his sons were Charles, Noah, Marcus, and Archibald. Charles returned East; Jared, Jr., moved north; Archibald is still a resident of the township. One daughter, Julia (Whitcomb), moved away.

In 1817 Thomas Howe, of Williamstown, Vermont, brought his family to this township, and settled in the southern part on lot eighty-five. He was born in Westmoreland, New Hampshire, in 1799, and in early life was a merchant. He carried on that business successfully a number of years in Williamstown. His wife, Clarissa, was born in Woodstock, Connecticut. Both were esteemed and honored throughout their lives. They had five children, all born in Vermont—Clarissa (Wilder), Thomas M., Dr. George W., Nancy (Green), and William H. Thomas M. and Mrs. Green are dead. The others all reside in Bloomfield. There was not a death in the Howe family until the youngest child was forty-six years old. Thomas M. lived in Pittsburg, and represented his district in Congress several terms. Dr. George W. has been a Representative to the Legislature, following in the footsteps of his father, and has held other honorable positions.

Hezekiah Howe came from Vermont in company with Asa Works, in 1817, and settled on lot sixty-five, where he still lives. He is now in the ninety-sixth year of his age. None of his sons now reside in the township.

Asa Works settled in 1817, where his only son Nelson now resides, on lot sixty-four.

Aaron Smith, about 1816, settled in the south of the township. Soon after his arrival he built a frame house, the first in the township. It is still standing, but has been removed to Bristol. Mrs. Smith's only child, a daughter, married Leonard Osborn and lives in Michigan.

Mayhew Crowell settled about a half a mile north of the center in 1815. His wife, Mehitabel (Howe) Crowell, died September 20, 1817, being the first death in the township. Her daughter Harriet was the first child born in the township. The Crowell family included five sons and three daughters, who arrived at mature years. All are now dead. Their names were as follows: Willard, Obadiah, Henry, Thomas, Roswell, Mehitabel (Bellows), Mercy, and Mary (Butler). Charles Thayer settled in the northwest of the township about the year 1816. None of the family now remain in Bloomfield. One son, Hiram, resides in Bristol.

John Bellows, about the same time, located one mile northwest of the center. One of his sons, Dr. Bellows, now resides in Michigan. William moved to Chagrin Falls. None are left here. The elder Mr. Bellows engaged in brick-making quite early. His brother Benjamin resided a while in this township.

Mr. Proctor, whose first name is not remembered, settled in the northern part of the township early. He was a strong Presbyterian and a good man. Two of his sons, Francis and Israel, lived and died in Bloomfield. Francis married Betsey Huntington, sister of 'Squire Brown's wife. She is still living. Mrs. Israel Proctor is also living.

Noyes Parker was a blacksmith and had a shop near Brown's mill. He made axes and scythes. One of his children was drowned in the mill-race about the second day after he came here to settle. Two or three years later an eight-year-old son was drowned in the river. This so disheartened the parent that he gave up his business and moved away.

This, we believe, about completes mention of the Vermont families who made the early settlement.

Later, a number of English families established homes in the township. This class now forms more than half the population. They are industrious, thrifty, and excellent citizens.

Mr. William Haine was among the first of the English settlers of the township, and still resides here.

ORGANIZATION AND FIRST OFFICERS.

This township was organized by a special act of the Legislature, and received its present name in 1816. The first township officers were chosen on the 9th of April, 1817, at an election held at the house of Ephraim Brown and were as follows: Aaron Smith, chairman; Leman Ferry and Jared Green, judges of election; Cyril Green, township clerk; Jared Kimball, David Comstock, and Leman Ferry, trustees; Mayhew Crowell and Timothy Bigelow, overseers of the poor; Leman Ferry, Jr., and Lewis Clisby, fence viewers; Jared Green, Jr., and John Weed, appraisers of property; Jared Green, Jr., lister; Jared Kimball, treasurer; Samuel Teed, constable; Mayhew Crowell and Leman Ferry, supervisors.

ANECDOTES AND INCIDENTS.

The following stories relative to early days in this township are taken mainly from a published historical sketch by Mr. George A. Robertson:

Many interesting incidents of early times are still remembered by the children of the early settlers, now gray-haired sires and grandsires, some of which deserve a place here.

The cows and hogs, while the settlers were commencing operations upon their farms, had nowhere to run except in the woods. The hogs were allowed much liberty during the summer, and in the fall as many of them as could be found were brought in and confined in rail pens to be fattened. But usually some of them would escape, and thus, in a comparatively short time, wild and ferocious hogs inhabited the forests; and when they had attained five or six years growth, their huge tusks and savage natures rendered them about as formidable as any wild beasts of the time. "Hunting the wild boar," the sport of the feudal and middle ages, so celebrated in the pages of song and romance, was occasionally revived here in the wilds of Ohio, and often many joined in it. Not unfrequently some unfortunate modern Adonis, would find himself too closely pursued and be compelled to take refuge in a tree to avoid destruction.

Mr. N. B. Ferry relates that often, when a boy, while hunting for the cows his dog would start a wild hog whose squealing would arouse others and attract them to the spot; and soon they would collect in such force as to drive him to a tree for safety, while the dog used every effort to keep from being rended in pieces by his savage pursuers.

TREED BY WOLVES.

One evening when Mr. N. B. Ferry was a boy he was out hunting for the cows, and not returning as soon as usual, his father started out to find him. Being unsuccessful in his search, he was returning to the house, and when within a short distance of it he was startled by the howling of wolves. Fearing that he would not be able to reach his home, he climbed a tree and shouted for help. Several men who were boarding at his house each seized a gun and hastened to the spot. The wolves were easily frightened away. It was afterwards learned that they were not at first in pursuit of Mr. Ferry. Jared Green had killed a deer that day and dragged it home; The wolves were following up the trail, and as Mr. Ferry unconsciously took the same course, they turned their attention to him.

TRAPPING A BEAR.

One night a cow belonging to Mr. Howe came up without her calf, to which she had given birth during the day. She was fastened for the night, and in the morning loosed, and the boys were directed to follow her as she would be sure to proceed to the spot where the calf had been left. The cow, on being untied, went some distance into the woods, and at length, coming to a clump of bushes, stopped and began lowing. This spot was undoubtedly the place where the calf had been left, but now it nowhere appeared. Traces of blood, and a trail where the calf had been dragged, pointed plainly to its fate. Following this trail a short distance, the boys found a portion of the carcass placed between two trees and covered over with leaves. They returned and related what they had seen to Mr. Norton, who had quite a reputation as a bear trapper. According he set a trap near the spot, and awaited developments. The next morning the trap was sprung, but the bear was not in it. The remains of the calf were gone, too, and for some distance, no trail was found. Mr. Norton directed that search be made in a circuit of some distance around the spot, as he believed that the bear would carry his burden a short distance, and then drag it. He was correct in his knowledge of the habits of the bear, and soon the trail was found. After following it up, they discovered the remaining portion of the carcass where it had again been deposited and covered with leaves. Here Norton set two traps, attaching heavy clogs to them.

Next morning young Howe found the ground around the spot torn up as though a drove of hogs had been there. One of the traps had been sprung, but the bear had managed to get his foot out of it. The other had gone and with it the clog. Following the course which the bear had taken a short distance, Howe soon heard the sharp clink of the trap against the stones in the creek bottom near by. Norton then came up, and put his dogs on the trail. Soon their barking was heard, and hastening on the hunters found the bear endeavoring to climb a tree with the trap on one of his fore paws. Hindered by this and by the dogs, he soon fell, shot by the rifles of the men. He weighed over four hundred pounds, and was well worth the trouble it had cost to capture him.

PRACTICAL JOKING.

In their hunting expeditions these pioneers would occasionally strive to make some new-comer the victim of their fondness for joking. A fellow had come to the township of whose courage a very poor opinion was entertained. He became at one time a member of a hunting party who engaged in a hunt of several days' duration, camping in the woods at night. It was determined to have a little fun with him, to pass away the time. One of the company accordingly went quietly outside of the camp, and after all were quiet, began making strange, unearthly noises. The men who were in the secret paid but little attention to the sounds, the most of them apparently being sound asleep. But the new member of the party became visibly alarmed, and enquired what the noise was. He was told that it sounded like the howl of a catamount, and at this, his fear and discomfort were so great that he requested that he be covered with a large trough which was near the camp, so that the animal could not get at him. A day or two later he learned the cause of his alarm, and much of his cowardice disappeared.

HOWE'S DOG ARGUS.

In the spring of 1815 several settlers came to Bloomfield from Vermont. By their request Mr. Howe allowed a valuable dog belonging to him to accompany them. Argus was his name. But somewhere in New York State the dog deserted the men and they saw nothing more of him. Some months later Howe drove through with a horse and sleigh. On stopping at a tavern he was much surprised to find Argus there, who received his old master with every manifestation of

delight. On asking the landlord how he came in possession of the dog, the landlord insisted that he had raised him from a puppy. Mr. Howe, though surprised at this claim, said, "The dog belongs to me and I can prove it. Here, Argus, get into that cutter and watch it; and now, landlord, if you can remove anything from the cutter the dog is yours, otherwise he is mine." "All right," replied the inn-keeper, as he approached the sleigh ; but by no amount of coaxing or threatening could Argus be induced to allow him touch the robe or the whip. When Howe was ready to start he told the landlord that he should not try to call the dog along, but Argus needed no special request, and readily became the traveling companion of his master. He reached the new settlement and there became a general favorite, acquiring much renown as a deer and bear dog.

RESCUE OF SLAVES.

As the people of Bloomfield were returning home from church one quiet Sabbath afternoon in the month of September, 1823, a negro with a woman and two children was seen on the turnpike. They appeared nearly worn out with much travel and almost ready to lie down and die. Those who saw them supposed, of course, that they were fugitive slaves, but communicated their suspicions to no one. About dark three men, the slave-owner, his son, and an attendant, rode up to the door of the tavern in the village, and inquired if the negroes had been seen. They were informed that they had gone on a short distance. The landlord advised the strangers to tarry with him all night, as they could easily overtake the objects of their pursuit in the morning. Having traveled very far that day and being much wearied, they consented. The slave-hunters retired early, asking the landlord to call them as early as possible in the morning. When it became known in the village that slave-hunters were at the tavern, the greatest excitement prevailed. The will to have the negroes escape was strong, and 'Squire Brown, backed by the public sentiment of almost the entire community, devised a plan to effect this result. He sent his covered wagon and a party of willing men, under cover of darkness, to overtake the runaways. About twelve miles from Bloomfield, in Rome, Ashtabula county, they learned that the objects of their search had been secreted in a certain house. They rode up to it, and on making known their object to its owner, were repulsed and ordered off his premises. Considerable expostulation and explanation ensued before he could be made to understand that their mission was a friendly one. But when satisfied of the sincerity of their intentions he allowed the Bloomfield men to take the negro family into the wagon. They then conveyed them south a short distance to a tavern kept by a Mr. Crowell, with a barn standing back of it in a field. Into this barn the wagon was driven and the doors securely closed.

Now let us go back to the Bloomfield tavern. Morning dawned, but for some inexplicable (?) reason the landlord and his family were not awake as soon as usual. In fact, the first to awake and arouse the household was the slave-owner. The landlord apologized; didn't know when such a thing as his oversleeping had happened before; said he was much ashamed of himself; and so on. He tried to dress, but one boot was missing. After much search it turned up in some unusual place. Then he proceeded to the barn; the door was locked and he had left the key in the house. Back to the house and then to the barn; the key didn't fit, and much time was wasted in unlocking the door. At length this was accomplished, and the horses were led out. Another discovery—each animal had lost a shoe and besides the hoof of one of them was badly broken. The owners thought the shoes of the horses were all right the night before; at least they had not noticed that any were missing. But they were missing now—that was evident, and the services of the village blacksmith were required before the impatient Virginians could proceed on their journey. Mr. Barnes, the smith, was not at his shop, and it required some time to hunt him up. Usually he was at his post early—a model of promptness. After he was found he had trouble in unlocking the door, and succeeded poorly in making a fire. He had not a nail in his shop, and used his last shoes in a job which he did the previous Saturday evening. Nails and shoes had to be made, but the blacksmith appeared in no hurry. At last the horses were shod, and about 9 o'clock the slave hunters started off. About noon they drove up to the tavern in front of the barn where

the wagon and the fugitives were. Through the cracks in the barn the happy negro family saw their pursuers start on. A little later the covered wagon emerged from its hiding place and returned to Bloomfield. Under the direction of 'Squire Brown a shelter for the fugitives had been prepared—a rude camp constructed between the roots of two upturned trees. Here the negroes remained, being supplied with food by the kind-hearted people of Bloomfield until all danger was past. Then they were brought to a log cabin near the center, where they resided for some time, the man being employed by 'Squire Brown. At length they were put on a vessel at Ashtabula harbor and reached Canada in safety.

When the slave-hunters returned to Bloomfield, after a fruitless search north of this place, they were arrested on a warrant charging them with having run a toll-gate north of Warren. Supposing that the objects of their pursuit would take the State road to Painesville instead of continuing on up the pike, they had paid toll only to the former road. They were fined five dollars each and costs. The village tavern-keeper refused to admit them, or to feed their horses. Some malicious mischief-maker removed the hair from the tails and manes of the horses while the owners of the team were at 'Squire Kimball's house, and pinned to one of the saddles a notice containing the following lines:

> Slave-hunters, beware !
> For sincerely we swear
> That if again here
> You ever appear,
> We'll give you the coat
> Of a Tory to wear.

This slave rescue was the first of a series of similar acts in which prominent citizens of Bloomfield took an active part. After the underground railroad was put in operation, it received sympathy and support from the good people of this region. Though there was hostility to the Abolitionists, and though liberal rewards were offered for the return of slaves to their owners, there never was, so far as known, an instance in which a runaway was betrayed.

EARLY EVENTS.

The first child born in this township was Harriet Crowell. The first male child was Charles Thayer.

The first death was that of Mrs. Mehitabel

Crowell, in 1817; the second, that of Mrs. Hannah Brown, April 28, 1818.

The first marriage ceremony was performed by Lyman Potter, Esq., of Bristol, in uniting John Weed and Jemima Bigelow.

The first sermon was preached by Mr. Cole, missionary, in Ferry's cabin in 1815. Mr. Badger, Congregationalist, preached soon after. The first sermon by a Methodist minister was preached in 1817 by Rev. Ira Eddy, in Mr. Thayer's house. Before any church was organized persons of different denominations united in holding meetings, where professors of religion offered prayer, and in the absence of a minister sermons were read and hymns were sung by those attending.

MILLS.

Aaron Smith was the first carpenter in the township, and in 1817 built for Ephraim Brown a saw-mill on Grand river, about two miles from the center. In 1819 a grist-mill was built upon the same stream, and managed by Leman Ferry, Jr., the first miller. This mill was in operation many years, with many changes in its ownership. It was in a bad site, and the cost of keeping up a dam was considerable.

Asa Law built for Mr. Brown a saw-mill on Center brook at an early day, about a half mile from the center.

William Haine's mill, in the northern part of the township, was built for him in 1855 by N. B. Ferry.

THE FIRST STORE

in the township was started by Ephraim Brown in 1816. He brought on a stock of goods from Boston, and having more than he could sell disposed of a part of them at Warren to Mr. Bentley. He built the store in Bloomfield, which is now French's shoe shop, and continued the mercantile business a number of years. Indians were sometimes his customers, trading venison for whiskey, tobacco, and other articles. A gallon of whiskey would purchase a side of nice venison.

William A. Otis was the second merchant. He made a good start here, removed to Cleveland and became a prominent and wealthy man. He came to Bloomfield about 1823. His son, Hon. Charles Otis, is an ex-mayor of Cleveland.

THE VILLAGE HOTEL.

In 1818 Samuel and John Teed undertook the building of this house, but as they had not the money to finish the work, they sold out to 'Squire Brown, who moved in and kept the house a year or so, while his own residence was building. In 1823 Milo Harris succeeded as landlord and remained several years.

THE POST-OFFICE

in Bloomfield, now known as North Bloomfield, was established about the year 1817, with Ephraim Brown as postmaster. Mail was carried to and from Warren once a week by a horseback rider. Judge Eliphalet Austin, of Austinburg, Ashtabula county, was the first mail contractor on the Warren and Ashtabula route.

EARLY SCHOOLS.

The first school-house was a log structure erected on Leman Ferry's farm in 1817. The first school was taught in that house by Chester Howard in the winter of 1817-18.

A school-house of logs was built at the center quite early. The first term of school, however, was taught in Lewis Clisby's log cabin in the winter of 1819, by Noah M. Green. Elizabeth M. Huntington, now Mrs. Proctor, also taught school in the same cabin. She is now living, over eighty-eight years of age.

Chester Howard was a brother of Major Thomas Howe's wife, and during his lifetime taught forty-two winter and twenty-six summer terms. Some of his pupils, now gray-haired old men, still live and hold him in grateful remembrance.

REPRESENTATIVES.

This township has sent the following men to the Legislature in the order named: Thomas Howe, 1819; Ephraim Brown, Augustus Otis, George W. Howe, and J. K. Wing. Some of them served several terms.

PHYSICIANS.

Soon after the settlement of the township Dr. Reynolds, of Mesopotamia, came here to practice. The population of the township being small, he found this an unpromising field and removed after a short stay.

Dr. Benjamin Palmer next came, as early as 1824, and practiced twenty years or more with distinguished success. He was a New Hampshire man, well educated. The surrounding townships having no physicians, he had a wide field for usefulness, and built up a large practice.

He left here having gained quite a large property for a country doctor.

The next physician was Dr. Hartman, now of Baltimore, Maryland. Other physicians have been quite numerous, as there has always been a doctor in the township since Dr. Palmer located.

Dr. G. W. Howe practiced in Bloomfield from 1847 till 1867. At the latter date he was appointed surgeon of the Pittsburg & Boston Mining company, and went to Lake Superior. Dr. A. O. Huntly assumed his practice, and is still continuing it successfully.

METHODIST EPISCOPAL CHURCH.

In 1818 Rev. Ira Eddy formed a class in this township. Charles Thayer was leader and seventeen members composed the organization. After a few years the religious interest died out somewhat, though occasional meetings were held by circuit preachers, generally in the old log schoolhouse in the southern part of Bloomfield. In 1830 a revival of interest took place and a number joined the church, which has since prospered steadily. Among the active members were Leonard Osborn and wife, Zimri Baker and wife, Willard Terrell and wife. Terrell was class-leader and a faithful worker. The church now has between one hundred and thirty and one hundred and forty members.

Through the combined efforts of the Methodists and Presbyterians, in about 1836 a house for public worship was erected, which was destroyed by fire later, through carelessness in taking up ashes and leaving them in the building.

In 1857 the two congregations built the church now standing, and continued to own and occupy it jointly until about seven years ago, when the Methodists bought the Congregationalists' share of the property. The house is a good one, pleasantly situated, and well furnished.

THE CONGREGATIONAL CHURCH.

This church was organized as Presbyterian September 9, 1821, by Rev. Giles H. Cowles, missionary, and consisted of the following members: Leman and Elizabeth Ferry, Jared Kimball, and Jemima Chapman. The following were afterwards received: October 22, 1822, Asa and Olive W. Smith; September 27, 1823, Sybil Brown; June 5, 1825, Deacon John Barnes and Lucretia Barnes, Francis and Nabby Proc-

tor, David Neal, William Root, and Charlotte Kendall; April 9, 1826, Noyes Parker, Ann Beckworth Bigelow; June 11, 1826, Calvin and Diadama Clark, Susan Parker; July 8, 1826, Eliza Otis; August 19, 1827, Philena Otis, Helen Hart, Sarah Comstock, David Comstock, Elijah Ballard, Joel Morley, Chauncy H. Latimer; October 5, 1828, George Haskell; January 4, 1829, Sally Teed, Pamelia Barnes, Mary Latimer, Julia Ann Wright. These were all the members prior to 1830.

Calvin Clark and Asa Smith were chosen deacons July 8, 1826. Elijah Ballard was chosen deacon January 14, 1832, and remained a faithful officer a long term of years until he was called from earth.

Among the early missionaries and preachers who ministered to this little flock were Revs. G. H. Cowles, J. W. Curtis, and Randolph Stone. Rev. Edson Hart was ordained pastor of the church June 6, 1827. In 1858 the church adopted the Congregational form of government. Slavery was the cause of the disruption. This society in conjunction with the Methodists built the house which the latter now occupy. During recent years they have met in the house built by the Disciples, from whom they purchased a half interest. The church is in a good condition morally and financially. There are about seventy members. Rev. E. B. Chase is the present pastor.

THE DISCIPLES' CHURCH.

About 1827 Benjamin Alton, of Genesee county, New York, settled in this township. He was a man of much religious zeal, and was quite early converted by the Methodists. In 1829 the citizens of Bloomfield at a public meeting resolved to unite in raising money to support preaching at the center school-house. This union was to allow the Presbyterians the use of the house one-half of the time, the Baptists and Methodists one-fourth, and the Unitarians one-fourth. Alton was engaged by 'Squire Brown to preach the portion of the time allowed to the Unitarians. He heard Thomas Campbell and became a convert to his views, and on announcing his belief the union exploded into fragments. Alton, however, continued to keep his appointments, and in 1830–31 converted several to his newly accepted doctrine. In 1832 he preached half of the time, holding meetings in a school-house. The first persons gathered into the Disciple fold were ten in number, viz: Mr. Nettlefield and wife, Benjamin Alton and wife, Mary Sager, Polly Green, Mehitabel Thayer, Nelson Works, Clarissa Wilder, William Parker. Revs. Hayden, Henry, Applegate, Bosworth and others visited the little band and by their labors added other worshipers. In 1836 Mr. Alton moved to Illinois, carrying with him the best wishes and the prayers of the church in Bloomfield. In October of the same year Rev. Marcus Bosworth visited this place and measures were taken to complete an organization, which was effected October 19, 1836. New names were then added as follows: Ruhama Luse, William M. Bellows, Benjamin Bellows, Josiah and Rachel Bellows, Mary Ann Bellows, Henry G. Neal, Clarissa Neal, William Parker, Charles Thayer, Candace Green, Anna Sager, and Mariam Smith. Early preachers were Revs. Hayden, Henry Applegate, Hartzell, Cyrus and Marcus Bosworth, Clapp, and Collins; a little later Lucy, Brockett, Perky, Calvin Smith, E. Wakefield, W. A. Belding, C. C. Foote, and H. Reeves.

In 1848, under the preaching of Rev. Isaac Errett the Disciples doubled their numbers. In 1849 the house at the center was built and Isaac Errett became the first pastor. He remained two years.

April 19, 1840, Nelson Works and H. G. Neal were appointed elders. In 1842 John Sager was elected deacon. April 19, 1854, the officers, who had thus far been unordained, were ordained. Edwin Wakefield was ordained "to the work of an evangelist;" Nelson Works and Charles Brown, elders; John Sager, David Snyder, Chester Howard, and N. B. Ferry, deacons; Cyrus Bosworth, M. S. Clapp, Isaac Errett, and B. F. Perky were the officiating ministers.

To the unwavering faithfulness of Nelson Works, now for many years an elder, the church owes much of its prosperity. The present membership is about eighty. The church edifice, erected in 1849, cost about $1,600. In 1875 half of the church building and grounds were sold to the Congregationalists, who now occupy it one-half of the time. Good will and harmony prevails. The two congregations have remodeled, enlarged and repaired the church, added a

steeple and bell, and made other improvements.

The Second Adventists have an organization and hold meetings at a school-house in the northern part of the township. This society has been in existence here some twelve or fifteen years and numbers some very good people among its members.

THE CEMETERY.

The chief burying-place in this township is the cemetery near the center. One acre of ground was given to the township by 'Squire Brown, and additional ground has since been purchased. The cemetery is a beautiful spot, thickly shaded by evergreens and other ornamental trees. Interments were made at an early day, and here repose the pioneers, their life struggles ended.

> Far from the madding crowd's ignoble strife,
> Their sober wishes never learned to stray;
> Along the cool, sequestered vale of life
> They kept the noiseless tenor of their way.

In the northern part of the township, a small piece of land was purchased and laid out as a graveyard. But few interments have been made here.

TOWNSHIP DIRECTORY.

Bloomfield center: stores, William C. Savage, D. W. Smith, and J. W. Haine. Post-office, George W. Howe. Hardware, tinware, and furniture, T. J. Sealey. Harness shop, R. Welchman. Manufacturer of wind-mills, H. F. Headley.

Cheese factories: Center Brook factory, center, Kincaid & Little. Clover Hill factory, north part of the township, George E. Haine.

Grist-mill: William Haine, in the north of the township.

Steam saw-mills: Russell & Ackley, east of the center, and A. Canfield in the north.

Hay-bailing: Steets & Davis, east of the center.

MASONIC.

Rural lodge No. 328, North Bloomfield, was granted a charter October 17, 1860. The following were the charter members: James Peirson, Horace Flower, George W. Howe, Chester Howard, Benjamin Cutter, Alvin A. House, Beriah Hill, Sumner Stoughton, Lucius S. Ball, William Harrington, Walker M. Price, and George W. Harrington. The lodge had been working under a dispensation from December 22, 1858. The lodge has steadily prospered ever since it was formed. At one time two hundred and eighty members belonged, but the organization of lodges in neighboring places caused several to withdraw, so that now only about seventy members are included in Rural lodge. The building in which the hall is, is owned by the lodge. They have pleasant rooms tastefully furnished, and are in excellent financial condition.

SCHOOLS.

The citizens of the village about fourteen years ago succeeded in establishing a special district at the center. A select school has been in progress about three years under the care of Professor Andrews. The school was divided into three grades, and Rev. Hiscock elected principal of the high school. He got the school into good working order, and it has since continued prosperous. Tuition scholars from abroad are received. Mr. Viets, the present principal, is now serving his second year in this school. The school-building is a substantial two-story frame house, used both for the school and as a town hall.

ROAD AND RAILROAD FACILITIES.

Bloomfield is on the Ashtabula & Warren turnpike, and is the southern terminus of the Painesville & Bloomfield plankroad from the northwest. The turnpike passes across the township from north to south, following a direct line a half mile west of the center line of the township. Just one mile east of the turnpike the Ashtabula, Youngstown & Pittsburg railroad crosses the township, uniformly straight, excepting one slight bend near the southern township line.

Before the railroad was opened, Bloomfield was comparatively far inland, and a journey to Warren, sixteen miles distant, was necessary whenever the inhabitants wished to go to market or visit the county-seat. Consequently the people formed the habit of living very much by themselves, and established stores and shops of almost every kind to avoid the necessity of frequent trips over the turnpike to Warren.

The railroad station, one mile east of the village, now affords great convenience to travelers and shippers of produce.

THE SWAMP.

The tamarack swamp was known far and wide as a favorite hunting ground for both white men and Indians. The tamarack trees grow very tall, and close together. Other kinds of soft wood are also found here. Fine oak timber, beech, maple, walnut, and hickory formerly covered the surface of the higher portions of the township, but tamarack, basswood, and poplar abound in and about the swamp. Whortleberry, or huckleberry bushes, covered many acres of ground, and almost fabulous numbers of quarts of berries were gathered in this swamp years ago. The ground has been burned over several times, and now but few berries can be found.

Formerly pigeons in countless numbers flocked to the swamp in autumn and spring, but hunting them has destroyed so many that only small flocks ever enter the swamp now.

The ground in this swamp was so wet in early years that a horse could nowhere cross it. Now it is easily crossed in almost any place, and if the process of draining continues to be carried on in a few years the great swamp will exist only in the memory of the oldest inhabitants. On an island, or rather a dry elevation in the midst of this moist land, the Mound Builders have left a memorial of themselves in the shape of three mounds. They are circular in form, and raised several feet above the adjacent surface. The largest is about fifteen feet in diameter, and five or six feet deep.

SETTLEMENT NOTES.

John Smith was born February 2, 1800, in Warwick, Massachusetts. His wife, Julia Ann Smith, *nee* Wright, was born at Northampton, Massachusetts, September 4, 1806. They were married December 31, 1829. Mr. Smith came to Ohio in an early day, and settled in Bloomfield township, south of the center. He cleared up a good farm, and lived upon it till his death. He died November 17, 1868; Mrs. Smith died April 16, 1870. Farming was Mr. Smith's occupation. He was well known as a surveyor; was justice of the peace many years, also town clerk. Mr. and Mrs. Smith were members of the Congregational church, formerly Presbyterian. There were four children in his family— Cornelia, born May 8, 1831; Justin E., born October 25, 1832; Dwight W., October 28, 1835; Mary Elizabeth, October 2, 1839; all born in Bloomfield. Justin is deceased; he died February 2, 1862, in hospital at Cincinnati.

Dwight Smith, son of John Smith, was born

in Bloomfield, October 28, 1835. He has always resided in the township; followed farming till 1872, then went into the mercantile business at the center. He was married May 28, 1856, to Miss Mary Richelieu, daughter of William P. Richelieu, of Scotland. William P. Richelieu was born November 5, 1805, in Scotland. Mrs. Richelieu was born May 28, 1817, in Scotland. Mr. and Mrs. Smith have had five children—John W., born April 10, 1857; Lazette and Lafayette (twins) born March 28, 1858; Martha C., April 8, 1864; Justin D., October 14, 1868. Lazette, died August 30, 1873; Lafayette, September 6, 1858. Mr. and Mrs. Smith, also two of the children, are members of the Congregational church.

Hon. Thomas Howe was born in Westmoreland, New Hampshire, on the first day of February, 1779. His opportunities for acquiring an education were meagre; however, he improved the chances presented him to the best possible advantage. Early in life he devoted himself to mercantile pursuits, and eventually settled in Williamstown, Orange county, Vermont, where he carried on the business of a merchant successfully. In 1817 he moved with his family to Bloomfield, Ohio,—a family comprising wife and five children; his wife survived the subject of our sketch about one year, and the children are all living. Clarissa, wife of Thomas Howe, was born in Woodstock, Connecticut. She was a woman of exalted virtue and unbounded benevolence, exerting a Christian influence on all with whom she had intercourse. Her memory is treasured by her children. The late Hon. Thomas Howe several times represented Trumbull county in the Ohio Legislature, honorably to himself and to the satisfaction of his constituents. He lived to be an octogenarian, and his whole life was one of exceeding worth, and fit for emulation by the youth and middle-aged, and even by those made venerable by the gray hairs of many years. The noblest tribute that either poet, sage, or sophist could not excel, is that expressed by his son, who has said that "he remembered no word or action of his lamented father he would wish changed for his memory's sake."

Dr. G. W. Howe, son of Hon. T. Howe, was born in Williamstown, Vermont, December 21, 1809. He was favored with the advantages for acquiring a good education, and he wisely improved the passing time. In the year 1817 he came to Bloomfield. During two winter seasons he taught school. September 25, 1832, he was united in marriage to Miss Julia A. Austin; from this union six children have been born; three are living. Mr. Howe studied medicine with Dr. Benjamin Palmer; followed his profession forty-four years; from 1862 to 1865 he was surgeon of board of enrollment; near the close of the service he received a communication from the assistant provost-marshal-general, certifying that the skill and fidelity manifested in the discharge of his official duties were highly creditable to himself, and deserving special commendation; that there was only one surgeon that stood as high as himself. Dr. Howe has twice represented his people in the Ohio Legislature.

William H. Howe was born January 5, 1817, in Williamstown, Vermont. His father, Thomas Howe, was one of the original owners of the township. Mr. William Howe came to Ohio with his father in 1817. In 1832 he went to Pittsburg where he was engaged in mercantile business till 1845. He then went to Michigan and was among the first miners of copper about Lake Superior. He remained here two years, then returned to Bloomfield and went into business for his brother George. In 1864 Mr. Howe returned to Lake Superior and was engaged in mining seven years. During the war he was clerk in the provost office at Warren. In 1871 he went to Corry, Pennsylvania, where he was an overseer in a manufactory of pails, tubs, etc., for five years, then returned to Bloomfield township, where he has since resided. He was married in 1850 to Miss Malvina Flower, daughter of Hiram Flower, of Bloomfield. They have had nine children, four of whom are living. Mrs. Howe is a member of the Congregational church.

Asa Works, an early settler of Bloomfield township, was born in 1775 in Richmond township, New Hampshire. He came to Ohio in 1817 and settled in Bloomfield upon the farm now occupied by his son, Nelson Works. He purchased two hundred acres of Brown & Howe. The county was an unbroken wilderness at this time. Asa Works died in 1826, March 3d, aged fifty-one years. There were four children in his family—Nelson, Sophia, Mary, and Martha. Sophia is deceased. Mr. Works was a hatter by trade. Mrs. Works died September 28, 1862, aged seventy-nine years. Mr. Works was a member of the Bible Christian church. Mrs. Works is a member of the Disciple church. Mr. Nelson Works has always lived in the township since he was six years old. Farming has been his chief business. He married Miss Delia Cleveland, daughter of William Cleveland, of Aurora. He had two children by his first marriage—Ellen A. and Laura J. Mrs. Works died January 25, 1852. Mr. Works was married again January 19, 1854, to Miss Harriet A. Booth, daughter of Peter Booth, of Greene township. She was born October 20, 1823. Mr. Nelson Works was born December 15, 1811, in Williamstown, Vermont. His family consisted of three children—Charles N., Lilian M., John B. Mr. and Mrs. Works are members of the Disciple church. Politically Mr. Works is a sound Republican. At the present time Charles is teaching in Youngstown; Lilian attending school at Hiram; John is at home; Ellen is teaching at Niles, and Laura is the wife of Dr. Ferrey, of Bloomfield.

William Haine, an old resident of Bloomfield township, was born in Somersetshire, England, February 8, 1806. His father, John Haine, was a native of England and lived and died in the old country. Mr. William Haine sailed from England April 11, 1835, landing on Prince Edward island after a passage of about thirty days. He soon went to Pictou, Nova Scotia, then to Castine, Maine, from there to Boston, from Boston to Ohio, where he had two sisters living in Bloomfield township, Trumbull county. Mr. Haine purchased one hundred and fifty acres of land of George Huntington, of Painesville, though the original deed was from 'Squire Brown. Mr. Haine began in the woods, or about the same, as there was but a small clearing in which he started. He has cleared most of his present farm by his own hard labor. He was married April 11, 1836, to Miss Mary Haine, daughter of Joseph and Sarah Haine, of Somersetshire, England. They have had ten children—William J., Sarah, Lottie, Emma, George, Ellen, John, Clara, Charles, and Ellen (deceased). Mr. and Mrs. Haine are members of the Methodist church, also the children. Politically Mr. Haine is a Republican.

John Sager was born April 12, 1810, in Bristol township. His father, William, was an early settler in Trumbull county. Mr. John Sager spent his entire life in Bristol and Bloomfield townships. He came to the latter in 1835 and settled upon the farm where his widow and daughter now live. The farm was formerly owned by George Norton. The many improvements now apparent have all been made by Mr. Sager. He was married April 12, 1835, to Miss Louisa Moffat, daughter of Hosea Moffat, of Bristol township. She was born July 11, 1816, in Orleans county, New York. They have had seven children—Mary, Martin, Sarah, Albert, Edwin, Sophronia, and Ella. Mr. Sager died April 2, 1881. Martin was killed at Malvern Hill, Virginia, July 28, 1864. He was in company A, Sixth Ohio cavalry. Sophronia died December 20, 1850. Ellen died May 29, 1871. Mr. John Sager was a member of the Disciple church, also Mrs. Sager and children.

Israel O. Proctor, an early resident of Bloomfield, was born February 4, 1796, in Manchester, Massachusetts. His father, Francis Proctor, was born February 28, 1758, at Ipswich, Massachusetts. His mother, Abigail Edwards, was born in Manchester, Massachusetts, August 30, 1784. There were twelve children in Francis Proctor's family: Isaac, Daniel, Francis, Israel, Arriel, Arriel William, Abigail, Abba, Eliza, Lucy, Ann, all of whom are dead. Mr. Israel Proctor came to Ohio in about 1819, and settled in Bloomfield township, and was a pioneer in this part of the county. He began in an unbroken forest and cleared up a good farm, which he worked till his death. He was married October 2, 1833, to Miss Delana Cornell, daughter of Richard Cornell, of Schenectady, New York. She was born March 24, 1813. Mr. Proctor died March 5, 1843. There are four children in the family: Abbie, born July 19, 1834; Richard, born December 29, 1835; Israel O., born September 27, 1837; Lucy D., born March 26, 1840. Abbie (widow Northway) is at home with her mother. Richard is in southern Illinois, Israel in Montana, Lucy (widow Pinney) is teaching in Massillon, Ohio.

Joseph Knowles Wing, a son of Barri and Lucy Clary Wing, was born in Wilmington, Vermont, July 27, 1810. At sixteen years of age he left his home for a clerkship in a store in Al-

Ephm Brown

Mary R. Brown

bany county, New York, and came from there to Bloomfield, Trumbull county, Ohio, in June, 1831, where he now resides. He married, October, 1842, Mary, the eldest daughter of Ephraim and Mary Huntington Brown, of Bloomfield, who was born May 28, 1812. He has spent some thirty years of his life as clerk and proprietor in mercantile pursuits. On the breaking out of the civil war he was commissioned by President Lincoln captain and assistant quartermaster of United States volunteers, and brevetted major and lieutenant-colonel; served on the staff of General G. M. Dodge until the taking of Atlanta, was then ordered to Newbern, North Carolina, as acting chief quartermaster of the district of North Carolina, remaining there until the close of the war. In 1869 he was elected a member of the House in the State Legislature, and re-elected in 1871. Their children are Mary Huntington, Elizabeth Brown, Virginia Passarant, died February 1871; George Clary, resides in Washington, D. C.; Francis Joseph, resides in Cleveland, Ohio; Julia King, and Anna Margaret.

William C. Savage, a well known merchant of Bloomfield, was born in Middletown, Connecticut, April 25, 1823. His father, Amasa Savage, was also a native of Connecticut. He was a ship carpenter by trade and followed this occupation many years, and was master-builder of many a craft upon the lakes after his coming to Ohio in 1831. He settled in Ashtabula county and lived there until his death, which occurred in 1855. The "fated schooner" Washington was probably the last he had charge of building, in 1838 or 1839. There were fourteen children in his family, eight girls and six boys, twelve of whom lived to maturity. Mrs. Savage died in 1865. Her maiden name was Sarah K. Hatch, of Weathersfield township, Connecticut. She was a devoted member of the Congregational church, as also was Mr. Savage in his latter days. William C. Savage, the subject of this sketch, came to Bloomfield in 1843. He has been engaged in mercantile business all his life. He was married in 1849 to Miss Martha L. Wright, daughter of Paul Wright, of North Hampton, Massachusetts. They have had but one child; this died in infancy. Mr. and Mrs. Savage are members of the Congregational church and are sincere Christians. Mr. Savage is a deacon of

the church. Politically he is a firm Republican and has held several of the township offices; has been town clerk, also was justice of the peace several terms and finally refused a re-election, thus showing the high esteem in which he is held by his fellow townsmen. He was also postmaster several terms.

Arthur V. Crouch was born in Washington county, Pennsylvania, August 2, 1827, oldest son of George and Mary Crouch. George Crouch, born in Washington county, Pennsylvania, in 1804, was a resident of Trumbull county some ten years. He married, in 1826, Mary, daughter of Arthur Van Wye, who was a pioneer in Weathersfield, where he settled about 1802. He was a soldier from Trumbull county in the War of 1812. Mrs. Crouch was born in Weathersfield in 1806 and died in 1848. A. V. Crouch in earlier years followed school-teaching some eight or ten years. Was a resident of Pittsburg some time where he was deputy county treasurer in 1858. From 1859 to 1874 he was connected with the Pittsburg Plow works, removing to Greene, Trumbull county, Ohio, in 1863, and conducting a branch business there, at the same time being engaged in farming and dairying. In April, 1881, he removed to Bloomfield, where he still resides. In 1858 he married Jennie F. McVey, who died in 1862. In 1864 he married Mrs. Mary F. Lewis, daughter of Captain Archibald Green, of Bloomfield, where she was born in 1842, and has six children, as follows: Martin L., Mary F., Florence M., Arthur V., Jr., Archibald G., and John B. Mr. Crouch was elected county commissioner for Trumbull county in 1878, and re-elected in 1881.

Alex. Wright was born in Ireland December 25, 1805, and came to America in 1819 in company with his mother. His father died before their coming to this country. Mr. Alex. Wright and mother came to Ohio and settled in Liberty township, Trumbull county, where he lived till he moved to Bloomfield township about 1853. His mother lived with her son John till her death in 1845. There were six children in her family —Nancy, Margaret, Jane, Mary A., John, and Alex. All are deceased. Mr. Alex. Wright located in Bloomfield township, about one mile north of the center. Farming was his chief occupation. He was married March 20, 1850, to Miss Eliza Gilmore, daughter of James Gilmore, of Portage county. She was born October 6, 1826. Mr. Wright died January 12, 1878. Mr. Wright was a member of the Methodist church. Mrs. Wright is also a member. Politically Mr. Wright was a firm Democrat. He was highly esteemed by all.

L. Wellington Mears was born February 8, 1817, in Poultney, Vermont. His father, Joseph, was also a native of Vermont. The family is of English descent. Mr. L. W. Mears came to Ohio in 1832, in company with his mother, and located in Hubbard township, Trumbull county. He remained in Hubbard several years, then went to Sharon, Pennsylvania, where he was engaged in the mercantile business about eight years. He was married in 1841, March 24th, to Miss Amanda Flower, daughter of Horace Flower, of Bloomfield township. They have had five children, three of whom are living—Byron, Albert, William, Horace, and Ida; Albert and Horace are deceased. Mr. and Mrs. Mears came to Ohio in 1848, and settled at first in Mesopotamia, and lived there about three years, then came to Bloomfield, where he has since resided. Mr. Mears is at the present time traveling in the West for a hardware house of Chicago. Mrs. Mears is a member of the Congregational church. In political matters he is a Republican.

BIOGRAPHICAL SKETCHES.

EPHRAIM BROWN.

It is impossible within the limits of a short sketch to give an adequate idea of the character, or to detail particular events in the life of Ephraim Brown. His father, whose name was also Ephraim, resided at Westmoreland, New Hampshire, and was much esteemed for his many excellent qualities. His mother was Hannah Howe, a woman of deep religious feeling. The family consisted of ten children, of whom Ephraim, born October 27, 1775, was the oldest. Mr. Brown owned a small farm and by adding to its productions the fruits of occasional labor in some mechanical pursuit, his large family was comfortably supported until he lost all his property by going security for a friend, a loss from

which he never recovered. It thus happened that the eldest son, at an early age, became the main support of a large family. This misfortune of his father offered him a field for the exercise of that indomitable perseverance which was so conspicuous an element of his character. At this formative period of his life the engrossing labor which circumstances threw upon him was not allowed to interfere with his intellectual culture. He read the best books obtainable, and sought the society of the best people in his neighborhood and wherever business called him. It is inferred from letters still in existence that he soon became a young man of some mark, for his advice was sought by elders, and his judgment received with much deference. Considerable of his correspondence at this early period related to moral, religious, and political subjects. He shows in these letters habits of earnest and honest thought, always ready to listen to argument, and when convinced of error always ready to renounce it. For example, when a young man he joined the Masonic fraternity, but years afterwards, when a young man sought his advice on the subject of joining he expressed the opinion that with advanced civilization the need of such societies was past.

Being a man of broad and tender sympathies Mr. Brown very early in life conceived a bitter hatred of the system of slavery, then fast growing into a political power, which sixty years it required the whole energy of the nation to suppress. In a letter written in 1807 to a Southern relative, who had located in the South and was endeavoring to persuade him to follow by arguing the superior facilities for making money in that section, Mr. Brown questioned the method by which wealth might be acquired so rapidly by "commerce in human flesh," and added, "I have been taught from my cradle to despise slavery, and will never forget to teach my children, if any I should have, the same lesson." The same letter contains sentiments thirty years afterwards given public utterance by William Lloyd Garrison and other distinguished abolitionists.

Mr Brown inherited from his mother deep religious feeling, which was strengthened by analytic habits of thought and extensive reading. But he distinguished between real piety and the mere semblance of religion, and his whole life was characterized by a high moral tone. His denunciation of evil was always vigorous and sometimes alarming to the more conservative and temporizing souls about him. His love of freedom and habits of thought prevented him from being closely associated with societies of any kind, though as an individual he was always industrious and kind.

As early as 1803 Mr. Brown became engaged in mercantile pursuits in connection with Thomas K. Green, of Putney, Vermont, who had charge of the business at that place, and Mr. Brown managed the branch at Westmoreland, and continued in business until his removal to Ohio in 1815. In the meantime he had represented his town in the Legislature several times. He was married on November 9, 1806, to Mary Buchanan, eldest daughter of Gordon and Temperance (Huntington) Buchanan. She was born at Windham, Connecticut, August 29, 1787; while yet a child her father and mother removed to Walpole, New Hampshire. She was a woman of talent, which she cultivated during her whole life. She taught school before her marriage; her attainments were therefore of a solid character.

In the year 1814 Mr. Brown formed a partnership with his uncle, Thomas Howe, and purchased of Peter C. Brooks, of Boston, township seven, range four, of the Western Reserve, since known as Bloomfield, to which place he removed his family in the summer of 1815. The journey was accomplished in six weeks and the family reached its future home July 16, some preparations having been previously made for its comfort and support. The two partners, Messrs. Brown & Howe, were in business temperament and character the antipodes of each other. The former was energetic, pushing, and fearless; the latter slow, hesitating and doubting. It is not strange that two such men should soon dissolve business relations. Mr. Howe after a short time retired from the partnership, and Mr. Brown assumed the burden of the debt, which in a few years, by the most scrupulous economy, unresting industry, and fortunate thriftiness was fully discharged.

A few years after Mr. Brown's settlement in Bloomfield (in 1819) the Ashtabula & Trumbull Turnpike company was formed and chartered under the laws of Ohio. Mr. Brown took an active part in pushing this enterprise, which at that time looked like an enormous undertaking, to a successful completion. For many years he maintained a ceaseless care for the interests of the company and the preservation of the road. The post-office at Bloomfield was secured through his influence. Within seven years after the first settlement of Bloomfield daily four-horse mail-coaches passed through the place on their route between the lake and the Ohio river. Land rapidly advanced in value, and the more thrifty settlers were soon able to improve their homes.

Mr. Brown was several times a member of the General Assembly, and always gave his potent influence to measures looking toward material improvement and educational advancement. His love of freedom was active, and influenced his whole conduct. The effort of a prominent religious sect in 1822 to dominate in politics, was condemned and resisted as strongly as the effort of the slave power to rule the country in after years. In his younger years he was a Jeffersonian Republican, and an avowed abolitionist always. He always offered assistance and protection to fugitive slaves, as is shown by instances elsewhere narrated.

The title of colonel was conferred upon Mr. Brown in New Hampshire, not, however, on account of any military service. He was captain of a company of militia, and promoted Governor's aid with the rank of colonel.

It has been said of Mr. Brown that he never sought or desired fame, but in a certain sense he won what was better than fame—the perfect respect and confidence of all who were capable of appreciating such a character. An intimate friend at the time of his death said in a letter, "In his social relations he was distinguished for his kindness, benevolence, and hospitality; in his business transactions for prudence, promptness, and integrity. Throughout a long and active life he eminently sustained the character of a patriot, philanthropist, and an honest man." He died of paralysis after a short illness, April 17, 1845, being in the seventieth year of his age.

Mrs. Brown was a woman of great excellence as wife, mother, neighbor, and friend. A life of well directed study gave her broad culture; a knowledge of the world widened her sympathies, and tenderness of feeling made her charitable. In her family she was gentle, loving, and interesting. In the social circle her influence was elevating and refining. Her death occurred January 26, 1862.

The family consisted of nine children: Alexander, born in 1807, lives in Bloomfield; George W., born in 1810, engaged in business in Pittsburg and died in Bloomfield in 1841; Mary, born in 1812, married to Joseph K. Wing and resides in Bloomfield; Charles, born in 1814, died in South Carolina in 1880; Elizabeth, born in 1816, resides in Bloomfield; James Monroe, born in 1818, died 1867 in Massillon; Marvin Huntington, born in 1820, resides in Painesville, Ohio; Fayette, born in 1823, resides in Cleveland, Ohio; Anne Frances, born in 1826, resides in Bloomfield.

HENRY CROWELL.

Henry Crowell was born in Grafton, Vermont, in the year 1802. His father, Mayhew Crowell, emigrated from Cape Cod, Massachusetts, residing in Grafton for a term of years and finally removed with his family to Bloomfield, Trumbull county, Ohio. His maternal relative, Mahitable Crowell, was the sister of Major Howe, formerly of Bloomfield, and cousin of Ephraim Brown, Esq., of the same township.

The subject of this biographical sketch removed with his parents from his Vermont home to Bloomfield in the year 1815. The journey was accomplished by means of ox teams and was necessarily slow and tedious, six weeks being consumed before they reached its termination, a distance which can now be overcome in less than twenty-four hours. For miles in many places they had to cut their way through dense forests, where the settler's axe had never before swung, bridging streams and camping out nights.

This journey proved no pleasure excursion. Few in these days of good roads and easy locomotion can appreciate the trials, privations, and suffering incident to pioneer life in those times when these little bands, severing the ties of old associations, poor in purse but strong in will, went forth in the early twilight of our Nation's history sowing the seeds of empire and breaking the way for future generations in the great West.

Arriving at Bloomfield, which at that time was a dense wilderness broken here and there only

by small clearings, few and far between, his father located a tract of land, a portion of which he ultimately sold to his son Henry, who, with characteristic industry, proceeded to clear and prepare it for cultivation, erecting a dwelling thereon. In the year 1832 he was united in marriage with Miss Almena Saunders, the result of which union was five sons and two daughters; five of these seven children are still living.

In the year 1865 he removed to Cleveland, Ohio. Here he afterwards resided until his death, which occurred September 20, 1881, in the eightieth year of his age, he being the last member of a family of twelve. His temperate, orderly life, combined with habits of well regulated industry, prolonged his years far beyond the average span of existence.

He was a man of sterling integrity, most eminently just in all his dealings, never having a quarrel or case of litigation in the entire course of his life. So sweetly ordered were all his ways that in the beaten path of his daily walk and conversation he never made an enemy or lost a friend. Peaceful, quiet, and unostentatious; firmly grounded in his religious convictions, beneath a calm exterior flowed the tides of kindly thought and feeling with scarce a surface ripple, but strong, resistless, pure, and holy. He lived a noble example of the possibilities of a religious culture which rounds into symmetrical beauty the best types of an exalted Christian manhood.

CHAPTER XI.
JOHNSTON TOWNSHIP.

The name of this township was doubtless derived from the original proprietor of the land, Captain James Johnston, of Salisbury, Connecticut, father of the late Edward Walter Johnston.

The township is in number six of the second range. It was surveyed by Nathan Moore and his assistant in the year 1802. It was then an unbroken wilderness uninhabited by any save the savage or wild beast of the forest. The first settler was a family by the name of Bradley, consisting of himself, Captain Bradley, his wife, Asenath, and their three sons, Thaddeus, Moore Bird, and Ariel. They bid adieu to their native town, Salisbury, Connecticut, on the 7th of June, 1803, and performed a journey of five or six weeks and six or seven hundred miles, reaching Canfield, this State, before they made a stop. Mr. James Bradley at that time was a man not far from fifty years of age, and his sons were young men just in the strength of early manhood.

Mr. Bradley and family remained at Canfield a few days to visit friends of former acquaintanceship, after which they resumed their journey by marked trees and bridle paths, making their way from one clearing to another, which however, were few and far between. After a few days they came to the last opening, about five miles distant from the locality selected for a home in the new township. The whole region at that time for a space of ten miles square around this spot selected for spending the remainder of their days, was an unbroken wilderness, uninhabited. Their neighbors were a family by the name of Barnes between this and Vienna, one family in the southwest part of Bazetta, between this and Warren, on what was known as the Quinby farm, a few families in Vienna, a few in Gustavus, and a few in Kinsman. They camped the first night in the township by a little stream, taking rest preparatory to the work of penetrating the unbroken forest still further on the morrow.

Captain Bradley and his family settled on a lot a little west of the center, but he subsequently removed to a farm in the west part of the township, where he lived about fourteen years, and died respected at the age of sixty-two. His widow lived fifteen years longer and died a venerable matron of four-score years, June 15, 1832. From the time she left the family of Mr. Barnes, in Fowler, and came into this township, it was a year and some months before she saw again the face of a white female.

Of the sons of Captain Bradley, Thaddeus, the eldest, spent much time from home aiding the family by such employment as he could find in Ravenna or the neighboring settlements in merchandising or teaching till he at length returned and settled in the west part of the township, where he died in October, 1865, at the old homestead which was afterwards owned by James D. Bradley, his oldest son. About six hundred acres of land was inherited by his three

children and a granddaughter. Moore Bird, the second son, after laboring a few years in clearing away the forest, turned his attention to the study of medicine. He was the first medical student under the instruction of Dr. Peter Allen, and after studying and reading with him for a time he practiced his profession in Mansfield and eventually settled in Pennsylvania, where he died, leaving a widow. Ariel, the youngest son, engaged in the more rugged employment of clearing the farm. He was the hero of the axe, who felled the first tree previously noted. But his strong constitution gave way under toil and disease and subsequently he too studied medicine, with his brother, and practiced as a physician. Late in life he married Miss Laura I. Barstow, who still lives, the widow of the first physician of the township.

The next arrivals were two young men, who were carpenters, without families. One was a mill-wright. They set themselves to work to look up a suitable location for a mill seat, and fixed upon a site in the northeastern part of the township. Those young men were Jared Hill and James Skinner. They came in July, 1804, and staid until winter, raised their saw-mill, then left until the next season. They went to Canfield, married, and soon after came back with their wives. When they moved in they came up through the first range, through Vernon, and cut a path a mile and a half to make an opening to get their teams through to their new abode in the wilderness. There they remained, and as the men were mechanics, their wives were sometimes left alone from Monday morning until Saturday night, their nearest neighbors being a camp of Indians a half mile down the stream from the mill.

In about a year and a half after their settlement Messrs. Hill & Skinner had their saw-mill in use to the very great accommodation of the settlement. They soon added a grist-mill which further accommodated the inhabitants. Before the erection of this mill their nearest place for grinding was at Orangeville, Pennsylvania. Of these families Miss Sallie Hill died July 1, 1822, aged forty years, and Jared Hill, Esq., died July 6, 1839, aged sixty-five years.

A few weeks after Hill and Skinner first came, in September, 1804, came a Mr. Jaqua with his family, which consisted of himself and wife and five children, two sons and three daughters. This family settled near the cross roads east of the center. In this family was the first marriage in the township. Solomon Brainard was married to Charity Jaqua. The exact date is not known, but it was in less than two years after the family came as it was before June, 1806. Mr. Jaqua was the first magistrate chosen in the township. His two sons died in a time of sickness which will be noted in the proper place. The family removed to Pennsylvania, where they lived the remainder of their days. Of the family of Solomon and Charity Brainard, the second son, John Brainard, after laboring for a time as a clothier and also as an engraver, occupied the chair of a professor in the homeopathic college in Cleveland.

In the spring of 1805 David Hine and a Mr. Hanchet, single men, came and put up a shanty where Mr. Henry K. Hulse afterwards lived, west of the center, but they did not remain.

Probably the next family which came in was that of Mr. Zebulon Walker. He came in the late part of the summer or in the fall of 1805. His family consisted of a wife and several children. He first settled near Mr. Jaqua, on the northeast corner of the cross-roads. He built a small house and made a little improvement, which he subsequently exchanged for a lot towards the north part of the township, to which he removed and afterwards left town. As near as can be ascertained the first white child born in the township was a child of Mr. Walker.

Most, or all of those mentioned in the above, were from Litchfield, Connecticut.

November 2, 1805, brought in quite an addition to the settlement: Four families came from Warren, Connecticut. Daniel Hine, Jr.; Erastus Carter, Howard Fuller, and Benjamin Andrews. There were also some young men who came with them, among whom were Augustus Adams, Josiah Finney, and a Mr. Breman. This company were three days coming from Youngstown. Mr. Carter settled near where Mr. Dunbar's tavern afterwards stood, and the others in different parts of the township. They engaged immediately in putting up their cabins for shelter for their families for the coming winter. While in the midst of their work in rolling up their logs for Mr. Fuller's house, Mr. Hine had his leg broken below the knee, which laid him up for most of the winter. When Mr. Hine first came he stored his goods in the shanty built by his brother and Mr. Hanchet, and it was there he was cared for until he recovered from his injury.

Mr. Carter did not unload his goods until he had rolled up a house for himself. About one year after Mr. Carter came into the township he lost his infant child. It was buried in what is now the graveyard for the township, and was the first grave made in the ground, and this was probably the first death which occurred among the early settlers. Mr. Hine dug the grave.

In June, 1806, the next year, added another company to the settlement. Daniel Hine, Sr., David Webb, William McKey, and Morris Smith arrived with their families. This company suffered from sickness on the road. Mrs. McKey was so unwell that she was obliged to stop at the house of Isaac Woodford, in Vienna, where they had serious sickness, the complaint being dysentery. Daniel Hine settled on the place afterwards owned by William Boor, but later, in a few years, left for Canfield, where he removed his family. David Webb settled on or near the place where his late widow, Sarah Webb, lived and died, afterwards occupied by Mr. Hale.

Mr. McKey settled where his son Henry McKey afterwards lived. These families furnished a large accession to the number of young people in the township. Mr. Hine had two sons and three daughters. Mr. Webb had five sons and two daughters, and Mr. McKey had three children. Daniel Abell, subsequently Major Abell, another single man, came in June, 1806. Nathan Webb, the eldest son of David Webb, a clothier* by trade, soon turned his attention to secure a site for his business. He first attempted to build a little below the mill of Messrs. Hill & Skinner. After he had spent one season in building a dam the result of his labor was swept away by a freshet, and he subsequently secured the privilege of the water-power at the mill of Hill & Skinner. He returned to Connecticut and married Miss Anna Gregory, from Milton, with whom he settled on the place which for many years he afterwards occupied. His wife was a professor of religion before she left Connecticut, and did much to advance the cause of Chris-

---

* A maker of cloth, as formerly used.

tianity in the new settlement. Mr. David Webb was found dead in his bed on the morning of March the 22d, 1827. He was seventy-one years old. His widow, Sarah Webb, was also found dead in bed on the morning of October 6, 1852. She was ninety-two years old.

Mrs. Laura Hine, wife of David Hine, Jr., died September 15, 1851, aged twenty-one years. She was honored in the memory of all who knew her.

Mr. Augustus Adams, who came in November, 1805, settled on the lot afterwards occupied by Frederick Stevens. He married one of the daughters of David Hine, Sr.

Mr. Abell commenced the improvement where Ebenezer Jackson afterwards lived, but went back and was married to Miss Root, and when he returned he settled on he place afterwards owned by Mr. Bennett.

About the time that Mr. Abell commenced his improvement on the west street the son of Captain Bradley commenced the improvement which they subsequently occupied near Mr. Abell. The improvement first commenced by Mr. Abell was afterwards occupied by Mr. Spencer, and still further north on the place occupied by a Mr. Dickerson, Mr. Consider Faunce settled. He remained there till his death, which ooccurred April 1, 1819, at the age of sixty-nine. His widow lived to an advanced age, much esteemed as a mother in Israel, and died at the house of her son, Joseph Barstow, March 19, 1848, aged ninety-eight years.

About this time also we find the family of Mr. Lilly settled at the center, on the place afterwards owned by Rev. O. S. Eells; also a son of his and a Mr. Hunt settled at the south part of the township on the center line, Mr. Hunt nearly opposite where Mr. E. Allen's barn stood and where the old mill was in use for a long time. Mr. Lilly was farther south.

In the fall of 1810 the widow Anna Jackson came in and settled first with her two sons, John and William, on the place, a long time afterwards owned by Mr. Amzi Webb; John was married and William was single at that time. They subsequently removed to the south part of the township, purchased the improvements made by Mr. Hunt and Mr. Lilly, and after about five or six years their older brother, Ebenezer, came, and settled where his widow fifty

years afterwards was living. Mrs. Anna Jackson died June 22, 1818, aged fifty-eight years. Mr. John Jackson moved east of the center.

About the same time, 1810, Mr. Amasa Hamlin settled in the west part of the township on the farm afterwards owned by Mr. Greer, formerly by Mr. Joseph Barstow. Mr. Hamlin afterwards left.

SICKNESS.

In the winter and spring of 1811 the settlement was visited with distressing sickness. It prevailed so extensively that the well were not enough in numbers to take care of the sick. While many recovered there were four young persons who died. Jesse Perry was the first. His parents lived somewhere near the center, but as he was not in a situation to be taken care of there he was removed to the house of David Webb, where he died.

The disease, typhus fever, prevailed in the family of Mr. Webb, and their daughter, Debby Webb, died May 2, 1811, aged eighteen years. Two sons of Mr. Jaqua died also about the same time, of the same disease, and also a young man, William Adams, who died of consumption. It has been stated that Mr. Adams was the first adult who died in the township. He died at the house of his brother, Augustus Adams. Also the wife of William Key died not far from this time. Her health was poor when she came into the county, and while here was always a feeble woman. These funerals were solemn and sad gatherings in the wilderness for the little community with scarcely enough to assist at the necessary preparations. Sometimes they had the aid of Mr. Crosby, a local Methodist preacher from Vernon, to conduct religious services. Sometimes some of the settlers offered a prayer, and sometimes the dead were taken up in silence and borne away to the grave. The first of the settlers who aided in a religious service at funerals was Mr. Hamlin. Said one of the witnesses on one of these occasions: "Although I had no particular interest in religious subjects at that time, I did feel thankful that we had some one among us who could pray at a funeral."

EARLY RELIGIOUS MEETINGS.

The first attempt to hold anything of the character of the social religious meetings on the Sabbath was not until some time after the arrival of the company in June, 1806. As we have remarked, there were a number of young people in the company, some of them singers, and nearly all accustomed to attend meetings on the Sabbath before they came West. Although not professors of religion, and none of them feeling qualified by religious experience to conduct the devotional exercises of religious worship, yet they agreed to meet on the Sabbath and join in the exercises. Mr. Daniel Hine, Jr., invited them to meet at his house the first Sabbath of their meetings. Dr. Wright, of Vernon, was providentially visiting the sick in the place, and learning of the meeting he attended and assisted by leading the congregation in prayer, in connection with their reading and singing. As there was, however, no one among them of sufficient confidence and Christian experience to lead the devotional exercises of public worship, after a few times these meetings were suspended, and no more regularly religious meetings were held on the Sabbath, till after the arrival of Mr. Hamlin, and as far as can be learned, not till after the season of sickness. Mr. Hamlin was a Methodist of very respectable qualifications, and consistent religious character, of a liberal mind and disposed to seek and promote religious society. After becoming acquainted with the community and ascertaining the willingness and desire to have meetings for worship on the Sabbath, he invited the people to meet together, and met with them.

By his influence and aid the meetings were conducted by prayer, singing, and reading discourses, and by such free conference as the members present were disposed to engage in. This was the beginning of the permanent establishment of public worship on the Sabbath in this place. It is believed that from this time it has been habitually maintained. There was at that time no ecclesiastical organization, but all met together simply for worship. The preachers of all denominations, either residing on the border or traveling through as missionaries, occasionally spent a Sabbath or called at other times and gave them a sermon.

Among the early preachers who visited them was Mr. Crosby from Vernon, already mentioned; Father Badger from Gustavus, and Mr. Robbins, a Congregational missionary from Vernon; Mr.

Darrow from Vienna, a Presbyterian; also Mr. Sheldon from Fowler, and Elder Rigdon, a Baptist missionary, and later, Mr. Simon Woodruff, and Mr. William Hanford, missionaries from the Connecticut Missionary society.

During the occasional visits and the labors of these men there was an interesting revival of religion, in which some of the leading heads of families were hopefully converted to Christ, and who have since been pillars in the different churches here. Mr. Crosby, after a few visits finding a number of the Methodist denomination, suggested to them that if they would request it of the conference they would probably send a circuit preacher, who would gather a class and make a regular preaching station at this place. It was accordingly done about the year 1812.

FIRST METHODIST EPISCOPAL CHURCH.

Rev. James McMahan is remembered as among the first circuit preachers, and he was on the circuit in 1813. It was then known as the Mahoning circuit, belonging to this conference, which was set off in 1812 from the Baltimore conference.

This was then a frontier circuit, extending north into Ashtabula, and west into Cuyahoga and Portage counties. The preachers sometimes got swamped between their appointments. One of them, somewhere in the valley of the Mosquito creek, was compelled to seek a dry spot in the midst of the wide waters and swamp for the night.

The meeting for forming the class was held at the house of Mr. Lilley, nearly across the street from the house now used. Among the male members were Mr. Hamlin, Mr. Spencer, and probably Mr. Dickinson, and soon after Mr. Judson Tyrrel. The wives of most of these were with their husbands. Other names were also associated, but the early records were lost and they can not be ascertained.

The Presbyterian or Congregational church was organized October 16, 1814, under the labors of Rev. William Hanford, a missionary of the Connecticut Missionary society. It consisted at first of six members—Solomon Brainard and his wife, Nathan Webb and wife, and Amzi Webb and wife. The church was organized in a log school-house, the first one built in the place. It stood on the south side of the street and nearly opposite the east school-house. Rev. Osias S. Eells was installed pastor of the Congregational church October 10, 1827. At the time he came they met in a hewed-log school-house, standing on the northwest corner at the center. At that time a frame meeting-house was in course of erection on the southeast corner, where Andrews & Finney's store afterwards was built.

Although the house above mentioned was the first school-house, a school was commenced before that house was built.

The first school was taught by Miss Elizabeth Hine, daughter of Daniel Hine, Sr., who afterwards became Mrs. Thaddeus Bradley. It is said that it did not begin until after the removal of Mr. Hine to Canfield, and that she was sent for to come back and teach the school. It was taught in the house built by Mr. Zebulon Walker on the corner opposite the house of Mr. Wilbur.

The log school-house was built in 18— and the next school-house was a hewed-log house and was built where the house and store of John Jackson, Esq., stood afterwards. This second school-house was built for the double purpose of school and church, and had a stand arranged for the minister's use.

This settlement, together with all the other new settlements, experienced some alarm from the war on the frontier at that time. War was declared January 19, 1812, and forces were raised by draft for the defense of the frontier. The militia mustered at that time under Colonel Hayes, of Hartford. At first both Mr. Hill and Skinner were drafted, but Mr. Skinner did not go on account of some lameness. About two months after the first draft a rumor was set afloat that the enemy were landing at Cleveland, and all the enrolled men were called out to go immediately. At that time nearly all the able-bodied men in the settlement left. Mr. Daniel Hine was never enrolled in the militia on account of his broken limb. He, together with some old men past the age of service, were about all who were left behind.

The alarm proving to be false, most of the men went no farther than Austinburg or Harpersfield, from whence they returned, but some of them went out to Erie county, to Camp Avery, near where Milan now stands, and were in the service about six months. Before this time Mr. Judson Tyrrell had come and settled in the township, and was among the men who remained in the service. Subsequently his brother, Sherman Tyrrell, came and settled near. The Dickenson family also were in the township. So also were the Halsteads, and many others whose history we are not able to get in full. Some families were brought in later by relatives or interests already here. A son and daughter of Captain Johnston, from whom the township was named, came in. Colonel Walter Johnston in 1828 settled first where Dr. Moore Bradley afterwards lived, but who subsequently left it for his brother-in-law, Captain Ebenezer Mix, who came in later, and Colonel Johnston moved into the house of his son, Herman Johnston. Captain Mix died November 21, 1839, aged sixty-three years. His wife, Sally Mix, died July 27, 1846, aged fifty-six years. Colonel Johnston died December 2, 1849, aged sixty-eight years. Mr. George Root, a brother of Mr. Abell, came into the country early and took up a lot of land, and returned, but did not come to take up his residence until eighteen years afterward. In the interval another brother came to make a permanent home.

LATER SETTLEMENTS.

About 1830, through the aid of Mr. John Boone, afterwards of Mecca, a very respectable emigration of Protestant Irish commenced a settlement in the northwest corner of the township, and though Mr. Boone himself resided in Youngstown he came, after a short time, and occupied a farm in the northwest corner of the township, and as the settlement increased they became organized into schools and a Methodist society, and afterwards secured for themselves a good substantial house of worship. The settlement embraced parts of Gustavus, Greene, and Mecca.

Mrs. Rosier, on the north line of the township, was there before the settlers came from Ireland.

In the southeast corner of the township commenced a settlement in 1840. Messrs. Thomas Tudhope and Alexander Curry were the first persons of the company who came.

The first family from Scotland was that of Mr. Robert Hamilton. They were afflicted in crossing the ocean by the loss of a son, whose mortal remains were consigned to the deep.

Mr. Dewy was in the neighborhood during the time the first Scotch settlement came. The district was afterwards almost exclusively Scotch. They established their school and often had religious worship among them. They were mostly Presbyterian. While Mr. Dewy resided in that district, and Mr. Halstead where Mr. Gomery afterwards lived, and Mr. Van Aikin where Mr. Stodard afterward lived, there was a meeting of United Brethren maintained, and also another class in the northeast, or what was called the Henry settlement, but their regular appointments have ceased.

ORGANIZATION OF TOWNSHIP.

Johnston was originally embraced in a poll district with Vernon, Hartford, and Fowler, elections being held in Hartford in the Hayes neighborhood. Subsequently Mecca and Bazetta were attached to Johnston, which formed a new election district. The first election for the township was held in this township October 9, 1816, at the house of Abijah Perry, near the center. Captain Jaqua was made chairman of the meeting, and Nathan Webb and Jared Hill judges. The election resulted as follows: · Jared Hill, clerk, Samuel Hine, Jr., David and John Jackson, trustees. Mr. Rose and Mr. Dawson, of Mecca and Bazetta, were among the officers elected.

BIOGRAPHICAL SKETCHES.

THE BUSHNELL FAMILY.

Lewis Bushnell was born in Johnston township, Trumbull county, March 23, 1818. December 30, 1841, he was married to Elizabeth A. Treat, of Vienna, who was born July 4, 1821. The father of Lewis (his name also was Lewis) was born April 12, 1787, in Hartland, Hartford county, Connecticut. When about sixteen years of age his father (Daniel B.) and family emigrated to Hartford, Trumbull county, Ohio, and he came with the family, of which he was the oldest. He (Lewis B., Sr.) was married to Sally Webb December 27, 1808. She also was born in Connecticut, on September 26, 1790, and had come with her people to Johnston, Trumbull

county, Ohio. Her father, David Webb, was one of the Revolutionary soldiers. After their marriage they lived in Hartford for several years and then removed to Johnston. They had four children, viz: Linus, who died September 22, 1828, aged nineteen years; Debby, who died October 3, 1812, aged nineteen months; Lorenzo, born January 29, 1813, who resided in Johnston until 1852, when he went to Waukon, Allamakee county, Iowa, where he has since lived; and Lewis, who has always resided in Johnston. Three months after the birth of Lewis, Jr., (June 29, 1818) his father died, and ten years later his mother was married to James Bascom, of Greene, Trumbull county. They also had four children. Linus and John, the two older sons, were in the army and there lost their lives. Linus died in the hospital on December 29, 1862, aged thirty-one years. His body was wounded in nine places, and like so many other brave soldiers his sufferings were beyond description. John went home from the hospital on a furlough in the fall to vote at the ensuing election, and died a few days after reaching there. His home was in Wisconsin. The other two children are living. Sarah D., born July 8, 1829, married Allen Mallory, and went to Massachusetts, where she has since lived, and Lyman W., born June 30, 1836, still resides in Johnston.

Young Lewis Bushnell spent the first part of his life with his mother, helping her to keep the "wolves from the door," and this phrase was at that time used in another sense than the figurative, for it was not an uncommon event for them to see wolves and bears, as for instance, his mother hearing a noise in the pig-pen one night, went out and found a bear there ready to help itself to the pork, but was frightened away by the light she carried in her hand. Mrs. Bascom died February 4, 1878, in her eighty-eighth year. At the age of twenty-three Lewis married. His wife's father, John Treat, was born February 15, 1795, in Milford, Connecticut. He came to Vienna, Trumbull county, in 1818. His wife, Mary Hummason, was born March 20, 1804, in Hartford, Connecticut. She was the daughter of Jacob Hummason, who was a merchant of that place. He emigrated to Brookfield about the year 1803, his wife and family coming a year or so later. They found a log house with split log floor, and greased paper for windows very different from the home they left, where plenty of luxuries reigned. Mr. Hummason was one of the best educated men of the county, one of the first teachers in the schools in Youngstown, and an active man in public life. They had six children, of whom Mary was the fifth. She was married to John Treat May 10, 1820, and they have since lived in Vienna. They had six children, viz: Elizabeth A.; Sidney C., born July 5, 1823, and now living in Hazelton, Mahoning county; Julius H., who died June 16, 1858, aged thirty years; Mary E., who died November 1, 1865, aged forty years, and Garry A., born April 17, 1830, and now living in Vienna. Mr. and Mrs. Treat have always been noted for their kindness, especially to the poor and friendless. In 1832 they united with what is now the Presbyterian (then Congregational) church of Vienna, and he has filled the office of deacon or elder since his election to it in 1848, till three years ago because of his age he insisted on laying aside those duties. In May, 1870, the fiftieth anniversary of their marriage was celebrated, and each of the eleven years since the children and grandchildren have spent a glad holiday with the aged couple. Though in their living together sixty-one years they have been more favored than most couples, we hope many more years may be added to their united lives. After the marriage of Lewis Bushnell with Elizabeth Treat they went to housekeeping in Johnston, and there they have lived, and their eight children were born. Hubert T., the oldest was born September 26, 1843. When seventeen years old he taught a term of school, and then returned to the store where he had clerked the previous year, and with the exception of the time spent in the army has since been engaged in mercantile business. He was a volunteer with the ninety-day men, and also in the nine months service.

On December 23, 1868, he was married to Jennie Hollett, of Watkins, New York. About two years after they went East, and are still residing in Hartford, Cortland county, New York. They have one child, Charles La Verne, born January 10, 1871.

Mary E. was born October 27, 1845. She began teaching at the age of seventeen, and followed it quite closely, and with evident success for about thirteen years. On the 15th of June,

1876, she was married to Frank C. Hinman, of Tallmadge, Summit county. Their home is in Easton, Wayne county. They have two children: Louis C., born September 28, 1877, and Flora E., born August 28, 1879.

Martha A. was born January 4, 1848. On the 10th of May, 1876, she was married to Sullivan Hutchins, of Hartford, and are still living upon their farm in that township. They have two children, Grace A., born June 18, 1877, and Mary E., born January 11, 1880.

Howard L. was born January 18, 1850. He has followed speculating much of the time. On September 18, 1876, he was married to Kit Clark, of Vienna. Their home is in that place. They have one child, Ira E., born July 17, 1880, also one adopted child, Freddie, born August, 1878.

Linus S. was born January 1, 1853. At sixteen years of age he began teaching, and followed it winters for several years. He was married to Emma A. Taylor, of Mecca, January 1, 1876. They have one child, Ida M., born March 8, 1877. They settled on a farm in Johnston.

Esther T. was born January 30, 1855. She has followed teaching several years, and at present is teaching in the graded schools of Orwell, Ashtabula county.

Sarah E. was born June 15, 1857. She has followed teaching a part of the time.

George A. was born April 20, 1861.

Though the persons named in this sketch have never gained world-wide fame, they have possessed honesty, energy, and enterprise, and rejoiced to see the many improvements of the country, and while they have helped to put down slavery, intemperance, or any other evil which assailed society, they have tried to strengthen that which is good and all that tended to the advancement of social and public interest.

NOTES OF SETTLEMENT.

Captain James Bradley and family were the first settlers of Johnston township. Mr. Bradley was born in Connecticut June 18, 1755, died March 3, 1817. His wife, Asenath Bird, was born June 10, 1752, in Connecticut, and died June 10, 1832. They had three children—Thaddeus, Dr. M. B., and Dr. Ariel. Dr. Ariel

Bradley was the first settled physician in Johnston township. Thaddeus Bradley was born in Vermont February 11, 1787, died October 7, 1865. He married Elizabeth Hine. She was born in Connecticut February 16, 1790, and died February 13, 1867. They had a family of six children— Mary, James D., Dr. Moor C., Lester, Timothy, and Myron. James D. Bradley, the son of Thaddeus and Elizabeth Bradley, was born March 14, 1817, died March 11, 1875. He married February 8, 1859, Laura A. Minor, born February 17, 1831. They have two children—Frank T. and Dudley A. Dr. Moore Bird Bradley, the second child of James and Asenath Bradley, was born in Vermont, May 2, 1790, died February 16, 1841. He was the father of eight children. Dr. Ariel Bradley, the third child of James and Asenath Bradley, was born in Vermont in July, 1792; died in Johnston township October 7, 1859. He came to Ohio with his parents at the age of nine years, where he lived until his death. He studied medicine and was the first practitioner in Johnston township. He was married in 1828 to Laura L. Barstow, daughter of Joseph and Betsey Barstow, both natives of Sharon, Connecticut. Laura was born in 1809, in Norway, New York, and came to Ohio with her parents in 1818 and settled in Johnston township where she still lives. Her father was born in 1781, October 2, died at the age of eighty-eight years. Her mother was born in 1787, died aged seventy-seven years. Ariel and Laura Bradley had one child, Reumah, born in March, 1829, died in 1854. She married Buell Pelton. They had two daughters, Emma A., and Reumah. Emma was born in June, 1851. Reumah was born in 1853. Ariel Bradley served in the War of 1812. Mrs. Bradley was one of a family of eight, as follows: John, Laura, Wallace, Samuel, Emma, Mary A., Adaline, and one that died in infancy.

George Root was born in Connecticut, 1789, died 1869. He came to Ohio in a very early day and purchased land in Johnston township. He returned to Connecticut and married Mary Johnston, born 1799, died 1853. They had nine children, all dead but three. Mr. and Mrs. Root were members of the Congregational church. Shortly after their settlement their little log hut was burned and they were left without shelter in the wilderness. Eunice C., the second

child, was born in 1819, in Connecticut, and came to Ohio with her parents and married in 1842, Giles L. Day, son of Giles and Hannah Day. He was born October 30, 1815, in Vermont, and came to Ohio with his parents. He died April 1, 1879, after a lingering illness of twelve years. They had six children, Mary R., deceased, Emma A., Cornelia R., Elvia V., Alvira, and Mary L. Mr. Day was lieutenant of the home guard. He was a member of the Disciple church for a number of years, then took up the faith of Spiritualism. His parents came to Ohio about the year 1829. They had a family of eleven children. Giles L. and Eunice C. Day have six grandchildren.

Hezekiah Green was born in Maryland in 1801, died in 1879. He married in 1828 Comfort Burnett, born in Hubbard township in 1804, the first white child born in Hubbard township; is still living. They had seven children. Seth, the second child, was born in 1832, and came to Johnston township with his parents in 1836. He married in 1860 Miss Sophia Skinner, daughter of Sherman and Betsey Skinner. She was born in Johnston township in 1840. They had four children, Carrie, Lydia, Harley and Arba. Mr. Green is a farmer. Mr. and Mrs. Green are members of the Methodist Episcopal church. Mrs. Green's grandparents, James and Nancy Skinner, were the first settlers in Johnston township. They came from Connecticut. Mr. Skinner was loved and esteemed by every one that knew him.

Rev. Ozias Eells came to Johnston township, Ohio, in March, 1827, and was soon employed to labor as a minister of the gospel. He enjoyed the privilege to live in the pious family of Deacon Nathan Webb. The house for public worship was constructed of hewed logs and stood on the northwest corner of the land in the center of the town. In this house he officiated twice on the Sabbath and attended a prayer-meeting in the house of a member of the church in the course of the week. He was influenced to locate in this locality on account of an expected donation of fifty acres of land, situated in Mecca, belonging to William Ely. This land, which he received, together with fifty acres obtained at a vendue sale, was a great pecuniary help to him. He visited the families and took a census of the town, and at that time there were sixty families.

He was to some extent engaged in the instruction of the young, and prepared three young men to enter the Western Reserve college, at Hudson. In addition to a subscription for the support of his work in Fowler, where he was also engaged to preach, assistance was furnished by a missionary society in Massachusetts. Mr. Eells says the church furnished suitable accommodations for him to live in a married state, and that a good Providence provided a suitable person for his wife, and they were married by Rev. Harvey Coe, of Vernon. He attended a meeting of the presbytery of Grand river, was examined and received as a member. After preaching about six months he received a call to take the pastoral charge of the church in Johnston and another in Fowler. The call was accepted and the installation services were held in Mr. Robert Morrow's house, Rev. Wells Andrews preaching the sermon. In 1831 the presbytery appointed him to attend the general assembly in Philadelphia. After the establishment of Oberlin college and young men from that institution could be obtained to preach, some of the members were desirous of procuring the services of one of them and Mr. Eells was dismissed. He accepted an invitation to preach in other towns and thus continued his ministerial labors. After fifty years of married life his golden wedding was celebrated, on which occasion a large number of neighbors and friends assembled, and pleasant it was to all, and a number of valuable gifts were presented to the esteemed couple.

Truman Buell was born in Litchfield, Connecticut, in 1784; died in 1867. He was married in 1804 to Nancy Hinman. She was born in 1785; died in 1866. They had eight children—George, Ezra, Albert, Alban, David, Lorain, Mary, and Angeline. George, the oldest son, was born in 1809, in Litchfield, Connecticut, and died in Johnston December 27, 1869. He married Mary Halcomb, of Connecticut. She was born November 28, 1806, and died in Johnston in 1867. She was the daughter of Amasa and Abigail Halcomb. George Buell came with his family of four children to Johnston in 1846. His children were as follows: Truman S., George F., James K., and Mary L. James K. was born December 31, 1842, and was married, in 1869, to Susan Moran, daughter of William and Elizabeth Moran. She was born in Ireland. They have three children—Georgiana, Mary V., and Carrie M. Mrs. Susan Buell's parents, William and Elizabeth Moran, were born in Ireland, Leitrim county. He was born in 1784, and died in the ninty-seventh year of his age; his wife was born in 1800, and died in her eightieth year. The had nine children—John, Alice, Mary A., Robert S., Eliza, Jane, William B., Francis E., and Susan M. They settled in Vernon in 1846. Warren Buell was born August 13, 1800, in Hartford county, Connecticut. He married, in 1823, Electa Squires, born in 1798 in Connecticut. They came to Ohio in 1832, and settled in Johnston township, where they still reside. They had seven children; six are living, and one died in infancy— Daniel W., Harvey L., Wayne, Zenas W., Norris L., Celestia A. Mr. Buell is a blacksmith. Harvey L., the second child, was born in Connecticut in 1827, and came to Ohio with his parents. He was married April 23, 1862, to Elizabeth M. Tennant, daughter of William H. and Elizabeth Tennant, born in Scotland, May 25, 1845. They have one daughter, Lizzie, born in 1869. Mr. Buell is a general farmer, and has a farm of fifty acres. William Buell, son of Norman and Emily Buell, was born in 1823, in Connecticut. He came to Ohio in 1841, and settled in Portage county, where he resided until 1851, then moved to Johnston township. He married, in 1848, Harriet Curtis, of Geauga county, Ohio, born in 1825. They have four children—Charles L., Flora (deceased), Ida, Franklin, and Frederick. Mr. Buell follows the lumber business. Mr. and Mrs. Buell are members of the Methodist Episcopal church.

Matthew Miller (deceased) was a native of Ireland, born in 1732, emigrated to Westmoreland county, Pennsylvania, about the year 1760; was a Revolutionary soldier; married in 1762, Margaret Corrnehan, and had a family of nine children, three boys and six girls, named as follow: Robert, William, and Isaac; Jenny, Betsey, Nancy, Mary, Margaret, and Dorcas, all of whom lived to be married and raise families, except William, who lived in Westmoreland county, Pennsylvania, until 1814, when he moved to Millersburg, Holmes county, Ohio, where he died in 1817, at the age of eighty-five years.

Isaac Miller, deceased, son of Matthew Miller,

52*

was born in Greensburg, Westmoreland county, Pennsylvania, February 8, 1798; was married to Sophia Dabney, January 26, 1819; moved to Holmes county, Ohio, where he lived thirteen years, thence moved to Youngstown, Mahoning county, in January, 1832. May 1, 1850, he moved to Farmington, Trumbull county, and resided there until November, 1854, and then moved to Johnston township, where he died April 2, 1875. He had a family of seven sons and five daughters: John, Lucinda, Robert, Nathaniel G., Margaret Mary, Elizabeth, Ebenezer D., William (first), Sophia, Catherine E., William (second), and Isaac J. Four are living and married; six died in childhood, and one in California in 1851, aged twenty-one years. Nathaniel G. was married to Maria Reader about 1848; lived in Bristol township, Trumbull county, and died at the age of thirty-four years; had a family of four boys, viz: Isaac Jefferson, Frank R., Charles, Clinton; three of whom are married and one single. Lucinda Miller was married to Jared Housel September 6, 1839, and lives in Farmington; has had a family of six children, five living and married, viz: Mary Jane, Isaac, George A., Sophia, and Ira. Sylvanus died in the Union army at the age of nineteen years. Margaret Miller was married to Ephraim Boon, and since then has lived in Gustavus township; has a family of three children, namely: Addie, Miller, and Thomas, of whom Addie and Thomas are married, and Miller is deceased. Catherine E. Miller was married to Frank B. Wood, August, 1857, and since has lived in Johnston township; has a family of three girls, one married and two single—Orissa A., Edna I., Maud E. Isaac J. Miller was married to Ella M. Fairchild, October 5, 1870, and has since resided in Johnston township, Trumbull county. He has a family of four children, as follow: Jay E., Katie E., Arvine D., Isaac J. The occupation of the sons and sons-in-law of the subject of this sketch is farming.

Isaiah Bartlett, born in Plimpton, Plymouth county, Massachusetts, June 12, 1793, married Miriam Mason, born in Litchfield county, Connecticut, in 1795. They resided in Litchfield until 1833, when they removed to Johnston, Trumbull county, Ohio, and settled where their son Robert now lives, and resided there until their death. Mr. Bartlett died in 1867; Mrs.

Bartlett in 1870. They had a family of five boys and three girls, as follows: Rev. P. M. Bartlett, president of Marysville (Tennessee) college; Jerusha (Jackson) deceased; Lucius, now in Warren; Rev. Alexander M., professor of Greek and Latin in Marysville college; Mary E. (Leroy) in Kansas; Emma C. (Root), and Robert A., on the home place in Johnston, and S. F., in Warren.

Harvey Selleck was born in Salisbury, Connecticut, in 1805, and came to Ohio in 1828 and settled in Johnston township. He married Lucia Landon, born in Salisbury in 1805, died in 1871. They had a family of two daughters, Samantha (deceased), and Harriet. Mr. and Mrs. Selleck are members of the Congregational church, being among the founders of the Congregational society of Johnston. Mr. Selleck is a general farmer.

Charles W. Brinsmade was born in Salisbury, Connecticut, in 1809. He came to Ohio in 1850 with his family, and settled in Medina county. He married Maria E. Lockwood, born June 12, 1813, died November 28, 1875. They had a family of nine children, viz: A. F., Alonzo L., Charles P., George E., Almira P., Frances M., Wesley H., and two that died in infancy. A. F. Brinsmade was born in 1834, in Salisbury, Connecticut, and came to Ohio with his parents and married Harriet S. Selleck. He is a farmer.

Daniel Hine was born in Litchfield county, Connecticut, in 1777; died in 1859. He married Laura Finney, who was born in Connecticut in 1779, and died in 1850. They came to Trumbull county and settled in Johnston township. They brought with them two children— Josiah and Wealthy. The remainder were born in Ohio, their names being Lester, Niram, Chancy, and Lucinda. Mr. Hine was married again in 1852 to Mary Palmer, who was born in 1785, and died in 1870. Mr. and Mrs. Hine were members of the first Congregational church. He was a farmer. His parents and four brothers followed him to Ohio. Lester, the third child, was born in Johnston township January 3, 1809. He was married in 1860 to Eliza Bradley, who was born in Connecticut, and died in 1864. Mr. Hine is a farmer. Josiah Hine was born May 23, 1803, and died July 26, 1879. He was married March 5, 1848, to Desire B. Pitcher. She was born January 27, 1822, in Norwich, Connecticut, and came with her parents to Ohio in

1846, and settled in Johnston township. They had five children, three of whom are living. The first and second were twins, born in 1848, both now deceased. George, born in 1850, resides in Colorado; Mary E., born in 1852, resides at home; Daniel E., born in 1860, resides at home.

Abiel Cram was born in New Hampshire in 1802, July 30th. His parents moved to Vermont and in 1817 came to Ohio, and settled in Monroe township, Ashtabula county, and in 1819 moved to Pennsylvania, where he was married, in 1827, to Sarah Madlam. She was born in Pennsylvania in 1810, and in 1865 came to Ohio and settled in Johnston township. They had eight children; two died in infancy, two in youth: Mary, John, Horace, Sarah, Hannah, Nancy. John died in the army, shot May 21, 1861; was in company L, Sixteenth Pennsylvania cavalry. The first, third, and fourth are living. Mr. Cram was a farmer. He died June 21, 1878. His wife survives him. They were members of the Methodist Episcopal church. Horace, the third child, was born September 30, 1832, in Pennsylvania. He married in 1858 Nancy Duffield. She was born in 1828, July 30. They have two children, William A. and Sarah E. Mr. Cram is a farmer. They are members of the Methodist Protestant church.

David Alling, a native of Connecticut, married Clementine Judd, of Connecticut. They came to Ohio in a very early day and settled in Vienna township, and afterwards moved to Johnston township. They had seven children. Edward, the second child, was born in Connecticut in 1807. He married Charlotte Roberts, born in Connecticut in 1811. They have three children, Luther, Lucius, and Charley. Mr. and Mrs. Alling are members of the Congregational church. He is a general farmer. Luther, the first child, was born in Johnston township in 1833. He married in 1854 Miss Jane Moran, daughter of Francis and Bridget Moran, born in Ireland in 1832. They have four children, Augustus, Estella, Frank, and Alvia. Mr. Alling is in the saw-mill business, and also manufacturing pumps.

Thomas Millikin was born in county Leitrim, Ireland, on the 16th day of May, in the year 1816; died in Johnston in the year 1875, December 19th. He came to America in 1831, and in 1842 married Tamar Clark, daughter of John and Mary Clark. She was born in Pennsylvania December 4, 1818, and came to Ohio in 1840 and in 1842 came to Johnston township. They have a family of eight children, all living: George R., John C., Thomas J., Richard, James T., Charles W., Allen, and Mary E. Mr. and Mrs. Millikin are members of the Methodist Episcopal church. He was a farmer; held the office of township trustee for several years.

James Currie was born in Scotland, where he died leaving a wife and nine children, who came to America in 1845, and settled in Johnston township, Trumbull county. Mrs. Currie's maiden name was Marian Hamilton. The children were Catharine, Margaret, Alexander, Ellen, Marian, Jeannette, John, James, Isabelle. Alexander and James reside in Johnston township and are unmarried. They follow farming on a farm of two hundred and forty-one acres. Alexander was born August 29, 1822, and James in 1835. They are extensive sheep raisers.

Reuben Mowrey was born in Connecticut in 1753, and died in Gustavus township in 1841. He married Lucy Couch, born in 1755, died in 1839; they had ten children. Isaac, the youngest child, was born May 9, 1800, and came to Ohio with his parents in 1812. He married Betsey Pelton, born August 22, 1803. They had ten children. Eunice, the fifth child, was born September 11, 1832, in Gustavus township, and married in 1854 T. A. Bradley. They have one child, Mary P., born May 20, 1867. They reside in Johnston township.

CHAPTER XII.

FOWLER.

This township, formerly known as Westfield, contains 16,500 acres. It was purchased from the Connecticut Land company by Samuel Fowler, of Westfield, Massachusetts, and sold to settlers under his direction. Titus Brockway was granted power of attorney to dispose of 10,000 acres. Abner Fowler, brother of the proprietor, in consideration of services rendered in surveying this land, received 100 acres at the center of the township.

The township was purchased by Mr. Fowler in 1798, for less than fifty cents per acre.

In 1806 Fowler was included in the Vernon election district, which was organized that year. In 1807 it was set apart as a distinct township and election precinct.

Fowler is a good farming region. Its soil is mostly a fertile clayey loam. The surface is generally slightly undulating. The western part of the township is drained by two small creeks which flow westward into Mosquito creek. Branches of Yankee creek form the watercourses of the eastern half.

Fowler center, a neat and enterprising little village, is situated about one mile west of Fowler station. Tyrrell Hill, a lively, growing little place, is on the southern township line, about one mile from the corner of Fowler and Hartford. The Youngstown branch of the Lake Shore railroad passes northward through the eastern half of the township.

Fowler is the fifth township of the second range, and is bounded on the north by Johnston, on the east by Hartford, on the south by Vienna, and on the west by Bazetta.

In 1880 this township produced 6,187 bushels of wheat, 76 bushels of rye, 38 bushels of buckwheat, 16,924 bushels of oats, 13,547 bushels of corn, 2,950 tons of hay, 213 bushels of flax seed, 23,746 pounds of butter, 272,970 pounds of cheese, and in 1881, 12,437 pounds of maple sugar, and 691 gallons of maple syrup.

PIONEER HISTORY.

Abner Fowler was the first settler. The first cabin was built by him in the spring of 1799, and stood on the site of the public square a little northeast of the cross-roads. Mr. Fowler's wife had died before he left Massachusetts and he lived alone in his pioneer dwelling until other settlers arrived. The Fowlers were descendants of one of the oldest of New England families and several of them were prominent both in the affairs of their native State and of the Nation. Abner Fowler acted as advance agent, or as a solicitor of settlers, and it was principally through his influence that the first families of the township were induced to locate here. Mr. Fowler lived to see his settlement fairly started and the foundations of permanent improvement laid. He died in 1806. This was the first death that occurred in the township. His body rests in the old graveyard at the center.

Only two of Abner Fowler's children settled here. Abner, Jr., came out in 1805, and Chester in 1806 or 1807. The first marriage ceremony was performed in August, 1807, in uniting Abner Fowler, Jr., and Esther Jennings. They were married by Titus Brockway, Esq., of Hartford. The wedding took place at the house of Wakeman Silliman, in Fowler. Abner moved to Brookfield in 1816 and there ended his days. Chester passed the most of his life in Fowler and died in Hartford.

The first family in the township was that of Levi Foote, from Westfield, Massachusetts. Foote located near the center in 1801. Lydia Foote, daughter of Levi and Milly (Allen) Foote, was the first white child born in the township. Her birth took place July 5, 1805. She died April 21, 1881. The Foote family was quite large. Levi Foote's mother was Miss Bathsheba Burr, a relative of Aaron Burr. She was born in Granby, Connecticut, in 1755, and lived to be one hundred years old, lacking five days. She was married three times. Her first husband was Asa Foote, her second Isaac Flower, and her third a Mr. Thompson. She died and was buried in Vienna. Auntie Thompson, as she was long familiarly called, experienced many of the hardships of pioneer life. It is said that the first wolf killed by a settler of Fowler was brought down by a gun in her hands. Her husband was absent when the hungry beast visited the pig pen and was bold and voracious enough to seize one of the little porkers in midday. When this fact was made known to Auntie Thompson, she seized a gun and fired. The wolf fell and was then carried to her doorstep by herself and thought to be dead, but to make sure of her work the wolf was struck with a club. This brought it to consciousness and it sprang to its feet and would have been off had she not hurriedly dispatched it. Mrs. Thompson spent the last years of her life at the home of Dexter Clinton, near Vienna center.

Only five families settled in the township before 1805. These were the families of Levi Foote, already mentioned; Lemuel Barnes, who lived one-half mile north of the center; John Morrow, at the center; Hillman Fisher, and Drake, who lived on the ridge.

In 1806 seven families arrived from Connecticut, having left that State in the fall of the same year. A month or six weeks later they arrived in New Connecticut. These emigrants were Elijah Tyrrell and wife, *nee* Clarissa Meeker, with her brothers, Justice, Daniel, Lyman, and William Meeker; John Vaughn and Wakeman Silliman. They all settled in the southeast of the township in the vicinity of Tyrrell Hill or Tyrrell corners.

This company first halted at the house of Joel Hummason, in Vienna, and the women and children remained there, while the men went forward into Fowler, cutting roads to their lands to build cabins. This work completed the families took up their abode upon the farms which they afterwards improved, and where most of them lived and died.

Elijah Tyrrell built his house at the corners, on the northwest of the same. The lot lines were established a few years later and the place has been called Tyrrell's corners and Tyrrell Hill ever since. The corners are one mile from the east line of the township, and a mile north of the Vienna line.

Justice Meeker built his house one-half mile north of the corners; Wakeman Silliman, a few rods further north; Lyman Meeker, three-fourths of a mile north, and his brother Daniel on the opposite side of the road. William Meeker settled half a mile south of Mr. Tyrrell's, and John Vaughn one-half mile east.

Miss Esther Jennings, afterwards Mrs. Abner Fowler, was one of this party of settlers, and soon after the families were established in their homes taught school—the first in the township—in the cabin of Wakeman Silliman. This cabin stood on the bank of Yankee creek—a stream named after the Yankee settlement made in its vicinity.

John Kingsley was one of the pioneers, and for many years was an honored citizen. He died in 1856 at the age of seventy-three. He was the first justice of the peace in Fowler.

The family of Matthias Gates was also in the township quite early. Later they removed to Hartford.

Elijah Tyrrell built the largest and most substantial cabin in that day. It was built of small logs, 18x24 feet, chinked and daubed with mud. The roof was made of clapboards, split out of oak logs, three and one-half feet long, and from six to eight inches wide. These were laid double and held down by weight-poles. The upper floor of this cabin was made of the same material; the lower or first floor was made of logs about eight feet long. These logs were split from four to six inches in thickness, and hewed on the upper side. The windows consisted of mere holes cut in the sides of the cabin, with upright and horizontal sticks placed across for sash, and over the whole of this net-work was pasted oiled white paper through which light was admitted. The door, rudely constructed, was hung by means of two large wooden hinges reaching across the door and pinned on with wooden pins. The hook or pin upon which the hinge played was of wood also. Neither nail nor spike was used in the construction of the building. The bedsteads were made in the corners of the rooms with one post for each bed, made of a round stick two and a half feet high, with two holes bored through it, one above the other and at right angles. Also two holes bored in the logs of the house, and poles placed in these holes, reaching from post to house logs. These posts formed the bed rails, and for bed cords hichory withes were used, laid across or stretched from side to side. The tables were made of four small poles, in pairs, crossed, which formed the legs. Through the center of each of these pair of legs a pole the length of the table was put, and then on top a puncheon was pinned fast for a leaf. In this way their tables were made, somewhat clumsily, to be sure, but very solid and durable.

The chairs were also of an odd construction, and were made of blocks of wood; in short the furniture was in every respect of the simplest manufacture, and was made more for use than for ornament. Their knives, forks, spoons, plates, and dishes were very limited as to number. These times, however, did not last long, for about the year 1807 Justice Meeker built a shop, in which he put his lathe, the only one then and for a long time afterwards used in the township. This lathe had a spring-pole fastened over head, with a buckskin string connecting the two, by which the motive power was communicated. With this machinery many and valuable were the articles manufactured, especially the wooden plates, bowls, spoons, and wooden dishes, also wooden knives and forks. The best of timber, generally maple, was used in the manufacture of these articles. These vessels were used for various purposes, in short, for as many purposes as the culinary art of that early day required.

In 1805 Hillman and Daniel Meeker were in the township before they moved their families, and at that time commenced the building of a saw-mill, but did not complete it until 1807, when the mill was put in operation, and from that time on the neighbors could secure boards instead of puncheons for their floors, and for many other purposes. This mill was the first one in the township. It was situated one-half mile north of the corners, and one-half mile east on Yankee creek. The stream becoming turbulent washed out the dam before the mill was set to running.

Groceries were hard to obtain in those days. Sometimes the neighbors would take their rifles and ox teams and go to Youngstown. These trips were not particularly dangerous, save for the troublesome wolves, that kept the men awake at night, and on guard, to protect themselves and their property. Salt was at that time worth $25 per barrel, and other necessaries of life were proportionally high and hard to obtain. In 1807 Harvey Hungerford built a flouring-mill on the north side of Yankee creek, on land subsequently owned by Milo Dugan, which was the first flouring-mill in the township. It was built on the south end of the dam of Meeker's saw-mill. Ebenezer Barnes made the mill-stones out of a large bowlder found in the woods, one-half mile west of Tyrrell Hill, or about two miles from the mill. Justice Meeker was the miller at that time.

Some time previous Elijah Tyrrell had increased the size of his blacksmith shop and was by this time largely increasing his business; in fact, the corners was becoming widely known. A saw-mill, a grist-mill, and a blacksmith shop being located here, drew custom from many of the townships, and even from Youngstown and other points. In 1812 Abijah Tyrrell moved to the township, and at first lived with his twin brother Elijah, until he could build himself a house, and went with Elijah Tyrrell's son, Asahel, now a resident of Tyrrell Hill, into the blacksmith shop. In this shop, which partook somewhat of the character of a machine-shop, they manufactured plows, shares, axes, scythes, shav-

ing knives, hoes, chains, etc. The Tyrrells made the first scythes manufactured in Trumbull county, and were largely patronized in this branch of industry until a Mr. Parker, of Kinsman, started up a scythe factory, that was run by water-power, by which the cost of manufacture was so much reduced that the Tyrrells discontinued their business.

In 1807 Rev. Joseph Badger, the noted pioneer missionary, visited the settlement and preached the first sermon.

About this time Seth and Enoch Perkins arrived and settled one mile west of Tyrrell Hill. Enoch Perkins soon after his arrival married Clarissa Barnes. This was probably the second wedding in the township.

Two settlers, Richard Houlton and Joseph Pittman, came in 1808. They built their cabins within a few rods of each other in the southern part of the township, dug a well, cleared some land, and after living here three or four years gave up pioneer life and returned to their former homes. Houlton, however, afterwards returned and settled in another part of the township. Solomon Dundee and Abraham Farrow came to Fowler with these men and became permanent settlers. They located east of Tyrrell corners.

Other early comers in the township made a few improvements, but becoming weary of life in the woods or discouraged by hardships, returned to civilization. Only stout hearts and determined spirits can endure the life of a pioneer.

Alfred Bronson settled at Tyrrell's corners in 1812, and for many years was a local preacher of the Methodist church. He is still living and resides in Prairie du Chien, Wisconsin. He is now in the ninetieth year of his age. While he resided in Fowler he was often the orator at Fourth of July celebrations.

There was a Mr. Stewart at the corners, who after clearing four or five acres and building a house already to raise, suddenly left and never came back. This property was afterwards taken by Alfred Bronson, the Methodist preacher. The property owned by William Meeker, previously mentioned, was cleared by a settler whose name has passed from recollection—fenced in part, logs cut and hauled ready for raising a house, when he suddenly left and never returned. This property, one hundred acres in all, was one-half mile south of the corners. The next lot south of this, now owned by Asahel Tyrrell, was at first taken by Hezekiah Reeder, who cleared and fenced about four acres, planted his garden, raised his house but never covered it, then left and never returned. This house was on the bank of a little brook, which has since been called Reeder's run. Mr. Reeder bought it in 1810, paying at that time $3 per acre. Mr. Tyrrell bought it in 1824 and paid $5 per acre. He was then thirty-two years of age and is now seventy-nine years old and has owned it ever since. But since that time what a change! Then it was all a wilderness; now the land is all cleared up, and a railroad runs through it within four rods of where the old Reeder house stood. The depot is about twenty rods from it. From four to six trains now pass daily on this road, and some of the land is laid out in village lots and a number of houses have already been built. Mr. Tyrrell built a large flouring-mill, a hotel, and a store. There are also some shops of different kinds, and a nail-keg head factory that is doing some business.

About the year 1813 John Webster and Newman Tucker moved into the place with their families. Webster moved into one end of John Vaughn's house, which stood a little west of the corners. He afterwards built a house three-fourths of a mile south of the corners on the east side of the road. Tucker moved into Alfred Bronson's house, while Bronson was out in the army. Tucker was taken sick, caused by a journey of forty-five days duration without intermission, except for a single day, and when Preacher Bronson came home the neighbors turned out (what few had not gone to the war) and built a brush house for Tucker. It was built in one day. Four posts were driven at suitable distances apart in the ground, the other ends being forked, and upon these forks poles were laid, reaching from one post to the other. Small poles were also pinned on the sides. Brush was then collected, and the roof and the sides of the shanty were plaited with leaves and twigs. The roof was covered with brush. A blanket was hung over the opening. Into this domicile the family moved, and lived two months. The Tucker family consisted of eight persons in all—the two old people and six children, four boys and two girls. The boys were Charles, Jabez,

William, and John. The girls were Betsy and Marilla.

Mr. Newman Tucker was the first male teacher in the township. He taught school in John Vaughn's house the winter after he came here.

THE WAR OF 1812.

There were but a few scattering families at this time in the township, and the militia of Fowler and Johnston townships was put under the command of Captain Elijah Tyrrell. Captain Tyrrell was ordered to draft one-half of his men, taking every other man in order as the names stood on the muster roll. This was the order given to each of the captains in the county. It caused considerable excitement and hardship, as half of the whole number of able-bodied men taken at such a time from their midst would leave them in straitened circumstances. There were nine in number drafted from Fowler township. Their names were: Captain Elijah Tyrrell, Alfred Bronson, Hoyt Tyrrell, Roswell Tyrrell, Isaac Farrow, Cable Meeker, and three of the Gateses. The service of these men was not very long, most of them coming home in three months. Some of the number staid six months. Roswell Tyrrell re-enlisted. John Gates was killed in the first engagement he was in.

Up to this time immigration was not very rapid, but after the war the people began to see better times, and settlers took up all the land except the swamps.

As late as the year 1826 there was no road passable for teams, and few settlers from the center of Fowler to the center of Hartford, and all the travel was done by the way of Tyrrell's corners from Bazetta, Fowler, and other places north to get to Hartford, or Burg Hill.

Mr. Asahel Tyrrell, then a mere a boy, usually went to mill for his father and the neighbors. His trips were made to Brockway's or to Bentley's, and sometimes to Sharon. The distance was great for a boy to make, and the wolves sometimes were so voracious as to cause him some apprehension for his safety. His father's old white mare which he rode, was the only one in the neighborhood.

PIONEER CUSTOMS.

In former times the women spun and wove what clothing was worn, excepting the buckskin breeches and jackets which were worn by the men in the winter. Linen was worn in the summer. Cotton was but little used in early days; the home-made linen served all purposes then. Many of the youngsters never wore boots or shoes, except wooden ones or moccasins, in their childhood and youth. Leggings were frequently worn. They were lashed tight over the shoes and tied with garters around the knees. Instead of glass they had wooden bottles that were often filled with whiskey from Mr. Bushnell's distillery in Hartford. It was nothing unusual to send a boy to the distillery for whiskey, with a bag thrown across a horse with a gallon wooden bottle in one end and a stone in the other to balance. These were times when a log-rolling, house-raising, or a corn-husking was not complete without the aid of this much-prized stimulant. These were times, too, when the daughters not only worked at the loom and spinning-wheel, but hoed corn, raked hay, bound grain, pulled flax, and did any other work, either out of or in doors, as the case seemed to demand. Stock, grain, or labor were used instead of money for exchange, cash price, or cattle at trade prices, or grain, cattle, or stock notes, were the terms used when making a "dicker," or driving a bargain.

WILD ANIMALS

were numerous and often troublesome. Stock, especially young cattle and sheep, had to be looked after very carefully or it would be destroyed. Hogs were sometimes allowed to run in the woods to feed upon acorns, and not unfrequently some of them became a prey to hungry bears.

Abner Fowler one day discovered a tree in the forest which was scratched from top to bottom, as though it had frequently been climbed by some sharp-clawed animal. Having a curiosity to know what beast, if any, used the hollow tree as a dwelling-place, Mr. Fowler cut it down. Out rushed a huge bear, which the pioneer soon succeeded in killing.

As an evidence that the women of pioneer days were possessed of the same courageous spirit that characterized the men, the following incident is related:

Mr. Ira Fowler, son of Abner Fowler, Jr., states that when he was about four years old, just as night was coming on one evening the family were disturbed by the howling of wolves. His father was away from home and only Mrs. Fowler and her three small children were in the house. Mr. Fowler had just purchased a few sheep and this night they had failed to come up to the house as usual. His mother, as soon as she heard the cries of the wolves, hastily undressed the children and put them in bed, commanding them on no account to rise until she returned. Then lighting a torch of hickory bark she went out into the fast gathering night alone to hunt up the sheep. She found them huddled together in the middle of a field with their heads erect. It was perfectly evident that they were aware that their foes were in search of them. The howls sounded nearer, but Mrs. Fowler began calling the sheep and they followed her obediently homeward. Arrived at the house she built up a bright fire in front of it. By this means the wolves were kept away and the sheep preserved.

SCHOOLS.

The first school, already mentioned, was for the benefit of the seven Connecticut families, though it may have been attended by children of the other settlers.

The first regular school for the accommodation of all was taught in a school-house built of logs, in the winter of 1814–15 by Polly Nichols. The next summer Phila Wright taught there, and the following winter Thomas Bushnell, of Hartford. The school-house was situated south of the center about one mile, on the east side of the road, opposite where the present school-house stands.

A DISTILLERY

was built in 1835 by Asahel Tyrrell. At that time there were a great many apples and peaches. He had been successful in securing a great many barrels (a statement is made of his having eight hundred barrels) of cider which he had stowed out doors, but the night previous to his starting the still some person cut holes in his barrels and vats and the cider was wasted. A loss of about $1,100 was sustained by Mr. Tyrrell by this malicious act. The next spring he manufactured two hundred barrels of cider, and afterwards stilled some more. In 1837 he built a storage house 30x40 feet, two stories high, adjoining his saw-mill (the saw-mill was built on Yankee creek in 1826, and had a capacity of ten thousand feet of lumber per day). The still had a capacity of twenty-five barrels per day and made about four gallons to the barrel, and in 1838 about two thousand barrels of cider was in this way used. In 1839 he built still larger rooms, where he could store three thousand barrels, but he made a mistake in cementing his vats with water-lime, which when taken up by the cider, destroyed it. He afterwards shipped brandies to New York but lost money on them. Later he sold some for home consumption, but the parties breaking up he sustained such a loss as to induce him to quit the business.

THE CONGREGATIONAL CHURCH.

This church was organized quite early, but at what date is not known. The house was built as early as 1836. There is but little known of its early history, save that the membership was at first so limited that when help by subscription was received the trustees appointed were instructed by previous arrangement to permit ministers of other denominations to preach in the house when the occasion so demanded. The organization after many years' existence was abandoned on account of the fewness of its members. Simon Aldrich, Charles Tucker, Henry Sanders, John Morrow, Carrie Barnes, of the Methodist Episcopal church, purchased the lot and paid for the same the sum of $25. Gideon Waterhouse and his wife, Phœbe, made the deed. The trustees of this church, Robert Morrow, Harry Beach, and Joseph Jones, in consideration of $160 received, transferred all right and title over to the Methodist Episcopal church. This was on the 18th day of August, in the year 1873, since which time the Methodist people have all claim to the church property of the former organization.

THE UNITED BRETHREN

have an organization formed some time about the year 1840, in the western part of the township.

THE METHODIST CHURCH.

This church was organized about the year 1815 by Rev. Alfred Bronson, and consisted of himself and wife, Abner Fowler and wife, Newman Tucker and wife, and Charles Tucker. These were all of the first members. Soon after

Rev. Joseph Davis, a local preacher, and his wife joined, and several members of the Barnes family. Their first church, a small frame building, was erected south of the center.

THE DISCIPLES CHURCH.

This organization took place at quite an early date. The ministers of this denomination first preached in the various homes of the new settlers, then in the warerooms near Mr. Clawson's store, and in the old carding-mill property now owned by Mr. Alderman, and used as a nail-keg-head factory. The society built their church during the year of the great hail storm in 1852. A. C. Williamson was the architect. The church is at the present time in a prosperous condition. The society have a church at the ridge. Rev. Mr. Bonewell is in charge.

PHYSICIANS OF FOWLER.

Dr. Porter was probably the first practicing physician who settled in the township. He came to the center about the year 1819, from New York State, practiced his profession a few years, and then bought a farm one and a half miles west of Fowler, where he lived the remainder of his days. The date of his death is not given. Following him Dr. Harry Beach came to this place in the year 1826, and practiced medicine in this whole country in all fifty-four years, when he moved to Cortland, Bazetta township, adjoining, in the year 1880, and where he is now in the full enjoyment of bodily health and vigor of mind, but retired from practice.

In 1853 there was a physician of the eclectic school who moved in and staid about fifteen years. Dr. Wells A. Horton moved to the center, but died in 1868. His family, consisting of his wife and two sons, then moved to Cleveland. There was one Dr. Tinker, who came to Fowler about the year 1868, and staid about four years, and following him came Dr. Arthur Hold, in 1872, but he only staid one year, since which time there have not been any physicians in the place, save Dr. Beach, who left in 1880. At this time there is no one practicing the profession of medicine in the township.

MISCELLANEOUS.

The first frame house in Fowler was built about 1814 by James Fowler, the son of Samuel Fowler, the proprietor of the land of the township. It stood on the southwest corner at the center and was used for many years as a dwelling. It is still standing, but has been removed from its original location and is now an out-building on a neighboring farm.

The first trial was an action for stealing, instituted against Abijah Bolton by his brother-in-law, Gates. Bolton was convicted and sent to the penitentiary. The township has been remarkably free from crimes of a violent character.

The first merchant was Elijah Barnes, who kept a store at Tyrrell Hill. Adam McClurg kept the first full stock of goods at the center. This was in 1838, when he opened up a full line of goods. Mr. George Halleck, however, kept a small line of goods, long before McClurg.

Fowler center is a small village near the center of the township. The store and post-office is kept by Mr. E. E. Clawson; a blacksmith shop by Warren Boston, and another by Mr. Josiah Enos; hotel by John F. Trowbridge; nail-keg heads are manufactured by Lewis Alderman on an extensive scale; a cheese factory, operated by C. A. Campbell, who manufactures about fifteen cheese per day. There are two good churches, one Methodist and one Disciple.

BIOGRAPHICAL SKETCHES.

ROBERT MORROW.

One of the earliest settlers of Fowler, and probably the earliest whose descendants remain residents of the township, was John Morrow. He was a native of Ireland, and after emigrating to this country with his parents became a settler of Washington county, Pennsylvania. While living there he married his wife, who was also a native of Ireland. In 1804, with their family, they removed to Fowler. There were at that time but four other families in the township. Mr. Morrow's family consisted of three sons and three daughters—Robert, James, John, Jane (Mrs. David Wright), Sarah (Mrs. William Jones), and Eliza. Mrs. Sarah Jones is the only survivor of the family. She resides in Fowler.

Robert, the oldest son of John Morrow, was born in Washington county, Pennsylvania, Oc-

tober 4, 1800, and was consequently but four years old when his parents came to the township. His boyhood, youth, manhood, and old age was spent on the same farm which he had helped to clear and prepare for cultivation. Like every other boy of the period Mr. Morrow experienced many hardships incident to pioneer life. People were poor, and their resources of a character that much labor was required to develop them. Mr. Morrow married, February 23, 1833, Harriet, daughter of Jared Hill, who came from Connecticut to Ohio in 1811. Mr. Hill's family consisted of six children by the first marriage and four by the second. Robert and Harriet Morrow have had a family of five children, three of whom are living—James, at Burg Hill; Jared, at Fargo, Dakota; and Martha, in Fowler.

Mr. Morrow became owner of the farm on which his father settled, and died on the same farm December 16, 1879. He was in every respect a man of good character and pure life. He was without aspirations further than to be a good man, and merit the respect of his neighbors. In early life he united with the Congregational church and lived faithful to his professions to the end of his life. Mrs. Morrow, who survives her husband, was a member of the same church, and a kind mother and loyal wife. She continues to reside on the old homestead.

One of Mr. Morrow's characteristics was a delight of story-telling. In this his Irish descent was traceable. With a rich Irish accent he was accustomed, in his older years, to narrate to his children and his neighbors' children experiences of the early day, when the woods, almost unbroken, were infested with wild animals and venomous reptiles. When his father first came to Fowler the family lived in the wagons till a cabin could be erected. One night after they had become settled in their little home the dog was heard to make an unusual noise, and something seemed to be crawling across the floor. No one was alarmed at the disturbance, or, indeed, paid any attention to it. But daylight revealed the fact that it was fortunate no one had arisen, for a snake seven feet long had invaded the house. It was tracked and killed but a short distance away.

Wolves were troublesome, and sheep had to be securely penned up every night. This work, of course, fell chiefly upon Robert. On one of

Robert Morrow

these errands he saw a panther, an animal very rare in this section of the West. He also took pleasure in the sports of the early period of settlement, and altogether had a large fund of interesting ancedotes.

SETTLEMENT NOTES.

William Jones (deceased) was a native of Massachusetts, born February 28, 1800. He was by occupation a farmer and stock dealer. He was married September 26, 1820, to Sarah, daughter of John and Hannah (Irwin) Morrow, natives of Ireland. She was born February 18, 1799, and came to Ohio with her parents in 1804; the family settling on a place now owned by Mrs. Robert Morrow. She taught school one or two terms prior to her marriage. Mr. and Mrs. Jones had ten children, six of whom are living—Edwin W., a farmer; Robert, also a farmer and stock dealer; James, now a resident of New Mexico; Aaron, a resident of Kansas; John D., and Frank at home. Mr. Jones settled on a farm one mile north of Fowler center, putting up a log-house. He died June 4, 1861. He was a member of the Congregational church (as is also his widow), and was a respected citizen and successful farmer. Mrs. Jones has a farm of fifty-two acres.

Asahel Tyrrell was born in Bridgeport, Connecticut, September 23, 1802; oldest son of Elijah and Clarissa (Meeker) Tyrrell, of Connecticut. His father was born March 8, 1775, and his mother May 21, 1774. They were married July 23, 1796, and came to Ohio in October, 1806, and located at Tyrrell's corners in Fowler township, Trumbull county. They were among the pioneers of the county, and worthy ones, too. They raised a family of eight children, six of whom are living. Elijah Tyrrell was a blacksmith by trade and also a successful farmer. He bought one hundred acres and cleared the same, now owned by A. H. Tyrrell. He was an active Whig. He died April 11, 1848. He was a soldier in the War of 1812, and his father, Asahel Tyrrell, was in the Revolutionary war and was killed at the surrender of Burgoyne, in October, 1777. Asahel Tyrrell, the subject of this sketch, was a scholar in the first school taught in Fowler township, taught by Miss Esther

Jennings, one of the original party consisting of seven families that came to the county with the Tyrrells. The heads of those families were all uncles of the subject of this sketch. Mr. Tyrrell's opportunities for obtaining an education were exceedingly limited, attending school but one month. He assisted his father in the blacksmith shop and also learned the trade of carpenter and joiner. He had built a saw-mill of green timber in the woods before coming of age. He erected a house for his father to compensate him for eight months of his time before reaching his majority. He followed building and contracting for some twenty years, erecting many of the finest residences in Fowler and surrounding townships. Mr. Tyrrell was first married in 1823, to Lucretia Webster, by whom he had four children, all living. One son, A. H., is a well-known resident of Fowler township. Mr. Tyrrell's first wife died November 10, 1871, and he has since been married twice. His present wife, to whom he was married February 20, 1875, was Polly Reeder, born in Connecticut September 1, 1811. Mr. Tyrrell has always been active in promoting every public enterprise, was prominent in the founding of Tyrrell Hill, and has taken an interest in the building of the railroad and other interests. He was formerly a Whig, but has been a Republican since the formation of the party. His home residence was erected in 1840. The farm consists of one hundred and forty-five acres, and he also owns three hundred and eighty acres in Vienna and Howland townships.

Asa Foote was born in Fowler township, Trumbull county, Ohio, August 31, 1807. The Foote family was among the earliest pioneers of the county, and the fifth family that settled in Fowler township. Levi Foote, father of Asa, moved with his family into that township in 1800. He served in the War of 1812. It is said that Lyda Foote (Barber), who died in the spring of 1880, was the first white female child born in Fowler. Asa was the oldest son of Levi and Amelia (Allen) Foote, and he distinctly recollects when the red men roamed through the forests of Fowler. He married November 12, 1840, Mary Dickinson, born in Connecticut, April 22, 1817, by whom he had six children. Levi was a member of the Forty-first Ohio volunteer infantry, and died in hospital January 23, 1862. Philip M. was a lawyer by profession;

died April 19, 1872. Curtis was a member of the One Hundred and Seventy-seventh Ohio votunteer infantry, and died at Nashville, Tennessee, February 27, 1865. He was married to Orell Baldwin, December 31, 1868. Lovilla died in infancy. Helen L. is the wife of L. G. Spencer, of Hartford township, and has two children, Bennie F. and Byron H. Aureil D., born September 27, 1857, wife of Frank E. Clark, resides on the home place. Mr. Foote was kicked a number of years ago on the head, by a horse, and severely injured, thirty pieces of broken bone being taken out, since which time he has been almost totally deaf. Mrs. Foote died March 15, 1872.

Leonard Clark, son of Abel and Eunice (Lamphear) Clark, was born in Petersburg, Rensselaer county, New York, February 27, 1808. His early educational advantages were limited, yet by self study he acquired a fair education for the times. He remained at home (but working for others) until he was twenty years of age. He was a resident of Pittsfield, Massachusetts, engaged in factory work for seven years. December 23, 1836, he was united in marriage to Miss Lucy Olds, who was born in Middlefield, Massachusetts, January 17, 1813. The following spring he removed to Ohio and settled upon the place where he still resides in Fowler township. The land was then wild, but he rapidly improved the place, supplanting the log house with his present residence in 1845. The farm is now fully improved, and comprises two hundred acres, having deeded three farms to his children. Mr. Clark is a prosperous, self-made man, and a gentleman of literary tastes. He was one of a family of twenty-two children. One of his brothers, Adam A., was a drum-major in the War of 1812, and was a celebrated drummer. Mr. Clark is the father of eight children, of whom six are living, as follow: Harriet E., born July 29, 1839, now wife of Emanuel Evarts, of Brookfield township; Leonard, born March 4, 1841, widow of Abner Viets, living in Fowler township; Lester A., born June 18, 1843, living on a farm adjoining the home place; George W., born December 17, 1845, a resident of Hartford township; Sherman S., born September 26, 1850, at home; Lucy, born November 5, 1852, wife of Henry Viets, of Fowler township. Since coming to Ohio Mr. and Mrs. Clark have been

members of the Methodist Episcopal church at Fowler center.

A. L. Stewart, son of Robert and Catharine (Sinclair) Stewart, was born in Huntingdon county, Pennsylvania, November 12, 1811. Robert Stewart was among the early settlers of Trumbull county, coming to Liberty township in the spring of 1812, and settling on a place where he spent the balance of his life. He died about 1850. When sixteen years of age our subject learned the blacksmith trade, at which he served an apprenticeship of two years; and afterwards working as a journeyman for five years. He started in the business in Liberty township in 1835, and has since carried on the business there and for many years in Vienna township, removing to Fowler township in the spring of 1872, purchasing the place where he still lives in the northeast corner of the square at Fowler center, where he owns sixty-nine acres of well-improved land, the house being originally built for a hotel by Alanson Smith. In connection with his trade he owned seventy-five acres of land in Vienna, upon which was discovered coal, which he sold, and the influx of miners caused him to seek a more retired home in Fowler. December 1, 1836, he married Miss Isabel, daughter of Thomas and Rebecca Wilson, early settlers in Liberty township. Mrs. Stewart was born there December 1, 1819. They are the parents of five children—Robert W., born October 3, 1837, residing in Iowa; Rebecca E., born April 9, 1842, now the wife of John P. Barber, and resides in Franklin Square, Ohio; Kate A., February 28, 1849, wife of Wilson S. Powers, and residing in Niles, Ohio; Ettalissa, October 13, 1851, wife of B. H. Long, of Hartford township; Emma, born June 26, 1859, died September 3, 1864.

Abner Leonard, youngest son of Caleb and Margaret (Morrow) Leonard, natives of Pennsylvania, was born in Bazetta township, Trumbull county, Ohio, February 27, 1823. Caleb Leonard was a mail-carrier from Ashtabula to Warren at an early day, making his trips on foot. He died about 1830. Abner was a pupil of the common school in Bazetta until reaching the age of about fifteen. In 1837 or 1838 he removed to Fowler township where he completed his attendance at school, living in the family of John F. Kingsley until becoming of age. He was married August 28, 1845, to Miss Delia Clark, who was born in Southwick, Massachusetts, in 1818. After his marriage Mr. Leonard purchased a place and settled in the northeast part of Fowler township. He carried on the dairy business on the J. S. Jones place. He was a resident of Hartford township for seven years, but about 1865 returned to Fowler township, purchasing the place where he still resides—the old Gersham Turner place. His farm consists of sixty-three acres of well-improved land. Mr. and Mrs. Leonard have an adopted son, Charles J., born February 22, 1861.

Phineas R. Tucker was born in Great Barrington, Berkshire county, Massachusetts, October 20, 1808, and came to Ohio with his parents in 1813. The family settled in the woods where the family homestead now is, the land then being in an entirely wild state. Newman Tucker, the father of Phineas, died in 1831. He raised a family of eight children, three of whom, besides the subject of our sketch, are living, viz: Betsey, widow of Isaac Leonard, residing in Hartford township; Marilla (born April 14, 1802), who still resides upon the home place, and Henry, a resident of Kansas. Phineas Tucker was brought up to farming, and enjoyed only the advantages of a common school education. He was married May 27, 1852, to Catharine B. Stevens, born in Howland township, Trumbull county, Ohio, June 25, 1823, daughter of Samuel Stevens, an early settler in Howland. Mr. and Mrs. Tucker were the parents of two sons: Nelson R., born November 8, 1853, and Homer P., born October 24, 1855. The latter was married to Hannah Stevens, March 19, 1879, and has one child, Wilbur S., born June 7, 1881. Both of the sons reside at home. Phineas Tucker was a successful farmer and an esteemed citizen. He died September 23, 1880. The home place consists of one hundred and seventy-nine acres, the present residence being built in 1828.

John Kingsley, only son of John F. and Sabrina (Gilbert) Kingsley, was born in Massachusetts, March 13, 1811. John F. Kingsley was one of the pioneers of Trumbull county, settling upon the place now owned by his son, in the spring of 1813, clearing up the farm, where he spent the balance of his life. He was a successful farmer and a prominent citizen. He held the office of justice of the peace for fifteen years, being elected five successive terms. He had a family of four children, of whom two survive. He died about the year 1856. John Kingsley received his education in the common schools of Fowler township, where he came with his parents in 1813. He was raised a farmer and remained at home until he was of age. He was married February 9, 1836, to Caroline Ames, born in Jefferson county, New York, March 11, 1817. Mr. and Mrs. Kingsley are the parents of twelve children, as follows: Jasper B., a resident of Vienna township; James, of Fowler township; Julia A., now wife of Jamen Cole, of Michigan; John, in some Western State; Jane, wife of Wilson Trumbull, of Fowler township; Flavel, a farmer of Fowler township; Hymen B., a resident of Vienna, owning a saw-mill; Randolph J., of Fowler; Helen M., wife of Gershom Turner, of the same township; Esther C., a school-teacher by profession, now teaching in Michigan; Frank W., at home, and Mary L., wife of Walter D. Campbell, of Fowler. Mr. Kingsley has resided in different places in Fowler township, settling in 1857 upon the family homestead, where he has since resided. The farm consists of one hundred and seventy-five acres. The house, originally built by his father in 1824, has been rebuilt and improved in later years by his son. Mr. Kingsley was township treasurer five years. He is a Republican in politics and was active during the war in raising troops.

N. C. Rhodes, son of Jonathan and Hannah (Davis) Rhodes, was born in Cazenovia, New York, April 13, 1806. With his parents he came to Ohio in 1816, settling in Fowler township, where he now lives. He helped his father clear off the farm, remaining at home until of age, and for a few years afterwards was in Pennsylvania employed in making shingles. February 17, 1831, he was married to Eliza Campbell, the result of which union was nine children, of whom four are living as follow: Catherine, wife of Addison J. Dawson, L. W., and Robert N., both farmers of Fowler township, and Orpha, wife of Calvin Tyrrell, of Tyrrell Hill. After his marriage in 1833 he settled on the place where he now resides. His farm consists of two hundred and eighteen acres, well improved, and he has given each of his sons a farm. His first wife died

July 18, 1853, and November 30, 1858, he married for his second wife Lucy M. Lewis, who was born in Connecticut March 30, 1820. By this marriage was born one son, Edwin Eugene, April 13, 1862; died October 18, 1868. Mr. Rhodes has been elected township trustee for several terms, first about 1840. Was elected justice of the peace in the spring of 1857, but after one year's service resigned the office.

George Alderman was a native of Brookfield, Trumbull county, Ohio, born in the year 1816. November 1, 1838, he married Mary M., daughter of John and Sarah (Webster) Greenwood, born in Trumbull county, June 21, 1823. Mr. Alderman remained upon his father's place in Brookfield until the spring of 1842, when he removed to Fowler township, settling on the place now owned by G. M. Greenwood, which place he cleared up. He subsequently resided in Brookfield again a year and a half. In the spring of 1856 he removed to the place which is now the family home. Mr. Alderman was an active, successful business man and a worthy citizen. He died November 5, 1871. Mr. and Mrs. Alderman were the parents of seven children, as follow: Harriet C., born April 25, 1840, now wife of Josiah Medley, residing in Vienna township; Eliza J., born December 3, 1841, died November 19, 1857; John S., born on the 22d day of November, in the year 1843, now of Michigan, married about the year 1869, and has four children; Erastus S., born October 9, 1848, now conducting the home farm, married October 3, 1877, to Miss Alice Thompson, born in Mercer county, Pennsylvania, March 11, 1855, and has one daughter and one son: Della, born August 14, 1878, and Roscoe, May 5, 1880; Worthy L., died in 1860, at the age of ten years; Betsey S., born March 12, 1852, wife of J. L. Kennedy, of Warren; Homer L., born April 2, 1859, also of Warren. After her husband's death Mrs. Alderman continued to carry on the farm which is now conducted by her son Erastus. In 1878 he raised on two acres the unprecedented crop of five hundred and thirty-eight bushels of corn, in the ear.

Samuel M. Meaker was born in Fowler township, Trumbull county, Ohio, April 9, 1817. He married, May 8, 1842, Perlia Clark, daughter of Samuel Clark, a well known citizen of Hartford township. Mrs. Meaker was born in Southwick, Hampden county, Massachusetts, January 6, 1821. After his marriage our subject settled in Fowler, on the farm still owned by his widow, occupying a log house which gave way to the present residence built in 1850. Only slight improvement had then been made. The farm consists of one hundred and fifty acres and is now fully improved. Mr. Meaker was an industrious, respected citizen, upright in all his dealings. He served as township trustee one term. He died November 17, 1876, aged fifty-nine years, seven months and eight days. Mrs. Meaker continued to reside on the home place until 1880, when she purchased the old Captain Jones' place, in Fowler center, where she now lives. There was built the first framed house in Fowler township. Mr. and Mrs. Meaker were the parents of one son and one daughter—Lucy, born August 11, 1843; died October 21, 1850, aged seven years, two months, and ten days; Isaac, born July 11, 1845, a promising, well educated young man, died October 10, 1871, aged twenty-six years, two months, and twenty-nine days. He attended a college in Cleveland two winters, fitting himself for a chemist. Mrs. Meaker came to Ohio with her parents in the winter of 1835, who settled in Hartford township. There were five children, four of whom are still living, viz: Mrs. Abner Leonard, Mrs. Orson Trumbull, and Mrs. Meaker, of Fowler township, and Mrs. Milton Goddard, of Iowa.

Alpheus R. Waters, son of Gideon and Phoebe (Rhodes) Waters, was born in Lee, Massachusetts, January 15, 1810. With his parents he came to Ohio in February, 1818, the family locating on the place now the home of James McCleery, in Fowler township. Gideon Waters was one of the hardy pioneers of the county; cleared up several farms. He was a cooper by trade. He was prominent in the militia, of which he was captain. He raised a family of seven children, five of whom are still living. He died about 1859. Alpheus was brought up to farming, but also learned the trade of cooper; remained at home until after becoming of age. About 1835 he bought a place adjoining his present home. November 9, 1837, he was married to Miss Mary R., daughter of Andrew C. Meaker, one of the original settlers of Fowler township. She was born September 3, 1818. One son was born of this marriage, James W., born December 15,

1838, married August 6, 1879, to Lina E. Murphy, born in 1860, and has one son, Ray A., born May 23, 1880. The first wife of our subject died January 7, 1839, and April 10th of the same year he married Rosamond P. Bushnell, a native of Connecticut, born August 22, 1809, by whom he has one child living, Julia P., born March 5, 1847. His second wife died August 17, 1857. Mr. Waters settled on the place where he now lives, in the spring of 1838, cleared up the farm and made all the improvements. James W. Waters enlisted in 1862 in the One Hundred and Seventy-first Ohio National guards, and was taken prisoner at Cynthiana, Kentucky; was paroled after three days, returned to Johnson's island and was finally mustered out at the close of term of service at Sandusky, Ohio.

Sandford L. Stewart was born in Fowler township, Trumbull county, Ohio, October 5, 1819, being the eldest son of Sandford and Bridget (Tew) Stewart. Sandford Stewart was born in Tolland, Massachusetts, about 1794; was married about the year 1811, and came to Ohio in 1815, first settling in Portage county, and then came to Trumbull county in 1817 and settled on the place now owned by his son, the subject of this sketch, which place he cleared up and improved. He was justice of the peace for his township in 1832. He died in 1837. Sandford L. worked out some three years after his father's death, and in 1842, January 5th, he was married to Clarinda, daughter of Linus Hall, who settled in Fowler township in 1815. She was born November 5, 1819, in Fowler township. After marriage he located on the homestead, which he still occupies, first occupying a log house built by his father, erecting the present dwelling in 1844. He was township trustee in 1862, and again in 1867. He has had a family of three children, only one of whom survives—Eliza C., born March 19, 1843, still at home. Pluma A. was the wife of Ahira Sigler, and died March 21, 1879. Lucy M. was born June 21, 1848, and died July 17, 1875. She was the wife of A. G. McCleery, and left one child—Nettie A., born September 1, 1874, who resides with her grandparents.

James McCleery, son of William and Margaret McCleery, was born in county Tyrone, Ireland, November 20, 1818. He came to this county with his parents in 1819, and the family the same year came to Trumbull county, locating in Liberty township. They afterwards removed to Bazetta township, where William McCleery cleared up a farm and spent the balance of his life. He died about 1856, and his wife in 1871. They were the parents of eight children, of whom three are living. James McCleery was married December 29, 1843, to Isabel C. Sigler, by whom he had four children—George A., born December 16, 1844, a resident of Fowler township; Isabel L., born January 26, 1848, was the wife of George A. Clark, and died August 23, 1877; James Luman and Andrew L., born June 18, 1850, both residing in Fowler. Mrs. McCleery died September 28, 1864, and November 22, 1865, he married a sister of his former wife, Mary C., daughter of Uriah Sigler, born in Fowler township January 3, 1819. Mr. McCleery, subsequent to his marriage, continued to reside on his original location until the spring of 1872, when he removed to the place where he now lives.

Henry Tew, a native of Rhode Island, was born in 1799. He came to Ohio about the year 1819, locating on the place now owned by his son, C. M. Tew, and where he spent the balance of his life. March 1, 1825, he married Mary Smith and raised a family of eleven children of whom five are now living. He died in 1873, and his wife in 1856. C. M. Tew, the youngest son, was born in Fowler township June 8, 1846; married May 27, 1877, Miss Alice M. Smith, daughter of William Smith of Bloomfield township, where she was born January 23, 1856. She died June 2, 1878, and he married as a second wife, May 12, 1880, Miss Susie, daughter of Thomas Bennett, born in Greene township, Trumbull county, Ohio, January 12, 1859. Mr. Tew has always resided on the family homestead which consists of one hundred acres, and is a successful farmer and dairyman.

Lewis Alderman, oldest son of Lyman and Lydia (Munson) Alderman, was born in Brookfield township, Trumbull county, Ohio, September 4, 1820. He was brought up to farming and remained at home until his marriage, January 17, 1849, to Annie Hutchins, of Hartford township. By this marriage he has one daughter, May, born May 8, 1850, and still at home. His first wife died May 17, 1850, and April 21, 1852, he married Miss Margaret Butts, daughter of Jonathan Butts, an early settler in Brookfield, where Mrs. Alderman was born May 1, 1826. This union has resulted in five children, as follow: Homer J., born January 15, 1853, living in California; Ella F., April 29, 1854, now wife of Charles Hallock, of Fowler township; Fred A., July 20, 1858; Harry H., May 1, 1868; Maria L., November 28, 1869. The three last named are at home. Homer J. married Ida J., daughter of Darius Baldwin. After his marriage Mr. Alderman settled at Tyrrell Hill, where he remained three years. He was a resident of Wisconsin a year and a half; was largely engaged in farming in Brookfield a couple of years. February, 1858, he located in Fowler center and engaged in the manufacture of cheese-box, shingles, and nail-keg heading, in which he did an extensive business. Mr. Alderman has been township trustee two terms, clerk two terms, and treasurer seven terms. He and his wife are members of the Disciple church and active in Sunday-school work.

Curtis Hall, oldest child of Amasa and Sarah (Remington) Hall, was born in Fowler township, Trumbull county, Ohio, March 21, 1820. Amasa Hall was one of the pioneers of Fowler, settling upon the place now owned by his son, F. A. Hall, in 1814. He raised a family of six children. He died in 1859. The subject of this sketch remained at home until his marriage, which took place October 24, 1839, when he settled on the farm where he now lives. His wife was Almira Sigler, daughter of George Sigler, Jr., by whom he has had three children. Two died in infancy. The daughter, Mary E., born October 29, 1843, became the wife of Allen Cadwallader, and died July 10, 1874, a few days after the birth of her son Elmer, born July 1, 1874. The subject of this sketch has been twice married. His first wife dying September 28, 1875, he married again January 23, 1878, Millie Barber, daughter of Romanta Barber, of Fowler township. She was born in 1840. Mr. Hall was first elected justice of the peace in 1859, and has held the office constantly since. He has also been township trustee at various times. During the war of the Rebellion he was active in raising volunteers.

Simeon Baldwin was born in Youngstown, Ohio, April 17, 1821. His parents were Jacob H. and Florinda (Waller) Baldwin, natives respectively of New York and Connecticut. Jacob H. Baldwin was a pioneer of Mahoning county, settling with his parents in Boardman township about 1804. He was a prominent citizen. He removed to Warren in an early day and was county auditor of Trumbull county for fifteen years, and held other offices. He died in December, 1880. Our subject derived his education at Warren. He was brought up to farming, and remained at home until his marriage in 1849. His wife was Lucy M. Baldwin, widow of Homer Baldwin and daughter of Richard Gates, an early settler in Hartford township, where she was born June 9, 1822. Mr. and Mrs. Baldwin are the parents of two children, one of whom is living—George L., born October 14, 1859, at present engaged in school-teaching, and Charles R., born October 14, 1850, and died in infancy. After his marriage Mr. Baldwin settled in Champion township, where he owned and improved a farm until 1854, when he removed to Fowler township and settled on the farm where he now lives, which consists of one hundred acres of land under a good state of cultivation. Mr. Baldwin is a Republican in politics and was active in raising recruits during the Rebellion.

Riley Hall, oldest son of Linus and Ruth (Barnes) Hall, was born in Fowler township, Trumbull county, Ohio, August 18, 1821. Linus Hall was born in Hampden county, Massachusetts, in 1797, and came to Ohio about the year 1815. He married about the year 1819, and had a family of nine children, six of whom are still living. He settled on the farm now owned by his son the subject of this notice, the same year that Amasa Hall settled on the adjoining farm. He cleared up the farm, first occupying a log house, building the dwelling now occupied by the son, about 1831. He died there in 1871. Riley Hall was united in marriage, December 19, 1844, to Lucy Merritt, by whom he had one son Linus, born November 20, 1847. His wife died February 17, 1848, and he was again married August 14th of the same year, to Mary J. Forward, daughter of George Forward. She was born in Hampden county, Massachusetts, January 5, 1827. The fruit of this union is one daughter and one son, Ella M., born August 30, 1849, now wife of Lucius Doud, of Howland, and Arthur, born December 8, 1850, residing in Mecca township. In 1861 our subject enlisted in the Sixth Ohio cavalry, and after some ten months' service, owing to an accident (his horse having fallen upon him) he was discharged. Returning to civil life he followed the carpenter and joiner business for some time. He purchased a place in Fowler, upon which he resided seven or eight years, then purchased another south of where he now lives. He was a resident of Ashtabula county some five years, returning to Trumbull in the spring of 1859, and most of the time since has resided on the old homestead.

Sylvester I. Rand, son of Daniel and Lois (Tanner) Rand, was born in Vienna township, Trumbull county, Ohio, May 1, 1823. Daniel Rand was an early settler in Vienna township. He died in 1851. Our subject was married to Clarinda Burns, April 8, 1851, by whom he had one daughter and two sons: Eva J., wife of Cyrus C. Butts, of Fowler township; Frank C., telegraph operator at Waterloo, Pennsylvania, Arthur M., at home. His first wife died March 13, 1864. His present wife, to whom he was married November 7, 1865, was Mrs. Lucy E. Applegate, daughter of Levi E. Hart, a settler in Brookfield township, where she was born September 10, 1833. By this second marriage he has had two sons: Charles S., born August 1, 1868, and Edward H., September 8, 1871. After his marriage he was a resident of Vienna, also of Champion and Vernon townships. In the spring of 1865 he purchased the old William Tanner place, and moved on to the same in 1866. Mr. Rand was the first man drafted in Vienna township. He was in camp one month, being finally rejected on account of physical disability. Mrs. Rand has one daughter by her first marriage: Ida M., now the wife of Darius B. Smith, of Fowler township.

Warren A. Hall, son of Amasa and Sarah (Remington) Hall, was born in Fowler township, Trumbull county, Ohio, March 20, 1831. He remained at home until about twelve years of age and subsequently resided with his uncle, Dr. Remington, of Hartford county, Connecticut, for three years. Returning to Ohio he shortly afterward commenced an apprenticeship, when about seventeen, of about four years at the harness and saddlery trade, at Bloomfield, Trumbull county. After acquiring a knowledge of the trade he worked as journeyman in the District of

Columbia, Pennsylvania, and Virginia, also in Ravenna for some six months. About 1856 he came to Warren, where he has since resided, with the exception of one year in Farmington. He was married July 16, 1859, to Dorcas E. Mackey, daughter of John Mackey, of Vienna township, born in July, 1841, and has two daughters: Allie I. and Blanche M., born respectively in 1861 and 1878. About 1864, in connection with his brother-in-law, F. J. Mackey, he commenced the harness and saddlery business in Warren, the firm name being Hall & Mackey. Mr. Hall has been councilman for a number of years and has also held other local offices. He is a member of the Masonic order, and has been an active Republican since the formation of the party.

Gersham Turner, son of Henry and Joanna (Roberson) Turner was born on Long Island, New York, July 1, 1803. He was brought up to farming; came to Ohio about 1823, and after attaining his majority he served an apprenticeship of two years at the blacksmith trade, at which he worked as journeyman a few years. He located upon the farm which he now owns, which was then but partially improved. He was married about 1828 to Mary A. Tyrrell, daughter of Abijah Tyrrell, and had six children, four now living; M. Junot resides on the home place; Henry R., a farmer, in Fowler; Betsy, wife of Henry Scofield, died in 1854; Harriet, wife of Alfred Lewis, residing in Fowler. Mr. Turner has resided on the place for the last twenty-seven years. He has made his own way in this world, having had no start in life. He is a successful farmer with pleasant surroundings. He is a member of the Methodist Episcopal church at Fowler center. Mrs. Turner is a member of the Disciples church.

Addison R. Silliman, oldest son of Abijah and Naomi Tyrrell Silliman, was born in Fowler township, Trumbull county, Ohio, July 2, 1823. Abijah Silliman was one of the early settlers of Fowler township, a prominent citizen and successful farmer. He was a director in the old Mahoning National bank, and held various township offices. He died March 14, 1865. His wife, Naomi Tyrrell, was a daughter of Abijah Tyrrell. She was born September 24, 1801, and is still living with her daughter in Mahoning county. A. R. Silliman was married November 28, 1848, to Lucy, daughter of Ephraim Baldwin, born June 21, 1827. They have had a family of ten children, of whom seven are living, viz: Willard C., a merchant of Cortland; Alice L., wife of L. Sigler, of Cleveland; Mary R., wife of Calvin Clawson, of Cortland; Afton E., born November 20, 1857; Olive M., born April 15, 1860; Carrie L., August 20, 1863; Lottie May, October 5, 1868. The three deceased are, Ella, born November 28, 1855, died May 12, 1857; Grant L., born May 1, 1866, died June 22, 1875; J. Edward, August 16, 1872, died in infancy. In January, 1849, Mr. Silliman settled on the family homestead in Fowler, which he occupied until the spring of 1881, when he moved to Warren, where he now lives. During his active business life Mr. Silliman was largely engaged in the buying and shipping live stock as well as in farming. The home place is now occupied by his son, Afton E. Silliman, who took charge upon the retirement of his father in the spring of 1881. December 23, 1880, he married Miss Georgie Hathaway, of Cortland, born March 14, 1862. The farm consists of two hundred and sixty acres, and is finely improved.

Ezra S. Ames, oldest child of Benjamin and Euretta (Shaff) Ames, was born in Jefferson county, New York, on the 7th of August, 1801. He came to Ohio with his parents in the spring of the year 1826, the family settling one-half mile north of his present residence in Fowler township. Benjamin Ames was a successful farmer, a school-teacher for several years, and also for several years township clerk. He reared a family of twelve children, of whom three only are living. He died on the farm which he had cleared up, about the year 1870, aged eighty-four. His wife died March 1, 1878, aged eighty-six. Mr. Ames was a soldier in the War of 1812, and was stationed at Sackett's Harbor. Ezra S. Ames was brought up upon a farm and enjoyed such educational opportunities—limited enough—as were to be had in that day. He married December 4, 1834, Catherine Campbell, born February 5, 1807. After his marriage he remained on the old home place one summer, removing to his present residence in the spring of 1836. His first wife died March 17, 1873, and on August 18, 1874, Mr. Ames married his present wife, Phila H. Stocking, born in Connecticut April 2, 1836. He is the father, by his first wife, of three sons, only one now living, to wit: William C., born August 22, 1837, died April 14, 1873; he married November 26, 1863, Lozetta H. Patch, and had two children. Horace B., born June 14, 1840, enlisted in the Forty-first Ohio volunteer infantry September 4, 1861, and was killed at Pittsburg Landing, his first battle, April 7, 1862. Cyrus D., born February 10, 1842, is a well known farmer of Fowler township. He married in 1875 Ellen Hoover. Mr. Ames, the subject of this sketch, has been township trustee some five or six years. During the Rebellion he was active in raising the quota. Mrs. Ames is a member of the Congregational church.

David M. Butts, oldest son of Jonathan and Eleanor Butts, was born in Washington county, Pennsylvania, December 4, 1818. With his parents he came to Ohio in the spring of 1819. The family settled in Brookfield township, Trumbull county, Ohio, where they remained till the spring of 1829, when they removed to Fowler township. David M. Butts obtained an ordinary education in the common schools, and at the age of fifteen began an apprenticeship, serving some six years at the blacksmith trade. He worked as journeyman one winter, when he commenced the business for himself at Fowler center, and continued for ten to fifteen years. March 15, 1842, he was married to Melissa, daughter of Gideon Watters, an early settler in Fowler township. Mrs. Butts was born in Fowler February 1, 1820. Mr. and Mrs. Butts have had three children, two daughters and one son—Malvina, born August 4, 1844, and died November 5, 1865; Cyrus C., born May 2, 1846, now a resident of Fowler center, and was married in 1878 to Eva J. Rand, daughter of Sylvester J. Rand, of Fowler, and has one daughter, Gracie B., born August 25, 1880; Phœbe Maria, born July 9, 1855, and died December 11, 1862. Mr. Butts settled upon the place where he now lives in the spring of 1850. He owns over one hundred acres of fine land, which is well improved. He was for four or five years engaged in milling. He was elected justice of the peace three terms at various times, and has been township treasurer five terms. Has also been trustee. The family are members of the Disciple church.

Austin N. Silliman (deceased), son of Abijah

Silliman, was born in Fowler township, Trumbull county, Ohio, December 18, 1829. He married in 1870 Lucy A., daughter of William H. and Melinda (Humason) Clawson, born in Vienna township, Trumbull county, August 25, 1842. With her parents she removed to Mercer county, Pennsylvania, about 1843, where they resided until the spring of 1865, when they returned to Trumbull county. Mr. Sillliman was a successful farmer and stock dealer of Fowler township, owning three hundred acres of land at the time of his death. He died March 17, 1875. He was the father of three children, two daughters and one son—Barton N., born December 28, 1870; Mella N., January 27, 1873; Hattie M., February 27, 1875. Since her husband's death Mrs. Silliman has resided at Fowler center, where she erected a substantial residence in 1880.

Edward Oatley was born in Bazetta township, Trumbull county, Ohio, May 15, 1830, youngest son of William and Sophia (Rhodes) Oatley. He resided at home until he was eighteen, when he commenced an apprenticeship of three years at the blacksmith trade in Farmington; worked as journeyman some four years in various places. He was united in matrimony April 18, 1856, to Helen Morse, born in Ashtabula county, Ohio, in 1832. The result of this union was six children, of whom are living as follows: Edward P., born January, 1859; Charlotte E., 1862; Leota, 1864; Abiah, October, 1871. The mother of these children died September 24, 1873. June, 1874, our subject was married to a daughter—Mary—of Rev. William Kincaid, a well-known resident of Farmington township, where Mrs. Oatley was born in 1838. Some three years after his marriage Mr. Oatley resided in Minnesota. In the spring of 1859 he made a trip to Pike's Peak. Returning to Trumbull county he engaged at his trade in Cortland, continuing there four years, when in the fall of 1864 he purchased fifty acres where he now lives in Fowler township, where he also established a shop and has since carried on the business in connection with farming.

Richard Steer, son of Elisha and Lois (Aldrich) Steer, was born in Hampden county, Massachusetts, November 4, 1800. He came to Ohio in the fall of 1830, settling on the farm where he still lives, in Fowler township. The farm was then but little better than a wilderness. He erected a log house which he occupied until about 1835, when the present residence was built. Mr. Steer was married to Anna Gillett January 6, 1829, by whom he had four children, viz: Mary, born January 25, 1830, now the wife of James Weir, of Johnsonville; Sarah A., July 4, 1832, wife of Rev. Milton Smith, a resident of New York State; Smith G., born March 15, 1836, living on a farm adjoining the homestead; Emma A., June 15, 1838, now the wife of John Steer, a resident of Massachusetts. Mr. Steer's first wife died March 19, 1852, and October 10th of the same year he married Mrs. Agnes Gillett, who was born in Massachusetts March 28, 1806. At the time of her marriage to Mr. Steer she was the mother of four children, three of whom survive. Mr. Steer owns one hundred and forty acres of land and has aided his children. He was justice of the peace during a residence of some six years in Geauga county. The family are members of the Methodist Episcopal church, himself an active member for over sixty years. His father was a Revolutionary soldier.

Isaac A. Smith, youngest son of William V. and Sarah E. (Townsend) Smith, was born in Beaver county, Pennsylvania, January 15, 1813. He remained at home until he was sixteen, when he served an apprenticeship of some three years in Pittsburg at the cabinet trade. He came to Trumbull county in 1831, settling at Fowler center in the fall of 1832, working for Wesley Hoge, the first cabinet-maker of that place. After working for him some two years he commenced the cabinet and undertaking business for himself at Fowler center, where he has since continued. He was married February 25, 1836, to Mary Hawley, daughter of Chandler Hawley, born November 13, 1818. He is the father of six children, of whom are living Sarah, wife of Hiram Post; Orpha, wife of Henry Sheldon; Emogene, wife of Marshall Scovill; Vanzant I., who conducts the home farm; and Adell Lily, wife of Artual Dawson. Mr. Smith was appointed postmaster at Fowler center at an early day, and was for twelve years township treasurer.

Orlin H. Hayes, oldest son of Enoch and Aseneth (Gillette) Hayes, was born in Hartford county, Connecticut, March 20, 1812. His father came with his family to Trumbull county in the fall of 1832, and settled on the place now occupied by James McIntyre. Enoch Hayes was the father of six children. Of these but two are living, the subject of this sketch and Richard A., a farmer of Mecca township. Mr. Hayes, Sr., died in 1867. Orlin purchased the farm where he still lives about 1837. He married January 6, 1841, Miss Mary Ann Fox, who was born in Hartford county, Connecticut, May 6, 1820, daughter of Joel and Jannet (Mason) Fox. Mrs. Fox was born in Chester, Connecticut, June 13, 1786, and is still living with her daughter, and is a remarkable specimen of mental activity and bodily vigor.

Lewis G. Lampson, eldest son of Milo and Martha A. (Cook) Lampson, was born in Fowler township, Trumbull county, Ohio, August 29, 1836. His father has been a resident of the county since 1823, when he settled on the ridge road, locating on his present place about 1850. He has raised a family of eight children, seven of whom are living. He is still a vigorous and hearty old gentleman. Lewis G. was educated in the common schools and obtained a fair education. He was brought up to farming, and worked out some for others. He now owns seventy-seven acres which he has acquired by his own industry. He bought his present place in 1865. He had some war experience during the rebellion, was in Kentucky, and was engaged in several skirmishes.

William Cratsley was born in Hunterdon, New Jersey, October 29, 1817; oldest son of Frederick and Emma (Chamberlain) Cratsley. The family removed to Ontario county, New York, in 1825, and thence to Ohio in 1837, locating in Vienna township, where the father died in 1859. William derived a good common school education and taught school during seven winters. November 4, 1841, he was married to Miss Sabrina Kingsley, daughter of John F. Kingsley, born in Fowler township in 1824. They were the parents of eight children, of whom six are living—Mary E., wife of Hugh Lowry, of Cortland; Martha J., wife of J. S. Webster, residing in Michigan; Olive M., wife of Moses Cooper, same State; Lucy, wife of Joseph Holland, also in Michigan; John F., a carpenter and joiner of Fowler center, born December 22, 1851, married in 1872 to Artelissa Rand, who was born in Mecca in 1853, and has two children ; Frank,

born December 29, 1855, a book-keeper in a large mercantile firm in Toledo. Mrs. Cratsley died in 1873. Our subject purchased a place and settled in Fowler township, and engaged in farming, clearing up a place and living there until about 1874. In 1878 he removed to Fowler center, where he has since resided and led a retired life. He was elected township clerk first in 1846, which office he held ten years; was elected justice of the peace in 1856, and served in that capacity fifteen years; was county commissioner in 1871; also assessor three years and notary public seven years.

Charles F. Hallock was born March 19, 1838, in Fowler township, Trumbull county, Ohio, youngest son of George and Phebe Hallock, of Long Island, New York. George Hallock was born November 23, 1798, and emigrated to the Reserve in the early years of the present century, locating in Brookfield township, Trumbull county, Ohio. He was engaged in mercantile business in Brookfield, and for two or three years subsequent to his removal to Fowler center. He located on the farm now owned by the subject of this sketch about the year 1836, where he spent the balance of his life. The place was then unimproved with the exception of a log house and a small clearing. He died April 18, 1870. He was a man well and favorably known throughout this region, and of more than ordinary energy of character. Was justice of the peace one or more terms. At a celebration July 4, 1824, held at Hartford, he was the orator of the day. His widow still resides on the home place, vigorous in mind and body. Charles Hallock remained at home until of age, when he took charge of a cheese factory at Fowler center, which he conducted successfully some ten years. He was married in 1872 to Miss Ella, daughter of Lewis Alderman, born April 29, 1854, and has one son, Asel J., born July 13, 1877. After his marriage he located upon the home place, where he still resides.

Noah Belford, youngest son of John and Sally (Tanner) Belford, was born in Fowler township, Trumbull county, Ohio, August 15, 1839. Mrs. Belford was a daughter of William Tanner, an early settler of Fowler. She died January 5, 1869. She made her home with her son, the subject of this sketch, during the latter years of her life. At fifteen Noah was thrown upon his own resources. At the age of eighteen he learned the carpenter trade; he continued that trade some eighteen years, during which time he has built many fine buildings in Fowler and elsewhere. In the fall of 1873 Mr. Belford purchased the Tyrrell Hill flouring mills, which had not been used as a mill for some years. He enlarged and remodeled the buildings, putting in modern machinery, including a new engine and boiler, and doing an extensive business.

Josiah Enos, son of John and Theodosia (Bushnell) Enos, was born in Genesee county, New York, July 18, 1818. John Enos was a soldier in the War of 1812. Josiah served an apprenticeship at the blacksmith trade at Buffalo when eighteen, and after learning the trade came to Ohio in 1839. He worked as journeyman at Warren, Trumbull county, for a time, where he was married December 12th of the same year to Sarah Neere born in Portage county, Ohio, by whom he has had six children—Mary A., born March 4, 1841, still at home; Elizabeth, born May 25, 1843; Emily, September 5, 1847; Cornelia, February 28, 1849, wife of John McFetridge, residing in Pennsylvania; Josephine, born September 5, 1852, wife of John Burnett, residing in Pennsylvania; Alice, June 7, 1855, wife of William Lewis, of Cleveland, Ohio. Mr. Enos commenced the blacksmith trade at Fowler immediately after his marriage, and has since carried on the business there. In 1861 Mr. Enos enlisted in the Eighty-seventh Ohio volunteer infantry, afterwards enlisting the Twelfth Ohio cavalry, and took part in some of the principal engagements of the war, such as the Second Bull Run, Pittsburg Landing, and other battles. He served until the close of the war, and was mustered out at Chattanooga, Tennessee, in September, 1865. He was present at the surrender of Joe Johnston. He has been a member of the Disciples church for thirty years, and his wife was also a member of the same church.

Lester A. Clark, oldest son of Leonard Clark of the preceding sketch, was born in Fowler township, Trumbull county, Ohio, June 18, 1843. He attended the schools in Fowler until he was eighteen, when he went to Hiram college one term. He was brought up on the farm, where he remained until he was twenty-two or twenty-three years of age. October 15, 1866, he married Ellen Coleman, born in Lorain county,

Ohio, in 1843, by whom he had three children, viz: Almira, born in 1867, died February 5, 1875; Coleman C., born August 1, 1870; Lillie M., born November 15, 1871. His first wife died November 3, 1875, and October 23, 1878, he was married to Miss Malinda, daughter of W. H. Clawson, of Fowler. She was born in Mercer county, Pennsylvania, June 8, 1851. One child is the fruit of this marriage, Lettie M., born October 8, 1878. After his marriage Mr. Clark remained on the homestead one year and was also a resident of Hartford one year. He located on his present place in the fall of 1868. In connection with farming he does an extensive business in the manufacture and sale of wood pumps.

Daniel Trowbridge was born in Palmyra, Portage county, Ohio, July 8, 1826, youngest son of Wheeler and Anna (Shaw) Trowbridge. He was thrown upon his own resources at an early age; worked out, and also bought live stock. He removed to Fowler township, Trumbull county, in the fall of 1845. He purchased the place where he now lives in the spring of 1854, then only partially cleared, now fully improved. June 21, 1854, he was married to Anna Baldwin, daughter of Ephraim Baldwin, one of the early settlers of Fowler township, where Mrs. Trowbridge was born in 1835. Mr. and Mrs. Trowbridge are the parents of six children, viz: John F., proprietor of Fowler hotel at Fowler center; Frederick M., Celestia M., Ernest A., Jessamine, and Carlton E.; the last five at home. Mr. Trowbridge has a farm of one hundred acres, and while engaged in farming has dealt largely in the business of buying and shipping live stock.

E. J. Forward, oldest son of George and Orphia (Hawley), Forward was born October 19, 1828, in Southwick, Hampden county, Massachusetts. Besides his attendance at the common school in his native State he went one term to an academy in Southwick. He came to Ohio in 1850, and January 19, 1853, was united in marriage to Maria Sigler, daughter of Philo and Esther Sigler, who settled in Fowler township, Trumbull county, as early as 1812. Mrs. Forward was born there January 30, 1833. After his marriage he settled on his father-in-law's place, where he remained till the spring of 1868. He is the father of five children, of whom one is deceased. The survivors are Alice M., born

October 5, 1853, now wife of Adelbert Card, of Fowler; Philo H., born March 30, 1858, now engaged in clerking; Minnie M., December 19, 1861; George M., August 13, 1863. Amelia A., died when five years old.

CHAPTER XIII.
LIBERTY.

In 1806 the people residing in range two (south) and town three, by petition to the proper authorities gained their Liberty, and the land situated south of Vienna, with Hubbard on the east, Mahoning county south, and Weathersfield west was organized as a township, taking the name of Liberty.

The north part of the township is generally level; the east and southeast rolling and more broken between Church Hill and Girard. In the north the soil is of heavy clay, but toward the east it is more of a gravel or sandy nature, and the south is generally of clay. The usual farm products are produced here with good average yield with other sections of the county. Coal is the chief production, and this is strictly a mining region, the chief industry being in this line. It was first discovered and the first mine was opened in 1860 on the farm of Alexander McCleery. The land was leased by one Strain, from Mr. McCleery, and operations were commenced. The first drilling was made without success; another start was made and a five foot vein was struck which was worked out, but as it did not prove to be profitable the lease was sold. Governor Tod afterward visited the mine, which was obstructed by "horse-backs." He made some effort to encourage the work by advising the owners to work around the obstructions, but the mine was abandoned.

About 1864-65 the Church Hill Coal company was formed and opened a bank at the village, which has been successfully operated since.

The Briar Hill company afterwards opened the Kline coal bank in 1868, which is also in successful operation.

The Garfield bank, on Wright's farm, the Hancock bank, on the farm of Calvin Denison, and Bank No. 9, have all been opened recently.

The Mahoning river flows across the southwest corner of the township, into which the land in the northwest part is drained by Squaw run. The western part is drained by Crab creek and its tributaries. The Lake Shore & Michigan Southern and the Atlantic & Great Western railroads extend across the southeast corner, and the latter has a branch, which with the Ashtabula, Youngstown & Pittsburg and Painesville & Youngstown railroads extends across the southwest.

POPULATION, ETC.

The mining interest has naturally attracted a large element of the working class who reside in close neighborhoods near the coal banks, and among which the foreign element predominates, in which the Welch is largely represented. Girard and Church Hill are villages of some note, the former being the larger and most important, neither of which have been incorporated.

The discovery of coal, and the manufacturing interests about Girard have been the means of increasing the population from 1,367 in 1860 to 2,420 in 1870, and 3,657 in the year 1880.

In very early times grist-mills were of great importance to the pioneer, and the introduction of a mill capable of grinding the corn for meal was hailed with special pleasure by the early settlers. One Mr. Steen in very early times built a mill near the forks of the road south of Powers' plat, which was propelled by water-power received from a tributary of Crab creek. This mill supplied as best it could, with the limited facilities, the wants of the settlers in this locality.

The first mill built on the Mahoning river at this point was erected by Mr. Wilkinson where the road crosses the river west of Tod's plat.

Another was erected near the present farm residence of E. Mahan, and another on Squaw creek, near Holliday's, in very early times. To these rude appliances for crushing corn and wheat the settlers made their regular visits with their frugal grists, and when a boy was old enough to go to mill he was then considered an important personage in the settlement, as the lonely journey required no little amount of courage, and the success of his journey a very important consideration to those who depended upon the scanty supply of meal for subsistence.

THE PLATS.

The several plats indicated on the map of this

township were laid out in anticipation of localities forming near the mines, and some of them have been successful in inducing settlements, but the uncertainty of coal mines have made it necessary for miners' families to be often removed, and hence there are many vacated premises. Tod's plat, Kline's plat, and Powers' plat were all designed for communities of workingmen, and are more or less settled.

EARLY SETTLEMENTS.

It is not known with absolute certainty who was the first settler in Liberty. The late Samuel Dennison is authority for the statement that Jacob Swager was the first, and as Mr. Dennison was about sixteen years of age when he came with his father in 1801, his recollections are entitled to great credit. Robert Stewart, now living in Brookfield, who came with his father in 1800, and was nine years old, thinks that Henry Swager, a cousin of Jacob's, was the first to commence the subjection of the wilderness of old Liberty.

Valentine Stull came in 1799, and from his grandson, John E. Stull, it is learned that when his grandfather came to Liberty there were but four families here, and that Henry Swager was one of them, and must have been here as early as 1798.

Mr. Swager settled on what was known afterwards as the Henry Ricard farm, immediately west of Church Hill, on the east and west center road, on the northeast corner of lot number eight. He lived here for several years, when he sold to Jacob Boyd and purchased a farm of one hundred acres in the southeast part of the township, where he lived until the age of over ninety-seven, when he died. He was a great hunter, and many were the bears, deer, wild turkeys, and other game that fell victims to the unerring aim of Liberty's pioneer marksman.

James Matthews came in 1798, and settled in the southwest part of the township on lot number one, where he continued to reside until 1825, when he removed to Warren township. Mr. Matthews kept the first public house in early days, and also erected and operated the first distillery in the township.

John Stull came in 1798, and settled about one-half mile from Girard toward Church Hill.

Valentine Stull came alone in 1799, and purchased a half section of land, lots eleven and twelve, to which he removed his family from Washington county; Pennsylvania, in 1800.

Archie Ralston emigrated from Virginia in 1802, and settled on the northwest part of lot nineteen, the same lot on which his grandson, James Nelson, died.

John Ramsey removed from Lancaster county, Pennsylvania, in 1800, and settled on lot number nine, south of Mr. Stull, and known afterwards as the George Herring farm. George Campbell, a native of Ireland, but for some years a resident of Lancaster county, Pennsylvania, came to Liberty as early as 1800-1, and settled on the north part of lot number seven, where he lived until his death in 1847. He was the father of eight sons and six daughters, all of whom lived until mature age. About this same time James Applegate came and settled on lot number five in the southeast part of the township, on the west side of the road where William Watson now lives, and who for some unknown reason committed suicide by hanging himself.

John Thorn, whose wife was a sister of James Matthews, came soon after his brother-in-law, and bought a lot of forty acres on the north side of the Mahoning river, on which he built a tannery. He was the father of James Thorn, who afterwards became a noted teacher in Liberty and Youngstown. It is related of this teacher that when a child he was twice rescued by his mother from drowning in the vats of his father's tannery, near which their dwelling was located.

William Stewart came from Huntingdon county, Pennsylvania, when his son Robert was nine years old, and cut his way through the trackless wilds of Liberty from Youngstown and settled where John B. McMurry now lives. They arrived in time of heavy rain and flood and were compelled to live in their wagons for some time.

Some time after their buildings were erected, the forest around them was so dense, the roads unbroken, the places of human habitation so few, and the marks of civilization yet so undefined that when any of the family were out at night but a little way from the cabins they would soon become lost and their cries would be answered by those in the house rapping on the roof for signals.

John and Abram Nelson came from Virginia about 1804 and settled in the northwest part of the township—lot twenty-one—where

Abram Storms now lives, and Abram Nelson built his cabin where Samuel Beemer now lives.

William Stewart's father settled near Sodom in very early times.

Samuel Dennison settled north of William Stewart on lot number fifteen, west part.

Neil McMullen settled near the farm residence of the late James Clark, west of Stewart.

The marriage of William McCombs, of Poland, to a sister of John Nelson, was (as is believed) the first wedding in Liberty.

James Nelson, brother of Abram and John, was accidentally killed by the fall of a tree while cutting a road from Painesville to Warren, and on the same day of his death Abram was engaged at work in the valley of Squaw creek, in Liberty, and he has often related that at this time he heard the voice of his brother James calling his name—Abram—three times in succession, when he left his work and went to his house expecting to find his brother James there, and was astonished to find that he had not been there. In a few days the news came of the accident that ended his brother's life, which happened on the day and hour that the voice was heard by Abram in the valley. This incident is sufficiently authenticated by undoubted authority and is here recorded for either an item of history or an illustration of wonderful hallucination.

Andrew Boyd came from Huntingdon county, Pennsylvania, and settled about one-half mile east of Church Hill, and started a tannery on the north side of the road, opposite the present residence of Mr. Leslie, which he operated about nine years.

James Anderson, a native of Ireland, removed with his family from Chester county, Pennsylvania, about 1804, and settled on the farm adjoining Valentine Stull on the north, where he lived until his death, in 1848.

William McClellan came with his family from Greene county, Pennsylvania, in 1805, and settled on land in lots numbers seven and eight, where he lived until 1843, when his decease occurred.

Nehemiah Scott came from Long Island in 1805 and made a settlement west of the present residence of Peter Kline, in a log cabin. He was a hatter by trade and carried on his trade at his shop, about one-fourth mile from the main road.

Robert Walker came in 1807-8 and settled near the present residence of Homer Walker, where he kept store until he moved to the center. His son, Dr. Robert H. Walker, kept the first store at Church Hill in 1832-33.

These were the early settlers of Liberty, or as many of them of whom anything can now be found. Others there may have been and doubtless were, but the memory of their names with the records of their history have passed into the grave with them, save what they may have left written not with the pen, but in the cleared farms and the early planted germs of civilization now blooming in full fruition in Liberty. Many of their graves are still kept green in the old burial grounds at Church Hill. Some of them in after years bade adieu to the scenes of early conflicts of pioneer life and found homes elsewhere. While time has crept on and changes have come, early footprints have long since been worn away, and the new generations are fast covering them deeper and deeper as the years bring wealth and prosperity. The log cabins have given way to many fine residences and beautiful rural homes, and the lightning express dashes over the blazed route of the pioneer. Mines of wealth that slumbered beneath the feet of the hunters and axmen of 1798 now give forth their hidden treasures to the giant power of steam and the cities of swarthy workmen gathered about the deepening tunnels.

CHURCH HILL

is located near the central part of the township, and derived its name from the eminence on which it stands and the location of the church at this point. The name was first selected for the post-office. Since then the name seems to have been very appropriately chosen, as there are now five churches located here: Old-school Presbyterian, Methodist Episcopal, Welch Methodist, Welch Baptist, and Welch Independent—the three latter are of recent origin. The village now has a union school, one dry goods store, drug store, book store, barber shop, wagon shop, blacksmith shop, shoemaker shop, ten saloons, and one hotel. Though the saloons outnumber the churches two to one yet the force and influence of the latter are amply strong, and the community of Church Hill, from all appearances, is a quiet and pleasant neighborhood.

The post-office was established in 1833, and

Matthew Walker was the postmaster. The office was first known as Liberty, but the official department at Washington, District of Columbia, sent back word that there was another office by that name. The Presbyterian church was then in course of erection, and as the location is on something of an elevation Church Hill was suggested and accepted.

THE PRESBYTERIAN CHURCH.

The pioneer religious organization of Liberty was effected by the Associate Presbyterian congregation. The history of this congregation begins with the early records of Liberty township, and indeed is one of the oldest organizations in this part of the Western Reserve. The last pastor, David Goodwillie, D. D., having voluntarily resigned his pastorate of fifty years in the year 1875, is now living in Girard, and kindly furnished the following history of the congregation: About the beginning of the present century a number of families located in this neighborhood while as yet it was an unbroken forest. Among these were William, James, Joseph, John, David, and Robert Stewart, from Marsh creek, Adams county, Pennsylvania. They were members of the Associate church. They settled in the northwest part of Coitsville and the southeast part of Hubbard. James Davidson, from Ireland, settled in the east part of Youngstown; James Applegate, from the Forks of the Youghiogheny, Pennsylvania, John Denison, from Washington county, Pennsylvania, and Alexander McCleery, from Ireland, in the east part of Liberty, and Samuel Ferguson, from Ireland, William Ralston, from Scotland, John Ramsey, from Washington county, Pennsylvania, and William McKinley, from Westmoreland county, Pennsylvania, in the west part.

These men and their families did not leave their religion behind them when they came to this wilderness, but in their log cabins they remembered the Lord God of their fathers, and in 1803-1804 they invited Rev. James Duncan, pastor of the Associate Congregations of Mahoning, Little Beaver, and Brush Run, to preach for them occasionally, which he accordingly did with great encouragement, holding the meetings in the log cabins, and in the woods.

In the year 1804 he organized a congregation in Poland, and during the same time preached one third of the time in Liberty, where in the

winter of the following year, 1805, he organized Liberty congregation. The congregation was then under the jurisdiction of Chartier's presbytery, but the records of the presbytery make no mention of any authority given Rev. Duncan to organize the congregations at Poland or Liberty, and it is supposed that he did this altogether on his own responsibility, and he seems to have regarded them as branches of the Mahoning congregation.

The organization was effected by the election and ordination as elders of William Stewart and James Davidson, the number joining in the organization supposed to be about thirty or forty.

One of the first things to engage their attention was the selection of a lot as the site for a meeting-house and graveyard. Their attention was first directed to a lot in the woods near the southeast corner of Liberty, offered by James Applegate, and now owned by his son Calvin. This was an elevated and beautiful site, and so confidently was it expected that it would be accepted that the remains of some persons were buried there, and the graves are yet to be seen. But at a meeting of the congregation at the house of Alexander McCleery, it was resolved to accept a lot offered by him, which is now occupied by the church and graveyard.

The deed for this lot was not made until March 15, 1828, twenty-five years after the purchase was made, and was given by Alexander McCleery to "Matthew Mitchell, James Boys, and William Geddes, trustees of the Presbyterian congregation of Liberty, belonging to the Associate Synod of North America."

In 1858, the Associate and Associate Reformed branches of the church having united, the congregation accepted the terms of said union and consequently became the United Presbyterian congregation of Liberty. In 1859 the congregation at Youngstown was formed from Liberty, eighteen or twenty members being disjoined for that purpose. The lot when procured was heavily covered by timber and the first thing done was the erection of a tent for preaching, which was built about where the northeast corner of the present church stands. It fronted to the east and the people were seated before it on temporary seats or on the ground. It was here the first communion of the Lord's supper was dispensed, on a table of rough boards, extending from the tent eastward. Here, under the shadow of the ancient trees of the forest, did the forefathers of Liberty assemble together from their cabin homes in the woods to celebrate for the first time in this wilderness the dying love of our great Redeemer; here, under the wide canopy of Heaven did they lift up their song of praise and their voice of prayer.

But it soon became necessary to clear the ground for the purpose of burying the dead, and the tent was moved to a piece of woods on the north side of the road, directly opposite the lot. Some time afterwards the ground was wanted for clearing, and the tent was removed to the woods, a short distance southeast of the cross-roads, and afterward carried back to the church lot, where it finally gave place to the first meeting-house. This house was constructed of round logs with clapboard roof, and stood on the northwest corner of the lot. It was a small building and not much used, as the private houses and the tent were yet used for preaching services. The second house was commenced in 1811 but the war came on the next year and the men were called away, so the house remained unfinished until the close of the war, being used, however, occasionally, in its unfinished state, the people sitting on the sleepers. It was constructed of very large hewed logs, many of them being nearly two feet through.

In 1825 the house was enlarged and otherwise improved, and in 1836 the present house of worship was built, which in 1869 was remodeled.

The ruling elders and deacons who from time to time exercised their office in the congregation were William Stewart, James Davidson, John Denison, James Applegate, John Abercrombie, James Stephenson (or "Steen" as he was usually called), Alex. Stewart, William Geddes, Samuel Denison, Joseph Stewart, John Milligan, William Smith, Robert Stewart, James Nelson, James Kennedy (Vienna), William Denison, John R. Kennedy, David Stewart, Armstrong Stewart, D. B. McGeehan, Stewart Denison, Joel K. Applegate.

The first pastor, Rev. James Duncan, preached for many years with acceptance and success, but at length days of difficulty and trouble came. He was charged before the presbytery at Cannonsburgh, Pennsylvania, in May, 1815, for preaching several grievous errors in relation to original sin, Christ's atonement and intercession, and publishing a book in their defense. He acknowledged his errors before the synod and received censure; but on his return to the congregation he denied his acknowledgment of error save in one particular. For public misrepresentations of his case he was suspended by the presbytery from the ministry and communion of the church. In personal appearance he was robust and corpulent; possessed a strong mind and great argumentative powers, and in private conversation was agreeable and instructive. He was careless in the management of his worldly affairs, and made poor provision for his family, and grossly addicted to tobacco. It was no uncommon thing for him while preaching to take a bite from his plug of tobacco, twisting it off in his hand. On one occasion, at least, he was known to have stopped in the midst of his discourse, go to one of the elders and borrow a chew of tobacco, and, returning to the tent, go on with his sermon. After his suspension little is known of his subsequent life. During the vacancy which occurred the congregation was supplied until 1820, when Rev. Robert Douglass was installed, who died in 1823, to whose memory the congregation erected a monument over his grave at Poland center.

On the 26th of April, 1826, Rev. David Goodwillie, D. D., was installed pastor of Poland, Liberty, and Deer Creek congregations. In 1833 he resigned the pastorate of Deer Creek, and for twenty-six years served Poland and Liberty. In 1859 he resigned Poland, and from that time until 1875 he was the pastor of Liberty alone. During his pastoral charge he has received into the church seven hundred and twenty-one; dispensed and assisted in dispensing sacraments three hundred and eighteen times; baptized thirty-six adults; solemnized two hundred and twenty-nine marriages, and preached no less than five thousand sermons. He was born at Barnet, Caledonia county, Vermont, August 28, 1802. His father was an able minister of the Associate church. He attended school at Cambridge academy, New York, four years, and then entered the sophomore class at Dartmouth, New Hampshire, and graduated there in 1820. He then attended the Eastern Theological seminary of the Associate church in Philadelphia, and was licensed to preach in 1823 at Ryegate, Vermont, and after some very extensive missionary work in various places he was called to the pastorate of Liberty, as above mentioned. On April 20, 1826, he was married to Francis Hamill, daughter of John Hamill, of Mercer county, Pennsylvania. Their eldest son is the Rev. D. H. Goodwillie, of Commerce, Michigan. The youngest son, Thomas, is a merchant of Cleveland, Ohio. The only surviving daughter is now Mrs. Rev. A. F. Ashton, of Monroe, Ohio. Dr. Goodwillie has formally retired from the pastorate, but in compliance with the wishes of his devoted people he has determined to end his days with them in quiet and peace.

METHODIST EPISCOPAL CHURCH, CHURCH HILL.

The original organization of this society was effected in 1821, under the ministry of Rev. Dillen Prosser. The first class numbered about sixty members, among whom were: Edward Moore and wife, Edward Mahan and wife, Peter Kline, wife and family (including his son Zenas, now one of the leading members), William Trotter and wife, John and Naomi Scott, Caroline Scott, William B. and Eliza Leslie, William Smith and wife, Matthew and Mary Trotter, Alexander Wright and wife, John and Miss Wright, John Hindman, William Henderson and wife, Jerome Monroe and wife, Irvin, William, Thomas, and Eliza Moore, Maria Wannamaker, Salome Henderson, Edward Irvin, John Clark, and William Trotter—the latter was the first class-leader and was succeeded by John Clark. The first building was erected the following summer, and is now used as town hall, and stands a short distance east of the original site. In this building the congregation worshiped until 1873, when the present church edifice was completed and dedicated. Among the ministers who have served this congregation were: Revs. Lane Plant, Ira Norris, William Day, Dr. Reeves, William Folgum, Peter Horton, Foutz, George Maltby, Holmes, Martin, Hurd, John Vance, Thomas Guy, Wesley Hill, Keller, Hubbard, Ezra Wade, William Hayes, Ely, Clark, C. F. Kingsberry, J. H. Starrett, T. Hodson, and Rev. McCleary, present pastor.

When first organized it belonged to Youngstown circuit, now known as Girard and Liberty.

As before stated the present church was dedicated under the ministry of Rev. Thomas Guy, Rev. Ives preaching the sermon.

The building is a frame of modern style of architecture, and cost $13,000; has an audience room with a seating capacity of four hundred, also lecture and Sabbath-school room, all heated by furnace and registers.

Soon after the society was organized the Sabbath-school was instituted by William Trotter and John Clark.

Special revivals were held by Revs. John Vance, Ely, and others; special accessions under Thomas Guy.

SCHOOLS.

The first school-house was located near Church Hill, at the west side of the cemetery. This house was rudely constructed after the well-known style of early times. The school was first taught by John Taylor, an elderly man about sixty years of age. Another house was then built about one-half mile east of Church Hill. Where William Sampson's barn now stands the principal school-house of the neighborhood was built in 1818. It was a huge log house covered with clapboards which were held to their places with weight-poles. Elias Grover was the first teacher. He came to the neighborhood as a stranger, announcing himself as being from the District of Maine. His school was very successful, and well attended. Many pupils came from a distance and boarded in the neighborhood for the purpose of attending this school. This teacher first made the advance in educational matters beyond the speller and "single rule of three," which then comprised the highest degree of pioneer education, and introduced grammar, geography, and surveying, which he successfully taught for some years.

A graded school was afterwards held in the house built for that purpose, now occupied by the Welsh Methodist church.

The present union school building was erected in 1871, and is a commodious building of three departments, and located at Church Hill. The school was organized under the superintendency of William Barrett, and is supported by the union of three districts, which now enumerates from five to six hundred children, of which, however, not more than one-half attend school.

The township besides supports nine school districts in which there are the usual provisions for ordinary schools.

THE PRESBYTERIAN CHURCH (OLD SCHOOL).

This congregation was originally organized from the congregation at Youngstown, where the original members first attended services. The organization was effected in 1832, in the fall of which year the frame of the present church building was erected. The presbytery of Beaver first sent Rev. James Satterfield, who succeeded in organizing the society. The first elders were John Nelson and James Anderson. The first settled pastor was Rev. John W. Scott, who afterwards became president of Washington college, Pennsylvania. He preached about four years and was followed by Rev. Joseph Kerr, who remained about ten years. He was followed by Rev. N. B. Lyon, who served the congregation three or four years, and was followed by Rev. T. C. Stewart, who preached about six years. The present pastor, Rev. J. H. Wright, resides in Hubbard and preaches at the latter place and Liberty. The membership now numbers about thirty-four.

GIRARD.

The settlement about the present village of Girard was later than the general settlement of the township, and was no doubt first made near the early mills located on the river. Special interests began to center here more extensively on the construction of the old Pennsylvania & Ohio canal, from Girard to Niles, in 1837.

About this time the original Girard plat was made by a company formed at Warren, among whom was Governor David Tod. Since then many additions have been made, principally along the lines of the railroads and bounded on the east by the State road. The Hartzell plat lies immediately north of the old Girard plat; north of this is the Stambaugh and Bush plats. The Osborn plat lies immediately south and Morris plat south of this. Between the latter and the Mahoning river Arms, Morris, and Tod made an additional plat, and across the river is Rayen's plat.

METHODIST EPISCOPAL CHURCH (GIRARD).

The first society of the Methodist Episcopal church in Girard was organized by Rev. Dillon Prosser in 1843. It consisted of Peter, Hannah, and Mary Carlton, Mary and Mrs. Hollingsworth, Abigail Osborn, Betsey McLean, and Samuel McMillan—the latter was appointed class-leader. The place of worship was a log school-house built on the ground now occupied by the residence of Obadiah Sheadle. Soon afterward they removed to a room in the store of Mr. Hollingsworth, afterwards the residence of George Spray, where services were held until the completion of the new frame school-house in which the meetings were then held. In 1852, after a great struggle to secure the necessary funds, a small chapel of very plain style was built without steeple, belfry or other mark to distinguish it from the surrounding buildings, except, perhaps, the two doors in front and windows above.

This was their home for twenty-seven years. The following have served this congregation: Dillon Prosser (1843), Ira Norris and Allen Foutz (1844), W. F. Day (1845), A. Norton, and J. L. Holmes (1846), A. Keller and S. Hubbard (1847), A. Keller and H. Kellogg (1848), W. N. Reno (1849), A. Reeves and W. N. Reno (1850), D. C. Wright and J. H. Vance (1851), J. H. Vance (1852), J. W. Weldon (1853), S. K. Paden (1854), N. C. Brown (1855), S. Heard (1856–57), J. W. Hill (1858–59), R. M. Bear (1860), E. Wade (1861–62), F. Vernon (1863), W. Hays (1864–65), J. H. Vance (1866–67, I. W. Ely (1868–69), W. A. Clark (1870), T. Guy (1871–73), C. T. Kingsbury (1874–76), J. H. Staratt, (1877–80), and Thomas McCleary, the present incumbent. The present house was dedicated January 18, 1880, by Rev. C. H. Payne, president of the Ohio Wesleyan university, from II. Chronicles, VI., 18, " But 'will God in very deed dwell with men on the earth?" This edifice is of Gothic style, with main audience room 40 x 50 feet, with transepts, right, left, and in front, 10 x 28 feet, cut off on the inside by folding doors which throw all the rooms together when required, with a seating capacity of four hundred, and costing about $4,500. The total indebtedness was discharged at the dedication exercises, and the building is certainly a fit temple for the purpose to which it is dedicated.

THE DISCIPLES CHURCH (GIRARD).

The first meetings of this denomination were held in the school hall, and among the ministers who preached during that time were Walter Hayden, Gideon Applegate, Orin Higgins, and others. The organization was effected February 5, 1867, by Orin Gates, who was sent by the missionary society of the church for that purpose. The original officials were Charles C. Fowler, James Shannon, and Ambrose Mason, elders; William Shannon, S. H. Miller, and John Patton, deacons. The original members of the church were Lucy Shannon, Laura Gilbert, Alice Harper, Louisa D. Fowler, Nancy Reel, Elizabeth Reed, Malinda and Minerva Phillips, Elizabeth Stanbaugh, Cynthia Young, Collins Atwood, Elizabeth Gantholtz, and Florence McLain. The present number of members is about sixty. The present church building was erected in 1871 at the time of Rev. N. N. Bartlett's ministry, and was constructed by William and James Shannon and John Reed, building committee, and Charles Fowler, contractor and carpenter. Among the ministers who have served this congregation from time to time were Henry Camp, James Van Horne, E. D. Wakefield, T. S. Hanselman, N. N. Bartlett, and S. S. Bartlett. The society is now in a good, prosperous condition, with a Sabbath-school of about fifty members. The present officials are James Shannon, Alanson Miller, and C. H. Stanbaugh, elders; William Wallace, and Frederick Coonly, deacons, and A. Wayne Kennedy, treasurer.

THE APOSTOLIC CHRISTIAN ASSEMBLY.

This society was organized in 1878 by Rev. J. Bollinger, who preached until last year, when he was succeeded by Rev. Joseph Bella.

Meetings of this denomination had been held previous to the organization at the residence of William Ludt, in Girard; and the first minister of this denomination was Rev. John Bakody. The original members were: Mr. and Mrs. William Ludt, Charles and Mrs. Schenoenfeld, and Mrs. Mary Fachield. The present beautiful little church at Girard was built in the year above mentioned at a cost of $1,600.

The society now numbers about fifty members, and is in a general state of prosperity, having regular services with the expectation of soon organizing a Sabbath-school. The society is composed of Germans who are wholly orthodox in their belief; and their efforts to maintain a church of their own people is commendable, and should be successful.

THE LUTHERAN CHURCH (GERMAN).

The building in which this society holds services at present, is situated on the State road about one-half mile north of Girard. The first house built by this society was a log building, and was situated on the site of the present church. The present house was erected in 1833; and among the early members of the church were Henry Barnhisel, Peter Reel, George Hood, Jacob Reel, and others. Among the ministers who have served this society were Rev. Morris Smith, Rev. Hess, Rev. Baker, Rev. Paultzgrow. The membership now numbers about forty, and services are held regularly at the above place, under the present ministry of Rev. Meisner. The cemetery grounds adjoining belong to the church.

THE GIRARD UNION SCHOOL.

The general movement for improvement of the educational facilities at Girard was begun about 1860. On March 12, 1861, the local directors of school district number two, Liberty township, namely, J. C. Allison, Abner Osborn, and Henry Barnheisel, with a committee appointed by the people consisting of William Johnson, Edward Ray, Martin Houston, Abner Rush, and H. P. Gilbert, met together for the consideration of a plan for the erection of a suitable school building. Abner Rush was appointed treasurer and clerk for the purpose of effecting this object. The present commodious brick building was then soon erected and completed at a cost of about $21,000, when Hugh Caldwell, now of Cleveland, Ohio, was first engaged as principal. In September, 1870, the present principal, A. Wayne Kennedy, took charge of the school with three assistants, and has continued in charge since with commendable success, the school increasing until now there are seven apartments with the following assistants: Miss Kit McGlarthery, Lara S. Schaeffer, Lizzie Kennedy, Della V. Reed, Mary E. Walker, and Louise M. Hauser. The whole number in the school is now three hundred and three. During the superintendency of Mr. Kennedy the following persons have been graduated from this school, namely: Charles Allison (engineer), William Lotze (telegraph operator), Evan Jones, and Ella Bowman. Frank E. Buntz was called away from his class just before graduation to enter the naval school at Annapolis, Maryland.

The curriculum of the school embraces philosophy, geometry, astronomy, and various higher branches of science and mathematics, and the school is now in the zenith of prosperity, and every indication bespeaks success. The building is conveniently and pleasantly located, and both in external appearance and the design for which it was built is a pride and honor to the people of Girard.

COURT LILY OF GIRARD NO. 6625.

This court of the Ancient Order of Foresters was organized January 31, 1880, when the following officials were elected : D. J. Woodford, C. R.; John Bevan, sub-C. R.; Morgan Thomas, F. S.; Morgan L. Jones, R. S.; Benjamin Parry, treasurer; William Moss, senior woodward; John Phillips, junior woodward; John Jinkins, senior beadle; L. D. Jones, junior beadle. The charter members were T. W. D. Jones, D. J. Woodford, and L. D. Jones. The society makes allowance of $5 per week in cases of sickness; also appointing attendants in cases of necessity. At this time it has a membership of twenty-eight, and meets every alternate Saturday night in Odd Fellows hall.

AMALGAMATED ASSOCIATION OF IRON AND STEEL WORKERS.

Shiloh lodge of Ohio No. 16, was organized August 4, 1876, with the following officials: Thomas S. Evans, president; John Bevans, vice-president; Thomas D. Davis, recording secretary; James Richards, guide; John Evans, I. G., Roderick Evans, O. G. The society is organized for mutual aid and protection, and holds its meetings in the Independent Order of Odd Fellows hall.

GIRARD LODGE NO. 432, INDEPENDENT ORDER OF ODD FELLOWS.

This lodge was instituted July 20, 1869, by Horace Beebe, special deputy G. M. The charter members were : S. J. Lambert, Calvin Eckman, Hugh Gilmore, Horatio M. Prindle, C. D. Goodrich, John P. Miller, L. Beaver, W. F. Adams, Jacob Stambaugh, Emanuel Hartzell, Jr., H. A. McCartney, Evan Morris, and C. S. Miller. The first officials were : Jacob Stambaugh, N. G.; Evan Morris, V. G.; S. J. Lambert, secretary; Hugh Gilmore, treasurer.

The lodge is now in a prosperous condition and holds its regular meetings in its own lodge-rooms on Liberty street, with the present officials : Robert Shaw, N. G.; John Allen, V. G.; Elias Lewis, secretary; C. G. Goodrich, F. S.; and E. Hartzell, Jr., treasurer ; with a present membership of fifty-nine.

FRIENDSHIP LODGE NO. 65, KNIGHTS OF PYTHIAS.

The above lodge was organized March 12, 1874, by Adams Emerson, G. C. The first officials were : E. Hartzell, Jr., C. C.; Joseph Hull, V. C.; M. L. Kazertee, K. of R. S.; L. S. Fowler, M. of F.; Edgar Cranton, M. of E.; S. E. Knight, prelate.

The following, including the above officials, were the charter members : James H. Gifford, E. Hartzell, Jr., J. Jones, C. D. Goodrich, John Wilkes, A. J. Jewell, James Jones, Robert Thompson, and Thomas Hughes. The lodge meets regularly in the Independent Order of Odd Fellows hall, and now has a membership of twenty-five, with the following officials : W. J. Walters, C. C.; A. E. Hartzell, V. C.; C. D. Goodrich, K. of R. and S.; A. J. Jewell, M. of F.; E. Hartzell, M. of E.; S. E. Knight, prelate.

THE GIRARD STOVE WORKS.

The above extensive manufactory is located on the west side of the river at Girard village. It was first established about 1867 by Lambert Crawford and C. B. Vanbroclin, who operated about six months when Crawford sold to George Johnson, and Faulkenstein about the same time became a member of the firm. About this time the works were closed and so remained about one year, when it passed into the hands of Hartzell, Lambert & May, who operated about one year. Hartzell then bought Lambert's interest, which was transferred to his son, Alonzo H. About this time A. J. Cartney and Jacob Stambaugh, were members of the firm, when C. R. Johnson purchased an interest of the latter; also Robert Walker and D. T. Kincaid purchased a one-fifth interest each. The company was then incorporated with Jacob Stambaugh president, C. R. Johnson, secretary, and S. H. Wilson, superintendent, the latter having purchased the interest belonging to Jacob May. The works are now owned by John R. Walker, John Stambaugh, A. J. McCartney, D. T. Kincaid, and S. H. Wilson. The foundry now requires from eight to ten moulders, one machinist, two stove mounters, one pattern maker, two blacksmiths and helpers, one engineer, two cupola tenders, and is now producing all kinds of work in this line. The utmost capacity is a five-ton casting. From seven to eight stoves are turned out per day, together with other odd castings to the amount of ten to twenty hundred pounds. A specialty is made of coal-bank cages and coal cars. Three and four of the latter are made per day. The works now have one fifty inch cupola running a daily heat and near full capacity. The engine used is a forty-horse power, and the works are in active and successful operation.

THE GIRARD FLOUR-MILL.

The present flouring-mills located at Girard were built about 1840-41 by Jesse Baldwin and Abner Osborn. The present company, under the name of Morris, Prindle & Co., runs the mill to a capacity of sixty or seventy barrels per day, having four run of buhrs propelled by water-power derived from the Mahoning river. The company is doing a general shipping and local custom trade.

GIRARD TANNERY.

The old tannery which stood on the site of the present extensive tannery of Krehl, Hauser & Co., was built and operated for some time by Elmadorus Cranden. The above company came into possession in 1860, and in 1873 very extensive improvements were made and other improvements have from time to time been made. The present capacity is six hundred sides of leather per week, requiring the assistance of twenty-five and more hands. The company now makes a specialty of harness and belt leather, also the manufacture of bands for driving machinery and fair line and collar leather. The present complete appliances are all new and the company is operating with every indication of success and increasing prosperity.

THE GIRARD SAVINGS BANK.

The bank was organized in 1873 under the general banking law of the State. The original officials were: R. H. Walker, president, and O. Sheadle, cashier. The latter has served in this capacity since, and is the present able and efficient cashier of the bank. The original company was composed of R. H. Walker, William B. Leslie, R. L. Walker, Evan Morris, John Morris, and O. Sheadle.

The incorporation was made with a capital of $50,000, and the deposits now amount to $100,000 with a surplus fund of $12,500.

The banking of this firm has been managed with commendable efficiency, and no losses have ever been experienced since the organization, and the operations have embraced a general banking business of almost ten years.

The present company is composed of R. L. Walker, William B. Sampson, Zenas Kline, I. R. Hayes, Rebecca and Margaret Leslie, and O. Sheadle, with the following officials: William D. Sampson, president, and O. Sheadle, cashier; the company owning its own banking house on Liberty street.

The present condition is in every way indicative of future success, and general confidence is felt in the condition and management of the bank.

THE CORNS IRON COMPANY ROLLING-MILLS.

These large and flourishing works were first established here in 1872-73 by a joint stock company, known as the Girard Rolling-mill company. The present company is operated by the following officials: Henry Wick, president; Myron C. Wick, secretary, treasurer, and general manager, who with John C. Wick compose the present company, the works now being superintended by T. H. Joy. The works now employ one hundred and fifty-three hands, and have fourteen puddling furnaces, three heating furnaces, one eighteen-inch muck-mill, one eight- and one ten-inch finishing-mill, two batteries, one of four and the other of two boilers. Special attention is paid to the manufacture of irons for agricultural implements, guard and finger irons, drag and brace bars, knife back, iron cylinder bar, and tooth iron for threshing machines, also chain, nut, and bolt iron. Present capacity nine to ten hundred tons per month.

THE GIRARD IRON COMPANY FURNACE.

The above furnace was first located here about 1866 by John Tod, J. G. Butler, William Richards, and Joseph Fleming. The present company is composed of A. M. Byers and Joseph Fleming of Pittsburg, Pennsylvania, with W. R. Drake, of Warren, as manager. The company has lately made considerable repairs and many improvements. The appliances now consist of the furnace sixty-six feet high with boilers of sixteen feet, two Robinson, Ray & Co. blowing engines of eighty-four-inch cylinders, four pumps, eight cylinder boilers forty-four feet long, a cast-iron tower with Crane Brothers' automatic hoist, a fine stock-house two hundred feet long and sixty wide; also two hot blasts. The furnace has a capacity of twenty thousand tons per month, and has convenient connections with the Ashtabula & Painesville, also the Mahoning division of the New York, Pennsylvania & Ohio railroads.

SODOM

is a small village in the northwestern part of the township. The settlement here was made more prominent about 1865 when the coal bank was opened. The place derived the name from the following incident: About 1840, when the temperance question was strongly agitated, Dr. Fisher gave a lecture on that subject at Church Hill, and those who were interested in the cause prevailed on the doctor to deliver a lecture in the school-house where the above village now stands. The lecturer did not meet with the success he anticipated, and at the next lecture at Church Hill he jocosely remarked that he had not been successful in his effort at the school-house and he feared that the locality was a perfect Sodom; and from that time this name has been retained. The village has some lines of trade represented but operations in mining are the main industrial pursuits.

The Methodist Protestant church is located at the village.

THE EVANGELICAL ASSOCIATION CHURCH.

This organization first held meetings at the house of George Herring, where Rev. Henry Yambert preached as early as 1822. A few years after a church was built on the south side of the road about one and one-fourth miles from Girard, between Church Hill and the former village. This building was afterwards moved to the present location, in the northeast part of the township.

Besides Rev. Yambert, who was the first preacher of this denomination in the township, there were many others who from time to time served this congregation. Among these were—Revs. Crossman, Staley, G. S. Domer, Long, Crowther, Rank, Van Dorsal, Beatty, Wyckle Hollinger, Somers, Brown, Poling, Dunlap,

Weaver, and C. F. Harting, the present pastor.

William Herring was one among the first class-leaders, also afterwards Jacob Miller. George Frazier, Simon Goist, and I. Smith served in this capacity. The present class-leader is George Frazier.

The present trustees are Jacob Miller, William Frazier, and Simon Goist, and the society is now under the jurisdiction of the Pittsburg conference.

THE METHODIST PROTESTANT CHURCH.

This society was organized February 22, 1862, by Rev. Henry Palmer. The original members were John and Phœbe Hawkins, Julius Truesdale and wife, Isaac D. Bard and wife, James H. Bard and wife, Abraham Storm and wife, Washington Powers and wife, John Barber and wife, Samuel McKenzie and wife, Wilson and Mary J. Powers, Henrietta and Sylvanus Moser, John S. Bennett and wife, Isaac Sutton, Cornelius Shook, Delilah Shook, Sarah Shook, Ann and Lucinda Storm, Arabella Denison, Harriet Goist, E. E. Goudy, Frank Allbright, Elizabeth and Julietta Miller, John Turner, Belinda Frazier, John Miller, Maria Hickox. John Hawkins was the first class-leader and J. H. Bard, steward. The church building was erected in 1872, dedicated on June 26th the same year. Rev. Thomas H. Colhour preached the dedication sermon. The building committee consisted of Isaac D. Bard, J. S. Denison, Wesley Triplet, Henry H. Jones, and A. S. Stewart. The following ministers have served this congregation: Henry Palmer, J. H. Mason, T. H. Colhour, C. P. Jordon, John Hodgkinson, C. P. Goodrich, McLaughlin, Henry Palmer, C. K. Stillwagon, William H. Gladden, E. A. Brindley. The society belongs to the Pittsburg conference, Trumbull circuit. The Sabbath-school was organized in 1862 with John Hawkins as superintendent. The first meetings of the society were held in the school-house of district number four for many years previous to the organization of the church proper. The revival of 1862, under Rev. Henry Palmer, was a special season of ingathering to the church, since which time there have been many revivals under the various ministers. The present membership numbers thirty-eight, and the society is in good condition.

Peter Kline

Mrs Esther Kline.

BIOGRAPHICAL SKETCHES.

PETER KLINE.

The subject of this sketch is the most extensive land owner in Liberty township. His father, Abram Kline, removed from Northampton county, Pennsylvania, to Ohio and settled in Youngstown township in the year 1806, on a farm opposite the mouth of Mill creek, on the Mahoning river. He was of German descent and a member of the Lutheran church. He was stern, generous, and enterprising, persevering in business, but always kind and social in his dealings. His death occurred in the year 1816, from a rupture of a blood vessel. He had accumulated a large estate, having farmed extensively and dealt successfully in live stock. The public sale of property after his death lasted three days. He had a love of blooded horses and one named Messenger was purchased by General Wadsworth, of Canfield, at the sum of $1,000. Mr. Kline was at the time of his death about forty-six years old. His family consisted of six children. Jonathan, the oldest son, settled at Canfield, where he died at the age of seventy-five years. He was small of stature, his weight being only one hundred and twenty-five pounds, but his frame was strong and his muscles wiry, being able to stand in a half bushel measure and shoulder three bushels of wheat without assistance. He left each of his four sons, who are all living, a good farm.

Solomon, the second son of Abram Kline, resides in Cortland, Trumbull county, and is extensively known as a man of large accumulations of money, and sagacious business talent. He has no children.

The three oldest children of Abram Kline were daughters—Polly married Conrad Neff and settled in Portage county, Sally married Daniel Everett and settled in Hubbard, Betsey married John Neff and settled in Canfield; all three are dead.

Peter Kline, the youngest son and subject of an illustration, was born in Northampton county, Pennsylvania, February 7, 1803. His early life was spent on his father's farm, and later in general farm labor for other people. In 1835 he purchased sixty-six acres of land in Liberty township, on which he settled. Having inherited a strong liking for stock, particularly cattle, and the kind of talent required for stock speculation, he turned his attention in that direction. He has been the most extensive cattle dealer in the southern part of Trumbull county, and his success is shown by the continued increase of his farm, which now embraces over seven hundred acres.

Mr. Kline was married in 1822 to Esther Brown, daughter of Rodger Brown, who with his family removed from Connecticut and settled in Coitsville township. Mrs. Kline was born in 1804 and died January 20, 1877. Their family consists of four children—Sarah, Zenas, Abram, and Jane. Sarah was born in 1823; she was married to John Lynch, who died at Meadville, Pennsylvania, leaving four children—Lucy, Lois, John, and Charles. Lois was married to John McMullen, and has one child living named Lois, a granddaughter of Peter Kline; Lucy is married to Lyman Lease. Sarah married for her second husband Joseph Wilson, of Weathersfield, where she resides.

Zenas, second child of Peter Kline, was born March 28, 1828; was married to Malinda Hooks and lives in Liberty township.

Abram Kline was born May 5, 1831; was married to Lucy McCartney, of Coitsville, and lives at Church Hill, in Liberty township.

Jane Kline was born August 27, 1836; was married to Rev. Charles W. Reeves, and resides in Warren.

Mr. Kline was married August 1, 1877, to Elizabeth Tayler, widow of George Tayler, of Warren, and daughter of Elliott Woodbridge, of Youngstown, and a great-granddaughter of President Jonathan Edwards, the illustrious New England preacher and philosopher. She was born April 9, 1819, and married to George Tayler, a sketch of whom will be found elsewhere in this volume. After his death, in 1864, she continued to reside in Warren until her marriage with Mr. Kline.

An excellent bed of coal was found on Mr. Kline's farm at Church Hill, in 1867, and a mine was opened the following year by Tod, Stambaugh & Co., lessees. It has been successfully and extensively operated ever since, bringing to its owner large revenues.

Mr. Kline is healthy, active, and strong.

Though eighty years of age he has the promise of several years of life yet. His physical powers have never been impaired by strong drink, as was too frequently the case with men of his business and period of early life. He has made total abstinence a life principle, and has rigidly adhered to that principle. His whole family in this respect have made him their example. He is using his large fortune liberally in the support of charities and for the benefit of his family.

NOTES OF SETTLEMENT.

John Denison settled in Liberty in the first settlement of the township. He was a native of county Down, Ireland. He erected a rude pole shanty in the east part of the township, in the place where Stewart Denison now lives; purchasing six hundred and forty acres of land, and lived there until his death, October 29, 1821. He was seventy-three years of age at the time of his death. His children were Samuel, James, Henry, John, David, and Margaret, all now dead. Samuel, the oldest of the children, married Betsy Stewart, and lived upon the old homestead. They were the parents of twelve children, of whom ten are yet living. Samuel Denison was a leading farmer in his township, and an influential and enterprising citizen. He held the office of justice of the peace for thirty-five years. He died in 1869 at the age of eighty-seven or eighty-eight. The surviving members of the family are Frances, John, Mary (Holland), Stewart, Calvin, Eliza (Applegate), Sarah (McMullen), Amy (Henderson), Esther (Bailey), and Margaret; all reside on a part of the original farm in Liberty except John, who resides in Champion, Mrs. Holland in Mahoning county, and Mrs. Applegate in Youngstown. John Denison is a farmer of Champion, born June 4, 1818. He has been married twice. Stewart Denison, born in 1822, married in 1845 Rosannah Russel, of Vienna.

Samuel Goist was born in Lancaster county, Pennsylvania, June 3, 1801. His father, George Goist, was a native of Pennsylvania. He came to Ohio in 1801 or 1802, in company with two of the family, coming on a flat-boat of their own construction as far as Beaver, then by teams through the wilderness to Liberty township, where they all settled. Mr. Goist began in the

woods but soon had a good farm under cultivation, and lived upon this until his death. There were six children in his family, three boys and three girls. All of the girls are living. Mr. Samuel Goist learned the wagonmakers' trade and followed this occupation until within a short time before his death, which accidentally occurred on November 7, 1878, caused by being thrown out of a buggy. Mrs. Samuel Goist, daughter of Isaac Hoffman, was born in Chester county, Pennsylvania, August 26, 1806. She is still living with one of her daughters, and is a smart, energetic lady. There were born to Mr. and Mrs. Goist eight children, five of whom are living. Mr. John M. Goist, one of the sons, of whom this information was obtained, resides in Liberty township. He was married in 1861 to Miss Rebecca Hoffman, daughter of Washington Hoffman, of Allegheny county, Pennsylvania. Three children were the fruits of this union. Mrs. Goist died in 1869. Mr. Goist was married in 1871 to Miss Mary A. Kirk, daughter of Josiah Kirk, of Jackson township, Mahoning county. One child by this marriage. He has made farming his chief occupation though has worked some at wagon-making and milling.

Simon Goist was born in Liberty township in 1835. His father, Samuel Goist, was one of the early settlers of the township. Mr. Goist has always lived in Liberty. Farming and milling have been his chief occupations. He was married in 1858 to Miss Mary A. Shiveley, daughter of Daniel Shiveley, of Liberty township. They have three children—Alice L., William H., and Iva F. Mr. Goist is a member of the Independent Order of Odd Fellows, and also of the Grangers.

John C. Wilkin, an old resident of Liberty township, was born in Allegheny county, Pennsylvania, October 16, 1804. His father, John, a native of Ireland, came to America in an early day and located in Allegheny county, where he was engaged in farming for many years. He died in Pittsburg, leaving a family of nine children, three of whom are living. Mr. Wilkin purchased land in Liberty, previous to 1800, though he soon sold it, as he did not care to go into a country where there were more Indians than white men. Mr. John Wilkin came to Ohio in 1834 and settled in Champion township,

Trumbull county. He here began in the woods, but soon had a good farm as a reward for his hard labors. He lived here ten years, and then moved to Howland township where he resided seven years, then back to Champion for seven years, then to Liberty, where we now find him. He has a good farm of one hundred acres. He was married in 1826 to Miss Mary Scott, daughter of William Scott, of Pennsylvania. He had nine children by this marriage. Mrs. Wilkin died in 1845. In 1847 Mr. Wilkin was again married—to Miss Rosannah Oaks, daughter of Isaac Oaks, of Pennsylvania. There were five children by this marriage. Mrs. Wilkin died in 1856. For his third wife Mr. Wilkin married in 1857 Miss Matilda Clark, daughter of William Clark, of Liberty township, by whom he had one child. She died in 1866. He was married the fourth time in 1867 to Miss Elizabeth Oaks, a sister of his second wife. Mr. Wilkin is a member of the Presbyterian church; Mrs. Wilkin of the Baptist church. Mr. Wilkin is still an active, energetic man, a good neighbor and citizen.

William Ward, a well-known resident of Trumbull county, was born in England in 1806, January 11th, and came to America in 1818 with his parents, William and Sarah Ward. They at once went to Pittsburg, Pennsylvania, where they lived till their deaths. Mr. Ward, the subject of this sketch, came to Ohio in 1826 and located at New Lisbon, where he was engaged in the iron business two years, then went back to Pittsburg, where he manufactured nails fourteen years. He then moved to Niles, Ohio, where he and his brother, James Ward, and Thomas Russell built the iron mills of James Ward & Co. Mr. Ward resided at Niles thirty-six years. He came to Girard in 1878, and is now engaged in farming. He was married in 1825 to Miss Ann McIntosh, daughter of Duncan McIntosh. Ten children were the fruits of this union, five of whom are living. Mr. and Mrs. Ward are members of the Presbyterian church. In politics he is a firm Republican. He has been one of the active business men of the county, and is held in esteem by all.

James B. McClelland, an old resident of Liberty township, was born in Liberty, April 10, 1811. His father, William McClelland, came from Pennsylvania or New Jersey, somewhere near Monmouth, though he was living in Greene county, Pennsylvania, when he came to Ohio, which was in 1805. He located in Liberty township, and was one of the early settlers, and knew well from experience what the trials and hardships were to which the pioneers were subject. He cleared up a good farm and resided upon it till his death, which occurred January 23, 1843. Mr. William McClelland was a member of the Presbyterian church, of which he was an elder for many years, being appointed when he was twenty-four years of age. Three of his children lived to maturity—Robert, Ann, James. Mr. James McClelland has always lived near his old home. He has made farming an occupation, though not exclusively. He has been justice of the peace six years, giving the best of satisfaction in his official position. He is a stanch Republican and a worthy citizen.

Abner Osborn, a well-known resident of Liberty township, was born in Youngstown township, September 5, 1810. His father, Joseph Osborn, was born in Virginia and came to Ohio in 1804, locating in Youngstown township, Trumbull county (now Mahoning), and was among the early pioneers. Like other old settlers in the wild country of Ohio at the time, he began in the woods with a dense wilderness about him in all directions, though he succeeded in making a good farm and lived upon this till his death, which occurred February 17, 1846, aged seventy-two years. There were eight children in his family, four of whom are now living. Mr. Abner Osborn came to Girard in 1841. He helped build the present grist-mill in company with Josiah Robins and Jesse Baldwin. Mr. Osborn has been engaged in various occupations. In connection with farming he is interested in coal business in Carroll and Columbiana counties. He was married in 1839, to Miss Abigail Allison, of New Lisbon, Columbiana county. Six children have been born to them, five of whom are living. One son was killed in the Rebellion. Mrs. Osborn is a member of the Methodist church. Politically Mr. Osborn is a good Democrat and is one of the enterprising men of the county.

Edward Mahan was born in 1812 in Ireland, and came to America in 1831, landing in Quebec after a perilous voyage of five weeks and four days. His father, Thomas, came to America about eighteen months afterwards, and at once came to Ohio where his son resided in Trumbull county. Here here mained several years, then went to Guernsey county, Ohio, where he died in 1841. There were nine children in his family, five boys and four girls. Six of the children came to this country. Mrs. Mahan died in Bristol some years after the death of Mr. Mahan. Mr. Edward Mahan has always lived in Liberty township since 1831, with the exception of eighteen months in Guernsey county. He learned the brickmakers' trade and followed this for over thirty years, then went upon the farm where we now find him. He was married in 1835 to Miss Lydia McFarland, daughter of William McFarland, of Coitsville, Mahoning county. They have had twelve children, all of whom are living and are the joy of their parents in their old age. Mr. and Mrs. Mahan are members of the Methodist church and are good citizens.

Gideon Carlton, an old resident of Trumbull county, was born in Austintown, June 10, 1812. His father, John C., a native of New Jersey, came to Ohio in a very early day, and was among the pioneers of the section. Mr. Gideon Carlton lived in Austintown till he was eighteen years of age, then went to Lordstown with his parents and resided there till 1845, when he moved to Champion township, living there five years, then came to Liberty township and made it his home till 1864, then moved to Weathersfield township and remained there till 1879, then moved back to Liberty, where we now find him on the north half of his father's old farm. He was married in 1835 to Miss Mary Brougher, daughter of John Brougher of Youngstown. By this union there were seven children. Mrs. Carlton died in March, 1850. Mr. Carlton was married the second time on October 10, 1850, to Mrs. Sarah McKinley, daughter of Archibald Prince, of Hubbard. He had four children by this marriage, two of whom are living. Mrs. Carlton is a member of the Disciple church. In politics Mr. Carlton is a firm Republican, and is held in high esteem by all

F. T. Adams, an old resident of Trumbull county, was born in Weathersfield township, September 23, 1817. His father, David A. Adams, came from Connecticut in an early day and located in Weathersfield township, and was one of the first settlers. He lived in Weathersfield

till his death on October 3, 1855. He was born February 10, 1784. Mrs. Adams was born April 26, 1794. She died December 21, 1864. There were seven children in the family—four boys and three girls. Mr. F. T. Adams has always lived in the county, is engaged in general farming, and has one hundred and fifty-eight acres of land. He was married in 1848 to Miss Elizabeth Nelson, daughter of John Nelson, of Liberty township. This union has been blessed with six children, two of whom are living—Charles F. and Calvin A. Mrs. Adams is a member of the Presbyterian church. Mr. Adams is a Republican and a good citizen.

John B. Tully, a well known resident of Liberty township, was born September 4, 1817. His father, James Tully, was born in Lancaster county, Pennsylvania, and came to Ohio in an early day. John P. Tully, father of James, came from Ireland before the Revolutionary war. He was a cooper by trade though he did not follow this exclusively, as he was upon the sea several years—made a voyage to the East Indies. During the Revolutionary war he was taken prisoner at Quebec. After the war he settled in Virginia for a short time, when, having trouble with the Indians, he moved to Westmoreland county, Pennsylvania, and from there to Washington county. He participated in the famous whiskey insurrection at Ginger Hill. In the spring of 1804 he came to Ohio and located in Liberty township upon the farm where Mr. J. B. Tully now lives, having previously purchased it. He cleared up a fine farm and lived upon it until his death, in 1830. There were seven children in the family. Mr. James Tully lived upon the farm until 1861, his death occurring in this year. Mrs. Tully died in 1852. There were four children in this family. Mr. John B. Tully, the subject of this sketch, lives upon the old home farm; he is engaged in general farming, though he works at his trade some—that of a carpenter, also wagon-making. He was married in 1850 to Miss May J. McGlathery, daughter of Joseph McGlathery, of Liberty township. Three children are the fruits of this marriage: Josephine A., Hagar, Austa. Hagar is deceased. Mrs. Tully and her daughter are members of the Disciple church. Mr. Tully is one of the substantial citizens of the township.

James Tully, brother of John B. Tully, was

born in Liberty township in 1824, and has always lived upon the old home farm. He has one hundred and thirty-two acres of excellent land. He was married in 1850 to Miss Emily, daughter of Samuel Geddis, of Liberty township. They have had five children, three of whom are living. In religion Mr. Tully is very liberal.

Jonathan Shook was born in 1823 in Columbiana county, Ohio. His father, Jacob Shook, was a native of Pennsylvania, and came to Ohio in an early day and settled in Columbiana county, where he resided several years, then moved to Liberty township, Trumbull county, where he lived until his death, in 1858; Mrs. Shook died in 1836 or 1837. Five children in the family, three of whom are living. Mr. John Shook is engaged in general farming and is one of the successful farmers of the township. He was married in 1845, to Miss Leah Hays, daughter of William Hays, of Liberty township. Seven children have been born to them, five of whom are living. Mrs. Shook died in 1878. Mr. Shook is one of the most enterprising men of the township, and is held in high esteem.

H. P. Gilbert was born in Austintown township in 1818. His father, Henry Gilbert, was born in Pennsylvania, and came to Ohio in company with his parents and settled in Austintown township, Trumbull county, now Mahoning. He moved to Liberty township in 1821, where he worked as a carpenter until 1837, when he went to Bazetta township and cleared up a farm, living there until his death, which occurred in 1855 or 1856. There were ten children in his family, four of whom are living. Mrs. Gilbert died in 1861. Mr. H. P. Gilbert has lived in Trumbull county since 1821, with the exception of a short time; was engaged in mercantile business at Austintown twenty-seven years, though is now interested in coal. He was married in 1845, to Miss Laura A. Rush, daughter of Abner Rush, of Liberty township. Five children have been born to them, three of whom are living. Mrs. Gilbert is a member of the Presbyterian church. Mr. Gilbert was in the One Hundred and Fifth Ohio infantry, was discharged in 1865 for disability. He is a Republican.

J. C. Bowman, M. D., an old physician of Girard, was born in Elkton township, Colum-

biana county, Ohio, in 1819. His father, David, was a native of York county, Pennsylvania, and came to Ohio in an early day, settling in Elkton township, where he lived till his death, which occurred in 1819. Dr. Bowman studied medicine with Dr. Hahn, of North Lima, Columbiana county; attended lectures at Ann Arbor, Michigan, and graduated at the Eclectic Medical institute in Philadelphia, in 1855. He practiced several years in Beaver township, Columbiana county, now Mahoning, before graduating. Since 1855 he has practiced in Southington, Beaver, and Girard, coming to Girard in 1862. He has a good practice. He was married in 1840 to Miss Sophia Hahn, daughter of John Hahn, of Beaver township. They have had seven children, three of whom are living. Mr. and Mrs. Bowman are members of the Evangelical Association. In politics Mr. Bowman was formerly a staunch Abolitionist, but is now a firm Greenbacker, being strongly opposed to National banks. He is a good physician, and is held in esteem by all.

William Rayen, one of the old residents of Girard, was born in Venango county, Pennsylvania, May 3, 1821. His father, John Rayen, was a Pennsylvanian and came to Ohio in 1827, and located at Youngstown when it was a very small place, and farmed upon what is now a part of the city. He lived here till 1833, when he moved to Champion township, where he resided till his death, which occurred in 1852, leaving a family of seven children and widow to mourn his loss. Two of the children died before this. Mrs. Rayen is still living. Mr. William Rayen came to Girard in 1853 or 1854, and has been engaged in business at this place ever since; first in the flax business, afterward in mercantile, in which we now find him. He was married in 1849 to Miss Lucy Moser, daughter of John Moser, of Liberty township. They have had three children, two of whom are living. Mr. Rayen is one of the active business men of the township. Politically he has been a Republican, though is inclined toward Greenbackism.

William Wilson was born in Weathersfield township in 1822. His father, Edward Wilson, was born in Youngstown township; he died in 1836, leaving a family of eight children. Mr. William Wilson, grandfather of Joseph, was born upon the ocean while his parents were on their way to America. He came to Ohio about 1800 and was among the pioneers of Ohio. There were two or three houses in Youngstown at that day. He cleared up a good farm, which remains in the family. Mr. Joseph Wilson was well known throughout this part of the Reserve as a great hunter. Mr. William Wilson came to Liberty township in 1847, from Niles, and settled in Girard. About five years ago he moved upon the farm where he now lives. He is a wagonmaker by trade, though he follows farming to some extent. He was married in 1845 to Miss Martha McCartney, daughter of Andrew McCartney, of Liberty township. They have had six children, four of whom are living. Mr. and Mrs. Wilson are members of the Methodist church. He is a Republican.

J. B. Hood was born in Liberty township, Trumbull county, in 1830. His father, Amos Hood, came from Washington county, Pennsylvania, to Ohio in 1808, in company with his father, George Hood, and settled in Liberty township near the center of the town. Mr. George Hood was a pioneer and passed through the trials and hardships incident to pioneer life. He began in the wilderness and cleared up a good farm. He died in 1846. There were nine children in his family, six boys and three girls. Mr. Hood was a farmer by occupation. Mrs. Hood died in 1852 or 1853. Mr. Amos Hood spent the most of his life in Liberty. He died in December, 1873. Mrs. Hood, wife of Amos Hood, died in May, 1864. There were five children in the family, three of whom are living. Mr. J. B. Hood has ever lived in Liberty township. He is engaged in general farming and is highly esteemed by all. He was married in 1856 to Miss Elizabeth Strock, daughter of John Strock, of Southington. They have two children—Vernetia and Ellis R. Politically Mr. Hood is a firm Democrat.

W. B. Sampson was born in Westmoreland county, Pennsylvania, in February, 1831. His father, William Sampson, was a native of Pennsylvania and lived and died there. Mr. W. B. Sampson came to Ohio in 1843, and has since lived at Church Hill, Liberty township. He married Miss Amanda Walker, daughter of Dr. R. H. Walker, of Church Hill, in 1855. They have had four children, Hattie J., John W., William H., and Robert H. Mrs. Sampson is a member of the Presbyterian church. Mr. Sampson is quite extensively engaged in stock business, and is one of the energetic, wide-awake farmers of old Trumbull. He is a staunch Republican.

Dr. John McCartney, a well-known physician of Girard, was born in Girard September 26, 1838. His father, James McCartney, a native of of Ohio, is now living at Girard. Dr. McCartney studied medicine with Isaac Barclay, M. D., and attended lectures at Cleveland Medical college, and graduated in 1861. He has since practiced at Girard with the exception of three years at Hubbard. Dr. McCartney has built up a good practice. He was married in 1872 to Mrs. Sarah Packard, daughter of John Crum, of Austintown township. Mrs. McCartney died in 1875. She was a member of the Lutheran church. Dr. McCartney is a Free Mason—politically a good Democrat.

George H. Beaver, a representative of an old family of Liberty township, was born in Liberty October 27, 1843. His father, Samuel Beaver, was a native of Perry county, Pennsylvania, and came to Ohio in 1822 in company with John Stambaugh, of Youngstown. He came to Liberty township in 1832 and settled upon a farm in the southeastern part of the township. He died in 1880. There were eleven children in the family, five of whom are living. Mrs. Beaver is still living. Mr. George Beaver has always lived in the county, residing in Hubbard twelve years and the remaining time in Liberty township. Farming has been his chief business, though he has been engaged in the stock and sheep business more or less. He was married in October, 1867, to Miss Rebecca D. Miller, daughter of Jacob Miller, of Liberty township. They have three children. Mr. Beaver has been township trustee two years, also school director and member of board of education.

John Walters was born in Germany December 9, 1820. He came to America about 1848, and at once came to Ohio and located in Warren, Trumbull county, residing here one year, then went to Youngstown, living there about twelve months, then to Liberty township, where he was engaged in the coal business for a short time, then came to Girard and went into mercantile business, in which he remained till his death, which was accidentally caused by the explosion of kerosene oil, December 10, 1861, leaving a family of nine children and a widow to mourn his loss. He was a member of the Lutheran church and was highly esteemed by his fellow-townsmen. He was married in 1846 to Miss Sophia Bishop, daughter of Jonas Bishop. She was born in 1826.

George Lotze was born in Germany in 1830, and came to America in 1850 landing in New York. He lived in Rochester and vicinity about two years, then moved to Sharon, Pennsylvania, where he resided three years, being employed as an engineer and manager in furnace in the meantime. He then came to Ohio in 1855 and worked one year in Vienna at his trade—blacksmithing. He then moved to Weathersfield township, living here one year, and in 1857 came to Girard and has since resided here. He is now engaged in the jewelry business in connection with the drug business, being assisted by his son. He was married in 1853 to Miss Catharine Kick, daughter of Henry Kick, of Germany. They have had seven children, six of whom are living. Mr. and Mrs. Lotze are members of the German Reform church. He is a member of the Knights of Pythias. Politically, a sound Democrat.

T. F. Hawley, a well known druggist of Girard, was born in Painesville, Ohio, in 1840. His father, Cyrus A. Hawley, was born in Fairfield county, Connecticut, and came to Painesville in 1834, and was among the first business men of the town. He was engaged in the drug business in Painesville till 1853, and then traveled six years through the South for a firm in Philadelphia. He came to Girard in 1867. Mr. T. F. Hawley has been engaged in the drug business at Girard since 1867. He was married in 1865 to Miss Flora Spencer, daughter of H. N. Spencer, of Geauga county, Ohio. They have two children. Mr. Hawley has been postmaster ten or twelve years, and is at the present time. He is a member of the Masonic lodge at Youngstown. He was in the Nineteenth Ohio infantry three months, and afterwards in the Forty-first Ohio, and served throughout the war, enlisting in 1861 and discharged in 1865. Mr. Hawley may well take pride in his military record. He was wounded six times and carries as many scars to this day.

Frederick Krehl, an enterprising business man of Girard, was born in Germany in 1840, and came to America in 1853. He at once came to Ohio and located in Canfield, Mahoning county, where he resided about four years, and then went to Poland township, remaining two years, when he came to Girard, where we now find him extensively engaged in the tannery business, employing between thirty-five and forty men most of the time. He rebuilt the tannery he now occupies in 1860, though he has made many additions, thus making one of the largest tannery establishments in northeastern Ohio. He was married in 1861 to Miss Sanzenbacher, daughter of Jacob Sanzenbacher, of Lawrence county, Pennsylvania. By this union there were three children. Mrs. Krehl died in 1870, and Mr. Krehl was married in 1872 to Miss Mary Krehl, daughter of Frederick Krehl, of Indiana. There were three children by this marriage. Mr. and Mrs. Krehl are members of the Lutheran church. Mr. Krehl is an active, wide-awake business man.

C. D. Goodrich was born in Hubbard in 1843. His father, Roswell Goodrich, was a native of Connecticut, and came to Ohio in 1838 or 1839, and settled in Hubbard, where he was engaged in a grist-mill until 1844, when he removed to Liberty township and purchased the Holliday mills. Mr. Goodrich resided here until 1852, then moved to Vienna township where he lived until his death, which occurred in 1853, aged seventy-three years. Mr. C. D. Goodrich, the subject of this sketch, came to Girard in March, 1860, and learned the cabinet-maker's trade, serving three years as an apprentice and one year as a journeyman, then began business for himself in 1864 in Hubbard and remained in it six months, then came back to Girard, where he has since been one of the active business men. He was married in 1864 to Miss Mary A. Keefer, daughter of John Keefer, of Mercer county, Pennsylvania. They have had seven children, six of whom are living. Mr. Goodrich is a Free Mason, Odd Fellow, and Knight of Pythias. He has been justice of the peace for ten years, also township trustee, and member of board of education; politically he is a Republican.

Dr. A. J. Brooks was born in Weathersfield township, Trumbull county, Ohio, September 11, 1844. His father, Thomas Brooks, a native of Ohio, is still living in Weathersfield. The family are among the early settlers of the township. Dr. Brooks studied medicine with Dr. Casper, of Niles, and graduated at the Cleveland Medical college in 1871, and has since practiced at Niles, Church Hill, and Girard, coming to the latter place in November, 1880. Dr. Brooks has a good practice and is well liked. He was married in 1873 to Miss Sylvia J. VanHorn, daughter of Abram VanHorn, of Carroll county, Ohio. They have two children, Hattie A. and Harvey T. Mr. and Mrs. Brooks are members of the Disciple church. He is a member of the Foresters; politically he is a Republican.

Isaac Hartzell, a well-known merchant of Girard, a member of the firm of Hartzell Bros., was born in Germany in 1851, and came to America in 1867, and at once came to Ohio and located at Girard, where he has been in business. The firm does an extensive business in dry goods, hats, caps, etc. He was married in 1877 to Miss Rachel Lambert, daughter of S. J. Lambert, of Kansas. They have one child, Blanche. In politics he is a Conservative. He is an active business man.

CHAPTER XIV.

VIENNA.

Vienna has a gently undulating surface and a fertile soil, consisting of clayey loam with some sand and gravel in places. Most of the land is free from excessive moisture, and is well adapted to agriculture and grazing. The drainage is by several small water-courses flowing toward all points of the compass.

The township is thickly populated and contains a large number of fine houses, large and well improved farms and other evidences of the thrift and prosperity of its farmers.

The mineral resources of Vienna have been found most valuable. A good quality of coal is found, and mining has been carried on quite extensively from 1868 until very recently. Quite a large mining village, which sprang up east of Vienna center, is now in a state of dilapidation, partly deserted, showing plainly that the coal interest is now on the wane, the best mines having been worked out.

Vienna center, a quiet and pretty country village, is on the mail route from Warren to Sharon. The place contains two churches, two hotels, four stores, a drug store, and a book store, as well as shops of various kinds. Brookfield station, on the Lake Shore & Michigan Southern road, three miles east, is the nearest railroad station for passengers. The Vienna branch of the New York, Pennsylvania & Ohio railroad passes near the village, but this road no longer runs passenger trains.

Vienna lies east of Howland township, north of Liberty, and south of Fowler. Brookfield adjoins it upon the east. Vienna is the fourth township in the second range.

SETTLEMENT.

The territory now known as Brookfield and Vienna was originally owned by Uriel Holmes, Ephraim Root, and Timothy Burr, of Connecticut. Mr. Holmes was principal agent, and in 1798 came out with a surveying party to lay out the farms. The part of the country chosen for the first settlement was Vienna. After spending some time here the party returned to the East, and in the spring of 1799 came again to Vienna bringing others with them, for the purpose of settlement. Isaac Flower and Dennis Palmer brought their families; no other families came until 1802.

Isaac Flower, according to good authority, made a permanent settlement in the year 1799. His second wife, the widow of Asa Foote, lived to be one hundred years old, and was the oldest person that ever died in the township. Dorothy Gates, mother-in-law of Solomon Payne, was the next oldest, and died at the age of ninety-nine. Lavinia Flower, daughter of Isaac and Bathsheba Flower, was the first white child born in Vienna. She was born in 1801, and died in 1881. She became Mrs. Steele and lived in Painesville, Ohio. Isaac Flower died in 1813, at the age of fifty-seven.

Levi Foote, step-son of Flower, came into this township early, but settled in Fowler.

Of Dennis Palmer but little is known, save that he was one of the surveying party in the employ of Mr. Holmes. Among this party was a young man named Samuel Hutchins, who had been brought up by Holmes. For his services rendered the surveyors he was allowed to choose one hundred acres from any part of the township. He selected land on the east and west

Ichabod Payne.

Mrs Betsy J. Payne

center road, three-fourths of a mile west of the place now known as Payne's corners; this was probably the first farm owned by any inhabitant of the township. In 1802 he married Freelove Flower, and settled upon his land, where he lived until too old to labor; then moved to Warren. His marriage was the first that took place in Vienna.

In 1802 Isaac Woodford and family settled south of the center on lot twenty-five. This made the third family in Vienna. They came from Connecticut by way of Pittsburg with ox teams and the old Yankee ox-cart, and the greater part of the way from Youngstown to Vienna, they were obliged to cut their way through the woods. Deacon Woodford, as he was generally called, was a pious, God-fearing man. At the age of twenty-four he united with the church in his native town, and throughout his life adhered to the motto, "As for me and my house, we will serve the Lord." After his arrival in the new settlement, he commenced holding regular religious services on the Sabbath. Up to this time there had been no religious meetings of any kind. He not unfrequently was the only one to take the lead in the meetings and the Sabbath-school. He was also instrumental in forming the Presbyterian church of Vienna. Deacon Woodford died at the age of sixty-four years.

The year 1802 also brought from Connecticut the families of Joel and Isaac Humason, Simeon Wheeler, Seth Bartholomew, and Sylvester Woodford. About the same time came Samuel Clinton, who located near the center. Joel and Isaac Humason settled on the farms now owned by George Patterson and Henry Fowler; Simeon Wheeler on the I. B. Payne farm; Woodford on the George Chamberlain farm; and Bartholomew on the Niles road. Some of these settlers had been in the township working upon their lands and preparing homes for their families every summer from 1798 until the time of their removal.

In 1803 or 1804 Samuel Lowrey and Samuel Lowery, Jr., settled on the Rogers farm west of the center. Other settlers of about the same period were Joseph and Abiel Bartholomew, Isaac Scott, William Clinton, and Calvin Munson. In 1805 these were followed by John Clark, Shelden Scofield, Andrew, Hugh, and

James Mackey, William Lafferty and his son John, Chauncy Hickox, and J. J. Truesdell. In 1807 Epenetus Rogers (one of the original surveying party) and Jesse Munson arrived. Few came in the years 1808-9-10. In 1811 Amasa Scoville and Job and Noah Wheeler settled.

Darius Woodford, who located on lot ten, a younger brother of Isaac Woodford, came to the township about the year 1804, and lived until he attained the ripe old age of eighty-eight years. He was among those who came in those very early days from Connecticut to Vienna, and by whose industry and energy the forests were converted into fruitful fields and comfortable homes, and a foundation laid for the present prosperity we find in all parts of the township. Mr. Woodford was one of the earliest temperance advocates in the township, and certainly this fact is worthy of record, for he lived when the times demanded for every half day of log-rolling or barn-raising a good quantity of whiskey. Those early pioneers were very friendly, and during the first years of the settlement liberally assisted each other in erecting houses, barns, stables. The people would turn out en masse and in a single day would perform wonders. It has been stated in a reminiscence given by I. B. Payne that when Samuel Hutchins' barn was struck by lightning the neighbors for quite a distance turned out, hewed the timber for another, framed it, raised the barn, put on the roof, and siding, shaving the shingles (from the tree) finishing it all up and hauling in a load of hay in a single day. The barn was 28 x 38 feet and is still standing and in good repair. He says a barn for Mr. Giddings and a house for Jared Spencer were built in the same way, one day for each building. These were in the west part of Brookfield township, which was then part of Vienna. These whole-souled men, generous to a fault, needed restraining influences of good men like the Woodfords to establish Christian principles for the coming generation.

James J. Truesdell, a native of Connecticut, came to the township in 1805, and settled in the southwestern part, where he remained until his seventy-seventh year, when he died in the year 1852. His was of the earliest families who came to the township. He was a prominent man of his day, and served as justice of the peace in all about eighteen years.

His son, Harry Truesdell, now residing a short distance north of Vienna center, is a representative of former times, having been born the 20th of August in the year 1799, and is now in the eighty-third year of age. In 1834 he was married to Miss Emeline Woodford, the oldest living representative of Deacon Woodford, and a relative of Governor Woodford of Connecticut. Mr. Truesdell served as justice of the peace twenty-one years between 1842 and 1872.

Mr. and Mrs. Truesdell are in the enjoyment of remarkable health and strength of mind for people of their age. They possess powers of recollection to a remarkable degree, and have been useful members of society in their long earthly sojourn in this land.

The foregoing list gives the names of those early settlers who came at a time when the township was an unbroken forest, abounding in all kinds of game—bear, wolves, deer, turkeys, etc.—from which the pioneers were supplied with all the meat they had. Rude cabins of logs were put up, covered with bark, greased paper serving in place of window-glass. Huge chimneys constructed of sticks and mortar, with a fire-place, served as a place to cook their frugal meals and to warm them, the light of the fire serving to light the whole cabin. Cabins being erected, the next thing was to clear some land, and they went at it with a will. The forest began to melt away before the woodman's ax and let the sun shine in and around the cabins. Corn was planted, but coons, squirrels, and other animals shared with the settlers, leaving but little oftentimes for the harvest. Wheat was sown afterwards and with better success, but the one great difficulty with the new comers was the need of a mill where wheat could be ground. The most convenient one in the whole country was at Beaver, Pennsylvania, and that was fifty miles away. The little settlement would send one of their number with an ox cart loaded with wheat made up by the different families, each sending a little, to be ground. This trip usually took about a week's time, but the journey was so long, tedious, and irksome, that the hand mill was resorted to. This mill was simply a large mortar into which the grain was put and pounded with a large pestle until fine enough for use. The block was cut from some huge tree, and then by burning and cutting away the center a large hole was made. The pestle was made from a sapling or piece of timber. The grain, after being pounded fine enough for cooking purposes, needed seasoning to render it palatable. For salt the settlers had to go to the salt springs in Weathersfield township with their kettles, and boil salt for a week or ten days, and then get but little.

About the year 1814 Alexander Stewart, from Center county, Pennsylvania, purchased quite a large tract of land in the southeast corner of the township and settled there with quite a large family. His descendants still living on the same lands are now quite numerous.

The settlement had received a serious back-set during the war with Great Britain, but after its conclusion many families arrived who, after hard labor, gained pleasant homes and prosperity.

ORGANIZATION.

In March, 1806, townships number four, in the first and second ranges, were separated from the remaining territory of Hartford and Vernon and constituted an election district under the name of Vienna. In 1810 this territory was divided and Vienna and Brookfield townships organized.

The commissioners of Trumbull county, on the 6th day of March, 1806, ordered that an election be held on the first Monday of April following at the house of Simon Wheeler, now Payne's corners. Accordingly the qualified electors met at the time and place appointed, and then and there proceeded to elect township officers. The meeting was called to order and elected Robert Hughes, chairman; Samuel Clinton and James Montgomery, judges; Dennis C. Palmer and Jacob Humason, clerks. The following is the ticket elected that day: Isaac Woodford, Isaac Flower, Jr., William Clinton, trustees; Robert Hughes, treasurer; Isaac Humason, constable; Dennis C. Palmer, township clerk; Samuel Hutchins, Robert Hughes, fence viewers; Joseph Bartholomew, Slevin Higby, overseers of the poor; Isaac Lloyd, lister; Isaac Lowrey, appraiser; Joel Humason, Jacob Middleswath, supervisors.

On the 7th day of July, 1809, Shelden Scofield was qualified as justice of the peace. The citizens of Brookfield obtained an order for the election of another justice to accommodate their part of the township; an election was held in July, 1809, and Robert Hughes, of Brookfield, was elected, and qualified on the 26th day of August the same year.

THE INDIANS

were quite numerous, though never troublesome, in the early years of the settlement. The forests lying between the Mahoning and Shenango rivers were favorite hunting-grounds with them. They left just before the war, and few, if any, ever returned.

HUNTING REMINISCENCES.

The pioneers of Vienna had the usual amount of trouble in keeping their hogs and sheep out of the clutches of the wild beasts. Unless sheep were put in strong pens every night some of the flock would surely be found missing in the morning. One Sunday Samuel Humason, who lived in the eastern part of the township, heard his hogs making a great outcry, and on going where they were saw a huge bear attacking them. He drove it away, then went to his neighbors, David Wheeler and Abner Alderman, both experienced hunters, and told them of the bear's actions. Both were soon on the ground with their dogs and guns. The dogs soon found the animal and the hunters killed it without much trouble. It weighed four hundred pounds and was the largest bear ever killed in Vienna.

One morning in summer two boys, Alfred Wheeler and Upson Andrews, were cutting brush, when they heard the squealing of a hog, and running to ascertain the cause, found that a large bear had killed a hog which had been allowed to run in the woods. At this time a Mr. Lewis, the owner of a large dog, was at Wheeler's house, and the boys having told him what they had seen he was anxious to give his dog a little experience in bear hunting. Accordingly he took his dog and went with Wheeler to see a dog-and-bear fight. When they reached the spot the bear was still enjoying his dinner of fresh pork, and seemed annoyed at being molested. Wheeler shot and wounded the bear, then Lewis let his dog go. The enraged beast gave the dog one blow with his strong paw, tearing nearly all the flesh from one side of his body, and having no further opposition, took to his heels and escaped.

Ring hunts were often engaged in, though but little game was killed on such occasions, on account of the great noise made by a large party of excited men, boys, and dogs. Notice of these hunts was usually given to all the neighbors in surrounding townships, and on the appointed day all who wished to engage in the hunt—and usually everybody who had received notice came —met at a certain place, selected leaders, and surrounded a large tract, sometimes a whole township, endeavoring to drive all the game within it toward a common point. It is strange that no serious accidents occurred where so many hunters were likely to shoot their bullets in almost every direction.

SOLDIERS OF THE WAR OF 1812.

The soldiers who left their homes in Vienna to serve in the War of 1812 were, as far as known —Captain, Asa Hutchins; privates, Isaac Humason, Chauncy Alderman, William Bartholomew, John Lafferty, Abijah T. Bolton, Isaac Woodford, Samuel Gleason, and probably some others.

FIRST EVENTS.

The first birth and the first marriage have already been mentioned.

The first death was that of Abiel Bartholomew, who was killed by a falling tree in January, 1805.

The first saw-mill was built by Samuel Lowery near the southwest corner of the township on Squaw creek.

The first store was opened in 1820, by Isaac Powers, at the center.

The first law-suit was tried before 'Squire Clinton in 1806. A wife entered complaint against her husband for maltreatment. Whiskey was the cause of the trouble.

The first orchard was set out by Simeon Wheeler on the I. B. Payne farm. Some of the trees are now fifty feet high and more than two feet in diameter. Fifty-six bushels of apples have been picked from a single tree.

The first frame building, a barn, was erected by Joel Humason, and the second frame barn by Simeon Wheeler. Both are still standing. Isaac Humason's frame house is said to have been the first erected in the township.

THE FIRST SCHOOLS.

The first school was taught a mile south of the centre in the summer of 1805, by Miss Tamar Bartholomew. It is stated that a hog-pen was temporarily used as a school-house. However this may be, it is certain that the building afterwards became a hog-pen. The following winter taught school in a log cabin on the farm of Samuel Clinton.

The first school-house built in the township was a frame building 20 x 26 feet, erected at the centre in 1806. Andrews Bushnell, of Hartford, taught a school in that house the following winter, it being the only school in the township. Now the township has eleven schools, all well filled with pupils.

THE PRESBYTERIAN CHURCH.

The organization of this society was effected by Rev. Thomas Robbins, a missionary from Connecticut, on the 22d of March, 1805, under the plan of union adopted by the Presbyterian and Congregational churches.

The original members were Isaac Flower, Rosanna Williams, Samuel Clinton, Ann Wheeler, Joseph and Sylvia Bartholomew, John and Lois Clark, Robert and Margaret Hughes, James and Jane Montgomery, and Isaac Woodford.

The meeting for the purpose of making the organization was held at the house of Samuel Clinton, where Ambrose Truesdell now lives, and for the first few years the services were held at private houses and school-houses. In 1810 Rev. Nathan B. Darrow was called to the pastorate of this society, and was installed as such the following year, and served four years, when he resigned in order to extend his usefulness as a missionary in Indiana. He returned in a few years, and labored both in the church and in the schools until his death, which occurred in 1828. He was born in New London, Connecticut, August 13, 1773, and spent his life as a faithful missionary of the gospel in the Western Reserve. Rev. John Core succeeded him in the pastoral charge, and was ordained at Youngstown as pastor over three churches—Youngstown, Vienna, and Brookfield. In 1830 Rev. Chester Birge was installed as pastor—November 17th—and remained until June, 1835, when he was succeeded by Rev. E. B. Chamberlain, who was installed in October, 1839.

In October, 1843, a call was made to Xenophon Betts, who was installed by the presbytery of Trumbull at Vienna. He served the congregation for nearly twenty-eight years, when his decease occurred, May 18, 1871.

On his funeral occasion the following resolution of respect was announced:

We acknowledge the grace and goodness of God in sparing our deceased brother to labor more than forty years in the work of the gospel ministry, enabling him to fulfil his course, setting us an example of Christian courtesy, patient continuance in well doing, devoted and self-sacrificing labor in his calling. In dying he leaves the church and people where he labored a precious legacy of Christian influence and of that faith which shall continue to speak to them long after their pastor's lips have been sealed in death.

The church was now for some time without a pastor, and among the supplies of this period were: Elder Wadsworth, of the Baptist church, Daniel Williams, and Willis Weaver.

On May 7, 1873, the present pastor, Rev. J. Rea Stockton, having been ordained April 24th of the same year by the Mahoning presbytery, at Canfield, was installed over the congregations of Vienna and Brookfield.

The first account of any officials of the church was in 1835, when Isaac Woodford was deacon; and in 1837 Samuel Hutchins appears in the records as deacon; the following year Dexter Clinton was elected to that office, and the following persons have served in that capacity since, namely: Daniel Griffis and Orris Woodford, 1839; John Treat, 1848; H. Truesdell, 1850; Ransom S. Deming, 1862; James G. Scott, 1871.

On the evening of January 18, 1853, the church building was burned down and everything in it destroyed, but they immediately began the present building, which was completed and dedicated May 3, 1854.

At a meeting held March 2, 1871, the following resolution was unanimously adopted:

Resolved, That this church adopt the Presbyterian form of government and discipline.

THE METHODIST CHURCH.

The Methodist Episcopal church of Vienna is quite an old organization but we have been unable to learn when the first class was formed. Meetings were held in the southwestern part of the township quite early, and the place came to be known as Methodist corners, a name which it still bears. Timothy B. Clark was an original member and a class-leader. A church was built at the corners. Ira Bartholomew, Elisha Booth, Maria Fuller, and Andrew Mackey were early members.

About 1820 Vienna became a circuit and was regularly supplied. Revs. Adams and Dunham were among the preachers of those days. The present meeting-house at the center was erected

Mrs. Eliza Numason.

about 1850. The society for many years has been large, strong, and flourishing.

THE CATHOLIC CHURCH.

Soon after the coal fields of Vienna began to be largely developed the advent of quite a body of foreigners caused the erection of a Catholic church east of the center. The Catholics, now much diminished in number, continue to have occasional services in this house.

THE CEMETERY.

The old cemetery at the center is the resting-place of many of the pioneers of Vienna. Root and Holmes, proprietors of the land of the township, donated to the Presbyterian church two acres to be used as a burial-place. The remains of Abiel Bartholomew were the first buried in this cemetery. His death occurred in 1805. Common flag-stone was the material used for the first head-stones. Rude lettering and still ruder attempts at ornamentation can still be seen upon some of these old stones, but the devastating hand of time has already rendered many inscriptions illegible. Costly monuments of polished marble and granite now stand side by side with these humbler testimonials of respect to the memory of those who for long years have been resting here—their generous toil and life's task completed.

In 1872 the old ground being nearly all filled, it was thought advisable to enlarge the size of the yard, and an additional acre of ground was according purchased.

ODD FELLOWS.

Trumbull lodge No. 532, Independent Order of Odd Fellows, Vienna, Ohio, was instituted July 24, 1872, with the following charter members: R. H. Law, J. L. Russell, H. H. Carey, J. B. McNaughton, H. Bittaker, George Young, L. Horn, W. Crollman, David Wilson, John P. Rosser, I. A. Beggs, John Bowen, A. C. Burnett, and E. E. Folsom. The first officers were I. A. Beggs, N. G.; J. B. McNaughton, V. G.; D. H. Wilson, secretary; J. L. Wilson, permanent secretary; and H. H. Carey, treasurer. The number who have been initiated as members of the lodge since its formation up to March, 1882, is one hundred and five. Fifteen or twenty have also been admitted by card. The number of members in good standing is sixty-two.

ROYAL TEMPLARS OF TEMPERANCE.

Enterprise council No. 15, Royal Templars of Temperance, was organized September 12, 1879, with fifteen members, and the following were elected officers: Lucius H. Hatch, S. C.; G. A. Treat, V. C.; W. I. Stewart, P. C.; W. H. Terry, recording secretary; N. C. Terry, financial secretary, and G. A. Treat, treasurer. The present membership is forty-two.

TEMPLE OF HONOR.

Laurel Temple of Honor and Temperance was formed in 1877. On the 30th of July a charter was granted to fifteen charter members. The first officers were as follows: J. B. Kingsley, W. C. T.; A. I. Powers, W. V. T.; Henry Powers, W. R.; J. L. Russell, W. A. R.; J. S. Bard, W. F. R., and K. Wortman, W. T. About sixty-five members of the order are now in good and regular standing, and the organization is in a healthy condition.

The Social Temple, a branch of the Temple of Honor, was formed in July, 1881, and is also prosperous.

COAL MINING.

The coal mines of this township have yielded a large return to their owners and operators in years past, but the chief ones are now nearly or quite exhausted. Coal mining was begun in this township about sixteen years ago. On the completion of the Vienna branch railroad to this township in 1869 the coal-fields began to be largely developed. In that year the Vienna Coal company, representing a capital stock of $300,000, opened Vienna mines numbers one and two, and soon were giving employment to three hundred men and producing four hundred to six hundred tons daily. The principal mining operations in this township have been carried on by the Vienna Coal company and by C. H. Andrews & Co.

The first mine was opened on a corner of Hampton Kerr's farm. I. B. Mackey was the contractor and sank the shaft.

Banks are being opened and some are still working, but probably the most valuable deposits are worked out.

MANUFACTURE OF RAKES.

The manufacture of revolving horse-rakes at the center of Vienna is an industry of considerable importance. The business was begun September 2, 1872, by Woodford, Humason & Co. The building occupied was formerly a planing-mill, which was rebuilt and enlarged by this firm. The following February the establishment was bought by Mrs. J. A. Humason, who has since conducted the business. From $8,000 to $12,-000 worth of horse-rakes and harrows are made and sold yearly. The industry is prosperous and the products find a ready sale in all parts of the country. About twelve men are employed on an average.

BIOGRAPHICAL SKETCHES.

ICHABOD B. PAYNE.

I. B. Payne was a prominent and influential citizen and a representative of one of the oldest families in Vienna township. His father, Soloman Payne, was a native of Amenia, Dutchess county, New York, and was born August 23, 1782. He was married to Polly Gates and removed to the Reserve, having purchased the farm on which Simeon Wheeler had made one of the first settlements in the township. Dortha Gates, Mrs. Payne's mother, at the time of her death, January 7, 1855, was the oldest person in the county, being in her centennial year. Solomon Payne died October 22, 1857. Polly Payne, his wife, died April 24, 1862, in her seventy-second year. The family consisted of seven children: David R. settled in Lawrence county, Ohio; Almon L. settled in Jefferson county, Indiana; Charlotte was married to Benjamin Brainard, who lived in Gustavus township; Elihu R. settled in Jefferson county, Indiana; Sally L. was married to Alfred Russell, and is the only one living—her home is at Clear Point, Ashtabula county; Theophilus G. settled in Jefferson county, Indiana; Ichabod B., the youngest son who grew to maturity, was born in Vienna township, February 18, 1824; he attended the district school till his eighteenth year and then began teaching; he taught about twenty terms in Brookfield, Weathersfield, Hartford, and Vienna townships. As a teacher he was held in high regard wherever known. Large and dignified, he governed a school with ease, and long practice made him efficient in giving instruction.

Mr. Payne married December 18, 1848, Betsy Jane Vinton. She was a daughter of John and

Sally Vinton, and was born March 10, 1826. Her parents removed to Brookfield township from Rochester, New York. They had ten children, seven girls and three boys, seven of whom are living: Mary (Alderman), deceased; Elcena (Miner), resident of Bloomfield; Hiram, Mercer county, Pennsylvania; Betsy Jane (Payne); Aaron, Vienna; Almira (Roy), Mercer county, Pennsylvania; Eliza (Snyder), Hartford; Harriet, died single; Arnitha (Seaburn), deceased; Homer resides in Brookfield. John Vinton was born August 7, 1794; he married Sally Madison January 13, 1820. She was born June 30, 1801, and still resides in Vienna.

Ichabod B. Payne was chosen from time to time to fill the several offices of his township, being justice of the peace several terms. In 1867 the Republican county convention placed him in nomination for county commissioner, an office to which he was elected, and again re-elected in 1869. He took to the office good business talent, and gave close and conscientious attention to the public affairs. During the war Mr. Payne took an active part in the recruiting service, and when Cincinnati was threatened by Kirby Smith with a strong rebel force, he hurried to the danger point in obedience to the call of Governor Tod, being one of that unorganized force known as "squirrel hunters." He contributed considerable time and money to clear the township of draft, and altogether his record was highly creditable. In politics Mr. Payne was an active and working Republican, and in religion was a Disciple. His connection with that denomination covered a period of twenty-two years. In appearance he was striking, being six feet four and a half inches tall, and well proportioned, having an average weight of two hundred and fifty pounds. He was always industrious, painstaking, and reliable in everything in which he engaged, whether private business or public affairs. He left at his death besides the record of an honorable life a competence for his family.

The family of I. B. and Mrs. Payne consists of four children—Jerusha P., wife of Benton Williams; Almon W., married to Rilla Card and lives in Vienna; Ellen G., and Cornelia M.

Mrs. Payne lives on the old homestead at Payne's corners, a place thus named on account of the prominence of this family.

JAMES J. AND ELIZA HUMASON.

James Julius Humason was born in the city of Hartford, Connecticut, September 27, 1801. His parents, James and Honor Humason, removed from Connecticut to Ohio and settled in Brookfield township. Their family consisted of Leonard, Henrietta, Maria, James J., Mary, and Laura Sterne. Soon after his settlement in Brookfield Jacob Humason died, and the family removed to Vienna, where Mrs. Humason died August 3, 1843, aged seventy-three years.

James Julius Humason taught district school and followed other employments in the summer. He was married April 12, 1829, to Eliza Woodford, a daughter of Darius and Bathiah Woodford. This introduces us to one of the largest and most respected families in the township. Four of the sons of Isaac Woodford settled in Trumbull county. Isaac, Jr., was for many years deacon in the Vienna Presbyterian church; he had a family of fourteen children. Sylvester Woodford had thirteen children; he removed from Vienna to Sandusky county in 1832 and died the following year. Sidney settled in Farmington township and afterwards removed to Mantua; he was one of the founders of West Farmington seminary. Darius was born at the old family seat in Farmington, Connecticut, in the year 1780. He was married in Connecticut to Bathiah Bass, and in 1805 removed to Vienna. Six of the family of thirteen children came to maturity, viz: Eliza (Humason), Celarcia (Hayes), Sophronia (McClung), Henry, Mary, and Darius. Mr. Woodford died March 28, 1867; Mrs. Woodford died December 11, 1877, aged ninety-three years.

Eliza, the oldest daughter, was born January 10, 1810. She attended district school and received instruction at Warren. The year 1828 she spent at Hartford and attended part of the time the seminary at that place while Catherine Beecher was principal and Harriet Beecher Stowe assistant. Mrs. Humason expresses preference for the former but retains a warm admiration of both these illustrious women. After leaving the seminary she learned the milliner and dressmaking trade in Hartford. The following year she was married and settled with her husband on the farm which she still owns, and which was given to her by her father. Mr. Humason taught school and gave some attention to the farm

during his lifetime. Since his death, which occurred April 13, 1853, the entire management has devolved upon his widow. She is a woman of extraordinary energy and strength; is intelligent and possesses a correct and radical judgment. She is a persistent temperance advocate. On the temperance question her family have a record. Her uncle, Deacon Sidney Humason, organized the first temperance society in the county, and one of the first in the State, in the year 1827. He soon prevailed upon his brothers and neighbors to abandon the free use of whiskey and gradually worked a revolution in public opinion on that topic. Mrs. Humason joined her uncle's society and her chief source of pride in the family is founded on the fact that none of them were drunkards. She hopes to have the privilege of casting a vote in favor of total abolition of the traffic.

James J. and Eliza Humason have had a family of four children—Celarcia is married to Miles Munson and lives in Fowler township; J. Eliza died in childhood; Martha Jerusha married Henry Fowler and lives in Vienna; James Henry married Juliette A. Betts and lives in Vienna.

SETTLEMENT NOTES.

Harry Truesdell was born in Connecticut in 1799, and came with his father, J. J. Truesdell, to Trumbull county in 1805, locating in Vienna township; married Miss Emaline Woodford in 1834. No children. Mr. Truesdell served as justice of the peace for twenty-one years; township clerk several years. Mr. Truesdell is excelled by few in correct business habits.

John Treat came from Milford, Connecticut, where he was born in 1795, to Trumbull county, in 1818, locating where Mr. Alexander Stewart now resides, in Vienna township. He married Miss Mary Humason in 1820. The names of their children are as follows: Elizabeth A. Bushnell, residing in Johnston township; Sidney C., residing in Hazelton; G. A., residing in Vienna township; one died in infancy; Mary E., died in 1865; Julius, died in 1858. Mr. Treat is now one of the oldest and most respected men in Vienna, having been a consistent member of the Presbyterian church since 1852.

J. H. Humason, born in Vienna in 1839,

married Miss Juliette A. Betts, and has five children—Martha, at home; James H., Charles, John, and Frank. Three died young. Mr. Humason is proprietor of the rake factory which was established in 1879, and employs from ten to fifteen hands; manufactured in 1880 about three thousand rakes. Present capacity about four thousand per annum. The rake manufactured by the Vienna Rake company is of superior quality and excellent finish, being manufactured from the best of slack timber. One of the most important features of this rake is the substitute of the steel spring by which the rake is completely under the control of the operator.

Calvin Munson was born near New Haven, Connecticut, in 1769. He came to Vienna township, Trumbull county, in September, 1804, locating on the farm now owned by his son Randil. He married Miss Sarah Hungelford. The fruits of this union were five children—Randil, residing in Vienna township; Killson, dead; Lucy Scoville, dead; Diadamia Reader, residing in Ashtabula county; Susanna Newbern, residing in Iowa. Randil Munson married Miss Lucinda Loveland in 1819. They have four children living—H. B., in Wisconsin; Erpi, residing in Bazetta township; H. N., in Mecca township; Charles, died in the army; and A. C. Mr. Munson has always been a farmer, and has worked on the farm where he now resides, ever since his first settlement in the county. He is the oldest settler (1881) now living in Vienna township.

R. Bartholomew, born August 13, 1831, in Vienna township, removed with his father to Cuyahoga county, when three years of age, where he remained until he was twenty-two years old, when he returned to Warren, where he resided fifteen years; returned again to Cleveland, where he was engaged in contracting about seven years, whence he returned to Vienna township, where he now resides. He married Miss Phila E. Truesdell, 1854. They have eight children: Ida A. Gillson, resides in Chicago; C. J., in Vienna; Mary E. Wemberg, Chicago; Milton O., William S., Frank P., Susan M., Eugene E., at home.

Isaac Woodford, Sr., came from Connecticut to Trumbull county in 1802, locating on the farm now owned by Albert Powers, Vienna township. He married Miss S. Cowles. There were twelve children; ten grew to maturity. Mr. Woodford was elder of the Presbyterian church from the time of its organization. His son Isaac married Miss Phebe E. Merritt. The names of their children are as follows: Frank, residing in Kansas; Jerusha M. Sanford, resides in Vienna; Isaac W., in Vienna; Lovilla M. Struble, dead; Eliza and Martha E. died young. Mr. Woodford has always been a farmer, having resided on the same farm forty-eight years.

Timothy Norton came from near Hartford, Connecticut, in 1819, locating in Vienna township. He married Annie Humason. They had eight children; six grew to maturity—Mrs. H. Greenwood, residing in Vienna township; Mrs. Nancy Greenwood, in Pennsylvania; Merit, in Vienna.

Merit Norton, born in Trumbull county in 1822, married, first, Diadamia Cratsley. Their children are: Edson, residing in Pennsylvania; Luther, in Akron; Rosaline Lampson, in Pierpoint, Ohio; Celestia Cowan, in Cortland; Emerson, at home; Allie, at home. Mr. Norton married for his second wife Mrs. Betsey Wilson; no children. Mr. Norton has never been an aspirant for office, preferring the quiet and independent life of a farmer. He has resided on the same farm twenty-nine years. His son Charlie was accidentally shot and killed August 27, 1879.

John Greenwood came from Massachusetts in 1813, locating where his son, Nathaniel C., now resides. He married Sarah Webster. They had eleven children, six only living: Nathaniel C., residing in Vienna township; Harriet, in Fowler; Morgan, in Fowler; Betsey, in Vienna; Oliver died in Indiana in 1879; Frank died in Indiana in 1880; the other children died young. Nathaniel C. Greenwood was born in Massachusetts in 1809. He married Miss Ladora A. Wright in 1833. They had four children, as follow: Leander, residing in Fowler; Hiram, in Howland; Holmes, in Vienna; Ellen Rogers, in Vienna. Mr. Greenwood followed the occupation of a gunsmith over five years. He is now engaged in farming.

Andrew Mackey, a native of Ireland, came into Trumbull county in 1805. He married Miss Mary Murray. They had six children, none of whom are now living. Andrew Mackey, Jr., was born in Bucks county, Pennsylvania, in

1779. He married Miss Jane Scott. They had seven children, six of whom are living, viz: Mary, residing on the old homestead; James; John died in 1853, aged twenty-eight years; Eleanor Munson, residing in Vienna; Robert, residing in Howland; A. H. residing in Vienna; Elizabeth, residing in Vienna. Mr. Mackey was one of the most enterprising farmers of Vienna township, having two hundred and twenty-five acres of land under cultivation at the time of his death.

Abraham Wartman was born in Pennsylvania in 1768 and came to Vienna in 1827, locating on the farm now owned by his son Solomon. He married Miss Ann M. Rhodes. They had eleven children, six of whom are living, viz: Catherine Hake, residing in Missouri; Rebecca Hake, residing in Vienna; Solomon, residing in Vienna; Sarah Shaffer, residing in Howland; Elizabeth Wehrenberger, residing in Lordstown; Rachael Hake, residing in Missouri; Marie Hake died in 1877; Jonathan, Abraham, Matthias, and Henry, are also dead. Solomon Wartman married Miss Louisa L. Whitten in 1839, September 27th. Five of their children are living: Cline, residing in Vienna; Elizabeth A. Hulse resides in Illinois; Solomon resides in Vienna; Mary A. is at home; Louisa L., Lucy, and James are dead. Mr. Wartman is a tanner by trade, having learned the trade from his father, but is now engaged in farming. He pays special attention to stock raising, dealing principally in fine stock, especially fine wooled sheep. He is also proprietor of the old saw-mill, which is located near his home.

Archibald McFarland came from Washington county, Pennsylvania, in 1808, into Vienna township. He married Miss Amelia Ball, by whom he has twelve children. The names of those living are Harvey, residing in Summit county; Robert, residing in Iowa; John, residing in Hartford township; Archie, residing in Fowler township; Emily A. married Edwin Griffin in 1850, has two children, and lives in Vienna township; Erastus and Augusta A. at home. Mr. Griffin was a natural mechanic, being able to make anything in wood and iron. He died in 1860, aged twenty-nine years. He was a man of remarkably even temper, never known to be thrown off his guard.

Joseph Rogers was born on Long Island in 1788, came to Trumbull county in 1812 and settled in Vienna township. He was drafted from Vienna in the War of 1812 and served in that war. He carried on a tannery in Vienna, also shoemaking in connection with farming. Later in his life he conducted a hotel at Vienna. After the War of 1812 he married Lydia Lowry and raised a family of two daughters and six sons all of whom are living. He lived to the advanced age of ninety-three, dying in 1881. His son, Royal L. Rogers, was born in Vienna, Trumbull county, Ohio, January 9, 1820. With his brother he began keeping hotel, and in 1834 was married to Caroline, daughter of Samuel Wise, an early settler in Youngstown, where Mrs. Rogers was born January 29, 1827. After marriage he continued in the hotel business and for sixteen years was located at Johnson centre. He resided in Ashtabula county for two years. In the spring of 1874 he came to Warren where he now resides. He is the owner of a large farm in Ashtabula county and another in Weathersfield, Trumbull county. He is the father of three children, Amarillis, James C., with his father in business, and Alley R., now a student at Oberlin College.

CHAPTER XV.

NEWTON.[*]

This is the extreme southwest township of the county, town three north, and range five. It lies immediately south of Braceville, with Lordstown on the east, Mahoning county south, and Portage county on the west; and contains fourteen thousand nine hundred and forty-six acres of land. The east branch of the Mahoning river (locally known as East river) extends from south to north across the township west of the central line. Kale creek, a tributary of the East river, flows from the southwest corner. The west branch of the Mahoning, called West river, flows across the northwest corner. Duck creek extends from south to north across the township along the western part. The township being thus well watered, and having much bottom land with rolling surface between the streams, the

*The thanks of the historian are due Dr. J. F. Porter, of Newton Falls, for much of the data contained in this sketch.

58*

agricultural advantages are superior, and it may be classed above the average township in the county. The usual products are found in abundance here, while great quantities of white oak ship-timber are exported from this locality for ship-building and other manufacturing purposes.

POPULATION.

The township has three distinct settlements— Deer Creek, the " River," and Newton Falls— which were more marked in early times than at present.

There is but one incorporated town, Newton Falls, in the township, in and around which the population and business interests now center.

According to the census reports of 1860 and 1870 the population decreased during that decade from fourteen hundred and ninety-six to twelve hundred and eighty, but in 1880 it increased again to thirteen hundred and fifty-eight.

ORGANIZATION AND PROPRIETORSHIP.

The township was organized in 1808, but having a larger political jurisdiction than at present, embracing Milton, now of Mahoning county, and Lordstown, in the same voting precinct under the same jurisdiction. This is evident from the fact that in 1814 John Johnson, of Milton, was elected justice of the peace and filed the date of his commission with the clerk of Newton; and as late as 1826 the road funds and job road work of Lordstown were under the control of the Newton trustees. Justin Ely, Elijah White, and Jonathan Brace were the original proprietors who drew this township in the partition made of the Western Reserve. On the 10th of December, 1800, they associated themselves with Roger Newberry, Enoch Perkins, and Jonathan Brace, who were the proprietors of Braceville, and made the conveyance of the lands of Newton as further described in the history of Braceville township. Why the township was called Newton is not now known, unless it was so called in honor of Sir Isaac Newton, the great philosopher.

At the time of the organization of the township (1808), a book was opened for the purpose of registering "ear-marks of cattle, sheep, and hogs. From this register are gleaned the following names of settlers in the township at that time: E. Hover, Robert Caldwell, Nathaniel Stanley, George L. Davison, Jacob Custard, Leonard Miller, George

Sheffelton, John Lane, Benjamin Davison, James Huffstetter, Daniel Dull, Jacob Winans.

JUSTICES OF THE PEACE.

The first justice, Benjamin Davison, was elected in 1808, and the following persons have been elected to that office in the township: Daniel Dull, 1810; G. L. Davison, 1813–16; John Johnson, 1814; Bildad Hine, 1814–17, and 1830; Dr. Tracy Bronson, 1819; Ezekiel, Hover, 1820–23; Stephen Oviatt, 1825–28; Charles Adgate, 1829; Alexander Sutherland, 1832–34; Austin Parker, 1833; Samuel Oviatt, Jr., 1834; William Porter, 1836–39; H. Hinman, 1838; Hiram Austin, 1838; U. D. Kellogg, 1841; J. I. Todd, 1842–45.

In 1826 the election of justice of the peace was contested between Ezekiel Hover and Stephen Oviatt before a jury and Hervey Stow, Esq., of Braceville, which resulted in favor of Oviatt on account of illegal voting. The second was between the same parties before Milton Rogers, of Milton, and resulted in the same way. The third contest between these parties is supposed to have resulted in favor of Oviatt, as the records do not show that Hover held a commission afterwards.

THE RIVER SETTLEMENT.

Perhaps a short time prior to the Duck creek settlement, a settlement was made on the Mahoning river in the present vicinity of Pricetown—now Callender's mills.

Jesse Halliday, Robert Caldwell, William and Nathaniel Stanley, David Carlile, Daniel Dull, Mr. Allen, and Benjamin Davison with their families composed this little colony.

Jesse Halliday paddled a canoe from Warren in about 1805, as far as the south line of Newton township, and finding rapids here, concluded he could build a mill which was in operation in 1807, and stood on the site of the present Callender mills (at Pricetown). This mill, however, being necessarily an imperfect structure, was often incapable of supplying the wants of the settlers, thus subjecting them to great inconvenience, as Garrettsville was the nearest mill, fifteen miles away. This, in the absence of any road except a blazed route, was something of a journey for a boy with his grist on horseback.

The Indians, owing to the trouble with the whites, were at this time fast leaving the country.

Their place of general rendezvous, salt springs, was readily reached from this settlement by the Indian trail, thus affording an important accommodation to the settlers in the way of procuring salt, as supplies had to be imported from Cleveland, or New Lisbon, twenty-five miles south.

The first marriage in this locality was Thomas McCoy to Polly Moore, and the first death was a child of Peter Decoursey.

In 1805 Isaac Hutson, from Huntingdon county, Pennsylvania, settled on Kale creek with a family of five sons and six daughters, and in 1811 John Hutson settled in the Lane neighborhood. Both had a large family of boys and girls. The boys were all good marksmen and "full-hands" at a hunt or shooting-match, and most of their names are found as contestants in a shooting-match on Christmas at Newton Falls, where Bildad Hine took this method of closing out his stock of goods—the first brought to the falls.

CHURCH AT "RIVER" SETTLEMENT.

The first Presbyterian church was organized in 1808 with a membership of seven—William Stanley and wife, John Sutherland and wife, Polly Wilson, Mrs. Davison, and Mrs. Gilmer.

After the death of Rev. Boyd, Rev. Hughes, from Beaver, preached occasionally, and Rev. Joshua Beer followed as next regular pastor. In 1809 the two settlements (Duck Creek and "River") united and built the frame church, which was removed a few years ago over into Milton township.

DUCK CREEK SETTLEMENT.

Alex. Sutherland settled at Duck Creek in 1802, and the only meat the family had the first year was deer and bear meat, furnished by the Indians in exchange for bread. The cabin in which he moved was made by setting posts in the ground, covered with bark on the sides and roof, and quilts hung up for doors.

There were five or six Indian camps near this cabin, and at one time an Indian chief named Kiogg came into the Sutherland cabin drunk and made threats of shooting some of them, but Ezekiel Hover broke a chair over his head, and another chief named Nickshaw afterwards settled the difficulty.

Alex. Sutherland and Ezekiel Hover marked the first path from Duck Creek settlement to Youngstown, to reach the nearest mill, a distance of almost twenty miles. Their nearest post-office was Warren—eight miles. Bears and wolves were very plenty, and the settlers were compelled to carry torches and keep their sugar-camp fires burning to keep them away.

Mr. Sutherland was elected county recorder soon after his arrival here. His son James carried the mail from Warren to Canton when there was no house from Duck Creek to Warren, or Quinby hill as it was then called. His son John, while mowing on the farm of E. Hover, cut off the head of a yellow rattlesnake seven and a half feet long. He skinned the reptile and made a cap of part of the hide, and Mr. Hover took a part for a shot pouch. The colors of the skin were very brilliant, being a light green and pale yellow, and glittered in the sunshine.

Ezekiel Hover built the first saw-mill where George Johnston's mill now stands.

James Gilmer and family settled in this locality April 30, 1807. The cabin home, which occupied the site of the present barn of John R. Johnson on the east bank of Duck creek, had been erected and roofed the previous autumn, and had served as shelter to a squad of Indians during the winter.

The settlement consisted of the following families: Thomas Reed, Peter Decoursey, Alexander Sutherland and his father, John, George Sheffelton, John Mashman and son, Alexander Mashman, Jacob Custard. Ezekiel Hover was then a young man holding the office of county surveyor.

SCHOOLS AT DUCK CREEK.

For several years after the first settlements were made the necessity for every man, woman, and child to assist in all kinds of labor, together with the scarcity of money, put the matter of school privileges out of the question. About 1812 or 1813 a log school-house was erected a short distance below where the saw-mill of G. R. Johnson now stands. It was a log cabin with rough stone chimney; a foot or two cut from the logs here and there admitted light through greased paper over the holes. A huge fire-place, puncheon floor, a few benches made of split logs, the flat side up, and a well-developed "birch," constituted all the requirements of the pioneer school-house. The first teacher was a young man by the name of Brooks, who received a compensation of $10 per month, payable in wheat, rye, or corn.

The usual methods of training the youthful minds common in early times were employed in these pioneer schools. The attendance of the scholars was necessarily irregular, and the appliances for imparting knowledge were exceedingly meager. Notwithstanding all this, however, it is found that the graduates from the log cabin colleges were good farmers, many of them adepts in mathematics, zealous and able ministers of the gospel, and successful business men.

RELIGIOUS ORGANIZATIONS.

The pioneers of Newton were not long without public religious exercises. John Sutherland, Sr., soon called those of his neighbors of like inclination, and organized a weekly prayer-meeting, which met alternately at the different houses. In the summer of 1808 Rev. James Boyd, a Presbyterian minister who was sent as a missionary to the Western Reserve from New England, found his way to the River settlement, preaching the first gospel sermon in the township, in the open air, on the farm now owned by Joseph G. Strock. An effort was then made to secure the services of Rev. Boyd as minister to the River and Duck Creek settlements and Warren, which was successful. He spent his life in ministerial labor with his people, and was laid to rest near the spot where he delivered his first sermon to the pioneers of Newton, in March, 1813. It is related of him that once as he was riding from this place to Warren to fill his appointment that day—it being Sunday—he happened to glance backward and saw a wolf following fast on his track. He put spurs to his horse, and on the way dashed through a swollen stream which otherwise would have been unfordable, and but for the wolf the congregation at Warren would have been without a preacher that day.

DISTILLERY.

In 1816 Stephen Oviatt moved his distillery from Braceville ridge, and established it in a rock excavation, where water was plenty, near the present site of Eagle mills. In 1818, with Bildad Hine as partner, it was moved to the east of the river to what has been known as the Patterson farm, and about 1823, seeking a central location, a brick distillery was erected on the Joseph Wilson

farm, which finally came into the possession of Judge Price.

INCIDENTS.

In 1813 the citizens of Newton and Braceville agreed to co-operate in procuring a supply of salt, and Newton furnished a wagon and one yoke of oxen, which were procured of John Lane. Braceville furnished a second pair, which constituted the joint team. A third pair of oxen were sent by Edmund Oviatt to trade for the salt at Fairport. Bildad Hine was selected as agent and ox driver, and after a week's absence returned alone on foot to the settlement and reported that he had traded the oxen for six barrels of salt, but that in crossing Eagle creek below Garrettsville the wagon stuck in the mud. The next day the citizens turned out in force and with teams, shovels, hoes, etc., proceeded to Eagle creek and brought home the salt in triumph.

About the year 1818 Robert Price, afterwards judge, bought the Holliday mills and logically claimed Holliday's interest in the Presbyterian church near by; and finding one Parker, a Helsian preacher whose views were sufficiently liberal, Price engaged him to preach the share of the time belonging to him as a separate congregation. On one Sunday morning when Father Beer had occupied the pulpit, and during the usual intermission preceeding the afternoon services, Price said to Parker: "Now go over and take the stand, and when you are through singing and praying I will come over and hear you preach." Parker went but found that he was too late as the afternoon services had begun, and he took a seat in the audience. Presently Price came in and seeing the Helsian seated as a hearer only, and thinking probably that he had been refused the pulpit, cried out, "What the h—l does this mean?" and forthwith mounted the pulpit and brought the minister down, struggling, under his arm. He then said to Parker, "Now my little man go up there and preach." Elder John Craig attempting to interfere was promptly ejected from the house, after which it is inferred that the services were allowed to proceed.

INDIANS.

The early settlers were often annoyed and sometimes not a little in fear of the depredations of bands of Indians that wandered up and down the river. In 1809 the Indian chief Paqua, with his squaw and a tribe of ten or twelve Indians and a white boy encamped for some time opposite where Kistler's saw-mill now stands and spent some days in drying venison into "jerk;" and in 1816 two Cornplanter Indians, called Abram and Jonathan, spent some time and became familiarly known at Newton Falls. The only monument of this race (of which a more general history will be found elsewhere in this work) in this locality was known as the "Indian grave." It was a structure of stone, evidently erected by human hands and ingenuity; built in the shape of a cone, fifteen feet in diameter and ten feet high. When first discovered this elevation was heavily covered with a growth of hemlocks, and was situated on the rock bank of the west branch of the Mahoning river, a few rods above where Porter's flour mill now stands. This was a favorite place for holiday resort for the children until in quarrying for stone to build the canal the mound was destroyed.

WILD GAME.

Eagle mill-pond afforded a sliding place for the children of early days in their winter sports. On one occasion when Noble Hine and a number of other boys and girls were skating on this pond, a large buck took refuge from the dogs by running to the children on the ice. The dogs were driven away, and the young folks amused themselves by sliding around the deer and pulling his hair. He might have been very indignant at this treatment, but could not help himself on the slippery ice. After tiring of the fun the deer, being too lean for table use, was driven to the shore and allowed to escape.

On another occasion Mr. Yale saw a fine deer chased into the river. It sought safety in an open hole in the ice. He shut down his mill, and after driving away the dogs he crept out to the opening in the ice and the deer swam to him. He helped it out of the water, and putting his arm over its shoulders, went up the bank with the deer at his side. The neighbors soon gathered and were desirous of dispatching the deer, to which Mr. Yale positively objected because it had come to him for safety. He ordered all to stand back, and then stepping backward a few feet he slapped his hands and the deer bounded into the forest.

Jacob Miller had a hand to hand engagement with a large buck which he caught in his arms as it attempted to jump a fence, and held it until Captain John Sheffleton cut its throat, but all that was left of Miller's clothes was "collar and hames."

The last deer seen in the township was killed by Judge Porter in 1835, on land now owned by William Green in the east part of the township.

Venison formed a large part of the provision of the early settlers, and the books of Messrs. Hine & Yale show that for many years it was an article of common traffic at from one to three cents per pound; and buckskin was a *quasi* legal tender.

SETTLEMENT AT NEWTON FALLS.

The proprietor of the lands in the locality of Newton Falls was Judson Canfield, of New Haven, Connecticut, who early contemplated the building of a rural city near the falls on the Mahoning river, in order to utilize the immense water-power which the two branches of the Mahoning river here afforded. For the purpose of inducing settlement the land was surveyed into lots of ten acres each, in the year 1807, and immigration was earnestly invited.

In the autumn of this year John Lane built his log-cabin residence in the new city, on the bank of the West river, on what is now Martin's grocery lot. On the 16th of June Bildad Hine and family arrived and were welcomed with true pioneer hospitality into the mansion of Mr. Lane. For this emergency the house seemed to have been especially planned, as it was one story high, 16x18 feet in size, and contained ample accommodation for a family of thirteen. The milk-house belonging to this house is now in good condition, except the door, it being a cave in the rock, projecting over the river, at the rear of Stocking's wagon factory.

In the summer of 1808 a Mr. Canfield, with Mr. Ruggles, built a saw-mill where Allen Hoyle's woolen factory now stands, and, according to the recollection of Barney C. Allen, in February, 1811, started the first grist-mill, and ground the first grist of wheat for Joseph Allen, the flour being afterwards bolted at home through a hair sieve.

The mill-stones were quarried in what was then called "Redding hill," in Hiram township. A part of one of these stones now lies at the door of Porter & Son's flour-mill.

The first mill was burned down in December,

1817, by a drunken man who had taken lodging in it for the night, who was obliged to wade the frozen river to escape the fire. The mill was not rebuilt, but, in 1829, Horace and Augustus Stephens erected the old Eagle mills, on the opposite side of the river.

James F. Porter & Sons afterwards erected the present flouring-mill adjoining the old one; the drawings of which were made by William H. Porter, son of J. F., who sent the drawings to Wilcox, Shinkle & Miller, who from these drawings alone made the works ready to be put in place; sent them on and erected the mill.

From the ledger of Benjamin B. Yale it is shown that he came to Newton in 1808 from Canfield, to the house of Samuel Oviatt, and was engaged as mill-wright at one dollar per day; was at the erection of the first mill, and afterwards was engaged as miller for Canfield & Ruggles, then for Canfield & Gilson in 1812; and in 1813 and 1815 he charges John Lane for work done on the grist- and saw-mill.

In 1814 he worked for Jesse Halliday in his mill, now owned by J. M. Callender, on the south line of the township, and from December, 1816, to July, 1817, operated the Falls mill for one Hopkins. The latter had purchased the mill from Cornelius Duboise, of New York, who had came into possession from a Mr. Fluellen, who had become indebted to him (Duboise) for goods. It seems that Mr. Hopkins was not accustomed to pioneer life or was very economical, for, as it was the custom as well as the necessity, to cut down the trees to furnish browse for the cattle, he could not quietly see the timber wasted, and he had it cut and carried home on the backs of his sons.

In 1813 the first bridge was built over the west branch by subscription, and about ten years after a second was built in the same way at the "narrows," above the Indian grave. In 1832 C. Duboise sent from New York the drawings of a lattice bridge, of which William North and Solon Trescott made a model of laths, and Barney C. Allen took the contract for the stone and timber work and completed the bridge—one hundred and twenty-five feet long—for $440; and $300 of this money was raised by subscription, the balance was paid by the county. This is said to be the first bridge of the kind in the county.

In these times wages as well as prices of all kinds were low, except salt, which, as will be seen, was very high. Mr. Yale in his ledger charges a customer $5.50 per bushel, and $16 per barrel. As late as 1823 the trustees resolved to allow fifty cents per day for a team of horses or oxen on the road, and the same for a wagon.

In addition to those already named as early settlers were Levi Jacobs, Jacob Storey, Ira Trescott, and Russell Trescott, who lived on the west side of the river. Henry Harsh, William Johnson, and John Bridges, soon after the above, arrived in the settlement. Of those who took part in the election of October, 1833, only four, William N. Hine, Joseph Nichols, and John Miller, are now living in the township.

NEWTON FALLS VILLAGE

is pleasantly situated between the east and west branches of the Mahoning river, in the northeastern part of the township. The falls in the west branch of the river, from which the village takes its name, were originally about six or seven feet high, and formed of layers of stone, thus affording natural foundations for a mill dam, for which it is now utilized. The village is the only center of trade in the township, and all the branches of merchandise are well represented, and the indications of active business operations are amply evident. The many branches of business cannot be here specialy noticed, but special lines of manufacture will be noticed elsewhere. Several attempts have been made in Newton Falls "to supply a long felt want" by the establishment of a newspaper, but without permanent success. The formal incorporation was made after some difficulty and no little strife; the achievement of the object, however, now meets with general approval, and the little city gives ample promise of future prosperity.

Newton Falls village was incorporated March 10, 1872, by T. I. Gilmore, J. N. Ensign, W. L. Hosier, and C. G. Graham, agents for the incorporation.

The first election was held April 1, 1872, which resulted in the election of the following officials: Lyman T. Soule, Henry Taylor, and James F. Porter, trustees; H. S. Robbins, marshall; C. G. Graham, clerk and treasuer.

J. N. Ensign became mayor by virtue of his office as justice of the peace.

The population of the village at the time of incorporation was five hundred and five, and in 1880 five hundred and seventy-four.

SURVEY OF VILLAGE.

In 1806 Ezekiel Hover made the first survey and plat for Mr. Canfield, and in 1829 Joshua Henshaw made a second for C. Duboise, and had much difficulty in finding the lines, and the number of the lots, and finally failed by many acres, in his estimate of the number of acres conveyed by Canfield and other parties. In 1836 the lines were adjusted by F. E. Stow for Dr. H. A. Duboise. The latter proposed to change the name of the village to Duboiseville, but afterwards put on record the amended map made by Mr. Stow, with the present name.

CHURCHES AT NEWTON FALLS.

The first church building at Newton Falls was erected by the Associate Reform (Seceder) church, under the pastorate of Rev. William Douthett. This society has long since passed away, and the house has since been occupied by the Regular Baptist society, which also has disappeared. Afterwards the Episcopalians remodeled the building, in which they held services, but they also have long since disbanded, and the building is now used as the town hall.

THE PRESBYTERIAN AND CONGREGATIONAL CHURCH ORGANIZATION.

On the 4th of September, 1836, agreeably to previous appointment a number of individuals favorably disposed to the cause of Christ, met at the house of Horace Stephens in the village of Newton Falls, for the purpose of consulting in reference to the establishment of a church in that place. Rev. John Treat, of the Presbyterian church, being present, presided over the meeting. Some fifteen or twenty persons were present, and an organization of a church of Jesus Christ was decided upon. It was also decided to invite Rev. Joseph Treat, of Portage presbytery, Rev. Josiah Town, of Trumbull presbytery, and Rev. Chapin, of Cleveland presbytery, to assist in the organization, and also that the church should take the form of worship of the Congregational church, and become attached to the Trumbull presbytery. Accordingly, December 4, 1836, the church was organized, called the Church of Jesus Christ. Joseph Treat and Chapin Clark were the ministers in charge, and

effected the organization. The following persons presented themselves for membership, viz: Hiram and Martha Hinman, of Dutch Reform church, Luther Lyman, of Congregational church, John Payne, of Presbyterian church, Amelia and Martha Beebe, of Presbyterian church, Lucy Babbitt, of Presbyterian church, Pamelia Kidder, of Congregational church, Amelia Stevens, of Presbyterian church. Also Horace Stevens, Reuben Babbitt, Henry Hutson, Emily Lyman, Amelia Stevens, and Susan and Margaret Patterson presented themselves for admission on confession of faith. The first public worship was held on December 15th, and the sermon was preached by Rev. Clark from Luke xiv: 28, "For which of you intending to build a tower sitteth not down first and counteth the cost."

The committee was appointed to prepare a Confession of Faith, which was presented, being the same, with some changes, as the one recommended by the presbytery of Portage, and was adopted at this meeting. December 24, 1836, a meeting was held at the house of Horace Stevens, and he was appointed clerk, and Hiram Hinman and Luther Lyman leaders, to conduct religious meetings and prepare rules for the regulation of the church.

RULES PRESENTED.

1. Standing committee not less than two or more than seven to take cognizance of public offenses and manage the prudential concerns.
2. Powers of the members of this committee same as elders in Presbyterian church to those avowing their preference to that church.
3. Committee to examine applicants for admission.
4. Inconsistent to admit members of distant churches to communion who have resided in community less than one year.
5. Prohibiting ardent spirits.
7. Prohibiting hauling hay or grain, making sugar, hauling milk or making cheese, attending any business, visiting friends, except in sickness, on Sunday.

The rules were presented by Hiram Hinman and Luther Lyman, committee. First delegate to presbytery was Luther Lyman, December 16, 1837, and at same meeting E. Lyman, M. Beebe, and H. C. Soule were appointed to secure "a supply of preaching," and Rev. C. R. Clark appears as the first "supply" in December, 1840, and Rev. Bennett Roberts the following year. February 19, 1840, a subscription paper was started to solicit aid in building a house for the use, as stated in the paper, of "the Presbyterian society and church of this village and vicinity," to be erected on the lot then owned by Isaac Stanley, where the house now stands. This subscription paper bears this motto in capitals—"Privilege to all—Exclusion to none." The church was dedicated March 16, 1842, by Professor Day, of Western Reserve college, preaching from the text—"And the glory of God filled the house."

Rev. Robert C. Learned was minister in 1842, and Daniel Emmerson in 1843. In the latter year the church adopted a rule giving the pulpit in charge of the minister, excluding from the house all shows, models of new inventions, exhibitions for the purpose of speaking dialogues, comedies, orations or the like, "decorations calculated to excite the gaze and call off the attention of the congregation," all political and other meetings, unless permission be given by a vote of three fourths of the congregation at a called meeting. In 1843 Rev. Solomon Stevens was called and his services began July 1st. Among the ministers who have served this society were Dr. Pratt, J. A. Woodruff, W. R. Stevens, Erastus Chester, Benjamin Walker, George Pierce, Augustus Cone, Isaac Hall, S. D. Taylor, Henry Farwell.

In 1868 it was proposed at a meeting called for that purpose to change the organization to a Presbyterian church, to which assent was made by a vote of thirty-three to eleven, and in the following June John Leonard, C. Price, William Herbert, S. A. Austin, and H. C. Soule were elected elders.

In 1879 a meeting was called, presided over by P. Baldwin, in which, by motion of J. W. Little, it was decided to change the organization to be known as the Congregational church, and the rules of the Windham Congregational church were adopted, and the organization now holds worship here under the pastorate of Rev. D. Waugh.

THE DISCIPLES CHURCH, NEWTON FALLS.

The organization from which this church is an offshoot was first effected as early as 1820. In the fall of 1819 Thomas Miller, a Baptist minister, preached at the house of Benoni Johnson in Braceville, where F. L. Mervin now lives, and Marcus Bosworth and wife were baptized. In the following year the church, under the ministry of Rev. Miller, was organized with Marcus Bosworth as deacon, and the following were the

original members: Marcus Bosworth and wife, Amos and Lucinda Clark, Henry and Elizabeth Harsh, Malinda Pells, Henry and Olive Hulen, Jane Pells, Deborah and Huldah Bosworth, Asaph and Rachel Stanley, Billius and Olive Newton, Benoni and Amanda Johnson, Diana Johnson, John and Eunice Conkling, Reuben North, Mindwell Roberts, Ursula Allen. Marcus Bosworth was the deacon and recognized leader in the church, and afterwards became an efficient minister. In 1825 Rev. Jacob Osborn came to this locality and gave a new impetus to scriptural investigation, resulting eventually in the reorganization of the church as "Christians," which was effected March 12, 1828, being the first formal adoption of the divine platform as the only basis, by the church in the Western Reserve; and Marcus Bosworth was elected overseer. In 1839 the church at Newton Falls was completed, when the congregation there began to worship, and of which Amos Clark, Joel Bradford, Henry Harsh, and Benoni Johnson served as overseers.

METHODIST EPISCOPAL CHURCH.

This church was originally organized in 1837 with seven members, as follow: William Earle and wife, Widow Harris, Mrs. John Hutson, and others whose names cannot now be recalled. The ministers forming the organization were Arthur M. Brown and E. J. L. Baker. The following winter they held a protracted meeting in the Disciples church and a great number were added to the church. In 1840 Lorenzo Rogers, assisted by John Robertson, conducted a meeting which resulted in eighty additions, and the present church building was erected. From this time until 1875 this society belonged to the same circuit with Braceville, and the same ministers served both churches.

In the above year the church at Newton was separated from Braceville with a membership of forty-six. The following ministers have served this congregation since that time: C. V. Wilson, J. H. Starrett, W. A. Clark, E. P. Edmunds, W. L. Davidson, John Tribby, and the present pastor, Rev. J. J. Wallace. The present membership is one hundred and forty-four, and the church is in a good state of prosperity.

THE LUTHERAN AND GERMAN REFORMED CHURCH.

This society was organized by Rev. F. C.

Becker, the present Lutheran pastor, in 1835. Rev. H. Huet and P. Mahnenschmid had preached here several times previous to the organization by Rev. Becker. The school-house in which the early meetings were held, and in which the organization was effected, was located about one-fourth mile from the present church building, which stands east of the center of the township.

The first officials were: Leonard Miller (Lutheran) and Jacob Feister (German Reform) as trustees. The original members were: Leonard, Jacob, and John Miller, George, Jacob, and David Longenberger (Lutherans), and Jacob Feister and John Loab (German Reformed). The first house of worship was erected in 1837, and the present one in 1850. Father Becker, the present pastor of the Lutheran church, has served this people for now almost fifty years, and is well known throughout the community as an able, zealous, and efficient pastor, and the work of his hands in the moral and religious welfare of his people will live after him.

The ministers who served the German Reformed congregation were: Revs. Mahnenschmid, Rahhauser, Ruhl, Reuter, Fair, Reuter, Fair, Grether, Perkins, and Otting. The two congregations hold services alternately in the present church building, which is locally known as Miller's church.

CEMETERY.

The original burial ground was donated by Bildad Hine and Jonathan Jacobs, each giving one-fourth of an acre. The first interment was that of Captain Reuben Bostwick, brother-in-law of Mr. Hine, who died July 16, 1813, aged seventy-eight years. With the later additions made to the grounds, in all about three acres, and many other improvements, they now present a very beautiful country cemetery, and will soon be incorporated under the jurisdiction of the township trustees.

SCHOOLS.

In the summer of 1812 the first school was taught at Newton Falls by Miss Draper, who afterwards became Mrs. Collar, a relative of Dr. Harmon. It is related of her that she forbade her scholars to kill innocent striped snakes and so strengthened her mandate by pleas of mercy and justice that two of her scholars, well-known

men in this community, Herbert Hine and Barney C. Allen, have never killed one from that day to this, and Mr. Allen has made it a rule to dismiss from his employ any one guilty of such an offense. In the winter of this same year the school was taught by Jonathan Trescott, and the following winter Hervey Stow, of Braceville, was teacher. Edmond Yale (deceased) used to tell how well he remembered getting a whipping from his teacher for refusing to sit between two little girls as a punishment for some previous offence.

Hon. Eben Newton, then a beardless boy, gave young America a winter's training in this school-room.

It seems he was more accomplished in literature than in navigation, as the following incident will illustrate. Having spent "an evening out" on the east side of the East river, in attempting to return at an *early* hour he became lost in a cranberry swamp and was compelled to remain under the shelter of a tree until morning, when, in great haste to get to his school, he came to the river, which had been swollen by the rain during the night and the current was rapid; he entered his boat, seized the only oar and attempted to cross. When about in the center of the stream the oar broke and the boat began drifting rapidly towards the falls. He saw no way of helping himself only to pull at the mooring rope and halloo for help. David Huffstetter was soon on the bank and directed the helpless teacher as follows: "Walk to this end of the boat and then run to the other," which he did, and the motion produced by the feet drifted the boat to the shore.

The house occupied by this first school stood near the site of the present south warehouse. From this beginning the schools began to appear as the township settled and became more numerously populated. The village is now supplied with a large school building in which the union school is now held, of three departments, and in which great pride is manifested by the community. This school has been very successful and has attracted pupils from distant parts of this section to take advantage of superior instruction here.

The following report of the condition of the school was made November 26, 1881.

Principal department 55
Second department 25

Grammar department........................ 33
High school department............................ 39

Total................................... 153
Average daily attendance......................... 144
Non-residents 19

Present board: W. W. Herbert, president; Max Matles, clerk; A. L. F. Albertson, treasurer; C. G Graham, N. Spencer, L. A. Robins, members.

JOHN E. MORRIS, Principal.

THE WOOLEN MILLS.

The present woolen mill was built by Augustus Stephens about 1825, and was enlarged and otherwise improved by H. C. Soule in 1843, who operated the mill until 1859, when he sold to Allen Hoyle, who now has the factory in charge manufacturing stocking-yarns and flannels. The mill has a capacity of one hundred pounds of wool per day. The spinning jack has one hundred and forty-four spindles on a forty-inch condenser, and the mill has two broad power-looms propelled by water-power from West river.

NEWTON FALLS FOUNDRY.

This foundry was begun some years ago and has undergone some changes of proprietorship. At present it is operated by lease from J. J. Pearson by Lewis Walters, who took possession in December, 1880. As operated at present two heats are made per week, and all kinds of ordinary work, such as stoves, plow-shares, plates of various kinds are moulded. The capacity of the foundry reaches fifteen hundred pound weight, but is not operated to full capacity. General custom and some shipping work is done, employing two and three hands. The present indications, under the efficient management of Mr. Walters, are promising for future success in this branch of industry.

NEWTON FALLS LODGE, FREE AND ACCEPTED MASONS, NO. 462.

This lodge was organized May 13, 1872, with the following charter members: Edward Spear, L. T. Soule, E. F. Shaw, Davis Lowry, W. L. Hosier, J. W. Little, L. C. Merrill, A. Elwell, L. F. Humphrey, I. E. Brown, N. C. Smith, M. Templeton, Mark Ames, John Patterson, E. W. Williams.

The first officials elected were: L. T. Soule, W. M.; L. F. Humphrey, S. W.; J. W. Little, J. W.; L. C. Merrill, secretary.

The first meetings were held over Herbert Bros.' store, and for the last two years the lodge has held its regular meetings in Ames' block, south side of Broad street.

The present number of Master Masons is forty-two, and the present officials are: L. C. Merrill, W. M.; T. H. Gilmer, S. W.; J. E. Griffrich, J. W.; J. W. Little, secretary; B. F. Rice, treasurer. Lodge is in good condition.

NEWTON FALLS LODGE, I. O. O. F., NO. 255.

The above lodge was instituted June 14, 1854, and the first officials were W. Tew, N. G.; Thomas R. Gaskell, V. G.; John Campbell, secretary; and S. J. Grinnell, treasurer. The charter members were composed of the above officials and J. S. Tompkins. The order held its first meetings over J. & W. Herbert's store, on the corner of Canal and Broad streets, but now meet in their own brick building on the north side of Broad street. One hundred and fifty persons have held membership in this lodge since its organization, and its present membership is thirty-three. It has expended in benefits and charities $1,500, besides attendance, and now owns real and personal property to the amount of $2,500. The present officials are L. C. Merrill, N. G.; R. F. Templeton, V. G.; H. M. Reecer, secretary; and H. Butts, treasurer. The lodge now enjoys a good degree of prosperity.

THE MAHONING VALLEY AGRICULTURAL AS-SOCIATION.

This association was organized September 22, 1871, with a capital stock of $3,000, which was divided into six hundred shares. The first election of officers occurred October 9, 1871, and resulted as follows: H. S. Robbins, president; William L. Hosier, first vice-president; John Snyder, second vice-president; Charles G. Graham, secretary; J. B. Stanley and C. W. Parsons, assistant secretaries; T. I. Gilmer, treasurer. The board of directors was composed of J. F. Porter, George Patterson, Charles Kistler, Elisha Walker, J. P. Baldwin, Azel Delin.

The association owns in fee-simple twenty-two acres of choice land, which lies immediately south of the village of Newton Falls and near the East branch of the Mahoning river. The grounds are substantially fenced and contain besides the necessary buildings a fine half-mile track, said to be one of the best in the State. The grounds and improvements cost over $4,000, and the annual exhibitions of the association have done much to foster and encourage agricultural industries in this locality and to stimulate local pride and energy among all classes. The annual meetings occur on the first Monday of February, and the present officials are L. C. Merrill, president; Henry Butt, vice-president; Charles G. Graham, secretary; D. H. Gardner, treasurer; and John Snyder, David Carlisle, William King, Henry King, C. M. Smith, B. F. Rice, and L. F. Merrill, compose the official board.

THE MAHONING VALLEY GRANGE, NO. 1272.

The organization of this Grange was effected April 18, 1876, by O. P. Laird, deputy for Trumbull county. The first officials were William King, W. M.; Hary King, overseer; L. D. Miller, lecturer; J. E. Johnson, steward; Isaac Hoyle, chaplain; S. M. McKibben, assistant steward; Calvin Lybolt, treasurer; William J. Ebert, gatekeeper; Mrs. Michael Bailey, Ceres; Mrs. Dallas Kistler, Pomona; Miss Maria King, Flora; Mrs. Mary A. Johnson, assistant steward. The charter members, including the above officers, were: Reuben Kale, Angeline Kale, Reuben Williams, W. D. Sutton, George Hewit, Hattie Ebert, Martha and James Lybolt, Mr. and Mrs. H. A. Leach, Mr. and Mrs. Charles Kistler, D. Lewis, Sarah Hoyle, Mr. and Mrs. Daniel Herner, Mrs. Henry King, Fred and Mary Sim, Mr. and Mrs. Michael Kistler, Mr. and Mrs. Daniel King, Mr. and Mrs. Owen Craver, Mrs. S. M. McKibben, Angeline McCollister, Esther and J. F. King, and Michael Bailey. The grange meets at Newton Falls, Ohio, on Saturday evenings, and at present has a membership of fifty-eight, embracing a very large proportion of the influential farmers of the neighborhood. The greater part of the members take advantage of the financial or business feature of the organization, purchases amounting to several hundred dollars per year.

Socially the grange is now confident of gaining ground in Newton, and if they have thus far failed in making "two blades of grass grow where but one grew before," they hope to do so in the future.

PHYSICIANS.

The first physicians of old Trumbull whose names have been handed down to posterity were General J. W. Seeley, of Howland; Enoch Leavitt, of Warren center; Peter Allen, of Kinsman; Dr. Dutton, of Youngstown; John B. Harmon, of Warren; Dr. Kirtland, of Poland; and Harry Beach, of Fowler. The profession thus ably represented was further strengthened in 1814 by the settlement of Dr. Tracy Bronson in Newton township. He was born in Middlebury, New Haven county, Connecticut, in 1791. After receiving an academic training he entered the medical department of Yale College, from which he graduated in 1813. On coming to Ohio the following year he purchased land near Price's mills, in Newton township, on which he settled, and soon was actively engaged in the practice of his profession. In 1817 Dr. Bronson married Mary Freeman, second daughter of Robert Freeman, of Braceville township. Her death occurred in May, 1833. He married for his second wife Sarah E. Stanwood, in 1834; she died in 1866. Dr. Bronson's family consisted of three sons and one daughter. James, the oldest son, was born in 1817, read medicine with his father, and practiced in Newton from 1845 until his death in 1872—he was a prominent member of the Independent Order of Odd Fellows; Henry W. was born in 1818, settled in Wisconsin in 1845, returned in 1872, and now resides in Newton township; Mary Freeman, the only daughter, was born in 1821, was married to S. W. Harris, of Warren, and died in Illinois in 1866; William, the youngest son, was born in 1832, and resides on the homestead farm in Newton township. Dr. Bronson continued the practice of his profession until a year previous to his death, which took place October, 1859. During the whole period of his professional career he maintained an honorable standing among his contemporaries and the full confidence of a large circle of friends. The duties of citizenship were not neglected by him. He served three times in the Ohio Legislature, having been elected first in 1836. In 1840 he was a member of the Whig National convention which nominated William Henry Harrison for President. He was frequently the recipient of local official honors.

SETTLEMENT NOTES.

Harvey Allen, a well known resident of Newton township, was born June 28, 1807, in Berkshire county, Massachusetts. His father, Joseph Allen, was a native of Massachusetts, who came to Ohio and settled in Braceville township, Trumbull county, in 1810. He reared a family of nine children, five of whom are now living, four sons and a daughter. All are now well advanced in years. Mr. Harvey Allen is the youngest son. The names of the children were, Sarah, born December 14, 1791; James, October 31, 1793; Amanda, September 29, 1795; Barney C., September 8, 1797; Amos, February 6, 1800; Barsha, January 3, 1802; Avery, August 21, 1804; Harvey, June 28, 1807; Eunice M., March 22, 1809. Joseph Allen was a shoemaker by trade; he also carried on a tannery several years. He died February 16, 1842. Mrs. Allen died October 12, 1853. Mr. Harvey Allen resided in Braceville township until 1875, then moved to Newton Falls. He has always been engaged in farming principally. He was married July 15, 1834, to Miss Mehitabel Frank. By this marriage he had one child. Mrs. Allen died December 15, 1840. He was again married November 15, 1843, to Miss Emeline Stanley. She died November 7, 1848. They had one child. He was married again November 8, 1849, to Mrs. Jane L. Tilley. She had four children by a former marriage. Mr. and Mrs. Allen belong to the Disciple church.

B. C. Allen, son of Joseph and Mary (Jacobs) Allen, was born in Berkshire county, Massachusetts, September 8, 1797. He came with his parents to Trumbull county in 1810. Joseph Allen left Massachusetts with his family on the 20th day of May, and arrived in Braceville, where they settled, on the 3d day of July. Of the twenty-two persons who came with Mr. Allen only five are now living. He settled in the southwest part of Braceville, where he spent the balance of his life. He died in February, 1842. His wife died in October, 1853. They had a family of nine children. Four sons and one daughter are still living, viz: B. C. Harvey, and Mrs. Eunice Minerva Sherman, at Newton Falls; Amos in Eaton county, Michigan; and Avery in Portage county. B. C. Allen was married first in 1822 to Ursula Newton, of Braceville, who died in February, 1850. He had ten children by that marriage, eight of whom are living. He married his present wife in 1868, Mrs. Martha M. Sherman, whose first husband, Dr. B. Sherman, died in the army in December, 1862. Mr.

Allen resided on the old homestead in Braceville until the spring of 1872, when he removed to Newton Falls, where he now lives nearly eighty-five years of age.

John Henry Hewit, a native of Maryland, moved with his family from Washington county, Pennsylvania, to Boardman township, now Mahoning county, in the spring of 1815. He was a minister of the Lutheran church, and the second clergyman of that denomination in this region. His work extended over a large extent of country, and his life was an active one and fruitful of good results. He died in Boardman, where he first settled, in 1854, his wife, Esther (Simon) dying two years after. They had a family of fourteen children. Five are still living—Mrs. Margaret Fiester; Samuel, in Newton; Catharine (Kale), in Milton, Mahoning county; Elizabeth, unmarried, in Newton; Lydia (Moyer), in Michigan. Samuel Hewit was born in Canton township, Washington county, Pennsylvania, December 21, 1800. He came to Trumbull county with his parents in 1815. He married in 1822 Sophia Berger, of Boardman, and in 1824 settled in Ellsworth township, and resided there until 1850, when he moved to Newton, locating where he now lives. His wife died February 19, 1876, in the seventy fifth year of her age. They have had a family of nine children, six of whom are living—John Henry, Hannah (widow of Daniel Bailey), Elias, Esther (Bailey), George, and Lewis, all living in Newton township, and all but one in the same neighborhood.

William Bronson, youngest son of Dr. Tracy and Mary (Freeman) Bronson, was born in Newton township, Trumbull county, June 23, 1832. Dr. Tracy Bronson was born in Connecticut in 1791. He was a graduate of Yale college. In 1814 he came to Ohio, and settled in Newton township, where he practiced his profession until 1850. He was the first physician in that township, and had an extensive practice. He married in 1815, Mary, daughter of Robert Freeman, one of the pioneers of Braceville township. He raised a family of four children, two of whom are living, viz: Henry W., a resident of Newton, and the subject of this sketch. Dr. Bronson died in October, 1859, and his wife in 1833. William was brought up on a farm, and during the construction of the Mahoning railroad he was engaged some four years in civil engineering. In

1854 he married Emeline E. Blair. They have had five children, viz: Mary Eugenia, who was the wife of L. N. Patterson, and who died in 1880, leaving two children; Hattie R., wife of George Patterson, residing in Titusville, Pennsylvania; Freeman, born November 18, 1865, died in August, 1867; Elizabeth M. and Tracy James are still at home. William Bronson was justice of the peace some fifteen years. In 1877 he was elected county commissioner for Trumbull county, and re-elected in the fall of 1880.

Henry Wilderson, one of the old residents of Newton, was born July 22, 1811, in York county, Pennsylvania, where he lived three years, and then went to Maryland in company with his parents, Charles and Christiana Wilderson. In 1832 Mr. Charles Wilderson came to Ohio, and settled in Beaver township, Columbiana county, now Mahoning county. He was a stone-mason by trade, though he made farming his business after coming to Ohio. He came to Newton in 1835, and located upon the farm where his son Henry now lives. Charles Wilderson died in 1863, surviving his wife several years. There were eleven children in the family. Mr. Henry Wilderson has lived in the township since 1835, upon the farm where we now find him pleasantly situated. He was married September 24, 1846, to Miss Rachel Barnhisel, daughter of Martin Barnhisel, of Weathersfield township. They have had seven children, six of whom are living: Ira N., Mary A., Martha M., Electa E., John H., Emma A., and Ella O. Mr. and Mrs. Wilderson are Methodists. Politically he is a Republican, and is highly esteemed.

David Carlisle, a well known resident of Newton, was born in Newton township upon the place where he now lives. His father, David, was a native of Mifflin county, Pennsylvania, and came to Ohio in 1806, and located in Newton township, and was one of the earliest settlers of the township. Beginning in a small clearing made by the Indians when the country was wild, he built up a nice farm, and lived here till his death, which occurred March 7, 1860. Mrs. Carlisle died in December, 1856. The family consisted of eight children, all of whom are living. Mr. David Carlisle, the subject of this sketch, is the youngest of the family. He has always lived upon the old home place. He was married December 3, 1857, to Miss Martha

Linn, daughter of William Linn, of Guernsey county, Ohio. They have had four children, three of whom are living—Frank L., William A., Charles, and one died in infancy. Mrs. Carlisle is a member of the Congregational church. Mr. Carlisle is a Republican, and is highly respected.

John Lewis, an early pioneer of Trumbull county, was born in 1801, in Washington county, Maryland. His father, Morris Lewis, was born in December, 1777. He was a farmer by occupation and died September 9, 1807, in Poland township, Trumbull county, now known as Mahoning county. Morris Lewis, Sr., father of Morris Lewis, was drowned in the Susquehanna river, when Morris Lewis was a boy. Mr. John Lewis, the subject of this sketch, had one brother and two sisters: William Lewis, born April 29, 1803, in Allegheny county, Maryland; Rachel, born February 18, 1806, died November 27, 1806; Rachel L. was born October 29, 1808, in Trumbull county, Ohio; she died April 21, 1880, in Kent county, Michigan. Mr. John Lewis came to Newton in 1843 from Portage county, Ohio, and lived upon the farm where his sons now live and was engaged in general farming until his death. He had a family of seven children, five of whom are living—Morris, William, Mary A., Isaiah, Andrew, Jonathan, and David. Isaiah and William are deceased. Mrs. Lewis died July 29, 1876. Mr. and Mrs. Lewis were members of the Lutheran church.

Samuel King was born in 1804, November 14th, in Lehigh county, Pennsylvania. His father, Jacob King, was a native of Pennsylvania, and spent his days in this State. He was a farmer by occupation, and died in 1829, leaving a wife and five children. Mrs. King died in 1837. Mr. Samuel King came to Ohio in 1837, and settled upon the farm where he now resides. He was married in 1824 to Miss Elizabeth Faulk, daughter of Daniel Faulk, of Lehigh county, Pennsylvania. They have had ten children, all of whom are living. Mrs. King died in 1850. She was a devoted member of the Lutheran church. Mr. King and family are also members of the same church, and are good citizens.

William King, one of the enterprising men of Newton township, was born July 24, 1827, in Lehigh county, Pennsylvania, and came to Ohio with his father, Samuel King, in 1837, and has since lived in the county. He learned the shoemaking trade when a young man, and served a little over a year as an apprentice. He began work for himself in 1847, and continued in the boot and shoe business for twenty-eight years, employing several hands at home. He had an extensive trade, extending over the southern part of Trumbull county, and was well known as an upright business man. His health failing he went to gardening, and has been engaged in horticulture for the past few years. He was married March 28, 1850, to Miss Esther Stroup, daughter of John Stroup, of Warren, Ohio. By this union there have been six children—Maria E., William H., John F., Harriet L., Clara S., and George N. Mrs. King is a member of the Lutheran church. Mr. King was formerly a member, though at the present time is very liberal in his views. In politics he is a conservative, voting for men rather than for party, and is one of the esteemed citizens of the township.

John N. Pearce was born in 1821 in Jackson township, Trumbull county, now Mahoning. His father, Joseph, was a native of New Jersey, and came to Ohio when he was about eight years of age. Mr. John N. Pearce has always lived in old Trumbull, living in Jackson until 1858 when he moved to Newton. General farming has been and is his occupation. He was married in 1845 to Miss Mary McConnell, daughter of James McConnell, of Jackson township. They have had ten children, seven of whom are living. Mrs. Pearce died in 1870. Mr. Pearce's second marriage occurred in 1872, to Mrs. Abram Ohl, of Jackson township. Mr. and Mrs. Pearce are members of the Disciples church. Politically he is a Republican.

Joseph Nicholls, the oldest living resident of Newton township, was born March 20, 1794, in Washington county, Pennsylvania. His father, Thomas Nicholls, was a native of Maryland, though lived a long time in Pennsylvania, and came to Ohio in 1812 and settled in Jefferson county, and was an early settler of this part of the State. He lived and died here. Farming was his chief occupation. He died in 1831, leaving a family of eight children. Mrs. Nicholls died in her ninety-first year. Mr. Joseph Nicholls came to Newton township in 1832, and has since resided in the township. He was married in 1815 to Miss Mercy Dowden, daughter of Michael Dowden, of Maryland.

They have had nine children, seven of whom are living. Mrs. Nicholls died in 1845. Politically Mr. Nicholls is a sound Democrat and is highly esteemed by all. He retains his sight remarkably and bids fair to round out the century.

Andrew J. Carlisle was born in 1827 in Lisbon, Columbiana county, Ohio. His father, Henry, came from New Jersey to Ohio in an early day and located in Columbiana county, where he lived until 1832, when he came to Newton Falls where he kept tavern for nineteen years. He died April 27, 1864. In the family there are four children. Mr. Andrew Carlisle has been engaged in farming chiefly. He was married January 8, 1858, to Miss Caroline De Forrest, daughter of Curtis De Forrest, of Portage county. They have two children, Curtis and Isabel. In politics Mr. Carlisle is a Democrat.

Joseph Strock was born September 25, 1831, in Austintown township, Trumbull county. His father, Samuel Strock, was a native of Pennsylvania, Cumberland county, and came to Ohio in 1814 with his father, Joseph, who first settled in Tuscarawas county for one season, then came to Trumbull county and settled in Austintown, where he lived till his death, which occurred in 1832, leaving a family of twelve children. Mrs. Strock died in a few weeks after the death of her husband. Mr. Samuel Strock came to Newton in 1840 and lived upon the farm where his son Joseph now resides, till 1878, and died in this year. Mrs. Strock died in 1868. Mr. Strock, the subject of this sketch, has always lived in what was old Trumbull. He has an excellent farm of two hundred and one acres. He was married in 1853 to Miss Susan Kistler, daughter of Michael Kistler, of Newton township. There were nine children by this marriage. Mrs. Strock died in 1868. His second marriage was in the fall of 1868 to Miss Almira Powers, daughter of William Powers, of Ohltown, Ohio. There were five children by this marriage. Mrs. Strock died in 1876. Mr. Strock is an enterprising man.

Joseph Wilson was born in 1818 in the county of Tyrone, Ireland, and came to America in 1834, and at once came to Austintown, Mahoning county, where he lived about twelve years, being engaged as a clerk for Caldwell Porter; also drove team and worked upon the farm. He then went to Youngstown where he acted as a clerk in the warehouse of Parks & Co. two and one-half years. He then bought the farm in Newton township where he now lives, and has since been engaged in stock-raising and general farming. He was married in 1850 to Miss Catharine Potter, daughter of Edward and Lucy Potter, of Warren. By this union there are four children—William F., Caldwell P., Lucy, and Elma J. Mrs. Wilson is a member of the Presbyterian church. In politics Mr. Wilson is a good Democrat.

Ferdinand Graber was born November 30, 1814, in Lehigh county, Pennsylvania. His father, Andrew Graber, was a native of Pennsylvania. The family is of German descent. Andrew Graber came to Ohio in 1815, and settled in Canfield township, Trumbull county, now Mahoning county. He was a farmer. He died in 1850, leaving a family of nine children and a widow. Mrs. Graber died in 1854. Both were members of the German Presbyterian church. Ferdinand Graber came to Newton in 1852, and settled upon the farm where we now find him. He was married in January, 1844, to Miss Sarah Wehr, daughter of Simon Wehr, of Boardman township, Mahoning county. They have had four children, three of whom are living—Ensign, Mary E., Anna M., Lucetta. Ensign is deceased. Mrs. Graber died December 24, 1877. She was a devoted member of the Presbyterian church. Mr. Graber is also a member of the same church.

Charles P. Wood was born April 20, 1811, in Canandaigua county, New York. His father, Josiah, was a native of New York, and came to Ohio in 1813 or 1814 and settled in Canfield, Trumbull county, now Mahoning county, and was among the early settlers. Mr. Charles P. Wood came to Newton in 1836 and located a year later upon the farm where his boys now live. Mr. Wood died May 29, 1880; Mrs. Wood died June 1, 1873. They had a family of five children—Josiah E., S. A. Wood, A. S., E. E., H. A. Mr. and Mrs. Wood were members of the Disciples' church.

Henry Taylor was born March 8, 1820, in Warren township, Trumbull county, Ohio. His father, Samuel, was a native of Maryland, and came to Ohio in an early day and was one of the pioneers of the Western Reserve. He was a shoemaker by trade, which occupation he fol-

lowed many years in Warren township, then went to Bazetta township, Trumbull county, where he pursued farming till his death, which occurred in 1835. There were seven children in the family—four boys and three girls. Mrs. Taylor died in 1829. Mr. Henry Taylor has always lived in Trumbull county. He learned the blacksmith trade when a young man, and has followed it as a vocation. He came to Newton Falls March 7, 1837. He was married in 1845 to Miss Margaret Cole, daughter of Peter Cole, of Newton Falls. They have had four children —William H., Charles, Mary, Addison S. Mr. and Mrs. Taylor are members of the Christian church. He is a staunch Democrat, and has held several of the township offices. He is esteemed and respected by all.

William Herbert, a well-known merchant of Newton Falls, was born March 17, 1837, in Portage county, Ohio. His father, Thomas Herbert, a native of Wales, came to America in 1823, and settled in Palmyra, Portage county, Ohio, and was one of the pioneers of this section. He was a tailor by trade, though followed farming chiefly as an occupation. He died in 1877, leaving a family of eight children and a widow to mourn his loss. Mrs. Herbert died in 1879. Mr. William Herbert is the oldest dry goods merchant at Newton Falls. He has been in business at this place twenty years, and has an extensive trade. He was married in 1864 to Miss Mary A. Jones, daughter of Richard D. Jones, of Mahoning county. Mrs. Herbert died January 1, 1865. He was again married in 1866, to Miss Marietta Hine, daughter of Noble Hine, of Ravenna, Portage county. They have three children. Mr. and Mrs. Herbert are members of the Congregational church, as is also their oldest son. In politics he is a firm Republican. He was second lieutenant in the One Hundred and Seventy-first Ohio infantry.

Alfred L. F. Albertson, M. D., a successful physician of Newton Falls, was born July 7, 1848, in Winslow, New Jersey. His father, Samuel Albertson, was a native of Pennsylvania, and for a long time was engaged in mercantile business. Dr. Albertson was raised in Philadelphia. He commenced to study medicine in 1868 with Dr. Kerr, of Philadelphia, and attended a course of lectures at the Jefferson Medical college; also a course in Cincinnati, and graduated in Cleveland in 1875, and has since practiced at Newton Falls, though he practiced here two or three years before going to Cleveland. He gives particular attention to the eye, and has been very successful in his practice thus far. He is a Free Mason, also an Odd Fellow. In politics a Republican.

H. M. Reeser was born in 1848 in Austintown, Mahoning county. His father, Andrew Reeser, was a native of Liberty township, Trumbull county. His grandfather, Daniel, was an early pioneer. Mr. H. M. Reeser lived in Pennsylvania several years, and came to Milton township in 1865, where he lived till 1873, when he was married to Miss Eunice A. Baldwin, daughter of J. P. Baldwin, of Newton township. They have one child—Lucius E. Mr. Reeser is engaged in teaching in connection with his farming, and is a wide-awake, enterprising man. He is an Odd Fellow.

CHAPTER XVI.
GUSTAVUS.

GEOGRAPHICAL AND PHYSICAL FEATURES.

Gustavus is the second of the northern tier of townships of Trumbull county, being the seventh township in the second range. It is north of Johnston, east of Greene, and west of Kinsman. Wayne township, Ashtabula county, adjoins it on the north.

The soil is good, and agricultural industry prospers. No railroad enters this township. Kinsman station on the Lake Shore branch road, four and a half miles from Gustavus center, is the nearest railroad point. Farming is the principal business of the inhabitants of this township. Two small villages, Hart's corners and the center, a mile apart, each contains a dozen or more houses, one store and a few shops. The surface is undulating with no particularly striking features. The soil is mostly sandy loam, somewhat gravelly in places. Some clayey spots are found near the streams. The drainage of the township is received by Pymatuning creek, which crosses the northeastern corner of the township, thence flows southeasterly through Kinsman and Vernon. Most of the streams are small, and are confined to the eastern half of the township. All flow toward the east.

NAME.

This township was surveyed and the lots numbered in 1800. Colonel Lemuel Storrs having purchased a part of lot number two, gave the township the name of his son, Gustavus.

SETTLEMENT.

Josiah Pelton, having purchased a tract of land north of the center of this township, came out in the year 1800, on horseback, to view his purchase and select a spot for a home. Having arrived in the unbroken wilderness, he turned his horse loose to graze along the Pymatuning creek. Mr. Pelton remained all summer, and during this time his horse had became so nearly wild that when he was wanted to carry his owner back to Connecticut in the fall, Mr. Pelton was obliged to catch him with a lasso, which proved a very difficult job. But at length having succeeded, Mr. Pelton made the return trip in company with a missionary who had no horse, but was allowed the use of this on a part of the way. Arriving at home in safety Mr. Pelton made an offer of one hundred acres of his land to the woman who would first engage to make her home in the wilds of Gustavus.

His son Jesse induced Ruhamah DeWolf, of Granby, Connecticut, to accept this offer, and she engaged to undertake with him the hardships of pioneer life. She came with her father's family to Vernon and there remained until a clearing had been made and a log cabin built upon the farm. The raising of this cabin took place the fourth day of June, 1802, Mr. Pelton being assisted in his labor by men from Vernon. A heavy fall of rain came on, and all who attended the raising were obliged to remain all night at the cabin. The next day they reached home, but were obliged to bridge some of the swollen creeks intervening by felling trees across them.

Mrs. Pelton did not take up her abode in the new cabin until the following December. Her husband meanwhile boarded himself, carrying his bread from Vernon. One day as he was going after a supply he saw a panther in a tree on the bank of the Pymatuning. He tied his hat and coat upon a bush, ordered his dog to watch them, and then returned to the center after his gun. The dog kept faithful watch until his master's return, when the panther was killed and found to measure nearly seven feet.

Elias Pelton, brother of Jesse, was the second man who settled in Gustavus with his family. His daughter Barbara, afterwards the wife of Hezekiah Barnes, was the first white child in the township who survived. She died in 1881. Her brother Storrs was the first male child.

Soon after these settlers arrived Josiah Pelton, the father, came here to reside. His sons were Jesse, Harvey, Elias, Zenas, Ithemur, and Julius. All remained a couple of years. Harvey died in Geauga county; Zenas moved to Michigan with his sons when an old man, and Jesse died in Pennsylvania. The others lived and died in Gustavus. All settled near the center on adjoining farms. Two daughters of Josiah Pelton, Mrs. John Lane and Eliphaz Perkins, also resided in this township. Of his grandchildren, Tenserd D. and Cynthia, children of Jesse Pelton, and Lysander, son of Julius, are still living in this township; also Mrs. Annis Barber, daughter of Julius.

In June, 1804, Obediah Gildersleeve and family came. They journeyed by team in company with Calvin Cone and others. Mr. Gildersleeve —the name is now abbreviated to Gilder—was from Hartland, Connecticut. He settled on a farm about one-half mile east of the center. Eight children were brought here and another was born after the arrival of the family. Mr. Gilder died in 1805 aged fifty years, and was among the first to be buried in the township graveyard north of the center. Mrs. Gilder lived to be seventy. The children were Bailey, Obed, Polly, Orril, Sally, Annis, Phebe, Chloe, and Betsey. Chloe was drowned in the creek when a child; Betsey also died young. The others all lived to mature years, and three, Obed, Orril, and Phebe, are still living, aged respectively eighty-nine, eighty-seven, and eighty years. The two former reside in Kinsman, and Phebe in Gustavus.

Thaddeus Selby, from Hartland, Connecticut, settled in 1804 one and one-half miles east of the center. One of his daughters, Mrs. M. S. Whittlesey, is living in Cleveland. The other members of the family were Jeremiah W., who died at St. Paul; Ephraim C., Laura E. (Beman), who lived in Gustavus, and Eliza (Ely),

who died in Illinois. Ephraim lived on the old homestead till 1861, and died in Gustavus in September, 1881. He married Wealthy Bishop, who is still living. Their family of five children all survive.

Calvin Cone, also of Hartland, settled in the eastern part of the township, but moved to Hartford township after some years. He was a State Senator from Trumbull county in 1806-9, and a very prominent man in his day. He was the first justice of the peace in Gustavus township, and was probably appointed to that office about 1808.

A little later Asa and Dosey Case, brothers, settled in the southwest of the township. Mrs. Totten and Mrs. St. John, daughters of Dosey Case, are the only representatives of the original families now in this township.

John Lane, about 1805, settled one mile north and a half-mile east of the center, where his son Cyrus now lives.

Six weeks or more were required for a journey from Connecticut to this township. Often the travelers had to build bridges and repair roads in order to proceed upon their way. The usual custom was to journey, a large company of emigrants to the West together, with ox teams and large covered wagons. Gipsy like, they ate and slept in these wagons.

After 1805 settlers continued coming gradually. Jehiel Meacham, better known as 'Squire Meacham, came at the request of Calvin Cone, Esq., who thought the settlement needed a blacksmith. Cone gave him fifty acres of land as an inducement to settle. Meacham accordingly came and located in a cabin across the road from Cone's. Land was then worth $2 per acre and upwards. Of the Meacham family, Jehiel, Jr., moved West when an old man and died; Ralph died in Mecca; Horatio is living; Edmund died in this township; Lydia (Allen) died in Kinsman; Patty (St. John) resides in Gustavus; Lucia (Moore) moved West.

Joseph Hart settled in Gustavus in 1811. His sons Nelson and Charles are still residents of the township.

Riverius Bidwell, of Canton, Connecticut, settled in the southeastern part of Gustavus in 1812. Other early settlers between the years 1810 and 1820 were Aaron Lyon, Lemuel Newton, William Linsley, Rufus Beman, and others, mostly from Connecticut. One of the later settlers and a thrifty farmer of Gustavus is Mr. C. E. Fisher. He was born in Germany in 1834. In 1847 he emigrated to America with his parents. He lived in Herkimer county, New York, about six years, and in California about as long. In 1861 he settled in Gustavus, on the fine farm which he now owns. Mr. Fisher married Aurelia Hafer, a native of Germany, in 1861, and has three children—George, Henry, and Andrew. In politics he is a Republican, in religion a Methodist.

ORGANIZATION.

This township was detached from Greene in 1821, and organized as a distinct township.

The first officers were elected September 11, 1821, and were as follows: Ithemur Pelton, Asa Case, Rufus Beman, trustees; William Roberts, Abraham Griswold, overseers of the poor; Ithemur Pelton, Walter W. Thornton, fence viewers; Jehiel Meacham, Jr., Lester Waters, constables; Joseph Hart, treasurer; Thaddeus Selby, township clerk; George Moses, lister; Marcus Andrews, Zenas Pelton, Thaddeus Selby, Joseph Hart, Harvey Pelton, Solomon Waters, Oliver Crosby, supervisors.

The first wedding was the marriage of Eliphaz Perkins and Zilpah, daughter of Josiah Pelton, April 6, 1804. The township had no justice of the peace at that time, and it is said that this couple waited a year for a missionary to come and perform the ceremony.

PIONEER REMINISCENCES.

The first few years of the settlement, Beaver, Pennsylvania, was the most convenient point at which there was a grist-mill. After a few years milling was done at Jamestown, Pennsylvania, fifteen miles distant.

Boiled wheat, with maple sugar or syrup, was a palatable and wholesome article of food much used by the early settlers on account of the difficulty they experienced in obtaining flour and meal.

The small amount of store trading done by the settlers of this township at the newly established store in Kinsman was by barter. Men were glad to receive pay for labor in provisions. A man's daily wages were forty cents; with a yoke of oxen, seventy-five cents. Women worked for seventy-five cents and one dollar per week, seldom receiving cash. Wheat was thirty cents per bushel; corn fifteen, and oats eight or ten cents. A good horse was worth $65. Of articles which had to be procured at the store the prices were about as follow: tea, $1.25 per pound; codfish, eighteen cents per pound; the poorest kind of brown sugar, twelve and a half cents.

EARLY SCHOOLS.

The first school ever taught in this township was held in the house of Elias Pelton. Roxy Brockway was the teacher. It was a private school, for the benefit of the Pelton children. The first public school was kept in John Lane's log barn about 1809, Sally Wakeman teacher. Children found their way to this dispensary of learning by following a path marked by blazed trees.

The first school-house was built upon the farm of Riverius Bidwell in 1813. Soon after Esther Bidwell taught school there. As all the children were not provided with hats and caps some came to school with handkerchiefs tied over their heads. Miss Bidwell was a very popular teacher.

TEMPERANCE.

The evils of intemperance were painfully evident among some of the early settlers. Rev. Joseph Badger was a rigid temperance man, and his influence caused some reformations. Marquis Andrews set on foot a temperance movement and called a meeting for the purpose of discussing the evils of immoderate drinking. He offered a resolution embodying his views, which the citizens so amended as to almost entirely obliterate its original meaning. Then a pledge was circulated so strongly worded that when it came to Andrews he would not sign it. Like many another temperance lecturer, he was not willing to practice total abstinence himself.

IN 1812.*

The call for troops for the war was received with enthusiasm, and nearly every able-bodied man in Gustavus volunteered for the service. The next day after the call was received here Marquis Andrews led towards Fort Stephenson at Lower Sandusky (now Fremont), a company armed and equipped. Among these volunteers

---

*For this and many other facts included in this chapter, the writer is indebted to a published article by Miss P. M. Barnes, of Gustavus.

were Joseph, Elias, and Julius Pelton, Lemuel Newton, Aaron Rice, Joseph Hart, John Lane, Thaddeus Selby, Aaron Lyon, Elam Linsley, and Lester Cone.

An amusing incident connected with the call was that when 'Squire Meacham learned that equipments were demanded as well as men, he proceeded to bury his two brass kettles in his corn-field. But his son Jehiel enlisted and the kettles had to be brought out for immediate use, as each man was required to furnish his own camp-kettle and blanket.

After the departure of the troops some experienced great anxiety through fear of an attack by the Indians, who were known to be the allies of the British. As the settlement was left almost wholly without arms and men this fear was not unnatural to the defenceless women and children left behind.

One day some boys killed a fawn in the western part of the township, and expressed their delight at their success in hunting by wild shouts and other boyish actions. Mrs. Newton, who lived two miles west of the center, was alone in her house with two small children. She heard the outcry and supposed that a band of Indians were raising the war-cry. Hastily taking up her children she left the house as secretly as possible and went to the center where her nearest neighbors lived. She and all others rejoiced when the true cause of her alarm became known.

A NIGHT WITH WOLVES.

It is almost unnecessary to state that the dense forests of this neighborhood were the lurking places of wolves and other wild animals in great numbers.

As a missionary Rev. Joseph Badger labored in Gustavus as early as 1804; but it was several years later that he entered the pulpit one Sunday morning and related the experiences of the previous night. Said he:

I had started to come through from Ashtabula, but there being no path I got ahead but slowly, and I cannot say how far I had come when darkness came upon me. As I could make no headway through a pathless wood, I tied my horse so that it could feed about some and then lay down on the ground to rest. Ere long I was aroused by the cry of a wolf. This cry was answered and soon it seemed that a hundred ravenous wolves were howling for their prey. I quickly arose, tied my horse more firmly, and, feeling about in the darkness, found a stout limb, which I cut for a cudgel, and prepared for an encounter with the enemy.

The wolves formed a circle about me. I drew near to my horse and walked around him constantly. The wolves came so near that I could hear the snapping of their jaws. All night long I kept up this walk, beating the trees with my stick and shouting to keep the hungry animals at bay. My horse trembled, but trusting in my protection did not try to get away.

In the first gray light of morning the wolves began to creep slowly away. Their cries grew fainter and fainter in the distance, and I found that they had left me. Blessing God for the countless manifestations of His goodness in preserving me through this and similar perils, I was again proceeding on my way when once more the barking of wolves resounded through the forest. There was little opportunity for me to hasten, as fallen trees, brush, and bushes were in the way. The pursuers were coming quite near, and their howling rent the air, when suddenly there was a crashing near me, and like a flash of light, a fine, full grown deer leaped out, bubbles of white foam falling from his mouth, and panting for breath. He thrust his head alongside my faithful horse and so came beside me until we reached a clearing probably four miles from the place where I had spent the night. The hungry wolves were again baffled, and retired to await the coming of another night in which to continue their search for food.

A BEAR STORY.

Ichabod Merritt was quite a noted hunter. He was out one day with an old man known as "Old" Wheeler, and tracked a bear to a large, hollow whitewood stump. The stump was too large and smooth for a man to climb, so a tree was cut and made to fall so as to lean against it. Merritt was then able to climb to the top of the stump, and, having reached this point, he pointed his rifle down the hollow trunk and discharged it. Before he could load again the old bear came rushing out of the top of the stump to avenge her own injuries and protect her young, which were in the hollow hiding-place. Merritt knew that to jump would be as certain death as to remain within reach of the bear. He crept out on a limb of the tree which he had cut, and so managed to keep out of her clutches. "Old" Wheeler, on the ground, nearly bereft of his wits, was shouting: "Oh dear! You'll be killed! you'll be killed!" in a voice loud enough to frighten anything except a maddened bear, and had not the presence of mind to use the gun he held in his hand. Ike Mowry happened to be not far away, and having heard Merritt's gun and the shouts of Wheeler, came to the rescue. With one shot he brought down the bear and released the hunter from his peril. A hole was then chopped into the stump and two little cubs were taken out.

POST-OFFICE.

A post-office was established in this township

a few years prior to 1830, and Riverius Bidwell, who lived in the southern part of the township, was appointed postmaster. The inhabitants of the center were not satisfied with the location of the office, and Rev. Joseph Badger sought to change it. He drew a map of the township showing the location of each house, thus proving that the center was the most convenient point for all to reach, and sent it to the department at Washington. Shortly after he was commissioned postmaster, and the office was moved to his house near the center. Now another difficulty began to trouble him. The weekly mail arrived on Sunday, and Rev. Badger had conscientious scruples against secular labor on that day. He, therefore, sent another remonstrance to Washington threatening to resign unless this arrangement was changed. His letter had the desired result, and the mail-carrier thereafter arrived in Gustavus on a week day. Mr. Badger resigned in 1830. While postmaster he kept the mail in a small hand-basket. Marvin was mail-carrier. This place now has a daily mail to and from Burg Hill, on the New York, Pennsylvania & Ohio railroad.

STORES.

The first store in this township was opened on the northeast corner at the center by George Hezlep, about 1828. He had been clerk for John Kinsman some years. Mr. Hezlep remained many years and was a successful merchant. Soon after he began business here Stoddard Stevens and Alvin Hayes opened a store in the eastern part of the township.

PHYSICIANS.

Dr. Allen, of Kinsman, was the first who practiced in this township. Not only the white people but Indians as well were his patients. Some of the latter who were living on the Pymatuning had the small-pox in early times. Dr. Allen attended them and controlled the disease so effectually that it never spread at all.

The first doctor who settled in this township was Naphtali Streeter, who came previous to 1812. Although his qualifications were limited, he nevertheless had some practice.

The only physician in the township at present is Dr. Isaac Barclay, who, during his residence here, has gained hosts of friends and an extensive practice. Dr. Barclay was born in old Trumbull county, in Poland, May 29, 1822. He is the son of Francis and Elizabeth Barclay, his father being a native of Pennsylvania and his mother of Virginia. Dr. Barclay is the youngest of twelve brothers. The whole family consisted of seventeen children, of whom eight are living, six sons and two daughters.

He studied medicine in Youngstown with Dr. Timothy Woodbridge, and graduated from the medical department of the Western Reserve college, Cleveland, in 1847. He was engaged in practicing in Youngstown nine years, in Girard five, and at Mineral Ridge four. In 1865 he came to Gustavus. Dr. Barclay was married in 1856 to Melvina Silliman, of Fowler township. She died in September following their marriage. He married his second wife, Mary Jane Holcomb, of Gustavus, in 1863. No children by either marriage.

THE FIRST SAW-MILL

in this township was built by Josiah Pelton on his own farm in early times. No water grist-mill was ever built in the township.

GUSTAVUS ACADEMY.

A good school exerts a powerful influence in any community. Its fruits are apparent even to the most careless observer, and we believe that it is a standard truth that in a rural town where a flourishing academy is located, the general morals, to say nothing of intelligence, are better than in places where no such schools are. Gustavus has shown commendable enterprise in educational mattters. The project of building an academy was started by Rev. Benjamin Fenn, Buell Barnes, S. C. Stevens, Stephen Linsley, E. H. Bishop, George W. Cowden, and other prominent citizens. In 1841 the matter took definite shape, and a subscription paper was circulated which received the signatures of a large number. Each subscriber agreed to take a certain number of shares of the stock, each share being $10. Some of the largest subscribers were Ebenezer H. Bishop, ten shares; S. C. Stevens, fifteen; Buell Barnes, twelve; Philo Gates, twelve; George Hezlep, twenty; James Q. Horner, fifteen.

Buell Barnes, then a member of the Legislature, succeeded in getting an act of incorporation passed. In 1843-44, a substantial two-story brick building was erected, and in the fall of 1844 the institution was opened with Franklin B. Hough principal. The school has been fairly successful considering the small population of the community on which it depends for support. The number of teachers has been large. James H. Brainard, John B. Beach, and E. P. Clisbee, each taught several terms. The present principal, Mr. L. P. Hodgman, has been at the head of the school two years. The usual number of pupils is from fifty to seventy-five.

In 1881 a building to be used as a boarding hall was erected. It cost, including furnishing, about $2,300.

MASONIC.

Gustavus lodge No. 442, Free and Accepted Masons, was organized under a dispensation April 19, 1870. A charter was granted October 19, 1870, to the following charter members: James S. Cowden, Robert Kennedy, Samuel Jones, Jr., A. P. Case, J. H. Fobes, William P. Fobes, Charles Wilder, C. C. Case, L. J. Morey, Edward Bladen, Thaddeus Morey, L. H. Fobes, A. D. DeBow, Charles Pease, J. R. Evans, John C. Smith, T. D. Pelton, L. D. Brainard, George C. Logan, Robert Sadler, David Allen, M. D. Cowden, H. J. Barnes, A. E. Brainard, Lauren Coleman, G. W. Harrington, J. H. Hubbard, R. C. Rice, Robert Evans, George W. Phillips, Marshall Lattin, L. B. Brainard, S. M. Hathaway, and Edward Spear.

The first officers were, Edward Spear, W. M.; Robert Kennedy, S. W.; A. P. Case, J. W.; Lauren Coleman, treasurer; John C. Smith, secretary; L. J. Morey, S. D.; M. Lattin J. D.; L. D. Brainard, tyler, and Rev. J. F. Hill, chaplain.

The past masters from the foundation of the lodge have been as follows: Edward Spear, Robert Kennedy, Lauren Coleman, John C. Smith, Richard K. Hulse, L. J. Morey, and F. A. Kinnear.

The lodge is at present in a good condition with fifty-four members.

CHURCH HISTORY.

The first sermon ever preached in this township was delivered by Rev. Thomas Robbins, at the house of Jesse Pelton, soon after the settlement began. Robbins was sent to the Reserve by the Connecticut Missionary society. He, Mr. Badger, Mr. Osgood, and others preached

occasionally in Gustavus until 1809, when Rev. Henry Cowles (Congregationalist), of Austinburg, preached during the summer at the house of Josiah Pelton, who paid him, principally, for his work.

METHODIST EPISCOPAL CHURCH.

The Methodist church at Gustavus center is a very old organization, and as all of its early records are lost, we have been able to gather very few particulars concerning it.

A class was formed about 1809, and among its members were Zenas, Polly, and Mercy Pelton, Eliphaz and Roger Perkins, and Thomas Partridge. Missionaries came but rarely to visit them, and when there was no preaching here the people met with the church in Kinsman. In summer it was customary for those who walked to church to carry their shoes and stockings in their hands until they came near to the meeting-house; then sitting down, they clothed their feet, and entered the sacred edifice with becoming reverence. In winter little tin foot stoves were carried to church. Warming the house by stoves was a later, and some thought a profane, innovation.

Singing was considered a part of the worship and was conducted with much earnestness and solemnity. "A joyful noise unto the Lord" was made by the harmonious blending of the voices of all the worshipers.

At an early date the Methodists erected a house of round logs one mile north of the center, where they continued to meet for some years. Their present church edifice at the center was erected about 1860, and is a very neat and comfortable house. The church is now large and prosperous. About two hundred members belong to it.

In the winter months of 1881 one of the greatest revivals ever known in this section took place in this church. One hundred persons experienced religion. Rev. W. J. Wilson, the present pastor, is grandly successful in his labors.

THE PRESBYTERIAN CHURCH.

A meeting was held for the purpose of forming a church organization April 27, 1825. After an introductory prayer by Rev. Joseph Badger a sermon was delivered by Rev. Ephraim T. Woodruff. Letters were read from the churches of Vernon and Wayne containing the following names of persons to be constituted a church in Gustavus: Jehiel and Rhoda Bidwell, Joseph and Eunice Hart, Asa and Hepsibah Case, Eliza Cowden, Naomi Gerrills, Faith A. Mills, William and Marquis Roberts, Aaron Lyon, Curtis B. Coe, Ira Skinner (died March 17, 1825), Hepsibah, Achsah, and Riley Skinner, Rufus and Alcinda Beman, Luther and Mary Jones, Seth St. John, Abner Waters and wife. Truman Cowden, Cyrus Bailey, and Abigail Bailey were examined for admission and baptized. The above-named persons were then solemnly organized into a Congregational church.

The above is from the church record, signed "Joseph Badger, moderator." The church was organized on the plan of union adopted by the most of the early Congregational and Presbyterian churches.

June 15, 1825, the first church officers were elected, as follows: Rufus Beman, clerk; Rufus Beman, Asa Case, and Abner Waters, standing committee; and Rufus Beman, deacon. At the same date it was voted that the presbytery be requested to take the church under its care. October 19, 1825, Rev. Joseph Badger was installed as pastor, Rev. Mr. Cowles preaching the sermon upon that occasion. Rev. Joseph Badger continued to supply this pulpit until 1835, when he resigned on account of the infirmities of age and a partial loss of his voice.

June 16, 1835, Rev. Benjamin Fenn was installed pastor, in the presence of Revs. Towne, of Warren; Bowton, of Farmington; McIlvaine, of Kinsman; Badger, former pastor; and Evans, of Vernon.

He was succeeded by Rev. E. B. Chamberlain, who was installed February 7, 1844. At this installation the following ministers were present and took part in the exercises: Revs. O. S. Eells, H. B. Eldred, T. J. Keep, A. Cone, B. Fenn, J. T. Pitkin, and H. Betts. Since that date the following have served as pastors and supplies: J. B. Allen, 1850; A. Cone, 1855–59; Joseph H. Spelman, 1860; E. B. Chamberlain, 1861; Henry B. Dye, 1865. Mr. Dye closed his labors in 1866, and the church has maintained no preaching since that date. Difference of opinion upon the slavery question caused the Congregationalists to withdraw and form a separate church. The Presbyterians, greatly reduced in numbers, managed to struggle on a while longer, but finally yielded to the might of necessity.

At one time the church was very prosperous. At the close of Rev. Badger's labors there were sixty-six members. The number continued to increase under his successors. A large and costly church edifice was erected at the center, which has never yet been disposed of by the church.

The Scotch Presbyterians formerly had a church organization in the eastern part of the township, but it is now extinct.

THE CONGREGATIONAL CHURCH

of Gustavus was organized September 5, 1852, by Rev. F. E. Lord, with seventeen members—Lucius and Huldah Badger, William Johnson, Samuel Krahl, Phebe Gilder, Sally Gilder, L. L., Theodosia, and Curtis P. Sheldon, William and Thersa Roberts, Mary A. Krahl, Huldah Humphrey, Adeline Meacham, Phebe Moses and Wealthy Burlingame. Lucius Badger was chosen deacon, November 25, 1852. In May, 1853, Abram Griswold was elected deacon. December 28, 1853, the following church officers were elected: William Johnson, Reuben Wakefield, and C. P. Sheldon, trustees; and L. L. Sheldon, clerk. The first pastor was Rev. E. H. Fairchild, followed by E. J. Comings, Johnson Wright, W. W. Foot, H. D. King, B. F. Markham, L. J. Donaldson, and E. P. Clisbee, who began his labors in 1879. The number of members is about fifty. The church has a very good house.

CHAPTER XVII.

BAZETTA.

The original proprietors of the land now contained in this township were David Huntington, Nathaniel Shalor, Samuel P. Lord, Sylvester Mather, and Richard McCurdy; and it embraces by the land company's survey 17,247 acres. Afterwards a special survey was made for these proprietors by David Wolcott, when it was found that the former survey was in error by two hundred and seventy-five acres short, the surplus accruing to the purchasers. The above-named persons formed a company and received the deeds of the lands from the Connecticut Land company, dated September 20, 1798. In 1802 the company formed by the proprietors, as above mentioned, had the land surveyed in separate portions and divided among themselves. Nathaniel Shalor received for his share the northern part of the tract beginning at lot number one and extending to lot number thirty-seven, inclusive, comprising in all 7,300 acres. David Huntington received lots numbers eight and thirty-four. Sylvester Mather received lots numbers thirty-nine and sixty-five, inclusive, and altogether amounting to 4,469 acres. Richard McCurdy received lots numbers sixty-six and ninety, and all inclusive, or 4,118 acres. S. P. Lord received lots numbers ninety-one and one hundred on the southern border, and all inclusive, or 1,635 acres. From these proprietors the early settlers made their purchases, and soon the settlement of Bazetta began.

LOCATION AND BOUNDARY.

This township is the central one of the twenty-five townships which now comprise Trumbull county, and its central point therefore is the center of the county. On this account some years ago an effort was made to have the county seat located here; but other influences were then more potent than the convenience of a central location for the court-house and the business of the county. The oldest settlement having been made at Warren, and the settlement of the township itself having been made in the northeast corner the project of removal of the court-house proved unsuccessful.

Bazetta as now constituted is bounded on the north by Mecca, east by Fowler, south by Howland, and on the west by Champion. The natural drainage is effected by Mosquito creek, which enters the township a short distance east of the central part of the north boundary, and after receiving several tributaries, mostly from the east, and flowing directly southward, leaves the township at a central point on the south.

This creek divides the township almost into halves, and in former times formed a boundary line of distinction between the settlers on the east and west side. Those of the west side were known as "west-siders," and those on the east as "east-siders."

Confusion run is a tributary of the Mosquito, and takes its rise in the northeast part of lot fifty-one, southeast of Cortland, and flowing southwest empties into the Mosquito in lot eighty-six. The singular name of this creek originated from the following incident of early times; Benjamin Rowlee, Henry K. Hulse, and another man whose name cannot now be remembered, were in the neighborhood on some expedition, and the wilderness was so dense, the roads unmarked, and the signs of civilization so undefined that they became lost, and in wandering through the woods would come upon this little stream, from which they would take their "bearings" and again attempt to find their way to the settlement, but time and again they lost their way and would find themselves at the creek again. So they very appropriately called it "Confusion," by which name it is known to this day.

The soil in the western part of the township is mostly clay; the eastern portion is a mixture of sand and gravel, and is generally productive. In 1880 the estimated products were 8,103 bushels of wheat, 14,223 bushels of corn, 2,433 tons of hay, 192 bushels of flax-seed, 28,155 pounds of butter, 298,558 pounds cheese, 21,005 pounds of maple sugar, and in the spring of 1881, 687 gallons of maple syrup. The timber is largely of maple, beech, and chestnut, and various other kinds common to this section of the State.

The Atlantic & Great Western railroad extends diagonally across the township from northeast to southwest, with the main station at Cortland. Several stone quarries have been opened in the township, especially in the southwest, from which the stone peculiar to this section, elsewhere described, is found in abundance.

POPULATION AND INDUSTRIES.

The first settlement having been made at what is now Cortland, this locality has still maintained the center of population in the township, while the west and southern parts, however, are thickly settled. Many large farms are located immediately east of Cortland, but west of the west center road they are divided into smaller tracts, growing larger, however, toward the south and southeast.

The industries are generally confined to the agricultural department, while there is some attention paid to stock-raising, grazing, etc.

MILLS AND FACTORIES.

The only flouring-mill in Bazetta is operated by J. H. & M. C. Post, and is located in the southeast part of the village of Cortland. The building is a frame, two stories high; has a basement wall of stone sixteen feet high, and three run of buhrs, with the usual capacity, propelled by both steam- and water-power. The same firm has also a steam saw-mill at the same place which has a capacity of three thousand feet per day. The trade is steady and increasing, necessitating the employment of five and six hands, and altogether embraces the most flourishing and successful industrial enterprise in the township.

THE DIAMOND CHEESE FACTORY

is now owned by Richard & Rose, and was built by David Everet in 1875. The factory now has a capacity of about ten boxes per day.

THE CORTLAND CHEESE FACTORY

is the largest factory in the township, and was built about 1868. It is now operated by a stock company, each stockholder a patron, partaking mutually and in proportion to the amount of milk he furnishes. At the present time the milk is brought in by farmers from a large section of the country, and representing the product from eight hundred cows, from which the factory, under the management of F. G. Kingdom, produces about twenty-three cheese per day. Butter is also extensively manufactured. Lewis Oatley is the business manager, who sells the products, the receipts of which—averaging about twenty-five cents for butter and ten cents for cheese—is divided among the stockholders.

EARLY SETTLEMENT.

The first settler in Bazetta was Edward Schofield, who came to the township about 1804, and settled on the farm now owned by N. A. Cowdery, on lot twenty-two. He was born in Connecticut in 1777, and came to the Reserve in 1797. He assisted in surveying lots in many of the townships and finally settled in Bazetta, alone, with his nearest neighbor five miles distant. In 1817 he was elected to the State Legislature. He was a pious man, often preaching the gospel to the early settlers, and was largely instrumental in founding the early religious organization of the township. He is remembered as a generous and liberal man, eminently given to hospitality.

About the same time with Schofield John Budd and family came and settled south of Schofield, on the farm now owned by William B. Kennedy—lot thirty-two. After him came Henry K. Hulse, and settled on the farm now owned by Ephraim Post—lot eight—north of Schofield and Budd; also Joseph Pruden came and settled north of Hulse, on the present William Davis farm—lot nine. John Godden came about this time, but he did not live long, having died about 1810, and was buried in the orchard lot on the Davis farm. Joshua Oatley and Moses Hampton also came about this same time.

These constituted the settlements made in Bazetta up to the year 1811. In the spring of this year William Davis, Sr., came from Pennsylvania and settled where Mr. Pruden had first settled, now owned by his son William, where he planted the first orchard in the township. He was accompanied to the new settlement in Ohio by his wife, who yet lives in Bazetta, and is the oldest living settler in the township. She was born in New Jersey July 1, 1784, and is a granddaughter of General Stark, of the Revolutionary war; her maiden name was Ann Luce. At the age of four years her father moved to Washington county, Pennsylvania, where she was afterward married to William Davis, January 1, 1804. She was soon left, by the misfortune of her husband, with a large family and considerable debt on the farm; but being possessed with remarkable energy, a good constitution, and health, she inspired her children with energy and perseverance that soon cleared the farm of debt. She was left a widow in 1860, the long illness of her husband finally ending in his death.

Mrs. Davis was one of the original members of the Disciple church, and is the only surviving member of that pioneer band. In addition to her own large family she gave a home to three orphan children, who were the subjects of her care with her own. She is now in her ninety-seventh year, and for several years a cataract in the eyes has almost totally destroyed her vision, and the past few years have rendered her frail in body and mind, but she has tender care from

William B. Kennedy.

.solicitous children, and her last days, so far as human hands can minister, will be smoothed peacefully down to the end.

Soon after Mr. Davis, Benjamin Rowlee came with quite a large family of young men and women, also widow Dixon and family, James Parker, and Moses McMahon with their families. In the following year (1812) the war commenced, which very much retarded the growth of the Bazetta settlement, and which also affected the prosperity of the pioneers for some time. The men of the settlement, with their neighbors throughout the section of country, who were capable of bearing arms, were soon called upon to leave their just begun work when most it needed their care, and go in defence of their country. The oat crop was then ready for gathering, and some of the fields had been mown down, and yet lay in the swath. Some was standing, but the men had to leave all and go.

In these early times very little could be lost without serious damage to the meager supply of the pioneer, whose simplest wants were hardly supplied by the hardest toil.

Let us turn back a leaf in the history of Bazetta, and see an example of patriotism, and especially of female courage and hardihood as shown by the early mothers of the township. The men were gone at their country's call, and the harvest stood half cut in the fields, and was fast going to waste, and they could ill afford to lose it. They saw that it depended upon them to save the harvest, while they already had the care of large families and the various other household duties to perform, but with commendable spirit and hardy ambition they repaired with their little ones to the fields, and having arranged for the keeping of the infants in the shades of the forest by the older children, they, with sickle, pitchfork, and rake in hand, entered the fields, and saved the grain. On the return of the men they found the harvest well cared for and the other work of the household and farm had suffered but little if any during their absence.

Among those who were called away at this time were Henry Hulse, Benjamin and Constant Rowlee, James and Walter Dixon, William Davis, and Samuel Tanner. After a few skirmishes with the Indians at Sandusky they all returned safely home except Walter Dixon, who

had been wounded but who subsequently recovered.

At this time the larger part of the township was almost an unbroken forest, with here and there a log hut, some of them without floor, save the ground; no doors except what were provided by hanging bed quilts across the opening. The windows were made by holes cut through the logs or the mud chinking, over which greased paper was pasted. The better cabins were provided with puncheon floors, but at best they were rude cabins and but meagerly furnished. The pioneer had little time and perhaps less desire to provide himself with luxurious comforts; his life was one of toil and privation, and was spent before the days of luxuries came. His strong frame, bent with toil, lies in the rural graveyard, and his hardened hands lie folded and quiet at last, while others reap where he has sown.

WILD ANIMALS

were very plenty, and every man was necessarily provided with a dog and gun; and most of the meat on which the pioneers subsisted was obtained from the wild animals of the forest. Deer, bear, wolves, turkeys, and other animals were common game in these days. The howling of the wolves made the night hideous, and it was with difficulty that the sheep and other domestic animals could be kept from being devoured by them. The pioneers were compelled then to keep a few sheep to provide wool for clothing, and for the purpose of keeping them from the wolves a high, closely-built pen had to be built in which, after being herded by the boys during the day, they were securely fastened at night. Many of the settlers were unable to provide enclosures for their stock, and were compelled to turn them loose in the forest to feed, first having put bells on them. William Davis relates that at one time he had so turned his horses out, and desiring to do some ploughing he started to find his horse, and following the sounds of the bell he found the mother of a young colt fighting five wolves that were tearing the colt to pieces. He procured one of the other horses and went immediately for his gun and dog, and when he returned the dog made an attack on the wolves, but was soon overpowered and returned beaten to his master; as the wolves followed the dog Mr. Davis killed one of them, and secured the hide and scalp, for which he afterwards received $7. Very often whole flocks of sheep were destroyed by the wolves, thus causing the early settlers no little annoyance and serious loss.

Bears were also very destructive to the swine that the owners were compelled to allow to run in the woods to procure their own feed upon which they were fattened. The sagacious brute after seizing its prey seemed to anticipate pursuit for his theft, and would seek some place where he would have a commanding view of his surroundings. One favorite place for one of these animals was on the roots of a tree in the vicinity of the Davis farm, where he would carry his victim and where the well-picked bones would afterwards be found. The bears when killed, as they often were, furnished meat if young, and if they were somewhat old they would be rendered into oil for the lamps.

Deer were very plenty in the fall, and the settlers killed very many of them for venison and from their hides manufactured their own clothing. The dressing of the hide was done by soaking it in a brine made by the brains of the animal and warm water. The hair was removed by rubbing with a kind of knife, after which the hide was allowed to remain in the brain water for some time, then taken out, stretched, pulled, and rubbed until it assumed the desired state ready for manufacturing into pants, jackets, etc., the common article of clothing for the early settlers.

Wild turkeys were more common than any game except squirrels, and the boys were compelled to keep watch over the buckwheat patches to prevent the wild turkeys from destroying the grain. When it is remembered that if the buckwheat crop was a failure, Pittsburg was the nearest market where grain could be bought, and that, with the scarcity of money, made the watch over the growing crops a very necessary precaution, upon which depended that very common pioneer article of diet, the old-time buckwheat cakes.

In 1816 Samuel Bacon and family came to Bazetta, and at that time there were very few more families here than those mentioned. He had formerly (1807) settled above Warren on the Mahoning, where he had purchased a farm of sixty acres, but in the above year he traded for the mill here, then owned by Bentley & Brooks,

which was operated by the family from that time until 1850, and was the only saw-mill in the neighborhood. They built the upper dam about 1829, the grist-mill having been built by Mr. Schofield about 1812.

The settlement made by Mr. Bacon was destined to become the starting point of the principal settlement and ultimately the only village of the township, indications of which were soon apparent. He had erected at this point the first frame building in the township, and soon after the community began to increase in population and the land was laid out in lots and other initial steps were taken for the building of a town. In 1829 Enos Bacon, son of Samuel, opened the first store in the little town—then and for a long time afterward known as Baconsburgh. After the completion of the railroad through the village the railroad company named the station at this place Cortland, since which time the town has been known by that name.

CORTLAND.

This is the only town in Bazetta township, and is pleasantly situated on the New York, Pennsylvania and Ohio railroad, in the northeastern part of the township. It is now a thriving town of six hundred and fourteen inhabitants, and contains three churches, two newspapers, stores, mills, and other industries and business operations and enterprises. Two hotels and two livery stables provide for the wants of the traveling public. H. G. Bacon in the principal dealer in groceries of all kinds, and C. C. Clawson is largely engaged in a dry goods and general mercantile business. J. A. Bradford deals in all kinds of furniture. These are a few of the prominent business firms of the village.

INCORPORATION.

The town was formally incorporated in 1874, and at the first election under the incorporation the following officials were chosen : Asa Hines, mayor; W. W. Post, clerk; E. A. Faunce, treasurer; Joseph Young, marshal; A. S. Gilbert, R. D. Larned, J. H. Post, M. Bacon, M. Craft, and A. G. Miller were elected councilmen.

NEWSPAPERS.

The Cortland Gazette was established May 19, 1876, and is devoted to general and local news, and has for its motto "One country, one currency, and a credit based upon coin." The paper was first started by W. A. Craft, publisher, and John Johnston, editor. The latter has since become sole proprietor.

The Cortland Era is a sprightly little paper, and has for its object "the greatest good to the greatest number." It is independent in politics and is issued by Caldwell & Hardy.

SCHOOLS.

Cortland is more noted for its educational advantages, her citizens having made special efforts in securing the location of a large and commodious union school-building, fitted with all the modern facilities for educational pursuits.

CORTLAND HIGH SCHOOL.

Cortland high school was established by a special act of the Legislature, and was opened for the admission of students September 3, 1877. The aim and scope of the school is, in many of its features, distinctly different from that of the ordinary high schools. The aim of the board of education is to furnish, not only to the citizens of Cortland, but also to the citizens of Trumbull and adjoining counties, a school of high standing, in which thorough preparation may be made for college, for the important work of teaching, or for the duties of active life. A liberal patronage and an increased interest in the great cause of education has rewarded their efforts.

The high school building stands upon an elevated plat of ground overlooking the village of Cortland and many miles of the surrounding country, affording scenery of great natural beauty. The building is new and commodious, consisting of five well heated, lighted, and ventilated rooms, furnished with comfortable sittings, and with charts, globes, and other apparatus necessary for the school-room. Attendance (1881), ladies 28, gentlemen 14, and non-residents 21.

EARLY SCHOOLS.

The pioneer school-house of Bazetta was built in the valley immediately above the present Cortland Cheese factory, on Walnut creek. This was a small, rude structure of unhewn logs, and as rudely furnished. The windows were made by cutting out a part of a log here and there, and over the apertures thus made oiled (real bear's oil) paper was pasted. The paper, however, had previously been used as copy books, and hence the windows of the pioneer academy were well

decorated with those hieroglyphic characters commonly known as "pot-hooks," and such familiar mottoes as "Honesty is the best policy."

The writing desks were constructed by boring holes in the wall, or logs, in which wooden pins were driven; on these boards were laid, and the desks were complete.

The course of study and supply of books were exceedingly limited, and embraced in the furthest advancement the well known acme of mathematical knowledge called the "single rule of three," now known as proportion.

When the old school-house was abandoned another one was built somewhat better, but after the same plan, and was erected about 1814. The cause of education soon received special and earnest attention from the people of this township, and as it became more settled and the population increased the various localities, as soon as circumstances would allow, were supplied with the usual common school facilities.

THE PRESBYTERIAN CHURCH.

The first meeting appointed for this society in Bazetta was held March 10, 1841. Morris Headley was appointed moderator, and J. W. Peck clerk. At the election which ensued J. A. Root, Constant Rowlee, and Lucius Peck were chosen as trustees; Silas Leonard and Joel Casterline, collectors; J. W. Peck and Joel Casterline, choristers. At this meeting the subject of building a house of worship was discussed and decided upon favorably. Nathan Latin presented a proposition to donate the site of the new church on his land at the center, and another was presented by Ezra Marvin for the erection of the house on the corner near his present residence.

A vote being taken it was decided to build the church at the center, which they immediately proceeded to carry into execution. The society was afterward incorporated under the act of the Legislature of the State, passed January 21, 1842.

The society was then incorporated as the First Presbyterian and Congregational church society of Bazetta, in which Lucius Peck, Joseph A. Root, and their successors in office were elected a body politic and corporate, known by the name above mentioned. The present pastor is Rev. R. A. Davis.

THE DISCIPLES CHURCH.

The pioneer religious organization was effected by the Baptists about 1818. The members of this pioneer society held their meetings at private houses and in the school-houses. Edward Schofield was the leading member of the society and frequently officiated as minister. Mrs. Ann Davis is the only person now living who belonged to this pioneer band. This organization was afterwards merged into what is now known as the Disciples church, and the well-known leaders in the new faith—Adamson Bentley, Walter Scott, Hayden, Headley, and others, often ministered to the members of this society.

The society is now in a flourishing condition in the village of Cortland.

The present church building was remodeled in 1875 and now has a baptistry and prayer-rooms, with ample seating capacity for the present membership of about two hundred. Rev. D. P. Thayer is the present pastor, and the present board of elders is composed of the following persons, namely: N. A. Cowdery, S. Hulse, and Aaron Davis; deacons, E. Barnes, H. McHanah, and H. G. Bacon. The Sabbath-school numbers about one hundred pupils.

This denomination also has another society at West Bazetta, which was organized December 16, 1848, by Calvin Smith. The official board is composed of Levi Bush and Alden Faunce, overseers; and Ellis Pierce, Joseph Sage, and Jacob Dice, deacons.

In 1853 this society was constituted an incorporate body, of which Stephen Mott, Hiram Wilber, and Joseph Dilley were chosen trustees, and John Diehl clerk.

The Disciples in the east part of the township met on September 7, 1852, and an organization was effected. At that time the association was called "The Church of God," and the official board was composed of Hervey Post, Moses Bacon, and Aaron Davis trustees, and Leman Palmer clerk.

These societies are now in a flourishing condition, and with commendable zeal bearing their respective part in the moral and religious work in this township.

THE METHODIST EPISCOPAL CHURCH.

From the best authority, in the absence of the records, the date of the organization of this society was about 1830. At this time the first building was erected, but the rapid growth of the society soon necessitated the building of a new edifice, and the old church was abandoned, and was refitted for a hall. The new building was begun in 1879, and is now (1881) finished. It is a large and commodious brick structure of modern architecture, with audience rooms having a seating capacity of over four hundred, also lecture room, basement, and other chambers, eight in all. The society now has a membership of about one hundred and twenty, formed into four classes, of which C. C. Clawson, Mahlon Craft, and F. A. Richards are the leaders. The board of trustees is composed of Solomon Cline, Mahlon Craft, C. C. Clawson, A. J. Larned, August Hayden, B. F. Meek, and F. A. Richards; and the present pastor is Rev. J. H. Starrett.

THE UNITED BRETHREN CHURCH.

This denomination has organized several societies in the township. The one in Cortland was organized in 1869, when the church building was erected. Rev. W. H. Millar was the first pastor. He came from Portage county, and took charge of this congregation, and the one in the south part of the township. The board of trustees, elected at the quarterly conference at the time of the organization, was composed of Rev. W. H. Millar, Rev. Silas Casterline, Thomas Kennedy, James Hulse, and D. P. Hayden. The latter was steward and David Wilson leader. The membership at that time numbered about twenty-seven, and was scattered over a great extent of territory. The church building was dedicated in January, 1870, and the dedicatory exercises were presided over by Bishop J. J. Glossbrenner, of Virginia. The present membership numbers about fifty, under the pastoral charge of Rev. D. A. Bonewell. The present officials are Silas Casterline, James Hulse, Thomas Kennedy, Fitch Mapes, and Orville Hayden, trustees. The latter is also class-leader and William Roberts steward.

THE TEMPLE, OR WEST BAZETTA CHURCH,

is located in the southwest part of the township, and was organized by Rev. W. H. Millar in 1856. The membership at the first organization exceeded one hundred, but at present is very much diminished in number.

Aaron Davis

THE INDEPENDENCE CORNER CHURCH

is located in the northeast corner of the township. The society was organized about 1840.

THE BAZETTA, OR KENNEDY CHURCH,

was established about 1840. Rev. D. A. Bonewell is the present pastor.

THE RIDGE CHURCH.

This church building was erected in 1842.

BIOGRAPHICAL SKETCHES.

AARON DAVIS.

This well and favorably known citizen of Bazetta township was the oldest son and third child of William Davis, who was born in Washington county, Pennsylvania, in the year 1782. His wife, Ann Luce, was a granddaughter of General Stark, of Revolutionary fame. She was born in 1783, and is yet living, being about ninety-nine years old, probably the oldest person living in the county. The extreme old age to which Mrs. Davis has lived will appear all the more remarkable when it is known that she has been the mother of fifteen children, named as follows: Mariah, Susan, Aaron, Matthias, Reuben, Mary, Permelia, Eliza, Sidney, William, Stockton and Judson (twins), Mariah, Lucy, and Elijah. Mr. Davis was a lieutenant of militia when the news of Hull's surrender of Detroit reached the Reserve, and at the first alarm prepared for action. The wildest confusion prevailed among the settlers, who seized all kinds of arms and had a volunteer army on foot in a miraculously short time, under command of General Perkins. Lieutenant Davis urged the necessity of guarding against an Indian incursion, and also made provision for the safety and support of the families of volunteers. After the war he engaged in the manufacture of potash on his farm. While thus employed he one winter suffered undue exposure to severe cold, and in consequence lost his native power and steadiness of mind. During the remaining years of his life he was at times demented and suffered constantly from feeble health. His death occurred in 1860.

Aaron Davis, the subject of an accompanying illustration, was born April 23, 1809. His early

life was spent on his father's farm. He was married September 13, 1832, to Alvira C. Knox, whose death occurred March 25, 1848. She left a family of six children—Lavina C., wife of Horace Detchon; Byron, resident of Mecca township; Theodocia, deceased; Newton, Mecca township; Mary, wife of Oswald Totton, Johnston township, and Marshall, Cortland.

Mr. Davis married for his second wife Mary Johnston, daughter of Colonel Walter Johnston, and granddaughter of James Johnston, a member of the Connecticut Land company and original proprietor of Johnston township. She was born March 4, 1824. The family by this marriage consisted of three children living—Ransom W., of Cortland; Eliza A., wife of Henry Day, of Gustavus township; Burritt, of Bazetta, and Jane M., deceased. Mr. Davis has held various local offices. He served two terms on the board of county commissioners, having been first elected in the year 1860. He was a competent and faithful officer. For more than two score of years he has been an active member of the Disciple church. He was selected one of the first board of trustees of Hiram institute, and was a member of the committee which located and purchased the ground. He served as trustee for a period of fifteen years, a part of the time with James A. Garfield, with whom he became well acquainted. He was a member of the board when Garfield was first employed as a teacher in Hiram. The following anecdote was related to Mr. Davis by the late President:

When I was a pupil in school in Geauga county I was, I suppose, an ungainly looking lad, at any rate I was the subject of a great many tricks and jokes. Once they sheared off my hair. I told the fellow who did the cutting that if I ever became able I would give him a sound thrashing. A year or two afterwards I fulfilled my promise. Several years later, while I was president of Hiram college, I was out lecturing, and one night saw this same fellow in one corner of the house. It was with difficulty I could keep from laughing out loud.

Mr. Davis has many other pleasant reminiscences of the Nation's late chief.

Mr. Davis is a ready hand at almost anything; while farming has engaged most of his attention, he has also worked at carpentering, cabinet work, etc. He is a quiet citizen, but always ready to respond to the call of duty. He has been overseer of the Disciple church for forty years, and is a practical Christian.

JAMES HERVEY POST.

The sons and descendants of Munson Post are among the most prominent and influential citizens of Bazetta township. The name is of Welsh origin. Joseph Post was one of the earliest settlers of Washington county, Pennsylvania, where Munson was born January 24, 1785. He was married February 7, 1811, to Elizabeth Cooper, who was born March 17, 1792. They lived in Washington county until the year 1826, the date of their settlement in Bazetta. Mr. Post was a man of quiet disposition, regular habits, and good business qualifications. He was universally respected, and died lamented, March 17, 1870, being eighty-five years old. Mrs. Post died July 18, 1874. Their family consisted of ten children, viz: Sarah, born December 27, 1811; Henry H., May 23, 1813; Joseph, August 20, 1815; Mary, February 22, 1818; James H., December 24, 1819; Moses C., May 23, 1822; Marcus, October 23, 1824; Elizabeth, November 15, 1826; Ephraim, November 13, 1828, and Emeline, December 7, 1832. All the daughters are dead. Three of the sons live in Cortland, and one near the village—all successful men and respected citizens.

James Hervey Post built the first mill in Cortland while it was yet known as Baconsburg. With the exception of an interval of three years he has been connected with the milling industry ever since. Since 1856 his brother, Moses C. Post, has been in partnership with him. The firm purchased the saw-mill in 1867, and in that branch have been doing an extensive business in sawing and prepared lumber, house-finishing materials, etc. Further particulars are given in the township history.

Mr. Post married in 1846, Miss Eliza Abell, daughter of Lewis Abell, of Bazetta township. She was born March 26, 1823. Their family consists of three children: Louis M., Florence E., and Calvin S.

Mr. Post is a man of good standing in his own community, but has never aspired to a wide popularity. He has been busily and successfully occupied with his business, and never aspired to public positions, though he has frequently been honored with local trusts. He has been treasurer of his township five years, and was formerly trustee for several terms. He also served one term on the county board of infirmary directors.

He is clear-headed and enterprising in business transactions, and upright and liberal in all his dealings. He is an active member and liberal supporter of the Disciple church in Cortland.

WILLIAM B. KENNEDY.

Samuel Kennedy, father of William B. Kennedy, was of Irish stock and was born in the year 1764. Jane Kennedy, his wife, was born in 1772. They lived in Northumberland county, Pennsylvania, until the year 1814, when with their family they removed to Howland township. Mr. Kennedy died two years later at the age of fifty two years. Mrs. Kennedy died in 1844. They had a family of eleven children, who at one time all lived within four miles of their mother's residence on the old homestead. Their names were as follows: Robert, Montgomery, Jane Maxwell (Mrs. D. B. King), Nancy (Mrs. Samuel King), Mary Barber (Mrs. William King), Tabitha (Mrs. Samuel Kennedy), James, Maxwell, Thomas, William B., Ann (Mrs. M. I. Iddings), and Elizabeth (Mrs. Montgomery Anderson). James, Nancy and Ann are living in Howland, Thomas and William B. in Bazetta. The remaining members of the family are deceased.

William B. Kennedy was born in Northumberland county, Pennsylvania, September 21, 1812, and was consequently two years old when his father removed to Ohio. In the year 1837 he was married to Eliza Davis, who was born in the year 1818. They have had a family of five children, the two youngest of whom, Ellen and Jud D., are deceased. Anthony Wayne, the oldest son, has been engaged in teaching since his eighteenth year, during the last ten years as principal of the schools at Girard. He has traveled extensively, having spent four years on the Rocky mountains. He is married to Eunice Kellogg. Ann, the only daughter of William and Eliza Kennedy living, is the wife of Kennedy Andrews, of Warren. Cassius Clay, third child of William and Eliza Kennedy, is married to Alice Kellogg. He owns one of the best farms in Bazetta township, and is a man of considerable local prominence. He has taught district school since the age of eighteen years.

Mr. Kennedy gave his children an early start in life, and has the satisfaction in his old age of

J. H. Post

seeing them in prosperous circumstances. He has lived on the same farm since 1837, and has devoted himself industriously to agricultural pursuits. He has lived for himself and family and by diligence, sobriety, and honesty has made himself a representative of that class of society known as the substantial common people, which gives soul and permanence to all industrial, moral, and political institutions.

NOTES OF SETTLEMENT.

Lebbeus Beach came from Hartland, Connecticut, and settled on a farm in Hartford township in 1812. He was born in the year of Independence—1776—and was married to Hope Spencer (who was born same year) in June, 1799. The children were—Harry, Seneca (deceased), Julia, now Mrs. M. Scott, of Gustavus; and Laura, now Mrs. Hulburt, of Ashtabula county. The family, with the exception of Laura, he brought with him; he was also accompanied by the aged father of his wife (Frederick) who was eager for the conquests of the new country. He lived in Hartford until 1855, eventually moving to Gustavus, where he lived with his daughter Julia until 1859, when he died. He was known as a farmer but held the office of justice of the peace for twenty-four years.

Dr. Harry Beach was born May 20, 1800, and was married to Mary Chew (born in 1805) in 1823. To them were born the following children: Emily, now Mrs. Ephraim Post; Leonora, deceased; Francis, of Meadville, Pennsylvania; Allison, of Wisconsin; Curtland, member of company A, Forty-first Ohio volunteer infantry, died at Nashville, Tennessee, in 1862. The doctor was, as is seen by the above, a farmer's son, but was given the advantage of the common school, of which he made the best use and was fit to begin the study of medicine, which he did in the fall of 1820, under Dr. Wilcox, of Hartford. There he remained two years, after which he studied under Dr. Fowler, of Brookfield, and commenced practice in the latter place in 1824, continuing two years. He then settled in Fowler, where he continued a successful practice for fifty years, until now at the age of eighty years he has retired from active life and lives with his daughter, Mrs. Post, in Cortland. He is widely known for a life of great usefulness in his profession, and also as the oldest living physician in Trumbull county.

Moses Cooper Post was born in Washington county, Pennsylvania, May 26, 1822, and came to Ohio with his father when about five years of age. He lived on the farm with his father until he was about twenty-one, when, May 28, 1843, he was married to Elvily C. Freer, who was born April 26, 1823. They are the parents of the following children: Olive Cornelia, born March 20, 1844, who was married to J. W. Hathaway, and moved to Marietta, where she died; Harriet Orissa (deceased), born March 26, 1846; Orpha Amanda, born September 29, 1848, now Mrs. Burt Swager; Wills Watson, April 10, 1851; Ella Ophelia, August 6, 1854, now Mrs. Lewis Hutton, of Bristol; Cora Estella, August 16, 1857, now Mrs. Homer Smith; Jennie E. (deceased), born July 22, 1860; Alta B., born May 21, 1864; and Candace E., born March 13, 1867. Soon after his marriage Mr. Post began life for himself, but with very little capital, in the milling business, having built his first mill on Walnut creek. He is now engaged with his brother Hervey in the milling business, operating the only flour-mills in Bazetta. He was captain of the Independent Rifle company that existed here in former years, whose musters occurred twice in the spring and once in the fall. His business relations have precluded his service in any public office except that of town trustee, which he held two terms; was elected to other offices, but for the above reasons he declined to serve. By hard work, industry, and economy, he has arrived at his present well-known position of affluence in this community, in which he has spent the quiet, but busy years of his manhood.

Ephraim Post was born November 13, 1828, and was married to Orpha Hawley, who was born February 14, 1826, and died September 2, 1870. He was again married September 11, 1872, to Emily (Beach) Trowbridge, who was born March 16, 1830. His children are Jay, born October 7, 1856; Viets C., born October 25, 1858, now living in Warren; Loren E., born May 3, 1861; Harry S., born August 28, 1864; Lizzie May, born November 5, 1867. Mrs. Emily Trowbridge, present wife of Mr. Post, had a family of four children, two now living: Charles A., born July 20, 1848, living in

Fowler; Edward M., deceased, born November 19, 1850; Frank B., deceased, born January 21, 1854; Nora, born December 11, 1857, now Mrs. C. C. Craft. Mr. Post, with whom the venerable Dr. Harry Beach (father of Mrs. Post) now makes his home, was born on the Post homestead farm, where he now lives, and where his youth and manhood years have been spent, and where he now expects to remain during life. He is a farmer by occupation, has held the office of councilman of the village of Cortland, and he and his wife are members of the Disciple church.

Deborah Latin came from New York in 1829 and settled in Bazetta. She was accompanied by her two sons, Eli and Shepherd, she being a widow. In 1831 her son Nathaniel came from the same State and settled on the present Latin homestead farm (lot fifty-five). He was a cabinet-maker by trade, which occupation he followed for some time, but subsequently gave it up and began farming. He first built a frame house on the site of his present residence, in which he and his family lived until 1840, when the present residence was erected. Laura Latin, his wife, engaged in tailoring and made the first ready-made gentlemen's clothing sold in Warren. She furnished the prominent men—the lawyers and doctors—with clothing, having in her employ several apprentices. Fifty years ago, when the Latin family came to Bazetta, there were no clearings or roads on the farm, and the wild animals were plentiful. The "whistle" of the deer was often heard from the door-stoop of the pioneer home, as they would come at night to the deer-lick only about forty rods in front of the house. At this lick Nathaniel Latin killed a deer weighing over two hundred pounds. What was then known as Bristol swamps abounded with bears and other wild animals that committed many depredations on the stock of the pioneers. Nathaniel Latin, deceased, was born August 25, 1801, and married May 30, 1822, to Laura Lonsberry, who was born March 15, 1802. To them were born the following children: Martin Hawley (deceased), born March 1, 1824; Warren A., February 1, 1826, now in Arizona; Susannah M., July 4, 1829, now Mrs. Samuel Bissel, of Pennsylvania; Lura C., August 30, 1831, now Mrs. O. B. Bissel, of Iowa; Sarah J. (deceased), born July 28, 1833; Oliver L., December 9, 1834, of Kansas; Delilah, February

17, 1837, now Mrs. Fisk of New York; Helen F., February 13, 1839, now Mrs. W. D. Kelly, of Kansas; Laura, November 25, 1843, now Mrs. William T. Wright, of Colorado; and Nathaniel, who was born December 10, 1847, and married Eliza Ellen Gilbert May 7, 1873, who was born September 22, 1851. To them was born one child, Gilbert S., born May 19, 1874; he now lives on the home farm in Bazetta.

Benjamin Rowlee was born in New Jersey, August 19, 1780, from whence he moved to Washington county, Pennsylvania, and afterwards to Ohio in 1805, and first settled on the farm now owned and occupied by his son Amos. He was married February 16, 1808, to Eunice Headley, who was born July 11, 1781. The family were John H., born January 18, 1813; Samuel, November 26, 1814; William, July 30, 1816; Hannah, September 25, 1817; Phebe, May 18, 1819; Mary, January 14, 1821; Abigail, September 25, 1823; Amos, October 9, 1824. He assisted in raising the first log-house in Mecca not long after he came to the State. His own house stood about forty rods north of the present residence of his son Amos, where in 1820 he built a brick house, where he lived until his death, which occurred December 15, 1841, followed by the death of his wife February 19, 1864. When he first came to his farm (1805), he deadened three trees. Two of them are now to be seen remaining on the farm. He paid for his farm by hard work, often cutting and splitting two hundred rails for a day's work, and then returning to his own work on the farm. Constant Rowlee built the first frame building in the township, which he erected over a spring for a milk-house, on the farm now owned by Solomon Cline, adjoining Cortland. Amos Rowlee was married in 1849, to Elizabeth Weir, who was born December 3, 1833. Their children are Lafayette, James, and Watson. He has served as constable, member of town council and board of education.

Samuel Bacon was the first of this family, except his sister, Rachel Rankin, to come to Ohio, where he arrived June 7, 1807, and settled on the banks of the Mahoning river, two and one-half miles north of Warren, having left Bridgetown, New Jersey, May 18, 1807. He left the following diary of the settlement: "And this we call a new country, only six years old, of settlers from New England, Pennsylvania, and New Jersey." He was born April 21, 1773, and was married in 1798 to Elizabeth Harris, who was born October 10, 1780. Their children were Charles, Enos, Richard, Moses, Phœbe, Grant, and Mary. Enos Bacon was born April 6, 1802, and was married in 1822 to Kiren Happuck, who was born May 1, 1801, and died in 1856. Their children were: Phœbe, Harrison, Laura, Almedia, Miles, Henry, Olive. He was again married to Elizabeth Forrester, who was born in 1818. About 1829 he and his father started the first store in Cortland, then known as Baconsburg. The building stood where Dutchon's house now stands, but was destroyed by fire in 1834 or 1835. When nineteen years of age he went to Lake Erie, and while there stepped on the deck of the first steamboat on the lake, called the Walk-in-the-Water. He and Aaron Davis erected the first houses in Baconsburg, he building a house and Davis a shop near the corner of Main and High streets, north of Main. Afterwards he went as contractor for bridges on the canal, and built the bridge at the mouth of Mosquito creek, and several others. About 1835 he returned to Bazetta and engaged in milling, and then erected a turning shop. Afterwards he went to Pennsylvania, returning to Cortland in 1873, where he now resides.

H. G. Bacon, son of Enos, was born May 23, 1835, in Cortland, and was married in 1856 to Catharine Grimm, who was born February 9, 1838. Their children are Ward L. and Alice. He assisted his father in the mill until 1867, when he began in the grocery business in Cortland, with A. D. Hathaway. He bought out his partner in 1872, and has continued business for himself since. He started with very small capital, but by personal effort and industry has succeeded in building up an excellent trade in his line. He was a member of the town council for two years. He has been a member and served as deacon in the Disciple church since 1856. Mr. Bacon has been efficient in building up his native town, having erected two stores and three residences within its limits. He disposed of his business interests here in 1876, and took a trip to Colorado; was absent two months, and then returned to his native town and former business at his old stand, where he is now located in a thriving grocery business.

62*

Joshua Oatley, the pioneer representative of this family, came from Virginia to Ohio about 1810. He was accompanied by his two sons, William and Edward, and they first cleared land on the farm now owned by Mrs. Abell, southwest of Cortland, afterwards entering the section on which Lewis now lives, and the cabin home was erected about thirty-five rods west of the present residence. On this lot afterwards three log houses were built and joined together, one for the parlor, one for the dining room and the other for the kitchen. The chimney was constructed of mud and sticks, after the pioneer style of architecture. At this time the Indians were frequent visitors to this locality, and were on friendly terms with the elder Oatley, to whose cabin they often came on friendly visits, thus affording him ample occasion to make himself familiar with the characteristics, the intents, and purposes of his red-skinned neighbors, and by careful management he succeeded in maintaining a friendly feeling with them, though they often passed his house painted in their fantastic colors indicative of war, and though turning their faces from him they passed his cabin in peace. The elder Oatley was fond of travel, and after some time had elapsed he went away from home, going, as he said, on a trip "down the river," since which time nothing has been heard of him. Edward sold his part of the farm and went to Ashtabula, and afterward to Michigan. William Oatley was born in Virginia in 1787 and died (in the house which he built, now the residence of his son Lewis) September 23, 1841. He was married in 1813 to Sophia Rhodes, who was born in Pennsylvania in 1788. To them was born the following family: Joshua was born April 2, 1814; Hannah, born April 27, 1817; Mary, born June 29, 1819; Anna, born April 25, 1821; Lewis; Melissa, born December 26, 1827, and Edward, born May 15, 1830. Lewis Oatley was born May 28, 1823, and was married March 11, 1860, to Thankful Brown, who was born July 22, 1837. Their family consists of the following children: Blanche, deceased, born June 3, 1861; Eva L., born October 15, 1863; Burke, born June 27, 1866; Anna B., born March 2, 1869, and Grace A., born May 14, 1873. Mr. Oatley has been chiefly engaged in farming, and by the hard work and economy of management necessary to his occupation he has succeeded in accumulating means sufficient to care for and properly educate his children, to which laudable purpose he is now earnestly devoted. In 1852 he made the trip to California via Nicaraugua, and engaged in prospecting and mining for four years, returning home in 1856. Three years after he went to Colorado, but returned in the fall of the same year, and in 1864 he visited Montana. During the late war he furnished a man for the regular army at an expense to himself of over $750, for which he never received any credit from the military committee of his town, though the man was accredited to Bazetta. Mr. Oatley is well known as one of the representative men of his town, and though not seeking any office he has served as town trustee and member of the Cortland school board.

William H. Clawson was born in Berkeley county, Virginia, March 20, 1815. He was named after his father, and his mother's maiden name was Betsey Whitmore. After living some time in Fayette county, Pennsylvania, he came to Ohio first at the age of twelve, where he remained about six years, in Fowler township, where his mother then lived. He then bound himself to Isaac Woods, of Uniontown, Pennsylvania, to learn the trade of harness making. He returned to Fowler when about nineteen and worked at the center. He was soon after married to Malinda Humason, who died about 1861. They had a family of the following children— William H., now living in Pennsylvania; Elizabeth, now Mrs. John Gievner, of Pennsylvania; Sylvia, now Mrs. T. R. Mackey, of Illinois; Allison M., of Mercer county, Pennsylvania; Lucy A., now Mrs. Austin Silliman; Charles, of Mercer county, Pennsylvania; Lewis, living in Fowler; Calvin C., of Cortland; Malinda, now Mrs. Lester Clark, of Fowler; Almira, now Mrs. Charles Trowbridge; Emerson E., of Fowler. The latter was born June 15, 1859, and attended school at Titusville. He is now extensively engaged in the dry goods and general mercantile business at Fowler center. Mr. Clawson was married the second time February 21, 1878, to Perlina Gates, with whom and their only child, Mina Josephine, he now lives on his farm near Fowler center.

Calvin C. Clawson, son of William H. Clawson, was born January 8, 1849, in Mercer county, Pennsylvania, and was married October 15, 1872,

to Mary R. Silliman, who was born May 6, 1853. To them were born three children, viz: William H., born July 16, 1874; Maud Belle, November 24, 1877; and Carrie May, December 5, 1880. He came to Cortland in 1874, and went in partnership with W. C. Silliman, in the general store and dry goods business, on the corner of Market and High streets. He purchased his partner's interest in 1875, and has continued the business since. He now carries a stock of from $8,000 to $10,000, and employs two clerks. He has held the office of treasurer of town and school board, the latter during the building of the new school-house, and is also a member of the Methodist Episcopal church, and the Independent Order of Odd Fellows. He also held the office of United States express agent at Titusville, Pennsylvania.

Martineus E. Freer came from New York and arrived in Bazetta July 7, 1832. He settled at the corners afterwards known as Freer's corners, taking the name from him. He was born January 10, 1771, and was married to Mary Deyo, who was born May 18, 1769. He died December 10, 1847, and her death occurred August 29, 1856. They were the parents of the following children: Hannah, Elizabeth, Gideon, Jane, Martha, Henry, William D., Josiah, Harry. Gideon Freer was born May 8, 1796, and came with his father from New York State to Ohio, and settled on the farm where he now lives. He was married December 1, 1818, to Jane Windnagle, who was born January 11, 1800, and died February 22, 1874. To them were born the following children: Eliza, Henry, Elvily, Hiram D., Jeremiah, and Harriet. Hiram D. Freer was born February 16, 1825, and was married March 5, 1848, to Caroline P. Brown, who was born July 6, 1826. Their family consists of the following children: Alice J., born April 14, 1849, now Mrs. Edwin Rathbun; Loice A. (deceased), born September 29, 1851; De Witt C., born January 25, 1853; Morgan M., born December 22, 1854; Nora, born November 23, 1859, now Mrs. Byron Tousley; Bertha, born October 7, 1862, now Mrs. James F. Andrews; Slade, born October 17, 1868. He came to Ohio with his father when about seven years of age, and at the age of twenty-three he married and moved to the log-house just west of his father's, where he lived about three years, after which he built his present residence, situated on his farm about three miles southwest of Cortland. He furnished a substitute during the late war, who served from 1862 to the close of the war. Mr. Freer has spent his life on the farm and belongs to a family of well-known citizens of this community.

James Atkinson, Sr., was a son of General Atkinson, of the Revolutionary war. He settled in Bazetta township, on the west side of Mosquito creek, where he lived for a number of years, afterwards moving to the western part of the State, where he died at the age of ninety-two. His son James came with his father when only three years of age. At about the age of fourteen he began work at the county infirmary, where he continued under employment until 1852, when he was made overseer of the institution. In 1852 he was married to Elizabeth Weiss, who died in 1857 or 1858. They were the parents of two children—Milton E., and Mary E. He was again married, in 1870, to Lucy A. Fox, to whom were born the following children : Charles W., James M., Millie W., Kittie, and Terry S. He was a farmer by occupation, also a member of the Independent Order of Odd Fellows. He died in Champion township at the age of fifty-three.

Milton Emon Atkinson, M. D., was born April 22, 1855, at the county infirmary, of which his father was overseer. He was married May 7, 1878, to Jennie E. Harsh, who was born in 1858. They are parents of two children, the first having died in infancy, and Lena May. He first attended school at the Western Reserve seminary, after which he began the study of medicine under Dr. D. B. Woods, of Warren. He then began the regular course at Ann Arbor university, Michigan, which was not quite completed when, at the death of his father, he returned home and afterwards finished his studies at Wooster. He located in his profession at Cortland in August, 1878, where he is now actively engaged in a successful and extensive practice.

John Bradford was born in Trumbull county, Ohio, and settled on a farm between Cortland and Warren, where he lived until his death, which occurred in 1853. He was married to Jane Meek, and to them were born the following children : William (deceased), James, Mary Ann, now Mrs. Ross Wakeman, of Iowa ; Olive, now

Mrs. H. K. Hulse, of Iowa ; Elizabeth, now Mrs. Napoleon Gretsinger, of Iowa. He was a stone-mason by occupation, and a member of the Baptist church. James Bradford was born April 20, 1842, and was married May 5, 1863, to Jennette Hulse. To them were born the following children : William, Lucy, Rhoda, James, and Rena. He was again married, to Mary Hulse, and they now have one child, Clara. Mr. Bradford was raised on the farm until about the age of sixteen years, when he went to work at the carpenter trade with Thomas Kennedy, working with him until he learned the trade. In 1866 he engaged for himself, and continued until 1878, when he commenced the furniture business in Cortland. He began with a capital of about $5,000. His trade has continued to increase, and he is now operating a business of $2,500 per annum. He is engaged in the general furniture trade on Market street, next door east of the post-office, and is a member of the Independent Order of Odd Fellows.

Charles Oliver, a native of Germany, left home when about eleven years of age, and went on the ocean as sailor. He afterwards rose to the position of mate, and followed seafaring life for thirteen years. He married when about twenty-five in New York, Mary Park, a native of Ireland, and with whom he became acquainted during a trip across the ocean. He came subsequently to Trumbull county, and settled in Bazetta, where he and his wife are still living. He continued his former occupation, being captain and mate on Lake Erie for number of years. He has nine children living, as follows: William, at Braceville center, born June, 1843, married Zelia Dice and has two children, Jennie (Clark) at Howland Springs, Maggie (Dice) in Braceville; Mary (Kean) and Minnie (Lawrence) in Carroll, Ohio; Frank in Bazetta, Emma, Ella, and Nettie at home.

CHAPTER XVIII.

MESOPOTAMIA.

INTRODUCTORY.

This is the northwestern township of Trumbull county, bounded on the north by Windsor, Ashtabula county, east by Bloomfield, south by Farmington, and west by Middlefield, Geauga county. The surface is more variable than that of most townships in the northern part of the county, east of the center being low, moist land, while the western and northwestern portions are high, arable land, composed mostly of a succession of hills and ridges of moderate elevation. The soil of Mesopotamia is fertile and well adapted to grazing. It is also the best wheat land in this part of the country. The soil, like the surface, varies much. The Grand River valley is sandy and clayey. The western portion of the township has but little clay on the surface, and sandy and gravelly loam predominates.

The principal water-course is the Grand river, which crosses a small corner of the southeastern part of the township, and after continuing its windings through Bloomfield, again enters Mesopotamia north of the center road, and pursuing a northerly course, passes out a short distance from the northeast corner of the township. Grand river is only a small stream in dry weather, but when it and its branches are swollen by rains it inundates a wide territory. Swine creek, Plum creek, and Mill creek are the principal streams flowing into the river. The two former drain the western and southern portions of the township, uniting in one stream about a mile and a half south of the east and west center road, and thence flowing northward about three miles, where they join the river. A short distance below the mouth of Swine creek, Mill creek enters the river from the northwest. Numerous springs and small creeks supply an abundance of water for stock, and the fertile meadows are excellent pasture lands for the same.

The only village in the township is at the center, and is about the size of the average "center" throughout the county.

ORGANIZATION.

In 1806 townships number seven in the fifth range, and number six in the fourth range were taken from the Middlefield election district and formed a portion of the district of Troy.

Township number seven, in the fifth range, was organized as a separate election precinct in 1819, and named Mesopotamia—the name requested in the petition to the Legislature.

FIRST OFFICERS.

At a meeting held in the district of Troy the 7th day of April, 1806, the following officers were chosen: Otis Guild, chairman; Hezekiah Sperry and Jonathan Higley, judges of election; Ephraim Clark, township clerk; William Cox, Gager Smith, and Jonathan Higley, trustees; S. D. Sackett and Abraham Daily, overseers of the poor; Griswold Gillette and Alpheus Sperry, fence viewers; Isaac Clark, appraiser and lister; Timothy Alderman, appraiser; Joseph Alderman, Jr., Amadeus Brooks, and William Reed, supervisors of highways; Griswold Gillette and Samuel Forward, constables; Ephraim Clark, treasurer.

After Mesopotamia became independent an election was held at the center school-house on the 5th day of April, in the year 1819, and the following officers elected, namely: Otis Guild, chairman; Zimri Baker and Moses Bundy, judges of election; Addison Tracy, clerk; Luther Frisby, Moses Bundy, and Elisha Sanderson, trustees; Reuben Joslin and Job Reynolds, overseers of the poor; John Sanderson and Amadeus Brooks, fence viewers; Lucius Frisby, appraiser and lister; Linus Tracy, appraiser; Matthew Laird, Job Reynolds, Zimri Baker, Noble Strong, Levi Pinney, Anson Hatch, and Guien Crawford, supervisors; Lucius Frisby, constable; Luther Frisby, treasurer.

OWNERSHIP.

This township was owned principally by Pierpont Edwards of New Haven, Connecticut, and his son, Colonel John Stark Edwards, acted as agent for its sale. After the death of the latter in 1813, Seth Tracy acted in that capacity.

SETTLEMENT.

The first settlers of this township came mainly from Connecticut. Some five or ten years after their arrival a few Pennsylvania families came in. At the time of the War of 1812 there were about a dozen families in Mesopotamia. The growth of the township was slow, and not until after 1820 was there any considerable addition to the number of settlers. The village was also built up very gradually.

Pierpont Edwards, owner of the township, through his son, John Stark Edwards, offered to give one hundred acres of land to each of the first five men who should purchase land, bring their families to this township and reside here a certain number of years (probably five); and to each of the first five single men who came and resided a like period he would give fifty acres. John S. Edwards visited the township in 1799, and put forth this offer on his return to Connecticut. He thenceforth resided upon the Reserve a portion of each year up to the time of his death (1813). From 1800 to 1804 his home was in Mesopotamia. Mr. Edwards was a graduate of Princeton college. From 1800 to 1813 he was recorder of Trumbull county. Among those who, as the heads of families, first settled in Mesopotamia were: Hezekiah Sperry, Otis Guild, Joseph Noyes, Joseph Clark, and Seth Tracy. Sperry, Guild, and Tracy remained permanently, and in due time came into possession of the hundred-acre gifts. What other settlers received premiums is no longer certain.

In the fall of 1800, Hezekiah Sperry, his son Alpheus, and his daughters, Martha and Cynthia, moved in, being the first family. He built the first cabin, on lot twenty-nine. The following year he returned to Woodbridge, Connecticut, his former home, and brought out his wife and the rest of his children. His cabin was situated upon the present Woodruff farm. His family consisted of four sons and nine daughters. Seven of the daughters lived to marry. The sons were: Alpheus, Hezekiah, Elias, and Lucius, all of whom lived and died in Mesopotamia. Lucius never married. The three others reared families, and some of their descendants are still in the township. Captain Sperry died in 1833, aged eighty-eight. His wife died in 1827.

The second arrival was that of Otis and Lois Guild and their family. They came from Sharon, Connecticut, to the Reserve in 1800, and after about one year's residence, came to Mesopotamia, and located on lot forty-one, near the center of the township. They had eight children, seven of whom grew to manhood and womanhood. Two sons and one daughter are still living. The names of the children were Jerusha, Oliver, Jairus, Albert, Charlotte, Oswin, Aurelia, first, and Aurelia, second. The young-

est daughters died, one at the age of two, and the other at the age of eighteen. The three now living are Oswin, and Mrs. Charlotte Sheldon, Mesopotamia, and Dr. Albert Guild, Boston.

Seth Tracy, from Pittsfield, Massachusetts, who had previously been here to locate a farm on which to settle, arrived in this township the 8th of May, 1801. With his family, and several teams, one of which was driven by Griswold Gillette, he started from Massachusetts, and journeyed as far as Whitestown, New York, by land. There he procured a boat, transferred his goods to it, and proceeded as far as Niagara Falls. At this point the boat was hauled around the falls on trucks, and again committed to the water. The voyagers then coasted along the south shore of Lake Erie until they came to the mouth of Grand river, which they entered, and followed to within one mile of the house of Judge Griswold in Windsor, whence they proceeded to Mesopotamia by land. The day after his arrival, Mr. Tracy erected a rude shelter of poles and bark which his family occupied until a log cabin was finished the following fall. During the season he cleared four acres sufficiently to admit of planting corn, and from this field secured an excellent crop. The large trees were girdled and left standing. The smaller ones were cut and burned. The method of corn planting deserves mention. After the ground had been cleared, holes were made in it by means of a pick-axe, and into each of these holes a few kernels were dropped. No cultivating or hoeing was allowed the crop, except hacking down a few weeds during the summer. Colonel Linus Tracy, then seven years of age, is still living, and has a vivid recollection of his pioneer labor, which he began under the direction of his father and the hired man, May 9, 1801.

Seth Tracy took up seven hundred acres of land in lots lying near the center. On the four acres first cleared the first orchard in the township was set out about the year 1806, in rows exactly two rods apart each way. Most of the trees are still living. They were procured from Detroit by David Barrett, who made a nursery on Mr. Tracy's land, and cultivated it until the trees were large enough to be planted in an orchard. Seth Tracy was the first justice of the peace in this section, and a very active man in his day. He died in 1827 at the age of seventy, and his wife when eighty-five. The family consisted of seven children, the youngest of whom was born in Mesopotamia: Clarissa, Pamelia, Sabrina, Sophia, Adeline, Linus and Addison. Clarissa married Griswold Gillette, and died in Cleveland. Pamelia married Deacon Horace Loomis, and resided in Mesopotamia. Sabrina married Horace Wolcott, of Farmington. Sophia married Dr. John S. Matson, of Mesopotamia. Adeline, youngest of the family, married Mr. Pelton and had one child. She died in Cleveland when a young woman. Excepting her all lived to rear families. Colonel Linus Tracy, the only survivor, was born in Massachusetts, March 2, 1794. He married Betsey Talcott, a native of Massachusetts, who lived to be seventy-five. She bore five daughters and two sons, all of whom are still living, two of the daughters in Mesopotamia and the two sons. One daughter resides in Madison and two in Cleveland. Mrs. Tracy died in 1873. Mr. Tracy, when a young man, entered the store of William Bell, at Warren, and after a service of six months went into the store of Judge King, where he remained five years. In 1818 he bought out Mr. King and removed the goods to Mesopotamia, where he continued the business several years. He served as a volunteer in the War of 1812, six months, and was chosen corporal. Subsequently (in 1825) he became a colonel of militia. The manner in which he studied military tactics was peculiar. While clerking for Judge King in Warren he procured a manual of military tactics, and had a hundred wooden figures turned, which he maneuvred upon a board until he became familiar with all the movements of troops. He served as lieutenant, major, and colonel of militia. In the time of the late war he also helped to train military companies. Both his sons were in the army. Colonel Tracy is as smart and active as many men who have not half his age, and is in full possession of all his faculties, with a vivid recollection of early events. He is one of the oldest residents of the county.

Joseph Noyes arrived in the township with his family the 6th of July, 1801, and settled a short distance west of the center. He had received a liberal education and graduated as a lawyer. Considerable wealth inherited from his father soon departed from him and he took to farming in the wilds of Ohio. After residing here a few years he exchanged farms with Isaac Clark, of Burton, and went to that township to live.

In July, 1801, Mr. Sperry harvested a good crop of wheat upon land which he had improved the previous year.

In August, 1801, Mr. Edwards wrote to his sister, from Mesopotamia, as follows:

My settlement is doing finely. We have this day had a lecture delivered by a clergyman. There were about forty people present. Every part of our country is rapidly increasing in numbers. You can have no idea of what pleasure is derived from the improvements that are daily making; every day brings a new inhabitant; a neighbor opens a new road, raises a new barn, or begins a new farm. Indeed, the Scripture is fulfilled where it says, 'The wilderness shall be made to blossom as the rose.' Our country does literally flow with honey. Bees are beyond calculation numerous. Go into a cornfield in blossom and you are stunned with their noise. Trees of them are found in every direction. The rich variety of flowers which our woods afford it would give you pleasure to see.

Dr. Joseph Clark, the first practicing physician, settled near the center in 1801, but did not long remain.

Isaac Clark located in 1804, on the northwest corner of the roads crossing at the center. His sons were Almon and Isaac. The former died in this township, and the latter in Bloomfield. His daughters were Electa and Susan. Electa married Rensselaer Smith, and lived in Bloomfield.

Gauger Smith settled in 1805 on the farm where his son Edmund now lives.

Thomas Bowyer, the first of the Pennsylvania settlers, located in the south part of the township early.

James Laird and family, from Washington county, Pennsylvania, arrived in this township April 15, 1811, making the thirteenth family in Mesopotamia. They lived in a log-cabin on the spot where Captain C. P. Lyman's house now stands, until October, 1814, when they removed the present J. H. Laird farm, lot thirty-nine. Of Mr. Laird's family of ten children eight came with him, viz: John, Matthew, Andrew, Margaret, Betsey, Polly, James, and William. His oldest daughter, Rachel Morrison, moved into this township with her husband in October, 1811. Josiah, the oldest son, settled in Beaver, Pennsylvania. Excepting him, the children spent most of their lives in this township, and all of them raised families but John and Rachel. Three, Matthew, James, and Mrs. Betsey Higby, passed their lives in this township ; Matthew upon the old place. Two only are now living, William, in Cleveland, and Mrs. Margaret Holbrook in Toledo. John and Rachel (Chambers) each married, but had no children. Andrew married Tabitha Parish in 1823, and settled one and one-half miles north of the center. He reared a family of four children, now all living. John resides in Stockwell, Indiana; Orris P., in Mesopotamia: Maria, single, in Fresno City, California; Mary is at present in New York city. James Laird, Jr., married Catharine Cox for his first wife, and had by her six children who reached mature years. For his second wife he married Lorain Joslin, who is still living. By his first wife his children were Stephen, Josiah, Ralph, Susannah, Minerva, and James. All are living but Ralph. Stephen resides is Mesopotamia, and is a member of the Ohio Legislature for 1881–82—the first Representative ever sent from this township. Josiah and James reside near Jesup, Iowa. Susannah (Griswold) and Minerva live at Hart's Grove, Ashtabula county. Orris P. Laird, the second son of Andrew, was born in Beaver county, Pennsylvania, in 1829. Six years later his father returned to Mesopotamia, where Mr. O. P. Laird has since resided. He was married September 9, 1857, to Betsey I. Atwood, of Licking county, Ohio. Their children are Louie (deceased), Marcy C., and Martin W., living. Both are being educated at Hiram college.

Seth Morrison, Laird's son-in-law, came about the same time with the Laird family, and settled on lot forty-two.

Zimri Baker, from Vermont, settled south of the center as early as 1812. None of the family are now in Mesopotamia. His son, Porter, lived on the old farm till his family were grown, when he moved away.

Amadeus Brooks, who married a daughter of Captain Sperry, settled on lot thirty previous to 1812, and remained a number of years. He moved to Bloomfield, and thence to Warren, where he died. He was a man of fine intelligence and a good citizen. Indeed, the same may be said of nearly every one of the pioneers of this township.

As early as 1815 Seth I. Ensign settled one and one-half miles south and a mile west of the center, where he lived and died. He was an early teacher in Bristol and a justice of the peace

in Mesopotamia a number of years. His daughter, Mrs. Parish, still lives upon the farm where he settled.

Reuben Joslin came here quite early, and settled on lot forty. He was a carpenter and had worked at his trade in Boston before coming here.

Moses Bundy settled in the southwest of the township at an early date, and lived and died here.

Elisha Sanderson settled on lot thirty-one previous to 1819. His widow, two sons, and two daughters are still living.

Alpheus Winter married a sister of 'Squire Isaac Clark, and settled on lot twenty-five previous to 1820.

In 1816 Joseph Eaton and a family consisting of nine children settled on lot twelve. They were from Massachusetts.

Job Reynolds, a soldier of 1812 and a native of Rhode Island, located in this township in 1817.

Flavel Sheldon, born in Massachusetts in 1791, died in Mesopotamia in 1832. He married Charlotte Guild, who is still living, the mother of three children.

Alva Lake settled in this township in 1817. He married Mary Hogan, a native of Vermont. He was born in Castleton, Vermont, in 1799.

FIRST EVENTS.

The first birth that took place in this township occurred in 1801, when a daughter was born to the wife of Dr. Joseph Clark. The child died young. The second child was born in September, 1801, and is still living. Her name is Charlotte, widow of Flavel Sheldon. She was the daughter of Otis and Lois Guild. Sardis Morse, son of Joseph Morse, was the first male child. His parents were here but a short time. The first death occurred in the spring of 1802. Mrs. Joseph Noyes died of consumption. The first wedding was in 1806, at the residence of the bride's father. The wedded couple were Griswold Gillette and Clarissa Tracy, and in addition to "giving away the bride," the father performed the marriage ceremony, having recently been elected justice of the peace. Mrs. Gillette lived to be ninety-one years of age and died in 1874.

The first frame house, as well as the first cabin, was built by Captain Sperry. Joseph

Morse was the first blacksmith. John Tomlinson made the first grave-stones from stone found in Mill creek. Some are still standing.

For several years each settler acted as his own shoemaker, making and mending boots and shoes for his family. Some time after the settlement Hezekiah Sperry, Jr., went to New Haven, Connecticut, and worked a year at shoemaking. He then returned and went from house to house working at his trade. He carried his tools with him and made pegs from maple. His shoe-thread was made by hand-spinning.

EARLY SCHOOLS.

In nothing is the progressive spirit of the early settlers more clearly shown than in the matter of schools. The first thought of the pioneer, after becoming established in his log house, seems to have been to provide for the education of his children. And though the speller, the reader, and the arithmetic—fortunate boy who possessed all three!—were the only books used in these early schools, many a pupil, who afterward became noted for intelligence and usefulness, received all of his educational training within the walls of rude log buildings.

The first school in Mesopotamia was taught by Samuel Forward, in 1803, in a room of Seth Tracy's house. Samuel Higley, of Windsor, taught the next winter term, which was followed by a summer school taught by Jerusha Guild.

The first school-house was built on the northern part of Seth Tracy's farm in 1806, a few rods south of the east and west center road. Linus Tracy, whose own schooling amounted to only about six months' attendance, taught school in this building in early days, and was a successful instructor. He has lived to see the most of those who were his pupils grow old and die and be gathered with their fathers in the quiet village churchyard.

CHURCH HISTORY.

It is said that the first sermon ever delivered in this township was preached by the pioneer missionary, Rev. Joseph Badger. The first church organized was the Presbyterian in 1817, with eight members. This organization still lives and prospers but is now Congregational. Among the early members were Deacon Zimri Baker and family, Mrs. Silvina Tracy, Mrs. Clarissa Gillette, Horace and Pamelia Loomis, Jairus, Laura, and Charlotte Guild, Israel Sheldon, Betsey Laird, Seth and Rachel Morrison, and John Crawford. The Presbyterians erected the first church edifice in 1822, at a cost of about $500. The house now in use was built in 1843 and cost about $2,500. The early preachers were Revs. Badger, Stone, Leslie, Cowles, Osborn, and others. Rev. Randolph Stone was the first pastor and remained a number of years. He was a talented man, liberally educated, and possessed great power and earnestness.

The first Methodist preacher was named Daniels. A class was formed quite early, but at exactly what date we cannot ascertain. The Methodists erected a house about 1830, which is still in use, having been twice rebuilt. Among the early members were Elisha Sanderson and wife, Matthew and Andrew Laird, John Easton and wife, Seth I. Ensign, Ira Parker, Benjamin Smith, and many others. The first quarterly meeting was held in Elisha Anderson's barn. Mrs. Sanderson was one of the most active and influential female members. Elders Mack, Ira Eddy, and William Brown were among the early preachers. In 1833 a great revival took place and about fifty persons experienced religion. Isaac Winans and James McMechan were on this circuit at that time.

The Universalists had quite a flourishing church in Mesopotamia, and built the edifice which is now the town hall. Wishing to outdo their orthodox brethren they built their church one foot larger each way than the Congregational house. Spiritualism and the lack of religious interest destroyed their organization.

BURIAL PLACES.

The first burials were made on a hill north of the center. Mrs. Noyes, a daughter of Mrs. Guild, and Mr. Crawford were buried there. Nothing now remains to indicate their resting-place.

The first of Captain Sperry's family who died were buried on his farm.

The first graveyard for the public was the present one at the village. It is a pleasant spot in the rear of the churches and is thickly marked with grave-stones. The first person buried there was the mother of Seth Tracy. She died in 1818, on the 4th of July.

MILLS, STORES, ETC.

The first saw-mill was built by John S. Edwards in the northwest of the township, on Mill creek, in 1803. In 1805 a grist-mill run by water from the same dam, was built. Fifteen years later Isaac Clark erected a grist-mill on the same stream, one mile below Crawford's. In the first mill William Crawford, a brother of John, was killed by falling between the water-wheel and the rocks.

The first store in the township was opened in 1818, by Linus Tracy, who with his brother Addison carried on the business a few years, then shut up the store until 1827, when Colonel Linus Tracy erected a new building for a store, and continued the business. The first store stood a few rods north of Colonel Tracy's present residence. Isaac Clark and his son Almon had a store a short time about 1830. Mr. Clark built the stone building on the southwest corner, which, enlarged and remodeled, is still standing.

Griswold Gillette had a small distillery, consisting of a copper boiler, in a log building near the center, in early times. This was the only establishment of the kind ever in the township. An old resident assures us that he made a first-rate article of whiskey, using only corn and rye in its manufacture.

Seth Tracy gave George Ives an acre of land on which to set up a tannery. He began the business about 1818, and carried it on successfully several years.

Dr. D. L. Newcomb, from New York, built and kept the first tavern about 1823. The present hotel was built by 'Squire Isaac Clark, and kept for a time by his son Hiram. The old tavern forms a part of it.

Mesopotamia center was never laid off into lots as a village. A piece of land fifteen rods wide and one hundred rods long was donated to the township as a public square, and around this, buildings have been erected at the pleasure of the inhabitants.

The first road through the township was laid out along the west end of the tier of lots fronting on the present road running south from the center.

THE INDIANS.

There were a few Indians in and about this township in early times. An old chief, Pauqua, sometimes came here, and though a "big Injun," he did not hesitate to beg food and drink. Before the War of 1812 all the Indians withdrew

from this neighborhood. After the war a small band encamped near Grand river, and engaged in hunting. Some of the settlers visited their camp one day, but found the Indians absent. They broke some of the kettles in the camp, drew the image of an Indian on the bark of a tree, shot a ball into the head of the figure, and returned to their homes. The Indians then cut the figure of a white man upon a tree, and made no mark upon it, in token of their friendliness. But the white men's warning, doubtless, had the desired effect, as the Indians left soon after.

SWINE CREEK.

It may be of interest to some of our readers to know the origin of the singular name of this stream. About the year 1802 a sow belonging to Seth Tracy wandered from his premises, and for some time the owner could learn nothing as to her whereabouts. Thinking that the Indians might perhaps discover her during some of their hunts, he caused the red men to be notified of his loss, and desired that they would report to him if they chanced to find the hog.

One evening an Indian came to the house while Mr. Tracy was away. He poked some ashes out upon the hearthstone, and drew a winding line in the ashes with his finger, talking in his own tongue meanwhile, and making frequent use of the words "coosh-coosh" and "pappoose coosh-coosh," but none of the family understood what he was trying to explain. When Mr. Tracy came home, the Indian again went through with his talk illustrating it as before. In the figure drawn in the ashes Mr. Tracy recognized the course of the creek, and at a certain bend which the Indian traced very minutely, he was made to understand that his lost hog was to be found. Mr. Tracy went the next day to the spot indicated, and there found his missing property with a fine litter of pigs. Accordingly he named the stream "Hog creek;" but some one more fastidious in the matter of names suggested the modification now in use, and it was immediately adopted.

THE EARLY RECORDS

of the township show that the system of "warning out" such persons as were considered likely to become township charges prevailed; and also that some of the men thus warned out remained and afterwards became prominent, wealthy, and respected citizens.

IN THE WAR OF 1812.

A military company had been formed under the command of Captain Hill, of Windsor. On the breaking out of the war a call was made for volunteers. Linus Tracy, Oliver Guild, Jairus Guild, and Whitney Smith volunteered; and afterward another call was made, when Matthew Laird, Elias Sperry, Griswold Gillette, Ebenezer K. Lamson, Amadeus Brooks, Lucius Sperry, and Isaac Clark went. Elias Sperry was wounded by the Indians in a fight on the "Peninsula." His brother Lucius took the fever, came home, and died, as did also two of his sisters, who attended him and took the fever from him.

STONE QUARRY.

An excellent quality of freestone is found in this township, and the business of quarrying it has been carried on quite successfully.

POST-OFFICE.

A post-office was established about 1809, Seth Tracy, postmaster. Mail was then brought once a week from Warren by a man who usually traveled on foot. Linus Tracy became postmaster in 1825 or 1826. Under Jackson's administration he was turned out, and Isaac Clark succeeded him. Mr. Tracy again received an appointment after 'Squire Clark had served his term, and kept the office many years.

THE SOLDIERS' MONUMENT.

This memorial of the brave boys in blue who served in the late war stands at the south end of the public square. It is of marble, eighteen feet high, surmounted by the image of an eagle. On the north side of the base are the words " Liberty and Union;" on the south, the name of the patriot president, Abraham Lincoln; on the east the date of the dedication of the monument, 1867; and on the west, " Honor the Brave." It was erected by the citizens of the township at a cost of $2,500.

TOWNSHIP DIRECTORY.

Mesopotamia center : General store, Elias Sperry ; hardware, C. E. Holcomb ; drug and grocery store, F. C. Peck. A fire in the fall of 1881, destroyed two stores.

Cheese factories : Highland factory, Pierce & Caldwell, in the northwest of the township ; Davis Brothers' factory one mile north and a half mile west of the center ; Center Brook factory, Jacob Lepper ; Cold Spring factory, E. C. Cox, center.

Hotel : Eagle house, E. P. Griffin, proprietor, center.

E. C. Cox has recently started a broom-handle factory at the center.

Feed-grinding-mill : Woodford Bros., center.

Steam saw-mills : Sperry & Wilcox, center ; A. R. Harshman, sawing-, planing-, and shingle-mill, west of the center ; Bridgen & Holcomb in the southeast of the township are sawing lumber for handles ; and in the northeast of the township Watson is sawing for Kirk & Christy, of Warren.

BIOGRAPHICAL SKETCHES.

ROSWELL A. BUTTON.

We can give in this volume but a brief outline of the career and experiences of Captain Button. His life has been written, and few more fascinating volumes have ever been published. It is the record of ten years of seafaring life in its most interesting phase. From the unpublished manuscript we derive our information for this sketch.

Captain Button is a descendant of Thomas Button, a mariner whose name is found in the record of North American discoveries and explorations in the seventeenth century. Among the descendants were several sailors, and of his father's family, consisting of ten children, there were three—James, Erasmus, and Roswell A. James was lost at sea near Kamtschatka. Erasmus became a partner of Roswell in the management of the merchant bark Clara Windsor.

Captain Button was born at Preston, New London county, Connecticut, June 28, 1822, and was the son of Allen and Anne A. (Witer) Button, both natives of Connecticut. He was quite young when his father died, and left without the means of acquiring an education. He attended the common schools, and early formed a taste for reading. He was especially interested in works of travel and adventure, which aroused his imagination and produced an ardent longing for the sea.

In 1843, having just passed his twenty-first

K. A. Button

year and ambitious for adventure, he enlisted as a common sailor before the mast on board the whaling vessel Lowell of New London, about to embark for the northwest coast of North America. Her course was by way of Cape of Good Hope, Indian ocean, and across the Pacific. After eight months voyaging the Isles of the Azores were reached, where the sea abounds in its "mightiest of monsters." Here the first prize of the seamen was spied, and after an exciting chase captured. This voyage occupied three years, during which time the vessel coasted among the Azores, around Australia, touched Van Dieman's Land, and coasted the Sandwich Islands. We quote a glimpse or two from the manuscript volume of which we have spoken:

One of the most interesting peculiarities of the whale is its immense loss of blood in death. It is presumed to have a large supply arteriorized in a reservoir, which is brought into use when that in general circulation becomes vitiated during a prolonged submergence. This reservoir is what whalemen term the life of the whale, and it is the spot sought by the harpoon and lance. When touched the bloody torrent surcharges the lungs and is expelled through the spout hole, suffocation and death following, but when the wound is slight the agonies of the dying beast are prolonged. The poor creature will lie on the surface feebly propelling itself onward, and with quick repeated sobs will pour out its life by slow degrees, coloring the surface of the ocean a deep crimson. From this stupor it is aroused to its last struggle. The head rises and falls, and the flukes, which are fifty feet long, thrash the water rapidly. With great speed it swims in a large circle two or three times, and then falls on its side dead.

The narrative of the first voyage concludes:

Now let us follow our old friend, the Lowell, on her way home. When we left her she was near New Zealand in about 35° south latitude; here two sperm whales were caught and then on she went into the southern sea, and then doubling the horn and stormy cape in latitude 57° south. After this her course lay through the north Atlantic, continuing her voyage until port New London was reached, where sails were furled, the anchor dropped, and to express their joy for safe return and good success in achieving the object of their expedition—a full cargo of oil and bone—they fired fifty-eight guns. Two weeks after their arrival their cargo was discharged and each man was paid off according to his share. Then the sailors visited their friends; the first voyage was ended.

After six weeks spent in rest at home the "Lowell of New London" again raised anchor and set sail for another voyage. After sailing six months Kamtschatka was reached, northeast of Asia, and the Yellow sea was traversed. At the end of this voyage four thousand barrels of oil, worth $50 per barrel, besides a large amount of bone, was brought home. This second voyage occupied the same period as the first with almost equal results, but Mr. Button, who was one of the experienced men, experienced more perils. He had two boats stove and was once thrown twenty feet into the water. He acquired the reputation (an enviable one among sailors) of being the strongest man in the whaling service. We again quote from Jones' manuscript biography of him:

The secret of Captain Button's wonderful strength lay in the possession of a naturally strong constitution, increasing instead of diminishing its energies by constant exercise and the regular observance of temperance habits.

After returning from the second voyage on the "Lowell" six more weeks were spent at home. The "Lowell" was sold and the Montezuma purchased for a third journey. On the second voyage he had been boat-steerer and was now advanced to second mate. While at the Sandwich islands Mr. Button left his own ship and engaged as first mate on the Clematis and after returning to this country abandoned the whaling service. His last seafaring was as captain of the "Clara Windsor," a merchant vessel which made regular trips between New York and St. Domingo.

In 1853 Mr. Button quit the sea for more quiet pursuits. He came to Ohio and settled on the farm he now owns, west of Mesopotamia center, and the following year married Miss Caroline S. Reynolds, whose acquaintance he had made in Connecticut. She was his perfect counterpart, and their married life was a season of unbroken happiness till the dread disease, consumption, began to show signs of its presence. Mr. Button traveled extensively in Cuba, Florida, and California, in company with his wife, in the hope of arresting the progress of the fatal disease, but without effecting the desired result. She died at Sacramento, California, December 28, 1873. From this time until his second marriage, October 6, 1881, Mr. Button lived entirely alone at Mesopotamia. The maiden name of his present wife was Louie Humphries, daughter of Richard and Ann H. Humphries, of Ashtabula county.

WILLIAM LAIRD.

William Laird, son of James Laird, was born in Washington county, Pennsylvania, November 20, 1809. He came to Mesopotamia in 1811. His father moving there at that time, and bringing his wife and eight children, was the eleventh settler in the township. His father and mother both died in 1826, and William, who was the youngest son, lived with an older brother until he arrived at the age of eighteen, when he commenced life for himself. He resided in Mesopotamia until 1874, at which time he went to Dakota Territory, where he pre-empted a claim in the Vermillion valley and became a citizen of that Territory. In 1832 he was married to Hannah Chambers, of Champion, Trumbull county, a daughter of John Chambers, with whom he lived forty-two years, and buried in Dakota, October 9, 1874. In 1877 he came to Cleveland, Ohio. In 1880 he was married a second time, to Mrs. Eliza Sartin, of Cleveland, and now resides at No. 34 Herman street, in that city. Of his children, five in number, Matthew A., the oldest son, married Rachel McDonald, of Toledo, Ohio, and is now a manufacturer and dealer in Kansas City, Missouri; John Chambers, his second son, died in 1855 at the age of eighteen and lies in Mesopotamia; Elizabeth M., his only daughter, married William B. Fauss, of Mesopotamia, and now resides with her husband and three children at Elk Point, Dakota, in the town where her mother is buried; Edwards W. married Ada E. Williams, daughter of Justin Williams—he is a member of the law firm of Marvin, Laird & Cadwell, of Cleveland, and resides at No. 266 Franklin avenue, in that city; Marcellus G., his youngest son, died in Dakota, August 20, 1874. Maggie Pierce, his wife, and daughter of Deacon Joseph Pierce, of Champion, Ohio, died September 21, 1874, in the same Territory, and son and daughter lie by the side of the mother in Elk Point. William Pierce, their son, and the namesake and only grandson, died in May, 1875, at the house of his grandfather, in Champion. Mr. Laird is of Scotch descent, being of the third generation born in this country. He has been a member of the Presbyterian church for more than fifty years, and was for many years one of its ruling officers. His early life as well as a part of his later years, has been spent on the frontier and his whole life has been an active one, yet at the age of seventy-three he is hale and hearty, retaining all his faculties. Though residing in Cleveland, he retains his old home in Mesopotamia, and says he will as long as he lives, and when he says home it means either Cleveland or Mesopotamia, the meaning of the word depending upon which place is spoken of.

SETTLEMENT NOTES.

Timothy Cox was born in York county, Pennsylvania, April 12, 1799. His father, John Cox, was of English descent. He removed from Pennsylvania to Ohio with his family in 1805 and settled in Bristol township, where he was one of the earliest pioneers. The family consisted of twelve children, three of whom are living. Mr. Cox was one of the most energetic farmers and pioneers in Bristol, where he died in 1856. Timothy Cox, the only surviving son, remained at home until the age of twenty-one years. He then took a contract to clear forty acres of land, receiving in payment forty acres of wild land. Mr. Cox married in 1824 Sarah Bonner, who was born in Pennsylvania in 1805. They had a family of ten children — Joseph A.; Ephraim; Mariah A., wife of Martin F. Smith, residents of Mesopotamia; Harriet, wife of Eben E. Caldwell, resident of Cleveland; Seymour A., killed in battle of Perryville, October 8, 1862; Clarissa P., wife of John Ritter, resident of Washington, District of Columbia; Louisa M., resident of Mesopotamia; Aaron P., resident of Cass county, Nebraska; Phebe, wife of Edwin Brigdon, of Mesopotamia; and Enos S., resident of Nebraska. Mrs. Cox died February 12, 1882. Mr. Cox lived in Bristol township until 1865, when he removed to Mesopotamia.

Chauncey Bates was born in Geauga county, Ohio, July 19, 1835. His father, William M. Bates, was a native of Norwich, Connecticut, the date of his birth being 1808. He came to Ohio and settled on a farm near his present residence in 1829. In 1831 he married Rachel, daughter of Alpheus Winter, one of the pioneers of Mesopotamia township. She was born January 28, 1810. The family of William and Mrs. Bates consisted of five children of whom four are living. Edwin, the oldest son, was a volunteer in the One Hundred and Seventy-ninth Ohio volunteer infantry, and died in the hospital at Nashville, Tennessee, in June, 1865. Chauncey Bates, after passing through the common schools attended the seminary at Orwell three terms. He subsequently taught school eighteen winters. He was married October 14, 1858, to Eliza H. Hart, a native of Geauga county. They have a family of three children—Frank A., born June 3, 1860; Earl H., born January 25, 1872; and Blanche E., born January 5, 1877. Mr. Bates enlisted in the United States service in 1865. He has served several years as clerk of the township, and has also filled other public positions. He is a member of the Congregational church, leader of the choir, and superintendent of the Sunday-school.

Edward P. Griffin, the son of Edward and Leah Griffin, was born in Mesopotamia township, Trumbull county, Ohio, in 1848. He followed farming until 1872, when he took charge of the hotel at Mesopotamia center, where he still continues. He married in 1870 Ella, daughter of Ellory and Saloma Williams. She was born in Mesopotamia in 1852. They have a family of three children, Lulu, Maud, and Walter.

Seba and Jane Ensign, with their family, came to Mesopotamia from Cattaraugus county, New York. They were among the early settlers of the township, settling in the northwest part. Seba Ensign, Jr., married Almira Smith, daughter of Edmond Smith, one of the early, and now one of the oldest residents of the township, having been born in 1800. His wife, Polly, is still living also. Mr. Ensign has been a carpenter and joiner by trade. For the past seventeen years he has been an invalid, being afflicted with dyspepsia, and has endured much suffering, on one occasion going without food for over twelve days. Mr. Ensign has a family of one daughter and two sons, viz: Julia, wife of Irvin E. Brigden, of Cleveland; Eugene J., in the same city, and Frank, engaged in merchandise in Garretsville, Ohio. The latter married Jessie Holcomb, of Cleveland. E. J. Ensign was born in Mesopotamia, June 23, 1850; married Betsey, daughter of Stephen W. Irwin, a well-known and early family of Mecca township. Two children have been born of this union, Leon E. and Carrie Bell. Mr. Ensign removed to Cleveland in 1881, and is now engaged in business there.

CHAPTER XIX.

BRACEVILLE.

The original proprietors of the lands of this township, who received their titles from the State of Connecticut, were Jonathan Brace, Enoch Perkins, and Roger Newberry, and the deed conveying the lands to these persons is dated April 22, 1799.

On the 10th of December, 1800, the above persons associated themselves with Justin Ely, who with Jonathan Brace was proprietor of Newton township, and they together conveyed their several interests to Pardon Brown for the purpose of reconveying the same lands to the grantors, which was done the same day, and the five proprietors above named became joint owners of the soil. At a later period the proprietors made a partition of their unsold lands, giving to each one a separate interest in different tracts. In 1802 the township was surveyed into lots or sections one mile square, and by the survey of the Connecticut Land company the township embraced an area of fifteen thousand and four acres of land. The first title deed made by the proprietors to a purchaser was made to Francis Freeman, on November 21, 1803, and is the same land on which Ralph Freeman settled, being the west part of section sixteen, in the southwest part of the township.

FIRST SETTLEMENTS.

In the spring of 1803, a man by the name of Millan, a "squatter," built a small log cabin on the ledge, on the township line between Braceville and Warren. After completing the cabin he left it for the purpose of bringing his family, but during his absence a fire was started in the woods, probably by the Indians, as it was a common thing in those days, especially on the hunting grounds, and the Millan cabin was burned down, and he, hearing of the disaster, never returned. From this incident the township was called Millantown, which it retained until its organization in 1811, when it was named Braceville, after Jonathan Brace, one of the proprietors, as before mentioned.

In July, 1803, Ralph Freeman and William Mossman, two unmarried men, came into the township and erected a log cabin on the bank of the Mahoning river near the former residence of Asa W. Parker, now the residence of John Hipple. Mossman had purchased one hundred acres of land on which the cabin was erected; Freeman becoming owner of the land deeded to his brother, as before mentioned, in section sixteen. They kept bachelor's hall for more than a year, chopping on their lands. They had one cow which fed on browse, and the milk they kept in a gourd; during the warm weather the handle of this gourd became infested with maggots, and to remedy the evil they cut it off, thus seriously damaging the usefulness of the vessel. The dishes belonging to the culinary department of this pioneer establishment were necessarily very few, and they partook of their plain fare in the well-known Pennsylvania fashion of "sup and bite."

William Mossman sold his interest in the land to Ralph Freeman and went to Warren, where he married and kept a public house for some years, afterwards moving to near Buffalo. Freeman remained on his farm alone and continued to make necessary improvements, and is therefore entitled to the honor of being the first pioneer settler of Braceville.

In 1804 Samuel Oviatt, Sr., of Goshen, Connecticut, purchased about one thousand acres of land in this township, and his sons, Samuel and Stephen, with their wives, moved into Braceville; these two women being the first white women in the township. Their journey was a long and tedious one, being over six weeks on the road, and coming over the Allegheny mountains by way of Pittsburg, to Warren, from which place they were compelled to cut a road through the wilderness, thus making the first wagon trail from Warren to Braceville. In this same year Jacob Earle came to the township. The winter of 1804-5 was one of great destitution to the pioneers of this township, there being as yet no mills and little grain. The Oviatt families subsisted principally on boiled corn and baked potatoes and such wild game as they could get, and for an entire week they subsisted on potatoes alone. At one time, becoming entirely destitute of provisions of any kind, just at sunset on a Sabbath evening, while they were reflecting on their destitute situation, as if sent by a kind Providence, a fine turkey gobbler perched upon a tree near their lonely cabin. One of the men seized his gun, and though it was now quite dark, he succeeded in bringing down his game,

and it is safe to say that that one turkey furnished ample provision for all Braceville. Mrs. Sally (Storn) Oviatt, wife of Stephen Oviatt, was the mother of the first white child born in the township—William J. Oviatt, who moved from here to Wisconsin.

An incident is related of Mrs. Oviatt, as follows: One day in the absence of the men a large deer came into the "chopping" near the cabin; she seized her husband's rifle and with unerring aim fired and brought down the game, a noble buck. She took an axe and hurried to where the deer lay, to make sure of the capture, and in her excitement, it is stated that she cut the animal's throat on the back of its neck; at least this is a standing joke on Mrs. Oviatt in the community.

In February, 1805, Joshua Bradford, with his sons, Joshua, Joel, and William, settled on lot fifteen; and in the spring of the same year Samuel Oviatt, Sr., and his sons, Edward (and wife), Seth, and Mark, also his two daughters, settled on lot twenty-three. At this time a small tribe of Indians, with their chief, Paqua, had a camp in the forks of the Mahoning river, where they remained until the spring of 1806. This is the same tribe with which General Cleveland held a council near Conneaut in 1796. They were friendly and inoffensive, but somewhat annoying to the whites on account of their constant begging for whiskey and powder. They were especially so to the elder Oviatt, who had brought a quantity of powder for the use of his sons in the new settlement.

Early in the spring after the difficulty at Deerfield—an account of which appears elsewhere in this work—this tribe disappeared down the river in their canoes. In searching through their camping-grounds, among other things was found a large iron kettle and other utensils for making maple sugar. The kettle is now kept as a relic, and is supposed to have belonged to General Parsons, who had used it in his operations at the old salt works in Weathersfield in 1789.

FIRST ELECTION OF JUSTICE OF THE PEACE.

The first election for justice of the peace was held April 22, 1812, and Fowler Merwin was declared elected, Solomon Oviatt being the opposing candidate. The election was contested and set aside on the ground that the successful candidate was the only clerk of election. On the

30th of May following another election was held with the same candidates in the field, resulting in the election of Solomon Oviatt. This election was also contested and set aside on account of informality. Forty votes were cast. The above are the only cases of contested elections or in which any election was set aside for any reason, whatever, in this township.

On the 4th of July following a third election was held, and the good people of Braceville becoming wearied of the contest between the two candidates for the office, and determining to have a justice of the peace they went into the election with that kind of patriotism common in early days on 4th of July occasions, embracing all the elements that the day and occasion usually required, and succeeded in electing Robert Freeman as the first justice of Braceville. When the result of the election was officially announced three cheers were given by the crowd, and the newly elected candidate was borne upon the shoulders of the inspired electors, into the school-house, where he made a very laconic speech, of which there is no further report, and according to the custom of the times called in a "jug and grog." This would seem a remarkable mode of procedure in Braceville now, but it was then the invariable rule for the successful candidate in any election to "treat."

Robert Freeman, Esq., lived with his son Ralph, and was affable and courteous in his manner, amiable in disposition, kind and generous as a neighbor, and prominent as a citizen. He was chairman of the organization and first election of the township; was one of the first trustees, and held the office of justice of the peace until his death, being the first adult person that died in the township. He was first interred on the Freeman farm, but was afterwards removed and placed in the public cemetery at Braceville center.

JUSTICES OF THE PEACE.

Robert Freeman, July 12, 1812; Auren Taft, May 1, 1813, three and one-half years; Edman Oviatt, September 1, 1813, six years; Philoceles Lewis, May 5, 1819, six years; Samuel Oviatt, July 22, 1820, six years; Hervey Stow, August 4, 1825, three years; Warren Arnold, June 20, 1826 (resigned); Seth Oviatt, September 2, 1826, three years; William Benedict, August 28, 1828, eighteen years; Benami Johnson, August 22,

1829, six years; William Griswold, August 2, 1835, two years; Uriah Merwin, November 10, 1837, six years; George Lyman, June 16, 1838, nine years; Franklin E. Stow, May 30, 1846, six years; Ancil Bosworth, April 5, 1847, three years; Parker Boynton, April 1, 1850, three years; Allison A. Preston, May 1, 1852, three years; Augustus Elwell, October 13, 1857.

CONSTABLES.

Harvey Allen served as constable of Braceville from 1820 to 1845; he was known as the standing constable of Braceville. He was pleased with the office and made an excellent officer, and might have served his township many years more had he not moved to Wisconsin where he has since died. Jacob S. Smith was elected in 1844 and served seven years. He was an efficient officer, and in 1859 was elected commissioner. John H. Clark served as constable from 1850 to 1860. The people of Braceville do not allow the question of politics to exclude a worthy man from holding township offices, and though the township is largely Republican, Franklin E. Stow as township clerk, and Nathan O. Humphrey as treasurer, each held their respective offices nine years, both being Democrats.

LOCATION—SURFACE FEATURES—POPULATION.

Braceville township is located in the southwestern part of the county—town four north, and range five west, and is bounded on the north by Southington, east by Warren, south by Newton, and on the west by Portage county.

The soil consists generally of sand and clay, productive of the ordinary cereals and superior quality of hay, and the surface generally rolling, is well adapted to all kinds of agricultural pursuits and grazing. The timber is of the general order, and varieties commonly found in this section of the State—oak, maple, etc.

The Mahoning river takes its winding zig-zag course from the central part of the south line, and flowing westward across the southeast corner, enters Warren township from section six, north of the central part of the west boundary line.

The northern part of the township is drained by Eagle creek and its tributaries, which takes its rise in the extreme northwest, and flowing in a southeasterly direction and crossing the west boundary in the north part of the township, and enters Warren where it empties into the Mahoning.

The Atlantic & Great Western railroad extends from east to west almost directly through the center, making the main station at Braceville. The Cleveland & Mahoning road enters about the central part of the west line, and takes a northwest course through the township, with a station at Phalanx, directly north of Braceville.

The Narrow Gauge extends through the central part of the township from north to south, connecting the stations Braceville and Phalanx, thus affording ample railroad facilities.

The population of the township is almost entirely rural, there being no incoporated towns, nor extensive manufacturing interests to collect communities of any considerable size.

Braceville center is the most important point of trade and local settlement, and has two churches, two small stores, a post-office, a wagon and smith shop, a town house, and a number of dwellings.

The township does not vary materially in the census reports of the past thirty years. In 1860 it was 1,049; in 1870, 958, and according to the last enumeration (1880) was 1,019.

POST-OFFICES.

Since the day of railroads, telegraphs, and other means of communication, the post-office loses some of its importance to the public, but in early times, when the mail-carrier was the only means of communication, its importance was well known and appreciated. In 1816 the first post-office was established at Braceville, of which Auren Stow was appointed postmaster, and on the 1st day of January the first mail for Braceville was received. The first postmaster served until 1850, when he was succeeded by Franklin E. Stow, who served until he was succeeded by G. C. Reed, who was followed by Isaac Ingraham, after which F. E. Stow again took the office, which subsequently passed to the hands of the present postmaster—Seth Lee.

SCHOOLS.

The people of this township early sought means for the proper education of their children, and as early as Braceville had any organization whatever she had a school. The first regularly organized school in this township, and among the first in Trumbull county, was taught by Hervey Stow at the center of Braceville, and though the township has not been able to sup-

port schools of higher grades than the common district schools, yet these have been supplied from time to time with ample facilities for an ordinary district school education, and the township now supports eight schools, situated in various localities of convenience throughout the township.

A TERRIFIC TORNADO.

The year 1860 will ever be remembered by the people of this locality as the year of the tornado. On July 23d of that year a tornado, of which the following is an account left among the papers of Franklin E. Stow, visited Braceville:

In the fore part of the day the clouds indicated rain, with a gentle southwest breeze. About 11 o'clock A. M. the wind lulled away and it became extremely hot and sultry. The first indication of an approaching storm, about 12 o'clock, was observed in the excited state of the clouds. Two dark clouds were seen rapidly approaching each other, one from the north and the other from the West; they came together and instantly a dark body was seen to fall rapidly toward the earth, about one mile northwest of Braceville Station, on the farm of Heman Rood, where the work of destruction commenced. The stoutest trees were twisted off and scattered like wisps of straw, rocks torn from their beds, fences swept away and scattered in every direction. The storm raged, whirling and roaring, and moving in a southeast direction with great rapidity. The first building in its course was Dr. Manly's farm-house, occupied by Gillette Griffin, which was torn to atoms. In the house were Mrs. Griffin, two children, and Mrs. Charles Mason; it was thrown six rods over a wood-pile seven feet high, and while the building was moving Mrs. Griffin jumped out and had her collar bone broken. Mrs. Mason and the children were buried in the ruins, the former having her skull fractured and was otherwise bruised; the children sustained but little injury; one of them, however, was so entangled in the ruins that it could not be extracted until the frantic mother ran to the station for help. Next was the house of Charles Mason, about twenty rods distant from Manly's, which was torn to fragments; the heavier timbers were scattered over a space of two acres, while the lighter materials were scattered far and wide.

The power and whirl of the wind is shown in

the fact that the first of these houses was taken to the south and the other to the northeast. The course of the storm was southeast, through Manly's woods, crossing the railroad, and into the woods belonging to F. E. Stow, upturning the strongest oaks, twisting and whirling the trees in every direction. Passing through the woods it struck with its greatest force the railroad station-house and an adjoining grocery store of Lucius Wood, the station agent. These buildings were raised several hundred feet high, and were revolved together, grinding and bursting into thousands of fragments, that were borne by the winds into regions unknown. The station-house contained several tons of freight. A box of hardware, containing bolts, buckles, etc., was strewn over the ground for a distance of half a mile; a bolt was found over half a mile distant driven into a tree to the depth of an inch; a two-pound weight was found over half a mile away; pennies and quarters were found in many places, and a hand-saw was carried over a mile distant. Opposite the station stood the dwelling and grocery of George Smith. The dwelling was raised from its foundations, carried several rods, and dashed to pieces. Mr. Smith was absent, but arrived home in time to give his family warning of the approaching storm. They immediately fled from the house, and when the storm came he clung to the woodpile; his son John held to a stump, and while clinging there for his life the violence of the wind would throw him off his feet, and he was repeatedly struck and badly bruised by falling rails, limbs of trees, boards, etc. Charles Moren fled from the grocery and took shelter under the station-house, and as it raised from its foundations he was stunned by falling debris, and was afterward picked up several rods distant.

Mrs. Jeremiah Galvin, living a few rods from the station, ran out with her umbrella to meet her little son but was overtaken by the storm and a limb or a rail was driven against her with such force as to carry her several rods and crush her skull, causing instant death. A freight car loaded and standing on the track was thrown a distance of sixty feet and totally wrecked. Another car was carried five hundred feet and dashed to atoms. The large brick house and frame barn of Mr. Wood were unroofed. Money packages from the express office amounting to

$700 were given to the winds and never found.

Continuing onward in its mad career, upturning and crushing the forest trees like reeds for a distance of two miles, it next spread devastation on the farm of Jesse Benedict, uprooting and destroying a large orchard. Among the trees of this orchard was the first tree planted in the township, having stood the blasts of fifty-five years. Deep furrows were plowed in the hardest ground, unripened fields of oats were mowed as with a scythe, and potatoes in the ground, hills, and all, were taken off to an unknown market by the swiftest express. Mr. Benedict's house and barn were unroofed and otherwise damaged.

The large frame dwelling of William Benedict was unroofed and shattered, the west side was pierced with rails and boards, presenting the appearance of having been bombarded with cannon. The chambers of the dwelling were rifled of clothing, a bureau and chest with their contents were carried completely away and never found. Two feather-beds and a pair of woolen blankets were picked up seven miles away. The gale then visited the Mahoning river, following the channel for nearly a mile, filling the stream with trees and branches, and sucking up the water and whirling and dashing it into foam and spray against the banks, and killing a great number of fish, from the minnow to the pike weighing several pounds. Leaving the river it tore up the orchard of Asa W. Parker, unroofing his house and barn. The dwelling of a German family named Kramer, in which were five persons, was demolished. Kramer and a small child were slightly injured, the wife had her collar-bone broken, and John Carpenter was thrown some sixty feet from the dwelling into a pile of stone and rubbish and severely injured. Continuing in the same direction through a corner of Warren and Lordstown, throwing down and unroofing buildings and doing great damage, it spread consternation and wild alarm throughout the whole country. At a distance of about fifteen miles from the beginning the wind rose gradually higher in the air, appearing like a dense cloud filled with branches of trees, leaves, shingles, boards, etc. Passing a little south of the village of Niles and over Girard, rising higher and higher, spreading wider, but moving slower the further it went, scattering the accumulated fragments, which descended over the townships of Hubbard and Coitsville and as far into Pennsylvania as New Castle, a distance of thirty-five miles from where the storm began. Way-bills from Braceville station, shingles, pieces of boards, etc., were scattered profusely over the whole country, where the fallen rubbish marked the path of the storm.

It commenced with the width of about ten rods, rising and falling as it advanced, varying the width and lessening the violence, being about forty rods in width where it left the earth. In 1823 a similar tornado visited this locality, commencing near Jesse Benedict's, overturning a barn, rooting up an orchard, and going north towards Champion, but confining its ravages to the forests.

CEMETERY.

The burial grounds at Braceville center were first laid out on grounds donated by Hervey Stow, to which his son, Franklin E., afterwards made valuable improvements, and beautified the grounds. The grounds were laid out in 1812, and the first interment was that of Saber Lane, wife of Isaac Lane, who died January 27, 1813. The cemetery is now under the jurisdiction of the township trustees, and is at present a well-kept and beautiful resting place for the dead, and many of the names of leading men and the old pioneers, who have ample mention in this history, may be found on these marble slabs. "Men die but their works live forever."

RELIGIOUS ORGANIZATIONS.

The first religious organization of this township was called the Bible Christian church, that for a few years held religious services in the old log school-house at the center, which was presided over by Father Ross, and his followers were locally denominated Rossites. Among those who belonged to this organization as zealous workers were Hervey Stow and Edman Oviatt. Barney C. Allen was here baptized— " in the faith of his father and mother "—by the venerable Ross, when but a small boy, but he yet remembers that he knelt on the floor and was copiously showered with water ; he remembers also that he had a very strong mental objection to the quantity of water thought to be necessary for his case. In 1812 Rev. William Penn, a Presbyterian, preached in the log school-house

and organized a society. This organization continued for many years, built a church, and, no doubt, effected many moral reforms and accomplished much good, but was finally disorganized, and the building which they erected now serves as the town hall at the center.

In 1814 the Congregational church of Braceville was organized, and was composed at this time of five members—Comfort Stow, William McWilliams, Rachel and Theda Stow, and Mary Oviatt. For seven years the responsibilities of committeeman, clerk, and deacon devolved upon Comfort Stow. Meetings were held in the school-house, now town hall, at the center, under the ministration of Revs. Joseph C. Curtis, Benjamin Fen, William Hanford, Joseph Treat, and others. In 1834 a society was formally organized, auxiliary to the church, and a house of worship was erected in 1835. The church has had several seasons of revival—notably among these was the one held in 1836, at which time twenty-seven were added to the church. In 1837 a call was made to Rev. Selden Haynes, who served one year, and was succeeded by Rev. Perry Platt in 1839, who did much to unite the church, endeared himself to the people, and at his death was buried in the Braceville cemetery. At this time the church numbered seventy-two members, but dissensions having already crept in were inflamed by the agitation of the slavery question, and the church in 1876 voted to sell its property and loan the funds to the American Missionary society.

METHODIST EPISCOPAL CHURCH.

In 1816 an itinerant Methodist preacher in the person of John McMann, found his way to this locality, and succeeded in organizing a class of that denomination. As remarked elsewhere, Hervey Stow and Edman Oviatt about this time were working together to effect a permanent organization of the Bible Christian church, but failing in this, Mr. Stow united with the Methodist, and his name appears first upon the church record. He was class-leader, steward, and trustee of the new church organization, and his house for twenty years was the regular preaching place, and for sixty years the itinerant preacher's home ; and the public singing of the congregation was led by him for twenty-five years. The circuit to which the Braceville church belonged was called Mahoning circuit, and embraced what now constitutes several districts.

In the early days such men as Elliott, Finley, Eddy, and a host of well-known pioneer itinerants threaded the wilds in the cause of the Master, and found ready welcome at the Braceville charge. The first church building was a large log house of hewn logs, substantially put together, and strong puncheon floor, of well-known pioneer architecture. Hervey Stow and Hervey Allen made the trip to Pittsburg in a road wagon, camping out on the way, to procure the glass and nails for this building. This house was occupied as a place of worship until the present house was built in 1838, which was remodeled in 1874.

When the class was organized at Newton Falls, the same ministers that served Braceville also preached there, and among the names of the ministers the following are those who are now remembered: Father Davis, Arthur M. Brown, T. B. Tate, G. W. Maltby, Lewis Clark, J. W. Lowe, E. B. Lane, Milo Butler, J. M. Plant, H. M. Loud, R. W. Crane, G. W. Chesboro, J. K. Hallock, H. B. Henderson, J. B. Grover, John H. Tagg, John Graham, Hiram Kellogg, E. D. McCreary, H. M. Chamberlain, C. C. Hunt, C. R. Waters, J. K. Shaffer, N. C. Brown, E. M. Nowlen, C. V. Wilson, and J. B. Corey.

Among the presiding elders were Ira Eddy, B. O. Plimpton, Hiram Kingsley, H. N. Stearns, Moses Hill, John Graham, J. Tribby, and A. D. Morton.

On June 15th, 1878, a reunion of the ministers of this circuit was held at Braceville, and was a meeting of great interest, and continued from Saturday until the next Tuesday evening. The programme consisted of special discourses, addresses to young people, memorials, reminiscences of early times, of pioneer members and pastors. This was was an occasion long to be remembered by the members of the church and the community in general.

Among the ministers who returned on this occasion to the scenes of their past labors, to renew pleasant memories of the past were T. B. Tate, W. H. Wilson, J. Tribby, H. P. Henderson, C. V. Wilson, J. B. Corey, H. M. Chamberlain, J. B. Grover, S. Graham, A. D. Morton, Stephen Heard, F. A. Archibald, R. M. Bear, J. Crum. Letters of regret at not being able to attend were received from G. W. Chesboro, D. Prosser, J. H. Tagg, J. K. Shaffer, and C. C. Hunt.

The meeting was held under the ministerial management of C. R. Waters, the pastor in charge.

The church at Braceville is now enjoying a good degree of prosperity, and bids fair to long continue to bear a good share in the moral and religious work in this community.

THE UNITED BRETHREN CHURCH.

The church building of this denomination is located on the center road in the north part of the township. The class was organized in 1857 and was composed of Eli Smith and wife, John Weaver and wife, Henry Fuhlwaler and wife, Benjamin Roberts and wife, Samuel Simpson, and others.

The first meetings were held in the old school-house that stood where the new school-house now stands, on Eagle creek. The following ministers have served this congregation: William Miller, Benjamin Smith, J. Noel, David Traver, I. M. Moody, J. Excell, Ebons Hotchkiss, Rufus Smith, C. Casterline, H. F. Day, and J. Shreffler. The present building was erected in 1875, under the direction of Jason Heard and Eli Smith, building committee, and was dedicated June 4, 1875, by Bishop Glossbrenner.

THE DISCIPLES (CHRISTIAN) CHURCH, BRACEVILLE CENTER.

The members of this congregation in appreciation of the importance of preserving the history of the church, lately appointed a committee consisting of Rev. J. S. Ross, Mrs. Lucinda A. Smith, and Mrs. Oliver M. Benedict, to gather the important facts connected with the early history of the congregation, and have them properly recorded. Free access to these records was cheerfully granted by Rev. Ross, and from the labors of this committee the following facts are noted.

During most of the year of 1867-68, Rev. J. N. Smith was employed one-half his time at Newton Falls; the remaining portion was secured to the District Missionary society of the denomination. Eliab W. Bosworth, of Newton Falls church, was corresponding secretary of the society district, and was authorized to direct the labors of Rev. Smith. In January, 1869, he arranged with Rev. Smith to hold a series of meetings in the town hall of Braceville center; which began early in the month, lasting over three Lord's days, and resulted in the conversion of the following persons: David Hagar, Julia Benedict (wife of George), Nancy and Martha Joy, and Mary Matthews; also Heaton and Elizabeth Joy were reclaimed.

The converts were baptized in the Mahoning river opposite the residence of George Benedict. While the meeting was in progress the question of organizing a church at this place was talked of among those interested, at various times, and as the meeting was still successfully protracted the feeling in favor of an organization grew stronger and definite action was finally resolved upon, when it was announced that Edward Shaffer, of Southington, and Solomon Brown, of Newton Falls, had declared their intention of uniting with the new organization at Braceville.

On the following Lord's day—January 31, 1869—the church was organized with the following charter members: Edward S. Shaffer and wife (Sarah), Belle and Louiza Shaffer, Seth and Susan Lee, David and Eleanor Hagar, Ezekiel and Elizabeth Woodward, Morley H. and Eliza Wirls, Heaton F. and Mary E. Joy, Julia A. Smith, Nancy and Martha Joy, Julia and Olive Benedict, Lucinda A. Smith, Lavina L., Mary E., and Salome Matthews, Maggie Austin, Lauriston Lane, Lucy (Woodward) Lane, Mary Levings, and Mary Wilson. Immediately after the organization John S. and Martha A. Myers, Frank Poreman, and A. Smith, were received into the church. At the first election the following officers were chosen: Edward Shaffer and Solomon Brown, overseers; Seth Lee and Ezekiel Woodward, deacons.

Solomon Brown did not become a member of the Braceville church, and Seth Lee was elected in his place as overseer. The following ministers have served this congregation: Rev. J. N. Smith, who organized the church, lived at Newton Falls, and moved from here to Lanark, Illinois; Rev. A. W. Olds, very soon after the organization was employed here for afternoon services, preaching in the morning at Newton Falls, where he resided; Rev. I. A. Thayer held services every fourth Lord's day from some time in 1869 to April, 1870. He was then just beginning his ministry, and offered to serve the congregation

for what they might be able to pay or raise for him. During the winter the church gave him a donation in addition to what was paid him from time to time. The donation party was held at Dr. Rice's, where William Oliver now lives. The following year he held services in the morning and evening every alternate Lord's day, and received another donation aggregating $70 and over. He resided in Southington, where he labored half his time, and also practiced medicine, being a physician of the Eclectic school.

Rev. Morgan P. Hayden, a student of Hiram college, was engaged the following year each alternate Lord's day, and was paid $6 per visit. During this fall Rev. N. N. Bartlett held a protracted meeting, which resulted in nine additions to the church. Afterwards he was engaged here one-half his time until 1872. He lived at Niles, where he also preached. In the fall of 1873 Rev. D. P. Thayer was engaged for services each alternate Lord's day, mornings and evenings.

At an early period Rev. Bartlett had suggested the building of a church, and about March, 1874, a meeting was called to decide the legal status of the organization, which met at the house of Augustus Elwell, and selected the following trustees: James Burnett, Seth Lee, and H. F. Austin. Efforts were made to purchase the old Presbyterian church, but were unsuccessful, and a purchase was made of the north side of the present lot for $200, to which, afterwards, an addition was made. The present church building was erected in the summer of 1874, and Rev. D. P. Thayer served the congregation the first year in the new building until 1875, when he was succeeded by Rev. O. C. Hill, a professor in Hiram college, who held services here until the following August.

The present pastor, J. S. Ross, began his work here in the fall of 1875, preaching his first sermon September 5th. He was at this time employed in the United States railway mail service, and the congregation engaged Elder Lyman Streator to hold a series of meetings which resulted in two accessions. In 1877 Elder D. C. Henselman held a meeting, with ten accessions; and in the winter of 1877–78 the pastor began a series of evening meetings, resulting in sixteen accessions to the church. Other special efforts have been made from time to time, especially during the last winter, with the assistance of Elder O. A. Richards, when twenty-five were received into the membership of the church, and the congregation is now enjoying a commendable degree of prosperity.

PHALANX FLOUR-MILL.

In the year 1811 Eli Barnum erected the first flour-mill on the site of the present Phalanx flour-mills on Eagle creek, in the northwestern part of the township. It afterwards passed into the hands of the Phalanx company, then to William Bail, of whom W. P. and A. E. Goodrich purchased. In 1865 A. G. Rood & Co. came into possession and operated about eight years, when the present company, F. A. & A. G. Rood, began operations. The capacity of the mills is about sixty bushels of wheat per day; has two run of stone—one for wheat and the other a chopper. They also have a saw-mill attached, and both propelled by water-power received from Eagle creek.

THE TRUMBULL PHALANX COMPANY.

In 1846 a company of about one hundred and fifty persons settled in the northwestern part of the township, and was known as the Trumbull Phalanx company. This company purchased the Eli Barnum flour-mill and five or six hundred acres of land, built a tannery, repaired the mill, erected a wooden bowl factory, wagon-shop, shoe-shop, and operated various other industries.

They erected one very long frame tenement house and several log dwellings for the accomodation of their families, and built a large school-house for educational purposes, and in which they held religious exercises and the free discussion of religious beliefs. The company was organized on the "mutual" plan, each one sharing equally from the dividends made from the proceeds of the various industries, and each person receiving credit for work done.

The company continued in operation here for about four years, when for some reason not now known was disbanded. But while here this was a place of considerable business activity as well as a resort for neighborhood social gatherings and other popular amusements common to rural neighborhoods.

From this company the locality received the name by which it is known and which it has transmitted to the railroad station and post-office.

The station known as Phalanx is located on the Cleveland & Mahoning railroad, and has but one store; it is a point for transferring coal and other railroad business. Phalanx post-office, of which Mrs. Samuel Barnum is postmistress, is located in convenience to this community.

THE CHEESE-BOX FACTORY.

This manufactory is located in the northern part of the township on the center road, and on the farm owned by the proprietor, Michael Templeton, who has operated in this locality for twenty-nine years. He first began making cheese boxes by hand, then horse power until 1870, when he began at the present location, where he is now extensively engaged using steam power, propelled by a forty-horse power engine. The capacity of the mill is about two hundred boxes per day. The saw-mill is used in connection with the factory, and also in doing general custom work.

EAGLE CREEK CHEESE FACTORY.

This factory is located near the Phalanx Flour-mill, and was first operated in 1872 by Charles Prentice, who continued about two years, when he sold to Mr. Peck, who worked the factory but one season, and sold to Walter Morton, who operated here until the past fall, when George Bear took possession, who operated with considerable success, using in the best season six or seven thousand pounds of milk per day, and realizing good prices for his product. There is another factory in the township located east of the center, but it is not now in operation.

SETTLEMENT NOTES.

The second family in Braceville was that of Samuel Oviatt. He removed from Goshen township, Connecticut, in 1805, and built a log-house across the river from where his grandson, Henry H., now lives. His father, Samuel Oviatt, Sr., came out a few years afterward and located where his son had settled, the latter then building the home west of the river, where he always lived afterward. He built, in 1808, the first frame barn in the township, which is still on the place, and in good preservation. His brother, Stephen Oviatt, and his young bride, they having been married the day they left Connecticut, came out at the same time. They lived in Braceville a short time, and then moved to Milton. Lucretia Oviatt, daughter of Samuel Oviatt, Jr., was the first female child born in Braceville, born about 1807. Samuel and Lois (Beckwith) Oviatt were the parents of nine children who grew to maturity of whom but four are now living, as follows: Mrs. Joseph James, in Charlestown, Portage county; Mrs. Thomas Douglass, of Warren, Ohio; Mrs. Nathan Wilson, of Ravenna, Ohio; and Mrs. Lucina Mitchell, living in Wisconsin. Moses L., the second child, who occupied the homestead until his death, was born in Connecticut, March 30, 1802. He married July 26, 1825, Lovina Purple, of Parkman, Geauga county, born July 25, 1803. They first settled at Newton Falls, where he operated a saw-mill and also engaged in farming. He afterwards settled on his father's place, which he purchased and occupied until his death, April 20, 1869. His wife survived him ten years lacking four days. They were the parents of twelve children, all of whom lived to reach manhood and womanhood, except one. The following are the survivors: E. L. Oviatt, of Marshalltown, Iowa; Mrs. Harriet L. Stow, of Braceville; Julia L. Humphrey, of Paris, Portage county; Ancil P., in Ravenna; Cornelia, wife of Comfort Ernest, of Warren township; Henry H., occupying homestead in Braceville; and Jemima (unmarried), in Ravenna. E. L. served in the Union army in the war of secession, and was a prisoner one year at Belle Isle and Andersonville. Henry H., born in August, 1844, married Esther A., daughter of B. C. Allen, and has three children living and two deceased.

Comfort Stow was born in Middletown, Connecticut, June 27, 1762. In 1783 he was married to Rachel Goodwin and in 1810 with his wife and oldest son, Hervey, removed to Braceville, Trumbull county, Ohio. The most prominent member of the family in this county was Franklin E. Stow. He was born in Braceville January 2, 1813. His father was Hervey Stow and his mother Lucretia Oviatt, who came to Braceville as early as 1805. Mr. Stow learned surveying, and in April, 1834, was appointed deputy county surveyor, and in 1835 was elected county surveyor, and re-elected in 1841. In 1842 he was elected justice of the peace, serving four terms; appointed postmaster in 1845, which office he resigned in 1850, when he was nominated for State Representative. In 1856 he was again appointed postmaster which

position he held until his death. In 1851 he was elected a representative to the State Legislature and served with fidelity and ability. In 1847 he was appointed district assessor for the purpose of valuing real estate. His district comprised six townships. His valuation was not changed by the board of equalization but was taken by them as a standard for the remainder of the county. In the fall of 1861 he raised a company of infantry which was attached to the Nineteenth regiment as company G. At the battle of Shiloh he distinguished himself for gallantry. He was subsequently prostrated by sickness as a result of that battle, and died on board the steamer Shenango, Tennessee river, April 30th. His remains were brought home for burial. He was married on the 15th of May, 1837, to Miss Mary Amy Heath, of Sandisfield, Massachusetts. One son was born in 1844. Mrs. Stow still resides in Braceville.

Ezra Roper was born in Connecticut in 1784; came to Ohio in an early day, and settled two miles west of the center of Braceville. He served in the War of 1812, and was wounded. He was twice married, first, to Abigail Lawson, by whom he had two children—Mary and Lorinda. His first wife died March 15, 1834, aged thirty-seven. He married for his second wife Lois Bristol, of Nelson, Portage county, and by this marriage had five children—Charles, living in Nelson; Lois (Doty), in Cleveland; George, at Braceville center; Aaron, in Youngstown, and Francis, in Cleveland. Ezra Roper died June 7, 1850. George Roper was born in 1841; married in March, 1862, Emeline Tousley, and has three children. He located at Braceville center twenty years ago, where he has carried on general blacksmithing and carriage and wagon-making for the past thirteen years.

Samuel Craig, son of Samuel and Elizabeth (Baxter) Craig, born January 18, 1811, in county Monaghan, Ireland, came to the United States in 1836, landing at Quebec. He came to Warren in July the same year, and worked on the Pennsylvania & Ohio canal as stone-cutter, which occupation he followed many years. He purchased the farm in Braceville now owned by William Anderson, about 1839, and erected the first house in that part of the township, which was then entirely a wilderness. He resided in Warren two years, afterwards purchasing where he now lives. He married in Pennsylvania in 1841, Margaret Darling, born in New York State in 1822. They are the parents of nine children, of whom five survive, viz: Samuel B., Benjamin, Josiah W., Maggie (Daugherty), and Charles F.

Robert A. Walker was born in Baltimore, Maryland, December 27, 1790, and went to Lancaster county, Pennsylvania, where he married Abbie Griswold, removing afterwards to Beaver county, where he resided until 1832, when he removed to Warren township, Trumbull county, Ohio. He had purchased land in Weathersfield and Warren a number of years before his removal. He resided in Warren, where he first settled, some twelve years, then moved to Braceville, and settled where George Benedict now lives. He afterwards moved to the northeast part of the township, where he spent the balance of his life. He died May 20, 1868. In the early part of his life he followed the trade of stone-mason. His wife died three years previous to his own death. Their family numbered nine children, all of whom grew to mature age. The survivors are Susan (Bartman) in Canfield, Mahoning county; Rachel Ann (Regal) at Baldwin's corners, Mahoning county; Elisha in Braceville, Trumbull county; J. P. in Cass county, Michigan; Abby (North) in Braceville; Robert A. in Jackson county, Michigan; William H. in Brookfield, Eaton county, Michigan.

Elisha Walker was born in 1822, July 4th, in Beaver county, Pennsylvania, and married in 1834, Lucy Ann Humphrey, who died in October, 1867. He again married in March, 1868, Maria Clark (Richards), born May 14, 1832. By the first marriage four children were born, viz: Franklin D., Abbie S. (Benedict), Robert Norris, Mary E. (Woodward). The result of the second marriage is one daughter, Effie B. Mr. Walker first settled in Warren township west of Leavittsburg, afterwards removing to Wyandot county, but after a short time returned to Trumbull county, locating in Braceville, where he has since resided.

John G. Gretzinger was born in Wurtemburg, Germany, April 28, 1811, and came to America about the year 1839. He went to Pittsburg, Baltimore, and other cities, following his business, which was that of butchering. He came to Trumbull county about 1842, and after residing in Warren township purchased a farm in Braceville, on Eagle creek, where he resided until his death, which took place October 2, 1880. Mr. Gretzinger was a hard-working and industrious man. He was sick and helpless the last twenty years of his life. He was first married in 1842 to Mrs. Rebecca Fry, who died in 1853. By this marriage he had six children, of whom five are living. He again married in 1856 Paulina Crouse, of Columbiana county, born in Wurtemburg, Germany, February 21, 1832, and coming to this country in 1855. Four children were the result of this marriage, three of whom are living—Paulina (Brown), Henry W., and Mary A. In the spring of 1882 Mrs. Gretzinger left the farm and removed to the center of Braceville, where she now lives.

Luther Matthews, son of James Matthews, was born in Liberty township, Trumbull county, Ohio, May 15, 1819. January 7, 1847, he married Lavinia Lightbourn, daughter of Joseph and Eleanor (Kyle) Lightbourn, who was born in Youngstown, Mahoning county, Ohio, June 29, 1825. Joseph Lightbourn was a native of Pennsylvania, born in 1795, came to Trumbull county in an early day, and located in Youngstown. He died in 1824. His wife survived him until October, 1856. After their marriage in 1847 Mr. and Mrs. Matthews settled on the place where she still lives, which they cleared up and improved. Besides general farming he also dealt in live stock. He died December 11, 1877. They were the parents of six children, of whom five are living—Ella S., born November 21, 1847, now the wife of Frank Brown, and residing in Meadville, Pennsylvania; Frances M., born October 30, 1849, wife of C. P. Rodenbaugh, of Kent, Ohio; Mary E., born March 18, 1852; Alfred E., May 4, 1866; Luther E., August 30, 1870.

William Ernest came to Trumbull county with his mother and step-father when fifteen years of age, in the fall of 1833. The family settled in Champion township. He was born in 1818; married in 1839 Nancy Leonard, and located in Warren. He learned the carpenter trade, and has followed it ever since. He has always been a hard-working, industrious man. He has three children, viz: Henry H., Comfort A., and Mary I., wife of John C. Pew, of Lordstown. Henry was born in Warren, Ohio, April 14, 1840, married Fidelia McKibbin, of Braceville, and until recently has lived in that township; has one child, Rowley Ward. Comfort A., born February 10, 1842, married Cornelia Oviatt, of Braceville, and has three children, viz: Albert, Hattie, and Jessie.

Christian Gleich was a native of Germany, and emigrated to this country with his parents when about eight years of age. His father, John Gleich, was a soldier under Napoleon, and was wounded in several engagements. He settled, on coming to Trumbull county, in Warren township, afterwards removing to Braceville. He died in Indiana at the age of ninety-three or ninety-four, having removed to that Sate in 1867. Christian Gleich married about 1847, Caroline Smith, of Braceville, and settled soon after where his son George now lives. He was engaged in farming and dealing in live stock during his life. He died in 1871, in the fiftieth year of his age. His widow is still living at Phalanx. They were the parents of five children. Two sons and two daughters are living, as follows: George, on the home place (married Almira C. Heintzleman, and has four children); Caroline (Weaver), in Braceville; Frank, at Phalanx; Eliza Ann living with her mother. Edward was killed by the kick of a horse in June, 1875, in his fifteenth year. George Gleich, who occupies the home place, is engaged in farming, and is an extensive dealer in live stock.

John G. Barkley, a native of Germany, emigrated to the United States in an early day and settled in Warren township. He married Christina Houseman, also born in Germany. He worked on the Pennsylvania & Ohio canal, and also followed farming. He lived on Duck creek, one mile south of Leavittsburg, and died there in 1848. His wife survived him, and died May 21, 1867. They were members of the Lutheran church. Gottleib D. Barkley, their second son, was born in Warren township, Trumbull county, in 1843; married Emma Josephine, daughter of Thomas Craig, of Warren township, and settled where he now lives in Braceville. He has one child living, and one deceased—John C., and Lucy J.

James Burnett was born in Kent, Portage county, Ohio, September 11, 1820. His father, Samuel Burnett, was born in Pennsylvania, May 11, 1792, and came to Ohio in 1804, locating in Portage county. He married in Trumbull county, Isabel Matthews, and removed to Weathersfield about 1835, and to Braceville in 1856, where they lived until their deaths—he died in August 1869, and his wife in 1861. James Burnett learned the blacksmith trade, and worked at his trade in Austintown, now Mahoning county, two years, then settled in Braceville, Trumbull county, where he remained until 1871, when he removed to Warren, purchasing the Dr. Leavitt place, where he still lives. For the past three years he has followed farming and stock-raising, owning two farms of one hundred and fifty-three and one hundred and thirty-five acres each. He was married December 29, 1844, to Miss Elizabeth, daughter of Joseph Lightbourn, who was born in Youngstown, Ohio, January 11, 1820. Two children were born of this union—Mrs. Reuben Johnson, born November 20, 1847, and Mrs. S. A. Elwell, December 20, 1854.

CHAPTER XX.

MECCA.

GENERAL FEATURES.

Mecca township is among the later settlements of this county, consequently its history is not as interesting in respect to pioneer life, adventures, and hardships as that of some of the older communities. A considerable portion of the township is well improved, and contains some excellent farming land. Mecca has no important manufacturing interests, no railroads, and no villages of importance, consequently it supports but a small population, which is chiefly engaged in agriculture.

The township is divided by Mosquito creek into two unequal portions. This stream enters the township from the north and pursues a course almost directly southward, entering Bazetta only a few rods east of the north and south center line of that township. About five-eighths of the land of Mecca lies west of the creek. Several small brooks from the east and one from the west join the Mosquito in this township. The bottom land of the creek is quite extensive. As it is low it is frequently overflowed. The surface is somewhat variable. A ridge extends through the township, north and south, on the east side of the creek; then come the bottom lands, and in the northwestern quarter of the township highlands more elevated than those east of the creek. The southwest of the township is like a level plain. It contains much

thus located, beginning at the north: Kirtland tract, Cowles tract, Kingsbury tract, Ely tract.

Judge Kirtland lived in Poland, and being anxious to have his tract settled, made very easy terms with the purchasers, leaving the payment of the principal optional with the contractor so long as the interest was kept up. Such easy

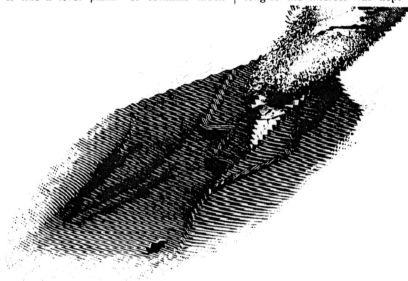

Lightning Source UK Ltd.
Milton Keynes UK
04 October 2010

160736UK00001B/5/P